Life Sketches of Lutheran Clergy,
North Carolina Synod
of the
Evangelical Lutheran Church in America
and Antecedents
1773-1999

Life Sketches of Lutheran Clergy, North Carolina Synod of the Evangelical Lutheran Church in America and Antecedents, 1773-1999

Historical Works Committee
North Carolina Synod
Evangelical Lutheran Church in America
1988 Lutheran Synod Drive
Salisbury, NC 28144

Published by North Carolina Synod, Evangelical Lutheran Church in America
1988 Lutheran Synod Drive
Salisbury, North Carolina 28144

Copyright © 2001 by North Carolina Synod, ELCA

Printed in the United States of America

First Edition, 2001

Library of Congress Catalog Card number: 2001093213

Historical Works Committee
North Carolina Synod
Evangelical Lutheran Church in America

ISBN 0-9641126-3-9

The Reverend Karl Monroe Park
1924-2000

Dedicated in
Memory of The Rev. Karl Monroe Park
Archives Helper and Assistant Archivist for the
North Carolina Synod
June 1987 until his death June 2000.

ACKNOWLEDGMENTS

Edited by
Eleanor E. Sifford and Bernard W. Cruse, Jr.

LIFE SKETCHES OF LUTHERAN CLERGY, NORTH CAROLINA SYNOD
OF THE
EVANGELICAL LUTHERAN CHURCH IN AMERICA
AND ANTECEDENTS, 1773-1999

HISTORICAL WORKS COMMITTEE MEMBERS

Clergy	Laity
Rev. Dr. Paul Barrier Beatty, Jr.	Bernard W. Cruse, Jr.
Dr. Raymond Morris Bost, Chair	Dr. Gary R. Freeze
Rev. Dr. Robert M. Calhoon	Gelene Lineberger
Rev. Cyrus Field Frazier	Catherine Safrit
Rev. Ted Wales Goins, Sr.	Eleanor E. Sifford
Rev. Luther Lavern Knauff	Mary Sullivan
Rev. Karl Monroe Park	Rebecca Wagoner
Rev. Donald Myron Phillips	
Rev. George Lamar Rhyne, Archivist	
Rev. Clarence Eugene Sifford, Jr.	
Rev. Joyce Elizabeth Taipale	

Planning Sub-Committee

Rev. Paul Barrier Beatty, Jr.	Rev. Karl Monroe Park
Rev. Luther Lavern Knauff	Eleanor E. Sifford

Editorial Committee

Rev. Dr. Raymond Morris Bost	Bernard W. Cruse, Jr.
Rev. George Lamar Rhyne	Eleanor E. Sifford

North Carolina Synod Staff Who Assisted With This Project

Glenda Lingle Ball	Tony V. Lippard
Peggy H. Bollinger	Iris M. McCullough
Melanie Jetton Bookout	Donna Davis Prunkl
Arline "Cookie" Elston	Diane Poole Ryan
Charlene D. Faggart	Tony Sherrill
Catherine Ficken Fink	Kelly H. Zalinsky

Director for Archives and Chief Historian, ELCA
Elisabeth C. Wittman
Assistant Archivist, Evangelical Lutheran Church in America
Diane Asseln

BISHOPS

Mark William Menees, D.D.	Leonard Homer Bolick, D.D.

Permission is on file from the following for use of materials in their publications:
North Carolina Synod - ELCA
South Carolina Synod - ELCA
Virginia Synod - ELCA
Olan Mills, Church Directory Division.

PREFACE

Following his transition in 1982 from a teaching ministry at Lenoir-Rhyne College to a ministry of oversight for the pastors and congregations of the North Carolina Synod of the Lutheran Church in America, the Reverend Michael C. D. McDaniel, Ph.D., moved early on as Bishop to reflect his broad knowledge of, and appreciation for, the history of the Church, especially as that history has been made manifest through the Lutheran tradition. With his strong support and encouragement, the Synod's Committee on Historical work proceeded to set for itself an ambitious agenda. That agenda included the publication of a narrative history of the synod to succeed its *History of the Lutheran Church in North Carolina* (1953), a useful work that clearly needed to be updated and expanded. A second item on the agenda was the publication of a new edition of *Life Sketches of Lutheran Ministers of the North Carolina and Tennessee Synods, 1773-1965* (1966), and, finally, the Committee projected the publication of a volume of historical sketches of the congregations making up the Synod.

Under the chairmanship of the late Pastor Karl M. Park, the Committee published in 1994 *All One Body: the Story of the North Carolina Lutheran Synod, 1803-1993*, a narrative history prepared by Raymond M. Bost and Jeff L. Norris. The volume you now hold is based on, and is the successor to, the 1966 edition of *Life Sketches*. The eight hundred sixty-five sketches appearing in the earlier volume have in many instances simply been reproduced as published earlier. In those instances where erroneous information crept into the earlier volume, or where materials have come to light that provide important new information, or where supplementary information has been made available to the Committee, earlier sketches have been modified. In the present volume, the number of sketches has been expanded to approximately fifteen hundred. It was the decision of the Committee on Historical Work that those sketches now appear in one continuous alphabetized roster rather than providing separate rosters for African-American pastors and oriental pastors, as was the case in the 1966 edition.

A word of explanation may be in order with regard to the two groups formerly rostered separately. Starting in the late 1860s, the Tennessee and North Carolina Synods made provision for licensing African-Americans to minister among Blacks in communities where there were Lutheran congregations. In 1880 the North Carolina Synod began ordaining African Americans, and in 1889 that synod assisted its Black pastors and lay representatives from their congregations in creating a synod of their own, "The Alpha Synod of the Evangelical Lutheran Church of Freedmen in America." In later years the congregations and pastors of the Alpha Synod united with the Lutheran Church-Missouri Synod.

As for the Asian pastors who were rostered by the North Carolina and Tennessee Synods, they were Chinese or Japanese persons ordained or enrolled as pastors by the synods at the request of mission boards. Such requests grew out of the desire to make provision for creating native pastors in the period prior to the actual establishing of branch denominational bodies on the mission fields. After sister churches were established on the mission fields in China and Japan, such pastors as had been rostered by the North Carolina and Tennessee Synods were transferred to the new church bodies in their homeland.

The most distinctive new feature of this edition of *Life Sketches* is its extensive index, a feature made possible with the advent of the computer and the substantial computer skills and dedication of Bernard William Cruse, Jr.

This volume was seven years in preparation, and several attempts have been made to secure updated information not only from pastors currently in the synod, but also concerning pastors who served in North Carolina but later transferred to other synods. Many pastors cooperated readily with the committee's efforts, and the committee is happy to acknowledge and express gratitude for that cooperation. But in other instances the committee was not able to secure the information it desired despite requests not only through the mail but also in many instances telephone calls. The cut off date for accepting information for the book was June 30, 1999.

As was the case with the earlier edition of *Life Sketches,* many of the pastors are represented not only by biographical sketches but by pictures as well. To have one's picture included in the new edition of *Life Sketches,* the committee concluded a pastor must: (1) have qualified for a picture in the 1966 edition of *Life Sketches*, (2) have held a major denominational office, or (3) have been ordained prior to June 30, 1959, (4) have served at least 20 years in ordained ministry in the North Carolina or Tennessee Synod and have a total of at least 40 years in ordained ministry. Pastors having served some of their ordained years in another denomination had those years counted toward the 40 year requirement provided their concluding years of ordained ministry were spent in the Evangelical Lutheran Church in America or a predecessor body. Armed Forces chaplains were credited with service in the North Carolina Synod for the time they were on the roster of the North Carolina Synod, irrespective of where they were assigned for duty.

It was not always possible to identify accurately congregations served by pastors in the early Nineteenth Century. It was commonplace for clergy to serve several congregations at one time, but the lines of such "parishes" were often fluid and subject to frequent modification. In some instances the "churches" served were not formally organized as congregations, some being what would later be designated "preaching points." Where preaching points did not develop into fully organized congregations, identification was especially problematic, despite the helpful assistance of current synodical officials.

The Office of the Bishop, now occupied by Leonard H. Bolick, D.Min., has continued its strong support for the work of the Committee. The Assistant to the Bishop helpfully working directly with the Committee on Historical Work during the final preparation of this volume was Pastor George L. Rhyne. While many persons have contributed to this volume by providing information, suggestions and recommendations, the organizing of the data and the preparation of the copy for printing has been chiefly the work of the editor, Eleanor E. Sifford, and the Committee's chief computer wizard, Bernard William Cruse, Jr. Their hours invested in this project have been extremely generous. Committee members during the period of this volume's preparation are noted in the Acknowledgments.

Those who prepared the 1966 edition of *Life Sketches* did their work well and that volume served its purpose for three and a half decades. It is the hope of the Committee on Historical Work that many using this volume will find it a worthy successor to its predecessor. With the publication of this volume, the Committee will now have as the primary focus for its work the preparation of the third volume of the trilogy envisioned in the 1980s, a volume of historical sketches briefly telling the story of the individual congregations comprising the synod.

Raymond M. Bost, Chair
The Committee on Historical Work
July, 2001

Bishop Michael Conway Dixon McDaniel
with LCA Ecumenical Director Dr. William G. Rusch
and Vatican Official Father John Rodano
and Pope John Paul II
at St. Peters Vatican in Papal Library, September 1985
First Visit Between Lutheran Bishop in USA and Pope

Ministers of the Evangelical Lutheran Tennessee Synod Convened at Holly Grove Church, Davidson County
November 8, 1889

1. John Melanchthon Smith
2. Robert Anderson Yoder
3. John Franklin Moser
4. William Pinckney Cline
5. Jacob Killian Efird
6. Andrew Leonhardt Crouse
7. Jerome Paul Stirewalt
8. Jason Chrysostom Moser

9. David Isaiah Offman
10. Robert Henry Cline
11. Eli Lot Lybrand
12. James Albert Cromer
13. Charles Herman Bernheim
14. John Nathaniel Stirewalt
15. John Anderson Rudisill
16. James Presley Price

17. Polycarp Cyprian Henkel
18. Irenaeus Conder
19. Timothy Moser
20. Jesse Reuben Peterson
21. William Leo Darr
22. Jefferson Polycarp Miller
23. John (Joseph) Miller, I
24. Marcus Lafayette Little

FOREWORD

"For I handed on to you as of first importance what I in turn had received: that Christ died for our sins in accordance with the Scriptures, and that he was buried, and that he was raised on the third day in accordance with the Scriptures, and that he appeared to Cephas, then to the twelve." 1 Corinthians 15:3-5

When Paul wrote those words to the church of God in Corinth, about 40 A.D., he provided our earliest written creed. That Good News of the Resurrection Faith has moved through the corridors of time. That News is who we are and what we share.

By 1743 Lutherans were sharing that Good News in permanent settlements in North Carolina, and in 1803 the North Carolina Synod was established. Five of the nine articles in the Constitution of the new synod dealt with the preparation for ordained ministry and providing pastors for congregations.

In these pages we note with thanksgiving those men and women who have answered the call of God through the church to share the faith of God's love through Christ as they celebrate Word and Sacrament. The North Carolina Synod is blessed beyond measure by those who serve as pastors, and by their families and the congregations and institutions they serve.

Bishop Leonard H. Bolick

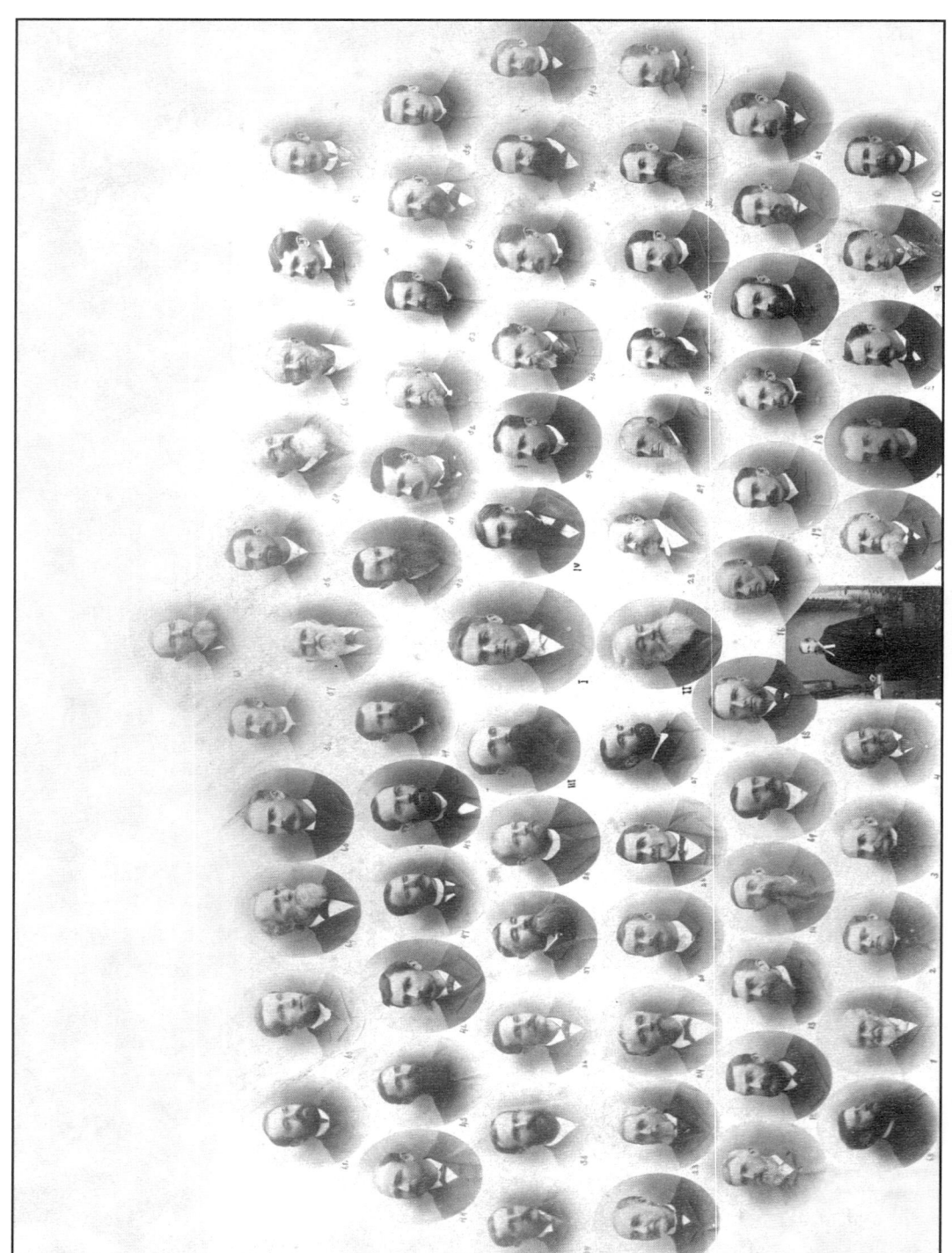

Evangelical Lutheran United Synod of the South
1891

OFFICERS:

I. Rev. E. T. Horn, D.D., President
II. Rev. W. B. Yonce, Ph.D., Vice President
III. Rev. A. L. Crouse, Secretary
IV. Prof. W. A. Barrier, Treasurer

DELEGATES:

1. Rev. W. Kimball
2. Rev. C. A. Rose
3. Capt. T. L. Seigle
4. Capt. J. A. Fisher
5. Rev. F. W. E. Peschau
6. Col. P. N. Heilig
7. Rev. W. G. Campbell
8. T. Z. Schultz, Esq.
9. W. H. Strauss, Esq.
10. Rev. L. A. Fox, D.D.
11. Capt. G. D. Groover
12. Rev. H. S. Wingard
13. Rev. W. S. Bowman, D.D.
14. Hon. H. C. McAllister
15. H. Vollers, Esq.
16. Rev. Geo. H. Cox
17. Rev. W. R. Brown
18. Rev. S. L. Keller
19. Rev. J. A. Bushnell
20. Rev. W. E. Hubbert
21. Hon. H. S. Trout
22. Hon. H. A. Meetz
23. Capt. H. H. Folk
24. C. Wulbern, Esq.
25. Rev. Dr. J. E. Berley
26. Maj. P. E. Wise
27. A. H. Kohn, Esq.
28. Rev. G. W. Holland, D.D.
29. Rev. J. Hawkins, D.D.
30. Rev. C. A. Marks
31. Dr. O. B. Mayer, Jr.
32. Rev. E. A. Wingard
33. J. Cappelman, Esq
34. Dr. R. F. Davis
35. Rev. W. J. Smith
36. Mr. W. M. Bucher
37. Rev. J. A. Snyder
38. Rev. L. G. M. Miller
39. Rev. L. L. Smith
40. Capt. T. H. Zittle
41. Rev. T. O. Keister
42. Mr. L. E. Grosch
43. Mr. C. W. Heater
44. Rev. J. H. Wilson
45. Rev. M. L. Little
46. C. M. Efird, Esq.
47. Rev. J. K. Efird
48. Rev. J. S. Koiner
49. Rev. J. C. Moser
50. Mr. T. S. Shank
51. A. L. Henkel, Esq.
52. Rev. C. H. Bernheim
53. Rev. W. P. Cline
54. Mr. J. S. Lipe
55. Rev. J. A. Rudisill
56. Rev. J. S. Moser
57. Col. C. E. Crowell
58. Mr. M. L. Mosteller
59. Rev. J. K. Hancher
60. Rev. A. J. Brown, D.D.
61. Rev. J. N. Derrick

VISITORS:

62. Rev. R. C. Holland
63. Rev. S. B. Barnitz
64. Rev. F. W. Conrad, D.D., L.L.D.
65. Rev. L. K. Probst
66. Rev. W. L. Darr

ABBE, PAUL VINSON
Date/Place of Birth: November 17, 1953; Omaha, Douglas County, Neb.
Parents: Reese Raymond Abbe and Janice Ann (Prentice) Abbe.
Spouse/Marriage Date: Marie (Lutz) Abbe; June 15, 1991 in Boca Raton, Fla.
Education: Washburn University; Appalachian Bible College; Miami Christian College, B.A. Biblical Studies 1985; Concordia Seminary; Chicago Seminary, M.Div. Systematic Theology 1991.
Ordination: August 28, 1992 by North Carolina Synod.
Calls: Holy Trinity, Raleigh, 1992-.
Other: United States Air Force, 1974-80.

ABEE, CRAIG KENNETH
Date/Place of Birth: February 12, 1962; Charlotte, N.C.
Parents: Russell Blair Abee, Sr., and Ethel (Dugas) Abee.
Spouse/Marriage Date: Ginny (Sigmon) Abee; May 7, 1994.
Education: Francis Marion University, B.A. History 1986; Philadelphia Seminary, 1987-88; Lutheran Theological Southern Seminary, M.Div. 1992.
Ordination: May 21, 1993 by North Carolina Synod.
Calls: Christ, Greensboro, 1993-.
Other: Lutheridge-Lutherock Staff; Youth Staffer for Iowa Synod, 1984-86; Lutheran Church in America Division for Parish Services, Coordinator of Youth Staffer Program, 1986-87; Youth Ministry Coordinator for South Carolina Synod, 1989-91.

ABRAHAM, JEROME MARTIN
Date/Place of Birth: April 5, 1950; Washington, D.C.
Parents: Sidney Abraham and Frieda (Bass) Abraham.
Spouse/Marriage Date: Jill Abraham; August 11, 1984 in Morehead City, N.C.
Education: University of Maryland, B.A. 1972; Gettysburg Seminary, M.Div. 1978; graduate work at State University of New York at Buffalo, M.A. 1982.
Ordination: 1978 in Pennsylvania by Upper New York Synod.
Calls: Kensington, Buffalo, N.Y., 1978-82; transferred to North Carolina Synod as Chaplain, U.S. Army, Fort Bragg, Fayetteville, 1983-86; transferred to Indiana-Kentucky Synod, 1986.
Other: Removed from roll 1993 Lake Worth, Fla. Pastor Abraham was a convert from Judaism.

ADDERHOLDT, CLARENCE CECIL
Date/Place of Birth: May 10, 1919; Hudson, Caldwell County, N.C.
Parents: Daniel Emmanuel Adderholdt and Alice (Brown) Adderholdt.
Spouse/Marriage Date: Youthalene (Nifong) Adderholdt; June 14, 1952 in Thomasville, N.C.
Children: Miriam Renee, Mark Pierre.
Education: Two years Mars Hill College; Appalachian State Teachers College, B.S. 1942; Gettysburg Seminary, B.D. 1949; graduate study at University of North Carolina and Duke University.
Ordination: 1949 by North Carolina Synod.
Calls: Lebanon-Silver Valley, Davidson County, 1949-52; Pastor to Lutheran students, Duke University, for five months in 1950; U.S. Air Force Chaplain, 1951-53;

Amity-Lebanon, Rowan County, 1953-54; St. David, Kannapolis, 1954-58; Messiah, Salisbury, 1959-63. Transferred to Southeastern Synod, Holy Trinity, Springfield, Ga., 1963. *Date of Death/Burial Location*: September 27, 1978; Tullahoma, Tenn.

ADDISON, FLOYD, JR.

Date/Place of Birth: December 18, 1937; Atlanta, Ga.
Parents: Floyd Addison, Sr. and LouRene (Marshall) Addison.
Spouse/Marriage Date: Judith (Fries) Addison; January 30, 1965 in Buffalo, N.Y.
Children: Mary Catherine Bergman; Andrew John Addison, David Michael Addison.
Education: Emory-at-Oxford and Emory University, B.A. 1958; Philadelphia Seminary, M.Div. 1962.
Ordination: June 17, 1962 by Georgia-Alabama Synod.
Calls: Holy Trinity, Elberton, Ga., 1962-64; Resurrection, Buffalo, N.Y., 1964-66; Emanuel, Corning, N.Y., 1966-72; Gilead-Evangelical-Raymertown, Troy, N.Y., 1972-77; Assistant Administrator of Lutheran Social Services, Jamestown, N.Y., 1977-86; Administrator of Hickory Unit of Lutheran Services for the Aging, Hickory, N.C., 1986-90; President-Chief Executive Officer of the Virginia Lutheran Homes, Inc., Roanoke, Va., 1990-.

ADDY, ROBERT ADAIR

Date/Place of Birth: May 29, 1935; Richland County, S.C.
Parents: J. G. Addy and Hazel (Odom) Addy.
Spouse/Marriage Date: Annie Ruth (Amick) Addy; June 8, 1958 in Lexington, S.C.
Children: Paul Robert, Cheryl Lynn.
Education: University of South Carolina, B.S. 1957; Lutheran Theological Southern Seminary, B.D. 1960.
Ordination: May 22, 1960, by South Carolina Synod.
Calls: Trinity, Fairfax, S.C., 1960-62; St. Nicholas, Fairfax, S.C., 1960-62; Faith, Newberry, S.C., 1962-66; Mt. Olive, Hickory, 1966-69.
Other: Evangelism Committee, 1968. Demitted October 1969.

ADERHOLDT, OSCAR WREY, SR.

Date/Place of Birth: July 15, 1883; Gaston County, N.C.
Parents: John A. F. Aderholdt and Barbara (Crouse) Aderholdt.
Spouse/Marriage Date: Genolia Ethel (Powlas) Aderholdt; 1909 in Barber, N.C.; sister of the wives of the Reverend Lawson Pettus Boland, the Reverend John Carnahan Peery, Sr., and the Misses Maude and Annie Powlas.
Children: Virginia Dare, John Paul, Oscar Wrey, Jr., Dorothy Ethel, Charles Bernard, Daniel Franklin.
Education: Lenoir-Rhyne, A.B. 1905; Chicago Seminary, B.D. 1909; Biblical Seminary; Midland College, D.D. 1934.
Ordination: 1909 by Tennessee Synod.
Calls: Chaplain, Passavant Hospital, Chicago, 1907-08; Salem-Grace, Rowan County, 1911-12; St. Mark-Bethel-Bethphage, Lincoln and Gaston Counties, and St. Paul, Crouse, 1915-20; St. John, Statesville, 1920-24; Organ, Rowan County, 1936-1954.   Also

churches in Virginia, Pennsylvania, New Jersey and Kansas. Organized and built two mission churches in Virginia and North Carolina. Retired to Salisbury, N.C., 1954.
Date of Death/Burial Location: Died March 7, 1955 on Ship *Liberte* at sea while returning from visit to a son in Germany; buried March 12, 1955 at St. Mark, Crouse, N.C.

AGNER, TERRY WAYNE
Date/Place of Birth: April 3, 1932; High Point, Guilford County, N.C.
Parents: Roy Augusta Agner and Elsie (Watson) Agner.
First Spouse/Marriage Date: Janice (Clodfelter) Agner; August 26, 1959 in Troutman, N.C.; died November 28, 1988.
Children of First Marriage: John Michael, Amy Gretchen.
Second Spouse/Marriage Date: Nancy (Blackwell) Bourne Agner, May 16, 1992 in Georgetown, S.C.
Education: Lenoir-Rhyne, A.B. 1954; Gettysburg Seminary, B.D. 1958; graduate work at Drew University, 1982-85 and University of North Carolina at Charlotte, 1977-78.
Ordination: June 8, 1958 by North Carolina Synod.
Calls: Board of American Missions, United Lutheran Church in America, Greenville, 1958-60; organized Our Redeemer, Greenville, 1960-62; St. John, Salisbury, 1962-63; St. Mark, China Grove, 1963-69; Secretary of Christian Education for North Carolina Synod, 1969-70; Administrative Assistant to President of North Carolina Synod, 1970-78; Emmanuel, Lincolnton, 1979-97; retired October 1997.
Other: Lutheridge Board of Trustees, 1967-76; Chair of Youth Ministry Committee, 1963-69; Lutheran Church in America Delegate five times; Delegate to North Carolina Council of Churches, nine years; Board of North Carolina Council of Churches, six years. Trustee, Lenoir-Rhyne. Chair of Task Force (Interdenominational) to introduce Good News Bible in North Carolina; Chair of Gaston-Lincoln Mental Health, Retardation and Substance Abuse Board; President, Lincolnton Rotary Club; Board of Habitat for Humanity; Board of Christian Ministry of Lincoln County; Board of Good Neighbor Shop of Lincolnton; Lincoln County Strategic Planning Task Force; Lincoln Medical Center Development Board.

ALDRICH, NICODEMUS (NATHAN, NICHOLAS)
Date/Place of Birth: January 14, 1816; Charleston, S.C.
Parents: Robert Aldrich and Ann H. (Lebby) Aldrich.
Spouse/Marriage Date: Elizabeth (Stroebel) Aldrich; November 1, 1838 in Charleston, S.C.
Children: Two sons.
Education: Prepared for college at the South Carolina Society School in Charleston, S.C. Attended Bristol College in Pennsylvania. Completed theological studies under Dr. Barnwell of The Episcopal Church in 1840.
License/Ordination: Licensed in 1840 by Dr. John Bachman and ordained in 1841 by South Carolina Synod.
Calls: In Georgia and South Carolina, 1841-59; Ascension, Savannah, Ga., 1841-47; supplied Lutherans in Graniteville area, 1854-56; Charleston, S.C., 1857-59; St. John, Salisbury, 1865-67; St. Mark's, Charlotte, 1865-74; Vandalia, Ill., 1874-77; St. Matthew,

Kings Mountain, 1880; in Virginia, 1880-84.

Other: President, North Carolina Synod, 1867, Secretary, 1868. President of the Organizing Convention, General Synod South in the Confederate States of America and first president, 1863. Delegate to General Synod South, 1868. Principal of Academy for Young Ladies at Edgefield, S.C., 1847-54. General Agent of the American Tract Society for South Carolina, 1856-58. Agent for Newberry College from 1858 until outbreak of the Civil War. In 1861 served as Chaplain of the First South Carolina Regiment. Chair of the Mecklenburg Bible Society and Editor of *The Evangelical Lutheran,* 1867. Co-editor, *The Southern Lutheran* and *The Evangelical Lutheran.*

Date of Death/Burial Location: Died 1886; Charlotte, N.C.

ALEXANDER, BEVERLY JANE DENNIS

Date/Place of Birth: October 15, 1953; Richland County, S.C.

Parents: Robert Z. Dennis Alexander and Helen (Balentine) Alexander.

Education: University of South Carolina, B.S. Biology 1975; graduate work at University of South Carolina, M.S. Biology 1977; Lutheran Theological Southern Seminary, M.Div. 1981.

Ordination: May 24, 1981 by South Carolina Synod.

Calls: St. Paul, Richland, S.C., 1981-85; Holy Trinity, Campus Pastor for North Carolina State University, Raleigh, 1985-.

ALEXANDER, JOHN NAIL

Ordination: May 25, 1980 by North Carolina Synod.

Other: Transferred to New Jersey Synod, June 8, 1980. Transferred to Waterloo Lutheran Seminary in Waterloo, Ontario, Canada.

ALKSNIS, TALLY

Date/Place of Birth: July 19, 1927; Riga, Latvia, and was a refugee after World War II, living in Charlotte, N.C.

Parents: John Alksnis and Elza (Upenieks) Alksnis.

Spouse/Marriage Date: Irene (Kazaks) Alksnis of Riga, Latvia, January 29, 1950 in Charlotte, N.C.

Child: Ingrid.

Education: University of Erlangen, Germany, 1946-49; Lutheran Theological Southern Seminary, B.D. 1953, graduate study also.

Ordination: 1953 by North Carolina Synod.

Calls: Pelion Parish, Pelion, S.C., 1953-55; Union-Mt. Hebron Parish, Leesville, S.C., 1956-66, transferred to Wisconsin Evangelical Lutheran Synod in 1966.

Other: Demitted July 3, 1966 at Menominee, Mich.

ALLEN, ROBERT EUGENE

Date/Place of Birth: September 1, 1940; Clinton, Laurens County, S.C.

Parents: Carl Andy Allen and Ollie (Wilkerson) Allen.

Spouse/Marriage Date: Nancy Lea (Huggins) Allen; June 11, 1966 in Hickory, N.C.

Children: Rachel Elizabeth, Timothy Paul.

Education: Lenoir-Rhyne, A.B. 1962; Lutheran Theological Southern Seminary, B.D. 1966; Emory- Columbia Presbyterian, M.Th. 1970.
Ordination: June 5, 1966 by South Carolina Synod.
Calls: Faith, Savannah, Ga., 1966-68; St. Paul, Decatur, Ga., 1968-72; St. Matthew, Kings Mountain, 1972- 77; St. James, Fayetteville, 1977-84; Ascension, Savannah, Ga., 1984-.
Other: Parish Education, World Missions, and Music and Worship Committees of the Southeastern Synod. Chair of the Music and Worship Committees of the North Carolina Synod, 1977-83; Chair-Coordinator for Induction of the Bishop, 1978, 1982; Chair of the Ordination Task Force, 1980-81; Convention Planning Committee, 1979-83; Chair of committee to introduce *Lutheran Book of Worship,* 1976-80; Cabinet for Parish Services, 1977-83; Task Force on Applying Our Theology to a Changing World, 1980-83; Chaplain-in- Residence, Lenoir-Rhyne, 1981. Chaplain, Music Week at Lutheridge, 1980-82; Guest Preacher, Convocations for Worship, Music and the Arts, Lutheran Theological Southern Seminary, 1980, and St. John, Salisbury, 1982; Contributing author to *Journal of Church Music; Pulpit Digest, Light for Today* and *Home Altar*; Mayor's Committee for Urban Renewal, Kings Mountain, 1973-77; Member, Lutheran Church in America, Drafting Committee of Lutheran-Episcopal Dialogue for Drafting the Theological Affinities between the Two Communions.

ALLRAN, WAYNE SULLIVAN

Date/Place of Birth: January 27, 1932; Cherryville, N.C.
Parents: Howard Wayne Allran and Dorothy (Sullivan) Allran.
Spouse/Marriage Date: Barbara Ada (Ritchie) Allran, daughter of the Reverend C. Ross Ritchie, November 17, 1961.
Education: Lenoir-Rhyne, A.B. 1954; Lutheran Theological Southern Seminary, B.D. 1957, M.Div.
Ordination: June 9, 1957 by North Carolina Synod.
Calls: Christ, East Spencer, 1957-58; First, Greensboro, 1958-61; Pastor-Developer, St. Timothy, Tarpon Springs, Fla., 1961-63; Trinity, Bradenton, Fla., 1963-.
Date of Death: October 27, 1994.

AMIDON, DAVID JON

Date/Place of Birth: February 14, 1953; Elyria, Ohio.
Parents: Roger Hallman Amidon and Julia Mae (Gotro) Amidon.
Spouse/Marriage Date: The Reverend Diane (Rose) Amidon; June 4, 1977 in Honolulu, Hawaii.
Children: Rebecca Elaine, Michael David.
Education: Juniata College, Pennsylvania, B.A. French/Education 1975; University of Strasbourg, France, 1973-74; University of Hawaii, M.A. French Literature 1977; Lutheran Theological Southern Seminary, M.Div. 1985.
Ordination: June 1985 by North Carolina Synod.
Calls: A Mighty Fortress, Charlotte, 1985-93; Redeemer, Charlotte; Co-Pastor with wife, Good Shepherd, Mt. Holly; Lutheran Church in France (Church of the Augsburg Confession of Alsace and Lorraine) through Division of Global Mission, 1993-96; St. Philip, Raleigh, 1996-.
Other: Chair, Committee on Worship, 1990-93; Lutheran Theological Southern Seminary Board of Directors, 1985-86.

AMIDON, DIANE ELAINE (ROSE)
Date/Place of Birth: May 23, 1950; Oklahoma City, Okla.
Parents: Gale Edwin Rose and Muriel Elaine (Ronk) Rose.
Spouse/Marriage Date: The Reverend David Jon Amidon; June 4, 1977 in Honolulu, Hawaii.
Children: Rebecca Elaine, Michael David.
Education: University of Southern California; University of Hawaii, B.A. Music, 1972; graduate work at University of Hawaii in Musicology, 1972-74; San Jose State, M.A. Vocal Performance 1975; Lutheran Theological Southern Seminary, M.Div. 1993.
Ordination: May 21, 1993 by North Carolina Synod.
Calls: Co-Pastor with husband, Good Shepherd, Mt. Holly; Lutheran Church in France (Church of the Augsburg Confession of Alsace and Lorraine) through Division of Global Mission, 1993-97.
Other: Choir Director at Christ the King, Cary; Music Director, Ascension Lutheran, Columbia, S.C.; CARE staff at Lutheridge, 1986-90.

AMOS, WILLIAM ROBERT
Date/Place of Birth: May 21, 1945 in Volusia County, Fla.
Parents: Robert Edwin Amos and Mary Elizabeth (Campbell) Amos.
Spouse/Marriage Date: Joyce Ann (Shroads) Amos; May 31, 1973 in Miami, Fla.
Education: University of North Carolina, B.A. 1966; Florida State University, M.S. 1967; Asbury Seminary, M.Div. 1971; graduate work at Lutheran Theological Southern Seminary, 1973-74, 1967.
Ordination: May 31, 1974 by North Carolina Synod.
Calls: Faith, Jacksonville, Fla. Transferred to American Evangelical Lutheran Church in 1979.

ANDERSON, BRUCE PALMER
Date/Place of Birth: May 4, 1933 in Hennepin County, Minn.
Parents: Robert Albin Anderson and Effie (Nugent) Anderson.
Children: Lisa Marie, Susan Anderson Guthrie, Jonathan Bruce.
Education: Carleton, B.A. 1955; Drew Seminary, B.D. 1960; Garrett Seminary, 1955-56; Chicago Seminary, 1956-7.
Ordination: 1960 by Ohio Annual Conference.
Calls: Christ the King, Centerville, Ohio, 1962-65; Gethsemane, Hopkins, Minn., 1965-66; Bethel, Salisbury, 1990-93; Philadelphia, Pa., 1993.

ANDERSON, LISA CHRISTINE
Date/Place of Birth: July 9, 1962; Brockton, Mass.
Parents: Frederick R. Anderson and Phyllis M. Anderson.
Education: Bridgewater State College, B.S. Professional Chemistry 1984; Lutheran Theological Southern Seminary, M.Div. 1998; graduate work at Worcester Polytechnic Institute and Bridgewater State College.
Ordination: June 6, 1998 by North Carolina Synod.
Calls: Augsburg, Winston-Salem, 1998-.

ANDERSON, ROBERT EMORY

Date/Place of Birth: December 13, 1919; Plymouth, Mass.
Parents: Carl Herman Anderson and Agnes (Olive) Anderson.
Spouse/Marriage Date: Maude A. (Nelson) Anderson; May 21, 1944 in Philadelphia, Pa.
Children: Richard H., Pamela Sigg, Christine Hatemi.
Education: Upsala College, A.B. 1947; Union Seminary, B.D. 1950.
Ordination: 1951 by Central Pennsylvania Synod.
Calls: Reformation, Media, Pa., 1950-1980, Pastor Emeritus, 1981.
Other: Transferred and retired to North Carolina Synod in 1985; Author of *Sentence Sermons*, 1972, and *Invitation to Commune*, 1980.
Date of Death/Burial Location: November 9, 1989; Evergreen City Cemetery in Charlotte, N.C.

ANTHONY, JACOB BROWN

Date/Place of Birth: October 30, 1808 and baptized about 1814 or 1815 by the Reverend Robert J. Miller.
Parents: Mary Anthony.
First Spouse/Marriage Date: Martha (Hardaway) Mitchell Anthony; January 31, 1836; died April 17, 1870.
Children of First Marriage: Emory Morris, Mary Agnes, William Dawson, Catherine Susan, Thomas Theophilus, Martha Roxana, Octavia Elizabeth, Jacob Bachman.
Second Spouse/Marriage Date: Nancy (Nunamaker) Anthony; December 17, 1876.
Ordination: By Methodist Church in 1832. Received by North Carolina Synod in 1844.
Calls: Reformation (New Jerusalem), Mocksville, 1834; St. John, Salisbury, 1845-47; Union, Rowan County, 1845-46; Beck's-Pilgrim, Davidson County, 1847-48; St. Luke, Tyro, 1847-48; New Bethel, Stanly County, 1860-66; St. John, Cabarrus County, 1860-67; St. Michael (Holy Trinity), Troutman, 1878-80; St. Paul, Iredell County, 1880-82. Served churches in South Carolina, 1849-58. According to Bernheim's history, served in Pennsylvania from 1867 to 1877. Also served in the Lovettsville Parish, Loudon County, Va., just south of Frederick, Md. in 1858-59, as a pastor of the North Carolina Synod.
Other: President, The Parent Education and Missionary Society of the North Carolina Synod, 1845, Vice President, 1846; President, North Carolina Synod, 1848 and 1865, Secretary, 1846 and 1864; Secretary, South Carolina Synod, 1851-54, President, 1855-57.
Date of Death/Burial Location: November 20, 1886; Mt. Pleasant, S.C.

AOYAMA, HIKOSHIRO

Date/Place of Birth: 1863; Okazaki, Japan, and baptized January 1877 in another Protestant Church.
Education: Graduated from Tsukiji University; and in theology from McCormick Seminary, Chicago, Ill.
Ordination: Previously ordained as non-Lutheran, 1892. In 1913 (?) was received into Lutheran Church, and in 1917 was enrolled by North Carolina Synod as an ordained minister.
Calls: In Japan labored as an evangelist at Ogura, Nagusaki Prefecture; taught in Wilhelmina Girls High School; Pastor, Hakata Church; Professor, Lutheran Seminary, Kumamoto, 1916; Pastor, Kobe Church, 1937-40. *Other*: One son became a Lutheran pastor in Japan. Treasurer, Joint Ministerium of Evangelical Lutheran Church in Japan, 1926.
Date of Death: December 21, 1944 at Kantizawa, Nagano Prefecture.

ARCHER, FREDERICK MELBOURNE
Date/Place of Birth: October 13, 1938; Rowan County, N.C.
Parents: Fred Marvin Archer and Margaret Pauline (Upright) Archer.
Spouse/Marriage Date: Alice Marie (Gragg) Archer; March 1, 1964 in Fletcher, N.C.
Child: Jennifer Lynne.
Education: Catawba College, A.B. 1961; Lutheran Theological Southern Seminary, B.D. 1964.
Ordination: 1964 by North Carolina Synod.
Calls: St. Luke, Catawba County, 1964-69; Grace, Hendersonville, 1969-72.
Other: Vice President, North Carolina Luther League, 1960-61. Demitted the Ministry, 1972. Became member of Church of the Lutheran Confession. Organized CLC congregation at Hendersonville.

ARENDS, JOHANN GOTTFRIED (Americanized to John Godfrey Arndt)
(See biography in first *Life Sketches, 1966*).
Date/Place of Birth: December 11, 1740; Goettingen, Germany territory of Hannover.
Parents: George Christoph Arends or Simon Christoph Arends (father and brother - not known which was parent).
Spouse/Marriage Date: Hannah Rudisill (Rutenseell) Arends of eastern Lincoln County, October 24, 1776; died 1831.
Children: Catherine Hoover, John, Elizabeth Smith, Hannah Hafner, Susan Sadler, Jacob, Frederick, Mary Cansler.
Education: May have attended the University at Goettingen; Hannover Teachers' Seminary.
Ordination: August 1775 at Second Creek (Organ) Church by Joachim Bulow.
Calls: Organ, Rowan County, 1775-1785; St. John, Salisbury, 1775-1785; Union, Rowan County, 1774-85; Low's, Guilford County, 1774-1789; Beck's, Davidson County, 1775-1785; Pilgrim, Davidson County, ca. 1778; Shiloh, Forsyth County, ca. 1777; Frieden's, Guilford County, 1775-1785; St. Paul, Alamance County, 1775-1789; Lutheran Chapel, China Grove, 1780-1789; Philadelphia, Gaston County, 1785-1807; Daniel's, Lincoln County, 1785-1807; Emmanuel, Lincolnton, 1785-1807; Grace, Catawba County, 1797-1807; Nazareth, Rural Hall, 1787-1788; St. Luke (Ore Bank), Lincoln County, 1785-1807; St. Paul, Newton, Catawba County, 1785-1807; St. John (The Lutheran Church-Missouri Synod), Catawba County, ca. 1790; Salem, Lincoln County, 1785-1807; Bethel, Gaston County, 1790-1807; St. Mark, Gaston County, 1791-1803; Zion, Catawba County, 1790-1807.
Other: First president of the North Carolina Lutheran Synod in 1803, the first Lutheran ordained in the state, and the "father of the Lutheran Church beyond the Catawba River." He was the teacher who came with Nussmann in a team from the German mother church in 1773 in response to the plea of the North Carolina Lutherans in 1771. May have also served as a practical physician, distributed books from Germany and served as an informal banker.
Date of Death/Burial Location: July 9, 1807; Emmanuel Church Cemetery, Lincolnton, N.C.

AREY, BENJAMIN
Date/Place of Birth: May 3, 1810, in Rowan County, of German ancestry, by way of Scotland, Wales, and Martha's Vineyard, Mass. His grandfather, Abram, settled in Rowan

County several years before the War of Independence. A sister, Amelia Rosetta, became the second wife of the Reverend Samuel Rothrock.

Parents: Peter Arey and Phoebe (Thomas) Arey.

Spouse: Martha Phoebe (Raynor) Arey of Philadelphia, Pa. April 19, 1836; died January 9, 1876.

Children: Theophilus and Charles M. (both died September 17, 1862 in battle at Antietam, Md.), Luther M. (died of war wounds, 1870), Harriett N., Edwin E., Alice M. Goodman, Benjamin E., Mary Jane White, Laura, Ellen E. Erwin, William H.

Education: Gettysburg College, 1833; Gettysburg Seminary, 1836.

Ordination/License: Licensed in 1836 and ordained in 1838 by North Carolina Synod.

Calls: Beck's-Pilgrim-St. Luke, St. Luke, Davidson County, 1837; New Bethel, Stanly County, 1837-38; St. Michael, Troutman, 1837-53; St. Matthew, Rowan County, 1838-41, St. Paul, Rowan County, 1843-45; St. Matthew, Davie County, 1840-45; organized St. Paul, Iredell County, 1840-46; Beth Eden, Newton, 1848-49. No record of pastoral service, 1853-82.

Other: Elected a delegate to the General Synod in 1849; President, North Carolina Synod, 1849; requested dismissal from the Lutheran clergy so that he could devote full time to farming and to providing a living for his large family. The 1860 Census lists him as being in Iredell County. After leaving the Lutheran clergy, he and family joined Bethesda Presbyterian Church, being a member for over 25 years and serving as a deacon.

Date of Death/Burial Location: February 12, 1882; Bethesda Presbyterian Church Cemetery, Iredell County, N.C.

ARMSTRONG, GEORGE ANDREAS

Date/Place of Birth: June 30, 1955 in San Francisco, Calif.

Parents: George A. Armstrong and ? (Schwab) Armstrong.

Spouse/Marriage Date: Gretchen (Kuhrmann) Armstrong; January 10, 1982 in Vienna, Va.

Children: Matthias Andreas, Marijke Rita.

Education: Newberry College, B.S. 1977; Trinity Seminary, M.Div. 1981.

Ordination: January 3, 1982 by Virginia Synod (American Lutheran Church-Eastern District).

Calls: St. John, (American Lutheran Church), Gillespie, Texas, 1982-86; Frieden's, Gibsonville, 1987-91. Transferred to Metro District of Columbia Synod 1991 to restart mission church, Holy Spirit, in Centerville, Va.

Other: Elections Chair of Southern District, American Lutheran Church, 1985.

ARNDT, JAMES ALLEN

Date/Place of Birth: April 29, 1871; Newton, N.C.

Parents: John M. Arndt and Malinda (Huit) Arndt. Great-grandson of the Reverend John Gottfried Arends.

Spouse/Marriage Date: Rosabelle (Reinhardt) Arndt; June 18, 1902 in Iron Station, N.C.

Education: Concordia College, Lenoir-Rhyne, A.B. 1892; Chicago Seminary, 1895.

License/Ordination: Licensed in 1895 and ordained 1898 by Tennessee Synod.

Calls: New Jerusalem, Davidson County; Emmanuel, Lincolnton; St. Luke, Iron Station; Salem, Lincoln County. Transferred to Southwest Virginia Synod, 1903; St. Paul, Rural Retreat, Va., 1903-05. Returned to Tennessee Synod 1906 and served Mt. Calvary, Claremont; St. James-Ebenezer, Newton, until his death.

Date of Death/Burial Location: June 30, 1909; St. James Cemetery, Newton, N.C.

ARNDT, JOHN GODFREY
(See Arends, Johann Gottfied)

ARRUZA, ANDREW LOUIS
Date/Place of Birth: January 26, 1940; Dutchess County, N.Y.
Parents: Leocadio Arruza and Margarite (Franco) Arruza.
First Spouse/Marriage Date: Esther D. (Holt) Arruza; April 24, 1960.
Second Spouse/Marriage Date: Palmer (Alsobrook) Arruza; August 3, 1973.
Children: Angela Theresa, Susan Elaine, Andrew Leocadio, Randall Lee Rich (stepson).
Education: Lenoir-Rhyne, A.B. 1974; Lutheran Theological Southern Seminary, M. Div. 1979.
Ordination: February 4, 1979 by North Carolina Synod.
Calls: Our Savior, Jacksonville, 1979-80; U.S. Army Chaplain, 1980-83.
Other: Coastal Committee Member, North Carolina Refugee Advocacy Committee. On leave from call, 1983-87.

ARTZ, WILLIAM A.
Date/Place of Birth: June 1, 1804; Maryland.
First Spouse/Marriage Date: Sarah (Sally) (Troxlar) Artz of Orange County; October 20, 1829; died September 20, 1867.
Children of First Marriage: Emily Huffman, Sarah A. Troxlar, William P., George, John D., Susan, Frances.
Second Spouse: Susan (Carriker) Artz of Cabarrus County.
Children of Second Marriage: Ann E. Lee, James, Tom, Daniel E.
Education: Gettysburg Seminary, 1829.
License/Ordination: Licensed in 1830 and ordained in 1831 by North Carolina Synod.
Calls: Frieden's-Coble's-Low's, Guilford County, 1829-53; Richland, Randolph County, 1830-52; St. Paul, Alamance County, 1830-52/54; Union, Rowan County, 1843; Lutheran Chapel, China Grove, 1859-61; St. Matthew, Rowan County, 1864; Organ, Rowan County, 1866-67.
Other: Ill health at times interrupted his labors. Not active after 1867. Served seven one-year terms as President of North Carolina Synod, 1836-59; Secretary, 1832-34, Treasurer, 1835. Member of original Board of Trustees, North Carolina College, 1859.
Date of Death/Burial Location: April 19, 1876; St. John, Cabarrus County, N.C.

ASCARZA, MARILYN T.
Spouse/Marriage Date: Manuel Ascarza.
Education: University of Virginia, M.A. 1971; University of Virginia, Ph.D. 1975.
Ordination: September 1990 by North Carolina Synod.
Calls: Christ Lutheran Church, Charlotte, 1990-.

ASHBY, MARTIN ALEXANDER
Date/Place of Birth: October 10, 1868; Culpeper, Va.
Parents: John A. Ashby and Nannie Virginia (Roudabush) Ashby.
Spouse/Marriage Date: Ida Rebecca (Pence) Ashby; June 1, 1893 in Broadway, Va.; died

February 11, 1950.
Children: Wilma Grant Rogers, Paul Revere.
Education: University of Richmond, A.B. 1892; D.D. 1936; Mt. Airy Seminary, 1895; University of Virginia, A.M. 1898; University of Chicago, Ph.D. 1901.
Ordination: 1895 by Joint Synod of Ohio.
Calls: Lutheran Chapel, Monterey, Va., 1895-97; Holy Trinity-Lutheran Chapel, Gastonia, 1912-13; Grace, Bessemer City, for six months in 1912; Humbolt Park, Chicago, Ill., 1898-1901; St. Paul, Grove Hill, Md. and St. Peter, Shenandoah, Va., 1801-1912; St. Paul, Alica, Va., and Toms Brook, Va., 1920-22; Boonsboro, Md., 1922-44; retired 1944 at Shenandoah, Va.
Other: President, Virginia Conference, Tennessee Synod; Delegate, Tennessee Synod, to merger convention, United Lutheran Church in America, 1918. President, Western Conference, Maryland. With Dr. Richard Sadeller Patterson, organized Maryland Synod Sunday School Association in 1927 and served as President, 1927-36.
Date of Death/Burial Location: October 5, 1956; Boonsboro, Md.

AULL, WILLIAM BOWMAN
Date/Place of Birth: March 19, 1870; Pomaria, S.C.
Parents: J. L. Aull and Julia (Haltiwanger) Aull.
Spouse/Marriage Date: Mabel (Deal) Aull from Landis, N.C., sister of the Reverend J. F. Deal; May 19, 1909.
Children: Sara, Eileen, Margaret, Mabel, Helen, Rowena, William, Arthur.
Education: Had three months of schooling each year until the sixth grade. Newberry College, A.B. 1897; Lutheran Theological Southern Seminary, 1901; Chicago Seminary, B.D. 1904; Lenoir-Rhyne, D.D. 1954.
Ordination: 1901 by Virginia Synod.
Calls: In Virginia, 1901-3; in South Carolina, 1904-7, 1910-13, and Walhalla, 1915-39, serving St. John some years and later as postmaster; in North Carolina: St. Mark, China Grove, 1907-10; Silver Valley, Davidson County, 1942-43; retired 1939 at Landis, N.C., and supplied for varying periods as many as twenty churches in Rowan and adjacent counties, until assuming pastorate at St. Paul, Iredell County, 1950-57.
Other: Secretary, South Carolina Synod, 1912-18. Author of booklet, "Thinking in Theology." President, Piedmont Conference of the South Carolina Synod.
Death/Burial Location: April 12, 1957; China Grove, N.C.

BADER, MARY ANNA
See Schimel, Mary Anna (Bader)
Date/Place of Birth: October 26, 1961; New York City, N.Y.
Parents: The Reverend Sylvester Bader and Anna (Nikodem) Bader.
Spouse/Marriage Date: Marty (Schimel) Bader; November 11, 1995.
Education: Houghton College, B.S. Psychology 1983; Lutheran Theological Southern Seminary, M.Div. 1987; Chicago Seminary, Th.M. 1993, Th.D. Hebrew and Hebrew Bible.
Ordination: 1987 by North Carolina Synod.
Calls: St. Paul, Durham, 1987-90; Pilgrim Lutheran, Chicago, Ill., 1991; Sts. Peter and Paul, Riverside, Ill., 1994-96.

BAILEY, CARL LYNN
Date/Place of Birth: March 12, 1944; Lubbock, Texas.
Parents: Carl Bailey and Marguerite (Sivells) Bailey.
Spouse/Marriage Date: Martha (Busby) Bailey; December 26, 1971.
Child: George Christopher.
Education: Texas Tech University, B.Mus. 1967; Lutheran Theological Southern Seminary, M.Div. 1984, D.Min. 1993; Union Seminary of New York, Master of Sacred Music 1970. Additional study at Royal Conservatory of Denmark; organ study in Paris.
Ordination: August 11, 1984 by North Carolina Synod.
Calls: Christ, Charlotte, 1984-90; Reformation, Columbia, S.C., 1990-95; St. Johannes, Charleston, S.C., 1995-.

BAILEY, STEPHEN C.
Date/Place of Birth: January 12, 1947; Long Beach, Calif.
Parents: Kenneth L. Bailey and Helen E. (Brehm) Bailey.
Spouse/Marriage Date: Jane (Wescott) Bailey; June 6, 1969 in Lincoln, Neb.
Child: Alyson Jean.
Education: University of Nebraska, B.S. 1970; Lutheran Theological Southern Seminary, M.Div. 1987.
Ordination: August 30, 1987 by South Carolina Synod.
Calls: St. Stephen, Lexington, S.C., 1987-1990; Faith, Conover, 1990-.
Other: Dropped from roll, February 16, 1996.

BAKER, BOBBY GENE
Date/Place of Birth: November 9, 1952; Concord, N.C.
Parents: Martin F. Baker and Rosa (Gregory) Baker.
Spouse/Marriage Date: Clara P. Baker; December 28, 1991.
Child: Matthew Gene.
Education: Lenoir-Rhyne, A.B. History 1975; Lutheran Theological Southern Seminary, M.Div. 1979; graduate work at The Citadel, 1984-85.
Ordination: June 10, 1979 by North Carolina Synod.
Calls: St. James, Rockwell, 1979-80; Cold Water, Concord, 1981; Good Shepherd, Walterboro, S.C., 1982- 89; Chester-York Parish, Chester-York, S.C., 1990-1991; Abiding Presence, York, S.C., 1992-.

BAKER, HOWARD GLENN
Date/Place of Birth: February 14, 1955; Concord, N.C.
Parents: Martin Flowe Baker and Rosa Jane (Gregory) Baker.
Spouse/Marriage Date: Susan Carol (Brown) Baker; July 12, 1980.
Children: Michael Jacob, Christy Dawn.
Education: Lenoir-Rhyne, A.B. History 1977; Lutheran Theological Southern Seminary, M.Div. 1981.
Ordination: 1981 by North Carolina Synod.
Calls: Holy Cross, Mocksville, 1981-83; Mt. Moriah, China Grove, 1983-89; Organ, Salisbury, 1991-1994; St. Stephen, Gold Hill and Organ, Salisbury, 1992; Mt. Olive, Mt. Pleasant, 1995.
Other: Eagle Scout, Vigil Honor, Order of Arrow, Boy Scouts.

BALLARD, BRIAN NEAL
Spouse/Marriage Date: Carolyn (Stenberg) Ballard; December 17, 1994.
Education: Lenoir-Rhyne, B.A. Psychology, 1992; Lutheran Theological Southern Seminary, M.Div. 1997.
Ordination: September 21, 1997 by North Carolina Synod.
Calls: Family of Faith, Harrisburg, 1997-.
Other: Volunteer with Habitat for Humanity in Guatemala; Mental Health Worker, Charter Hospital, 1992- 93.

BALLARD, RICHARD GENE
Date/Place of Birth: January 15, 1959; Asheville, N.C.
Spouse/Marriage Date: The Reverend Ruth A. (Holland) Ballard; December 27, 1981 in Asheville, N.C.
Education: Mars Hill College, B.A. Religion and Philosophy 1979; Clinical Pastoral Education at North Carolina Memorial Hospital, Chapel Hill, Summer, 1980; Lutheran Theological Southern Seminary, M.Div. 1983, D.Min. 1989; University of South Carolina, M.Ed. Secondary Guidance and Counseling 1986.
Ordination: July 3, 1983 by North Carolina Synod.
Calls: Mt. Olivet, Chapin, S.C., 1983-1988; Mt. Hermon, Peak, S.C., 1983-1988; St. Matthew, Granite Falls, 1988-.

BALLARD, RUTH A. (HOLLAND)
Date/Place of Birth: July 21, 1955; Illinois.
Parents: James N. Holland and Eleanor (Carpenter) Holland.
Spouse/Marriage Date: The Reverend Richard Gene Ballard; December 27, 1981 in Asheville, N.C.
Education: Old Dominion, B.S. 1977; Southeastern Seminary, M.Div. 1980; Lutheran Theological Southern Seminary, Certificate, 1980-81.
Ordination: July 10, 1988 by South Carolina Synod.
Calls: Mt. Olive, Hickory, 1988-91; transferred to Lower Susquehanna Synod, 1991.

BALLENTINE, JACOB LUTHER
Date/Place of Birth: August 1, 1916; Lingle, Miss.
Parents: The Reverend Arthur W. Ballentine and Anna Elizabeth (Derrick) Ballentine.
Spouse/Marriage Date: Frances Lou (Dickson) Ballentine; June 11, 1941 in Columbia, S.C.
Children: Carol Evelyn Steele, Anne Dickson McClellan, Frances Roberta Metts.
Education: Roanoke College, A.B. 1937; Lutheran Theological Southern Seminary, B.D. 1940; graduate study, Chicago Seminary and Lutheran Theological Southern Seminary.
License/Ordination: Licensed 1940 and ordained 1941 by Virginia Synod.
Calls: Corinth-Kimberling-Pleasant Hill, Rural Retreat, Va., 1940-43; St. Mark-St. Andrew, Blythewood, S.C., 1943-48; Christ's, Columbia, S.C. and St. Paul-Bachman Chapel, Pomaria-Prosperity, S.C., 1948-51; Redeemer, Kannapolis, 1951-58; Trinity, Elloree, S.C., 1958-80. Interim pastor for various congregations.
Other: South Carolina Synod Stewardship Committee and Continuing Education Committee; President and Chaplain, Elloree Lions Club. President, Lake Marion Chapter

American Association Retired Persons in Santee, S.C.
Date of Death/Burial Location: April 1, 1986; Trinity Lutheran Church Cemetery, Elloree, S.C.

BAME, PAUL JONAS
Date/Place of Birth: September 20, 1883; Rowan County, N.C.
Parents: Samuel Bame and Laura Jane (Goodman) Bame.
Spouse/Marriage Date: Vallie F. (Barnhardt) Bame; May 14, 1913 in Charlotte, N.C.
Children: Charlotte Berlyn (married the Reverend George W. Lingle), Laura Elizabeth, Eugenia Rodelle, Martha Conrad (married the Reverend B. Paul Huddle).
Education: Newberry College, A.B. 1910; Lutheran Theological Southern Seminary, 1913, B.D., 1927.
Ordination: 1913 by North Carolina Synod.
Calls: Augusta, Ga., 1913-17; in North Carolina, 1917-28; First, Lexington; St. Andrew, Hickory; in Virginia, 1928-59. Retired 1959 at Faith, N.C.
Other: Member, Lenoir-Rhyne Board.
Date of Death/Burial Location: April 23, 1960; Rowan Memorial Park, Salisbury, N.C.

BAME, RICHARD LOUIS
Date/Place of Birth: March 28, 1862; Rowan County, N.C.
Parents: Edward Bame and Margaret L. (Brown) Bame.
Spouse/Marriage Date: Alda C. (Still) Bame; September 20, 1894 in Cabarrus County, N.C.
Children: Elmer A., Mary E., Bertha L.
Education: North Carolina College.
Ordination: 1893 by North Carolina Synod.
Calls: In Illinois, 1894-97; in North Carolina: Bethany, Davidson County; Nazareth-Shiloh, Forsyth County, 1897-99; transferred to Virginia Synod, 1899.
Other: Later joined The Episcopal Church.
Date of Death/Burial Location: August 20, 1915; Little Rock, Ark.

BANSEMER, C. F.
Date/Place of Birth: October 27, 1811; Prussia.
Education: Lutheran Theological Southern Seminary, 1841; North Carolina College, D.D. 1882.
Ordination: 1842 by South Carolina Synod.
Calls: In South Carolina, Mt. Pleasant, Ehrhardt and St. Nicholas, Fairfax, 1842; Principal of a school in the lower part of the state, 1843-circa 1845; Principal in an academy in Chester, 1846-49; Winnsboro, 1849-circa 1853; connected with a private school and Pastor of St. John, Walhalla, 1853-59; Professor Latin and Greek at Newberry College, 1860-63. In Augusta, Ga., 1863-67. President of North Carolina College, 1867-68. In Savannah, Ga., 1869-77. In Florida, 1877-89.
Other: Left Augusta, Ga., 1867 to reportedly become President of North Carolina College, but apparently to succeed Bikle as Principal of The Female Academy. In 1868 wrote to the North Carolina Synod to explain his absence from the convention and to also explain his

reason for not requesting a transfer of his clerical membership from the South Carolina to the North Carolina Synod. "Your committee has no suggestions to make in reference to Bro. Bansemer's letter, but recommend that it be read in open Synod." *Minutes, North Carolina Synod, 1868,* p. 13. The convention accepted Bansemer's reasons for delaying his affiliation, excused his absence, and gave him until the 1869 convention to unite with the North Carolina Synod. *Ibid.,* p. 14.

Date of Death/Burial Location: 1889; buried possibly in Jacksonville, Fla.

BARB, JAMES COLUMBUS

Date/Place of Birth: December 16, 1832; McMinn County, Tenn.

Parents: Abraham Barb and Mary Ann (Miller) Barb.

First Spouse/Marriage Date: Hanna Adeline (McDonald) Barb; June 17, 1862; died July 4, 1891.

Children From First Marriage: Four daughters, two sons, one of them the Reverend Ernest Barb, pastor in Joint Synod of Ohio.

Second Spouse/Marriage Date: Frankie E. (Moser) Barb, January 15, 1896 in Monroe County, Tenn.

Education: Largely self-taught; received D.D. while serving in Indiana.

Ordination: December 19, 1859 by Tennessee Synod.

Calls: Sinking Springs Church, Greene County, Tenn., 1862; Salem, Parrottsville, Tenn., Holston Synod, 1871-76; also served at Solomon in Greene County; St. Mark, Whitestown, Ind., 1883-95; Reformation, Greeneville, Tenn., 1895; in Holston Synod, including Caney Branch Parish in Virginia, at time of death. Also was for two years at Our Saviour, Johnson City and three years at Trinity (later, Good Shepherd), Morristown, Tenn.

Other: Began his career as a teacher in 1848. An organizer of Holston Synod, several times its President. Also, taught in Hiwassee College, Wesleyan Institute, and Mosheim Institute, in Tennessee. Was first Secretary of the Holston Synod. In 1877 became the second president of Mosheim Mosheim Male and Female Institute. Also served as Professor of Moral and Mental Science, and Mathematics. He had his master's degree at this time. Resigned as President of Mosheim Institute (also known as Holston Synodical College), 1880. Reported that he taught at Hiwassee College, Madisonville, Tenn. and at Wesleyan Institute, Athens, Tenn. prior to 1877.

Date of Death/Burial Location: January 23, 1900; Mosheim, Tenn.

BARGER, GLENN LEROY

Date/Place of Birth: May 26, 1905; Faith, N.C.

Parents: Charles Jacob Barger and Carrie Roxie (Kluttz) Barger.

Spouse/Marriage Date: Mary Ethel (Fisher) Barger; October 10, 1933 in Cabarrus County, N.C.

Children: Charles Glenn, Mary Ann, John Michael and Jacob Leroy (twins) died day after birth.

Education: Lenoir-Rhyne, A.B. 1929; Lutheran Theological Southern Seminary, B.D. 1932; graduate study Hamma Divinity School, 1949.

Ordination: July 10, 1932 by North Carolina Synod.

Calls: Trinity-St. Enoch, Concord, 1932-37, Trinity only, 1937-40; Calvary, Concord, 1949-50; St. Stephen, Hickory, 1954-56; St. Andrew, New Bern, 1956-58; Frieden's,

Guilford County, 1959-64. Also, in South Carolina 1940-42 and in Indiana 1947-49. U.S. Navy chaplain in World War II, 1943-47, and Korean Conflict, 1950-54. While at Camp Lejeune assisted in developing Jacksonville Mission, Our Savior, 1952-54; Frieden's, Gibsonville, 1962-64; Trinity, New Smyrna, Fla., 1965-67.
Other: Board, Children's Home of the South, 1962-64; Social Ministry Committee, 1962-3, and North Carolina Council of Churches, 1962-63. Retired December 1967 to Pompano Beach, Fla.
Date of Death/Burial Location: October 27, 1990; Pompano Beach, Fla.

BARNHART, DAVID RALPH

Date/Place of Birth: November 23, 1939; Armstrong County, Pa.
Parents: Ralph J. Barnhart and Helen (Caldwell) Barnhart.
Spouse/Marriage Date: Mary (Nelson) Barnhart; August 16, 1958 in Apollo, Pa.
Children: Ralph Michael, Charles Arthur, Richard Edward.
Education: Clarion State, B.S. 1961; Lutheran Theological Southern Seminary, B.D. 1964, and graduate work.
Ordination: May 25, 1964 by South Carolina Synod.
Calls: Grace Lutheran, Erie, Pa., 1964-66. Redeemer, Charlotte, 1967-71; transferred to Central Pennsylvania Synod, 1971.

BARRIER, JACOB W.

Date/Place of Birth: September 1840; Cabarrus County, N.C.
Parents: David Barrier and Sophia (Bost) Barrier.
Spouse/Marriage Date: Laura M. (Brown) Barrier; April 28, 1864 in Rowan County while on furlough from war; died November 25, 1889.
Child: Mary Ida.
Education: Western Carolina Male Academy (North Carolina College); studied theology under other ministers.
Licensed: Examined by Central Conference of the North Carolina Synod meeting at Organ, Salisbury, and licensed ad interim until the regular annual meeting. Licensed in 1867.
Calls: Trinity-St. Enoch, Concord, 1866-67, less than a year.
Other: Left North Carolina College to enlist in the Confederate States Army 1861 and rose to rank of Second Lieutenant. In April 1865 was wounded and captured.
Date of Death/Burial Location: July 20, 1867 from typhoid fever; St. John Cemetery, Cabarrus County, N.C.

BARRINGER, BENJAMIN ALFRED, SR.

Date/Place of Birth: November 8, 1892; Mt. Pleasant, N.C.
Parents: Marshall Otho Barringer and Alice Annette (Cook) Barringer.
Spouse/Marriage Date: Lorena Smith (Arndt) Barringer, a descendant of the Reverend John Gottfried Arends; June 18, 1925, in Claremont, N.C.
Children: Benjamin Alfred, Jr., Paul Arndt, George Herbert, Joseph Allen, Jackson Lee.
Education: Mount Pleasant Collegiate Institute; Roanoke College, A.B. 1918; Lutheran Theological Southern Seminary, 1922, B.D. 1927; University of South Carolina, M.A. 1922.
Ordination: Licensed 1918 by Virginia Synod and ordained 1922 by North Carolina Synod.

Calls: Grace-Richland-Melanchthon, Liberty, 1922-27; in Virginia, 1927-31. Left active ministry and became a teacher and principal in North Carolina public schools, 1931-1959.
Other: Lieutenant of Infantry, U.S. Army in World War I. Conducted Sunday school and church services in own home in Havelock, New Bern, and Jacksonville, before missions were begun.
Date of Death/Burial Location: December 2, 1959; Jacksonville, N.C.

BARRINGER, HUGH PERRY

Date/Place of Birth: April 14, 1905; Somerset, Ky.
Parents: Perry L. Barringer and Lena (Rudisill) Barringer.
Spouse/Marriage Date: Edna (Coogler) Barringer; June 29, 1932 in Irmo, S.C.
Children: Hubert Paul, Larry Edward.
Education: Lenoir-Rhyne, A.B. 1926; Lutheran Theological Southern Seminary, 1932; American Bible College, Th.D. 1947.
Ordination: 1932 by North Carolina Synod.
Calls: Bethel-Bethphage-St. Mark-St. Paul, Gaston and Lincoln Counties; St. Paul, Rowan County; Grace, Bessemer City.
Date of Death/Burial Location: March 6, 1956; Gaston Memorial Park, Gastonia, N.C.

BARRINGER, JOHN DANIEL

Date/Place of Birth: April 7, 1915; Mt. Pleasant, Cabarrus County, N.C.
Parents: D. L. Barringer and Mamie (Rowland) Barringer.
Spouse/Marriage Date: Evelyn E. (McLemore) Barringer; December 6, 1940 in Columbia, S.C.
Children: Elaine Elizabeth, Martha Sue, Sheila Ann.
Education: Pfeiffer, Lenoir-Rhyne, A.B. 1937; Lutheran Theological Southern Seminary, B.D. 1940.
Ordination: 1940 by North Carolina Synod.
Calls: Zion, Catawba County, 1940-42; Grace, Hendersonville, 1946-48; Chaplain, U.S. Army World War II, 1942-46; Chaplain, U.S. Air Force, 1948-66; Morning Star, Matthews, 1966-70; Kure Memorial, Kure Beach, 1970-75; Lutheran Church of the Living Word, Laurinburg, 1975-77; Supply Pastor to various congregations. Transferred to Southeastern Synod, 1963. Retired May 1, 1977.
Other: Member, Evangelism Committee of North Carolina Synod; Chair, Committee on Service to Military Personnel of Synod.
Date of Death/Burial Location: August 25, 1980; St. John, Cabarrus County, N.C.

BARTHOLOMEW, CRAIG E.

Date/Place of Birth: May 3, 1942; Rochester, N.Y.
Parents: C. Earl Bartholomew and Laura O. Bartholomew.
Spouse/Marriage Date: LaVaughn (Boyle) Bartholomew; November 27, 1964 in Meadville, Pa.
Child: Christopher.
Education: Allegheny College, A.B. 1964; Philadelphia Seminary, B.D. 1967.
Ordination: June 9, 1967 by Upper New York Synod.

Calls: St. Mark, Mayville, N.Y., 1967-70; St. Mark, Albany, N.Y., 1970-74; Holy Spirit, Albany, N.Y., 1974- 97.
Other: Retired to North Carolina in 1997.

BARTOS, JAMES ANDREW

Date/Place of Birth: October 14, 1938; Dayton, Ohio.
Parents: Andrew Bartos and Helen (Gribbon) Bartos.
Spouse/Marriage Date: Carl Ann (Bayer) Bartos; August 22, 1959.
Children: Elizabeth Ann, Jeffrey Andrew, Timothy Scott.
Education: Wittenberg University, B.A. 1960; Hamma Divinity School, M.Div. 1964; graduate work at Trinity Seminary, Mt. Mary's College, and Lutheran Theological Southern Seminary.
Ordination: May 1964 by Ohio Synod.
Calls: Our Saviour, Lancaster, Ohio, 1964-66; Mt. Lebanon United, Pittsburgh, Pa., 1966-68; Zion Church, Wheeling, W.Va., 1968-73; Lutheran Campus Ministry, Oshkosh, Wis., 1973-79; The Village Church, Milwaukee, Wis., 1979-93; Holy Trinity, Charlotte, 1993-. Interim Pastor, Incarnation, Charlotte, 1994-95.
Other: District Dean while serving as campus pastor at the University of Wisconsin-Oshkosh. Served as Chaplain to the Wisconsin Synod Assembly in Stevens Points, Wis. (Lutheran Church in America) and was preacher and celebrant for the Northern Wisconsin District Assembly (American Lutheran Church) at Oshkosh. Wrote the prayers of the faithful for the installation of Bishop Peter Rogness in Milwaukee. Poem published in *Sojourners* magazine. Was a Merrill Fellow at Harvard Divinity School in fall term of 1985.

BATTERMAN, WILLIAM HENRY

Date/Place of Birth: September 4, 1941; Grand Coulee, Wash.
Parents: Henry Otto Batterman and Alice Christina (Anderson) Batterman.
Spouse/Marriage Date: Mary Amy (Matthews) Batterman; June 29, 1968 in York, S.C.
Step-Children: Keith Douglas Clark, Mark Earl Clark.
Education: Karl Ruprecht University (Heidelberg, Germany), 1961-62; Pacific Lutheran University, A.B. 1963; Harvard Divinity School, M.Div. 1967; Episcopal Seminary in Virginia, D.M. 1996.
Ordination: May 6, 1968 by North Carolina Synod.
Calls: New Covenant, High Point, 1968-70; Mission Developer, Columbia, S.C., 1970-73; St. James, Chilhowie, Va., 1973-77; Pleasant View, Staunton, Va., 1977-83; Our Redeemer, Petersburg, Va., 1983-93; St. Andrew, Portsmouth, Va., 1993-.

BAUER, LOUIS EDWIN, JR.

Date/Place of Birth: July 28, 1941; Akron, Ohio.
Parents: Louis E. Bauer, Sr. and Esther I. (Brown) Bauer.
Spouse/Marriage Date: B. Susan (Bilton) Bauer; June 15, 1968 in Akron, Ohio.
Children: Jason David, Megan Elizabeth.
Education: Valparaiso University, B.A. 1963; Yale Divinity School, M.Div. 1967; graduate work at St. Elizabeth Hospital, Washington, D.C., 1972-74, and University of Tennessee, 1983-86.
Ordination: September 10, 1967 by New England Synod.

Calls: Concordia, Manchester, Conn., 1967-70; St. Paul, Gloucester, Mass., 1970-72; St. Elizabeth Hospital, Washington, D.C., 1972-74; Messiah, Knoxville, Tenn., 1974-86; Holy Trinity, Chapel Hill, 1986-97. Vice Pastor at various congregations.

Other: Teacher, Paulinum Seminary, Otjimbingwe, Nambia, 1997-.

BAUMGARTNER, HUGH EDWARD, JR.

Date/Place of Birth: July 12, 1921; Brunswick, Ga.

Parents: Hugh E. Baumgartner, Sr. and Thelma (Conyers) Baumgartner.

Spouse/Marriage Date: Frances (Wisdom) Baumgartner; November 6, 1946 in Elberton, Ga.

Children: William Edward, Patricia Lee Bowles, Andrew Conrad, Paul Wisdom, Carla Frances, Hugh Eric.

Education: Lenoir-Rhyne, A.B. 1944; Lutheran Theological Southern Seminary, B.D. 1945; Newberry College, D.Div. 1973.

Ordination: February 7, 1945 by Georgia-Alabama Synod.

Calls: Redeemer, Atlanta, Ga., 1945; Holy Trinity, Elberton, Ga., 1945-47; St. Paul, Mobile, Ala., 1947-50; Mission Developer, Tuscaloosa, Ala., 1950; Trinity, Anniston, Ala., 1950-53; Redeemer, Macon, Ga., 1953-59; Mt. Olive, Hickory, 1959-1965; St. Paul, Savannah, Ga., 1965-71; Resurrection, Augusta, Ga., 1971-79; Redeemer, Newberry, S.C., 1979-86.

Other: Board, Lutheran Theological Southern Seminary; Board, Newberry College; Executive Board, Georgia, Alabama and Southeastern Synods; Statistician, Georgia-Alabama Synod; President, Lutheran Theological Southern Seminary Alumni Association; Delegate, Baltimore and Dallas Conventions; Chair, South Carolina Synod Examining Committee, Consultation Committee, and Discipline Committee. Retired in 1986 to Dayspring-White Rock, S.C.

BAYNE, JAMES DEOULIA

Date/Place of Birth: May 30, 1925; Henderson County, N.C.

Parents: James Columbus Bayne and Carrie Viola (McDowell) Bayne.

Spouse/Marriage Date: Faith Katherine (Auvil) Bayne; December 19, 1947 in Brevard, N.C.

Children: Cynthia Diana Johnson, Clara Denise Reid, James Nicholas, Philip Michael.

Education: Brevard College, Lenoir-Rhyne, B.A. 1956; Lutheran Theological Southern Seminary, M.Div. 1960.

Ordination: 1960 by North Carolina Synod.

Calls: Bethany-Holy Communion (Watauga Parish), Watauga County, 1959-61; Trinity-Good Hope, Saluda, S.C., 1961-64; Good Shepherd, Walterboro, S.C., 1964-67; Chaplain, U.S. Army, 1967-72; St. John- Providence, Lexington, S.C., 1972-75; St. John, Lexington, S.C., 1975-77.

Other: Served two one-year tours in Vietnam as U.S. Army Chaplain. Received Bronze Star for meritorious service.

Date of Death/Burial Location: April 3, 1977; St. John Cemetery, Lexington, S.C.

BEAM, KEITH JUNIOUS

Date/Place of Birth: September 28, 1926; Lincoln County, N.C.

Parents: J. Ray Beam and Mae (Sorrels) Beam.

Spouse/Marriage Date: Alpha Jane (Hamilton) Beam; August 30, 1948 in Spartanburg, S.C. *Children*: Jonathan Mark, Noel Alisane.
Education: Lenoir-Rhyne, A.B. 1949; Lutheran Theological Southern Seminary, B.D. 1952.
Ordination: 1952 by North Carolina Synod.
Calls: Frieden's, Guilford County, 1952-55; Good Shepherd, Brevard, 1955-1957; St. John, Walhalla, S.C., 1957. Chaplain, U.S. Army.
Date of Death/Burial Location: June 17, 1973; Cherryville, N.C.

BEARD, ROBERT QUINCY
Date/Place of Birth: December 7, 1929; Iredell County, N.C.
Parents: Robert Ezeakial Beard and Nola (Hoover) Beard.
Spouse/Marriage Date: Carrie Felicity (Stewart) Beard; August 12, 1950 in Statesville, N.C.
Children: Kathryn Ann Little, Janet Lynne Leinbach, Mary Faith.
Education: Lenoir-Rhyne, A.B. 1955; Lutheran Theological Southern Seminary, M.Div. 1958.
Ordination: June 8, 1958 by North Carolina Synod.
Calls: Interim Pastor, St. Mark, Blowing Rock, 1954-55; Grace, Liberty, 1958-60; Faith, Conover, 1960-62; St. Paul, Startown, 1963-73; Alamance, Alamance, 1977-78; President and Chief Executive Officer, Lutheran Services for the Aging, Inc., 1978-92; Holy Trinity, Troutman, 1992-94; St. John, Lenoir, 1994-.
Other: Elected to North Carolina General Assembly, House of Representatives, Catawba County, Republican, for three terms, 1968-73. Appointed by Governor Holshouser as Executive Director, North Carolina Office for Aging, 1973-77. Received Distinguished Citation, Lenoir-Rhyne, 1976; Inducted into the Joe Kappler Senior Citizens Hall of Fame, Everett, Wash., 1976; Member, Synod Nominating Committee, 1963; Lutheran Church in America Voting Member, 1974. Retired 1992.

BEARDEN, GEORGE STEELE
Date/Place of Birth: February 29, 1868; South Carolina.
Parents: George W. Bearden and Ellen A. (Steele) Bearden.
Spouse/Marriage Date: Sarah Catherine (Luther) Bearden; November 6, 1895 in Prosperity, S.C.
Child: Elizabeth.
Education: Newberry College, A.B. 1893; Lutheran Theological Southern Seminary, 1895.
Ordination: 1895 by South Carolina Synod.
Calls: In South Carolina, 1895-1904, 1917-21. In North Carolina, 1905-09; Augsburg, Winston-Salem; St. Matthew, Wilmington. In Virginia, 1922-25.
Other: Published *A Study of the Lord's Prayer,* and a novel.
Date of Death/Burial Location: December 5, 1928; Elmwood Cemetery, Columbia, S.C.

BEATTY, HAROLD ELMER, SR.
Date/Place of Birth: 1880; Rowan County, N.C.
Parents: John F. Beatty and Martha (Barrier) Beatty.

Spouse/Marriage Date: Catherine (von Ohsen) Beatty; 1917 in Orangeburg, S.C.
Children: Helen C., Harold E., Jr., Barbara, Louis B., John V.
Education: Roanoke College, A.B. 1907, A.M., 1919; Lutheran Theological Southern Seminary, 1910.
Ordination: 1910 by North Carolina Synod.
Calls: St. Matthew, Wilmington, 1910-13; Orangeburg, S.C., 1913-17; St. Luke, Florence, S.C., 1917-22; Muhlenberg, Harrisonburg, Va., 1922-27; Georgetown, Washington, D.C., 1927-56, Pastor Emeritus, 1957.
Date of Death/Burial Location: December 2, 1966; Washington, D.C.

BEATTY, PAUL BARRIER, JR.

Date/Place of Birth: November 17, 1931; China Grove, Rowan County, N.C.
Parents: Paul Barrier Beatty, Sr. and Wilkie Lenora (Patterson) Beatty.
Spouse/Marriage Date: Elma Jean (Piester) Beatty; September 9, 1962 in Newberry, S.C.
Children: John Christian; Daniel Christopher, Mark Stephen.
Education: Lenoir-Rhyne, A.B. 1953; Lutheran School of Theology at Chicago, M.Div., 1957, S.T.M., 1968; graduate work at Drew University, D.Min. 1990.
Ordination: 1957 by North Carolina Synod.
Calls: Luther Place Memorial, Washington, D.C., 1957-58; St. Paul, Hamlet, 1959-63. Mission service in Guyana, South America by Lutheran Church in America Board of World Missions, 1964-74; St. Luke, Monroe, 1974-1993; Reformation, Taylorsville, 1994-98. Retired 1998.
Other: Two of his sisters married the Reverends George C. Kahl, Chaplain, and Carroll Lee Robinson, respectively. Publications: *A History of the Lutheran Church in Guyana,* 1970; *Forming a New Vision for the Future Through a Study of the History of St. Luke's Lutheran Church - Monroe, N.C., 1990.*

BEAVER, BEN ROBERT

Date/Place of Birth: June 2, 1945; Charlotte, N.C.
Parents: Ben Rubin Beaver and Mae (Allen) Beaver.
Spouse/Marriage Date: Nancy (Chambers) Beaver; May 25, 1968.
Children: Jennifer Anne; Amanda Allen.
Education: Lenoir-Rhyne, B.A. History 1967; Lutheran Theological Southern Seminary, M.Div. 1971; graduate work at University of South Carolina, 1967-79; Clinical Pastoral Education at Hall Institute, Columbia, S.C., 1973-74.
Ordination: June 6, 1971 by North Carolina Synod.
Calls: Lutheran Church of the Living Word, Laurinburg, N.C., 1971-73; Chaplain, Pee Dee Mental Health Center, Florence, S.C., 1974-79; Chaplain, McLeod Regional Medical Center, Florence, S.C., 1979-80; Abiding Presence, Burke, Va., 1980-84; Macedonia, Burlington, 1984-87; Vice President, Development, Lutheran Social Services, York, Pa., 1987-93; Director, Lutheran Homes of South Carolina Foundation, Columbia, S.C., 1994.

BEAVER, ERVIN TAYLOR

Date/Place of Birth: March 20, 1910; Concord, N.C.
Parents: Taylor Reese and Betty (Collette) Beaver.
Spouse/Marriage Date: Iris (Chewning) Beaver; May 24, 1938 in Mullins, S.C.
Children: Michael Ervin, David Pritchard.
Education: Mount Pleasant Collegiate Institute, Newberry College, Lenoir-Rhyne, A.B. 1935; Lutheran Theological Southern Seminary, 1938.
Ordination: 1938 by North Carolina Synod.
Calls: None in North Carolina; Board of American Missions in Pennsylvania, New Jersey, Wisconsin, New York City, Maryland, Florida, and Mississippi. In 1965 was in St. Matthew, Princeton, Ill.
Date of Death: May 24, 1982.

BEAVER, GRADY WILSON (BUDDY), JR.

Date/Place of Birth: June 18, 1945; Mooresville, Iredell County, N.C.
Parents: Grady Wilson Beaver, Sr., and Adelina (Vernon) Beaver.
Spouse/Marriage Date: Judy (Smith) Beaver; April 10, 1966.
Children: Jerry Lane, Nicole Michelle.
Education: Lenoir-Rhyne, A.B. Religious Studies 1979; Lutheran Theological Southern Seminary, M.Div. 1984.
Ordination: August 15, 1984 by North Carolina Synod.
Calls: Lebanon, Cleveland, 1984-87; Holly Grove, Lexington, 1987-89; Lebanon-St. Paul Parish, Lebanon Church, Va., 1989-93; Coble's, Julian, 1993-; Vice Pastor at various congregations.
Other: American Missions Committee, 1985-89.

BEAVER, PERRY LEE

Date/Place of Birth: February 22, 1943; Mooresville, N.C.
Parents: Carl D. Beaver and Margaret McNeely Beaver.
Spouse/Marriage Date: Sarah B. (Scarritt) Beaver; June 21, 1969.
Child: Michael Andrew.
Education: Lenoir-Rhyne, A.B., 1965; Lutheran Theological Southern Seminary, M.Div. 1969.
Ordination: 1969 by North Carolina Synod.
Calls: Christ, West Boylston, Mass., 1969-72; St. Paul, Middletown, Conn., 1972-87; Immanuel, Meriden, Conn., 1987-.
Other: Chaplain, Lutheran Home for Aged, Middletown, Conn., 1974-; President, North Carolina Luther League, 1964-65; Executive Committee, Luther League, Lutheran Church in America, 1963-66.

BEAVER, ROGER LEE

Date/Place of Birth: February 25, 1945; Concord, N.C.
Parents: William Lewis Beaver and Frances (Faggart) Beaver.
Spouse/Marriage Date: Dorothy Jean (Drennan) Beaver; August 13, 1967.
Child: Christopher Andrew.
Education: Catawba College, B.A. Religion/Philosophy 1966; Lutheran Theological

Southern Seminary, M.Div. 1971.

Ordination: June 6, 1971 by North Carolina Synod.

Calls: Mt. Gilead, Mt. Pleasant, 1971-74; St. Timothy, Hickory, 1974-.

Other: Adjunct Chaplain, Catawba Memorial Hospital, 1983-; Secretary, Carolina Moonlighters - a Barbershop Singing Chorus of International Singing Chapters; Secretary/Treasurer of ministerial group; past leader of a tutor program at Arndt Middle School, Hickory; Secretary, Music Boosters Club at St. Stephen High School, Hickory; North Carolina Real Estate Brokers License.

BEAVER, SUSAN MITCHAM (BUTLER)

Date/Place of Birth: July 12, 1946; Lancaster County, Neb.

Parents: Dean Wood Butler and Laura (Buddin) Butler.

Spouse/Marriage Date: Gordon Alexander Beaver; February 11, 1978 in Tullahoma, Tenn.

Children: Christopher, Butler.

Education: Middle Tennessee State College, B.S. 1969; Lutheran Theological Southern Seminary, M.Div. 1976.

Ordination: September 18, 1977 by Southeastern Synod.

Calls: St. Andrew, Plains, Ga., 1977-79; St. Thomas, Charlotte, 1982-84; part-time at Good Shepherd, Charlotte, 1984; transferred to American Lutheran Church, Charlotte, 1984.

BEAVER, TOMMY KALE

Date/Place of Birth: September 17, 1942; Cabarrus County, N.C.

Parents: Lewis Alfred Beaver and Della (Allman) Beaver.

Spouse/Marriage Date: Rosalind (Reinhardt) Beaver; December 20, 1964 in Raleigh, N.C.

Children: Gregory Thomas; Jennifer Elise.

Education: Appalachian State University, B.S. 1964; Lutheran Theological Southern Seminary, M.Div. 1969.

Ordination: June 1, 1969 by North Carolina Synod.

Calls: Bethel, Lincolnton, 1969-74; Mission Developer, Christ the King, Whiteville, 1974-79; A Mighty Fortress, Summerville, S.C., 1979-85; St. Peter, Salisbury, 1985-94; Holy Trinity, Troutman, 1994-; Vice pastor at various congregations.

Other: Member, Summerville Kiwanis Club, Salisbury Kiwanis Club and Troutman Lion's Club.

BECK, ALFRED RILEY
Date/Place of Birth: February 17, 1867; Davidson County, N.C.
Parents: William Austin Beck and Elizabeth (Hedrick) Beck.
Spouse Name/Marriage Date: Carrie Belle (Leonard) Beck;
December 28, 1893 in Davidson County, N.C.
Children: Twin sons died in infancy, Waldo McRae.
Education: Concordia College, Lenoir-Rhyne, A.B. 1892, D.D.
1926; one year each at Chicago and Philadelphia Seminaries.
Ordination: 1892 by Tennessee Synod.
Calls: In Virginia, 1892-93, 1904-11, 1919-21. Bethel and three
missions, Manassas, St. Mary and Solomon, Mt. Jackson (on
leave 10 months to study at Chicago Seminary, and serve St. James, Chicago, Ill.); St.
Peter-St. James-St. Paul-St. Luke, Page County; in South Carolina, 1896-1903; St. Peter-
St. John, Lexington County. In North Carolina, 1893-96, 1903-04, 1911-19, 1921-44;
Holly Grove-Pilgrim-Beck's-New Jerusalem, Davidson County; First, Albemarle; Holly
Communion-Philadelphia-Antioch-St. Paul, Gaston County; St. John, Statesville; St.
Timothy, Catawba County, and Beth Eden, Newton.
Other: Retired 1944 at Newton, later at Lowman Home, S.C. President, Tennessee Synod,
three one-year terms, and Secretary, one year. Member, Boards of Lenoir- Rhyne College,
Lutheran Theological Southern Seminary, and Lowman Home. Editor, *The Catawba
Lutheran*, 1922-23; Editor, *The North Carolina Lutheran*, 1923-37. Member, Ways and
Means Committee for organizing of United Lutheran Church in America, 1918.
Date of Death/Burial Location: December 17, 1954; Holly Grove Church, Davidson
County, N.C.

BECK, HAROLD GENE
Date/Place of Birth: May 7, 1937; Charleston, W.Va.
Parents: Liston Calvin Beck and Fanny Ethyl Beck.
Spouse/Marriage Date: May Frances (Jantzen) Beck; August 11, 1963 in Charleston, S.C.
Children: Shaw Frances Price, Tara Elizabeth Allen, Ernest Liston Beck.
Education: Guilford College, Lenoir-Rhyne, A.B. 1960; Lutheran Theological Southern
Seminary, M.Div. 1964.
Ordination: June 14, 1964 by North Carolina Synod.
Calls: Pilgrim, Davidson County, Lexington, 1964-67; Wittenberg, Leesville, S.C., 1967-
73; St. Paul's Lutheran Church, Mt. Pleasant, S.C., 1975-78. Retired in 1998.

BECK, WALTER HERMAN
Date/Place of Birth: November 7, 1898; Milwaukee, Wis.
Parents: Carl Beck and Ottilia (Hinz) Beck.
Spouse/Marriage Date: Ruth E. (Smyre) Beck; June 5, 1929 in Greensboro, N.C.
Child: Dorothy Ann Voyta.
Education: Concordia College, Northwestern College, A.B. 1919; Wisconsin Lutheran
Synod (Wauwatosa), B.D. 1922; Philadelphia Lutheran Seminary, S.T.M. 1935;
University of Wisconsin, M.A. 1929; Temple University, Ed.D. 1937.
Ordination: September 10, 1922 by The Lutheran Church-Missouri Synod for the
Synodical Conference.
Calls: Mt. Zion Lutheran Church (Synod Conference Negro Mission), New Orleans, La.,

1922-25; Immanuel Lutheran College Theological Seminary, Greensboro (Synod Conference Negro Mission); 1925-37; supply pastor in High Point and Southern Pines, 1928-31; Concordia Lutheran Teachers' College, 1937-44. Resigned position to affiliate with United Lutheran Church in America in 1944; Midland College in Fremont, Neb., 1944-47; Texas Lutheran College in Seguin, Texas, 1947-55; Refugee Service Lutheran Welfare, Milwaukee, Wis., 1955-57; Refugee Service Lutheran Welfare and Pastor of Faith, South Beloit, Ill., 1956-60; Newberry College, S.C., 1960-65. Retired to Wilmington, N.C., 1965 then Lakeland, Fla.

Date of Death/Burial Location: March 31, 1979; Penny Farms, Fla.

BEEBE, MARK A.

Date/Place of Birth: April 25, 1955; Cincinnati, Ohio.

Parents: Donald F. Beebe and ? (Laker) Beebe.

Spouse/Marriage Date: Barbara (Wilcox) Beebe; October 24, 1981 in New Orleans, La.

Child: Erin Lee

Education: Valparaiso University, B.A. 1976; Trinity Seminary, M.Div. 1981; Graduate work at St. Louis University, M.A. English Literature 1976.

Ordination: 1982 by Southern District, American Lutheran Church.

Calls: Holy Cross, Harris, Texas, 1982-86; Atascocita, Harris, Texas, 1986-87; Organizing Pastor Inwood, Harris, Texas, 1987-88; Family of Faith, Harrisburg, 1988-97; Christ, Hilton Head, S.C., 1997-.

BELL, CHARLES KRAUTH

Date/Place of Birth: December 11, 1870; Smithsburg, Md.

Parents: The Reverend Lewis Jacobs Bell and Charlotte Ann (Marbourg) Bell.

Spouse/Marriage Date: Alice Virginia (Fox) Bell, daughter of the Reverend Luther Augustine Fox; January 31, 1900 in Salem, Va.; died 1961.

Children: None.

Education: Gettysburg College, A.B. 1895; Gettysburg Seminary, M. A. 1898; Lenoir-Rhyne College, D. Div. 1915.

Ordination/License: Licensed 1897 and ordained 1898 by Maryland Synod.

Calls: College Church, Salem, Va., 1898-1905; St. Matthew-St. Luke, Kings Mountain, 1905-19.

Other: Professor of Practical Theology, Lutheran Theological Southern Seminary, 1919-46, then supply teaching to March 1948. Retired 1948 at Smithsburg, Md.; Secretary, Tennessee Synod, 1906-08; President, 1914-16; Member, Board of Home Missions, United Synod South, 1912-18, and of Board of American Missions, United Lutheran Church in America, 1918-22; Member from the United Synod South on Commission to draft Constitution of United Lutheran Church in America, 1918.

Date of Death/Burial Location: September 17, 1962; Smithsburg, Md.

BELL, GLYNN MICHELE (SWAIM)
Date/Place of Birth: February 9, 1954; Greensboro, N.C.
Parents: William D. Swaim and Anne (Coble) Swaim.
Spouse/Marriage Date: Bruce Henry Bell; December 30, 1989.
Education: University of North Carolina-Greensboro, B.A. *magna cum laude*, 1976; Pacific Lutheran Theological Seminary, M.Div. with Honors, 1993.
Ordination: April 28, 1994 by North Carolina Synod.
Calls: Holy Cross, Mocksville, 1994-.

BELL, JOHN ERIC
Date/Place of Birth: March 6, 1964; Summit, N.J.
Parents: Robert A. Bell and Patricia E. (Johnson) Bell.
Spouse/Marriage Date: Bonnie (Grubb) Bell; September 30, 1995.
Education: Lenoir-Rhyne, B.A. 1986; Lutheran School of Theology at Chicago, M.Div. 1991.
Ordination: May 31, 1991 by New Jersey Synod.
Calls: Bethphage, Lincolnton, 1991-.

BELL, JOSEPH EDWARDS
Date/Place of Birth: August 22, 1789; Virginia.
Ordination/License: Licensed 1816 by North Carolina Synod. Ordained by the Reverend Philip Henkel, 1819 with ratification by the North Carolina Synod in 1820. Withdrew in 1821 to join newly formed Tennessee Synod.
First Spouse/Marriage Date: Nancy (White) Bell; 1809.
Second Spouse/Marriage Date: Mary Ann (Farnsworth) Bell; 1832.
Third Spouse/Marriage Date: Hepzibah (Woolsey) Bell; 1855.
Children: Fifteen children.
Calls: In Tennessee: Solomon, Greene County; Lick Creek Church, Greene County; Union Church, Greene County; Hopewell Congregation, Washington County. None in North Carolina.
Other: With Philip Henkel, operated Tennessee Academy (later called Henkel and Bell Seminary), teaching Greek, Hebrew, and English. At some time joined Presbyterian Church and had charge of a church in Lincolnton. After Tennessee Synod Reorganized was formed, joined that body, and in 1867 joined the Holston Synod. Practiced medicine in Tennessee; Principal, Lincolnton Female Academy in 1820; Agent, Lincolnton Bible Society in 1826.
Date of Death: February 7, 1871.

BENDERT, WILLIAM MARK
Date/Place of Birth: September 17, 1958; Aberdeen, Md.
Parents: Edwin William Bendert and Barbara (Eddinger) Bendert.
First Spouse/Marriage Date: Kimberly Ann (Wilson) Bendert; August 23, 1980 in Bel Air, Md.
Second Spouse/Marriage Date: Theresa Marie (Esper) Bendert; April 30, 1988 in Bel Air, Md.
Child by Second Marriage: Rachel Katherine.
Education: Concordia College, A.A. 1978; Concordia Teachers College, B.A. 1980;

Lutheran Theological Southern Seminary, M.Div. 1984.
Ordination: August 12, 1984 by Southeastern Synod.
Calls: Our Saviour, Welcome, 1984-86; Lutheran Church of the Living Word, Memphis, Tenn., 1987-92; Pilgrim, Marysville, Mich., 1992-.

BENNICK, JOHN SYLVANUS
Parents: Philip Bennick and Susan (Henkel) Bennick, daughter of Pastor David Henkel.
Spouse: Miss Wise of Virginia.
Child: A son was later a prominent lawyer in New Market, Va.
License/Ordination: Licensed in 1865 and ordained 1868 by Tennessee Synod in Salem Church, Lincoln County.
Calls: Worked in Virginia Conference of Tennessee Synod, in and around New Market, Va.; Rader, Timberville, 1869-81; St. Mary, Forestville, 1869-81; Zion, Edinburg, 1870-76; Solomon, Forestville, 1869- 81; St. Paul, Jerome, 1870-79; and organizing pastor for Prince of Peace, Powder Springs, 1870-81.
Other: Treasurer, Tennessee Synod, 1869 and again in 1872.
Date of Death: 1882 prior to October 14.

BERNARDS, VOLDEMARS TEODORUS
Date/Place of Birth: October 1, 1907; Cesis, Latvia.
Family: Had no family in the United States, but considered Kamilla Shulman of Syracuse, N.Y., a foster sister since they escaped to the West together and maintained contact with each other until his death.
Education: State University in Riga, Latvia, Licentiate in Theology. Earned the Ph.D. degree in linguistics at Columbia University.
Ordination: February 13, 1944; Evangelical Lutheran Church of Latvia in the Dome Cathedral of the Archdiocese of Riga.
Calls: Assistant Pastor of St. Gertrude Church, an academic parish in Riga. Joined faculty of Lenoir-Rhyne, providing instruction in Latin, Greek, German and Russian.
Other: Fled from his homeland to escape living under communist rule. Arrived in the United States in 1950 and became a naturalized citizen June 3, 1958. Received personal greetings from Archbishop Arnolds Lusis of the Latvian Lutheran Church in the Free World, Toronto, Canada. Translated Bible into White Russian for a Bible Society. Retired from Lenoir-Rhyne faculty in 1973. Lenoir-Rhyne College presented him with a Trustee Award in 1980.
Date of Death/Burial Location: July 29, 1988; Latvian-American Disabled Veterans Cemetery in Elka Park, N.Y.

BERNHARDT, CHARLES EDWARD
Date/Place of Birth: December 18, 1921; Salisbury, N.C.
Parents: Ira Leo Bernhardt and Maggie Elizabeth (Parks) Bernhardt.
Spouse/Marriage Date: Gladys Irene (Boggs) Bernhardt; September 15, 1944 in Claremont, N.C.
Children: Barbara Elizabeth Bell, Charles David, Timothy Paul.
Education: Lenoir-Rhyne, A.B. 1942; Lutheran Theological Southern Seminary, B.D. 1945.

Ordination: April 4, 1945 by North Carolina Synod.
Calls: Christ's-St. Luke, Stanley, 1945-51; St. John, Asheboro, 1951-53; St. Matthew, Wilmington, 1954-58; St. John's, Cherryville, 1958-68; Mt. Tabor, West Columbia, S.C., 1969-75; Martin Luther, Charleston, S.C., 1975-83; Pine Grove, Lone Star, S.C., 1984-86; Vice pastor at various congregations. Retired December 31, 1986 at Sherrill's Ford, N.C.
Other: Board, North Carolina Lutheran Homes; Board, Lutheran Theological Southern Seminary; Dean of the South Carolina Synod Coastal District; Board, Franke Home.

BERNHARDT, CHRISTIAN EBERHARD

Date/Place of Birth: 1763; Stuttgart, Germany.
Spouse/Marriage Date: Sometime in 1788-89, in the Forsyth-Stokes counties area.
Ordination: According to one source, ordination was in Germany in 1785; according to another source, he was ordained in October 1791 by the North Carolina "Ministerium" at its organizational meeting.
Calls: Came to Savannah, Ga., in 1786, and preached to the Salzburgers at Ebenezer, Ga. From there moved to Rowan County, N.C., in 1787. That year Nussmann wrote to Germany: "Bernhardt is a young educated man from Wuerttemberg with considerable ability, about 24 years old, in whom I see daily that the gospel truths, which he preaches, are a vital matter in his own young life. He preaches for the lower Second Creek Charge in Peint (Pine) Church (Union, Rowan County), and in several other churches." Other churches served: Beck's-Pilgrim-St. Luke, Davidson County, 1787-88; in Forsyth and Stokes Counties, 1788-89; Frieden's-Low's, Guilford County, and St. Paul, Alamance County, 1789-1800. From 1800 to his death served churches in Lexington District, S.C.
Other: He and his churches approved of organization of the North Carolina Synod in 1803, becoming members. In 1794 one of the five resident pastors in North Carolina (Nussmann, Arends, Storch, and Roschen being the others), who examined and ordained Robert J. Miller as an Episcopal minister. Secretary of the North Carolina Synod, 1806-08. Father of the Reverend David Bernhardt, one of first graduates of Lutheran Theological Southern Seminary.
Date of Death/Burial Location: August 27, 1809; St. Michael Church, near Columbia, S.C.

BERNHEIM, CHARLES HERMAN

Date/Place of Birth: April 6, 1831; Cologne, Germany. In his infancy his family settled in Western Pennsylvania.
Parents: The Reverend John Herman Bernheim and Lisette (Dellman) Bernheim. His father, of a distinguished Berlin Jewish family, was a convert from Judaism, and became a Lutheran minister. His older brother was the Reverend G. D. Bernheim.
Spouse Name and Marriage Date: Jane E. (Todd) Bernheim; Charleston, S.C.
Children: Several children.
Education: Theological Seminary and Classical Institute, Lexington, S.C., 1855.
Ordination/License: Licensed 1855 and ordained 1858 by South Carolina Synod.
Calls: In 1856 was growing discouraged because of his inability to preach acceptably in German for the folk in Augusta. His "Vestry" was threatening to resign. Was away from the parish for a time in the fall because of illness. Returned to the field voicing the conviction that the field should either be turned over to a German pastor or abandoned. In March 1867 was united with the Methodist Episcopal Florida Conference and therefore no

more a minister of the Lutheran Church. In May 1867 from *The Lutheran Visitor,* "We are glad to be able from reliable authority, to say to our readers that this brother has only gone into the Methodist Episcopal Church in order to be usefully employed in the Master's work till a field presented itself in the Lutheran Church." His address remained Apalachicola, Fla. In April 1868 was united with the North Carolina Synod at its convention at Lau's, Guilford County and was listed as serving Gibsonville. He presented a "certificate of withdrawal from the Florida Conference of the Methodist Episcopal Church South." He was assigned the responsibility of supervising the ministry of Michael Coble, a black licentiate. In North Carolina, from 1868: Frieden's, Guilford County; St. Paul, Alamance County; St. James, Concord; Pilgrim-Lebanon-St. Luke, St. Luke, Bethany, and Beck's-New Jerusalem, Davidson County; Nazareth-Shiloh, Forsyth County. In 1880 transferred to Tennessee Synod, and served Beth Eden, Newton; St. John and St. Timothy, Catawba County; supplied Mt. Pleasant, Watauga County; St. Martin-Sharon, Iredell County; and Shiloh and Friendship, Alexander County.

Other: Secretary, North Carolina Synod, two terms; President, Tennessee Synod, 1884; financial agent, and later professor, Concordia College, Conover. In 1897 withdrew from Tennessee Synod to unite with The Lutheran Church-Missouri Synod. Proposed the name "The United Synod of the Evangelical Lutheran Church in the South" for the general body of Southern synods organized at Salisbury in 1886. Treasurer, Synodical Missionary Society, 1869. Was asked to serve as Secretary pro-tem at the opening session of the synodical convention at Lutheran Chapel, China Grove in 1870.

Date of Death/Burial Location: January 20, 1901; near Conover, N.C.

BERNHEIM, GOTTHARD DELLMAN

Date/Place of Birth: November 8, 1827; Iserlohn, Westphalia, Prussia.

Parents: The Reverend John Herman Bernheim and Lisette (Dellman) Bernheim. With parents and younger brother, the Reverend Charles H. Bernheim, came at age five to Western Pennsylvania. His father of a distinguished Berlin Jewish family, was educated to be a rabbi, converted to the Christian faith and became a Lutheran minister.

First Spouse/Marriage Date: Elizabeth Crowe (Clayton) Bernheim; April 25, 1854 in Charleston, S.C.

Children from First Marriage: Eight.

Second Spouse/Marriage Date: Amanda Ella (Lease) Bernheim; April 22, 1897; Nokomis, Ill.

Children from second marriage: Five.

Education: From Pennsylvania, rode horseback to enter Theological Seminary and Classical Institute, Lexington, S.C., graduating in 1849. Received D.D. degree.

Ordination/License: Licensed 1843 and ordained 1853 by South Carolina Synod.

Calls: Zion (later called Wentworth Street, then St. Andrew's), Charleston, S.C., 1851-57. Transferred 1858 to North Carolina Synod: St. John, Cabarrus County-New Bethel, Stanly County; organized and was second pastor of St. Mark's, Charlotte, 1861-65; St. Michael, Troutman; organized and served Ebenezer, Rowan County; St. Paul, Wilmington, to 1881. Transferred to Ministerium of Pennsylvania, 1883; Grace, Phillipsburg, N.J., nine years. Transferred back to North Carolina Synod, 1892; first pastor, St. Matthew, Wilmington, 1892-1901; supplied St. Paul in 1892; supplied St. Luke-Morning Star, Monroe, 1905-07.

Other: In 1866 was authorized by the Conference to assist some members of Organ in establishing a new congregation nearer where they lived. In 1869 was elected to a three-year term on the Board of Trustees of North Carolina College. Was also elected Recording Secretary of the Synodical Missionary Society. Was elected as a delegate to the Winchester convention of the General Synod South. Secretary, North Carolina Synod, 1861; president, two years. Service in educational institutions. Financial agent of North Carolina College, 1858, member of first board 1859 and college President, 1882-83; dean, later principal, Mt. Pleasant Female Seminary, 1868-70; dean and professor of Bible, Elizabeth College, Charlotte. Author of *The Success of God's Work, Localities of the Reformation, History of the German Settlements in North and South Carolina, The First Twenty Years of the History of St. Paul, Wilmington, N.C.,* and with the Reverend George H. Cox, *History of the Evangelical Lutheran Synod and Ministerium of North Carolina* (1902); contributed many articles to church periodicals. Retired in 1901 to Charlotte.
Date of Death/Burial Location: October 25, 1916; Charleston, S.C.

BERNLOHR, JACK

Date/Place of Birth: November 2, 1934; Columbus, Ohio.
Parents: William Bernlohr and Ruth (Russell) Bernlohr.
Spouse/Marriage Date: Doris Ruth (Lamb) Bernlohr; August 4, 1956.
Children: Lisa Ann Krzan, Kurt.
Education: Capital University, B.S. Education 1956; Evangelical Lutheran Theological Seminary, Columbus, Ohio, B.D. 1961.
Ordination: 1961 by American Lutheran Church.
Calls: St. Paul, Canonsburg, Pa., 1961-64; Immanuel, Deshler, Ohio, 1964-69; First, Detroit, Mich., 1969-74; Emmanuel, Warren, Ohio, 1990-98; Interim St. Philip, Raleigh, 1998-.
Other: Transferred from North East Ohio to North Carolina Synod in March 1998.

BEYER, LOUIS RUDY

Date/Place of Birth: December 17, 1942; Chattanooga, Tenn.
Parents: Louis A. Beyer and Georgia Mae (McGuffey) Beyer.
Spouse/Marriage Date: Judith (Albohm) Beyer; June 24, 1967.
Children: Louis Jonathan, Elizabeth R.
Education: Valparaiso University, B.A. Philosophy-Psychology 1965; Concordia Seminary, M.Div., 1969; graduate work at Springfield College, Massachusetts, 1980-84.
Ordination: June 22, 1969 by New England Synod.
Calls: St. Paul's, New Hartford, Conn., 1969-74; Grace, The Lutheran Church-Missouri Synod, West Springfield, Mass., 1974-1993; St. James, Fayetteville, 1993-97; Immanuel, Amherst, Mass., 1997-.
Other: Chaplain, Air National Guard, U.S. Air Force, 1983-93.

BICKLEY, JOHN JACOB

Date/Place of Birth: March 16, 1873; Lexington County, S.C.
Parents: Silas Franklin Bickley and Eliza Ann (Lindler) Bickley.
Spouse/Marriage Date: Corrie Ella (Wessinger) Bickley; January 21, 1903 in Chapin, S.C.

Children: Rose Evelyn, Barney Lee, Vernon Lamar.
Education: Attended Newberry College; University of Georgia, Medical School, M.D.; studied at Chicago Seminary, 1917-18.
Ordination: 1918 by Tennessee Synod.
Calls: Mt. Calvary, Claremont; Trinity, Vale-Cedar Grove, Lincoln County; Sardis, Catawba County; Philadelphia, Granite Falls-St. John, Hudson-St. Matthew, Caldwell County to 1925. Transferred to South Carolina Synod, 1925; returned to North Carolina Synod 1928 and served churches until death: Bethphage-St. Paul, St. Mark, Lincoln County; Bethel, Gaston County; Holy Communion, Dallas-Christ's, Stanley.
Other: Practiced medicine, 1899-1917.
Date of Death/Burial Location: September 30, 1944; St. Thomas Church, Chapin, S.C.

BIKLE, LOUIS ALBERT, SR.
Date/Place of Birth: November 6, 1834; Mechanicsville, Md.
Parents: Christian Emmanuel Bikle and Barbara (Fichte) Bikle. An older brother of the Reverend Philip M. Bikle.
Spouse/Marriage Date: Sara Ann (Chritzman) Bikle; December 27, 1859 in Gettysburg, Pa.; died February 8, 1900.
Children: George, Lulu Kate, Louis Albert, Jr.
Education: Gettysburg College, A.B. 1857; Gettysburg Seminary, 1859; Franklin and Marshall College, D.D. 1874.
License/Ordination: Licensed 1859 and ordained 1862 by North Carolina Synod.
Calls: Ebenezer, Rowan County, 1870-75; St. James, Concord, 1875-80; supplied Cold Water, Cabarrus County, 1877; St. Matthew, Kings Mountain, 1884-1904; organized St. Luke, Cleveland County, 1895-1904; with the Reverend M. L. Little supplied Holy Communion, Dallas, 1886-91; supplied Emmanuel, Lincolnton, 1890.
Other: Pastoral work done chiefly along with school work. Professor of Latin and Greek, North Carolina College, 1859-61, the College closing in 1861 because of war; President of same, 1866-67, 1868-74, 1878-81. Elected to the first Board of Trustees for Mont Amoena, 1868. Elected to a three-year term on the Board of Trustees of Mt. Pleasant Female Seminary, 1869. Served as Secretary of the Ministerium and a member of the Synod's Examining Committee, 1869. Elected as one of the North Carolina Synod's four pastoral delegates to the next convention of the General Synod South which was scheduled to meet at Newberry, S.C., 1868. Elected corresponding delegate to the Tennessee Synod, 1868. Elected a delegate to the Winchester convention of the General Synod South, 1869. Professor, Gaston Female College, Dallas, six years; Principal, Kings Mountain High school, five years. Secretary, North Carolina Synod, four terms; President, four terms. Chaplain, N.C. 20th Infantry Regiment, 1863-65. Retired 1904 at Concord. After retirement taught school at various times for ten years.
Date of Death/Burial Location: June 29, 1931; Oakwood Cemetery, Concord, N.C.

BIKLE, PHILIP MELANCHTHON
Date/Place of Birth: December 1, 1844; Smithsburg, Md.
Parents: Christian Emmanuel Bikle and Barbara (Fichte) Bikle. A younger brother of the Reverend Louis A. Bikle, Sr.
First Spouse/Marriage Date: Anna M. (Wattles) Bikle; December 28, 1869 in Gettysburg,

Pa.; died July 8, 1872.
Child of First Marriage: Horace Wattles.
Second Spouse/Marriage Date: Emma J. (Wolf) Bikle; January 2, 1877; Mifflinburg, Pa.; died November 27, 1918.
Children of Second Marriage: Henry Wolf, Paul H., Philip R.
Education: Gettysburg College, A.B. 1866, D.D. 1914; Gettysburg Seminary, 1869; Roanoke College, Honorary Ph.D. 1884.
Ordination: 1869 by North Carolina Synod.
Calls: No record of his pastoral ministry.
Other: Professor of Latin and Greek, North Carolina College, 1869-70. Transferred to Maryland Synod, 1870; vice-principal and teacher, Maryland College, Lutherville, Md., 1870-73. At Gettysburg College, Professor of Physics and Astronomy, 1874-81, Professor of Latin, 1881-1925, Dean, 1889-1925, Professor Emeritus, 1925 to death. Co-editor, later Editor, *The Lutheran Quarterly*, 1880-1907. Author of *Faraday, the Scientist and Christian, Our Present Knowledge of the Sun, Educating Young Men for the Ministry, Jesus, the Son of God,* translator from Latin of Philip Melanchthon's *Apology of the Augsburg Confession.*
Date of Death/Burial Location: January 19, 1934; Mifflinburg, Pa.

BITTLE, DANIEL HOWARD

Date/Place of Birth: June 6, 1819; Middletown, Md.
Parents: Thomas Bittle and Mary (Baer) Bittle. Younger brother of the Reverend Dr. David F. Bittle, President of Roanoke College.
Spouse/Marriage Date: Susan E. (Biglow) Bittle; November 1849 in Collamer, Ohio; died at age of 90.
Education: Gettysburg College, A.B. 1843; Lane Seminary, 1849; Roanoke College, D.D. 1869.
Ordination: 1849 by Miami Synod.
Calls: In Ohio, Indiana, Maryland, Pennsylvania, West Virginia, last in Savannah, Ga., 1871-74.
Other: First President, North Carolina College, 1859-61 (College closed in 1861 because of war); principal of a female seminary, Austin, Texas, 1861-65; Agent, Wittenberg University, Hagerstown Female Seminary, and Roanoke College, where taught, 1865-67.
Date of Death/Burial Location: January 14, 1874; Savannah, Ga.

BLACK, PAUL HOWELL

Date/Place of Birth: December 30, 1947; Gastonia, N.C.
Parents: Paul G. Black and Mattie Lou (Burgin) Black.
Spouse/Marriage Date: Gail Irene (Meyer) Black; June 14, 1975.
Children: Nathan Howell, Allyson Nicolle.
Education: Lenoir-Rhyne, B.A. 1971; Lutheran Theological Southern Seminary, M.Div. 1975; graduate work with Pacific Lutheran Seminary extension, 1977.
Ordination: June 8, 1975 by North Carolina Synod.
Calls: St. John, Gardena, Calif., 1975-77; Mission Developer/Pastor, Spirit of Joy, Mesa, Ariz., 1978-90; House of Prayer, Escondido, Calif., 1990-.
Other: Chair, Synod Nominating Committee; Chair, Synod Bishop Nominating Committee; Dean, Harvest Conference, North, in San Diego County, Calif.

BLACKWELDER, GAITHER GIBSON
Date/Place of Birth: October 19, 1935; Charlotte, N.C.
Parents: Frank M. Blackwelder and Frances (Morton) Blackwelder.
Spouse/Marriage Date: Alice Linda (Buff) Blackwelder; May 31, 1959 in Charlotte, N.C.
Children: Donald Wayne, Susan Frances.
Education: Lenoir-Rhyne, A.B. 1958; Lutheran Theological Southern Seminary, B.D. 1962.
Ordination: 1962 by North Carolina Synod.
Calls: St. Paul, Burlington, 1962-65; Vice Pastor, Mt. Pleasant, 1963-64; Vice Pastor, Alamance, Alamance, 1963; Atonement, Wilkesboro, 1965-73.
Other: District Chair, *The Lutheran Magazine,* 1968-73. Resigned from the ministry, 1976.

BLACKWELDER, GLENN HERMAN
Date/Place of Birth: February 27, 1952; Salisbury, N.C.
Education: University of North Carolina at Chapel Hill, A.B. 1974; Chicago Seminary, M.Div. 1978.
Ordination: 1978 by North Carolina Synod.
Calls: Associate Pastor Holy Trinity, Glenview, Ill., 1978-82; St. Mark, Chicago, Ill., 1982-.

BLACKWELDER, LEROY EMERSON
Date/Place of Birth: February 1, 1896; Cabarrus County, N.C.
Parents: Asa Blackwelder and Louisa (Litaker) Blackwelder.
Spouse/Marriage Date: Mildred (Blomgren) Blackwelder, August 17, 1927 in Mt. Pleasant, N.C.; died March 14, 1985.
Child: Phyllis Svanhild.
Education: Mount Pleasant Collegiate Institute, Newberry College, A.B. 1922, D.D. 1956; Lutheran Theological Southern Seminary, B.D. 1927.
Ordination: 1927 by North Carolina Synod.
Calls: Faith, Faith, 1927-33; St. Mark's, Mooresville, 1933-48; Vice Pastor, St. Paul, Dallas; Vice Pastor, Grace, Bessemer City; Vice Pastor, St. John's, Cherryville.
Other: Taught at Mount Pleasant Collegiate Institute, 1922-24. Superintendent, Lowman Home for the Aged and Helpless, 1949-51; Member, Board of Lowman Home, 1941-48. Retired 1961 at Gastonia. Active in Piedmont (South Carolina) Council, Boy Scouts of America, 1943-48; awarded Silver Beaver, 1946. Executive Committee, North Carolina Synod, 1933-35; Delegate to Convention of Lutheran Church in America, 1942, 1948.
Date of Death/Burial Location: September 2, 1983; Mt. Hermon Lutheran Church Cemetery, Concord, N.C.

BLACKWELDER, OSCAR FISHER
Date/Place of Birth: March 6, 1898; Newberry, S.C.
Parents: John Alexander Blackwelder and Dora Esther (Fisher) Blackwelder, a great-great-granddaughter of the Reverend Adolph Nussmann.
Spouse/Marriage Date: Geneva (Lionberger) Blackwelder; June 28, 1926 in Roanoke, Va.
Children: Theodore Fisher, The Reverend David Lewis.
Education: Mount Pleasant Collegiate Institute, Roanoke

College, A.B. 1917, L.L.D. 1942; Lutheran Theological Southern Seminary, 1920; graduate study, Union Seminary and Columbia University; Susquehanna University, D.D. 1928.
Ordination: 1920 by North Carolina Synod.
Calls: Supply Pastor, St. Martin, Stanly County, 1920; Christ, Roanoke, Va.; Christ, Baltimore, Md.; Reformation, Washington, D.C., 1933-54, Pastor Emeritus, 1954-1961.
Other: Retired early because of ill health. In United Lutheran Church in America, served on Board of Publication, Executive Board, as convention delegate, and chaplain in 1948. Washington correspondent, *The Lutheran*, about twenty years. Preacher, National Preaching Mission, 1936-37, and Sunday Vespers, ABC Radio; Co-author, *Reality in Preaching;* contributed *Exposition on Galatians* in Interpreter's Bible.
Date of Death/Burial Location: April 6, 1961; Roanoke, Va.

BLAKE, CHARLES KING

Date/Place of Birth: March 14, 1954; Baltimore, Md.
Education: St. Paul College, A.A. Foreign Language 1975; Concordia College, B.A. Education 1977; Gettysburg Seminary, M.Div. 1993.
Ordination: 1994 by Maryland Synod.
Calls: Prince of Peace, Greensboro, 1994-95.
Other: Moved to Maryland. Dropped from roll January 19, 1997.

BLUME, HARVEY LUDWICK

Date/Place of Birth: May 16, 1936; Concord, N.C.
Parents: Fred William Blume and Mary Bell (Chambers) Blume.
Spouse/Marriage Date: Susanne (Snyder) Blume of Bryn Mawr, Pa.; August 20, 1960 in Hickory, N.C.
Children: Karen Blume Feezor, Carol Blume Everhart, Lara Blume Garrett.
Education: Lenoir-Rhyne, A.B. English 1958; Lutheran Theological Southern Seminary, M.Div. 1961; graduate work at Lutheran Theological Southern Seminary and Drew University.
Ordination: June 11, 1961 by North Carolina Synod.
Calls: St. Luke-Salem Parish, Lincolnton, 1961-63; St. Mark, Lumberton, 1963-70; St. Mark, China Grove, 1970-91; Sardis, Hickory, 1991-98. Retired 1998. Vice Pastor at various congregations.
Other: Chair, Synodical Youth Committee; Chair, Synodical Campus Ministry Committee; Chair, Special Synodical Committee on Election of the President; Synodical Stewardship Committee; American Missions Committee; Secretary, Central Conference; President, Rowan Cooperative Christian Ministry.

BOAZ, CHARLES HARTER

Date/Place of Birth: May 14, 1921; Downers Grove, Ill.
Parents: Mr. and Mrs. Ralph Warren Boaz.
Spouse/Marriage Date: Doris Mabel (Balleine) Boaz; August 17, 1946.
Children: Carol Sue, Betty Balleine, Charlinna Alberta, Debra Lee.
Education: Armour Institute, Chicago, 1939-40; Capital University, Columbus, Ohio, B.A. 1954; Evangelical Lutheran Theological Seminary, Columbus, Ohio, Diploma 1956.
Ordination: June 24, 1956 by American Lutheran Church.

Calls: Christ the King, Kenner, La., 1956-59; Grace, Abilene, Texas, 1959-62; Old St. Paul, Newton, 1962- 70; Atonement, Jacksonville, Fla., 1970-79; St. Peter, Baltimore, Md., 1979-88.
Other: Retired in 1988.
Date of Death/Burial Location: May 1, 1992. N.C.

BOCK, HOWARD WALTER

Date/Place of Birth: April 10, 1919; Hazelton, Pa.
Parents: John Howard Bock and Anna (Stoltz) Bock.
Spouse/Marriage Date: Margaret (Miller) Bock; December 3, 1940 in Wilmington, Del.
Children: William George, Margaret Ann, Catherine Elizabeth.
Education: Muhlenberg College, A.B. 1939; Philadelphia Seminary, two years; Temple University Seminary, S.T.B. 1946; graduate study, Gettysburg Seminary.
License/Ordination: Licensed 1946 and ordained 1947 by Central Pennsylvania Synod.
Calls: In Pa.: Garrett Parish, Garrett, 1947-48; St. Paul, McSherrystown, 1948-1951; St. James, Ashland, 1951-53; Windsor Park Parish, York, 1953-1957. In N.Y.: Zion, Clarence Center, 1957-59; St. Paul, Syracuse, 1959-61. Durham, N.C. on disability, 1961-62; Our Redeemer, Greenville, 1962-63.
Date of Death/Burial Location: February 25, 1963; Greenwood Cemetery, Greenville, N.C.

BOCKELMAN, PAUL LOUIS

Date/Place of Birth: August 16, 1931; Toledo, Ohio.
Parents: Louis Christopher Bockelman and Bessie Lavern (Laubenthal) Bockelman.
Spouse/Marriage Date: Ruth Madilyn (Troutman) Bockelman; June 27, 1954.
Children: Debra J. Schmidt, Paul Dean, Mark Alan, Timothy Lee.
Education: Capital University, B.S. Music 1953; Trinity Seminary, M.Div. 1962.
Ordination: June 10, 1962 by Ohio District, American Lutheran Church.
Calls: Bethel, Russell, Ky., 1962-66; Atonement, Muskego, Wis., 1966-70; Hope, Fostoria, Ohio, 1970-85; Abiding Savior, Asheville, 1985-1991; Trinity, Vale, 1991-95.
Other: Retired July 2, 1995 in Mooresville. U.S. Army, 1953-55. Music Teacher in Onsted, Mich., 1955-56, and Deshler, Ohio, 1956-58.

BODIE, EARL KENNAN

Date/Place of Birth: November 8, 1896; Orangeburg, S.C.
Parents: The Reverend Nathan Davis Bodie and Lilla E. (Vansant) Bodie.
Spouse/Marriage Date: Annie Belle (Dantzler) Bodie; October 19, 1922 in Cameron, S.C.
Children: Ehrline (died after four days), Geraldine, Rosalind Bowling, Jacqueline Parsavand.
Education: Mount Pleasant Collegiate Institute, Newberry College, A.B. 1917; Lutheran Theological Southern Seminary, 1920; Philadelphia Seminary, B.D. 1921.
Ordination: June 10, 1921 by North Carolina Synod.
Calls: St. Stephen-Mt. Olive, Cabarrus County, 1921-24; Pine Grove, Lone Star, S.C., 1924-30; St. Matthew, Wilmington, 1930-38; St. Luke, Bear Poplar, 1938-43; Bethany, Kannapolis, 1943-52; Sharon-Peace, Gibsonville, 1952-56; Nazareth, Rural Hall, 1956-

64. Vice Pastor at various congregations.

Other: Board of Children's Home of the South, 1953-60. Retired 1963 near Elon College. Historical Works Committee of North Carolina Synod, 1969-74.

Date of Death/Burial Location: September 26, 1987; Alamance Memorial Gardens, Burlington, N.C.

BODIE, NATHAN DAVIS

Date/Place of Birth: January 25, 1862; Saluda County, S.C.

Parents: Obediah Bodie and Annie Elizabeth (Chapman) Bodie.

Spouse/Marriage Date: Lilla E. (Vansant) Bodie; December 24, 1895 in Saluda, S.C.

Children: The Reverend Earl Kennan, Ralph Gilbert, Muriel, Winifred, Henry Cromer, Nathan Vansant.

Education: Newberry College, A.B. 1893, A.M.; Lutheran Theological Southern Seminary, 1895, B.D. 1926.

Ordination: 1894 by South Carolina Synod.

Calls: In South Carolina, 1894-98, 1907-12. In Georgia, 1898-1903. In North Carolina in 1903-07 and 1912-26: Christiana, Granite Quarry-Union, Rowan County; St. Luke-Pilgrim, Davidson County- Reformation, Davie County; Christiana-Wittenberg, Granite Quarry-St. James, Rockwell; Grace, Thomasville; second time, Union, Rowan County.

Other: Retired 1927. Pioneer in Sunday School teacher training. Member and Chair, Boards of Mount Pleasant Collegiate Institute and Mont Amoena Seminary. Joint Communion Basis and Constitution for Merger of North Carolina and Tennessee Synods, 1919-21.

Date of Death/Burial Location: October 9, 1934; Union Church, Rowan County, N.C.

BOGER, RICHARD EDWIN, JR.

Date/Place of Birth: May 13, 1952; Atlanta, Ga.

Parents: Richard E. Boger, Sr. and Marie (Leonard) Boger.

Spouse/Marriage Date: Jill Roberta (Howard) Boger; April 26, 1980 in Peachtree City, Ga.

Child: John Michael Howard.

Education: Lenoir-Rhyne, A.B. Philosophy 1973; Hamma Divinity School, Pacific Lutheran Theological Seminary, M.Div. 1978.

Ordination: August 31, 1980 by Southeastern Synod, Lutheran Church in America.

Calls: Our Savior, Jacksonville, 1980-90; Nazareth, Rural Hall, 1990-. Vice Pastor at various congregations.

Other: President, Forsyth Lutheran Council, 1993; Vice President, 1995; President, Rural Hall-Stanleyville Ministerial Association, 1995; North Carolina Synod Worship and Music Committee, 1982, 1984-86, 1994; *Who's Who in Religion*, 1992-93.

BOGER, WILLIAM JENNINGS
Date/Place of Birth: July 13, 1869; Cabarrus County, N.C.
Parents: Daniel Philip Boger and Nannie Estelle (Crowell) Boger.
Spouse/Marriage Date: Mary Jane Christine (Cook) Boger; December 7, 1897 in Mt. Pleasant, N.C.
Children: Daniel Jennings, William Jonas, Charles Cook, Henry Crawford.
Education: North Carolina College, A.B. 1893; Philadelphia Seminary, 1897; Lenoir-Rhyne, D.D. 1926.
Ordination: 1897 by Tennessee Synod.
Calls: Good Shepherd, Mt. Holly-Lutheran Chapel, Gastonia, 1897-1909; Good Shepherd only, 1909-13; organized and served Holy Comforter, Belmont, 1910-12; with the Reverend W. A. Deaton, organized and supplied Holy Trinity, Gastonia, 1898-1900, 1901-02; St. Luke-Morning Star, Monroe, 1913-18; St. Paul, Startown-St. James-Ebenezer, Newton, 1918-27; St. James only, 1927-36.
Other: Retired 1936 to live in Mt. Pleasant, N.C.; President, Tennessee Synod, 1910-11; Member, 1903-32, and President, 1926-32, Board, Lenoir-Rhyne; Member, original (1914-15) Joint Commission to Propose Union of North Carolina and Tennessee Synods.
Date of Death/Burial Location: January 29, 1949; Mt. Pleasant, N.C.

BOGGS, JACOB MARION
Date/Place of Birth: June 23, 1941; Rowan County, N.C. *Parents*: Harvey William Boggs and Mary Jane (Younce) Boggs.
Spouse/Marriage Date: Jane Eleanor (Goodman) Boggs; March 4, 1962 in Salisbury, N.C.
Children: Tamara Letitia, Derek Anthony, Amanda Kristina.
Education: Pfeiffer; Lenoir-Rhyne, B.A. History/Sociology 1964; Lutheran Theological Southern Seminary, M.Div. 1968; San Francisco Theological Seminary, 1975-76.
Ordination: June 8, 1968 by North Carolina Synod.
Calls: Holy Cross, Mocksville, 1968-71; Vice Pastor/Interim of various congregations; Chaplain, U.S. Air Force, 1971-97; Colonel, Chief of Chaplain Support Element, Office of the Air Force Chief of Chaplains, Washington, D.C.; retired, 1997 to Salisbury; Amity, Cleveland, 1998-.
Other: Transferred to Southern California (West) Synod, 1988; Board of Trustees, Lutheran Theological Southern Seminary, 1970-72.

BOGGS, JAMES RUSSELL
Date/Place of Birth: November 18, 1923; Catawba County, N.C.
Parents: Fitzhugh Boggs and Verdie Lee (Loftin) Boggs.
Spouse/Marriage Date: Mary Olivia (Cloninger) Boggs; December 27, 1943 in Claremont, N.C.
Children: Olivian Russell, Terry Kristen.
Education: Lenoir-Rhyne, A.B. 1944; Lutheran Theological Southern Seminary, M.Div. 1946; U.S. Army Chaplains School; Newberry College, D.D. 1990.
Ordination: July 14, 1946 by North Carolina Synod.
Calls: Grace-Melanchthon-Richland, Liberty, 1946-48; Cedar Grove, Leesville, S.C.,

1949-53. Mission Developer and first Pastor, Our Redeemer, Montgomery, Ala., 1953-57. Active duty U.S. Army Chaplain, 1957-77, retiring as Colonel in 1977. Director of the Chaplaincy and Chaplain to the Corps of Cadets, The Citadel, Charleston, S.C., 1977-80; Director of Church Relations and Planned Giving, Newberry College, 1980-88; Pastor, preaching point, Holly Hill, S.C., then Mission Developer and first pastor of Hope Lutheran Church, Vance, S.C., 1988-93, Pastor Emeritus.

Other: Retired 1987 and moved to Claremont, N.C. in 1993. Distinguished Service Citation, Lenoir-Rhyne, 1975. Vietnam Service Medal with Bronze Service Star and Legion of Merit. Contributor of articles for *The Lutheran, Parish School Magazine and Luther Life.*

BOGGS, WILLIAM GILMER

Date/Place of Birth: August 1, 1927; Rowan County, N.C.

Parents: Harvey William Boggs and Mary Jane (Younce) Boggs.

Spouse/Marriage Date: Peggy Jolene (Lipe) Boggs; December 19, 1948 in China Grove, N.C.

Children: Dwight Randall, Sydna Jolene Shaw, Karen Denise Wagner, Kevin Gilmer.

Education: Lenoir-Rhyne, A.B. 1947; Lutheran Theological Southern Seminary, M.Div. 1950; graduate work at Union Seminary, N.Y.; Duke University and at University of Southern California, 1967; Baptist Hospital, Winston-Salem, Clinical Pastoral Education 1969; numerous military schools.

Ordination: June 25, 1950 by North Carolina Synod.

Calls: Christiana, Granite Quarry, 1950-56. Chaplain, U.S. Air Force, 1956-87.

Served as Interim Pastor at various congregations.

Other: President, Luther League, Northern District; Chair, Evangelism Committee of North Carolina Synod; U.S. Air Force Award for Humanitarian Service; Outstanding Young Chaplain of U.S. Air Force in European Theater; Chair, Japan District, Boy Scouts; Legion of Merit; Presidential Unit Citation; U.S. Air Force Commendation Medal, received three; U.S. Air Force Meritorious Service Medal, received four; Edwin Chess Award for Excellence of Service Involving Sensitivity of Human Needs; National Defense Service Medal; Chaplain, Arlington National Cemetery and Air Staff at the Pentagon; visited sites for White House; Senior Inspector for world-wide Chaplain Service, 1978-80. Served as Senior Chaplain at installations from 1968-87. Retired March 1987 from Shaw Air Force Base, S.C., to China Grove, N.C.

BOHR, CHRISTINE LADONNA

Date/Place of Birth: January 3, 1949; York County, Pa.

Parents: William Robert Bohr and Lottie Marie (Koller) Bohr.

Education: Catawba College, A.B. 1970; Richland Memorial Hospital, Columbia, S.C., Clinical Pastoral Education 1976; Lutheran Theological Southern Seminary, M.Div. 1979; graduate work at University of North Carolina at Chapel Hill, 1972-74.

Ordination: June 10, 1979 by North Carolina Synod.

Calls: St. David, Kannapolis, 1979-82; Christ, Brooklyn, N.Y., 1982-

BOLAND, ARTHUR GLENN

Date/Place of Birth: August 6, 1940; Columbia, S.C.

Parents: Arthur Clyde Boland and Mary Evelyn (Riser) Boland.

Spouse/Marriage Date: Carole Elaine (Albert) Boland; June 23, 1962.

Child: Lane Albert.

Education: Newberry College, A.B. 1962; Lutheran Theological Southern Seminary, M.Div. 1966; graduate work at University of Georgia, 1968; and in Pastoral Care at Lutheran Theological Southern Seminary, 1967- 69.

Ordination: June 1966 by South Carolina Synod.

Calls: St. Michael, Moncks Corner, S.C., 1966-70; Resurrection, Kings Mountain, N.C., 1971-78; Haven, Salisbury, 1979-83; Holy Trinity, Charlotte, 1983-91; Grace, Rock Hill, S.C., 1991-95; Kimball, Kannapolis, 1995-.

Other: Member, Youth Ministry Committee, South Carolina Synod, 1967-69. In North Carolina Synod: Member, Educational Ministry Committee, 1973-79, Chair, 1975-79; Educational Ministry Coordinator, 1977- 78; Evangelical Outreach Consultant, North Carolina Synod, 1981; Member, Parish Life and Ministry Development Team, North Carolina Synod, 1983; Evangelism Committee, 1988; Member, Carolina's Evangelism Conference Task Group; Chair, Evangelism Rally Task Group; Metrolina AIDS Project, Charlotte; American Red Cross, Mecklenburg County, AIDS Education Task Force, 1989; Workshop Leader for *Faces of AIDS* Conference, Metrolina AIDS Project and University of North Carolina at Charlotte, 1989. Hospice; Board, Brothers, Inc.; Board, Lutheran Children's Home of the South, 1975-78; Director, Lutheran Family Services of North Carolina, 1979-85, 1986-89, Chair, 1980-82, Finance Committee Chair, 1979, Personnel Committee Chair, 1987-89, AIDS Task Group, 1988. Member of Steering Committee to plan and implement ministry to children and their families in South Carolina, 1989.

BOLAND, LAWSON PETTUS

Date/Place of Birth: February 12, 1875; Little Mountain, S.C.

Parents: Middleton Boland and Annie Barbara (Frick) Boland.

First Spouse/Marriage Date: Orra Elizabeth (Phillips) Boland, May 30, 1901 in Springfield, S.C.; died August 1, 1903.

Child of First Marriage: Blandina, who died in 4th year, two years after her mother's death.

Second Spouse/Marriage Date: Margaret Elizabeth (Powlas) Boland; May 8, 1906 in Barber, N.C.; sister to wives of the Reverends O. W. Aderholdt and John C. Peery and of Misses Maude and Annie Powlas, missionaries to Japan.

Children of Second Marriage: Juanita, Margaret Elizabeth, Annie Barbara, Lawson Powlas.

Education: Newberry College, A.B. 1897; Lutheran Theological Southern Seminary, Mt. Pleasant, 1901.

Ordination: 1901 by Mississippi Synod.

Calls: In Mississippi, 1901-03. In South Carolina, 1903-04. In North Carolina: Lebanon-Providence, Rowan County-St. Matthew, Davie County, 1904-08. In South Carolina: Pine Grove, Lone Star-Trinity, Elloree, 1908- 16; St. James-Beth Eden-Colony, Newberry County, 1916-24. In North Carolina: St. Enoch, Enochville- Trinity, Concord, 1924-32; St. John-Friendship-Shiloh, Taylorsville, 1932-40. After retirement in 1940 supplied Lebanon, Rowan County, 1942-44.

Other: Board, Summerland College, 1910-24; Board, Children's Home of the South, 1929-33; Member, Ordination Board Examining Committee, middle 1930s.
Date of Death/Burial Location: October 30, 1966; Lebanon Lutheran Church Cemetery, Cleveland, N.C.

BOLAND, MARION QUINCY

Date/Place of Birth: 1873; Newberry County, S.C.
Parents: Daniel C. Boland and Caroline (Meetz) Boland.
Education: Newberry College, A.B. 1896; Lutheran Theological Southern Seminary, 1902.
Ordination: 1902 by Tennessee Synod.
Calls: St. Luke-Morning Star, Monroe, 1902-03. Transferred to Southwest Virginia Synod, 1903. Pastoral service of short duration. Taught school before entering and after leaving ministry.
Date of Death/Burial Location: 1948; St. Peter Church, Chapin, S.C.

BOLDT, KARL L. J., SR.

Date/Place of Birth: October 22, 1864; Mecklenburg-Schwerin, Germany.
Parents: Henry Boldt and Wilhelmina (Westendorff) Boldt. *Spouse/Marriage Date*: Jeanette Caroline (Otgen) Boldt; February 17, 1891 in Charleston, S.C.
Children: Henry G. A., Edward William, Karl Theodore, Lisette H. (married the Reverend Henry J. Black, President of South Carolina Synod), Dorothy J. C., Karl L. J., Jr.
Education: University of Rostock, Germany; Concordia Seminary.
Ordination: 1890 by New York and New Jersey Synod.
Calls: St. Johannes, Charleston, S.C., 1890-93, 1897-1903. In North Carolina: St. Paul, Wilmington, 1893-97.
Other: Taught Greek and Catechetics, Lutheran Theological Southern Seminary, while pastor at St. Johannes.
Date of Death/Burial Location: January 9, 1903; Bethany Cemetery, Charleston, S.C.

BOLICK, ERNEST BERNARD, JR.

Date/Place of Birth: May 7, 1933; Watauga County, N.C.
Parents: Ernest Bernard Bolick, Sr. and Virginia (Moretz) Bolick.
Spouse/Marriage Date: Theresa (Feezor) Bolick; June 11, 1955, in Lexington, N.C.
Child: Maria Theresa.
Education: Lenoir-Rhyne, B.A. 1955; Lutheran Theological Southern Seminary, 1958; University of North Carolina at Chapel Hill, M.A., in History, 1966; University of North Carolina at Greensboro, Doctorate in Education, 1978.
Ordination: 1958 by North Carolina Synod and transferred to Florida Synod.
Calls: Good Shepherd, Sanford, Fla., 1958-63; St. Paul, Clearwater, Fla., 1966-68.
Other: Dean, Eastern District, Florida Synod, 1962-63; History Instructor at University of North Carolina, 1963-66; Listed in *Who's Who in the South and Southwest,* 1965; History Instructor and Dean of Students, Louisburg College, Louisburg, N. C. 1968-69; Education instructor and Research assistant, University of North Carolina-Greensboro, 1974-78 . Resigned in 1969 from Florida Synod; retired 1998 from N.C. Synod.

BOLICK, LEONARD HOMER
Date/Place of Birth: July 17, 1946; Lenoir, N.C.
Parents: Homer Jethro Bolick and Naomi Florence (Bradshaw) Bolick.
Spouse/Marriage Date: Rita Marie (Abee) Bolick; June 15, 1974.
Children: Joseph Leonard, Sarah Rita.
Education: Appalachian State University, B.S. 1968; Lutheran Theological Southern Seminary, M.Div. 1972; McCormick Theological Seminary, D. Min. 1982; graduate Theological Foundation (Notre Dame), D.Min. 1989.
Ordination: June 4, 1972 by North Carolina Synod.
Calls: Calvary, Concord, 1972-84; St. James, Fayetteville, 1984-86; Assistant to Bishop, 1986-96; Bishop of the North Carolina Synod, 1996-. Vice Pastor at various congregations.
Other: Board, Lutheran Theological Southern Seminary; President, Concord Bible Teaching Association; Secretary, Concord Ministerial Association; Lecturer, Hood Theological Seminary; Consultant, Evangelical Lutheran Church in America Colleague Program; Faculty member for SEARCH Bible Study; Staff of Evangelical Lutheran Church in America Start-Up Workshop; Chair, Parish Life of Ministry Development; Adult Leader for Youth Convo; Stewardship Visitation team; Honorary Life Member, Lutheran Men in Mission; Contributions to *Light For Today, Pulpit Digest* and *Graduate Theological Foundation Yearbook.*

BOLIEK, ABNER LAFAYETTE
Date/Place of Birth: June 21, 1862; Alexander County, N.C.
Parents: Anderson Abraham Boliek and Sarah (Docery) Boliek.
First Spouse/Marriage Date: Lula C. (Smyre) Boliek; April 13, 1890 in Conover, N.C.
Children of First Marriage: Gaither Lafayette, Leo Ernst, Paul Marcellus.
Second Spouse/Marriage Date: Fannie Elizabeth (Gaither) Boliek; September 28, 1898 in Rockingham County, Va.
Children of Second Marriage: The Reverend Wynne Colford, Luther Gerberding, the Reverend John Glenn.
Education: Concordia College, Lenoir-Rhyne, A.B. 1891; Rutherford College, Honorary A.M. 1891.
Ordination: 1891 by Indiana Synod.
Calls: In Indiana, 1891-93, 1902-06. In Virginia (Tennessee Synod), 1893-1902, 1921-25, 1925-46. In North Carolina, 1906-21: Beck's-Holly Grove-Emmanuel-Lebanon-New Jerusalem, Davidson County; Friendship-Shiloh, Alexander County, supplying Mt. Pleasant, Watauga County, 1912; organized and served St. Matthew, Caldwell County; St. Timothy-St. Paul, and Bethlehem, Catawba County; Christ's, Stanley; Lutheran Chapel, Gastonia.
Other: Retired 1946 at Luray, Va.; Secretary, Tennessee Synod, one term.
Date of Death/Burial Location: March 8, 1946; Zion Church, near Edinburg, Va.

BOLLES, EDWIN ABIEL
Date of Birth: May 10, 1812.
Education: Tutored by Dr. John Bachman of Charleston; graduated in second class (1835) at Lutheran Theological Southern Seminary.
License/Ordination: Licensed 1836 by North Carolina Synod. Ordained in 1837 by South Carolina Synod in Ebenezer Church, Effingham County, Ga.
Calls: Supplied St. John, Salisbury, 1835-36. Transferred 1836 to South Carolina. Served in Georgia 1837- 43. Supplied churches in the Charleston, S.C. area, 1844-46. Taught school and supplied in Aiken, also supplying Beth Eden and St. James, Newberry, S.C., 1848-52.
Other: Served as Agent of the American Bible Society, 1852-61, 1866-76; Agent of the Confederate States Bible Society, 1863-66; Chaplain of the South Carolina State Mental Hospital, 1876-92; Vice President of the South Carolina Synod, 1874-75, and President, 1876-77.
Date of Death/Burial Location: 1893; Columbia, S.C.

BOLLINGER, JOHN HENRY
Date/Place of Birth: September 17, 1930; Rowan County, N.C.
Parents: Henry Leroy Bollinger and Anne E. (Gardner) Bollinger.
Spouse/Marriage Date: Nancy Jane (London) Bollinger; December 15, 1956 in Mt. Ulla, N.C.
Children: Susan Lynn, John Mark, Steven Craig.
Education: North Carolina State University, B.S. 1954; Lutheran Theological Southern Seminary, B.D. 1958.
Ordination: June 1958 by North Carolina Synod.
Calls: Gladesboro, Hillsville, Va., 1958-62; Prince of Peace, Salisbury, 1962-64. Board of World Missions School of Missions, Lutheran Church in America, 1964-65; Grace, Snyder, Texas, 1965-69; Board of World Missions, Guyana, South America, 1969- 72; St. Paul, Dallas, 1972-93. Vice Pastor at various congregations.
Other: Retired, 1993 to Sugar Grove, N.C. World Missions Committee Chair, Texas-Louisiana Synod; Camp Committee, North Carolina Synod; Lutheran Outdoor Ministries Board, North Carolina Synod, chair for three years.

BOLLINGER, LAWRENCE HUGH
Date/Place of Birth: July 21, 1930; Catawba County, N.C.
Parents: Russell Winston Bollinger and Jessie Elizabeth (Harris) Bollinger.
Spouse/Marriage Date: Cora Alice (Wilson) Bollinger; December 25, 1948 in Hickory, N.C.
Children: Alice Karen Wright, Jan Marie Wright, Paul Stephen, Timothy Hugh, Judy Elise Brown, Nathan Russell.
Education: Lenoir-Rhyne, A.B. 1952; Lutheran Theological Southern Seminary, B.D. 1955.
Ordination: 1955 by North Carolina Synod.
Calls: Bethlehem, Leesville, S.C., 1955-57; Coble's, Guilford County, 1957-62; St. James, Newton, 1963; Holy Trinity, Springfield, Ga., 1971-74; Organ, Rockwell, 1974-81; St. Luke, Mt. Ulla, 1981-83.
Other: Retired 1984. Demitted ministry April 1963 and restored to roll in 1971.
Date of Death/Burial Location: December 24, 1993; Catawba Memorial Park, Hickory, N.C.

BOLLINGER, SCOTT HUNT

Date/Place of Birth: May 7, 1958; Hickory, N.C.
Parents: Ray Hunt Bollinger and Elene (Yount) Bollinger.
Spouse/Marriage Date: Cynda (Harkness) Bollinger; January 21, 1989.
Child: Riley.
Education: Appalachian State University, B.S. in Business Administration 1980; Lutheran Theological Southern Seminary, M.Div. 1993.
Ordination: June 19, 1993 by North Carolina Synod.
Calls: Associate Pastor, Beth Eden, Newton, 1993-98; St. Mark, Claremont, 1998-.
Other: Board, Family Care Center of Catawba Valley, Inc., 1993-98.

BOLLINGER, STEVEN CRAIG

Date/Place of Birth: January 11, 1962; Salisbury, N.C.
Parents: The Reverend John H. Bollinger and Nancy Jane (London) Bollinger.
Spouse/Marriage Date: Marilyn Kay (Purdham) Bollinger; August 3, 1985 in Virginia Beach, Va.
Children: Steven John, Sarah Elizabeth.
Education: Lenoir-Rhyne, B.A. Health and Physical Education 1984; Lutheran Theological Southern Seminary, M.Div. 1988.
Ordination: June 5, 1988 by North Carolina Synod.
Calls: St. Mark's Lutheran, Charlotte, 1988-92; Developer-Pastor, Christ the King, Charlotte, 1992-.

BOLLINGER, THOMAS EUGENE

Date/Place of Birth: January 12, 1932; Turrell, Ark.
Parents: John Thomas Bollinger and Lorez (Simpson) Bollinger.
Spouse/Marriage Date: Rita Louise (Pierce) Bollinger; August 11, 1952 in Memphis, Tenn.
Children: Catherine Elaine, Lydia Ruth, David Michael, Virginia Lee.
Education: Memphis State College, B.S. 1951; Hamma Divinity School, B.D. 1954; University of South, S.T.M.
Ordination: 1954 by Kentucky-Tennessee Synod.
Calls: St. Paul, Louisville, Ky., 1954-56. In North Carolina: Messiah, Salisbury, 1956-58.
Other: Demitted Lutheran ministry, October 1958. Later took orders in The Episcopal Church.
Date of Death: October 24, 1983.

BOLTON, DENNIS RUDOLPH

Date/Place of Birth: March 24, 1953; High Point, N.C.
Parents: Rudolph Alexander Bolton and Gerda Sophie (Gemar) Bolton.
Spouse/Marriage Date: Angela (Polk) Bolton; May 25, 1974.
Children: Jessica Kristen, Brittany Megan.
Education: University of South Carolina at Columbia, B.A. Religious Studies 1975; Lutheran Theological Southern Seminary, M.Div. 1979; Union Seminary, D.Min. 1984; Duke University Medical Center, Clinical Pastoral Education 1988-89.
Ordination: June 3, 1979 by South Carolina Synod.

Calls: Shepherd of the Sea, Atlantic Beach, 1979-81; Christus Victor, Durham, 1981-88; Lutheran Chapel, Gastonia, 1989-95; Mt. Tabor, West Columbia, S.C., 1995-.
Other: Publications - *Lectionary Homiletics; Biblical Preaching Journal; Preaching; Journal of Pastoral Care; Currents; Pulpit Digest.* Editor for Academy of *Parish Clergy Journal - Sharing and Practice.* Chair, Christian Education Committee, 1987-91.

BONHAM, NEHEMIAH, JR.

Date/Place of Birth: November 1, 1765; New Jersey.
Parents: Nehemiah Bonham, Sr. and Elizabeth (Martin) Bonham.
First Spouse: Betsy (Williams) Bonham of New Jersey.
Children of First Marriage: Israel W., James H., Zedekiah Asbury, Nancy, Lucy, Benjamin, Luther.
Second Spouse: Rachel (Karr) Bonham.
Child of Second Marriage: Polly, born in 1792.
Education: Educated in theology under the Reverend Paul Henkel.
License/Ordination: Licensed 1790 and ordained 1791 by Maryland and Virginia Synod.
Calls: In Virginia, itinerating extensively in Grayson, Bland, Wythe, Smyth, and Tazewell Counties. Transferred in 1824 to Tennessee Synod while preaching in Tazewell County, Va. Until his horse died, he made periodic trips from his home west of Canton to visit Tennessee Synod congregations in Virginia, eastern Tennessee and Piedmont North Carolina.   After visiting his most southerly stop in North Carolina (Morning Star, Matthews, he went on south to visit Lutherans near the present city of Lancaster, S.C. Among his stops in North Carolina were: Mt. Moriah, Rowan County, 1830; Morning Star, Mecklenburg County, 1831; occasional supply, St. Martin, Stanly County, 1831-38, and Trinity, Vale, 1833.
Other: He has been described as "a young English preacher who left the Methodist Church at the time when they began to introduce their new mode of shouting and tumult."
Date of Death/Burial Location: November 5, 1846; Morning Star Church, Haywood County, which he organized and served until 1844.

BOOZER, VIRGIL YOUNG, SR.

Date/Place of Birth: June 24, 1868; Newberry County, S.C.
Parents: Henry Sheppard Boozer and Mary Jane (Young) Boozer.
Spouse/Marriage Date: Essie Gertrude (Wyse) Boozer; November 4, 1896 in Prosperity, S.C.
Children: Herman Wyse, Pauline (married the Reverend H. A. Schroder), Mary Elizabeth, Virgil Young, Jr.
Education: Newberry College, A.B. 1891, M.A. 1908, D.D. 1917; Lutheran Theological Southern Seminary, 1894.
Ordination: 1894 by North Carolina Synod.
Calls: In North Carolina, 1894-1916: Salem-Grace-Lebanon, Rowan County; Macedonia, Burlington; organized and built Peace, Guilford County; Bethel-St. Paul, Rowan County; supplied Faith, Faith, two years; St. John, Cabarrus County; First, Lexington; organized, built church, and supplied Grace, Thomasville, four years. In South Carolina and Virginia, 1916-26. In North Carolina, 1926-35: Lutheran Chapel, East Gastonia; Salem, Rowan County, again.

Other: Retired 1935 at Leesville, S.C. Later at Lowman Home. Secretary, 1903-08, President, 1908-10, of North Carolina Synod. Member, Boards of North Carolina College, 1910-16, Lutheran Theological Southern Seminary, 1909-20, 1927-30, and Lowman Home, 1924-26. Member and one-time president, Board of Home Missions, United Synod South, and delegate to seven biennial conventions.

Date of Death/Burial Location: January 6, 1956; Wittenberg Church, Leesville, S.C., which he had served.

BOSCHEN, HENRY JOHN

Date/Place of Birth: February 4, 1937; New York, N.Y.
Parents: Henry Boschen and Dorothee (Rippe) Boschen.
Spouse/Marriage Date: Martha (Burkhard) Boschen; January 25, 1959.
Children: Paul, Ruth Berkelhammer, Elizabeth Stamm, Lois.
Education: Fordham University, B.S. Pharmacy 1957; Trinity Seminary, M.Div. 1963.
Ordination: June 9, 1963 by Eastern District - American Lutheran Church.
Calls: Lutheran General Hospital Chaplain, Park Ridge, Ill., 1963-64; Mission Developer and First Pastor of Hope Lutheran Church, Selden, N.Y., 1964-71; Mission Developer and First Pastor of Community of Christ, Billerica, Mass., 1971-1975; Christ Lutheran, Greensboro, 1975-97; Mission Director, Division for Outreach, Evangelical Lutheran Church in America, serving North Carolina and Virginia Synods, 1997-.

BOST, FLOYD WILLIAM

Date/Place of Birth: July 11, 1928; Rowan County, N.C.
Parents: Holland R. Bost and Grace (Freeze) Bost.
Spouse/Marriage Date: Bonnie Lee (Edwards) Bost; July 20, 1947 in Rowan County, N.C.
Children: Karen Lynn Deal, Wanda Faye Thomas, Dana William.
Education: Newberry College, A.B. 1952; Lutheran Theological Southern Seminary, M.Div. 1955.
Ordination: June 12, 1955 by North Carolina Synod.
Calls: Immanuel, Rockwell, 1955-58; Christ, Fairfax, Va., 1958-64; St. Paul, Rowan County, 1964-81; Zion, Hickory, 1981-91; Prince of Peace, Salisbury, 1991-94; Interim Pastor at various churches.

Other: Retired in 1993 to Salisbury, North Carolina, Dean of Central District and Western District, North Carolina Synod, seven years combined; Chair, Evangelism Committee, North Carolina Synod, six years; Board, North Carolina Lutheran Homes, 1970-80; Executive Board, North Carolina Synod, four terms. Lutheran Church in America Delegate, 1970.

BOST, GENE COLEN

Date/Place of Birth: November 19, 1939; Rowan County, N.C.
Parents: Holland R. Bost and Grace (Freeze) Bost.
Spouse/Marriage Date: Myra (King) Bost; December 20, 1959 in Kannapolis, N.C.
Children: Barry Gene, Keith Alan, Bonnie Sue Benson, Benjamin.
Education: University of North Carolina at Charlotte, B.A. History 1969; Lutheran

Theological Southern Seminary, M.Div. 1973.

Ordination: June 1973 by North Carolina Synod.

Calls: Cross of Christ, Concord, 1973-80; Grace, Salisbury, 1980-; Vice pastor at various congregations.

Other: Historical Works Committee, 1975-79; Lutheran Family Services Board, 1980-92; Delegate to Evangelical Lutheran Church in America Constituting National Convention, 1988.

BOST, LARRY WAYNE

Date/Place of Birth: December 11, 1942; Rowan County, N.C.

Parents: Clarence Edwards Bost and Ruby (Owens) Bost.

First Spouse/Marriage Date: Dr. Mary Lynn (Sidler) Bost; August 15, 1965; died October 2, 1997.

Child: Jonathan Elliott.

Second Spouse/Marriage Date: Linda (Bethea) Bost; April 8, 2000.

Education: Catawba College, A.B. 1964; Lutheran Theological Southern Seminary, M.Div. 1968, D. Min. 1985.

Ordination: June 9, 1968 by North Carolina Synod.

Calls: Amity, Cleveland, 1968-79; Developer-Pastor in Columbia, S.C., to organize a Lutheran witness with the deaf population of the midlands of South Carolina with a home base at St. Paul, Columbia, 1979-85; Pastor, Ministry with the Deaf Lutheran Church, 1985-, the only Evangelical Lutheran Church in America organized deaf congregation in the South.

Other: Instructor in deaf ministry for Lutheran Theological Southern Seminary; resource person for Evangelical Lutheran Church in America and South Carolina Synod for deaf ministry; Global Mission Events Resource person for deaf ministry. Retired 1998.

BOST, RAYMOND MORRIS

Date/Place of Birth: August 18, 1925; Maiden, Catawba County, N.C.

Parents: Loy Robert Bost, Sr. and Virginia Marie (Anderson) Bost.

Spouse/Marriage Date: Margaret Martha (Vedder) Bost; August 16, 1947 in Hartford, Conn.

Children: Timothy Lee, Penelope Ruth Judd, Peter Raymond, Jonathan Otto.

Education: The Citadel, 1942-43; in military service, 1943-47; Lenoir- Rhyne, A.B. 1949, D.D. 1976; Lutheran Theological Southern Seminary, B.D. 1952; Biblical Seminary, New York City; Yale University, M.A. 1959, Ph.D. 1963; Institute for Educational Management, Harvard University, Certificate, 1975; University of Puerto Rico, Certificate, 1983.

Ordination: June 1952 by North Carolina Synod.

Calls: Nativity, Spartanburg, S.C., 1952-53; Holy Trinity, Raleigh, 1953-57; Campus Pastor, North Carolina State University, 1953-57; Campus Pastor, Yale University, 1957-60; Reader, American Studies, Yale University, 1959-60.

Other: Professor of Church History and Director of Field Education at Lutheran Theological Southern Seminary, 1960-66; Part-time Instructor at Benedict College, 1964;

Part-time Instructor at Columbia College, 1963-64; Instructor at Columbia U.S. Army Reserve School, 1961-65; Instructor at U.S. Army Chaplain School, 1964-66; Academic Dean, Professor of History and President, Lenoir-Rhyne, 1966-76; Philadelphia Seminary, President, 1976-85; North Carolina Synod Historian, 1985-87. Academic Dean; Director for Center for Ethical Development; President, Newberry College, 1987-89, 1990-92, 1992-95. Chair, Conference of Directors of Internship, Lutheran Church in America, 1965-66. Contributor to *Christian Unity in North America,* ed. by I. Robert Nelson; *A History of the Lutheran Church in South Carolina,* ed. by P. McCullough; *Essays and Reports, The Lutheran Historical Conference; A Truly Efficient School of Theology,* ed. H. George Anderson and Robert M. Calhoon. Listed in *Who's Who in the South and Southwest; Dictionary of American Scholars; Who's Who in America.* Author with Jeff L. Norris, *All One Body: The Story of the North Carolina Lutheran Synod, 1803-1993.* U.S. Marine Corps, 1943-47; U.S. Army Reserve, Chaplain Branch, 1956-67; South Carolina Synod - Committee on Church Vocations, Historical Works Committee; North Carolina Synod - Chair of the Committee on Continuing Education for Ministers, Examining Committee, Committee for Professional Leadership, Delegate to Lutheran Church in America Conventions in 1970-76. Trustee, Lutheran Theological Southern Seminary, Secretary, Board of Trustees; Lutheran Church in America Board of Theological Education, 1969-70; Lutheran Church in America Standing Committee on Approaches to Unity, 1971-72; Lutheran Church in America Board of Publication, Vice President, 1976-84; Chair, Committee on Public Affairs, North Carolina Council of Churches; President, Raleigh Ministerial Association; Board of Directors, Lutheran Educational Conference in North America, 1970-74, 1983-84; Participant in the Lutheran-United Methodist Dialogues, 2nd series, 1985-87; Board of Directors, Lutheran Historical Conference, 1995-; Vice Chair, Commission on the Future, LECNA; President, Piedmont University Center of North Carolina; President, Independent College Fund of North Carolina; Executive Committee, North Carolina Association of Independent Colleges and Universities. President, Board of Trustees, James R. Crumley, Jr., Archives, 1995-96. Contributor to histories of Lutheran Theological Southern Seminary, the South Carolina Synod and the North Carolina Synod; historical essays published in *The Lutheran Quarterly, Concordia Historical Institute Quarterly,* and in the *Proceedings of the Lutheran Historical Conference.* Chair, Higher Education Tuition Grants Committee for the State of South Carolina. Retired January 1997 in Newton, N.C.

BOSTIAN, MICHAEL DAVID

Date/Place of Birth: August 26, 1954; Cabarrus County, N.C.
Parents: Sylvester Bostian and Arlene (Overcash) Bostian.
Spouse/Marriage Date: Barbara (Holderby) Bostian; October 18, 1980 in Kannapolis, N.C.
Children: Matthew David, Laura Elizabeth, Erica Leigh.
Education: Duke University, B.A. 1975; Lutheran Theological Southern Seminary, M.Div. 1980.
Ordination: June 15, 1980 by North Carolina Synod.
Calls: Assistant Pastor, Trinity, Des Plaines, Ill., 1980-82; St. Andrew, West Chicago, Ill., 1982-90; Chaplain, Director Pastoral Care Craven, Regional Medical Center, New Bern, 1991-; Interim Pastor, St. Timothy, Havelock, 1994-.

BOUKNIGHT, LOUIS ELBERT
Date/Place of Birth: July 25, 1908; Little Mountain, S.C.
Parents: Thomas Augustus Bouknight and Mamie Lilla (Cannon) Bouknight.
Spouse/Marriage Date: Mildred Lee (Sayre) Bouknight; June 23, 1937 in Augusta County, Va.
Children: Ray Stephen, Allen Thomas.
Education: Newberry College, A.B. 1931; Lutheran Theological Southern Seminary, B.D. 1934.
License/Ordination: Licensed in 1935 and ordained 1936 by Virginia Synod.
Calls: In Virginia, 1935-49. In West Virginia, 1949-52. In North Carolina: St. Mark's, Mooresville, 1952-59. Transferred to Virginia Synod 1959. Rader-St. John-St. Paul, Timberville, Va., 1965-66.
Other: Retired in 1966.
Date of Death/Burial Location: January 26, 1968; Riverview Cemetery, Waynesboro, Va.

BOVINGDON, MICHAEL WILLIAM
Date/Place of Birth: August 12, 1957; Atlanta, Ga.
Parents: James William Bovingdon and Alice Diane Bovingdon.
Spouse/Marriage Date: Paulette (nee Turq)(Weathers) Bovingdon; June 6, 1982 in East Point, Ga.
Step-*Children*: Shannon Neal Weathers, Darren Robert Weathers.
Education: Lenoir-Rhyne, A.B. 1979; Lutheran Theological Southern Seminary, M.Div. 1983.
Ordination: 1983 by South Carolina Synod.
Calls: Good Shepherd, Hickory, 1983-88; Bethel, Springfield, Ga., 1988.

BOWDEN, GEORGE STEWART, JR.
Date/Place of Birth: September 23, 1920; Charleston, S.C.
Parents: The Reverend George Stewart Bowden, Sr. and Laura Heilig (Lentz) Bowden.
Spouse/Marriage Date: Lois (Wandel) Bowden; June 6, 1945 in Hagerstown, Md.
Children: Twins, George Stewart, III, and Lois Wandel.
Education: Lenoir-Rhyne, A.B. 1941; Lutheran Theological Southern Seminary, B.D. 1944.
Ordination: 1944 by North Carolina Synod.
Calls: Christ, East Spencer, 1944-47. Transferred to Virginia Synod, 1947; St. Peter-St. Matthew, Toms Brook, Va.; Zion-St. James, Waynesboro, Va.; last parish, St. Paul, Funkstown, Md., 1952-64.
Date of Death/Burial Location: March 30, 1964; Resthaven Cemetery, Hagerstown, Md.

BOWDEN, GEORGE STEWART, SR.
Date/Place of Birth: May 11, 1892; Wilmington, N.C.
Parents: Robert Cowan Bowden and Catherine Elizabeth (Bryant) Bowden.
Spouse/Marriage Date: Laura Heilig (Lentz) Bowden; May 22, 1919 in Mt. Pleasant, N.C.; died July 22, 1965(?).
Children: The Reverend George Stewart, Jr., Catherine Barrier.
Education: Mount Pleasant Collegiate Institute, 1914; Newberry College, A.B. 1916;

Lutheran Theological Southern Seminary, 1919.
Ordination: 1919 by North Carolina Synod.
Calls: St. Barnabas, Charleston, S.C., 1919-22; St. Paul, Strasburg, Va., 1922-29; Holy Trinity, Gastonia, 1929-44.
Other: Board, Children's Home of the South, 1926-29.
Date of Death/Burial Location: August 12, 1944; Gastonia, N.C.

BOWLES, JOHN D.
Date/Place of Birth: January 25, 1832; Newberry County, S.C.
Spouse/Location of Marriage: Margaret Carolina (Fellers) Bowles in Newberry County, S.C.
Children: Ella (daughter-in-law of the Reverend W. A. Julian), Monroe, Jeff, Ida M.
Education: Perhaps at Newberry College, Lutheran Theological Southern Seminary, 1860.
Ordination: 1861 by Georgia Synod.
Calls: In Georgia, 1861-69. Transferred to North Carolina Synod, 1869; Nazareth-Shiloh, Forsyth County; Beck's-Bethany-Lebanon-Pilgrim-St. Luke, Davidson County; Reformation, Davie County. Transferred to South Carolina Synod, 1874.
Other: President, North Carolina Synod, 1873.
Date of Death/Burial Location: June 20, 1914; Colony Church, Newberry, S.C.

BOWMAN, WILLIAM SPENCER
Date/Place of Birth: August 3, 1830; Powell's Fort Valley, Shenandoah County, Va.
Parents: George Bowman and Susan Bowman.
First Spouse: Mary Virginia (Andrews) Bowman; died April 21, 1869.
Second Spouse/Marriage Date: George Anna (Hacker) Bowman; August 8, 1871 in Charleston, S.C.; died April 4, 1880.
Third Spouse/Marriage Date: Catherine Anna (Bonchert) Bowman; January 10, 1882; died September 22, 1891.
Fourth Spouse: Margaret Catherine (Barrier) Bowman; August 18, 1896 in Cabarrus County, N.C.
Education: In common schools, and as apprentice to cabinet maker; followed that trade for a few years; studied theology under tutors; Newberry College, D.D. 1870.
License/Ordination: Licensed in 1854 and ordained 1856 by Virginia Synod.
Calls: In Virginia, 1854-59; St. Andrew's, Charleston, S.C., 1859-80; Ascension, Savannah, Ga., 1880-90. In North Carolina: St. Mark's, Charlotte, 1890-97. It is said that in 1860-61 in Charleston, he baptized, received by certificate, and communed Negroes.
Other: President, 1871, Vice President, 1876, South Carolina Synod; President, Board of Newberry College, and twice was offered college presidency, but declined. President, General Synod South 1884.
Date of Death/Burial Location: March 26, 1900; Charleston, S.C.

BOYD, JOHN EBENEZER, JR.
Date/Place of Birth: February 7, 1943; Statesville, N.C.
Parents: John Ebenezer Boyd, Sr. and Evelyn (Walker) Boyd.

Spouse/Marriage Date: Lynda Diane (Strange) Boyd; November 24, 1967 in Florence, S.C.
Children: Kristen Louise, Amanda Elizabeth.
Education: Catawba College, A.B. 1965; Lutheran Theological Southern Seminary, M.Div. 1970; Columbia Theological Seminary, D.Min. 1990.
Ordination: June 7, 1970 by North Carolina Synod.
Calls: Grace Lutheran, Rock Hill, S.C., 1970-75; Ascension, Savannah, Ga., 1975-76; Holy Trinity, North Augusta, S.C., 1976-1985; Calvary, Concord, 1985-. Vice Pastor at various congregations.
Other: Examining Committee, 1972-76; Board, Lutheridge, 1973-76; 1977-90, President, 1982-90; North Carolina Synod Education Committee, 1991-, Chair, 1991-; Co-author of the North Carolina Synod Call Process; Hospice of Cabarrus County Board of Trustees and Board Chair, 1987-93; Published works include D.Min. Dissertation: *A Workshop for Training Lay Members to Work with the Terminally Ill, 1990.* Honors include Distinguished Service Award, Rock Hill Jaycees; Honorary Life Member, Lutheran Men in Mission.

BOYE, RICHARD ERIK

Date/Place of Birth: September 10, 1928; Kansas City, Mo.
Parents: Erik C. Boye and Helen (Jackson) Boye.
Spouse/Marriage Date: Mary Fonda (Setzer) Boye, daughter of the Reverend Roy B. Setzer and sister of the Reverend Peter Setzer; June 1, 1952 in Louisville, Ky.
Children: Carol Borovatz, Leanne Buckley, The Reverend Erik J., Kirsten Herman.
Education: Wittenberg University, B.A. 1949; Hamma Divinity School, M.Div. 1952; graduate work at Union Seminary, 1954, and Chicago Seminary, 1957.
Ordination: May 14, 1952 by Illinois Synod of the United Lutheran Church.
Calls: Amity Lutheran Church (now Good Shepherd), Lena, Ill., 1952-56; Trinity, Carthage, Ill., 1956-60; Good Shepherd, Southampton, Pa., 1960-80; St. Mark's, Charlotte, 1980-83; Elim, Robbinsdale, Minn., 1983- 93.
Other: Retired October 31, 1993; Pastor Evangelist of the Lutheran Church in America; Two sermon books published - *I Saw a New Heaven* and *Affirming Life.* Board of Social Missions, Illinois Synod; Examining Committee, Illinois Synod; Secretary-Chair of the Committee of American Missions, Southeast Pennsylvania Synod; Instructor at Carthage College for two years.

BRAKE, DENNY JUNIOR

Date/Place of Birth: July 10, 1927; Columbus, Ohio.
Parents: Charles Denman Brake and Hazel (Mock) Brake.
Spouse/Marriage Date: Sarah Jane (Berg) Brake; August 28, 1949.
Children: Donald David, Jeanette Marie Kuchenreuther, Joseph Charles.
Education: University of Southern California, B.A. Education; Luther Seminary, M.Div. 1961; graduate work at various places.
Ordination: June 1961; Los Angeles, Calif.
Calls: Looney Valley - Cedar Valley Parish, Houston, Minn., 1961-67; Elgin Highland Parish, Elgin, Iowa, 1967-71; Ascension, Marion, Iowa, 1971-75; St. Peter, Denver, Iowa; Messiah, Janesville, Iowa, 1975-84; St. John, Pomeroy, Iowa, 1984-92. Interim Pastor at Abiding Presence, Fuquay-Varina, 1992-93.
Other: Retired to Raleigh in September 1992. Had newspaper column in five of the towns

where he served. Had radio program each weekday morning in Twin Lakes, Iowa. Two books: *Christ in Our Vacation* and *Prayer and Praise Along the Way.*

BRASWELL, JAMES C., JR.

Date/Place of Birth: September 10, 1945; Washington, D.C.
Parents: James C. Braswell, Sr. and Wilda (Guy) Braswell.
Spouse/Marriage Date: Jeryl (Slaughenhaupt) Braswell; July 5, 1966.
Children: Amy Lynn Graham, Teresa Guy Saleeby, James C., III, David Henry, Leah Christine.
Education: Smithdeal-Massey, Business Administration 1965; University of North Carolina at Charlotte, Psychology 1982; Lutheran Theological Southern Seminary, M.Div. 1985.
Ordination: 1985 by North Carolina Synod.
Calls: St. Luke, Mt. Ulla, 1985-88; Mt. Calvary, Mt. Jackson, Va., 1988-90; Our Savior, Jacksonville, 1990- 96; St. Matthew, Herron, Md., 1996-.

BRENDLE, IVERSON McKOY, JR.

Date/Place of Birth: June 25, 1930; Burke County, N.C.
Parents: The Reverend Iverson McKoy Brendle, Sr. (Methodist minister) and Mozelle (Esker) Brendle.
Education: Lenoir-Rhyne, A.B. 1954; Lutheran Theological Southern Seminary, B.D. 1959.
Spouse/Marriage Date: Margaret Gayle (Bess) Brendle; June 25, 1950 in Lincoln County, N.C.
Children: Lewis Manuel, Sandra Naomi, Caryl Elizabeth.
Ordination: 1959 by North Carolina Synod.
Calls: St. Martin, Stanly County, 1959-63; Sardis, Catawba County, 1963-74; Immanuel, Rockwell, 1974-81. Vice Pastor at various congregations.
Other: Dropped from roll, May 25, 1984.

BRINK, CARL ALBIN

Date/Place of Birth: November 2, 1927; Hartford, Conn.
Parents: John A. Brink and Hildur (Anderson) Brink.
Education: University of Connecticut, B.A. 1951, graduate study, 1957-58; Augustana Seminary, S.M. 1955.
Ordination: 1955 by Augustana Lutheran Church.
Calls: In Minnesota, New Jersey, and Michigan, 1955-62. Since 1962 U.S. Navy Chaplain. Transferred May 31, 1963 to North Carolina Synod, while stationed at Camp Lejeune, from Wisconsin-Upper Michigan Synod, and to New England Synod, July 5, 1963.

BRITTON, CHARLES THOMAS

Date/Place of Birth: May 15, 1950; Greensboro, N.C.
Parents: Elmer W. Britton and Frances (Gilbert) Britton.
Education: Lenoir-Rhyne, B.A. English Literature 1972; Chicago Seminary, M.Div. 1976; graduate work at University of Chicago, 1974-76; graduate work at Philadelphia Seminary,

1977; graduate work at Cambridge University, England, 1978; graduate work at Princeton University, S.T.M. 1981; graduate work at Strasbourg, France.

Ordination: June 13, 1976 by North Carolina Synod.

Calls: Grace, Malvern, Pa., 1976-81; Headmaster Lutheran Parish School and Pastor/Minister Frederick Evangelical, St. Thomas, U.S. Virgin Islands, 1981-83; Grace, Liberty, 1984-90; Kure Memorial, Kure Beach, 1990-92; Greensboro.

Other: Chaplain, Pastoral Care Department, Baptist Hospital, Winston-Salem, N.C., 1974; *Driftings, Quasars and Daffodils, Gathering Up the Fragments* by Maude O. Powlas editor and ghost writer, World Hunger Activity Poster for Children with Dr. Allan Hart Jahsmann; *Imagination in the Poetry of Gerald Manley Hopkins.* Chair, Hospice Care Unit, Paoli Memorial Hospital, Paoli, Pa., 1981; Assistant Editor, Program Resources, Division for Parish Service, Lutheran Church in America, 1974-75. Editor, *Seeker,* Journal of Lutheran School of Theology at Chicago, 1974-76; Director of Music, Yellowstone National Park, Wyo., 1972; Intern in Religious Journalism, *The Lutheran,* 1973; Business and Tour Manager, Lenoir-Rhyne Choir, 1969-72; Senior Research Assistant, Humanities Division, Lenoir-Rhyne, 1968- 71; Director of Music-Organist, Church of the Master United Church of Christ, 1968-72; *Outstanding Young Men of America,* 1976; Annual Award for Outstanding Service to Campus and Community, Lenoir-Rhyne, 1972. Publications in various magazines. The Greater Malvern Ministerium, President, 1980- 81; Southeastern Pennsylvania Synod Worship Commission, Secretary, 1980-81; Southeastern Pennsylvania Youth Ministry Committee, 1977-79; Synod Lay School of Theology, Steering Committee, 1979-81, Instructor in Worship, 1981; Editor, *Soli Deo Gloria,* quarterly journal in worship, music and the fine arts. Editor, *We Believe in One God,* Essays in Honor of Michael McDaniel, 1992-93; *Worship Alive: The Care and Feeding of Christians;* World Peace Through World Law Speech Award, 1968. Demitted August 1992. Counselor, Triad Health Project, 1993-96.

Date of Death: January 2, 1998; Memorial Service at First Lutheran, Greensboro, N.C.

BROKHOFF, JOHN RUDOLPH

Date/Place of Birth: December 19, 1913; Pottsville, Pa.

Parents: John H. Brokhoff and Gertrude A. (Heiser) Brokhoff.

First Spouse/Marriage Date: Helen (Leininger) Brokhoff; June 20, 1938 in Pottsville, Pa.

Children of First Marriage: Wendy Ann, Helen Elaine, Virginia Sue, John William, Jodi.

Second Spouse/Marriage Date: The Reverend Barbara J. Brokhoff; June 9, 1972.

Education: Muhlenberg College, A.B. 1935, D.D. 1951; Philadelphia Seminary, M.Div. 1938; University of Pennsylvania, M.A. 1938.

Ordination: 1938 by Ministerium of Pennsylvania.

Calls: Assistant at First English, Richmond, Va., 1938-40; Ebenezer, Marion, Va., 1940-42; Christ, Roanoke, Va., 1942-45; Redeemer, Atlanta, Ga., 1945-55; St. Mark's, Charlotte, 1955-62; Trinity, Lansdale, Pa., 1962-65. Professor of Homiletics, Candler School of Theology, Emory University, 1965-78; Theologian in Residence, St. Paul United Methodist, Largo, Fla., 1993-.

Other: Board, Marion College and Children's Home of the South. United Lutheran Church in America counselor to National Lutheran Council. Called often for preaching in missions and at colleges. Executive Committee, North Carolina Synod, 1959-62; President, Mecklenburg Ministers, Charlotte, 1960-61; WBTV, Charlotte, *Pastors Face Your Questions,* 1955-62; weekly columnist, *The Charlotte Observer,* 1955-62. Author of 35 books; contributor to religious periodicals. George Washington Medal Award by Freedom

Foundation of Valley Forge for sermon, *Human Rights or Duties?*, 1966. One of 50 *Leaders of Tomorrow* by *Time* magazine, 1955. Chaplain, Pennsylvania House of Representatives, 1963-74; *Who's Who in the South,* 1978; Guest Columnist, *The Atlanta Constitution,* 1953-55; weekly column in *The North Penn Reporter,* Lansdale, Pa., 1962-65; Contributing Editor, *The Pulpit Digest,* 1977; Certificate of Merit for Outstanding Service to the Community in the Field of Religion by the Charlotte Junior Women's Club, Charlotte, 1961.
Retired: December 1978.

BROOKS, CHARLES EARNEST

Date/Place of Birth: September 8, 1938; Gaston County, N.C.
Parents: Barnet B. Brooks and Almeddy (Sprinkle) Brooks.
Spouse/Marriage Date: Jo Anne (Cloninger) Brooks; August 28, 1960 in Dallas, N.C.
Children: Nina Marcelle, Carol Anne.
Education: Lenoir-Rhyne, A.B. 1961; Lutheran Theological Southern Seminary, B.Div. 1964; University of North Carolina at Chapel Hill, MSPH 1972, DPH 1974.
Ordination: 1964 by North Carolina Synod.
Calls: Assistant Pastor, St. John, Salisbury, 1964-68; First, Carlisle, Pa., 1968-70; Staff, Tresslor Lutheran Services Association, Williamsport, Pa., 1972-76, Administrative Counseling Programs, 1976-83; Vice President, Lutheran Service Association, Hartford, Conn., 1983-.
Other: Youth Ministry, North Carolina Synod, 1967-68.

BROWDER, RICHARD ALLEN

Date/Place of Birth: August 18, 1943; Madison, Ind.
Parents: Clarence Browder and Mary Browder.
Spouse/Marriage Date: Belinda Jo (Cronkhite) Browder; June 7, 1964.
Children: Richard Wayne, Amy Jo, Caroline Elizabeth.
Education: Indiana State University, B.S. 1965; Evangelical Theological Seminary, M.Div. 1971.
Ordination: June 27, 1971 by Eastern District of the American Lutheran Church.
Calls: Mt. Pisgah, Hickory, 1971-88; Faith, Suffolk, Va., 1989-.

BROWER, SALLY (MORGAN)

Date/Place of Birth: May 22, 1949; Norfolk, Va.
Parents: Chester D. Morgan and Priscilla H. Morgan.
Spouse/Marriage Date: A. Brent Brower; June 19, 1971.
Children: Staley Erin, Stephen Ross.
Education: Virginia Commonwealth University, BFA-Design 1971; North Carolina State University, M.S. Psychology 1978, Ph.D. Psychology, 1987; Erskine Theological, M.Div. 1998; Lutheran Theological Southern Seminary, 1997-99.
Ordination: May 23, 1999 by North Carolina Synod.
Calls: Christ, Charlotte, July 1999-.

BROWN, ABEL J.
Date/Place of Birth: March 27, 1817; near Lincolnton, N.C.
Parents: Absolom Brown and Elizabeth (Killian) Brown.
First Spouse: Julia (Teeter) Brown; died a year later.
Second Spouse/Marriage Date: Nancy (Teeter) Brown, 1842.
Children: Charles A., (may be son of first wife), Agnes, Lizzie, Joe.
Education: Emory and Henry College, A.B., A.M.; Roanoke College, D.D. 1873.
License/Ordination: Licensed 1836 (at age 19) and ordained 1837 by Tennessee Synod.
Calls: In North Carolina: organized Lutheran Chapel, Gastonia, 1838, (*History of the Lutheran Church in North Carolina, (1803-1953)* says, 1828; but he was born in 1817); with other pastors, Morning Star, Mecklenburg County, 1836-39. Moved to Sullivan County, Tenn., where he served Tennessee Synod and later Holston Synod churches, including Immanuel and Buehlers, 1858-94.
Other: Head of Jefferson Male Academy, Blountville, Tenn., five or six years; taught at Tusculum College, Greeneville, Tenn., two years; again at the former school. Secretary, Tennessee Synod, six one-year terms, 1838-52, President, 1854, 1858. One of ten Tennessee Synod pastors organizing Holston Synod, 1860-61, writer of its Constitution, and often its President; with two others lived to celebrate its 25th anniversary in 1886. One-time President of General Synod South; had a leading role in organizing United Synod South, and presided over organizing *Diet at Salisbury,* 1886. Twice elected President of North Carolina College, but declined. Also declined editorship of *The Lutheran Standard* in Ohio At age 21 wrote *A Vindication of the Evangelical Tennessee Synod,* in reply to a sermon by the Reverend Dr. John Bachman. Also, while still young, wrote articles for *The Lutheran Observer* on the Lord's Supper, which the editor, Dr. Kurtz, criticized in lengthy editorials, also complimenting the young writer's talent, but pitying his misdirected zeal. Dr. Brown lived to see his views accepted by great majority of American Lutherans. Contributed to Lutheran magazines; many scholarly sermons issued in pamphlet form.
Date of Death/Burial Location: Collapsed and died shortly after, July 17, 1894 while delivering a funeral discourse at Buehlers Church on *Nightless Day in the Home of the Blest.* Buried at Blountville, Tenn.

BROWN, BACHMAN SAMUEL
Date/Place of Birth: November 19, 1854; in Rowan County, N.C.
Parents: Alexander Brown and Mary (Kistler) Brown.
Spouse/Marriage Date: Mary Catherine (Brown) Brown; November 19, 1878 in Wytheville, Va.
Children: Lillian, Edna, Mary Elizabeth, Monica, the Reverend Bachman Storch, Sr., Eugene Luther, Myron Day, Frank Hatcher.
Education: North Carolina College, Roanoke College, A.B. 1875, D.D. 1925; Lutheran Theological Southern Seminary, 1878.
Ordination: 1878 by North Carolina Synod.
Calls: In Mississippi, 1879-80. In North Carolina, 1881-88: St. Paul-Lutheran Chapel,

Rowan County; Center Grove, Cabarrus County; Holy Trinity-Zion, Hickory. In Virginia: 1888-92, 1911-12. In North Carolina, 1892-1910: Holy Trinity-Prosperity, Mt. Pleasant; First, Albemarle; St. Michael-St. Paul-Amity, Troutman; St. Matthew, Davie County; Providence, Rowan County; St. Luke-Concordia, Rowan County; Salem-Grace, Rowan County; Trinity-Concordia, Landis, 1912-15; and St. Martin, Stanly County, 1920-21. In Tennessee, 1918-20. Supplied Ebenezer, Rowan County, 1927-30.
Other: Retired 1921 at China Grove. Executive Committee, North Carolina Synod, Secretary, 1885, President, 1894-96. Contributor to church periodicals.
Date of Death/Burial Location: June 9, 1934; St. Luke Church, Bear Poplar, N.C.
Note: 1965 *Life Sketches of Lutheran Ministers* lists him as B. S. Brown, Sr. to distinguish him from Bachman Storch Brown, Sr. who was younger and serving during the same time.

BROWN, BACHMAN STORCH, SR.
Date/Place of Birth: October 6, 1889; Madison, Va.
Parents: The Reverend Bachman Samuel Brown and Mary Catherine (Brown) Brown.
Spouse/Marriage Date: Beulah L. (Isenhour) Brown, October 14, 1924 in Concord, N.C.; died June 10, 1991.
Children: Bachman Storch, Jr., Charles Eugene.
Education: Roanoke College, A.B. 1913; Philadelphia Seminary, 1916; Lenoir-Rhyne, D.D. 1944.
Ordination: 1916 by Holston Synod.
Calls: Salem and Luther Memorial, Parrottsville, Tenn., 1916-24. In North Carolina, 1924-59: First, Lexington, fifteen years; Daniel's-Grace, Lincoln County, seven years; Lutheran Chapel, China Grove, thirteen years.
Other: Retired 1959 at Kannapolis. President, Holston Synod, 1919-21. Executive Committee, North Carolina Synod, 32 years, 1925-29, 1935-63; Board, Lenoir-Rhyne, 1930-36, 1949-52; Board, Lutheran Theological Southern Seminary, 1952-55. Chair, special Committee to Study Conditions at Lutheran Theological Southern Seminary, 1951. With Drs. Jacob L. Morgan and John Hall, an Editor of *History of the Lutheran Church in North Carolina, (1803-1953)*. Collaborated with other members of the Historical Works Committee in producing the *History of the North Carolina Synod, (1953-63) Supplement* and *Life Sketches of Lutheran Ministers, North Carolina-Tennessee Synod, 1773-65*. Contributed article for *Lutheran World Encyclopedia*. Served as Vice Pastor at various congregations.
Date of Death/Burial Location: March 9, 1978; Lutheran Chapel, China Grove, N.C.
Note: 1965 *Life Sketches of Lutheran Ministers* lists him as B. S. Brown, Jr. to distinguish him from Bachman Samuel Brown who was older and serving during the same time.

BROWN, CHRISENBERRY ALEXANDER

Date/Place of Birth: December 6, 1859; Rowan County, N.C.
Parents: John D. A. Brown and Sarah Cladora (Fisher) Brown.
Spouse/Marriage Date: Emily Athalinda (Propst) Brown; September 10, 1890 in Rowan County, N.C.
Children: Lala Cladora, Edna Propst, Thelma Ruth, Herman Alexander, Armand Chrisenberry, and an un-named son (last two died in infancy).
Education: Roanoke College, 1887; Gettysburg Seminary, 1890.
Ordination: 1889 by North Carolina Synod.
Calls: In Virginia, 1890-92. In North Carolina, 1892-1932: Grace-Concordia, Rowan County; Christiana-Union, Rowan County; St. Andrew-Mt. Hermon, Concord; Frieden's-Sharon, Gibsonville; Ebenezer-Organ, Rowan County; Center Grove, Kannapolis-Lutheran Chapel, China Grove; organized and supplied Kimball Memorial, Kannapolis, four months; Grace, Rowan County; Prosperity, Cabarrus County.
Other: Retired January 1, 1932 at China Grove. President, North Carolina Synod, 1915-19, re-elected for four years, but declined.
Date of Death/Burial Location: October 8, 1932; China Grove, N.C.

BROWN, HENRY MAXWELL

Date/Place of Birth: April 2, 1845; Rowan County, N.C.
Parents: Solomon Brown and Amy (Miller) Brown. A younger brother of the Reverend R. L. Brown, and an uncle of the Reverend P. D. Brown.
Spouse/Marriage Date: Lucetta Jane (Fisher) Brown; 1873 in Cabarrus County, N.C.
Children: Dora, Lular Rosa, Mary Lucetta (married the Reverend R. R. Sowers), Bachman H., Lillie Eudora, Nathan Maxwell, Myrtle M., Jason S., Clarence E., Clyde G.
Education: North Carolina College, 1873, studying theology there also.
Ordination: 1873 by North Carolina Synod.
Calls: Bethel pastorate, Rowan County, and Reformation, Davie County, 1873-1912; Christ, East Spencer; St. Michael-St. Paul-organized Amity (1885), Iredell County; St. Matthew, Davie County; Nazareth-Shiloh, Rural Hall; Low's, Guilford County; Richland, Liberty; St. Martin, Stanly County. Transferred to South Carolina Synod, 1913.
Other: Author of *The Scriptural Mode of Baptism,* and *Seven Sermons on Creation.*
Date of Death/Burial Location: July 23, 1913; Organ Church, Rowan County, N.C.

BROWN, JOHN DANIEL

Date/Place of Birth: January 27, 1934; Concord, N.C.
Parents: Robert Hall Brown and Cordelia (Cox) (Ritchie) Brown. A great-grandson of the Reverend George H. Cox.
Spouse/Marriage Date: Betty Waddill (Murchison) Brown (daughter of the Reverend J. M. Murchison, Presbyterian minister); June 7, 1957 in Concord, N.C.
Children: Karen Cox, Evelyn Christian.
Education: Lenoir-Rhyne, A.B. 1956; Lutheran Theological Southern Seminary, B.D.

1959; Princeton Seminary, Th.M. 1960; Drew University, Ph.D. 1965.
Ordination: 1959 by North Carolina Synod.
Calls: St. Stephen-Mt. Olive, Cabarrus County, 1959; Grace, Thomasville, 1960-62. Transferred 1965 to South Carolina Synod. Returned to North Carolina Synod, 1967.
Other: Professor, Department of Religion, Converse College 1965-67; Professor, Department of Religion and Philosophy, Catawba College, Salisbury, 1967-97. Demitted February 26, 1970.

BROWN, PETER MARCHMAN

Date/Place of Birth: February 16, 1952; Miami, Fla.
Parents: Oscar L. Brown and Ladye L. Brown.
Spouse: Ann (Alderson) Brown.
Children: Benjamin, Timothy, Christopher.
Education: Texas Lutheran, B.A. 1974; Trinity, M.Div. 1978; graduate work at Trinity College.
Ordination: June 11, 1978 by Florida-Bahamas Synod.
Calls: Prince of Peace, Kalamazoo, Mich., 1978-81; Faith, Orlando, Fla., 1981-83; Director of Recruitment, Trinity Seminary, 1983-84; Epiphany, Toledo, Ohio, 1984-94; St. Paul, Startown, 1994-.
Other: Instructor, Religion-Philosophy Department, Lenoir-Rhyne College.

BROWN, PLEASANT DAVID

Date/Place of Birth: November 26, 1886; Granite Quarry, N.C.
Parents: Nathan Brown and Rosa S. (Agner) Brown. Two uncles were the Reverends H. M. and R. L. Brown.
Spouse/Marriage Date: Florence Adelle (Bodenhorn) Brown; August 20, 1913 in Philadelphia, Pa.; died December 27, 1990.
Children: Robert Meredith, Janice Adelle, Barbara Louise, Lois Elizabeth.
Education: Mount Pleasant Collegiate Institute, Roanoke College, A.B. 1909, A.M. 1910; Philadelphia Seminary, 1913; Newberry College, D.D. 1926.
Ordination: 1913 by North Carolina Synod.
Calls: Women's Memorial (Emmanuel), High Point, Guilford County, 1913-21; Ebenezer, Columbia, S.C., 1921-39; St. John, Salisbury, 1939-52.
Other: Elected second full-time President, North Carolina Synod, 1949, but declined. Board, Lutheran Theological Southern Seminary, 1940-52, President, 1943-52; Elected President of Lutheran Theological Southern Seminary, 1938, but declined. From four to twelve years, member of United Lutheran Church in America boards and commissions including Executive Board, Parish & Church School, Social Missions, Education, Church Papers, Theological Education, and National Lutheran Council. Also of Committee to Study Change of Officers' Titles to Conform to Ecclesiastical and Historical Usage. Delegate from South Carolina and North Carolina Synods to twelve United Lutheran Church in America conventions; Chaplain at the 1946 convention. United Lutheran Church in America delegate to Lund, Sweden, Lutheran World Federation Convention, 1947. Author of *The Christian Home* (study text); *Christ in the Home: The Family Altar* (L.L.M. leaflet); *Things We Ought to Know* (pamphlet on church worship); and *The Widow's Mite*

(meditation in *God's Moment*); also, Editor, September 1936 issue of *Light For Today*.
Date of Death/Burial Location: August 3, 1952; City Memorial Park, Salisbury, N.C.

BROWN, RICHARD L.
Date/Place of Birth: March 18, 1842; Rowan County, N.C.
Parents: Solomon Brown and Amy (Miller) Brown. The older brother of the Reverend H. M. Brown, and an uncle of the Reverend P. D. Brown.
Spouse/Marriage Date: Nancy E. (Agner) Brown, January 31, 1866 in Rowan County, N.C.
Children: Mary L. R., David Solomon, Lewis D. Henry, John Richard, Maxwell Melanchthon, Cora Ann (five of whose seven sons became Lutheran pastors), Marcus Calvin.
Education: North Carolina College, A.B. 1867; self-taught in theology.
License/Ordination: Licensed 1868 and ordained 1871 by North Carolina Synod.
Calls: 1867-1903: St. Stephen, Cabarrus County; Luther's-St. Matthew, Rowan County; Christiana-Union, Rowan County; Reformation-St. Matthew, Davie County; Providence, Rowan County; Prosperity (now Cross of Christ), Cabarrus County; Emmanuel, Rowan County; organized Faith, Faith; supplied St. Peter, Rowan County. No record of pastoral activity after 1903.
Other: Secretary, North Carolina Synod, 1875. Wrote a history of the Michael Brown Family.
Date of Death/Burial Location: 1923; Christiana Church, Granite Quarry, N.C.

BROWN, THOMAS SHANNON, SR.
Date/Place of Birth: November 24, 1857; Wytheville, Va.
Parents: Joseph Brown and Sarah (Hudson) Brown.
Spouse/Marriage Date: Lucy Ashton (Dillard) Brown; 1886 in Charlotte, N.C.
Children: Thomas Shannon, Jr., Mattie Jordan, Jennie Bass, Sarah Josephine, Ellen Gladys, Lucy Mabon.
Education: Roanoke College, A.B. 1879; Gettysburg Seminary, 1882.
License/Ordination: Licensed 1881 and ordained 1882 by Southwest Virginia Synod. *Calls*: St. Mark's, Charlotte, 1882-90. In Virginia, 1890-95. In Pennsylvania, 1895-1909. In South Carolina, 1909-12, 1922-26. In North Carolina: Macedonia, Burlington; Peace, Guilford County, 1913-22. In Savannah, Ga.; Ascension, 1926, and Reformation, 1927-40.
Other: Retired 1940 at Savannah, Ga.; Secretary, North Carolina Synod, 1884. Member, North Carolina Synod committee (with Pastors W. G. Campbell, F. W. E. Peschau, and George H. Cox), which organized four licensed Negro ministers and their congregations of North Carolina Synod into "The Alpha Synod of the Evangelical Lutheran Church of Freedmen in America," 1889.
Date of Death/Burial Location: July 18, 1941; Elmwood Cemetery, Columbia, S.C.

BROWN, WILLIAM ROEDEL

Date/Place of Birth: August 9, 1859; Wytheville, Va.
Parents: Rufus Brown and Margaret (Earhart) Brown.
Spouse/Marriage Date: Mary Eve (Cassell) Brown; March 1, 1888 in Rural Retreat, Va.
Children: Anna Margaret, Florence Earhart, Paul Cassell, Josephine Virginia.
Education: Roanoke College, 1883; Philadelphia Seminary, 1886.
Ordination: 1886 by Ministerium of Pennsylvania.
Calls: In Virginia: Kimberling Parish (Kimberling, St. Paul, Pleasant Hill), Wythe County, 1894-98; Grace, Waynesboro, Augusta County, 1898-1900; Bethlehem, Waynesboro, Augusta County, 1899-1900. In North Carolina: Organ-Ebenezer, Rowan County, 1886-94. Retired 1900.
Other: Retired 1900 because of ill health, but did supply preaching and served as Treasurer, 1907, Southwest Virginia Synod. Member, Board of Marion College, 1893-1937, and Board President, 1917-32.
Date of Death/Burial Location: December 29, 1937; Kimberling Church, Wythe County, Va.

BRUCE, GENE WAYNE

Date/Place of Birth: November 8, 1942; Rowan County, N.C.
Parents: Armond Glenn Bruce and Lillian (Jacobs) Bruce.
Spouse/Marriage Date: Patricia (Moore) Bruce; July 25, 1965.
Children: David Armond, Daniel Moore, Elizabeth Monroe.
Education: Lenoir-Rhyne, A.B. Sociology 1965; Lutheran Theological Southern Seminary, M.Div. 1969.
Ordination: June 1, 1969 by North Carolina Synod.
Calls: St. Paul, Crouse, 1969-74; Grace, Newton, 1974-92; St. Mark, Salisbury, 1992-. Vice Pastor at various congregations.
Other: Summers of 1978-79, served as Protestant Chaplain at Philmont Boy Scout Ranch; Protestant Chaplain for four National Boy Scout Jamborees, 1977, 1981, 1985, 1989; Lutheran Outdoor Ministries Board of North Carolina Synod; Lamb Award and the Silver Beaver Award by Boy Scouts of America, 1988, 1989. Lenoir-Rhyne Alumni Distinguished Service Award, 1989; Catawba County Distinguished Public Service Award, 1992; President, Eastern Catawba County Cooperative Christian Ministry; President, Catawba County Heart Association; President, Catawba County Council on Aging; President, Aging Advisory Council, Unifour Council of Governments; President, Adult Life Programs, Catawba County. Catawba Memorial Hospital Chaplaincy Committee; Catawba County Nursing and Domiciliary Home Community Advisory Committee.

BRUCE, JIMMY LANE
Date/Place of Birth: December 1, 1937; near Faith, N.C.
Parents: Armond Glenn Bruce and Lillian (Jacobs) Bruce.
Spouse/Marriage Date: Martha Susan (Link) Bruce (daughter of the Reverend J. Lester Link); August 7, 1960 in Hickory, N.C.
Children: Jonathan Mark, Martha Constance Reuter.
Education: Lenoir-Rhyne, A.B. Sociology 1960; Lutheran Theological Southern Seminary, B.D. 1963.
Ordination: 1963 by North Carolina Synod.
Calls: St. James, near Chilhowie, Va., 1963-68; St. Peter, Shenandoah, Va., 1968-71; Holy Trinity, Martinsville, Va., 1972-80; St. Paul, Startown, N.C., 1980-86; Lutheran Church of the Living Word, Laurinburg, 1986-. Vice Pastor at various congregations.

BRUHWEL, BRUCE ARTHUR
Date/Place of Birth: November 5, 1942; Cheektowaga, Nassau County, N.Y.
Parents: Arthur J. G. Bruhwel and Anna (Jacobsen) Bruhwel.
Spouse/Marriage Date: Annabel (Boozer) Bruhwel; June 29, 1963 in Charlotte, N.C.
Children: Krister Bruce, Nicole Marie, Emily Anne, Scott Arthur.
Education: University of North Carolina, B.A. 1964; Harvard Divinity School, B.D. 1967.
Ordination: June 30, 1968 by North Carolina Synod.
Calls: Resurrection, Erie, N.Y., 1968-70; Advent, Spindale, N.C., 1987-.
Other: Board, Lutheran Theological Southern Seminary, 1994.

BUCK, JAMES LAFAYETTE
Date/Place of Birth: September 19, 1846; Wythe County, Va.
Spouse/Marriage Date: Callie Louise (Cobb) Buck; October 23, 1883 in Guilford County, N.C.
Children: Bachman Krauth, James Seiss, Beale Cobb, Callie Virginia, Carl Russell.
Education: Roanoke College, A.B.; Lutheran Theological Southern Seminary, 1878.
License/Ordination: Licensed 1877 and ordained 1878 by Southwest Virginia Synod.
Calls: In Virginia, 1878-81. In North Carolina, 1881-90: Frieden's, Guilford County; St. Paul, Alamance County; Macedonia, Burlington; Lutheran Chapel, China Grove; Center Grove, Cabarrus County. Again in Virginia, 1890-93. After 1893 in Pennsylvania, Florida, South Carolina and Mississippi.
Other: Secretary, North Carolina Synod, 1886-88. Retired 1911 at Jacksonville, Fla.
Date of Death/Burial Location: March 29, 1920; Evergreen Cemetery, Jacksonville, Fla.

BUCK, WILLIAM CROCKETT
Date/Place of Birth: April 9, 1878; Rural Retreat, Va. *Parents*: John Abe Buck and Josephine (Wiseley) Buck.
Spouse/Marriage Date: Ora Leigh (Conduff) Buck; September 7, 1910 in Willis, Va.
Children: Helen Maxine, Mildred Lavane, Virginia Jeanette.
Education: Roanoke College, A.B. 1905, A.M. 1912; Southern Seminary, 1909, B.D. 1927.

Ordination: 1909 by Southwest Virginia Synod.

Calls: In Virginia, 1909-10. In North Carolina, 1910-25: St. Matthew-St. Peter, Rowan County; Reformation, Davie County; St. Luke-Pilgrim, Davidson County; Nazareth-Shiloh, Forsyth County. Again in Virginia, 1927-31.

Other: Retired 1931 at Rural Hall because of ill health, but supplied churches and taught school until 1947.

Date of Death/Burial Location: November 25, 1959; Mountain View Memorial Park, Rural Hall, N.C.

BULOW, JOACHIM

Child: Ann Elizabeth Geddes.

Calls: A descendent, John Bulow Campbell, writing in the early 1920s credited him with founding "the Lutheran Church in Newberry District in 1765." Was preaching at St. Paul, Pomaria, S.C. in 1775 and "owned 200 acres of land on Crim's Creek and had a mill on Bush River." Ordained Johann Gottfried Arends on August 28, 1775 at Second Creek, Rowan County, N.C. Velthusen reported the arrival in Germany of a letter from Nussmann dated May 4, 1784 a letter reporting the ordination of Arends as the Revolution was getting under way. "They had this man ordained on the Saludi River in South Carolina by a certain Mr. Buelow (a former clerk in a store who had done some preaching.)" This suggests that the deacons at Organ may have taken Arends down to Pomaria where he was examined and ordained before Bulow's congregation. This reading seems supported by the ordination certificate with its commendation of the new pastor to "all Christians at the North." This reading, "at the North", would refer to Christians generally in the state of North Carolina. But if the ordination certificate is also correct in describing the event as taking place at "Second Creek, Rowan County, N.C.," then one must assume that the examination took place in South Carolina, the ordination in North Carolina, and the commendation to Christians "at the North" recognized the existence of denominational bodies like the Pennsylvania Ministerium which had their base of operation "at the North." Served St. Paul, Pomaria, S.C., ca. 1775-78. Moved to Charleston after American Revolution.

Date of Death: Summer of 1795.

BUMGARNER, ELVIN LOY, JR.

Date/Place of Birth: May 7, 1927; Tulsa, Okla.

Parents: Elvin Loy Bumgarner, Sr. and Leslie Imhilda (Primm) Bumgarner.

Spouse/Marriage Date: Martha Elizabeth (Ross) Bumgarner; May 30, 1953 in Washington, D.C.

Children: Thomas Loy, Mark Fleming.

Education: Midland Lutheran College, B.A. 1950; Philadelphia Seminary, M.Div. 1954.

Ordination: June 27, 1954 by Kansas and Adjacent States, United Lutheran Church in America.

Calls: St. Paul, Valley Falls, Kan., 1954-56; organized Our Saviour, Johnson City, Tenn., 1956-60; Immanuel, Blountville, Tenn., 1960-68; St. Stephen, Lenoir, 1968-82; St. Paul, Burlington, 1982-92. Interim and Vice Pastor at various congregations.

Other: Retired June 30, 1992 to Hickory, N.C. U.S. Army in Korea; Church Vocations

Committee, Virginia Synod, 1956-62; Christian Education Committee, North Carolina Synod, 1970-78.
Date of Death/Burial Location: June 20, 1997; Stuart Cemetery, Stuart, Va.

BUMGARNER, LETHCO C.
Date/Place of Birth: May 10, 1901; Catawba County, N.C.
Parents: Elsie Eugene Bumgarner and Lillie G. (Sigmon) Bumgarner.
Spouse/Marriage Date: Martha Ellen (Rimmer) Bumgarner (native of England); July 8, 1937 in Concord, N.C.
Children: Joseph Eugene, Alice Dianne Eidson.
Education: Lenoir-Rhyne, A.B., A.Mus. 1924; Lutheran Theological Southern Seminary, B.D. 1928.
Ordination: May 24, 1928 by North Carolina Synod.
Calls: St. Andrew, Concord, 1928-47; Lutheran Chapel, East Gastonia, 1947-52; St. Paul, Rowan County, 1952-58; Co-pastor, Augsburg, Winston-Salem, 1958-71. Served as Vice Pastor at various congregations.
Other: Secretary, Southern Conference, 1936-48. Chair, Parish Education Committee, 1948-62. Member, Lutheridge Board, 1951. Retired in 1971.
Date of Death/Burial Location: December 26, 1982; Parklawn Memorial Gardens, Winston-Salem, N.C.

BURNS, ERNEST TARVER
Date/Place of Birth: February 21, 1920; Springfield, Ga.
Parents: Ellis R. Burns and Bessie Louise (Gnann) Burns.
Spouse/Marriage Date: Kathryn (Neidlinger) Burns; April 21, 1943 in Springfield, Ga.
Children: Sheron Padgett, Donita Linder.
Education: Newberry College, A.B. 1954; also attended Georgia Teachers College; Lutheran Theological Southern Seminary, B.D. 1957.
Ordination: June 2, 1957 by Georgia-Alabama Synod.
Calls: Good Shepherd, Walterboro, S.C., 1957-58; Trinity, Anniston, Ala., 1958-60; Ehrhardt Parish, S.C., 1960-63; St. Andrew, Concord, 1963-64; Trinity, Anniston, Ala., 1964-66; Summer Memorial, Newberry, S.C., 1966-67; Fairfax Parish, Fairfax, S.C., 1967-76; St. Andrew, Plains, Ga., 1976-77; Mt. Pleasant, Ehrhardt, S.C., 1977-82. Interim Pastor to various congregations.
Other: Retired December 31, 1982. World Missions Committee, 1964.
Date of Death/Burial Location: January 20, 1995; Bethel Lutheran Church Cemetery, Springfield, Ga.

BURT, DAPHNE
Date/Place of Birth: May 27, 1956; Cleveland, Ohio.
Parents: Kenneth Burt and Sally (Robinson) Burt.
Education: Yale University, B.A. Religious Studies 1978; Catholic University, M.Div. 1983. Continuing Education and graduate studies at Duke University, Lutheran Theological Southern Seminary.
Ordination: February 1, 1987 by Southeast Synod.

Calls: Christ Lutheran, Bristol, Tenn., 1987; Campus Pastor and Director of Placement Services, Newberry College, 1987-89; Bethany, Boone, 1989-92; Part-time Minister of Christian Education, Grace, Raleigh, 1992; Assistant Pastor, Holy Trinity, Hickory, 1992; Secretary of North Carolina Synod, 1991-93; Campus Minister of Campus Christian Community, Mary Washington College, Fredericksburg, Va., 1994-.

Other: Publications - *Ten Ways to Welcome a Supply Pastor, On the Death and Dying of a Congregation, You Can Help Save a Life, When a Church Dies.* Vice Chair, North Carolina Lutheran-Roman Catholic Covenant Committee, 1991; Worship Subcommittee, 1990-91; Board, Lutheran Outdoor Ministries, 1990-91; Pastor in Residence, Lenoir-Rhyne, 1992; Chaplain, North Carolina Women of the Evangelical Lutheran Church in America, Synodical Organization annual convention, 1991; Chaplain, North Carolina Lutheran Youth Organization Junior High Youth Winter Retreat, 1991; Yale Alumni Association Board of Governors, 1992; Watauga County Diagnostic Team on Sexual Abuse of Children, 1989- 92; Boone Area Coalition of Churches, Board Member, 1989-92; Watauga County Hunger Coalition, Board Member, 1989-92.

BUSBY, LEVI E.

Date/Place of Birth: September 5, 1849; Lexington District, S.C.

Parents: Benjamin C. Busby and Eva (Folk) Busby.

Spouse/Marriage Date: S(allie ?) A. Goode; June 20, 1878 in Craig County, Va.

Children: Sallie Virginia, John Carroll, William, Julian Goode.

Education: Newberry College, A.B. 1875; Lutheran Theological Southern Seminary, 1878; North Carolina College, D.D. 1901.

License/Ordination: Licensed 1877 by Southwest Virginia Synod and ordained 1878 by South Carolina Synod.

Calls: In Giles County, Va., 1875-76. Four months as missionary for Southwest Virginia Synod in 1878. In South Carolina, 1878-96, succeeding the Reverend E. Caughman as pastor of Pastorate #14 in South Carolina, which included Wittenberg, Leesville, Good Hope, Saluda, St. Peter, Batesburg, Union, Bethlehem. In North Carolina: Mission work, Asheville; St. John, Salisbury, 1896-1902; Holy Trinity, Mt. Pleasant, 1902-03.

Other: With G. F. McAllister, opened Carolina English and Classical School in 1902-3. Established Leesville (South Carolina) English and Classical Institute; Secretary, South Carolina Synod, 1881; Secretary, North Carolina Synod, 1898-1900; President, South Carolina Synod, 1892-93.

Date of Death/Burial Location: March 14, 1903; Mt. Pleasant, N.C.

BUTT, JAMES CARROLL

Date/Place of Birth: September 11, 1950; Charleston, S.C.

Parent: Dr. Justus Butt *Spouse/Marriage Date*: Linda (Rowe) Butt; September 7, 1974 in Columbia, S.C.

Children: Jonathan, Helen, Michael Vincent.

Education: Newberry College, A.B. 1972; Lutheran Theological Southern Seminary, M.Div. 1977. Campbell University, JD 1985.

Ordination: May 1977 by South Carolina Synod.

Calls: St. John-Beth Eden, Louisville, Miss., 1977-78; Good Shepherd, Sandy Run, Swansea, S.C., 1978-79; Lebanon, Cleveland, N.C., 1980-84. Served as Vice Pastor in various congregations. Chaplain, United States Navy, 1986-89.

Other: Stewardship Committee, South Carolina Synod, 1979; transferred to The Lutheran Church-Missouri Synod, 1992.

BYRNE, ROBERT THOMAS

Date/Place of Birth: May 4, 1950; Cleveland, Ohio.
Parents: Frank John Byrne and Elizabeth (Chisholm) Byrne.
Spouse/Marriage Date: Christine (McCutcheon) Byrne; September 11, 1971.
Children: Michael John, Steven Thomas.
Education: Wittenberg University, B.A. Economics/Accounting 1972; graduate work at Iowa State University, 1972; Case Western Reserve University, M.A. Management Economics, 1976; Lutheran Theological Southern Seminary, M.Div. 1995.
Ordination: May 1995 by North Carolina Synod.
Calls: Christ's, Stanley, Gaston County, 1995-98; Ebenezer, Columbia, S.C., 1998-.

CAMPBELL, JAMES WILSON, JR.

Date/Place of Birth: June 5, 1948; Catawba County, N.C.
Parents: James Wilson Campbell, Sr. and Jahaza (Yoder) Campbell.
Spouse/Marriage Date: Sylvia (Nelson) Campbell; August 23, 1980 in Columbia, S.C.
Children: Zachary Nelson, Colleen Nelson-Campbell, Amber Nelson.
Education: Appalachian State University, B.S. 1972; Lutheran Theological Southern Seminary, M.Div. 1981.
Ordination: February 19, 1984 by North Carolina Synod.
Calls: Peace, Gibsonville, 1984-1990; Frieden's, Gibsonville, 1987-90; St. David, Kannapolis, 1990; Interim Pastor at St. Matthew, Salisbury; St. John, Pomaria, S.C., 1996-.

CAMPBELL, LARRY DAVID

Date/Place of Birth: July 10, 1937; Hickory, N.C.
Parents: Conrad Sylvester Campbell and Mary Lee (Waller) Campbell.
Spouse/Marriage Date: Gaynell (McEntire) Campbell; June 24, 1960 in Wilkesboro, N.C.
Children: Lisa Gaye, Larry Edward, Mary Kaye, William Brandon Lee.
Education: Lenoir-Rhyne, B.A. History/Political Science 1960; Lutheran Theological Southern Seminary, B.D. 1963; continuing education work at Michigan State University in counseling, 1966-68, and at Maryland Community College, 1989.
Ordination: 1963 by North Carolina Synod.
Calls: Holy Communion, Watauga County, 1963-. Vice Pastor at various congregations.
Other: Served as Lutheran Church in America-North Carolina Synod representative on Committee on Religion in Appalachia; Social Ministry Committee, 1969-74. Original Director and developer of Watauga Center for Exceptional Children. Organized and chartered Foscoe Fire Department and served as President for twenty years; Training officer 1971-95; Arson Investigator, 1980-; Chief, 1975-1994. North Carolina Department of Insurance Fire Fighter Instructor, 1991-; part-time faculty, Caldwell Community College and Technical Institute.

CAMPBELL, RICHARD ROSS, SR.
Date/Place of Birth: December 4, 1944; Lewistown, Pa..
Parents: Clyde S. Campbell and Anna M. (Trumpler) Campbell.
Spouse/Marriage Date: Rebecca (Cromer) Campbell (daughter of the Reverend Voigt R. Cromer); July 16, 1968 in Hickory, N.C.
Children: Richard Ross, Jr., Christopher Scott.
Education: Lenoir-Rhyne, A.B. 1967; Lutheran Theological Southern Seminary, M.Div. 1971; graduate work at American University, 1969-70.
Ordination: June 6, 1971 by North Carolina Synod.
Calls: Associate Pastor, Ebenezer, Columbia, S.C., 1971-74; Christus Victor, Durham, 1974-79; Holy Trinity, Charlotte, 1979-82; Assistant to the Bishop, North Carolina Synod, 1982-86; St. Matthew, Charleston, S.C., 1986-.
Other: Board of Division of Congregational Ministries; Partner in Evangelism; Secretary, Eastern District, 1978; Chair, Youth Ministry Committee, 1979-81; Regional Planning Committee and Chaplain, Southeast Regional Youth Event, 1980; Adult Advisor, North Carolina Delegation to Youth Convo, 1980; Planning Committee, Southeast Regional Youth Event, 1983; Board, Lutheridge, 1982; Evangelical Outreach Coordinator, 1982; President, Charlotte Area Lutheran Clergy Association; One of three original authors of and involved in development of *Confirmation Ministry Program*.

CAMPBELL, WRIGHT GATEWOOD, SR.
Date/Place of Birth: April 1, 1849; Strasburg, Va.
Parents: The Reverend John Francis Campbell and Martha C. (Gatewood) Campbell.
Spouse/Marriage Date: Mary A. (Ott) Campbell; February 4, 1875 in Woodstock, Va.
Children: Elizabeth Anne, Mary, Helen, Frank, Wright G., Jr. (last four died in infancy).
Education: Roanoke College, 1870.
License/Ordination: Licensed 1877 by Southwest Virginia Synod; ordained 1877 by Virginia Synod.
Calls: In Virginia, 1877-83; in Pennsylvania, 1883-86, and after 1893. In North Carolina: St. James, Concord, 1886-93; in 1890 organized and supplied mission which in 1893 became St. Andrew, Concord.
Other: Member of the Committee that organized four licensed Negro ministers and their congregations of North Carolina Synod into "The Alpha Synod of the Evangelical Lutheran Church of Freedmen in America", 1889. Professor, Irving Female Seminary, 1895. U.S. Army Chaplain in Cuba, 1898.
Date of Death/Burial Location: 1925; Woodstock, Va.

CANNIFF-KUHN, MARY
Date/Place of Birth: November 17, 1956; Mooresville, N.C.
Parents: Isaac Kuhn and Gilda Kuhn.
Spouse/Marriage Date: The Reverend Tim Canniff-Kuhn; August 22, 1981.
Children: Matthew Scott, Jesse Michael, Nathan Isaac.
Education: Wake Forest University, B.A. Art/Psychology 1979; Lutheran Theological Southern Seminary, M.Div. 1988.
Ordination: May 31, 1988 by North Carolina Synod.
Calls: Apostles, Brandon, Fla., 1988-94; Program Director, Lutheridge Conference Center and Camp, 1994-.

CANNIFF-KUHN, TIM
Parents: Roger Canniff and Lois Canniff.
Spouse/Marriage Date: The Reverend Mary Canniff-Kuhn; August 22, 1981.
Children: Matthew Scott, Jesse Michael, Nathan Isaac.
Education: University of Wisconsin, B.A. Social Work, 1981; Lutheran Theological Southern Seminary, 1988.
Ordination: May 21, 1988 by Wisconsin-Upper Michigan Synod.
Calls: Apostles, Brandon, Fla., 1988-94; Program Director, Lutheridge Conference Center and Camp, 1994-.

CANUP, MARTIN LUTHER
Date/Place of Birth: March 10, 1879; Rowan County, N.C.
Parents: Caleb Canup and Julia Ann (Brown) Canup.
Spouse/Marriage Date: Inez (Bollinger) Canup; June 19, 1918 in Lancaster, Pa.
Child: William Caleb.
Education: Mount Pleasant Collegiate Institute, Roanoke College, A.B. 1904; Philadelphia Seminary, 1907; Wittenberg College, D.D. 1930.
Ordination: 1907 by Virginia Synod.
Calls: Woman's Memorial (now Emmanuel), High Point, 1909-12; First, Greensboro, 1909-10; New York City, 1912-40; St. Louis, Mo.; Pastor to Lutheran students at Wayne University, Detroit, and soldiers and sailors in training there during World War II.
Other: Retired 1940 at Detroit. Engaged in personnel work for Chrysler Corporation, 1940-53.
Date of Death/Burial Location: January 22, 1956; St. Paul, Rowan County, N.C.

CARLSON, DAVID ALFRED
Date/Place of Birth: July 23, 1923; Bradford, Conn.
Parents: The Reverend Gustave A. G. Carlson and Grace (Romberg) Carlson.
Spouse/Marriage Date: Gloria Arlene (Eakins) Carlson; March 23, 1957 in Houston, Texas.
Child: Timothy Arvid. *Education*: Iowa State University, B.S. 1948; Central Seminary, B.D. 1961; Michigan Technical University, M.B.A. 1974.

Ordination: 1963 by Texas-Louisiana Synod.
Calls: Mt. Zion-New Bethel, Stanly County, 1962-65; Prince of Peace, Kinston, 1965-66; Bethany, Siren, Wis., 1966-74; Our Redeemer, Newberry, Mich., 1974-79.
Other: Employed in chemical research, with some patents awarded, by Standard Oil Company of California, E. I. du Pont de Nemours & Company and Texas Butadiene and Chemical Corporation, 1948-57. Retired in 1983.

CARLSON, HENRY G., JR.

Date/Place of Birth: March 4, 1945; Cuyahoga County, Ohio.
Parents: Henry G. Carlson, Sr. and Dorothy (Youngberg) Carlson.
Spouse/Marriage Date: Anne Page (Lowy) Carlson; April 24, 1971 in Cincinnati, Ohio.
Education: Augustana, Illinois, B.A. 1967; Hamma, M.Div. 1971.
Ordination: May 31, 1971 by Ohio Synod.
Calls: St. Paul Cross Roads, Batesville, Ind., 1971-73; St. Paul Smyrna, Greensburg, Ind.; New Covenant, High Point, 1973-76.
Other: Member, Commission on Mission, World Missions Task Force, 1971-73. Dropped from roll, 1980.

CARPENTER, CECIL WALTER

Date/Place of Birth: May 26, 1919; Chapin, S.C.
Parents: The Reverend Rubertus Melanchthon Carpenter and Blanche Viola (Thornburg) Carpenter. A grandfather was the Reverend Michael Luther Carpenter.
Spouse/Date of Marriage: Dorothy M. (Roesel) Carpenter; June 11, 1947 in Augusta, Ga.
Children: Cecilia Roesel Frutz, Walter Alan, Tina Marie.
Education: Lenoir-Rhyne, A.B. 1940; Lutheran Theological Southern Seminary, B.D. 1943.
Ordination: 1943 by North Carolina Synod.
Calls: None in North Carolina. In South Carolina: Bethlehem Parish, Pomaria, 1943-44; St. Paul, Mt. Pleasant, 1943-47. In Georgia: Reformation, Savannah, 1947-53; Messiah, Decatur, Ga., 1954-65.
Other: Stewardship Regional Director for Division of Parish Services, Ga.
Date of Death: February 17, 1985.

CARPENTER, MICHAEL LUTHER

Date/Place of Birth: January 4, 1853; Lincoln County, N.C.
Parents: Michael Carpenter and Rebecca Carpenter.
Spouse/Date of Marriage: Mary Christine Caroline (Senter) Carpenter; 1876 in Gaston County, N.C.
Children: The Reverend Rubertus Melanchthon, Jonas Michael, Violet Rebecca May, Martin Luther, George Loy, Malinda Caroline E., Walter T., Anna Pearl. The Reverend Cecil W. Carpenter is a grandson.
Education: Catawba College, at Newton; no formal seminary training.
Ordination: 1875 by Joint Synod of Ohio.
Calls: Gaston County Parish of Tennessee Synod Reorganized; Joint Synod churches in Virginia. Transferred 1912 to Tennessee Synod; Holy Communion-Mt. Pleasant,

Watauga County, 1913-18.
Date of Death/Burial Location: January 9, 1918; Bethel Church, Gaston County, N.C.

CARPENTER, RUBERTUS MELANCHTHON

Date/Place of Birth: December 28, 1877; Lincoln County, N.C.
Parents: The Reverend Michael Luther Carpenter and Mary Christine Caroline (Senter) Carpenter.
Spouse/Marriage Date: Blanche Viola (Thornburg) Carpenter; October 4, 1905 in Dallas, N.C.; died April 17, 1976.
Children: Elmer Louis, Bleeka Irene, Frieda Isabelle, Helen Viola, the Reverend Cecil Walter.
Education: St. Paul Practical Seminary, Hickory, graduating in 1897.
Ordination: 1897 by Joint Synod of Ohio, his father officiating, and the same day installing him in first charge.
Calls: Of Joint Synod: In West Virginia, 1897-1907. In North Carolina: Alexander County and Claremont, 1907-16. In Tennessee Synod: Chapin, S.C., 1916-23. In North Carolina Synod, 1923-50: Daniel's, Lincoln County; Grace, Catawba County; Bethany, Hickory; Philadelphia, Granite Falls; St. John, Hudson; St. Matthew, Caldwell County; Mt. Hermon-Sharon-St. Paul, Iredell County. Regular supply, St. Matthew, Caldwell County, 1950-64.
Other: Retired 1950 at Hickory. Secretary, Tennessee Synod, 1918-20. Delegate, Tennessee Synod to United Lutheran Church in America merger convention, 1918. Board, Lenoir-Rhyne, and Secretary, 1928-30.
Date of Death/Burial Location: January 25, 1967; Fairview Cemetery in Hickory, N.C.

CARR, WILLIAM BURNEY

Date/Place of Birth: October 23, 1922; Wadley, Ga.
Parents: William Joseph Carr and Belle (McGowan) Carr.
Spouse/Marriage Date: Betty Jean (Hill) Carr; June 9, 1951 in Atlanta, Ga.
Child: Jeffrey Daniel.
Education: University of Georgia, B.S. 1954; Lutheran Theological Southern Seminary, M.Div. 1954; Philadelphia Seminary, one year.
Ordination: August 1954 by Southeastern Synod.
Calls: Reformation, Savannah, Ga., 1954-56; Bethel Parish, Springfield, Ga., 1957-62; Grace, Thomasville, 1963-65; Philadelphia, Dallas, 1965-71; Prince of Peace, Salisbury, 1972-76; Shepherd of the Sea, Atlantic Beach, 1976-78; St. Luke, Conover, 1979-80. Supply Pastor at St. Andrew, Blythewood, S.C., 1989-94.
Other: World War II, in South Pacific, U.S. Navy and U.S. Marine Corps. Retired in 1980 at Moncks Corner, S.C.

CARSWELL, ROBERT WAYNE

Date/Place of Birth: September 25, 1933; Lincoln County, N.C.
Parents: Lester F. Carswell and Bryte (Wilson) Carswell.
Spouse/Marriage Date: Elizabeth Rhodes (Cromer) Carswell (daughter of the Reverend Voigt Rhodes Cromer); August 15, 1956 in Hickory, N.C.

Children: Sara Lynn, David Voigt.
Education: Lenoir-Rhyne, A.B. 1955; Lutheran Theological Southern Seminary, B.D. 1958.
Ordination: 1958 by North Carolina Synod.
Calls: Faith, Warner Robins, Ga.; Shades Valley, Birmingham, Ala.; St. Andrew's, Columbia, S.C., 1966-.
Other: Resigned 1975 in Chapin, S.C.

CARTER, GAROLD RAYMOND

Date/Place of Birth: August 29, 1925; Wellington, Kan.
Parents: Albert Logan Carter and Izetta Ruth (Plemmons) Carter.
Spouse/Marriage Date: G. Yvette (McMillen) Carter; September 1, 1950.
Children: Philip L., Patricia A. Murdoch.
Education: East Carolina University, B.A. 1971; Lutheran Theological Seminary, Columbus, Ohio, M.Div. 1974.
Ordination: 1974 by North Carolina Synod.
Calls: Holy Cross, Mocksville, 1974-80; St. Luke, Conover, 1980-91. Retired in 1991 and resumed service as Mission Developer, Living Faith, Newport, 1993-. Interim pastor at various congregations.
Other: American Missions Committee, 1978-79; World Missions Committee, 1977-85; Committee for Global Mission Event, 1984-85; District Youth Advisor, 1982-83. Retired September 30, 1991 in Newport, N.C.

CASTOR, BRADSHAW DeKIME

Date/Place of Birth: March 10, 1898; Cabarrus County, N.C.
Parents: David Bradshaw Castor and Barbara Bertie (Kime) Castor. Brother, Henry Carmen Castor, was also a pastor in the United Lutheran Church in America, serving in Ohio and in Virginia.
Spouse/Marriage Date: Olga Caroline (Linsemeyer) Castor; December 15, 1926 in Bluefield, W.Va.
Children: Charles Robert, the Reverend David Frederick.
Education: Roanoke College, Lenoir-Rhyne, A.B. 1923; Lutheran Theological Southern Seminary, 1926; graduate study, University of South Carolina.
License/Ordination: Licensed 1926 and ordained 1927 by Virginia Synod.
Calls: In Tennessee and Virginia, 1926-47. In North Carolina since 1947: Trinity, Cabarrus County, 1947-53; St. Martin, Stanly County, 1953-58; Shiloh, Forsyth County, 1958-62; Lebanon, Rowan County, 1962-66. Vice pastor at various congregations.
Other: Board, Children's Home of the South, 1929-31; Board, Williams-Henson Home for Boys, Knoxville, Tenn., 1929-35. In the Virginia Synod served on the Executive Council, Stewardship Committee, and was President of the New Market Conference. Business-circulation Manager, the *North Carolina Lutheran*, 1958-68. Retired in 1966 at Kannapolis, N.C.
Date of Death/Burial Location: October 3, 1968; Center Grove Cemetery, Kannapolis, N.C.

CASTOR, DAVID FREDERICK

Date/Place of Birth: November 4, 1930; Parrottsville, Tenn.
Parents: The Reverend Bradshaw DeKime and Olga Caroline (Linsemeyer) Castor.
First Marriage: Dorothy Claire (Swan) Castor; August 24, 1952 in Tampa, Fla.
Children of First Marriage: Jane Caroline, Mary Claire, Jonathan Todd.
Second Marriage: Robin (Bjorlo) Castor.
Child of Second Marriage: Jeremy.
Education: Lenoir-Rhyne, A.B. 1952; Lutheran Theological Southern Seminary, B.D. 1955, S.T.M. 1959; University of Florida, M.Ed.
Ordination: 1955 by North Carolina Synod.
Calls: St. Michael, Columbia, S.C., 1955-59; St. John, Jacksonville, Fla., 1959-63; University Campus Ministry, Gainesville, Fla., 1963-74; Campus Ministry, Colorado State University, Fort Collins, Colo., 1974- 92.
Other: Retired December 31, 1992. Active in Global Missions. Director, Global Mission Event, 1991.

CASTOR, DAVID LARRY

Date/Place of Birth: March 8, 1934; Concord, Cabarrus County, N.C.
Parents: Ross A. Castor and Helen E. (Smith) Castor.
Spouse/Marriage Date: Faye Romona (Critcher) Castor; August 25, 1957 in Boone, N.C.
Children: Christopher David, Cynthia Alane, Mark Gregory.
Education: Lenoir-Rhyne, B.A. 1957; Lutheran Theological Southern Seminary, M.Div. 1960.
Ordination: June 5, 1960 by North Carolina Synod.
Calls: St. Paul, Burlington, 1960-62; Philadelphia, Granite Falls, 1962-65; Resurrection, Kings Mountain, 1965-70; St. Stephen, Hickory, 1970-73; Executive Director, Lutheran Outdoor Ministry, North Carolina Synod, 1973-. Vice Pastor at various congregations.
Other: Served as Executive Director during development of Kure Beach and Agape Camp. Region 9 Lutheran Outdoor Ministries Facilitator; Lutheran Outdoor Ministry Region 9 Past President and Treasurer; Lutheran Church in America National Committee for Development of Lutheran Outdoor Ministry in the Evangelical Lutheran Church in America; Committee on Nominations, 1968; District Secretary, 1965; Lutheridge Committee, 1972-74. Retired December 1996 to Cary, N.C.

CAUBLE, FRANKLIN PIERCE, JR.

Date/Place of Birth: November 20, 1905; Lincoln County, N.C.
Parents: Franklin Pierce Cauble, Sr. and Mary Ellen (Coon) Cauble.
Spouse/Marriage Date: Lela Custis (Melton) Cauble; September 1, 1934 in Badin, N.C.
Child: Lela Ellen.
Education: Lenoir-Rhyne, B.A. 1926; Lutheran Theological Southern Seminary, M.Div., 1929; University of South Carolina, M.A. 1929; University of North Carolina, Ph.D. 1934.
Ordination: 1931 by North Carolina Synod.
Calls: Pastor to Lutheran students at University of North Carolina, 1931-32; St.

Matthew-St. Peter, Rowan County, 1932-38; Lutheran Chapel, Gastonia, 1938-41; St. Andrew, Hickory, 1941-53; Pastor-Developer Haven, Hagerstown, Md., 1953-57; Pastor-Developer, Bethlehem, Lynchburg, Va., 1958-71.

Other: Retired January 1971 at Lynchburg, Va. Board, Children's Home of the South, 1938-41; Board, Lenoir-Rhyne, 1941-53. Instructor, Lenoir-Rhyne, 1942-43. Author of *Centennial History of St. Matthew's Lutheran Church, Rowan County*. Published mimeographed biographies of Walter W. Lenoir, 1973 and Daniel E. Rhyne, 1974. Contributor to The Lutheran and other Lutheran periodicals.

Date of Death/Burial Location: July 7, 1993; Lynchburg, Va., area.

CAUBLE, HERMAN WOODROW, SR.

Date/Place of Birth: November 11, 1918; Salisbury, N.C.

Parents: Luther Charles Cauble and Pearl (Safrit) Cauble.

Spouse/Marriage Date: Anna Elizabeth (Petrea) Cauble (daughter of the Reverend B. E. Petrea); January 1, 1944 in Salisbury, N.C.

Children: Herman Woodrow, Jr., Charles Eugene, Cynthia Elizabeth Perry, Susan Dale Brown.

Education: Lenoir-Rhyne, A.B. 1940; Lutheran Theological Southern Seminary, B.D. 1943, and graduate work also; graduate study, Chicago Seminary, 1946-47, and University of South Carolina, 1942-43; Newberry College, D.Div. 1970.

Ordination: July 11, 1943 by North Carolina Synod.

Calls: Assistant Pastor, St. John, Salisbury, 1943-44; St. John, Cabarrus County, 1944-49; Ascension, Columbia, S.C., 1949-65; Secretary, South Carolina Synod, 1965-71. President of South Carolina Synod, 1971- 80; Bishop of South Carolina Synod, 1980-1987, Bishop Emeritus, 1988.

Other: Retired December 31, 1987 in Columbia, S.C. Distinguished Service Award - Newberry College, 1987; Algernon Sydney Sullivan Award, 1990; honorary member of Columbia Rotary Club; Lutheran Church in America Pension Board, and Boards of Lutheran Theological Southern Seminary, Newberry College, Lutheridge, Lowman Home, and Children's Home of the South. Representative to The Lutheran Council - U.S.A. Committee Chair for building chapel and president's home at Lutheran Theological Southern Seminary. Advisor of youth work in North Carolina Synod and South Carolina Synod. Chair, Synodical Committee on Student Work; Chair, Synodical appeal for campus ministry facilities at Clemson University. Delegate to the bi-annual convention of Lutheran Church in America, 1968 and 1970. Secretary and President, Central Conference of United Lutheran Church in America, South Carolina Synod. President, Lutheran Ministers' Association of Columbia and President, Columbia Social Missions Society. Board Member and President, Travelers Aid Society. United Service Organization Committee of Greater Columbia. Chaplain and Vice President of Post B, T.P.A.

CAUBLE, JOHN L.
Date/Place of Birth: January 8, 1905; Salisbury, N.C.
Parents: Henry Washington Cauble and Katherine B. (Parker) Cauble.
Spouse/Marriage Date: Jenny L. (Lineberger) Cauble; June 25, 1930 in Mt. Holly, N.C.
Children: John Robert, Walter Lee, Clifford Paul.
Education: Lenoir-Rhyne, A.B. 1927; Lutheran Theological Southern Seminary B.D. 1930; Midland College, D.D. 1958.
Ordination: June 25, 1930 by North Carolina Synod.
Calls: Goodman, Miss.; Terre Haute, Ind.; Juneau, Alaska; Longview, Wash., and St. Mark, Salem, Ore., 1951-68.
Other: President, Salem Ministerial Association, 1955, 1966; Lutheran Board of American Missions, 1960- 68; Executive Board, 1962-68. Executive Committee, Pacific Northwest Synod; Board, Willamette Chapter, American Red Cross; Executive Board, United Fund.
Date of Death/Burial Location: July 23, 1968; Belcrest Cemetery, Salem, Ore.

CAUBLE, RANDALL ALAN
Date/Place of Birth: September 19, 1960; Salisbury, N.C.
Parents: Ray E. Cauble and Mary (Jones) Cauble.
Spouse/Marriage Date: Vicki Elizabeth (Davis) Cauble; November 17, 1990 in Salisbury, N.C.
Education: University of North Carolina at Charlotte, B.A. Political Science, 1982; Lutheran Theological Southern Seminary, M.Div. 1986.
Ordination: June 29, 1986 by North Carolina Synod.
Calls: Calvary, Spencer, 1986-91; New Jerusalem, Hickory, 1991-. Vice Pastor at various congregations.

CHANG, HSINNG SAN
Ordination: December 29, 1935 at annual meeting of the Tsimo District Conference, Kiachow, China by the Reverend L. Grady Cooper, by order of North Carolina Synod.
Calls: Pastor of Lutheran Mission at Tsimo, Shantung, China.
Date of Death/Burial Location: 1944; China. Note from Dr. L. Grady Cooper: "In 1944, was living in Tsingtao, Shantung, China...was trying to preserve church building at his home town, Pang Chia Lan, by keeping the military out, when he was taken and beaten so seriously that he died from this mistreatment."

CHAPMAN, LEMUEL HEZEKIAH DREHER (H.D.)
Date/Place of Birth: November 29, 1875; Little Mountain, S.C.
Parents: J. L. Chapman and Almenia (Dreher) Chapman.
Spouse/Marriage Date: Clara Mabel (Easler) Chapman; May 2, 1915 in Spartanburg, S.C.
Children: Jacob Dreher, Verna Mabel, Hugh David, Norman Stanley, Virginia Ruth, Mary Ann, Clara Elizabeth.
Education: Roanoke College, 1904-06; University of South Carolina, 1907-09; Lutheran Theological Southern Seminary, 1915, B.D. 1927.
Ordination: 1915 by Virginia Synod.
Calls: In Virginia and Holston Synods, 1915-21; at Rockingham, Va., Tennessee Synod church, when North Carolina and Tennessee Synods merged, 1921. Transferred to Virginia Synod, 1924 with other North Carolina Synod pastors and congregations in Virginia. Last

parish, Sharpsburg, Md., 1925-44.
Date of Death/Burial Location: January 19, 1944; Sharpsburg, Md.

CHIGA, TORANOSUKE

Date/Place of Birth: May 9, 1863; Nagasaki, Japan and was baptized in 1883 by a Methodist missionary.
Education: Chinzei Gakuin, Nagasaki; in theology at Aoyama Gakuin, Tokyo (both Methodist institutions). Taught in academic department of the latter.
Ordination/Calls: Was ordained in 1897 as Methodist minister. In 1904 began pastoral ministry in Methodist Church, serving in Tokyo, Kumamoto, Kagoshima, and Naha; then taught in Lutheran Boys' School, Kynshu Gakuin, Kumamoto. In 1915 became a helper in Lutheran Church, Nagoya; in 1918 resigned from Methodist Church, joined Lutheran Church and in 1918 was enrolled as ordained by North Carolina Synod; worked together with the Reverend E. T. Horn, establishing the work in Nagoya in 1915; later transferred to Fukuoka. Pastor, Hakata Church; Pastor, Church at Karatsu, 1929-34.
Other: Held several positions in Joint Ministerium of Evangelical Lutheran Church in Japan in 1925; on Joint Constitution Revision Committee; Joint Executive Committee; Ordination Examining Committee; took leave of absence in 1930 due to serious eye trouble. Professor, Aoyama Gakuin, Tokyo.
Date of Death: May 9, 1934.

CHILTON, DELMER LOWELL

Date/Place of Birth: March 2, 1954; Stuart, Va.
Parents: Gaston Lowell Chilton and Dorothy (Hubbard) Chilton.
Spouse/Marriage Date: Deborah (Hollowell) Chilton; December 29, 1974 in Goldsboro, N.C.
Children: David Lowell, Joseph Franklin.
Education: Guilford College, 1972-74; Southeastern Baptist Theological Seminary, 1976-77. University of North Carolina at Chapel Hill, A.B. Sociology 1976; Duke Divinity School, M.Div. 1980; Lutheran Theological Southern Seminary, Certificate in Lutheran Studies, 1983.
Ordination: September 15, 1984 by North Carolina Synod.
Calls: As Methodist Pastor - N.C. Conference: Rock Creek, Snow Camp, 1977-78 and Hightower, Mebane, 1978-82. As Lutheran Minister: Lutheran Chapel, China Grove, 1984-88; Gloria Dei, Luthonsia, Ga., 1989-93; Holy Trinity, Nashville, Tenn., 1993-.
Other: Southeast Synod: Chair, Multi-Cultural Committee; Chair, North Georgia Conference; Chair, Middle Tennessee Conference. Executive Director, Caswell Cooperative Parish, 1981-82; N.C. Synod World Missions Committee, 1985-88.

CHU, DANIEL, SR.

Date/Place of Birth: March 20, 1918; Sinyang, Honan, China.
Parents: The Reverend Chu Hao Ran and Wang Hsuch Tao.
Spouse/Marriage Date: Shirley (Liu) Chu; December 25, 1941 in Kityang, China.
Children: Franklin, William, Daniel, Jr., Elizabeth.
Education: Cheloo University, China; Wittenberg University, B.A. 1950; Hamma Divinity School, B.D. 1951.

Ordination: 1953 in Hong Kong, for North Carolina Synod by the Reverend Charles Reinbrecht, at request of United Lutheran Church in America Board of Foreign Missions. *Calls*: Pastor in United Lutheran Church in America Mission in Malaya, 1953-55; St. Luke Church, Springfield, Ohio, 1955-66; Bethlehem, Mt. Clemens, Mich., 1966-73; Transfiguration, Taylor, Mich., 1973- 77; Resurrection, Tacoma, Wash., 1977-80; Pastor-Developer, Grace, Seattle, Wash., 1980-83; retired 1983.

CHURCH, RONNIE LINDSEY, JR.
Ordination: June 6, 1998 by North Carolina Synod for Nebraska Synod.
Calls: First, Fremont, Neb., 1998-.

CLAPP, NATHAN
Place of Birth: Alamance County, N.C.
Ordination: 1884 by North Carolina Synod, in Ebenezer Church, Rowan County.
Calls: Springdale, Samuel Holt Chapel, and Elon College School House, all presumably in Alamance County.
Other: One of organizers of the Alpha Synod of the Evangelical Lutheran Church of Freedmen in America, May 8, 1889.

CLARK, BENJAMIN McLAURIN
Date/Place of Birth: July 31, 1895; Chapin, S.C.
Parents: J. H. Clark and Janie (Alewine) Clark.
Spouse/Marriage Date: Nellie Irene (Gilbert) Clark; May 14, 1924 in Statesville, N.C.
Children: Betty Kathryn.
Education: Newberry College, A.B. 1920, D.D. 1961; Lutheran Theological Southern Seminary, 1923, B.D. 1925; University of South Carolina, A.M. 1922.
Ordination: 1923 by North Carolina Synod.
Calls: St. Matthew-St. Peter, Rowan County, 1923-28. In South Carolina: St. John, Walhalla, 1928-54; Grace, Prosperity, 1954-65. Pastor to Lutheran students at Clemson University.
Other: Board, Children's Home of the South, 1943-55, Retired 1965 at Walhalla, South Carolina.
Date of Death/Burial Location: 1968; Walhalla, S.C.

CLAUSEN, FREDERICK BERNARD
Date/Place of Birth: February 25, 1880; New York City, N.Y.
Parents: John F. Clausen and Susan (Abel) Clausen.
First Spouse/Marriage Date: Freda (Reineck) Clausen; March 1, 1905 in Rochester, N.Y.
Child of First Marriage: Frederick R., Marguerite.
Second Spouse/Marriage Date: Rose (Enssle) Clausen; January 31, 1931 in Waterloo, Canada.
Education: Wagner College, A.B. 1900; Philadelphia Seminary, 1903; Hartwick College, D.D. 1933.
Ordination: 1903 by Ministerium of Pennsylvania.
Calls: In New York City, 1903-12, 1918-31. In North Carolina: St. Paul, Wilmington,

1912-18. President and Dean, Waterloo College and Seminary, Kitchener, Ontario, Canada, 1931-42.
Date of Death/Burial Location: August 5, 1942; New York City, N.Y.

CLECKLEY, EDWARD WALTER, JR.

Date/Place of Birth: June 5, 1956; Charlotte, N.C.
Parents: Edward Walter Cleckley, Sr. and Elizabeth (Fanning) Cleckley.
Spouse/Marriage Date: Susan (Mansley) Cleckley; February 13, 1983.
Child: Charlotte Randall.
Education: Lenoir-Rhyne, B.A. English 1978; Gettysburg Seminary, M.Div. 1983.
Ordination: July 17, 1983 by New Jersey Synod for North Carolina Synod.
Calls: St. Stephen, Edison, N.J., 1983-86; Union, Salisbury; 1986-91; St. Paul, Lititz, Pa., 1991-.
Other: Evangelism Committee for North Carolina Synod; Directing Committee for Lutheran Campus Ministry, Rutgers University, New Brunswick Campus, 1983-84; Minutes Committee, Communications Committee for New Jersey Synod. Cabinet Member, Central District of New Jersey Synod, 1984. Editor/Founder of *Anima* College Literary Magazine.

CLEMMER, PALMER DEKALB

Date/Place of Birth: June 5, 1952; Gastonia, N.C.
Parents: John Franklin Clemmer, Jr. and Mary Louise (Fulton) Clemmer.
Spouse/Marriage Date: Cynthia Louise (Long) Clemmer; July 12, 1975 in Raleigh, N.C.
Education: Lenoir-Rhyne, B.S. 1974; Lutheran Theological Southern Seminary, M.Div. 1978.
Ordination: June 11, 1978 by North Carolina Synod.
Calls: Co-Pastor, Kimball, Kannapolis, 1978-81; King of Glory, North Myrtle Beach, S.C., 1981-87; Our Saviour, Southern Pines, 1987-93; Grace, Hendersonville, 1993-.

CLINE, JOHN PHILIP

Date/Place of Birth: October 1, 1803; Woodstock, Va.
Parents: Henry Klein and Mary Klein.
Spouse/Marriage Date: Melinda (Zirkle) Cline; October 1, 1929.
Education: Studied theology under the Reverend S. S. Schmucker at New Market, Va.
License/Ordination: Licensed May 10, 1826 at Salem and ordained 1829 by North Carolina Synod at St. John, Wythe County, Va.
Calls: St. Peter and St. Paul, Rockingham County (later Page County, Va.) in 1926. In Virginia, 1828-34, 1847-66: St. Matthew, New Market; Solomon, Forestville; Zion, Edinburg; Emanuel, Woodstock. Represented North Carolina Synod at annual convention of the Synod of Maryland and Virginia in 1828. Leitersburg and Waynesboro, Md., congregations, 1834-47.
Other: Taught school near Woodstock, Va. in 1825. He and the Reverend Socrates Henkel were assistants to the Reverend Ambrose Henkel. With other North Carolina Synod pastors and laymen in Virginia, assisted in organizing Virginia Synod in 1829 and in drafting its constitution. Served as President of Synod, 1848-50.
Date of Death/Burial Location: July 20, 1866; Lutheran Cemetery in New Market, Va.

CLINE, ROBERT HENRY
Date/Place of Birth: November 1, 1859; Startown, Catawba County, N.C.
Parents: Eli Davidson Cline and Roxanna (Star) Cline. The Reverend W. P. Cline was an older brother.
Spouse/Marriage Date: Sara Alice Cline; February 23, 1886 in Newton, N.C.
Children: T. H., Miriam, Anna Myrtle, Carl P., William Russell, Harry Glen, Robert Frederick, Ed Wynn.
Education: Catawba College, Roanoke College, A.B. 1885; studied theology under course of Tennessee Synod Board of Education; North Carolina College, M.A.; Roanoke College, D.D. 1940.
Ordination: 1885 by Tennessee Synod.
Calls: Mt. Moriah, Rowan County, 1886-90. In Virginia, 1890-1900. In North Carolina, 1900-15: St. John's, Cherryville; St. Mark, Crouse, supplied St. Paul, Crouse; Cedar Grove, Lincoln County, supplied Sardis, Catawba County; Trinity, Vale; St. Luke-Morning Star, Monroe; Christ's, Stanley. Transferred to Virginia Synod, 1915.
Other: Retired 1934 at Roanoke, Va.; Secretary, Tennessee Synod, 1890-92.
Date of Death/Burial Location: January 3, 1951; Evergreen Cemetery, Roanoke, Va.

CLINE, WILLIAM PINCKNEY
Date/Place of Birth: March 21, 1853; Startown, Catawba County, N.C.
Parents: Eli Davidson Cline and Roxanna (Star) Cline. The Reverend R. H. Cline was a younger brother.
Spouse/Marriage Date: Julia Catherine (Bost) Cline; 1880 in Newton, N.C.
Children: First four died in infancy; Julia Ethel, the Reverend William Preston, Frances Naomi, Robert Benjamin.
Education: Catawba College, Roanoke College, University of North Carolina, Ph.B. 1878; studied theology under the Reverend A. J. Fox; Lenoir- Rhyne, D.D. 1913.
Ordination: 1881 by Tennessee Synod.
Calls: 1880-1907: Supplied St. Matthew, Kings Mountain; St. Luke, Lincoln County; Beck's-Pilgrim-New Jerusalem, organized Holly Grove, Davidson County; Mt. Olive, Hickory; organized St. Martin, Maiden; supplied St. John, Statesville, four years; St. Martin, Iredell County; supplied Emmanuel, Lincolnton; again St. Luke, Lincoln County; Sardis, Catawba County; Philadelphia, Granite Falls; Mt. Olive (again); St. Andrew, Hickory; organized Bethlehem, Catawba County, 1907.
Other: Transferred to South Carolina Synod, 1907. President, Tennessee Synod, 1890-91. One of founders and professor, Lenoir-Rhyne, 1891-1901. Board Member and President of Board of Lenoir-Rhyne. Founder of Holly Grove Academy, 1885-1891. Superintendent, Lowman Home, 1911-22. President, Board of Publication, United Synod South, 1909-18.
Date of Death/Burial Location: September 11, 1925; Hickory, N.C.

CLONINGER, CHARLES JEFFREY

Date/Place of Birth: July 15, 1953; Newton, Catawba County, N.C.
Parents: Walter Glenn Cloninger and Pauline (Martin) Cloninger.
Spouse/Marriage Date: Mildred Sue (Caldwell) Cloninger; December 16, 1973 in Conover, N.C.
Children: Hannah Kristen, Andrea Erin.
Education: Lenoir-Rhyne, A.B. 1975; Lutheran Theological Southern Seminary, M.Div. 1979.
Ordination: June 10, 1979 by North Carolina Synod.
Calls: Holly Grove, Lexington, 1979-82; Emmanuel, Lincolnton, 1982-84; St. Paul, Statesville, 1984-86; St. Michael, High Point, 1986-89.
Other: Resigned April 1989.

CLONINGER, JACOB

Date/Place of Birth: October 26, 1826; Gaston County, N.C. Grew up in Georgia, then moved to Tennessee after marriage.
Spouse/Marriage Date: Mary E. (Lineberger) Cloninger; 1847 in Gaston County, N.C.
Children: One son, two daughters.
Education: Studied theology under the Reverend J. R. Peterson.
License/Ordination: Licensed 1859 and ordained 1861 by Tennessee Synod.
Calls: No record.
Other: In Monroe and McMinn Counties, Tenn. Transferred to and took part in organization of Holston Synod, 1861; one of three organizers living in 1886 to celebrate its 25th anniversary. A teacher of sacred vocal music.
Date of Death/Burial Location: May 29, 1890; St. Paul Church, Monroe County, Tenn.

CLONINGER, LEONARD GLENN, SR.

Date/Place of Birth: January 24, 1907; Gaston County, N.C.
Spouse/Marriage Date: Grace (Hollenbeck) Cloninger; July 18, 1936 in Milwaukee, Wis.
Children: Leonard Glenn, Jr., Paul Norman, John Mark.
Education: Lenoir-Rhyne B.A. 1930; Northwestern Seminary, M.Div. 1933; Carthage College, D.D. 1964.
Ordination: September 3, 1933 by Northwestern Synod.
Calls: Church of the Redeemer, Milwaukee, Wis., 1933-36; First English Church, Billings, Mont., 1936-42; St. Luke, Waukesha, Wis., 1942-73; St. Matthew, Kings Mountain, 1973-78.
Other: Retired in 1978. Vice President, Wisconsin Conference; Chair, Synodical Foreign Mission Committee; President, Board of Lutheran Homes in Oconomowoc, Wis.; Board, Carthage College.
Date of Death/Burial Location: December 11, 1991; St. Paul, Dallas, N.C.

CLONINGER, PAT CASWELL

Date/Place of Birth: October 3, 1929; Gaston County, N.C.
Parents: Augustus Eugene Cloninger and Margaret Kathleen (Plonk) Cloninger.
Spouse/Marriage Date: Eva Janet (Lineberger) Cloninger; January 26, 1958 in Maiden, N.C.
Education: Lenoir-Rhyne, A.B. 1951; Lutheran Theological Southern Seminary, 1954.

Ordination: June 20, 1954 by North Carolina Synod.
Calls: St. James, Catawba County, 1954-57; Trinity, Vale, 1957-63.
Other: Demitted January 13, 1963.

COBB, JAMES GURLEY

Date/Place of Birth: September 29, 1947; Hickory, N.C.
Parents: The Reverend James Kivett Cobb and Sara Ellen (Wingard) Cobb. Grandson of the Reverend William Gurley Cobb; nephew of the Reverends John W. Cobb, John D. Mauney, W. Dexter Moser.
Spouse/Marriage Date: Judith Ann (Dawson) Cobb; May 19, 1973 in Gettysburg, Pa.
Children: Christopher James, Stephen Andrew.
Education: William and Mary, B.A. 1969; graduate work at Catholic University, 1973-74; Gettysburg Seminary, M.Div 1973, D.Min. 1980.
Ordination: June 3, 1973 by North Carolina Synod.
Calls: Assistant Pastor, St. Martin, Annapolis, Md., 1973-74; Christ, Fredericksburg, Va., 1974-81; Trinity, Grand Rapids, Mich., 1981-88; First, Norfolk, Va., 1988-.
Other: Evangelical Lutheran Church in America Church Council, 1987-95; Evangelical Lutheran Church in America, Study of Ministry, 1988-93; Evangelical Lutheran Church in America, Ecumenical Affairs Advisory Committee, 1993-; Evangelical Lutheran Church in America Ecumenical Overseas Visitation Delegation, 1995; various synodical leadership roles in Michigan and Virginia; writer for various publications.

COBB, JAMES KIVETT

Date/Place of Birth: August 30, 1918; Rural Retreat, Wythe County, Va.
Parents: The Reverend William Gurley Cobb and Emma Lillian (Akard) Cobb. The Reverend John W. Cobb is an older brother.
Spouse/Marriage Date: Sarah Ellen (Wingard) Cobb; October 18, 1945 in Columbia, S.C.
Children: The Reverend Dr. James Gurley, Bessie Kathryn Glenham, Ellen Dianne Rimmer.
Education: Lenoir-Rhyne, A.B. 1942; Lutheran Theological Southern Seminary, B.D. 1945.
Ordination: April 4, 1945 by North Carolina Synod.
Calls: St. Andrew's-St. Michael, Columbia, S.C., 1945-46. Pastor-Developer, Reformation, Taylorsville, 1946-49; St. John, Hudson-St. Matthew, Caldwell County, 1949-50; Philadelphia, Granite Falls, 1949-52. Rader, Timberville, Va., 1951-54; Board of American Missions Developer, Knoxville, Tenn., 1954-55; Immanuel, Blountville, Tenn., 1955-58; Emmanuel, Roanoke, Va., 1958-65; Good Shepherd, Goldsboro, 1972- 74; Faith, Newberry, S.C., 1974-82; Supply Pastor for Mt. Olivet, Prosperity, S.C., 1982-90. Retired from South Carolina Synod to Stanfield, N.C., 1998.
Other: Devotions for *Light for Today*. Retired 1982 to Stanfield. Member of the Stewardship, Evangelism, and World Missions Committee in the Virginia Synod.

COBB, JOHN MOSER

Date/Place of Birth: August 3, 1944; Roanoke, Va.
Parents: The Reverend Dr. John William Cobb and Rachel Carolyn (Moser) Cobb.
Spouse/Marriage Date: Irene Elizabeth (Szues) Cobb; May 11, 1974.
Children: Jolan Elizabeth, Johannes Moser.

Education: Lenoir-Rhyne, 1963; University of North Carolina, B.A. 1968, M.A. 1972; Waterloo Seminary, 1970-72; Lutheran Theological Southern Seminary, M.Div. 1976; University of Manitoba, Ph.D. Candidate.
Ordination: 1976 by North Carolina Synod.
Calls: Trinity, Poueka, Alberta, Canada, 1976-81.
Other: Transferred to Western Canada Synod, 1976. Part-time Chaplain, Alberta Hospital. Professional Leadership Committee, Western Canada Synod, 1980-81. Worship and Music Portfolio, 1979; Secretary/Treasurer, Canadian Lutheran Historical Association, 1981-83; Editor *For the Record, Journal of Canadian Lutheran Historical Association, 1985-87*. Active in bi-lingual ministry (German- English) in Canada. Author of *History of St. Paul Evangelical Lutheran Church, Savannah, Georgia, 1977*.

COBB, JOHN WILLIAM
Date/Place of Birth: December 6, 1916; Blountville, Tenn.
Parents: The Reverend William Gurley Cobb and Emma Lillian (Akard) Cobb. The Reverend James K. Cobb is a younger brother.
Spouse/Marriage Date: Rachel Carolyn (Moser) Cobb; June 16, 1942 in Greensboro, N.C.
Children: John Moser, William Jerry.
Education: Lenoir-Rhyne, A.B. 1936, D.D. 1967; Lutheran Theological Southern Seminary, B.D. 1939; graduate study, Chicago Seminary, 1952.
Ordination: June 1939 by North Carolina Synod.
Calls: Trinity, Rocky Mount, 1939-43. Luther Memorial, Blacksburg, Va., 1943-47; Campus Pastor, Virginia Polytechnic Institute, 1943-47; Grace, Bethlehem, Pa., 1947-57; Holy Trinity, Raleigh, and Pastor to Lutheran students at North Carolina State University and other institutions, 1957-80. Vice Pastor at various congregations.
Other: Retired February 1, 1980 to Cherryville, N.C. Board, Children's Home of the South, 1960-64; Dean, Eastern District, 1962-68; Executive Board, 1964-70, 1976; Publications and Publicity Committee, 1963-64; American Missions, 1971-72, 1974; Committee on College and University Work, 1963; Delegate, North Carolina Council of Churches, 1963-65; Delegate, Lutheran Church in America Convention, 1962, 1966, 1968, 1970; Examining Committee, 1970-75, Chair, 1972-73. Freedoms Foundation Award for sermon preached, 1956. Shelton Communication Award, North Carolina Council of Churches, 1977 (the only individual ever to be so honored); Second Vice President of the Luther League of America, 1937-39; President, Roanoke Conference, Virginia Synod, 1945-47; President Eastern Conference, 1962; Dean, Eastern District, 1963-69; Trustee Michael Peeler Fund, 1975-; Executive Director, North Carolina Lutheran Men in Mission, 1982-; President, Raleigh Ministerial Association, 1961-62; Chair, State and Local Affairs Committee and Chair of Christian Nurture Committee, North Carolina Council of Churches. Nominating Committee, Lutheran Church in America Kansas City Convention, 1966; Chair, Task Force on World Missions and Ecumenism for Committee on Structure and Function, Lutheran Church in America, 1971-72; Steering Committee for Lutheran Men in Mission, Evangelical Lutheran Church in America, 1986-88.

COBB, PAUL BRYSON

Date/Place of Birth: September 22, 1922; Greensboro, N.C.
Parents: Afton C. Cobb and Hyacinth (Mangum) Cobb.
Spouse/Marriage Date: Edna Louise (Bowers) Cobb of Newberry, S.C.; October 14, 1947 in Concord, N.C.
Children: Rosalyn Louise, Martha Ellen Yates.
Education: Duke University, A.B. 1943; Lutheran Theological Southern Seminary, M.Div. 1945; University of North Carolina at Charlotte, M.Ed. 1973.
Ordination: October 7, 1945 by North Carolina Synod.
Calls: Calvary, Concord, 1945-49; Cold Water, Cabarrus County, 1946-49; Alamance, Alamance, 1949-53; Ascension, Shelby, 1953-60. Woman's Memorial (now Trinity), Pulaski, Va., 1960-64; St. Thomas, Charlotte, 1964-84; Part-time pastor to sick and shut-in members at St. Mark's, Charlotte. Vice Pastor to various congregations.
Other: Retired in 1984 in Charlotte, N.C. Synodical Committee on Christian Education; Board, Lutheran Theological Southern Seminary. Served 25 years on Advisory Council of the Salvation Army Adult Rehabilitation Center in Charlotte.

COBB, WAYNE SINCLAIR

Date/Place of Birth: November 18, 1954; Salisbury, N.C.
Parents: Curtis E. Cobb, Sr. and Dorothy Lee (Barber) Cobb.
Spouse/Marriage Date: Ann (Lomax) Cobb; January 29, 1977.
Children: Adam Sinclair, Elizabeth English.
Education: University of North Carolina at Chapel Hill, 1974-76; Christopher-Newport College, 1978-80; University of North Carolina at Asheville, B.A. Independent Studies, 1982;Lutheran Theological Southern Seminary, M.Div. 1986.
Ordination: May 1986 by North Carolina Synod.
Calls: The Lutheran Church of the Good Shepherd, Brevard, 1986-92; St. Stephen, Hickory, 1992-98; St. James, Concord, 1998-.

COBB, WILLIAM GURLEY

Date/Place of Birth: December 30, 1887; Guilford County, N.C.
Parents: John Calvin Cobb and Mary Emma (Starr) Cobb.
Spouse/Marriage Date: Emma Lillian (Akard) Cobb; March 3 1916 in Sullivan County, Tenn.; died November 7, 1978.
Children: The Reverend John William, the Reverend James Kivett, Mary Emma (married the Reverend J. D. Mauney, Jr.), Margaret Elizabeth (married the Reverend W. D. Moser, Jr.), Martha Louise, Mildred Marie, Frances Irene.
Education: Elon College, Newberry College, A.B. 1911; Lutheran Theological Southern Seminary, 1914, B.D. 1927; graduate study, Chicago Seminary.
Ordination: 1914 by North Carolina Synod.
Calls: Holston Synod in Tennessee, 1914-17; Southwest Virginia Synod, 1917-22. In North Carolina, 1922-54: Salem-Grace, Rowan County; then, Salem alone; supplied Lebanon, Rowan County, one year; Zion- Bethlehem-New Jerusalem, Catawba County; St.

John's, Cherryville, 1924-51; St. David, Kannapolis, 1951-54. Developed and organized Our Saviour, Gaston County, 1957. Regular supply preacher to various congregations.
Other: Retired 1954 at Cherryville, N.C. Secretary, Holston Synod, 1914-17. Committee on Merger of Holston, Southwest Virginia and Virginia Synods. Board, Lowman Home, 1928-42, Secretary 1937-39; Board, Children's Home of the South, 1942-53.
Date of Death/Burial Location: May 18, 1960; St. John's Church, Cherryville, N.C.

COBLE, GARY STEPHEN

Date/Place of Birth: December 20, 1950; Greensboro, N.C.
Parents: Barney Jason Coble and Ila Mae (Hemphill) Coble.
Spouse/Marriage Date: Hope (Basnight) Coble; June 30, 1973.
Children: Carol Anne, Victoria Elizabeth.
Education: Lenoir-Rhyne, B.S. Physics 1973; Lutheran Theological Southern Seminary, M.Div. 1977.
Ordination: June 12, 1977 by North Carolina Synod.
Calls: Holy Trinity, Reidsville, 1977-81; Mt. Hebron, Hildebran, 1981-.
Other: Icard Township Fire Department Captain and Assistant Team Leader for First Responders; Board of Directors for Fire Department.

COBLE, MICHAEL

Place of Birth: Guilford County, N.C.
License: 1868 by North Carolina Synod.
Calls: Preached to Negroes in and around Concord, mostly in homes of the people, for want of church buildings. After a few years joined the Methodists.
Other: Member of Alpha Synod.

COFFEY, ARTHUR WADE, JR.

Date/Place of Birth: November 19, 1946; Norfolk, Va.
Parents: Arthur Wade Coffey, Sr. and Elizabeth (Cohn) Coffey.
Spouse/Marriage Date: Kathleen Stella (Johnson) Coffey; July 12, 1969.
Children: Julie Elizabeth, Jonathon Brooke, Isaac, Adam.
Education: Appalachian State University, B.A. 1969; Lutheran Theological Southern Seminary, M.Div. 1973.
Ordination: June 3, 1973 by North Carolina Synod.
Calls: Trinity, Roanoke, Va., 1973-83; Bethany, Lexington, Va. and New Mt. Olive, Fairfield, Va., 1985-93. Chaplain, Army Reserve.
Other: Removed from roll, February 8, 1993 in Raphine, Va.

COFFMAN, J. H.

Date/Place of Birth: 1827; probably in North Carolina.
First Spouse/Marriage Date: Elizabeth "Bettie" Ann (Locke) Coffman (Died July 12, 1851 possibly in giving birth to son. Buried in the Lutheran Cemetery, Salisbury, N.C.); October 23, 1850.
Child of First Marriage: Henry Locke.
Second Spouse/Marriage Date: Margaret C. (Anderson) Coffman; December 23, 1851.

Education: Attended Roanoke College and Lutheran Theological Southern Seminary.
License: Licensed 1848 by North Carolina Synod, but never ordained. Submitted a letter of resignation to the Ministerium and turned in his license in 1852.
Calls: St. Enoch, Rowan County, 1849-50; St. John, Salisbury, 1848-52.
Other: Operated/managed a book/stationery department in Salisbury. Elected Vice President of the Missionary and Education Society of the North Carolina Synod in 1850. Moved to South Carolina, 1852.

COGAN, THOMAS FRANKLIN

Date/Place of Birth: August 16, 1952; Washington, D.C.
Parents: Joseph Edward Cogan and Evelyn Georgianna (Hayes) Cogan.
Spouse/Marriage Date: Robin Cordelia (Hall) Cogan; June 7, 1980.
Children: Amanda Lea, Joshua Edward.
Education: James Madison University, B.A. 1974; Trinity Seminary, M.Div. 1981.
Ordination: June 13, 1982 by American Lutheran Church.
Calls: Providence (American Lutheran Church), Winston-Salem, 1981-83; Holy Trinity, Troutman, 1984-92; St. Luke, Conover, 1992-. Vice Pastor at various congregations.
Other: Minutes and Unfinished Business Committee; Board, Lutherock, 1981-83; North Carolina Lutheran Marriage Encounter.

COLLEY, THOMAS NEWELL

Date/Place of Birth: June 10, 1948; Nashville, Tenn.
Parents: Newell G. Colley and Mildred M. Colley.
Spouse/Marriage Date: Gail Ruth (Keller) Colley; August 15, 1970.
Children: Janine Webb, Julie, Joanna.
Education: Concordia Junior College, Bronxville, A.A. 1968; Concordia Senior College, Fort Wayne, B.A. 1970; Christ Seminary, M.Div. 1974, Drew University, Doctorate in Pastoral Ministry, 1993.
Ordination: July 21, 1974 by American Evangelical Lutheran Church.
Calls: Prince of Peace, Claremont, N.H. (American Evangelical Lutheran Church) 1974-80; Trinity, Vernon, Conn. (American Evangelical Lutheran Church), 1980-83; St. Thomas, Charlotte, 1985-89; Nativity, Arden, 1989-95; Mt. Olive, Hickory, 1995-.
Other: Board of Governors, Mental Health Region II, N.H.; Board, Group Foster Home, Claremont, N.H.; advisor to youth groups on district level.

COLLINS, MICHAEL EVANS

Date/Place of Birth: December 15, 1957; Arlington, Va.
Parents: Robert R. Collins and Sali E. Collins.
Spouse/Marriage Date: Elizabeth Anne (Pharr) Collins; August 12, 1978 in Raleigh, N.C.
Children: Joshua Michael, Katherine Elizabeth, Hannah Quaid.
Education: Lenoir-Rhyne, B.A. 1980; Gettysburg Seminary, M.Div. 1984.
Ordination: May 25, 1984 by North Carolina Synod.
Calls: Christ's, Stanley, 1984-87; First, Lexington, 1987-92; St. John's, Cherryville, 1993-. Vice Pastor at various congregations.

COLLINS, MICHAEL LEE, SR.
Date/Place of Birth: March 14, 1952; Hickory, N.C.
Parents: Hume S. Collins, Sr. and Naoma C. Collins.
Spouse/Marriage Date: Sheila (Harris) Collins; November 11, 1981 in Charlotte, N.C.
Children: Courtney Michelle, Michael Lee, Jr., Candace Marie, Chase Lucas.
Education: Appalachian State University, B.S. Social Science, 1974; Lutheran Theological Southern Seminary, M.Div. 1978; Graduate Theological Foundation, D.Min. 1989.
Ordination: June 11, 1978 by North Carolina Synod.
Calls: Christ, Winston-Salem, 1978-81; A Mighty Fortress, Charlotte, 1981-84; Calvary, Morganton, 1984- 89; Emmanuel, Naples, Fla., 1989-.
Other: *Preaching Helps, Currents in Theology and Mission; A Christmas Day Journey; A Journal for Preachers; Christ Did Not Come to Bring Peace; 1989 Fellows Yearbook.* First Editor for *Soli Deo Gloria* (North Carolina Worship newsletter distributed nationally); Recipient of Human Rights Award, 1988; *Who's Who in American Religion, 1992-3; Good Guy Award, Naples, 1996;* Board, Lutheridge-Lutherock, 1983-1991; Educational Ministry Committee; Family Life Council; Stewardship Interpreter; Confirmation Ministry Facilitator; Chair, Worship and Music Committee; Cabinet on Congregational Life.

CONDER, IRENAEUS
Date/Place of Birth: October 17, 1832; Union County, N.C.
Parents: Philip Conder and Sophia (Byrum) Conder.
Spouse/Marriage Date: Susan Catherine (Conrad) Conder; 1866 in Forsyth County, N.C.
Children: Ella E., Frances L., Anna S., Conn Luther.
Education: Davidson College, North Carolina College, (closed 1861 before his graduation because of the war), Honorary A.M. 1872; studied theology under the Reverend Polycarp C. Henkel.
License/Ordination: Licensed 1859 and ordained 1861 by Tennessee Synod.
Calls: 1861-66: Mt. Moriah, Rowan County, one year; Beck's-Pilgrim-New Jerusalem, Davidson County. In Tennessee Synod in Virginia, 1867-94. Secretary, Tennessee Synod, three one-year terms; President, 1893.
Other: A son of old Morning Star Church near Matthews. Author of a book, *A Plea for Teaching the Decalogue in the Public Schools.* Contributor to *Our Church Paper,* New Market, Va. Retired 1898 in McGaheysville, Va.
Date of Death/Burial Location: August 31, 1928; Mt. Olivet Cemetery, McGaheysville, Va.

CONE, JAMES HOWELL
Date/Place of Birth: April 12, 1953; San Francisco County, Calif.
Parents: William Henry Cone and Edith Cleve (Turner) Cone.
Spouse/Marriage Date: Yvonne Chalee (Boyle) Cone; May 27, 1979 in Jacksonville, Fla.
Children: Stephanie Kate, Christopher William James.
Education: Newberry College, A.B. 1975; Lutheran Theological Southern Seminary, M.Div. 1979.
Ordination: June 10, 1979 by North Carolina Synod.
Calls: St. Peter, Southport, 1979-82; Bethany, Kannapolis, 1982-87; Holy Trinity, Hickory, 1987-91; Mt. Calvary, Claremont, 1991-.

CONE, WILLIAM HENRY

Date of Birth: December 11, 1825.

First Spouse/Marriage Date: Carmilla (Cornelia) C. (Miller) Cone; December 21, 1865; died February 4, 1875.

Second Spouse/Marriage Date: Barbara A. (Shirley) Cone; December 7, 1876 in New Market, Va.; died April 3, 1926.

Child: Son, Shirley Z., who died at 25 years of age.

Ordination: 1858 by Southwest Virginia Synod.

Calls: Organized Bethel, Edinburg, Va. in 1858-65. Supplied Bethlehem, Luray, Va. for four years and also was supply for St. James, Hudson's Cross Roads, Va. Transferred to North Carolina Synod, 1866. Churches served in North Carolina, 1864-81: Beck's-Pilgrim-St. Luke-Lebanon, Davidson County; Union, Rowan County; Organ, Rowan County; St. John, Salisbury; supplied St. James, Concord, three years; St. Peter, Rowan County; St. Matthew; Luther's, Richfield,, 1875-77; Lutheran Chapel, China Grover, 1877-81; Center Grove; St. Paul.

Other: Served as agent for Roanoke College. President, North Carolina Synod, 1872-73. Moved to New Market, Va., his wife's home city, and engaged in her family's business of making carriages and wagons. Served a three-year term on the Board of Trustees of North Carolina College. Served a three-year term on Board of Trustees of Mt. Pleasant Female Seminary. Elected Corresponding Secretary for Synodical Missionary Society, 1869. Corresponding Delegate to the Tennessee Synod, 1969.

Date of Death/Burial Location: December 22, 1902; St. Matthew Church, New Market, Va.

CONNELLY, RACHEL LEAH

Date/Place of Birth: March 17, 1963; Macon, Ga.

Parents: The Reverend James R. Connelly and Faith (Bunger) Connelly.

Spouse/Date of Marriage: Michael Alan Goyne; June 16, 1990.

Child: Jacob Diedrich Goyne.

Education: Newberry College, B.S. Business Administration, 1985; Lutheran Theological Southern Seminary, M.Div. 1990.

Ordination: June 8, 1990 by North Carolina Synod.

Calls: Good Shepherd, Goldsboro, July 1990-.

Other: Executive Committee, Lutheran Theological Southern Seminary; Evangelism Committee; Goldsboro AIDS Task Force; Evangelical Lutheran Church in America Assembly Delegate.

CONRAD, DAVID FRYE

Date/Place of Birth: July 26, 1921; Hickory, N.C.

Parents: The Reverend Dr. Flavius Leslie Conrad, Sr. and Mary (Huffman) Conrad. Older brother is the Reverend F. L. Conrad, Jr., and younger brother the Reverend Paul L. Conrad; one of their sisters is wife of the Reverend Philip L. Wahlberg, Jr.

Spouse/Marriage Date: Janis (Patton) Conrad; June 24, 1948 in Birmingham, Ala.

Children: David Mark, Timothy Patton, Hugh Victor, Charles Kristian.

Education: Lenoir-Rhyne, A.B. 1942; Lutheran Theological Southern Seminary, B.D. 1945.

Ordination: April 4, 1945 by North Carolina Synod. Transferred to Georgia-Alabama Synod.
Calls: Christ the King, Birmingham, Ala., 1945-52; National Lutheran Council, Educational Secretary in Negro Work, 1952-54; Grace, Houston, Texas, 1954-72; St. Luke's, Charlotte, 1972-85.
Other: Retired 1985 in Oneonta, Ala.

CONRAD, E. PARKER

Date/Place of Birth: July 29, 1879; Davidson County, N.C.
Parents: George W. Conrad and Mary Anne (Leonard) Conrad.
Spouse/Marriage Date: Myrtle (Graeber) Conrad; May 27, 1908 in China Grove, N.C.
Children: Faith, Hope, Charity.
Education: Lenoir-Rhyne, A.B. 1900; Chicago Seminary, 1903/04.
Ordination: 1904 by North Carolina Synod.
Calls: Augsburg, Winston-Salem, 1904-05. Transferred to Chicago Synod, 1905. Churches in Indiana and Ohio. Supply preaching to 1955.
Other: Retired 1956 at Middle Point, Ohio.
Date of Death/Burial Location: June 24, 1956; Ridge Cemetery, Van Wert, Ohio.

CONRAD, FLAVIUS LESLIE, JR.

Date/Place of Birth: May 5, 1920; High Point, N.C.
Parents: The Reverend Flavius Leslie Conrad, Sr. and Mary W. (Huffman) Conrad. Two brothers are the Reverends David F. and Paul L. Conrad, one of his sisters is the wife of the Reverend Philip L. Wahlberg, Jr.
Spouse/Marriage Date: Mary Elizabeth (Isenhour) Conrad; November 4, 1944 in Salisbury, N.C.
Children: Elizabeth Ann Meisner, Susan Leslie Amis.
Education: Lenoir-Rhyne, A.B. 1941; Lutheran Theological Southern Seminary, B.D. 1944; Temple University, S.T.M. 1955, S.T.D. 1958.
Ordination: July 16, 1944 by North Carolina Synod.
Calls: St. Timothy, Catawba County, 1944-49; Holy Comforter, Belmont, 1949-50; St. Luke, Richardson, Texas, 1960-86, Pastor Emeritus.
Other: Executive Secretary, Luther League of America, 1950-60. Published more than 1,100 sermons, articles, book chapters, encyclopedia write-ups, devotional booklets, book reviews, poems and hymns. Prepared several series of Augsburg Sunday School Quarterlies. Developed and directed the Lutheran Youth Caravan Program, 1950-59. Supervised new Constitution and By-Laws for Luther League of America. Authored two books *Four Non-Denominational Youth Movements* and *Poetic Potshots at Preachers and People*. Synodical Delegate to several conventions of the Lutheran Church in America. Member of General Board and General Assembly of National Council of Churches. Winner, National Poetry Contest, 1960. Member of Lutheran Church in America Board of Publications, 1974-82. Assistant Editor, *Church Management Magazine*, 1964-77. Correspondent, *The Lutheran*, 1962-87. Columnist, *Texas-Louisiana Lutheran*, 1961-87. Listed in *Who's Who in the East, Who's Who in Religion, Who's Who in America, Who's Who in the World*, and *Who's Who in the South and*

Southwest. Dean, Dallas and North Texas Conference of the Texas-Louisiana Synod, 1975-78. Retired December 1986 in Richardson, Texas.

CONRAD, FLAVIUS LESLIE, SR.

Date/Place of Birth: May 23, 1894; Davidson County, N.C.
Parents: Charles F. Conrad and Frances E. (Fritz) Conrad.
Spouse/Marriage Date: Mary W. (Huffman) Conrad; June 24, 1919 in Hickory, N.C.
Children: The Reverend Flavius Leslie, Jr., the Reverend David Frye, Rachel (married the Reverend Philip L. Wahlberg, Jr.), Rebekah Meller, the Reverend Paul Luther.
Education: Lenoir-Rhyne, A.B. 1916, D.D. 1941; Lutheran Theological Southern Seminary, 1919, B.D. 1926; graduate study University of South Carolina.
Ordination: September 12, 1919 by Tennessee Synod.
Calls: Philadelphia, Granite Falls; St. John, Hudson; St. Matthew, Caldwell County, 1919-21; Emmanuel, High Point, 1921-49. Secretary, North Carolina Synod, 1937-49. President, North Carolina Synod, 1949-62. Vice Pastor to various congregations.
Other: Editor, *Catawba Lutheran,* 1920-21. Board, Lenoir-Rhyne, 1935-49. In United Lutheran Church in America, member of Board of American Missions, and other boards and committees, and delegate to conventions, 1937-62. Retired December 31, 1962 at Kure Beach, N.C. Honored by having his name given to Conrad Hall (dormitory) at Lenoir Rhyne College, and to Conference Room in the Church House at Salisbury.
Date of Death/Burial Location: November 8, 1987; Holly Grove Cemetery, Lexington, N.C.

CONRAD, GEORGE DWIGHT

Date/Place of Birth: September 21, 1912; Thomasville, N.C.
Parents: Curtis H. Conrad and Mary Ellen (Clemmons) Conrad.
Spouse/Marriage Date: Ruth Matilda (Shoaf) Conrad; May 21, 1939 in Thomasville, N.C.
Children: Linda Ruth Pilotti, Rebecca Elaine Rhyne, Martha Annette, Timothy Dwight.
Education: Lenoir-Rhyne, A.B. 1936; Lutheran Theological Southern Seminary, B.D. 1939.
Ordination: June 1, 1939 by North Carolina Synod.
Calls: Assistant Pastor, St. Mark's, Charlotte, 1939-40; Bethany, Hickory, 1940-66; Mission Developer, Redeemer, Gastonia, 1966-73; St. Paul, Startown, 1973-79. Vice Pastor at various congregations.
Other: Board, Lenoir-Rhyne, 1963-75. Social Ministry, Mission and Evangelism Committees for North Carolina Synod. Author of devotions for *Light For Today* and *Word In Season.* Preached in twelve states on preaching missions and in Germany and India. Retired December 31, 1979.
Date of Death/Burial Location: July 18, 1985; Catawba Memorial Park, Hickory, N.C.

CONRAD, PAUL LUTHER

Date/Place of Birth: April 20, 1931; High Point, N.C.
Parents: The Reverend Flavius Leslie Conrad, Sr. and Mary W. (Huffman) Conrad. Two older brothers are the Reverends Flavius Leslie, Jr., and David F. Conrad.
Spouse/Marriage Date: Laura Katherine "Kay" (Oxner) Conrad; June 23, 1956 in West Columbia, S.C.
Children: Tina Marie Kestner, Laurie Janise Spain, Jonathan Paul.
Education: Lenoir-Rhyne, A.B. 1953, D.D., 1990; Lutheran Theological Southern Seminary, M.Div. 1956.
Ordination: June 10, 1956 by North Carolina Synod.
Calls: Concordia, China Grove, 1956-59; Prince of Peace, Kinston, 1959-64; St. Paul, Statesville, 1964-73; Epiphany, Winston-Salem, 1973-93. Vice Pastor at various congregations.
Other: Assistant Editor, *North Carolina Lutheran*, 1959-66; Editor, 1967-68. Correspondent for *The Lutheran* from North Carolina Synod for eighteen years. Social Ministry, Publications, Lutheran Theological Southern Seminary, Auxiliaries, Nominating and World Missions Committees for the North Carolina Synod. Jaycees' Distinguished Service Award "Young Man of the Year," 1961. In Statesville, President, City of Progress Kiwanis Club; Recipient, Civitan Club's Distinguished Citizenship Award, 1972; Statesville Chamber of Commerce's Outstanding Citizenship Award, 1972. In Winston-Salem, Board, Goodwill Industries and Industries for the Blind, Chair in 1981; President, Stratford Kiwanis Club, 1977; Kiwanian of the Year, 1981- 82; Chair, Winston-Salem-Forsyth County Community Partnership Committee for the International Year of Disabled Persons, 1981. President, Forsyth Lutheran Council, 1985. Chaplain volunteer, Piedmont Aerospace Institute, 1978-84. President, Lenoir-Rhyne Alumni Association, 1978-79. Recipient of Lenoir-Rhyne Alumni Association Service Award, 1981. Board of Trustees, Lenoir-Rhyne. Contributing writer to the *Lutheran Women* magazine, *The Lutheran,* and *The Winston-Salem Sentinel* newspaper. Chair, Lenoir-Rhyne Alumni Association "Loyalty Fund," 1985. Retired June 30, 1993 in Winston-Salem, N.C.

COOK, CARLA (LANG)

See Lang, Carla

COOK, DENNIS LEE

Date/Place of Birth: September 5, 1946; Minneapolis, Minn.
Parents: Ralph Cook, Jr. and Jean (Brickson) Cook.
Spouse/Marriage Date: Shirley Jean (Seppi) Cook; June 7, 1970 in Stillwater, Minn.
Children: Jennifer, Jonathan.
Education: Winona State University, B.A. Social Science/Social Work, 1968; Northwestern Seminary, M.Div. 1972.
Ordination: June 4, 1972 by Minnesota Synod.
Calls: Grace, Louisville, Ky., 1972-75; St. Thomas, Brookville, Ind., 1975-79; Cokato Swedish Evangelical Lutheran Church, Cokato, Minn., 1979-87; Christ, Durham, 1988-97; Christus Victor, Fayetteville, 1997- .

Other: District Coordinator, Strength for Mission; District Youth Task Force, Indiana-Kentucky Synod. Chair, Family Life Committee, North Carolina Synod. Contributor to *Light For Today,* 1973, 1994.

COOK, EDWIN ALEXANDER

Date/Place of Birth: April 22, 1928; Cabarrus County, N.C.
Parents: Frank McDonald Cook and Mary Jane (Castor) Cook.
Spouse/Marriage Date: Verna Mae (Troutman) Cook; March 16, 1957 in Kannapolis, N.C.
Children: Rebecca Ann, David Alexander, Lydia Jane Craven.
Education: Lenoir-Rhyne, A.B. 1960; Lutheran Theological Southern Seminary, M.Div. 1963.
Ordination: June 9, 1963 by North Carolina Synod.
Calls: Coble's, Guilford County, 1963-67; St. Luke, Monroe, 1967-74; Ascension, Wilson, 1974-79; Antioch, Dallas, 1979-93. Vice Pastor at various congregations.
Other: Pastors' Support Committee, 1972-74. Retired August 1, 1993.

COOK, FRANK P.

Date/Place of Birth: May 23, 1854; Mt. Pleasant, N.C.
Parents: Matthew Cook and Mary Magdalene (Costner) Cook. His father, a native of Germany, was "Baptized a Roman Catholic, buried in Lutheran Cemetery, Mt. Pleasant, 1894."
Spouse/Marriage Date: Emma M. (Melhorn) Cook, sister of the Reverend Dr. N. R. Melhorn, long-time editor of *The Lutheran;* June 24, 1885 in Ada, Ohio. Her father was born and baptized a Roman Catholic, but was confirmed into the Lutheran faith by his son-in-law.
Children: Martha A., Mary A.
Education: North Carolina College, A.B. 1874; Philadelphia Seminary, 1877.
Ordination: 1877 by North Carolina Synod.
Calls: Assistant to Dr. G. D. Bernheim, St. Paul, Wilmington, 1877-78. Transferred to Ohio Synod, 1878. In Ohio, 1878-1910; in Pennsylvania, 1910-19.
Date of Death/Burial Location: December 13, 1919; Woodlawn Cemetery in Ada, Ohio.

COON, ROBERT GEORGE

Date/Place of Birth: August 28, 1946; Lincolnton, N.C.
Parents: Robert Clarence Coon and Nellie (Brown) Coon.
Spouse/Marriage Date: Ann Hampton (Barker) Coon; July 6, 1968 in Staunton, Va.
Children: Elizabeth Ann, Robert Wade.
Education: Lenoir-Rhyne, B.A. 1968; Lutheran Theological Southern Seminary, M.Div. 1972.
Ordination: June 4, 1972 by North Carolina Synod.
Calls: Associate Pastor/Pastor Trinity, Greenville, S.C., 1972-. *Other*: President, South Carolina Synod Lutheran Conference and Retreat Centers, 1989-92; Chair, South Carolina Synod Youth Ministry Committee, 1974-79; President, United Ministries, 1993-94; Chair, Community Foundation of Greater Greenville, 1995.

COOPER, DAVID FRANCIS

Date/Place of Birth: May 1, 1917; High Point, N.C.

Parents: Hubert F. Cooper and Lula Pearle (Bostian) Cooper. Uncles were the Reverends E. C., G. H., and L. G. Cooper.

Spouse/Marriage Date: Lillian Josephine (Goodwin) Cooper; January 2, 1943 in Charlotte, N.C.

Children: The Reverend David Mark, The Reverend Paul Robert, The Reverend Stephen Goodwin, Michael James.

Education: High Point College, A.B. 1938; Lutheran Theological Southern Seminary, B.D. 1941.

Ordination: June 1941 by North Carolina Synod.

Calls: Assistant Pastor St. Mark's, Charlotte, 1941-43; St. David-Redeemer, Kannapolis, Rowan County, 1943-47; Holy Trinity, Mt. Pleasant, 1947-49. Organized and developed Good Shepherd, Brevard, 1950-54. Transferred to Texas-Louisiana Synod, 1954; Messiah, Austin, Texas, 1955-62; St. Paul, Baton Rouge, La., 1962-69; St. John, Grand Prairie, Texas, 1969-77; Our Saviour, Tyler, Texas, 1977-85.

Other: Director for Christian Higher Education Year, employed by Lenoir-Rhyne, 1949-50. Editor, *North Carolina Lutheran* and North Carolina Correspondent for *The Lutheran*, 1951-54. President, Interdenominational Pastor's Association at Brevard, N.C. President of the Board, Baton Rouge Parish Senior Citizens Commission. Named "Man of the Year" for Community Service, Kannapolis, N.C., 1946. Distinguished Churchman Award from Texas Lutheran College; Executive Board, Louisiana Council of Churches; Executive Council, Texas-Louisiana Synod. Dean, Dallas-Ft. Worth District and Dallas Area. Synod Convention Chaplain at San Antonio, 1954 and at New Orleans Convention 1967. Synodical delegate to eight United Lutheran Church or Lutheran Church in America conventions. Editor, *Texas-Louisiana Lutheran,* for 36 years, the paper winning twenty-six awards in journalistic judged competition sponsored by the Lutheran Church in America's Department of Press, Radio and Television. *Who's Who in Religion, 1975-76.* Retired February 1985.

Date of Death/Burial Location: April 2, 1990; Our Saviour, Tyler, Texas.

COOPER, EDGAR CLAUDIUS

Date/Place of Birth: March 29, 1887; China Grove, N.C.

Parents: John Francis Jacob Cooper and Martha Jane (Page) Cooper. Two younger brothers were The Reverends G. H. and L. G. Cooper.

Spouse/Marriage Date: Vera Lavene (Mauney) Cooper, sister of the Reverend J. D. Mauney, Sr., and aunt of the Reverends J. Luther Mauney, J. D. Mauney, Jr., and Marshall Mauney; September 11, 1913 in Kings Mountain, N.C. *Children*: Jacob Mauney, Margaret Juletta Plonk, the Reverend Edgar Mauney.

Education: Roanoke College, A.B. 1907; Princeton University, M.A. 1909; Philadelphia Seminary, 1912; Hartford Seminary, Ph.D. 1927.

Ordination: 1912 by Southwest Virginia Synod.

Calls: Holy Trinity, Lynchburg, Va., 1912-14; Advocate, Germantown, Pa., 1914-23. First, Albemarle, 1923-25; synodical missionary, 1927-39, serving and developing Holy Comforter, Belmont; Bethany, Kannapolis; St. Luke-Morning Star, Monroe; Calvary, Morganton; Watauga County Parish; Ascension, Shelby, 1932-37. Director of Religious

Training, and Chaplain of Raleigh prisons, North Carolina State prison system, 1937-39. President and part-time professor, New Testament Introduction and Interpretation, Lutheran Theological Southern Seminary, 1939-45. Served Holy Trinity, Chapel Hill, 1946-53, raising part of funds and building church and parsonage, also served as pastor to Lutheran students at University of North Carolina. Chaplain, U.S. Penitentiary, Atlanta, Ga., 1945-46.

Other: Retired 1953 at Kings Mountain, N.C. Later, guest professor of New Testament and Greek, Dana College, Blair, Neb., and Pacific Seminary, Berkeley, Calif. Author of *Jude—Author of Hebrews,* in *The Lutheran Quarterly,* and of book in manuscript, *The Source Value of John's Gospel,* which he was working on at death.

Date of Death/Burial Location: May 26, 1963; Mountain Rest Cemetery, Kings Mountain, N.C.

COOPER, GEORGE HERMAN

Date/Place of Birth: February 17, 1894; China Grove, N.C.

Parents: John Francis Jacob Cooper and Martha Jane (Page) Cooper. Two brothers are the Reverends E. C. and L. G. Cooper.

Spouse/Marriage Date: Doris Victoria (Ritchie) Cooper; September 25, 1924 in Richfield, N.C.

Children: Doris Jean, Ruth Victoria.

Education: Roanoke College, University of North Carolina, A.B. 1916; Lutheran Theological Southern Seminary, 1920, B.D. 1924; Chicago Seminary, S.T.M. 1928; graduate study, University of Chicago.

Ordination: 1920 by North Carolina Synod.

Calls: 1920-26: St. Matthew-St. Peter, Rowan County; Haven, Salisbury. Transferred to Illinois Synod, 1926: Chicago, Joliet, and Wheaton; Pastor Emeritus of church in Wheaton, 1960.

Other: Retired at Salisbury, N.C. Chaplain, U.S. Army 1941-46 retiring as Lieutenant Colonel in Reserves. President, National Chaplains Association.

Date of Death/Burial Location: May 15, 1961; Greenlawn Cemetery, China Grove, N.C.

COOPER, LUTHER GRADY

Date/Place of Birth: July 10, 1902; China Grove, N.C.

Parents: John Francis Jacob Cooper and Martha Jane (Page) Cooper. Older brothers were the Reverends E. C. and G. H. Cooper.

Spouse/Marriage Date: Miriam Roberta (Greever) Cooper, daughter of the Reverend Walton H. Greever; December 30, 1936 in Columbia, S.C.

Children: Kathryn Anne (married the Reverend William Homer Link), John Walton, Virginia Roberta Schott.

Education: Roanoke College, A.B. 1922; University of South Carolina, A.M. 1924; Lutheran Theological Southern Seminary, B.D. 1925; Hartford Seminary, Ph.D. 1927; Union Seminary, S.T.M. 1957; Newberry College, D.D., 1977.

Ordination: 1927 by North Carolina Synod.

Calls: Newport-Pembroke, Newport, Va., 1923-24; Rader, Timberville, Va., 1925; supply pastor at various congregations. Marburg University, Germany, 1927-28. United Lutheran

Church in America missionary, Shantung, China, 1928-48. During attack of Pearl Harbor was imprisoned by Japanese for seven months until prisoner exchange. Secretary and President of Shantung Lutheran Mission. President of American Lutheran Church, Tsingtao, Shantung, China, 1940-47. Transferred to South Carolina Synod, 1948. Holy Trinity, Little Mountain, S.C., 1948-53; Trinity, Elloree, S.C., 1953-57.

Other: Professor and head of Department of Bible and Religious Education, Newberry College, 1957-73, Professor Emeritus, 1972. Retired August 1971.

Date of Death/Burial Location: March 15, 1991; Memorial service at Lutheran Church of the Redeemer, Newberry, S.C.

COOPER, PAUL ROBERT

Date/Place of Birth: December 27, 1945; Kannapolis, N.C.
Parents: The Reverend David F. Cooper and Jo (Goodwin) Cooper.
Spouse/Marriage Date: Deborah Jean (Ash) Cooper; June 6, 1970 in Columbia, S.C.
Children: Mary Ashley, David S., Raymond Paul.
Education: Lenoir-Rhyne, A.B. 1968; Lutheran Theological Southern Seminary, M.Div. 1972; Drew University, D. Min. 1983; graduate work at University of Houston, 1988.
Ordination: June 4, 1972 by Texas-Louisiana Synod.
Calls: St. Paul, Roanoke, Va., 1972-77; Immanuel, Bluefield, W.Va., 1977-82; United Dr. Martin Luther, Shiner, Texas, 1982-90; Cross of Christ, Concord, 1990-97; Holy Trinity, Anderson, S.C., 1997-.

COPELAND, JUDY (LEWIS)

Date/Place of Birth: September 10, 1963; Charleston, S.C.
Parents: William Joseph Lewis and Sandra (Saulisbury) Lewis.
Spouse/Marriage Date: The Reverend Keith Thomas Copeland; August 26, 1989 in Charleston, S.C.
Child: Joshua Lewis.
Education: Newberry College, B.A. 1985; Lutheran Theological Southern Seminary, M.Div. 1989.
Ordination: September 17, 1989 by South Carolina Synod.
Calls: Atonement, Laurens, S.C., 1989-90; Twin Lakes Retirement Center, 1990-91; Administrative Assistant, Region 9, 1991-92; Messiah, Burlington, 1992-93; Mt. Zion, Conover, 1993-.

COPELAND, KEITH THOMAS

Date/Place of Birth: August 19, 1962; Chicago, Ill.
Parents: Charles Copeland and Judith Copeland.
Spouse/Marriage Date: The Reverend Judy (Lewis) Copeland; August 16, 1989 in Charleston, S.C.
Education: University of South Florida, B.A. Finance, 1984; Lutheran Theological Southern Seminary, M.Div. 1992.
Ordination: June 27, 1992 by North Carolina Synod.
Calls: Messiah, Burlington, 1992-93; Mt. Zion, Conover, 1993-. Interim Pastor at various congregations.

COPELAND, MARIA-ALMA (RAINEY)

Date/Place of Birth: October 13, 1931; York, S.C.
Parents: Mason Rainey, Sr. and Arleva Mobley.
Spouse/Marriage Date: Richard Earl Copeland-Thomas; 1968 in El Paso, Texas.
Child: Carla Michele.
Education: Alaska Business College-Anchorage Community College, 1961-63; Augsburg College, 1978-79; MacAlester College, 1979; Pacific Lutheran University, B.A. 1979; Luther-Northwestern Seminary, M.Div. 1985; graduate work in Mitaka, Japan, 1984; Florida Junior College, 1986.
Ordination: June 30, 1985 by Southeast Minnesota Synod.
Calls: Associate Minister, Ebenezer African Methodist Episcopal Zion Church, Seattle, Wash., 1977-78; Fellowship Lutheran, Duval, Fla., 1985-87; Good Shepherd, Cuyahoga, Ohio, 1987-89; 106th Trans. Bn., Azbill Barracks, Russelheim, Germany, 1982-84. Assistant to North Carolina Synod Bishop, 1989-91. Transferred to Central States Synod, 1992.
Other: Federal Chaplaincy Advisory Board, 1988-; Presided, Constituting Convention Women of the Evangelical Lutheran Church in America, 1987; President and Vice President Protestant Women of the Chapel, Mainz, Germany, 1972-74, 1982-84; Hospital Supply Chaplain for Florida State Mental Hospital; Television Talk Show Hostess; Newswriter for *Jacksonville Times Union;* Outstanding Civilian Worker, Mainz, Germany; First black female ordained by the American Lutheran Church. Northeast Ohio Synod Ministry Committee; Aleyeska Toastmistress International.

CORBELL, THOMAS WRIGHT

Date/Place of Birth: February 3, 1944; Richmond, Va.
Parents: Robert Thurston Corbell, Jr. and Evelyn (Harkness) Corbell.
Spouse/Marriage Date: L. Anne (Tysinger) Corbell; August 3, 1968 in Salisbury, N.C.
Children: Kristen Anne, Jennifer Wright. *Education*: Pfeiffer College, B.A. 1969; Lutheran Theological Southern Seminary, M.Div., 1969.
Ordination: June 3, 1973 by North Carolina Synod.
Calls: Reformation, Lancaster, S.C., 1973-79; St. Stephen, Lexington, S.C., 1979-90; St. John, Statesville, 1990-.
Other: Chair, North Carolina Synod AIDS Task Force; Officer in Ministerial Associations.

COSTNER, JACOB

Date/Place of Birth: August 27, 1788.
Spouse/Marriage Date: Mary Ann (Rudisill) Costner; February 10, 1810.
Children: Ten children, five of whom survived him.
Ordination: Was authorized at third session (1822) of Tennessee Synod, his ordination as deacon, by the Reverends Paul and David Henkel, or one of them. No record of his having been ordained as pastor.
Calls: No record of churches served.
Date of Death: March 19, 1862 as appended to the Minutes of the Tennessee Synod for 1862.

COULTER, MARK A.

Date/Place of Birth: August 31, 1958; Roanoke Rapids, N.C.
Parents: Rufus Guy Coulter and Minnie Marjorie (Harris) Coulter.
Spouse/Marriage Date: Kathy Ellen (Weishuhn) Coulter; September 24, 1983 in Arden, N.C.
Children: Paige Lynette, Robin Amanda, Janna Elizabeth.
Education: University of North Carolina at Chapel Hill, B.A. Psychology, 1980; Lutheran Theological Southern Seminary, M.Div. 1984.
Ordination: May 25, 1984 by North Carolina Synod.
Calls: Co-pastor, Emmanuel, Lincolnton, 1984-1988; St. James, Lexington, S.C., 1988-.

COUNTS, ERNEST KARL

Date/Place of Birth: January 28, 1897; Little Mountain, Newberry County, S.C.
Parents: Joseph Andrew Counts and Mary Ada (Aull) Counts.
Spouse/Marriage Date: Nellie L. (Derrick) Counts; May 23, 1922 in Columbia, S.C.
Children: Mary Elizabeth Koon, Etta Ruth, Inez Ernesteen Richardson.
Education: Newberry College, A.B. 1919; Lutheran Theological Southern Seminary, 1922.
Ordination: 1922 by North Carolina Synod.
Calls: St. Martin, Stanly County; St. Martin, Concord, 1922-25. Transferred to Mississippi Synod, 1926. Board of American Missions, Zion, Lingle, Miss., 1926-27; Trinity, Jackson, Miss., 1927-34. In South Carolina Synod: Bethlehem Parish, Pomaria, and St. Matthew, Pomaria, S.C., 1934-43; St. John-Mt. Calvary, Johnston, 1944-48; Silverstreet, Silverstreet, 1948-54; Mt. Pleasant, Saluda, 1954-63; Assistant Pastor, Ebenezer, Columbia, 1964; Supply Pastor for various congregations including Swansea, Swansea & Sandy Run, Swansea, 1965-72.
Other: Assistant Dean, Lutheran Leadership Training School for Central Dutch Fork and Newberry Conference; Chair, Stewardship Committee of South Carolina Synod; Committee, Pastoral Arrangements; Chair, Synodical Committee on Deaconess Work. Taught Bible at Silverstreet High School for five years. Chaplain, American Legion, Saluda, S.C. Active in Boy Scouts. Statistical Secretary, Mississippi Synod, 1928- 32; Secretary, Newberry Conference, 1940-53, 1951-53; Vice President, Newberry Conference, 1943-44, 1953, 1954; Acting President, 1954. Retired at West Columbia, S.C.
Date of Death/Burial Location: May 17, 1983; Pomaria Church Cemetery, Pomaria, S.C.

COUNTS, ROBERT PAUL

Date/Place of Birth: April 26, 1928; Lingle, Miss.
Parents: The Reverend Fulton B. Counts and Mattie E. (Roberts) Counts. The Reverend Henry P. Counts was his grandfather, and the Reverend Paul M. Counts, an uncle.
Spouse/Marriage Date: Shirley Marie (Ziemer) Counts; January 3, 1954 in Atlanta, Ga.
Children: Rebecca Ann, Karlena Naomi, Lisa Louise, Sheila Rae.
Education: Newberry College, B.S. 1950; Lutheran Theological Southern Seminary, B.D. 1953.
Ordination: 1953 by Georgia-Alabama Synod.
Calls: Holy Trinity, Marietta, Ga., 1953-56; Christ, Cullman, Ala., 1956-60. In North Carolina: St. Enoch, Kannapolis, 1960-64. In Tennessee: Our Savior, Memphis, Tenn., 1964-70. Prince of Peace, Huntsville, Ala., 1970-.

Other: Social Missions Committee, Georgia-Alabama Synod, 1957-60; District Secretary, North Carolina Synod, 1962-64. Removed from roll November 24, 1992 in Hazel Green, Ala.

COX, CLARENCE BROWN, SR.

Date/Place of Birth: April 18, 1873; Knox County, Tenn.
Parents: The Reverend George Henry Cox and Nancy (McPherson) Cox. A grandson is the Reverend J. Daniel Brown.
First Spouse/Marriage Date: Cordelia E. (Spangler) Cox; April 12, 1899 in Gettysburg, Pa.
Children of First Marriage: Cathrine, Cordelia.
Second Spouse/Marriage Date: Blanche Bard (Mearig) Cox; May 21, 1912 in Norfolk, Va.
Children of Second Marriage: Elizabeth Martha, Clarence Brown, Jr., Mary, Alfred Bard.

Education: North Carolina College, A.B. & A.M. 1895; Gettysburg Seminary, 1898; Wittenberg University, D.D. 1924.
Ordination: 1898 by North Carolina Synod.
Calls: Mission (later discontinued), 1899-1901; in Tennessee, 1901-03. In North Carolina: Macedonia, Burlington; Peace, Guilford County, 1903-12. In Virginia: 1912-36.
Other: Retired 1937 at Highland Springs, Va. President, Marion Junior College, 1916-28. President, Virginia Synod, 1922-26. Delegate to 1918 United Lutheran Church in America merger convention.
Date of Death/Burial Location: April 4, 1942; Burlington, N.C.

COX, GEORGE HENRY

Date/Place of Birth: August 9, 1838; Boston, Mass., youngest of fourteen children, and only one of seven sons to reach maturity.
Parents: Lemuel Cox and Mary (Tras) Cox. Father, perhaps a Quaker, died three weeks before son's birth. Mother was a Methodist. Baptized at age 22 in Presbyterian Church in Elizabethton, Tenn., having moved to Tennessee at sixteen with family of one of his sisters.
First Spouse/Marriage Date: Nannie E. (McPherson) Cox of, but formerly of Chatham County, N.C.; January 1866; died October 5, 1889.

Children of First Marriage: Effie Best (mother of the Reverend C. Ross Ritchie, Sr.), the Reverend C. Brown.
Second Spouse/Marriage Date: Mrs. Ellen (Kesler Barringer) Cox; April 1896 in Rowan County, N.C.
Children of Second Marriage: No record.
Education: In Boston, Mass., schools. Taught school in Tennessee, and studied theology under the Reverend Abel J. Brown. Received D.D. Degree.
License/Ordination: He, a Presbyterian, and first wife, a Methodist, made a comparative study of doctrines of churches in their Tennessee community, and under guidance of the Reverend A. J. Brown read in *The Book of Concord*. They were confirmed into Lutheran faith by Dr. Brown in October 1870 in Immanuel Church, Sullivan County, Tenn. Licensed

1871 and ordained 1872 by Holston Synod.

Calls: Of Holston Synod in Tennessee, to 1887; also owned and operated a female seminary at Morristown, Tenn., with as many as 175 students. In December 1887 rode horseback to North Carolina. In North Carolina, 1888-1922: Mt. Olive-St. Stephen, Cabarrus County; New Bethel, Stanly County; organized and supplied St. Andrew, Concord. In Rowan County: Organ-Ebenezer; organized Immanuel, and Wittenberg, Granite Quarry; supplied First, Albemarle; St. Enoch, Rowan County; Trinity, Cabarrus County; Christ, East Spencer; Cold Water-St. John, Cabarrus County; and supplied Lebanon, Rowan County.

Other: Secretary, Treasurer, President of the Holston Synod. President, North Carolina Synod, 1890-93, 1904-08. Volunteer in Confederate States Army 1861 to war's end; wounded several times; captured three times and each time escaped. Author, with Dr. G. D. Bernheim, of *History of the Evangelical Lutheran Synod and Ministerium of North Carolina,* (1902). Besides his son and grandson, two great-grandsons entered the Lutheran ministry, the Reverends C. Ross Ritchie, Jr., and J. Daniel Brown. Retired 1922 at Salisbury.

Date of Death/Burial Location: December 7, 1928; Mt. Pleasant, N.C.

COZART, JOHNNY CLAYTON

Date/Place of Birth: October 29, 1947; Rowan County, N.C.
Parents: Clay Wilburn Cozart and Rebecca (Brown) Cozart.
Spouse/Marriage Date: Mary Belinda (Bernhardt) Cozart; June 21, 1970 in Salisbury, N.C.
Children: Ashley Cameron, Bradley Parks, Amanda Gayle.
Education: Davidson County Community College, A.A. 1968; Lenoir-Rhyne, A.B. 1970; Lutheran Theological Southern Seminary, M.Div. 1974.
Ordination: May 31, 1974 by North Carolina Synod.
Calls: St. Luke, Mt. Ulla, 1974-80; Cross of Christ, Concord, 1980-85; St. Mark's, Mooresville, 1985-. Vice Pastor at Lebanon, Cleveland.

CRAUN, WILLIAM ARTHUR

Date/Place of Birth: November 28, 1880; Rockingham County, Va.
Parents: Charles Edward Granville Craun and Sarah Etta (Early) Craun.
Spouse/Marriage Date: Rosa B. (Lowman) Craun; June 24, 1914 in Brunswick, Ga.
Children: Alvin Edward, Dwight Marvin.
Education: Roanoke College, A.B. 1911; Lutheran Theological Southern Seminary, 1914; University of South Carolina, A.M. 1914; Chicago Seminary, B.D. 1922.
Ordination: 1914 by Virginia Synod.
Calls: In Virginia, 1914-21; in Indiana, 1922-24. In North Carolina: Calvary, Morganton; Mt. Hebron, Hildebran, 1924-27. Transferred to South Carolina Synod, 1927.
Date of Death/Burial Location: December 21, 1931; Mt. Sidney, Va.

CRAWFORD, CLAUDE EVERETTE, JR.

Date/Place of Birth: January 27, 1936; Charleston, S.C.

Parents: Claude Everette Crawford, Sr. and Alma Mildred (Halsall) Crawford.

Spouse/Marriage Date: Mary Aletha (Wacker) Crawford; February 28, 1959 in Charleston, S.C.

Children: Cynthia Hulda Earl, Ashley Brailsford Guilbert, Timothy Wacker.

Education: Newberry College, B.A. 1958; Lutheran Theological Southern Seminary, M.Div. 1961.

Ordination: September 10, 1961 by South Carolina Synod.

Calls: St. Paul, Louisville, Ky., 1961-62; St. Mark/St. Andrew, Blythewood, S.C., 1963-65; Corinth/St. Mark, Prosperity, S.C., 1965-68; Holy Spirit, Baltimore, Md., 1968-72; Pilgrim, Lexington, 1973-77; Lebanon and New Jerusalem, Lexington, 1978-87; Lebanon only, Lexington, 1987-88; Vice Pastor at various congregations.

Other: Retired in Charleston, S.C., in 1991.

CRIGLER, JOHN FIELDING, SR.

Date/Place of Birth: October 13, 1869; Madison County, Va.

Parents: Jason Cornelius Crigler and Mary Elizabeth (Aylor) Crigler.

Spouse/Marriage Date: Edith Norris (Wolf) Crigler, born in Guntur, India, daughter of the Reverend Luther BeNaiah Wolf; October 7, 1903 in Lutherville, Md.; died September 14, 1972.

Children: Elizabeth Aylor, Catherine Wolf Gebhart, Eleanor Fielding Aldinger, John Fielding, Jr., Norris Wolf, Benner Bittinger.

Education: Roanoke College, A.B. 1892, D.D. 1924; Gettysburg Seminary, B.D. 1896.

License/Ordination: Licensed 1895 and ordained October 11, 1896 by Maryland Synod.

Calls: St. Paul, Lutherville, Md., 1896-1915. Instructor in Bible in Maryland College, Lutherville, Md., 1900-15. Organized Holy Comforter, Baltimore, Md. in 1911 and served as supply until 1913; St. Mark's, Charlotte, 1915-48.

Other: Secretary, Maryland Synod, 1913-15. Member, Board of Deaconess Work, and Committee on Evangelism, United Lutheran Church in America. Board, Lenoir-Rhyne; Board, Lutheran Theological Southern Seminary. Author of a religious drama published, *Saul of Tarsus;* contributor of articles and poems to church periodicals. Retired 1948 at Charlotte, N.C.

Date of Death/Burial Location: August 26, 1962; Hebron Church, Madison County, Va.

CRIM, JACOB

License/Ordination: Licensed 1837 by South Carolina Synod. Transferred to North Carolina Synod 1839 and ordained in 1841.

Calls: In South Carolina, 1837-39. In North Carolina: Nazareth-Shiloh, Forsyth County, 1839-40; Beck's-Pilgrim-St. Luke, Davidson County, 1839-42; New Jerusalem (1843-60)-St. Matthew (1845-61), Davie County; organized Bethel (1851-58, 1861-62)-Salem (1860-62), Rowan County.

Other: Secretary, 1850, President, 1864, North Carolina Synod. Member, first Board of North Carolina College, 1859.

Burial Location: Buried in Texas.

CROMER, JAMES ALBERT

Date/Place of Birth: August 18, 1847; Lexington County, S.C.
Parents: Daniel Cromer and Julia Ann (Monts) Cromer.
Spouse/Marriage Date: Mary Jane (Roof) Cromer; 1871 in Lexington County, S.C.
Children: Silas Dean, the Reverend Joseph Lee (father of the Reverend Voigt R. Cromer), Lottie Cornelia, Cyprian I., Hattie Irene, Charles Webster, Robert Yoder, Julian Daniel.
Education: North Carolina College, 1876; studied theology under the Reverend Daniel Efird.
License/Ordination: Licensed 1876 and ordained 1878 by Tennessee Synod.
Calls and Other: Of the Tennessee Synod, which after merger of North Carolina and Tennessee Synods became South Carolina Synod churches, in home area of Lexington County, S.C. 1876-1921 as follows: Emmanuel, Zion, St. Peter, organized Pilgrim (1899), organized Grace (1893), and organized Mt. Hermon (1910); also St. Andrew, Richland County; served some of them for 20 to 25 years. At age 16 enlisted and served six months in Confederate States Army near close of War Between the States. At 26 with wife and two children, mortgaged farm and attended North Carolina College, to prepare for ministry. Along with pastoral ministry, pioneered in truck farming near Columbia, S.C., and thus primarily supported family. One church requiring forty miles of travel per month paid him $22.00 per year. Member, committee for establishing and locating Summerland College, Batesburg, S.C.
Date of Death/Burial Location: January 1, 1922; Zion Church, Lexington County, S.C.

CROMER, JOSEPH LEE

Date/Place of Birth: September 7, 1874; Lexington County, S.C.
Parents: The Reverend James Albert Cromer and Mary Jane (Roof) Cromer.
Spouse/Marriage Date: Lillie Mae (Rhodes) Cromer; November 1, 1899 in Gaston County, N.C.
Children: Prima, Alene, the Reverend Voigt Rhodes, John Albert.
Education: Lenoir-Rhyne, A.B., A.M. 1895; studied theology during college course.
Ordination: 1895 by Tennessee Synod.
Calls: In North Carolina, 1895-1913: Beth Eden-St. James, Newton; St. Timothy, Catawba County; supplied, with others, Shiloh, Alexander County; Ebenezer, Catawba County; St. Martin, Maiden, 1900-01, 1905-13; Philadelphia, Granite Falls; Holy Trinity, Gastonia; Rhodhiss, Caldwell County; Mt. Hebron, Hildebran; Salem, Lincoln County. Tennessee Synod churches in South Carolina, at Gilbert and Chapin, 1913-20. After North Carolina-Tennessee Synods merger, transferred to South Carolina Synod, 1922.
Other: Retired 1931 because of ill health. Delegate to merger convention, United Lutheran Church in America, 1918. Board, Lenoir-Rhyne College, and college Business Manager, 1920-22. Principal, Grady's Academy while pastor at St. James, Newton. Secretary of the North Carolina Conference of the Tennessee Synod, 1906. Editor and Business Manager, *South Carolina Lutheran,* several years. Planned and built five

churches and two parsonages. Mt. Tabor, Prosperity, S.C., was dedicated free of debt immediately upon completion. It was built by a rural congregation. Pastor Cromer used the unique method of asking housewives to give their Sunday eggs, the proceeds being put into the building fund. The farmers were given cotton seed to plant, and receipts went into the building fund. Members gave timber for the building. Added to these gifts were liberal contributions in money by the members.

Date of Death/Burial Location: June 21, 1939; Lincolnton, N.C.

CROMER, VOIGT RHODES

Date/Place of Birth: July 31, 1906; Rhodhiss, Caldwell County, N.C.

Parents: The Reverend Joseph Lee Cromer and Lillie Mae (Rhodes) Cromer. Grandfather was the Reverend James Albert Cromer.

Spouse/Marriage Date: Sara Elizabeth (Dreher) Cromer; August 17, 1932 in Lexington, S.C.; died January 2, 1986.

Children: Elizabeth Rhodes (married the Reverend R. W. Carswell), Rebecca Ruth (married the Reverend Richard Campbell).

Education: Lenoir-Rhyne, A.B. 1925, D.D. 1947; Lutheran Theological Southern Seminary, B.D. 1928; University of South Carolina, M.A. 1927; Hartford Seminary, S.T.M. 1929; Union Seminary, 1939; Gettysburg College, Honorary L.L.D. 1956.

Ordination: May 1928 by South Carolina Synod.

Calls: St. Luke, Summerville, S.C., 1929-30. In North Carolina: Emmanuel-St. Luke, Lincolnton, 1930-36; St. James, Concord, 1936-41; Holy Trinity, Hickory, 1941-47. President, North Carolina Synod, succeeding Dr. Jacob L. Morgan, 1947-49. President, Lenoir-Rhyne, 1949-67. Vice Pastor to various congregations.

Other: President, Western Conference of North Carolina Synod, 1946. Secretary, Southern Conference of the North Carolina Synod. President, Alumni Association of Lutheran Theological Southern Seminary, 1937- 1940. Attended as delegate from the North Carolina Synod most conventions of the United Lutheran Church in America and the Lutheran Church in America from 1936-66. President Emeritus and Administrative Consultant, Lenoir-Rhyne, 1968; Board, Lenoir-Rhyne, 1936-49. United Lutheran Church in America Commissioner to National Lutheran Council, 1948-54. Member, United Lutheran Church in America Boards–Social Missions, 1948-60 and American Missions, 1960-62; Joint Communion on Lutheran Unity, 1958-62. Member, Executive Council, Lutheran Church in America, 1963-66. President, Lutheran Educational Conference in North America, 1955-56. President, Conference of Church-Related Colleges in the South, 1954-55. Member, United Lutheran Church in America Commission on The Doctrine of the Ministry. Active in community affairs in the Rotary Club and in other service organizations. Author of *Christian Action in Human Relations;* contributor of sermon to *This Holy Venture* (Muhlenberg Press). Preacher, *CBS Church of the Air, The United Lutheran Hour,* and at college commencements at Lenoir-Rhyne, Clemson, Gettysburg, and Newberry. Retired 1967 to Hickory, N.C.

Date of Death/Burial Location: May 31, 1980; Hollybrook Cemetery, Lincolnton, N.C.

CRONK, BENJAMIN WESLEY

Birth/Place of Birth: August 6, 1857; Floyd County, Va.
Parents: Eli H. Cronk and Mary E. (Griggs) Cronk. A brother was the Reverend E. C. Cronk of the Southwest Virginia Synod.
Spouse/Marriage Date: Alice Eliza (Snidow) Cronk; June 15, 1887 in Pembroke, Va.
Child: Earle Tabor Walker.
Education: Roanoke College, B.A. and M.A. 1883; Lutheran Theological Southern Seminary, 1883.
License/Ordination: Licensed 1884 and ordained 1885 by Southwest Virginia Synod.
Calls: In North Carolina: Coble's-Low's-Richland, Guilford County, 1887-91; Salem-St. Luke, Rowan County, 1891-93; organized Lebanon, Rowan County, 1893-94. Transferred to South Carolina Synod 1894. Parishes in South Carolina, Virginia and Tennessee.
Other: Superintendent, Children's Home of the South, Salem, Va. for several years. Retired 1932 at Pembroke, Va.
Date of Death/Burial Location: October 13, 1934; Pembroke, Va.

CROTTY, EDWARD JOHN

Date/Place of Birth: September 14, 1942; Boston, Mass.
Parents: William J. Crotty and Helen F. Crotty.
Spouse/Marriage Date: Anne (Lafferty) Crotty; January 23, 1973.
Children: Susan K., Marian G., Elizabeth M.
Education: Boston University, B.S. Education 1965; Trinity Seminary, M.Div. 1987; University of Georgia, M.Ed. 1966; University of North Carolina Law School, J. D. 1972.
Ordination: June 6, 1987 by Southwest Pennsylvania Synod.
Calls: Lynnwood, Belle Vernon, Pa., 1987-89; Forks-Zion, Leechburg, Pa., 1989-96; St. Thomas, Charlotte, 1996-.

CROUSE, ANDREW LEONHARDT

Date/Place of Birth: June 8, 1849; Randolph County, N.C.
Parents: The Reverend Thomas Crouse and Barbara (Fox) Crouse.
First Spouse/Marriage Date: Tirza Carolina (Darr) Crouse; September 8, 1870.
Child of First Marriage: Thomas Henry.
Second Spouse/Marriage Date: Mary Lavinia (Bilbo) Crouse; December 24, 1873 in Greensboro, N.C.
Children of Second Marriage: Luther Augustus, Carl Froelich, Luda Amelia.
Education: Perhaps at Concordia College; studied theology under father and the Reverend A. J. Fox.
Ordination: 1871 by Tennessee Synod.
Calls: In South Carolina, and mission work in Alabama, 1872-82. In Virginia and West Virginia, 1882-89. In North Carolina: Friendship, 1890-91, 1897-1905, and Shiloh, 1894-96, Alexander County; Mt. Olive-St. Stephen, Hickory, 1890-1903; organized St. Andrew, Hickory, 1893-94. Joined The Lutheran Church- Missouri Synod, 1903.
Other: One of founders, and professor (German, English), Lenoir-Rhyne. After joining The Lutheran Church- Missouri Synod taught theology, Concordia College, at Conover.

Secretary, Tennessee Synod, several terms; President, two terms. Secretary, United Synod South, several terms. Author of *A Christian Catechism for Children, The Modern Evangelistic System, Pulpit and Altar Fellowship, Historical Sketches of Alexander County.* German editor, *Our Church Paper,* New Market, Va.
Date of Death/Burial Location: October 13, 1915; St. Stephen Church (The Lutheran Church-Missouri Synod) in Hickory, N.C.

CROUSE, THOMAS
Date/Place of Birth: June 6, 1822; Davidson County, N.C.
Parents: Andrew and ? (Daniels) Crouse.
First Spouse/Marriage Date: Barbara (Fox) Crouse; Randolph County, N.C.; died after eight years.
Children of First Marriage: The Reverend Andrew Leonhardt, Sarah, Luther, Joseph Augustus.
Second Spouse/Marriage Date: M. Caroline (Fox) Crouse, sister of the Reverend A. J. Fox, M.D.
Child of Second Marriage: Alfred.
Education: Professor Dusenberry's School, Lexington; was tutored in theology.
License/Ordination: Licensed 1845 and ordained 1850 by Tennessee Synod.
Calls: Cobles, Guilford County; Melanchthon, Randolph County, 1856; Mt. Pleasant, Alamance County, 1848-57, 1863-66; Beck's-New Jerusalem-Pilgrim, Davidson County, 1866-75.
Other: Treasurer, Tennessee Synod, 1862. Attended North Carolina Synod Convention in 1868, and was invited to a seat as an advisory member of Synod.
Date of Death/Burial Location: April 11, 1876; Beck's Church, Davidson County, N.C.

CROWTHER, JOSEPH GREGORY
Date/Place of Birth: September 4, 1963; Rowan County, N.C.
Parents: Milton Crowther and Louise (Brown) Crowther.
Spouse/Marriage Date: Carrie (Bradshaw) Crowther; October 26, 1985 in Salisbury, N.C.
Children: Joseph Grant, Rachael Lauren.
Education: Catawba College, B.A. Psychology 1985; Gettysburg Seminary, M.Div. 1989; graduate work at Lutheran Theological Southern Seminary.
Ordination: August 6, 1989 by North Carolina Synod.
Calls: St. Luke, Mt. Ulla, 1989-91; St. Paul, Roanoke, Va., 1991-.

CRUSE, GUY CALVIN

Date/Place of Birth: May 9, 1927; Cabarrus County, N.C.

Parents: Oscar Orlin Cruse and Ila Maggie (Kluttz) Cruse.

Spouse/Marriage Date: Cary (Dowd) Cruse of Carthage; June 17, 1953 in Concord, N.C.

Children: The Reverend Guy Reginald, Kim RenÈ (died two days after birth), Karen Lisa Peterson, Joy Theresa Lee, Joel Keith.

Education: Lenoir-Rhyne, A.B. 1948; Lutheran Theological Southern Seminary, B.D. 1951; graduate work, Lutheran Theological Southern Seminary, 1958-63.

Ordination: July 8, 1951 by North Carolina Synod.

Calls: Mt. Olive-St. Stephen, Gold Hill, 1951-54; Cedar Grove, Leesville, S.C., 1954-59; Bethel, White Rock, S.C., 1959-92.

Other: Retired June 30, 1992 in White Rock, S.C.

CRUSE, GUY REGINALD

Date/Place of Birth: August 14, 1955; Richland County, S.C.

Parents: The Reverend Guy Calvin Cruse and Cary (Dowd) Cruse.

Spouse/Marriage Date: Janice Amanda (West) Cruse; May 26, 1979 in West Columbia, S.C.

Children: Joshua Aaron, Rebekah Caroline.

Education: Newberry College, B.A. 1977; Lutheran Theological Southern Seminary, M.Div. 1981.

Ordination: May 24, 1981 by South Carolina Synod.

Calls: Grace, Liberty, 1981-84; St. Martin, Maiden, 1984-88; Redeemer, Kannapolis, Rowan County, 1989- 91. St. Nicholas/Trinity, Fairfax, S.C., 1991-.

CUMBEE, LURIA ERASTUS, JR.

Date/Place of Birth: September 13, 1931; Aiken County, S.C.

Parents: Luria Erastus Cumbee, Sr. and Hazel V. (Bryant) Cumbee.

Spouse/Marriage Date: Sylvia Faye (Pitts) Cumbee; June 11, 1955 in Newberry, S.C.

Children: Michael Paul, Stephen Craig, Allison Faye.

Education: Newberry College, B.S. 1955; Lutheran Theological Southern Seminary, B.D. 1957, also graduate study.

Ordination: June 1957 by South Carolina Synod.

Calls: Pilgrim, Lexington, 1957-58; New Jerusalem, Hickory, 1958-62; Christus Victor, Fayetteville, 1962-81; Messiah, Hanahan, S.C., 1981-. Vice Pastor at several congregations.

Other: U.S. Army Reserve Chaplain, First Lieutenant; instituted religious services, for Sunday drills, for three U.S. Army Reserve and National Guard units in Hickory area, 1955-71. Nominations Committee, North Carolina Synod, 1974. Military Personnel Committee, North Carolina Synod, 1968-72; Chaplain, Franke Home in Charleston, S.C., 1981-. One of two pastors involved in the founding of Lutheran Social Services of Greater Charleston, 1984-. Chair, Cumberland County Parks and Recreation Commission.

CUTHBERTSON, RUFUS BRAXTON, JR.

Date/Place of Birth: July 3, 1920; Charlotte, N.C.

Parents: Rufus Braxton Cuthbertson, Sr. and Euphemia Clementine (Robinson) Cuthbertson.

Spouse/Marriage Date: Dorothy Jean (Wandel) Cuthbertson; June 6, 1945 in Hagerstown, Md.

Children: Jean Elizabeth, Dorothy Euphemia, Charles Paul, Philip Martin.

Education: Brevard College; Lenoir-Rhyne, A.B. 1941; Lutheran Theological Southern Seminary, B.D. 1944, S.T.M. 1965.

Ordination: July 16, 1944 by North Carolina Synod.

Calls: St. Paul, Hamlet, 1944-48; Mission Developer/Pastor, St. Andrew, New Bern, 1948-51; Christ's, Stanley, 1951-57; St. Luke, Lincoln County, 1951-52; Good Shepherd, College Park, Ga., 1957-67; Associate Secretary, Board of Social Ministry, New York City, N.Y., 1967-73; Mission Developer/Pastor, Church of the Incarnation, Silver Springs Shores, Fla., 1975-82.

Other: Retired 1982 to Dahlonega, Ga.

DANIEL, VANCE MILLER

Date/Place of Birth: August 5, 1918; Salisbury, N.C.

Parents: B. K. Daniel and Lorena (Miller) Daniel.

Spouse/Marriage Date: Margaret Burke (Poole) Daniel; June 3, 1944 in Salisbury, N.C.

Children: Rebecca Jane, David Walter.

Education: Lenoir-Rhyne, A.B. 1940; Lutheran Theological Southern Seminary, B.D. 1943.

Ordination: 1943 by North Carolina Synod.

Calls: Organized Messiah, Salisbury, 1942-44; Trinity, Sanford, 1944-51; organized Resurrection, Kings Mountain, 1951-53; St. Paul, Decatur, Ga., 1953-58; Grace, Harlingen, Texas, 1958-64; St. Martin, Houston, Texas, 1964-72; Hutto, Hutto, Texas, 1972-84; Gethsemane, Austin, Texas, 1984-86.

Other: Retired 1986 in Austin, Texas.

DARR, WILLIAM LEO

Date/Place of Birth: January 7, 1864; Davidson County, N.C.

Parents: Henry Darr and Salome (Goodman) Darr.

First Spouse: Lillie (Sligh) Darr; died 1898.

Child of First Marriage: Rebecca.

Second Spouse: Aquila (Ergle) Darr of South Carolina.

Third Spouse: Mae (Dellinger) Darr of Virginia.

Children of Third Marriage: Ursula, Krauth, Revere.

Education: Concordia College, 1889.

Ordination: 1889 by Tennessee Synod.

Calls: Tennessee Synod in South Carolina: Bethlehem, Irmo, 1888-96; St. Thomas, Chapin, 1888-96, Mt. Horeb-St. Jacob, Chapin, 1891-95. In North Carolina., of those known, all were in Iredell County; St. Martin; organized Mt. Hermon, 1896-1906; Sharon, 1898-1907; St. John, Statesville, 1898-1905. Transferred to Virginia Synod, 1922.

Date of Death/Burial Location: September 4, 1938; St. Martin Cemetery, Iredell County, N.C.

DASHER, BERGMAN SHADRACK

Date/Place of Birth: September 28, 1881; Effingham County, Ga.
Parents: Shadrack E. Dasher and Salina E. (Nease) Dasher.
Spouse/Marriage Date: Beulah (Vansant) Dasher; October 26, 1913 in Ward, S.C.
Education: Newberry College, A.B. 1908; Lutheran Theological Southern Seminary, 1911.
Ordination: September 1, 1911 by Virginia Synod.
Calls: In Virginia, Augusta County, 1911-13; in North Carolina, 1913-24: Frieden's-Sharon, Gibsonville; Calvary-St. Andrew, Concord; St. Enoch, Rowan County; Trinity, Cabarrus County.
Transferred to Georgia Synod and adjacent states, 1924. Later served parishes in Tennessee, Virginia, and South Carolina.
Other: Retired 1949 in Guyton, Ga.
Date of Death/Burial Location: 1968; Marlow, Ga.

DASHER, EVERETT AUSTIN

Date/Place of Birth: December 7, 1918; Marlow, Ga.
Parents: Olin George Dasher and Caroline Salome (Zittrauer) Dasher. Two brothers are the Reverends L. O. and O. G. Dasher.
Spouse/Marriage Date: Helen Mae (Stoudemayer) Dasher; May 20, 1946 in West Columbia, S.C.
Children: Larry Austin, Eileen Susan Chapman, Eva Ruth White.
Education: Newberry College, A.B. 1940; Lutheran Theological Southern Seminary, B.D. 1948.
Ordination: 1948 by Georgia-Alabama Synod.
Calls: Trinity-St. Nicholas, Fairfax-Hampton, S.C., 1948-50. In North Carolina: St. Peter, Rowan County, 1950-53; Bethlehem, Catawba County, 1954-58; St. Matthew, Wilmington, 1959-61. Mt. Horeb, Chapin, S.C., 1961-73; St. Timothy, Camden, S.C., 1974-81. Served as interim pastor at Good Hope, Ward, S.C., 1982-93.
Other: Retired December 31, 1981.

DASHER, LEWIS OTTO

Date/Place of Birth: December 30, 1902; Marlow, Ga.
Parents: Olin George Dasher and Caroline Salome (Zittrauer) Dasher. Older brother of the Reverends Olin G. and Everett A. Dasher.
Spouse/Marriage Date: Ruth Irene (Coon) Dasher; May 12, 1931 in Lincoln County, N.C.; died July 27, 1986.
Child: The Reverend Robert Lewis.
Education: Lenoir-Rhyne, one year, Muhlenberg College, A.B. 1927; Lutheran Theological Southern Seminary, B.D. 1930.
Ordination: June 3, 1930 by Georgia-Alabama Synod.
Calls: Ebenezer Parish, Rincon, Ga., 1930-39; St. David's Parish, West Columbia, S.C., 1939-47. In North Carolina: Mt. Calvary, Claremont, 1947-56. Reformation, New Market, Va., 1957-69. Vice Pastor at various congregations.
Other: Member, Committee On Arrangements for Savannah, Ga., United Lutheran Church in America convention, 1934. Retired January 1, 1970 to Arden, N.C.
Date of Death/Burial Location: August 17, 1992; Daniel's, Lincolnton, N.C.

DASHER, ROBERT LEWIS

Date/Place of Birth: July 27, 1934; Rincon, Ga.

Parents: The Reverend Lewis Otto Dasher and Ruth Irene (Coon) Dasher.

Spouse/Marriage Date: Ann Secrist (Krider) Dasher; July 2, 1958 in Concord, N.C.

Children: Ann Roberta, Charles Lewis.

Education: Lenoir-Rhyne, A.B. 1956; Lutheran Theological Southern Seminary, B.D. 1959; University of South Carolina, M.Ed.

Ordination: June 14, 1959 by Virginia Synod.

Calls: Lutheran Chapel, China Grove, 1959-63; Our Redeemer, Greenville and pastor to Lutheran students at East Carolina University, 1963-68; Campus Pastor, University of South Carolina, Columbia, S.C., 1969-84; Assistant to the Bishop, South Carolina Synod (Lutheran Church in America and Evangelical Lutheran Church in America) 1985-96. Vice pastor to various congregations.

Other: Executive Board, South Carolina Synod; Chaplain, South Carolina Synod Lutheran Church in America Convention; Board, North Carolina Lutheran Homes; Delegate, churchwide conventions/assemblies; Transition Team, South Carolina Synod; Evangelical Lutheran Church in America Church Council; Dean, Central District, North Carolina Synod, 1962-63, Secretary, 1965-68; Pastors' Support Committee, North Carolina Synod, 1967-69. President, Lenoir-Rhyne Alumni Association, 1995-96; Man of the Year Award, South Carolina Synod Lutheran Men, 1994; retired September 1996 in Columbia, S.C.

DAUBENSPECK, WAYNE MARTELL

Date/Place of Birth: November 25, 1904; Selinsgrove, Pa.

Parents: The Reverend Lloyd Mashine Daubenspeck and Della A. (Burns) Daubenspeck. An uncle was also a minister.

First Spouse/Marriage Date: Ethel (Mason) Daubenspeck; July 15, 1931 in Omaha, Neb.; died December 17, 1973.

Children of First Marriage: Richard Edward, Ruth Elizabeth, Henry Mason.

Second Spouse/Marriage Date: Ollie B. (Allman) Daubenspeck; January 18, 1976 in Kannapolis, N.C.; died April 4, 1978.

Third Spouse/Marriage Date: Christine Helen (Dunn) Daubenspeck; February 17, 1980 in Kannapolis, N.C. *Education*: Susquehanna University, A.B. 1927, B.D. 1930; clinical training, Greystone Mental Hospital, N.J., 1938; Chaplain School, Harvard University, 1943.

Ordination: May 1930 by Central Pennsylvania Synod.

Calls: St. Mark, Oshkosh, Neb., 1930-35. In North Carolina: St. David, Kannapolis, 1964-69, Pastor Emeritus. Chaplaincy service in the U.S. Army, Nebraska Conservation Construction Corps, 1936-38. Service pastor, Lutheran Service Commission, in Japan and Korea, 1954-64. Interim Pastor for various congregations. Chaplain, Veterans of Foreign Wars, 1967-76, 1978.

Other: U.S. Penal System, Lewisburg, Pa., and Narcotics Prison at Ft. Leavenworth, Kan., 1938-40; U.S. Army with service in Alaska and Europe, 1940-54, retiring from Reserves in 1964 as Colonel. Received Army Bronze Star and several service medals. *Who's Who in the South and Southwest; Personalities of the South; Two Thousand Men of Achievement; Men of Achievement; Community Leaders and Noteworthy Americans; Notable Americans of the Bicentennial Era; Dictionary of International Biography, Book of Honor.* Retired December 31, 1969.

Date of Death/Burial Location: August 19, 1981; National Cemetery, Salisbury, N.C.

DAVIS, JACK LANE
Date/Place of Birth: September 4, 1934; China Grove, N.C.
Parents: Rosco Alexander Davis and Frances Beatrice (Melchor) Davis.
Spouse/Marriage Date: Jane McMillan (Bryant) Davis; June 4, 1957 in Marion, S.C.
Children: Julia Lane, Mark Melchor, Matthew McMillan, Lynn Marie.
Education: Lenoir-Rhyne, B.A. Religious Education 1956; Lutheran Theological Southern Seminary, B.D. 1959, S.T.M.; graduate work at University of St. Andrew, Scotland, 1967-8.
Ordination: June 1959 by North Carolina Synod.
Calls: Holy Trinity, Mt. Pleasant, 1959-63; Mission Developer, 1964; organized St. Michael, High Point, 1965-67.
Other: Publications and Publicity Committee, 1964-66. Member, Piedmont Personnel Association; Catawba County Chamber of Commerce; Hickory Choral Society; Hickory Community Theatre, Best Actor of Year Award. Resigned from the ministry, 1969.

DAVIS, JOHN BARTON
Date/Place of Birth: May 26, 1808; Winchester, Va.
First Spouse: Unknown.
Second Spouse/Marriage Date: Anna Caroline (Sieg) Davis; died 1896.
Children: Luther, Paul B., Mary, Richard, John, Jefferson.
Education: Gettysburg College, A.B. 1835, A.M. 1853; Gettysburg Seminary; North Carolina College, D.D. 1873.
License/Ordination: Licensed 1834 and ordained 1837 by Virginia Synod.
Calls: In 1840 assisted at the organizing of St. Peter, Wardensville, W.Va. In Virginia, 1834-75: Trinity, Stephens City, 1834-50; Mt. Tabor, Augusta County; St. Peter's, Churchville; Christ, Staunton; St. Paul, Strasburg, 1834- 44; and St. John, Gravel Spring Parish, Frederick County, near Winchester. Transferred 1875 to North Carolina Synod: President, North Carolina College, 1875-77. Served Holy Trinity, Mt. Pleasant, 1881-85; Mt. Olive, Cabarrus County, 1884-85. Assisted in organizing, but was not pastor, Grace, Rowan County, 1880.
Other: President, Virginia Synod, 1838-41, 1844-47, 1855-56. Professor (Natural Science), Roanoke College, 1865-75. Author of *A Botany of the Bible, A Chemistry of Life, The Cosmogony of Moses, Unity of the Human Race From a Christian Standpoint, Papers on the Mineral Kingdom, The Vegetable Kingdom of Nature, The History of Theological Seminaries,* and *The Intellectual Triumphs of Youth and Age Compared.*
Date of Death/Burial Location: January 3, 1896 (Synod Minutes say February 26, 1895); East Hill Cemetery, Salem, Va.

DAVIS, JOHN FRANK
Date/Place of Birth: March 2, 1903; Gaston County, N.C.
Parents: Frank O. Davis and Alice (Jenkins) Davis.
First Spouse: Mildred (Propst) Davis of Concord, N.C.; died January 23, 1932.
Second Spouse/Marriage Date: LeRhea (Counts) Davis; June 15, 1937 in Columbia, S.C.
Child of Second Marriage: Gwendolyn Woodmansee.

Education: Lenoir-Rhyne, A.B. 1925, D.D. 1955; Lutheran Theological Southern Seminary, B.D. 1929; University of South Carolina, M.A. 1929; graduate study, Union Seminary, Yale University.

Ordination: May 29, 1929 by North Carolina Synod.

Calls: In North Carolina, 1929-43: Pastor to Lutheran students, University of North Carolina at Chapel Hill; Bethany, Kannapolis, 1929-30; supply, Calvary, Concord, 1934-5; Lutheran Chapel, Gastonia, 1935-39; Ascension, Shelby, 1933-34, 1939-44. Assistant Pastor, Holy Trinity, New York City, N.Y., 1943-44; Resurrection, Augusta, Ga., 1944-49; St. Paul, Wilmington, N.C., 1949-68. Interim pastor at 65 congregations.

Other: Stewardship Committee, 1962-64; Historical Works Committee, 1973-75; Board, Newberry College, 1944-48; Board, Lenoir-Rhyne, 1964-68. Sermon in *This Holy Venture* (Muhlenberg Press). Preacher, Protestant Radio Hour. Contributor to Lutheran periodicals. Retired, March 1968.

Date of Death/Burial Location: May 9, 1986; Elmwood Cemetery, Columbia, S.C.

DAVIS, WALTER CLEVELAND, JR.

Date/Place of Birth: November 3, 1917; Knoxville, Tenn.

Parents: The Reverend Walter Cleveland Davis, Sr. and Fannie (Ghormley) Davis.

Spouse/Marriage Date: Ruthanna (Gotherman) Davis; February 17, 1940 in Carrollton, Ky.; deceased.

Children: Barbara Ann Falb, Helen Louise Yoder, Walter C., III.

Education: Wittenberg University, A.B. Economics 1939; Chicago Seminary, B.D. 1942; graduate work at Ball State University, Purdue University, Washington University, Chicago Seminary, and Lutheran Theological Southern Seminary.

Ordination: May 1942 by Indiana Synod of United Lutheran Church in America.

Calls: Jay County Parish, Ind., (Zion, Portland; Faith, Bryant; New Zion, New Corydon), 1942-48; Pastor/Developer, Tuscaloosa, Ala., 1948-49; Unity, St. Louis, Mo., 1949-52; St. Luke, Logansport, Ind., 1952-65; Oak Grove, Bristol, Va. and Faith, Bristol, Tenn., 1965-68; St. Matthew, Rowan County, 1965-81.

Other: Committee on Continuing Education for Ministers, 1973-74; Committee for Pastoral Preparation, 1974-81; Rowan County Lutheran Ministers Association and Chair of its Continuing Education Committee.

Date of Death/Burial Location: April 17, 1981; St. Matthew Church Cemetery, Rowan County, N.C.

DAY, CHARLES HOWARD

Date/Place of Birth: September 14, 1863; near Baltimore, Md.

Parents: Nathaniel Day and Caroline Day.

Spouse/Marriage Date: Charlotte (Dickie) Day; October 12, 1910 in Black Lick, Pa.

Child: Charles William.

Education/Ordination: Educated for ministry in Methodist Church and ordained in 1886 by that church. Presumably affiliated with Lutheran Church about 1911.

Calls: In Kansas, 1911-14; in Virginia, 1914-17. In North Carolina: St. Andrew-Calvary, Concord 1918-20; supplied Cold Water, Cabarrus County, 1919-20; Pilgrim-St. Luke, Davidson County, 1920-21. Transferred 1922 to Central Pennsylvania Synod.

Other: Retired 1925 at Riverside, Calif.

Date of Death/Burial Location: May 12, 1932; Riverside, Calif.

DEAL, CLAUDE VICTOR, JR.

Date/Place of Birth: May 11, 1937; Monroe, N.C.

Parents: The Reverend Claude Victor Deal, Sr. and Barbara (Setzer) Deal.

Spouse/Marriage Date: Helen Elizabeth (Herion) Deal; August 26, 1961 in Mt. Pleasant, N.C.

Children: Jeffery Alan, Brian Andrew, Douglas Victor.

Education: Lenoir-Rhyne, A.B. English 1959; Lutheran Theological Southern Seminary, M.Div. 1963; University of North Carolina School of Public Health, M.S.P.H. 1974; graduate work at Duke Divinity School.

Ordination: June 9, 1963 by North Carolina Synod.

Calls: Christ, Winston-Salem, 1963-67; Associate Director of Chaplaincy, North Carolina Memorial Hospital, Chapel Hill, 1970-74; Director of Chaplaincy Services, The Williamsport Hospital, Williamsport, Pa., 1974-89; Chaplain, Duke University Medical Center, Durham, 1989-.

Other: Board of Lutheran Children's Home of the South, 1970-74; Association for Clinical Pastoral Education, Accreditation Commission, 1976-82, Chair, 1983-85; Standards Committee, 1990-96; North Carolina Synod AIDS Task Force, 1992-; North Carolina Synod Social Ministry Committee, 1993; Adult Advisor, Executive Committee, Luther League, 1963-64; Continuing Education for Ministers Committee, 1970-76, Chair, 1972-76. Task Force on Men and Women, Central Pennsylvania Synod of the Lutheran Church in America, 1985-6.

DEAL, CLAUDE VICTOR, SR.

Date/Place of Birth: March 5, 1906; Hickory, N.C.

Parents: John Q. Deal and Ida C. (Yount) Deal.

Spouse/Marriage Date: Barbara (Setzer) Deal; September 12, 1931 in Hickory, N.C.

Children: The Reverend Claude Victor, Jr., Barbara Hahn Land (married the Reverend Robert E. Land), Cornelia Katherine Land.

Education: Lenoir-Rhyne, A.B. 1930; Lutheran Theological Southern Seminary, B.D. 1934.

Ordination: May 1934 by North Carolina Synod.

Calls: St. Luke-Morning Star, Monroe, 1934-41; surveyed and supplied Hamlet, 1941; Lutheran Chapel, Gastonia, 1941-42. World War II, U.S. Army Chaplain, 1942-47. Trinity, Landis, 1947-61; Mission Developer/Pastor, Incarnation, Charlotte, 1961-68; Grace, Salisbury, 1968-74.

Other: Commission in U.S. Army Chaplains Reserves. Executive Board, 1956-60; 1963-68; Board, Lenoir- Rhyne, 1968-74; Board, Lutheran Theological Southern Seminary, 1948-51; American Missions, 1969-74; Committee on Military Personnel, 1969-72. North Carolina Synod's Special Committee on the North Carolina Council of Churches, 1951-59.

Date of Death/Burial Location: May 15, 1974; Grace Lutheran Church Cemetery, Salisbury, N.C.

DEAL, DONALD RAY

Date/Place of Birth: April 15, 1934; Rowan County, N.C.
Parents: Charlie Thomas Deal and Margie Elizabeth (Wilhelm) Deal.
Spouse/Marriage Date: Nancy Lyerly (Cline) Deal; August 4, 1957 in Cabarrus County, N.C.
Children: David Eugene, Brenda Kay, Melvin Wayne, Alan Ray.
Education: North Carolina State University, Lenoir-Rhyne, A.B. 1956; Lutheran Theological Southern Seminary, M.Div. 1959.
Ordination: June 7, 1959 by North Carolina Synod.
Calls: Lebanon, Rowan County, 1959-61; Our Saviour, Dallas, 1961-71; Holy Trinity, Mt. Pleasant, 1971-. Vice Pastor at various congregations.
Other: Lutheran World Relief Committee, Chair, 1959-83; Board, North Carolina Lutheran Homes and Lutheran Services for the Aging, 1980-87, 1989-.

DEAL, GARY MICHAEL

Date/Place of Birth: November 3, 1948; Concord, N.C.
Parents: Fred J. Deal, Jr. and Billie Elizabeth Linker (Blume) Deal.
Spouse/Marriage Date: Ruth (Daniel) Deal; April 3, 1988 in Hickory, N.C.
Children: Richard Michael, Lanita G. Deal-Pirkle, David Stewart.
Education: Pfeiffer College, B.A. 1972; Emory University at Candler, M.Div. 1977; Lutheran Theological Southern Seminary, M.Div. 1993.
Ordination: June 10, 1977 by Western North Carolina Annual Conference - The United Methodist Church; May 8, 1993 by North Carolina Synod.
Calls: The Lutheran Church of the Good Shepherd, Brevard, 1993-.
Other: Chair, Transylvania County Lutheran-Angelican-Roman Catholic-United Methodist; Executive Officer, Transylvania Christian Ministry, Inc.; Clergy Representative, Transylvania Christian Ethics Committee; Hospital Chaplain Volunteer.

DEAL, HAROLD GERHARDT, JR.

Date/Place of Birth: April 8, 1923; Hickory, N.C.
Parents: Harold Gerhardt Deal, Sr. and Margaret A. (Wannemacher) Deal. A grandson of the Reverend J. H. Wannemacher.
Spouse/Marriage Date: Miriam Elizabeth (Morgan) Deal, daughter of the Reverend John L. Morgan; June 2, 1947 in Hickory, N.C.
Children: The Reverend David Morgan, Stephen Michael, Carol Rebekah. *Education*: Lenoir-Rhyne, A.B. 1945; Lutheran Theological Southern Seminary, B.D. 1947; Union Seminary, STM 1954; Chicago Seminary, D.Min. 1984.
Ordination: April 16, 1947 by North Carolina Synod.
Calls: As missionary in Japan, 1947-61. Holy Trinity, Houston, Texas, 1961-64; St. John, Winter Park, Fla., 1964-68; St. Paul, Pensacola, Fla., 1968-78; Grace, Houston, Texas, 1978-82; Luther Place Memorial, Washington, D.C., 1982-88; Director of Special Needs, St. Luke, Silver Spring, Md., 1988-96. Interim Pastor at Prince of Peace, Gaithersburg, Md., 1993-94.
Other: Secretary, Japan Lutheran Missionaries Association, 1950-52. Member and English Secretary, Executive Board, Japan Evangelical Lutheran Church, 1952-53; President, Japan Lutheran Missionaries Association, 1955-57. Board, Lutheran Theological Southern

Seminary; Chair, Youth Ministry Committee, Florida Synod; Chair, Task Group for Legislative Action, Florida Synod; Chair, World Missions Committee, Texas-Louisiana Synod; Chair, Cluster of Lutheran Churches, Washington, D.C. Contributed articles from Japan to *The Foreign Missionary, Lutheran Woman's Work*, and *The Lutheran. The Lord's Supper in the New Testament - An Inquiry into the New Testament Grounds for Doctrine of the Real Presence,* translated into Japanese and published in *Japan Lutheran Quarterly,* 1957. Retired February 29, 1996 in Hickory, N.C.

DEAL, JACK DONALD, SR.

Date/Place of Birth: March 8, 1932; Hickory, N.C.
Parents: Vernon H. Deal and Violet (Munday) Deal.
Spouse/Marriage Date: Carolyn J. (Hollar) Deal; December 26, 1949 in Hickory, N.C.
Children: Jack Donald, Jr., Cathryn L., Paul L., Stephen C.
Education: Florida Southern College, B.S. 1959; Lutheran Theological Southern Seminary, B.D. 1962.
Ordination: June 17, 1962 by North Carolina Synod.
Calls: Mission Developer/Pastor, Our Saviour, Southern Pines, 1962-66; St. John, Concord, 1966-73. Interim Pastor at various congregations. Pastor-Developer, Ladson, S.C., 1975; Peace, Charleston Heights, S.C., 1975-.
Other: Social Ministry Committee, 1965-66; Pensions Committee, 1969-72; Stewardship Committee, 1971- 73; Continuing Education for Ministers, 1970-73.

DEAL, JAMES FRANCIS, SR.

Date/Place of Birth: December 18, 1877; Rowan County, N.C.
Parents: Calvin J. Deal and Sarah J. (Coleman) Deal.
First Spouse/Marriage Date: Kate Elizabeth (Peterson) Deal; July 7, 1909 in Stanly County, N.C.; died October 22, 1917.
Children of First Marriage: James Francis, Jr., Charles C., Elizabeth, Sarah Lillian.
Second Spouse/Marriage Date: Myrtle Hoyt (Lowe) Deal; 1923 in Ohio; died 1935.
Third Spouse/Marriage Date: Nena E. (White) Deal; December 25, 1937 in Albemarle, N.C.
Education: Lenoir-Rhyne, A.B., A.M. 1896; Philadelphia Seminary, 1899.
Ordination: 1899 by Tennessee Synod.
Calls: Some dates are questionable. In South Carolina, 1899-1901: St. Jacob-Mt. Horeb-St. Thomas-Bethlehem, Chapin. In North Carolina, 1902-12: St. Martin-Mt. Gilead, Cabarrus County; Trinity, Vale-Cedar Grove-David Chapel, Lincoln County; Sardis, Catawba County; Christ's, Stanley 1906-09; St. Luke, Lincoln County, 1910-12; Beck's-Holly Grove-New Jerusalem-Emmanuel-Lebanon, Davidson County; St. Luke, Lincoln County; St. John, Hudson; St. Stephen, Lenoir. In Virginia, 1912-17: Bland and Giles Parishes.
Other: Retired 1918 at Landis; engaged in business; in later years lived at St. Petersburg, Fla.   Secretary, Tennessee Synod, 1903-06; Treasurer, North Carolina Conference, Tennessee Synod. Board, Lenoir-Rhyne.
Date of Death/Burial Location: February 19, 1962 at St. Petersburg, Fla. ; Mt. Moriah Church, Rowan County, N.C.

DEATON, JOHN LEROY

Date/Place of Birth: September 4, 1862; near China Grove, N.C. Twin brother of the Reverend W. A. Deaton. Twin brother's son, the Reverend John Leroy Deaton, D.D., was named for him.

Parents: John E. Deaton and Nancy Elizabeth (Crosby) Deaton.

First Spouse/Marriage Date: Laura (Lipe) Deaton; May 4, 1886 (died that summer of typhoid fever) in Landis, N.C.

Second Spouse/Marriage Date: Laura (Hoke) Deaton; November 15, 1900 in Lincolnton, N.C.

Child: Georgiana.

Education: North Carolina College, A.B. 1888, winning first honor by a little over twin brother; Philadelphia Seminary, 1891.

Ordination: 1891 by Ministerium of Pennsylvania and transferred to Tennessee Synod.

Calls: Mt. Moriah-St. Mark, Rowan County, 1891-93, 1900-02. Missionary in Seattle, Wash., and other places in Pacific Northwest, succeeding the Reverend E. F. Keever, 1893-95. Health failing, returned to North Carolina, 1895-1900. Organized and built church, Mt. Zion, Watauga County; Mt. Pleasant; Holy Communion; also preached in schoolhouses and churches of other denominations at Blowing Rock, Boone, Deep Gap, and Cove Creek. Supplied New Jerusalem, Davidson County, 1897. In Virginia, 1902-06: St. Jacob-Zion-Salem-Morning Star-Powder Springs, Edinburg.

Other: Retired 1906 due to declining health, near Lincolnton. The twin brothers observed 82 birthdays together until the other died in 1945.

Date of Death/Burial Location: September 22, 1951 after long invalidism following a farm accident; Hollybrook Cemetery, Lincolnton, N.C.

DEATON, WILLIS ALEXANDER

Date/Place of Birth: September 4, 1862 near China Grove, N.C. Twin brother of the Reverend John Leroy Deaton.

Parents: John E. Deaton and Nancy Elizabeth (Crosby) Deaton.

First Spouse/Marriage Date: Margaret Pauline (Miller) Deaton; July 14, 1891 in Cabarrus County, N.C.; died 1922.

Children of First Marriage: Miriam Ophelia (married the Reverend Hugo L. Dressler), the Reverend John Leroy, Oscar Claudius, Wilhelmina (died at age 2), Paul Willis, James Krauth (died at age twenty months), Louis Edwin.

Second Spouse/Marriage Date: Catherine Elizabeth (Moretz) Deaton; January 23, 1924 in Boone, N.C.; died June 12, 1981.

Education: Roanoke College, (junior year), North Carolina College, A.B. 1888, losing first honor by an edge to twin brother; Philadelphia Seminary, 1891; Lenoir-Rhyne, D.D. 1911.

Ordination: 1891 by North Carolina Synod.

Calls: St. Andrew-St. Michael, Lexington County, S.C.; Holy Communion, Dallas; Philadelphia-Antioch, Gaston County; Christ's, Stanley, Gaston County, 1897-1906; with the Reverend W. J. Boger, organized and supplied Holy Trinity, Gastonia, 1898-1900, 1901-02. As Tennessee Synod synodical missionary, 1906-19, organized and served: Trinity, Vale, 1907; St. Stephen, Lenoir, 1908-09, Calvary, Morganton, 1910-17, and Bethany, Hickory, 1910-25; Mt. Hebron, Hildebran, 1913-20; St. Matthew, Caldwell County, 1917-19; and in Watauga County: Old Mt. Pleasant, 1923-32, 1933-34; Mt. Zion, 1925-31, 1934; Holy Trinity, Mt. Pleasant, 1925-32.

Other: Retired 1932 at Boone, N.C. President, Tennessee Synod, 1901 and 1921 at time of merger of North Carolina and Tennessee Synods. Chair, Joint Commission on Basis and Constitution for Merger of North Carolina and Tennessee Synods, 1919-21. Member, and sometime Chair, Board, Lenoir-Rhyne, 1898-1901, 1909-26. Co-editor of *The Catawba Lutheran,* 1909. Business Manager, 1912. Board, Lutheran Theological Southern Seminary, 1906. Board, Foreign Missions, United Synod South, 1904. Served two terms in House of North Carolina General Assembly, 1923-26, from Catawba County. Celebrated 82 birthdays with twin brother, who survived him by six years.
Date of Death/Burial Location: June 18, 1945; Oakwood Cemetery in Hickory, N.C.

DEESE, PHILLIP WAYNE

Date/Place of Birth: December 15, 1937; Rowan County, N.C.
Parents: John A. Deese and Lillian A. (Overcash) Deese.
Spouse/Marriage Date: Linda Merchant (Lockrow) Deese; June 10, 1961 in Winston-Salem, N.C.
Children: Deborah Carole, David Charles.
Education: Lenoir-Rhyne, A.B. 1960; Lutheran Theological Southern Seminary, B.D. 1963.
Ordination: June 9, 1963 by North Carolina Synod.
Calls: Advent, Spindale, 1963-66; Our Saviour, Southern Pines, 1966-71; Assistant Pastor, First Lutheran, Greensboro, 1971-78. Vice Pastor to various congregations.
Other: Youth Committee, 1967-73, Chair, 1969-73, 1969-70; Foundation for Lutheran Campus Ministry in Central North Carolina, 1972-77; Chair, Campus Ministry, 1973-78.
Date of Death/Burial Location: May 16, 1978; Forsyth Memorial Park, Winston-Salem, N.C.

DeRASMO, FREDERICK JOSEPH, JR.

Date/Place of Birth: July 21, 1957; Long Branch, N.J.
Parents: Frederick Joseph DeRasmo, Sr. and Diana (Boynton) DeRasmo.
Spouse/Marriage Date: Karen Louise (Korting) DeRasmo; May 29, 1982.
Child: Joseph Michael.
Education: Upsala College, B.A. Psychology 1979; Lutheran Theological Southern Seminary, M.Div. 1984.
Ordination: June 17, 1984 by New Jersey Synod.
Calls: Mt. Olive, Mt. Pleasant, 1984-88; Trinity, Landis, 1988-90; St. Michael, Unionville, Pa., 1991-. Vice pastor at various congregations.
Other: Lutheran World Relief Committee of the North Carolina Synod; Worship Committee of the Southeast Pennsylvania Synod.

DERHAMMER, G. A.

Other: Nothing is known of him, except that he served the following churches, 1900-02: Luther's Chapel, Lincoln County; Bethel, Gaston County; and St. Paul, Crouse.

DERRICK, CLARENCE KESLER, JR.

Date/Place of Birth: March 21, 1921; Kings Mountain, Cleveland County, N.C.

Parents: The Reverend Clarence Kesler Derrick, Sr. and Myrtle (Davis) Derrick.
Spouse/Marriage Date: Mary Ethel (Hutto) Derrick; June 26, 1956 in Jacksonville, Fla.
Children: Paul Hutto, Margaret Elizabeth, James Lee, The Reverend John David, Mark Christopher, Michael Andrew.
Education: Newberry College, A.B. 1954; Lutheran Theological Southern Seminary, B.D. 1957.
Ordination: June 9, 1957, by Georgia-Alabama Synod.
Calls: Mission Developer/Pastor, Our Saviour, Albany, Ga., 1957-63; Our Savior, Gatlinburg, Tenn., 1963- 68; Apostle, Atlanta, Ga., 1968-71; Beth Eden, Newton, 1971-86; St. Michael, Moncks Corner, S.C., 1986-91; Pisgah, Lexington, S.C., 1991-96.
Other: Campus Ministry Committee, 1973-76; Southeastern Synod: American Missions Committee, Executive Board; District Dean in Southeastern, North Carolina and South Carolina Synods.

DERRICK, CLARENCE KESLER, SR.

Date/Place of Birth: October 26, 1901; near Columbia, S.C.
Parents: Julius Clarence Derrick and Martha Elizabeth (Kesler) Derrick.
Spouse/Marriage Date: Myrtle Ada (Davis) Derrick; October 4, 1927 in Columbia, S.C.
Children: Infant son, infant daughter (both lived only a few hours), the Reverend Clarence Kesler, Jr., Myrtle Davis (lived three days), Mildred Elizabeth.
Education: Newberry College, A.B. 1924, D.D. 1951; Lutheran Theological Southern Seminary, B.D. 1927; graduate study, Vanderbilt University and Union Seminary.
Ordination: 1927 by South Carolina Synod.
Calls: Pelion Mission in South Carolina (four churches), 1927-30. St. Andrew's, Charleston, S.C., 1935-45. St. John, Atlanta, Ga., 1945-55. In North Carolina: St. Matthew-St. Luke, Kings Mountain, 1930-35. Mayer Memorial, Newberry, S.C., 1961-67. Interim Pastor, St. Mark, Blythewood, S.C., 1967-.
Other: Chair, Board of Lowman Home. Chaplain (Captain), South Carolina State Guard. Executive Committee and first Director, Lutheran World Action, South Carolina Synod; Secretary, Board of Trustees of Newberry College. In Georgia Synod: Executive Committee and President, Central Conference, 1953-54.
Date of Death/Burial Location: July 30, 1977; Little Mountain, S.C.

DERRICK, JOHN DAVID

Date/Place of Birth: July 3, 1960; Albany, Ga.
Parents: The Reverend Clarence Kesler Derrick, Jr. and Mary (Hutto) Derrick.
Spouse/Marriage Date: Amanda (Caughman) Derrick; December 19, 1984 in West Columbia, S.C.
Children: Anna Catherine, Sarah Elizabeth. *Education*: Lenoir-Rhyne, 1978-80; Newberry College, A.B. 1983; Lutheran Theological Southern Seminary, M.Div. 1988.
Ordination: June 5, 1988 by North Carolina Synod.
Calls: Associate Pastor, St. John, Salisbury, 1988-91; Pastor-Developer Resurrection, Newnan, Ga., 1991-98; Lexington, S.C., 1999-.
Other: Chaplain, Rowan Memorial Hospital; Review Board, Department for Social Services, Rowan County; Past Vice President, Rowan Lutheran Ministers Association; Salisbury-Rowan Human Relations Council; Advisory Board, Rowan Helping Ministries Homeless Shelter; Chair, Homeless Shelter Policies and Procedures Committee; Kiwanis;

Mentor, Coweta County School; Executive Committee, Lutheran Theological Southern Seminary Alumni Association; Pastoral Advisory Committee, Lutheran Theological Southern Seminary Capital Campaign.

DERRICK, JOHN LUTHER

Date/Place of Birth: March 25, 1929; Woodstock, Va.
Parents: John Perry Derrick and Agnes Hannah Derrick.
Spouse/Marriage Date: Carol (Martin) Derrick; August 29, 1964 in Wilkes-Barre, Pa.
Children: John Alan, David Christopher, Paul Andrew.
Education: Roanoke College, B.A. 1951; Mt. Airy, Philadelphia Seminary, M.Div. 1960.
Ordination: September 11, 1960 by Virginia Synod.
Calls: St. Paul, Wilkes-Barre, Pa., 1960-66; Christ, Durham, 1966-76; Muhlenberg, Harrisonburg, Va., 1976- 91; Trinity Ecumenical, Moneta, Va., 1991-93.
Other: Parish Education Committee, 1967-69; Lutheran Student Foundation of Durham, 1967-76; Campus Ministry Committee, 1969-74; Lutheran Campus Ministry in Central North Carolina, 1972-74. Retired 1993 to Harrisonburg, Va.

DERRICK, PATRICK HENRY ELMORE

Date/Place of Birth: November 20, 1856; Lexington County, S.C.
Parents: Fred Derrick and Lucinda (Unger) Derrick.
Spouse/Marriage Date: Ellen Baker (Geiger) Derrick; October 8, 1891 in St. Matthews, S.C.; died February 28, 1949.
Children: Anna Geiger, Elizabeth Horlbeck, Emma Julia Blum, Margaret Baker.
Education: Newberry College, A.B. 1882, Honorary A.M. 1894; Lutheran Theological Southern Seminary, 1889.
Ordination: 1889 by South Carolina Synod.
Calls: In South Carolina and Florida, 1889-94. In North Carolina: Mt. Olive-St. Stephen, Cabarrus County, 1895-97; supplied Holy Trinity, Mt. Pleasant, while teaching mathematics at North Carolina College, 1897; Luther's, Rowan County 1898-99.
Other: Transferred to South Carolina Synod, 1899. Retired 1911 in Blythewood, S.C. Taught public school after retiring.
Date of Death/Burial Location: October 1, 1920; Sandy Run Church, Calhoun County, S.C.

DEY, KEITH HOWARD

Date/Place of Birth: October 30, 1955; Toledo, Ohio.
Parents: Warren Bertrand Dey and Yvonne Beatrice (Cherel) Dey.
Spouse/Marriage Date: Brenda Jean (LaChine) Dey; August 27, 1977 in Northwood, Ohio.
Children: Stephanie Lynn, Christine Leigh.
Education: The University of Toledo, B.A. 1980; Trinity Seminary, M.Div. 1990.
Ordination: June 3, 1990 by Northwestern Ohio Synod.
Calls: Holly Grove, Lexington, 1990-96; Ascension, Wilson, 1996-. Vice Pastor to various congregations.

DICKERT, JAMES CANNON

Date/Place of Birth: August 5, 1915; Columbia, S.C.

Parents: Andrew Herbert Dickert and May Ella (Cannon) Dickert.
Spouse/Marriage Date: Nell (West) Dickert; June 28, 1941 in Columbia, S.C.
Child: Andrew Calvin.
Education: University of South Carolina, B.S. Business Administration 1938; Lutheran Theological Southern Seminary, B.D. 1941.
Ordination: June 23, 1941 by South Carolina Synod.
Calls: Grace, Richland, Melanchthon, Liberty, Randolph County, 1941-46. St. John, Clinton, S.C., 1946-52; Organizer/Pastor, Ascension, Augusta, Ga., 1952-57; Reformation, Lancaster, S.C., 1957-72; Ehrhardt Memorial, Ehrhardt, S.C., 1972-80.
Other: Retired August 1980 to White Rock, S.C.; Assistant Chaplain, Lowman Home, 1981-84.
Date of Death/Burial Location: February 12, 1998; Elmwood Memorial Gardens, Columbia, S.C.

DICKSON, CHARLES WILLIAM, SR.

Date/Place of Birth: August 14, 1936; Jamestown, N.Y.
Parents: Elmer Axel Dickson and Edna P. Dickson.
Spouse/Marriage Date: Marilyn (Canady) Dickson; February 19, 1964.
Children: Sheri Lynn, Charles William, Jr.
Education: St. Petersburg Junior College, 1955; University of DuBuque; University of Tampa, B.A. 1958; Lutheran Theological Southern Seminary; Wartburg Seminary, M.Div. 1961; Stetson University, M.A. 1966; University of Florida, Ph.D. 1969.
Ordination: July 9, 1961 by Florida Synod.
Calls: Abiding Saviour, Winter Haven, Fla., 1961-66; Chaplain, University of Florida Medical Center, Gainesville, Fla., 1968-70; Christ, Jacksonville, Fla., 1970-72; St. John, Lenoir, 1975-81; Shiloh, Hickory, 1981-85; St. John, Taylorsville, 1985-. Vice Pastor at various congregations.
Other: Instructor of Science, Lake City Community College, Lake City, Fla., 1968-70; Instructor of Science, Florida Community College, Jacksonville, Fla., 1970-72; Staff, Frye Regional Medical Center, Hickory, 1972- 81; Instructor of Chemistry, Catawba Valley Community College, Hickory, 1973-; Instructor, Lenoir-Rhyne, Hickory, 1972-76; Chemist for Engineering Department, City of Hickory, 1985-. Executive Board, North Carolina Council of Churches, 1982-85; Chair, Ecumenical Affairs, North Carolina Council of Churches, 1982- 85; Chair, Ecumenical Relations Committee of the North Carolina Synod, 1983-85; Contributing Editor, *Queen Magazine,* 1992-. Regular contributing writer to four National Roman Catholic Magazines. Also writes Teen Materials for Southern Baptists and Assembly of God. Author of more than 300 magazine articles in Business, Science, and Religious areas. Author of two books: *A Chemistry Lab Manual,* and *Religion Book on Mariology.* Retired September 1991.

DIEFENDORF, CHAUNCEY

Date/Place of Birth: February 1, 1838; New York.
Parents: Daniel Diefendorf and Nancy Barbara (Wieting) Diefendorf.
Spouse/Marriage Date: Melissa Louise (Wetherwax) Diefendorf; June 8, 1871 in West Sand Lake, N.Y.
Children: Edna Margaret, Elizabeth Lusetta, Clarence Wetherwax, Grace Louise.
License/Ordination: Licensed 1873 and ordained 1875 by Franckean Synod.

Calls: In New York to 1905. St. Matthew, Rowan County, 1905-07. Transferred 1907 back to Franckean Synod.
Other: Grandfather of the Reverend Paul C. Empie, Executive Director of National Lutheran Council.
Date of Death/Burial Location: November 19, 1909; Fort Plain, N.Y.

DIEGEL, RONALD LYELL

Date/Place of Birth: July 3, 1937; Albany, N.Y.
Parents: Lyell Erwin Diegel and Miriam D. (Kronan) Diegel. *Spouse/Marriage Date*: Charlotte Anne (Lesemann) Diegel; September 11, 1965 in Charleston, S.C.
Children: Ronald Barton, Charlotte Rebecca Jernigan.
Education: Hudson Valley Technical College, 1956-58; Hartwick College, B.A. Psychology 1962; Lutheran Theological Southern Seminary, M.Div. 1965; University of South Carolina, M.Ed. Education and Counseling 1980.
Ordination: June 6, 1965 by North Carolina Synod.
Calls: St. Paul, Burlington, 1965-69; Chaplain, U.S. Army, Vietnam Veteran, 1969-72; Pastor-Developer, Bethlehem, Irmo, S.C., 1972-.
Other: Bronze Star Medal, Air Defense Medal.

DIETZ, JOHN CALVIN

Date/Place of Birth: March 3, 1876; Catawba County, N.C.
Parents: Washington Marion Dietz and Susan Jan (Propst) Dietz.
Spouse/Marriage Date: Minnie Rose (Rudisill) Dietz; September 19, 1900 in Maiden, N.C.
Children: Paul Hunt, Henry W.
Education: Lenoir-Rhyne, A.B. 1898, D.D. 1936; Chicago Seminary, 1900.
Ordination: 1900 by Tennessee Synod.
Calls: Emmanuel, Lincolnton; St. Luke-Salem, Lincoln County, 1900-03. In Indiana, 1903-06; in South Carolina, 1906-09. Again in North Carolina, 1909-44: St. John's, Cherryville; Bethphage, Lincoln County; St. Mark, Gaston County; St. Paul, Crouse; Bethel, Gaston County; Grace, Bessemer City; Holy Trinity, Gastonia; Union, Rowan County, (twice); Mt. Calvary, Claremont; St. Luke, Catawba County; Good Hope, Hickory; St. Paul, Startown; St. Martin, Cabarrus County; St. Martin, Stanly County; First, Lexington.
Other: Retired 1944 at Gastonia, N.C. Chair, Committee on Arrangements, and temporary Chair, Merger Convention, North Carolina and Tennessee Synods, 1920-21. Secretary, second to be elected, of the United North Carolina Synod, 1923-37. Board, Lenoir-Rhyne.
Date of Death/Burial Location: February 12, 1954; Gaston Memorial Cemetery, Gastonia, N.C.

DITTMAN, GARY ALLAN

Date/Place of Birth: January 15, 1962; Dayton, Ohio.
Parents: Robert Alan Dittman and Mina Marie Dittman.
Spouse/Marriage Date: Karen Rose (Brumby) Dittman; July 28, 1984 in Manchester, Ga.
Education: Young Harris College, A.A. 1982; LaGrange College, B.A. Religion, Speech

and Drama 1984; Chicago Seminary, M.Div., 1988.
Ordination: 1988 by Southeastern Synod.
Calls: Emmanuel, Lincolnton, 1988-.
Other: Chair, Youth Ministry Committee, 1992-.

DOERMANN, MARTIN JOHN

Date/Place of Birth: December 6, 1925; Blue Island, Ill.
Parents: The Reverend Gerhard H. Doermann and Mary Josephine (Messarvey) Doermann. Father had first chair, Christian Education, at the Evangelical Lutheran Seminary.
Spouse/Marriage Date: Barbara Katherine (Reck) Doermann; January 26, 1949.
Children: Geoffrey Martin, Deborah Faith Burch, James M.
Education: Dartmouth College, Cornell U.S. Naval Reserve Midshipman School, 1945; Capital University, A.B., 1947; Evangelical Lutheran Seminary (now Trinity), B.D., 1952; Harvard Divinity School, 1963.
Ordination: 1952 by American Lutheran Church-Ohio Synod.
Calls: Chaplain, U.S. Navy, 1952-75; Emmanuel, Sugar Grove, Ohio, 1975-78; and with The Lutheran Church-Missouri Synod: Good Shepherd, Gulf Breeze, Fla., 1987-88; and Galilean, Biloxi, Miss., 1987-88.
Other: Combat Action Ribbon; Meritorious Unit Citation; Vietnam Campaign Ribbon; Vietnam Service Medal with six bronze stars; Bronze Star with Combat "V"; Korean Service Medal; Vietnam Gallantry Cross Unit Citation; Vietnam Presidential Unit Citation; Naval Reserve Medal; National Defense Service Medal with Bronze Star; United Nations Service Medal. Retired 1988 to Hillsborough, N.C.

DOGGETT, LEWIS BELTON, JR.

Date/Place of Birth: October 3, 1946; Charlotte, N.C.
Parents: Lewis Belton Doggett, Sr. and Mary E. (Houser) Doggett.
Spouse/Marriage Date: Margo (Myers) Doggett; December 23, 1978 in Rock Hill, S.C.
Child: Joy Elizabeth.
Education: University of North Carolina, A.B. Sociology 1968; Lutheran Theological Southern Seminary, M.Div. 1972.
Ordination: June 4, 1972 by North Carolina Synod.
Calls: Prince of Peace, Chester, S.C., 1972-75; Cedar Grove, Vale, 1979-84; Associate Chaplain, Mary Washington Hospital, Fredericksburg, Va., 1986-.
Other: Clinical Counselor at Catawba Center for Growth and Development, Rock Hill, S.C., 1976-79. Social Ministry Committee; Task Force on Alcohol and Drug Abuse; President, Lincoln County Ministerial Association; Associate Volunteer Chaplain, Cleveland Memorial Hospital, Shelby, N.C.; Executive Board, Lincoln County Christian Ministries. Removed from roll September 1991 in Culpeper, Va.

DORSEY, TERRY MICHAEL

Date/Place of Birth: August 1, 1956; Cuyahoga, Ohio.
Parents: George R. Dorsey and Wilma (O'Dea) Dorsey.
Education: University of Toledo, Ohio, B.A. 1978; Trinity Seminary, M.Div. 1990; graduate work at Chandler (Emory) School of Theology, 1983, and Lutheran Theological Southern Seminary.
Ordination: August 10, 1990 by Southeastern Synod.
Calls: Christ the King, Cary, 1990-94; Mission Developer, Circle of Grace, Apex, 1995-.

DORTON, LEWIS FRANKLIN

Date/Place of Birth: June 27, 1931; Cabarrus County, N.C.
Parents: Ted R. Dorton and Rebecca (Castor) Dorton. Older brother is the Reverend Richard B. Dorton.
Spouse/Marriage Date: Alice (Blackwelder) Dorton; September 5, 1951 in Concord, N.C.
Children: James Timothy, Ted Mark, Elissa Ann.
Education: Lenoir-Rhyne, A.B. 1952; Lutheran Theological Southern Seminary, B.D. 1955; Chapel Hill Pastoral Clinical School, 1970; Pittsburgh Seminary, D.Min. 1990.
Ordination: 1955 by North Carolina Synod.
Calls: Amity-Lebanon, Cleveland, 1955-57; St. Luke, Conover, 1957-61; Christiana, Granite Quarry, 1961-69; Chaplain, North Carolina Memorial Hospital, Chapel Hill, 1969-70; Our Saviour, Welcome, 1970-73. Vice Pastor at various congregations. Messiah, Casselberry, Fla., 1973-90.
Date of Death/Burial Location: December 10, 1991; Florida.

DORTON, RICHARD BRADSHAW, SR.

Date/Place of Birth: May 3, 1929; Concord, N.C.
Parents: Ted Richardson Dorton and Rebecca (Castor) Dorton. Younger brother is the Reverend L. Franklin Dorton.
Spouse/Marriage Date: Mary Elizabeth (Hardy) Dorton; June 22, 1958 in Lincolnton, N.C.
Children: Richard Bradshaw, Jr., Fonda Elizabeth.
Education: Lenoir-Rhyne, A.B. 1951; Lutheran Theological Southern Seminary, B.D. 1954; graduate work at Clinical Pastoral Education, Baptist Hospital, Winston-Salem and at North Carolina Memorial Hospital, Chapel Hill.
Ordination: June 20, 1954 by North Carolina Synod.
Calls: Friendship, Taylorsville, 1954-65; St. Enoch, Kannapolis, 1965-78; Chaplain, North Carolina Memorial Hospital, Chapel Hill, 1978-80; Mt. Olive, Mt. Pleasant, 1980-83. Vice Pastor at various congregations.
Other: Social Ministry Committee; President, Kannapolis Ministerial Association.
Date of Death/Burial Location: December 23, 1983; Mt. Olive Lutheran Church Cemetery, Mt. Pleasant, N.C.

DOSH, THOMAS WILLIAM LUTHER

Date/Place of Birth: November 21, 1830; Strasburg, Va.
Parents: Thomas William Dosh and Mary (Swan) Dosh.
Spouse/Marriage Date: Catherine (Brown) Dosh; November 3, 1864 in Winchester, Va.

Children: Katharine, William Henry, Portia Baker (died in infancy), Fanny Bachmann (died in infancy), Virginia, Mary Ellen, Olive Augusta (married the Reverend N. Burch Tucker), Bowman Campbell, Mary Krauth (married the Reverend C. E. Krumbholz).

Education: Gettysburg College, A.B. 1856; Gettysburg Seminary, 1858; Roanoke College, D.D. 1875.

License/Ordination: Licensed 1858 and ordained 1859 by Virginia Synod.

Calls: In West Virginia and Virginia, 1859-72; St. John's, Charleston, S.C., 1872-76. In North Carolina: St. John, Salisbury, 1876-77. Transferred to Virginia Synod, 1877; Burkittsville, Md., 1885-89.

Other: President, Roanoke College, 1877-78. Professor, Southern Seminary in Salem, Va., 1878-84. Editor, *The Lutheran Visitor*, 1874-78; Editor, *The Lutheran Home*, 1876-86. President of the Evangelical Lutheran General Synod North America.

Date of Death/Burial Location: December 24, 1889; Winchester, Va.

DOUGHERTY, JAMES LIONEL

Date/Place of Birth: February 25, 1955; Norfolk, Va.

Parents: Edgar Pierce Dougherty and Thelma Viola (Hilt) Dougherty.

Education: Florida State University, Newberry College, B.A. Religion, Philosophy, History, 1976; Clinical Pastoral Education, Valley Baptist Medical Center, Harlingen, Texas, 1979; Lutheran Theological Southern Seminary, M.Div. 1980; University of North Carolina at Charlotte, M.Ed. 1982-85.

Ordination: June 1, 1980 by South Carolina Synod.

Calls: Reformation, Lancaster, S.C., 1980-81; St. James, Concord, 1981-85; Christus Victor, Fayetteville, 1985-90; St. Paul, Salisbury, 1990-92; St. Matthew, Kings Mountain, 1995-. Vice Pastor at various congregations.

DRAWDY, CHARLES FULTON, II

Date/Place of Birth: June 4, 1948; Burlington, N.C.

Parents: Charles Fulton Drawdy, Sr. and Margaret (Smith) Drawdy.

First Spouse/Marriage Date: Lynda A. (Gilpin) Drawdy.

Child of First Marriage: Shannon Christine.

Second Spouse/Marriage Date: Lynne Barbara (Johnson) Drawdy; August 3, 1975 in Deerfield Beach, Fla.

Child of Second Marriage: Alaina Lynne.

Education: Greensboro College, B.A. 1970; Lutheran Theological Southern Seminary, M.Div. 1974; Clinical Pastoral Education certificate from South Carolina State Mental Hospital; Drew University, D.Min. 1980.

Ordination: May 31, 1974 by North Carolina Synod.

Calls: Mission Developer, St. Timothy, Havelock, one summer. Zion, Deerfield Beach, Fla., 1974-76; Our Saviour, Southern Pines, 1976-81. Vice Pastor at various congregations. Transferred to Southeast Synod in 1981.

Other: Operational Committee on Evangelism, North Carolina Synod, 1977. While in Florida: Secretary/Treasurer of Ministerial Association; Deerfield Beach Human Services Council. Resigned in October 1985.

DREHER, DANIEL ISAIAH

Date/Place of Birth: October 10, 1824; Lexington District, S.C.
Parents: Jeremiah Dreher and Lydia Dreher.
First Spouse/Marriage Date: Mildred C. (Kerr) Dreher; died November 10, 1859.
Child of First Marriage: Sally.
Second Spouse/Marriage Date: Martha Ann K. (Heilig) Dreher; January 3, 1866 in Rowan County, N.C.; died May 8, 1913.
Children of Second Marriage: Augustus Heilig, Jeremiah H., Mary Lydia.
Education: Professor, White's Academy, Lexington, S.C.; Lutheran Theological Southern Seminary, 1853; North Carolina College, D.D..
License/Ordination: Licensed 1853 by South Carolina Synod and ordained by North Carolina Synod in 1856.
Calls: Liberty Hill, S.C., church later moved to Jalapa, S.C., and named St. James; St. James, Concord, 1854-69; Union, Rowan County, 1867.
Other: Taught private school at Newberry, S.C., 1853; Principal and Professor, Mt. Pleasant Female Seminary, Mt. Pleasant, 1870-71. Member, first Board, North Carolina College, 1859; Board, North Carolina College, 1869. Secretary, North Carolina Synod, 1857-59, 1860-61; President, 1862-63. Delegate Chair to General Synod South Convention, 1867, 1868. Corresponding Secretary of North Carolina Synod, 1868, 1869.
Date of Death/Burial Location: February 18, 1871; Organ Church, Rowan County, N.C.

DREHER, GODFREY

Date/Place of Birth: December 4, 1789; Irmo, Lexington District, S.C.
Parents: John Dreher and Ann (Hollinshed) Dreher.
First Spouse: Anna E. (Sailor) Dreher.
Second Spouse: Mary Catherine (Miller) Dreher, daughter of the Reverend Robert J. Miller, one of organizers of North Carolina Synod in 1803.
Children of Second Marriage: Caroline, Margaret Ann, Henrietta (married the Reverend Daniel Efird), Mary, John Robert, Luther, Solomon, Osman, Elisha.
Third Spouse: Mrs. Peggy (Leaphart) Dreher.
Child of Third Marriage: John Walter.
Education: Self-educated.
License/Ordination: Licensed 1810 in Organ Church, Rowan County, by North Carolina Synod, and ordained 1812 in Bethel Church, White Rock, S.C., by a special committee of North Carolina Synod, as the Lutheran churches in South Carolina, were members of North Carolina Synod until 1824 when South Carolina Synod was organized.
Calls: Fourteen churches served (1810 to about 1852) within horseback riding range of his home in Lexington District, S.C. Co-pastor with other pioneer Lutheran ministers. In South Carolina: St. Peter, Lexington, 1810, 1837-51; St. Peter, Piney Woods, 1833-52; St. Michael, Irmo, 1814-?; Bethlehem, Irmo, 1810, ?-1851; Sandy Run, Swansea, 1824-26; St. Paul, Gilbert, 1837-51; Mt. Calvary, Johnston, 1833; Bethlehem, Leesville, 1829-40; Nazareth, Lexington, 1827-28; Zion, his home church, near Lexington, 1810- 54; St. John, Pomaria, about 1850-?; Cedar Grove, Leesville, 1852-54; St. John, Lexington, about 1831?.
Other: Like other pioneer ministers served for freewill offerings, living chiefly from his farm. Leading pastor among six who organized South Carolina Synod in 1824; elected first

President in 1824 and Treasurer 1825-34. Active in forming the Lexington Sunday School Union and served on the board of directors that founded a seminary in 1830 and led a successful campaign to locate the seminary near his congregations in Lexington. He ended his relationship with the South Carolina Synod in 1837, becoming "an independent Lutheran pastor" without synodical affiliation. In 1852 the congregations he had served joined the Tennessee Synod, but he did not, preferring to remain"independent." Paralysis ended his active ministry in 1854. When the Tennessee Synod met in South Carolina in 1858, it named Dreher "an honorary member." (See p. 211, *Encyclopedia of Religion in the South*. 1984, by Hugh George Anderson, Samuel S. Hill, ed., Macon: Mercer University Press.)
Date of Death/Burial Location: July 28, 1875; St. Michael Church, Irmo, S.C.

DREHER, JOHN

License: Licensed 1815 by North Carolina Synod, but not subsequently ordained.
Calls: No record available of any churches that he served in North Carolina or in South Carolina.
Date of Death/Burial Location: 1847; Lexington District, S.C.

DRESSLER, HUGO LUTHER

Date/Place of Birth: September 1, 1891; Vernon Mills, N.Y.
Parents: The Reverend William George Dressler and Mary K. (Hoke) Dressler.
Spouse/Marriage Date: Miriam (Deaton) Dressler, daughter of the Reverend W. A. Deaton; September 26, 1918 in Hickory, N.C.; died September 26, 1981.
Child: Dorothy Miriam.
Education: Wittenberg University, A.B. 1913; Chicago Seminary, B.D. 1918.
Ordination: 1918 by Ohio Synod.
Calls: In Ohio and Pennsylvania, 1918-21; Atonement, Buffalo, N.Y., 1921-47. In North Carolina: Holy Trinity, Hickory, 1947-52.
Other: Prominent in work of New York Synod. Taught sixteen years in leadership training school at Holy Trinity, Buffalo, N.Y. Member, Board of Parish Education, United Lutheran Church in America, sometime Vice President, Chair of Committee on Field Work, and Board Representative to Constituting Convention of National Council of Churches of Christ, 1950. Contributor of articles and book reviews to *The Lutheran Quarterly, Ecclesia Plantanda,* and other periodicals. Board, Wagner College.
Date of Death/Burial Location: November 10, 1952; Oakwood Cemetery, Hickory, N.C.

DREWS, ROGER PHILLIP

Date/Place of Birth: January 23, 1937; Summit County, Ohio.
Parents: Edwin Drews and Ruth (Heise) Drews.
Spouse/Marriage Date: Patricia Ann (Grasse) Drews; January 23, 1960.
Children: Daniel Scott, Joel David, Mark Roger, Jonathan Phillip, Laural Ruth, Linda Ruth, Jennifer Marie.
Education: Northwestern University, B.A. 1960; Wisconsin Lutheran Seminary, B. Th. 1965; Luther Northwestern, Historical Theology, 1972; Lutheran Theological Southern Seminary, 1991.
Ordination: July 18, 1965 by WELS Synod.

Calls: Good Shepherd, Burnsville, Minn., 1965-72; St. John, Oak Creek, Wis., 1972-83; St. John, Woodbury, Minn., 1984-85; Mt. Moriah, China Grove, 1991-93. Transferred to Indiana-Kentucky Synod to Christ, Madisonville, Ky., 1993-.

DRUM, HAROLD A.

Date of Birth: July 9, 1933.
Spouse: Janet Drum.
Children: Adrienne, Margaret.
Education: Lenoir-Rhyne, B.A. 1955; Evangelical Lutheran Seminary, Columbus, Ohio, M.Div. 1959.
Ordination: June 7, 1959 by American Lutheran Church.
Calls: St. Mark, Ridge, Long Island, N.Y., 1959-64; established Galilee, Pasadena, Md., 1964-70; Stewart Avenue, Pittsburgh, Pa., 1970-80; Greenville, S.C., 1980-82; Mt. Hope, Pontiac, Mich., 1982-98; Interim, Mt. Zion, Conover.

DRUM, MAURY

Date/Place of Birth: June 7, 1928; Conover, N.C.
Spouse/Marriage Date: Mary (Richardson) Drum; 1954.
Education: Lenoir-Rhyne College, B.A. 1949; Evangelical Lutheran Theological Seminary, Columbus, Ohio, B.Th., 1953, New York Theological Seminary, M.S.T. 1972.
Ordination: 1953.
Calls: Grace, Scarsdale, N.Y., 1953-58; Christ, Greensboro, 1958-68; Our Savior's, Glen Head, N.Y., 1968- 79. Retired.
Other: Staff, Eastern District, American Lutheran Church, 1979-

DUKE, DANIEL WHITE

Date/Place of Birth: April 27, 1961; Charlotte, N.C.
Parents: Dr. Robert L. Duke and Jo Ann (Williams) Duke.
Education: Belmont Abbey College, B.A. 1983; Gettysburg Seminary, M.Div. 1991.
Ordination: August 9, 1992 by North Carolina Synod.
Calls: St. Enoch, Kannapolis, 1992-99; Grace, New Orleans, La., 1999-.

DUKE, JAMES M., III

Date/Place of Birth: September 7, 1953;
Spouse: Glenda (Mitchell) Duke.
Child: Julie.
Education: Undergraduate work at University of Tennessee, Belmont College, and Carson Newman College in Psychology. Scarritt College, B.A. Religion 1978, M.A. Church and Community 1979; Boston University School of Theology, M.Div. *magna cum laude* 1981 candidate in Doctor of Ministry degree program, Pastoral Counseling. Extended unit of basic Clinical Pastoral Education through Massachusetts General Hospital Department of Pastoral Care, 1981.
Ordination: United Methodist Church, Deacon's Orders, June 1981; Elder's Orders, June 1983. Received from United Methodist Church to Southeastern Synod, Evangelical Lutheran Church in America, 1988.

Calls: St. Stephen United Methodist Church, Marblehead, Maine, 1980-81; Port Royal United Methodist Church, Clarksville, Ind., 1981-84; United Methodist Urban Ministry, Clarksville, Ind., 1984-86; Wesley Foundation at Austin Peay State University, Campus Minister, 1984-88; Peace Lutheran, Memphis, Tenn., 1988-91. Grace, Raleigh, 1991-.

Other: Member of Clarksville Area Ministerial Association, Vice President and Treasurer; designed and led Spiritual Formation Retreats for clergy in the Middle Tennessee area; Committee Member, Clarksville District Leadership Development Team; Member and Treasurer East Montgomery Civitan Club; Task Force Member - Vollintine-Evergreen Community Association Children's Project; First Vice President, Lutheran Council of Greater Memphis; Evangelical Lutheran Church in America Liaison Person with Shelby County Inter-Faith Association; lecturer and panelist in various discussion groups. Clarksville District Council on Ministries, District Camping Coordinator, Urban Ministries representative, Higher Education Chair; First Chair, Clarksville District Urban Ministries Task Force; first Executive Director, United Methodist Urban Ministries-Clarksville District.

DUKES, JAMES EDWARD, JR.

Date/Place of Birth: February 18, 1938; Columbia, S.C.
Parents: James Edward Dukes, Sr. and Avis (Bolen) Dukes.
Spouse/Marriage Date: Gladys Irene (Canada) Dukes; December 21, 1968 in Nashville, Tenn.
Children: Barbara Diane, Marjorie Christina.
Education: University of Florida, B.A.E. 1961; Candler-Emory University, B.D. 1965; Lutheran Theological Southern Seminary, Certificate, 1975; University of South Carolina, M.A. 1971.
Ordination: June 1, 1975 by South Carolina Synod.
Calls: New Bethel, Richfield, 1975-78; St. Mark, Lumberton, 1978-83; Christus Victor, Bonita Springs, Fla., 1983-.

DuMOND, JAMES X.

Date/Place of Birth: August 7, 1957; Miami, Fla.
Parents: Joseph DuMond and Patricia DuMond.
Spouse/Marriage Date: Alice (Stroberg) DuMond; August 8, 1981.
Children: Jennifer, Christine.
Education: Southern Connecticut State College, B.S. Economics 1979; Lutheran Theological Southern Seminary, M.Div. 1998.
Ordination: August 9, 1998 by North Carolina Synod.
Calls: Redeemer, Gastonia, 1998-.

DUNCAN, BILL JUNIOR

Date/Place of Birth: February 9, 1956; Hickory, N.C.
Parents: Billy Leroy Duncan and Frances (Icard) Duncan.
Spouse/Marriage Date: Karen Freda (Bentley) Duncan; June 18, 1983 in Miami, Fla.
Education: Newberry College, B.A., 1979; Lutheran Theological Southern Seminary, M.Div. 1983.
Ordination: May 19, 1983 by North Carolina Synod.

Calls: St. Stephen, Gold Hill, 1983-87; Emmanuel, High Point, 1987-89; Vice Pastor at various congregations. Transferred to Indiana-Kentucky Synod, 1990.
Other: Executive Board, North Carolina Lutheran Men, 1983-90; President, Cabarrus-Stanly Ministerial Association, 1984-86. Resigned 1994.

DUNCAN, CHARLES RICHARD

Date/Place of Birth: October 6, 1941; Hickory, N.C.
Parents: Willard L. Duncan and Mary Ellen (Isenhour) Duncan.
Spouse/Marriage Date: Charlotte Ann (Bridges) Duncan; June 9, 1963.
Child: Richard David.
Education: Lenoir-Rhyne, A.B. Sociology, 1964; Lutheran Theological Southern Seminary, M.Div. 1968; Central Michigan University, M.A. Management, 1977; Duke University, Th.M. Ethics, 1983.
Ordination: June 9, 1968 by North Carolina Synod.
Calls: Redeemer, Pearisburg, Va., 1968-70; Holy Trinity, Charlotte, 1970-74; Vice Pastor at various congregations; U.S. Navy Chaplain Corps, 1974- with stations in Japan, Florida, Iceland, Camp Lejeune, Duke University, Virginia. Chief of Chaplains Office, Washington, D.C. 1991-94; Fleet Chaplain, U.S. Naval Forces, Europe, London, United Kingdom, 1994-.
Other: Legion of Merit Award, Meritorious Service Medal, Navy/Marine Corps Commendation Medals (3).

DUNCAN, JOHN WALTON, JR.

Date/Place of Birth: March 1, 1953; Charlotte, N.C.
Parents: John Walton Duncan, Sr. and Mary Frances L. Duncan.
Spouse/Marriage Date: Cynthia (Oates) Duncan; June 8, 1974.
Children: Christopher John, Lori Denise, Megan Lee.
Education: North Carolina State University, B.S. 1975; Clemson University, M.B.A. 1984; Lutheran Theological Southern Seminary, M.Div. 1996.
Ordination: August 17, 1996 by North Carolina Synod.
Calls: Holy Cross, Lincolnton, 1996-.

DUNCAN, SILAS STEVEN, JR.

Date/Place of Birth: April 4, 1943; Hendersonville, N.C.
Parents: Silas Steven Duncan, Sr. and Agnes (Specht) Duncan.
Spouse: Hazel Eileen (Mackie) Duncan; August 13, 1966.
Child: Stephanie Heather.
Education: Lenoir-Rhyne, A.B. 1965; Lutheran Theological Southern Seminary, M.Div. 1969; graduate work at Memphis Institute of Medicine and Religion, C.P.C., 1970; Pastoral Counseling and Consultation Center of Greater Washington, two-year clinical studies, 1977; North Carolina Baptist Hospital, Life Enrichment Center of Raleigh, two-year Pastoral Counseling Residence, 1980; Union Seminary, Va., D.Min. 1985.
Ordination: July 1971 by North Carolina Synod.
Calls: Our Saviour, Warrenton, Va., 1971-78; Vice Pastor at various congregations; Director, Pastoral Care and Counseling Center of Wilkes, Inc., 1985-.

DUNN, KARL UMBARGER
Date/Place of Birth: August 8, 1927; Bland, Va.
Parents: Guy Brown Dunn and Mary Letitia (Umbarger) Dunn.
Spouse/Marriage Date: Sadie Rae (Rawl) Dunn; June 9, 1954 in Columbia, S.C.
Children: Deborah Rae, Christine Elizabeth, Mary Letitia, Karla Lynn.
Education: Newberry College, A.B. 1951; Lutheran Theological Southern Seminary, B.D. 1954.
Ordination: May 31, 1954 by Virginia Synod.
Calls: Mt. Zion-New Bethel Richfield, 1954-57; Ebenezer, Rowan County, 1957-1965; Bethphage, Lincoln County, 1965-73; St. Stephen, Hickory, 1973-91. Vice Pastor at various congregations.
Other: Stewardship Committee, 1969-73; Lutheran World Relief, 1965-70; Pastors' Support Committee, 1967-71. Retired November 3, 1991.

DUTTON, WADE HAMPTON
Date/Place of Birth: February 24, 1890; Rural Retreat, Va.
Parents: The Reverend William Addison Dutton and Mary Louisa (Crawford) Dutton.
Spouse/Marriage Date: Ida Mae (Riser) Dutton; January 2, 1919 in Saluda County, S.C.
Children: Mary Crawford, Virginia C., Sarah Esther, Rebekah, Paul Riser, John Addison, Naomi Louise, Mark Daniel.
Education: Mount Pleasant Collegiate Institute, 1912, Newberry College, A.B. 1914; Lutheran Theological Southern Seminary, 1917.
Ordination: 1917 by South Carolina Synod.
Calls: In Newberry, S.C., 1917-27. In North Carolina: St. Stephen-Mt. Olive, Cabarrus County, 1927-38; Mt. Hermon-Sharon-St. Paul, Iredell County, 1938-43; St. Martin, Cabarrus County; St. Martin, Stanly County, 1943-47; Antioch-Philadelphia, Gaston County, 1947-53; again, Mt. Hermon, Iredell County, 1953-58.
Other: Member and Chair, Examining Committee. Author of treatise, *Five Revelations of the Cross*. Retired February 1958.
Date of Death/Burial Location: May 7, 1958; Mt. Hermon Church, Iredell County, N.C.

DUTTON, WILLIAM ADDISON
Date/Place of Birth: April 16, 1859; near Rural Retreat, Va.
Parents: William Reece Dutton and Saphronia (Wolf) Dutton. A grandson is Lutheran pastor, the Reverend F. C. Jones, Jr,, M.D., Atlanta, Ga.
First Spouse/Marriage Date: Mary Louisa (Crawford) Dutton; 1886/87, in Mississippi; died 1892.
Children of First Marriage: Vance Orton, the Reverend Wade Hampton, Mary Blake.
Second Spouse/Marriage Date: Lena Brown (Umberger) Dutton; September 15 1892.
Children of Second Marriage: Carrie Fay (died in infancy), Lena May, Roy Milton, Lex Byron, Max Carlile, Banks Addison.
Education: No formal education, except short time in medical school, Baltimore, Md.

Studied theology privately.

License/Ordination: Licensed 1893 and ordained 1897 by Southwest Virginia Synod.

Calls: In Nebraska, 1895; Price's Fork, Va., 1896-1900. In North Carolina: St. Stephen-Mt. Olive, Cabarrus County, 1900-07; New Bethel-Mt. Zion-Luther's, Richfield, 1907-12. In South Carolina, 1912-22.

Date of Death/Burial Location: August 15, 1926; Ebenezer Church, Columbia, S.C.

EARP, JOHN CURTIS

Date/Place of Birth: September 3, 1949; Danville, Pa.

Parents: Harry E. Earp and Paulyne S. Earp.

Spouse/Marriage Date: Sally (Fox) Earp; November 2, 1985.

Education: University of South Florida, Lenoir-Rhyne, B.A. 1971; Lutheran Theological Southern Seminary, M.Div., 1976.

Ordination: June 20, 1976 by Florida Synod.

Calls: Prince of Peace, Fernandina Beach, Fla., 1976-80; St. Stephen, Pinellas Park, Fla., 1983-87; St. James, Fayetteville, 1987-92; Macedonia, Burlington, 1992-98. Vice Pastor at various congregations.

EASLEY, CHARLES WARD, SR.

Date/Place of Birth: May 25, 1931; Georgetown, S.C.

Parents: Lefflette Teed Easley and Louise (Colbert) Easley.

Spouse/Marriage Date: Emma Lou (Bossart) Easley from Arona, Pa.; June 29, 1951 at Columbia, S.C.

Children: Charles Ward, Jr., David Harry (died at age 6), Irene Louise Moye, William Teed, Penelope Ruth Burton.

Education: Newberry College, B.S. 1953, D.D. 1986; Lutheran Theological Southern Seminary, B.D. 1956.

Ordination: June 10, 1956 by South Carolina Synod.

Calls: Our Saviour, Albany, Ga., 1956-58; St. Peter, Lexington County, S.C., 1958-61. In North Carolina: Center Grove, Kannapolis, 1961-64; St. Matthew, Kings Mountain, 1964-72; First, Albemarle, 1972-75. Vice Pastor at various congregations. Mt. Tabor, West Columbia, S.C., 1975-86; St. Mark, Roanoke, Va., 1986-93; Virginia Lutheran Homes, 1993. Retired to Lexington, S.C.

Other: Chair, Publications and Publicity, 1962-66; Examining Committee, 1968-70; Secretary, American Missions Committee, 1968-70; Church Vocations Committee, 1971-76.

EASTERLY, GEORGE

Date/Place of Birth: December 20, 1781; Shenandoah County, Va.

Parents: George Easterly and Ann Maria (Neas) Easterly.

Spouse/Marriage Date: Lydia (Harpine) Easterly; March 3, 1804 in Shenandoah County, Va.

Children: Rachael, Abraham, Elizabeth, Jonathan, Philip H., Magdalin, Ambrose G., Reuben M., Rufus.

Education: Henkel and Bell Seminary, Greene County, Tenn.

License/Ordination: Licensed 1820, by Tennessee Synod at first regular session of Synod in Solomon Church, Greene County, Tenn. Ordained 1822 by Tennessee Synod.

Calls: In North Carolina: supplied with others, Mt. Moriah, Rowan County, 1831 and Trinity, Vale; St. Paul, Newton (Startown) 1832; Bethel-Philadelphia, Gaston County, 1832. In East Tennessee: 1820-1830, 1833-1850.

Other: In 1848 disagreeing with positions of Tennessee Synod, helped in the effort to organize "The Reorganized Evangelical Lutheran Tennessee Synod" (1848-84), which led to removal of his name from roll of the Tennessee Synod, October 20, 1849.

Date of Death/Burial Location: March 29, 1850; St. James Church, Greene County, Tenn.

EASTES, DAVID RUSSELL

Date/Place of Birth: June 27, 1947; Three Rivers, Mich.

Parents: Earl Glenn Eastes and Ethelyn Grace Eastes.

Spouse/Marriage Date: Linda Joy (Connors) Eastes; May 23, 1981 in Richmond, Va.

Child: Dawn Renee Granger.

Education: Brevard Community College, A.A. 1968; University of South Florida, B.A. 1970; Lutheran Theological Southern Seminary, M.Div. 1974.

Ordination: June 13, 1970 by Florida Synod.

Calls: St. John, Nappanee, Ind., 1974-78; Trinity, Logansport, Ind., 1978-80; St. Andrew, New Bern, 1982- 96; Director of Pastoral Care, Randolph Hospital, Asheboro, 1998. Vice Pastor at various congregations.

Other: Dean and Secretary of Coastal Conference, North Carolina Synod; Call Process Revision Committee; Ecumenical Affairs Committee; Lutheran-Roman Catholic Covenant Committee.

EBENER, WILLIAM CLARK

Date/Place of Birth: October 23, 1944; Greenville, S.C.

Parents: Joseph Bret Ebener and Faye (Clark) Ebener.

Spouse/Marriage Date: Margaret (Busbee) Ebener; April 2, 1967.

Children: Kenneth William, Karen Margaret Young.

Education: Newberry College, A.B. 1966; Lutheran Theological Southern Seminary, M.Div. 1970; graduate work at University of South Carolina, 1989-91.

Ordination: June 1, 1970 by South Carolina Synod.

Calls: St. Paul's, Mt. Pleasant, S.C., 1971-74; Associate Pastor, St. Mark's, Charlotte, 1974-78; Faith, Batesburg, S.C., 1978-81; Redeemer, Atlanta, Ga., 1981-84; Transfiguration, Cayce, S.C., 1984-91; Union, Leesville, S.C., 1993-.

Other: Director of Lexington County Aging Program, South Carolina, 1991-96.

EBERT, FRANK EDWARD, JR.

Date/Place of Birth: July 30, 1929; Battle Creek, Mich.

Parents: Frank Edward Ebert, Sr. and June M. (Thomas) Siddell.

Spouse/Marriage Date: Lois C. (Adrain) Ebert; February 15, 1956 in Valdosta, Ga.

Children: Terri Ann Woodall, Paul Thomas.

Education: University of South Florida, B.A. 1969; Lutheran Theological Southern Seminary, M.Div. 1972.

Ordination: May 28, 1962 by Florida Synod.

Calls: Trinity, Rocky Mount, 1972-74; St. Timothy, Havelock, 1974-94. Vice Pastor at various congregations.
Other: Synodical Evangelism Committee; Synod Council. Retired August 21, 1994 in Havelock, N.C.

ECK, DAVID WILSON

Date/Place of Birth: April 7, 1962; Pittsburgh, Pa.
Parents: Herbert Walter Eck and Linda Joan (Butera) Eck.
Education: University of Pittsburgh, B.S. Chemistry 1984; Gettysburg Seminary, M.Div., 1988.
Ordination: July 24, 1988 by Southwest Pennsylvania Synod.
Calls: Mt. Zion, Conover, 1988-93; Abiding Savior, Asheville, 1993-.
Other: Synod Council, 1995-; Worship and Music Committee, 1993-95; AIDS Task Force, 1992; Editorial Board, Soli Deo Gloria, 1990-; Songwriter/Performing Artist with five cassettes of original music and one publishing project, *Guitar Hymns; Who's Who in Religion, 1992-93; Who's Who in the South and Southwest, 1995-96; Who's Who in the World, 1996.*

ECKARD, GLENN STINE

Date/Place of Birth: March 30, 1907; Hickory, N.C.
Parents: Jefferson Polycarp Eckard and Lyda Ola (Fry) Eckard.
Spouse/Marriage Date: Ruby Pearl (Sandel) Eckard; January 31, 1933 in Chapin, S.C.
Children: Seth Lyman, Glenn Jerome, Elaine Winona.
Education: Lenoir-Rhyne, A.B. 1928; Lutheran Theological Southern Seminary, B.D. 1931.
Ordination: 1931 by South Carolina Synod.
Calls: In South Carolina, 1931-42. U.S. Navy Chaplain 1942-1953 retiring as Lieutenant Commander. Christ Mission, Norwich, N.Y., 1946; Alamance, Alamance, 1953-63; Good Shepherd, Goldsboro, 1963-67; Advent, Spindale, 1967-73. Vice Pastor at various congregations. Retired April 30, 1973 and transferred to South Carolina Synod.
Date of Death/Burial Location: April 11, 1976; St. Stephen, Hickory, N.C.

ECKARD, RALPH EDGAR

Date/Place of Birth: June 22, 1927; Alexander County, N.C.
Parents: Frederick Lee Eckard and Vertie Veronica (Price) Eckard.
Spouse/Marriage Date: Betty Jayne (Froehlich) Eckard; June 10, 1950 in Chicago, Ill.
Children: Nancy Ellen Verderosa, Ruth Ann Anderson, Linda Jane.
Education: Lenoir-Rhyne, A.B. 1947, D.D., 1974; Chicago Seminary, B.D. 1950.
Ordination: June 25, 1950 by North Carolina Synod.
Calls: In Iowa, 1950-56. Assistant Pastor, St. John, Council Bluffs, Iowa, 1950-51; First,

Newton, Iowa, 1951-56; Secretary, Iowa Synod, 1953-55, Vice President, 1953-56. Trinity, Kirkwood, Mo., 1956-60; Wilmette, Wilmette, Ill., 1960-61; Secretary for Stewardship, Illinois Synod, 1961-62; Administrative Assistant to President Franklin Clark Fry, President Robert James Marshall and President-Bishop James Robert Crumley, Jr., 1962-89, over a period of 26 years and 8 months, covering the last 2fi months of the United Lutheran Church in America, the 25 years of the Lutheran Church in America, and 1 1/2 years of the Evangelical Lutheran Church in America. Retired June 25, 1989 to Hickory, N.C. Vice Pastor at St. Matthew, Granite Falls, 1992.
Other: Editor, *The Gleaner;* Board Member and Director, Chicago Seminary; President, Southern Conference, Illinois Synod; Executive Board, Illinois Synod.

ECKERT, RUSSELL ADOLPH
Date/Place of Birth: May 3, 1927; Racine, Wis.
Parents: Ted Eckert and Flora (Frank) Eckert.
Spouse/Marriage Date: Barbara (Stewart) Eckert; March 24, 1956 in Portsmouth, Va.
Children: Scott, Robin, Russell.
Education: Dana College, B.A. 1950; Northwestern Seminary, B.D. 1954; graduate work at University of Minnesota, 1957.
Ordination: 1956 by Wartburg Synod.
Calls: U.S. Army Chaplain, 1956-59; Trinity, Roanoke, Va., 1960-66; Christ, Lewisburg, Pa., 1966-67; Bethel-Mt. Zion, Houtzdale-Glasgow, Pa., 1967-69; Messiah-St. John, Bedford-Cessna, Pa., 1971-73; Good Shepherd, Hickory, 1973-82. Ebenezer, Catawba County, 1985-89.
Other: Retired November 1, 1989.

EDSELL, ROBERT WILLIAM, SR.
Date/Place of Birth: May 16, 1932; Concord, N.C.
Parents: Roy Lee Edsell and Blanche (Cress) Edsell.
Spouse/Marriage Date: Martha Rose (Miller) Edsell; June 25, 1958 in Mt. Pleasant, N.C.
Children: Robert William, Jr., Maria Elizabeth Lambert, (twins) Amy Louise Poteat and Anna Linnett Willis.
Education: Lenoir-Rhyne, A.B. 1955; Lutheran Theological Southern Seminary, B.D. 1958.
Ordination: June 8, 1958 by North Carolina Synod.
Calls: Peace, Gibsonville, 1958-60; Mission Developer/Pastor, Messiah, Burlington, 1960-68; Our Father, Greensboro, 1968-71; St. Mark's, Mooresville, 1971-77; Our Saviour, Dallas, 1978-80; Interim Pastor, Mt. Gilead, Mt. Pleasant, 1982-87; Interim Pastor, Amity, Cleveland, 1987-95.
Other: Retired 1995 in Mooresville, N.C., Youth Committee, Evangelism Committee, American Missions Committee.

EDWARDS, TED ELKIN
Date/Place of Birth: October 22, 1933; Pickens County, S.C.
Parents: Lowe Kline Edwards and Alice Elizabeth (West) Edwards.
Spouse/Marriage Date: Beverly Ann (Smeltz) Edwards; June 24, 1967.

Children: David Elkin, Michael Elkin, Stephen Elkin.

Education: Lenoir-Rhyne, A.B. 1956; Lutheran Theological Southern Seminary, M.Div. 1959; McCormick Theological Seminary, D.Min. 1982.

Ordination: June 7, 1959 by North Carolina Synod.

Calls: St. Timothy, Norfolk, Va., 1959-63; Chaplain, U.S. Navy, 1963-70; Messiah, Monroe, La., 1970-73; St. Stephen, Pinellas Park, Fla., 1973-79; Staff Chaplain, Veterans Administration Medical Center, Canandaigua, N.Y., 1980-88; Chief, Chaplain Service, Veterans Administration Medical Center, Beckley, W.Va., 1988-.

Other: Retired as Captain Chaplain Corps, U.S. Naval Reserve with 28 years of service. Awarded Navy Commendation Medal with Gold Star in lieu of second award. Distinguished Service Award by Military Chaplains' Association, 1995. Adjunct Clinical Lecturer in Pastoral Care, West Virginia School of Osteopathic Medicine, Lewisburg, W.Va.; Adjunct Faculty, The College of West Virginia, Beckley, W.Va., teaching Introduction to Philosophy and Medical Ethics. Navy Armed Forces Expeditionary Medal for service in South Viet Nam.

EFIRD, ADAM

Date/Place of Birth: April 20, 1821; Stanly (then a part of Montgomery) County, N.C.

Parents: Martin Efird and Mary (Coble) Efird. A younger brother was the Reverend Daniel Efird.

Spouse/Marriage Date: Catharine Louise (Miller) Efird, August 12, 1851 in Rowan County, N.C.

Children: The Reverend Jacob Killian, whose second wife was Lula J. (Julian) Efird, daughter of the Reverend W. A. Julian, Albert Erastus, Jesse Windle (died in infancy), Abel Brown, Jason Adam, Francis Bruner, Garriefelia (mother of the Reverend Cecil Clarendon Hine).

License/Ordination: Licensed 1847 and ordained 1850 by Tennessee Synod.

Calls: All Tennessee Synod: St. Martin, Stanly County, 1848-50; Beck's-Pilgrim, Davidson County, 1849-54; Mt. Moriah, Rowan County, 1851-52; and Sharon, Iredell County, with his brother Daniel between 1846 and 1850. In Lexington County, S.C., 1854-70: Zion; organized Emmanuel, near Lexington; Cedar Grove, Leesville; St. Paul, Gilbert; and one other.

Other: Treasurer, Tennessee Synod, 1852; President, 1859, 1861, 1866. Committee to Examine and Report on the Book of Concord, 1851, published by Henkel Press. Served two years in South Carolina Legislature during War Between the States; and as probate judge for Lexington County, 1864-70. Collected considerable sums of money to aid sick and wounded soldiers of Confederate Army. As many early pastors, had to depend on farming and business for support, owning a large plantation, slaves, mansion house, and fine horses, also operating a rice mill, grist mill, and general store. Sherman's Army plundered his property but did not burn the home. Mrs. Efird thought it was because she held her infant son Bruner in her arms.

Date of Death/Burial Location: September 13, 1870; Zion Church, Lexington County, S.C.

EFIRD, DANIEL
Date/Place of Birth: November 10, 1824; present day Stanly County, N.C. formerly Montgomery County
Parents: Martin Efird and Mary (Coble) Efird. An older brother was the Reverend Adam Efird.
Spouse/Marriage Date: Henrietta M. (Dreher) Efird, youngest daughter of the Reverend Godfrey Dreher; July 1, 1852 in Lexington County, S.C.
Children: Alice M., Mary Jane, Cyprian M., D. Franklin, Emilie, Belle; of the daughters only the first lived beyond age nine; the two sons were prominent lay leaders in South Carolina Synod.
Education: Studied privately and taught school; studied theology under the Reverends P. C. Henkel and Timothy Moser.
License/Ordination: Licensed 1850 and ordained 1852 by Tennessee Synod.
Calls: Sharon, Iredell County, 1850-51; St. Martin, Stanly County, 1850-51. His son C. M. says, "He regularly supplied Flat Rock, Stanly County; Morning Star, Mecklenburg County; Immanuel, Luther's, and Union in Rowan County, and Bethlehem, Lancaster County, S.C." In 1851 after a preaching journey to South Carolina, moved there to assist the Reverend Godfrey Dreher in serving churches in Lexington County, S.C., 1851-54; and later was associated with brother, the Reverend Adam Efird, and others to 1882 serving St. John, Pomaria; Bethlehem, near Irmo; St. Jacob and St. Peter, near Chapin; Zion and Emmanuel, near Lexington; St. Paul, Gilbert; and Cedar Grove, near Leesville. Churches served by Pastors Dreher and Efird, on petition, were received into Tennessee Synod at Salem Church, Lincoln County, 1852. His entire ministry after 1851 was spent in South Carolina.
Other: Corresponding Secretary and Examining Committee, Tennessee Synod, 1867; Treasurer, Tennessee Synod, 1877. Promoted Pine Ridge Academy, Lexington County, S.C.
Date of Death/Burial Location: June 1, 1891; St. Michael Church, near Irmo, S.C.

EFIRD, FRANK KIMBALL, SR.
Date/Place of Birth: November 1, 1916; Wadesboro, N.C.
Parents: Frank Martin Efird and Beulah Pauline (Kimball) Efird. A great-grandson of the Reverend Whitson Kimball.
Spouse/Marriage Date: Sybil Eloise (Trexler) Efird; November 14, 1942 in Concord, N.C.
Children: Frank Kimball, Jr., Sybil Jane Hvizdak.
Education: Lenoir-Rhyne, A.B. 1938, D.D. 1957; Lutheran Theological Southern Seminary, M.Div. 1941.
Ordination: May 1941 by North Carolina Synod.
Calls: St. Luke-Morning Star, Monroe, 1941-43; organized and supplied St. Paul, Hamlet, 1941-42; Holy Trinity, Wytheville, Va., 1943-46; Christ, Roanoke, Va., 1946-53; St. John, Salisbury, 1953-63, Pastor Emeritus, 1987-99; Luther Memorial, Madison, Wis., 1963-73; Holy Trinity, Akron, Ohio, 1973-83.
Other: Editor, *The Virginia Lutheran, 1948-53*. Virginia and North Carolina correspondent to *The Lutheran*, 1947-63. Member, 1953-63, and Vice Chair, 1960-63, Board, Lenoir-Rhyne; also, Chair, Capital Funds Directing Committee, 1955, 1963; United Lutheran Church in America Board of Parish Education, 1954-62; Chair, Joint Board Committee for new parish education curriculum, 1960-62. Board of Parish Education, Lutheran Church in

America, 1968-72.   Member, Board of Pensions, Lutheran Church in America, 1978-84. Member, Executive Council, Lutheran Church in America, 1962-68. Lutheran Church in America delegate to Lutheran World Federation Assembly, Helsinki, Finland, 1963. Counselor of United Lutheran Church in America at National Lutheran Council, and Member, Executive Committee, 1958-62. Preacher in England and Scotland 1961 in exchange program of National Council of Churches, U.S.A., and British Council of Churches. Author of *Meditations and Prayers,* delivered as Chaplain at United Lutheran Church in America 1960 and 1962 conventions; "Observe a Week of National Penitence," in *The National Lutheran,* June 1961; sermons in *The Christian Century* and *Pulpit.* Built and operated Lutheran Service Center for Camp Sutton for National Lutheran Council. In Wytheville: Chair of the County Red Cross Chapter. In Roanoke, Va.: Rotary; Board, Roanoke Area Council Boy Scouts and Red Cross; President, Children's Home Society; Roanoke J. C. "Man of the Year" in 1953. In Salisbury: President, Rotary Club; President, Rowan County Mental Health Association; President, Ministerial Association; helped organize United Fund. In Wisconsin: President, Madison West Rotary Club; President, Lutheran Social Services Wisconsin-Upper Michigan; President, Wisconsin Council of Churches, 1970-72; Madison Human Rights Commission, 1963-64; Board, Trustees, Carthage College, 1965-66; Wisconsin-Upper Michigan Synod Executive Board, 1966-72. In Ohio: Akron Rotary; Good Will Industries Board, 1978-82; Board, Hamma School of Theology, 1974-78. Author of national Sunday School lessons and devotional materials. Retired 1983 in Salisbury, N.C.
Date of Death/Burial Location: March 15, 1999; ashes interred at St. John Columbarium, Salisbury, N.C.

EFIRD, JACOB KILLIAN

Date/Place of Birth: June 28, 1852; Davidson County, N.C.
Parents: The Reverend Adam Efird and Catherine Louise (Miller) Efird.
Spouse/Marriage Date: Lula (Julian) Efird, daughter of the Reverend W. A. Julian; November 7, 1877 in Rowan County, N.C.
Children: Lester, Winford, Charles, at least a son and a daughter more (names unknown).
Education: North Carolina College; studied theology under his uncle, the Reverend Daniel Efird.
Ordination: 1878 by Tennessee Synod.
Calls: Of Tennessee Synod in South Carolina, 1878-92: St. Paul-Cedar Grove, Lexington County; St. Peter (Piney Woods)-St. John (White Church), Newberry County; organized and served Holy Trinity, Little Mountain, 1890-92. Transferred to Northwest Synod, serving in state of Washington, 1893. Transferred back to Tennessee Synod 1895 serving in Virginia and West Virginia. Member of South Carolina Synod 1901-05 serving again Holy Trinity, Little Mountain, which had changed synodical affiliation, and Macedonia, near Prosperity; also served Bethel Parish, Manassas, Va., 1905-12. Transferred 1912 to New York Synod.
Other: In retirement lived at Lowman Home, White Rock, S.C. Treasurer, Tennessee Synod, 1885-87.
Date of Death/Burial Location: 1924; St. Peter (Piney Woods) Church, near Chapin, S.C.

EHLERS, EDWIN LORD

Date/Place of Birth: July 7, 1929; Jersey City, N.J.
Parents: Julius A. Ehlers and Anna (Siefert) Ehlers.

Spouse/Marriage Date: Jane Louise (Bills) Ehlers; September 1, 1951 in Akron, Ohio.
Children: Linda S. Baver, The Reverend Stephen E., Mark J.
Education: Wittenberg University, B.A. 1951; Hamma School of Theology; M.Div. 1953; graduate work at Philadelphia Seminary, 1958-64, and Temple University, 1965-70; Wittenberg University, D.D. 1971; Upsala College, D.D. 1972.
Ordination: May 1953 by New Jersey Synod.
Calls: St. James, Phillipsburg, N.J., 1953-61; St. Matthew, Moorestown, N.J., 1961-68; Assistant to President of the New Jersey Synod (Lutheran Church in America), 1968-70; President, New Jersey Synod, 1970-78; Trinity, Worcester, Mass., 1978-81; Redeemer, McLean, Va., 1981-91; Interim Pastor at various congregations in North Carolina.
Other: Retired July 31, 1991 to Hendersonville, N.C. Boards of Upsala College, Philadelphia Seminary; Lutheran Church in America Board of Publication, Lutheran Church in America Commission on Women in Church and Society; Metro Washington, D.C. Synod Council. President of New Jersey Council of Churches; Chair of the Board of Washington Theological Consortium; President, Lutheran Outdoor Ministries of Virginia; President, Henderson County, N.C., Habitat for Humanity. *Who's Who in Religion,* first and second edition.

EHLERS, STEPHEN EDWIN

Date/Place of Birth: November 5, 1955; Easton, Pa.
Parents: The Reverend Edwin Lord Ehlers and Jane Louise (Bills) Ehlers.
Spouse/Marriage Date: Sheila Gwen (Good) Ehlers; August 6, 1977 in Hickory, N.C.
Children: Curtis Edwin (deceased), John Stephen, Kristin Elizabeth.
Education: Lenoir-Rhyne, B.A. 1978; Lutheran Theological Southern Seminary, M.Div. 1982.
Ordination: June 6, 1982 by North Carolina Synod.
Calls: Our Father, Greensboro, 1982-88; Vice Pastor at various congregations in North Carolina. St. James, Brunswick, Ga., 1988-.
Other: Youth Director at St. Andrew, Hickory. Clinical Pastoral Education Training at Memorial Hospital in Worcester, Mass. Lenoir-Rhyne Boatman Greek Award for community service. President of student body at Lutheran Theological Southern Seminary, 1981-82. Resigned from the ordained ministry December 1, 1995.

EIBLING, ROBERT ANTHONY

Date/Place of Birth: June 8, 1921; Somerset, Ohio.
Parents: The Reverend and Mrs. H. W. Eibling.
First Spouse/Marriage Date: Arlene (Rinck) Eibling; June 29, 1947.
Children of First Marriage: David E., Ruth E., Elizabeth A., Philip E.
Second Spouse/Marriage Date: Marion S. (Farb) Eibling; 1986.
Education: Capital University, Ohio, A.B. 1944; Evangelical Lutheran Theological Seminary, Columbus, Ohio, M.Div. 1947; Florida Atlantic University, Boca Raton, Fla., M.Ed. 1970.
Ordination: 1947 by American Lutheran Church.
Calls: St. John, New Bedford, Ohio, 1947-49; Miller's, Hickory, 1949-61; Abiding Savior, Fort Lauderdale, Fla., 1961-83.
Other: Retired 1983.

EICHORN, CHRISTIAN DAVID

Date/Place of Birth: July 5, 1959; Levittown, Pa.
Spouse/Marriage Date: Pamela L. (Barksdale) Eichorn; 1983.
Child: Jennifer Elizabeth.
Education: Philadelphia Seminary, M.Div. 1986; graduate work at Drew University.
Ordination: Ordained 1986 by Lutheran Church in America.
Calls: Associate Pastor, Macedonia, Burlington, 1986-88; Christ's, Stanley, 1988-93. Transferred to Northeastern Pennsylvania Synod.

EICHHORN, GARY WAYNE

Date/Place of Birth: March 16, 1953; Camden, N.J.
Parents: Whitmore T. Eichhorn and Phyllis J. (Bald) Eichhorn.
Spouse/Marriage Date: Deborah Anne (Meek) Eichhorn; June 25, 1977 in Cincinnati, Ohio.
Children: Stephen Joseph, Megan Caitlin.
Education: Hanover College, B.A. History 1975; Philadelphia Seminary; Lutheran Theological Southern Seminary, M.Div. 1979.
Ordination: June 3, 1979 by South Carolina Synod.
Calls: Christ, Charlotte, 1979-82; St. Stephen, Lenoir, 1982-89; Associate Pastor and Pastor, Our Savior, Dayton, Ohio, 1989-.

EISEMANN, RICHARD GEORGE

Date/Place of Birth: June 26, 1927; Mineola, N.Y.
Parents: Richard W. Eisemann and Beatrice Catherine Eisemann.
Spouse/Marriage Date: Shirley Nadinne (Hehl) Eisemann; June 14, 1953 in Pontiac, Mich.
Children: Chris Ann Melvin, Kim Lee, Lynn Marie, Richard Gregory, Jeffrey Paul.
Education: Wittenberg University, B.A. 1952; Hamma School of Theology, B.D. 1955; University of Southern California, M.Ed. 1970; Boston University, M.A. 1985.
Ordination: May 18, 1955 by Ohio Synod.
Calls: Pleasant Valley, Lucas Parish, Lucas, Ohio, 1955-59; Associate Pastor, Trinity, Ashland, Ohio, 1960-62; U.S. Air Force Chaplain, 1961-86; Interim Pastor at various congregations in North Carolina.
Other: Retired September 1, 1988 in Louisburg, N.C.

EITRHEIM, NORMAN DUANE

Date/Place of Birth: January 14, 1929; Baltic, S.D.
Parents: Daniel T. Eitrheim and Selma (Thompson) Eitrheim.
Spouse/Marriage Date: Clarice (Pederson) Eitrheim; August 23, 1952.
Children: Daniel, David, John, Marie.
Education: Augustana College, B.A. 1951, Doctor of Humane Letters, 1988; Luther Seminary, B.Th. 1956.
Ordination: June 3, 1956 by South Dakota District.
Calls: First English, Tyler, Minn., 1956-63; St. Philip, Fridley, Minn., 1963-76; Assistant to the President - Luther-Northwestern

Seminary, St. Paul, Minn., 1976-80; Bishop, South Dakota District, American Lutheran Church, Sioux Falls, S.D., 1981-87; Bishop, South Dakota Synod, Evangelical Lutheran Church in America, Sioux Falls, S.D., 1988-95; Interim Bishop, North Carolina Synod, Evangelical Lutheran Church in America, Salisbury, N.C., 1996-97.
Other: Retired August 1995 in Sioux Falls, S.D.

EKLUND, MARJORIE (LYONS)
Date/Place of Birth: June 5, 1929; Minneapolis, Minn.
Parents: Clarence Wood Lyons and Signe Annette (Anderson) Lyons.
Spouse/Marriage Date: Clyde E. Eklund; June 28, 1952 in Minneapolis, Minn.
Children: Carole Lee, Ann L. Harless, Joy E. Philipp.
Education: Macalester College, B.A. 1951; Roosevelt University, Paralegal Certification-Litigation 1976; Lutheran Theological Southern Seminary, M.Div. 1990.
Ordination: June 8, 1990 by North Carolina Synod.
Calls: Ascension, Wilson, 1990-95; Interim, Our Redeemer, Greenville, 1995-96. Vice Pastor at various congregations.
Other: Ecumenical Committee; Educational Committee, 1995 Synod Assembly Chaplain; Reference and Counsel - Synod Assembly, 1993-94; Bishop's Consulting Committee, 1995-96; Minister of Music, Richfield, Minneapolis, Minn.
Date of Death/Burial Location: October 3, 1996; Reformation, Upper Providence, Pa.

ELKINS, EDGAR G.
Date/Place of Birth: September 14, 1953; Fayetteville, N.C.
Parents: James L. Elkins and Ruby D. Elkins.
Spouse/Marriage Date: Joanne (Baggett) Elkins; November 15, 1975.
Children: Jamin E., Joshua E., Joel C.
Education: Sandhills Community College, A.A. Mental Health 1974; Methodist College, B.A.S. 1981; Duke University, M.Div. 1985; Lutheran Theological Southern Seminary, D.Min. 1991-94.
Ordination: 1987 by North Carolina Synod.
Calls: Lees's Chapel and Warren's Grove, United Methodist Church, Roxboro, 1981-85; Asbury and Pineview United Methodist Church, Lumberton 1985-6. St. Paul, Vonore, Tenn., 1986-87; St. Mark, Lumberton, 1987-91; Our Redeemer, Greenville, 1991-95.

ELLINGSEN, MARK
Date/Place of Birth: June 18, 1949; Brooklyn, N.Y.
Parents: Emil Ellingsen and Edna Ellingsen.
Spouse/Marriage Date: Betsey (Shaw) Ellingsen; August 18, 1973 in Farmington, Conn.
Children: Patrick John, Elizabeth Ann, Peter.
Education: Gettysburg College, B.A. *magna cum laude* 1971; Yale Divinity School, M.Div. *magna cum laude*, 1974; Yale University, M.A. 1975, M.Phil., 1976, Ph.D. 1980.
Ordination: July 18, 1976 by Northeastern Pennsylvania Synod.
Calls: St. Luke, Hellertown, Pa., 1975-77; Central Pocono Lutheran Parish, Scotrun, Pa., 1977-78; Haven, Salisbury, 1988-90; St. John, Asheboro, 1990-93.
Other: Assistant Professor of Systematic Theology, Luther-Northwestern Seminary, 1979-82; Associate Professor, Institute for Ecumenical Research, Strasbourg, France, 1982-88;

Part-time Instructor Randolph Community College, Asheboro, 1992-93; Assistant Professor of Church History, Interdenominational Theological Center, Atlanta, Ga., 1993-. 1995 *Marquis' Who's Who in the South and Southwest;* Phi Beta Kappa. Books include: *Doctrine and Word; The Evangelical Movement: Growth, Impact, Controversy, Dialog; The Integrity of Biblical Narrative: Story in Theology and Proclamation; Preparation and Manifestation: Reflections on Lent and Easter; The Cutting-Edge: How Churches Speak on Social Issues; A Common Sense Theology: The Bible, Faith, and American Society.* Has written over 100 articles in various publications and many book reviews, paper presentations and workshops. Analyst for Lutheran Church in America Lutheran Listening-Post Survey VII, 1979; participant in Twin Cities' Lutheran-Roman Catholic Dialogue, 1980; Open Hearing Leader at Lutheran World Federation Assembly, 1984; panelist on *The Ministry of the Laity* at a workshop of the North Carolina Synod, 1988; guest on various radio talk-show interviews; panelist on radio documentary program, *Religion in the 1980s,* in Detroit, Michigan, 1989; panelist on *Research, Writing and Publication,* at Theta Phi Symposium on Theological Education and Excellence, 1994.

EMMERT, JACOB B.

Date/Place of Birth: May 7, 1815; Carter County, Tenn.
Ordination: Ordained Deacon 1850 and Pastor 1853 by Tennessee Synod.
Calls: Did not hold a regular pastorate but preached at outposts, and assisted other pastors.
Other: His post office was Holston Furnace, Tenn., near Elizabethton. He was one of a number of men who were ordained from time to time to meet the urgent need for ministers. One of the organizers of the Holston Synod, 1860-61.
Date of Death: October 16, 1873.

ERICSON, MARK JOHN

Date/Place of Birth: July 28, 1956; Staten Island, N.Y.
Parents: Charles John Ericson and Marilyn Francis (Zoubek) Ericson.
Spouse/Marriage Date: Joyce (Wilson) Ericson; May 24, 1980.
Education: Broward Community College, A.A. 1976; Florida Atlantic University, B.A., 1978; Lutheran Theological Southern Seminary, M.Div. 1982, D.Min. 1995; South Carolina State Hospital, Clinical Pastoral Education, 1982; Carolinas Medical Center, Charlotte, Residency Clinical Pastoral Education, 1992-93.
Ordination: October 3, 1982 by Florida Synod.
Calls: Morning Star and Bethlehem (Blue Ridge Lutheran Parish), Luray, Va., 1982-85; Associate Pastor, St. Paul, Wilmington, 1985-86; St. Mark, Cherryville, 1986-91; Incarnation, Charlotte, 1995-98; St John, Concord, 1999-.
Other: Chaplain-Coordinator at Hospice of Gaston County, Gastonia, 1994-95. *Engraved in Rock,* booklet dealing with tombstones at St. Mark in Cherryville Cemetery, 1988. *The Use of Oral History to Facilitate the Transition of a Pastor Into a New Parish Setting,* 1995.

ERNST, MATTHEW L.

Date/Place of Birth: October 28, 1939; Spokane, Wash.
Parents: Henry J. Ernst and Bertha Ernst.
Spouse/Marriage Date: Karen (Gerhard) Ernst; July 17, 1965.
Children: Heide, Kristin Wolf, Jonathan.

Education: Pacific Lutheran University, B.A. 1961; Wartburg Seminary, M.Div. 1965.
Ordination: September 10, 1967 by American Lutheran Church.
Calls: First St. John's, Pittsburgh, Pa., 1967-71; St. Luke, Baltimore, Md., 1974-81; All Saints, Lilburn, Ga., 1981-93; Living Saviour, Charlotte, 1993-98; St. Luke, Ocean Isle Beach, 1998-.
Other: Lutheran Social Services of Maryland, Baltimore, Md., 1965-67; Lutheran Service Society, Pittsburgh, Pa., 1971-73.

EVANS, JOHNNIE PIERCE, JR.

Date/Place of Birth: March 8, 1938; Augusta, Ga.
Parents: Johnnie Pierce Evans, Sr. and Sarah (Kilpatrick) Evans.
Spouse/Marriage Date: Clarice (Shealy) Evans; October 9, 1966 in Little Mountain, S.C.
Children: Trudy Anne (deceased), Sarah Jo.
Education: St. Petersburg Junior College, Newberry College, A.B. 1961; Lutheran Theological Southern Seminary, B.D. 1966.
Ordination: May 23, 1966 by Florida Synod.
Calls: Ebenezer, Catawba, 1966-68; Summer Memorial, Newberry, S.C., 1968-75; St. James, Leesville, S.C., 1975-83; Trinity, Concord, 1983-98; Faith, Newberry, S.C., 1998.
Other: In South Carolina Synod, served on Social Ministry and American Missions Committees.

EVANS, WILLIAM MICHAEL

Date/Place of Birth: March 18, 1952; Denver, Colo.
Parents: Hurvey Mason and Margaret Alice (Schmoker) Evans.
First Spouse/Marriage Date: Carol Nannette (Butcher) Evans; July 2, 1972.
Children of First Marriage: Diane Jeanette, Megan Lynnette, Jennifer Nannette.
Second Spouse/Marriage Date: Annemarie Evans; June 18, 1993.
Education: Friends University, A.B. Religion/Philosophy 1974; Gettysburg Seminary, M.Div. 1979; Loyola College, M.S. Pastoral Counseling 1990.
Ordination: July 29, 1979 by Rocky Mountain Synod.
Calls: St. John, Lanham-Zion, Hollenberg, Kan., 1979-83; Our Lord, Oklahoma City, Okla., 1984-87; Capon- North River Parish, Wardensville, W.Va., 1988-92; Pastoral Counselor, Winchester, Va., 1992-93; Interim, Our Redeemer, Greenville, N.C., 1996-97; Holly Grove, Lexington, 1997-.
Other: Board, Job Training Program, Oklahoma City, Okla.

FAGGART, BRADY YOUNG, JR.

Date/Place of Birth: April 17, 1930; Concord, N.C.
Parents: Brady Young Faggart, Sr. and Annie Lee (Aycock) Faggart.
Spouse/Marriage Date: Lois Barrier (McEachern) Faggart; August 1, 1952 in Concord, N.C.
Children: Laura Beth Zahran, Lois Anne Brouillette, Luther Brady.
Education: Lenoir-Rhyne, A.B. History 1952, D.D. 1972; Chicago Seminary, M.Div. 1956.

Ordination: June 10, 1956 by North Carolina Synod.

Calls: Mission Developer/Pastor, Good Shepherd, Hickory, 1956-59; St. Mark, China Grove, 1960-63. Synodical Secretary, Christian Education, Salisbury, 1963-66; Executive Director, Lutheridge, 1967-68; Assistant to the President, Lutheran Church in America, 1969-75; First, Greensboro, 1975-93. Interim pastor at various congregations.

Other: Committee on Appeals, Evangelical Lutheran Church in America, 1991; Executive Council, Lutheran Church in America, 1978-86; Lutheran Church in America Chair, Committee on Planning; Management Committee, Division for Professional Leadership, Lutheran Church in America, 1976-78; Board, Lenoir- Rhyne, 1977-80, 1983-92; Executive Committee, Lenoir-Rhyne; Chair, Promotion and Development; Chair, Centennial Campaign Phase II; Adjunct Chaplain, Wesley Long Hospital, 1978-91; Resource Developer, Lutheran Family Services in the Carolinas, 1993-; Interim Executive Director, Lutheridge-Lutherock Ministries, Inc., 1993; Executive Committee, Luther League of America, 1965-67; Lutheran Church in America Delegate, 1964; North Carolina Council of Churches, 1962-63; District Secretary, 1962; Chair, Committee for Professional Service; Chair, Triad Refugee Interfaith Program, 1987-88. Donald H. Larsen Award, Lutheran Immigration and Refugee Service, 1992. Retired 1993 in Greensboro, N.C.

FALTIN, LINDA ANN

Date/Place of Birth: January 3, 1942; York, Pa.

Parents: Hans George Faltin and Katharine (Faul) Faltin.

First Spouse: Carl Allen Sutton, Sr., deceased.

Second Spouse: Robert Charles Griffin.

Children: Carl Allen Sutton, Jr., Hope Elisabeth Sutton, Mark Rollin Sutton, Paul Anthony Griffin.

Education: Wagner College, B.S.N., 1963; Lutheran Theological Southern Seminary, M.Div. 1990; graduate work at University of Maryland, 1974-75.

Ordination: August 12, 1990 by North Carolina Synod.

Calls: New Covenant, Archdale, 1990-. Interim Pastor at various congregations.

FARRIS, MELBOURNE RUDISILL

Date/Place of Birth: July 19, 1905; Cherryville, N.C.

Parents: William A. Farris and Etta Viola (Rudisill) Farris.

Spouse/Marriage Date: Elizabeth (Lingle) Farris, daughter of the Reverend G. H. L. Lingle; June 30, 1931 in Salisbury, N.C.

Children: Mary Melbourne Zinn, Hama Elizabeth Holloway.

Education: Lenoir-Rhyne, A.B. 1928; Lutheran Theological Southern Seminary, 1931.

Ordination: September 1931 by North Carolina Synod.

Calls: Holy Comforter, Belmont, 1931-36; Salem, Rowan County, 1936-43; Peace-Sharon-Frieden's, Gibsonville, 1943-49; Frieden's only, 1949-51; First, Lexington, 1951-69; Trinity, Landis, 1969-73. Vice Pastor at various congregations.

Other: Officers and Staff Salaries Committee, 1966-67; Auxiliaries Committee, 1969; Executive Board, 1962-64; Examining Committee, 1965-66. Retired December 31, 1973 to Salisbury, N.C.

FAUBLE, DONALD ROGER

Date/Place of Birth: March 11, 1926; Cleveland, Ohio.
Parents: Clarence R. Fauble and Hazel May (Hanson) Fauble.
Spouse/Marriage Date: Emma Adelaide (Fletcher) Fauble; February 4, 1953.
Children: Timothy Roger, Jonathan David.
Education: Wittenberg University, A.B. 1946; Hamma Divinity School, M.Div. 1949; graduate work at University of Tennessee and Lutheran Theological Southern Seminary.
Ordination: January 30, 1949 by Ohio Synod.
Calls: St. Paul, Paulding, Ohio, 1949-51; Assistant Pastor, St. John, Knoxville, Tenn., 1951-52; Holy Trinity, Kingsport, Tenn., 1952-59; Lutheran Church of the Ascension, Chattanooga, Tenn., 1959-66; St. Timothy, Hendersonville, Tenn., 1966-73; Reformation, Greeneville, Tenn., 1973-83, Pastor Emeritus; Director of Development, Lutheridge, 1983-88; Grace Mountainside Church (Lutheran and Episcopal Fellowship), Robbinsville, 1990-. Interim Pastor at various congregations.
Other: Executive Board, Southeastern Synod, 1976-79, 1982-83; Editor *Southeastern Lutheran,* 1964- 76; Delegate, Lutheran Church in America Conventions, 1972, 1986; Trustee, Williams-Henson Lutheran Home for Children, Knoxville, Tenn., 1974-79, 1980-86, President, 1981-83; Trustee, Lutheran Children's Home of the South, 1962-80, Chair, Finance Committee, 1964-80; Trustee, Protestant Radio and TV Center, Atlanta, Ga., 1964-85; President, Tennessee Council of Churches, 1961-63. Retired July 1, 1988 to Arden, N.C.

FELDMAN, GEORGE ROBERT, SR.

Date/Place of Birth: September 9, 1941; Baltimore, Md.
Parents: Herman O. Feldman and Thelma M. Feldman.
Spouse/Marriage Date: Catherine (Beckwith) Feldman; June 17, 1967.
Children: George Robert, Jr., John B.
Education: Concord College, B.A. 1970; Gettysburg Seminary, M.Div. 1972.
Ordination: July 17, 1972 by Virginia Synod.
Calls: Mt. Tabor, Middlebrook, Va., 1972-74; U.S. Army Chaplain, 1974-83, stationed at Ft. Bragg, 1978-82; St. James, Chilhowie, Va., 1983-88; St. Peter, Toms Brook, Va., 1988-. While stationed in North Carolina, did extensive supply work for various congregations.
Other: Worked with North Carolina Synod Committee to discover ways for local congregations to minister to military families in their areas, 1978-80.

FESPERMAN, FRANCIS IRVING

Date/Place of Birth: October 19, 1921; Draper, Rockingham County, N.C.
Parents: Luther A. Fesperman and Beulah (Beaver) Fesperman.
Spouse/Marriage Date: Kathleen (Castor) Fesperman; October 7, 1939 in Cabarrus County, N.C.
Children: Martha Lou Marky, Luther Paul.
Education: Lenoir-Rhyne, A.B. 1941; Lutheran Theological Southern Seminary, M.Div. 1945; Chicago Seminary, S.T.M. 1962; Vanderbilt University, Ph.D. 1969.
Ordination: April 4, 1945 by North Carolina Synod.

Calls: In Florida: Bethlehem/St. Luke Parish, Lake City, 1945-49; Mission Developer, University Lutheran, Gainesville, 1950-51; Mission Developer/Pastor St. Andrew, St. Petersburg, 1951-57.

Other: Chaplain and Faculty, Newberry College, 1957-64, Faculty Member, 1964-92, Professor of Religion Emeritus. Secretary, Florida Synod United Lutheran Church in America, 1947-57. Author *From Torah to Apocalypse,* 1983. Retired 1992 to Newberry, S.C.

FESPERMAN, JOSEPH HAMILTON

Date/Place of Birth: July 7, 1841; Rowan County, N.C.
Parents: Michael Fesperman and Cynthia Fesperman.
Spouse/Marriage Date: Crissie Ann (Lentz) Fesperman; September 19, 1866 in Rowan County, N.C.
Children: Bikle Hamilton, Augustus Love, Claudia Brown, Lula Irene, Joseph Eugene, Florence Bell, Arthur Ney.
Education: No formal education; studied theology under older ministers.
License/Ordination: Licensed May 3, 1868 and ordained 1871 by North Carolina Synod.

Calls: Two in Davie County; Beth Eden, Newton; organized Providence "in Scotch-Irish township", Rowan County, 1871-76; St. Michael, Troutman, 1871-77, St. Paul, Iredell County, 1871-74.

Other: Retired about 1877 because of ill health. Author of *The Life of a Sufferer, An Autobiography, Practical Lessons and Devotional Thoughts, A Sufferer's View of Christ and the Scriptures, or The Sick Man's Friend.*

Date of Death/Burial Location: April 26, 1917; St. Michael Cemetery, Troutman, N.C.

FICKEN, CARL FREDERICK WILHELM, JR.

Date/Place of Birth: September 16, 1935; Augusta, Ga.
Parents: Carl Frederick Wilhelm Ficken, Sr. and Jean (Mobley) Ficken.
Spouse/Marriage Date: Anne (Holderfield) Ficken; June 16, 1962 in La Grange, Ga.
Children: Catherine Anne Fink, Mark Jonathan.
Education: Lenoir-Rhyne, A.B. 1957; Philadelphia Seminary, B.D. 1960; University of South Carolina, Ph.D. 1972; Lutheran Theological Southern Seminary, S.T.M. 1968; Lenoir-Rhyne, D.D. 1995.
Ordination: May 1960 by South Carolina Synod.
Calls: St. Mark, Sullivan's Island, S.C., 1960-62; Campus Pastor, Lutheran Student Center, University of South Carolina, 1962-68; Assistant to Pastor, Macedonia Church, Burlington, 1973-75; Faculty, Lutheran Theological Southern Seminary, 1976-79; Professor, Theology and Culture 1984-97; Director of Lutheran Theological Center in Atlanta, 1988-97; Vice Pastor at various North Carolina congregations; Associate Pastor, Redeemer, Atlanta, Ga., 1997-.
Other: Faculty, Lutheran Theological Southern Seminary, 1966-67, 1968-70; Assistant Professor English, Elon College, 1972-75. North Carolina Synod Historical Works Committee, 1973-82. Board, Lenoir-Rhyne, 1982-91; Candidacy Committee, North Carolina Synod, Evangelical Lutheran Church in America representative, 1989-; Bread for the World Chapter, Coordinator, Columbia, S.C., 1981-88; Interfaith Coalition,

Atlanta, Ga., 1990-; Author, *God's Story and Modern Literature,* 1985, and articles on American literature and Lutheran history.

FINCK, WILLIAM JOHN
Date/Place of Birth: July 1, 1861; Trenton, N.J.
Spouse/Marriage Date: Anna Louise (Kretschmann) Finck; May 8, 1888 in Philadelphia, Pa.; died May 3, 1943.
Children: George Ernest, Margaret (married the Reverend Henry H. Bagger), the Reverend Theodore Kretschmann, Elmer Frederick.
Education: Muhlenberg College, A.B. 1884, D.D. 1915; Philadelphia Seminary, 1887, graduate study, Indiana University.
Ordination: 1887 by Ministerium of Pennsylvania.
Calls: In Pennsylvania and Indiana, 1887-1906; St. Matthew, Augusta, Ga., 1906-12; Emmanuel-Mt. Zion, New Market, Va., 1912-31 (1912-21 in Tennessee Synod, 1921-24, in United North Carolina Synod, transferred to Virginia Synod, 1924).
Other: Member, United Lutheran Church in America West Indies Board. Author of *Lutheran Landmarks and Pioneers in America,* 1913. Collaborator in writing histories of synods. Left unpublished research in early American Lutheran Church history, especially on the eastern seaboard.
Date of Death/Burial Location: October 3, 1945; Riverview Cemetery, Wilmington, Del.

FINK, KENNETH WAYNE
Date/Place of Birth: July 8, 1950; Rowan County, N.C.
Parents: Worth Monroe Fink and Clarence Elizabeth (Harwood) Fink. Brother of The Reverend Ronald W. Fink.
Spouse/Marriage Date: Vicki Gail (Bowman) Fink; June 1, 1974 in Hickory, N.C.
Children: John Christopher, Matthew Wayne.
Education: Lenoir-Rhyne, A.B. Mathematics 1972; Lutheran Theological Southern Seminary, M.Div. 1976.
Ordination: June 13, 1976 by North Carolina Synod.
Calls: St. Paul, Crouse, 1976-80; Redeemer, Kannapolis, Rowan County, 1980-87; Mary and Martha, Durham, 1987-94; St. Luke, Monroe, 1994-. Vice Pastor at various congregations.
Other: Lutheran World Relief-World Hunger Committee, 1978-85, Chair, 1983-85; Cabinet, Social Ministry, 1982-85; Committee, Minutes and Unfinished Business, Chair, 1985; Lutheran Church in America World Hunger Appeal Conference, 1979, 1981, 1984; Lutheran Church in America World Hunger Appeal Consulting Committee meetings, 1980, 1983; Social Ministry Action Education Project, 1984, 1985.

FINK, RONALD WORTH

Date/Place of Birth: April 18, 1947; Albemarle, N.C.
Parents: Worth Monroe Fink and Clarence Elizabeth (Harwood) Fink. Brother of The Reverend Kenneth W. Fink.
Spouse/Marriage Date: Swannetta Eileen (Boone) Fink; August 10, 1968 in Alamance, N.C.
Child: Susan Renee.
Education: Lenoir-Rhyne, B.A. History/Political Science 1969; Lutheran Theological Southern Seminary, M.Div. 1973.
Ordination: June 3, 1973 by North Carolina Synod.
Calls: Our Saviour, Welcome, 1973-79; Good Hope, Hickory, 1979-92; Haven, Salisbury, 1992-. Vice Pastor at various congregations.
Other: Communications Committee, 1975-85, 1988-, Chair, 1982-85, 1988-; Editor of North Carolina Synod Communications Handbook; Board, Lutheran Services for the Aging, 1987-92; Stewardship Committee, 1985- 87; EMR Growth (Stewardship Program) Resource Person; Secretary, Western District; Synod Correspondent to *The Lutheran* magazine; Installation Committee, 1991; Synod Council, 1992-94; Secretary, North Carolina Synod, 1994-; meditation columns for various newspapers; devotions for radio and television; script consultant/editor for North Carolina Synod video, *Walking Together.* Board and Treasurer, Davidson County Council on Aging; President, North Davidson Ministerial Association; CONTACT Telephone Ministry, Lexington; Catawba County Rest Home-Nursing Home Advisory Committee, Chair for one year; President, Hickory Ministerial Association; Officer, Catawba Valley Lutheran Ministers' Fellowship; Board and Committee Chair, Cooperative Christian Ministry; Civitan Club Member.

FINK, WILLIAM H.

License: Licensed in 1847 by North Carolina Synod and in 1848 by the South Carolina Synod, but never ordained. License not renewed by South Carolina in 1850.
Calls: St. Paul, Iredell County, 1846-47. Transferred 1848 to South Carolina Synod; served Beth Eden, St. James, Jalapa, Newberry County, S.C., 1848-50.

FINKBEINER, ROBERT GLYNN

Date/Place of Birth: December 26, 1941; Laurens, S.C.
Parents: Robert Adam Finkbeiner and Madera (Glynn) Finkbeiner.
Spouse/Marriage Date: Phyllis Kay (Wade) Finkbeiner; April 11, 1964 in Greenville, S.C.
Children: Paul Glynn, Christine Lynn, Amy Lee.
Education: Newberry College, A.B. 1964; Lutheran Theological Southern Seminary, B.D. 1968.
Ordination: May 28, 1968 by South Carolina Synod.
Calls: Holy Cross, Lincolnton, 1968-71; St. John, Beaufort, S.C., 1971-72; Immanuel, Jamestown, N.Y., 1972-80; Assistant Executive Director, Social Services of Upper New York, Jamestown, N.Y., 1980-84; Executive Director, Lutheran Social Services, South Region, York, Pa., 1985-94.
Other: Removed from roll, May 18, 1994.

FISCHER, JOHN FREDERICK

Date/Place of Birth: December 6, 1934; Charleston, S.C.

Parents: Henry P. Fischer and Blanche (O'Neill) Fischer. Mother and wife's father were Roman Catholic; her mother Methodist; his father Lutheran.

Spouse/Marriage Date: June Loretta (Pop) Fischer; August 24, 1958 in Mt. Pleasant, S.C.

Children: John Christopher, Timothy Shawn, Shannon Ross, Jamie Matthew, Jonathan Kirk.

Education: College of Charleston, B.S. 1958; Lutheran Theological Southern Seminary, B.D. 1961.

Ordination: May 1961 by South Carolina Synod.

Calls: Atonement, Wilkesboro, 1961-64; St. Paul, Gilbert, S.C., 1964-65; St. Timothy, Goose Creek, S.C., 1966-82; Nativity, Spartanburg, S.C., 1982-.

Other: Demitted May 18, 1994.

FISHER, CARL HILBERT, SR.

Date/Place of Birth: November 19, 1910; Salisbury, N.C.

Parents: Luther Vastine Fisher and Cora Ann (Brown) Fisher. A grandson of the Reverend Richard L. Brown. Brothers were the Reverends Earle Hugo, Herman George, Ray Richard and Roscoe Brown Fisher.

Spouse/Marriage Date: Lena Belle (Gobble) Fisher; December 21, 1935 in East Spencer, N.C.

Child: Carl Hilbert, Jr.

Education: University of North Carolina, A.B. 1932; Lutheran Theological Southern Seminary, B.D. 1937.

Ordination: 1937 by North Carolina Synod.

Calls: Grace-Melanchthon-Richland, Liberty, 1937-39; St. Matthew, Wilmington, 1939-46; Good Shepherd, Mt. Holly, 1946-55. Transferred 1955 to Kentucky-Tennessee Synod; Mission Developer, St. John, Nashville, Tenn.; Our Saviour, Albany, Ga. Interim Pastor at St. Stephen, Warren, Mich.

Other: Secretary, Southern Conference; American Missions Committee of the Southeastern Synod; Southeastern Synod Consultation Team; Worship Committee; Ministerial Association President in each community of his five pastorates.

Date of Death : February 17, 1981.

FISHER, CARL MELCHIOR, SR.

Date/Place of Birth: February 4, 1933; Davidson County, N.C.

Parents: The Reverend Roy Linn Fisher and Ethel Frances (Blackwelder) Fisher.

Spouse/Marriage Date: Miriam (Eleazer) Fisher; June 21 1959 in Orangeburg, S.C.

Children: Carl M., Jr., Jeremy Eleazer, Janthi Elizabeth, The Reverend William Gene Linn.

Education: Sophia University, Tokyo, Japan; Lenoir-Rhyne, A.B. 1955, D.D. 1973; Lutheran Theological Southern Seminary, M.Div. 1958; Chicago Lutheran School of Missions, 1961-62; Chicago Seminary, S.T.M. 1967.

Ordination: June 8, 1958 by North Carolina Synod.

Calls: Trinity, Cabarrus County, 1958-61. Lutheran Church in America missionary in Malaysia, 1962-77; Bishop, Lutheran Church in Malaysia and Singapore, 1969-77. Ascension, Savannah, Ga., 1978-81; Director, Service and Development of Lutheran World Ministries, N.Y., 1981-86; Pastor-Developer, Cross and Crown, Matthews, 1986-98; retired 1998 to Charlotte, N.C.

Other: Lutheran World Federation Staff, Department of Studies, 1972-77; President, Association of Missionaries in Malaysia and Singapore, 1967-72; President, Conference of Lutheran Churches in Malaysia and Singapore, 1970-77; Chair, Board of Governors, Trinity Seminary, Singapore, 1971-73; *Dictionary of International Biography*, Meritorious Service as a Church Leader; Organizer of All-Asia Lutheran Conference, 1976; Chair, World Missions and Ecumenical Committee of the Southeastern Synod, 1980-81; Delegate of Lutheran Church in America Convention, Southeastern Synod, 1980. Named Bishop Americus of Lutheran Church in Malaysia and Singapore, 1997. Co-Executive Director, North Carolina Lutheran Men, 1998-.

FISHER, CHARLES LEE THORNTON

Date/Place of Birth: April 4, 1857; Rowan County, N.C.

Parents: Peter Alexander Fisher and Camilla Elizabeth (Brown) Fisher. A younger brother was the Reverend J. H. C. Fisher.

Spouse/Marriage Date: Mary Caroline (Horner) Fisher; August 28, 1886 in Gettysburg, Pa.

Children: Pauline Tyrone, Homer Charles.

Education: North Carolina College, Gettysburg College, A.B. and A.M. 1882; Gettysburg Seminary, 1885.

License/Ordination: Licensed 1884 and ordained 1885 by Maryland Synod.

Calls: In Maryland and Nebraska, 1885-89. Transferred to North Carolina Synod, 1890. With the Reverend J. D. Shirey, Holy Trinity, Mt. Pleasant, 1890-92; Luther's, Rowan County, 1903; supplied six months, Mt. Zion, Richfield, 1904; Holy Trinity-Mt. Gilead, Mt. Pleasant, 1923-25; again supplied, Holy Trinity, Mt. Pleasant, 1926. While in educational work and after retiring In 1926 at Lynchburg, Va., his pastoral service was chiefly on supply basis.

Other: Professor (Latin, Greek), North Carolina College, 1889-92. Principal, Mont Amoena Seminary, 1892-97. Vice President, Elizabeth College, Charlotte, 1897-1904.

Date of Death/Burial Location: March 10, 1936; Lynchburg, Va.

FISHER, CLIFFORD PAUL, II

Date/Place of Birth: October 16, 1918; China Grove, N.C.

Parents: The Reverend Clifford Paul Fisher, Sr. and Zelia Gladys (Pless) Fisher.

Spouse/Marriage Date: Martha Lou (Mauney) Fisher; June 30, 1943 in Kings Mountain, N.C.

Children: Martha Jean Cook, Zelia Elizabeth Frick, Clifford Paul, III.

Education: Lenoir-Rhyne, A.B. 1940; Lutheran Theological Southern Seminary, B.D. 1943.

Ordination: July 11, 1943 by North Carolina Synod.

Calls: Prosperity (Cross of Christ), Cabarrus County, 1943-49; St. James, Rockwell, 1949-62; Transfiguration, Cayce, S.C., 1962-83. Transferred to North Carolina Synod, 1983. Interim Pastor at various congregations.

Other: Secretary, Lowman Home Board; President, Northern Conference; Chair, Seminary Appeal. In South Carolina, Professional Leadership Preparation Committee and Examining Committee. Retired June 1983 at Rockwell, N.C.

FISHER, CLIFFORD PAUL, SR.

Date/Place of Birth: July 29, 1877; Cabarrus County, N.C.

Parents: Thomas Fisher and Margaret (Barringer) Fisher.

Spouse/Marriage Date: Zelia Gladys (Pless) Fisher; April 22, 1908 in Rowan County, N.C.

Children: Vern Weidner, Ertha Margaret, the Reverend Clifford Paul, II, Mary Gladys.

Education: North Carolina College, A.B. 1900; Chicago Seminary, B.D. 1903; Lenoir-Rhyne, D.D. 1943.

Ordination: 1903 by North Carolina Synod.

Calls: Faith-Immanuel, Faith, 1903-18; St. Mark, China Grove, 1918-26; St. James-Immanuel, Rockwell, 1926-30; Trinity-Concordia, Landis, 1930-45; also, supplied the following: Wittenberg, Granite Quarry, 1930-40; Mt. Olive, Cabarrus County, 1910; Grace, Rowan County, 1922, 1923-25; Prosperity, Cabarrus County, 1924; New Bethel, Stanly County, 1925.

Other: Board, Lenoir-Rhyne, 1931-45.

Date of Death/Burial Location: October 26, 1945; Faith Church, Faith, N.C.

FISHER, EARLE HUGO

Date/Place of Birth: March 24, 1913; Salisbury, N.C.

Parents: Luther Vastine Fisher and Cora Ann (Brown) Fisher. A grandson of the Reverend Richard L. Brown. Brothers were the Reverends Carl Hilbert, Sr., Herman George, Ray Richard and Roscoe Brown Fisher.

First Spouse/Marriage Date: Eileen (Argabright) Fisher.

Children of First Marriage: Earle Michael, Patrick Shannon.

Second Spouse/Marriage Date: Kaja (Westergard) Fisher; October 9, 1954 in Brooklyn, N.Y.; died February 1994.

Child of Second Marriage: Faith Cora.

Education: Roanoke College, B.S. 1936; Lutheran Theological Southern Seminary, 1939.

Ordination: 1939 by North Carolina Synod.

Calls: Assistant Pastor, Ebenezer, Columbia, S.C. 1939-40; Reformation, Greeneville, Tenn., 1940-44; Ascension, Chattanooga, Tenn., 1944-48; Giles Parish, Pembroke, Va., 1948-53; Newport, Newport, Va., 1946-51; Salem Danish, Brooklyn, N.Y., 1943-54; Chapel of Faith (Non-synodical), Charlotte, 1955-.

Other: After 1954 not in Lutheran ministry. Affiliated with The Episcopal Church. Virginia Synod: Chair, Committee on Auxiliary Organization, 1944-47; Chair, Lutheran World Action for Knoxville Conference, 1941-43; President, Roanoke Conference, 1949-53. National Lutheran Commission on Evangelism for Virginia, North Carolina, Synods, 1951-53.

Date of Death/Burial Location: November 14, 1997; Holy Comforter Episcopal, Charlotte, N.C.

FISHER, HERMAN GEORGE, SR.
Date/Place of Birth: March 25, 1906; Salisbury, N.C.
Parents: Luther Vastine Fisher and Cora Ann (Brown) Fisher. Twin brother is the Reverend Ray R. Fisher. Other brothers were the Reverends Carl Hilbert, Sr., Earle Hugo and Roscoe Brown Fisher. A grandson of the Reverend Richard L. Brown.
First Spouse/Marriage Date: Ruby Brooks (Lowder) Fisher; September 9, 1930 in Burlington, N.C.; died January 2, 1976.
Children of First Marriage: Herman George, Jr., Araminta Ann, Ruby Vance, John Hilbert.
Second Spouse/Marriage Date: Helen Ruth (Rimer) Fisher; June 30, 1977.
Education: Roanoke College, A.B. 1928; Lutheran Theological Southern Seminary, B.D. 1931.
Ordination: 1931 by North Carolina Synod.
Calls: Alamance, Alamance, as student supply 1929-31; as Pastor 1931-38; Redeemer, Macon, Ga., 1938-40; St. Matthew-St. Luke, Kings Mountain, 1940-44; Concordia, Rowan County, 1944-48; Advent, Spindale, 1948-53; St. John, Spartanburg, S.C., 1953-63; Faith, Evansville, Ind., 1963-65; St. Mark's, Mooresville, 1965-71; Pilgrim, Lexington, 1971-73. Vice Pastor at various congregations.
Other: Retired December 31, 1973.
Date of Death/Burial Location: October 19, 1992; Organ, Salisbury, N.C.

FISHER, JAMES HENRY CORNELIUS
Date/Place of Birth: March 30, 1859; Rowan County, N.C.
Parents: Peter Alexander Fisher and Camilla Elizabeth (Brown) Fisher. An older brother was the Reverend C. L. T. Fisher.
Spouse/Marriage Date: Leah J. (Blackwelder) Fisher; 1897 in Mt. Pleasant, N.C.
Children: Katherine B., Amy Louise, Mary Virginia, Henry Lee.
Education: North Carolina College, Gettysburg A.B. 1887; Gettysburg Seminary, 1890.
License/Ordination: Licensed 1889 and ordained 1890 by Maryland Synod.
Calls: New Bethel, Stanly County, 1893-94; Luther's, Rowan County, 1894-96; Immanuel, Rowan County, 1900-02; Prosperity, Cabarrus County, 1900-19; supply, St. Andrew, Concord, 1914; Mt. Hermon-Cold Water, Cabarrus County, 1925-30; supply, Mt. Gilead, Cabarrus County, 1926-32.
Other: Principal, Preparatory Department, North Carolina College, five years. Principal, Mont Amoena Seminary, 1902-14, 1921-27. Retired at Mt. Pleasant, N.C.
Date of Death/Burial Location: April 10, 1933; Mt. Pleasant, N.C.

FISHER, PATRICK SHANNON
Date/Place of Birth: October 1, 1943; Greeneville, Tenn.
Parents: The Reverend Earle Hugo Fisher and Eileen Ann (Argabright) Fisher.

Spouse/Marriage Date: Sarah McAllister (Parsons) Fisher; June 12, 1965 in Wytheville, Va.

Children: Christopher Shannon, Gregory Scott.

Education: Davidson College, A.B. History 1965; Lutheran Theological Southern Seminary, M.Div. 1969; University of North Carolina at Charlotte.

Ordination: June 8, 1969 by North Carolina Synod.

Calls: St. James, Chilhowie, Va., 1969-73.

Other: Resigned from ministry to enter secular work as a Certified Public Accountant in Charlotte, N.C.

FISHER, RAY RICHARD

Date/Place of Birth: March 25, 1906; Salisbury, N.C.

Parents: Luther Vastine Fisher and Cora Ann (Brown) Fisher. Twin brother is the Reverend Herman George Fisher. Other brothers were the Reverends Carl Hilbert, Sr., Earle Hugo and Roscoe Brown Fisher. A grandson of the Reverend Richard L. Brown.

Spouse/Marriage Date: Ruth (Lyerly) Fisher; June 24, 1933 in Salisbury, N.C.

Children: Ray Richard, II, Rebecca Ruth.

Education: Roanoke College, Catawba College, A.B. 1928; studied law one year, University of North Carolina; Lutheran Theological Southern Seminary, 1933; Lenoir-Rhyne, D.D. 1960.

Ordination: June 25, 1933 by North Carolina Synod.

Calls: Mt. Pleasant, Good Hope, Trinity in Saluda County, S.C., 1933-37. In North Carolina: St. Mark, Asheville, 1937-42; Augsburg, Winston-Salem, 1942-71. Vice Pastor at various congregations.

Other: Board, Lutheridge, 1949-58; Board, Lutheran Theological Southern Seminary, 1958-64; President, Ministerial Association in Saluda, S.C., Asheville and Winston-Salem; sermons published in *Ministers Annual, Preaching Today, Pulpit Preaching* and *The Expositor.* President, Eastern Conference. Radio and TV preacher for WSJS in Winston-Salem. Retired April 12, 1971.

Date of Death/Burial Location: June 22, 1975; Parklawn Memorial Gardens, Winston-Salem, N.C.

FISHER, ROSCOE BROWN

Date/Place of Birth: November 21, 1909; Salisbury, N.C.

Parents: Luther Vastine Fisher and Cora Ann (Brown) Fisher. Brothers were the Reverends Carl Hilbert, Sr., Earle Hugo, Herman George and Ray Richard Fisher. A grandson of the Reverend Richard L. Brown.

Spouse/Marriage Date: Pauline (Little) Fisher; August 28, 1935 in Statesville, N.C.

Children: Luther Brown (died in 8th year), Martha Little Ouderkirk, Mary Pauline Lemons, Miriam Ann Elizabeth Honeycutt, Mildred Brown "Millie" Milam, Luther Brown, II.

Education: University of North Carolina, A.B. Sociology 1931; Lutheran Theological Southern Seminary, 1934; Columbia University; Emory University; Union Seminary; McCormick Seminary, D.Min., 1978.

Ordination: 1934 by North Carolina Synod.

Calls: Lutheran Churches: Assistant, St. John, Salisbury, summer 1934; Pastor to Lutheran students, University of North Carolina at Chapel Hill, 1934-35; developed and organized St. James, Fayetteville, 1935-38, also St. John, Asheboro, 1938-42. Also called to St. Paul, Hamlet, 1942-44; St. Stephen-St. John, Lenoir, 1944-52; Good Shepherd, Brooklyn, N.Y., 1952. Received into the Presbyterian Church in 1962 and served churches in Badin, Raleigh, Cooleemee, Statesville, and Harmony.

Other: Editor, *North Carolina Lutheran;* Correspondent to *The Lutheran.* Member, radio and TV committees of synods and councils of churches. Not in Lutheran ministry after 1954. Author, *A History of the Michael Brown Family, Michael Braun of the Old Stone House - His Influence and Descendants.* Author, *The James Carling Illustrations of Edgar Allen Poe's The Raven.* Author of a 25-year newspaper column *Bits of Life.* Editor, *The Presbyterian News.* Historian, Michael Braun Family Association. Past President, Trustee, North Carolina Society of County and Local Historians. President, Fisher Publications. Listed in *Dictionary of International Biography,* 1971, and *2000 Men of Achievement,* 1972. Member, National Writer's Club. Has written for numerous magazines and religious periodicals including *Readers' Digest, Coronet*, and *Ladies Home Journal.*

Date of Death/Burial Location: October 27, 1993; Oakwood Cemetery, Statesville, N.C.

FISHER, ROY LINN

Date/Place of Birth: July 31, 1901; Rowan County, N.C.
Parents: Linn A. Fisher and Maggie (Penninger) Fisher.
Spouse/Marriage Date: Frances Ethel (Blackwelder) Fisher; May 28, 1929 in Cabarrus County, N.C.
Children: Doris Roselyn Misenheimer, Daphne Jean Poole, the Reverend Carl Melchior, Dr. Marjorie Ethel Matthews.
Education: Mount Pleasant Collegiate Institute, 1923; Lenoir-Rhyne, B.A. 1925; Lutheran Theological Southern Seminary, B.D. 1928; graduate study, University of South Carolina; Chaplain School at Harvard University, 1943; Erlangen University, Germany; Indiana University, 1956-58; Chicago Seminary, 1958-61.

Ordination: May 1928 by North Carolina Synod.

Calls: Holly Grove-Beck's-New Jerusalem-Lebanon, Davidson County, 1928-42; organized Silver Valley, Davidson County, 1940-42; St. Paul-Bethphage-St. Mark-Bethel, Crouse, 1942-43. Chaplain, U.S. Army, 1943-54; Chaplain, State Hospital, Logansport, Ind., 1955-66.

Other: Awarded five theatre ribbons. Retired 1966 in Rockwell, N.C., Chaplain for Rockwell Civitans, Miller-Russell American Legion Post and the Veterans of Foreign Wars. Volunteer in service organizations in Rowan County.

Date of Death/Burial Location: January 18, 1975; St. James Cemetery, Rockwell, N.C.

FISHER, WALLACE E.

Date/Place of Birth: March 29, 1918; Greensburg, Pa.
Parents: Daniel Rhoads Fisher and Rose Elizabeth (Brantner) Fisher.
Spouse/Marriage Date: Margaret Elizabeth (Stauffer) Fisher; September 2, 1942 in Pittsburgh, Pa.
Child: Paul Mark.

Education: Gettysburg College, A.B. 1940; Philadelphia Seminary, B.D. 1943; University of Pittsburgh, M.A. 1945; graduate work at University of Pennsylvania.
Ordination: May 28, 1943 by Pittsburgh Synod.
Calls: In Pennsylvania: St. John, Dravosburg, 1943-44; First English, Sharpsburg, 1944-46; English, Zelienople, 1946-47; Gettysburg College, Gettysburg, 1947-49; Christ, Gettysburg, 1949-52; Holy Trinity, Lancaster, 1952-82, Pastor Emeritus.
Other: Retired September 1982 to Pinehurst, N.C. June 1996 removed from North Carolina Synod to Lower Susquehanna Synod. Author of numerous publications.
Date of Death/Burial Location: October 25, 1997; Lancaster, Pa.

FISHER, WILLIAM GENE LINN

Date/Place of Birth: December 12, 1970; Orangeburg, S.C.
Parents: Dr. Carl Melchior Fisher and Miriam (Eleazer) Fisher.
Education: Lenoir-Rhyne, A.B. Political Science, 1993; Lutheran Theological Southern Seminary, M.Div. 1997.
Ordination: May 30, 1997 by North Carolina Synod.
Calls: Pastor-Developer, Amazing Grace, Waxhaw, N.C., 1997-.

FITZSIMMONS, MARK ELMER

Date/Place of Birth: February 29, 1960; Hamilton County, Ohio.
Parents: Elmer Scott Fitzsimmons and Margaret Ida (Staehli) Fitzsimmons.
Spouse: Dana Fitzsimmons.
Education: University of North Carolina at Chapel Hill, B.A. 1982; Lutheran Theological Southern Seminary, M.Div. 1986; graduate study, M.A. Counseling.
Ordination: May 30, 1986 by North Carolina Synod.
Calls: Bethany, Boone, 1986-89; Christus Victor, Durham, 1989-90; Associate Pastor, Grace, Winchester, Va., 1991-96; Nativity, Arden, 1996-. Vice Pastor at various congregations.

FLEENOR, ADAM

Date/Place of Birth: November 3, 1826; Washington County, Va.
Parent: Abraham Fleenor.
Spouse/Marriage Date: Lavinia (Ottinger) Fleenor; 1852 in Cocke County, Tenn.
Children: Joseph, Mary, Sarah, Narcissus, Adam.
Ordination: Ordained Deacon 1852 in Salem Church, Lincoln County and Pastor 1856 in Melanchthon Church, Randolph County, by Tennessee Synod.
Calls: In vicinity of Parrottsville, Tenn., where settled, 1852-70; Sinking Springs, Greene County, Tenn., 1868-9.
Other: One of organizers of Holston Synod, 1860-61. Author of motion to begin Sunday School work in that synod.
Date of Death/Burial Location: Died April 14, 1870; Salem Church, Cocke County, Tenn.

FLEENOR, JAMES

Date/Place of Birth: September 30, 1806; Washington County, Va.
First Spouse/Marriage Date: Catherine (Horn) Fleenor in 1830; died 1852.

Children of First Marriage: Five sons, four daughters.
Second Spouse/Marriage Date: Ludia (Vicars) Fleenor; died 1877.
Children of Second Marriage: One son, one daughter.
Ordination: Entered ministry in middle forties, ordained Deacon in 1850 and Pastor in 1853 by Tennessee Synod.
Calls: Rich and Poor Valleys, Washington County, Va.
Other: One of ten organizers of Holston Synod, 1860-61.
Date of Death/Burial Location: June 29, 1889; presumably, in Washington County, Va.

FLOWERS, WILLIAM CARROLL

Date/Place of Birth: January 11, 1928; Hickory, N.C.
Parents: Carroll Flowers and Ola E. (Huffman) Flowers.
Spouse/Marriage Date: Delorys (Duncan) Flowers; May 15, 1949 in Hickory, N.C.
Children: Joyce Davis, Tina McMeans, Denise Sease.
Education: Lenoir-Rhyne, 1966; Lutheran Theological Southern Seminary, M.Div. 1969.
Ordination: June 1, 1969 by North Carolina Synod.
Calls: St. Andrew, New Bern, 1969-79; Pastor-Developer Christ the King, Whiteville, 1981-83; Bethany, Newberry, S.C., 1983-92. Vice Pastor at various congregations.
Other: Before entering the seminary, he joined the Federal Bureau of Investigation, served in the Army, and was a printer and freelance photographer for *Hickory Daily Record*. Retired 1992 due to health problems.
Date of Death/Burial Location: March 7, 1993; Newberry Memorial Gardens, Newberry, S.C.

FOGLEMAN, JON RICH

Date/Place of Birth: December 21, 1943; Burlington, N.C.
Parents: A. Brown Fogleman and Gwendolyn P. Fogleman.
Spouse/Marriage Date: Dianne (Dixon) Fogleman; June 6, 1966 in Burlington, N.C.
Children: Jon Mark, Karen Dianne.
Education: Lenoir-Rhyne, A.B. 1966; Chicago Seminary, M.Div., 1970.
Ordination: June 11, 1970 by North Carolina Synod.
Calls: Redeemer, Kannapolis, 1970-76; Holy Trinity, Campus Ministry, Chapel Hill, 1976-81; St. Paul, Guelph, Ontario, Canada, 1981-.
Other: North Carolina Synod: Social Ministry Committee, 1973-74; Lutheran World Relief, 1973-76. Delegate to Constituting Convention of the New Canadian Church.

FOLK, EDWARD LESSING

Date/Place of Birth: October 4, 1858; near Shepherdstown, W.Va.
Parents: Jacob Folk and Martha Jane (Lingamfelter) Folk.
Spouse/Marriage Date: Lucy Flaherty (Riner) Folk; June 13, 1888 in Riner, Va.
Children: Martha Melissa, Edward Riner.
Education: Shepherd Normal School, graduating 1879; several years at Roanoke College, and Southern Seminary while at Salem, Va.; one year at Philadelphia Seminary, graduating 1885.
Ordination: 1885 by Southwest Virginia Synod.
Calls: In Virginia and Pennsylvania, 1885-1900; Augsburg, Winston-Salem, 1900-02;

again in Virginia, 1902-15; First, Greensboro, 1916-17; in Maryland, 1918-21.
Other: Retired 1921 in Washington, D.C., supplying churches, sometimes for a year. Contributed poems to *The Poetry Digest,* annual anthology of verse (1939), also to *The Lutheran* and other periodicals. Book of poems, *Lutheran Lyrics, An Anthology of Aesthetic, Moral, and Religious Poems.*
Date of Death/Burial Location: April 14, 1939; Elmwood Cemetery, Shepherdstown, W.Va.

FORD, CRAVEN GLENN

Date/Place of Birth: December 17, 1950; Durham, N.C.
Parents: L. Glenn Ford and Lelia (Clemmer) Ford.
Spouse/Marriage Date: Sharon (Boone) Ford; August 29, 1971 in Alamance, N.C.
Child: Ella Elizabeth.
Education: Appalachian State University, B.S. Economics and Business 1973; Gettysburg Seminary, M.Div. 1983.
Ordination: May 1983 by North Carolina Synod.
Calls: Atonement, Wilkesboro, 1983-90; Mission Developer/Pastor, Abiding Presence, Fuquay-Varina, 1990- 93; First, Lexington, 1993-.
Other: Justice and Social Change Committee, 1984-85; Candidacy Committee, 1987-.

FORD, DANIEL THOMAS, JR.

Date/Place of Birth: January 24, 1947; Salisbury, N.C.
Parents: Daniel Thomas Ford, Sr. and Edna Elizabeth (Hagler) Ford.
Spouse/Marriage Date: Elsie Josephine Heinsen (Mertes) Ford; August 27, 1967 in Winston-Salem, N.C.
Children: John Walter, Anne Elizabeth.
Education: Lenoir-Rhyne, B.A. English, 1969; California State University at San Bernardino; University of California at Riverside; Chicago Seminary, M.Div. 1973; Fuller Seminary, Certificate in Fund Raising; Chicago Theological Seminary, Catholic Theological, McCormick Theological, Th.D class work, New Testament, 1978-79.
Ordination: June 3, 1973 by North Carolina Synod.
Calls: Grace, Liberty, 1973-76; Pastor-Developer, Lord of Life, Garner, 1976-78; Interim Pastor at various congregations; Clinical Pastoral Education Resident-Lutheran Chaplain, North Carolina Memorial Hospital, Chapel Hill, 1981; Our Saviour, Fort Collins, Colo., 1982-84; Director, Development and Pastoral Counselor, Habitat for Humanity, Americus, Ga., 1985-86; Lutheran Social Services of Southern California, Area Director, 1986-91; Associate Director of Development, Lutheran Theological Southern Seminary, 1993; Executive Director, The Kansas City Metropolitan Lutheran Ministry, 1993-. Preached in churches in North Carolina, South Carolina, Georgia, Virginia, West Virginia, California, Colorado, Wyoming, Kansas, Missouri, Connecticut, Illinois, Iowa, Wisconsin, New York.
Other: Board of Directors, Lutheran Human Relations Association of America, Habitat for Humanity. North Carolina Synod: Process of Electing a Bishop Committee, 1976; Consulting Committee, Justice and Social Change, 1977-78. Board, Lutheran Campus Ministry of Colorado, 1982-84; Secretary, Northern Colorado- Southern Wyoming District, Rocky Mountain Synod - Lutheran Church in America, 1983-84. Publications: Devotions for *The Home Altar;* book reviews for *The North Carolina Lutheran;* articles for *Habitat World.* Lutheran Youth Leadership Award, Lutheran Brotherhood, 1965; Bread for the

World; The Fellowship of Reconciliation; Association for Clinical Pastoral Education; Lutheran Peace Fellowship, Amnesty International.

FORESTER, DAVID

License/Ordination: Licensed 1826 and ordained 1828 by Tennessee Synod in St. Paul Church, Newton (Startown, now known as Old St. Paul's).
Calls: Served a number of Tennessee Synod churches until about 1850 when affiliated with Joint Synod of Ohio.

FOX, ALFRED J.

Date/Place of Birth: September 6, 1817; near Staley in Chatham County, N.C.
Parents: David Fox and Elizabeth (Moretz) Fox.
Spouse/Marriage Date: Lydia (Bost) Fox; April 5, 1842 in Cabarrus County, N.C.
Children: The Reverend Luther Augustine, Isabella Jane, Albert C. (M.D.), Eugene (M.D.), Ida Catherine, Emma Frances, Laura E., the Reverend Junius Bost, John Frank (M.D.), Claud Porterfield (M.D.), Lawrence Sylvester (D.D.S.). Two cousins and a grandson were Lutheran pastors, and a cousin, Rebecca Fox, married the Reverend Polycarp C. Henkel.
Education: In 1836 moved in with his uncle Daniel Moser to study theology. About 1850-51 graduated with M.D. from University of Georgia Medical School, Augusta, Ga. Received D.D. degree.
Ordination: Ordained Deacon 1837 and Pastor 1838 by Tennessee Synod.
Calls: In North Carolina, 1837-42: with other pastors, Flat Rock, Stanly County, Lutheran Union, Cabarrus County; Morning Star, Mecklenburg County; Mt. Moriah, Rowan County; St. Martin, Cabarrus County; St. Martin, Stanly County. In Tennessee, 1844-46: Blue Springs, Sinking Springs, Cone Creek, and Salem. In Alabama, as Tennessee Synod missionary, also privately studying medicine under Drs. Francis and Clark. Later at Augusta, Ga., as noted above. Practiced medicine, in Alabama, for several years. Returned to North Carolina in 1854 to serve churches and practice medicine: In Watauga County, Mt. Pleasant, 1869; in Lincoln County: Trinity, Vale, 1854-74; Daniel's-St. Luke, 1855-75; organized Bethphage, 1858-73; and Salem, 1860-84. In Gaston County: Christ's, Stanley, 1854; and St. Mark, 1868-72; in Catawba County: Grace, 1855-54; Sardis, 1867-72; and Holy Trinity, Hickory, 1880-84; in Iredell County: Sharon-St. Martin, 1874-76; and St. Matthew, Kings Mountain, 1884.
Other: In addition to ministry and medical practice, also taught school at times in North Carolina, Tennessee, and Alabama, Secretary; Tennessee Synod, three one-year terms, 1843-64; President, six one-year terms, 1857-81; and Treasurer, 1871, 1876. Member, Tennessee Synod Committees: To Prepare Order for Licensure of Ministers, 1865; To Examine Books of Worship and Recommend One for Use in Tennessee Synod (*The Church Book of General Council* was recommended); On Joint Committees of North Carolina and Tennessee Synods to Present Basis for Union 1871 adopted by both synods, but later North Carolina Synod voted "to postpone all action in regard to union with other ecclesiastical bodies for five years," but a merger was effected 50 years later (1921); and To Submit Policy to Avoid Conflicts in the Work of the Two Synods, 1882.
Date of Death/Burial Location: June 10, 1884; Salem Church, Lincoln County, N.C.

FOX, CLARENCE MERKEL
Date/Place of Birth: August 11, 1870; Strasburg, Pa.
Parents: The Reverend Luther Augustine Fox and Marie Henrietta (Glossbrenner) Fox.
Spouse/Marriage Date: Minnie (Frye) Fox; May 8, 1901 in Cripple Creek, Va.
Children: Dorothy Clay, Luther Augustine, Thurston Givens, John Alfred.
Education: Roanoke College, A.B. 1890; Southern Seminary, Salem, Va.
License/Ordination: Licensed 1892 and ordained 1893 by Southwest Virginia Synod.
Calls: In South Carolina, 1894-97. In North Carolina: Coble's-Low's-Richland-St. Paul, Guilford and Alamance Counties, 1906-07; St. Enoch, Rowan County and Trinity, Cabarrus County, 1908-09; St. Stephen-Mt. Olive, Cabarrus County, 1914-16; Luther's-New Bethel-Mt. Zion, Richfield, 1916-18; supplied Lebanon, 1921; Grace 1922; and Concordia 1930 Rowan County; also churches in Tennessee and Virginia.
Date of Death/Burial Location: March 10, 1936; Salisbury, N.C.

FOX, DANIEL E.
License/Ordination: Licensed as Deacon 1863 by the Reverend P. C. Henkel on order of Tennessee Synod, and ordained as Pastor 1865 by Tennessee Synod.
Calls: Jackson Church (Mt. Pleasant), Watauga County.
Other: Served with the 38th North Carolina Regiment in the Confederate States of America. A nephew of the Reverend A. J. Fox.
Date of Death/Burial Location: 1866; St. John Church, Conover, Catawba County, N.C.

FOX, JUNIUS BOST, SR.
Date of Birth: June 17, 1860.
Parents: The Reverend Alfred J. Fox and Lydia (Bost) Fox. Younger brother of the Reverend L. A. Fox.
Spouse: Nancy (Mayes) Fox.
Children: Junius Bost, Jr., Nancy Elizabeth, William Mayes.
Education: Pennsylvania College, A.B., Ph.D.
Ordination: Examined and ordination authorized in 1883 by special committee, Tennessee Synod.
Calls: St. Matthew, Kings Mountain, 1881-83; first regular pastor, Good Shepherd, Mt. Holly, 1882-84; Transferred to Holston Synod, 1884; on clerical roll of South Carolina Synod, 1886-99. Organized Mt. Hermon, Peak, S.C., 1889; Redeemer, Newberry, S.C., 1893-99; St. Philip, Newberry, S.C., 1888.
Other: Author of a biography of the Reverend Alfred J. Fox, M.D., his father. Professor, Newberry College, 1885-92; Professor, Lutheran Theological Southern Seminary, 1889.
Date of Death/Burial Location: 1900; Newberry, S.C.

FOX, LUTHER AUGUSTINE
Date of Birth: August 8, 1843.
Parents: The Reverend Alfred J. Fox and Lydia (Bost) Fox. A younger brother was the Reverend Junius Bost Fox.
Spouse: Marie Henrietta (Glossbrenner) Fox.
Children: The Reverend Clarence Merkel, Alice Virginia (married the Reverend C. K. Bell), Horace, Alfred J.
Education: Attended North Carolina and Newberry Colleges; Roanoke College, A.B. 1868, D.D. 1881; Susquehanna University, L.L.D. 1915. No formal seminary training; studied theology under his father, Dr. Alfred J. Fox.
License/Ordination: Licensed 1863 and ordained 1864 by Tennessee Synod.
Calls: St. Mark, Gaston County, 1866; New Jerusalem, Davidson County, 1867. Transferred, 1868 to Southwest Virginia Synod. Transferred back to Tennessee Synod, 1871 from Ministerium of Pennsylvania. Transferred again to Southwest Virginia Synod, 1886.
Other: Professor, Roanoke College, 1882-1924; Secretary of Tennessee Synod, four one-year terms, 1866-81; President, 1874-75. President, Board, Lutheran Children's Home of the South, 1904-14. Associate Editor, *Our Church Paper*.
Date of Death/Burial Location: July 9, 1925; East Hill Cemetery, Salem, Va.

FOX, MICHAEL LEONARD
Date/Place of Birth: January 13, 1827; Randolph County, N.C.
Parents: Christian Fox and Charity (Moser) Fox.
Spouse: Sarah (Lutterloh) Fox; died 1899.
Children: William A., Julia, Leonard Michael, Cora M., Sally Ann, Dennis L., Thomas Israel, Junius C. Two sons followed father in medical profession.
Education: A medical doctor with M.D. degree who later studied theology, perhaps under guidance of second cousin, the Reverend Alfred J. Fox; received D.D. degree.
License/Ordination: Licensed 1867 and ordained 1871 by Tennessee Synod.
Calls: Coble's, Guilford County; Melanchthon, Randolph County; Mt. Pleasant, Alamance County, 1867-88.
Other: Had extensive medical practice in home county, Randolph, and adjoining counties, but fulfilled obligations to his parish. Representative, one term in North Carolina General Assembly.
Date of Death/Burial Location: July 22, 1888; Melanchthon Church, Randolph County, N.C.

FRANK, CHARLES H., SR.
Date/Place of Birth: May 28, 1912; Crestline, Ohio.
Parents: Charles William Frank and Priscilla Mae (Fletcher) Frank.
Spouse: Christine (Schilling) Frank; October 17, 1937 in Parkersburg, W.Va.
Children: The Reverend Paul Schilling, The Reverend Mark Henry, Charles H., Jr.
Education: Wittenberg University, B.A. 1934; Hamma Divinity School, B.D. 1937.
Ordination: 1938 by Ohio Synod.
Calls: Corinth, Rural Retreat, Va., 1967-72; Advent, Spindale, 1974-77.
Other: Transferred to Florida Synod, 1977. Retired June 1977.
Date of Death: August 16, 1982.

FRANKLOW, JOHN PHILIP
License/Ordination: Licensed April 1812 and ordained October 1812 in Lau's (Low's) Church, Guilford County, by North Carolina Synod.
Calls: Served in South Carolina until 1824 when the South Carolina Synod was organized: St. Matthew, Cameron, 1799-1814; Bethel (High Hill), Richland County, where preached in German, while the Reverend Godfrey Dreher preached in English; Zion, Lexington County; St. Michael, near Irmo.
Other: One of six North Carolina Synod pastors in South Carolina; the others, the Reverends John Y. Meetze, Godfrey Dreher, Michael Rauch, Jacob Moser, and Samuel Herscher, with their lay delegates, organized South Carolina Synod at St. Michael, near Irmo, S.C., in 1824.
Date of Death/Burial Location: September 4, 1829; Lexington County, S.C.

FRANZEN, DAVID MICHAEL
Date/Place of Birth: August 24, 1944; Britton, S.D.
Parents: Harold Gustar Franzen and Marian Eunice Franzen.
Spouse/Marriage Date: Janie Marie (Tunheim) Franzen; August 14, 1965.
Children: Signe Ruth, Kurt David.
Education: Gustavus Adolphus College, B.A. 1966; Chicago Seminary, M.Div. 1970; University of Virginia Medical Center, 1974-77; Duke University Divinity School, Th.M. 1984.
Ordination: July 12, 1970 by Red River Valley Synod.
Calls: Zion and Calvary, Winter, Wis., 1970-74; Lutheran Chaplain Supervisor, Duke University Medical Center, Durham, 1977-88; Lutheran Pastoral Counselor, Counseling Services, Inc., 1988-95. Vice Pastor at various congregations.
Other: Chair, Service to Leadership Committee, 1978-80; Chair, Candidacy Committee, 1984-. President, North Carolina Association of Pastoral Counselors; Certified Supervisor, Association for Clinical Pastoral Education; Certified Fellow, American Association of Pastoral Counselors; North Carolina State Certified Fee- Based Practicing Pastoral Counselor; Certified Fellow, The College of Chaplains, A.P.H.A.; North Carolina Chaplains' Association.

FRAZIER, CYRUS FIELD, JR.
Date/Place of Birth: August 23, 1927; Claremont, Catawba County, N.C.
Parents: Cyrus Field, Sr. and Zelda Belle (Huffman) Frazier.
First Spouse/Marriage Date: Ann Ranes (Cline) Frazier (deceased); April 15, 1958 in Charlotte, N.C.; died July 18, 1984.
Children of First Marriage: Laura Cline Merritt, Cyrus Field, III, Matthew Woody.
Second Spouse/Marriage Date: Ann (Hartsfield) Frazier; April 28, 1990.
Education: Lenoir-Rhyne, A.B. 1953; Lutheran Theological Southern Seminary, B.D. 1956.
Ordination: June 10, 1956 by North Carolina Synod.
Calls: Good Shepherd, Mt. Holly, 1956-93; Pastor Emeritus. Interim Pastor at various congregations.

Other: Retired August 30, 1993 in Mt. Holly. Board, Lutheran Children's Home of the South, 1965-77; Secretary, Southwestern District, 1964-70; Board, Stanly Total Living Center, 1986-; Committees: Chair, World Missions, 1970; Nominating Committee; American Missions; Youth Committee; Historical Works Committee.

FREDERICK, DANIEL HENRY

Date/Place of Birth: October 4, 1909; Luckey, Ohio.
Parents: The Reverend Martin Luther Frederick and Mary (Kruckeberg) Frederick.
Spouse/Marriage Date: Miriam (Beal) Frederick; July 7, 1940, in Bucyrus, Ohio.
Children: Daniel Martin, Robert Milton, Cherrie Ann Murphy.
Education: Capital University, A.B. 1934; Capital University Seminary, B.D. 1937; University of Texas, Counseling, 1956.
Ordination: October 17, 1937 by Michigan Synod.
Calls: St. Paul-Emmanuel (ALC), Leesville-Hopewell, Ohio, 1937-39; St. Paul-St. John, Celina, Ohio, 1939- 46; Chaplain during WWII; St. Paul, Dayton, Ohio, 1946-51; U.S. Air Force Chaplain, 1951-66; Addis Ababa - Ethiopia International Lutheran Church, 1966-68; Shepherd of the Sea, Atlantic Beach, 1973-76. Vice Pastor at various congregations.
Other: Received Bronze Star, American Defense Service Medal, American Campaign Medal, Asiatic-Pacific Theater of Operations Service Medal, Philippines Liberation Medal, World War II Victory Medal, Air Force Commendation Medal, Asiatic Victory Medal, Longevity Medal. Retired as Colonel, U.S. Air Force. Taught Air Force Reserve Officer Training Corps program and Junior Reserve Officer Training Corps at West Carteret High School, Morehead City. First Chaplain and Director of the Ministry to Seamen at Morehead City, 1976- 81. Retired November 1976 to Wilson, N.C. and New Smyrna Beach, Fla.
Date of Death/Burial Location: March 31, 1999.

FREED, WALTER BITNER, SR.

Date/Place of Birth: September 29, 1909; Johnstown, Pa.
Parents: Benjamin F. Freed and Leanora (Walter) Freed.
Spouse/Marriage Date: Natalie (Selser) Freed; June 21, 1938 in Mercersburg, Pa.
Children: Rosann Mary Whitten, Barbara Bitner Barnhart, Walter Bitner, Jr.
Education: Gettysburg College, A.B. 1930, D.D. 1948; Gettysburg Seminary, B.D. 1933.
License/Ordination: Licensed 1932 and ordained May 17, 1933 by Allegheny Synod.
Calls: Trinity, Greencastle, Pa., 1933-37. In North Carolina: St. Paul, Wilmington, 1937-48; St. Mark's, Charlotte, 1948-54; Luther Place Memorial, Washington, D.C., 1954-60; Zion, Sunbury, Pa., 1960-65; Reformation, Rochester, N.Y., 1965-80.
Other: Board, Lenoir-Rhyne, 1946-54; Special lecturer in preaching, Lutheran Theological Southern Seminary, 1953-54; President, United Lutheran Church in America and Lutheran Church in America Board of Parish Education, 1954-65; Trustee, Susquehanna University, 1965-80; Delegate to numerous National Conventions, United Lutheran Church in America and Lutheran Church in America; contributor to religious

and secular magazines; sermons published; religious radio and television. Retired in 1980.

Date of Death/Burial Location: October 9, 1988; Rochester, N.Y.

FREEZE, GRAY LAWRENCE

Date/Place of Birth: September 23, 1925; Kannapolis, Cabarrus County, N.C.

Parents: William Reynolds Freeze and Effie (Gatton) Freeze.

Spouse/Marriage Date: Florence Estelle (Yarbrough) Freeze; May 28, 1950 in Salisbury, N.C.

Education: Brevard College, two years, Catawba College, A.B. 1947; Lutheran Theological Southern Seminary, B.D. 1950.

Ordination: June 25, 1950 by North Carolina Synod.

Calls: Assistant Pastor, First English, Richmond, Va., 1950-51; St. Andrew, New Bern, 1951-54; St. Stephen-Mt. Olive, Gold Hill, 1954-58; Christ, East Spencer, 1958-64; St. Luke, Monroe, 1964-67; Immanuel, Cairo, Ill., 1967-70; Calvary, Chicago, Ill., 1970-76; Calvary-Trinity, Chicago, Ill., 1976-92. Retired to Saratoga, Fla., November 1, 1992.

FRESEMAN, DAVID RICHARD

Date/Place of Birth: September 11, 1947; Lodi, Ohio.

Parents: The Reverend Richard D. Freseman and Doralee (Hoffman) Freseman.

Spouse/Marriage Date: Susan Elaine (House) Freseman; December 21, 1969 in Westerville, Ohio.

Children: Kathryn, Deborah, Adam.

Education: Capital University, B.A. 1969; Trinity, M.Div. 1973.

Ordination: June 24, 1973 by Ohio Synod.

Calls: First, Avoca, Neb., 1973-82; Calvary, Scottsbluff, Neb., 1982-90; Pastor-Developer Community, Greensboro, 1990-96.

Other: Nebraska Synod Council; Nebraska Synod Transition Team; North Carolina Synod Council. Resigned from ministry December 5, 1996.

FRICK, VERNON ARDELL

Date/Place of Birth: July 7, 1925; Chapin, S.C.

Parents: Jonas Berley Frick and Annie Mae (Riddle) Frick.

Spouse/Marriage Date: Ethel (Clamp) Frick; June 2, 1946 in Prosperity, S.C.

Children: Humis Dawn Merrell, Kristie Vernell Wells, Amy Doratha.

Education: Newberry College, A.B. 1950; Lutheran Theological Southern Seminary, B.D. 1953.

Ordination: June 7, 1953 by South Carolina Synod.

Calls: In South Carolina: Lexington Parish, Lexington, 1953-57; Nativity, Spartanburg, 1957-61. In North Carolina: Union, Rowan County, 1961-71; Frieden's, Gibsonville, 1971-78; Holy Trinity, Troutman, 1978-83. Vice Pastor at various congregations.

Other: U.S. Navy during World War II.

Date of Death/Burial Location: May 15, 1983; Union Church Cemetery, Salisbury, N.C.

FRICK, WOODROW FELTON
Date/Place of Birth: December 7, 1946; Newberry, S.C.
Parents: Wyman Stone Frick and Myra Ruth (Shealy) Frick.
Spouse/Marriage Date: Zelia Elizabeth (Fisher) Frick; April 15, 1971 in Cayce, S.C.
Children: Rebekah Elizabeth, Benjamin Woodrow.
Education: University of North Carolina at Charlotte, B.A. History 1969; Lutheran Theological Southern Seminary, M. Div. 1973.
Ordination: June 3, 1973 by North Carolina Synod.
Calls: St. Mark, Lumberton, 1973-77; Colony, Newberry, S.C., 1977-81; St. James, Rockwell, 1981-1995; Unity, Hickory, 1995-; Vice Pastor, Christ the King, Whiteville, 1973-77.
Other: Historical Works Committee, 1984-85.

FRITZ, CHARLES EVERETT
Date/Place of Birth: June 25, 1891; Davidson County, N.C.
Parents: William Fritz and Albertine (Grimes) Fritz. An older half-brother was the Reverend R. L. Fritz.
Spouse/Marriage Date: Rose Margaret (Stump) Fritz (daughter of the Reverend Joseph Stump); April 26, 1917 in Maywood, Ill.; died August 29, 1958.
Children: Charles Joseph, the Reverend William Richard, Sr., Alice Albertine, the Reverend Robert Douglas, Sr., Elizabeth Anne.
Education: Lenoir-Rhyne, A.B. 1914, D.D. 1939; Chicago Seminary, 1917.
Ordination: 1917 by Tennessee Synod.
Calls: Holy Communion-Antioch-Philadelphia-St. Paul, Dallas, 1917-19. In Indiana, 1919-22; in Wisconsin, 1922-35; First, Greensboro, 1935-39. In South Carolina: Ebenezer, Columbia, S.C., 1940-49. In Georgia: Peachtree Road, Atlanta, Ga., 1949-50.
Other: President, Georgia-Alabama Synod, 1950-57. Delegate of Tennessee Synod to United Lutheran Church in America merger convention 1918 and other conventions; Board, Lenoir-Rhyne, 1937-39; United Lutheran Church in America Board of Adjudication. Published pamphlets, and contributed articles to periodicals.
Date of Death/Burial Location: November 6, 1957; Columbia, S.C.

FRITZ, ROBERT DOUGLAS, SR.
Date/Place of Birth: January 18, 1927; Waukesha, Wis.
Parents: The Reverend Charles Everett Fritz and Rose Margaret (Stump) Fritz.
Spouse/Marriage Date: Anne Estelle (McClintock) Fritz; June 8, 1952 in Montreat, N.C.
Children: Robert Douglas, Jr., David Alan.
Education: Lenoir-Rhyne, A.B. 1947, D.D. 1971; Lutheran Theological Southern Seminary, B.D. 1950.
Ordination: June 5, 1950 by Georgia-Alabama Synod.
Calls: In North Carolina: Mt. Hebron, Hildebran, 1950-54; Resurrection, Kings Mountain, 1954-58. In Kentucky-Tennessee Synod: Bethany,

Memphis, Tenn., 1958-1962. In North Carolina: St. John, Salisbury, 1962-75. In Florida: King of Glory, Port Richey, 1975-80.
Other: Board, Lenoir-Rhyne, 1965-68, 1973-76; Chair, Evangelism Committee, Southeastern Synod; Executive Board, North Carolina Synod, 1968-73; Lutheran Church in America Delegate, 1966; American Missions Committee, 1964-68. Co-founder, Rowan Cooperative Christian Ministry. Retired January 1, 1981 in Columbia, S.C.

FRITZ, ROBERT LINDSAY, SR.
Date/Place of Birth: February 2, 1869; Davidson County, N.C.
Parents: William Fritz and Lucretia (Bowers) Fritz. Mother died day of his birth. The Reverend Charles E. Fritz was a younger half-brother.
Spouse/Marriage Date: Ora Leslie (Huit) Fritz; April 30, 1896 in Catawba County, N.C.
Children: Robert Lindsay, Jr., Herbert Huit, Ruth Katharine, Ora Louise, Mary Lucretia, William Abel, Jacob L., John Richard, Dorothy Esther, Lula Elizabeth, and Conrad Bowers.
Education: Roanoke, Concordia, and Lenoir-Rhyne, A.B. 1891; studied theology at Concordia and Lenoir College; Lenoir-Rhyne, Honorary M.A. 1895, D.D. 1913, L.L.D. 1941; graduate study, Johns Hopkins University, and University of North Carolina.
License/Ordination: Licensed 1891 and ordained 1894 by Tennessee Synod.
Calls: Chiefly supply work, due to teaching and administrative duties in colleges: Salem, Lincoln County; St. Paul, Catawba County, 1897; with others, Shiloh, Alexander County, 1896-1907; St. Andrew, Hickory, 1894-95; Good Hope, Hickory.
Other: For 56 years, except 1897-1901 (when on faculty of Elizabeth College, Charlotte), served at Lenoir- Rhyne, as teacher, 1891-97; President and Professor, 1901-20; Professor and Head, Mathematics Department, 1920-47; Professor Emeritus, 1947-61. Retired 1947 at Hickory. Men's dormitory at college is named in his memory. Member: Mu Sigma Epsilon, Chi Beta Phi, North Carolina Academy of Science, Mathematics Association of America, and (life) National Education Association; listed in *Who's Who in America*. Last survivor of original faculty and of first graduating class of Lenoir-Rhyne.
Date of Death/Burial Location: October 6, 1961; Oakwood Cemetery, Hickory, N.C.

FRITZ, WILLIAM RICHARD, JR.
Date/Place of Birth: February 7, 1949; Columbia, S.C.
Parents: William Richard Fritz, Sr. and Evelyn Rogers (Ackerman) Fritz.
Spouse/Marriage Date: Cecilia Roesel (Carpenter) Fritz (daughter of the Reverend Cecil Walter Carpenter); August 14, 1976.
Children: Paul Christian, Kathlyn Elizabeth Marie.
Education: Yale University, B.A. Philosophy 1972; Lutheran Theological Southern Seminary, M.Div. 1977.
Ordination: May 19, 1977 by South Carolina Synod.
Calls: Bethany, Lexington, Va. and New Mt. Olive, Fairfield, Va., 1977-80; St. John and St. Matthias, Norfolk, Va., 1980-83; Ascension, Danville, Va., 1983-95; St. Andrew, Hickory, 1995-.

FRY, HOMER EDGAR

Date/Place of Birth: November 5, 1927; Newton, Catawba County, N.C.
Parents: George Franklin Fry, Sr. and Mattie Anna (Miller) Fry.
Spouse/Marriage Date: Alice Eldora (Barnhardt) Fry; May 27, 1956 in Concord, N.C.
Children: Trudy Ellen Reese, Franklin Edgar, Nelson Earl.
Education: Lenoir-Rhyne, A.B. 1951; Lutheran Theological Southern Seminary, B.D. 1955.
Ordination: 1955 by North Carolina Synod.
Calls: Luther's, Richfield, 1955-57; Christ's, Stanley, 1957-62; Holly Grove, Lexington, 1962-64; Cross of Christ (formerly Prosperity), Concord, 1964-71; New Covenant, High Point, 1972-73; Reformation, Taylorsville, 1973-75; Sardis, Hickory, 1975-85. Vice Pastor at various congregations.
Other: Retired in 1985 in Newton, N.C.; Board, North Carolina Lutheran Homes, 1971-73.

FRY, THOMAS

Place of Birth: Lincoln County, N.C.
License: At 1865 Tennessee Synod Convention he applied for licensure. A committee of the Reverends P. C. Henkel and J. M. Smith, examining him, found that he could not read or write, and was not otherwise qualified to be licensed.
Calls: Even though not licensed, for most of his life he ministered to his own people in Catawba and Lincoln Counties, and organized St. Peter in Catawba County, N.C.
Other: Member of Alpha Synod.

FRYE, MICHAEL WAYNE

Date/Place of Birth: May 27, 1947; Cabarrus County, N.C.
Parents: Martin Luther Frye and Mary Alice (Clontz) Frye.
Spouse/Marriage Date: Judy Vernice (Sloop) Frye; August 16, 1969 in Kannapolis, N.C.
Children: Elizabeth Anne, Jennifer Leigh.
Education: Lenoir-Rhyne, A.B. History 1969; Lutheran Theological Southern Seminary, M.Div. 1973; Eastern Baptist Seminary, D.Min. 1987.
Ordination: June 3, 1973 by North Carolina Synod.
Calls: Gloria Dei, Salisbury, 1973-77; Mission Developer/Pastor Living Saviour, Charlotte, 1977-92; Christ, Dallas, Texas, 1992-94; Lutheran Chapel, Gastonia, 1995-. Vice Pastor at various congregations.
Other: President, North Carolina Luther League Unit, 1997-98; Chair, Youth Ministry Committee; Chair, Family Life Committee, 1990-92; Delegate to Lutheran Church in America Assembly, 1972, Evangelical Lutheran Church in America Assembly, 1990; Board, Lutheran Children's Home of the South; Board, Lutheran Family Services in North Carolina.

FULENWIDER, EDWARD, SR.

Date/Place of Birth: November 29, 1876; Salisbury, N.C.
Parents: G. O. Fulenwider and Millie (Earnhardt) Fulenwider.
Spouse/Marriage Date: M. Venora (Blackwelder) Fulenwider; May 6, 1903 in Mt. Pleasant, N.C.
Children: Paul Edward B., George Osborne, Mary Houseal (died at age 3), Edward, Jr.
Education: North Carolina College, A.B. 1899; Lutheran Theological Southern Seminary, 1902; Newberry College, D.D. 1925.
Ordination: 1902 by North Carolina Synod.
Calls: St. Andrew-Mt. Hermon, Concord, 1902-04; as synodical missionary, organized and served First Church, Lexington, 1904-08; Redeemer, Newberry, S.C., 1908-20; St. John, Salisbury, 1920-30; Macedonia, Burlington, 1930-40; Holy Trinity, Troutman, 1940-47. Supplied Mt. Gilead, Cabarrus County, 1947-53; also, 1954-55; Faith, Faith; Luther's, Rowan County; and St. Andrew, Concord.
Other: Retired 1947 at Mt. Pleasant, N.C.; later resided at Union, S.C. Board, Lenoir-Rhyne; President, South Carolina Synod, 1916-18. Delegate, organizing convention (1918) and other United Lutheran Church in America conventions.
Date of Death/Burial Location: May 1, 1962 at Union, S.C.; Rosemont Cemetery, Newberry, S.C.

FULMER, CLARENCE LUTHER, JR.

Date/Place of Birth: August 18, 1929; Augusta, Ga.
Parents: Clarence Luther Fulmer, Sr. and Julia (McCarty) Fulmer.
Education: Junior College of Augusta, two years, Newberry College, A.B. 1951; Lutheran Theological Southern Seminary, B.D. 1954.
Ordination: 1954 by Georgia-Alabama Synod.
Calls: Ebenezer, Rowan County, 1954-57; St. Timothy, Forest Park, Ga., 1957-61; Associate Pastor, Holy Trinity, Buffalo, N.Y., 1961-.
Date of Death: August 12, 1985.

FULMER, VERLEY LORENZO

Date/Place of Birth: September 11, 1887; Lexington County, S.C.
Parents: Sidney C. Fulmer and Ada (Wessinger) Fulmer.
Spouse/Marriage Date: Edith P. (Shell) Fulmer; July 15, 1913 in Hickory, N.C.
Children: Alice Rebecca, Rachel Shell, Ruth Virginia, John Henry, Edith Lorene, James Verley.
Education: Lenoir-Rhyne, A.B. 1910; Lutheran Theological Southern Seminary, 1913, B.D. 1927; Franklin and Marshall College, M.A. 1926.
Ordination: 1913 by South Carolina Synod.
Calls: Bethel Parish, White Rock, S.C., 1913-15; Beth Eden, Newton, 1915-20; New Jerusalem-Zion, Catawba County, 1915-17; St. Timothy, Catawba County, 1916-20; Rader-St. Paul-St. John, Timberville, Va. 1920-23; Zion, Marietta, Pa.

Other: Board, Lowman Home, 1914-15. Author of several church and family histories. Business Manager for the *Catawba Lutheran* in 1917; Editor, 1918.
Date of Death/Burial Location: March 5, 1959; Zion Church, Leacock, Pa.

FUTCHS, JOHN FREDERICK
Date/Place of Birth: June 10, 1906; Wilmington, N.C.
Parents: John William Henry Futchs and Mary (Strunck) Futchs.
Spouse: Selma Ruth (Bergner) Futchs; October 2, 1945 in Chicago, Ill.
Child: Mariya Johanna (Futchs) Fine.
Education: Wagner College, A.B. 1927; Philadelphia Seminary, B.D. 1930; Midland, D.D.
Ordination: July 9, 1931 by Ministerium of Pennsylvania.
Calls: Zion-St. Matthew, Weatherly, Pa., 1930-31; Burkes Garden Parish, Burkes Garden, Va., 1940-42; Trinity, Boulder, Colo., 1942-51; President, Rocky Mountain Synod, 1951-57; St. Paul, El Paso, Texas, 1957- 63; Messiah, Denver, Colo., 1963-71. Interim Pastor at St. Paul, Wilmington.
Other: Retired June 1971 to Wilmington, N.C. Organized chapter of Common Cause in Wilmington.
Date of Death/Burial Location: August 27, 1998; Wilmington, N.C.

FUTTERER, JOHN WINDUS, SR.
Date/Place of Birth: February 12, 1959; Rockingham, N.C.
Parents: William Frances Futterer, Jr. and Mary (Warrick) Futterer.
Spouse/Marriage Date: Anne (Martin) Futterer; May 14, 1983 in Hamlet, N.C.
Child: Annie Carlon.
Education: University of North Carolina at Charlotte, B.A. Religion 1981; Duke University, M.Div. 1984; graduate work at Lutheran Theological Southern Seminary, 1984-86.
Ordination: May 30, 1986 by North Carolina Synod.
Calls: Kimball Memorial, Kannapolis, 1986-89; Resurrection, Kings Mountain, 1989-95; First, Albemarle, 1995-. Vice Pastor at various congregations.

GANTT, JAMES RICHARD
Date/Place of Birth: September 11, 1933; High Point, N.C.
Parents: Claude Miles Gantt, Sr. and Martha Margaret (Ledbetter) Gantt.
Spouse/Marriage Date: Connie Lee (McElveen) Gantt; August 30, 1958 in Atlanta, Ga.
Children: Donna Celeste Bauer, Kellie Dianne Racine, Allison Dawn Hagan.
Education: Lenoir-Rhyne, B.A. 1956; Lutheran Theological Southern Seminary, M.Div. 1959, S.T.M. 1970; Newberry College, D.D. 1990.
Ordination: June 7, 1959 by North Carolina Synod.
Calls: St. Andrew, Concord, 1959-62; Mission Developer/Pastor, Our Saviour, Tampa, Fla., 1962-67; Good Shepherd, College Park, Ga., 1967-73; Regional Director, Division for Mission in North America, Lutheran Church in America, 1973-87; Mission Director, Division for Outreach, Evangelical Lutheran Church in America, 1988-98. Retired October 31, 1998.
Other: Church Extension Committee; Mission Planning Task Force; Multi-Ministry Task Force; Synod Council of the Southeastern Synod; Board of Trustees, Lutheran

Theological Southern Seminary; Senior Consultant for Kairos and Associates, Leesburg, Va. 1999-.

GANTT, JONATHAN

Spouse: Pamela Gantt.
Education: Lenoir-Rhyne, B.A. Christian Education 1992; Gettysburg Seminary, M.Div. 1996.
Ordination: September 15, 1996 by North Carolina Synod.
Calls: St. Paul, Hamlet, 1996-98; St. Mark's, Mooresville, 1998-.
Other: Habitat for Humanity, Williamsport Food Bank.

GARDNER, JEFFREY ERIK

Date/Place of Birth: April 15, 1961; Elyria, Ohio.
Parents: Stewart Phillips Gardner and Janis (Benson) Gardner.
Spouse/Marriage Date: Michelle (Martin) Gardner; August 17, 1985 in Greensboro, N.C.
Children: Jacob Erik, Ashley Martin.
Education: University of North Carolina at Chapel Hill, B.A. Religious Studies 1983; Lutheran Theological Southern Seminary, M.Div. 1988; Doctorate studies at Drew University.
Ordination: June 5, 1988 by North Carolina Synod.
Calls: Beth Eden, Newton, 1988-92; St. John, Concord, 1992-96; Christ Lutheran, Charlotte, 1996-.
Other: Chair, Youth Ministry Committee, 1991, 1992; Project Leader, Cabarrus Lutheran Habitat for Humanity House, 1994; Chair, Catawba County CROP Walk, 1989; Vice President Eastern Catawba Cooperative Christian Ministry, 1991-92; Spiritual Director for Western North Carolina Lutheran Via de Cristo movement; author, *Our Church's One Foundation - Jesus Christ; A Brief History of St. John Lutheran Church, Concord.*

GEORGE, JOHN JACOB, SR.

Date/Place of Birth: June 15, 1866; Lexington County, S.C.
Parents: Nelson Benjamin George and Isabel (Shealy) George.
Spouse/Marriage Date: Frances Pearl (Mauney) George; July 29, 1896 in Cherryville, N.C.
Children: Virgil and Virgie (twins, died day of birth), Frances Linchen, Melba Kerne, Prentis Legare, Katherine Isaminnie, Samuel Delmas, John Howard, Mary Reba, Marjorie, Sidney Spitzer (died at six months), Garcie Celestine, Ruth Mauney, John Jacob, Jr.
Education: Newberry College, Concordia College, Lenoir-Rhyne, A.B. 1892; graduate study one year, Columbia University.
Ordination: 1893 by Tennessee Synod.
Calls: Churches served in North Carolina, 1893-99: St. Mark, Crouse; Bethphage, Lincoln County; St. John's, Cherryville.
Other: Engaged in business in Cherryville after 1899. Treasurer, Tennessee Synod, 1896-97; Member, as layman, of two joint (North Carolina and Tennessee Synods) Committees: To Develop Summer School for Church Workers, 1907; and On Arrangements for North Carolina and Tennessee Synods Merger Convention in 1921.
Date of Death/Burial Location: September 16, 1932; Cherryville, N.C.

GERBERDING, WILLIAM PASSAVANT, SR.
Date/Place of Birth: April 4, 1892; Fargo, N.D.
Parents: The Reverend J. H. Gerberding and Annie (Danver) Gerberding.
First Spouse/Marriage Date: Name Unknown.
Children of First Marriage: John H., Dorothy Grohs, Myrtha Sailand, William Passavant, Jr., Donna Cheatham.
Second Spouse/Marriage Date: Mildred (Ott) Gerberding; October 8, 1947 in St. Paul, Minn.
Child of Second Marriage: Thomas.
Education: Thiel College, A.B. 1915, Honorary A.M. 1918, D.D. 1951; Chicago Seminary, 1918.
Ordination: 1918 by Pittsburgh Synod.
Calls: In Pennsylvania and Wisconsin, 1918-26; St. Mark, Fargo, N.D., 1926-38; Holy Trinity, St. Paul, Minn., 1938-51. In North Carolina: St. Matthew, Kings Mountain, 1951-1964. Retired 1964 at Winter Park, Fla.
Other: Member 1940-52 and Vice President 1946-52 United Lutheran Church in America Board of Foreign Missions; Commissioner, Board of Missions in Liberia, Africa, 1945; Examining Committee, 1962-65.
Date of Death/Burial Location: August 23, 1965; Woodlawn Cemetery, St. Petersburg, Fla.

GERHARD, STEPHEN PAUL
Date/Place of Birth: November 13, 1945; Woodbury, N.J.
Parents: The Reverend Harry Paul Gerhard and Helen (Munch) Gerhard.
Spouse/Marriage Date: Barbara Jeanne (Foreman) Gerhard; August 24, 1968 in Camp Hill, Pa.
Children: Christopher Paul, Meredith Courtney.
Education: Thiel College, A.B. English Literature 1967; Philadelphia Seminary, M.Div. 1971; Pittsburgh Seminary, Th.M. 1976.
Ordination: June 13, 1971 by Western Pennsylvania-West Virginia Synod.
Calls: Messiah, Moundsville, W.Va., 1971-74; Lutheran Campus Ministry, Raleigh, 1974-79; Holy Trinity, Raleigh (Associate 1974-79, Senior Pastor 1980-95); Epiphany, Winston-Salem, 1995-.
Other: Board, Lenoir-Rhyne, 1981-90; Dean, Eastern Conference, 1988-92; Synod Council, 1992-95; First Chair of Board, Raleigh Urban Ministries, 1981; President, Raleigh Ministerial Association, 1986; Chair, North Carolina State University Cooperative Campus Ministry, 1978; Synodical Committees: Candidacy, Stewardship, Campus Ministry. Publication of articles in *Lutheran Women Today* and *Soli Deo Gloria*.

GERHARDT, WILLIAM
Date/Place of Birth: October 28, 1817; Beuern, Hesse Darmstadt, Germany.
Parents: Baltzer Gerhardt and Anna Maria (Henz) Gerhardt.
First Spouse/Marriage Date: Lucinda A. (Riley) Gerhardt; November 9, 1844 in Fairfield, Pa.
Children of First Marriage: Lewis DeWitt.
Second Spouse/Marriage Date: Mrs. C. A. (Mantz) Gerhardt; 1887.

Education: Gettysburg College, A.B. 1841; Gettysburg Seminary, 1847; North Carolina College, D.D. 1880.

License/Ordination: Licensed 1847 and ordained 1850 by Ministerium of Pennsylvania.

Calls: Mt. Carmel, near Mt. Pleasant, which later was merged with Lutheran Union Church (Tennessee Synod) to form Mt. Gilead Church, Cabarrus County; Supply, St. Paul, Iredell County, 1859. In Pennsylvania, 1860-67; Martinsburg, W.Va., 1867-90.

Other: Taught school several years in Maryland and Ohio, and educational positions held in Pennsylvania, 1847-55; first Principal and Professor Western Carolina Male Academy (name changed to North Carolina College in 1859), Mt. Pleasant, 1855-59; President, North Carolina Synod, 1856-57. Principal, Franklin Academy, Concord, 1859-60; Principal, schools in Martinsburg, W.Va., 1867-90.

Date of Death/Burial Location: December 6, 1917; Martinsburg, W.Va.

GERSCHWITZ, PAUL RAY

Date/Place of Birth: June 13, 1929; Gibsonville, N.C.

Parents: O. H. Gerschwitz and M. E. (Starke) Gerschwitz.

Spouse/Marriage Date: Erika (Steiniger) Gerschwitz; January 16, 1964 in Melbourne, Australia.

Children: Dieter Paul, Heidi, Krista.

Education: Adelaide University, Australia; Augsburg, Minneapolis, B.A. 1967; Gettysburg Seminary; M.Div. 1970.

Ordination: June 14, 1970 by Central Pennsylvania Synod.

Calls: Sharon, Gibsonville, 1970-72.

Other: Transferred to Lutheran Church in Australia, 1972.

GIESLER, HENRY D.

Date of Birth: February 2, 1833.

Ordination: Ordained Deacon September 10, 1859 by Tennessee Synod, in Bethlehem Church, Augusta County, Va. and Pastor by Holston Synod, January 2, 1861 at its first convention.

Date of Death: 1865 presumably, while serving as Secretary Pro-tem of Holston Synod. The Reverend J. K. Hancher conducted his funeral at 1865 synod convention.

GILBERT, JACKSON GEORGE, JR.

Date/Place of Birth: November 5, 1951; Charlotte, N.C.

Parents: Jackson George Gilbert, Sr. and Helen (Branner) Gilbert.

Spouse/Marriage Date: Linda (Hicks) Gilbert; August 7, 1976 in Charlotte, N.C.

Children: Jackson George, III, Derrick Andrew.

Education: Lenoir-Rhyne, A.B. 1973; additional study at University of North Carolina at Charlotte, 1977; Lutheran Theological Southern Seminary, M.Div. 1987; doctorate studies at Drew University.

Ordination: May 19, 1987 by North Carolina Synod.

Calls: Our Saviour, Welcome, 1987-89; Redeemer, Charlotte, 1989-96; Pastor-Developer, Grace Mission, Charlotte, 1996-. Vice Pastor at various congregations.

Other: President, Lutheran Clergy Association of Charlotte, 1991-94; President, Lutheran Clergy (Evangelical Lutheran Church in America and The Lutheran Church-Missouri

Synod) Association of Mecklenburg County, 1994-; Board Member, Presbyterian Career and Personal Counseling Service, Charlotte (Lutheran Board Member), 1993-; Spiritual Director, Lutheran Via de Cristo Secretariat, 1993-; Head Spiritual Director, Western North Carolina Lutheran Via de Cristo Secretariat, 1995-; Board, Treasurer, Charlotte Area Clergy Association, 1992-94.

GILLIKIN, KENNETH CRAIG

Date/Place of Birth: August 2, 1963; Baltimore, Md.
Parents: Lowell Thomas Gillikin and Donna Marie Gillikin.
Spouse/Marriage Date: Margaret (Wilson) Gillikin; July 24, 1993.
Education: Valparaiso University, B.S.W. 1985; Lutheran Theological Southern Seminary, M.Div. 1994.
Ordination: October 12, 1994, by North Carolina Synod.
Calls: St. John, Asheboro, 1994-.

GILREATH, GARY ALLAN

Date/Place of Birth: March 3, 1951; Wilkes County, N.C.
Parents: Claude Williams Gilreath and Lela Faye (Parris) Gilreath.
Spouse/Marriage Date: Mary Eloise (Ritchie) Gilreath; June 19, 1976 in Lexington, N.C.
Children: Erin Marie, Joshua Carl Williams.
Education: Lenoir-Rhyne, B.A. 1979; Lutheran Theological Southern Seminary, M.Div. 1983.
Ordination: July 9, 1983 by North Carolina Synod.
Calls: Holy Cross, Mocksville, 1983-86.
Other: Supervisor, Police Chaplaincy Services, City of Tallahassee, Fla. Police Department, 1981-82; Departmental Chaplain of Police, Town of Mocksville Police Department, 1983-86; Pioneer in establishing standard institute for educating and certifying Police Chaplains, 1981-86; Member, International Association of Police Chaplains, 1981-86; Member, Executive Committee for Continuing Education; established Police Chaplaincy Services with various law enforcement agencies throughout Southeast, 1981-86. Retired disabled 1986 to North Wilkesboro, N.C.

GITLIN, EMMANUEL

Date/Place of Birth: November 9, 1922; Zdolbunow, Poland, now in the Ukraine.
Parents: Moses H. Gitlin and Clara S. (Pikman) Gitlin.
First Spouse/Date of Marriage: Ethel (Ruppenthal) Gitlin; February 7, 1946.
Children of First Marriage: Sharon Jane Robertson, David Ernest.
Second Spouse/Date of Marriage: Helen Warren (Edmiston) Gitlin; December 19, 1961 in Daytona Beach, Fla.
Education: Columbia International University; University of South Carolina; Texas Christian University, B.A. History 1946; Duke University Divinity School, M.Div. 1946; graduate work at Divinity School, University of Chicago, 1944-45; Johns Hopkins University (Oriental Institute), 1946-48; Duke University, Ph.D. 1953.

Ordination: Ordained by the Minnesota Conference, United Methodist Church, 1951; North Carolina Synod, June 1, 1969.

Calls: Associate Minister, First Methodist, Austin, Minn., 1950-53; St. John Methodist, St. Louis, Mo., 1953; Associate Minister, Chapel Hill Methodist Circuit, Chapel Hill, 1956-57. Vice Pastor at various congregations in North Carolina. Five-year term of missionary service in Croatia and Poland under the Mennonite Central Committee, Akron, Pa., teaching in theological seminaries.

Other: Phi Beta Kappa at Duke University. Teaching appointments under Methodist Bishops at University of North Carolina at Chapel Hill, 1953-57; Perkins School of Theology, Southern Methodist University, Dallas, Texas, 1947-61; Bethune-Cookman College, Daytona Beach, Fla., 1961-63; University of Florida, Gainesville, Fla., 1963-67. Teaching appointment as Professor of Biblical Studies, Lenoir-Rhyne, under the North Carolina Synod, 1968-91. Lecturer for Lutheran and Baptist seminary programs in Russia in the Russian language.   Two three-month terms of pastoral service in Israel, 1970s. Articles on *Biblical Theology in Judaism, Motive, Christianity in Life, Western Humanities Review, Eternity, The Episcopalian, Dialog, Encounter, Christian Advocate,* and other theological journals in English, Russian, Polish, Croatian and Hebrew languages.   Director of Hebrew-Christian Center in Pittsburgh, Pa.   Published book: *The Little Flock: Jews in the Church of Christ.* Teacher, New Testament course at Caldwell Community College and Talmud-Torah class at the Jewish-Reformed Temple Beth Shalom. Lectured at Mansfield College, Oxford University, England. Retired June 1991 in Hickory, N.C.   More than 20 years of his over 40 years as an ordained clergy were served in North Carolina.

GLASS, JOSEPH DINSON, JR.

Date/Place of Birth: December 29, 1935; Kannapolis, N.C.

Parents: Joseph Dinson Glass, Sr. and Lelia (Shive) Glass.

Spouse/Marriage Date: Carolyn (Wise) Glass; July 26, 1958 in Asheville, N.C.

Children: Joseph Dinson, III, Sharon Carole, Mark Rembert.

Education: Duke University, A.B. 1957; Lutheran Theological Southern Seminary, B.D. 1960. Yale University, M.A. 1962, Ph.D. 1964.

Ordination: June 5, 1960 by North Carolina Synod.

Calls: Assistant, Beth Eden, Newton, 1960-61. Professor of Christian Education, Lenoir-Rhyne, 1964-. Vice Pastor at various congregations.

Other: Lutheridge Committee, 1968-75.

GLENHAM, TIMOTHY HOWARD

Date/Place of Birth: November 30, 1947; Charlotte, N.C.

Parents: Marvin Talbot Glenham and Virginia (Barefoot) Glenham.

Spouse/Marriage Date: Nancy (Herdje) Glenham; June 17, 1972 in Charlotte, N.C.

Children: Michael Todd, Christopher Trey.

Education: Gardner Webb, A.A. 1969; Lenoir-Rhyne, B.A. 1971; Lutheran Theological Southern Seminary, M.Div. 1975.

Ordination: May 14, 1975 by North Carolina Synod.

Calls: Good Shepherd, Goldsboro, 1975-80; Associate Pastor, Augsburg, Winston-Salem, 1981-89; Morning Star, Matthews, 1989-. Vice Pastor at various congregations.

Other: Board of American Missions; Chair, Youth Ministry Committee; Board, Lutheran Outdoor Ministries.

GOBINS, VITOLDS

Date/Place of Birth: June 9, 1927; Latvia, Eastern Europe.
Parents: Andrejs Gobins and Emilija (Osins) Gobins. Father was Lutheran; mother Russian Orthodox.
Spouse/Marriage Date: Milena (Moll) Gobins, born in Yugoslavia of Roman Catholic parents; June 12, 1953 in Buffalo, N.Y.
Education: High schools in Latvia and Germany; entered University of Erlangen, Germany, 1947; Lutheran Theological Southern Seminary, B.D. 1953.
Ordination: 1953 by North Carolina Synod.
Calls: St. Andrew, Andrews, 1953-60. Transferred to Central Pennsylvania Synod, 1960; serving Zion-St. Peter, Trevorton, Pa., 1960.
Other: Came to U.S.A. in late 1940s. Retired in Winfield, Pa.

GOERES, RICHARD JOHN

Date/Place of Birth: December 26, 1956; San Antonio, Texas.
Parents: Richard Valentine Goeres and Gloria (Gavett) Goeres.
Spouse/Marriage Date: Neva (Mathews) Goeres; December 5, 1981 in Columbia, S.C.
Children: Gloria Elisabeth, Richard James.
Education: James Madison University, B.S. Psychology 1979; Lutheran Theological Southern Seminary, M.Div. 1984; Drew University, D.Min. 1994.
Ordination: June 17, 1984 by North Carolina Synod.
Calls: Holy Cross, Lincolnton, 1984-86; Assistant to the Bishop, North Carolina Synod, 1986-89; Incarnation, Columbia, S.C., 1989-.
Other: Vice President, Christian Ministry of Lincoln County; Chair, Emergency Services Ministry Group, Lincoln County; Vice President, Lincoln County Ministerial Association; Adjunct Chaplain, Gaston Memorial Hospital. North Carolina Synod Committees: World Missions Committee; Registrar, Mini-Global Mission Event at Lenoir-Rhyne.

GOINS, SAMUEL EDWIN, SR.

Date/Place of Birth: August 21, 1932; Vale, N.C.
Parents: Maurice Henry Goins and Mary Vena (Wood) Goins. An older brother is the Reverend Ted W. Goins.
Spouse/Marriage Date: Barbara Ann (Lyerly) Goins; June 11, 1960 in East Spencer, N.C.
Child: Samuel Edwin, Jr.
Education: Lenoir-Rhyne, A.B. 1954; Chicago Seminary, B.D. 1958; graduate work at Lutheran Theological Southern Seminary, 1967.
Ordination: June 8, 1958 by North Carolina Synod.
Calls: St. Matthew, Rowan County, 1958-61; Good Shepherd, Goldsboro, 1961-63; Mission Developer/Pastor, A Mighty Fortress, Charlotte, 1963-69; St. Thomas, Sunset Hills, Mo., 1969-78; First Lutheran, Paxton, Ill., 1978-90.
Other: North Carolina Synod: Stewardship Task Force; Camp Committee; Evangelism Committee, 1968. Illinois Synod: Strength for Mission; Social Ministry. Retired September 30, 1990 to Leesburg, Fla.

GOINS, TED WALES, SR.
Date/Place of Birth: December 6, 1930; Vale, N.C.
Parents: Maurice Henry Goins and Mary Vena (Wood) Goins. A younger brother is the Reverend Samuel E. Goins.
Spouse/Marriage Date: Frances Queen (Summey) Goins of Gaston County; December 25, 1952 in New York City, N.Y.
Children: Mary Vena Clemmer, Ted Wales, Jr., John David.
Education: Lenoir-Rhyne, A.B. 1953; Lutheran Theological Southern Seminary, B.D. 1956.
Ordination: June 10, 1956 by North Carolina Synod.
Calls: Sharon, Iredell County, 1956-60; Good Hope, Hickory, 1961-67; St. Luke, Lexington, 1967-73; St. John, Concord, 1973-88; St. Paul, Crouse, 1988-98; Retired 1998 to Dallas. Vice Pastor at various congregations.
Other: Evangelism Committee, 1963-67; American Missions, 1971-73; Historical Works Committee; Professional Leadership; Lutheran Institutional Chaplaincy; Delegate to Lutheran Church in America Convention, 1978; Lutheridge Board.

GOODMAN, DAVID A.
Date of Birth: November 8, 1837.
Parents: The Reverend Henry Goodman and Esther (Faggart) Goodman.
First Spouse: Susan (Leonard) Goodman (born 1837 died 1880); Davidson County, N.C.
Children of First Marriage: Alpheus, Minnie, Dora.
Second Spouse: Mrs. Martha (Seitz) (Yoder) Goodman; Catawba County, N.C.
Child of Second Marriage: Victor.
License/Ordination: Licensed 1864 and ordained 1882 by Tennessee Synod.
Calls: Mt. Pleasant, Watauga County, 1881-82, 1887; Philadelphia, Granite Falls, 1882-84. United with The Lutheran Church-Missouri Synod 1907 and afterwards preached at Trinity, Glen Alpine, and at preaching points at Bridgewater and Drowning Creek. After retiring, served several churches until health failed.
Other: Retired at Connelly Springs, N.C.
Date of Death/Burial Location: March 15, 1917; St. John Church, Conover, Catawba County, N.C.

GOODMAN, GILBERT BROWN, SR.
Date/Place of Birth: January 5, 1912; Mt. Pleasant, N.C.
Parents: The Reverend Reuben Alonzo Goodman and Nena A. (Troutman) Goodman.
First Spouse/Marriage Date: Grace (Smith) Goodman, died September 1, 1973; November 6, 1937 in Concord, N.C.
Children of First Marriage: Clyde Reuben, Mary Lois, Gilbert B., Jr.
Second Spouse/Marriage Date: Kathleen (Ragan) Goodman; October 4, 1975 in Boone, N.C.

Education: Newberry College, A.B. 1933; Lutheran Theological Southern Seminary, B.D. 1936.

Ordination: May 28, 1936 by North Carolina Synod.

Calls: Calvary, Concord, 1936-45; Supply, Cold Water, Cabarrus County, 1940-45; St. Enoch, Kannapolis, 1945-56; Advent, Spindale, 1956-62; Mission Developer at Elkin, 1962-66; Bethany, Boone, 1966-77.

Other: Lutheran World Relief Committee, 1965-69

Date of Death/Burial Location: May 16, 1977; St. Michael, Troutman, N.C.

GOODMAN, HENRY

Date/Place of Birth: April 9, 1798; Cabarrus County, N.C.

Parents: Michael Goodman and Elizabeth Goodman.

Spouse/Marriage Date: Esther (Faggart) Goodman; July 20, 1819.

Children: Fourteen, several dying in infancy or early childhood. Michael, Salome, Oliver, Jacob L., Mary Ann, Betsse, John E., Margaret, Easter, Daniel H., the Reverend David A., Catherine, Adeline, Robert Luther. Two sons and two grandsons were Lutheran ministers.

Education: Probably was self-educated.

License/Ordination: Licensed 1831 and ordained 1832 by Tennessee Synod.

Calls: Supply, St. Martin, Stanly County, 1831-32; Supply, with others, Mt. Moriah, Rowan County, 1832; Beck's-Pilgrim, Davidson County, 1832-49; St. Martin, Iredell County, 1833-41, 1871-73; Supply, with others, Morning Star, Mecklenburg County, 1833-39; Coble's, Guilford County; Melanchthon, Randolph County; Mt. Pleasant, Alamance County, 1844; Mt. Pleasant, Watauga County, 1849-52, 1870-72; St. James, Catawba County, 1851; Zion, Catawba County, 1852-65; St. Stephen, Hickory, 1864; Friendship, Taylorsville, 1869-70; organized Philadelphia, Granite Falls, 1876; St. Martin, Cabarrus County. From home near St. Martin, Iredell County, made long itinerating evangelistic journeys in North Carolina, and adjoining states. Having urged the Synod to recognize the importance of providing a ministry to persons in the military, he himself visited and preached to Confederate Army combat soldiers.

Other: Treasurer of Synod, 1857. Appointed to the committee created to review the proposed revision of the Synod's constitution in the light of the communications received by the convention on that subject, 1859. Synod Examining Committee, 1964.

Date of Death/Burial Location: January 26, 1878; St. Martin Cemetery, Iredell County, N.C.

GOODMAN, REUBEN ALONZO

Date/Place of Birth: July 23, 1881; Amity, Iredell County, N.C.

Parents: Joseph A. B. Goodman and Margaret O. (Lipe) Goodman.

Spouse/Marriage Date: Nena Avis (Troutman) Goodman; December 28, 1910 in Troutman, N.C.

Children: The Reverend Gilbert Brown, Sr., Margaret Jane, Mary Helen, Joseph Augustus (died on 17th day after birth), Sgt. William Bennet, U.S. Air Force (lost in bomber training flight over Gulf of Mexico, April 23, 1944).

Education: Roanoke College A.B. 1906, D.D. 1928; Lutheran Theological Southern Seminary, 1909.

Ordination: 1909 by North Carolina Synod.

Calls: Christ-Calvary, Spencer, 1909-11; Holy Trinity, Mt. Pleasant, 1911-21. Transferred to South Carolina Synod 1921. Supplied many churches, 1921-57, including Redeemer, Newberry, S.C., especially four years in World War II in pastor's absence as Army Chaplain; named Pastor Emeritus of Redeemer, 1952.

Other: Instructor (Greek, Latin), Mount Pleasant Collegiate Institute, 1911-13; and principal and teacher, Mont Amoena Seminary, 1913-21; Professor (Bible, Christian Ethics, Greek), Newberry College, 1921-57, and Secretary of faculty 25 years. Contributed articles to *The Lutheran Church Visitor, The Lutheran,* and other periodicals. Wrote chapter *Voigt as Writer* in *A. G. Voigt—Moulder of Southern Lutheranism,* biography of Dr. A. G. Voigt, long-time head of Lutheran Theological Southern Seminary. Listed in *Who's Who in the South and Southwest,* 1950. Retired 1957 at Troutman, N.C. Retained clerical membership in South Carolina Synod.

Date of Death/Burial Location: August 22, 1969; St. Michael Cemetery, Troutman, N.C.

GOTWALD, FREDERICK GEBHART, II

Date/Place of Birth: May 4, 1922 in Kodaikanal, South India.

Parents: Luther Alexander Gotwald, III, and Ethel Grace (Baer) Gotwald.

Spouse/Marriage Date: Margaret Leila (Miller) Gotwald; October 10, 1947 in Silver Spring, Md.

Children: Frederick Kimball, Paul Michael, Luther Alexander, Victoria Anne Rufty.

Education: Gettysburg College, B.A. 1943; Gettysburg Seminary, B.D. 1946.

Ordination: February 27, 1947 by New York and New England Synod United Lutheran Church in America.

Calls: Assistant Pastor, Reformation, Rochester, N.Y., 1946-49; Our Saviour, Croton-on-Hudson, N.Y., 1949-70; Assistant to Bishop, Upper New York Synod, Syracuse, N.Y., 1970-83; Associate Pastor, St. John, Salisbury, 1983-87. Permanent Interim Pastor at Lebanon, Lexington. Retired at Salisbury, N.C., 1987.

Other: Circle in front of church at Croton on Hudson and Youth Education Building named in honor of Pastor Gotwald, 1994. Completed ten volumes of work on Nero Wolfe, Brainchild of Rex Stout. Created filmstrips, *The First Easter Bunny* and Ixthy, *The Talking Goldfish,* an explanation of baptism for primary children. Multimedia shows, *He Had a Face, Jesus Christ Super Star,* and *Godspel.*

GOYNE, RACHEL LEAH (CONNELLY)

See Connelly, Rachel Leah

GRAEBER, HENRY

Date/Place of Birth: January 28, 1793; York County, Pa.

Spouse/Marriage Date: Anna Maria (Morelock) Graeber; 1820/21 in Carroll County, Md.

Children: Alexander Henry, Jeremiah L., Augustus Franklin, Jonathan, Louisa Rebecca Harriet, Sarah Ann Elizabeth Belinda, Mary Salome Florentina.

Education: In private schools and by tutors; studied and practiced medicine; later to enter ministry, at Gettysburg Seminary. Held both M.D. and D.D. degrees.

License/Ordination: Licensed 1818 and ordained 1821 by Ministerium of Pennsylvania.
Calls: In Maryland, 1818-27. In North Carolina: pastor of six churches in Lincoln and Catawba Counties that preferred the North Carolina to the Tennessee Synod, 1827-32, including St. Paul and Grace, Catawba County, and Daniel's, Lincolnton; Organ, Rowan County; St. John, Cabarrus County, 1832-43; Luther's, Rowan County, 1833-41; Lutheran Chapel, China Grove, 1833-37.
Other: President, North Carolina Synod, five one-year terms; Secretary, three one-year terms, 1832-41. Along with pastoral ministry, practiced medicine chiefly for benefit of parishioners.
Date of Death/Place of Burial: September 11, 1843; Organ Church, Rowan County, N.C.

GRAF, RICHARD BYRON, JR.

Date/Place of Birth: September 27, 1939; Charlotte, N.C.
Parents: Richard Byron Graf, Sr. and Helen (Stilwell) Graf Sharpe.
Spouse/Marriage Date: Shirley Alene (Whitley) Graf; June 10, 1961 in Bessemer City, N.C.
Children: Eric Michael, Kristin Suzanne.
Education: Lenoir-Rhyne, B.A. History 1961; graduate work, Appalachian State University, 1969; Gettysburg Seminary, M.Div. 1965; Pittsburgh Theological Seminary, D.Min. 1980.
Ordination: June 6, 1965 by North Carolina Synod.
Calls: Grace, Boone, 1965-67; Campus Pastor, University of Miami, Coral Gables, Fla., 1967-70; St. Thomas, Miami, Fla., 1970-73; St. Stephen, Tallahassee, Fla., 1973-75; Secretary and Assistant to the Bishop, Florida Synod, Lutheran Church in America, 1975-77; Macedonia, Burlington, 1977-83; St. Paul, Wilmington, 1983-92; St. Paul, Columbia, S.C., 1992-98; St. Martin, Concord, 1998. Retired, 1999. Vice Pastor at various congregations.
Other: Campaign Director/President, United Way, Cape Fear Area, N.C.; President, Wilmington Kiwanis Club; Adjunct Professor in English, Elon College; Visiting Professor in Homiletics, Lutheran Theological Southern Seminary, 1994-97; Radio Commentary (daily), 1993-97; Listed in *Community Leaders and Noteworthy Americans,* 1976; *Personalities of the South,* 1975; *Clergyman of the Year,* Tallahassee, Fla., 1973; Junior Chamber of Commerce Outstanding Young Man Award, 1966; *Who's Who Among Students in American Colleges and Universities,* 1961; Marquis *Who's Who in Religion in America,* since 1985; Special Consultant to New Hanover County Commissioners on Hospital Reorganization; Outstanding Community Service Award, Wilmington, 1990; North Carolina Governor's Award for Volunteer Service - twice; Board, Brigade Boys Club of Wilmington; Development Board, Lenoir- Rhyne; Development Board, North Carolina Lutheran Homes, Wilmington Project; Chamber of Commerce; New Hanover County Task Force on Tourism; Thalian Association Board; Evangelism Committee. Publications: *Rediscovering Direction in Lutheran Campus Ministry; A Radio Ministry to Elderly Homebound Persons; The Preacher's Name is Judas; It Ain't Always Easy; Jump.*

GRAGG, STEPHEN T.
Date/Place of Birth: November 2, 1948; Hickory, N.C.
Parents: Thomas L. Gragg and Kathleen (Troutman) Gragg.
Spouse/Marriage Date: Kathryn Susan (Yost) Gragg; August 29, 1971 in Hickory, N.C.
Children: Nathan Thomas, Bonnie Brook, Rachel Kathryn.
Education: Montreat-Anderson Junior College, A.A. 1969; Newberry College, B.A. 1971; Lutheran Theological Southern Seminary, M.Div. 1975; Southern Baptist Center for Biblical Studies, D.Min. 1984, U.S. Marine Corps Command and Staff College, 1997.
Ordination: June 8, 1975 by North Carolina Synod.
Calls: Philadelphia, Granite Falls, 1975-79; Christus Victor, Durham, 1979-80; Salem, Dakota City, Neb., 1980-85; Holy Trinity, North Augusta, S.C., 1986-. U.S. Navy Chaplain Corps, Reserve, 1985-.
Other: Lutheran Church in America Stewardship Motivator, Nebraska Synod.

GREEN, GAREY
Date/Place of Birth: August 16, 1935; Duval, Fla.
Parents: John Capehart Green and Henrietta Green.
Spouse: Carolyn (Davis) Green.
Children: Gwendolyn D., Garry, Gail, Gregory, Gerald, Gilbert, Michelle.
Education: Benedict College, B.A. 1967; Virginia Union University, M.Div. 1970; University of South Carolina, M.Ed., M.CRJV; D.D., Friendship Junior College, 1978; Lutheran Theological Southern Seminary, D.Min. 1981.
Ordination: May 27, 1983, by South Carolina Synod.
Calls: Resurrection, Queens, N.Y., 1982-84; Hope, Raleigh, 1984-87; Ascension Evangelical, Toledo, Ohio, 1987-88.
Other: Removed from roll, 1991.

GREEVER, JOHN JACOB
Date/Place of Birth: April 27, 1811; near Burkes Garden, Va.
Parents: Philip Greever and Mrs. Margaret (Bates) Hayter Greever. A great-uncle of the Reverend Walton H. Greever.
First Spouse/Marriage Date: Margaret Gose (Peery) Greever; April 2, 1840 in Burkes Garden, Va.
Children of First Marriage: Elizabeth, Ann L., Agnes, the Reverend Joseph Brown, Philip Melanchthon, George, Thomas (the last two died in childhood).
Second Spouse: Catherine (Peery) Greever; Wythe County, Va.
Children of Second Marriage: Dr. C. W. and Margaret (twins), John H., James Alexander, Nannie E., Lettie C., M. Angeline (married the Reverend David S. Fox).
Education: Walked from home to Gettysburg Seminary, for theological training.
License/Ordination: Licensed 1840 by North Carolina Synod; ordained by Southwest Virginia Synod at organizing convention, 1842.
Calls: North Carolina Synod churches in Virginia, to 1842; thereafter churches of Southwest Virginia Synod; periodically held two-week meetings in churches in Bland, Wythe, Smyth, and Tazewell Counties, Va. Pastor of a union congregation, majority of members being Lutherans, until later when Lutherans built new church.
Date of Death/Burial Location: June 3, 1877; Burkes Garden, Va.

GRIESON (GREESON), JACOB
Date/Place of Birth: April 24, 1768; Guilford County, N.C.
Spouse: Barbara Grieson.
Children: Leah, Elizabeth (married the Reverend Jacob Scherer).
License: Licensed 1810 by North Carolina Synod but never ordained.
Calls: Chiefly as assistant to the Reverend Jacob Scherer in Guilford, Alamance, and Randolph Counties; Low's, 1810-54; Frieden's-Richland-St. Paul, 1834-39.
Date of Death/Burial Location: August 13, 1854; Low's Church, Guilford County, N.C.

GRIFFIN, JOSEPH LEROY
Date/Place of Birth: October 1, 1922; Rural Hall, N.C.
Parents: Jesse Lee Griffin and Ola (Styers) Griffin.
Spouse/Marriage Date: Rita (Wallace) Griffin; July 15, 1944 in Concord, N.C.
Children: Joseph Laird, Lea Duncan.
Education: Lenoir-Rhyne, A.B. 1943; Lutheran Theological Southern Seminary, B.D. 1948; University of South Carolina, M.A. Social Service, 1947; Newberry College, D.D. 1963.
Ordination: April 7, 1948 by North Carolina Synod.
Calls: St. Andrew, Concord, 1948-50; St. Mark, China Grove, 1950-53; St. Paul, Savannah, Ga., 1953-65; Holy Trinity, Gastonia, 1965-70; Emmanuel, High Point, 1970-80; Mission Developer/Pastor, Cross and Crown, Florence, S.C., 1980-82; Shepherd of the Hills, Sylva, 1982-86; Chaplain, Lutheran Nursing Home, Albemarle, 1986-. Vice Pastor for various congregations.
Other: Board, Lutheran Theological Southern Seminary; Chair, Executive Committee; Evangelism, Social Missions, Vocational, Examining Committees. Lutheran World Action - three-month travel scholarship throughout Germany observing benefits of Lutheran World Action; Lutheran Campus Pastor for seven colleges and universities; Allocations Commission, United Lutheran Church in America; Commission on Evangelism, Lutheran Church in America; Board, Protestant Radio-Television Center, Atlanta, Ga.; Guest Missioner for 21 Missions in North Carolina, South Carolina, Georgia, Alabama and Florida. Paratrooper in World War II; *Who's Who in the South and Southwest; Directory of International Biography.* Retired March 15, 1986.

GRIFFIN, LINDA ANN (FALTIN)
See Faltin, Linda Ann

GRIMES, ADAM
License: Licensed 1821 by North Carolina Synod but never ordained.
Calls: Organized and served a small congregation fourteen miles from his home at Hay Meadows, Wilkes County. In Forsyth County: Nazareth, 1832-36, 1837-47; Shiloh, 1832-36, 1840-47.
Date of Death/Burial Location: March 22, 1868; Wilkes County, N.C.

GRISLIS, EGIL

Date/Place of Birth: February 19, 1928; Mitau, Latvia.

Parents: Robert Kristian Grislis and Lucia-Maria (Stankewitz-Einfeld) Grislis.

Spouse/Marriage Date: The Reverend E. Lorraine (Sommers) Grislis; June 30, 1956 in Marquette, Mich.

Children: Karen Ann, Kristin Eva Taylor, Erik Lauri.

Education: Gymnasium in Latvia and Germany; Divinity School Heidelberg University, 1948-49; Gettysburg College, A.B. 1950; Gettysburg Seminary, B.D. 1953; Yale University, Ph.D., 1958.

Ordination: June 19, 1957 by New York Synod.

Calls: Emanuel, Hudson-Emanuel, Harlemville, N.Y., 1957-59. Associate professor of Historical Theology, Duke University Divinity School, 1959-69. Professor of Historical Theology, Hartford Seminary Foundation, Conn., 1969-73; Theology Department of Fordham University, Bronx, N.Y., 1973-76; Department of Religion, University of Manitoba, Winnepeg, Manitoba, Canada. Vice Pastor to Holy Cross Latvian Evangelical Lutheran Church in Winnipeg, Manitoba, Canada, 1976-.

Other: Examining Committee, 1962-65, 1967-69; Board of Governors, Saskatoon Seminary, Saskatchewan, Canada; regular contributor to *Canada Lutheran;* teaching Fellow at the Graduate Theological Foundation in Notre Dame, Ind.; Chair, Graduate Studies in Religion at the University of Manitoba. Publications: *Luther's Understanding of the Wrath of God, The Journal of Religion; Calvin's Doctrine of Baptism, Church History; Richard Hooker's Method of Theological Inquiry, Anglican Theological Review; Richard Hooker's Image of Man, Renaissance Papers;* co-editor with Robert E. Cushman, *The Heritage of Christian Thought: Essays in Honor of Robert Lowry Calhoun;* contributor, *The Role of Consensus in the Theology of Richard Hooker; Conservatives and Liberals Need Each Other, Christianity Today; Ernest L. Hazelius: Ecumenical Theologian of the Southern Lutheran Church, Lutheran Theological Seminary Bulletin; Martin Luther's View of the Hidden God: The Problem of Deus abscouditus in Luther's Treatise De Servo Arbitrio, McCormick Quarterly; Calvin's Use of Cicero in the Institutes I: 1-5 - A Case Study in Theological Method, Archiv fuer Reformationsgeschichte; The Hermeneutical Problem in Richard Hooker,* and *Richard Hooker: An Annotated Bibliography by Egil Grislis and W. Speed Hill, Richard Hooker: Essays Preliminary to an Edition of His Works; Richard Hooker: A Selected Bibliography* by Egil Grislis and W. Speed Hill.

GROSECLOSE, LEVI C.

Date/Place of Birth: June 6, 1820; Smyth County, Va.

Parents: John Groseclose and Mary (Snavely) Groseclose.

Spouse: Betty (Honeycutt) Groseclose; Rowan County, N.C.

Children: John, William, Anna.

Education: Wittenberg College.

License/Ordination: Licensed 1849 and ordained 1850 by Southwest Virginia Synod.

Calls: Beck's-Pilgrim-St. Luke, Davidson County, 1849-54; St. John, Salisbury; Union (supplied 1851), Rowan County, 1857-65; New Jerusalem, Davie County, 1861-63; St. Stephen, Cabarrus County, 1865-66, also supplying Frieden's, Guilford County, and St. Paul, Alamance County; St. Matthew, Rowan County, 1866; Luther's, Rowan County, 1866-67;

St. John, Cabarrus County; Co-organized Holy Trinity, Mt. Pleasant (1868)-New Bethel, Stanly County, 1867-72.
Other: Transferred 1873 to Southern Illinois Synod. Secretary, two one-year terms, North Carolina Synod, President one term; Secretary, Synod's Missionary and Education Society; Board, North Carolina College, 1867-69; Agent, *The Lutheran Visitor,* 1868; Board, Mt. Pleasant Female Seminary, 1869-72; Joint Committee to Recommend Terms for Union of North Carolina and Tennessee Synods, 1870.
Date of Death/Burial Location: May 2, 1905; Eureka, Kan.

GROSSMAN, MOSES
Ordination: Ordained in 1893 by Susquehanna Synod.
Calls: In Lycoming and York Counties, Pa., 1895-99. Transferred in 1900 from the West Pennsylvania Synod to Tennessee Synod, and served Bethel-Trinity, Manassas, Va., 1900-04. Transferred to Allegheny Synod, 1904 again serving in Pennsylvania; later served parish in Indiana of Olive Branch Synod, 1911-.

GROTH, JOHN HENRY CHRISTOPHER
Date/Place of Birth: June 26, 1954; Waterloo, Iowa.
Parents: Ulrich F. Groth and Ruth (Johnson) Groth.
Spouse: Cheryl Ann Groth.
Children: David, Eric Samuel.
Education: Wartburg College, B.A. 1976; Wartburg Seminary, M.Div. 1981; graduate work at Trinity Seminary.
Ordination: July 11, 1982 by Iowa Synod.
Calls: St. John, Preston, Iowa, 1981-82; St. John, Lithopolis, Ohio, 1982-88; Old St. Paul, Newton, 1988-93. Resigned in 1994.

GRUBER, HARRY LAWRENCE, SR.
Date/Place of Birth: December 24, 1925; Womelsdorf, Berks County, Pa.
Parents: Claude Lewis Gruber, Sr. and Evelyn Mae (Moyer) Gruber.
First Spouse/Marriage Date: Helen Lorena (Howe) Gruber; August 3, 1952 in Newton, N.C.
Child of First Marriage: Harry Lawrence, Jr.
Second Spouse/Marriage Date: Edna Grace (Kreider) Gruber; January 7, 1984.
Children of Second Marriage: Irene Kreider Stump, Grace Kreider Heberlins.
Education: Albright College, A.B. 1948; Lutheran Theological Southern Seminary, B.D. 1952.
Ordination: June 1952 by North Carolina Synod.
Calls: Grace, Catawba County, 1952-58; Calvary, Spencer, 1958-64; St. Andrew, Concord, 1964-83. Vice Pastor for Christ Lutheran, Bellegrove, Pa., 1985-95.
Other: Retired 1983.
Date of Death/Burial Location: April 21, 1995; Gaston Memorial Park, Gastonia, N.C.

GRUNKE, RONALD CLAY

Date/Place of Birth: July 22, 1950; Mora, Minn.
Parents: Harvey Fred Grunke and Dorothy C. Grunke.
Spouse/Marriage Date: Virginia Ann (Dunkley) Grunke; December 21, 1973 in Durham, N.C.
Child: John Aaron.
Education: Concordia College, A.A. Religion 1970; Duke University, B.A. Sociology, 1972; Duke Divinity School, M.Div. 1975.
Ordination: June 13, 1976 by North Carolina Synod.
Calls: Redeemer, Kannapolis, 1976-79; Lord of Life, Garner, 1979-84; Our Saviour, Victoria, Texas, 1984- 93; Holy Trinity, Marietta, Ga., 1993-.

GUY, FREDERICK PAIGE

Date/Place of Birth: October 14, 1947; Newport News, Va.
Parents: Alma Paige Guy and Mabel Emily (Morgan) Guy.
Spouse/Marriage Date: Elizabeth Friel (Killinger) Guy; August 23, 1969.
Children: Morgan Paige, Ryan Frederick.
Education: Emory and Henry College, B.A. Interdisciplinary Social Science 1970; Gettysburg Seminary, M.Div. 1986; Radford College, M.S. Educational Media 1978; graduate work at Old Dominion University, Educational Administration and Supervision.
Ordination: June 7, 1986 by Virginia Synod.
Calls: Holy Trinity, Lynchburg, Va., 1986-89; Messiah, Virginia Beach, Va., 1989-96; Associate Pastor, Holy Trinity, Hickory, 1996-.
Other: Dean, Tidewater Conference, Virginia Synod, 1994-96. Chaplain, Police-Community Relations, Virginia Beach, Va.; Chair, Winter Task Force for the Homeless, Virginia Beach, Va.; Head Chaplain, Windemere Nursing Home, Virginia Beach, Va.; Allocations Chair, South Hampton Roads Campaign for the Homeless; Elementary Public School Teacher, Northampton County, Va.; Instructional Specialist, Gifted and Talented Education and Staff Development, Campbell County, Va.; Chair, Committee on Homeless Priorities, Virginia Beach, Va.

HAAS, CLYDE PINKNEY, JR.

Date/Place of Birth: May 27, 1933; Baltimore, Md.
Parents: Clyde Pinkney Haas, Sr. and Frieda (Jubb) Haas.
First Spouse/Marriage Date: Juanita (Wood) Haas; December 22, 1954.
Children of First Marriage: Eric C., Timothy A.
Second Spouse/Marriage Date: Barbara (Armstrong) Haas; November 24, 1989.
Child of Second Marriage: David.
Stepchildren: Beth Morphis, Susan Loper, David Minter.
Education: Lenoir-Rhyne, B.A. History and Government, 1964; Lutheran Theological Southern Seminary, M.Div. 1969; one year Clinical Pastoral Education.
Ordination: June 1, 1969 by North Carolina Synod.
Calls: Lebanon, Cleveland, 1969-71; St. Paul, Hamlet, 1971-77; Pilgrim, Lexington, 1977-82; St. David, Kannapolis, 1982-88; Chaplain, Davidson County Correctional Center, 1992-98. Vice Pastor at various congregations.
Other: U.S. Navy, Korean War; Central Carolina Civitan Club; Human Relations Committee in Hamlet, 1975-77; Fellow College of Chaplains, 1995.*Date of Death/Burial Location*: October 12, 1998; St. Paul Lutheran Church Cemetery, Startown, N.C.

HAAS, HAROLD IRWIN

Date/Place of Birth: September 26, 1925; Buffalo, N.Y.
Parents: Elmer John Haas and Gladys Kingdon (Ford) Haas.
Spouse/Marriage Date: Ruth (Miller) Haas; September 6, 1952 in Buffalo, N.Y.
Children: Rachel Ann, Peter John, Sara Sorensen, Lois Gartner, Elizabeth Ann.
Education: Concordia College, 1945; Concordia Seminary, B.A. 1946, M.Div. 1949; Washington University, M.A. 1949; University of Buffalo, Ph.D. 1956.
Ordination: October 1950 by The Lutheran Church-Missouri Synod.
Calls: Faith, Penfield, N.Y., 1956-7; Concordia Senior College, Fort Wayne, Ind., 1957-77; Valparaiso University, 1977-79; retired May 1997.
Other: Faculty, Lenoir-Rhyne, 1979-97. Publications - *The Christian Encounters: Mental Illness; Pastor Counseling with People in Distress.*

HAAS, TIMOTHY ALBERT

Date/Place of Birth: June 18, 1958; Newton, N.C.
Parents: Clyde Pinkney Haas, Jr. and Juanita (Wood) Haas.
Education: Lenoir-Rhyne, B.A. 1980; Lutheran Theological Southern Seminary, M.Div. 1984.
Ordination: June 24, 1984 by South Carolina Synod for North Carolina Synod.
Calls: Christ's, Columbia, S.C., 1984-87.
Other: Removed from roll, November 19, 1991 in Atlanta, Ga.

HACKNEY, HAROLD STEPHEN

Date/Place of Birth: October 27, 1948; Rowan County, N.C.
Parents: Harold B. Hackney and Ruth (Bost) Hackney.
Education: Western Carolina, B.A. 1971; Lutheran Theological Southern Seminary, B.D. 1975.
Ordination: June 1975; Hickory, N.C.
Calls: Bethel, Lincolnton, 1975-80; St. John, Taylorsville, 1983-85.
Other: Dropped from roll May 1985.

HADDOCK, GARY STEVEN

Date/Place of Birth: August 24, 1953; Fayetteville, N.C.
Parents: Henry Haddock and Leole Haddock.
Spouse/Marriage Date: Rebecca A. (Harriss) Haddock; May 17, 1975 in Wilmington, N.C.
Children: Aaron Michael, Rachel Elizabeth, Benjamin Nathaniel.
Education: Campbell College, B.A. 1976; Yale University Divinity School, M.A.R 1981, M.Div. 1982, C.P.E.; graduate work at Duquesne University.
Ordination: June 6, 1982 by North Carolina Synod.
Calls: Shepherd of the Sea, Atlantic Beach, 1982-84; Trinity, Verona, Pa., 1984-89; Interim Pastor at Reconciliation, Wilmington; Associate Pastor, Holy Trinity, Hickory, 1992-95; St. Mark, Butler, Pa., 1995-.

Other: President, Bogue Banks Surplus Food Distribution Program, 1983-84; Social Justice Committee - West Virginia - Western Pennsylvania Synod, 1986-87; Co-Chair, Task Force for the Family Violence Project of Catawba County; President of Board, Celebration Theater of Wilmington, 1990-92. Publications: Article, "The Easter Vigil As Primary Celebration and Formation;" poem, *Vigil*.

HAHN, ARTHUR LEROY, SR.

Date/Place of Birth: January 5, 1905; Mt. Pleasant, N.C.
Parents: Richard Whitfield Hahn and Mary Elizabeth (Pickler) Hahn.
Spouse/Marriage Date: Mary Virginia (Richard) Hahn, daughter of the Reverend Marion G. Richard; October 12, 1929 in Collingdale, Pa.
Children: James Richard, Virginia Estelle Melchor, The Reverend Arthur Leroy, Jr.
Education: Mount Pleasant Collegiate Institute, four years, Lenoir-Rhyne, A.B. 1926; Lutheran Theological Southern Seminary, B.D. 1929; graduate work at Philadelphia Seminary, 1952-55.
Ordination: May 29, 1929 by North Carolina Synod.
Calls: None in North Carolina. In Virginia: Washington County, 1929-33; Salem, Mt. Sidney, 1933-39; Trinity, Newport News, 1939-46. Chaplain, College of William and Mary, Williamsburg, Va., after World War II. In Pennsylvania: Calvary, Philadelphia, 1946-60; Zion, Zion Hills, 1960-66; Dinkey Memorial-St. Paul, Lehighton, 1966-70. Vice Pastor/Supply at various congregations. Retired 1970.
Date of Death/Burial Location: December 28, 1985; Topton Union Cemetery, Topton, Pa.

HAHN, LESTER CLEMENT, SR.

Date/Place of Birth: July 5, 1914; Mt. Pleasant, N.C.
Parents: Jason Farry Hahn and Minnie Esther (Hall) Hahn.
Spouse/Marriage Date: Helen Elizabeth (Yoder) Hahn; May 18, 1940 in Catawba County.
Children: Lester Clement, Jr., Rachael Elizabeth Kennedy, Gerald Michael, John Allen.
Education: Pfeiffer College, one year, Lenoir-Rhyne, A.B. 1937; Lutheran Theological Southern Seminary, B.D. 1940, graduate study 1955-58.
Ordination: May 29, 1940 by North Carolina Synod.
Calls: St. Andrew and St. Mark, Plains, Ga., 1940-43. Ebenezer, Rowan County; Mt. Hermon, Cabarrus County, 1943-47; Ebenezer only, 1947-50; Bethphage-Cedar Grove, Lincoln County, 1951-54; Mt. Hebron, Hildebran, 1954-69, Bethlehem, Hallandale, Fla., 1969-84.
Other: Director for North Carolina Synod, Christian Higher Education Year campaign for funds, 1951-52. North Carolina Lutheran Homes Committee, 1962-64; Retired May 31, 1984.
Date of Death/Burial Location: April 8, 1998; Mt. Hermon Cemetery at Concord, N.C.

HAHN, SAMUEL WAIGHTSTILL

Date/Place of Birth: May 23, 1895; Hickory, N.C.
Parents: Daniel Efird Hahn and Laura Susan (Yoder) Hahn.
Spouse/Marriage Date: Doris (Becker) Hahn; October 29, 1919 in Columbia, S.C.
Children: Samuel Wilfred, Marjorie Eleanor, Dorothy Augusta, M.D.
Education: Lenoir-Rhyne A.B. 1915, D.D. 1941; Lutheran Theological Southern Seminary, 1919; graduate study, University of South Carolina; Union Seminary, Columbia University, 1953.
Ordination: 1919 by Southwest Virginia Synod.
Calls: Burkes Garden, Va., 1919-22; Grace, Prosperity, S.C., 1922-25; Augsburg, Winston-Salem, 1925-42; St. James, Concord, 1942-50. Professor, Lutheran Theological Southern Seminary, 1950-62.
Other: High school teacher one year. Retired 1962 at Leesville, S.C. Member, Board of Lutheridge, 1946-50. Transferred to South Carolina Synod, 1963.
Date of Death/Burial Location: 1981; Elmwood Cemetery, Columbia, S.C.

HAIGLER, JESSE BOWMAN

Date/Place of Birth: December 5, 1863; Cameron, S.C.
Parents: Jesse Newel Haigler and Frances Caroline Haigler.
Spouse/Marriage Date: Emma (Havird) Haigler; January 3, 1894 in Newberry, S.C.
Children: Oliver Newel, Helen.
Education: Newberry College, A.B. 1889; Philadelphia Seminary, 1892.
Ordination: 1892 by Ministerium of Pennsylvania.
Calls: In Pennsylvania, Nova Scotia, South Carolina, Georgia, and Virginia, 1892-1919. In North Carolina: Union, Rowan County, 1919-22. Transferred to South Carolina Synod 1922 where he served Bethlehem, Pomaria, 1922-26; Mt. Horeb, Chapin, 1926; Bethel, White Rock, 1926-30. Retired 1930 at Newberry, S.C.
Date of Death/Burial Location: July 14, 1932; Rosemont Cemetery, Newberry, S.C.

HAITHCOX, HENRY CLAY

Date/Place of Birth: February 17, 1843; Iredell County, N.C.
Parents: James Allen Haithcox and Mary (Lentz) Haithcox.
First Spouse/Marriage Date: Martha Ann (Hoover) Haithcox; May 18, 1862 in Iredell County. Died January 13, 1914.
Children of First Marriage: Eva and Eta (twins), Lulu, Henry James, William Hayes, Mae Belle, Martha Anna, Sophronia.
Second Spouse/Marriage Date: Mrs. Margaret (Miller) (Lied) Haithcox; July 11, 1917 in Freeport, Ill.
Education: Missionary Institute, Susquehanna, Pa., one year; Susquehanna University, A.B. 1869, D.D. 1894; Susquehanna Seminary, 1872.
Ordination: 1872 by Susquehanna Synod.
Calls: Presumably in Pennsylvania and Ohio, 1872-1890. Transferred to North Carolina Synod in 1890 from Eastern Ohio Synod; Salem-St. Luke, Rowan County, 1890. Transferred to Northern Illinois Synod, 1890. In Pennsylvania, Illinois, Ohio, Kansas, Indiana, and West Virginia. Retired 1923 at Lanark, Ill.

Other: Contributed to the *Augsburg Teacher, The Lutheran Quarterly,* and other periodicals.
Date of Death/Burial Location: February 2, 1926; Freeport, Ill.

HALEY, JAMES LAWTON, JR.

Date/Place of Birth: July 26, 1932; Lincolnton, N.C.
Parents: James Lawton Haley, Sr. and Sallie Mae (Mosteller) Haley.
Spouse/Marriage Date: Mary Eleanor (Homes) Haley; January 11, 1963.
Child: David Michael.
Education: University of North Carolina at Chapel Hill, A.B. History 1954; Philadelphia Seminary, B.D. 1958; Yale University, M.A. 1963, Ph.D. Church History, 1967.
Ordination: June 4, 1958 by New York-New England Synod.
Other: St. Paul, Ithaca, N.Y., 1958-61; Professor, Concordia College, Minnesota, 1965-97. Red River Valley Synod: Committee on Worship; Lutheran Church in America Centennial Committee. Post-doctorate study with Nikolas Zernov and Bishop Kallistos Ware at Oxford University, England. Adjunct Professor of Church History, St. Petersburg Academy and Seminary. Retired August 1998 to Marion, N.C. Publications: *The Religious Heritage and Education of Samuel Simon Schmucker: A Study in the Rise of American Lutheranism; Stumbling Toward Zion: A Mosteller Chronicle; J. George Schmucker and the Roots of His Spirituality* article in *Lutheranism and Pietism.*

HALL, BRYANT C.

License/Ordination: Licensed 1855 and ordained 1858 by North Carolina Synod.
Calls: In Rowan County: Lutheran Chapel, 1855-57, St. Paul, 1855-59, and Union, 1856; supplied Salem, Lincoln County, 1859; Coble's-Low's, Guilford County, 1859-64; Richland, Randolph County, 1864.
Date of Death/Burial Location: 1864; Low's Church, Guilford County, N.C.

HALL, JOHN

Date/Place of Birth: April 21, 1878; Chillicothe, Ohio.
Parents: Elias Hall and Elizabeth (Downey) Hall.
Spouse/Marriage Date: Lela Fisher (Yoder) Hall, daughter of the Reverend R. A. Yoder; June 4, 1901 in Catawba County, N.C.
Children: Lela Elizabeth, John Robert, Margaret Ellen Wight, Charles Noah, the Reverend William Edward.
Education: Lenoir-Rhyne, A.B. 1900, D.D. 1938; Lutheran Theological Southern Seminary, 1903, B.D. 1927; graduate study, University of Pennsylvania and Philadelphia Seminary.
Ordination: 1901 by Tennessee Synod.
Calls: Watauga Parish, five churches, including Holy Communion, Mt. Pleasant, and Mt. Zion, 1901-05; Holy Trinity, Gastonia-Grace, Bessemer City, 1905-12; Lutheran Chapel, Gastonia, 1910-12; Holy Trinity, St. Petersburg, Fla., 1913-17. Chaplain, U.S. Army, 1917-40. Supplied various churches for periods up to one year; supplied in Georgia, 1941-61.
Other: Field Secretary, Lenoir-Rhyne, 1912-13. President, Secretary, North Carolina Conference of the Tennessee Synod. Initiated leadership training of church workers in Tennessee Synod, jointly with North Carolina Synod, 1907. Joint Editor, the *History of the*

Lutheran Church in North Carolina, (1803-1953), and writer of section "Educational Developments." Contributed to *Lutheran Church Visitor, The Lutheran,* and other church periodicals.
Date of Death/Burial Location: November 18, 1968; Arlington National Cemetery, Arlington, Va.

HALL, STANFORD ROY

Date/Place of Birth: May 3, 1933; Chicago, Cook County, Ill.
Parents: Roy Irving Hall and Pearl Astrid (Lindstrom) Hall.
Guardians after death of parents: Roy Peter Anderson and Lillie S. (Lindstrom) Anderson.
Spouse/Marriage Date: Charlotte Anne (Hafford) Hall; June 4, 1954 in Davenport, Iowa.
Children: Mark Bryant, Nancy Jane, Julie Anne, Mary Ellen.
Education: Augustana College, A.B. 1954; Augustana Seminary, B.D. 1958; graduate work at Chicago Seminary 1961 and University of Utah, 1964-68.
License/Ordination: Licensed 1955 by Augustana Synod and ordained June 22, 1958 by Augustana Synod.
Calls: First Lutheran, Ault, Colo., 1958-62; Campus Ministry, Greeley, Colo., 1961-62; Holy Trinity, Salt Lake City, Utah, 1962-65; Campus Ministry, Salt Lake City, Utah, 1962-68; Lutheran Student Foundation, Durham, N.C., 1968-75.
Other: Executive Secretary, Utah Council of Churches, 1968; North Carolina Synod Music and Worship Committee, 1974-76. Resigned from ministry, 1975.

HALL, WILLIAM EDWARD

Date/Place of Birth: February 25, 1922; Koblenz, Germany, while father was on duty as U.S. Army Chaplain.
Parents: The Reverend John Hall and Lela Fisher (Yoder) Hall. Grandson of the Reverend R. A. Yoder.
Spouse/Marriage Date: Mary Beth (Kuhn) Hall; December 31, 1946 in Hickory, N.C.
Children: John Franklin, Robert Edward, Rebecca Ann Sharpe, Martha Elizabeth.
Education: Lenoir-Rhyne, A.B. 1944; Philadelphia Seminary, B.D. 1949.
Ordination: June 5, 1949 by North Carolina Synod.
Calls: St. Andrew, Andrews, 1949-52. Chaplain, Fort Bragg, 406th Engineer Brigade, 1952-53; Organ, Rowan County, 1954-63; Our Savior, Jacksonville, 1964-65; Holly Grove, Davidson County, 1965-70; Christiana, Salisbury, 1970-76; Sharon, Statesville, 1976-80. Vice Pastor at various congregations.
Other: U.S. Army 17th Infantry Regiment, in Korea (combat service), 1953-54; received two Bronze Star combat medals. Board of Directors, Lowman Home, 1964-66. Retired March 1, 1982.
Date of Death/Burial Location: August 30, 1993; Organ, Salisbury, N.C.

HALLMAN, SAMUEL THOMAS
Date/Place of Birth: September 3, 1844; Lexington County, S.C.
Parents: David Hallman and Annis (Kirton) Hallman.
First Spouse/Marriage Date: Sarah Jane (Wingard) Hallman.
Died in Concord in 1882 and is buried there.
Child of First Marriage: Milledge Solomon.
Second Spouse/Marriage Date: Lillian Luetta (Brown) Hallman,
niece of the Reverend Samuel Rothrock; July 18, 1883 in
Concord, N.C.
Children of Second Marriage: Lillie Belle, Elmer Berly, Jenny
Louise, Charlie Raymond, Samuel Schaeffer, Ruth Aurelia, Kate
Amelia, Nelly Brown.
Education: Newberry College, until it closed in 1861; Lutheran Theological Southern
Seminary, 1868; Newberry College, Honorary M.A. and D.D.
License/Ordination: Licensed 1868 and ordained 1869 by South Carolina Synod.
Calls: In South Carolina, 1868-80. In North Carolina: St. James-Cold Water-Mt. Hebron,
Concord, 1880-83. Transferred to South Carolina Synod, 1883-1927.
Other: Enlisted in Confederate States Army. President, North Carolina Synod, 1882-83;
Board, North Carolina College. President three years, Secretary eight years, South Carolina
Synod. Secretary, United Synod South, ten years. Board, Newberry College, 43 years, ten
years as Secretary. Editor of the following: *The Lutheran Visitor,* 1895-1904; *The Southern
Lutheran* (later called *Tidings*), 1894-1904; and *History of the Evangelical Lutheran Synod
of South Carolina,* (1824-1924). An avocation was the making and repairing of violins.
Date of Death/Burial Location: March 8, 1927; Oakwood Cemetery, Spartanburg, S.C.

HALTIWANGER, WILLIAM DARR
Date/Place of Birth: August 3, 1889; Chapin, S.C.
Parents: Andrew William Haltiwanger and Elizabeth Caroline
(Hiller) Haltiwanger.
Spouse/Marriage Date: Bessie Lee (Herman) Haltiwanger; April
24, 1921 in Newton, N.C.
Education: Newberry College, A.B. 1909; Lutheran Theological
Southern Seminary, 1912, B.D. 1927.
Ordination: 1912 by Tennessee Synod.
Calls: Sharon-Mt. Hermon-St. Martin, Iredell County, 1912-17;
Zion-New Jerusalem-Bethlehem, Catawba County, 1917-25.
Transferred 1925 to South Carolina Synod.
Date of Death/Burial Location: March 20, 1957; Mt. Horeb Church, Chapin, S.C.

HALVERSON, ROBERT ANTHONY, SR.
Date/Place of Birth: January 31, 1931; Chicago, Ill.
Spouse/Marriage Date: Barbara C. (Clark) Halverson; April 20, 1963.
Children: Heidi Marie, Robert Anthony, Jr., Kurt Andrew, Michael Alan.
Education: Luther College, B.A. 1960; Northwestern Seminary, B.D. 1964.
Ordination: June 3, 1964 by Minnesota Synod.
Calls: Associate Pastor, St. Stephen, Erie, Pa., 1964-66; Christus Victor, Fort Wayne, Ind., 1966-68; St. Luke's, Charlotte, 1968-72. Transferred to New Jersey Synod, 1972.
Other: Press, Radio and TV Committee, Associated Churches of Fort Wayne, 1967; Chair, Protestant Committee on Scouting for Erie and Crawford Counties, Pa., 1965-66; Lay Delegate, Constituting Convention, Minnesota Synod, 1963; Brotherhood Cabinet, City of Chicago, 1949; Secretary, Lutheran Brotherhood, 1949; Lutheran Pastors' Associations in Indiana, Pennsylvania and Charlotte, N.C.; Associate Member, Lutheran Church Historical Association; Lutheran Society for Worship, Music and the Arts; Society of Biblical Literature and Exegesis; North Carolina Synod Publications and Publicity Committee, 1968-72; Charlotte Lion's Club. Removed from roll October 31, 1988 at Cape May Courthouse, N.J.

HAMM, LUTHER BOYD
Date/Place of Birth: March 24, 1900; Newberry County, S.C.
Parents: Drayton Luther Hamm and Nancy (Long) Hamm.
Spouse/Marriage Date: Mildred (Wheeler) Hamm; October 12 1931 in Macon, Ga.
Children: Ruth Oneita Nichols, Nancy Patricia Wagner, Sarah Virginia Shirley, Carol Boyd Strickland.
Education: Newberry College, A.B. 1925, D.D. 1950; Lutheran Theological Southern Seminary, B.D. 1928; graduate study, Chicago Seminary, 1944.
Ordination: January 26, 1928 by Georgia-Alabama Synod.
Calls: Redeemer, Macon, Ga., 1928-35; St. Matthew-St. Luke, Kings Mountain, 1935-40; Macedonia, Burlington, 1940-46; St. Paul, Columbia, S.C., 1946-51; St. John, Hagerstown, Md., 1951-57; Wittenberg, Leesville, S.C., 1958-65; Assistant Pastor, Bethany, Hickory, 1965-66; Assistant Pastor, Holy Trinity, Gastonia, 1966-78. Vice Pastor at various congregations.
Other: Secretary, Georgia-Alabama Synod, 1929-35; Board, Newberry College; Board, Lowman Home; Board, Lutheran Theological Southern Seminary; United Lutheran Church in America Board of Parish Education. Retired January 1966.
Date of Death/Burial Location: June 6, 1978; Silverstreet, S.C.

HAMSHER, PAUL O.
Calls: Transferred from Southeast Pennsylvania Synod to St. Paul, Hamlet, 1970-71. Vice Pastor at Lutheran Church of the Living Word, Laurinburg, 1971. Transferred to Central Pennsylvania Synod, 1971.
Date of Death: March 6, 1993.

HANBERRY, DONALD EDWIN
Date/Place of Birth: July 28, 1933; Clyo, Effingham County, Ga.
Parents: Henry Theodore Hanberry and Lottie Belle (Porterfield) Hanberry.
Spouse/Marriage Date: Janet (Arnsdorff) Hanberry; June 4, 1955 in Springfield, Ga.
Children: Dr. Candace Regina, Andrew Donald, Randall Theodore, Sanford Gordon.
Education: Reinhardt Junior College, Waleska, Ga., two years, Newberry College, B.S. 1954; Lutheran Theological Southern Seminary, B.D. 1958, S.T.M.
Ordination: June 1, 1958 by Georgia-Alabama Synod.
Calls: Good Shepherd, Garden City, Ga., 1958-61; Trinity, Landis, 1961-68. Vice pastor of various congregations. Transferred to Southeast Synod, 1968: Advent, Augusta, Ga., 1968-73; Trinity, Lilburn, Ga., 1973-.
Other: Southeast Synod: Parish Education Committee, 1959-60; Home Missions Committee, 1960-61; Vice President, Ebenezer Conference, 1960-61. North Carolina Synod: American Missions, 1962-63; North Carolina Council of Churches, 1962-63; Parish Education Committee, 1962-63; District Secretary, 1963; District Dean, 1964-68.

HANCHER, JAMES KNICELEY
Place of Birth: Sullivan County, Tenn.
Parents: Father was the Reverend William Hancher.
First Spouse/Marriage Date: Unknown.
Second Spouse: Sarah (Bushong) Hancher.
Children of Second Marriage: William, Belle, Ida N. B. (mother of Miss Martha Akard, pioneer woman missionary in Japan of United Synod South), the Reverend G. B., Joseph.
Third Spouse: Martha (Rankin) Hancher.
Child of Third Marriage: The Reverend A. D. R. Hancher.
Ordination: Ordained Deacon 1845 and Pastor 1847 by Tennessee Synod.
Calls: In East Tennessee and Southwest Virginia, including Solomon, Greene County, 1846-65; Sinking Springs, Greene County, 1846-62; Salem, Cocke County, 1846-51; Zion, Sullivan County, 1865-66; Holston Grove, Sullivan County; Oak Grove, Washington, 1890-94; New Haven, Sullivan County, 1890-94.
Other: President, Tennessee Synod, 1856-57. One of organizers of Holston Synod 1861 and first President.
Date of Death/Burial Location: August 28, 1897; Mosheim, Tenn.

HANCHER, WILLIAM
Date/Place of Birth: September 7, 1788; Frederick County, Va., and moved in 1812 to Sullivan County, Tenn. Several years later by profession of faith became Lutheran.
Child: One son is known, the Reverend James Kniceley, two of whose sons were the Reverends C. B. and A. D. R., and a daughter, Ida, was the mother of Miss Martha Akard, pioneer and long-time Lutheran missionary in Japan.
Ordination: Ordained Deacon 1835 and Pastor 1836 by Tennessee Synod. First ordained minister of Tennessee Synod to preach exclusively in English.
Calls: Churches served were in East Tennessee in Sullivan, Washington and Carter counties.
Other: One of ten Tennessee Synod ministers organizing Holston Synod, January 2, 1861.
Date of Death/Burial Location: September 5, 1870; Sullivan County, Tenn.

HANDSCHIN, RICHARD
Spouse/Marriage Date: Karen.
Ordination: 1971
Calls: St. Luke's, Charlotte, 1998-.

HANSEN, ALLISON AINSWORTH
Date/Place of Birth: September 28, 1922; Sioux City, Iowa.
Parents: Mr. and Mrs. Harold A. Hansen.
Spouse/Marriage Date: Marie C. (Nelson) Hansen; June 18, 1948.
Children: Sharon Kay, Randy Allen, Sandra Mae.
Education: Kansas State University; Dana College, Blair, Neb., B.A. *cum laude*, 1948; Trinity Seminary, Blair, Neb., M.Div. 1853.
Ordination: June 21, 1953 by American Lutheran Church.
Calls: Bethany, Minden, Neb., 1953-57; Fredericksburg, Minden, Neb., 1953-57; First, Denver, Calif., 1957- 58; Trinity, Westbrook, Maine, 1959-65; Good Shepherd, Charlotte, 1965-69; St. Paul, Hull, Iowa, 1969-73; Zion, Hull, Iowa, 1969-73; Nazareth, Coulter, Iowa, 1973-81; Our Savior, Leland, Iowa, 1981-84; West Prairie, Leland, Iowa, 1981-84; Visitation Pastor Blue Ridge Trinity, Raytown, Mo., 1984-.
Other: Member, District Appeals and Adjudication Committee, 1961-61; Member North East Conference District Home Missions Committee, 1963-65.

HARBINSON, CLINE WHITENER
Date/Place of Birth: September 9, 1912; Maiden, N.C.
Parents: Grover Lee Harbinson and Nancy (Cline) Harbinson. A younger brother is the Reverend James A. Harbinson.
Spouse/Marriage Date: Madeleen (Campbell) Harbinson; December 27, 1940 in Taylorsville, N.C.
Children: Dr. Jane Campbell Teague, Philip Carroll, John Mark, Joel Cline.
Education: Lenoir-Rhyne, A.B. 1937; Lutheran Theological Southern Seminary, B.D. 1940.
Ordination: May 30, 1940 by North Carolina Synod.
Calls: Friendship-St. John-Shiloh, Alexander County, 1940-43; St. Stephen, Hickory, 1943-47; Shiloh, Alexander County; St. Luke, Catawba County, 1947-57; Shiloh only, 1957-64. Call to serve a tent-making ministry at St. Mark, Blowing Rock, 1967-77. Retired October 1977. Vice pastor at various congregations.
Other: Officer of West Conference, 1945-57, seven years as Secretary, two as Vice President, and three as President.
Date of Death/Burial Location: September 8, 1987; Shiloh Cemetery, Hickory, N.C.

HARBINSON, JAMES ALEXANDER, SR.
Date/Place of Birth: September 21, 1934; Maiden, Catawba County, N.C.
Parents: Grover Lee Harbinson and Nancy (Cline) Harbinson. An older brother is the Reverend Cline W. Harbinson.

Spouse/Marriage Date: Geraldine (Ramseur) Harbinson, sister of the Reverend Fred M. Ramseur, Jr.; June 14, 1959 in Maiden, N.C.

Children: James A., Jr., Nancy G. Salmon, Jonathan Andrew.

Education: Lenoir-Rhyne, A.B. 1956, D.D. 1992; Lutheran Theological Southern Seminary, M.Div. 1959, S.T.M., 1967.

Ordination: June 7, 1959 by North Carolina Synod.

Calls: Holy Communion, Dallas, 1959-69; Incarnation, Charlotte, 1969-94; Vice Pastor at various congregations; Director of Capital Development, Lutheran Theological Southern Seminary, 1994-97; retired September 1997.

Other: American Missions, 1967-69; Worship and Music, 1967-69, 1970-73; Board, Lenoir-Rhyne, 1970-71, 1984-87; Nominations Committee, 1962; District Dean, 1970-78; Executive Board, 1971-80; Lutheran Church in America Delegate, 1974, 1976, 1978; Chair, "One in Mission" Appeal, 1987-90; President, Lenoir-Rhyne Alumni Association, 1975-76; President, Lutheran Theological Southern Seminary Alumni Association, 1977-80; Chair, Cabinet for Mission, 1978-84; Chair, Campus Ministry Committee, 1993; Coordinator of Campus Ministry Study, 1993-96; President, Mecklenburg Lutheran Campus Ministry Foundation, 1970-71; President, Charlotte Lutheran Ministers Association.

HARDY, DAVID EDMOND, III

Date/Place of Birth: November 23, 1946; Rochester, N.H.

Parents: David Edmond Hardy, Jr. and Ellen Louise (Banker) Hardy.

Spouse/Marriage Date: Marlene Isabell (Cressman) Hardy; July 24, 1971 in Waterloo, Ontario, Canada.

Children: Allison Victoria, Kathryn Ellen, Matthew David, Michael Christopher.

Education: Lenoir-Rhyne, B.A. 1968; Waterloo Seminary, M.Div. 1972; additional study at Wilfred Laurier University, 1968.

Ordination: July 16, 1972 by North Carolina Synod.

Calls: Trinity, St. Johns, Newfoundland, 1972-76; Zion, Sault St. Marie, Ontario, 1976-87; Executive Director, Canadian Lutheran World Relief, Winnipeg, Manitoba, 1987-.

Other: Lutheran Church in America Delegate, 1976, 1982; Lutheran Church in America-Canada Conventions, 1979, 1981, 1983, 1984. Signed the merger documents as an Lutheran Church in America-CS Counselor.

HARMS, PAUL W. F.

Date/Place of Birth: December 24, 1923; Ambur, India.

Parents: John C. W. Harms and Eva Ella Erna (Miller) Harms.

Spouse/Marriage Date: Phyllis Rae (Mahnke) Harms; June 24, 1950 in Milwaukee, Wis.

Children: The Reverend Steven Paul, Rae Antoinette Neunaber, Claudia Nanette Theis, Nathan Scott, Caleb Dietrich, Seth Siegfried.

Education: St. John's College, Winfield, Kan., A.A. 1943; Concordia Seminary, B.A. 1945, M.Div. 1948, S.T.M. 1954; Northwestern University, M.A. 1957, Ph.D. 1973; graduate work at Washington University, University of Minnesota, University of Portland and Portland State University.

Ordination: September 1949 by Oregon Syn

Calls: Grace, Ashland, Ore., 1949-52; Interim pastor at various congregations; Counselor, Southern Oregon Circuit, Northwest District, The Lutheran Church-Missouri Synod, 1951-52.

Other: Professor of English and Speech at Concordia College in Portland, Ore. and Concordia Senior College in Ft. Wayne, Ind. Professor of Homiletics and Dean of Community Life at Evangelical Lutheran Seminary and Trinity Seminary, 1976-84. Board for Missions, The Lutheran Church-Missouri Synod, 1964-77; Member, Standing Committee Lutheran Campus Ministry, Lutheran Council, U.S.A., 1965-69; Member, Homiletical Literature Committee, Commission on Church Literature, The Lutheran Church-Missouri Synod, 1965-71. Assigned to North Carolina Synod as representative from Trinity Seminary.

HARPER, WILLIAM EDWARD, JR.

Date/Place of Birth: September 12, 1938; Rocky Mount, Nash County, N.C.
Parents: Wiley R. Williams (step-father) and Inez White (Foy) Harper.
Spouse/Marriage Date: Ruby Faye (Goff) Harper; July 22, 1962 in Rocky Mount, N.C.
Children: Tracy Lynn Radican, Deborah Faye Couvertier.
Education: Lenoir-Rhyne, A.B. History 1961; Lutheran Theological Southern Seminary, B.D. 1964.
Ordination: June 14, 1964 by North Carolina Synod.
Calls: Christ, East Spencer, 1964-67; Trinity, Roanoke, Va., 1967-72; Holy Cross, Herndon, Va., 1972-88; Macedonia, Burlington, 1988-92; Zion, Hickory, 1992-.
Other: Virginia Synod: Youth Ministry Committee, 1968-72; resource person for Lutheran Church in America's "Strength for Missions;" Chair, World Missions Managing Group, 1983-86; Coordinator of Summer Assembly of the Virginia Synod; Virginia Synod Policy Making Committee for the "One in Mission" Appeal; Board, Lutheran Social Services, Washington, D.C., area.

HARR, FRANCIS MARION

Date/Place of Birth: February 21, 1857; Sullivan County, Tenn.
Spouse/Marriage Date: Catherine (Wolford) Harr; October 1, 1885 in Blountville, Tenn.
Children: Claude F., Clarence E., Ruth Agnes.
License/Ordination: Licensed 1881 and ordained 1891 by Holston Synod.
Calls: Greene County, Tenn., to 1903. In North Carolina, 1903-09: St. Matthew-St. Peter, Rowan County; Frieden's-Sharon, Gibsonville; others in Tennessee and Virginia.
Date of Death/Burial Location: February 17, 1942; Immanuel Church near Blountville, Tenn.

HARR, JOSEPH

Ordination: Ordained Deacon 1821 by Tennessee Synod at its second convention, in Zion Church, Sullivan County, Tenn.
Calls: Ministry was short, as he died in 1823.
Date of Death: 1823.

HARRIS, W. BENNETT

Date/Place of Birth: December 16, 1957; Edgecombe County, N.C.
Parents: Wilbur Clyde Harris and Carol Ann (Pitt) Harris.
Spouse/Marriage Date: Robin (Hendrix) Harris; June 8, 1991 in Gettysburg, Pa.
Child: Anna Elisabeth.
Education: Lenoir-Rhyne, A.B. Philosophy/Theology 1987; Gettysburg Seminary, M.Div. 1991.
Ordination: May 19, 1992 by North Carolina Synod.

Calls: St. Matthew, Granite Falls, 1992-94; Daniel's, Lincolnton, 1994-.
Other: Adjunct Faculty, Lenoir-Rhyne, 1992-1994.

HARRIS, ZACHARIAH, III

Date/Place of Birth: November 19, 1962; Pensacola, Fla.
Parents: Zachariah Harris, Jr., and Audrey (Vogel) Harris.
Spouse/Marriage Date: Stephanie (Bloom) Harris; August 18, 1990 in Goldsboro, N.C.
Education: North Carolina State University; Lenoir-Rhyne, B.A. 1985; Gettysburg Seminary, M.Div. 1991, graduate work toward S.T.M.
Ordination: July 20, 1991 by North Carolina Synod.
Calls: Christus Victor, Fayetteville, 1991-96; Pastor-Developer, Holy Cross, Mebane, 1996-. Vice Pastor at various congregations.

HARRY, J. H.

Place of Birth: Ohio.
Ordination: 1874 North Carolina Synod.
Calls: St. James, Concord, 1874-75. He returned then to his native state because of illness.

HARTER, WILLIAM GEORGE

Date/Place of Birth: September 25, 1811; Barnwell District, S.C.
Parents: George Harter and Margaret (Platts) Harter.
First Spouse/Marriage Date: Margaret Virginia (Nuttall) Harter of Richmond, Va.; December 30, 1846 in Salisbury, N.C.
Children of First Marriage: Laura Louisa Euphrasine, William Olinthus Fontaine, Edwin Hazelius Nuttall (died in infancy), Marie Susan Virginia, and infant daughter (died 33 days after birth).
Second Spouse/Marriage Date: Charlotte E. (Hine) Harter; January 6, 1858 in Silver Run, Ohio.
Children of Second Marriage: George Elwyn, Margaret Estilla, Carrie Lamenta.
Education: Classical and Theological Institute (Lutheran Theological Southern Seminary), 1837.
License/Ordination: Licensed 1837 and ordained 1838 by South Carolina Synod.
Calls: In South Carolina, 1836-41. In North Carolina, 1841-56: Cold Water, Cabarrus County; organized St. James, Concord, 1843, and served to 1854, and Mt. Carmel; St. Enoch, Union, and Luther's in Rowan County; New Bethel, Stanly County; supplied St. Paul, Iredell County; also served churches in Kentucky, 1857-64.
Other: Traveled for the home mission cause in Pennsylvania, Maryland, Virginia, Kentucky, Tennessee, and North Carolina. Secretary, five one-year terms, and President 1850-51 North Carolina Synod. On synod committee 1844 to visit destitute people in Lincoln and Catawba Counties. Fraternal Delegate 1844 to Southwest Virginia and South Carolina Synods. Author of *The Abrahamic Covenant, A Treatise on Infant Baptism.*
Date of Death/Burial Location: July 31, 1864; Hopeful Church, Florence, Ky.

HARTSELL, LARRY FRANK

Date/Place of Birth: September 22, 1947; Marquette, Mich.

Parents: Lester Curtis Hartsell and Anne Blanche (Libick) Hartsell.
Spouse/Marriage Date: Pamela Jean (Zeigler) Hartsell; June 22, 1974 in Rincon, Ga.
Children: Jonathan Andrew, Caleb Benjamin.
Education: East Tennessee State University, A.B. 1969, M.A. 1974; University of Georgia, Dramatic Literature, 1975; Lutheran Theological Southern Seminary, M.Div. 1979.
Ordination: June 13, 1979 by Southeast Synod.
Calls: St. Andrew, New Bern, 1979-82; Campus Pastor, Holy Trinity, Chapel Hill, 1982-98; University Lutheran, Clemson, S.C., 1998-.

HARTWIG, GEORGE H.

Date/Place of Birth: 1879 at Canajoharie, N.Y.
Spouse: Margaret (Valborg) Hartwig.
Children: Katherine, Dorothy, Robert.
Education: Wagner College, A.B. 1898; Leland Stanford Junior University A.B.; Philadelphia Seminary, 1901; graduate study at Cornell, Harvard, and Chicago Universities.
Ordination: 1901 by New York Synod.
Calls: In New York and Nova Scotia, 1901-08. Transferred to Tennessee Synod, 1909.
Other: Professor and Head of English Department, Lenoir-Rhyne, 1908-16. Transferred to Pacific Synod, 1917. Later taught at St. Olaf, Wittenberg, Dana, and Midland Colleges. Retired in 1949.
Date of Death/Burial Location: July 31, 1956; funeral, Lake of the Isles Church, Minneapolis, Minn.

HASKELL, WILLIAM CLARK, JR.

Date/Place of Birth: August 6, 1949; Lakeland, Polk County, Fla.
Parents: William Clark Haskell, Sr. and Lina (Parrish) Haskell.
Education: Auburn University, B.S. Business Administration 1971; Southern Baptist Seminary, M.Div. 1977; Lutheran Theological Southern Seminary, 1978.
Ordination: September 16, 1979 by Indiana-Kentucky Synod.
Calls: St. Stephen, Hickory, 1979-81; Christus Victor, Fayetteville, 1981-84; St. Paul, Hamlet, 1984-89; Lutheran Chapel, China Grove, 1989-. Vice Pastor at various congregations.
Other: In Fayetteville at Christus Victor, helped found Alms House, a Crisis-outreach ministry in southern Cumberland County along with the clergy and congregations of the Roman Catholic, Episcopal, United Methodist and Presbyterian churches in the area. In Hamlet at St. Paul, active in ecumenical events, area soup kitchens, shelter program for victims of domestic violence in Richmond County. Youth Convo Planning Committee; Synodical Communications Committee.

HAUER, D. J.

Education: Received D.D. degree.
License/Ordination: Licensed 1826 and ordained 1828 by North Carolina Synod.
Calls: Assistant to the Reverend Jacob Scherer at Low's, Guilford County, 1827-28; Frieden's, Guilford County; Richland, Randolph County; St. Paul, Alamance County, 1828-29. Transferred to Maryland and Virginia Synod, 1829. Served at Manchester, Carroll

County, Md., but in the 1860s moved to Adams County, Pa., before beginning ministry in Hanover, York County, Pa.

Date of Death/Burial Location: 1901; Hanover, Pa.

HAUSENFLUCK, JOHN WILLIAM

Date/Place of Birth: February 14, 1848; Shenandoah County, Va.
Parent: Simon Hausenfluck.
Spouse/Marriage Date: Mary Catherine (Lohr) Hausenfluck; March 27, 1877 in Shenandoah County, Va.
Children: Luther A., Mary Virginia Roudabush, Carrie L., William A., Solon A.
Education: Polytechnic Institute, New Market, Va.; in theology under Dr. Socrates Henkel.
License/Ordination: Licensed and ordained 1877 by Tennessee Synod.

Calls: In East Tennessee, except one church in West Virginia, though he resided in Virginia, 1877-1917. Served in Virginia: Page County, 1877-92; Augusta County, 1878-1912; Shenandoah County, 1892-1900, 1913-16; Rockbridge County, 1891-97; Rockingham County, 1892-1913.

Other: Retired 1917 because of failing health.

Date of Death/Burial Location: September 26, 1922; Washington, D.C.

HAWKINS, ELIJAH

Date/Place of Birth: March 3, 1812; Newberry District, S.C.
Education: Classical and Theological Institute, (later Newberry College and Lutheran Theological Southern Seminary), member of first seminary class, 1836.
License/Ordination: Licensed 1836 by South Carolina Synod. Transferred to North Carolina Synod, 1837 and ordained 1838.
Calls: In North Carolina Synod churches, Smyth County, Va., 1837-42. Served churches of Southwest Virginia Synod, 1842-68; Rural Retreat, Va., 1855-68.
Other: One of organizers of Southwest Virginia Synod, 1842; President, four terms, 1845-59. Fraternal Delegate to North Carolina Synod, 1850 and 1858. Delegate to General Synod Convention, 1850 and 1856.
Date of Death: March 5, 1868.

HAWKINS, ROBERT WILLIAM

Date/Place of Birth: January 14, 1950; Burlington, N.C.
Parents: Cameron Wilton Hawkins and Mae Dew (Pittman) Hawkins.
First Spouse/Marriage Date: Tina Nanette (Dennis) Hawkins; April 1, 1978 in Columbia, S.C.
Child of First Marriage: William John.
Second Spouse: Jamie (Bennett) Hawkins; July 8, 1995 in Sandy Run, S.C.
Education: Lenoir-Rhyne, A.B. English 1973; Lutheran Theological Southern Seminary, M.Div. 1981.
Ordination: May 24, 1981 by North Carolina Synod.
Calls: Reformation, Taylorsville, 1981-85; Providence, Lexington, S.C., 1985-90; Resurrection, Columbia, S.C., 1990-92; Clinical Pastoral Education, Baptist Hospital, 1992-93; Sandy Run, Swansea, S.C., 1993-.

Other: Global Mission Committee; Associate Minister, Lexington Hospital.

HAWN, JOHN MARTIN

Date/Place of Birth: March 14, 1937; Lincoln County, N.C.
Parents: John Victor Hawn and Annie Lee (Finger) Hawn Powell.
Spouse/Marriage Date: Leta Lynn (Kendall) Hawn; June 25, 1961 in Charlotte, N.C.
Children: Mark Kendall, Brian Martin.
Education: Lenoir-Rhyne, A.B. 1959; Lutheran Theological Southern Seminary, M.Div. 1963.
Ordination: June 9, 1963 by North Carolina Synod.
Calls: Grace, Hendersonville, 1963-69; St. Mark, Asheville, 1969-76; First, Albemarle, 1976-94; Vice Pastor at various congregations; St. Mark, Roanoke, Va., 1994-.
Other: In North Carolina Synod: Synod Executive Board, 1972-5; Lutheran Homes Board, 1967-8; District Dean; Chair, Social Ministry Committee, 1967-70; World Missions Committee, 1965-68; President's Task Force - Priority Program (Justice and Social Committee), 1970-74; Delegate to Lutheran Church in America Convention, 1972; Board, Lenoir-Rhyne. Retired to North Carolina.

HAWTHORNE, HARRY DAVID, SR.

Date/Place of Birth: December 29, 1918; Lancaster, Pa.
Spouse/Marriage Date: Alice Josephine (Whitener) Hawthorne; August 1, 1943 in Hickory, N.C.
Children: Harry David, Jr., Susan Leigh Cain.
Education: Lenoir-Rhyne, A.B. 1941, D.D. 1964; Lutheran Theological Southern Seminary, M.Div. 1943; graduate study, Chicago Seminary; S.T.M. resident work completed, 1953; graduate study School of Theology, University of the South, three summers; Canisius College, M.S.Ed. 1969; State University of New York, M.A. 1981.
Ordination: July 11, 1943 by North Carolina Synod.
Calls: St. Luke-Morning Star, Monroe, 1943-44; Beth Eden, Newton, 1945-49, Pastor Emeritus; Emmanuel, High Point, 1949-63; Pastor to Lutheran Students at High Point College; transferred to New York Synod, 1964; First English, Lockport, N.Y., 1964-70; Ascension Lutheran, Snyder, N.Y., 1971-83, Pastor Emeritus; Pastor to Lutheran Students at Daemon College, Snyder, N.Y.; Vice Pastor and Interim Pastor at various congregations in New York and in North Carolina. Retired December 31, 1983.
Other: Instructor in Bible, Monroe High School. National Lutheran Counseling Service Pastor, Camp Sutton, 1943-44, holding services also for German prisoners of war. Pastor to Lutheran students, High Point College, 1949-63. President, Lenoir-Rhyne Alumni Association, 1948-50; Board, Lenoir-Rhyne, 1956-63; North Carolina Council of Churches, 1963. Served as Advisor of the North Carolina Synod's Women of the Church for six years. Regional Coordinator, Lenoir-Rhyne Centennial Appeal. In High Point: Board, School for Exceptional Children; Board, United Fund; Board, Family Service Bureau; Adviser, Society for Crippled Children and Adults; Adviser, Guilford County Domestic Relations Court; Dean, Northern District, 1962-63; Vice Chair, Board, Lutheran Church Home, Buffalo, N.Y., 1971-83; President, Kiwanis Club, High Point and Hickory, N.C.; President, High Point Executive's Club. *Who's Who in the South and Southwest,* Volumes 6 and 7; *Who's Who in Religion,* 1976, 1977, 1978, 1992, 1993.

HAYNES, CARL MICHAEL
Date/Place of Birth: January 13, 1956; Salisbury, N.C.
Parents: Carl Rogers Haynes and Betty (Cress) Haynes.
Spouse/Marriage Date: Kathy Sue (Morrow) Haynes; June 19, 1977 in Rowan County, N.C.
Children: Suzanna Louise, Natalie Michelle, Emily Kathryn.
Education: Catawba College, A.B. Religion 1978; Lutheran Theological Southern Seminary, M.Div. 1982.
Ordination: June 6, 1982 by North Carolina Synod.
Calls: Our Saviour, Dallas, 1982-91; Christiana, Salisbury, 1992-.
Other: Lutheran Family Services Board; Secretary, President, Board, Lutheran Support Group of Gaston, Inc.; Outreach Committee; Pastor Advisor, Lutheran Men in Mission.

HEAVNER, CHRISTOPHER STOWE
Date/Place of Birth: February 10, 1957; Lincolnton, N.C.
Parents: Ralph Foster Heavner and Georgia Kathleen (Beam) Heavner.
Spouse/Marriage Date: The Reverend Laura Marion (Hunter) Heavner; June 11, 1983 in Lawrenceville, Ga.
Children: Miriam Kathleen, Smith Foster, Caleb Stowe.
Education: North Carolina State University, B.A. Education 1979; Chicago Seminary, M.Div. 1983.
Ordination: May 29, 1983 by North Carolina Synod.
Calls: Bethel, Salisbury, 1983-86; Good Shepherd, Houghton, Mich., 1986-93; Lutheran Campus Ministry, Clemson, S.C., 1993-.
Other: Interim Dean of Students, Lutheran School of Theology at Chicago, 1987.

HEAVNER, LAURA MARION (HUNTER)
Date/Place of Birth: November 6, 1958; Atlanta, Ga.
Parents: Charles Smith Hunter and Miriam (Kaufold) Hunter.
Spouse/Marriage Date: The Reverend Christopher Stowe Heavner; June 11, 1983 in Lawrenceville, Ga.
Children: Miriam Kathleen, Smith Foster, Caleb Stowe.
Education: Gordon Junior College, A.A. 1978; University of Georgia, B.F.A. 1982; Chicago Seminary, M.Div. 1987.
Ordination: July 5, 1987 by North Carolina Synod.
Calls: Good Shepherd, Houghton, Mich., 1987-93. On leave from call, 1993-.

HEDRICK, JOHN M.
Calls: Transferred 1878 to Virginia Synod from Susquehanna Synod, and served churches in Augusta County, Va., 1877-84. Transferred to North Carolina Synod, 1884. Churches served in North Carolina: 1884-87: Christiana and Union, Rowan County; Reformation, Davie County; Pilgrim-St. Luke, Davidson County. Transferred to Carroll County, Southwest Virginia Synod, 1887, and again to North Carolina Synod, 1889: Mt. Hermon-Cold Water-Prosperity, Cabarrus County, 1888-93.
Date of Death/Burial Location: February 17, 1895; Charlottesville, Va.

HEFNER, DOUGLAS EDWARD (See Page 547)

HEFNER, LORI ANN (VAN RAVESTEIN) (See Page 547)

HEFNER, VIRL RICHARD

Date/Place of Birth: March 21, 1919; Catawba County, N.C.
Parents: Robey Albert Hefner and Rosa Luetta (Lail) Hefner.
Spouse/Marriage Date: Dorothy Jane (Gockenbach) Hefner; September 18, 1945 in Columbus, Ohio.
Children: John Mark, Silvia Marie Finelli, Verla Jane Ubert, Margaret Rose Wagner, Elizabeth Ann Lutz.
Education: Lenoir-Rhyne, A.B. 1942; Evangelical Seminary, Capital University, M.Div. 1945; graduate work at National Institute of Mental Health, Bethesda, Md., Alcoholism Counselor, 1968; graduate work at Wartburg Seminary, 1962; D.D., Otay Mesa Ministry of Salvation Bible College and Seminary, San Diego, Calif.
Ordination: September 30, 1945 by North Carolina Synod (American Lutheran Church).
Calls: Trinity-St. James Parish, Fort Recovery, Ohio, 1945-49; First, Portsmouth, Ohio, 1949-53; St. John, Ellicott City, Md., 1953-71; Mt. Hebron, Hildebran, 1974-81. Retired, March 1981.

HEGLAR, DEWEY LEE, SR.

Date/Place of Birth: February 2, 1902; Cabarrus County, N.C.
Parents: Victor C. Heglar and Julia (Cohen) Heglar.
Spouse/Marriage Date: Elsie Louise (Counts) Heglar, daughter of the Reverend Henry P. Counts, October 16, 1932 in Haralson, Ga.
Child: Dewey Lee, Jr.
Education: Mount Pleasant Collegiate Institute, 1924; Lenoir-Rhyne, A.B. 1926; Lutheran Theological Southern Seminary, B.D. 1929.
Ordination: 1929 by North Carolina Synod.
Calls: None in North Carolina; in Georgia, South Carolina, Virginia, and since 1960 Trinity, Chattanooga, Tenn. Retired to Knoxville, Tenn., 1970.
Date of Death/Burial Location: January 15, 1982; Knoxville, Tenn.

HEILIG, JOHN SAMUEL

Date/Place of Birth: January 8, 1820; Rowan County, N.C.
Parent: John Heilig.
Education: Gettysburg College, A.B. 1848; Lutheran Theological Southern Seminary, 1851.
License/Ordination: Licensed 1851 and ordained 1854 by North Carolina Synod.
Calls: St. Enoch, 1852-66; Salem, 1853-58, Rowan County; organized Trinity, Cabarrus County, 1857-66; St. Paul, Iredell County, 1865. Transferred to Maryland Synod, 1866. In West Virginia and Kentucky. Returned to North Carolina, and served Cold Water, Cabarrus County, 1884.
Other: Secretary, North Carolina Synod, 1859-60, 1879-80.
Date of Death/Burial Location: August 12, 1885; Concord, N.C.

HEINZE, RONALD OWEN

Date/Place of Birth: January 5, 1940; Cumberland, Md.

Parents: The Reverend Edward P. Heinze and Viola Eva (Potts) Heinze.

Spouse/Marriage Date: Charlotte Frances (Law) Heinze; June 19, 1965 in North Augusta, S.C.

Children: Mark Edward, Christopher Ronald.

Education: Gettysburg, A.B. 1962; Gettysburg Seminary, B.D. 1966; University of North Carolina at Charlotte, M.Ed. 1976.

Ordination: September 11, 1966 by Maryland Synod.

Calls: Advent, Doraville, Ga., 1966-72; Associate Pastor, Beth Eden, Newton, 1972-76; Redeemer, Charlotte, 1977-89; Philadelphia, Granite Falls, 1989-95; Our Saviour, Freeport, Grand Bahamas, 1995-.

HELLAND, CARL K.

Date/Place of Birth: March 17, 1853; Queen Ann Prairie, Ill.

Parents: Rasmus Helland and Kari (Scheie) Helland.

Spouse/Marriage Date: Hattie F. (Hall) Helland (died 1922); 1885.

Education: Augustana College (Marshall, Wis.), 1877-81; Augustana Seminary (Beloit, Iowa), 1881-84.

Ordination: In 1890 he shifted from the Norwegian Augustana Lutheran Church which ordained him to the United Norwegian Church.

Calls: Marshville, Wis., 1894-96; Superintendent, Homme Children's Home, Wittenberg, Wis., 1896-99. Where he served from 1899 to 1902 is not known, but in 1902 began his ministry at Frankfort, Tenn.; Thorsby, Ala., 1905-1908; transferred 1908 to North Carolina Synod from Norwegian Synod, and served St. Matthew, Rowan County, 1908-09. In 1909 transferred back to Norwegian Synod. In 1912 began a four-year ministry in Shelby, Mich. and a four-year ministry in New Era, Mich. Served in Tomahawk, Wis., 1920-22 and in Chicago, Ill., for five years.

Other: While in Thorsby, Ala., served on City Council and the School Board; Trustee, Norwegian Augustana Synod; public school teacher, Vermillion, S.D.

Date of Death: July 23, 1940.

HELMS, ROBERT ANDREW

Ordination: 1896 by Virginia Synod

Calls: Buena Vista Parish, Virginia, following ordination. Also conducted occasional services for Zion, Glen Wilton, probably being the last pastor to serve this now disbanded congregation. Transferred to North Carolina Synod serving 1899-1900: St. Michael, Troutman; Providence, Rowan County; St. Matthew, Davie County; St. Paul, Iredell County. Transferred to North West Synod 1903 serving churches in Minnesota, and from 1912 churches of Northern Illinois Synod. In 1920 was in Oshkosh, Neb. and the following year in Hardy. In 1924 he was in Stella and in 1927-28 was a member of the Iowa Synod located in Fernald, Iowa.

HELTON, ROBERT LEE, JR.

Date/Place of Birth: January 31, 1952; Jacksonville, Fla.

Parents: Robert Lee Helton, Sr. and Ruth (Cloaninger) Helton.

Spouse/Marriage Date: Marilynn (Jones) Helton; January 11, 1975.
Child: Amanda Lynn.
Education: Lenoir-Rhyne, A.B. Religious Studies, 1975; Lutheran Theological Southern Seminary, M.Div. 1979.
Ordination: June 10, 1979 by North Carolina Synod.
Calls: Prince of Peace, Kinston, 1979-82; Vice Pastor at various congregations; Special Call to U.S. Army Chaplaincy Major, 1982-, serving at Ft. Carson, Colo., Heidelberg, Germany, Ft. Monmouth, N.J., Ft. Benning, Ga. Six-month duty in Desert Storm - one year as Airborne School Chaplain and one year as the Chaplain Budget Officer. Also served in Mons, Belgium, for The Supreme Headquarters, Allied Powers Europe, and Vicenze, Italy, at U.S. Army Headquarters in The Southern Region and Italy.

HENKEL, AMBROSE
Date/Place of Birth: July 11, 1786 near Solomon Church, eight miles Northwest of New Market, Va.
Parents: Third son of the Reverend Paul Henkel and Elizabeth (Negeley) Henkel.
First Spouse: Catharine (Hoke) Henkel in Lincoln County, N.C.
Child of First Marriage: Noah Isaiah.
Second Spouse: Mary (Kite) Henkel of Page County, Va.
Children of Second Marriage: Mary Catharine, Arianna Elizabeth, Eleanora Caroline, Paul Philip.
Third Spouse: Veronica Hoyle (Heyle) Henkel in Lincoln County, apparently sister of his brother David's wife, Catharine.
Children of Third Marriage: Gerhart Ambrose, Hieronymus.
License/Ordination: Licensed 1823 and ordained 1824 by Tennessee Synod.
Calls: All in Virginia: Trinity (Koiner's), 1823-25; Mt. Calvary, Page County, 1823-37; Emmanuel, New Market, 1825-38; St. Mary, near Mt. Jackson, 1825-55; St. Paul's, Jerome, 1827-36; Rader, Timberville, 1829-37; and Zion, near Edinburg, 1854; St. Jacob, Edinburg, 1855-57.
Other: Learned printer's trade at Hagerstown, Md., having walked there from home in Virginia, 1802; established first Lutheran printing shop in America at New Market, Va., 1806. Published a German language paper, *The Virginia and New Market Popular Instructor and Weekly News,* 1807-09. Edited a New Market newspaper for 62 years, and was referred to as "perhaps the oldest practical printer in Virginia." Sold printing shop to older brother, Solomon, a physician, who thus became a publisher also. The Henkel Press was long an outstanding force in the development of the Lutheran Church in worship, confessional strength, education, and practices throughout the South. Literary contributions: Prepared and published *Church Hymn Book,* 1838; was Chair of Committee of Tennessee Synod to prepare *Book of Forms* (liturgy and orders), published in 1843; aided in translating into English, Lutheran symbols, and publishing *The Christian Book of Concord,* 1851; translated into English and published serially, Vol. 1, Luther's *Church Postil* (Epistles), 1857-58; Secretary, Tennessee Synod, 1829, 1831, 1833; President, 1853.
Date of Death/Burial Location: January 6, 1870 at New Market, Va.; Emmanuel Church in New Market, Va.

HENKEL, ANDREW
Date/Place of Birth: October 21, 1790; New Market, Va., fourth son of the Reverend Paul and Elizabeth (Negeley) Henkel.
First Spouse/Marriage Date: Margaret (Trout) Henkel; 1815.
Second Spouse: Mrs. Elizabeth (Swartzell) Henkel.
Children: Hiram, Philip, Julia, Paul, Margaret, Vandalena, Sabina, George, William, Edward.
License: Licensed 1811 by Ministerium of Pennsylvania and transferred 1814 to North Carolina Synod.
Calls: No record of any churches served in North Carolina. In 1826 he accepted a call to the Lutheran Church at Germantown, Ohio, and also in Goshen, Ind., and Lewisburg, Ohio.
Date of Death/Burial Location: April 23, 1870; Germantown, Ohio.

HENKEL, CHARLES
Date/Place of Birth: May 18, 1798; New Market, Va., sixth son of the Reverend Paul and Elizabeth (Negeley) Henkel, and youngest of the five minister sons.
First Spouse: Mary C. (Siegrist) Henkel of Madison County, Va.
Children of First Marriage: The Reverend David Melanchthon, Mary Elizabeth, Charles Ambrose.
Second Spouse: Mary (Warner) Henkel in Columbus, Ohio.
Calls: No churches served in North Carolina. President, Ohio Synod and was founder of numerous churches. Translated the *Augsburg Confession* (1831) which was afterwards published by the order of the Tennessee Synod.
Date of Death/Burial Location: February 2, 1841; Perry County, Ohio.

HENKEL, DAVID
Date/Place of Birth: May 4, 1795, fifth son of the Reverend Paul and Elizabeth (Negeley) Henkel, in Augusta County, Va.
Spouse: Catharine Hoyle (Heyle) Henkel of Lincoln County, N.C., a sister of Veronica Hoyle, his brother Ambrose's third wife.
Children: Susan, Elizabeth, Leah, the Reverend Polycarp Cyprian, Cicero, Flora, Eleanora, the Reverend Socrates. Two grandsons were the Reverends Augustus R. Bennick (Methodist) and John S. Bennick (Lutheran).
Education: Private study in German, English, Latin, Greek, Hebrew, Theology, and Lutheran confessions and practices. Before he was licensed, his father arranged for him to work with Pastor Godfrey Dreher in South Carolina congregations.*License/Ordination*: Licensed 1813 at the age of 18 and ordained 1819 by North Carolina Synod.
Calls: Daniel's, Lincoln County, 1814-25; St. Luke, organized Trinity, Vale, 1821-30; St. Mark, Gaston County, 1814-30; Bethel-Philadelphia, 1821-30; and White Haven (a group from original White Haven organizing separately about a mile away under Henkel and served by him), 1814-31; Morning Star, Mecklenburg County, 1815-18, 1830; St. Paul, Newton, 1820-31; supplied St. Martin, Cabarrus County, 1821; occasional supply, St. Martin, Stanly County, 1820-28; organized Mt. Moriah, Rowan County, 1823-24.

Other: Not present for organization of Tennessee Synod in 1820 but having agreed to it, was recognized as a charter member; served as Secretary 1824, 1826, 1827. Literary contributions: drafted constitution of Tennessee Synod; translated into English Luther's Small Catechism, with an appendix, *An Essay on Regeneration;* also wrote *A Treatise on the Person and Incarnation of Jesus Christ, in Which Unitarian Arguments are Examined and Answered;* and a number of other treatises on doctrinal subjects.
Date of Death/Burial Location: June 15, 1831; St. John, Catawba County, N.C.

HENKEL, DAVID MELANCHTHON

Parents: The Reverend Charles Henkel and Mary C. (Siegrist) Henkel, and grandson of the Reverend Paul Henkel.
Spouse: Heleah Anna Maria (Henkel) Henkel, youngest child of his uncle Solomon Henkel; September 11, 1849.
Children: Six, of whom Leah Ellen, the third child, married the Reverend A. L. Yount, D.D.
Education: Received a D.D. Degree.
Ordination: Ordained Deacon 1848 and Pastor 1849 on day of marriage, by Tennessee Synod.
Calls: Transferred 1855 to Virginia Synod. In 1860 was located in Danville, Montour County, Pa., where he served for a number of years before moving to Richmond, Va. Transferred back to North Carolina Synod, 1873. St. John, Cabarrus County; Holy Trinity, Mt. Pleasant, 1872-75. Transferred to Indiana Synod, 1876.
Date of Death/Burial Location: November 8, 1904; Catawissa, Pa.

HENKEL, DAVID SOCRATES

Date/Place of Birth: August 24, 1846; North Carolina.
Parents: The Reverend Polycarp C. Henkel and Rebecca (Fox) Henkel, and great-grandson of the Reverend Paul Henkel.
First Spouse/Marriage Date: Rebecca (Henkel) Henkel, daughter of Solomon D. Henkel; 1871.
Children of First Marriage: Sallie, Alice, Beatrice, Tilden, Clinton, Roscoe, Herbert, George, Charles, Laura.
Second Spouse: Elizabeth (Vaughan) Henkel.
Child of Second Marriage: One son.
License: Licensed 1863 by Tennessee Synod, but not ordained.
Calls: St. Martin, Stanly County, 1865-67; Mt. Moriah, Rowan County, 1867-69.
Other: Treasurer, Tennessee Synod, 1867. After pastorate at Mt. Moriah, went to New Market, Va., and read law with Judge George R. Calvert and practiced law for about twenty years, serving in the Virginia Legislature. Left the Lutheran Church and became affiliated with the Disciples of Christ. Organized and served congregations in that church in Virginia, at Waynesboro, Basic City, Harrisonburg, Newport News, and Chatham from 1892-1914.
Date of Death/Burial Location: February 7, 1914; Emmanuel Church, New Market, Va.

HENKEL, EUSEBIUS
Parents: The Reverend Philip L. Henkel and Catherine (Rupert) Henkel, and grandson of the Reverend Paul Henkel.
Ordination: Deacon by Tennessee Synod in 1833.
Calls: As Tennessee Synod missionary in Indiana, 1833-35. With the Reverend Christian Moretz (Tennessee Synod) and the Reverend John Ludwig Markert (North Carolina Synod), assisted in organizing Indiana Synod in 1835. Markert was chosen first President of that synod.

HENKEL, PAUL
Date/Place of Birth: December 15, 1754; on Dutchman's Creek, sixteen miles from Salisbury, in then Rowan County (now a part of Davie County), N.C. Was the first Lutheran pastor born in North Carolina.
Parents: Jacob Henkel and Mary Barbara (Teeter) Henkel.
Spouse/Marriage Date: Elizabeth (Negeley) (sometimes spelled Negly, Nagly) Henkel; November 20, 1776.
Children: Solomon (a physician) and five minister sons, Philip L., Ambrose, Andrew, David and Charles; Hanna (married the Reverend John N. Stirewalt), Naomi, and Sabina.
Education: In 1776 he began his study in theology and the classics under the guidance and sponsorship of the Reverend John Andrew Krugh, Fredericktown, Md.
License/Ordination: Licensed by the Ministerium of Pennsylvania June 1783 with renewal annually until ordination by the same Synod on June 6, 1792.
Calls: In Virginia, and perhaps in other states, from his home in New Market, Va., until 1806 when he was appointed "traveling preacher," and was allowed $40 a month for the time he was actually engaged in his work. The next year (1807) he reported that he traveled 128 days in the service of the Synod and baptized 158 children and received $106.05 on this journey. In 1808 he was appointed missionary for Virginia, North Carolina and Tennessee, and from records it appears that he was re-appointed annually with his field widened to "territory of his own selection." It seems reasonable to assume that during the years he was traveling preacher he would have lived in North Carolina from 1800 to 1805 while serving the following churches in this state: Dutchman's Creek Church (later called New Jerusalem, then Reformation from 1870 to disbanding in 1925), Davie County, 1800-05; Beck's-Bethany-Pilgrim, St. Luke, Davidson County; Nazareth-Shiloh, Forsyth County, 1800-05; also, in same area after 1820 occasional supply with other Tennessee Synod pastors. Assistant to Johann Gottfried Arends (Arndt), Emmanuel, Lincolnton-Zion, Catawba County, 1803; and supply, St. Mark, Gaston County, 1803. Because of malarial climate moved back to New Market, Va., 1805. Made repeated missionary tours in North Carolina, South Carolina, Virginia, Tennessee, Ohio, Kentucky, and Indiana.
Other: While preparing to become a minister and in his early ministry supported his family by working at the cooper's trade. One of four pastors with fourteen laymen, organizing the North Carolina Synod in 1803. Assisted in organizing Ohio Synod in 1818 but did not become a member. Also an organizer of Tennessee Synod, with six other North Carolina Synod pastors, including sons Philip and David. Wrote and published the following: A work on Baptism and the Lord's Supper in German, 1809, later translated into English; a German hymnbook with 246 hymns, 1810, with some hymns (perhaps in both books) written by himself. Also German and English catechisms based on Luther's *Small*

Catechism. Preached in both German and English. The records of the Ministerium of Pennsylvania show that he attended its convention at Lancaster, Pa., in 1820, for the last time.

Date of Death/Burial Location: November 17, 1825; Emmanuel Church, New Market, Va.

HENKEL, PHILIP L.

Date/Place of Birth: September 23, 1779; Pendleton County, Va.
Parents: Second son of the Reverend Paul and Elizabeth (Negeley) Henkel.
Spouse: Catharine (Rupert) Henkel.
Children: Three sons are known, The Reverend Eusebius, the Reverend Irenaeus, Ambrose Dedric; but records state that at his death he was survived by his wife and seven children.
License/Ordination: Licensed 1800 by Ministerium of Pennsylvania, and ordained in 1805 by North Carolina Synod.
Calls: Frieden's-Low's, Guilford County; St. Paul, Alamance County, 1800-05; as assistant to Johann Gottfried Arends (Arndt), Emmanuel, Lincolnton; Daniel's, Lincoln County; Grace-St. Paul, Catawba County, 1805-14, as Pastor, 1808-14; also as Arends' assistant, Zion, Catawba County, 1805-07, as Pastor, 1807-12; Bethel-Philadelphia, Gaston County; St. Luke, Lincoln County, 1808-14; also St. John, Catawba County, 1805- 14. In later years of ministry apparently did mostly supply work, 1825-33, at Cobles, Guilford County; Mt. Pleasant, Alamance County; Mt. Moriah, Rowan County, with other Pastors, 1825, 1831-32, alone in 1833; and Trinity, Vale. Pastor In Tennessee and did missionary work in other states, particularly in Indiana, where he organized five churches in the period from 1814-25.
Other: Secretary 1811 and President 1815 North Carolina Synod. With other pastors, including his father and brother David, was an organizer of Tennessee Synod, 1820 in Solomon Church, Greene County, Tenn., of which he was Pastor at the time; Secretary 1830 and was elected President one month before death.
Date of Death/Burial Location: October 9, 1833, aged 54, after short illness, while on pastoral tour to churches in Guilford and Randolph Counties, having preached last sermon on September 21, 1833 in Richland Church, Randolph County, N.C., where he is buried.

HENKEL, POLYCARP CYPRIAN

Date/Place of Birth: August 20, 1820; Lincoln County, N.C.
Parents: The Reverend David Henkel and Catharine (Heyle/Hoyle) Henkel. A grandson of the Reverend Paul Henkel, and older brother of the Reverend Socrates Henkel.
Spouse/Marriage Date: Rebecca (Fox) Henkel; 1843 in Randolph County, N.C.
Children: The Honorable David S., Catharine C. (Lail).
Education: Received a D.D. degree.
Ordination: Ordained Deacon 1843 and Pastor 1846 by Tennessee Synod.
Calls: Christ's, Stanley, 1846; Daniel's, Lincoln County, 1847-55; Friendship, Alexander County, 1847-61; St. Paul, Newton, 1849-69; St. Stephen, Hickory, 1849-64, 1865-73, 1877-89; Mt. Olive, Hickory, 1889; St. Martin, Iredell County, 1876-81; Philadelphia, Granite Falls, 1878; St. John, Catawba County, 1843-ff.; Mt. Pleasant, Watauga County, 1880, 1883, 1885. In Missouri, 1870-77 (conflict with some preceding dates), helped to organize English District of The Lutheran Church-Missouri Synod; transferred to it in 1873. Returned to Tennessee Synod 1877 to serve again in North Carolina.

Other: One of founders of Concordia College, Conover, in 1878 and its President until resigning in 1885 due to failing health. Secretary 1858, and President 1878, Tennessee Synod. On Committee to Prepare a Plan for Missionary Work in Confederate States Army, 1863; on Committee to Submit a Form for Public Licensing of Men for the Ministry, 1865; on Joint Committee (North Carolina and Tennessee Synods) to Submit Policy to Prevent Conflicts in Work of the two Synods, 1882.

Note: There is a question as to whether his proper name was Cyprian Polycarp rather than Polycarp Cyprian, since he was known universally as "P.C." According to David Henkel's diary the name was Cyprian Polycarp with "P.C." standing for Poly Carp. There is some confusion because Henkel's signatures and even his tombstone are "P.C."

Date of Death/Burial Location: September 26, 1889; St. Peter Church, Catawba County, N.C.

HENKEL, SOCRATES

Date/Place of Birth: March 23, 1823; Lincoln County, N.C.

Parents: The Reverend David Henkel and Catharine (Heyle/Hoyle) Henkel. A grandson of the Reverend Paul Henkel, and a younger brother of the Reverend Polycarp C. Henkel.

Spouse/Marriage Date: Eleanora C. (Henkel) Henkel, daughter of the Reverend Ambrose Henkel; 1850.

Children: Ambrose L., Elon O., Otto H. Probably others, names not known. Ambrose and Elon were proprietors of the Henkel press in New Market, Va.

Education: Received a D.D. degree.

Ordination: Ordained Deacon 1850 and Pastor 1851 by Tennessee Synod.

Calls: All in Virginia. This is all we have about his ministry: "He entered the ministry of the Tennessee Synod in 1850 and took charge of Emmanuel congregation of New Market. It was the congregation of which his illustrious grandfather, The Reverend Paul Henkel, was pastor for many years. Dr. Henkel was pastor of Emmanuel for a period of forty-five years. In 1895 he was compelled to resign because of impaired health, but retained his pastorate as Emeritus until his death." (*The Henkel Memorial 1717-1912*, First Series, Number Four, p. 128.)

Other: Voluminous writer. Treasurer, Tennessee Synod, 1855, 1875, 1879, 1881; Secretary, 1859, 1869, 1870; President, 1871, 1876, 1877, 1880, 1882; Member of Committee to Recommend a *Book of Worship*, 1871. This committee recommended the *General Council Church Book*, which was approved and used until 1919 when the *Common Service Book* was published. One of six Tennessee Synod clerical and three lay delegates to Diet at Salisbury in 1885 to consider Basis for closer cooperation among Southern Lutheran Synods, which resulted in the organization of the United Synod South in 1886, Tennessee and North Carolina Synods becoming members. Among literary contributions: *History of the Evangelical Lutheran Tennessee Synod;* translation from German and Latin into English, with others, of the *Book of Concord*, 1851, of which he was editor-in-chief, the first translation of that volume into the English language.

Date of Death/Burial Location: June 20, 1901; Emmanuel Church, New Market, Va.

HERB, DONALD WARREN

Date/Place of Birth: March 23, 1923; Reading, Pa.
Parents: Peter Paul Herb and Marguerite (Angstadt) Herb.
Spouse/Marriage Date: Nancy Elizabeth (Miner) Herb; August 26, 1944 in Gettysburg, Pa.
Children: Sandra Rae Aueritt, Paul Charles, Peter Warren.
Education: Gettysburg College, A.B. 1943; Gettysburg Seminary, Philadelphia Seminary, M.Div. 1945; Columbia University, Michigan State University, Ph.D. 1961.
Ordination: November 4, 1945 by Central Pennsylvania Synod.
Calls: U.S. Naval Reserve Chaplain, 1945-47. St. Matthew, Lancaster, Pa., 1947-50. Lutheran pastor to students in greater New York City, 1950-57, while member of New York and New England Synod. Campus pastor, Michigan State University, 1957-61, while member of Middle District, American Lutheran Church; Southeast Regional Director, National Lutheran Campus Ministry at Chapel Hill, 1961-66; St. John, Lindenhurst, N.Y., 1973-88. Transferred 1963 to North Carolina Synod. Retired in 1988. Supply, Our Saviour, Welcome, 1989.
Other: Associate Professor, Pastoral Theology, Gettysburg Seminary, 1966-68; Executive Secretary, Division of Educational Services, Lutheran Council, 1968-73.

HERBERTSON, DAVID HILLEN

Date/Place of Birth: September 12, 1941; Pensacola, Fla.
Parents: David Springer Herbertson and Helen Kathleen (Hillen) Herbertson.
Spouse/Marriage Date: Ann Powel (Debele) Herbertson; August 17, 1963 in Columbia, S.C.
Children: David Kirk, Carol Ann.
Education: Georgia Institute of Technology, two years; Davidson College, A.B. English 1963; Lutheran Theological Southern Seminary, M.Div. 1967; Southeastern School of Alcohol Studies, 1969; Hospital Chaplaincy Training, South Carolina Department of Mental Health.
Ordination: May 26, 1967 by South Carolina Synod.
Calls: St. Timothy, Camden, S.C., 1967-73; Emmanuel, Lincolnton, 1973-78.
Other: Secretary, Treasurer, Vice President, President of the, 1967-72; Chaplain, U.S. Army Reserve; Committee on *The Lutheran;* American Field Service, Kershaw County Chapter Board of Directors, Family Liaison Officer, 1968-69; President, 1970, Kershaw County Mental Health Association, 1967-71; Board, Kershaw County Association for Retarded Children; Advisor, Youth for Action in Christ, Camden High School; Board, Kershaw County Activities Center for the Retarded; Executive Board, Kershaw County Memorial Hospital Chaplaincy Program; Chaplain, Kershaw County Memorial Hospital and Camden Military Academy; Chair, Evangelism Committee, 1974-77; Carolinas' Evangelism Conference Planning Committee, 1974-77; Radio Ministry in Lincolnton, N.C.; Chaplain, Lincoln County and Crowell Memorial Hospitals; Organizing and Nominating Committees of the Christian Ministries of Lincoln County; Board, Good Neighbor Shop, 1974-78; Lincoln County Ministerial Association, 1973-78, President, 1976-77; Conference and Workshops Task Group, Continuing Education Committee, Lutheran Theological Southern Seminary; Synod Evangelism Committee of the North Carolina Synod. Dropped from roll, 1979. Organized an independent- interdenominational congregation in Charleston, S.C., 1979.

HERMAN, FLOYD LADELL, JR.
Date/Place of Birth: October 17, 1938; Hickory, N.C.
Parents: Floyd Ladell Herman, Sr. and Beatrice (Long) Herman.
Spouse/Marriage Date: Barbara (Allran) Herman; June 25, 1967 in Cherryville, N.C.
Education: Lenoir-Rhyne, B.A. 1961; Lutheran Theological Southern Seminary, M.Div. 1969.
Ordination: June 1, 1969 by North Carolina Synod.
Calls: Sharon, Statesville, 1969-76; Vice Pastor, St. John, Taylorsville, 1976-79, 1980-83.
Other: Staff, Hickory Museum of Art.

HERSCHER, SAMUEL
License: Licensed 1822 by North Carolina Synod and ordained at the organizing convention of the South Carolina Synod in 1824.
Calls: Served churches in Orangeburg District, S.C. Transferred 1824 to South Carolina Synod, along with five other North Carolina Synod ministers, namely, the Reverends John P. Franklow, John Y. Meetze, Godfrey Dreher, Michael Rauch, and Jacob Moser, who with laymen from their churches organized the South Carolina Synod in 1824. St. Paul, near Pomaria, S.C., 1824-25. Removed from ministerial roll, 1825.
Other: Secretary-Treasurer, 1824-25, South Carolina Synod, and Secretary, 1825.

HESS, BERNARD WAYNE
Date/Place of Birth: October 24, 1940; Youngstown, Ohio.
Parents: Father, Bernard Frances Hess and Elizabeth Louise (Whitehouse) Hess; Step-Father, George Leroy Brainard.
Spouse/Marriage Date: Grace Ann (Farnum) Hess; June 12, 1966 in Unionville, Conn.
Children: Cheryl Lynn Pressley, Michael Steven.
Education: Youngstown University, B.A. Philosophy 1964; Hamma School of Theology, Certificate of Graduation, 1968; Ashland Seminary, M.Div. Counseling 1975; Extended Clinical Pastoral Education at Wesley Long Hospital.
Ordination: September 9, 1968 by Ohio Synod.
Calls: St. Michael, Mifflin, Ohio, 1968-74; St. Andrew, North Olmsted, Ohio, 1974-1978; Advent, Charlotte, 1978-85; Prince of Peace, Greensboro, 1985-92; Interim Specialist, Our Father, Greensboro, 1992-97, Pastor, 1997-.
Other: Greensboro Human Relations Commission, 1989-95, Chair, 1993-95.

HEWITT, ABEL KENNETH, JR.
Date/Place of Birth: August 9, 1926; Hickory, N.C.
Parents: The Reverend Abel Kenneth Hewitt, Sr. and Jane (Dixon) Hewitt.
Spouse/Marriage Date: Mary Helena (Waters) Hewitt; September 5, 1948 in Konnarock, Va.
Education: Roanoke College, Newberry College, B.A. 1951; Lutheran Theological Southern Seminary, B.D. 1958.
Children: A. Kenneth, III, Owen Lee, Mary Malissa.
Ordination: Ordained 1958 by Virginia Synod.
Calls: Daniel's, Lincoln County, 1956-58; Mission Developer/Pastor, Christ, Durham, 1958-60. Transferred 1960 to South Carolina Synod. Summer Memorial, Newberry, S.C., 1960-65; Bethel, Manassas, Va., 1965-.
Date of Death/Burial Location: August 14, 1994; Manassas, Va.

HEWITT, ABEL KENNETH, SR.
Date/Place of Birth: July 5, 1901; Marion, N.C.
Parents: Albert Cullen Hewitt and Maude (Buffaloe) Hewitt.
First Spouse/Marriage Date: Jane (Dixon) Hewitt; January 2, 1919 in Guilford County, N.C.
Children of First Marriage: Sarah Catharine, Jane Dixon, the Reverend Abel Kenneth, Jr.
Second Spouse/Marriage Date: Bonnie (Buford) Hewitt; 1977.
Education: Lenoir-Rhyne, A.B. 1926, D.D. 1950; Lutheran Theological Southern Seminary, B.D. 1929.
Ordination: 1929 by North Carolina Synod.
Calls: St. Matthew-St. Peter, Rowan County, 1929-32; Rural Retreat, Va., 1932-40; Superintendent, Southern Mountain Missions, 1940-50; Haven, Salisbury, 1950-54; Reformation, Columbia, S.C., 1954-67.
Other: Regional Director, Christian Higher Education Year Campaign; President, Board, Lutheran Theological Southern Seminary; Director, Development Fund Campaign, Lutheran Theological Southern Seminary, 1958; Director of Development, Lutheran Theological Southern Seminary, 1967-73.
Date/Place of Burial: July 20, 1983; Elmwood Cemetery, Columbia, S.C.

HEYDENREICH, LOUIS W.
Date/Place of Birth: June 22, 1805; Weissenburg, France.
Marriage Date: 1831 at Strasbourg, France.
Children: Two sons, one of them named Victor served on the Board of Hartwick Seminary, and four daughters.
Education: At a university in France.
Ordination: Ordained 1827 at Strasbourg, France.
Calls: Came to Pennsylvania, settling near Philadelphia, 1851. Received as member of Ministerium of Pennsylvania, 1852. Supplied briefly a church at Manayunk, Pa. Transferred 1867 to Eastern Pennsylvania Synod. Transferred to North Carolina Synod, 1868.
Other: Professor (Modern Languages), Moravian Female Seminary, Bethlehem, Pa. Taught about one year in Wilmington. Transferred 1869 to Maryland Synod, and taught in a female seminary, Hagerstown, Md. Published *An Elementary German Reader* and *The Life of Gustavus Adolphus*. Contributed articles to *The Evangelical Review, The Quarterly Review,* and the *Lutheran Observer*. Retired 1872 at Brooklyn, N.Y., assisting sons in business.
Date of Death/Burial Location: March 18, 1879; Brooklyn, N.Y.

HILBERT, LOUISE (CARTER)
Date/Place of Birth: December 26, 1947; Jacksonville, Fla.
Parents: Nathaniel Harrison Carter and Lorna Louise (Tillman) Carter.
Spouse/Marriage Date: Larry Earl Hilbert; December 28, 1968 in Jacksonville, Fla.
Children: Laura Emily, Luther David, Lewis Howard.
Education: Florida State University, B.S. 1968; Lutheran Theological Southern Seminary, M.Div. 1989.
Ordination: June 11, 1989 by South Carolina Synod.

Calls: St. David's, West Columbia, S.C., 1989-91; Christus Victor, Durham, 1991-.
Other: Certified Lay Professional, Trinity, Jacksonville, Fla., 1982-85.

HILBINGER, JOHN SCOTT
Date/Place of Birth: May 23, 1962; Baltimore, Md.
Parents: Charles Frederick Hilbinger, Jr. and Virginia Lee (Franz) Hilbinger.
Spouse/Marriage Date: Cindy (Antle) Hilbinger; June 8, 1985.
Child: Katherine Bess.
Education: University of North Carolina at Greensboro, B.S. Business Administration 1984; Lutheran Theological Southern Seminary, M.Div. 1989.
Ordination: September 17, 1989 by South Carolina Synod.
Calls: Associate Pastor, Ebenezer, Columbia, S.C., 1989-96; Assistant Pastor, First, Greensboro, 1997-.
Other: South Carolina Synod: Spirituality Committee, 1994-96; Co-Chaplain - Lutherans Concerned of South Carolina, 1993-96.

HILL, GARTH LEE, SR.
Date/Place of Birth: April 25, 1924; Salisbury, N.C.
Parents: Charles Lee Hill and Daisy Lee (Arey) Hill.
Spouse/Marriage Date: Frances Patricia (Steadman) Hill; October 11, 1947 in Ridge Spring, S.C.
Children: Garth Lee, Jr., Leslie Marlynn Ruff, Richard Anderson, Karen Elizabeth Weller, Mary Patricia, Michael David.
Education: Lenoir-Rhyne, A.B. 1945; Lutheran Theological Southern Seminary, D.Min. 1948.
Ordination: April 1948 by North Carolina Synod.
Calls: St. James-Ebenezer, Newton, Catawba County, 1948-54; Holy Trinity, Little Mountain, S.C., 1954-69; Zion, Lexington, S.C., 1969-81.
Other: Board, Newberry College, twelve years, Secretary, eight years; President, Newberry District, South Carolina Synod, six years; President, Western District, South Carolina Synod, three years; Scouting Committee, South Carolina Synod; Recipient of Silver Beaver Award; Delegate, Lutheran Church in America Convention in Kansas City; Director, Lutheridge Senior Citizen Week, fourteen years; Board of American Missions, South Carolina Synod, six years; Charter Member, Newberry County, S.C. Development Board, four years; President, Lexington, S.C. Lions Club; President, Gilbert, S.C. Ruritan Club; Charter Member, Driver and Chaplain of Little Mountain, S.C. Volunteer Fire Department. Retired in 1981 in Gilbert, S.C.

HILL, JESSE DAVID
Date/Place of Birth: November 10, 1950; Laurinburg, N.C.
Parents: Jesse Hill and Annie Laura (Grant) Hill.
Spouse/Marriage Date: Beth (Bennett) Hill; May 16, 1982 in Durham, N.C.
Child: Adair Marie.
Education: Western Carolina University, B.S. Education 1974; Southeastern Baptist Seminary, M.Div. 1977; Lutheran Theological Southern Seminary, Advanced Study, 1985; Graduate Theological Foundation, D.Min. 1996, Ph.D. Candidate.

Ordination: 1985 by North Carolina Synod.

Calls: Pastor-Developer Living Waters, Cherokee Indian Reservation, 1985-90; Calvary, Morganton, 1990- 97. Interim pastor at various congregations. Transferred to University Lutheran Chapel and Student Center, Ohio State University, Department of Campus Ministry of Evangelical Lutheran Church in America, 1997-.

Other: Voting member, Evangelical Lutheran Church in America Assembly, 1988; Chaplain, 1988 North Carolina Synod Assembly; Chair, Multicultural Committee; Board, Evangelical Lutheran Missions in Appalachia; North Carolina Synod Council; Dean, Mountain Conference. First Lutheran Pastor to be invited into training of Spiritual Directors by the Charlotte Diocese of Roman Catholic Church, through the ecumenical movement begun by Bishop McDaniel (Evangelical Lutheran Church in America) and Bishop Donohue (Roman Catholic).

HILL, RALPH GULLORD

Date/Place of Birth: March 9, 1962; Vallejo, Calif.

Parents: Carroll Herbert Hill and Belvin (Sease) Hill.

Spouse/Marriage Date: Cynthia (Powell) Hill; January 3, 1987.

Child: Andrew Powell.

Education: University of South Carolina, B.S. Biology 1985; Lutheran Theological Southern Seminary, M.Div. 1990.

Ordination: May 26, 1990 by South Carolina Synod.

Calls: St. John, Lexington, S.C., 1990-1994; Associate Pastor, Grace, Hendersonville, 1994-.

HILLER, WILLIAM HASKEL, SR.

Date/Place of Birth: October 22, 1868; Lexington County, S.C.

Parents: Joseph Isaiah Hiller and Catherine Susan (Caughman) Hiller.

Spouse/Marriage Date: Addie Esther (Patterson) Hiller; February 25, 1903 in Concord, N.C.

Children: Mary Catherine, William Haskel, Jr.

Education: Newberry College, A.B. 1894; Lutheran Theological Southern Seminary, 1898; Columbia University, A.M. 1911.

Ordination: 1898 by Georgia Synod.

Calls: In Georgia and South Carolina, 1898-1902. In North Carolina: St. James, Concord, 1902-05; St. John, Cabarrus County, 1905-06. In South Carolina Synod, 1906-14. In Florida Synod, 1914-31. Pilgrim-St. Luke, Davidson County, 1931-33. Retired 1933 at Goldsboro. Held services for Lutherans in Goldsboro prior to Synod's developing Good Shepherd, 1936-37.

Other: Promotion in Mid-West for United Lutheran Church in America Pension Fund Endowment, 1928.

Date of Death/Burial Location: October 11, 1954; Oakwood Cemetery, Concord, N.C.

HIMES, JOHN ROBERT

Date/Place of Birth: July 11, 1912; Newark, Ohio.
Parents: The Reverend Winfred Keith Himes and Mabel Margaret (Winn) Himes.
Spouse/Marriage Date: Ruth Marie (Dickerson) Himes; August 4, 1938 in London, Ohio.
Child: Ruth Anne Click.
Education: Wittenberg University, A.B. 1935; Hamma Divinity School, 1938; Duke Divinity School, B.D. 1964, Th.M. 1965.
Ordination: July 3, 1938 by Ohio Synod.
Calls: In Ohio: St. Paul, Marion, 1938-41, St. Paul, Bellville, 1941-42, St. John, Johnsville, 1941-42; Chaplain, U.S. Army, 1943-63; Our Savior, Jacksonville, N.C. 1971-72.
Other: Faculty, Thiel College, 1967-68; Professor, Lutheran Theological Southern Seminary, 1968-71. Retired and transferred to South Carolina Synod, 1977.
Date of Death/Burial Location: June 15, 1994; Florence National Cemetery, Florence, S.C.

HINSHAW, WILLIAM BRIAN

Date/Place of Birth: Kannapolis, N.C.
Education: Lenoir-Rhyne, A.B. 1961; Lutheran Theological Southern Seminary, B.D. 1964.
Ordination: August 23, 1964 by New York Synod at North Carolina Synod's request after being examined and approved for ordination at North Carolina Synod Convention in May 1964.
Calls: Assistant Pastor, Ascension, Franklin Square, N.Y., 1964; faculty, Roanoke College, 1969-74.
Other: Resigned February 5, 1974 in Salem, Va.

HINTZE, FREDERICK MOHR, JR.

Date/Place of Birth: December 15, 1929; Wilmington, N.C.
Parents: Frederick Mohr Hintze, Sr. and Swindell K. (Johnston) Hintze.
First Spouse/Marriage Date: Priscilla Talbutt (Williams) Hintze; July 3, 1954 in Wilmington, N.C.
Children of First Marriage: Christoph Heinrich, George Frederick.
Second Spouse/Marriage Date: Margerette (Stultz) Hintze; May 26, 1973.
Step-Children: Matthew Glen Clark, Michael Charles Clark.
Education: Wilmington Junior College, 1948; Lenoir-Rhyne, A.B. Sociology/Religious Education 1961; Lutheran Theological Southern Seminary, M.Div. 1964; Mental Health Training Institute, East Carolina University, 1971; Georgia Mental Health Institute, Division of Mental Health, Atlanta, Ga., 1971; Eastern Regional School of Alcohol Studies, East Carolina University, 1971, 1972; Drug Abuse School, Duke Medical School Department of Psychiatry, 1973; University of Georgia, Southeastern School of Alcohol Studies, 1974; Duke Divinity School, 1984.
Ordination: June 14, 1964 by North Carolina Synod.
Calls: Daniel's, Lincoln County, 1964-66; Our Savior, Jacksonville, 1967-71; Haw Branch United Methodist Church, Richlands, 1983-.
Other: U.S. Navy Submarine Service, Korean War, 1952-54; served Bethany, Watauga County, July 1958-June 1959; Elkin Mission, August 1959-July 1960; Chaplain, North Carolina Department, American Legion, 1959-60; Military Personnel Committee, 1967-69; North Carolina Council of Churches on Christian Education, Advisor on Scouting, 1968-71; Alcoholism Professionals of North Carolina and Alcohol and Drug Problems

Association of North America. Resigned in 1971 to be Alcoholism and Drug Abuse Counselor with Onslow Mental Health Center, Jacksonville, N.C. Mental Health Clinic Steering Committee of Onslow County; Treasurer, Onslow County Mental Health Association; Board, Onslow County Mental Health Clinic, Executive Committee, Professional Advisory Committee, and Budget Committee; Crippled Children and Adults Society, Onslow Chapter, 1969-71; Rotary Club of Jacksonville, 1970-74, Board, 1971-72; Advisory Board, Department of Social Services, Jacksonville, 1971-75; Board, American Red Cross, Jacksonville, 1971-72; Chair, Boy Scouts District Training Committee, 1967-71, District Chair, 1970-71, Executive Committee, East Carolina Council, 1970-72, Adult Trainer, Adult Leadership Training, Philmont Scout Ranch, 1970, Onslow District Committee, 1967-75, Leadership Training Award, Woodbadge Training Award, Onslow Award, East Carolina Council Compass Award, Green Band Award, Silver Lamb Award, Eagle Scout, Order of the Arrow; American Legion Post Chaplain, Concord, 1956-60, North Carolina Department Chaplain, 1959-60; Richlands Chamber of Commerce.

HITCHCOCK, WALTER LEVANOIS, JR.
Date/Place of Birth: April 5, 1928; Poughkeepsie, N.Y.
Parents: Walter LeVanois Hitchcock, Sr. and Louisa W. (Smith) Hitchcock.
Spouse/Marriage Date: Naomi Jane (Orr) Hitchcock; August 18, 1956 in Altoona, Pa.
Children: Pamela Jane Richin, Mary Ann Gosnell, David Walter, Stephen Andrew.
Education: Muhlenberg, M.A. Sociology 1954; Philadelphia Seminary, Th.M. 1957; Spanish Language Institute, Costa Rica, Diploma 1964.
Ordination: 1957 by Ministerium of Pennsylvania and Adjacent States.
Calls: St. Paul, Lansdowne, Pa., 1957-59; Mission Developer/Pastor, Trinity, Fairless Hills, Pa., 1959-64; Missionary, Santiago, Chile, 1965-69; Missionary In Residence, Southeast Synod, Evangelical Lutheran Church in America, 1969; Mt. Olive, Hickory, 1970-93. Retired in August 1993 in Hickory, N.C.
Other: Chair, World Missions Committee, 1972-75; Evangelism Committee, 1973-74; American Missions Committee; Consultation Committee, Refugee Resettlement; Area Director, Forward Together; Area Director, Love In Action; Campus Ministry Committee; Companion Synod Committee.

HITE, ENOCH
Date/Place of Birth: April 27, 1873; Lexington County, S.C.
Parents: Joseph Hite and Martha Ann (Oxner) Hite.
Spouse/Marriage Date: Mattie Anna (Roof) Hite, sister of the Reverends F. K., W. H., and W. J. Roof; November 20, 1906 in Lexington County, S.C.
Children: Violet Thesta, Wilbert M., Jayne.
Education: Summit Academy, Lexington, S.C.; Lenoir-Rhyne, A.B. 1903; Lutheran Theological Southern Seminary, 1906.
Ordination: 1906 by Tennessee Synod.
Calls: In South Carolina: St. Jacob, Chapin, 1906-09; Bethlehem-St. Matthew, Pomaria, 1918-20; Silverstreet, 1925-28. In Virginia: Emmanuel, New Market, 1909-11. In North

Carolina: Emmanuel, Lincolnton, 1911-18; St. Luke, Lincoln County, 1915-18; St. Stephen-Mt. Olive, Hickory, 1920-25; Mt. Moriah-St. Mark, China Grove, 1928-31; Frieden's-Peace-Sharon, Gibsonville, 1931-35.
Other: Built churches in several parishes. Taught school four years in home county.
Date of Death/Burial Location: August 31, 1935; Frieden's Church, Guilford County, N.C.

HIX, PAM (MITCHAM)
Date/Place of Birth: October 9, 1952; Kings Mountain, N.C.
Spouse: D. Michael Hix.
Education: University of North Carolina, B.Mus.Ed. 1974; Lutheran Theological Southern Seminary, M.Div. 1987.
Ordination: 1987 by North Carolina Synod.
Calls: Associate Pastor, Mt. Tabor, West Columbia, South Carolina Synod, 1987-.

HIZER, HAROLD J.
Date/Place of Birth: December 12, 1930; Pittsburgh, Pa.
Parents: Mr. and Mrs. Edward Hizer.
Spouse/Marriage Date: Patricia Ann (Eynon) Hizer; December 27, 1952.
Children: Todd James, Tracey Lynn, Tennyson Carolina, Trenton Eynon.
Education: Duquesne University, Pittsburgh, Pa., A.B. 1961; Evangelical Lutheran Theological Seminary, Columbus, Ohio, B.D. 1967.
Ordination: June 11, 1967 by American Lutheran Church.
Calls: Providence, Winston-Salem, 1967-74; Grace, Chesapeake, Va., 1974-.
Other: Signal Corps, two years.
Date of Death/Burial Location: September 14, 1995.

HODGES, CHARLES EUGENE
Date/Place of Birth: May 7, 1958; Akron, Ohio.
Parents: Gene Hodges and Catherine (Culler) Hodges.
Spouse/Marriage Date: Kristin Lora (Henderson) Hodges; June 22, 1985 in Gainesville, Fla.
Education: University of Florida, B.A. Political Science 1985; University of District of Columbia; Lutheran Theological Southern Seminary, M.Div. 1990.
Ordination: June 28, 1990 examined by Florida Synod and transferred and ordained August 1990 by North Carolina Synod.
Calls: Pilgrim, Lexington, 1990-93; Grace, Thomasville, 1990-93. Luther Place Memorial, Washington, D.C., 1998-.

HOFFNER, BILL RAY
Date/Place of Birth: January 30, 1940; Salisbury, N.C.
Parents: Robert Leonard Hoffner and Mary (Kluttz) Hoffner.
Spouse/Marriage Date: Carolyn Bell (Eleazer) Hoffner; June 18, 1966 in Columbia, S.C.
Children: Andrea Linn, Alek Leonard.
Education: Lenoir-Rhyne, B.A. 1962; D.D., 1995; Lutheran Theological Southern Seminary, M.Div. 1966.

Ordination: June 5, 1966 by North Carolina Synod.
Calls: Our Saviour, Johnson City, Tenn., 1966-72; St. Paul, Savannah, Ga., 1972-95.
Other: St. Paul Fellowship Center dedicated to him in September 1994; Dean, Ebenezer Area Lutheran District.
Date of Death/Burial Location: September 28, 1995; Hillcrest Abbey Memorial Park, Savannah, Ga.

HOFFNER, JEFFREY LYNN

Date/Place of Birth: December 10, 1961; Salisbury, N.C.
Parents: J. L. Hoffner and Colleen (Haynes) Hoffner.
Spouse/Marriage Date: Lee-ann (Shotts) Hoffner; September 4, 1989 in Ft. Lauderdale, Fla.
Education: University of North Carolina at Chapel Hill, B.A. Psychology/Sociology 1985; Lutheran Theological Southern Seminary, M.Div. 1989; Chaplain Intern, Central State Hospital, Milledgeville, Ga., 1989-90.
Ordination: October 22, 1990 by North Carolina Synod.
Calls: Peace, Gibsonville, 1990-93; Church of the Resurrection, Rocky Mount, 1993-96; Shiloh, Hickory, 1996-.
Other: Adult Assistant, Lutheran Youth of North Carolina, 1994-95.

HOLLAND, ROBERT CHRISTIAN

Date/Place of Birth: April 30, 1840; near Staunton, Va.
Parents: Robert H. Holland and Eliza Ann Holland. An older brother was the Reverend George W. Holland, D.D., one-time President of Newberry College.
First Spouse: Kate B. (Shirey) Holland.
Second Spouse: Mary Virginia (McClanahan) Holland, sister of the Reverend G. W. McClanahan.
Education: Roanoke College, A.B. 1860, D.D. 1890; University of Virginia, B.L. 1866.
License/Ordination: Licensed 1868 and ordained 1869 by Virginia Synod.
Calls: In West Virginia and Virginia, 1869-88. St. Andrew's, Charleston, S.C., 1888-98. In North Carolina: St. Mark's, Charlotte, 1898-1906. President, North Carolina Synod, 1902-04.
Other: Faculty, North Carolina College, 1860-61. At the outset of the War Between the States, enlisted as a member of Picket's celebrated Division and was wounded three times, in both arms, at the Battle of Gettysburg. After the war, practiced law for two years before preparation for ministry. Vice President, Roanoke College, 1878-81. General Secretary, Board of Foreign Missions, United Synod South, 1906; Board, Lutheran Theological Southern Seminary. Suggested organization of Women's Missionary Society, United Synod South, 1906.
Date of Death/Burial Location: November 17, 1915; East Hill Cemetery, Salem, Va.

HOLLAR, JERRY LEONARD, SR.

Date/Place of Birth: March 9, 1933; Kannapolis, N.C.

Parents: Ellard David Hollar and Daisy Belle (Miller) Hollar.
Spouse/Marriage Date: Wilma Geraldine (Holshouser) Hollar; November 13, 1954 in Faith, N.C.
Children: Jerry Leonard, Jr., Jan Leigh.
Education: Lenoir-Rhyne, B.A. 1958; Lutheran Theological Southern Seminary, B.D. 1961.
Ordination: June 11, 1961 by North Carolina Synod.
Calls: Lutheran Chapel, Gastonia, 1961-67; St. John, Knoxville, Tenn., 1967-.
Other: American Missions Committee, 1964-65.

HOLLAR, WILLIAM KENNETH, JR.

Date/Place of Birth: May 16, 1939; Newton, N.C.
Parents: William Kenneth Hollar, Sr. and Henrietta (Poovey) Hollar.
Spouse/Marriage Date: Carol Joyce (Luke) Hollar; August 24, 1963 in Rochester, N.Y.
Children: Dawn Christine Weisenberger, David William, Jeffrey Martin, Michael Kenneth.
Education: Lenoir-Rhyne, A.B. 1961; Trinity Seminary, M.Div. 1965; Drew University, D.Min. 1977.
Ordination: June 27, 1965 by Eastern District, American Lutheran Church.
Calls: Fellowship, Jacksonville, Fla., 1965-70; Prince of Peace, Norristown, Pa., 1970-76; Church of the Resurrection, Rocky Mount, 1976-88; Redeemer, Succasunna, N.J., 1988-.
Other: Florida Lutheran Bible Camp Committee; Jacksonville, Fla., Urban Ministry Board; Florida Chair, Conference on the Inner-city, American Lutheran Church, 1970-71. Chair, Eastern Pennsylvania-New Jersey Conference, 1972-74; Conference Chair, Eastern Carolina Conference, 1984-85; Hospice of Nash County Board; Chair, Pastoral Care Committee of Nash General Hospital; President, Rocky Mount Ministers' Association; Camp Beisler Camp Committee, New Jersey; Board, New Jersey Social Ministries. Articles for *The Lutheran Standard.*

HOLLIFIELD, WILLIAM RAYMOND

Date/Place of Birth: December 7, 1940; Rutherfordton, N.C.
Parents: Walter R. Hollifield and Mary Louise (Hill) Hollifield.
Education: Belmont Abbey, A.B. 1965; Lutheran Theological Southern Seminary, M.Div. 1970.
Ordination: June 7, 1970 by North Carolina Synod.
Calls: St. Luke, Fort Wayne, Ind., 1970; St. Matthew, Charleston, S.C., 1971-75; Trinity, Anniston, Ala., 1975-76; Messiah, Salisbury, 1980-88; Messiah of the Mountains, Burnsville, 1988-. Vice Pastor to various congregations.

HOLMES, LAWRENCE FREDRICK

Date/Place of Birth: September 10, 1946; Dansville, N.Y.
Parents: Frederick C. Holmes and Martha M. Holmes.
First Spouse/Marriage Date: Barbara A. (Sabol) Holmes; July 12, 1969.
Second Spouse/Marriage Date: Ilene M. (Maurer) Holmes; July 2, 1983.
Education: King's College, Wilkes-Barre, Pa., B.S. Business Administration 1969; Lutheran Theological Southern Seminary, 1997-98; Duke University, M.Div. 1998.
Ordination: June 6, 1998 by North Carolina Synod.
Calls: Associate Pastor, Holy Trinity, Raleigh, 1998-.

HOLT, SAMUEL
Place of Birth: Alamance County, N.C.
Ordination: 1884 by North Carolina Synod.
Calls: Organized and served several churches in Alamance and Guilford Counties, including Samuel Holt Chapel at Elon College.
Other: An organizer and first treasurer of Alpha Synod, 1889.
Date of Death/Burial Location: April 2, 1914/15; Samuel Holt Chapel, Elon College, N.C.

HOMESLEY, GEORGE SCOTT
Date/Place of Birth: November 2, 1959; Shelby, N.C.
Parents: George C. Homesley and Clara L. Homesley.
Spouse/Marriage Date: Robin (Horton) Homesley; June 14, 1981.
Children: Nicholas Scott, Jeremy Trent, Elisa Jeanette.
Education: Lenoir-Rhyne, B.A. Music Education, 1983; Lutheran Theological Southern Seminary, M.Div. 1996.
Ordination: May 31, 1996 by North Carolina Synod.
Calls: Associate Pastor, Our Saviour, Southern Pines, 1996-.

HONEYCUTT, CARL ADAMS
Date/Place of Birth: June 19, 1905; Cabarrus County, N.C.
Parents: John W. Honeycutt and Frances M. (Moose) Honeycutt.
Spouse/Marriage Date: Mary Elizabeth (Barre) Honeycutt; June 7, 1934 in Columbia, S.C.
Children: Mary Carolyn, Katherine.
Education: Mount Pleasant Collegiate Institute, 1928; Roanoke College, A.B. 1930, D.D. 1947; Lutheran Theological Southern Seminary, B.D. 1933.
Ordination: 1933 by North Carolina Synod.
Calls: Burkes Garden, Tazewell, Va., 1933-35; Ebenezer, Marion, Va., 1935-39; Grace, Winchester, 1939-43. Zion, Sunbury, Pa., 1943-49; Ebenezer, Columbia, S.C., 1949-63; Good Shepherd, Tampa, Fla., 1963-70. Retired January 1970.
Other: United Lutheran Church in America representative to Federal Council of Churches of Christ in America, 1946-49; President, Board, Lutheran Theological Southern Seminary, 1954-63; Chair, Lutheran Service Center, Columbia, S.C., 1950-55.
Date of Death/Burial Location: February 25, 1983; Elmwood Cemetery, Columbia, S.C.

HOOK, WADE F.
Date/Place of Birth: October 15, 1922; West Columbia, S.C.
Parents: Sandel W. Hook and Mary Ann (Dreher) Hook.
Spouse/Marriage Date: Melverda R. (Padget) Hook; June 29, 1950 in Saluda, S.C.
Child: Melanie Padget.
Education: Newberry College, A.B. 1943; Lutheran Theological Southern Seminary, B.D. 1949; University of South Carolina, M.A. 1950; Duke University, Ph.D. 1957.
Ordination: June 1949 by South Carolina Synod.
Calls: Grace, Hendersonville, 1949-51; Campus Pastor to Lutheran students, Duke University, 1951-53; Holy Trinity, Chapel Hill, and Campus Pastor to Lutheran students, University of North Carolina, 1953-59. Vice Pastor at various congregations. Transferred to Central Pennsylvania Synod, 1967.

Other: Professor and Head of Department of Sociology, Lenoir-Rhyne, 1959-67. Lutheran Theological Southern Seminary Board, 1964-67; Examining Committee, 1962-66; College and University Work Committee, 1966-68; Professor, Gettysburg College, Gettysburg, Pa., 1967-95. Retired.
Date of Death/Burial Location: January 27, 1998; near Columbia, S.C.

HOPKINS, BURRELL N.

License: Licensed in 1849 by North Carolina Synod, but never ordained.
Calls: St. Paul, Iredell County, 1849-52; organized Beth Eden, Newton, 1850-53; previously a mission of the Reverend Benjamin Arey's parish; organized Salem and served St. Enoch, Rowan County, 1850-52.
Other: Name removed from clerical roll in 1853.

HORA, GALEN FLOYD

Date of Birth: September 19, 1940; Anamosa, Iowa.
Parents: Mr. and Mrs. Leonard Hora
First Spouse/Marriage Date: Nava Carol (Smith) Hora; June 17, 1962.
Child of First Marriage: Daniel Kevin.
Second Spouse/Marriage Date: Christina (Byers) Hora; 1976.
Education: Wartburg College, Waverly, Iowa, B.A. in Greek and Psychology 1962; Wartburg Seminary, Dubuque, Iowa, B.Div. 1967; Union Seminary, Richmond, Va., Th.Min. 1958.
Ordination: June 9, 1968 by American Lutheran Church.
Calls: Christ, Greensboro, 1968-70; Campus Pastor, University of Miami, Miami, Fla., 1970-75; Campus Pastor, University of Pittsburgh, Pittsburgh, Pa., 1975-77; Campus Pastor, South Dakota State University, Brookings, S.D., 1977-82; Campus Pastor, University of Michigan, Ann Arbor, Mich., 1982.

HORNE, EVERETT ENOCH

Date/Place of Birth: November 15, 1928; Hickory, N.C.
Parents: James Albert Horne, Sr. and Annie Earl (Cordell) Horne.
First Spouse/Marriage Date: Bonnie Mae (Hayworth) Horne; March 27, 1949 in Hickory, N.C.
Children of First Marriage: Teresa Gale, Timothy Craig.
Second Spouse/Marriage Date: Mary Catherine (Blancher) Horne; September 24, 1977 in Wilmington, N.C.
Step-Child: James A. Farrior.
Education: Lenoir-Rhyne, A.B. 1953; Lutheran Theological Southern Seminary, B.D. 1962.
Ordination: June 17, 1962 by North Carolina Synod.
Calls: Low's, Guilford County, 1962-65. Ebenezer, China Grove, 1965-73; Kure Memorial, Kure Beach, 1973-74; Christ, Elkin, 1978-81. Vice Pastor at various congregations. Transferred to Central Pennsylvania Synod, 1981; St. Matthew, Plainfield, Pa., 1981-85.
Date of Death/Burial Location: July 15, 1985; Plainfield, Pa.

HOSS, WILLIAM NEIL
Date/Place of Birth: October 22, 1933; Kansas City, Mo.
Parents: William J. Hoss and M. V. (Fitzwater) Hoss.
Spouse/Marriage Date: Sandra Kay (Grigg) Hoss; August 27, 1983 in Charlotte, N.C.
Step-Children: Angela Dawn Teague, Billy Vance Teague.
Education: Syracuse University; University of North Carolina at Charlotte; Chicago Seminary, M.Div. 1987.
Ordination: June 20, 1987 by Illinois Synod.
Calls: Sharon, Gibsonville, 1987-93; St. Stephen, Gold Hill, 1993-98; St. Martin, Albemarle, 1998-.

HOUCK, MARY ANN
Ordination: June 6, 1998 by North Carolina Synod for Pennsylvania Synod.
Calls: Emanuel, Bradford, Pa., 1998-.

HOUCK (HAUCK), WILLIAM A.
Child: The Reverend William A. Houck in South Carolina Synod, 1853-74, may have been his son. Dr. Samuel Rothrock in diary says he married the William A. Houck to Catherine L. Fisher in 1852 presumably in North Carolina.
License: Licensed 1810 by North Carolina Synod in Organ Church, Rowan County. Application for ordination in 1812 was refused by North Carolina Synod, because he was a member of the Reformed Church.
Other: He was "a great leader and preacher in the Reformed Church" in North Carolina for 25 years, and was elected first President of their Classis (Synod) at its organization.

HOVIS, MARCUS BENJAMIN, III
Date/Place of Birth: July 18, 1958; Gastonia, N.C.
Parents: Marcus Benjamin Hovis, Jr. and Bonnie Jean (Casner) Hovis.
Spouse/Marriage Date: Vanessa (Davis) Hovis; July 25, 1987 in Lincolnton, N.C.
Child: Meredith Elaine.
Education: Winthrop College, B.A. 1985; Lutheran Theological Southern Seminary, M.Div. 1990; McCormick Theological Seminary (Chicago, Ill.) 1999 D.Min.
Ordination: June 7, 1991 by North Carolina Synod.
Calls: St. Paul, Statesville, 1991-93; St. Paul, Salisbury, 1994-.

HOWARD, ROBERT FRANCIS
Date/Place of Birth: December 29, 1946; Evanston, Ill.
Parents: Homer H. Howard and Wilma L. Howard.
Spouse/Marriage Date: Robin Ann (Foster) Howard; June 9, 1979.
Children: Hannah Elizabeth, David Robert.
Education: Roanoke College, B.A. 1979; Lutheran Theological Southern Seminary, M.Div. 1983.
Ordination: November 13, 1983 by Virginia Synod.
Calls: McConnellsburg Parish, McConnellsburg, Pa., 1983-87; Salem, Reamstown, Pa., 1987-94; Ebenezer, China Grove, 1994-.

HOYLE, CHARLIE LEMUEL

Date/Place of Birth: November 28, 1931; Catawba County, N.C.
Parents: Lemuel Veta Hoyle and Alpha Emma (Rudisill) Hoyle.
First Spouse/Marriage Date: Constance Ruth (Bertolet) Hoyle of Trenton, N.J.; May 31, 1955 in Konnarock, Va.
Children of First Marriage: Peter Marvin, Timothy Stuart, Rebecca Annette, Jonathan Charles.
Second Spouse/Marriage Date: June (Handley) Hoyle; June 13, 1987.
Step-Children: Lind Woodall, Perry Howell.
Education: Lenoir-Rhyne, A.B. History 1954; Lutheran Theological Southern Seminary, M.Div. 1958; graduate study at Lutheran Theological Southern Seminary; Baptist Hospital, Pastoral Counseling, 1974; Duke Medical Center, 1988.
Ordination: June 8, 1958 by North Carolina Synod.
Calls: Sardis, Hickory, 1958-61; Bethphage, Lincolnton, 1961-65; Good Shepherd, Hickory, 1965-71; Holly Grove, Lexington, 1971-79; Alamance, Alamance, 1979-87; St. Michael, High Point, 1990-96. Vice pastor at various congregations.
Other: Board, North Carolina Lutheran Homes, 1971-78, Secretary, 1976-78; Professional Preparations Committee, 1971-79; organizer of "Contact" Telephone Ministry, Lexington, 1974-79, Chair of Training Committee, 1976-79; District Dean of the Northern District, 1978-82; Board of Access of Alamance County, 1980-86, Chair, 1985-86; Delegate to the Conventions of The Lutheran Church in America, 1982, 1984; Board, of Lutheridge Retreat Center, 1982-88; Chair, The Study and Action Committee on Alcoholism and Chemical Dependency, 1982-88. Retired in 1996 in High Point, N.C.

HUBBERT, WILLIAM EFFIAH

Date/Place of Birth: October 23, 1844; Roanoke County, Va.
First Spouse/Marriage Date: Mittie (Pettit) Hubbert (died within a few months).
Second Spouse/Marriage Date: H. Virginia (Ribble) Hubbert; 1873 in Montgomery County, Va.
Children: William E., Florence.
Education: Roanoke College, A.B. 1867, A.M.; Philadelphia Seminary, 1871.
License/Ordination: Licensed 1868 and ordained 1870 by Southwest Virginia Synod.
Calls: Ebenezer, Marion, Va., 1868-71. Member of North Carolina Synod 1871-77, while professor (Ancient Languages) at North Carolina College. New St. Peter, Blacksburg and New River Parish, Va., 1877-87; Trinity (Woman's Memorial), Pulaski, Va., 1887-89.
Other: Served and was wounded in War Between the States. Assistant Editor, *Our Church Paper*, New Market, Va. Later, Editor, *The Lutheran Church Visitor*. Secretary, Southwest Virginia Synod. Delegate to last convention of General Synod South 1886 in Salisbury, and to first and second conventions, United Synod South, Savannah, Ga., 1887, and Wilmington, 1889.
Date of Death: 1916.

HUDDLE, DAVID KELLER
Date/Place of Birth: September 14, 1941; Cabarrus County, N.C.
Parents: The Reverend K. Y. Huddle and Frances (Castor) Huddle.
First Spouse/Marriage Date: Betty (Roof) Conner; June 8, 1963 in Granite Quarry, N.C.
Children of First Marriage: Deborah Kelley, Lisa Suzanne, Jonathan David.
Second Spouse/Marriage Date: Patricia (Kuebler) Huddle; November 2, 1991.
Education: Lenoir-Rhyne, A.B. 1963; Lutheran Theological Southern Seminary, M.Div. 1966.
Ordination: June 5, 1966 by North Carolina Synod.
Calls: Philadelphia, Granite Falls, 1966-75; St. John, Salisbury, 1975-90; Beck's Lutheran, Lexington, 1990-. Vice Pastor at various congregations.
Other: Chair, Camp Committee and President, Board of Trustees, Lutheran Outdoor Ministries, 1970-; Lamb Award, Boy Scouts of America; National Committee on Outdoor Ministries; Executive Council of North Carolina Synod; Delegate, Lutheran Church in America Conventions.

HUDDLE, KELLER YONCE
Date/Place of Birth: April 24, 1912; Ceres, Bland County, Va.
Parents: The Reverend Marion David Huddle and Mary Belle (Rosenbaum) Huddle. Older brother of the Reverend B. Paul Huddle and Miss Elizabeth Huddle, Lutheran missionaries in Japan.
Spouse/Marriage Date: Sarah Frances (Castor) Huddle, sister of the Reverend B. D. Castor; October 14, 1936 in Kannapolis, N.C.
Children: Sarah Frances II (married the Reverend Ralph J. Wallace), The Reverend David K., The Reverend Stephen Michael, Samuel Mark.
Education: Junior College of Goodman, Miss.; Lenoir-Rhyne, A.B. 1933; Lutheran Theological Southern Seminary, B.D. 1936, M.Div. 1976.
License/Ordination: Licensed 1936 and ordained January 27 1937 by Virginia Synod.
Calls: Rockingham County, Va., 1936-38. In North Carolina: St. Andrew, Andrews, 1938-40; Trinity, Cabarrus County, 1941-46; St. Matthew, Wilmington, 1946-53; St. Matthew, Rowan County, 1953-57; St. James, Newton, 1958-62; Christ's, Stanley, 1962-72; St. Martin, Albemarle, 1972-79. Retired 1979. Vice Pastor at various congregations.
Other: Member, Press, Radio, and Television Committee; Port representative for National Lutheran Council, Wilmington, 1948-53. Instrumental in beginning countywide inter-racial Reformation Service, New Hanover County, 1951; Board of Trustees, North Carolina Lutheran Homes; Educational Ministry Committee; Professional Preparation Committee; American Missions Committee.
Date of Death/Burial Location: May 23, 1985; Center Grove Lutheran Church Cemetery, Kannapolis, N.C.

HUDDLE, STEPHEN MICHAEL
Date/Place of Birth: June 27, 1943; Concord, N.C.
Parents: The Reverend K. Y. Huddle and Sarah Grances (Castor) Huddle.
Ordination: June 15, 1969 by North Carolina Synod.
Calls: Assistant Pastor, First, Norfolk, Va., 1969-70.

Other: Resigned December 31, 1970 in Norfolk, Va.

HUDDLE, WILLIAM PETER

Date/Place of Birth: February 20, 1862; Wythe County, Va.
Parents: Peter Huddle and Sallie (Staley) Huddle.
Spouse/Marriage Date: Sarah Caroline (Coley) Huddle; December 28, 1887 in Rural Retreat, Va.
Children: Eula Miriam, Ruth Elizabeth, William Chalmers, Carl Max, Sarah Christine, Charles Edwin.
Education: Roanoke College, A.B. 1882; Gettysburg Seminary, one year; also studied theology under the Reverends J. J. Scherer, Sr., and J. B. Greiner.
License/Ordination: Licensed 1885 and ordained 1888 by Southwest Virginia Synod.
Calls: In Virginia, 1885-93. In North Carolina: St. Matthew-St. Peter, Rowan County, 1893-97. Transferred to Virginia Synod 1897 and served Madison Parish, 1897-1921, and Churchville Parish, Augusta County, Va., 1921-28.
Other: Board, Lowman Home; Author, *The History of Hebron Lutheran Church, Madison, Virginia,* (1717-1907).
Date of Death/Burial Location: August 29, 1939; Thornrose Cemetery, Staunton, Va.

HUFFMAN, ARTHUR MILTON

Date/Place of Birth: July 12, 1892; Hickory, N.C.
Parents: William Pinckney Huffman and Mary Cornelia (Fry) Huffman. A sister, Mary, married the Reverend F. L. Conrad, Sr.
Spouse/Marriage Date: Pauline Geneva (Miller) Huffman; October 24, 1921 in Raleigh, N.C.
Children: Mary Miller, James O. (adopted), Virginia Baker (married the Reverend Robert Paul Stroup).
Education: Lenoir-Rhyne, A.B. 1912, A.M. 1914; Lutheran Theological Southern Seminary, 1917; Columbia University, M.A. 1927; Wittenberg University, D.D. 1947.
Ordination: 1917 by South Carolina Synod.
Calls: St. Barnabas, Charleston, S.C., 1917-18; U.S. Army Chaplain, 1918-19. In North Carolina: Holy Trinity, Raleigh, 1919-24; developed and organized St. Paul, Durham, 1923; and St. Matthew-St. Luke, Kings Mountain, 1924-29; St. John, Knoxville, Tenn., 1929-43; First, Louisville, Ky., 1943-55.
Other: Retirement due to ill health. Member, United Lutheran Church in America Board of Pensions. President, Kentucky-Tennessee Synod, 1947-49.
Date of Death/Burial Location: October 3, 1956; Cave Hill Cemetery, Louisville, Ky.

HUFFMAN, DAVIDSON CORNELIUS

Date/Place of Birth: June 29, 1853; Catawba County, N.C. Uncle to the Reverend Arthur M. Huffman.

Parents: Langdon W. Huffman and Amy (Miller) Huffman.

First Spouse/Marriage Date: Nancy C. R. (Hunt) Huffman; January 6, 1875 in Catawba County, N.C.

Children of First Marriage: Ossie P., Olive V. (died in infancy).

Second Spouse/Marriage Date: Harriet Malinda (Miller) Huffman; February 26, 1880 in Catawba County, N.C.

Children of Second Marriage: Vance Oliver, George Lee, William Plato, Mattie May Belle, John Davidson, Beulah Aurora, Paul Cornelius, David Crouse.

Education: Rutherford College; also studied medicine later.

Ordination: 1877 by Joint Synod of Ohio.

Calls: Transferred to Tennessee Synod, 1886. Held no regular pastorates, but in Catawba County, organized Mt. Olive 1885 and St. Timothy 1887 serving those and other churches in Catawba, Alexander, and Burke Counties.

Other: About 1881 began practice of medicine, and had an extensive practice in Catawba and adjoining counties.

Date of Death/Burial Location: May 14, 1898; St. Stephen Church, Hickory, N.C.

HUFFMAN, LESTER LEE

Date/Place of Birth: June 19, 1890; near Alma, Page County, Va.

Parents: David Huffman and Ada (Dovel) Huffman.

Spouse/Marriage Date: Minna (Beam) Huffman; November 6, 1916 in Gastonia, N.C.

Children: Richard Long, Harold Lee (born almost four months after father's death).

Education: Lenoir-Rhyne, A.B. 1910; Chicago Seminary, B.D. 1914.

Ordination: 1914 by Tennessee Synod.

Calls: Lutheran Chapel, Gastonia; Grace, Bessemer City, 1914-15; four churches, Toms Brook, Va., 1915-18.

Other: Promotional work for Lenoir-Rhyne. Instrumental in arranging 400th Anniversary Reformation Service in Harrisonburg, Va., 1917.

Date of Death/Burial Location: Died October 13, 1918 a victim of influenza, in fifth year of ministry; Alma Church, Page County, Va.

HUGGINS, CHARLES RUSSELL

Date/Place of Birth: June 14, 1936; Lenoir, N.C.

Parents: Russell Jefferies Huggins and Bleeka Irene (Carpenter) Huggins. Grandson of the Reverend R. M. Carpenter.

Spouse/Marriage Date: Linda Sue (Cline) Huggins; August 9, 1959 in Hickory, N.C.

Children: Susan Elaine Grainger, Mark Richard.

Education: Lenoir-Rhyne, A.B. 1958; Lutheran Theological Southern Seminary, M.Div. 1961; Union Seminary, Va., D.Min. 1981.

Ordination: June 10, 1961 by North Carolina Synod.

Calls: Mission Developer/Pastor, New Covenant, High Point, 1961-67; Trinity, Sanford, 1967-.

Other: Nominating Committee, 1963; Camp Committee, 1970-75; Parish Education Committee, 1969-74, Chair, 1971-72; World Missions Committee, 1969; Secretary,

American Missions Committee, 1975-80; Eastern Conference Dean, 1986-88, 1991-95, Secretary, 1981-84; Youth Ministry Consultant, P.L.M.D. Task Force, six years. President, High Point Ministerial Alliance, 1967; Board, Lee County Group Homes; Board, President, Lee County American Red Cross.

HULL, J. W.

License: Licensed by Tennessee Synod, 1841 but never ordained.
Calls: Mt. Moriah, Rowan County, 1841-42; St. Martin, Iredell County, 1841-48; organized Sharon, 1842-46, Iredell County; St. Martin, Stanly County, 1842-47, St. Peter, Rowan County, 1842-45.

HUNT, GEORGE L.

Date/Place of Birth: January 5, 1832; Sullivan County, Tenn.
Other: Presumably was a member of the Joint Synod of Ohio, who served several churches in Gaston and Lincoln Counties, which later affiliated with Tennessee Synod. Not listed on clerical roll in *History of the Lutheran Church in North Carolina*, (1803-1953), but name occurs in relation to pastoral ministry in following churches: Supply pastor, with others, including the Reverends Andrew Rader and Adam Miller, Jr., Antioch, Gaston County, 1853-; Bethel, Gaston County, 1853-77; Ebenezer (later St. Paul), Crouse, 1853-77.
Date of Death/Burial Location: Died November 11, 1910; St. Paul near Newton.

HUNT, LAWRENCE EVERETT

Date/Place of Birth: July 12, 1938; Baltimore, Md.
Parents: Mr. and Mrs. Edward O. Hunt, Sr.
Spouse/Marriage Date: Carolyn Mary (Keeley) Hunt; June 4, 1961.
Children: Douglas Lawrence.
Education: Capital University, Columbus, Ohio, A.B. 1958; Evangelical Lutheran Theological Seminary, Columbus, Ohio, C.T., 1962.
Ordination: October 14, 1962 by American Lutheran Church.
Calls: Assistant Pastor, Advent, Milwaukee, Wisc., 1962-63; Church of Abiding Savior, Durham, 1965-68; Lutheran Inner-City Ministry of Racine, Wisc., 1968-70.
Other: Removed from roll, December 31, 1977.

HUNTON, JOHN HENRY

Ordination: Ordained 1858 at a special meeting of Virginia Conference of the Tennessee Synod, in Rader Church, Timberville, Va.
Calls: In Virginia: Edinburg, 1857-61; St. Matthew, Toms Brook, 1861; Emmanuel, Shenandoah County, 1856; Woodstock.
Other: Transferred 1861 to Pittsburgh Synod. In 1866 moved to Canada. Secretary, Special Virginia Conference, Tennessee Synod 1856-61 its first five years.

HURLOCKER, TOMMY WAYNE

Date/Place of Birth: May 29, 1939; Concord, N.C.

Parents: Thomas G. Hurlocker and Lillie (Winecoff) Hurlocker.

Spouse/Marriage Date: Constance Ann (Richmond) Hurlocker; August 6, 1961 in Salisbury, N.C.

Children: Eric Wayne, Tamara Denise Peele.

Education: Lenoir-Rhyne, A.B. 1960; Gettysburg Seminary, M.Div. 1964; Shippensburg State University, M.S. 1984; Susquehanna University, D.D. 1990.

Ordination: June 13, 1964 by North Carolina Synod.

Calls: Evangelical, Reedsville, Pa., 1964-67; First, Carlisle, Pa., 1967-71. Vice President, Tressler Lutheran Service Associates, Camp Hill, Pa., 1972-85; President/CEO, 1985-.

Other: Board, Lutheran Immigration and Refugee Services; numerous consultations to Lutheran Social Ministry Organizations; Curriculum Consultation - Gettysburg Seminary (Social Ministry).

IDDINGS, JOHN WHITE, SR.

Date/Place of Birth: December 29, 1904; Rowan County, N.C.

Parents: Charles Lafayette Iddings and Sallie Louise (Watson) Iddings.

Spouse/Marriage Date: Pauline (Kuhn) Iddings; June 18, 1931 in Hickory, N.C.

Children: John White, Jr., William Robert.

Education: Lenoir-Rhyne, A.B. 1927, D.D. 1958; Lutheran Theological Southern Seminary, M.Div. 1930; Yale University, C.P.E. 1962; Duke University, Certified Chaplain by American Hospital Association, 1965.

Ordination: June 25, 1930 by North Carolina Synod.

Calls: Ebenezer, Rowan County-Mt. Hermon, Cabarrus County, 1930-38; Christiana, Granite Quarry, 1938-43; St. Mark, Asheville, 1943-49; First, Albemarle, 1949-65; first institutional Chaplain, Durham Area, 1965-79; Staff Chaplain, Duke Medical Center, 1965-79; Interim Pastor, St. John, Salisbury, 1980-90; Pastor Emeritus; first Chaplain, Trinity Oaks Retirement Center, Salisbury, 1992-. Vice pastor at various congregations. Retired May 1, 1977.

Other: Board, Lenoir-Rhyne, 1949-65, Secretary, 1955-65; Chair, Committee on Social Ministry, 1963-65; Continuing Education for Ministers Committee, 1967-72; Lutheran Church in America Delegate, 1964; Lenoir- Rhyne Development, 1979-80. Published series of newspaper articles on Revised Standard Version of Bible, 1952. After study tour of Southern Europe, Egypt, and Holy Land, three months in 1954, and observing operations of Lutheran World Federation, LWA, and LWR in Middle East, published six articles on religious and political situation in Near and Middle East countries. Lecturer at University of Cairo, Egypt and Augusta Victoria Hospital, 1958. President, Rotary Club, Albemarle, N.C.; Paul Harris Fellow, Salisbury Club.

Date of Death/Burial Location: March 1, 1999; Christiana, Granite Quarry, N.C.

JEFFCOAT, HERBERT WARREN

Date/Place of Birth: October 9, 1859; Pike County, Ala.
Parents: The Reverend James O. J. T. Jeffcoat and Rachael (Zodie) Jeffcoat. Father and both grandfathers were Methodist ministers.
First Spouse/Marriage Date: Eve Ella (Epting) Jeffcoat; April 23, 1882 in Springfield, S.C.
Children of First Marriage: William Cecil (father of the Reverend Luther H. Jeffcoat), Cora Pearl, George Holland.
Second Spouse/Marriage Date: Bettie C. (Hendrix) Jeffcoat; 1896 in Davie County, N.C.
Third Spouse/Marriage Date: Mrs. Rose (Fisher) (Moose) Jeffcoat; 1899 in Cabarrus County, N.C.
Education: Newberry College, A.B. 1890; Lutheran Theological Southern Seminary, 1894.
Ordination: 1894 by North Carolina Synod.
Calls: Concordia-St. Luke, Rowan County, 1894-1900; Amity, Iredell County, 1894-95; Haven (first church built), Salisbury; Christ, East Spencer, 1900-01; transferred 1901 to Georgia Synod; back in 1909 to North Carolina Synod from Mississippi Synod; St. Michael, Troutman; St. Paul, Iredell County, 1909-12; Coble's-Low's, Guilford County; St. Paul, Alamance County, 1914-21; Grace, 1916-20; and Richland, Liberty, 1914-15; Christiana, Granite Quarry, 1922-23; in Watauga County: (Watauga Mission), Holy Trinity-Holy Communion-Mt. Pleasant-Mt. Zion-St. Mark; organized Grace, Boone (1925), 1923-26; St. Martin, Cabarrus County; St. Martin, Stanly County, 1926-29. Retired 1929 at Boone.
Other: Secretary, Mississippi Synod.
Date of Death/Burial Location: April 5, 1937; St. Mark Church, Blythewood, S.C.

JEFFCOAT, LUTHER HALL

Date/Place of Birth: March 7, 1908; Burlington, N.C. His great-grandfather Jeffcoat and two great-great-grandfathers were Methodist ministers.
Parents: Dr. William Cecil Jeffcoat and Jessie May (Gnann) Jeffcoat. Grandfather was the Reverend H. W. Jeffcoat.
Spouse/Marriage Date: Dorothy Maulsby (Platt) Jeffcoat; April 12, 1936 in Columbia, S.C.
Children: Dorothy Louise, Reverend William Ernest.
Education: Appalachian State Teachers College, two years; Lenoir-Rhyne, A.B. 1933; Lutheran Theological Southern Seminary, B.D. 1937.
Ordination: 1937 by North Carolina Synod.
Calls: In South Carolina: St. James and St. Matthew, Lexington, 1937-41; Trinity, Elloree, 1941-45; Mt. Horeb, Chapin, 1946-51; Macedonia, Prosperity, 1948-51; St. Barnabas, Charleston, 1951-59; Mission Developer, Board of American Missions, 1959-60; Holy Communion, Spartanburg, 1960-68.
Date of Death/Burial Location: July 25, 1968; Elmwood Cemetery, Columbia, S.C.

JEFFCOAT, WILLIAM ERNEST

Date/Place of Birth: February 29, 1944; Orangeburg, S.C.
Parents: The Reverend Luther H. Jeffcoat and Dorothy (Platt) Jeffcoat.

Spouse/Marriage Date: Virginia (Gaffos) Jeffcoat; August 27, 1983 in Camden, S.C.
Children: Kimberly Ann Baxter, Angelin Elain, Jamey Jones, Virginia Nikkolette Jones.
Education: Newberry College, B.A. Sociology 1967; Lutheran Theological Southern Seminary, M.Div. 1971.
Ordination: 1971 by South Carolina Synod.
Calls: St. Matthew, Lexington, S.C., 1971-76; Mt. Hebron, Leesville, S.C., 1985-90; St. Paul, Hamlet, 1990- 95; St. Matthew, Salisbury, 1995-.

JENKINS, DANIEL

Place of Birth: Maryland.
Education: Gettysburg College, A.B. 1831.
License: Licensed 1834 by North Carolina Synod but never ordained.
Calls: During 1833-36: Union, Rowan County, Beck's-Bethany-St. Luke, Davidson County; New Bethel, Stanly County.
Other: Moved back to Maryland in 1836.

JENKINS, WILLIAM

Spouse: Mary (Euliss) Jenkins.
Children: J. W., others not known.
License/Ordination: Licensed 1824 and ordained 1828 by North Carolina Synod in Union Church, Rowan County.
Calls: In 1824 was sent to minister to scattered Lutheran settlers from North Carolina, on Duck River in Bedford County, Tenn. John Shofner, a surveyor in that county, came from North Carolina about 1803 and his father, Martin Shofner (1758-1838), followed in 1808. The latter, as patriarch of Lutherans in the area, preached some; old records refer to him as "Rev. Shofner." Inquiring his way at a camp meeting, Jenkins was piloted by Nimrod Burrow, a Methodist, to the Lutheran settlement where the Shofners lived. He held his first service in October 1824 and first Communion service in March 1825 with 38 persons communing, five of them slaves. He served this parish until his death, except for four years at Lovettsville, Va., during the War Between the States. He preached at times to as many as ten congregations, some doubtless not organized.
Other: His library and personal records were destroyed by fire in his son J. W.'s home in 1912. In 1823 the Reverend Jacob Scherer visited the Duck River settlements to minister to the people. Presumably hearing his report, North Carolina Synod sent Pastor Jenkins there in 1824 and also the Reverend Jacob Medtart held a Communion service for fourteen persons on May 30, 1824. Jenkins continued a member of North Carolina Synod until 1835 when he became a charter member of the "Synod of the West," forerunner of the Olive Branch Synod, of which he was a member at death.
Date of Death/Burial Location: 1877; Shelbyville, Tenn.

JENNINGS, WILLIAM HANSEL, JR.

Date/Place of Birth: September 14, 1934; Thomasville, Ga.
Parents: W. H. Jennings, Sr. and Maude (Thornton) Jennings.
Spouse/Marriage Date: Frances (Motsinger) Jennings; August 19, 1956 in High Point, N.C.
Children: Catherine, Sherry.

Education: Lenoir-Rhyne, A.B. 1956; Lutheran Theological Southern Seminary, B.D. 1959; Yale University, Ph.D. 1966.
Ordination: June 7, 1959 by North Carolina Synod.
Calls: St. Andrew, New Bern, 1959-62.
Other: Resigned January 1972. Professor of Religion, Muhlenberg College, Allentown, Pa.

JERNIGAN, WILLIAM EARL, SR.

Date/Place of Birth: January 26, 1937; Columbia, S.C.
Parents: William Boyd Jernigan and Janie Viola (Roof) Jernigan.
Spouse/Marriage Date: Betty Jean (Hartman) Jernigan; May 29, 1958 in Pomaria, S.C.
Children: William Earl, Jr., Sharon Marie.
Education: Newberry College, B.S. 1959; Lutheran Theological Southern Seminary, B.D. 1963.
Ordination: May 26, 1963 by South Carolina Synod.
Calls: Macedonia, Newberry County, S.C., 1963-64; Holy Trinity, Mt. Pleasant, 1964-66; Chaplain, U.S. Army, 1966-72; Cedar Grove, Vale, 1972-79. Transferred to South Carolina.
Other: Resigned 1983 in Whitmire, S.C. Later entered the ordained ministry of another denomination. Emergency Medical Technician at Newberry County Memorial Hospital.

JOHANSSON, PAUL STEPHEN

Date/Place of Birth: August 25, 1953; Quincy, Mass.
Parents: The Reverend Carl J. Johansson and Alice K. (Sandberg) Johansson.
Spouse/Marriage Date: Martha Elizabeth (Weatherspoon) Johansson; August 30, 1986.
Children: Stephen Carl, Andrew Paul.
Education: Canadian Lutheran Bible Institute, two years; Gordon Conwell Theological Seminary, one year; University of Minnesota, B.A. 1978; Luther Northwestern Seminary, M.Div., 1984.
Ordination: January 1985 by Minnesota Synod.
Calls: St. Mark's, Charlotte, 1985-87; Emanuel, Manchester, Conn., 1987-93; Salem, St. Cloud, Minn., 1993- .

JOHNSON, CHRISTOPHER LANE

Date/Place of Birth: August 3, 1966; Fairfax, Va.
Parents: Robert Allen Johnson and Sue Gay (Lane) Johnson.
Spouse/Marriage Date: The Reverend Kristina Natale (Madsen) Johnson; August 26, 1989 in Red Bank, N.J.
Education: William and Mary, B.A. Psychology 1988; Gettysburg Seminary, M.Div. 1993.
Ordination: June 29, 1993 by North Carolina Synod.
Calls: St. Andrew, Mt. Airy, 1993-.

JOHNSON, DAVID FRONTIS

Date/Place of Birth: July 25, 1917; Saluda County, S.C.
Parents: George Tolbert Johnson and Lida Mae (Denny) Johnson. Half-brother to the Reverend T. C. Plexico.

Spouse/Marriage Date: Eleanor Louise (Weir) Johnson; August 16, 1942 in Columbia, S.C.

Children: James David, John Foster.

Education: University of South Carolina, A.B. 1938; Lutheran Theological Southern Seminary, B.D. 1942; Lenoir-Rhyne, D.D. 1980.

Ordination: May 31, 1942 by South Carolina Synod.

Calls: Gladesboro Parish, Hillsville, Va., 1942-47; St. Matthew, Rowan County, 1947-52; Kure Memorial, Kure Beach, 1952-57; Kimball Memorial, Kannapolis, 1957-61.

Other: Rural Church Committee, Virginia Synod, 1944-47; Stewardship Committee, North Carolina Synod, 1950-51; Brotherhood Committee of the Lutheran Brotherhood, 1956-60; Board, Lowman Home, 1957-59; Allocation Commission of the United Lutheran Church in America, 1959; Mission Committee of the North Carolina Synod, United Lutheran Church in America, 1960-62; Delegate to the Convention of the Lutheran Church in America, 1960, 1962; Regional Secretary, Southeastern Synod, 1963-71; Committee on Architecture and Fine Arts, North Carolina Synod, 1971-72; President's Task Force on the Priority Program, 1970; Superintendent of Missions, North Carolina Synod, 1961-63; Regional Secretary, Lutheran Church in America Board of American Missions, for North Carolina and Southeast Synods, 1963-72; Regional Director, North Carolina and South Carolina, Division of Mission in North America of Lutheran Church in America, 1973-81. Served as a building consultant for over 80 building programs and organized approximately 70 mission congregations. Chair, North Carolina and South Carolina Inner Faith Committees; National Council of Churches of Christ in the United States of America Commission on Town and Country, and of Commission on Appalachia and of Commission on Religion in Appalachia (interdenominational). Wrote feature stories in *The Lutheran* magazine and in *Deaf-Mute Publications*. Taught deaf-mute sign language classes and conducted public worship for deaf in sign language.

Date of Death/Place of Burial: August 6, 1981; Carolina Memorial Park, Concord, N.C.

JOHNSON, HARRY WILLIAM, JR.

Date/Place of Birth: January 19, 1930; Sumter, S.C.

Parents: Harry William Johnson, Sr. and Ethel (Seastrunk) Johnson.

Education: University of South Carolina, A.B. 1952; Lutheran Theological Southern Seminary, B.D. 1956.

Ordination: 1958 by South Carolina Synod.

Calls: Kure Memorial, Kure Beach, 1956-57; Advent, Mattituck, N.Y. in 1965.

Other: Retired to Kansas City, Mo., Central States Synod.

JOHNSON, JOHN ARTHUR

Date/Place of Birth: July 9, 1931; Erie, Pa.

Parents: Arthur Severin Johnson and Loretta Catherine (Miller) Johnson.

Spouse/Marriage Date: Dona Louise (Adamson) Johnson; November 27, 1943 in Dravosburg, Pa.

Children: Elizabeth Katherine, Krister Gustav Edward, Heidi Linnea Rhyne.

Education: Thiel College, B.S. 1953; Philadelphia Seminary, B.D. 1959, S.T.M. 1961.

Ordination: March 19, 1961 by Pittsburgh Synod.

Calls: Holy Trinity, Montgomery, Pa., 1961-62; Muhlenberg Memorial, Philadelphia, 1962-65; Trinity, McKean, Pa., 1965-67; St. Stephen, Erie, Pa., 1968-85; St. Mark, Lumberton, 1985-86; Holy Cross, Mocksville, 1986-92.

Date of Death/Burial Location: February 16, 1992; Memorial Service at Holy Cross, Mocksville, N.C.

JOHNSON, KRISTINA NATALE (MADSEN)

Date/Place of Birth: December 23, 1963; Summit, N.J.
Parents: Eric Viggo Madsen and Gertrude E. (Fletcher) McLaughlin Madsen.
Spouse/Marriage Date: The Reverend Christopher Lane Johnson; August 26, 1989 in Red Bank, N.J.
Education: Wake Forest University, B.A. Spanish, 1987; Gettysburg Seminary, M.Div. 1993; graduate work at La Universidad de Salamanca in Spain and Penn State University in Spanish Literature; Clinical Pastoral Education residency as hospital chaplain at Baptist Hospital, Winston-Salem.
Ordination: June 29, 1993 by North Carolina Synod.
Calls: St. Andrew, Mt. Airy, 1993-94.
Other: Participated in ecumenical Hispanic ministry and has served as a clinic translator.

JOHNSON, MARK CYRUS

Date/Place of Birth: May 6, 1943; Lenoir, N.C.
Parents: Roy Leonard Johnson and Violet (Smith) Johnson.
Spouse/Marriage Date: Willie Ruth (Spoon) Johnson; February 25, 1967 in Gibsonville, N.C.
Child: Christy Yvette.
Education: Mitchell College, A.A. 1963; Lenoir-Rhyne, A.B. 1965; Lutheran Theological Southern Seminary, M.Div. 1969; University of North Carolina at Greensboro, M.Ed. 1976; College for Financial Planning, Certified Financial Planner, 1990.
Ordination: June 1, 1969 by North Carolina Synod.
Calls: Mt. Gilead, Mt. Pleasant, 1969-71; Our Saviour, Southern Pines, 1971-76; Administrator, North Carolina Lutheran Home in Albemarle, 1979; Administrator, North Carolina Lutheran Home in Hickory, 1981; Resurrection, Greensboro, 1992-97. Vice Pastor at various congregations.

JOHNSON, STEPHEN BROR

Date/Place of Birth: February 1, 1933; Winnebago, Wis.
Parents: Royce E. Johnson and Olga (Wellberg) Johnson.
Spouse/Marriage Date: Joan (Dixon) Johnson; June 8, 1957 in Arthur, Ill.
Children: Julia Attaway, Ralph, Elizabeth Lennox.
Education: Northwestern University, B.A. 1955; Augustana Seminary, M.Div. 1959; Yale Divinity School, S.T.M. 1961; graduate work at Kaiser Wilhelm Univeritat zu Munster, 1959-60; Princeton Seminary, D.Min. 1981.
Ordination: June 1961 by Augustana Synod.
Calls: Trinity, Centerbrook, Conn., 1961-66; St. Paul, Old Saybrook, Conn., 1961-66; Chaplain, Upsala College, East Orange, N.J., 1966-72; St. Luke, Dunellen, N.J., 1972-79; St. John, Easton, Pa., 1979-88; Pastor- Developer, Gloria Dei, Gastonia, 1988-. Vice pastor at various congregations.
Other: Civil Rights Volunteer, Mississippi, 1964; Chair, Ecumenical Committee, North East Pennsylvania Synod; Founder, Day Shelter at St. John, Easton, Pa.; planned religious

programming for Association of Retarded Citizens, New Jersey, 1974-79; President, Child Guidance Clinic, Lehigh Valley (United Way Agency), 1986-88; President, Project of Easton, Pa. (Interfaith Service Agency for poor), 1987-89; Co- organizer, Interfaith Association, Gaston County, 1992-; AIDS Council, Gaston County, 1992-; Co-author with Gary Weant, *Seeking Common Ground,* study of relation of church and religion to public education.

JOHNSON, WILLIAM MELVIN, SR.

Date/Place of Birth: April 29, 1930; Columbia, S.C.
Parents: John Wesley Johnson and Genora (Cloninger) Johnson.
Spouse/Marriage Date: Madeline (Fink) Johnson; June 7, 1953 in Faith, N.C.
Children: William Melvin, Jr., Harry Andrew, Lonora Gay.
Education: Augusta (Georgia) Junior College, Catawba College, A.B. 1957; Lutheran Theological Southern Seminary, B.D. 1960, D.Min. 1982.
Ordination: June 5, 1960 by North Carolina Synod.
Calls: Grace, Catawba County, 1960-64; Gloria Dei, Salisbury, 1964-72; Vice Pastor at various congregations; Holy Cross, Spring Hill, Fla., 1972-95. Retired April 30, 1995 in Spring Hill, Fla.
Other: Part time Chaplain at Veterans Administration Hospital in Salisbury, 1964-72; Chair, Stewardship Committee; President, Milford Hills Lions Club, Salisbury; President, Rowan County Ministerial Association; President, Rowan County Lutheran Ministerial Association; President, Spring Hill Ministerial Association; Piedmont Council of the Boy Scouts in America; Public Relations Committee, Boy Scouts of America; Evangelism Committee; Chair, Evangelism (Outreach) Committee, Florida Synod; Board of Trustees, Board of Visitors and Advisory Board, Lutheran Theological Southern Seminary, 1995-. U.S. Air Force, three years as instructor in Air Force School of Electronics, Cheyenne, Wyo., then employed as electrician by Atomic Energy Commission, Savannah River Project, Aiken, S.C.

JONES, JOHN ROYAL, III

Date/Place of Birth: July 2, 1945; Hickory, Catawba County, N.C.
Parents: John R. Jones, Jr. and Marie (Teague) Jones.
Spouse/Marriage Date: Rachel (Moretz) Jones; August 21, 1965 in Catawba County, N.C.
Children: Kimberly Rachel, Jennifer Marie, Ashley Elizabeth.
Education: Lenoir-Rhyne, B.A. 1970; Lutheran Theological Southern Seminary, M.Div. 1973.
Ordination: June 3, 1973 by North Carolina Synod.
Calls: Assistant Pastor, Bethany, Hickory, 1973-75; Bethel, Salisbury, 1976-82. Vice Pastor at various congregations.
Other: Removed from roll May 1986.

JORDAN, TIMOTHY CHARLES

Date/Place of Birth: September 19, 1960; LaPorte, Ind.
Parents: Charles F. Jordan and Doris Christine (Yochum) Jordan.
Spouse/Marriage Date: Cheryl Lynne Jordan; June 4, 1983 in Cleveland, Ohio.
Child: Michael Aaron.

Education: Capital University, B.G.S. 1983; Trinity Seminary, M.Div. 1987.
Ordination: June 14, 1987 by Illinois District Synod.
Calls: Co-Pastor, Mt. Pisgah, Alexander County, 1987-89; Trinity, New Era, Mich., 1989-.

JULIAN, WILLIAM ALEXANDER
Date/Place of Birth: November 28, 1830; Salisbury, N.C.
Parent: Father was William Julian.
Spouse/Marriage Date: Emily Caroline (Reid) Julian; August 9, 1853 in Salisbury, N.C.
Children: Henry T., Louisa J. (married the Reverend J. Killian Efird), Abner J. P., Horace M., William L., Charles A., Carrie Emma (married the Reverend S. C. Ballentine).
Education: North Carolina College, 1855.
License/Ordination: Licensed 1856 by North Carolina Synod and ordained 1859.
Calls: Beck's-Lebanon-St. Luke,-Pilgrim, Davidson County, 1854-63; Coble's-Low's, Guilford County; Richland, Randolph County, 1865-70; St. Enoch, Rowan County; Trinity, Cabarrus County, 1874-79; St. Luke, Davidson County, 1878-84; Reformation, Davie County, 1880-84; and last pastorate, organized Haven, Salisbury and Christ, East Spencer, 1899-1900; in Florida, 1863-65; in New York and New Jersey, 1870-74; in Georgia, South Carolina, and Florida, 1884-99. Retired 1900 and resided at Mason City, Fla. and later at Leesville, S.C. Supplied church in Wythe County, Va., 1907.
Other: Secretary, North Carolina Synod, 1867; President, 1869.
Date of Death/Burial Location: August 19, 1913; Wittenberg Church Cemetery, Leesville, S.C.

JUNGKUNTZ, DANIEL LOUIS, SR.
Date/Place of Birth: March 10, 1936; Watertown, Wis.
Parents: Otto William Jungkuntz and Clara Martha (Lange) Jungkuntz.
First Spouse: Janet (Harder) Jungkuntz.
Children of First Marriage: Harry Harder, Stella Obeuthul.
Second Spouse/Marriage Date: Patricia (McClelland) Jungkuntz; December 26, 1977.
Children of Second Marriage: Rachel, Daniel L., Jr., David.
Education: Northwestern College, B.A. 1957; Wisconsin Lutheran Seminary, B.D. 1961; Eden Seminary, D.Min. 1972; University of Wisconsin at Madison, M.A. Classics 1958; graduate work at University of Southern California, Andrus Gerontology Center.
Ordination: June 10, 1962 by Wisconsin Synod.
Calls: Assistant Pastor, St. Paul, Saginaw, Mich., 1962-63; Our Savior, Topsfield, Mass., 1963-66; Chaplain, Lutheran Mission Association, St. Louis, Mo., 1967-76; Christian Seminary, 1976-79; The Pastoral Institute, Columbus, Ga., 1979-82; North Carolina Baptist Hospital, Pastoral Counseling Director of Training, Winston- Salem, 1982-87; Lutheran Family Services, Triad Lutheran Center, Winston-Salem, 1987-89; Peninsula Pastoral Counseling, Newport News, Va., 1989-.
Other: North Carolina Transition Team, AELA Member, 1986-87; North Carolina Synod Council, 1987-88; Leadership Support, Virginia Synod, 1990-96; GEM Coordinating Committee, 1992-; Evangelical Lutheran Church in America Work Group on Science and Technology - Coordinating Consultant, 1990-96; Diplomat, American Association of

Pastoral Counselors; Approved Supervisor and Clinical Member, American Association of Marriage and Family Therapy; North Carolina and Virginia Licensed Marriage and Family Therapist; American Association for the Advancement of Science; National Interfaith Coalition of Aging, Teaching Member. Numerous publications: *Minnie Remembers . . . Religion, Sexuality and Successful Aging; Listening to Pain; Spiritual Aspects of the Care of the Geriatric Patient.*

JUST, DONALD RAY

Date/Place of Birth: November 23, 1939; McIntosh County, N.D.
Parents: Julius A. Just and Helen K. (Dockter) Just.
Spouse/Marriage Date: Helen (DuPre) Just; January 1, 1987 in Hickory, N.C.
Children: Sharon Virginia Linder-Sandifer, Charles Joseph Linder.
Education: Concordia Junior College, St. Paul, Minn., A.A. 1959, Concordia College, (Minn.), B.A. 1961 Concordia Seminary, (Ill.), B.D. 1965; North Carolina State University, M.Ed. 1972; School of Theology, Claremont, Calif., Ph.D. 1981.
Ordination: September 5, 1965 by North Dakota District, The Lutheran Church-Missouri Synod.
Calls: Redeemer/Peace, Victoria, British Columbia, Canada, 1965-67; Chaplain, U.S. Army, 1967-72; Trinity-St. Paul-St. Matthew, Wis., 1981-82; Dean of Students, Concordia College, (Wis.), 1975-80; Chaplain, Lenoir-Rhyne, 1983-95. Vice Pastor at various congregations. Messiah, Austin, Texas, 1995-.
Other: Campus Ministry Committee, North Carolina Synod, 1983-94, Chair, 1993-94; Board, Family Care Center, Hickory, 1989-94, Chair, 1992-94; Candidacy Committee, Texas, 1995-; Ecumenical Ministry Committee, Texas, 1995-. Founded the Pathway (Spiritual Renewal) Program for students at Lenoir-Rhyne College, 1991.

KADEL, THOMAS EDWARD

Date/Place of Birth: November 11, 1947; Champaign County, Ohio.
Parents: Ralph Edward Kadel and Phyllis (Knull) Kadel.
Spouse/Marriage Date: Paula Ruth (Ritchie) Kadel; September 23, 1969 in Salisbury, N.C.
Education: Lenoir-Rhyne, A.B. 1969; Lutheran Theological Southern Seminary, M.Div. 1973.
Ordination: June 1973 by North Carolina Synod.
Calls: Peace, Philadelphia, Pa., 1973-77; Upper Dublin, Pa., 1977-89.
Other: Removed from roll June 16, 1992 in Harleyville, Pa.

KAEMPHER, JACOB

Date/Place of Birth: July 23, 1800; Shenandoah County, Va.
Spouse: Lydia (Oswald) Kaempher near Hagerstown, Md.
Children: Five sons and one daughter reached maturity; three children died in infancy.
Education: Gettysburg Seminary, 1829.
License/Ordination: Licensed 1829 and ordained 1831 by North Carolina Synod.
Calls: In Rowan County: Organ, 1829-32; Luther's-Lutheran Chapel, 1830-33. Transferred to Pennsylvania Synod in 1833 and served parishes in Synods of Western Pennsylvania, Maryland, Central Pennsylvania and Eastern Pennsylvania, 1833-72, chiefly rural churches. Retired 1872 at Glen Rock, Pa.
Date of Death/Burial Location: January 19, 1880; Beaver Springs, Snyder County, Pa.

KAESER, DAVID WALLACE
Date/Place of Birth: December 7, 1942; Canton, Stark County, Ohio.
Parents: Werner David Kaeser and H. Berdene (Arner) Kaeser.
Spouse/Marriage Date: Edwina (Hyde) Kaeser; December 26, 1965 in Collins, Ohio.
Children: Kristen Natalie, Matthew David.
Education: Capital University, B.A. 1964; Trinity Seminary, M.Div. 1968.
Ordination: June 16, 1968 by American Lutheran Church.
Calls: St. Stephen/St. Peter, Camp Douglas, Wis., 1968-71; Vernon, Mukwonago, Wis., 1971-75; St. John, Reedsburg, Wis., 1975-78; Chaplain, U.S. Army, 1978-81; Prince of Peace, Kalamazoo, Mich., 1981-83; Vice Pastor, St. James, Fayetteville; Ascension, Wilson, 1984-89; Mission Developer, Grace, Washington, 1989-97. Vice pastor at various congregations.
Date of Death: March 3, 1997.

KAHL, GEORGE CALVIN, SR.
Date/Place of Birth: June 26, 1922; Hagerstown, Md.
Parents: George Henry Kahl, Jr. and Ruth Mae (Bream) Kahl.
Spouse/Marriage Date: Rachel Lenora (Beatty) Kahl, sister of the Reverend P. B. Beatty, Jr.; December 21, 1948 in Charlotte, N.C.
Children: Ruth Lenora, George Calvin, Jr., Anita Catherine Baum, The Reverend John Beatty.
Education: Lenoir-Rhyne, A.B. 1950; Lutheran Theological Southern Seminary, M.Div. 1953.
Ordination: June 14, 1953 by North Carolina Synod.
Calls: St. Jacob Parish, Chapin, S.C.; St. John, Pomaria, S.C.; Mt. Olivet, Spring Hill, S.C., 1953-54; Atonement, Laurens, S.C., 1954-58; Chaplain, U.S. Army, 1958-75; Good Shepherd, Brevard, 1975-81. Retired in 1981.

KAHL, JOHN BEATTY
Date/Place of Birth: December 13, 1960; Frankfurt, West Germany.
Parents: The Reverend George Calvin Kahl, Sr. and Rachel Lenora (Beatty) Kahl.
Spouse/Marriage Date: Cindy Lou (Schwarz) Kahl; May 26, 1984.
Children: Joshua Michael, Lisa Denise, Amanda Michelle.
Education: Lenoir-Rhyne, B.S. 1983; Lutheran Theological Southern Seminary, M.Div. 1992.
Ordination: May 29, 1992 by North Carolina Synod.
Calls: Mt. Zion, Richfield, 1992-. Interim pastor at First, Albemarle, 1994-95.

KANUPP, PAUL R.
Date/Place of Birth: March 5, 1943; Catawba County, N.C.
Parents: E. E. Kanupp and Clara (Killian) Kanupp.
Spouse/Marriage Date: Linda (Propst) Kanupp; June 25, 1967 in Hickory, N.C.
Children: Matthew P., Jeffrey D.
Education: Lenoir-Rhyne, B.A. 1966; Trinity Seminary, M.Div. 1970.

Ordination: July 12, 1970 by Eastern District, American Lutheran Church.
Calls: St. Matthew, Baltimore, Md., 1970-87; Miller's, Hickory, 1987-95; Holy Communion, Dallas, 1995- .*Other*: Secretary, Baltimore Conference; Editor, Eastern District *Echoes* (Synod Newsletter); President, Chaplaincy Committee and Member of the Medical Ethics Advisory Committee of Franklin Square Hospital, Baltimore, Md., Dean, Western Piedmont Conference, North Carolina Synod; Chaplain, Active Firefighter, Bowley's Quarters VFD, Baltimore, Md.; Board, Cooperative Christian Ministry of Greater Hickory.

KARRIKER, LONNIE WILLIAM

Date/Place of Birth: March 11, 1934; Rowan County, N.C.
Parents: Thebus Bernard Karriker and Blanche (Deal) Karriker.
Spouse/Marriage Date: Bobbie Jo (Overcash) Karriker; September 9, 1956 in Rowan County, N.C.
Children: Scott Hamilton, Audrey Alese Brown, Tara Leigh Kallam.
Education: Lenoir-Rhyne, A.B. 1958; Lutheran Theological Southern Seminary, B.D. 1961.
Ordination: June 11, 1961 by North Carolina Synod.
Calls: St. Matthew, Rowan County, 1961-64; Center Grove, Kannapolis, 1965-76; Mission Developer, Lake Norman Area, 1976-77; Community in Christ, Huntersville, 1976-. Vice Pastor at various congregations.
Other: World Missions, 1967-70; Nominating Committee, 1968; American Missions Committee, 1968-74.

KAUFMAN, JEROME BOWER STAMBACH

Date/Place of Birth: September 20, 1908; Somerset County, Pa.
Parents: Charles Kaufman and Peony M. (Stambach) Kaufman.
Spouse/Marriage Date: Ruth G. (Dively) Kaufman; June 21, 1932 in Berlin, Pa.
Children: Patricia Ann Schiemann, Michael Jean, Nicholas Linwood, Christina Gail Micek, Stephen Charles William.
Education: Susquehanna University, B.A. 1928; Chicago Seminary, M.Div. 1932.
Ordination: 1932 by Allegheny Synod of Lutheran Church in America.
Calls: St. John, East Juniata, Pa., 1932-36; Multi-Parish Service in Syracuse, Ind., 1936-39; Faith, Flat Rock, Mich., 1939-45; Grace, Villa Park, Ill., 1945-57; Lutheran Social Services of Illinois in Park Ridge, Ill., 1957-81. Supplied in North Carolina after retirement.
Other: Retired in 1981.
Date of Death/Burial Location: January 8, 1991; Kaufman Cemetery in Davidsville, Pa.

KAYLOR, RAY BUFORD

Date/Place of Birth: February 24, 1939; Catawba County, N.C.
Parents: Frank Kaylor and Ida M. (Willis) Kaylor.
Spouse/Marriage Date: Gloria R. (Abercrombie) Kaylor; July 30, 1966 in Columbia, S.C.
Children: Suzanne R., Jonathan B.
Education: East Carolina University, B.S. 1963; Lutheran Theological Southern Seminary, M.Div. 1968.

Ordination: May 26, 1968 by South Carolina Synod.
Calls: Immanuel, Blountville, Tenn., 1968-71; St. Paul, Maryville, Tenn., 1971-77; Redeemer, Gastonia, 1978-97; retired to Gastonia, N.C.
Other: Campus Ministry Committee, 1972-74; World Missions Committee, 1975-77; Adjunct Chaplain, Gaston Memorial Hospital; Chaplain, Civil Air Patrol; Blount County Counseling Center, Maryville, Tenn., 1974-76; Lions Club; President, Blount County Ministerial Association; Board, Blount School for Children with Perceptual Learning Disabilities.

KEARNEY, GRACE ELIZABETH (KUHN)

Date/Place of Birth: March 17, 1952; Mooresville, N.C.
Parents: Isaac F. Kuhn and Gilda Griffin (Koontz) Kuhn.
Spouse/Marriage Date: The Reverend Walter Douglas Kearney; June 1, 1974 in Newton, N.C. The first clergy couple ordained in North Carolina Synod.
Children: Mary Kathryn, Douglas Micah.
Education: Wake Forest University, B.A. 1974; Lutheran Theological Southern Seminary, M.Div. 1981.
Ordination: May 24, 1981 by North Carolina Synod.
Calls: St. Paul, Crouse (Co-Pastor), 1981-86; Epiphany, Winston-Salem (Co-Associate), 1986-92; Assistant to Bishop, North Carolina Synod, 1992-.
Other: Delegate, Lutheran Church in America Assembly, 1986; Voting member, Evangelical Lutheran Church in America Assembly; North Carolina Synod Council, 1988-92.

KEARNEY, WALTER DOUGLAS

Date/Place of Birth: December 16, 1952; Clearwater, Fla.
Parents: James F. Kearney and Lois Anita (Waterson) Kearney.
Spouse/Marriage Date: The Reverend Grace Elizabeth (Kuhn) Kearney; June 1, 1974 in Newton, N.C. The first clergy couple ordained in North Carolina Synod.
Children: Mary Kathryn, Douglas Micah.
Education: Wake Forest University, B.A., 1974; Lutheran Theological Southern Seminary, M.Div. 1981.
Ordination: May 24, 1981 by North Carolina Synod.
Calls: St. Paul, Crouse (Co-Pastor), 1981-86; Epiphany, Winston-Salem (Co-Associate), 1986-92; Interim Ministry by North Carolina Synod Council with intentional interims at Ebenezer, China Grove, 1992-94, and Family of Faith, Harrisburg, 1994-.

KEASEY, LESTER DEAN

Date/Place of Birth: May 6, 1920; Blair County, Pa.
Parents: William Orlando Keasey and Edna (Miller) Keasey.
Spouse/Marriage Date: Joy (Silvis) Keasey; June 28, 1947 in Greensburg, Pa.
Children: John Mark, Paul Allen.
Education: Pennsylvania State University, one year; Gettysburg College, A.B. 1943; Gettysburg Seminary, B.D. 1945; University of Southern California; Biblical Seminary; New York University, M.A. 1949; University of Pittsburgh, Ph.D., 1955; University of Minnesota, Marriage Counseling Training Program, 1964-65.

License/Ordination: Licensed 1945 and ordained January 27, 1946 by California Synod.
Calls: In California, New York City, Pennsylvania, 1945-55.
Other: In 1955 became Associate Professor of Sociology and Religious Studies, Lenoir-Rhyne. Regularly supplied churches. Subject of doctoral dissertation: *The Readability of the "Christian Growth Series" of Lutheran Church School Lessons.* Executive Director and psychiatric social worker, Family Guidance Center, Hickory, 1959-61. Left Lenoir-Rhyne to join the faculty at Appalachian State University. Dropped from roll. Became United Methodist Minister, 1973.
Date of Death: June 1999.

KECK, ALBERT HENRY, JR.
Date/Place of Birth: March 23, 1910; Aurora, Ill.
Parents: The Reverend Dr. Albert Henry Keck, Sr. and Charlotte (Zimmerman) Keck.
Spouse/Marriage Date: Virginia Elizabeth (Rhodes) Keck, daughter of the Reverend George H. Rhodes; August 16, 1934 in Albemarle, N.C.
Children: The Reverends George Albert and David Rhodes, Timothy Alan, Barbara Jane Pitts.
Education: Wittenberg University, A.B. 1931 D.D. 1959; Hamma Divinity School, two years, Chicago Seminary, B.D. 1934.
Ordination: May 15, 1934 by Michigan Synod.
Calls: St. John, Sterling, Ill., 1934-45; Emmanuel-St. Luke, Lincolnton, 1945-48; supplied Luther's Chapel, Lincoln County, 1947-48. St. Andrew, Hickory, 1953-75, Pastor Emeritus, 1976-. Supply pastor for various congregations.
Other: Professor of Practical Theology, Lutheran Theological Southern Seminary, 1948-53. Secretary, Board, Chicago Seminary, 1940-45; Board, Lenoir-Rhyne, 1955-82, Secretary, 1965-82. United Lutheran Church in America Commission on Worship, 1952-54; American Missions Committee, 1965-68; North Carolina Council of Churches, 1964-67; Commission on Ministry, Lutheran Church in America, 1966-70; Board of Publications, Lutheran Church in America, 1969-80; Examining Committee of South Carolina Synod, 1968-73; Delegate to six Conventions of United Lutheran Church in America and five of the Lutheran Church in America; Preaching Missions in 52 congregations in 11 states; Writer of tract on the Call to the Ministry and Commentary on a quarter's Sunday School lessons on the gospel of John; Recipient of the Distinguished Service Award, Lenoir-Rhyne Alumni Association, 1973; Lenoir-Rhyne Trustee Award, 1984. Retired March 31, 1975 in Hickory, N.C.

KECK, DAVID RHODES, JR.
Date/Place of Birth: June 7, 1965; Greensboro, N.C.
Parents: The Reverend David Rhodes Keck, Sr. and Diana (Rudisill) Keck.
Spouse/Marriage Date: Nina (Cunningham) Keck; May 21, 1994.
Education: Lenoir-Rhyne, B.A. 1987; Lutheran Theological Southern Seminary, M.Div. 1996.
Ordination: August 15, 1996 by North Carolina Synod.
Calls: Good Shepherd, Raleigh, 1996-.

KECK, DAVID RHODES, SR.
Date/Place of Birth: November 24, 1938; Sterling, Ill.
Parents: The Reverend Albert H. Keck, Jr. and Virginia (Rhodes) Keck. Grandfathers were the Reverends Albert H. Keck and George H. Rhodes; older brother is the Reverend George Albert Keck.
Spouse/Marriage Date: Rachel Diana (Rudisill) Keck; June 10, 1961 in Cherryville, N.C.
Children: The Reverend David Rhodes, Jr., Dr. Charlotte Karriker, Frances Patterson.
Education: Lenoir-Rhyne, A.B. 1960; Salutatorian, D.D. 1994; Lutheran Theological Southern Seminary, B.D. *cum laude* 1964.
Ordination: June 14, 1964 by North Carolina Synod.
Calls: Our Father, Greensboro, 1964-67; Grace, Boone, 1967-76, Campus Pastor at Appalachian State University; Kimball Memorial, Kannapolis, 1976-94; Our Saviour, Southern Pines, 1994-.
Other: Synod Council, 1988-94; Outreach Committee, 1994-; Synod Executive Committee, 1983-88; Board, Lenoir-Rhyne, 1974-83; Voting member, Evangelical Lutheran Church in America Assemblies, 1993, 1989, 1987; Lutheran Church in America Convention Delegate 1987, 1984; Southern District, Lutheran Church in America, Dean, 1986-88, Secretary, 1982-86; Parish Education Committee, 1966-67; Chair, Lutheran Family Services "Love in Action" Congregational Phase, 1994-97.

KECK, GEORGE ALBERT
Date/Place of Birth: April 8, 1936; Sterling, Ill.
Parents: The Reverend Albert Henry Keck, Jr. and Virginia Elizabeth (Rhodes) Keck. Grandfathers were the Reverends Albert H. Keck and George H. Rhodes; younger brother is the Reverend David Rhodes Keck, Sr.
Education: Lenoir-Rhyne, A.B. 1958; Lutheran Theological Southern Seminary, B.D. 1962; University of North Carolina at Greensboro, B.A. Art, 1975, M.F.A. Studio Art, 1976.
Spouse/Marriage Date: Margo W. (Sicha) Keck; June 12, 1960 in Hickory, N.C.
Child: Laura Marie.
Ordination: June 17, 1962 by North Carolina Synod.
Calls: St. Stephen, Lenoir, 1962-67; Epiphany, Winston-Salem, 1967-73. Vice pastor at various congregations.
Other: Delegate, Lutheran Church in America Convention, 1972; Adjunct Chaplain to Lutheran students at Wake Forest University, 1967-73. Several hymns published by the North Carolina Synod and the Lutheran Church in America Board of Parish Education. Board, Lutheridge, 1965-68; Youth Ministry, 1963-68; Parish Education, 1969-70; Music and Worship, 1972-73; Architecture and Fine Arts, 1967-72. Resigned in 1976 to pursue lifelong interest in the visual arts.

KEEVER, EDWIN FRANCIS
Date/Place of Birth: May 18, 1864 of Scotch-Irish and Saxon ancestry; Reading, Pa.
Spouse/Marriage Date: Sadie Elizabeth (Durr) Keever; November 18, 1897.

Children: Two daughters, one (name not known) who married John C. Leathem; Marion, who married John E. Walker, Sr.; one son, Paul.

Education: Muhlenberg College, A.B. 1886; Philadelphia Seminary, 1889; Muhlenberg College, D.D., 1913.

Calls: Seattle, Wash., 1889-93, and General Council Missionary in Oregon, Washington and Utah, 1893-94; St. Mark, Boston, Mass.; Holy Trinity, Catasauqua, Pa., and Redeemer, Utica, N.Y., 1907-16; Campus Lutheran Pastor, Harvard University, 1919-21. In North Carolina: St. Paul, Wilmington, 1922-37, Pastor Emeritus.

Other: President, New York and New England Synod, 1912-14. Chaplain, U.S. Army in World War I, 1917-19. "First Citizenship Award" by Wilmington Exchange Club, thereafter to be given yearly to that citizen of New Hanover County, "whose life most resembles in act and deed that of Dr. Keever."

Date of Death/Burial Location: December 17, 1949; Oakdale Cemetery, Wilmington, N.C.

KEGLEY, CHARLES R. W.

Date/Place of Birth: August 14, 1875; Wytheville, Va.

Parents: Stephen A. Kegley and Sarah E. (Umberger) Kegley.

Spouse/Marriage Date: Orpha M. (Koch) Kegley; April 1903 in New Bern, N.C.

Child: The Reverend Charles William.

Education: Roanoke College, A.B. 1898, M.A. 1902; Lutheran Theological Southern Seminary, 1901.

Ordination: 1901 by Southwest Virginia Synod.

Calls: St. Matthew, Wilmington, 1901-07; Bluefield, W.Va., 1907-11; Chicago, Ill., 1911-19. Transferred to Tennessee Synod 1919 and served Holy Trinity, Hickory, 1919-23. Transferred to Illinois Synod, 1923; served Hope-Epiphany, Chicago, Ill., and was pastor to Lutheran students, 1923-32.

Date of Death/Burial Location: December 29, 1932; Wytheville, Va.

KEISER, ALBERT, SR.

Date/Place of Birth: December 7, 1887; Neufirrel, Ostfriesland, Germany.

Spouse/Marriage Date: Lena Virginia (McGukin) Keiser; June 6, 1942 in Anderson, S.C.

Child: Albert, Jr.

Education: Wartburg College, A.B. 1911; Wartburg Seminary, 1913; University of Montana, A.M. 1915; University of Illinois, Ph.D. 1918; graduate study after 1918, University of Minnesota; University of Wisconsin; Harvard University.

Ordination: 1913 by Iowa Synod (American Lutheran Church).

Calls: Missionary of Iowa Synod in Montana, 1913-15; St. Paul, Beloit, Wis., 1918-20. Supplied churches in North Carolina in summers and sometime for months while professor at Lenoir-Rhyne; Friendship, Shiloh, and St. John, Alexander County; Emmanuel, Lincolnton; Grace, Bessemer City, and others.

Other: Acting professor (Classics), Newberry College, 1915-16; Acting Professor (English), Beloit (Wisconsin) College, 1918-19. Professor and Head of Department of English, Augustana College, Sioux Falls, S.D., 1920-25. Professor and Head of Departments of English and Public Speaking, Lenoir-Rhyne, 1925-57. Retired 1957 at

Hickory, N.C. Archivist, North Carolina Synod, 1955-59. Founder and Director, South Atlantic Forensic Tournament, 1933-59. Modern Language Association of America; American Association of University Professors; North Carolina and Catawba Poetry Societies; North Carolina Intercollegiate Forensic Association; Pi Kappa Delta Honorary Forensic Fraternity; Honorary Thunderbird Clan of Winnebago Indian Tribe (for meritorious service). Publications: *Influence of Christianity Upon the Vocabulary of Old English Poetry; Lutheran Mission Work Among the American Indians; The Indian in America's Literature; Parliamentary Law for Students; College Names: Their Origin and Significance; The Way Up* (autobiography published posthumously, Richard R. Smith, 1961). *Who's Who in America,* 1925-ff; honorary Litt.D., Lenoir-Rhyne, 1958.
Date of Death/Burial Location: December 5, 1959; Oakwood Cemetery, Hickory, N.C.

KEISLER, FRANK LAVAUGHN, SR.

Date/Place of Birth: February 7, 1930; Lexington County, S.C.
Parents: Frank L. Keisler and Gevena (Fraley) Keisler.
Spouse/Marriage Date: Elizabeth Jean (Haigler) Keisler; July 4, 1954 in Cameron, S.C.
Children: Frank L., Jr., Kerry H.
Education: Newberry College, A.B. 1951; Lutheran Theological Southern Seminary, B.D. 1954.
Ordination: May 1954 by South Carolina Synod.
Calls: St. Mark, Sullivan's Island, Charleston, S.C., 1954-56; Bethlehem Parish, Irmo, Richland, S.C., 1956- 62. In North Carolina: St. Luke, Monroe, 1962-63; St. Paul, Hamlet, 1968-69. In South Carolina: Pilgrim, Lexington, 1963-66; Mt. Hebron and Union Parish, Leesville, 1971. Interim Pastor at various congregations. Part-time Chaplain at South Carolina State Hospital, Columbia, S.C., 1967. Retired.

KEISLER, JAMES ALBERT, JR.

Date/Place of Birth: August 20, 1909; Lexington County, S.C.
Parents: James Albert Keisler, Sr. and Easter Elizabeth (Shull) Keisler. An older brother is the Reverend E. Bryan Keisler.
Spouse/Marriage Date: Violet Kathleen (Huffman) Keisler; August 20, 1935 in Hickory, N.C.
Child: Catherine Dianne Steward.
Education: Newberry College, A.B. 1932, D.D. 1952; Lutheran Theological Southern Seminary, B.D. 1935.
Ordination: October 6, 1935 by South Carolina Synod.
Calls: In South Carolina: St. Paul, Pomaria, 1935-37; in Virginia: St. Peter, Toms Brook, 1937-42, Christ, Radford, 1942-43; in South Carolina: Mt. Tabor, West Columbia, 1943-51; St. Andrew's, Charleston, 1951-55. Southeastern Area Director for Evangelism, United Lutheran Church in America Board of Social Missions, 1955-59; in Florida: St. James, Jacksonville, 1959-62; Kimball Memorial, Kannapolis, 1962-65; Grace, Prosperity, S.C., 1965-69; St. John, Wytheville, Va., 1969-70; Mt. Hebron, Hildebran, 1970-73. Retired August 1, 1973. Supply Pastor for various congregations.
Other: Board, Newberry College, 1947-59; Visitor, Lutheran World Federation Assembly, Hannover, Germany, 1952. Board, Lutheran Theological Southern Seminary; Board, Children's Home of the South; North Carolina Evangelism Committee; Virginia Synod Stewardship Committee; South Carolina Synod: President, Central Conference; Board of

Foreign Missions; Board of Home Missions; Chair, Evangelism Committee of Florida Synod; Delegate to three United Lutheran Church in America Conventions; Board, Franke Home for the Aged; Regional Director of Evangelism for the Southeastern area of the United States, Puerto Rico and St. Thomas, U.S. Virgin Islands.
Date of Death/Burial Location: September 30, 1996; St. Paul, Gilbert, S.C.

KELLER, SAMUEL LUTHER, SR.
Date/Place of Birth: January 15, 1859; near Edinburg, Va.
Parents: Aaron C. Keller and Eliza E. (Coffman) Keller.
Spouse/Marriage Date: Elizabeth R. (Miller) Keller; March 10, 1889 in Cabarrus County, N.C.
Children: Lucille M., Samuel L., Jr., Leila J.
Education: Roanoke College, A.B. 1882; Philadelphia Seminary, 1887.
Ordination: 1887 by Ministerium of Pennsylvania.
Calls: Transferred to North Carolina Synod, 1888. St. John, Cabarrus County, 1887-90; Prosperity, Cabarrus County, 1887-88. In South Carolina: Orangeburg, Orangeburg, 1890-93; St. James, Graniteville, 1890-91. In West Virginia and Ontario, Canada; Zion-St. James, Augusta County, Virginia, 1900-09; Nebraska, 1890-1914.
Other: Retired 1914 due to physical disability, in Fremont, Neb.
Date of Death/Burial Location: 1940; Riverview Cemetery, Waynesboro, Va.

KENNEDY, TIMOTHY JOHN
Date/Place of Birth: February 17, 1945; Buffalo, N.Y.
Parents: Lester John Kennedy and Marjorie Helen (Dayer) Kennedy.
Spouse/Marriage Date: Nellena Mabel (Reinhardt) Kennedy; May 30, 1970.
Children: Christopher Dale, Michael Charles, Sara Rebecca.
Education: Lenoir-Rhyne, A.B. 1970; Lutheran Theological Southern Seminary, M.Div. 1974.
Ordination: May 31, 1974 by North Carolina Synod.
Calls: Gloria Dei, Huntington Station, N.Y., 1974-78; Grace, Yorktown Heights, N.Y., 1978-.

KEPLEY, ROBERT HUGH
Date/Place of Birth: September 6, 1903; Davidson County, N.C.
Parents: Robert Leonard Kepley and Julia A. (Younts) Kepley.
Spouse/Marriage Date: Lois Lucille (Bolick) Kepley; May 26, 1931 by Claremont, N.C.
Child: The Reverend Robert Julius.
Education: Lenoir-Rhyne, A.B. 1927; Lutheran Theological Southern Seminary, B.D. 1930.
Ordination: 1930 by North Carolina Synod.
Calls: Mt. Hermon-Sharon-St. Paul, Iredell County, 1930-32; Lebanon-Providence, Rowan County; Amity, Iredell County; St. Matthew, Davie County, 1932-35; St. Stephen, Hickory, 1935-43; Holy Comforter,

Belmont, 1943-49; St. Paul, Startown, 1949-55. Transferred to Georgia-Alabama Synod, 1955; Zion, Guyton, Ga., 1965. Returned to North Carolina Synod upon retirement in 1970. Vice Pastor at various congregations.

Other: Merger Committee, Southeast Synod, 1962.

Date of Death/Burial Location: March 13, 1972; Claremont Cemetery, Claremont, N.C.

KEPLEY, ROBERT JULIUS

Date/Place of Birth: March 18, 1936; Hickory, N.C.

Parents: The Reverend Robert Hugh Kepley and Lois Lucille (Bolick) Kepley.

Spouse/Marriage Date: Susan Louise (McGee) Kepley; July 29, 1961 in Minneapolis, Minn.

Children: Robert Joel, Anne-Marie Kepley.

Education: Lenoir-Rhyne, A.B. 1958; Lutheran Theological Southern Seminary, B.D. 1962.

Ordination: June 17, 1962 by North Carolina Synod.

Calls: Mission Developer/Pastor, St. Philip, Raleigh, 1962-98; retired 1998 to Raleigh.

Other: Evangelism Committee, 1963-72, 1973-74; Publications and Publicity Committee, 1966-74; Sub- Committee Chair, *The Lutheran,* 1971-74; Raleigh Ministerial Association; Communications Committee.

KERN, JAMES SUMMERS

Date/Place of Birth: January 2, 1903; Rowan County, N.C.

Parents: John Augustus Kern and Josephine (Summers) Kern.

Education: Lenoir-Rhyne, A.B. 1923; Philadelphia Seminary, 1926; graduate study, University of Denver, Master Social Work 1938; University of Chicago 1952-54.

Ordination: 1928 by North Carolina Synod

Calls: Transferred to Ministerium of Pennsylvania; served St. Paul, Millville, N.J., 1928-34. Voluntarily demitted ministry, 1935.

Other: Faculty, University of Denver as Professor of Social Work, since 1939 except for Army service as U.S. Army sergeant in Chaplaincy Section, 1942-45.

KESTER, MOSES LEE

Date/Place of Birth: March 25, 1885; near Salisbury, N.C.

Parents: John Anderson Kester and Frances (Swink) Kester.

Spouse/Marriage Date: Annie (Little) Kester; June 4, 1913 in Statesville, N.C.

Children: Ruth Pauline, Virgil Carl, Mary Elizabeth, Carroll Little, John Lee.

Education: Mount Pleasant Collegiate Institute, Newberry College, A.B. 1909, D.D.; Lutheran Theological Southern Seminary, 1912, B.D. 1925.

Ordination: 1912 by North Carolina Synod.

Calls: Haven, Salisbury, 1912-13; St. Luke-Pilgrim, Davidson County; Reformation, Davie County, 1918-19; St. Stephen-Mt. Olive, Cabarrus County, 1919-20; St. Andrew-Calvary, Concord, 1920-28; St. Luke, Bear Poplar, 1928-31; Bethany, Kannapolis, 1931-35. In South Carolina: St. John, Mt. Calvary, Johnston; Good Hope, Saluda, 1913-18;

Beth Eden, St. James, Colony, Newberry, 1935-42; Emmanuel, Ridge Spring, St. Peter, Batesburg; Enon and Bethlehem, Leesville, 1943-46; Good Shepherd, Walterboro, 1946-52; Ehrhardt Memorial and Mt. Pleasant, Ehrhardt, 1952-54. Retired 1953 at Walterboro, S.C.
Other: Board, Lutheran Theological Southern Seminary.
Date of Death/Burial Location: February 16, 1961; Greenlawn Memorial Park, Columbia, S.C.

KETCHIE, WILLIAM RUFUS

Date/Place of Birth: February 13, 1839; China Grove, N.C.
First Spouse: Sallie Jane (Patterson) Ketchie in Rowan County, N.C.
Children of First Marriage: William Franklin Hubbert, Fannie Jane.
Second Spouse: Ann Catherine (Plaster) Ketchie in Enochville, N.C.
Child of Second Marriage: Mary Edna (married the Reverend H. E. H. Sloop).
Third Spouse: Salena Jane (Hoover) Ketchie in Statesville, N.C.
Education: North Carolina College; tutored privately in theology.
License/Ordination: Licensed in 1868 and ordained in 1871 by North Carolina Synod.
Calls: St. Matthew, Davie County, 1866-82; New Jerusalem, Davie County, 1869-70; St. Stephen, Cabarrus County; New Bethel, Stanly County, 1873; Organ, Rowan County, 1873-74; St. Paul, Iredell County, 1875-79; Providence, Rowan County, 1878-88, supplied 1892, 1897; Nazareth-Shiloh, Forsyth County, 1887-88. Retired 1888 at Mocksville, N.C.
Other: Secretary, North Carolina Synod, 1874-75.
Date of Death/Burial Location: April 6, 1921; Greenlawn Cemetery, China Grove, N.C.

KETCHIE, WILLIAM STEWART

Date/Place of Birth: February 1, 1949; Salisbury, N.C.
Parents: William Wesley Ketchie and Mary Frances (Roseman) Ketchie.
Spouse/Marriage Date: Kathy Marlene (Brown) Ketchie; August 30, 1970 in Faith, N.C.
Children: Christine Michelle, William Christopher.
Education: Lenoir-Rhyne, B.A. Sociology, 1971; Lutheran Theological Southern Seminary, M.Div. 1975.
Ordination: June 8, 1975 by North Carolina Synod.
Calls: Reformation, Columbia, S.C., 1975-77; St. John, Asheboro, 1977-89; St. Paul, Salisbury, 1989-.

KEYS, R. L.

Ordination: May 24, 1959 by Florida Synod.
Calls: Interim Pastor at Our Savior, Jacksonville, September-October 1966.
Other: Chaplain, (Lt.), U.S. Navy.

KEYSER, CAMERON POWELL
Date/Place of Birth: September 6, 1950; Charleston, W.Va.
Parents: Harry Cameron Keyser and Rosalie Virginia Barlow Keyser.
Spouse/Marriage Date: Ronda Ann (Walker) Keyser; May 5, 1975.
Children: Christopher Patrick, Ashley Lynn.
Education: University of the State of New York, B.S. Political Science 1979; Lutheran Theological Southern Seminary, M.Div. 1993.
Ordination: May 16, 1993 by North Carolina Synod.
Calls: Good Shepherd, Mt. Holly, 1993-98; St. Peter, Pawleys Island, S.C., 1998-.
Other: Communications Committee; Board, Habitat for Humanity, Mt. Holly; Mt. Holly Rotary Club.

KIBLER, MARTIN
Place of Birth: Was a native of Ohio.
License: Licensed 1820 by North Carolina Synod. In October 1820 applied to Virginia-Maryland Synod to ordain him, but the Synod declined.
Other: Moved to Maryland in 1821.
Calls: No record of churches served in North Carolina.

KIEFER, ROBERT
Calls: Interim Pastor, Our Savior, Jacksonville, May-December 1963.
Other: Chaplain.

KIESLER, S. S.
Education: While living in Ops, Ark., was a beneficiary student of Tennessee Synod, 1889-94.
Ordination: 1894 by Tennessee Synod.
Calls: None in North Carolina. Ops, Ark., 1894-96, presumably St. John, near Little Rock.
Other: In 1895 requested letter of dismissal not naming to what synod; request was not complied with. At same time an official of St. John asked to withdraw the congregation, to unite with English Synod of The Lutheran Church-Missouri Synod. In 1898 he requested his name to be removed from Tennessee Synod roll.

KILLIAN, JACOB
Date/Place of Birth: June 8, 1818; Lincoln County, N.C.
Spouse: Julia (Koiner) Killian in Koiner's Church community, Augusta County, Va.
Children: Three sons and one daughter survived him.
Ordination: Ordained Deacon 1836 by Tennessee Synod in Philadelphia Church, Lincoln (now Gaston) County. Ordained Pastor in 1839.
Calls: Koiners Church, Augusta County, Va., 1837. Histories of North Carolina and Virginia Synods are in conflict concerning churches he served. North Carolina History shows him serving Mt. Moriah, 1837, and St. Peter, 1837-38, Rowan County; and Morning Star, Mecklenburg

County, 1840-55, in same period that Ephraim Rudisill is also listed as pastor. *History of the Lutheran Church in Virginia and East Tennessee* says that he served the following churches in Virginia: Koiner's, Augusta County, 1837, (ordination) to 1871 (death); St. Paul, Mt. Solon, 1838-41; McGaheysville, 1864.

Other: President, Tennessee Synod, 1851, 1852, 1858; Secretary, 1855. Secretary, Virginia Special Conference of Tennessee Synod, 1859; President, six one-year terms, 1857-69.

Date of Death/Burial Location: July 5, 1871; Bethlehem Church, near Waynesboro, Va.

KILVER, MARTEEN DICK

Date/Place of Birth: December 16, 1906; Winchester, Ill.

Parents: Herman Kilver and Lena (Marsch) Kilver.

Spouse/Marriage Date: Elsa Pauline (Hoener) Kilver; June 22, 1932 in Carthage, Ill.

Children: Mary Ann Kilber, Rose Marie Gooding.

Education: Carthage College, B.A. 1929; Chicago Seminary, B.D. 1932.

Ordination: May 1932 by Illinois Synod.

Calls: Trinity, Milledge, Ill., 1932-37; Zion, Liberty, Ill., 1938-42; Chaplain, Central Conference, 1942-46; Christ, Sharon, Wis., 1946-48; Grace, Muscatine, Iowa, 1948-52; St. Mark, Indianapolis, Ind., 1952-58; St. Mark and Marquardt, Monroeville, Ind., 1952- 58; Mt. Zion, LaGrange, Ind., 1961-71. Retired in 1971 to Saluda, N.C. and transferred to North Carolina Synod March 31, 1979.

Other: Board, Carthage College; Board, Wittenberg University.

Date of Death/Burial Location: September 2, 1987; Grace Lutheran Church Memorial Garden in Hendersonville, N.C.

KIMBALL, WHITSON

Date/Place of Birth: March 28, 1828; Dunn's Mountain (now Granite Quarry), N.C.

Parents: Colyer Kimball and Catharine (Cauble) Kimball.

Spouse/Marriage Date: Patience Evelyn (Foil) Kimball; March 15, 1854 in Rowan County, N.C.

Children: Elizabeth Catharine, Colyer Michael, Henry B., Mary Jane, Leah Louisa Anzonetta (married the Reverend H. R. Overcash), William Luther Melanchthon, Talitha Augusta, Neifer W., Charles J. Three great-grandsons are the Reverends Frank K. Efird, John K. Lasley, and Ernest L. Misenheimer, Jr.

Education: Taught school nine years from age 21 continuing to study. In theology was tutored by his pastor, the Reverend Simeon Scherer.

License/Ordination: Licensed 1860 and ordained 1862 by North Carolina Synod.

Calls: Twenty-eight churches in nine North Carolina counties, 1860-98. In Forsyth County: Nazareth and Shiloh; in Davie County: St. Matthew and Reformation; in Rowan County: St. Matthew, St. Paul, Lutheran Chapel, 1861-77, Ebenezer, organized Center Grove, 1876, Providence, Concordia, Grace, and Christ (East Spencer); in Iredell County: St. Michael, Amity, and St. Paul; in Guilford County: Frieden's; in Alamance County: Macedonia (Burlington) and St. Paul; in Cabarrus County: St. Stephen, Mt. Olive, Mt. Hermon, and Cold Water; Stanly County: organized First (Albemarle), 1880, and New Bethel; and in Davidson County: Pilgrim, St. Luke, St. Luke, and Bethany. Most of pastorates were from two to five years, and he repeated pastorates in several instances.

Other: President, North Carolina Synod 1870-71 and Secretary, three one-year terms, 1866-77. Served as financial agent for North Carolina College, 1880, preached in every congregation of synod and raised $15,000. In 38 years of ministry never missed a synod convention, attending his last two weeks before death. Performed the marriage ceremonies of all nine of his children.
Date of Death/Burial Location: May 23, 1898; Greenlawn Cemetery, China Grove, N.C.

KINARD, JAMES DAVID
Date/Place of Birth: July 1, 1866; Prosperity, S.C.
Parents: David Belton Kinard and Mary Anne (Long) Kinard. An older brother was the Reverend M. M. Kinard.
Spouse/Marriage Date: Margaret (Wilson) Kinard; March 25, 1896 in Peak, S.C.
Children: Junius H., the Reverend Karl W., Sr., Mazie W.
Education: Newberry College, A.B. 1891/92, D.D. 1917; Lutheran Theological Southern Seminary, 1894.
Ordination: 1895 by South Carolina Synod.
Calls: In South Carolina, 1895-1924; St. John, Statesville, 1924-29. Retired 1930 in Columbia, S.C. Supplied St. Andrew's-St. Michael, Columbia, S.C., 1930-42.
Other: Secretary, Board, Newberry College, 1904-24; Secretary, South Carolina Synod, 1905-07, and President, 1909-11; Board, Lutheran Theological Southern Seminary.
Date of Death/Burial Location: July 4, 1942; Wittenberg Church, Leesville, S.C.

KINARD, MICHAEL MIDDLETON
Date/Place of Birth: February 19, 1856; Prosperity, S.C.
Parents: David Belton Kinard and Mary Anne (Long) Kinard. A younger brother was the Reverend James D. Kinard.
Spouse/Marriage Date: Joanna Dorothea (Seeba) Kinard; October 1887 in Walhalla, S.C.
Children: Albert Junius, Seeba David (died in 4th month of age), Marie Eloise (died at age 22).
Education: Newberry College, A.B. 1885, D.D. 1912; Lutheran Theological Southern Seminary, 1887; University of South Carolina, M.A.; Pennsylvania (Gettysburg) College, Honorary Ph.D. 1894.
Ordination: 1887 by South Carolina Synod.
Calls: Ebenezer, Columbia, S.C., 1887-1903; St. John, Knoxville, Tenn., 1903-06. In North Carolina: St. John, Salisbury, 1906-20; Augsburg, Winston-Salem, 1920-24.
Other: Vice President and President, South Carolina Synod, 1894-97; Board, Newberry College, 1890-96; Board, Lutheran Theological Southern Seminary, 1914-20; President, Holston Synod, 1903-05; President, North Carolina Synod, 1911-15; President, United Synod South, 1918-20; United Lutheran Church in America Board of Foreign Missions, 1918-22.
Date of Death/Burial Location: 1924; Ebenezer Churchyard, Columbia, S.C.

KING, CARL STANLEY
Date/Place of Birth: February 9, 1934; Salisbury, N.C.
Parents: The Reverend Clayborne Stanford King and Vivian P. (Kester) King.
Spouse/Marriage Date: Harriette N. (Collins) King; May 22, 1955 in Hickory, N.C.
Children: Elizabeth Carol, Patricia Leigh.
Education: Lenoir-Rhyne, A.B. 1955; Lutheran Theological Southern Seminary, B.D. 1958; Long Island University, M.A. Sociology, 1972.
Ordination: June 8, 1958 by North Carolina Synod.
Calls: Mt. Zion-New Bethel, Richfield, 1958-59; Mission Developer/Pastor, St. Thomas, Charlotte, 1959-63; U.S. Army Chaplain, 1963-. Transferred to Central States Synod, 1963.
Other: Resigned January 1979 in Sierra Vista, Ariz.

KING, CHARLES BANKS, JR.
Date/Place of Birth: October 19, 1858/9; Giles County, Va.
Parents: Charles Banks King, Sr. and Elizabeth (Martin) King.
Spouse/Marriage Date: Annie (Watts) King; 1889 in Baltimore, Md.
Children: Mary Elizabeth, Clara Ann, Gerard Watts, Charles Banks, III, George Watts.
Education: Roanoke College, also D.D.; Gettysburg Seminary.
License/Ordination: Licensed 1885 and ordained 1887 by North Carolina Synod.
Calls: St. John, Salisbury, 1886-96; supplied St. Mark's, Charlotte, 1897-98, also St. Michael, Troutman, 1901.
Other: Founder and first President, Elizabeth College, Charlotte, N.C. (named for his and his wife's mothers), 1896-1914/5. Secretary, North Carolina Synod, 1888-96, 1900-03.
Date of Death/Burial Location: August 28, 1919; Elmwood Cemetery, Charlotte, N.C.

KING, CLAYBORNE STANFORD
Date/Place of Birth: July 18, 1906; Durham, N.C.
Parents: William Stanford King and Emma J. (Dodson) King.
Spouse/Marriage Date: Vivian P. (Kester) King; June 1, 1929 in Spencer, N.C.
Children: The Reverend Carl Stanley, William Joseph, Ph.D.
Education: Wake Forest College, 1924-25; University of North Carolina, A.B. Education, 1929, also graduate study (summers); Lutheran Theological Southern Seminary, M.Div. 1949.
Ordination: 1949 by North Carolina Synod.
Calls: Organized Good Shepherd, Tampa, Fla., 1951-52; in North Carolina; Grace, Rowan County, 1949-50; St. Stephen-St. John, Lenoir, 1952-56; St. Stephen only, 1956-61; St. Luke, Catawba County, 1961-63; Messiah, Salisbury, 1963-68; Christ, Winston-Salem, 1968-71; New Jerusalem, Lexington, 1971-74; retired, 1974. Supply Pastor, Ohio Synod, 1974-84.
Other: Taught school seventeen years in East Spencer, Spencer, and Woodleaf (also principal at Woodleaf four years), before entering seminary.

KING, MARGARET JILL

Education: Western Carolina University, B.S. Education 1981, M.A. Education 1985; Lutheran Theological Southern Seminary, M.Div. 1994.
Ordination: May 17, 1998 by North Carolina Synod.
Calls: Christ, Durham, 1998-.
Other: Chaplain, Spartanburg Regional Medical Center, 1995. Former teacher and assistant principal, Cumberland County.

KING, WILLIAM HOWARD

Date/Place of Birth: October 5, 1952; New Orleans, La.
Parents: Joe M. King and Mary E. (Pettigrew) King.
Spouse/Marriage Date: Beverly Gail (Scott) King; August 10, 1975 in Monetta, S.C.
Children: William Scott, Laura Marie.
Education: Furman University, B.A. 1974; Louisiana State University, Baton Rouge, M.A. 1976; Lutheran Theological Southern Seminary, M.Div. 1980.
Ordination: June 1, 1980 by South Carolina Synod.
Calls: Our Saviour, Welcome, 1980-84; Lutheran Campus Ministry, Virginia Polytechnical Institute, 1984-; Director for Campus Ministry, Region 9, 1994-. Vice Pastor at various congregations.
Other: Publications - *Science and Religion*; "Starting the Conversation," *The Christian Century,* 1986; *Paradoxes of Paradise;* "Christians in a Technological Age," "Currents in Theology and Missions," 1992; "Learning to Read: Science, Technology and Theological Education," *Lutheran Partners,* July/August 1988.

KINNEY, GEORGE GLADSTONE

Date/Place of Birth: March 5, 1940; Concord, N.C.
Parents: The Reverend Paul Gladstone Kinney and Annie Mae (Patterson) Kinney. An older brother is the James William Kinney.
Spouse/Marriage Date: Priscilla Katherine (Schlenker) Kinney; July 4, 1964 at Perkasie, Pa.
Children: Annie Elizabeth Esquire, Katherine Melissa.
Education: University of North Carolina at Chapel Hill, B.S. Industrial Relations 1962; Lutheran Theological Southern Seminary, M.Div. 1966; Chicago Seminary, S.T.M. 1971; Andover Newton Theological School and Institute of Religion and Health, D.Min. 1977; Clinical Pastoral Education, Institute of Religion and Memorial Baptist Hospital, Houston, Texas. graduate work at New York University, 1967-68.
Ordination: May 7, 1968 by North Carolina Synod.
Calls: Board of American Missions Atlanta, Community of Hope and Community Center, 1968-72; St. John, Jersey City, N.J., 1972-75; St. Paul, Terryville, Conn., 1976-79; Emanuel, Worcester, Mass., 1980-91; Associate Pastor, Trinity, Reading, Pa., 1991-94; Bethel, Leesport, Pa., 1995-.
Other: Part-time Counseling Practice, Bristol, Conn., 1975-79; New Jersey City, N.J., 1975; Shillington, Pa., 1996-; Worcester Pastors Counseling Center, 1983-91. First Lutheran Church in America Pastor to enter an African American community since the War Between the States; Executive Board, New England Synod; Dean, Central Massachusetts Conference; Evangelism Committee, New Jersey Synod; Officer, Board, Urban Training Organization of Atlanta, Georgia; Board, Southwest Atlantans for Progress; Officer, Clergy

Association of Southwest Atlanta, 1968-72; Heights Interfaith Council and Evangelism Committee, New Jersey Synod, 1972-75; Officer, Greater Bristol, Conn., New England Synod Continuing Education Committee, 1976-79; Chair, Division for Professional Leadership; Officer, Quinsigamond Clergy Association, 1980-87; Global Missions and Continuing Education Committee, New England Synod; Chair, Professional Development Committee, Northeast Synod; American Association of Pastoral Counselors; American Association of Marriage and Family Therapists; Association of Couples and Marriage Enrichment, President and Founder, Emmanuel Development Corporation, Worcester. Vice President, Urban Training Center of Atlanta, Reading Emergency Shelter.

KINNEY, JAMES WILLIAM

Date/Place of Birth: November 12, 1937; Winston-Salem, N.C.
Parents: The Reverend Paul Gladstone Kinney and Annie Mae (Patterson) Kinney. A younger brother was the George Gladstone Kinney.
Spouse/Marriage Date: Lois Marie (Bouknight) Kinney; June 23, 1962 in Rock Hill, S.C.
Children: Martha Elizabeth, Gordon Andrew.
Education: University of North Carolina at Chapel Hill, A.B. English 1960; Lutheran Theological Southern Seminary, M.Div. 1963; graduate work at St. Mary University, 1971.
Ordination: June 9, 1963 by North Carolina Synod, and transferred to Southeast Synod.
Calls: Mission Developer, Lutheran Church in America Board of American Missions, Greeneville, Tenn., 1963-65; St. Timothy, Hendersonville, Tenn., 1965-66; Sharon, Statesville, 1966-68; Chaplain, (Lt. Col.), U.S. Air Force, 1968-96. Chief of Medical Group Ministries at Keesler Air Force Base. Retired March 1, 1996 in Ocean Springs, Miss.
Other: Received Meritorious Service Medallion of the Evangelical Lutheran Church in America for service as a military chaplain, March 1996; Military Decorations: Bronze Star, Air Force Meritorious Service Medal with Six Oak Leaf Clusters; Air Force Commendation Medal with three Oak Leaf Clusters and the Air Force Achievement Medal. Publications: *Chaplain, Please Pray*, 1985.

KINNEY, PAUL GLADSTONE

Date/Place of Birth: March 22, 1903; Alamance County, N.C.
Parents: James Clingman Kinney and Sarah Leah (Keck) Kinney.
Spouse/Marriage Date: Annie Mae (Patterson) Kinney; June 27, 1933 in Burlington, N.C.
Children: The Reverend James William, The Reverend George Gladstone, Sarah Mae.
Education: Lenoir-Rhyne, two years, Elon College, A.B. 1928; Lutheran Theological Southern Seminary, B.D. 1931; graduate study Duke University, 1935-36, serving also as pastor to Lutheran students at University of North Carolina at Chapel Hill.
Ordination: September 22, 1931 by North Carolina Synod.
Calls: St. Luke, Bear Poplar, 1931-35; Ebenezer, Rowan County - Mt. Hermon, Cabarrus County, 1938-43; Christiana, Granite Quarry, 1943-49; St. Paul-Mt. Pleasant, Alamance County, 1949-56; St. Enoch, Rowan County, 1956-60; St. Paul, Iredell County, 1960-62. Retired 1962 near Burlington, N.C.
Date of Death/Burial Location: June 5, 1973; St. Paul Cemetery, Burlington, N.C.

KISTLER, HENRY ALFRED, SR.

Date/Place of Birth: December 30, 1879; Lincolnton, N.C.

Parents: Adolphus Monroe Kistler and Mary Suana (Robinson) Kistler.

Spouse/Marriage Date: Myrtle Blanche (Clark) Kistler; December 23, 1912 in Blountville, Tenn.

Children: Myrtle Blanche, Henry Alfred, Jr., (died in service World War II, April 15, 1943), Adolphus Job.

Education: Lenoir-Rhyne, A.B. 1902; Lutheran Theological Southern Seminary, 1905, B.D. 1926; graduate study, Chicago Seminary; University of Georgia, Ph.D. 1930.

Ordination: 1905 by Tennessee Synod.

Calls: Holy Communion-Mt. Pleasant-Mt. Zion, Watauga County, 1905-10; in Tennessee, Holston Synod, 1910-20; in South Carolina, in Tennessee Synod, Pomaria and St. Matthew, 1920-22, and in South Carolina Synod at Zion, Pilgrim, Lexington, 1922-34. Again in North Carolina (Watauga Parish): Mt. Pleasant-Holy Trinity-Mt. Zion-Old Mt. Pleasant, Watauga County, 1934-37; Lebanon-Providence, Rowan County; Amity, Iredell County; St. Matthew, Davie County, June 1937-May 1938.

Other: Vice President, Holston Synod. Board, Lutheran Theological Southern Seminary; Board, Summerland College.

Date of Death/Burial Location: May 7, 1938; Daniel's Church, Lincoln County, N.C.

KISTLER, PAUL

Place of Birth: Near Bear Poplar, Rowan County, N.C.

Parents: John Kistler and (?) Barringer.

First Spouse: (?) (Wingard) Kistler of South Carolina.

Child of First Marriage: Albert.

Second Spouse: Thursa (Cloy) Kistler of South Carolina, daughter of the Reverend Robert C. Cloy.

Children of Second Marriage: Victoria, Mary, Kate, Belle, John.

Education: Lutheran Theological Southern Seminary, 1841.

License/Ordination: Licensed 1841 and ordained 1843 by South Carolina Synod.

Calls: In South Carolina at Mt. Calvary, Johnston and Trinity, Saluda, 1841-56; in North Carolina, 1856-58: Beth Eden, Newton; St. Michael, Troutman; St. Paul, Iredell County.

Other: In 1859 united with Methodist Church.

KITE, WILLIAM JACKSON, JR.

Date/Place of Birth: May 26, 1933; Fayetteville, N.C.
Parents: William Jackson Kite, Sr. and Flora Mae (Lawson) Kite.
Spouse/Marriage Date: Barbara Jean (Conner) Kite; March 1, 1955 in Hickory, N.C.
Children: Karen Jane, William Lindon, Christopher Lee, Barbara Renee, Lester Dean.
Education: Lenoir-Rhyne, A.B. 1955; Lutheran Theological Southern Seminary, B.D. 1958.
Ordination: June 8, 1958 by North Carolina Synod.
Calls: Mt. Hermon, Iredell County, 1958-59; Reformation, Taylorsville, 1959-73.
Other: Demitted ministry, 1973.

KLAPPENBACH, DAVID EDWARD

Ordination: June 6, 1998 by North Carolina Synod for Ohio Synod.
Calls: Trinity, Malinta, Ohio, 1998-.

KLATT, ALICE BATTELLE (DEFOREST)

Date/Place of Birth: July 13, 1933; Houston, Texas.
Parents: The Reverend Lionel Theodore DeForest and Agnes Battelle (Bonell) DeForest.
Spouse/Marriage Date: Emil H. Klatt, Jr.; June 27, 1953.
Children: Eric William, Emil H., III, Amber Suzanne Thompson.
Education: Monticello College, University of South Carolina, B.A. 1982; Lutheran Theological Southern Seminary, M.Div. 1986.
Ordination: October 10, 1986 by South Carolina Synod.
Calls: Sandy Run, Swansea, S.C., 1986-92; Gloria Dei, Salisbury, 1992-98. Retired 1998 to South Carolina Synod.
Other: Task Force on North Carolina Synod Structure, 1994; College Group Leader, North Carolina Synod 1995; North Carolina Synod Nominating Committee, 1995; South Carolina Synod Council, Voting member, Churchwide Assembly; South Carolina Chair, Bishop's Advisory Committee on Ecumenism; Chair, South Carolina Synod Nominating Committee.

KLUTTZ, MILES JOSEPH

Date/Place of Birth: March 26, 1893; Rowan County, N.C.
Parents: H. A. Lewis Kluttz and Mary E. (Walton) Kluttz.
Spouse/Marriage Date: Sarah Pearle (Lyerly) Kluttz; November 19, 1922 in Rowan County, N.C.
Children: Pearle Lyerly McCall, Miles Joe, Sarah Elaine.
Education: Mount Pleasant Collegiate Institute, Lenoir-Rhyne, A.B. 1916; Lutheran Theological Southern Seminary, 1919; Philadelphia Seminary, B.D. 1920.
Ordination: 1919 by North Carolina Synod, and transferred to New York and New England Synod.
Calls: Ascension, Brooklyn, N.Y., 1920-24; St. Luke, Bear Poplar, 1924-27; Augusta County Parish, Waynesboro, Va., 1927-35; Washington County Parish, Damascus, Va., 1935-40; Wittenberg, Granite Quarry, 1940-52.

Other: Retired 1952 to Granite Quarry, N.C. Published in *Lutheran Church Quarterly* article titled *Rural Church Problems and Their Solutions.* President, Staunton Conference, Lutheran Synod of Virginia.
Date of Death/Burial Location: April 22, 1963; Union Church, Rowan County, N.C.

KNAUFF, JOHN LOWELL
Date/Place of Birth: March 13, 1936; Ravenna, Ohio.
Parents: The Reverend and Mrs. Walter F. Knauff.
Spouse/Marriage Date: Juanita Yvonne (Rogers) Knauff; August 23, 1958.
Children: Mark David, Paul Roger, John Andrew.
Education: Capital University, Columbus, Ohio, A.B. Social Science, 1958; Evangelical Lutheran Theological Seminary, Columbus, Ohio, M.Div., 1962.
Ordination: June 24, 1962 by American Lutheran Church.
Calls: Mission Church, Grace, Raleigh, 1962-68; Resurrection, Weirton, W.Va., 1970-77; Hope, Annandale, Va., 1977-.

KNAUFF, LUTHER LAVERN
Date/Place of Birth: July 23, 1922; Venus, Pa.
Parents: The Reverend George M. Knauff and Luella E. Wagner.
Spouse/Marriage Date: Mildred R. (Albrecht) Knauff; May 25, 1946 in Galion, Ohio.
Children: Karen Louise, Mark John, Philip Luther, Lois Ann, Craig Martin.
Education: Capital University, B.A. 1943; Trinity Seminary, B.D. 1946; Graduate Institute on Judaism, Vanderbilt Divinity School, 1972.
Ordination: June 9, 1946 by American Lutheran Church, Michigan Synod.
Calls: Gethsemane, Warren, Mich., 1946-48; Nazareth, Chatfield, Ohio, 1948-57; Perry Highway-St. John of Lovi, Wexford, Pa., 1957-59; St. Martin, North Tonawanda, N.Y., 1959- 71; Old St. Paul, Newton, 1971-87.   Retired, July 1987. Vice pastor at various congregations.
Other: Chair, North Amherst Cooperative Ministry, 1967-71; Vice President, Eastern District, American Lutheran Church, Washington, D.C., 1967-69; Trustee, Buffalo Council of Churches, 1968-71; Chair, Catawba Valley Lutheran Fellowship, 1978-84; Chair and Treasurer, Catawba County Historical Society, 1984-90.

KNIGHT, OSCAR KENNETH
Date/Place of Birth: January 18, 1924; Caldwell County, N.C.
Parents: Oscar K. Knight and Lula Kate (Beaty) Knight.
Spouse/Marriage Date: Jeanne Marie (Stengle) Knight; July 18, 1944 in the Bronx, New York, N.Y.
Children: Jack Oscar Kenneth, Kate Elizabeth Marie, Kevin Douglas Anthony, Carl Kerron William.
Education: U.S. Merchant Marine Academy, Kings Point, Long Island, N.Y., 1942-44; Lenoir-Rhyne, A.B. 1949; Lutheran Theological Southern Seminary, B.D. 1952.

Ordination: 1952 by North Carolina Synod.
Calls: Daniel's, Lincoln County, 1952-55. Transferred 1956 to Pacific Southwest Synod.
Other: Demitted ministry for secular employment as a social worker, December 1959.

KOHN, ERNEST HOUSEAL
Date/Place of Birth: November 7, 1863; Little Mountain, S.C.
Parents: Aaron Hamilton Kohn and Martha Elizabeth (Feagle) Kohn.
Spouse/Marriage Date: Catharine (Ehrhardt) Kohn; May 16, 1895 in Philadelphia, Pa.
Children: Gertrude Elizabeth, Paul Houseal (died in infancy), Grace Koiner, Ruth, Faith, George Ehrhardt.
Education: Newberry College, A.B. 1885, A.M., Ph.D., D.D.; graduated Philadelphia Seminary, 1893.
Ordination: 1893 by Ministerium of Pennsylvania.
Calls: In Virginia, Southwest Virginia, and Tennessee Synods, Burkes Garden 1893-1907, and Emmanuel, New Market, 1887-1902; St. Peter, Natrona, Pa., 1902-04; Harrold-Seenors Parish, Pa., 1911-13; in North Carolina: St. John's, Cherryville; Bethphage, Lincoln County; St. Paul-St. Mark, Crouse, 1904-09; Good Shepherd, Mt. Holly; Holy Comforter, Belmont, 1913-27; Good Shepherd only, 1927-46; St. James, Sumter, S.C., 1909-11. Retired 1946 at Mt. Holly, later at Gastonia.
Other: Joint Committee (for Tennessee Synod) to Consider Proposal to Unite all Lutherans in North Carolina in one Synod, 1915; Secretary, Tennessee Synod, 1898-99, President, 1899-1900; First Statistical Secretary, United North Carolina Synod, 1921-33.
Date of Death/Burial Location: November 11, 1950; Mt. Holly, N.C.

KOINER, JUNIUS SAMUEL
Date/Place of Birth: July 9, 1849; Flatwoods, Va.
Education: University of Virginia, 1874; Philadelphia Seminary, 1880.
Ordination: 1881 by Tennessee Synod.
Calls: Zion, Hickory, Catawba County, 1881-83; other Tennessee Synod churches in South Carolina: Bethlehem, Irmo; St. Jacob and St. Thomas, Chapin; and in Virginia: Bethel, Manassas, 1890-92, and Mt. Nebo, Madison, 1888-92.
Other: Educator at Gustavus Adolphus College, 1881; taught theology at Concordia College in Conover; President, Tennessee Synod, 1887-88; in 1899 left Tennessee Synod to join The Lutheran Church-Missouri Synod.
Date of Death: 1915.

KOONTZ, DAVID JAMES

Date/Place of Birth: 1846; Davidson County, N.C.
Children: Jesse, Perry, John, Mamie, Elizabeth, and Lillie.
Ordination: Ordained at Mt. Pleasant by North Carolina Synod May 1, 1880.
Calls: Organized and served Negro churches in Cabarrus, Rowan, and Davidson Counties.
Other: Jensson says of him: "He was confirmed by the Reverend W. A. Julian, who also installed him as pastor of Pleasant Grove Church, . . . the first colored Lutheran Church the North Carolina Synod organized and received. He laid the foundation for the congregations in the Alpha Synod, and lived to see two young men, whom he had baptized, instructed and confirmed, in the Lutheran ministry, one of which was W. P. Phifer, Secretary of the Alpha Synod." *(American Lutheran Biographies)*. An organizer of Alpha Synod in 1889 and its first president.
Date of Death/Burial Location: May 27, 1890; Old Lutheran Cemetery, Concord, N.C.

KOSS, LAWRENCE L.

Date of Birth: November 23, 1927.
Spouse/Marriage Date: Nancy Koss.
Education: University of Iowa, B.A. with Honors in English 1955; Trinity Seminary, Certified for Ordination, 1985; Florida Beacon, MRE, 1978.
Ordination: September 15, 1985 by American Lutheran Church, Florida Synod.
Calls: Pastoral Associate, Peace, Palm Bay, Fla., 1980-85, Assistant Pastor, 1985-87; Triumphant Cross, Dothan, Ala., 1987-93. Transferred to North Carolina Synod from Southeastern Synod 1993 and then to Florida-Bahamas Synod, in 1995.
Other: Retired, 1993.

KOVITCH, JOSEPH GERARD

Date/Place of Birth: April 21, 1964; Euclid, Ohio.
Parents: Joseph Robert Kovitch and Angela Jeanne Kovitch.
Spouse/Marriage Date: Marie (Rosenberg) Kovitch; April 5, 1986.
Children: Zachary Joseph, Jesse Michael.
Education: Malone College, Cleveland State University, B.A. Communications, 1989; Trinity Seminary, M.Div. 1993.
Ordination: June 12, 1993 by North Carolina Synod.
Calls: St. Mark's, Charlotte, 1993-96; New Hope, Kannapolis, 1996-.
Other: Co-Chair, Multicultural Synodical Committee; President, Charlotte Evangelical Lutheran Clergy Association; Board, Youth Innovation 2000; Race Relations Task Force, Mecklenburg Ministry.

KRAFT, CHRISTOPHER KENNETH

Date/Place of Birth: November 20, 1949; Rochester, N.Y.
Parents: Donald G. Kraft and Ethel K. Kraft.
Spouse/Marriage Date: Ann (Courson) Kraft; May 24, 1970.
Child: Michael Gordon.
Education: Brevard Community College, Cocoa, Fla., A.A. Marketing, 1977; University of Central Florida, B.A. Marketing/Business Administration, 1981; Trinity Seminary, M.Div. 1991.

Ordination: August 4, 1991, by Florida-Bahamas Synod.
Calls: Associate Pastor, Lutheran Ministry in Christ, Coral Springs, Fla., 1991-96; Trinity, Vale, 1996-.

KRAFT, NANCY KURTZ
See Kurtz, Nancy (Kraft)

KRAFT, ORION RALPH, JR.
Date/Place of Birth: June 15, 1965; Savannah, Ga.
Parents: Orion Ralph Kraft, Sr. and Alice Faye (Buck) Kraft.
Education: University of Georgia, B.S. Agriculture 1989; Lutheran Theological Southern Seminary, M.Div. 1995.
Ordination: October 8, 1995 by North Carolina Synod.
Calls: Calvary, Spencer, 1995-.
Other: Eagle Scout.

KRAUSHAAR, GEORGE H.
Date/Place of Birth: March 15, 1948; San Francisco County, Calif.
Parents: Harold F. Kraushaar and Juanita (Pelot) Kraushaar.
Spouse/Marriage Date: Ruth Louise (Onsum) Kraushaar; December 31, 1970 in Bellingham, Wash.
Children: Marcus Keith, Sara Kristina.
Education: Seattle Pacific University, B.A. 1970; Concordia and Lutheran Theological Southern Seminary, M.Div. 1976.
Ordination: September 1, 1976 by Southeast Synod.
Calls: Knox Lutheran Parish, Knox, Pa., 1976-78; Salem and Mt. Zion, Smicksburg, Pa., 1978-82; St. Andrew, Andrews, 1982-84.
Other: Resigned from ministry August 1984.

KUHN, HARVEY ALVIN, JR.
Date/Place of Birth: June 11, 1925; Lincoln County, N.C.
Parents: Harvey Alvin Kuhn, Sr. and Elizabeth (Noe) Kuhn.
Spouse/Marriage Date: Eva Jean (Foltz) Kuhn; August 25, 1949 in Shenandoah, Va.
Children: Brenda Jean Kuhn-Yale, Pamela Jo Catron.
Education: Texas A & M, Lenoir-Rhyne, A.B. 1948; Philadelphia Seminary, B.D. 1951.
Ordination: 1951 by North Carolina Synod.
Calls: Trinity, Sanford, 1951-55. Mission Developer/Pastor, Redeemer, McLean, Va., 1955-67; Staff, Commission on Evangelism, Lutheran Church in America, 1967-71; St. Stephen, Wilmington, Del., 1971-77; Peace, Alexandria, Va., 1977-84; St. Paul, Hampton, Va., 1984-.
Other: Executive Board, Virginia Synod, 1981-87; Examining Managing Group, Virginia Synod, 1979-87; Delegate, Lutheran Church in America Convention, 1986; Pastor/Evangelist, Lutheran Church in America, 1975-77; retired to Williamsburg, Va.

KUHNS, SAMUEL WASHINGTON
Place of Birth: January 10, 1848; Clarion County, Pa.
Parents: John Kuhns and Sarah (Knight) Kuhns.
Spouse: Marziena (Saeger) Kuhns in Saegertown, Pa.
Child: Elizabeth Sarah.
Education: Muhlenberg College, 1872; Philadelphia Seminary, 1875.
Ordination: 1875 by Pittsburgh Synod.
Calls: Grace, Franklin, Pa., 1875-80; First, Columbus, Ohio, 1880-84; St. John, Duluth, Minn., 1894-1901. Transferred to North Carolina Synod from Northwest Synod, 1910. Supplied Concordia, Rowan County, 1909. Later served Emanuel, Woodstock, Va., 1911-22 and Maryland.
Other: Retired 1924 at Frederick, Md.
Date of Death/Burial Location: 1928; Emlenton, Pa.

KUPKE, HAROLD G.
Date/Place of Birth: November 4, 1920; Ogallala, Neb.
Parents: The Reverend George J. Kupke and Rose A. (Rottmann) Kupke.
Spouse/Marriage Date: Beatrice W. (Stenke) Kupke; April 15, 1952 in Detroit, Mich.
Children: David W., Kathryn A. Manthei, Carol L. Lang, Kenneth G., Lois L. Vaughn.
Education: St. Paul College, A.A. 1940; Concordia Seminary (Mo.), B.D. 1945; Wayne State, M.A. 1955; Graduate work at University of Southern California, 1958-60; University of Nebraska, Ph.D. 1969.
Ordination: February 1945 by The Lutheran Church-Missouri Synod.
Calls: St. Luke, Bazine, Kan., 1945-48.
Other: Instructor of Religion, Languages, Lutheran High School, Detroit, 1948-54; Instructor of Religion, Social Studies, Lutheran High School, Los Angeles, 1954-63; Professor of Sociology, Concordia College, Nebraska, 1963-72; Professor of Sociology, Lenoir-Rhyne, 1972-84. Publications: *Child Rearing and the Christian Educative Process, Issues*, Fall, 1971; *Parent-Child Relationships and Value Formation, Issues*, Spring, 1972; Quality of Life Study, Catawba County, 1978. Transferred to North Carolina Synod, 1983. Retired, 1984.
Date of Death/Burial Location: December 8, 1989; Catawba Memorial Park, Hickory, N.C.

KURTZ, MILBERT ELDON
Date/Place of Birth: January 25, 1938; Mitchell, S.D.
Parents: Rudolph Kurtz and Erna (Weise) Kurtz.
Spouse/Marriage Date: Janet Gail (Olsen) Kurtz; June 28, 1970.
Child: Mark Milbert.
Education: Augustana College (S.D.), B.A. 1960; Wartburg Seminary, B.M. 1964.
Ordination: June 7, 1964 by American Lutheran Church.
Calls: Bethlehem, Glenwood and Troy, Crosby, N.D., 1964-67; St. Paul and Christ, Center, N.D., 1968-74; St. John, Dickinson, N.D., 1975; Emmanuel, Gackle, N.D., 1975-79; St. Matthew and Rosendal, Thompson, N.D., 1979-83; Ness, Meckinock, N.D., 1985; Christ, Winston-Salem, 1986-93; St. Luke, Mt. Ulla, 1993-.

KURTZ, NANCY (KRAFT)

See also Kraft, Nancy Kurtz

Date/Place of Birth: November 10, 1952; Hamilton, Ohio.

Parents: Robert O. Kraft and Ellen (Wakefield) Kraft.

First Spouse: Richard Wayne Ferris.

Children of First Marriage: Gretchen Ferris, Benjamin Ferris.

Second Spouse/Marriage Date: Stephen A. Kurtz; 1996.

Child of Second Spouse: Stephen Kurtz.

Education: Bowling Green State University, B.S. in Education/English, 1974; Trinity Lutheran Seminary, M.Div., 1979; University of Pittsburgh, Ph.D./Christian Education, 1992.

Ordination: March 11, 1979 by American Lutheran Church.

Calls: Assistant Pastor, Trinity, Jamestown, N.D., 1979-84; Trinity/Emmanuel Lutheran, Carrollton-Kilgore, Ohio, 1984-86; Assistant to the Bishop, Northeastern Ohio Synod, 1988-91; Advent, Uniontown, Ohio, 1991-97; Advent, Charlotte, 1998-.

KYLES, CHARLES FAY

Date/Place of Birth: February 28, 1902; Iredell County, N.C.

Parents: William Curry Kyles and Mary V. (Barnhardt) Kyles.

Spouse/Marriage Date: Mary Ida (Fink) Kyles; June 19, 1930 in Cleveland, N.C.

Children: Ruth Marie Gunter, the Reverend Lewis Lee.

Education: Lenoir-Rhyne, A.B. 1924; Lutheran Theological Southern Seminary, 1929.

Ordination: May 29, 1929 by North Carolina Synod.

Calls: Lebanon-Providence, Rowan County; Amity, Iredell County; St. Matthew, Davie County, 1929-32; Grace, Rowan County; Prosperity, Cabarrus County, 1932-40 and Prosperity only, 1940-43; Beck's-Holly Grove-Lebanon-New Jerusalem, Davidson County, 1943-47; Friendship, Taylorsville, 1947-53; Low's, Guilford County, 1953-58; Luther's, Rowan County, 1958-63; Cold Water-St. Martin, Cabarrus County, 1963-67. Vice Pastor at various congregations.

Other: Taught high school for two years. Synod Examining Committee, Parish Education Committee.

Date of Death/Burial Location: March 5, 1984; Cross of Christ (Prosperity), Concord, N.C.

KYLES, LEWIS LEE

Date/Place of Birth: November 2, 1932; Rowan County, N.C.

Parents: The Reverend Charles Fay Kyles and Mary Ida (Fink) Kyles.

Spouse/Marriage Date: Barbara Ann (Dobson) Kyles; June 24, 1962 in Marion, N.C.

Education: Lenoir-Rhyne, A.B. 1954; Lutheran Theological Southern Seminary, B.D. 1957.

Ordination: June 1957 by North Carolina Synod.

Calls: St. Paul, Milan, Ind., 1957-58; Morning Star, Mecklenburg County, 1958-63; Mt. Hermon, Cabarrus County, 1963.

Other: Demitted the ministry for youth work at the Charlotte Young Mens' Christian Association, 1963.

Date of Death/Burial Location: July 13, 1984; Lord of Life, Garner, N.C.

LACKEY, JACOB LAFAYETTE

Date/Place of Birth: May 9, 1916; Cleveland County, N.C.
Parents: James Rufus Lafayette Lackey and Sara Josephine (Oats) Lackey.
Spouse/Marriage Date: Helen Lucille (Safrit) Lackey; June 4, 1944 in Cabarrus County, N.C.
Children: Miriam Angela, Gloria Ann.
Education: Salisbury Business College, 1936; Lenoir-Rhyne, A.B. 1941, D.D. 1975; Lutheran Theological Southern Seminary, B.D. 1944; Columbia University, M.A. 1953.
Ordination: July 16, 1944 by North Carolina Synod.
Calls: Mt. Zion-Luther's-New Bethel, Richfield, 1944-47; Mt. Hermon (first full-time pastor), Cabarrus County, 1947-49; St. Timothy, Catawba County, 1949-54; Mission Developer/Pastor, Christ, Charlotte, 1954-83. Vice Pastor at various congregations. Retired July 1983 in Charlotte, N.C.
Other: Board, Lenoir-Rhyne; Board, North Carolina Lutheran Homes; Parish Education Committee, 1963-65; Publications and Publicity Committee, 1968-73; Chair, Sub-Committee of *North Carolina Lutheran*, 1968-69; Secretary, Southern District, 1965-70; Lutheran Church in America delegate, 1962; President, Southern Conference; President, Pastors' Association, Hickory, Charlotte; Chair, Constitution Committee to enable lay persons to be part of the Pastors' Association. Author of *A Church is Born, History of Christ Lutheran Church,* (1954-83). Invited to participate in Model II Metropolitan Church Study at Philadelphia, Pa., 1981. Attended Lutheran World Federation in Helsinki, Finland, as a visitor, 1963.

LAFFON, MICHAEL REID

Date/Place of Birth: March 18, 1959; Hickory, N.C.
Parents: Reid Eugene Laffon and Mary Beckom (Abernathy) Laffon.
Education: Wake Forest University, B.A. 1981; Lutheran School of Theology at Chicago, M.Div. 1989.
Ordination: May 21, 1989 by North Carolina Synod.
Calls: Zion, Jersey City, N.J., 1989-95.
Other: Retired on disability as of January 17, 1995.

LAND, ROBERT EDGAR

Date/Place of Birth: June 20, 1937; Buffalo, N.Y.
Parents: Lt. Col. Walter C. Land and Helen (Beck) Land.
Spouse/Marriage Date: Barbara (Deal) Land; January 1, 1964 in Hickory, N.C.
Children: Barbara Katherine, Allison Scott.
Education: Lenoir-Rhyne, A.B. Music, 1963; Lutheran Theological Southern Seminary, M.Div. 1968; University of North Carolina at Charlotte, 1977.
Ordination: June 9, 1968 by North Carolina Synod.
Calls: Assistant Pastor, St. Paul, Liverpool, N.Y., 1968-70; Immanuel, Jamestown, N.Y., 1970-75; Morning Star, Matthews, 1977-80; Pastor, Augustana, Detroit, Mich., 1985-86; Associate Pastor, St. Paul, Orlando, Fla., 1988-90; Interim Pastor at Bethlehem, Hallandale, Fla., 1990-92, Atonement, Orlando, Fla., 1993, and Faith, Conover, N.C., 1993-95; Messiah, Burlington, 1995-.

Other: New York State LIRS Consultant (Lutheran Council in the United States of America), 1976-77; Director, Refugee Resettlement, Florida Council of Churches, 1980-82; Director, Miami Office of the Episcopal Presiding Bishop's Fund for World Relief, 1982-83; Dean of Students, Luther High School, Orlando, Fla., 1983-85; Ecumenical Representative of the Broward Conference, Florida-Bahamas Synod; Chair, Florida-Bahamas Synod Multi-cultural Commission.

LANDERS, TIMOTHY L.

Date/Place of Birth: December 10, 1956; Cincinnati, Ohio.
Parents: Robert Landers and Bertha (Klocker) Landers.
Spouse/Marriage Date: Theresa Landers; June 17, 1982 in Jonesboro, Ga.
Children: Jamie, Jacki, Justin, Jenna.
Education: St. Meinrod College, B.A. 1978; Atlanta University, M.S.W. 1980; Lutheran Theological Southern Seminary, M.Div. 1990.
Ordination: January 6, 1991 by Southeast Synod.
Calls: Rock of Ages, Stone Mountain, Ga., 1991-92; Our Saviour, Dallas, 1992-94. Transferred to West Virginia-Western Maryland Synod, 1994.

LANG, CARLA

Date/Place of Birth: May 29, 1951; Chicago, Ill.
Parents: Arthur Carl Lang and Ucma (Homsey) Lang.
Spouse/Marriage Date: Garry David Cook; March 31, 1989 in Winston-Salem, N.C.
Step-Child: Amy Cook.
Education: North Park College, B.A. Biology, 1972; North Park Seminary, M.Div. 1976; Loyola University, M.A. Counseling Psychology, 1979; Emory University, Ph.D. studies, 1979-82.
Ordination: June 12, 1980 by Evangelical Covenant Church; January 21, 1990 by Evangelical Lutheran Church in America.
Calls: Lutheran General Hospital, Pastoral Counseling Center, 1978; Georgia Association for Pastoral Care, Atlanta, Ga., 1979; Pastoral Counseling, Baptist Medical Center, Birmingham, Ala., 1986-88; Group Practice, Atlanta, Ga., 1980-86. In Evangelical Covenant Church: Mt. Pilgrim, Haralson, Ga., 1985; Christ, Jasper, Ala., 1986-88. In Evangelical Lutheran Church in America, Pastoral Counseling Center, North Carolina Baptist Hospital, Winston-Salem, 1988-.

LANGE, MELVIN SYLVANUS

Date/Place of Birth: June 22, 1911; Denver, Colo.
Parents: Didrik Lange and Martha (Villa) Lange.
Spouse/Marriage Date: Helen (Knight) Lange; October 17, 1937 in Elkhart, Ind.
Children: Beth Ellen, Paul Melvin.
Education: Akron University (Ohio), Wittenberg University, A.B. 1934; Hamma Divinity School, B.D. 1937. Clinical training, Augustana Hospital, Chicago, Ill. Roanoke College, D.D., 1951.
Ordination: 1937 by Ohio Synod.

Calls: Redeemer, Parma, Ohio, 1937-39; Mission Developer, Board of American Missions, Upper Arlington, Va., 1939-41; Christ, Staunton, Va., 1941-53; Holy Trinity, Hickory, 1953-58; Resurrection, Arlington, Va., 1958-72. Retired January 1, 1974.
Other: Executive Council, Virginia Synod, 1959-62; Executive Board, Virginia Synod, 1965-68, 1970-73; Trustee, Marion College, 1962-67.

LANGSDORF, KENNETH ALAN
Date/Place of Birth: April 27, 1966; Madison, Wis.
Parents: Jon H. Langsdorf and Mary Lynn (Ellis) Langsdorf.
Spouse/Marriage Date: Catherine Lee (Mauney) Langsdorf; January 9, 1988 in Arlington Heights, Ill.
Education: Carthage College, B.A. Religion 1988; Chicago Seminary, M.Div. 1992.
Ordination: August 2, 1992 by South Central Wisconsin Synod.
Calls: Epiphany, Winston-Salem, 1992-94; St. Peter, Southport, 1994-. Served as Lutheran Campus Pastor at Wake Forest University, 1992.

LASLEY, JOHN KERR
Date/Place of Birth: November 15, 1913 at China Grove, N.C.
Parents: William Blair Lasley and Pauline (Thom) Lasley. A great-grandson of the Reverend Whitson Kimball.
Spouse/Marriage Date: Helen Lee (Misenheimer) Lasley; June 7, 1938 in Richfield.
Children: Jackie Lee, Frances Thom.
Education: Lenoir-Rhyne, A.B. 1935, D.D. 1965; Lutheran Theological Southern Seminary, B.D. 1938.
Ordination: 1938 by North Carolina Synod.
Calls: Mission Developer/Pastor, Good Shepherd, Goldsboro, 1938-45; St. John, Statesville, 1945-71.
Other: Member, Board of North Carolina Lutheran Homes, 1961-71. Resigned from ministry, 1971.
Date of Death/Burial Location: November 28, 1984; Pine Hill Cemetery, Burlington, N.C.

LAUGHLIN, ARTHUR JAMES, JR.
Date/Place of Birth: November 23, 1928; Zanesville, Ohio.
Parents: Arthur James Laughlin, Sr. and Louella Gaile (Denny) Laughlin.
Spouse/Marriage Date: Mary Elizabeth (Caldwell) Laughlin; July 14, 1951 in Columbus, Ohio.
Children: James Stephen, Jeffrey Lee, Heather Colleen.
Education: Capital University, B.M., Church Music 1950; Hamma Divinity School, B.D. 1953; Newberry College, D.D. 1973.
Ordination: 1953 by Ohio Synod.
Calls: St. John, Vandalia, Ohio, 1953-58; Associate Pastor, St. Mark's, Charlotte, 1958-59; Haven, Salisbury, 1959-64; St. Matthew, Charleston, S.C., 1964-74; Holy Trinity, Manhattan, New York, N.Y., 1974-82; Christ, Ft. Lauderdale, Fla., 1982-92.
Other: Chair, Music Commission, for 1958, (Dayton) United Lutheran Church in America convention; Worship Commission, United Lutheran Church in America, 1960-62; Director,

Lutheridge School of Church Music, 1959-73; Board, Lutheridge, 1963-64; National Board, The Liturgical Conference, 1978-82; National President, Lutheran Society for Worship; National Vice President, Lutheran Society for Worship, Music and the Arts, 1977-78. Over 100 articles for *Church Music, Liturgy,* and North Carolina and South Carolina Synodical papers, 1960-78. Author of *Music in the Lutheran Church,* 1959. Writer of monthly column, *The Worship Corner,* in *The North Carolina Lutheran.* Assisted in introducing new musical settings of liturgy of *Service Book and Hymnal* to North Carolina Synod congregations. Metro New York Bishop's Representative as Dean for the 100th Anniversary of St. Patrick Cathedral, New York City. Asked by New York Council of Churches to preach on Easter Sunday, 1978, at the Cathedral Church of St. John the Divine, New York City.
Date of Death: July 4, 1992; Ft. Lauderdale, Fla.

LAUTENSCHLAGER, PAUL E.

Date/Place of Birth: June 6, 1902; Glenford, Ohio.
Parents: The Reverend C. J. E. Lautenschlager and Emma (Elsass) Lautenschlager.
Spouse/Marriage Date: Mary Eveline (Dougherty) Lautenschlager, 1927.
Education: Spokane College, 1921; Capital University, Columbus, Ohio, B.A., 1925; Evangelical Lutheran Theological Seminary, Columbus, Ohio.
Ordination: 1928 by Ohio Synod.
Calls: Thorn Creek Parish, Franklin, W.Va., 1928-39; St. John's, Ellicot City, Md., 1939-45; Israel, Paris, Ohio, and Mapleton, Ohio, 1946-50; St. Luke, Baltimore, Md., 1950-53; St. Luke, Taylorsville and Mt. Pisgah, Hickory, 1954-67.
Date of Death: May 10, 1968.

LEAS, STANLEY JAY

Date/Place of Birth: December 15, 1946; Reading, Pa.
Parents: Harold W. Leas and Lois J. (Shontz) Leas.
Spouse/Marriage Date: Nancy M. (Craft) Leas; January 19, 1974 in Inverness, Fla.
Children: Jessica Orene, Erica Ayn.
Education: Drexel Institute of Technology; Drexel University; Lutheran Theological Southern Seminary, M.Div. 1993.
Ordination: May 9, 1993 by North Carolina Synod.
Calls: Good Shepherd, Raleigh, 1993-95; St. Paul, Hickory, 1995-1999; St. Martin, Albemarle, 1999-.
Other: Lay Conference Convener, Coastal Conference, Southeast Texas-Southern Louisiana Synod.

LEAVITT, CHARLES EARL, SR.

Date/Place of Birth: October 3, 1931; Juliaetta, Idaho.
Parents: Charles O. Finney, Stepfather, and Zella Mae (McVicker) Finney.
Spouse/Marriage Date: Eva Rebecca (Priddy) Leavitt; March 12, 1966 in Harleyville, S.C.
Children: Charles Earl, Jr., Karen Gwennette, Craig Alan, Dana Rebecca.
Education: Baptist College, Charleston, S.C., B.A. 1971; Lutheran Theological Southern Seminary, M.Div. 1975.
Ordination: June 1, 1975 by South Carolina Synod.

Calls: Christ, Cullman, Ala., 1975-82; Bethel, Lincolnton, 1982-97; retired, 1997 to Lincolnton, N.C.

Other: Stewardship Committee, North Carolina Synod, 1984; Chair, Stewardship Committee, Southeastern Synod, 1981-82; Program Co-ordinator, Southeastern Synod, 1981-82; Evangelical Outreach Committee, Southeastern Synod, 1980, 1982; President, Cullman Area Cerebral Palsy.

LEAZER, CARL WAYNE

Date/Place of Birth: January 3, 1932; Salisbury, N.C.

Parents: Carl Edgar Leazer and Edna (Cauble) Leazer.

Spouse/Marriage Date: Beverly (Janes) Leazer; November 18, 1972 in Richmond Hill, N.Y.

Children: Kristin Beverly, Sonia Marta.

Education: Murray State College, B.M.E. 1954; Eastman School of Music, M.M. 1956; Lutheran Theological Southern Seminary, M.Div. 1961; Kirchenmusikschule, Hannover, Germany, 1968-69.

Ordination: June 11, 1961 by North Carolina Synod.

Calls: Assistant Pastor and Director of Music, Holy Trinity, Hickory, 1961-63; Associate Pastor and Director of Music, St. Paul, Savannah, Ga., 1963-64; Ascension, Columbus, Ga., 1964-68; Calvary, Bronx, N.Y., 1970- 79; Prince of Peace, Brentwood, N.Y., 1979-.

Other: Composer of anthem, published by Concordia Publishing House; listed in *Who's Who in the South and Southwest*. Commission on Worship for Lutheran Church in America, 1964-73; Director of A Capella Choir, Lutheran Theological Southern Seminary, 1960-61; Worship Committee, North Carolina Synod, Southeastern Synod and Metro New York Synod; numerous vocal recitals benefitting various causes; Christmas anthem published by Concordia Publication House. Life Member of Phi Mu Alpha Sinfonia professional music fraternity.

LECKY, HUGH FRANKLIN, JR.

Date/Place of Birth: November 3, 1931; Newark, Ohio.

Parents: Hugh Franklin Lecky, Sr. and Hazel Marie (Barrett) Lecky.

Spouse/Marriage Date: Janet Lee (Storms) Lecky; June 21, 1952 in Shaker Heights, Ohio.

Children: Richard Louis, Carol JoAnne Thompson, Harold Franklin, Jeffrey Hugh.

Education: Baldwin Wallace, A.B. 1953; Hamma Divinity, M.Div. 1956; Miami, Ohio, M.Ed. 1957; Duke University, Th.M. 1969, Ph.D. 1970; Boston University, M.Ed. 1975; Armed Forces Staff College, 1979.

Ordination: May 20, 1956 by Ohio Synod.

Calls: St. John, Findlay, Ohio, 1956-57; Lutheran Student Foundation Campus Ministry, Faith, Oxford, and St. Matthew, Darrtown, Ohio, 1957-60; U.S. Navy Chaplaincy, 1960-85; Messiah Lutheran, Burlington, 1985- 91; Interim Pastor, Macedonia, Burlington, 1992-93; Interim Pastor, St. John, Asheboro, 1993-94. Retired 1992 in Durham, N.C.

Other: Author: *Homiletic Resources*, 1983; *Family Therapy*, 1970; *Management of Ministry*, 1975. Director, U.S. Navy Chaplain Resource Board, 1981-84.

LEFSTEAD, WALDEMAR HIRAM

Date/Place of Birth: September 9, 1903; Thorsby, Ala.
Parents: Ole Andreas Lefstead and Johanna (Paulsen) Lefstead, who immigrated from Norway.
Spouse/Marriage Date: Mary (Mellon) Lefstead; November 14, 1929 in Lexington, N.C.
Child: Paul Mellon.
Education: Birmingham-Southern College, A.B. 1923; Lutheran Theological Southern Seminary, B.D. 1927; University of South Carolina, M.A. 1927; Newberry College, D.D. 1956.
Ordination: 1927 by North Carolina Synod.
Calls: St. Andrew, Andrews, 1927-29; Bethel-St. Paul, Rowan County, 1929-30; St. Luke, Summerville, S.C., 1931-50; St. Paul, Mobile, Ala., 1950-61; Faith, Birmingham, Ala., 1961-62; Assistant to President, Southeast Synod, Atlanta, Ga., 1963-69. Retired to Atlanta, Ga., 1969.
Other: Secretary, Board, Newberry College, 1953-62.
Date of Death: July 14, 1983.

LEINS, CURTIS EDWARD

Date/Place of Birth: November 27, 1952; Washington, D.C.
Parents: J. Edward Leins, Jr. and Helen Louise (Young) Leins.
Spouse/Marriage Date: Deborah Ann (Kelley) Leins; September 1, 1974 in Hickory, N.C.
Children: Robert Paul-Francis, Peter Kris-Matthew, Christopher John-Kelley.
Education: Lenoir-Rhyne, A.B. Philosophy and Sociology, 1974; South Carolina Baptist Hospital, Clinical Pastoral Education, 1976; Lutheran Theological Southern Seminary, M.Div. 1978; Duke University Divinity School, Th.M. Church History, 1984; Temple University, Candidate for Ph.D. in Church History.
Ordination: June 11, 1978 by North Carolina Synod.
Calls: St. Luke, Lexington, 1978-80; St. James, Fayetteville, 1980-81; Good Shepherd, Goldsboro, 1981-84; Zion, Wilmington, Del., 1984-92. Vice Pastor at various congregations. Resigned October 1992 in Wilmington, Del.
Other: *Who's Who in American Colleges and Universities*; North Carolina Synod Educational Ministry Committee, 1982-84; Educational Ministry Resource Team Coordinator and Administrative Consultant for Eastern and Coastal North Carolina, 1979-84; L.E.A.D. Congregational Consultant, 1980-82; Pastor/Advisor for District Youth Ministry Cabinet, 1981-82; Youth Convention Pastor, North Carolina Synod, 1979; Goldsboro Protestant School Vice Chair and Protestant School Personnel Committee Chair, 1981-83; CROP Walk of Goldsboro, Public Relations Committee, 1982; Contact Telephone Ministry Phone worker and instructor; Contact Pastor to Lutheran Military Personnel, Seymour Johnson Air Force Base, 1981-84; active in various chorus groups and dramatic productions.

LENTZ, CALEB

Date/Place of Birth: April 12, 1825; Rowan County, N.C. A son of Organ Church.
Parent: Henry Lentz.
Spouse: Sarah (Dreher) Lentz of South Carolina.
License/Ordination: Licensed 1856 and ordained 1859 by North Carolina Synod.

Calls: Beth Eden, Newton 1859 in list of pastors referred to as "Prof. Lentz;" New Jerusalem, Davie County, 1863.
Other: Directed funds appeal for Western Carolina Male Academy (later North Carolina College), Mt. Pleasant 1858 and was a professor there.
Date of Death/Burial Location: September 30, 1863; Davie County, N.C.

LENTZ, JOHN

Other: The only data with reference to him is found on pages 333 and 334 in the *History of the Lutheran Church in North Carolina,* (1803-1953), as follows: "St. Paul Church is located in Rowan County, five miles south of Salisbury just off the old Concord Road. The Church was organized with seventeen members on March 30, 1830 by Rev. John Lentz, as a part of a union church where different denominations worshiped at different times." Served the church from 1830 to 1834. Name does not appear in list of licensed and ordained ministers found in the above-quoted history.

LEONARD, HENRY BELK

Date/Place of Birth: February 18, 1920; Hickory, N.C.
Parents: Vernon O. Leonard and Augusta (Kyaw) Leonard.
Spouse/Marriage Date: Elizabeth Smith (Bearden) Leonard; May 19, 1943 in Columbia, S.C.
Children: Linda Ann Swartzendruber, Cynthia Elizabeth.
Education: Lenoir-Rhyne, A.B. 1940; Lutheran Theological Southern Seminary, B.D. 1943.
Ordination: July 11, 1943 by North Carolina Synod.
Calls: (Watauga Parish), Holy Trinity-Mt. Zion-Mt. Pleasant-Old Mt. Pleasant, Watauga County, 1943-44; Friendship-Shiloh-St. John, Alexander County, and developed Reformation, Taylorsville, 1944-46; St. John, Louisville, Miss., 1946-50; Kimberling, Wythe County, Va., 1950-57; Rockingham, 1957-60; Morning Star-Prince of Peace, Orkney Springs, Va., 1960-67.
Other: President, Mississippi Synod, 1948-50.
Date of Death/Burial Location: August 19, 1967; Grace Lutheran Church Cemetery, Newton, N.C.

LERCH, MALCOM ANDREW

Date/Place of Birth: April 14, 1938; Buffalo, N.Y.
Parents: George Andrew Lerch and Serena Louise (Brown) Lerch.
Spouse/Marriage Date: Edith Kathryn (Putman) Lerch, June 17, 1961 in Middletown, Conn.
Child: Mary Edith.
Education: Syracuse University, A.B. 1960; Philadelphia Seminary, M.Div. 1964.
Ordination: August 23, 1964 by New York Synod.
Calls: Assistant Pastor, Christ, Nassau, N.Y., 1964-68; St. Andrew, Yorktown Heights, N.Y., 1968-77; Stephen City Parish, Frederick, Va., 1977-85; St. Andrew, Andrews, 1985-96; St. James, Newton, 1996-
Other: Campus Ministry Management Group, Virginia Synod, 1978-85; Youth Ministry Committee, 1968- 70; Secretary, Mountain Conference, North Carolina Synod, 1995-96;

President, Secretary, Cherokee County Ministerial Association; part-time Campus Pastoral Co-ordinator, Lord Fairfax Community College, Middletown, Va., 1979-82, 1984-85; part-time Adjunct Faculty, Tri-County Community College, Murphy, English, Religion, Guided Studies, 1988-96.

LESHER, ROBERT ROYAL, JR.

Date/Place of Birth: June 24, 1948; Des Moines, Iowa.
Parents: Robert Royal Lesher, Sr. and Ann (Winter) Lesher.
First Spouse/Marriage Date: Marie Agnes (Zeisig) Lesher; August 14, 1970 in Houston, Texas.
Children of First Marriage: Erica Michelle, Erin Marie.
Second Spouse: Susan Beth Lesher.
Education: Carthage, B.A. History, 1970; Lutheran Theological Southern Seminary, M.Div. 1976; Chicago Seminary, D.Min. 1992.
Ordination: August 15, 1976 by North Carolina Synod.
Calls: Daniel's, Lincolnton, 1976-78; Christ Hospital, Oak Lawn, Ill., 1980-81; Tabor, Rockford, Ill., 1981- 84; Mt. Zion, Oak Lawn, Ill., 1984-88; Our Lord, Chicago, Ill., 1989-93; Edison Park Home, LSSI, Park Ridge, Ill., 1993-.
Other: Evangelism Committee, 1987-93, Chair, 1991-93; Uproot and Build Anti-Racism Trainer, 1991-; Dean, Central Conference, 1991-93; Chair, Oak Lawn Clergy Association, 1986-87; Board, Southwest Suburban Fair Housing, 1987, 1988.

LESLIE, ELMER WALSTINE

Date/Place of Birth: November 21, 1871; Bedford County, Va.
Parents: David A. Leslie and Elizabeth (Lemon) Leslie.
Spouse/Marriage Date: Araminta Antoinette (Obenshain) Leslie; December 24, 1895 in Botetourt County, Va.
Foster Child: Mrs. Mary O. Nichols.
Education: Roanoke College, A.B. 1905, A.M.; privately instructed in theology.
Ordination: 1898 by Southwest Virginia Synod.
Calls: Wythe County, Va., 1898. In North Carolina: St. Matthew-St. Peter, Rowan County, 1898-1902; supplied Luther's, Rowan County, 1901-02; again in Virginia: Pembroke, 1902-10, Harrisonburg, 1921-22, and near Salem, 1924-26; in South Carolina: Grace-Mt. Tabor, Prosperity, 1911-21; Trinity, Elloree-Pine Grove, Lone Star-St. Mark, Fort Motte, 1916-21; Graniteville-Aiken Parish 1926-41 then St. James, Graniteville only, 1942-43. Retired 1943 at Graniteville, S.C.
Other: Published *History of The Lutheran Church in Botetourt County, Virginia,* (1910). Superintendent, Children's Home of the South, Salem, Va., 1922-24.
Date of Death/Burial Location: September 27, 1950; Graniteville, S.C.

LETTS, HAROLD CHESTER

Date/Place of Birth: July 28, 1911; Seward, Schoharie County, N.Y.
Parents: William M. Letts and DeEtte (Lawyer) Letts.
Spouse/Marriage Date: Isobel Louise (Smith) Letts; 1937 in Springfield, Mass.
Children: Cynthia Jean Adcock, Laurence Alan, David William.

Education: Colgate University, B.A. 1933; Union Seminary, N.Y., D.Min. 1937; Mt. Airy Seminary, S.T.M. 1942; Wagner College, D.D. 1955.
Ordination: October 3, 1937 by New York Synod.
Calls: Calvary, Jersey City, N.J., 1937-43; St. Peter, Jamaica, N.Y., 1943-47. Retired December 31, 1976. Transferred to North Carolina Synod June 28, 1978 and to Northwest-Washington Synod in 1990.
Other: Board of Social Missions, Secretary for Social Action, 1947-57; Associate Director, Division of Christian Life and Work, National Council of Churches of Christ in the United States of America, 1957-67; Director, Long Range Planning, National Council of Churches, 1967-70; Board of Social Ministry, 1970-72; Committee for Social Concerns, 1972-76. Board, Lutheridge.
Date of Death: August 20, 1992.

LINDLER, COLIE EDGAR
Date/Place of Birth: May 18, 1926; Chapin, S.C.
Parents: Virgil O'Neal Lindler and Anna (Miller) Lindler.
Spouse/Marriage Date: Mary Elaine (Stroke) Lindler; July 31, 1953 in Parr, S.C.
Child: Luther Edgar.
Education: Newberry College, A.B. 1950; Lutheran Theological Southern Seminary, B.D. 1953.
Ordination: June 7, 1953 by South Carolina Synod.
Calls: In South Carolina: St. James, Lexington County, 1953-55; Silverstreet, Silverstreet, 1955-58; in North Carolina: St. Martin, Maiden, 1958-64; Mt. Moriah, Rowan County, 1964-74; Friendship, Taylorsville, 1974-89. Retired 1989.
Other: Worship and Music Committee, 1964-72. Published articles in *South Carolina Farm Paper.* Writer of sermons for the *Rowan Times-Herald, China Grove.*

LINDLER, DAVID FRANKLIN
Date/Place of Birth: January 3, 1958; Cabarrus County, N.C.
Parents: The Reverend John David Lindler and Gwendolyn (Chapman) Lindler.
Spouse/Marriage Date: Barbara Jean (Herbst) Lindler; September 1, 1984 in Newton, N.C.
Children: Sarah Elizabeth, Michael Andrew.
Education: Lenoir-Rhyne, B.A. 1980; Lutheran Theological Southern Seminary, M.Div. 1984.
Ordination: May 25, 1984 by North Carolina Synod.
Calls: Beth Eden, Newton, 1984-87; St. Andrew, Mt. Airy, 1987-92.
Other: Removed from roster March 5, 1997.

LINDLER, HORACE J. C.
Date/Place of Birth: September 15, 1909; Chapin, S.C.
Parents: Charlie F. Lindler and Bessie Ida (Shealy) Lindler.
Spouse/Marriage Date: Mary Eve (Shealy) Lindler; October 20, 1934 in Chapin, S.C.
Children: James Monroe, Beverly Lavenia Ludwig, Mary Judith Key.

Education: Newberry College, A.B. Philosophy 1943; Lutheran Theological Southern Seminary, B.D. 1945, also graduate work, 1956-63.
Ordination: September 28, 1945 by Georgia-Alabama Synod.
Calls: In Georgia: Ebenezer Parish, Effingham County (Jerusalem and St. John, Rincon, Ga. and Grace, Stillwell, Ga.), 1945-48, and 1960-63; in South Carolina: Kendall Parish, Newberry County, 1948-54; Zion, Lexington County, 1954-60; Christ's, Columbia, 1963-65; in North Carolina: St. Matthew, Rowan County, 1965-66; again in South Carolina: St. Barnabas, Charleston, S.C., 1967-69; Silverstreet, Silverstreet, S.C., 1969-74. Retired October 1974. Supplied various congregations after retirement.
Date of Death/Burial Location: January 21, 1985; Mt. Horeb Lutheran Church Cemetery, Chapin, S.C.

LINDLER, JOHN DAVID

Date/Place of Birth: December 17, 1924; Little Mountain, S.C.
Parents: Daniel Evans Lindler and Carrie Lucile (Eargle) Lindler.
Spouse/Marriage Date: Gwendolyn (Chapman) Lindler; June 11, 1956 in Peak, S.C.
Children: The Reverend David Franklin, John Paul Chapman, Ruth Ann.
Education: Newberry College, A.B. 1949; Lutheran Theological Southern Seminary, B.D. 1952; graduate study, 1955-60, courses for S.T.M. completed.
Ordination: June 1, 1952 by South Carolina Synod.
Calls: Grace, Hendersonville, 1952-53; Mt. Gilead, Cabarrus County, 1954-63; St. James, Newton, Catawba County, 1963-73; Shiloh, Lewisville, 1973-76.
Other: Evangelism Committee, 1969-72. Active in scouting program.
Date of Death/Burial Location: March 16, 1976; Peak Cemetery, Peak, S.C.

LINEBERGER, CORLEY ROOSEVELT

Date/Place of Birth: January 4, 1919; Detroit, Mich.
Parents: The Reverend Fred Louis Lineberger and Mava (Corley) Lineberger. Father was pastor of The Lutheran Church-Missouri Synod Church in Wilson; two brothers, Henry F. and Robert B., also became ministers of North Carolina Synod.
First Spouse/Marriage Date: Giuseppina Degli (Abbati) Lineberger; August 1, 1945 in Rome, Italy, while in United States Army service in Italy during World War II.
Child of First Marriage: Lynne Ambler Stewart.
Second Spouse/Marriage Date: Rebecca (Stewart) Lineberger; August 19, 1957 in Wilson, N.C.
Children of Second Marriage: LuAnne Wixon, Corley Van, Frederick Wike.
Education: Concordia College, Conover, and Atlantic Christian College, A.B. 1949; Lutheran Theological Southern Seminary, B.D. 1951, also graduate work; South Carolina State Hospital, Clinical Pastoral Education 1968.
Ordination: July 8, 1951 by North Carolina Synod.
Calls: St. Martin, Maiden, 1951-54; Grace, Hendersonville, 1954-57; Kure Memorial, Kure Beach, 1957-60. Immanuel (Virginia Synod), Bluefield, W.Va., 1960-67; Prince of Peace, Salisbury, 1967-71; St. Mark, Kansas City, Mo., 1971-73; First, Lafayette, La., 1973-82; Ebenezer, Catawba, 1988-92. Retired July 1, 1982 in Lafayette, La., but moved to Catawba, N.C. Vice pastor at various congregations.

Other: Contact pastor to Women's Federal Prison, Alderson, W.Va., 1960-67. Contact pastor for Bluefield State College, Bluefield, W.Va., Concord College, Athens, W.Va., and Bluefield State College, Bluefield, W.Va., 1960-67. Clinical Pastoral Education at South Carolina State Hospital, Columbia, S.C., 1967-68. Contact person for University of Southwestern Louisiana, Lafayette, La., 1973-87.

LINEBERGER, ERNEST ROBINSON, JR.

Date/Place of Birth: April 4, 1926; Asheville, N.C.
Parents: The Reverend Ernest Robinson Lineberger, Sr. and Irene Victoria (Buckman) Lineberger.
Spouse/Marriage Date: Sarah S. (Ridenhour) Lineberger, daughter of the Reverend M. L. Ridenhour; August 17, 1948 in Kannapolis, N.C.
Children: Mary Christian (died at birth), Vicki Irene, Katherine Ruth, Sara Lynn, Ernest Robinson, III.
Education: Lenoir-Rhyne, A.B. 1947; Lutheran Theological Southern Seminary, B.D. 1950; graduate study, University of South Carolina, Harvard University.
Ordination: 1950 by North Carolina Synod.
Calls: Trinity, Rocky Mount, 1950-51. Chaplain, Commander, United States Navy, since 1951. Transferred to Southwest Pacific Synod, 1963. Retired, Merced, Calif.

LINEBERGER, ERNEST ROBINSON, SR.

Date/Place of Birth: January 12, 1892; Gaston County, N.C.
Parents: John Sylvanus Lineberger and Laura C. (Wallace) Lineberger.
Spouse/Marriage Date: Irene Victoria (Buckman) Lineberger; May 23, 1925 in Newport News, Va.
Children: The Reverend Ernest Robinson, Jr., Ruth May.
Education: Lenoir-Rhyne, A.B. 1922; Lutheran Theological Southern Seminary, B.D. 1925; University of South Carolina, M.A. 1925.
Ordination: 1925 by North Carolina Synod.
Calls: St. Mark, Asheville, 1925-36, also serving the mission of Andrews for one year; St. James-Ebenezer, Catawba County, 1936-47; Christ, East Spencer, 1948-51; Mission Developer/Pastor, St. Mark, Lumberton, 1951-62. Vice Pastor for various congregations. Retired 1962 at Lumberton, N.C.
Other: Field Secretary for synodical Luther League, 1921-22. President, Western Conference, 1939-40; Board, Lenoir-Rhyne, 1953-56; Ministerial Education Committee; Examining Committee; Stewardship Committee.
Date of Death/Burial Location: October 3, 1967; Peninsula Memorial Park, Newport News, Va.

LINEBERGER, EVERETTE LEWIS

Date/Place of Birth: February 16, 1929; Dallas, Gaston County, N.C.
Parents: Graham Lewis Lineberger and Sarah Ann (Lewis) Lineberger.
Spouse/Marriage Date: Elizabeth Ann (Dry) Lineberger; August 16, 1953 in Albemarle, N.C.
Children: Deborah Ann Galli, Stephen Lewis, John David.

Education: Lenoir-Rhyne, A.B. 1951; Lutheran Theological Southern Seminary, B.D. 1954; S.T.M. 1962.
Ordination: June 20, 1954 by North Carolina Synod.
Calls: Grace, Rock Hill, S.C., 1954-58; Redeemer, Charleston, S.C., 1958-63; St. John, Spartanburg, S.C., 1963-90.
Other: Member, Synodical Executive Council; voting member to several Lutheran Church in America Conventions. Retired December 1990. Former chair of five synodical committees.

LINEBERGER, HENRY ANDREW

Date/Place of Birth: April 17, 1945; Monroe, N.C.
Parents: The Reverend Henry F. Lineberger and Phyllis (Guren) Lineberger.
Spouse/Marriage Date: Jacqueline Florence Lineberger; November 29, 1970 at Augusta, Ga.
Children: Andrew Glenn, Matthew Joseph, Aaron Michael.
Education: Atlantic Christian College, B.S. Art 1967; Lutheran Theological Southern Seminary, B.D. 1971.
Ordination: July 6, 1971 by North Carolina Synod.
Calls: Assistant Pastor, Holy Trinity, Hickory, 1971-73; Messiah, Burlington, 1973-82. Transferred to Florida Synod, 1982.
Other: Removed from roll August 24, 1989 in Sarasota, Fla.

LINEBERGER, HENRY FORD

Date/Place of Birth: December 10, 1916; Detroit, Mich.
Parents: The Reverend Fred L. Lineberger and Mava (Corley) Lineberger. Two younger brothers are the Reverends Corley R. and Robert B. Lineberger. Father was pastor of The Lutheran Church-Missouri Synod Church in Wilson.
Spouse/Marriage Date: Phyllis (Guren) Lineberger of Minnesota; September 17, 1943 in Wilson, N.C.
Children: The Reverend Henry Andrew, Gerald Wayne, Philip Stephen, David Wade.
Education: Concordia College, Conover; Concordia College, (Ind.), and Concordia College, (Ill.); also University of South Carolina, but received no degree; Lutheran Theological Southern Seminary, one year, 1944-45.
Ordination: 1945 by North Carolina Synod.
Calls: St. Luke-Morning Star, Monroe, 1945-49; Prosperity, Cabarrus County, 1949-52; Ebenezer, Rowan County, 1952-53; Lebanon-Silver Valley, Davidson County, 1955-57.
Other: Removed from the clerical roll due to disability.

LINEBERGER, ROBERT BROWN

Date/Place of Birth: July 18, 1930; Columbia, S.C.
Parents: The Reverend Frederick Louis Lineberger and Nettie Mava (Corley) Lineberger. Father was pastor of The Lutheran Church-Missouri Synod Church at Wilson, N.C. Two older brothers Henry F. and Corley R., were North Carolina Synod pastors.
Spouse/Marriage Date: Catherine L. (Steele) Lineberger; August 17, 1952 in Gibsonville, N.C.
Children: Lela Catherine Groene, Sara Elizabeth Mendes, Peter Robert.

Education: Lenoir-Rhyne, A.B. 1952; Lutheran Theological Southern Seminary, B.D. 1955; also graduate study.

Ordination: June 1955 by North Carolina Synod.

Calls: Morning Star, Mecklenburg County, 1955-58; Assistant Pastor, St. John, Salisbury, 1958-62; St. Paul, Hampton, Va., 1962-77; Our Saviour, Richmond, Va., 1977-86; Immanuel, Bluefield, W.Va., 1986-89; Christ the King, Columbia, S.C., 1989-95. Retired July 31, 1995 in Columbia, S.C.

Other: Contact Pastor for Ft. Jackson, S.C.; Langley Air Force Base, Va.; Ft. Monroe, Va.; Kecoughtan Veterans Administration Hospital, Hampton, Va.; Hampton Institute, Hampton, Va. In Virginia Synod: Member, Executive Committee; Chair, Home Missions, Evangelism and Stewardship Committees; Chair, Personnel Committee of Outdoor Ministries.

LINGLE, DEAN ROLLIN

Date/Place of Birth: November 14, 1948; Rowan County, N.C.

Parents: Carr H. Lingle and Helen (William) Lingle. Brother of The Reverend Jeffery Lane Lingle.

Spouse/Marriage Date: Matilda E. (Doyle) Lingle; July 6, 1968 in Salisbury, N.C.

Children: Philip Charles, Carrie Rosetta, Jenny Marguerite.

Education: Lenoir-Rhyne, B.A. 1971; Lutheran Theological Southern Seminary, M.Div. 1975.

Ordination: June 8, 1975 by North Carolina Synod.

Calls: Evangelical Lutheran, Worthington, Pa., 1975-80; Holy Trinity, Raleigh, 1980-84.

Other: American Missions Committee of the Western Pennsylvania, West Virginia Synod.

Date of Death/Burial Location: September 16, 1984; Faith Lutheran Church Cemetery, Faith, N.C.

LINGLE, FLOYD BOST

Date/Place of Birth: August 13, 1890; Rowan County, N.C.

Parents: Littleton William Lingle and Margaret Ellen Elizabeth (Bost) Lingle.

Spouse/Marriage Date: Annie Elizabeth (Cooper) Lingle, sister of the Reverends E. C., G. H., and L. G. Cooper; September 15, 1921 in China Grove, N.C.

Child: Jane Elizabeth.

Education: Mount Pleasant Collegiate Institute, Newberry College, A.B. 1915; Lutheran Theological Southern Seminary, 1918.

Ordination: 1918 by North Carolina Synod.

Calls: Calvary-Christ, Spencer, 1918-31; St. Paul, Strasburg, Va., 1931-49.

Date of Death/Burial Location: July 23, 1949; Chestnut Hill Cemetery, Salisbury, N.C.

LINGLE, GEORGE HENRY LEWIS

Date/Place of Birth: June 4, 1878; Rowan County, N.C.
Parents: L. R. Lingle and Polly (Peeler) Lingle.
Spouse/Marriage Date: Hama (Kime) Lingle; May 1905 in Liberty, N.C.
Children: W. Rudolph, Elizabeth (married the Reverend M. R. Farris), the Reverend George W., John M.
Education: North Carolina College, A.B. 1901; Lutheran Theological Southern Seminary, 1904.
Ordination: 1904 by North Carolina Synod.
Calls: Frieden's-Sharon, Gibsonville, 1904-06; St. Luke, Pilgrim, Davidson County, 1906-10; Reformation, Davie County, 1907-09; St. Stephen-Mt. Olive, Cabarrus County, 1910-14; Haven, Salisbury, 1914-22; St. Mark's, Mooresville, 1922-27; Zion-Bethlehem-New Jerusalem, Catawba County, 1927-31; St. Paul-Bethel, Rowan County, 1931-39; Bethel only, 1939-50. Supplied churches in Rowan and other counties 1950-54 for 3- to 6-month periods.
Other: Retired 1950 at Salisbury, N.C. Secretary, North Carolina Synod, 1915-21; Joint Committee for Merger of North Carolina and Tennessee Synods, and Committee on Arrangements for Merger Meeting, 1921; Board, North Carolina College; Board, Mount Pleasant Collegiate Institute; Secretary, Board, Lenoir-Rhyne.
Date of Death/Burial Location: January 11, 1962; Christiana Church, Granite Quarry, N.C.

LINGLE, GEORGE WOODLEY, SR.

Date/Place of Birth: February 15, 1915; Rowan County, N.C.
Parents: The Reverend G. H. L. Lingle and C. Hama (Kime) Lingle.
Spouse/Marriage Date: Charlotte B. (Bame) Lingle, daughter of the Reverend P. J. Bame; May 23, 1939 in Newport News, Va.
Children: George Woodley, Jr., The Reverend John Paul, William Rudolph, Charlotte Virginia, Angela Vallie, Robert Louis.
Education: Lenoir-Rhyne, A.B. 1936; Lutheran Theological Southern Seminary, B.D. 1939.
Ordination: 1939 by North Carolina Synod.
Calls: St. James, Fayetteville, 1939-45; Holy Trinity, Gastonia, 1945-64; Vice Pastor at various congregations in North Carolina Synod; St. Mark, Jacksonville, Fla., 1964-69; Mt. Zion-St. Luke, Oglethorpe, Ga., 1969-76.
Other: In North Carolina Synod: Executive Committee, 1953-58; Board, North Carolina Lutheran Homes, 1960-63; Board, Lenoir-Rhyne, 1962-64; Church House Building Committee; and Little Joint Commission on Lutheran Unity, 1962-63; Chaplain, Constituting Convention, North Carolina Synod of Lutheran Church in America, 1962; Dean, Southwestern District, 1962-64.
Date of Death/Burial Location: May 3, 1976; Oakwood Cemetery, Gastonia, N.C.

LINGLE, JAMES LEON (CHIP), JR.

Date/Place of Birth: April 22, 1954; Salisbury, N.C.
Parents: James Leon Lingle, Sr. and Izetta (Holler) Lingle.
Spouse/Marriage Date: Katherine Ruth (McCombs) Lingle; June 13, 1976 in West Columbia, S.C.

Children: James Leon, III, Robert Benjamin.
Education: North Carolina State University, B.A. Psychology 1976; Lutheran Theological Southern Seminary, M.Div. 1980.
Ordination: May 25, 1980 by North Carolina Synod.
Calls: Daniel's, Lincolnton, 1980-82; Kimball Memorial, Kannapolis, 1982-85; Transferred to Martin Luther, Charleston, S.C., 1985; Faith, Savannah, Ga., 1998.
Other: North Carolina Synod: Historical Works Committee, 1981-84; Board, Lutheran Theological Southern Seminary, 1981-85; Task Force for the Formation of Lutheran Youth of North Carolina, 1984-85; Synod Youth Convo Pastor, 1984-85.

LINGLE, JEFFREY LANE

Date/Place of Birth: June 21, 1953; Salisbury, N.C. Brother of the Reverend Dean Rollin Lingle.
Parents: Carr H. Lingle and Helen (William) Lingle.
Spouse/Marriage Date: Sally (Darsey) Lingle; August 6, 1977.
Children: Darsey Ann, Margaret McCall.
Education: Lenoir-Rhyne, A.B. Sociology 1975; Lutheran Theological Southern Seminary, M.Div. 1979.
Ordination: June 10, 1979 by North Carolina Synod.
Calls: St. Andrew, Hickory, 1979-81; Developer/Pastor, Advent, LaGrange, Ga., 1982-89; Developer/Pastor, Epiphany, Rock Hill, S.C., 1989-.
Other: Board of Directors, Lutheran Ministries of Georgia, 1987; South Carolina Synod Council, 1993-.

LINGLE, JOHN PAUL

Date/Place of Birth: December 30, 1942; Fayetteville, N.C.
Parents: The Reverend George Woodley Lingle, Sr. and Charlotte (Bame) Lingle, daughter of the Reverend P. J. Bame.
Spouse/Marriage Date: Alice Marie (Templeton) Lingle; February 6, 1965 in Jacksonville, Fla.
Child: Paul Edward.
Education: Lenoir-Rhyne, A.B. English 1964; Lutheran Theological Southern Seminary, M.Div. 1968.
Ordination: June 9, 1968 by North Carolina Synod.
Calls: Ascension, Shelby, 1968-73; Incarnation, Charlotte, 1973-76; St. Mark, Asheville, 1976-82; Mt. Zion- St. Luke, Oglethorpe, Ga., 1982-88; Daniel's, Lincolnton, 1988-94; St. Paul, Dallas, 1994-98; St. Martin, Maiden, 1998-.
Other: Evangelism Committee; Parish Life and Ministry Development guide and area leader of youth ministry events; Youth Adult Leadership Labs; Lutheridge summer staff for six years.

LINK, ADAM S.

Place of Birth: Ohio.
License: Licensed 1837 by Tennessee Synod.
Calls: None in North Carolina. Preached in what is now Pendleton County, W.Va. about two years.

Other: Name removed from roll in 1839 when affiliated with Joint Synod of Ohio. Moved to Ohio and preached for some twenty years. In 1860 was located in Hummelstown, Dauphin County, Pa.

Date of Death/Burial Location: March 30, 1862; Ohio.

LINK, JOHN WILLIAM, SR.

Date/Place of Birth: February 10, 1882; Darke, W.Va.

Parents: William Harmon Link and Martha Rebecca (Daniels) Link.

Spouse/Marriage Date: Helen Elizabeth Link; June 10, 1913 in Uvilla, W.Va.

Children: John William, Jr., Elizabeth Melvin, Arthur Stanley, Elinor Louise.

Education: Shepherd College, 1904; Roanoke College, A.B. 1907; Philadelphia Seminary, 1910.

Ordination: 1910 by Southwest Virginia Synod.

Calls: In Tennessee (Redeemer, Bristol; Buehler's, Sullivan County) and Virginia(St. Peter, Toms Brook), 1910-18; Camp Pastor, Camp Sevier, S.C., and Camp Lee, Va., 1918-19; churches again in Virginia (New Market Parish; Ascension, Danville), 1919-27; in North Carolina: Holy Trinity, Mt. Pleasant, 1927-47; Mt. Gilead, Cabarrus County, 1933-47.

Other: Retired June 30, 1947 at Shepherdstown, W.Va.

Date of Death/Burial Location: 1975; Elmwood Cemetery, Shepherdstown, W.Va.

LINK, WILLIAM HOMER

Date/Place of Birth: October 25, 1935; Volusia County, Fla.

Parents: The Reverend James Lester Link and Martha Constance (Coiner) Link.

Spouse/Marriage Date: Kathryn Ann (Cooper) Link, daughter of The Reverend Dr. L. Grady Cooper; September 14, 1962 in Columbia, S.C.

Children: Susan Christine Lowman, Mary Virginia Getz, David Jonathan.

Education: Lenoir-Rhyne, B.A. 1958; Lutheran Theological Southern Seminary, M.Div. 1961.

Ordination: June 25, 1961 by Virginia Synod.

Calls: St. Matthew/Faith, Konnarock/Whitetop, Va., 1961-64; Bachman Chapel, Prosperity, S.C., 1964-73; Sharon, Gibsonville, 1973-77; Luther's, Richfield, 1977-89. Transferred to South Carolina Synod, Pine Grove, Lone Star, 1989-94; St. Matthew, Pomaria, S.C., 1994-.

LINN, CHARLES ADOLPHUS

Date/Place of Birth: October 27, 1890; Mt. Pleasant, N.C.

Parents: The Reverend Josephus Adolphus Linn and Mary Cordelia (Miller) Linn. Brothers in the Lutheran ministry are the Reverends John K. and J. Arthur Linn.

Spouse/Marriage Date: Jennie Holmes (Snider) Linn; June 12, 1919 in Salisbury, N.C.

Child: Jennie Holmes.

Education: Mount Pleasant Collegiate Institute, Roanoke College, A.B. 1915; Philadelphia Seminary, B.D. 1918; Hartford Seminary, S.T.M., 1924, and Ph.D., 1931; Newberry College, 1942, D.D.

Ordination: 1918 by Ministerium of Pennsylvania.

Calls: Holy Trinity, Wildwood, N.J., 1918-20; Redeemer, Macon, Ga., 1920-22; Holy Trinity-Mt. Gilead, Mt. Pleasant, 1922-23; St. John's, Cherryville, 1924-27; Ascension, Savannah, Ga., 1927-47.

Other: President of Georgia-Alabama Synod, several terms; and first full-time President, 1947-50; Chair, United Lutheran Church in America, Committee on Church Papers, 1935-50; Vice Chair, Board, Lutheridge, 1947-50. Researched Saltzburger Settlement on Savannah River in Georgia. Author of *The History of the German Friendly Society of Savannah, Georgia,* (1837-1937).

Date of Death/Burial Location: September 11, 1950 at Atlanta, Ga.; Salisbury, N.C.

LINN, HUBERT CONRAD

Date/Place of Birth: May 19, 1924; Tokyo, Japan.

Parents: The Reverend Justin Arthur Linn and Mabel Kinder (DeMent) Linn. A grandson of the Reverend Josephus Adolphus Linn.

Spouse/Marriage Date: Phyllis Irene (Boddiger) Linn; October 27, 1951 in Polo, Ill.

Children: James Andrew, Deborah Irene Sekelewski, Martin Arthur, John Charles.

Education: Lenoir-Rhyne, A.B. 1948; Lutheran Theological Southern Seminary, M.Div. 1951.

Ordination: July 8, 1951 by North Carolina Synod.

Calls: (Watauga Parish), Holy Trinity-Mt. Pleasant-Mt. Zion-Old Mt. Pleasant, Watauga County, 1951-53; Advent, Spindale, 1953-56; St. John-Beth Eden, Louisville, Miss., 1956-59; Assistant Pastor, Messiah, Philadelphia, Pa., 1960-64; Living Word, Roslyn, Pa., 1964-88. Retired June 30, 1988 in Roslyn, Pa.

Other: Southeast Pennsylvania Synod: World Missions and Ecumenism Committees, Alcohol and other Drug Dependencies Committee.   President, Eastern Montgomery County Ministerial Association; President, Organizer of Fellowship of Roslyn Area Churches; COMAC, a community organization of Abington Township, Pa., which worked with local drug concerns; various scouting programs including Camping and Activities Chair in Spindale, N.C.; Convener of IPEC Cluster Group of clergy, the first cluster group of its kind organized in the Lutheran Church in America; Attended Lutheran Church in America Global Mission Events seven times. Secretary of Mississippi Synod, 1957-59; Chaplain, Lutheran Retirement Community, Peak Run, Philadelphia, Pa., 1991-93.

LINN, JOHN KENNETH, SR.

Date/Place of Birth: April 29, 1889; Mt. Pleasant, N.C.

Parents: The Reverend Joseph Adolphus Linn and Mary Cordelia (Miller) Linn, sister of the Reverend C. B. Miller. Older brother of the Reverends C. A. and J. Arthur Linn.

Spouse: Lucy Laurie (Ligon) Linn, daughter of the Reverend Richard C. Ligon (Presbyterian); June 30, 1915 in Pomaria, S.C.

Children: Mary Louise (died in third year), John Kenneth, Jr., Ph.D., Marion Ligon Horine.

Education: North Carolina College, one year, Mount Pleasant Collegiate Institute, three months, Roanoke College, A.B. 1911; Philadelphia Seminary, 1915. Graduate study: Japanese Language School in Tokyo, 1915-17; Kennedy School of Missions (Hartford Seminary Foundation), 1919; Yale Divinity School, 1926-27.

Ordination: May 30, 1915 by Ministerium of Pennsylvania.

Calls: General Council missionary in Japan, 1915-18; United Lutheran Church in America missionary in Japan, 1918-40: Tokyo, Toyohashi, and Saga, 1915-22; Professor of New and Old Testament, Japan Lutheran Seminary, Kumamoto, later Tokyo, 1922-40; resident supply, Trinity, Greenville, S.C., 1941-42; Professor of New and Old Testament, Lutheran Theological Southern Seminary, 1942-52; Grace, Liberty, 1952-56. Retired 1956 at Hyattsville, Md.; later moved to Columbia, S.C.

Other: Secretary, Japan Lutheran Mission, and English Secretary, Japan Lutheran Church; Acting President, Japan Lutheran Seminary, 1927-28, 1935-36; Secretary, Faculty of Lutheran Theological Southern Seminary, 1943-52.

Date of Death/Burial Location: June 19, 1976; Greenlawn Memorial Park, Columbia, S.C.

LINN, JOSEPH ALEXANDER

Date/Place of Birth: May 26, 1820; Rowan County, N.C. Referred to as J. A. Linn, Sr., in *History of the Lutheran Church in North Carolina*, (1803-1953).

Parents: Samuel G. Linn and Elizabeth Linn.

First Spouse: Miss Shuler from South Carolina.

Child of First Marriage: John.

Second Spouse: Margaret Ann (Bernhardt) Linn in Cabarrus County.

Child of Second Marriage: The Reverend Josephus Adolphus Linn (in *History of the Lutheran Church in North Carolina*, (1803-1953), J. A. Linn, Jr.). The Reverends J. K., C. A., and J. Arthur Linn are grandsons, and the Reverend H. C. Linn is a great-grandson.

Education: Lexington (South Carolina) Classical and Theological Institute (forerunner of Newberry College and Lutheran Theological Southern Seminary), and Gettysburg Seminary.

License/Ordination: Licensed 1844 and ordained 1845 by North Carolina Synod.

Calls: In Rowan County: St. Matthew, 1844-64; St. Paul, 1845-55; Luther's, 1846-52, 1856-63; St. Peter, 1853-55; in Cabarrus County: St. Stephen, 1856-63; in Iredell County: St. Paul, supply, 1860.

Other: North Carolina Synod President, three one-year terms, 1851-58; and four terms as Secretary, 1847-62. In his President's 1852 report urged establishing of a High School of collegiate character, resulting in founding of Western Carolina Male Academy in 1855 at Mt. Pleasant, which became North Carolina College in 1859; Committee on Church Relations, 1861.

Date of Death/Burial Location: While returning from a church service March 13, 1864 on horseback was thrown and suffered skull fracture, which resulted in his death three days later on March 16, 1864; Organ Church, Rowan County, N.C.

LINN, JOSEPHUS ADOLPHUS (J. A. Linn, Jr. in *History of the Lutheran Church in North Carolina,* (1803-1953).
Date/Place of Birth: January 22, 1853; Rowan County, N.C.
Parents: The Reverend Joseph Alexander Linn and Margaret Ann (Bernhardt) Linn.
First Spouse: Alice F. (Nunamaker) Linn.
Children of First Marriage: Myron Oscar, Marie Lucille, Margaret Alice, Joseph (died in third month; mother died thirteen days after his birth, 1887).
Second Spouse: Mary Cordelia (Miller) Linn, sister of the Reverend C. B. Miller; July 1888 in Rowan County, North Carolina.
Children of Second Marriage: The Reverends John Kenneth, Charles Adolphus, and Justin Arthur, and Hubert Miller, who also planned to be a minister, but drowned 1922 just after graduating from Gettysburg College. A grandson is the Reverend H. C. Linn.
Education: North Carolina College, A.B. 1874; Philadelphia Seminary, 1877.
Ordination: 1877 by North Carolina Synod.
Calls: St. Matthew-St. Peter-Luther's, Rowan County, 1877-80; Beth Eden, Newton, 1881-83; First, Albemarle, 1887-88, Supply 1890; Trinity, Versailles, Ohio, 1893-98; Holy Trinity, Mt. Pleasant-New Bethel-Mt. Zion, Stanly County, 1898-1902; St. James, Holston Synod, Greeneville, Tenn., 1903-05; St. Peter, Rowan County, 1907-09; organized St. James, Rockwell, 1907-11; Christiana-Wittenberg, Granite Quarry, 1909-11; Bethlehem, Pomaria, S.C., 1912-14. After retiring, served Luther's, Rowan County-New Bethel-Mt. Zion, Stanly County, 1914-15.
Other: President, North Carolina Synod, 1884-85; Secretary, 1880-81, 1883-84; Principal, Mont Amoena Seminary, 1885-91.
Date of Death/Burial Location: March 25, 1923; Mt. Pleasant, N.C.

LINN, JUSTIN ARTHUR
Date/Place of Birth: October 27, 1893; Versailles, Ohio.
Parents: The Reverend Josephus Adolphus Linn and Mary Cordelia (Miller) Linn, sister of the Reverend C. B. Miller. Younger brother of the Reverends J. K. and C. A. Linn.
Spouse/Marriage Date: Mabel Kinder (DeMent) Linn; August 16, 1922 in Rockwell, N.C.
Child: The Reverend Hubert Conrad.
Education: Roanoke College, A.B. 1917; Philadelphia Seminary, B.D. 1922.
Ordination: June 7, 1922 by Ministerium of Pennsylvania.
Calls: United Lutheran Church in America missionary in Japan (Tokyo and Moji), 1922-33; St. Luke, Bear Poplar, 1935-38; Grace, Hendersonville, 1938-45; Mt. Olive, Hickory, 1946-52; Lakeland, Fla., 1952-56, and Oglethorpe, Ga., 1956-58. Retired 1959 at Hickory. Vice Pastor at various congregations.
Other: Served in U.S. Marine Corps in World War I, and was wounded. Transferred back to North Carolina Synod, 1960. Treasurer, Japan Lutheran Mission and Japan Lutheran Church, 1931-33. Board, Lutheran Theological Southern Seminary, 1947-52; Secretary, North Carolina Synod's Christian Higher Education Year Appeal, and Hickory District Chair, 1950-51; Chaplain, North Carolina Lutheran Homes, Hickory. Delegate to United Lutheran Church in America Convention, 1950; President, Western Conference, 1948-51.

Date of Death/Burial Location: November 10, 1985; Holy Trinity Lutheran Cemetery in Mt. Pleasant, N.C.

LIPPARD, ALBERT WIKE

Date/Place of Birth: April 11, 1898; Statesville, N.C.
Parents: Albert Henry Lippard and Maggie (Kimball) Lippard. An older brother was the Reverend Carl O. Lippard.
Spouse/Marriage Date: Dorothea (Quante) Lippard; 1935 in Savannah, Ga.
Children: Margaret Helen Gentry, Albert Henry.
Education: Lenoir-Rhyne, A.B. 1926, D.D. 1961; Lutheran Theological Southern Seminary, B.D. 1929.
Ordination: 1929 by North Carolina Synod.
Calls: Grace, Hendersonville, 1929-37; St. Martin, Maiden-Luther's Chapel-Salem, Lincoln County, 1938-42; Calvary, Morganton, 1942-49; Chaplain, Broughton State Hospital, Morganton, 1949-64; regular supply, St. Matthew, Granite Falls; retired 1964 at Hickory. In retirement, served two years on the staff of Holy Trinity, Hickory.
Other: First full-time chaplain in North Carolina State mental institutions; Board, Sipe's Orchard Home for Boys; Board, Ministry to Aging and Helpless, which proposed the establishing of North Carolina Lutheran Homes and a member of the North Carolina Lutheran Homes Board, 1961-63; President, Western Conference, 1942-44.
Date of Death/Burial Location: May 10, 1979; Catawba Memorial Park, Hickory, N.C.

LIPPARD, CARL ORESTES

Date/Place of Birth: September 14, 1888; Iredell County, N.C.
Parents: Albert Henry Lippard and Maggie (Kimball) Lippard. A younger brother is the Reverend A. Wike Lippard.
Spouse/Marriage Date: Lucy Emma (Yoder) Lippard; June 30, 1920 in Catawba County, N.C.
Education: Lenoir-Rhyne, A.B. 1915; Lutheran Theological Southern Seminary, 1918, B.D. 1929.
Ordination: 1918 by Southwest Virginia Synod.
Calls: Virginia Heights (renamed Christ), Roanoke, Va., 1918-20; Crouse Parish: St. Paul-Bethel-St. Mark-Bethphage, Lincoln and Gaston Counties, 1920-24; Trinity-Concordia, Landis, 1924-30; Philadelphia-St. John-St. Matthew, Granite Falls, 1930-32; Lutheran Chapel, Gastonia, 1932-33.
Date of Death/Burial Location: September 11, 1933; Oakwood Cemetery, Hickory, N.C.

LIPPARD, CEPHAS KELLY

Date/Place of Birth: April 9, 1871; Statesville, N.C.
Parents: Henry Lippard and Susanna (Bowman) Lippard.
Spouse/Marriage Date: Mary Emma (Gerberding) Lippard, daughter of the Reverend G. H. Gerberding, and sister of the Reverends R. H. and W. P. Gerberding; September 15, 1900 in Chicago, Ill.
Children: Faith (married the Reverend Walter Krumwiede), Lois, Violet (married the Reverend C. Donald Heft), Elizabeth.
Education: Lenoir-Rhyne, A.B. 1895, D.D. 1908; Chicago Seminary, 1899, B.D. 1900.
Ordination: 1900 by Tennessee Synod.
Calls: Missionary in Japan of United Synod South, 1900-18, then of United Lutheran Church in America, 1918-30, 1932-39, serving in Omuta, Moji, Kobe, and Osaka. Pastor of Good Shepherd, Philadelphia, Pa., 1930-32. Retired 1941 at Philadelphia, Pa., later at Oaklyn, N.J.
Date of Death/Burial Location: July 20, 1964; Philadelphia, Pa.

LIPPARD, LUTHER AARON

Date/Place of Birth: May 9, 1924; Rowan County, N.C.
Parents: Luther Alexander Lippard and Maggie Jane (Park) Lippard.
Spouse: Doris Elizabeth (Miller) Lippard, daughter of the Reverend Paul L. Miller; February 16, 1950 in Hickory, N.C.
Children: The Reverend Michael Aaron, Janice Elizabeth.
Education: Catawba College, A.B. 1948; Lutheran Theological Southern Seminary, B.D. *cum laude* 1956.
Ordination: June 10, 1956 by North Carolina Synod.
Calls: Shiloh, Lewisville, 1956-58; St. Timothy, Havelock, 1958-60; Cedar Grove, Lincoln County, 1960-71; Union, Salisbury, 1971-85; Prince of Peace, Salisbury, 1985-86; Vice pastor at various congregations.
Other: Served in United States Army Air Corps, 1943-45, fifteen months in South Pacific as engineer gunner, 42 combat missions; was discharged as Technical Sergeant. Between college and seminary, 1948-53, worked in textile chemistry field as laboratory technician, color matcher, and dye house shift foreman, in Charlotte, Elberton, Ga., and Pilot Mountain. Professional Preparation and Service to Professional Leaders Committees; Board, North Carolina Lutheran Homes, Inc.; Dean, Central District.
Date of Death/Burial Location: February 15, 1986; Union Cemetery, Salisbury, N.C.

LIPPARD, MICHAEL AARON

Date/Place of Birth: January 27, 1951 in Elberton, Ga.
Parents: The Reverend Luther Aaron Lippard and Doris (Miller) Lippard.
Spouse/Marriage Date: Jane Herman (Rhodes) Lippard; May 29, 1976 in Arden, N.C.
Child: Emily Erin.
Education: Davidson College, Hollins College, Catawba College, B.A. 1974; Lutheran Theological Southern Seminary, M.Div. 1978.
Ordination: 1978 by North Carolina Synod.

Calls: St. James, Chilhowie, Va., 1978-82; Pastor-Developer Christiansburg, Va., 1982-83; Our Saviour, Christiansburg, Va., 1984-. Residing in Tupelo, Mich. in 1998.
Other: In Virginia Synod: Campus Ministry Managing Group, 1979-80, 1985-; Home Mission Managing Group, 1980-82; Social Action Managing Group, 1983-85; Peacemaking Task Force, 1983-85.

LISCHER, RICHARD ALAN

Date/Place of Birth: November 12, 1943; St. Louis, Mo.
Parents: Herbert F. Lischer and Edna E. (Alsbrook) Lischer.
Spouse/Marriage Date: Tracy (Kenyon) Lischer; June 4, 1966 in St. Louis, Mo.
Children: Sarah Kenyon, Richard Adam.
Education: Concordia College (Ind.), B.A. 1965; Concordia Seminary (Mo.), M.Div. 1969; Washington University, M.A. 1967; King's College, University of London, Ph.D. 1971; Counseling Supervision, Norfolk, Va., 1976-77.
Ordination: January 2, 1972 by The Lutheran Church-Missouri Synod.
Calls: Emmaus, Dorsey, Ill., 1972-74; Prince of Peace, Virginia Beach, Va., 1974-79.
Other: Faculty, Duke Divinity School, 1979-. Publications: *Speaking of Jesus*, 1982; *Marx and Teilhard*, 1979; *A Theology of Preaching*, 1981; numerous published articles, sermons, and reviews. *Who's Who in Religion*, 1977. Member of American Academy of Religion and Academy of Homiletics; Advisory Committee on Doctrine and Conciliation, The Lutheran Church-Missouri Synod, 1974-76; Planning participant, Lutheran World Ministries Marxism Consultation, 1979; Board, CONTACT, Virginia Beach, Va., 1978-79. Joined the North Carolina Synod in 1982.

LITTLE, MARCUS LAFAYETTE

Date/Place of Birth: October 17, 1848; Catawba County, N.C.
Parents: Peter Little and Harriet Louisa (Smith) Little.
Spouse/Marriage Date: Candace Mary Almetta (Herman) Little; May 4, 1871 in Newton, N.C.
Children: The Reverend Carroll Herman (father of the Reverends Arthur B. and J. Frederick Little), Etta Blanche, Clarence Smith, the Reverend William Herbert, Mabel Pearl and Grace Pearl (twins), Alla Pearl, Marcus Leopold, Arthur Bikle, Jennie Lee, Hermine.
Education: Catawba College, A.B. 1867, Honorary A.M. about 1886; studied theology under the Reverend J. M. Smith, 1869-72.
License/Ordination: Licensed 1873 and ordained 1876 by Tennessee Synod.
Calls: Catawba County: Sardis, 1872-82; Lincoln County: Trinity, Vale, (supply also, 1873-76); Bethphage, 1881-91; Daniel's, 1882-83; and Emmanuel, Lincolnton, 1889; Mt. Pleasant, Watauga County, supply, 1882; Gaston County: St. Mark, Crouse, 1874-88; first pastor of both St. John's, Cherryville, and Antioch, bringing the latter into Tennessee Synod, 1881-91; Lutheran Chapel, Gastonia, 1883-91; organized College Chapel Church, Dallas, later named Holy Communion, 1885, and supplied with the Reverend L. A. Bikle, pastor at Kings Mountain, 1886-91.
Other: Head and teacher: Pleasant Hill Seminary and Hickory Tavern High School, Catawba County, 1867-73; Ridge Academy and Daniel's Academy, Lincoln County, 1873-82; and Gaston High School, Dallas, 1882-84; founder and president, Gaston College,

Dallas, 1885-89, which then became Gaston Female College. Pioneered in education for women in Piedmont North Carolina. Assisted in project of founding Lenoir-Rhyne, at Hickory out of Concordia College, Conover; Secretary, Tennessee Synod, 1879; Treasurer, 1882.
Date of Death/Burial Location: February 16, 1891; Oakwood Cemetery, Hickory, N.C.

LITTLE, RICHARD CLARENCE

Date/Place of Birth: July 2, 1944; Lincolnton, N.C.
Parents: C. Rhyne Little and Jane Heim (Page) Little.
Spouse/Marriage Date: Cheryl Lynn (Rudisill) Little, daughter of the Reverend Glenn H. Rudisill; July 27, 1968 in Dumont, N.J.
Children: Shane Page, Kerri Lynn.
Education: Davidson College, B.A. History 1966; Gettysburg Seminary, M.Div. 1970.
Ordination: June 7, 1970 by North Carolina Synod.
Calls: St. David, Kannapolis, 1970-73; Prince of Peace, Greensboro, 1973-78; Administrative Assistant for Outreach Ministries, South Carolina Synod, 1978; Assistant to Bishop, 1978-82, 1982-86; Advent, Charlotte, 1986-.
Other: Voting member to Lutheran Church in America Assembly, 1982, 1984, 1986; Voting member to Evangelical Lutheran Church in America Constituting Assembly, November 1987; Voting member to Evangelical Lutheran Church in America Assembly, Orlando, 1991; Executive Committee, North Carolina Council of Churches, 1989-92.

LITTLE, THOMAS SHELTON, SR.

Date/Place of Birth: June 14, 1936; Hickory, N.C.
Parents: Wilbert Harold Little and Nell L. (Wilkinson) Little. Grandson of the Reverend W. H. Little and great-grandson of the Reverend M. L. Little.
Spouse/Marriage Date: Elizabeth Annette (Howell) Little; June 26, 1960 in East Spencer, N.C.
Children: Thomas Shelton, Jr., and Marian Elizabeth (Mari-Beth).
Education: Lenoir-Rhyne, A.B. 1959; Lutheran Theological Southern Seminary, B.D. 1963. Clinical Pastoral Education in Spartanburg, S.C.
Ordination: June 9, 1963 by North Carolina Synod.
Calls: Good Shepherd, Morristown, Tenn., 1963-64; St. Luke, Thunderbolt, Ga., 1964-66; Good Shepherd, Florence, Ala., 1966-67; Psychiatric Chaplain, Highland Rim School for Girls, Tullahoma, Tenn., 1977-83; Full time Supply/Vice Pastor at Christ-Crowell, Shelbyville, Tenn., 1983-84; Staff Chaplain, Lutheran Chaplaincy Service of Greater Cleveland, Ohio; Chaplain, Cuyahoga County Juvenile Court Detention Center, 1984-87; Social Ministry Committee, Southeastern Synod, 1977-83, Chair, 1981.
Other: Demitted ministry to teach school 1967-71 and to serve as Supervisor of Emergency Medical Training, North Carolina State Board of Health, 1973-76; Instructor, Emergency Medical Training, Spartanburg Technical College.
Date of Death/Burial Location: April 14, 1992; Cleveland, Ohio.

LITTLE, WILLIAM HERBERT

Date/Place of Birth: March 15, 1876; Lincoln County, N.C.
Parents: The Reverend Marcus Lafayette Little and Candace A. (Herman) Little.
First Spouse/Marriage Date: Mary Elizabeth (Bessie) (Rudisill) Little; June 3, 1903 in Lincolnton, N.C.
Children of First Marriage: Wilbert Harold, Evangeline Rudisill, Marcus Lafayette, Lillian Augusta, Franklin Herman.
Second Spouse/Marriage Date: Mary Elvira (Sheely) Little; April 24, 1926 in Columbia, S.C.
Children of Second Marriage: Mary Sheely, William Frederick, Arthur Herbert, Carroll Curtis.
Third Spouse/Marriage Date: Carolyn Rhodes (Deal) Little; 1950 in Dallas, N.C.
Education: Gaston College, Lenoir-Rhyne, A.B. *magna cum laude* 1896; honorary A.M. 1900; Philadelphia Seminary, 1900; graduate study, Dallhousie University, Halifax, Nova Scotia, 1907-08; University of Wisconsin, summer 1916.
Ordination: 1900 by Tennessee Synod.
Calls: St. Martin-Mt. Gilead, Cabarrus County; St. Martin, Stanly County for four months.
Other: From 1901 to 1918, except for one year leave, served in several capacities at Lenoir-Rhyne: Professor (German, French, History, Bible); Secretary of Faculty, Treasurer, Business Manager, Field Representative, 1901-15; Dean, 1908-18; Acting President, 1915-17. Superintendent, Bethany Orphan's Home of Nova Scotia Synod, United Lutheran Church in America, Bridgewater, Nova Scotia, 1907-08. After 1918 managing executive of savings and loan association in Hickory; also active in supplying pulpits, teaching Bible classes, and writing poetry. Author of *A Verse a Day*, devotional poems on Scripture verses; and *God's Plan for Man*, Christian doctrines in verse.
Date of Death/Burial Location: September 24, 1969; Oakwood Cemetery, Hickory, N.C.

LLEWELLYN, MARVIN LANNESS, JR.

Date/Place of Birth: February 3, 1938; Gadsden, Etowah County, Ala.
Parents: Dr. Marvin Lanness Llewellyn, Sr. and Jane (Stallworth) Llewellyn.
Spouse/Marriage Date: Dorothy (Beeland) Llewellyn; December 28, 1958 in Greenville, Ala.
Children: Mary George Bake, Jennifer Clarletta, Susan Preege.
Education: Marion Institute, United States Naval Academy, University of Alabama, B.S. Aerospace Engineering 1962; Chandler School of Theology, Lutheran Theological Southern Seminary, M.Div. 1980.
Ordination: June 1, 1980 by Southeastern Synod.
Calls: Ebenezer, China Grove, 1980-84; Jerusalem, Rincon, Ga., 1984-88; Prince of Peace, Columbus, Mo., 1988-94. Retired to Kennesaw, Ga.

LOADHOLDT, DONALD BRANTLEY

Date/Place of Birth: June 1, 1931; Fairfax, S.C.
Parents: Albert M. Loadholdt and Lillian (Miller) Loadholdt. An older brother is the Reverend Earl H. Loadholdt.
Spouse/Marriage Date: Pauline Elizabeth (Betty) (Brunson) Loadholdt; June 14, 1957 in Summerton, S.C.
Children: Donna E., William A., Catherine Ann, Mary Beth.
Education: Newberry College, B.A. 1954; Lutheran Theological Southern Seminary, B.D. 1957.
Ordination: November 1957 by South Carolina Synod.
Calls: Holly Grove, Davidson County, 1957-61; Kure Memorial, Kure Beach, 1961-62; St. John, Pomaria, S.C., 1962-67; Immanuel, Rockwell, 1967-74; St. James, Newton, 1974-94. Vice Pastor at various congregations. Retired October 1, 1994 to Summerton, S.C.
Other: Lutheran World Relief, 1972.

LOADHOLDT, EARL H.

Date/Place of Birth: July 13, 1928; Fairfax, S.C.
Parents: Albert M. Loadholdt and Lillian (Miller) Loadholdt. A younger brother is the Reverend Donald B. Loadholdt.
Spouse/Marriage Date: Marcia (Marth) Loadholdt; August 15, 1950 in Atlanta, Ga.
Children: Paul Stephen, Jan Elise, The Reverend Gary Alan.
Education: Newberry College, A.B. 1949; Lutheran Theological Southern Seminary, B.D. 1952, also graduate study.
Ordination: 1952 by South Carolina Synod.
Calls: In South Carolina (St. John, Johnston), 1952-60; Grace, Hendersonville, 1960-62; Our Saviour, West Columbia, S.C., 1962-69; Advent, Charleston Heights, S.C., 1969.
Other: President, Luther League of South Carolina, 1951-52.
Date of Death: March 23, 1981.

LOCKLEY, JAMES DANIEL

Date/Place of Birth: March 11, 1951; New Castle, Pa.
Parents: J. E. Lockley and Elizabeth (Thompson) Lockley.
Spouse/Marriage Date: Mary Margaret (Maurie) (Wigman) Lockley; January 17, 1971 in Wilmington, Pa.
Child: Elizabeth Margaret.
Education: Slippery Rock University, B.S. Education 1974; Gettysburg Seminary, M.Div. 1988.
Ordination: May 31, 1988 by North Carolina Synod.
Calls: Alamance, Alamance, 1988-; Vice Pastor at various congregations.
Other: Chair, Ecumenical Affairs Committee; Spiritual Director, Eastern North Carolina Lutheran Via De Cristo.

LOHR, DAVID LINDSEY

Date/Place of Birth: February 21, 1941; Lincolnton, N.C.
Parents: George Edmund Lohr and Gladys (Lackey) Lohr; grandson of The Reverend Dr. Luther Lindsay Lohr.

Spouse/Marriage Date: Betty (Pugh) Lohr; June 26, 1966 in Asheboro, N.C.
Children: Cynthia Jeanette, Mary Christine.
Education: Lenoir-Rhyne, B.A. 1964; Chicago Seminary, M.Div. 1967.
Ordination: June 4, 1967 by North Carolina Synod.
Calls: Wittenberg, Granite Quarry, 1967-72; Mt. Pleasant, Saluda, S.C., 1973-78; Ascension, Shelby, 1978- 82; Advent, Spindale, 1982-87; Ascension, Shelby, 1987-.

LOHR, LUTHER LINDSAY

Date/Place of Birth: October 1, 1860; Lincoln County, N.C.
Parents: Joshua Lohr and Emeline (Edmunds) Lohr.
First Spouse/Marriage Date: Jessie Cora (Zinn) Lohr; July 15, 1891 in Gettysburg, Pa.
Children of First Marriage: Minnie Marie, Lawrence Luther, Elida Emeline, George Edmund.
Second Spouse/Marriage Date: Mrs. Mary Jane (Schlegel) Lohr; December 28, 1907 in Williamsport, Pa.
Third Spouse/Marriage Date: Lula (Fritz) Lohr in Hickory, NC.
Education: Gaston College, A.B. 1887; Gettysburg Seminary, 1894; Lenoir-Rhyne, D.D. 1914.
Ordination: 1891 by Tennessee Synod.
Calls: In North Carolina, 1890-93: St. Luke-Bethphage in Lincoln County; St. John's, Cherryville; Lutheran Chapel, Gastonia; St. Mark-Antioch in Gaston County; in Pennsylvania, 1893-1908: Manheim, Mahanoy City, and Williamsport; Daniel's, Lincoln County; Grace, Catawba County, 1908-18, 1919-22; Organ, Rowan County, 1918-19; Trinity-Cedar Grove, Vale-Sardis, Catawba County, 1927-30; in Virginia: Rader, Timberville, 1923-25; in South Carolina: Fairfax, 1925-27, and 1930-31; retired 1931 at Lincolnton.
Other: Instructor 1887-91 and co-principal 1891 Gaston College; Secretary, Susquehanna Synod, three years; Board, Lenoir-Rhyne, 10 years; Secretary, Board of Education, United Synod South, four years; President, Tennessee Synod, 1912-14.
Date of Death/Burial Location: August 24, 1937; Daniel's Church, Lincoln County, N.C.

LONDON, GLENN LEMUEL, JR.

Date/Place of Birth: November 12, 1946; Hamlet, N.C.
Parents: Glenn Lemuel London, Sr. and Mildred (Brice) London.
Spouse/Marriage Date: Eugenia Anne (McDonald) London; July 26, 1970.
Children: Jonathan Scott, Brice McDonald.
Education: Lenoir-Rhyne, A.B. English 1969; Lutheran Theological Southern Seminary, M.Div. 1973.
Ordination: June 6, 1973 by North Carolina Synod.
Calls: St. John, Wytheville, Va., 1973-75; St. Michael, Blacksburg, Va., 1976-85; Grace, Waynesboro, Va., 1985-89; Redeemer, Bristol, Va., 1989-.
Other: Virginia Synod Executive Board; Intern Supervisor; Lutheran Family Services of Virginia, Inc.; Board, Children's Home of the South.

LONG, ERNEST EDWARD
Date/Place of Birth: May 28, 1932; Catawba County, N.C.
Parents: Albert E. Long and Jeanette (Wilson) Long.
Spouse/Marriage Date: Jewel Drucilla (Deal) Long; October 28, 1951 in Newton, N.C.
Children: Gary Shannon, Derek Keith.
Education: Lenoir-Rhyne, A.B. 1959, D.D. 1979; Lutheran Theological Southern Seminary, B.D. 1962, graduate study.
Ordination: June 17, 1962 by North Carolina Synod.
Calls: Mt. Moriah, Rowan County, 1962-64; Board of World Missions, Lutheran Church in America, to overseas mission service in Liberia, West Africa, 1964-71; Nativity, Arden, 1971-73; St. John, Salisbury, 1973- 81; St. John, Hollywood, Fla., 1981-87; Developer/Pastor, Living Springs, Columbia, S.C., 1987-95. Retired July 1, 1995.
Other: United States Navy, 1952-56; Board, North Carolina Lutheran Homes, 1978-80. Evangelism Committee, 1971-72; World Missions Committee, 1971-81.

LONG, GEORGE EDWARD
Date/Place of Birth: October 24, 1872; Newberry County, S.C.
Parents: George Adam Long and Emmaline (Fulmer) Long. Grandfather of the Reverend Ernest Edward Long.
Spouse/Marriage Date: Alice Catherine (Yount) Long; December 27, 1891 in Conover, N.C.
Children: Robert Gehardt, Stella Lois, George Everett, John Vernon, Walter Eugene, Charles Winfred, Lena Evelyn, Albert Emil, Marian Catherine.
Education: Newberry College, Concordia College (N.C.), and graduated in the first class of Lenoir-Rhyne College in 1891.
Ordination: Ordained 1893 in Emmanuel Church, New Market, Va. by Tennessee Synod.
Calls: Friendship-Salem-St. Paul, Taylorsville; name was removed from the clerical roll of Tennessee Synod after uniting with The Lutheran Church-Missouri Synod in 1897; served St. Stephen, Augustana and Christ Church, Hickory; Bethel and Emmanuel, Catawba County; Mt. Olive, Hickory.
Other: County Superintendent of School, Catawba County, 1907-25.
Date of Death/Burial Location: January 10, 1936; Conover, N.C.

LONG, IRVING ERNEST
Date/Place of Birth: June 19, 1882; Prosperity, S.C.
Parents: Luther I. Long and Eva M. (McCullough) Long.
Spouse/Marriage Date: Erline Charlotte (Weinheimer) Long; October 19, 1910 in Charleston, S.C.
Children: Azile Elizabeth, Russell Dalton, Charles Harold.
Education: Newberry College, A.B. 1907, D.D. 1930; Lutheran Theological Southern Seminary, 1910.
Ordination: 1910 by South Carolina Synod.
Calls: St. Mark's, Mooresville; St. Luke, Bear Poplar, 1911-16; Augsburg, Winston-Salem, 1916-20; St. Johannes, Charleston, S.C., 1920-57; Pastor Emeritus, 1957-58; retired 1957 at Charleston, S.C.

Other: Board, Mount Pleasant Collegiate Institute, 1914-18; Board, Children's Home of the South, Salem, Va., 1930-36; North Carolina Synod delegate to merger (1918) Convention, United Lutheran Church in America.
Date of Death/Burial Location: September 11, 1958; Charleston, S.C.

LONG, JOHN JACOB
Date/Place of Birth: November 5, 1871; Newberry County, S.C.
Parents: Luther M. Long and Ann (Schumpert) Long.
First Spouse: Nannie (Livingston) Long in Newberry County, S.C.
Children of First Marriage: Olin Bearden, the Reverend John Virgil.
Second Spouse: Bessie M. (Blair) Long in Silverstreet, S.C.
Children of Second Marriage: Ann Margaret, Sarah Mildred.
Education: Newberry College, A.B. 1895, D.D., 1922; Lutheran Theological Southern Seminary, 1898.
Ordination: 1898 by South Carolina Synod.
Calls: In South Carolina (Mayer Memorial, Newberry; Mt. Olivet, Prosperity), 1898-1910, (Holy Trinity, Little Mountain; Macedonia, Prosperity; Trinity, Mt. Pleasant; Saluda, Bethel, White Rock), 1912-42; St. John, Cabarrus County, 1910-12.
Other: President, Summerland College, 1928-30.
Date of Death/Burial Location: July 14, 1942; Rosemont Cemetery, Newberry, S.C.

LONG, TERRELL GLENN, JR.
Date/Place of Birth: December 10, 1950; Gastonia, N.C.
Parents: Terrell Glenn Long, Sr. and Mary Sue (Rutledge) Long.
Spouse/Marriage Date: Myra Louise (Rogers) Long; December 30, 1978.
Children: Leah Marie, Miriam.
Education: Lenoir-Rhyne, A. B. Sociology 1973; Lutheran Theological Southern Seminary, M.Div. 1977.
Ordination: June 12, 1977 by North Carolina Synod.
Calls: New Covenant, Archdale, 1977-89; Messiah, Salisbury, 1989-96; Philadelphia, Granite Falls, 1996-. Vice Pastor at various congregations.
Other: Stewardship Committee; American Missions Committee; conducted elections for two years at Synod Assembly; Chair, Nominations Committee;
Lutheran World Relief Committee; Training Committee for Synod Appeals *One in Mission* and *Forward Together.*

LONGAKER, FRANK CARROLL
Date/Place of Birth: December 10, 1872; Limerick, Pa.
Parents: Abraham Haldeman Longaker and Susanna (Carroll) Longaker.
Spouse/Marriage Date: Ellen (Espenship) Longaker; May 11, 1897.
Education: Muhlenberg College, A.B. 1894, A.M. 1897; Hamma Divinity School, 1897; University of Pittsburgh, 1911-13; University of Pennsylvania, 1923; Ph.D. 1929.
Ordination: 1897 by Wittenberg Synod.

Calls: In Kentucky, Michigan, Pennsylvania, and Ohio in 1897-1915. Transferred 1916 to Tennessee Synod from Miami Synod. Supplied St. Martin, Iredell County, 1917, and Augsburg, Winston-Salem, 1924.

Transferred 1925 to Virginia Synod from United North Carolina Synod.

Other: Professor (Greek, History, Economics), Lenoir-Rhyne, 1915-25; Professor (Philosophy, Religion), Roanoke College, 1925; President, Miami Synod, 1901-03; Translator of *Loehe's Agenda* and *First Page of the Bible;* Author: *Behold, the Lamb of God, Some Counterfeit Religions, Syllabus of a Course in Psychology, A Message of the Old Testament,* and *A Psychological Study of Martin Luther.* Retired at Graterford, Pa.

Date of Death/Burial Location: April 24, 1948; Litchfield, Ill.

LORIMER, PAUL ALFRED

Date/Place of Birth: May 7, 1913; Eau Claire, Wis.

Parents: The Reverend Julius E. Lorimer and Anna V. (Erlander) Lorimer. Father, three uncles, two brothers and a son served as Lutheran ministers.

Spouse/Marriage Date: Genevieve M. (Larson) Lorimer; June 11, 1940 in Wahoo, Neb.

Children: The Reverend Steven Paul Lorimer, Faith Annette Fisher, Curtis John.

Education: Temple University, B.S. 1936; Augustana Seminary, B.D. 1940; graduate work at Boston University School of Theology.

Ordination: June 9, 1940 in Rock Island, Ill.

Calls: Augustana, Omaha, Neb., where services were conducted in Swedish; churches in Florida, Massachusetts, Connecticut, New York, Pennsylvania, Georgia, Texas. Assisted for six months at St. Luke, Charlotte. Retired in 1975. Transferred to North Carolina Synod in January 1997.

Other: Stewardship Director, New York Conference; Faculty, Lake George Leadership Institute; Chair, Vocations Committee, Metro New York Synod; President, New Haven Council of Churches; President, Long Island, N.Y., Council of Churches; President, Board, Lutheran Residences, Inc. of St. Petersburg, Fla. Publications: *Advice for Pastors Who Minister to the Aging.*

Date of Death: December 15, 1997. Memorial service held at St. Luke, Charlotte, N.C.

LORIMER, STEVEN PAUL, SR.

Date/Place of Birth: June 23, 1941; Ft. Lauderdale, Fla.

Parents: The Reverend Paul A. Lorimer and Genevieve (Larson) Lorimer.

First Spouse/Marriage Date: Sonja Kay (Dyck) Lorimer; May 28, 1962 in Lindsborg, Kan.

Children of First Marriage: Kristen Denise, Theresa Peck, Timothy.

Second Spouse/Marriage Date: Fancita (Beyer) Lorimer; January 11, 1974 in Atlanta, Ga.

Child of Second Marriage: Steven Paul, Jr.

Education: Bethany College, B.A. 1963; Augustana, Gettysburg Seminary, M.Div. 1966.

Ordination: June 2, 1966 by New York Synod.

Calls: St. Michael, High Point, 1967-71; Bethany, Miami, Fla., 1971-74; Living Word, Atlanta, Ga., 1975-81; Holy Trinity, Kingsport, Tenn., 1981-85; St. Luke's, Charlotte, 1985-; Vice Pastor at various congregations.

LOVE, CALVERT BERNARD, JR.

Date/Place of Birth: January 21, 1926; Chicago, Ill.

Parents: Mr. and Mrs. Calvert Bernard Love, Sr.

Spouse/Marriage Date: Clara May (Klug) Love; October 8, 1950.

Children: Paula Christine, Janet Katherine.

Education: Capital University, Columbus, Ohio, B.A., 1946; Evangelical Lutheran Theological Seminary, Columbus, Ohio, 1949.

Ordination: March 6, 1949 by American Lutheran Church.

Calls: Christ, Elvaton, Md., 1949-56; Old St. Paul, Newton, 1956-62.

LUCKEY, RONALD GRINNELL

Date/Place of Birth: October 3, 1947; Atlanta, Ga.

Parents: Wilbur Vernon Luckey, Sr. and Hannah Eve (Grinnell) Luckey.

Spouse/Marriage Date: Pacita Yvonne (Robinson) Luckey, daughter of The Reverend Harry H. Robinson, Jr.; August 26, 1967 in Durham, N.C.

Children: Jason Isaac, Joshua Adam, Bryna Eve, Daniel Alexander.

Education: Lenoir-Rhyne, A.B. 1969; Lutheran Theological Southern Seminary, M.Div. 1973; Lexington Seminary, D.Min. 1993; graduate work in Theology at Emory University; Graduate work in English Literature at Clemson University.

Ordination: May 27, 1973 by Southeastern Synod.

Calls: Christ's, Stanley, 1973-77; University, Lutheran Campus Center, Clemson, S.C., 1977-87; Faith, Lexington, Ky., 1987-.

Other: Publications: various sermons and articles in *Biblical Preaching Journal, Master Sermon Series,* and *The Lutheran* magazine; Retreat leader; Chaplain, South Carolina Synod Convention; Chaplain, South Carolina Synod Women's Convention.

LUDDER, CARSTEN JUDD

Date/Place of Birth: September 22, 1951; Miami, Fla.

Parents: The Reverend Carsten H. Ludder and Doris (Vezie) Ludder.

Spouse/Marriage Date: Bina (Antle) Ludder; October 9, 1977.

Child: Emily Lauren.

Education: University of Florida, Lenoir-Rhyne, B.A. 1974; Lutheran Theological Southern Seminary, M.Div. 1983.

Ordination: June 12, 1983 by Florida Synod.

Calls: Grace, Hendersonville, 1983-92; Christ the King, South Miami, Fla., 1992-. Prince of Peace, Largo, Fla., 1998.

LUDWIG, RUDOLPH FRIDOLIN

Date of Birth/Burial Location: October 29, 1911; West New York, Bergen County, N.J.

Parents: Rudolph J. Ludwig and Anna (Truempy) Ludwig.

Spouse/Marriage Date: Grace Carol (Morgan) Ludwig, daughter of the Reverend C. I. Morgan; August 30, 1939 in Leesville, S.C.

Children: Rudolf Carol, Peter Martin, Anna Wilson, Luther Paul, Margaret Rebekah.

Education: Wagner College, A.B. 1934; Philadelphia Seminary, 1937.

Ordination: July 17, 1938 by New York Synod.

Calls: Prince of Peace, Binghamton, N.Y., 1938-40; St. John, Potter, N.Y., 1940-42; Cripple Creek Parish, Crockett, Va., 1942-45; Bethel, Manassas, Va., 1945-47; Quicksburg Parish, Quicksburg, Va., 1947-48; Konnarock Parish, Konnarock, Va., 1948-51; St.

Matthew, Rowan County, 1952-53; Konnarock Parish, Konnarock, Va., 1952-56; St. Paul, Bridgeport, Conn., 1956-60; Our Saviour, Johnson City, Tenn., 1960-65; Emmanuel, Roanoke, Va., 1965-69; Corinth/St. Mark, Prosperity, S.C., 1969-76. Vice Pastor at various congregations; retired to North Carolina, 1976.

Date of Death/Burial Location: January 26, 1993; Memorial service at St. Paul, Durham, N.C.

LUMAN, RALPH IFARD

Date/Place of Birth: July 13, 1918; Akron, Ohio.
Parents: Simon Luman and Mary Jane (Jackson) Luman.
Spouse/Marriage Date: Sarah Johnson (Odom) Luman; June 28, 1948 in Oak Ridge, Tenn.
Children: Paul Martin, Mary Elisabeth.
Education: Pennsylvania State University, B.S. 1940; Lutheran Theological Southern Seminary, M.Div. 1956.
Ordination: June 10, 1956 by South Carolina Synod.
Calls: St. Stephen, Lexington, S.C., 1956-60; Good Shepherd, Lorain, Ohio, 1960-62; Holy Comforter, Charleston, S.C., 1962-65; Bethel, Miami, Fla., 1965-66; Holy Trinity, North Augusta, S.C., 1966-70; Bethany, Hickory, 1970-76; Good Shepherd, Sanford, Fla., 1976-84; St. John (part time as visitation pastor), Winter Park, Fla., 1985-90; Chaplain (part time), Florida Lutheran Retirement Center, Deland, Fla., 1990-. Retired December 31, 1984 to Deland, Fla.
Other: Cabinet, Lutheran Ministries of Florida, Central Area.

LUTZ, CY EMMET

Date/Place of Birth: July 26, 1897; Vale, Lincoln County, N.C.
Parents: Silas E. Lutz and Emma M. Lutz.
Spouse/Marriage Date: Ruth May (Karriker) Lutz; June 12, 1928 in Rowan County, N.C.
Children: William Roeford, Paul E., Ph.D., James David, Harold Wayne.
Education: Lenoir-Rhyne, A.B. 1924; Lutheran Theological Southern Seminary, 1927.
Ordination: 1927 by North Carolina Synod.
Calls: Friendship-Shiloh-St. John, Alexander County, 1927-31; Zion-Bethlehem-New Jerusalem, Catawba County, 1931-40; Grace, Rowan County, 1940-48; Concordia, Rowan County, 1948-54; Antioch-Philadelphia, Gaston County, 1955-64; Mt. Gilead, Cabarrus County, 1964-67; retired July 1967 in China Grove, N.C.
Other: Directed seven building projects in churches served.
Date of Death/Burial Location: May 28, 1968; St. Enoch Church Cemetery, Kannapolis, N.C.

LUTZ, WILLIAM ALONZO

Date/Place of Birth: June 10, 1850; Newton, N.C.
Parents: Jacob Lutz and Harriet (Mahaffey) Lutz.
First Spouse/Marriage Date: Mrs. Esther C. (Peeler) (Stafford) Lutz, who had two daughters; October 31, 1878 in Davidson County, N.C.

Second Spouse/Marriage Date: Mrs. Martha (Houseal) (Wertz) Lutz, widow of the Reverend J. Q. Wertz; September 19, 1919 in Newberry, S.C.

Education: Catawba College, A.B. 1874; Philadelphia Seminary, 1877; Gaston College, A.M. 1882.

Ordination: 1877 by North Carolina Synod.

Calls: Forsyth County Mission (Nazareth-Shiloh-Hopewell, and Bethany, Davidson County), 1877-80; St. Enoch-Trinity, Enochville, 1880-92; organized Concordia, Rowan County, 1882-83; organized Augsburg, Winston-Salem 1891 and served 1892-1900; Grace, Prosperity, S.C., 1902-05; St. John, Statesville, 1905-16; supplied Mt. Olive, Hickory, 1905; first regular pastor, Holy Trinity, Charlotte, 1916-24; St. James, Brunswick, Ga., 1924-26; retired 1926 at Charlotte, later lived at Salisbury and Lenoir.

Other: President, North Carolina Synod, 1885-86; President, North Carolina College, 1900-02.

Date of Death/Burial Location: July 12, 1941; Winston-Salem, N.C.

LYBRAND, ELI LOT

Date/Place of Birth: June 22, 1852; Lexington County, S.C.

Parents: Godfrey Lybrand and Barbara Lucinda (Kelly) Lybrand.

Spouse/Marriage Date: Charlotte Barbara (Roof) Lybrand; September 7, 1876 in Lexington County, S.C.

Children: Jesse Carroll, Barbara Magnolia, Maxcy Henkel.

Education: North Carolina College, two years. With J. A. Cromer left college to serve Tennessee Synod churches in Lexington County, S.C., on their appeal, as only one pastor was active there then. They preached and catechized in churches, and studied theology under the Reverend Daniel Efird, who supervised their work.

Ordination: 1878 by Tennessee Synod.

Calls: In South Carolina: Emmanuel-Zion-St. Peter, Lexington County, 1878-81; St. James, Summit; Cedar Grove, Leesville; St. Paul, Gilbert, 1881-95; with the Reverend J. A. Cromer organized and served St. Andrew, near Blythewood, 1878-80; organized and served Bethlehem, near Pelion, and Mt. Tabor, New Brookland (now West Columbia), and served St. Andrew again, 1880-1915; Pastor Emeritus of Mt. Tabor, 1919; retired at New Brookland, S.C., 1919.

Other: Studied and graduated in medicine; practiced among parishioners, until latter part of career, when he devoted full time to pastoral ministry. Also a school teacher. State legislator, South Carolina Legislature, one term, and member of South Carolina State Constitutional Convention, 1895.

Date of Death/Burial Location: January 23, 1922; Mt. Tabor Church Cemetery, West Columbia, S.C.

LYBRAND, RUFUS EDWARD, JR.

Date/Place of Birth: April 23, 1949; Aiken, S.C.

Parents: Rufus Edward Lybrand, Sr. and Lucy (Friar) Lybrand.

Spouse/Marriage Date: Jacquelyn (Wilson) Lybrand; June 3, 1973 in Newberry, S.C.

Children: Jennifer Mauri, Brett Edward.

Education: Newberry College, B.A. 1971; Lutheran Theological Southern Seminary, M.Div. 1975.

Ordination: June 1, 1975 by South Carolina Synod.

Calls: Trinity, Georgetown, S.C., 1975-78; Resurrection, Columbia, S.C., 1978-82; Grace, Rock Hill, S.C., 1982-88; Holy Trinity, Gastonia, 1988-.

Other: Publications: *Home Is A Four-Letter Word; Holy Communion Is;* contributing author to *Emphasis* for two years; two sermons published in *Dynamic Preaching*.

LYERLY, CALVIN C.

Place of Birth: Montgomery County, Ill.

Parents: Solomon Lyerly and Delilah (Williams) Lyerly. In a letter of a relative the name is spelled "Lyerla".

Spouse: Wife's given name was Lavica.

Children: Elmer, Effie.

License/Ordination: Licensed 1881 and ordained 1886 by Southern Illinois Synod.

Calls: Presumably in Illinois, 1881-90; transferred 1890 to North Carolina and served in North Carolina, 1890-97: New Bethel, Stanly County; Luther's, Rowan County; organized and built Mt. Zion, Richfield, 1895-97. Transferred 1897 back to Southern Illinois Synod. Served churches in Illinois and Missouri; last charge was Sargent Chapel and Sedgewickville, Sedgewickville, Mo.; retired in Texas with one of his children.

Date of Death/Burial Location: 1928; Sargent Chapel Church, Sedgewickville, Mo.

LYERLY, FRANK EDWARD

Date/Place of Birth: February 26, 1930; Salisbury, Rowan County, N.C.

Parents: Burley Franklin Lyerly and Mary Elizabeth (Trexler) Lyerly.

Spouse/Marriage Date: Barbara Alice (Brown) Lyerly; May 25, 1955 in Prosperity, S.C.

Children: Charles Franklin, Barbara Elizabeth Boyd, Richard William.

Education: Catawba College, B.A. 1952; Lutheran Theological Southern Seminary, B.D. 1955.

Ordination: June 12, 1955 by North Carolina Synod.

Calls: St. Martin, Maiden, 1955-58; Gloria Dei, Anna Maria Island, Fla., 1958-63; Mt. Pleasant, Saluda, S.C., 1963-66; Ascension, Columbia, S.C., 1966-73; St. Johannes, Charleston, S.C., 1973-74; Gloria Dei, Anna Maria Island, Fla., 1974-92; retired May 31, 1992 to Ceres, Va.

LYERLY, GARY RAY

Date/Place of Birth: June 19, 1943; Rowan County, N.C.

Parents: Carr R. Lyerly and Pearl (Holshouser) Lyerly.

Spouse/Marriage Date: Dorothea (McCarter) Lyerly; August 26, 1967 in Gastonia, N.C.

Children: Cory Ray, Carla Ruth.

Education: University of North Carolina, Lenoir-Rhyne, A.B. *cum laude* 1965; Lutheran Theological Southern Seminary, M.Div. *cum laude* 1969; Clinical Pastoral Education Residency, Spartanburg Regional Medical Center, Advanced Clinical Pastoral Education Certification, 1996; Clinical Pastor Education, Yale-New Haven Hospital, New Haven, Conn.

Ordination: June 1, 1969 by North Carolina Synod.

Calls: St. Timothy, Havelock, 1969-71; Pastor-Developer, Shepherd of the Sea, Atlantic Beach, 1969-71; St. John, Asheboro, 1971-77; Pastor-Developer, Cross and Crown, Florence, S.C., 1977-80; Our Saviour, Johnson City, Tenn., 1980-94; Good Shepherd, Virginia Beach, Va., 1994-95. Relocated to White Rock, S.C.

Other: Dean, Holston Area of Southeastern Synod, 1984-94; Chair, Stewardship Committee, 1984; Covenant Consultation, 1984, Chair, 1985. As part of North Carolina Synod: Christian Education Committee, Publications and Publicity Committee. Task forces in both North Carolina and Southeastern Synods.

LYERLY, JOHN WILF0RD

Date/Place of Birth: March 31, 1915; Granite Quarry, N.C.
Parents: John Calvin Lyerly and Mary Frances (Trexler) Lyerly.
Spouse/Marriage Date: Betty Jane (Conley) Lyerly; September 8, 1979.
Education: Lenoir-Rhyne, A.B. 1935, D.Div. 1970; Roanoke College, summer session; Lutheran Theological Southern Seminary, B.D. 1938; Union Theological Seminary, (N.Y.), The Biblical Seminary (N.Y.), (now New York Theological Seminary), and Columbia University, M.A. 1950; Clinical Pastoral Education, North Carolina Baptist Hospital and Bowman Gray School of Medicine, 1969; additional graduate studies at The Biblical Seminary, now New York Theological Seminary.

Ordination: 1938 by North Carolina Synod.

Calls: Mission Pastor, he organized Mt. Hebron, Hildebran, 1938-44, and Messiah, Salisbury, 1944-56; Mission Developer/Pastor, Christ, Winston-Salem, 1956-62; Secretary, North Carolina Synod, 1953-72 (ten years part time and ten years full time), last ten years served as Director of Public Relations, Necrologist, Archivist, Assistant in Home Missions; Pastor-Developer Christ, Elkin, 1966-67; Pastor-Developer, St. Andrew, Mt. Airy, 1968, 1972-86; Chaplain, Northern Hospital of Surry County, 1973; Good Shepherd, Galax, Va., 1992-94 (Episcopal-Lutheran Congregation). Vice Pastor at various congregations; retired March 31, 1986 to Mt. Airy, N.C.

Other: Board, Lowman Home, 1952-53; Historical Works Committee, 1963-72; One of founders of Hospice, Surry County; Delegate to United Lutheran Church in America and Lutheran Church in America conventions 1954-66 except in 1956; Protestant Hour preacher (United Lutheran Church in America series), 1954. Booklets published: *In the School of Suffering, Daily Reading and Holy Living, God's Best Answer for You*. Board, Lenoir-Rhyne, 1972-76; North Carolina Council of Churches, 1962-63; Church Vocations Committee, 1972.

LYERLY, QUINCY OSCAR

Date/Place of Birth: February 13, 1893; Rowan County, N.C.
Parents: John Albert Lyerly and Augusta Elizabeth (Wyatt) Lyerly.
First Spouse/Marriage Date: Berta Silvesta (Bradford) Lyerly; May 25, 1926 in Iredell County, N.C.
Children of First Marriage: William Voigt, James Albert, David Mark.

Second Spouse/Marriage Date: Lola Margaret (Park) Lyerly; July 5, 1958 in Rowan County, N.C.
Children of Second Marriage: Roger Franklin, Rose Elizabeth.
Education: Crescent Academy, Roanoke College, A.B. 1917; Lutheran Theological Southern Seminary, B.D. 1925; graduate study, University of South Carolina.
Ordination: 1925 by North Carolina Synod.
Calls: Mt. Hermon-Sharon, Iredell County, 1925-28; Grace-Richland, Liberty, 1928-36; one of several pastors to preach occasionally at Alamance before organization of church; Holy Trinity, Troutman, 1936-40; Coble's-Low's, Guilford County, 1940-52; Pilgrim, Davidson County, 1952-56; Mission Developer/Pastor, Prince of Peace, Rowan County, 1956-60. Vice Pastor at various congregations; retired 1961 near Salisbury.
Other: Served as infantry officer in World War I; Board, Lowman Home, 1947-49, 1951-52, 1955-59; Board, Lenoir-Rhyne, 1952-55. Delegate to United Lutheran Church Convention, 1952.
Date of Death/Burial Location: November 7, 1969; St. Peter Church Cemetery, Salisbury, N.C.

MacLAUGHLIN, CHARLES PETER

Date/Place of Birth: 1870; Allegheny County, Pa.
Parents: The Reverend Alexander MacLaughlin and Emma Sara (Fox) MacLaughlin. Father was born in County Kent, Ireland.
Spouse/Marriage Date: Annie (Phillips) MacLaughlin, born in Carmarthen, Wales; January 30, 1901 in Selinsgrove, Pa.
Children: Mary Emma, Dorothy Ruth, Charles Phillips, Alexander Henry.
Education: Susquehanna University, A.B. 1898, D.D. 1909; Gettysburg Seminary, 1901.
Ordination: 1901 by Illinois Synod.
Calls: In Illinois and Pennsylvania, 1901-10; St. James, Concord, 1910-16; organized and supervised student supply, Calvary, Concord, 1913-14; supplied Mt. Hermon, Cabarrus County, 1914-16; First, Pittsburgh, Pa., 1916-21; Redeemer, Atlanta, Ga., 1924-28.
Other: Compiler of a Good Friday (three hour) Service long used by St. James, Concord.
Date of Death/Burial Location: November 13, 1928; Atlanta, Ga.

MacMURPHY, CHARLES BOWICK

Date/Place of Birth: June 6, 1933; Augusta, Ga.
Parents: Charles Edgar MacMurphy and Elizabeth (Bowick) MacMurphy.
Spouse/Marriage Date: Phyllis (Karriker) MacMurphy; June 14, 1958.
Children: Shawn Lee, Kevin Deal, Charles Preston.
Education: Junior College of Augusta, Diploma, 1952; Lenoir-Rhyne, A.B. 1954; Chicago Seminary, B.D. 1960; graduate work at School of Missions, Diploma 1961 and Japanese Language Diploma 1962.
Ordination: June 12, 1960 by Southeastern Synod.
Calls: Board of World Missions, Lutheran Church in America, Missionary to Japan, 1960-66; Trinity, Anniston, Ala., 1966-70; St. Matthew, Columbus, Ga., 1970-95; Part time at Christ, Winston-Salem, 1995-.

McCARTER, RUFUS (RUS) LARRY

Date/Place of Birth: January 10, 1940; Gastonia, Gaston County, N.C.
Parents: Alva Lee McCarter and Ruth (Hallman) McCarter.
Spouse/Marriage Date: Linda Joyce (Lockard) McCarter; August 26, 1962 in Winston-Salem, N.C.
Children: Luther Glenn, Loren Michael.
Education: Lenoir-Rhyne, A.B. History and Social Studies 1961; Lutheran Theological Southern Seminary, M.Div. 1964; Drew University, Ph.D. Theology and Culture 1971.
Ordination: June 4, 1967 by North Carolina Synod.
Calls: Redeemer, Irvington, N.J., 1964-66; Wheatland, Buchanan, Va., 1967-71; St. Michael, High Point, 1971-75.
Other: Visiting lecturer at Philadelphia Seminary, 1966-67; Synod Coordinator, Virginia Synod Justice and Social Change Program; Instructor of Religion, Guilford College and High Point College; Guilford Technical Institute; Davidson County Community College; Trainer, Consultant, and Counselor for Wholistic Living Center. Dropped from roll June 10, 1979. Community Development Specialist, 1975-78, Youth Services Bureau Program Coordinator/Director; Trainer and Program Coordinator, 1978-79, Youth Services Bureau, Director, Best Friends (Big Brother/Big Sister) Program. Author: *T.L.C. Parenting Manual* and *T.L.C. for Singles*.

McCARTHY, EDWARD G.

Date/Place of Birth: November 1, 1956; Nassau, N.Y.
Parents: Edward McCarthy and ? (Herr) McCarthy.
Education: Concordia College (N.Y.), B.A. 1983; Gettysburg Seminary, M.Div. 1987.
Ordination: January 17, 1988 by North Carolina Synod.
Calls: Nazareth, Rural Hall, 1987-90; Prince of Peace, Ida, Mich., 1989-90; Clinical Pastoral Education Residency, Nassau County Medical Center, N.Y., 1990-91.
Other: Member, Planning Committee for North Carolina Synod Winter Youth Retreat, 1988.

McCARTHY, MICHAEL ALAN PETER

Date/Place of Birth: January 31, 1953; Chicago, Ill.
Parents: John F. McCarthy and June (Peterson) McCarthy.
Spouse/Marriage Date: Catharin Elizabeth (Coley) McCarthy; October 6, 1990.
Child: Patrick Ryan.
Education: Duke University, A.B. 1975; Case Western Reserve University, 1978-79; Yale Divinity School, M.Div. 1984.
Ordination: November 27, 1987 by North Carolina Synod.
Calls: Assistant Pastor, Holy Trinity, Hickory, 1987-91; Faith, Little Rock, Ark., 1991-.
Other: Chaplaincy Committee, Frye Regional Medical Center, 1987-91; Chair, Board, Oasis Renewal Center, Little Rock, Ark., 1989-91; Global Missionary Committee, Arkansas-Oklahoma Synod, 1992-95; 1992-95, Chair, Executive Committee, Stillpoint School for Spiritual Formation and Direction, Little Rock, Ark.

McCAULEY, ERNEST ROEDEL

Date/Place of Birth: June 13, 1869; Salem, Va.

Parents: William McCauley and Margaret Jane (Shirey) McCauley. Two brothers were the Reverends Victor and J. William McCauley.

Spouse/Marriage Date: Grace Beth (Ford) McCauley; July 1897 in Cedar Rapids, Iowa.

Children of First Marriage: William Ford, Frederick Dixon.

Second Spouse/Marriage Date: Mrs. Annie (Meeder) (Cheatham) McCauley of Ridgeway; March 7, 1930 in Rocky Mount, N.C.

Education: Roanoke College, A.B. 1892, M.A. 1895; Gettysburg Seminary, 1895; Susquehanna University, D.D. 1908.

License/Ordination: Licensed 1892 by Southwest Virginia Synod; ordained 1895 by Allegheny Synod.

Calls: In Iowa, Pennsylvania, and Virginia (First, Norfolk), 1895-1922; general evangelistic work, 1922-24; Holy Trinity, Raleigh, 1924-30; All Saints, Baltimore, Md., 1930-48, Pastor Emeritus, 1948-57; retired 1948 at Baltimore, Md.

Other: Board, Lutheran Theological Southern Seminary; Board, Children's Home of the South; Board, Jewish Missions, United Lutheran Church in America; Editor, The Augsburg Teacher, adult department, eight years; contributed *Saturday Sermons* in *Norfolk (VA) Ledger Dispatch.* Author, brochure, *Resurrection of the Body;* Lecturer, *Science and the Bible,* in churches and colleges.

Date of Death/Burial Location: November 7, 1957; East Hill Cemetery, Salem, Va.

McCLANAHAN, GEORGE WALKER, JR.

Date/Place of Birth: March 6, 1863; Beeville, Texas.

Parents: George Walker McClanahan, Sr. and Mary Doretha (Harris) McClanahan. Father was reared in Craig County, Va., and mother in Charlotte, N.C. Orphaned in childhood, he, two brothers, and sister (Mary Virginia, who married the Reverend Robert C. Holland) were brought to Salem, Va., and were reared and educated by their uncle, the Reverend William S. McClanahan, with proceeds from their father's estate.

First Spouse/Marriage Date: Eliza Ann (Robertson) McClanahan of Lynchburg, Va.; June 1893 in Strasburg, Pa.

Second Spouse/Marriage Date: Cedelia May (Lovell) McClanahan of Farmersville, Texas; November 24, 1915 in Columbia, S.C.

Education: Roanoke College, A.B. 1889, A.M. 1892, D.D. 1944; Philadelphia Seminary, 1892.

Ordination: 1892 by Ministerium of Pennsylvania.

Calls: Salem (Frankford), Philadelphia, Pa., 1892-97; St. Michael, Strasburg, Pa., 1897-1912; St. Matthew, Wilmington, 1913-21; Frieden's-Peace-Sharon, Gibsonville, 1921-31; Christiana, Granite Quarry, 1931-38; Grace, Bessemer City, 1938-48; retired 1948 near Salisbury.

Other: Board, Children's Home of the South, 1926-49; Necrologist, North Carolina Synod, 1936-49; Delegate from North Carolina Synod to 1918 (merger) Convention, United Lutheran Church in America. Author of brochure, *Bible Questions and Answers,* (five editions).

Date of Death/Burial Location: October 12, 1949; East Hill Cemetery, Salem, Va.

McCLEARY, DAVID A.

Date/Place of Birth: March 3, 1931; Carroll County, Ind.
Parents: John M. McCleary and Dessie (Hunter) McCleary.
Spouse/Marriage Date: Winifred (Stough) McCleary; November 17, 1956 in Maywood, Ill.
Children: Christina Ruth, Craig David, Sheryl Diane, Theresa Lynn, Jeffrey Carl.
Education: Carthage College, A.B. 1953; Chicago Seminary, M.Div. 1957.
Ordination: May 1957 by Illinois Synod.
Calls: St. John-Trinity, Meredosia, Ill., 1957-59; St. John, Sterling, Ill., 1959-65; Incarnation, Burbank, Ill., 1965-71; Mission Developer/Pastor, Christ the Redeemer, Bloomingdale, Ill., 1971-79; Mission Developer, New Orleans, La., 1979-80; Mission Developer/Pastor, King of Glory, Clemmons, N.C., 1980-87; Vice Pastor at various congregations.
Date of Death: October 26, 1987; Memorial service on November 1, 1987 at Augsburg, Winston-Salem. Disposition of ashes unknown.

McCOMBS, CHARLES AUGUSTUS, SR.

Date/Place of Birth: November 11, 1929; Kannapolis, N.C.
Parents: Marvin F. McCombs and Connie (Foster) McCombs.
Spouse/Marriage Date: Elizabeth (Robinson) McCombs; November 19, 1950 in Hickory, N.C.
Children: Nora Ann, Connie Chloe, Charles Augustus, Jr.
Education: Lenoir-Rhyne, A.B. 1952; Lutheran Theological Southern Seminary, B.D. 1955.
Ordination: 1955 by North Carolina Synod.
Calls: Bethel, Rowan County and St. Matthew, Davie County, 1955-59; Bethel only, 1959-61; St. Matthew, Wilmington, 1961-73.
Other: Committee on Brotherhood Work, 1958; Committee on Manifest Life of the Church, 1959-62, Chair, 1960-62; Committee on Stewardship, 1960; Special Committee on Group Insurance, 1961-62; Board, Lutheridge, 1962-65; Nominating Committee, 1969; Committee on Social Ministry, 1966-69; Camp Committee, 1971-73.
Date of Death/Burial Location: January 21, 1973; Oleander Memorial Park Cemetery, Wilmington, N.C.

McCOMBS, ROBERT EARL, JR.

Date/Place of Birth: March 23, 1929; Rowan County, N.C.
Parents: Robert Earl McCombs, Sr. and Katherine (Smith) McCombs.
Spouse/Marriage Date: Martha Ann (Barnhardt) McCombs; June 10, 1951 in Rowan County, N.C.
Children: Katherine Ruth, Robert Earl, III, Mary Ann Cooper.
Education: Lenoir-Rhyne, A.B. 1952; Lutheran Theological Southern Seminary, B.D. 1955.
Ordination: 1955 by North Carolina Synod.
Calls: St. Andrew, Concord, 1955-58; Faith, Faith, 1958-65; Epiphany, Winston-Salem, 1965-66; St. David's, West Columbia, S.C., 1966-80; Immanuel, Greenwood, S.C., 1980-; Vice Pastor at various congregations; retired.
Other: Evangelism Committee, 1962-63; Stewardship Committee, 1966. In South Carolina Synod: American Missions Committee, Educational Ministry Committee, Spiritual Growth Workshop Leader.

McCREARY, GEORGE BOAL
Date/Place of Birth: March 19, 1900; Beaver County, Pa.
Parents: Charles Krauth McCreary and Sarah Effie (Boal) McCreary.
Spouse/Marriage Date: Florence Edwina (Bost) McCreary; June 27, 1931 in Greenville, Pa.
Children: Dr. Charles Bost, John Bost, Sarah Bost Davis, David Bost, James Bost.
Education: Thiel College, A.B. 1922, A.M. 1923; Northwestern Seminary, 1931, B.D.; University of Pittsburgh, L.L.B. 1927; Carthage College, D.D. 1953.
Ordination: June 18, 1931 by Pittsburgh Synod.
Calls: St. John, Phillips, Wis., 1931-34; Developer/Pastor, First, Sheboygan, Wis., 1934-50; Stewardship and Evangelism Secretary, Assistant to the President, and Editor, *Northwest Synod, Bulletin,* 1950-62; Salem, Minneapolis, Minn., 1963-65. Retired 1965 to Oriental, N.C.
Other: Welfare Division of the National Lutheran Council; Board, Lutheran Welfare Society of Wisconsin; Board, Nachusa Childrens Home; Board, Lutheran Home for the Aged, Fond du Lac, Wis.; Board, Northwestern Seminary; Stewardship Committee of the Northwest Synod for twenty years. Editor, daily devotional booklet, *The Word in Season.*
Date of Death/Burial Location: September 6, 1985; National Cemetery, New Bern, N.C.

McCULLOUGH, HENRY ANTINE, JR.
Date/Place of Birth: March 19, 1909; Albemarle, N.C.
Parents: The Reverend Henry Antine McCullough, Sr. and Lily Amelia (Blackwelder) McCullough.   Two brothers were the Reverends Paul G. and John B. McCullough.
Spouse/Marriage Date: Mary Katherine (Johnston) McCullough; October 17, 1933, in Marion, Smyth County, Va.
Children: William Henry, David Legarde, Katherine Elizabeth Trexler.
Education: Mount Pleasant Collegiate Institute, Newberry College, A.B. 1929, D.D. 1962; Lutheran Theological Southern Seminary, B.D. 1932, graduate study at Lutheran Theological Southern Seminary and Chicago Lutheran Seminary.
Ordination: June 1, 1932 by South Carolina Synod.
Calls: Ascension, Chattanooga, Tenn., 1932-43; Ascension, Columbia, S.C., 1943-48; Emmanuel, Lincolnton, 1948-59; Supply, Luther's Chapel, Lincoln County, 1948-49; Redeemer, Newberry, S.C., 1959-74; Supply Pastor, Mt. Olivet, Prosperity, S.C., 1975-81; retired June 1974 to Newberry, S.C. and to Durham, N.C. in 1983.
Other: Executive Boards of North Carolina and South Carolina Synods, 1953-69; Ministerial Examining Committee for Professional Leadership of the Southeastern Lutheran Synod, 1971-74; Board, Lenoir-Rhyne; Board, Lutheran Theological Southern Seminary; Board, Lowman Home for Aged and Helpless. Involved in grass-roots organization and development of Interfaith Community Social Services organization and Developmentally Disabled Adults Agency and program; Boy Scout Councils, Recreation Commission, United Fund in Lincolnton; Young Men's Christian Association in Chattanooga, Tenn., 1933-59; Mayor's Biracial Commission in Newberry, S.C., 1963-65; Executive Secretary, Newberry County United Way, 1974-77; Board, United Way of

Midlands; Newberry Kiwanis Club, 1959-93; *Who's Who in the South and Southwest*, 1963; *Personalities of the South*, 1974.

McCULLOUGH, HENRY ANTINE, SR.

Date/Place of Birth: December 18, 1865; Newberry County, S.C.

Parents: John   McCullough   and   Margaret   (McNeill) McCullough.

Spouse/Marriage   Date: Lily   Amelia   (Blackwelder) McCullough; May 30, 1899 in Mt. Pleasant, N.C.

Children: The Reverend Paul G., Miriam Niobe, Hazel Parham, the Reverend Henry A., Jr., Sarah Elizabeth, Margaret Amelia, the Reverend John B.

Education: Newberry College, A.B. 1893, Honorary M.A.,1905, D.D., 1917; Lutheran Theological Southern Seminary, 1895; Chicago Seminary, B.D. 1901.

Ordination: 1895 by South Carolina Synod.

Calls: St. Andrew-Mt. Hermon-Cold Water, Concord, 1895-98; Holy Trinity, Mt. Pleasant, 1903-07; First, Albemarle, new site bought and church built, 1907-11; St. Matthew-Mt. Lebanon, Cameron, S.C., 1898-1903; St. Paul, Columbia, S.C., 1911-45; retired 1945 at Columbia, S.C.

Other: Co-principal of Mount Pleasant Collegiate Institute, 1903-07; Secretary, North Carolina Synod, 1908-11; President, Board, Lutheran Theological Southern Seminary; Board, Newberry College.

Date of Death/Burial Location: May 8, 1958; Elmwood Cemetery, Columbia, S.C.

McDANIEL, KEITH ALEXANDER

Ordination: May 1980 by North Carolina Synod.

Other: Transferred to Southeast Synod, July 1980. Resurrection, Augusta, Ga., 1980-84; Trinity, Columbia, S.C., 1984-91. Resigned September 30, 1991 in Columbia, S.C.

McDANIEL, MICHAEL CONWAY DIXON

Date/Place of Birth: April 8, 1929; Mt. Pleasant, N.C.

Parents: John Henry McDaniel and Mildred Juanita (Barrier) McDaniel.

Spouse/Marriage Date: Marjorie Ruth (Schneiter) McDaniel; November 26, 1953 in Jeffersontown, Ky.

Child: John Robert Michael.

Education: University of North Carolina, B.A. English 1951; Hamma Divinity School, B.D. 1954; University of Chicago, M.A. Systematic Theology 1969, Ph.D. Christian Theology 1978; Lenoir-Rhyne, D.D. 1983, Professor Emeritus, 1995; Belmont Abbey, Honorary L.L.D. 1984; Goethe Institute for German Language and Culture, West Germany, Certificate of Excellence 1968; Post-graduate study, University of Hamburg (Hamburg, Germany), 1968-69.

Ordination: June 20, 1954 by North Carolina Synod.

Calls: Faith, Faith, 1954-58; Ascension, Savannah, Ga., 1958-60; Associate Director, Department for Evangelism, United Lutheran Church in America, New York City, N.Y., 1960-62; Edgebrook, Chicago, Ill., 1962-67; Interim University Pastor and Guest Professor, Wittenberg University, 1970-71; Bishop, North Carolina Synod, 1982-91; Vice Pastor at various congregations; retired June 1, 1995 in Hickory, N.C.

Other: Military Service in the U.S. Army in Korea, 1946-48; Professor, Lenoir-Rhyne, 1971-82; Director, Center for Theology and Theologian in Residence, Lenoir-Rhyne, 1991-95. Distinguished Alumnus, Trinity Seminary, 1990; Cuthbert Allen Award for Contributions to Ecumenism by Ecumenical Institute of Wake Forest University and Belmont Abbey College, 1993; Evangelical Lutheran Church in America Committee on Appeals, 1993; Round Two of Lutheran-Orthodox Dialogue in U.S.A., 1982; Chair, Task Force on Ecumenism, CNLC; First delegation of Lutheran Bishops to visit the Pope, the Patriarch, and the Archbishop of Canterbury; Board of Publication, Lutheran Church in America; First chair, Advisory Bishops on Church Council, Evangelical Lutheran Church in America. Appointed by Lutheran World Federation as Lecturer and Tutor, Oxford University, 1989. Crafted Covenant with Roman Catholic dioceses in North Carolina, 1991 and with Southeast District, The Lutheran Church-Missouri Synod. Publications: *Welcome to the Lord's Table,* 1971; *The Pastor as Liturgical Leader,* 1989; *Teaching Authority in the Evangelical Lutheran Church in America: Who Calls the Shots on Matters of Doctrine?,* 1990; *Salvation as Justification and Theosis,* 1992.

McKAY, HENRY MANN, JR.

Date/Place of Birth: April 13, 1937; Macon, Ga.

Parents: Henry Mann McKay, Sr. and Eleanor (Schroder) McKay.

Spouse/Marriage Date: Judy (Schott) McKay, daughter of the Reverend Franklin Herbert Schott; December 28, 1966 in Jackson, Miss.

Children: Dorothy Elizabeth, Henry Franklin.

Education: Lenoir-Rhyne, A.B. 1960; Lutheran Theological Southern Seminary, M.Div. 1964; University of North Carolina at Charlotte, M.Ed. 1971; Jesuit School of Theology, Berkeley, D.Min. 1981.

Ordination: May 31, 1964 by Southeastern Synod.

Calls: Ascension, Jackson, Miss., 1964-67; Mission Developer/Pastor, Advent, Charlotte, 1967-73; Executive Director, Lutheran Outdoor Ministry of Southern California for Pacific Southwest Synod, 1973-80; Area Director, Inland Empire Area, Lutheran Social Services, Riverside, Calif., 1980-81; First, Watsonville, Calif., 1981-85; Executive Director, Lutheran Social Services of Central South Carolina, 1985-.

Other: President, Family Service Center of Pajaro Valley, Calif., 1984; Bishop's Ecumenical Council R. C. Dioceses of Monterey, Calif., 1984; Consultant on Church Growth to Lutherkirch, Heidenau, East Germany, 1990; South Carolina Synod Committee on HIV/AIDS Ministry, 1992; Clinical Member, American Association of Marriage and Family Therapy; Licensed Professional Counselor, State of South Carolina.

McKINLEY, EDWIN WAYNE

Date/Place of Birth: November 16, 1937; Cabarrus County, N.C.

Parents: Kenneth Wright McKinley and Janie Ruth (Rodgers) McKinley.

Spouse/Marriage Date: Norma Lucille (Langford) McKinley; July 25, 1964 in West Columbia, S.C.

Child: Kenneth Norman.
Education: Pfeiffer, A.B. 1962; Lutheran Theological Southern Seminary, B.D. 1966.
Ordination: June 5, 1966 by North Carolina Synod.
Calls: Assistant Pastor, Incarnation, Columbia, S.C., 1966-74; Our Saviour, Dallas, 1974-75.
Other: Dropped from roll, July 1, 1975.

McLAUGHLIN, PATRICK JAMES

Date/Place of Birth: April 20, 1961; Milwaukee, Wis.
Parents: James A. McLaughlin and Jane (Schoeni) McLaughlin.
Spouse/Marriage Date: Leigh (Phipps) McLaughlin; April 23, 1987 in Columbia, S.C.
Children: Mariah Phipps, Jane Elizabeth, Megan Leigh.
Education: Western Carolina University, University of South Carolina - Spartanburg, B.A. 1983; Lutheran Theological Southern Seminary, M.Div. 1989.
Ordination: May 22, 1989 by Virginia Synod.
Calls: St. Timothy, Vinton, Va., 1989-90; St. Enoch, Kannapolis, 1990-91; Chaplain, United States Navy, 1992-.

McMAKIN, MICHAEL

License: Licensed 1817 by North Carolina Synod.
Other: Moved to Tennessee soon after becoming licensed. No records of his ever serving churches in North Carolina or Tennessee Synods.

McMANUS, CHARLES RAY

Date/Place of Birth: December 7, 1933; Gastonia, N.C.
Parents: Charles E. McManus and Irene Laura (Shoemaker) McManus.
Spouse/Marriage Date: Ann Elizabeth (Moser) McManus; December 22, 1957 in Winston-Salem, N.C.
Children: Paul Mark, Elizabeth Sudonna Handy, Stephanie Ann Fortenberry.
Education: Lenoir-Rhyne, A.B. 1956; Lutheran Theological Southern Seminary, B.D. 1959, graduate study, 1965; at University of Chicago, 1962.
Ordination: June 7 1959 by North Carolina Synod.
Calls: Mt. Hermon, Cabarrus County, 1959-62; St. James, Rockwell, 1962-74; Lutheran Chapel, Gastonia, 1974-89; St. Peter, Southport, 1989-93; Vice Pastor at various congregations; retired 1993 in Bolivia, N.C.
Other: Executive Board of Synod; World Missions Committee, 1963-70, Chair, 1965-70; Christian Education Committee, 1964-72, Chair, 1965-72; Board, Lutheran Family Services; Personnel Committee for Parish Education, 1969; Board, Lutheridge, 1962-65.

McREE, OSWALD THEODORE

Date/Place of Birth: June 23, 1910; Catawba County, N.C. Brother of the Reverend George V. McRee.

Parents: William Tate McRee and Sally Ola (Deal) McRee.
Spouse/Marriage Date: Elizabeth (Coyner) McRee; September 10, 1933 in Conover, N.C.
Children: Charlotte Jane Kolzow, Ruth Ann Schultz, Richard Theodore, Walter Adrian.
Education: Concordia College, Conover; Concordia Seminary, (Mo.), 1932.
Ordination: July 8, 1934 by The Lutheran Church-Missouri Synod.
Calls: Organized, built and served Bethany, Trenton, N.J., 1933-49; established Messiah, Princeton, N.J., 1947; Dean, Philadelphia, Pa., The Lutheran Church-Missouri Synod, 1947-49; Executive Secretary, English District, The Lutheran Church-Missouri Synod Office, Detroit, Mich., 1949-58; Resurrection, Yardley, Pa., 1958-76; Eastern Vice President English District, The Lutheran Church-Missouri Synod, 1960-70; Church of the Savior, Newland, 1978-84; Co-organizer of American Evangelical Lutheran Church, 1976; retired to Newland, N.C. in 1976.
Other: Agent, Aid Association for Lutherans, North Carolina and Illinois, 1932-33.
Date of Death/Burial Location: December 28, 1992; Mt. Olive Church Cemetery, Newton, N.C.

McSWAIN, HAROLD LOVE

Date/Place of Birth: February 17, 1939; Albemarle, Stanly County, N.C.
Parents: Wyatt McSwain and Martha (Tucker) McSwain.
Spouse/Marriage Date: Mary Margaret (Gribble) McSwain; June 23, 1962 in Kannapolis, N.C.
Children: Heather Lee, Dr. Mark Wyatt.
Education: Lenoir-Rhyne, A.B. 1961; Lutheran Theological Southern Seminary, B.D. 1964.
Ordination: June 14, 1964 by North Carolina Synod.
Calls: Luther's, Richfield, 1964-68; Ascension, Wilson, 1968-73; St. Matthew, Wilmington, 1973-94; Vice Pastor at various congregations.
Other: Executive Board, North Carolina Synod, two terms; Dean, Coastal District; Delegate to Lutheran Church in America conventions in 1982, 1986; Voting member to Evangelical Lutheran Church in America Churchwide Assembly, 1993; Board, Lutheran Theological Southern Seminary; Chair, Candidacy Committee; President, New Hanover Minister's Association; Program Director, Wilmington Lion's Club.
Date of Death/Burial Location: September 2, 1994; St. Martin's Church Cemetery, Albemarle, N.C.

MANOUSO, DAVID

Calls: Interim Pastor, St. Timothy, Havelock, 1996.

MANSFIELD, MILTON JAMES, JR.

Date/Place of Birth: December 4, 1939; Omaha, Neb.
Parents: Milton James Mansfield, Sr. and Cleola M. (Dawson) Mansfield.
Education: Creighton University, two years, Gustavus Adolphus College, two years, A.B. 1961; U.S. Army Chaplain School, 1963; Lutheran School of Theology at Chicago (Rock Island Campus), B.D. 1965.
Ordination: 1965 by Nebraska Synod.

Calls: St. Timothy, Havelock, 1965-68; Shepherd of the Sea Mission, Atlantic Beach, 1965-68; Assistant Pastor, St. James, Concord, 1968-69.
Other: Officer, U.S. Army Reserve. Demitted Ministry, 1969.

MARCARD, ADAM NICHOLAS
Spouse: Mary Elizabeth (Coleman) Marcard.
Child: Jacob, born November 21, 1799 in Cabarrus County, N.C.
Calls: St. John-Cold Water-St. Martin, Cabarrus County; Morning Star, Mecklenburg County, 1797-1800.
Other: Kept a diary in German of his ministry with record of ministerial acts.
Burial Location: Lexington District, S.C.

MARKERT, JOHN LUDWIG (LEWIS)
Date/Place of Birth: Ohio.
License/Ordination: Licensed 1804 and ordained 1808 by North Carolina Synod.
Calls: Beck's-Bethany-Pilgrim-St. Luke, Davidson County; Dutchman's Creek, Davie County, 1805-16; Frieden's-Low's, Guilford County; St. Paul, Alamance County; Richland, Randolph County, 1805-10.
Other: First Missionary of North Carolina Synod to Ohio, Indiana, and Illinois, and after 1829 of Tennessee Synod, remaining in that area to aid pastors and churches in pioneer period of Lutheran Church. An organizer and first President of Indiana Synod, 1848. Third Secretary, North Carolina Synod, 1809. "Probably the first clergyman to visit St. John (in Union County, Ill.) was the Reverend John Lewis Markert, then a member of the North Carolina Synod. It was probably he who directed its organization, for he visited the colonies north of the Ohio in 1818 and also in 1819 following a heart-affecting memorial to the North Carolina Synod pleading for ministers." Note: "Lewis" was used instead of "Ludwig" as his middle name.
Date of Death/Burial Location: November 22, 1850; Portland Mills, Ind.

MARKS, CHARLES ALEXANDER, SR.
Date/Place of Birth: October 2, 1848; Stephens City, Va.
Parents: Jacob Alexander Marks and Elizabeth A. (Schryock) Marks.
First Spouse: Name unknown.
Second Spouse/Marriage Date: Mary Edith (Weade) Marks; January 18, 1911 in Waynesboro, Va.
Children: Charles A., Jr., Mary E.
Education: Roanoke College, Lutheran Theological Southern Seminary, 1878.
License/Ordination: Licensed 1876 and ordained 1877 by Southwest Virginia Synod.
Calls: In Virginia, Carroll, Botetourt and Floyd counties, 1876-86; Grace, Prosperity, S.C., 1886-89; in North Carolina: Lutheran Chapel-Center Grove, Rowan County, 1889-96; organized and built church, St. Mark, China Grove, 1894-96; Mt. Tabor, Augusta County, Va., 1896-99; First English, Richmond, Va., 1899-1906; Zion-St. James, Waynesboro, Va., 1910-20; retired 1920.
Date of Death/Burial Location: January 29, 1926; Waynesboro, Va.

MARTIN, CLAUDE JACKSON

Date/Place of Birth: June 21, 1927; Hillsville, Carroll County, Va.

Parents: William Martin, Sr. and Fannie Emaline Martin.

First Spouse/Marriage Date: Shirley Lorraine (Ellinger) Martin; July 4, 1954 in Norfolk, Va.

Children of First Marriage: William Joseph, Mary Lynn Bre, Susan Marie.

Second Spouse/Marriage Date: Alvina Murial (Gunderson) Martin; May 15, 1988 in Ft. Valley, Va.

Education: Roanoke College, B.A. 1949; Lutheran Theological Southern Seminary, M.Div. 1953, graduate work; graduate study at Gettysburg Seminary.

Ordination: June 21, 1953 by Virginia Synod.

Calls: Mission Developer/Pastor, St. John, Norfolk, Va., 1953-60; Bethany, Kannapolis, 1960-64; Muhlenberg, Harrisonburg, Va., 1964-79; Staff of Division for Mission in North America, Lutheran Church in America, 1979-88; Mission Developer/Pastor, St. Luke, Shallotte, 1988-90; retired December 31, 1990 to Harrisonburg, Va.

Other: As a seminarian, organized Kure Memorial, Kure Beach, 1951; Rural Church Program Committee, 1955; Lutheran World Action Committee, 1955-56; President, Tidewater Conference of the Virginia Synod, 1958-59; United Lutheran Church Men Executive Committee, 1960; American Missions Committee, 1963-64; Summer Assemblies Committee, 1965; Stewardship Committee, 1966-67; Roanoke College Appeal Committee and Conference Director, 1966-67; Chair, Committee on Men's Work, 1966-67; Dean, Central District of the Virginia Synod, 1968-71; Task Force, Priority Program on Justice and Social Change, 1969-70; Regional Panel for the Commission on Function and Structure of the Lutheran Church in America, 1970; Committee on Continuing Education for Pastors, 1970-71; Task Force, Study of Mission and Structure of the Virginia Synod, 1970-71; Board, Virginia Synod Lutheran Homes, 1966-75, 1978-82; Synodical Director for Virginia Synod Lutheran Homes LOVE Appeal, 1971-72; Chair, Council for Parish Life, 1971-72; Delegate, Lutheran Church in America Convention, 1972; Regional Task Group to study Lutheran Theological Education in the Southeast, 1973; Chair, Council for Missions, 1973-77; Board, Virginia Synod Executive 1972-77; Regional Panel meeting in Atlanta, Ga., to study minority concerns in the Lutheran Church in America, 1976; Synodical Director, Strength for Mission Appeal, 1977-78; Chair, Career Planning and Development Managing Group of Council for Ministry, 1978-79; President, Ministerial Associations of Kannapolis (1963-64) and Harrisonburg, Va. (1966-67); Synodical Representative to Virginia Council of Churches, 1975-76. Publications: *The First Hundred Years of Gladesboro Lutheran Church; The History of Muhlenberg Lutheran Church.*

MARTIN, DAVID LOUIS

Date/Place of Birth: June 21, 1941; Danville, Pa.; grandson of the Reverend Dr. David Sylvester Martin.

Parents: The Reverend Dr. Richard Byers Martin and Larue (Wetzel) Martin.

Spouse/Marriage Date: Debbra Lois (Sisk) Martin; April 21, 1974 in Dallas, N.C.

Children: Suzanna Leigh, Adrienne Elizabeth.

Education: Elizabethtown College, B.A. English 1964; Gettysburg Seminary, M.Div. Systematic Theology 1968; Union Seminary, (Va.), Th.M. Pastoral Care 1972; Clinical Pastoral Education, North Carolina Memorial Hospital, Chapel Hill, 1971.

Ordination: June 9, 1968 by Central Pennsylvania Synod.

Calls: Good Shepherd, Goldsboro, 1968-71; Assistant to the Bishop of the North Carolina Synod of the Lutheran Church in America, Secretary of Synod, Archivist, Minister for Professional Leadership, 1972-82; Associate Director of Leadership Support of the Division for Professional Leadership of the Lutheran Church in America, Philadelphia, Pa., 1982-84; St. Paul, Durham, 1984-91; St. Mark, Asheville, 1991-.

Other: Committee on American Missions, 1970-71; Chaplain, Hickory Jaycees, 1966-67; Goldsboro Human Relations Commission, 1969-70; Board, Wayne County Mental Health Association, 1969-71; Co-Chair, Wayne County Mental Health Month, 1970; Founder and first President of Dial Help, Inc. of Wayne County; Governor's Award, 1972; Wayne County Mental Health Association and Board Member of the Year Award, 1971; Board, Dial Help of Rowan County, 1973-74; United Way of Rowan County, Unit Chair, 1976; Publications: *Forgotten Members: The Pastor's Family,* a chapter in the book, *Growth In Ministry*, 1979.

MARTIN, MICHAEL TIMOTHY

Date/Place of Birth: April 8, 1965; Gastonia, N.C.
Parents: Franklin Eugene Martin and Frances Elizabeth (Houser) Martin.
Education: Lenoir-Rhyne, A.B. Music 1987; Gettysburg Seminary, M.Div. 1991.
Ordination: July 14, 1991 by North Carolina Synod.
Calls: Low's, Liberty, 1991-.

MARTIN, RICHARD BYERS

Date/Place of Birth: April 27, 1909; New Freedom, Pa.
Parents: The Reverend David Sylvester Martin, D.D. and Mary (Byers) Martin.
Spouse/Marriage Date: Larue Koontz (Wetzel) Martin, daughter of Dr. G. Lewis Wetzel; June 21, 1935 Silver Run, Md.
Children: Richard Hugo, the Reverend David Louis.
Education: Gettysburg College, A.B. 1931, D.D. 1958; Gettysburg Seminary, B.D. 1934, S.T.M. 1936; graduate studies at University of Edinburgh, Scotland and at Union Seminary, (N.Y.), 1943.
Ordination: April 16, 1936 by Central Pennsylvania Synod.
Calls: Trinity, Shamokin, Pa., 1936-44; Augsburg (now Lakeside), Harrisburg, Pa., 1944-61; St. Paul, Williamsport, 1961-72; retired in 1972 and transferred to North Carolina Synod.
Other: Central Pennsylvania Synod Committee of Higher Educational Institutions, 1946-53; Board, Susquehanna University, 1953-72; Dean, Williamsport District of Central Pennsylvania Synod, 1969-72; Delegate to the Minneapolis Convention of the Lutheran Church in America in 1970. Publications and articles: *History of Trinity Lutheran Church, Shamokin, Pennsylvania,* (1840-1940); *Highlights of a Century in St. Paul Lutheran Church, Williamsport, Pennsylvania;* meditations in *Light for Today* and articles in *Luther League Topics* and *Parish and Church School Magazine*.
Date of Death/Burial Location: September 21, 1975; St. Mary's Lutheran and Reformed Cemetery, Silver Run, Md.

MARZ, WALTER GEORGE

Date/Place of Birth: June 11, 1928; Derita, N.C.
Parents: Ferdinand Henry (known as Fred) Marz and Emma (Schroeder) Marz.

First Spouse/Marriage Date: Gretchen (Grau) Marz; September 13, 1955.
Children of First Marriage: David Michael, Jonathan Martin.
Second Spouse/Marriage Date: Marianna Lee (Billing) Marz; January 27, 1985.
Education: North Carolina State University, one year, Lenoir-Rhyne, A.B. 1949;
Philadelphia Seminary, M.Div. 1952.
Ordination: June 1952 by North Carolina Synod.
Calls: Assistant Pastor, St. Mark's, Charlotte, 1952-54; Assistant Pastor, Luther Place
Memorial, Washington, D.C. 1954-56 and Pastor to Lutheran students at George
Washington University; Christ the King, Daytona Beach, Fla., 1956-. Retired.
Other: President, Lutheran Servicemen's Lounge, Washington, D.C., 1955-56; President,
North Conference, Florida Synod, 1959-62; Dean, East Central District, Florida Synod,
1963-66.

MATOUSH, JOSEPH RICHARD

Date/Place of Birth: March 20, 1948; Cook, Ill.
Parents: Joseph Matoush and Elsie Matoush.
Spouse/Marriage Date: Helen Maria Matoush; June 15, 1985 in Jacksonville, N.C.
Children: Gwen Marie, Joseph Patrick.
Education: University of Illinois, B.A. 1970; Wartburg, M.Div. 1974; University of
Oklahoma, 1979.
Ordination: June 6, 1974 by Southern Wisconsin American Lutheran Church Synod.
Calls: St. John, Mazomanie, Wis., 1974-78; Immanuel, Merrimac, Wis., 1976-78; U.S.
Navy Chaplain, 1978- 92, assigned to Jacksonville and Elizabeth City.   Transferred to
California Synod.

MATTHIAS, HENRY JULIAN

Date/Place of Birth: October 3, 1871; Lexington County, S.C.
Parents: David Joseph Matthias and Margaret Catherine (Kleckley) Matthias.
Spouse/Marriage Date: Minnie Bell (Shell) Matthias; 1898 in Conover, N.C.
Children: Herman, Mabel, Julian, one other died in infancy.
Education: Concordia College (N.C.), Lenoir-Rhyne, two years, Newberry College, A.B.
1895; Lutheran Theological Southern Seminary, 1898.
Ordination: 1898 by South Carolina Synod.
Calls: In South Carolina, 1898-1903: St. Michael, Irmo; St. Lukes, near Prosperity, and St.
Andrew, Lexington County; Tennessee Synod churches in North Carolina: Emmanuel,
Lincolnton; Salem-St. Luke, Lincoln County, 1903-05; transferred 1905 to Chicago Synod;
served churches in Florida, Tennessee, Indiana, Washington, and California; last parish at
San Bernardino, Calif.
Other: U.S. Army Chaplain in World War I.
Date of Death/Burial Location: May 19, 1927; San Bernardino, Calif.

MATTHIAS, ROBERT W.

Date of Birth: July 27, 1937.
Parents: The Reverend and Mrs. P. C. Matthias. A brother is The Reverend Paul F.
Matthias.
Spouse: Laura (Werner) Matthias.
Children: Philip, Mark, Lauri, Katee, Bryon.

Education: Wartburg College, B.A. English 1959; Wartburg Seminary, M.Div. 1963; Clinical Pastoral Education - two quarters.
Ordination: September 8, 1963.
Calls: Our Savior, Lansing and Waterville, Iowa, 1963-66; Chaplain, U.S. Navy, 1966-91; Our Savior's, Sun Prairie, Wis., 1991-93; Bethlehem, Santa Rosa, Calif., 1993-96; Kure Memorial, Kure Beach, 1996-.

MAUNEY, JACOB LUTHER, JR.

Date/Place of Birth: December 21, 1937; Pulaski, Va. Grandfather was the Reverend John David Mauney, and two uncles are the Reverends John D. Mauney, Jr., and Marshall F. Mauney.
Parents: The Reverend Jacob Luther Mauney, Sr. and Ruth Boger (Barrier) Mauney.
Spouse/Marriage Date: Judy Nelle (Patterson) Mauney; June 20, 1964 in China Grove, N.C.
Children: Daniel Wayne, Timothy Jacob.
Education: Roanoke College, A.B. 1960; Lutheran Theological Southern Seminary, M.Div. 1964, D.Min. 1980; Virginia Commonwealth University, Certificate in Patient Counseling, 1971.
Ordination: June 14, 1964 by Virginia Synod.
Calls: Grace, Catawba County, 1964-68; Chaplain, Medical College of Virginia, 1970-1996.
Other: Associate Professor, Virginia Commonwealth University. Publications and Publicity Committee of North Carolina Synod, 1967-68; Chaplain and Director of Pastoral Services, Westbrook Psychiatric Hospital, Richmond, Va.; Pastoral Counselor, Virginia Institute of Pastoral Care, Richmond, Va., 1971-79; Board, Lutheran Family Services of Virginia, 1985-89.

MAUNEY, JACOB LUTHER, SR.

Date/Place of Birth: May 22, 1907; Newton, N.C.
Parents: The Reverend John David Mauney and Bessie Miller (Frantz) Mauney. Younger brothers are the Reverends J. D. Mauney, Jr., and Marshall F. Mauney.
Spouse/Marriage Date: Ruth Boger (Barrier) Mauney; September 3, 1935 in Mt. Pleasant, N.C.
Children: The Reverend Jacob Luther, Jr., Mary Ruth Wells, Grace Virginia.
Education: Roanoke College, A.B. 1930, L.H.D. 1962; Lutheran Theological Southern Seminary, B.D. 1934; Lenoir-Rhyne, D.D., 1948.
Ordination: 1934 by North Carolina Synod.
Calls: None in North Carolina. In Virginia: Zion-St. James, Waynesboro, 1934-37; Woman's Memorial, Pulaski, 1937-42; Ebenezer, Marion, 1942-53; Resurrection, Arlington, 1953-58; President (part-time), Virginia Synod, 1948-58; full-time, 1958-76, President Emeritus, 1976. Retired in 1976
Other: Board of Parish Education of the Lutheran Church in America; Court of Adjudication of the Lutheran Church in America; Board of Pensions of the Lutheran Church in America; Board, Marion College; Board, Roanoke College; Board, Lutheran Theological Southern Seminary, President; Board, Ex-officio member, Lowman Home and Children's Home of the South; Board of Visitors, Emory and Henry College, 1950-54; President, Virginia Council of Churches, 1962-65; Roanoke College Board.
Date of Death/Burial Location: January 29, 1990; Mt. Rest Cemetery, Kings Mountain, N.C.

MAUNEY, JOHN DAVID, JR.
Date/Place of Birth: May 6, 1918; Augusta, Ga.
Parents: The Reverend John David Mauney, Sr. and Bessie Miller (Frantz) Mauney. Older brother is the Reverend J. Luther Mauney and younger one the Reverend Marshall F. Mauney.
Spouse/Marriage Date: Mary Emma (Cobb) Mauney, daughter of the Reverend W. G. Cobb; July 1, 1939 in Cherryville, N.C.
Children: John David, III, William Marshall, Richard Louis (died sixteen hours after birth), Margaret Carolyn, Richard Benjamin.
Education: Lenoir-Rhyne, A.B. 1940, D.D. 1972; Lutheran Theological Southern Seminary, B.D. 1943.
Ordination: July 11, 1943 by North Carolina Synod.
Calls: Mt. Olive, Hickory, 1943-45; St. James, Fayetteville, 1945-77, where he ministered to Lutheran chaplains, officers and soldiers based at Fort Bragg during three wars; Shepherd of the Hills, Sylva, 1977-82; Vice Pastor at various congregations; Part time Pastor, Messiah of the Mountains, Burnsville, 1983-88 (Organized the congregation, 1985); retired January 1982 in Sylva, N.C.
Other: Treasurer, Synodical Parish Education Committee, 1950-59; Lutheridge Planning Council, 1951-54, Chair, 1952-54; North Carolina Missions Committee, 1955-61, 1964-67, Secretary, 1965-67, Consulting Member, 1978-82, Chair, 1982-85; President, Eastern Conference, 1957-58; Board, Lutheran Theological Southern Seminary, 1958-64; Chair, Committee on Auxiliaries, 1963-66; Board, Lenoir-Rhyne, 1964-67, 1976-79; Dean, Eastern District, 1967-74; Recipient of Lamb Award, 1971; Camp Committee, 1976-79; World Missions Committee, 1976-79; Chair, Southern Highlands Area Mission Strategy Study, 1983-84, for Division for Mission in North America.

MAUNEY, JOHN DAVID, SR.
Date/Place of Birth: October 15, 1878; Kings Mountain, N.C.
Parents: Jacob S. Mauney and Margaret Juletta (Rudisill) Mauney.
Spouse/Marriage Date: Bessie Miller (Frantz) Mauney; November 12, 1901 in Salem, Va.
Children: Dorothy Virginia, the Reverend Jacob Luther, Margaret Louise, Elizabeth Marshall, Mary Vera, the Reverend John David, Jr., the Reverend Marshall Frantz.
Education: Roanoke College, A.B. 1901, M.A. 1903; Philadelphia Seminary, 1906.
Ordination: 1906 by Tennessee Synod.
Calls: Beth Eden, Newton; Zion-New Jerusalem, Catawba County, 1906-09; St. Andrew-Mt. Olive-St. Stephen, Hickory, 1911-17; first regular Pastor, Grace, Hendersonville, 1921-28; St. Andrew, Hickory, 1928-40 (educational building named in his memory); St. Paul, Columbia, S.C., 1909-11; St. Matthew, Augusta, Ga., 1917-21; retired 1940 in Hendersonville, N.C.
Other: Professor (Bible), Lenoir-Rhyne, 1913-17; Secretary, Tennessee Synod, 1911-13; Board, Lutheran Theological Southern Seminary.
Date of Death/Burial Location: June 13, 1947; Kings Mountain, N.C.

MAUNEY, MARSHALL FRANTZ

Date/Place of Birth: December 8, 1920; Augusta, Ga.

Parents: The Reverend John David Mauney, Sr. and Bessie Miller (Frantz) Mauney. Two older brothers are the Reverends J. Luther Mauney, Sr. and J. D. Mauney, Jr.

Spouse/Marriage Date: Laura Virginia (Foltz) Mauney; June 24, 1948 in Shenandoah, Va.

Children: Virginia Marshall Fox, The Reverend James Foltz, Robert Frantz, Carol Mae Robinson.

Education: Lenoir-Rhyne, A.B. 1942; Lutheran Theological Southern Seminary, B.D. 1945; Roanoke College, D.D.

Ordination: April 4, 1945 by North Carolina Synod.

Calls: None in North Carolina; St. Peter and St. Matthew, Toms Brook, Va., 1945-47; Holy Trinity, Lynchburg, Va., 1947-61; Mt. Tabor, West Columbia, S.C., 1961-67; First, Norfolk, Va., 1967-87; retired June 30, 1987 in Norfolk, Va.

Other: Executive Council, Lutheran Church in America, 1976-86; Editor, *The Virginia Lutheran*; Board, American Missions, 1975-84, President, 1978-84; Board, Lutheran Theological Southern Seminary; Board, Newberry College; Chaplain, Lutheran Church in America Convention in Chicago, 1978; Preacher for *Lutheran Section of the Protestant Hour*, 1979-83.

MAXWELL, ROBERT MELVYN

Date/Place of Birth: December 20, 1944; Dallas, N.C.

Parents: August Jerome Maxwell and Ida (Hoover) Maxwell.

Spouse/Marriage Date: Deanna Sue (Moore) Maxwell; August 20, 1966 in Gastonia, N.C.

Children: Paul Jerome, Peter Michael, Phillip Justin.

Education: Lenoir-Rhyne, A.B. 1967; Lutheran Theological Southern Seminary, M.Div. 1971.

Ordination: June 6, 1971 by North Carolina Synod.

Calls: Holy Cross, Lincolnton, 1971-73; St. David, Kannapolis, 1973-78; retired, August 1981.

Date of Death/Burial Location: October 3, 1996; location for disposition of ashes unknown.

MAYER, JACOB LEGRANDE, JR.

Date/Place of Birth: January 22, 1942; Clinton, S.C.

Parents: The Reverend Jacob LeGrande Mayer, Sr. and Ruth (Wilson) Mayer.

Spouse/Marriage Date: Karen Margaret (Dohrmann) Mayer; June 14, 1964 in Charlotte, N.C.

Children: Kristin Louise Fischer, Andrew LeGrande.

Education: Lenoir-Rhyne, A.B. Sociology 1964; Lutheran Theological Southern Seminary, M.Div. 1968.

Ordination: June 9, 1968 by North Carolina Synod.

Calls: St. Paul, Strasburg, Va., 1968-72; Muhlenberg, Harrisonburg, Va., 1972-75; Grace, Salisbury, 1975-79; Messiah, Mechanicsville, Va., 1979-85; St. Michael, Blacksburg, Va., 1985-.

Other: Publication: *History of the Lutheran Church in Wythe County, Virginia*.

MAYER, JACOB LeGRANDE, SR.
Date/Place of Birth: April 23, 1910; Prosperity, S.C.
Parents: Andrew T. Mayer and Leila (Shealy) Mayer.
Spouse/Marriage Date: Ruth Lexine (Wilson) Mayer; July 18, 1936 in Columbia, S.C.
Children: Brenda Ruth Lown, The Reverend Jacob LeGrande, Jr.
Education: University of South Carolina, A.B. 1932; Lutheran Theological Southern Seminary, B.D. 1935.
Ordination: June 14, 1936 by South Carolina Synod.
Calls: Trinity, Elloree, S.C., 1936-39; St. John, Clinton, S.C., 1939-43; Redeemer, Charleston, S.C., 1943-51; Grace, Prosperity, S.C., 1951-53; St. Luke's, Charlotte, 1953-67; Trinity, Rocky Mount, 1967-71; Calvary, Spencer, 1971-75; Vice Pastor for various congregations; retired April 1975.
Other: Supply, St. Matthew-St. Luke, Kings Mountain, N.C., 1935; Supply, St. John's, Charleston, S.C., 1936.
Date of Death/Burial Location: March 25, 1993; Grace Lutheran Church Cemetery, Salisbury, N.C.

MEDLIN, WILLIAM FRANK
Date of Birth: December 12, 1924.
Parents: Fred Medlin and Rosa Ella (Garrett) Medlin.
Spouse/Marriage Date: Mary K. (Purser) Medlin; October 1950 in Raleigh, N.C.
Education: Lenoir-Rhyne, A.B. 1947; Lutheran Theological Southern Seminary, B.D. 1950; New York University, M.A. 1955.
Ordination: 1950 by North Carolina Synod.
Calls: Immanuel-New Haven-Zion, Blountville, Tenn., 1950-54.
Other: Left parish ministry for graduate study, leading to Ph.D. degree in counseling and religious education.

MEETZE, JOHN YOST
Date/Place of Birth: December 2, 1756; Hesse, Germany.
License/Ordination: At age of 46 in 1812 licensed by North Carolina Synod at Low's, Guilford County, and ordained in 1822 by the Reverends Godfrey Dreher and Michael Rauch, by order of North Carolina Synod, in Lexington District, S.C.
Calls: 1812 to 1824 in North Carolina Synod churches located in South Carolina: St. Paul, Newberry County; Bethel (High Hill), Richland County; and Zion, Lexington District. Churches served 1824 to 1833 were of South Carolina Synod: Sandy Run, Calhoun County; Nazareth-St. Peter (called "Meetze's"), Lexington County, and St. Michael, Richland County, where the South Carolina Synod was organized. In some churches was co-pastor with the Reverend Godfrey Dreher.
Other: One of Hessian troops, with many others against his will, hired to Great Britain to fight American colonials in Revolutionary War; deserted to American forces at siege of Charleston, S.C., 1780. After war settled in Lexington District, S.C., married, and had children. In 1824 one of six North Carolina Synod pastors who organized South Carolina Synod.
Date of Death/Burial Location: May 7, 1833; buried perhaps at St. Michael Church, Lexington County, S.C. where he was serving at time of his death.

MELESCHNIG, FRANK J.
Date/Place of Birth: June 7, 1931; Hartford, Conn.
Parents: Frank Meleschnig and Katherine (Pfitz) Meleschnig.
Spouse/Marriage Date: Norma (Kemner) Meleschnig; June 1, 1957 in Philadelphia, Pa.
Children: Lydia Katherine, Priscilla Anne, Peter Jon, Maria Louise, Paul David.
Education: University of Connecticut, A.S. 1953; Chicago Seminary, M.Div. 1957.
Ordination: August 10, 1957 by Illinois Synod.
Calls: Acacia Park, Norridge, Ill., 1957-66; Immanuel, Naugatuck, Conn., 1966-78; First, Southington, Conn., 1978-88; retired to Hendersonville, N.C. in 1988; Vice pastor at various congregations, including Nativity, Arden.

MENEES, MARK WILLIAM
Date/Place of Birth: January 3, 1950; Nashville, Davidson County, Tenn.
Parents: The Reverend John William Menees, Jr. and Nancy Rae (Walker) Menees.
Spouse/Marriage Date: Martha Jo (Staley) Menees; November 25, 1971 in Kingston Springs, Tenn.
Children: Matthew Shae, Kerri Beth.
Education: Martin College, 1970; Austin Peay State University, B.S. 1972; Vanderbilt School of Theology, M.Div. 1975; Lenoir-Rhyne, D.D. 1991.
Ordination: May 13, 1979 by North Carolina Synod.
Calls: Mt. Olive, Hickory, 1979-82; Administrative Assistant to Bishop, Minister for Leadership, North Carolina Synod, 1982-91; Bishop, North Carolina Synod, 1991-96. Vice Pastor for various congregations.
Other: Resigned May 25, 1996.

MENGERT, JOHN H.
Date/Place of Birth: 1813; Bremen, Germany.
Marriage/Child: Married and had one son.
Education: Attended University of Bonn.
License/Ordination: Licensed 1836 and ordained 1839 in Germany.
Calls: Served as missionary in Indiana; transferred 1859 from Indiana Synod to North Carolina Synod; first regular pastor and built church, St. Paul, Wilmington, 1858-62. From 1864 to 1870 lived at Ocala and Gainesville, Fla., still a member of North Carolina Synod, but no record of ministry in Florida. Transferred 1870 to Maryland Synod. Served in Washington, D.C., 1873-76.
Date of Death/Burial Location: October 26, 1876; Baltimore, Md.

MERCK, JOHN FRANKLIN

Date/Place of Birth: July 19, 1938; St. Petersburg, Fla.

Parents: Horace Raymond Merck and Dorothy (Melzer) Merck. An older brother is the Reverend Kenneth Horace Merck.

First Spouse/Marriage Date: Betty Suzanne (Funderburke) Merck; August 28, 1960 in Concord, N.C.

Children of First Marriage: John David, Paul Kenneth, Ann Elizabeth.

Second Spouse/Marriage Date: Nancy (Lowery) Merck; August 2, 1997.

Education: Lenoir-Rhyne, A.B. 1960; Lutheran Theological Southern Seminary, M.Div. 1964; Bowman Gray School of Medicine Clinical Pastoral Care, North Carolina Baptist Hospital, 1967; graduate studies at Lutheran Theological Southern Seminary, 1971; McCormick Seminary, D.Min. 1991.

Ordination: June 14, 1964 by North Carolina Synod.

Calls: Mission Developer/Pastor, Resurrection, Greensboro, 1964-69; Holy Communion, Dallas, 1969-89; Faith, Faith, 1989-97; A Mighty Fortress, Charlotte, 1997-. Vice Pastor at various congregations.

Other: Worship Leader, World Missions Event, 1981; Chair, Social Ministry Committee; Key '73 Planning Committee; Board, North Carolina Lutheran Homes, Inc. 1973-82; Board, Lutheran Services for the Aging, 1986-93, Vice President, 1990-93; Chair, Professional Services Committee, 1983-86; Chaplain, 1980 Convention of Synod; Regional Coordinator, Strength for Mission Appeal; District Dean of Southwestern District, 1978-85; Conference Dean for Central Conference, 1990-.

MERCK, KENNETH HORACE

Date/Place of Birth: April 24, 1933; Jacksonville, Fla.

Parents: Horace Raymond Merck and Dorothy (Melzer) Merck. Brother is the Reverend John Franklin Merck.

Spouse/Marriage Date: Judith (Coryell) Merck; June 9, 1956 in Indianapolis, Ind.

Children: Karen Marie, Gregory Norman, Eric Raymond.

Education: Lenoir-Rhyne, A.B. 1956; Lutheran Theological Southern Seminary, one year, Northwestern Seminary, B.D. 1960; Indiana University, Ph.D. Counseling/Psychology 1965.

Ordination: May 18, 1960 by Northwest Synod.

Calls: Redeemer, Milwaukee, Wis., 1960-61; Peace, Guilford County, 1961-62; Mission Developer, Nativity, Arden, 1962-63. Chaplain, Indiana University Medical Center, 1963-65.

MERRIMAN, NEDRA (PENROD)

Date/Place of Birth: September 20, 1951; Shelby, Tenn.

Parents: Ned Penrod and Iris (Witherspoon) Penrod.

Spouse/Marriage Date: David Berry Merriman; February 9, 1971 in West Lafayette, Ind.

Child: Emily Penrod.

Education: Vanderbilt University, B.A. 1977; Vanderbilt Divinity School, M.Div. 1988.

Ordination: November 10, 1988 by North Carolina Synod.

Calls: Grace, Raleigh, 1988-92; St. Michael, Doraville, Ga., 1992-.

METZ, GEORGE ALBERT

Date/Place of Birth: August 20, 1905; Charleston, S.C.
Parents: George John Louis Metz and Elsie (Lange) Metz.
Spouse/Marriage Date: Lucile (Heinz) Metz; July 25, 1935.
Children: Gerald Arthur, David Charles, John Richard, Paul Douglas.
Education: Newberry College, B.A. 1926; Lutheran Theological Southern Seminary, B.D. 1929; graduate studies at University of North Carolina at Chapel Hill.
Ordination: 1929 by South Carolina Synod.
Calls: Campus pastor to Lutheran students at University of North Carolina at Chapel Hill, before organization of Holy Trinity, 1929-31.
Other: Demitted ministry, 1931.
Date of Death/Burial Location: January 31, 1981; Charleston, S.C.

MEUTER, FREDERICK WILLIAM, III

Date/Place of Birth: September 13, 1957; Arlington, Va.
Parents: Frederick William Meuter, Jr. and Lillian Marie (Paul) Meuter.
Spouse/Marriage Date: Debra Lynn (Krumrey) Meuter; December 30, 1989.
Child: April Lynn.
Education: Lenoir-Rhyne, B.A. Theology, 1979; Chicago Seminary, M.Div. 1983, D.Min. 1996.
Ordination: May 29, 1983 by North Carolina Synod.
Calls: Advent, Spindale, 1983-86; Good Shepherd, Buena Park, Calif., 1987-90; Christ, Fort Lauderdale, Fla., 1991-. In 1998 was serving Immanuel, Ceresco, Neb.
Other: Lutheran Disaster Response.

MEYER, JOHN WILLIAM

License: Licensed 1812 by North Carolina Synod, but never ordained.
Calls: Beck's-Pilgrim-St. Luke, Davidson County, 1816-17; New Bethel, Stanly County, 1814-17.
Other: Name removed from roll in 1817. Spent life teaching in Davidson County in the days when there were no public schools.

MEYER, LAWRENCE FREDERICK

Date/Place of Birth: May 26, 1937; Oceanside, Long Island, N.Y.
Parents: The Reverend T. Rene Meyer and Janet M. Meyer.
Spouse/Marriage Date: Linda Carolyn (Barton) Meyer; December 28, 1984 in Ravenna, Ohio.
Children: Matthew, Erika Hite, Brian Hite, John.
Education: Capital University, Columbus, Ohio, B.S. 1959; Trinity Seminary, M.Div. 1963.
Ordination: June 15, 1963 by Ohio Synod, American Lutheran Church.
Calls: Puritas, Cleveland, Ohio, 1963-68; St. John, Canal Fulton, Ohio, 1968-77; Interim, Advent, Solon, Ohio, 1978-79; St. Paul, Ravenna, Ohio, 1979-86; St. Paul, Hickory, 1986-91; Reconciliation, Wilmington, 1991-.
Other: Chaplain, Constituting Convention, May 1987.

MEZEZERS, VALDIS

Date/Place of Birth: January 24, 1910; Riga, Latvia; came to this country from Germany in 1949.

Parents: Janis Steimachers Mezezers and Emilia (Bartuseviz) Mezezers.

Spouse/Marriage Date: Erika (Albina) Mezezers; June 23, 1940 in Riga.

Education: Gymnasium Jelgava, Latvia, 1936; University of Riga, 1940 Licentiate of Theology, 1943; graduate study, Johns Hopkins University, Temple University, Philadelphia, S.T.M. 1961, also doctoral studies to 1966; Berean Christian Seminary, Wichita, Kan., Th.D. 1974.

Ordination: 1940 by Archbishop of Latvian Lutheran Church.

Calls: In Latvia, 1941-44; two mission churches, Emmanuel, Stoney Creek, and Magothy-Chelsea Community, and evening services at the Latvian church group, Baltimore, Md., 1950-58; Latvian, Applebachsville, Pa., 1949-50; Tuckerton Parish, Pa., 1958-60; St. Paul, Sassamansville, Pa., 1960-65; Antioch, Dallas, 1965-75. Retired in 1975. Served as Interim Pastor at St. Luke from 1975-82.

Other: Professor (Religion, History) Displaced Persons Junior College, Wuerzburg, Germany, 1945-49 (under U.S. Military Government). Literary works: In Latvian: Editor, publisher, literary-religious monthly, *The Way,* 1945-48, sponsored by U.S. Military Government in Germany; several hymns in Latvian Church Hymnal; three plays: "The Hour of Sunrise," "When the Apple Tree Was Blooming," and "The People of the Farm;" two volumes of poems in English; Sermons, "God and Man," 1956; sermons and meditations, "The Great Life," 1957; "Jesus' Concept of Wealth and Poverty," 1961 (Temple University); Dissertation, "The Herrnhuterian Pietism in the Baltic."

Date of Death/Burial Location: June 6, 1982; St. Luke Cemetery, Lincolnton, N.C.

MICHAEL, DANIEL WILLIAM, SR.

Date/Place of Birth: December 18, 1857; Davidson County, N.C.

Parents: Jacob Michael and Rebecca (Long) Michael.

First Spouse/Marriage Date: Laura (Gorsett) Michael (died 1894).

Children of First Marriage: Eddy, Ney, Ralph, Willie Kate, Fred, Helen Blanche.

Second Spouse/Marriage Date: Lena (Troutman) Michael; 1895 (died a few months later).

Third Spouse/Marriage Date: Maude L. (Brill) Michael; December 23, 1896 in Intermont, W.Va.

Children of Third Marriage: May, Lois, Daniel W., Jr., Grace Elaine, Vida Ruth.

Education: Trinity College (forerunner of Duke University), A.B.; Lutheran Theological Southern Seminary; studied law one year at University of North Carolina, admitted to the bar.

Ordination: 1887 by North Carolina Synod.

Calls: Pilgrim-St. Luke, Davidson County, 1887-91; Amity, Iredell County, 1890-94; St. Michael, Troutman-St. Paul, Iredell County, 1891-95; from 1895 to 1921: Wardensville, W.Va.; Donegal, Pa.; Duluth, Minn.; Pleasant Unity and Scottdale, Pa.; Aurora and Chicago, Ill.; Myerstown, Pa.; and Tacoma, Wash.

Date of Death/Burial Location: December 12, 1921 in Tacoma, Wash.; Greenwood Cemetery, Superior, Wis.

MICHAEL, DON MALCOLM, SR.

Date/Place of Birth: September 16, 1925; Lexington, Davidson County, N.C.

Parents: James Archie Michael and Thelma (Fritts) Michael.

Spouse/Marriage Date: Helen Frances (Waggoner) Michael; August 21, 1948 in Salisbury, N.C.

Children: Don Malcolm, Jr., Julia Lynn.

Education: Lenoir-Rhyne, A.B. 1946; Lutheran Theological Southern Seminary, M.Div. 1949; graduate study, Harvard Divinity School, 1959.

Ordination: June 5, 1949 by North Carolina Synod.

Calls: Zion, Catawba County, 1949-51; Chaplain, U.S. Navy, 1951-78; Gloria Dei, Salisbury, 1978-87; retired 1987 in Salisbury, N.C.; Vice Pastor to various congregations.

Other: Member and Chair, Parish Life in Ministry Committee; Professional Services Committee; retired as Navy Chaplain July 31, 1978 and presented Meritorious Service Medal.

MIELKE, DAVID NATHANIEL

Date/Place of Birth: January 2, 1945; Brooklyn, N.Y.

Parents: Dr. Robert H. E. Mielke and Norma (Bachler) Mielke.

Spouse/Marriage Date: Margaret Sue (Barnes) Mielke; March 30, 1969 in Blountville, Tenn.

Children: Matthew David, Laura Lynn.

Education: East Tennessee State University, B.S. 1967; Gettysburg Seminary, Second Career Certificate, 1986; University of Tennessee, M.S., 1971, Ed.D. 1977.

Ordination: October 26, 1986 by North Carolina Synod.

Calls: St. John, Lenoir, 1986-91; Atonement, Wilkesboro, 1991-97; Our Savior, Jacksonville, 1997-; Vice Pastor at various congregations.

Other: Professor, Appalachian State University, Department of Leadership and Educational Studies, 1972-.

MILHOLLAND, PAUL BENJAMIN

Date/Place of Birth: May 16, 1961; Burlington, N.C.

Parents: The Reverend Dr. William F. Milholland, Sr. and Mary Anne (Beaver) Milholland.

Education: Lenoir-Rhyne, B.A. Religion and Theology, 1985; Clinical Pastoral Education, Lutheran Medical Center, Brooklyn, N.Y., 1986; Gettysburg Seminary, M.Div. 1989; graduate work Presbyterian School of Christian Education, 1994.

Ordination: June 2, 1989 by North Carolina Synod.

Calls: St. John, Concord, 1989-91; St. Paul, Hampton, Va., 1991-96; Christ the King, Miami, Fla., 1995-98; Messiah, North Fort Myers, Fla., 1998-.

Other: Youth Director, St. John, Fairfield, Pa., 1988-89; permanent Supply Preacher, Luther Chapel, Petersville, Md., 1988-89; Cabarrus County Council on Aging Advisory Board, Chair, Retreat Committee; County Task Force for Long Range Planning for Aging; Board, Cooperative Christian Ministry of Greater Hickory, N.C.; Board, Lutheridge, 1980-89; Youth Staffer with Metro New York Synod, 1982-83; Region 9 Evangelical Lutheran Church in America Steering Committee, 1982-83; Region 9 Evangelical Lutheran Church in America - Chair, Continuing Education Committee, 1982-83; Board and Executive

Committee, Virginia Synod Lutheran Family Services; President of Board, Hampton Ecumenical Lodgings and Provisions (homeless ministry); Publications: five articles on "Youth Ministry for Parish Teacher Journal," 1993, 1994; "Year of Evangelism for Voices of Congregational Life of Evangelical Lutheran Church in America."

MILHOLLAND, WILLIAM FRANKLIN, JR.

Date/Place of Birth: October 25, 1953; Salisbury, N.C.
Parents: The Reverend William Franklin Milholland, Sr. and Mary Anne (Beaver) Milholland.
Spouse/Marriage Date: Susan (Morris) Milholland; August 8, 1976 in Wilmington, N.C.
Children: Sarah Catherine, Joel Benjamin.
Education: Lenoir-Rhyne, B.A. History 1978; Lutheran Theological Southern Seminary, M.Div. 1987.
Ordination: May 29, 1987 by North Carolina Synod.
Calls: Bethel, Salisbury, 1987-89; Zion, Lexington, S.C., 1989-98; Community, Summerville, 1998-.
Other: Board, Lenoir-Rhyne, 1982-; Board, Alumni Association, Lenoir-Rhyne, 1979-81.

MILHOLLAND, WILLIAM FRANKLIN, SR.

Date/Place of Birth: August 21, 1929; Statesville, Iredell County, N.C.
Parents: Ira Franklin Milholland and Mabel Pressley (Stikeleather) Milholland.
Spouse/Marriage Date: Mary Anne (Beaver) Milholland; March 20, 1952 in Salisbury, N.C.
Children: The Reverend William F., Jr., David Clifford, The Reverend Paul Benjamin, John Christopher.
Education: Catawba College, A.B. Business 1951; Lutheran Theological Southern Seminary, M.Div. 1958; Lenoir-Rhyne, D.D., 1988.
Ordination: June 8, 1958 by North Carolina Synod.
Calls: Macedonia, Burlington, 1958-61; Christ, Roanoke, Va., 1961-68; St. Paul, Wilmington, 1968-75; St. Andrew, Hickory, 1975-94. Retired in 1994.
Other: Board, Lutheran Children's Home of the South, Salem, Va.; Chair, Evangelism Committee, Virginia Synod; North Carolina Synod Executive Board; Board, Lutheran Theological Southern Seminary; Chair of Board, Lenoir-Rhyne; Chair, Professional Preparation Committee; while at St. Andrew in Hickory, organized Lutherhaus (home for elderly and handicapped) and Luther Hope Apartments (housing for homeless); Delegate to three Lutheran Church in America Conventions.

MILLER, ADAM, JR.

Date/Place of Birth: February 23, 1801.

Parent: John Miller. Nephew of Adam Miller, Sr.

First Spouse/Marriage Date: Mary Ann (Rudisill) Miller; 1829.

Children of First Marriage: Catherine, S. Gerard and Frances (died at sixteen years).

Second Spouse/Marriage Date: Susan (Carpenter) Miller; 1857.

Children of Second Marriage: Gertrude and Candace.

Ordination: Ordained Deacon, 1825 and Pastor 1826 by Tennessee Synod.

Calls: Fifteen in North Carolina, 1831-46, most from six to ten years; Grace, St. John, St. Paul, and St. Stephen in Catawba County; Daniel's, Emmanuel, St. Luke, St. Paul, and Trinity in Lincoln County; Antioch and Bethel in Gaston County; Morning Star in Mecklenburg County; Mt. Moriah in Rowan County; Friendship in Alexander County; St. Martin in Stanly County.

Other: Secretary, Tennessee Synod, 1835. Withdrew from Tennessee Synod in October 1846, with others in project to organize The Reorganized Evangelical Lutheran Tennessee Synod, a small synod that eventually united with The Joint Synod of Ohio. Petitions for his reinstatement from St. James, Greene County, Tenn., and Salem, Cocke County, Tenn., were submitted to 1847 Convention of Tennessee Synod and considered, but the Synod declined request. Later joined Joint Synod of Ohio.

Date of Death/Burial Location: February 13, 1868; St. Paul Cemetery, near Newton, N.C.

MILLER, ADAM, SR.

Date/Place of Birth: April 18, 1760; York County, Pa. Uncle, not father of Adam Miller, Jr. Felt called to ministry because of dearth of pastors in East Tennessee and at age 53 preached first sermon.

Parents: Jacob Miller (Muller) and Mrs. Miller.

First Spouse/Marriage Date: Maria or Mary Ann (Wirtmiller) (Wirtmuller) Miller; around 1785.

Second Spouse/Marriage Date: Catherine (Fleenor) Miller; 1834.

License/Ordination: Licensed 1815 by North Carolina Synod, and ordained 1820 at age 60, at organizing convention of Tennessee Synod at Solomon Church, Greene County, Tenn.

Calls: Credited with having organized Miller Lutheran Church, which was received into the North Carolina Synod in 1811; a school teacher and cattleman, he was living in Sullivan County, Tenn., where he was, since Lutheran clergy were so few and so rarely available, prevailed upon by friends to preach his first sermon at age 53 in 1813. With the Reverend David Henkel, St. Martin, Cabarrus County, 1821; Immanuel, near Blountville, Tenn., 1815-29; Miller (apparently Lonas Chapel, Millertown) and Zion, Knox County, Tenn., 1818; Buehler's, Sullivan County, Tenn., 1819; St. Martin, McMinn County, Tenn., 1830; Washington County, Va.; supplied Old Pine Church in Shenandoah County, Va., 1826; St. Paul, Monroe County, Tenn., 1843; preached last sermon in Poor Valley Church, Washington County, Va., six days before death, caused by violent attack of scarlet fever.

Other: Around 1808 may have spent some time in the Knoxville area as a teacher. Secretary, Tennessee Synod, 1822-23.

Date of Death/Burial Location: July 6, 1844; Poor Valley Church, Washington County, Va.

MILLER, CALVIN LUTHER, SR.

Date/Place of Birth: April 30, 1870; Rockwell, N.C.
Parents: Crawford A. Miller and Mary M. (Peck) Miller.
Spouse/Marriage Date: Martha Lee (Pharr) Miller; September 21, 1898 in Concord, N.C.
Children: Calvin Luther, Jr., Mary B., Steven Franklin, Martha Alexander.
Education: Roanoke College, A.B. 1895, A.M. 1897; Chicago Seminary, B.D. 1901; Lenoir-Rhyne, D.D. 1924.
Ordination: 1898 by North Carolina Synod.

Calls: Beck's-Holly Grove-Emmanuel-Lebanon-Pilgrim-New Jerusalem, Davidson County, 1898-1903; Haven, Salisbury; Christ, East Spencer, 1903-05; organized and served, New Jerusalem, Catawba County, 1905-06; St. Andrew-Mt. Olive-St. Stephen, Hickory, 1905-10; Trinity, Greenville, S.C., 1912-22; Ascension, Chattanooga, Tenn., 1922-31; Supply, St. James, Fayetteville, 1938-39; supplied Lutheran churches (some from three to nine months) and a few of other denominations; Pastor Emeritus of Holly Grove, a church in first parish, which with New Jerusalem he last supplied (1948).
Other: Professor (Bible), Lenoir-Rhyne, 1905-10; and financial agent, 1910-12, raising funds to equip a dormitory, build Yoder Science Hall, and began an endowment fund; Superintendent, Iron Mountain School for Boys, Konnarock, Va., 1931-38; retired 1940 at Bennettsville, S.C.; Secretary, Tennessee Synod, 1901-02; founder and editor, *The Catawba Lutheran;* United Lutheran Church in America Board of Pensions, 1918-25; builder of eight churches; researcher in history of Lutheran Church in North Carolina and the South; contributor of articles, especially on home missions and church histories to religious and secular periodicals.
Date of Death/Burial Location: October 11, 1953; Oakwood Cemetery, Concord, North Carolina.

MILLER, CHARLES BEAUREGARD

Date/Place of Birth: March 24, 1861; Rowan County, N.C.
Parents: Charles R. Miller and Sarah Elizabeth (Sifferd) Miller. Maternal uncle of the wives of the Reverends L. P. Boland, O. W. Aderholdt, and John C. Peery (second wife), the Misses Maude and Annie Powlas, long-time missionaries in Japan, and the Reverends John K., Charles A., and J. Arthur Linn, and granduncle of the Reverends Hubert C. Linn and William P. Peery.
Spouse: M. Irene (McCutchan) Miller; February 19, 1889 near Middlebrook, Va.

Child: James Bennett.
Education: North Carolina College, Roanoke College; Gettysburg Seminary, 1887.
Ordination: 1887 by North Carolina Synod.
Calls: Concordia, Rowan County, Supply 1886, 1908-09; Macedonia, Burlington, 1890-95; Frieden's, Guilford County, 1890-92; St. Paul, Alamance County, 1890-93; St. James, Concord, 1896-1902; First, Albemarle, 1901-02; St. Mark, China Grove, 1902-07; Newport, Augusta County, Va., 1888-90; Hebron, Madison, Va., 1895-96; retired 1907 in China Grove, and engaged in secular employment; supplied Christiana, Granite Quarry, 1919-21.

Other: President, North Carolina Synod, 1900-02.
Date of Death/Burial Location: October 1, 1936; Charlotte, N.C.

MILLER, DAVID LEANDER

Date/Place of Birth: December 30, 1875; Catawba County, N.C.
Parents: Lemuel Cicero Miller and Caroline Jemima (Huffman) Miller.
Spouse/Marriage Date: Edith Maude (Price) Miller; November 30, 1909 in Luray, Va.
Children: Helen Virginia, Paul Edwin, Ruth Caroline, Carroll David.
Education: Lenoir-Rhyne, A.B. 1903; Chicago Seminary, 1907.
Ordination: 1907 by Tennessee Synod.
Calls: Mt. Calvary-Grace-Morning Star-Beth Eden, Page County, Va., 1907-09; Donegal, Pa., 1909-12; Solomon, St. Mary, Shenandoah County, Va., 1912-15; Trinity, Vale-Sardis, Catawba County-Cedar Grove, Lincoln County, 1916-18; Mt. Gilead-St. Martin, Cabarrus County, 1919-21; Mt. Hermon-Sharon-St. Martin, Iredell County, 1921-24; St. Peter-St. Thomas, Lexington County, S.C., 1924-34. Retired 1934 at Luray, Va.
Date of Death/Burial Location: May 29, 1949; Evergreen Cemetery, Luray, Va.

MILLER, EARLEAN

Date/Place of Birth: November 22, 1935; Robbins, Ill.
Parents: Early Witcher Miller, Sr. and Rosalie Bernice (Beard) Miller.
Education: Roosevelt University, 1975; Chicago Seminary, M.Div. 1979.
Ordination: August 26, 1979 by Indiana-Kentucky Synod.
Calls: Prince of Peace, Greensboro, 1979-84; Calvary, Minneapolis, Minn., 1984-97; Hope, Columbus, Ohio, 1998-.
Other: First black woman to be ordained into ministry in a Lutheran church. Task Force on Drug Abuse; Task Force on New Church Designs for the Commission for a New Lutheran Church.

MILLER, GILMER CLINTON, JR.

Date/Place of Birth: June 25, 1943; Salisbury, N.C.
Parents: Gilmer Clinton Miller, Sr. and Dorothy (Kluttz) Miller.
Spouse/Marriage Date: Nancy Hudson (Grier) Miller; December 27, 1972 in Charlotte, N.C.
Child: Gilmer Clinton, III.
Education: Lenoir-Rhyne, B.A. Sociology, 1965; Lutheran Theological Southern Seminary, M.Div. 1969.
Ordination: June 1, 1969 by North Carolina Synod.
Calls: St. Luke, Conover, 1969-76; St. Michael, High Point, 1976-81; New Jerusalem, Hickory, 1981-90; St. Stephen, Lenoir, 1990-; Vice Pastor at various congregations.
Other: Synod Council, 1992-ff.; Chair, Ecumenical Affairs Committee, 1988-ff.

MILLER, GLENN ALLEN

Date/Place of Birth: November 7, 1909; Rockwell, N.C.
Parents: Calvin Middleton Miller and Maggie Lee (Bost) Miller.
Spouse/Marriage Date: Virjilia Ruth (Hollis) Miller; May 25 1941 in Waynesboro, Tenn.
Children: The Reverend Hollis Allen, Marilyn Lee, Cheryll Jill.
Education: Lenoir-Rhyne, A.B. 1930; graduate study for "A" grade high school principal's certificate; Lutheran Theological Southern Seminary, 1934.
Ordination: 1934 by North Carolina Synod.
Calls: Calvary, Concord, 1934-36; Mt. Olive-St. Stephen, Cabarrus County, 1944-50; Trinity, Vale, 1950-59; St. Peter, Rowan County, 1959-75; retired December 31, 1975.
Other: Landis high school teacher and coach, 1930-31; Southmont High School teacher and coach, 1939-43, and principal, 1943-44; nominated for Lenoir-Rhyne and North Carolina State Sports Halls of Fame.
Date of Death/Burial Location: May 13, 1981; St. Peter Cemetery, Salisbury, N.C.

MILLER, HENDERSON NEIFFER

Date/Place of Birth: June 8, 1872; Salisbury, N.C.
Parents: Calvin J. Miller and Jessie S. (Ketchie) Miller.
Spouse/Marriage Date: Cora L. (Patterson) Miller; 1894 in China Grove, N.C.
Children: Cora Louise, the Reverend Frank Henderson, Nellie Jones, Ethel Roberta.
Education: North Carolina College, A.B. 1891; Gettysburg Seminary, 1894; Gettysburg College, Ph.D. 1896.
Ordination: 1894 by Maryland Synod.
Calls: Grace-Lebanon-Salem, Rowan County, 1895-97; Holy Trinity, Mt. Pleasant, 1897-98; in Ohio, Georgia, (Holy Trinity, Wytheville, Va., 1916-17) and Pennsylvania, 1902-33.
Other: Principal, Mont Amoena Seminary, 1897-1902; President, Marion Junior College, 1913-16; Superintendent, Artman Home, Ambler, Pa., 1930-34; Secretary, North Carolina Synod, 1897-98; retired 1933.
Date of Death/Burial Location: 1939; China Grove, N.C.

MILLER, HOLLIS ALLEN

Date/Place of Birth: December 29, 1942; Lexington, N.C.
Parents: The Reverend Glenn A. Miller and Ruth Vergilia (Hollis) Miller.
Spouse/Marriage Date: Susan (Gribble) Miller; August 8, 1965 in Kannapolis, N.C.
Children: Jeffrey Allen, Jonathan Andrew.
Education: Lenoir-Rhyne, A.B. Sociology 1965; Lutheran Theological Southern Seminary, M.Div. 1969; Drew Theological School, D.Min. 1984.
Ordination: June 1, 1969 by North Carolina Synod.
Calls: Associate Pastor, St. John, Salisbury, 1969-73; Mission Developer/Pastor, St. Peter, Southport, 1973- 76; Grace, Rock Hill, S.C., 1976-81; Zion, Lexington, S.C., 1981-89; St. James, Concord, 1989-96.
Other: Contributing writer for Emphasis: *A Preaching Journal for the Parish Pastor;* Delegate and visitor to Lutheran Church in America conventions and Evangelical Lutheran Church in America Churchwide Assemblies; Board, Lutheran Theological Southern

Seminary; President of Board, Camp and Conference Ministries, South Carolina Synod; Dean, North Carolina and South Carolina Synods; Parish Education and American Missions Committees and Task Force on Justice and Social Change, North Carolina Synod; Evangelism and Stewardship Committees, South Carolina Synod; Chair, Professional Leadership Service Committee, South Carolina Synod; Board, Lenoir-Rhyne Alumni Association; Chair, Lenoir-Rhyne Alumni Appreciation Day; voting member, two National Assemblies, Evangelical Lutheran Church in America; Concord Rotary Club; Concord Human Relations Board.

Date of Death/Burial Location: June 30, 1996; Carolina Memorial Park in Concord, N.C.

MILLER, JACOB

License/Ordination: Licensed 1812 in Low's Church, Guilford County, and ordained 1822 in Pilgrim Church, Davidson County.

Calls: No record of his ministry or other activity earlier than 1821. Listed as pastor of St. Luke, Davidson County, 1821-27, and of Beck's-Pilgrim, Davidson County, 1824-27. Gaps in the listing of pastors of the last two churches would justify assumption that he served them, too, from 1821.

Other: Presumably went to Indiana as missionary from North Carolina Synod and labored there, where preachers were so badly needed; took a leading part in organizing Indiana Synod; transferred to it in 1840 from North Carolina Synod.

Burial Location: Indiana.

MILLER, JEFFERSON POLYCARP

Date/Place of Birth: May 12, 1866; Catawba County, N.C.

Parents: John Monroe Miller and Harriet Camilla (Isenhower) Miller.

Spouse/Marriage Date: Emma Eleanora "Ella" (Carpenter) Miller; November 20, 1899 in Catawba County, N.C.

Children: Robert Leroy, Grace Virginia.

Education: Concordia College (N.C.); Chicago Seminary; Wittenberg University, D.D. 1921.

Ordination: 1889 by Tennessee Synod.

Calls: Friendship-Shiloh, Alexander County, 1891-93; Sardis, Hickory, Catawba County, 1891-94, and St. Timothy, 1893-95, Catawba County; Mt. Moriah, Rowan County, 1895-99; St. Mark, Rowan County, 1895-1901; Union-Christiana, Rowan County, 1900-02; Supply, Christ, East Spencer, 1902; Orangeburg, Orangeburg, S.C., 1902-05; Burkes Garden, Burkes Garden, Va., 1905-07; Holy Trinity, Mt. Pleasant; Holy Trinity, Wytheville, Va., 1907-11; Supply, St. Andrew-Mt. Hermon, Concord, 1909; Supply, Holy Trinity, Charlotte; in South Carolina and Virginia, (Burkes Garden, Tazewell County, Va.), 1902-07; First Lutheran, Tyrone, Pa., 1915-19; St. Paul, Redmond, Ind., 1919-28; Holy Trinity, Wytheville, Va., 1928-31; retired at Radford, Va.

Other: Secretary, Tennessee Synod, 1894-96; Instructor (Greek), Lenoir-Rhyne; Instructor, Mount Pleasant Collegiate Institute, and Mont Amoena Seminary, 1907-11; Field Representative, Elizabeth College, 1914-15; President, Marion College, 1911-13; President, Indiana Synod.

Date of Death/Burial Location: May 11, 1939; Sunset Cemetery, Christiansburg, Va.

MILLER, JOHN ABNER LOCKE

Date/Place of Birth: August 9, 1858; Zeb, Rowan County, N.C.

Parents: Captain Alfred Alexander Miller and Mary Elizabeth (Hall) Miller. Father was killed in combat at Fredericksburg, Va. on December 12, 1862; mother died three months after father's death.

Spouse/Marriage Date: Mary Ann (Pinkston) Miller; December 28, 1876 near Salisbury, N.C.

Children: Bernard Alonzo, William Alfred, Samuel Cyrus, Mrs. Sallie Leora Muller Pike, Robert Love, Charles Elmer.

Education: Franklin Academy, Zeb, where classmates were the Reverends H. A. Trexler and H. M. Brown; while engaged in secular work, he read and studied theology at night for a period of twenty years under the guidance of neighboring pastors; when examined for ordination in 1910 he was found well-prepared.

Ordination: 1910 at age 52 by North Carolina Synod.

Calls: Hopewell-Nazareth-Shiloh, Forsyth County, 1909-14; St. Martin, Stanly County, 1914-19; served in Virginia, at Bridgewater, Middlebrook, Price Fork, and Willis, 1919-30; retired 1930 to live with daughter at Concord; transferred back to North Carolina Synod, 1932; supplied Cold Water, Cabarrus County, 1934-40 to age 82.

Date of Death/Burial Location: October 23, 1945; Bethel Church, Rowan County, N.C.

MILLER, JOHN (JOSEPH), I

Date/Place of Birth: June 2, 1830; Rockingham County, Va.

Parents: Joseph Miller and Elizabeth (Link) Miller. Younger brother of the Reverend Peter Miller.

Spouse/Marriage Date: Miss Hules; October 2, 1860 in Baltimore, Md.

Education: Roanoke College; received D.D. degree in 1886; attended Gettysburg Seminary.

Ordination: 1859 by Maryland Synod.

Calls: In West Virginia: Shepherdstown; in Maryland: Clearspring; in Virginia: Buena Vista, Luray, Browntown, Staunton, and Churchville; in South Carolina: Cedar Grove, Lexington County, and St. James, Graniteville; none in North Carolina. Member of Tennessee Synod, 1885-94.

Other: In Staunton, Va., seventeen years, five years as pastor and twelve years as first Principal of Staunton Female Seminary, 1870-82; operated Von Bora College for Girls, while pastor at Luray, Va.; also a girls' school at Buena Vista, Va., for a few sessions; publisher and editor of *The Lutheran Visitor* at Staunton, Va., a few years until taken over in 1868 by General Synod South; Secretary, 1861-62, President, 1866-67, Virginia Synod.

Date of Death/Burial Location: 1912; Virginia.

MILLER, LAWRENCE W.

Date/Place of Birth: February 8, 1903; Lecksville, Ohio.

Parents: William Miller and Minnie Miller.

Spouse/Marriage Date: Vivian (Newton) Miller.

Children: Janice Miller Romeo, Carolyn Miller, William Miller.

Education: Capital University Theological Seminary, 1928; Chicago Lutheran Seminary, Doctor of Sacred Theology, 1942.

Ordination: June 15, 1928 by Joint Synod of Ohio.

Calls: St. Mark, Claremont, 1928-59.

Other: Author of two books: *The Christian's Resurrection Body, Its Nature and Characteristics* and *Jesus Christ is Alive.*

Date of Death/Burial Location: March 29, 1959; Claremont, N.C.

MILLER, LEROY SUMMIE

Date/Place of Birth: March 13, 1896; Catawba County, N.C.

Parents: William Absalom Miller and Laura Blanche (Isenhour) Miller.

Spouse/Marriage Date: Erin Estelle (Payne) Miller; November 9, 1920 in Hickory, N.C.

Child: Freda Estelle Thompson.

Education: Lenoir-Rhyne, A.B. 1916; Chicago Seminary, 1920.

License/Ordination: Licensed 1920 and ordained 1921 by the Ohio Synod.

Calls: In Ohio: Adamsville, 1920-24; Toledo, 1924-28; in North Carolina: St. Stephen-St. John, Lenoir, 1928-43; Bethel-Bethphage-St. Mark-St. Paul, Crouse (at last named, built new church after fire, 1949), 1943-50; same parish without Bethphage, 1950-61; retired 1961 at Lenoir; St. Stephen, Lenoir, 1961-69, Pastor Emeritus.

Other: Principal, Enochville High School, 1916-17; President, Western Conference, United Evangelical Lutheran Synod of North Carolina, 1940-42; contributed articles to *The Lutheran* from 1930-40; President, Lenoir and Catawba County Lutheran Ministers' Associations.

Date of Death/Burial Location: April 9, 1969; Oakwood Cemetery, Hickory, N.C.

MILLER, LESTER DAVID, JR.

Date/Place of Birth: April 15, 1919; Lenoir, N.C.

Parents: The Reverend Lester David Miller, Sr. and Lola Anna (Miller) Miller.

Spouse/Marriage Date: Annie R. (Lytle) Miller; November 25, 1942 in Hickory, N.C.

Children: Anita Lytle Rich, Andrea Frye.

Education: Lenoir-Rhyne, A.B. 1939, Mus.D. 1960; Lutheran Theological Southern Seminary, B.D. 1942; School of Music, Union Seminary (N.Y.), M.S.M. 1947; post graduate work, Kirchenmusikschule, Hannover, Germany, 1959.

Ordination: June 4, 1942 by North Carolina Synod.

Calls: Assistant Pastor, Macedonia, Burlington, 1942-44; Assistant Pastor, Holy Trinity, New York City, N.Y., 1944-47; Associate Pastor, Trinity, Fort Wayne, Ind., 1947-54; St. Mark, Van Wert, Ohio, 1954-55; Professor of Church Music, Hamma School of Theology, 1955-78; Professor of Church Music, Lutheran Theological Southern Seminary, 1978-86, Professor Emeritus, 1986; retired in 1986.

Other: Director and Dean, 1955-78, School of Music, and Choir Director, Wittenberg University; Executive Committee and Consulting Committee, United Lutheran Church in America Department of Worship, 1955-62; Author-composer of *Psalms for Today* and *A Call to Remembrance* for speech choir, published by United Lutheran Church in America Women's Missionary Society; *A Book of Descants,* for publication by Lutheran Church in America Board of Publication; hymn tune, *Fortitudo,* for No. 502 (Service Book and Hymnal); and seven hymn tunes in *Lutheran Hymnal of Japan, Service Book and Hymnal, Church School Hymnal for Children; Who's Who in America, 1969; Dictionary of*

International Biography, 1970; Who's Who in Religion; Citation for Distinguished Service by Choral Conductors Guild in America, 1960; Luther Medallion Award from Evangelical Lutheran Church of Germany for outstanding leadership in church music, 1969; Distinguished Alumnus Award, Lenoir-Rhyne, 1972; Distinguished Service Award, Wittenberg University, 1974; Distinguished Service Award, Newberry College, 1992; Award for Outstanding Excellence in Religious Music by Protestant Radio and Television Center, 1988; Designated Fellow of Hymn Society in the United States of America and Canada, 1997; Department of Worship, United Lutheran Church in America, 1956-63; Chair, Music Committee of Department of Worship, 1959-63; Commission on Liturgy and Hymnal, National Lutheran Council, 1958-63; Lutheran Representative on Worship and the Arts, National Council of Churches, 1960-63; Executive Committee, Hymn Society of America, 1972-80, President, 1976-80; Commission on Worship, Lutheran Church in America, 1978-85; Board, Liturgical Conference, 1979-84; Worship and Music Committees in Indiana, Ohio, and South Carolina Synods; author of articles in *The Lutheran, Luther Life, High Ideals, Parish School Magazine, Resource, Lutheran Church Quarterly, Journal of Church Music, The Hymn, The American Organist;* Author: *Hymns, The Story of Christian Hymns, Psalms for Today;* Composer of 50 Descants for Hymns of the Church, 12 Descants in Armed Forces Hymnal, 1973; Director of choirs at Constituting Convention, Lutheran Church in America; Lutheran Youth Convocations in Kansas and Miami, Fla.; Organist, Lutheran World Federation, Helsinki, 1963; directed Wittenberg Choir on Lutheran Series of Protestant Hour for twenty consecutive years; directed Wittenberg Choir on National Broadcasting Corporation series, National Radio Pulpit, Great Choirs of America, and CBS Church of the Air, Armed Forces Radio Network throughout the world for twenty years; Organizer/Director of Lutheran Student Choir of Greater New York, 1944-47; Organizer/Director, Lutheran Bach Choir of Columbia, S.C., 1980-87; Guest Clinician Choral Music, Organ Playing at Music Week, Lutheridge, 1955, 1957, 1960, 1962, 1965, 1968, 1970, 1972, 1975, Chaplain, 1994; honored by U.S. Congress with Resolution commending him and the Wittenberg Choir for World Tour of 1966 as "Ambassadors of Song and Goodwill to the World for the United States," Congressional Record, 89th Congress, Second Session, Resolution 963; Board, Chantry Music Press, 1960-78.

MILLER, LESTER DAVID, SR.
Date/Place of Birth: February 11, 1883; Catawba County, N.C.
Parents: Philo Lee Miller and Candace L. (Frye) Miller. A younger brother is the Reverend Paul L. Miller.
Spouse/Marriage Date: Lola Anna Miller; June 23, 1907 in Hickory, N.C.
Children: Frances Louise (married the Reverend M. L. Stirewalt, Jr.), the Reverend L. David, Jr.
Education: Lenoir-Rhyne, A.B. 1906, D.D. 1943; Lutheran Theological Southern Seminary, 1909.
Ordination: 1909 by Tennessee Synod.
Calls: Mt. Gilead-St. Martin, Cabarrus County, 1909-18; St. Stephen, Lenoir, 1918-24; St. John, Cabarrus County, 1924-44; supplied Mt. Hermon, 1916-18, and Cold Water, 1924, 1930-33, Cabarrus County.
Other: Board, Lenoir-Rhyne, and Executive Committee of Synod; retired 1944 at Hickory.
Date of Death/Burial Location: September 8, 1955; St. Timothy Church, Catawba County, N.C.

MILLER, MARTIN MONROE

Date/Place of Birth: September 9, 1833; Cabarrus County, N.C.; later resided in Zeb/Franklin, Rowan County.
Parents: John Cyrus Miller and Sophia (Propst) Miller.
Spouse: Sarah Rebecca (Winkler) Miller.
Child: Margaret "Maggie" Monroe.
Education: Attended Gettysburg College, 1858-59.
License: According to *History of the Lutheran Church in North Carolina,* (1803-1953), was licensed in 1861 (probably earlier).
Calls: Shiloh, Forsyth County, 1861; "Old Dutch Church," Nazareth, Rural Hall, N.C.
Other: Career was cut short by war service, which was marked in 1862 by enlistment in Confederate States Army on March 5, capture at Sharpsburg, Md., September 17, and exchanged November 10 and in 1863 by wounds at Gettysburg on July 2 capture at Hagerstown, Md. July 5 and parole and exchange in August. From wounds at Gettysburg, he had lost sound use of a leg, and wrote Governor Vance (North Carolina), requesting appointment as chaplain for the Salisbury Wayside Hospital, or a post as a commissary clerk. Presumably he did not receive one.
Death/Burial Location: Mortally wounded at Cold Harbor, Va., June 7, 1864 in 31st year. Buried at Bethel Church, Rowan County, N.C.

MILLER, MATTHEW LANE

Date/Place of Birth: July 17, 1967; Salt Lake City, Utah.
Parents: James R. Miller and Nan (Phillips) Miller.
Spouse/Marriage Date: Tracy Suzzane Carrier-Miller, December 19, 1992.
Education: Appalachian State University, B.S. Art 1991; Lutheran Theological Southern Seminary, M.Div. 1995.
Ordination: May 19, 1995 by North Carolina Synod.
Calls: Center Grove, Kannapolis, 1995-98; Atonement, Wilkesboro, 1998-.

MILLER, PAUL LEOPOLD

Date/Place of Birth: May 11, 1895; Catawba County, N.C.
Parents: Philo Lee Miller and Candace (Frye) Miller. An older brother was the Reverend Lester D. Miller, Sr.
Spouse/Marriage Date: Willie (Deal) Miller; May 1921 in Hickory, N.C.
Children: Rebecca Evelyn Wolfe, Mary Louise Greene, Doris Elizabeth (married the Reverend L. Aaron Lippard).
Education: Lenoir-Rhyne, A.B. 1918; Lutheran Theological Southern Seminary, 1921.
Ordination: June 10, 1921 by North Carolina Synod.
Calls: St. Luke-Morning Star, Monroe, 1921-22; Organ-Ebenezer, Rowan County, 1922-27; Organ only, 1927-36; Good Hope, Hickory-St. Paul, Startown, 1936-44; Good Hope only (church built on new site), 1944-60; retired 1960 at Hickory; resident supply, St. Andrew, Andrews and Vice Pastor at various congregations.
Date of Death/Burial Location: September 23, 1982; St. Timothy Cemetery, Hickory, N.C.

MILLER, PETER
Date/Place of Birth: September 18, 1828; Rockingham County, Va.
Parents: Joseph Miller and Elizabeth (Link) Miller. Older brother of the Reverend J. I. Miller. A grandson of their parents was the Reverend C. Armand Miller.
License/Ordination: Licensed 1858 and ordained 1860 by Virginia Synod.
Calls: Missionary work in Capon-North River Parish in Harden and Hampshire Counties, West Virginia, 1858-71, 1884-90, and after division into two parishes: North River, 1898-1914, and Capon, 1915-18, organized a number of churches; Mt. Jackson, Orkney Springs, Woodstock, Toms Brook, Floyd County, and Churchville, all in Virginia, 1871-80, 1894-98; served churches in South Carolina, 1880-84; in North Carolina: St. John, 1890-93; Mt. Hermon, 1893-94, Cabarrus County.
Other: Secretary 1867-68, President 1871-72, 1903-04, Virginia Synod.
Date of Death/Burial Location: April 21, 1918; Woodstock, Va.

MILLER, PETER LINK
Date/Place of Birth: June 9, 1855; Rockingham County, Va.
Parent: The Reverend Peter H. Miller.
Spouse/Marriage Date: Alice (Coffman) Miller; 1883.
Child: Milton L., Dr. J. R.
Education: No formal college or seminary training, but studied theology under the Reverend A. A. J. Bushong, Woodstock, Va.
License/Ordination: Licensed 1891 and ordained 1895 by Virginia Synod.
Calls: From 1891 in West Virginia, Virginia, Ohio, and Tennessee; in North Carolina: First, Albemarle 1898-1901; Christ, East Spencer (church built on new site), 1898-99; Luther's, Rowan County, 1899; transferred to Wittenberg Synod, 1901; retired at Point Pleasant, W.Va.
Date of Death/Burial Location: June 9, 1936; Point Pleasant, W.Va.

MILLER, RICHARD J.
Date/Place of Birth: December 15, 1947; Richmond County, N.Y.
Parents: Henry J. Miller and Margaret I. Miller.
Spouse/Marriage Date: Linda Gayle (Graham) Miller; November 21, 1970 in Geary, Okla.
Education: Wagner College, B.A. 1973; Lutheran Theological Southern Seminary, M.Div. 1977.
Ordination: May 29, 1977 by South Carolina Synod.
Calls: St. Paul, Burlington, 1977-82; transferred to Central States Synod on January 4, 1982.
Other: Resigned February 9, 1990 in Springfield, Mo.

MILLER, ROBERT JOHNSTONE
Date/Place of Birth: July 11, 1758 near Dundee, Scotland.
Parents: George Miller and Margaret (Bathier) Miller.
Spouse: Mary (Perkins) Miller.
Child: A daughter, Catherine, married the Reverend Godfrey Dreher, a pioneer Lutheran pastor of North Carolina Synod serving in South Carolina.
Education: Dundee Classical School.
License/Ordination: Licensed by Methodist Church, and served in western counties of North Carolina. Among churches served were Whitehaven, Lincoln County, nominally Episcopal but with Lutherans and perhaps Reforms worshiping there. On their petition, no Episcopal diocese then being in North Carolina, he was examined and ordained May 20, 1794 by resident Lutheran pastors Nussmann, Arends, Roschen, Bernhardt, and Storch, in St. John, Cabarrus County; perhaps the first English-speaking and first Episcopal minister to be ordained in North Carolina (*History of the Lutheran Church in North Carolina,* (1803- 1953), p. 25).
Calls: Dutchman's Creek (later named Reformation), Davie County; organized St. Michael, Troutman, 1815-21.
Other: Came in 1774 to Charlestown, Mass., to assist an older brother in East and West India trade. Served in Colonial Army in battles of Long Island, Brandywine, White Plains, and Valley Forge; was discharged in the South. Took part in organizing North Carolina Synod in 1803; first Secretary, 1803-05; President, 1812; offered to be and was appointed itinerant missionary, 1810; traveling five months in Virginia, East Tennessee and the Carolinas, Miller covered an estimated 3000 miles. In 1813, he made another missionary tour for the Synod which covered 1082 miles in two months and twelve days. Withdrawing from Lutheran Church activity, in 1821 was ordained priest by Episcopal bishop in Raleigh, and served Episcopal churches in Lincoln, Burke, Iredell, and other counties, 1821-34. Author of the catechism, *An Introduction to the Knowledge of the Christian Religion,* published in Salisbury in 1789.
Date of Death/Burial Location: 1834; Lenoir, N.C.

MILLER, ROBERT THOMAS
Date/Place of Birth: October 30, 1930; Greenville, S.C.
Parents: Robert E. Miller and Zunie (Stewart) Miller.
Education: Lenoir-Rhyne, A.B. 1953; Lutheran Theological Southern Seminary, B.D. 1956.
Ordination: 1956 by North Carolina Synod.
Calls: Assistant Pastor, First, Norfolk, Va., 1956-58; Holy Trinity, Newport, Tenn.; Millers-Zion, near Knoxville, Tenn.
Other: Demitted ministry October 10, 1961 at Knoxville, Tenn.

MILLER, THOMAS W.
License/Ordination: Licensed 1832 and ordained 1833 by Virginia Synod.
Calls: In Virginia, 1832-50: St. Jacob, Fincastle; Zion, Burke Ford; Floyd County; Hebron, Madison; St. Peter, Blacksburg; Zion, Roanoke County, and Zion, Edinburg.
Other: President, Virginia Synod, 1834-35; transferred to Virginia Special Conference of Tennessee Synod 1865 of which was President in 1873; no record of Tennessee Synod

churches, probably in Virginia, which he served; Treasurer, Tennessee Synod, 1870-71. Transferred back to Virginia Synod, 1878.
Date of Death/Burial Location: November 1, 1880; Summsville, Va.

MILSTEN, JEFFREY ALAN
Date/Place of Birth: December 5, 1961; Tacoma, Wash.
Parents: Alfred Milsten and Ramona Milsten.
Education: Pierce College, A.A. 1982; University of Virginia, B.S. 1984; Gettysburg Seminary, M.Div. 1992.
Ordination: July 18, 1993 by North Carolina and Southwest Washington Synod.
Calls: St. James, Concord, 1993-97; Clearwater Parish, Orofino, Idaho, 1997-.

MIMS, BILLY BURNS, JR.
Date/Place of Birth: June 18, 1946; Greensboro, N.C.
Parents: Billy Burns Mims, Sr. and Virginia (Umbaugh) Mims.
Spouse/Marriage Date: Sherry Lynne (Foust) Mims; December 21, 1968.
Children: John Thomas, Stephen Frederick.
Education: University of North Carolina at Chapel Hill, B.A. Psychology 1968; Lutheran Theological Southern Seminary, M.Div. 1972; Union Seminary, (Va.), D.Min. 1983.
Ordination: June 4, 1972 by North Carolina Synod.
Calls: Wittenberg, Granite Quarry, 1972-74; Incarnation, Columbia, S.C., 1974-79; Orangeburg, Orangeburg, S.C., 1979-87; Beth Eden, Newton, 1987-; Vice Pastor at various congregations.
Other: In South Carolina: Chair, Professional Leadership Service Committee; Dean, Amelia District; in North Carolina: Part-time faculty, Lenoir-Rhyne, 1995-; Board, Lutheridge, Vice President and Chair of Program Committee, 1981-91; Board, Lutheridge-Lutherock Ministries, President, 1991-; Dean, Western Piedmont Conference, 1992-; Worship Committee, 1990-93; Delegate, 1986 Lutheran Church in America Convention; President, Newton-Conover Rotary Club; Clarinetist with Lenoir Rhyne Wind Ensemble, Western Piedmont Chamber Orchestra; *Who's Who in Religion*, 1985.

MISENHEIMER, CLYDE ALTON
Date/Place of Birth: January 5, 1914; Rockwell, N.C.
Parents: John A. Misenheimer and Margaret (Miller) Misenheimer.
Spouse/Marriage Date: Edith (Ritchie) Misenheimer; June 7 1944 in Richfield, N.C.
Child: Cynthia Rose Fritts.
Education: Lenoir-Rhyne, A.B. 1935; Lutheran Theological Southern Seminary, B.D. 1938.
Ordination: June 2, 1938 by North Carolina Synod.
Calls: Lebanon-Providence, Rowan County; Amity, Iredell County; St. Matthew, Davie County, 1938-39; St. Stephen-Mt. Olive, Cabarrus County, 1939-43; St. Luke, Bear Poplar, 1943-56; Mission Developer/Pastor, Faith, Conover, 1956-60; Concordia, Rowan County, 1960-78; Vice Pastor at various congregations.

Other: Board, Children's Home of the South, 1952-60; Board, Lowman Home, 1963-66; American Missions Committee, 1962-63; Stewardship Committee, 1962-68; Board, Lenoir-Rhyne, 1968-71; Executive Board of Synod, 1973-77; Delegate to Convention of Lutheran Church in America, 1966.
Date of Death/Burial Location: February 7, 1978; Concordia Cemetery, China Grove, N.C.

MISENHEIMER, DAVID LENTZ

Date/Place of Birth: March 19, 1946; Rockwell, N.C., brother of The Reverends James Stephen and John Charles Misenheimer.
Parents: The Reverend Dr. Ernest Luther Misenheimer, Jr. and Margaret (Lentz) Misenheimer.
Spouse/Marriage Date: Jacqualyn Collins (Wells) Misenheimer; June 28, 1969 in Seaford, Del.
Child: Jennifer Lauren.
Education: Lenoir-Rhyne, A.B. 1968; Lutheran Theological Southern Seminary, M.Div. 1972; University of South Carolina, M.A. 1968-70.
Ordination: June 4, 1972 by North Carolina Synod.
Calls: Associate Pastor, Mt. Tabor, West Columbia, S.C., 1972-74; A Mighty Fortress, Charlotte, 1974-80; St. Martin, Houston, Texas, 1980-83; Christ, Charlotte, 1983-97.
Other: Removed from roll, 1997.

MISENHEIMER, ERNEST LUTHER, JR.

Date/Place of Birth: March 10, 1915; Richfield, Stanly County, N.C. Great grandson of the Reverend Whitson Kimball, Lutheran Pastor and former President of the North Carolina Synod.
Parents: Ernest Luther Misenheimer, Sr. and Ora (Whitley) Misenheimer.
Spouse/Marriage Date: Margaret (Lentz) Misenheimer; July 11, 1941 in Mt. Ulla, near Salisbury, N.C.
Children: Ernest Luther, III, The Reverend David Lentz, The Reverend John Charles, The Reverend James Stephen.
Education: Lenoir-Rhyne, A.B. 1937, D.D. 1959; Lutheran Theological Southern Seminary, B.D. 1940.
Ordination: May 30, 1940 by North Carolina Synod.
Calls: Assistant Pastor, St. John, Salisbury, 1940-43; St. James-Immanuel, Rockwell, 1943-49; St. Mark's, Mooresville, 1949-51; Center Grove, Kannapolis, 1951-55; Assistant to President of Synod, Dr. F. L. Conrad, 1955-62, and Dr. George R. Whittecar, 1963-78, as Director for Evangelism, Stewardship and Social Ministry; Bishop of North Carolina Synod, 1978-82; retired August 31, 1982; Vice Pastor for various congregations.
Other: Chair, Stewardship Committee, 1948-55; Delegate to fourteen United Lutheran Church in America and Lutheran Church in America Conventions, 1948-82; North Carolina Council of Churches, 1962-63; Board, Lutheran Services for the Aging, 1978-98; Chair, North Carolina Lutheran Homes Appeal Committee, 1984- 87; North Carolina Lutheran Homes Appeal Follow-up Director, 1985-87; Chair, North Carolina Synod Transition Team Preparatory to Merger, 1986-87; Presiding officer for Constituting Conventions for Florida and North Carolina Synods, 1987; Author, "Christ Gives You the

Green Light," stewardship tract, published by Lutheran Laymen's Movement for Stewardship.

MISENHEIMER, JAMES STEPHEN

Date/Place of Birth: January 16, 1954; Mooresville, Iredell County, N.C., brother of The Reverends David Lentz and John Charles Misenheimer.
Parents: The Reverend Dr. Ernest Luther Misenheimer, Jr. and Margaret (Lentz) Misenheimer.
Spouse/Marriage Date: Jeanne (Keener) Misenheimer; December 30, 1983 in Granite Falls, N.C.
Children: Tiffany, Joshua Stephen.
Education: Lenoir-Rhyne, B.A. 1976; Clinical Pastoral Education, M.D. Anderson Cancer and Tumor Hospital, Houston, Texas, 1980; Lutheran Theological Southern Seminary, M.Div. 1982.
Ordination: June 6, 1982 by North Carolina Synod.
Calls: Philadelphia, Granite Falls, 1982-88; St. John, Knoxville, Tenn., 1988-.
Other: In Southeastern Synod: Budget and Finance Committee Member, Chair; Discipline Committee; Stewardship Committee; Evangelism Rally speaker; Williams-Henson Lutheran Home for Children Board; Bishop's Consultation Committee, 1994-2000; Board, Lutheran Theological Southern Seminary, 1994-97; Western North Carolina Via de Cristo, Pilgrim 1991, Spiritual Director, 1992, 1994; Board, Children's Hospital of Knoxville Pastoral Care; Knoxville Area Rescue Ministry Spiritual Life Task Group; Knoxville Inner City Churches United for People Board; Lutheran Community Services; Ecumenical Service Planning Group; Cardiac Residence for Clergy Program, Ft. Sanders Health Systems. In North Carolina Synod: Evangelism Committee, 1984-85, Chair, 1985-86; Ministry of the Laity Task Force; Granite Falls Ministerial Association, Vice President, 1983-84; Granite Falls Optimist Club, Vice President, 1983-84, President, 1984- 85; Board, South Caldwell Christian Ministries, President, 1984-85; Board, Caldwell County American Red Cross, 1983-86; Hospice of Caldwell County Task Force; Team Chaplain for South Caldwell High School Football Team, 1982; North Carolina Representative to Evangelism Practicum in Orlando, Fla., 1986; Region 9 Evangelism Transition Team; National Youth Ministry Commission of the Lutheran Church in America, 1968-72.

MISENHEIMER, JOHN CHARLES

Date/Place of Birth: March 24, 1948; Salisbury, N.C., brother of The Reverends James Stephen and David Lentz Misenheimer.
Parents: The Reverend Dr. Ernest L. Misenheimer, Jr. and Margaret (Lentz) Misenheimer.
Spouse/Marriage Date: Martha (Rudisill) Misenheimer; June 26, 1971 in China Grove, N.C.
Children: Marcus John, Jessica Lynn.
Education: Lenoir-Rhyne, B.A. 1970; Lutheran Theological Southern Seminary, M.Div. 1974.
Ordination: May 31, 1974 by North Carolina Synod.
Calls: Mt. Hermon, Concord, 1974-81; First, Lexington, 1981-86; Bethany, Hickory, 1986-94; St. Paul, Wilmington, 1994-.
Other: Executive Board, North Carolina Synod, 1986; Synod Council, 1988-93; Evangelism Committee, 1986-93; Spiritual Director, Western and Eastern North Carolina Lutheran Via de Cristo.

MITCHAM, JANE AMELIA (POPE)

Date/Place of Birth: June 16, 1939; Statesville, N.C.
Parents: Carl M. Pope, Sr. and Pauline F. Pope.
Spouse/Marriage Date: The Reverend L. William Mitcham, Jr.; May 27, 1961.
Children: Tamera Lynne Shealy, Jonathan Todd.
Education: Lenoir-Rhyne College, A.B. 1961; Pacific Lutheran Seminary, 1998; University of South Carolina, M.A.T. 1973, Ed.D. 1981.
Ordination: June 6, 1998 by North Carolina Synod.
Calls: Bishop's Staff, North Carolina Synod, 1998-.
Other: Vice President of North Carolina Synod, 1991-92; Synod Council, 1988-92; author of various Sunday School materials; Evangelical Lutheran Church in America consultation team for developing Sexual Misconduct Prevention Strategies; Presenter/therapist - Women of the Evangelical Lutheran Church in America Triennial Assembly, 1993, 1996; Voting Member - Constituting Assembly of Evangelical Lutheran Church in America, 1987. Bishop's Staff, North Carolina Synod, as lay person in 1992-98.

MITCHAM, LOYD WILLIAM, JR.

Date/Place of Birth: May 14, 1938; Kings Mountain, N.C.
Parents: Loyd William Mitcham, Sr. and Oveda (Ross) Mitcham.
Spouse/Marriage Date: The Reverend Jane Amelia (Pope) Mitcham; May 27, 1961 in Statesville, N.C.
Children: Tamera Lynne Shealy, Jonathan Todd.
Education: Lenoir-Rhyne, A.B. 1960; Lutheran Theological Southern Seminary, B.D. 1964; University of South Carolina, M.Ed. Counseling, 1974; Eastern Theological Seminary, Philadelphia, D.Min. Marriage and Family, 1984.
Ordination: June 14, 1964 by North Carolina Synod.
Calls: Assistant Pastor, Reformation, Columbia, S.C., 1964-66; Faith, Newberry, S.C., 1966-68; Assistant to the Bishop, South Carolina Synod, 1968-84; Director, Family Counseling, Lutheran Family Services, Charlotte, 1984-.
Other: Author of curriculum for Lutheran Church in America and Evangelical Lutheran Church in America; President, North Carolina Association for Family Therapy, 1993-94; Vera and David Mace Award for outstanding contributions to the field of marriage and family therapy, 1992.

MITCHELL, CARVETH PEARN

Date/Place of Birth: May 4, 1911; Cornwall, England.
Parents: Carveth Mitchell and Helena (Pearn) Mitchell.
Spouse/Marriage Date: Kathryn (Rogers) Mitchell; June 21, 1937 in Zanesville, Ohio.
Children: The Reverend Sanford Carveth, Kathryn Ann Rogers Taylor.
Education: Wittenberg University, A.B. 1934, D.D. 1955; Hamma Divinity School, B.D. 1937.
Ordination: June 10, 1937 by Ohio Synod.
Calls: Assistant Pastor, First, Dayton, Ohio, 1937-38; Hilltop, Columbus, Ohio, 1938-45; First, Mansfield, Ohio, 1945-63; St. Mark's, Charlotte, 1963-79; retired 1980; Vice Pastor at various congregations.

Other: Secretary, Ohio Synod, 1943-45; Board, Wittenberg University and Hamma School of Theology, 1947-63; Board of Social Missions, United Lutheran Church in America, 1952-62, Chair, Evangelism Division; Board of Social Ministry, Lutheran Church in America, 1962-65; Executive Board, Ohio Synod, 1966-69, North Carolina Synod, 1969-72; Board, Lutheran Theological Southern Seminary; Chair, Board, Lutheran Church in America Foundation; Board, Children's Home of the South, 1964-66; Lutheran Church in America Delegate, 1970; co-editor with son, Sanford, of *Homiletics*.

MITCHELL, SANFORD CARVETH

Date/Place of Birth: February 28, 1942; Columbus, Ohio.
Parents: The Reverend Dr. Carveth Pearn Mitchell and Kathryn (Rogers) Mitchell.
Spouse/Marriage Date: Judith Ann (Weber) Mitchell; August 14, 1965 in Findlay, Ohio.
Children: Jeffrey Carveth, Rodney Lewis.
Education: Wittenberg University, B.A. 1964; Lutheran Theological Southern Seminary, two years; Hamma School of Theology, M.Div. 1967; Bowling Green State University, M.A. 1971; Ashland Seminary, D.D. 1990.
Ordination: June 4, 1967 by North Carolina Synod.
Calls: First, Findlay, Ohio, 1967-71; Zion, Defiance, Ohio, 1971-79; Trinity, Ashland, Ohio, 1979-.
Other: Pastor/Evangelist Lutheran Church in America, Partner in Evangelism Evangelical Lutheran Church in America, fourteen years. Editor of Clergy Journal, *Homiletics*. Professional Leadership Unit of the Ohio Synod, fourteen years; Numerous positions on Christian Education, Lakeside and various youth committees of the Synod; Transition teams for Ohio Synod and the new Northeast Ohio Synod.

MITCHUM, ROBERT CLINTON, JR.

Date/Place of Birth: March 21, 1939; Lincoln County, N.C.
Parents: Robert Clinton Mitchum, Sr. and Margaret Baine (Rudisill) Mitchum.
Spouse/Marriage Date: Lois Ann (Veler) Mitchum, daughter of the Reverend Robert W. Veler; November 17, 1962 in Columbus, Ohio.
Children: Robert Andrew, Sarah Elizabeth.
Education: Lenoir-Rhyne, A.B. 1961; Hamma School of Theology, B.D. 1965.
Ordination: June 6, 1965 by North Carolina Synod.
Calls: Trinity-St. Paul, Frederick County, Va., 1965-68; All Saints, Covington, Va., 1968-72; Good Hope and Paradise, North Lima, Ohio, 1972-74; Good Hope, North Lima, Ohio, 1974-75.
Other: Resigned June 1979 in Newton, N.C.; employed by Catawba County Department of Social Services, 1976-87, as case worker with family and children's services.

MITSCHKE, ROBERT FREDERICK, JR.

Date/Place of Birth: March 28, 1952; Charlotte, N.C.
Parents: Robert Frederick Mitschke, Sr. and Edith (Sheppard) Mitschke.
Spouse/Marriage Date: Anne Nash (White) Mitschke; July 29, 1972.
Children: Elisha Adraiana, Robert Frederick, III.
Education: Pembroke State University, B.A. 1974; Lutheran Theological Southern Seminary, M.Div. 1978; Gaston College, Level II Fire Service Instructor, 1991.

Ordination: June 11, 1978, by North Carolina Synod.
Calls: Sharon, Gibsonville, 1978-86; Grace, Bessemer City, 1986-.
Other: Environmental Concerns Committee; Award for Heroism, Gibsonville Fire Department, 1985; Firefighter of the Year, Tryonota Volunteer Fire Department, 1993.

MOCKICIN, SOL BIRD
Date/Place of Birth: June 1, 1942; Delaware County, Okla.
Parents: James Boyd Gibson and Tennis Mockicin.
Child: Zitka Bird.
Education: Dana College, B.A. Sociology, 1964; graduate work at Black Hills State in Bilingual Education.
License: Commissioned by North Carolina Synod on May 4, 1991.
Calls: Living Waters, Swain County, 1991-.
Other: Social worker at American Lutheran Church Children's Home, 1964-69; Teacher, Augustana Academy, American Lutheran Church High School, 1969-70; Social worker, Lutheran Social Services, South Dakota, 1970-72; faculty, American Lutheran Church College, Augustana, S.D., 1972-74. Bilingual Educator of the Year, 1978, in San Juan, Puerto Rico; Outstanding Alumnus Recipient, Dana College, 1985; *Who's Who in American Politics, 1972*; Administrator of the Decade, Cherokee Nation; Oklahoma Commission for Children and Youth, Governor's Appointment; National Indian Lutheran Board, President and Charter Member; Executive Board, Family Services of America, Inc.; Association of American Indian Social Workers, Charter Member; Founder and first Chair and President, South Dakota Indian Education Association; President, Sioux Falls Human Relations Commission; President, Rapid City Human Relations Commission; Board, American Indian Services Center, Sioux Falls, S.D.; Executive Board, Oaks Indian Center; National Secretary, Native American Lutheran Association.

MOEBIUS, JOHN CHARLES, SR.
Date/Place of Birth: December 7, 1920; Buffalo, N.Y.
Parents: John E. Moebius and Esther (Young) Moebius.
Spouse/Marriage Date: Edith (Buerger) Moebius; March 17, 1945 in Niagara Falls, N.Y.
Children: Wendy Baver, John Charles, Jr., Anne J. Cooper, Paula E., Joel C.
Education: Capital University, B.A. 1949; Columbus, Ohio. Seminary, B.D. 1952; graduate work at Town and Country Leadership School at West Virginia University.
Ordination: August 3, 1952 by Eastern District, American Lutheran Church.
Calls: South Park, Buffalo, 1952-56; Holy Trinity, Laurel, Md., 1956-1962; Miller's, Hickory, 1962-86; retired August 6, 1986 in Hickory, N.C.; Vice Pastor at various congregations.
Other: Eastern District, American Missions Committee, 1964-70; American Lutheran Church. Regional Stewardship Committee, 1974-80; Lutheran Representative on Commission on Religion in Appalachia, 1976- 82.

MOHR, ROBERT EDWIN
Date/Place of Birth: April 12, 1921; Buffalo, N.Y.
Parents: Edwin Julius Mohr and Mabel D. (Knorr) Mohr.
Spouse/Marriage Date: Janet C. (Lauterbach) Mohr; September 5, 1953 in Woodhaven, N.Y.
Children: Robert Wayne, Carolyn Anne, Nancy Jeannie Baker, Linda Christine Hessong.
Education: Cornell University, B.S. 1943; Philadelphia Seminary, B.D. 1945. graduate work at Union Seminary, 1947.
Ordination: November 4, 1945 by New York Synod.
Calls: Zion, Niagara Falls, N.Y., 1945-50; St. Luke, Woodhaven, N.Y., 1950-62; St. Stephen, Wilmington, Del., 1961-70; Trinity, Hagerstown, Md., 1970-81; Christ, Durham, 1981-87. Retired, 1987.
Other: President, Long Island District and the Brooklyn-Queens District, New York Synod. Commission on Stewardship of the Lutheran Church in America; Delegate to Lutheran Church in America Conventions.
Date of Death/Burial Location: May 7, 1988; Resthaven Cemetery, Hagerstown, Md.

MOKRY, RICHARD MICHAEL
Date/Place of Birth: June 1, 1955; Rome, N.Y.
Parents: Albert Andrew Mokry and Florence Renee (Perkosky) Mokry.
Spouse/Marriage Date: Miriam Ruth (Kohlmeier) Mokry; April 11, 1982 in Rome, N.Y.
Children: Jacob Aaron, Nathaniel Andrew, Leah Elizabeth, Anna Rachel.
Education: Concordia College (N.Y.), A.A. 1975; New York University, B.A. 1977; Christ Seminary, M.Div. 1981.
Ordination: June 17, 1982 by North Carolina Synod.
Calls: Calvary, Spencer, 1982-85; Shepherd of the Sea, Atlantic Beach, 1985-95; transferred to New England Synod in 1995; Zion, Stamford, Conn., 1998-.

MONROE, PAUL EUGENE, JR.
Date/Place of Birth: June 23, 1922; Gastonia, N.C.
Parents: Paul Eugene Monroe, Sr. and Mary Bradley (Jones) Monroe. The Reverend Pleasant Edgar Monroe, D.D., was his uncle.
Spouse/Marriage Date: Josephine Louise (Beck) Monroe; June 16, 1945 in Warren, Ohio.
Children: Lynn Suzanne Bolick, Marcia Louise Lyle, Paula Ruth McAllister, Jonathan Beck.
Education: Lenoir-Rhyne, A.B. 1943; Hamma Divinity School, B.D. 1945, S.T.M. 1953.
Ordination: May 23 1945 by Ohio Synod.
Calls: Assistant Pastor, Luther Place Memorial, Washington, D.C., 1945-47; Redeemer, Newberry, S.C., 1947-58; First, Nashville, Tenn., 1958-64; Emmanuel, High Point, 1964-69.
Other: Board, Lutheran Theological Southern Seminary, 1956-58; Board, Newberry College, 1963-64; Executive Board, Kentucky-Tennessee Synod, 1960-62; United Lutheran Church in America delegate, Assembly of National Council of Churches, St. Louis, 1954, and San Francisco, 1959; part-time teacher (German, Bible, Sociology), Newberry College, 1950, 1954, 1957; contributor to *The Lutheran* and other Lutheran

periodicals, and of sermon to Peabody College Reflector; S.M.T. thesis subject, "History of Southern Lutheranism." Board of Newberry County, S.C., Red Cross, 1950-56, and Chair of Blood Donor Program. Retired, 1969.
Date of Death/Burial Location: March 23, 1989; Emmanuel Church Cemetery, High Point, N.C.

MONROE, PLEASANT EDGAR
Date/Place of Birth: December 18, 1875; Rowan County, N.C.
Parents: Thomas Burton Monroe and Catherine Victoria (Cress) Monroe.
Spouse/Marriage Date: Julia Houseal (Hentz) Monroe; April 2 1902 in Pomaria, S.C.
Children: Carl Hentz (died at age of 9), Mary Kathryn Gwin.
Education: North Carolina College, A.B. 1898; Chicago Seminary, B.D. 1901; Newberry College, M.A., D.D. 1919, L.L.D. 1947.
Ordination: 1901 by Southwest Virginia Synod.
Calls: In Virginia: Woman's Memorial-Christ, Pulaski, 1901-02; in South Carolina: Ehrhardt Memorial-Mt. Pleasant-St. Nicholas, Ehrhardt, 1902-08; St. John-Mt. Calvary-Good Hope, Johnston, 1908-13; in North Carolina: Holy Trinity, Hickory, 1924-30; St. James, Concord, 1930-34; retired 1949 at Hickory, N.C.
Other: President, Summerland College for Girls, Batesburg, S.C., 1913-24; Acting President, Lenoir-Rhyne, 1925-26; President, Lenoir-Rhyne, 1934-49, President Emeritus, 1949; Member of Board, 1931-34, Secretary, 1911-12, President, 1914-16, South Carolina Synod; Board of Foreign Missions, United Lutheran Church in America, 1930-42; President, North Carolina College Conference (embracing 44 colleges), 1945; delegate to conventions of United Synod South, and United Lutheran Church in America.
Date of Death/Burial Location: July 31, 1954; Oakwood Cemetery, Hickory, N.C.

MOORE, GEORGE TRUETT, SR.
Date/Place of Birth: August 25, 1920; Greenville, S.C.
Parents: The Reverend James Furman Moore and Eunice (Peeler) Moore. Father was a Baptist minister.
Spouse/Marriage Date: Nellie Elizabeth (Stevens) Moore; January 12, 1943 in Savannah, Ga.
Children: George Truett, Jr., Johnnie Stevens, William Spencer, Alex Arthur.
Education: Clemson University, B.S. Architecture 1942; Lutheran Theological Southern Seminary, M.Div. 1957, also graduate study.
Ordination: June 9, 1957 by Georgia-Alabama Synod.
Calls: After one year in seminary, served, 1953-55, in Liberia, Africa, as mission builder under Board of Foreign Missions, United Lutheran Church in America; after seminary graduation and ordination, served again in Liberia, but as an evangelistic missionary, July 1957 to December 1958. Health problems forced resignation. Churches served in North Carolina: Resurrection, Kings Mountain, 1959-65; Calvary, Spencer, 1965-70; Zion, Hickory, 1970-76; St. Matthew, Charleston, S.C., 1976-80; Grace, Prosperity, S.C., 1980-85; retired December 31, 1985 in Greenville, S.C. and then to Leesville, S.C.; Vice Pastor at various congregations.

Other: Pursued his profession of architect, 1942-52; Board, Lowman Home, 1962-77; Chair, Committee on World Missions, 1960-65; Chair, Architecture and Fine Arts Committee, 1967-72; Dean, Central District, 1968-69; Education Committee for Ministers, 1962; American Missions Committee.

MOORE, JOYCE (LINDH)

Date/Place of Birth: October 9; Latrobe, Pa.
Parents: John P. Lindh and Gladys V. (Shultz) Lindh.
Spouse/Marriage Date: Charles Eugene Moore; September 18, 1964.
Children: Michael Gene, Jon Lynn.
Education: Thiel College, Miami University of Ohio, B.A. English; Pittsburgh Seminary, M.Div.; graduate work at University of Pittsburgh.
Ordination: June 9, 1979 by Western Pennsylvania-West Virginia Synod.
Calls: Bethel, Latrobe, Pa., 1979-84; First, Greensboro, 1989-90; Holy Trinity, Reidsville, 1990-98; Vice Pastor at various congregations.
Other: Chaplain, Triad Health Project, Greensboro, 1986; AIDS Ministry Internship, San Francisco General Hospital, 1994; Clinical Pastoral Education Residency, Wesley Long Hospital, Greensboro, 1990.

MOOSE, JOHN BAXTER

Date/Place of Birth: May 27, 1885; Cabarrus County, N.C.
Parents: Giles Monroe Moose and Rose Cameline (Misenheimer) Moose.
Spouse/Marriage Date: Bernice Marie (Hummer) Moose; May 14, 1930 in Reading, Pa.
Education: Mount Pleasant Collegiate Institute, Newberry College, A.B. 1908, A.M. 1914, D.D. 1937; Lutheran Theological Southern Seminary, 1913; Chicago Seminary, B.D. 1915; graduate study at Columbia University, 1914, Northwestern and Chicago Universities, 1925; Hartford Seminary, 1923-25, Ph.D., *summa cum laude*.
Ordination: 1913 by North Carolina Synod.
Calls: Mt. Zion-Luther's-New Bethel, Richfield, 1913-14; Immanuel, Bluefield, W.Va.-Wartburg, Graham, Va., 1915-17; Synodical Missionary, Grace, Thomasville, 1917-18; Prosperity-Mt. Hermon, Cabarrus County, 1918-23, and supplied Cold Water, 1920-22; Supply St. Paul, Hartford, Conn., 1924-25. Supplied (three to eight months) churches in and near Columbia, S.C., 1933-53, while professor at Lutheran Theological Southern Seminary. Organized Christ's, Columbia, 1944; Supply, St. Matthew, Lexington County, S.C., 1953-60; retired 1953 at Leesville, S.C.
Other: Professor (Bible, Greek, Latin), Mount Pleasant Collegiate Institute, 1909-10; same (Bible, Greek, History), 1918-23. Professor (Historical Theology), Chicago Seminary, 1925-33. Professor (Historical Theology), Lutheran Theological Southern Seminary, 1933-53, and Dean, 1943-46; Author, *Adolph Nussmann, Pioneer Lutheran Preacher in North Carolina;* American Society of Church History, American Society for Reformation Research, American Association of University Professors (Emeritus), and President, United Lutheran Church in America Theological Seminary Professors.

Date of Death/Burial Location: June 3, 1963 at White Rock, S.C.;   St. John Church, Cabarrus County, N.C.

MOOSE, JOHN SHELTON, SR.

Date/Place of Birth: February 17, 1913; Hickory, N.C.
Parents: John Wesley Moose and Daisey Mae (Healan) Moose.
First Spouse/Marriage Date: Hazel (Ott) Moose; May 1943 in Lexington County, S.C.
Children of First Marriage: Hazel Jane Martz, John Shelton, Jr., William Hamilton.
Second Spouse/Marriage Date: Evelyn Hamilton (Wingard) Moose; May 29, 1966 in Columbia, S.C.
Education: Newberry College, A.B.; D.D. 1961.
Ordination: August 1939 by South Carolina Synod.
Calls: St. Jacob Parish, Chapin, S.C., 1939-43; St. John, Clinton, S.C., 1943-45; Pastor/Organizer, Atonement, Laurens, S.C., 1945-50; Pastor/Organizer St. Timothy, Camden, S.C., 1950-53; South Carolina Synod Field Worker, 1953-62; Regional Secretary, Board of American Missions-United Lutheran Church in America-Lutheran Church in America, 1962-66; First, Garland, Texas, 1966-68; Pastor/Developer, Board of American Missions, Charlotte, 1968-72; Our Father, Greensboro, 1972-79; retired 1979; Reformation, Columbia, S.C., 1979-83.
Other: Executive Board, South Carolina Synod, 1952-62.
Date of Death: April 28, 1994.

MOOSE, PAUL EDWARD

Date/Place of Birth: July 25, 1910; Catawba County, N.C.
Parents: Eddie Lawrence Moose and Willie Ellen (Huitt) Moose.
Spouse/Marriage Date: Aura Lee (Bowman) Moose; June 25, 1935 in Hickory, N.C.
Children: Paul Lawrence, The Reverend Stephen Lee.
Education: Lenoir-Rhyne, A.B. 1932; Lutheran Theological Southern Seminary, B.D. 1935.
Ordination: May 23, 1935 by North Carolina Synod.
Calls: Mt. Hermon-Sharon-St. Paul, Iredell County, 1935-38; Mt. Zion- Luther's-New Bethel, Richfield, 1938-43; Salem (built new church after fire), Rowan County, 1943-66; Low's, Liberty, 1966-75; retired August 1975; Vice Pastor at various congregations.
Other: Board, Children's Home of the South, 1951-71; Pensions Committee, 1963-72, Chair, 1965-72.
Date of Death/Burial Location: August 5, 1996; Mt. Calvary, Claremont, N.C.

MOOSE, STEPHEN LEE
Date/Place of Birth: April 28, 1943; Albemarle, N.C.
Parents: The Reverend Paul Edward Moose and Aura Lee (Bowman) Moose.
Spouse/Marriage Date: Dorothy Montgomery (Pritchett) Moose; August 7, 1965 in Bethesda, Md.
Children: Grace Elise, Andrew Lee.
Education: Lenoir-Rhyne, B.A. 1965; Lutheran Theological Southern Seminary, M.Div. 1969, D.Min. 1985.
Ordination: June 1, 1969 by North Carolina Synod.
Calls: Daniel's, Lincolnton, 1969-76; St. Philip, Roanoke, Va., 1976-81; St. Andrew, Portsmouth, Va., 1981-; Vice Pastor at various congregations.
Other: Board, Lutheran Theological Southern Seminary; Chair, Consulting Committee on Justice and Social Change, North Carolina Synod; Area Dean, Virginia Synod; Virginia Synod Professional Preparation Managing Group; Virginia Synod Council for Ministry.

MOREHEAD, FLAY CURTIS, JR.
Date/Place of Birth: April 30, 1918; Shelby, N.C.
Parents: Flay Curtis Morehead, Sr. and Minnie (Herman) Morehead.
Spouse/Marriage Date: Martha Mae (Hines) Morehead; August 23, 1944 in Hickory, N.C.
Children: Flay Curtis, III, Martha Irene, and John Leslie.
Education: Lenoir-Rhyne, A.B. 1941; Lutheran Theological Southern Seminary, B.D. 1944.
Ordination: July 16, 1944 by North Carolina Synod.
Calls: As a seminarian, spent a summer serving Trinity, Rocky Mount and another at Trinity, Pulaski, Va.; Mt. Hebron, Hildebran, 1944-50; St. John, Hudson, 1950-67; Haven, Salisbury, 1967-77; retired May 14, 1981.
Other: President, Lenoir-Caldwell Ministerial Association, Secretary, Western and Central Conference; Discussion group leader at the anniversary convention of the Luther League of America, Lawrence, Kan., 1957; Vice Pastor at various congregations.

MORETZ, CHRISTIAN
Note: In *History of the Lutheran Church in North Carolina, (1803-1953)*, designated "Christian Moretz," while his brother John's son was designated "Christian Moretz, Jr."
Date/Place of Birth: November 30, 1797; Randolph County, N.C.
Parents: Christian Moretz and Molly (Fox) Moretz. May have been related to the Reverend Alfred J. Fox through both father's and mother's families.
Marriage: Unknown.
License/Ordination: Licensed 1822 and ordained 1824 in Greene County, Tenn., by Tennessee Synod.
Calls: Possibly the first Lutheran to preach in Missouri. In 1821 first Tennessee Synod pastor to preach in Gravelton, Mo., in English. Served as missionary in Missouri, Kentucky, and Indiana, 1823-35; one church known: Zion, Gravelton, Mo., 1823-28.
Other: Aided in organizing Indiana Synod in 1835 and thereafter a member of it.

MORETZ, CHRISTIAN

Note: In *History of the Lutheran Church in North Carolina,* (1803-1953), listed as Christian Moretz, Jr., but nephew, not son, of Christian Moretz, Jr., as noted in above sketch).

Date/Place of Birth: July 29, 1827; Catawba County, N.C.

Parents: John Moretz and Catharine (Hefner) Moretz (second wife).

First Spouse: Frances Eleanor (Stirewalt) Moretz of Catawba County, N.C., sister of the Reverend Miles J. Stirewalt.

Children of First Marriage: Fourteen, of whom eleven were: Jerome Chrysostom, Alice Luretta, John Michael, Paul Jacob, Sarah Caroline, Mary Ellen, Martin Luther, Frances Adaline Jamima, Melchi Melanchthon, Christian Le Roy, Sion Gideon.

Second Spouse/Marriage Date: Mrs. Carolyn (Phillips) (Faw) Moretz; July 24, 1889 in Ashe County, N.C.

Children of Second Marriage: Laura Elizabeth, Polly Mabel, Zora Cisco, Amelia Blanche, Ann Dezo.

Education: Self-taught, but was said to have been brilliant, with many books for his day.

License/Ordination: Licensed 1852 and ordained 1856 by Tennessee Synod.

Calls: Mt. Pleasant, Watauga County, fourth pastor, 1852-68 (a John Moretz, Sr., was one of two councilmen chosen at its organization in 1845); St. Martin, Stanly County, 1855. In 1858 Bethlehem, Lancaster, S.C. reported their satisfaction with the service he had provided and asked that they be continued. Morning Star, Matthews, provided a similar letter. Other pastorates are not known, but mail addresses (1857-72) were Moretz Mills, Rose Vale, Taylorsville, and Boone.

Other: Secretary, Tennessee Synod, 1865, 1886. Name was removed from roll in 1874.

Date of Death/Burial Location: October 19, 1905; Moretz Cemetery on Grassy Creek, Watauga County, N.C.

MORETZ, WALTER JENNINGS, JR.

Date/Place of Birth: January 23, 1933; Columbia, S.C.

Parents: The Reverend Walter Jennings Moretz, Sr. and Opal A. (Ledford) Moretz.

Spouse/Marriage Date: Sara Anne (Phelps) Moretz; December 27, 1955 in Wilmington, N.C.

Child: Catherine Hand.

Education: Lenoir-Rhyne, A.B. *cum laude* 1955; Lutheran Theological Southern Seminary, M.Div, 1959, S.T.M.; graduate work at Duke University; Florida State University, Ph.D.

Ordination: 1959 by Florida Synod.

Calls: St. Timothy, Camden, S.C., 1959-61; Chaplain to Lutheran Students at North Carolina State University, part time during graduate work; Haven, Salisbury, 1964-67.

Other: College Student Work Committee; Chair, Elections Committee, 1967; established and served as Director for Counseling and Psychological Services Center, George Mason University, 1970-75; Assistant Professor of Education/Psychology, George Mason University, 1970-73; Associate Professor, Psychology, George Mason University, 1973-; American Psychological Association; Society for the Scientific Study of Religion; *Who's Who in American Colleges and Universities;* Duke University - Martin Luther Fellow, University Fellow; Florida State University - University Fellow, NDEA Fellow, Delta Tau Kappa. Publications: Various articles and presentations. Demitted February 16, 1971.

MORETZ, WALTER JENNINGS, SR.
Date/Place of Birth: October 5, 1896; Watauga County, N.C.
Parents: S. E. Moretz and May Virginia (Houck) Moretz.
Spouse/Marriage Date: Opal A. (Ledford) Moretz; June 30, 1928 in Rural Hall, N.C.
Children: The Reverend Walter Jennings, Jr., Ph.D., Rufus Ledford, Ph.D., Bettie Opal, Ph.D.
Education: Lenoir-Rhyne, A.B. 1924; Lutheran Theological Southern Seminary, B.D. 1927.
Ordination: 1927 by North Carolina Synod.
Calls: Nazareth-Shiloh, Forsyth County, 1927-31; Orange Chapel, Springfield-Good Shepherd, Swansea, S.C., 1932-43; Ehrhardt Memorial-Mt. Pleasant, Ehrhardt, S.C., 1943-48; in Florida: Trinity, Bradenton, 1948-63; Ebenezer, Pierson, 1963.
Other: Board, Lutheran Theological Southern Seminary.
Date of Death/Burial Location: June 9, 1963; Pierson Lutheran Cemetery, Pierson, Fla.

MORGAN, CARROLL IRVING
Date/Place of Birth: September 1873; Lexington County, S.C.
Parents: Jeremiah Winn Morgan and Grace Eugenia (Craps) Morgan.
Spouse/Marriage Date: Lillie Russell (Tyson) Morgan; December 26, 1911 in Salisbury, N.C.
Children: Margaret Russell (died three days after birth), Grace Carol (married the Reverend Rudolph Ludwig).
Education: Lenoir-Rhyne, A.B. 1900; Lutheran Theological Southern Seminary, 1903; Chicago Seminary, B.D. 1909.
Ordination: 1902 by Tennessee Synod.
Calls: Holy Trinity, Gastonia, 1902-05; organized and built Grace, Bessemer City, 1903-05; Haven, Salisbury, 1905-11; supplied Christ, East Spencer, 1908-09; Macedonia, Burlington, 1912-13; Ebenezer-St. James and supplied St. Paul, 1917, Catawba County, 1913-17; Trinity, Landis and Concordia, Rowan County, 1917-21; in Virginia at Mt. Calvary, Morning Star, Grace, Page County, 1921-25; in South Carolina at Mt. Hebron and Union in Leesville and St. Mark, Prosperity, 1925-36.
Other: Instructor in Bible, Summerland College, Batesburg, S.C., 1925-28.
Date of Death/Burial Location: January 1948; Leesville, S.C.

MORGAN, FRANCIS GROVER
Date/Place of Birth: November 19, 1889; Lexington County, S.C.
Parents: Henry S. Morgan and Amanda (Hare) Morgan.
Spouse/Marriage Date: Mary Letitia (Doak) Morgan; August 14, 1912 in Wytheville, Va.
Children: Frances Letitia, William David Edward, Marian, James Henry, Virginia Caroline (married the Reverend Paul David Townsend), Joanna Doak.
Education: Lenoir-Rhyne, A.B. 1909; Lutheran Theological Southern Seminary, 1913, B.D. 1925; University of South Carolina, M.A. 1913, Ph.D. 1928.
Ordination: 1913 by Tennessee Synod.

Calls: Supply, Grace, Hendersonville, 1915-16; Hebron, Madison, Va., 1919-21; Interim Pastor at various congregations.

Other: Instructor in Bible, Lenoir-Rhyne, 1915-17; President, Summerland College, 1921-27; Professor of Religious Education, Converse College, 1927-32; same, Lenoir-Rhyne, 1932-48; Chaplain, U.S. Marine Corps in World War I, 1917-19.

Date of Death/Burial Location: June 17, 1948; St. Stephen Church, Hickory, N.C.

MORGAN, JACOB LEVI

Date/Place of Birth: February 7, 1872; Rowan County, N.C.

Parents: Jacob Morgan and Sally Amanda (Hodge) Morgan.

Spouse/Marriage Date: Elizabeth Virginia Clay (Shoup) Morgan, daughter of the Reverend J. B. Shoup, who performed the ceremony; May 25, 1903 in Mt. Pleasant, N.C.

Children: Gladys, M.D., (medical missionary in India, married William Happer, M.D., Ruth (died at age 2), Karl Ziegler (Ph.D.), Katherine, Lois.

Education: North Carolina College, A.B. 1899; Lutheran Theological Southern Seminary, 1902; Lenoir-Rhyne, D.D. 1921, L.L.D. 1945.

Ordination: 1902 by North Carolina Synod.

Calls: Haven, Salisbury and Christ, East Spencer, 1902-03; St. Enoch-Trinity, Enochville, 1903-07; as synodical missionary, 1907-17, developing, organizing, serving and building churches for five: Emmanuel, High Point and First, Greensboro, 1907-09; St. Mark's, Mooresville and Trinity, Landis, 1909-11; and Richland (supply)-Grace, Liberty and Holy Trinity, Raleigh, 1911-17; the last only as full-time pastor, 1917-19; pastor to Lutheran students in Raleigh, and visiting pastor to Lutheran students at University of North Carolina at Chapel Hill, 1911-19; Pastor to Lutheran soldiers, Camp Polk, Raleigh, 1917-19.

Other: Vice President, North Carolina Synod, 1918-19; first full-time President of same 1919-21 and of the merged synod (United Evangelical Lutheran Synod of North Carolina), 1921-47, President Emeritus, 1947-60; *ex officio* Chair, Synodical Executive, Mission, and Ministerial Education Committees, and *ex officio* member of all synodical boards and committees; delegate, conventions of United Synod South 1904-18, except for one, and of United Lutheran Church in America conventions, 1918-46, 1950. While synodical missionary, 1907-17, and Synod President, 1919-47, led synod in organizing some 40 congregations. Recommended and promoted Brotherhood Loan and Gift Fund for aiding North Carolina missions, instituted in 1922; United Lutheran Church in America boards: Foreign Missions, 1927-30, Executive, 1930-38, and American Missions, 1946-52; Chair, Historical Works Committee, and chief editor of the *History of the Lutheran Church in North Carolina,* (1803-1953); retired 1947 at Salisbury, N.C., but was active in efforts to collect and preserve sources of synod's history.

Date of Death/Burial Location: December 27, 1960; Chestnut Hill Cemetery, Salisbury, N.C.

MORGAN, JOHN LUTHER, SR.
Date/Place of Birth: April 3, 1885; Rowan County, N.C.
Parents: Moses L. Morgan and Julia Ann Elizabeth ("Betty" Morgan) Morgan. Mother was sister of the Reverend Jacob L. Morgan.
Spouse/Marriage Date: Annie Louise (Lowman) Morgan; January 23, 1918 in Columbia, S.C.
Children: John Luther, Jr., Voigt Fritz, the Reverend Paul Lowman, Miriam Elizabeth (married the Reverend Harold G. Deal, Jr.).
Education: Lenoir-Rhyne, A.B. 1913, D.D. 1959; Lutheran Theological Southern Seminary, 1916; University of South Carolina, M.A.
Ordination: May 14, 1916 by North Carolina Synod.
Calls: St. Michael, Troutman (merged with St. Martin, 1923, under name of Holy Trinity)-St. Paul-Amity, Iredell County, 1916-27; Supply, Lebanon, Rowan County, 1925; Holy Trinity, Charlotte, 1928-34; Faith, Faith, 1934-36; Frieden's-Sharon-Peace, Gibsonville, 1936-43; Lutheran Chapel, Gastonia, 1943-47; Mt. Zion-New Bethel-Luther's, Richfield, 1947-53; Sardis, Catawba County, 1954-57; first pastor, Our Saviour, Gaston County 1958-61 Pastor Emeritus, 1962.
Other: Known as "The Builder" of six church edifices and three parsonages, and worked on eight other churches and three other parsonages, and improved thirteen cemeteries; retired at Richfield, N.C., in 1961; President, Western Conference; Board, Lenoir-Rhyne; Board, North Carolina Lutheran Homes; served as last appointed Archivist of the synod, 1962.
Date of Death/Burial Location: April 6, 1982; Rowan Memorial Park, Salisbury, N.C.

MORGAN, PAUL LOWMAN
Date/Place of Birth: March 16, 1923; Troutman, N.C.
Parents: The Reverend John Luther Morgan, Sr. and Annie Louise (Lowman) Morgan.
Spouse/Marriage Date: Bess Marie (Silman) Morgan; October 15, 1945 in Gastonia, N.C.
Children: Paul Z., Paula Marie, Sheila Elizabeth Stahlberger.
Education: Lenoir-Rhyne, A.B. 1944, D.D. 1967; Lutheran Theological Southern Seminary, M.Div. 1945.
Ordination: 1945 by North Carolina Synod.
Calls: United Lutheran Church in America Missionary in India, 1946-47; St. Peter, Rowan County, 1948-49; Good Shepherd, Goldsboro, 1949-52; Philadelphia, Granite Falls, 1952-55; Center Grove, Kannapolis, 1955-61; First, Greensboro, 1961-74; Incarnation, Columbia, S.C., 1974-77; Christ, Roanoke, Va., 1977-85; Vice Pastor for various congregations; retired 1985 in High Point, N.C.
Other: Executive Committee, North Carolina Synod, 1960-63; Board, Lenoir-Rhyne, 1966-72; President, Lenoir-Rhyne Alumni Association; Dean, Northern District, 1964-70; Pastor Chair for Campus Campaign, 1965; District Secretary, 1962-63; Lutheran Student Foundation, 1966-72; United Lutheran Church in America and Lutheran Church in America Delegate, eight times. South Carolina Synod: Board, Lowman Home; Social Ministry Committee. Virginia Synod: Dean, Southern District; Managing Group on

Evangelism; Managing Group on Home Missions; General Chair, One in Mission Campaign for Synod.

MORGAN, WILLIAM CHAPIN
Date/Place of Birth: July 2, 1939; Pittsboro, N.C.
Parents: W. B. Morgan and Elizabeth (Chapin) Morgan.
Education: University of North Carolina at Chapel Hill, A.B. 1961; Lutheran Theological Southern Seminary, M.Div. 1964.
Ordination: December 6, 1964 by North Carolina Synod.
Calls: Prince of Peace, Salisbury, 1964-67. As an Episcopal priest, served Christ, Savannah, Ga. and Prince of Peace, Salisbury, N.C. Left Episcopal priesthood to become a Pentecostal minister.
Other: Publications and Publicity, 1966-67. Demitted, May 9, 1967.

MORTENSEN, FRED SVEND
Date/Place of Birth: April 28, 1950; Sandusky, Ohio
Parents: Christ Mortensen and Bodel (Jensen) Mortensen.
Spouse/Marriage Date: Karen (Bescherer) Mortensen; 1974.
Education: Capital University, Columbus, Ohio, B.A. in Speech, 1972; Evangelical Lutheran Theological Seminary, Columbus, Ohio, M.Div., 1977.
Ordination: August 14, 1977.
Calls: Assistant Pastor, Christ, North Miami, Fla., 1977-81; St. Luke, Taylorsville, 1981-84; Associate Pastor, Advent, Boca Raton, Fla., 1984-95.
Other: Resigned, August 14, 1995.

MORTON, WALLACE EDWARDS, SR.
Date/Place of Birth: August 4, 1920; Glencoe, Calhoun County, Ala.
Parents: Milton L. Morton and Gertrude (Hindman) Morton.
Spouse/Marriage Date: Lucille (Redmond) Morton; July 26, 1945 in Anniston, Ala.
Children: Wallace Edwards, Jr., Kathy Lynn Wilson, Stephen Carey.
Education: Jacksonville State University, B.S. 1942; Southern Baptist Seminary, M.Div. 1945; Lutheran Theological Southern Seminary, Special Study, 1972; Atlanta Law School, Doctor of Laws 1954.
Ordination: Baptist, June 8, 1941; Lutheran, June 3, 1973 by Southeastern Synod.
Calls: Salem and Luther, Parrottsville, Tenn., 1972-75; Bethany, Kannapolis, 1976-81; St. Enoch, Kannapolis, 1981-89; St. James, Chilhowie, Va., 1989-92; New Bethel, Richfield, 1993-; retired June 30, 1992; Vice Pastor at various congregations.
Other: Southeastern Synod: Stewardship Committee, Nominating Committee, Dean's Cabinet. North Carolina Synod: Stewardship Committee, Dean's Cabinet. President, Ministerial Associations in Gadsden, Ala., Columbus, Ga., Knoxville, Tenn., and Kannapolis, N.C. Created Kannapolis Preaching Mission, 1978. Vice President, President, Cabarrus and Stanly County Lutheran Pastor's Conference; Lions Club, Kiwanis Club,

Rotary Club; President, Cocke County Senior Citizens, Newport, Tenn. Chair, Board, Cocke County Senior Citizens, Newport, Tenn. Director, United Way Campaign, Cocke County, Newport, Tenn., 1974; Outstanding Tennessee Clergyman, University of Tennessee, Knoxville, Tenn., 1974. *Who's Who in Religion in America*, 1977, 1985.

MOSER, ADAM DAVID LUTHER

Date/Place of Birth: September 9, 1836; South Carolina.
Parents: The Reverend Jacob Moser and Peggy (Counts) Moser of South Carolina.
Spouse/Marriage Date: Eliza Frances (Suber) Moser; September 22, 1859 in South Carolina.
Children: Mary Elizabeth, Lillian Theodosia, Gustavus Adolphus.
Education: Newberry College, and Lutheran Theological Southern Seminary, course interrupted by War Between the States.
License/Ordination: Licensed 1863 and ordained 1866 by South Carolina Synod.
Calls: Trinity, Saluda County, S.C., 1866; Beck's-Pilgrim-St. Luke, Davidson County, 1867-68; Trinity, Cabarrus County and St. Enoch, Rowan County, 1868-73; in South Carolina: Lexington County, 1873-83; again in North Carolina: Coble's-Low's, Guilford County, 1883-86, and Richland, Randolph County, 1883-84; First, Albemarle, 1884-86; New Bethel, Stanly County, 1885-87; St. Stephen-Mt. Olive-Mt. Hermon-Cold Water (1888), Cabarrus County, 1886-87.
Other: Secretary, North Carolina Synod, 1873-74.
Date of Death/Burial Location: July 26, 1893; Elmwood Cemetery, Charlotte, N.C.

MOSER, DANIEL

Date/Place of Birth: May 8, 1790; Orange (now Alamance) County, N.C.
Parents: Michael Moser and Sophia (Reinhardt) Moser.
Spouse: Mary Barbara (Moretz) Moser of Lincoln (now Catawba) County, daughter of the Reverend Christian Moretz.
Children: The Reverend Timothy Moser, (whose two sons were the Reverends Jason C. and John F. Moser), the Reverend Jonathan, Rebecca, Marcus.
Education: No formal college or seminary education.
License/Ordination: Licensed 1812 and ordained 1819/20 by North Carolina Synod.
Calls: Zion, Catawba County, 1812-39; Bethel-Philadelphia, Gaston County, 1814-21; Emmanuel, Lincolnton-St. Luke, Lincoln County-St. Paul, Newton, 1815-20; St. John, Conover, Catawba County; Mt. Moriah, Rowan County, Supply 1824, 1832 with others, 1826-29; Daniel's, Lincoln County, 1825-34; St. Peter, Catawba County, 1825-39; Cobles, Guilford County-Melanchthon, Randolph County-Mt. Pleasant, Alamance County, 1831; organized St. Stephen, Catawba County, 1837-39.
Date of Death/Burial Location: July 11, 1839; St. John Church, Lincoln (now Catawba) County, N.C.

MOSER, JACOB

Place of Birth: Orange (now Alamance) County, N.C.
Parents: Michael Moser and Sophia (Reinhardt) Moser.
Spouse: Peggy (Counts) Moser, perhaps of Newberry County, S.C.

Children: Michael (died in infancy or early childhood), Elizabeth, Mary (died in young womanhood), Rebecca, the Reverend Adam David Luther.

License/Ordination: Licensed 1820 by North Carolina Synod; transferred to South Carolina Synod 1824 and ordained In April 1824 by that Synod.

Calls: As member of North Carolina Synod was preaching as early as 1810 in South Carolina; Newberry County, St. Matthew, St. John, St. James, and Beth Eden, S.C.; St. Jacob, Chapin, S.C.; Mt. Calvary, Johnston, S.C.

Other: Took part in organizing of South Carolina Synod in January and November 1824 as one of the six North Carolina Synod pastors.

Date of Death: 1865/66.

MOSER, JASON CHRYSOSTOM

Date/Place of Birth: November 18, 1849; Cabarrus County, N.C.

Parents: The Reverend Timothy Moser and Margaret M. (Hedrich) Moser. The Reverend Daniel Moser was his grandfather, the Reverend Jonathan Moser an uncle, and the Reverend John F. Moser his brother.

Spouse/Marriage Date: Elizabeth Colclough (Lee) Moser; December 25, 1873 in Union County, N.C.

Children: Arthur Lee, Claude Albert, Leslie Rupert, Virginia Beatrice.

Education: North Carolina College, A.B. 1873, D.D.; studied theology under his father.

Ordination: Ordained Deacon 1873 and Pastor 1876 by Tennessee Synod.

Calls: In his ministry of 38 years he served twenty churches in nine North Carolina counties: (1873-82) Mt. Moriah, Phaniel, and organized St. Mark, Rowan County; Morning Star, Mecklenburg County; Emmanuel, Union County, 1883-88; St. Martin-Sharon, Iredell County; St. John, Concordia, and Zion, Catawba County; re-organized Beth Eden, Newton; Holy Trinity, Hickory, 1888-1911; St. Paul, Newton (two years); and Calvary, Claremont-Salem, for nine months before his death; Supply, Mt. Pleasant, Watauga County, 1889; Philadelphia, Granite Falls; Supply with the Reverend W. P. Cline, St. John, Statesville; organized Mt. Hebron, Hildebran, 1904-06; Friendship, Alexander County, 1906-07.

Other: Professor, later President, of Concordia College, at Conover, 1882-88. Taught school at China Grove in first pastorate, and at other times. A founder, with the Reverends W. P. Cline, A. L. Crouse, and R. A. Yoder, of Lenoir-Rhyne, 1891; Professor (Latin), 1891; and Member of Board of same, 1891-1906, Chair, 1891-1901; President, Tennessee Synod 1888, 1897, 1900, 1908; and Secretary, 1880.

Date of Death/Burial Location: November 12, 1911 the day his resignation was read in his church at Claremont; Oakwood Cemetery, Hickory, N.C.

MOSER, JOHN FRANKLIN

Date/Place of Birth: April 4, 1854; Mecklenburg County, N.C.

Parents: The Reverend Timothy Moser and Margaret (Hedrick) Moser. The Reverend Daniel Moser was his grandfather. An older brother was the Reverend Jason C. Moser.

Spouse/Marriage Date: Laura Hester (Watkins) Moser of near China Grove; December 26, 1881.

Children: Frank Llewellyn, Hazel, Earle Edwin, Max Ivan, Ruth, Carl Luther, John Frederick.
Education: North Carolina College, A.B. 1874.
Ordination: 1889 by Tennessee Synod.
Calls: St. Luke (organized and built church), Monroe-Morning Star, Mecklenburg County, 1889-95; Emmanuel, Lincolnton, 1892-95; Lutheran Chapel, Gastonia, 1895-97; Good Shepherd, Mt. Holly, 1892-97.
Other: Teacher, Concordia College, 1884-89; taught schools in Salisbury and near Mt. Moriah Church, Rowan County, presumably between 1874 and 1884; President, Tennessee Synod, 1894-95.
Date of Death/Burial Location: February 3, 1897; Mt. Holly, N.C.

MOSER, JONATHAN R.

Place of Birth: Lincoln (now Catawba) County, N.C.
Parents: The Reverend Daniel Moser and Mary Barbara (Moretz) Moser. Mother's father was the Reverend Christian Moretz. A younger brother was the Reverend Timothy Moser.
Spouse/Marriage Date: Barbara (Thomas) Moser; September 7, 1848.
Children: Anna Caroline, Selina Catherine, Abel John Franklin, Sarah Rebecca, Philo Washington.
Education: Educated for the ministry by his father.
License/Ordination: Licensed 1836 and ordained 1837 by Tennessee Synod.
Calls: St. Peter, Rowan County, 1836-37; Coble's, Guilford County; Melanchthon, Randolph County; Mt. Pleasant, Alamance County, 1838-39; Friendship, Alexander County, 1844-45; organized Mt. Pleasant, Watauga County, first called Jackson Church after meeting place, Jackson School, 1845-46; St. Martin, Cabarrus County-St. Paul, Newton (Startown), 1847-48. Moved in 1851 to Missouri, and served Tennessee Synod churches until 1873 when was dismissed with the Reverend P. C. Henkel to unite with The Lutheran Church-Missouri Synod; helped to organize the English Conference of that Synod.
Other: Secretary, Tennessee Synod, five terms, 1836-48. In 1844 member of first common school board in Catawba County, and along with brothers, the Reverend Timothy Moser and Marcus M. Moser, an early public school teacher in that county.
Death: Data not available.

MOSER, TIMOTHY

Date/Place of Birth: May 17, 1817; Lincoln (now Catawba) County, N.C.
Parents: The Reverend Daniel Moser and Barbara (Moretz) Moser. An older brother was the Reverend Jonathan R. Moser. Great-Great-Grandson is The Reverend Clarence Eugene Sifford, Jr.
Spouse/Marriage Date: Margaret Malinda (Hedrick) Moser; September 8, 1848.
Children: The Reverend Jason Chrysostom, Titus A., the Reverend John Franklin, Barbara Jane, Ida Caroline, Rosa B.
Education: Educated under the instruction of his father.
License/Ordination: Licensed 1844 and ordained 1847 by Tennessee Synod.

Calls: Mt. Pleasant, Watauga County, 1847; Zion, Catawba County, 1847-52; St. Martin, Cabarrus County, 1848-87; St. Martin, 1848-57, Supply 1873, and Sharon, 1850-58, Iredell County; Morning Star, Mecklenburg County, 1856-57; St. Martin, Stanly County, 1856-59, 1867-88; St. Peter, Catawba County, 1849-56; Friendship, Alexander County, 1862-67; first pastor, Luther Union Church (merged church of Lutheran Union, Tennessee Synod, and Mt. Carmel, North Carolina Synod, voting by majority of one to affiliate with Tennessee Synod), name later changed to Mt. Gilead, Cabarrus County, 1887-88.

Other: Tennessee Synod Secretary 1856, President 1862, Treasurer 1868.

Date of Death/Burial Location: July 25, 1900; St. Martin Church, Cabarrus County, N.C.

MOSER, WILLIAM DEXTER, JR.

Date/Place of Birth: April 20, 1918; Burlington, N.C.

Parents: Dr. William Dexter Moser, Sr. and Cornelia (Hancock) Moser.

Spouse/Marriage Date: Margaret Elizabeth (Cobb) Moser, daughter of the Reverend W. G. Cobb and Lillian (Akard) Cobb; February 27, 1943 in Cherryville, N.C.

Children: Ronald Dexter, Davis Denton, Martha Elizabeth.

Education: Wake Forest College, 1938-41; Lenoir-Rhyne, A.B. 1947; Lutheran Theological Southern Seminary, M.Div. 1950.

Ordination: June 25, 1950 by North Carolina Synod.

Calls: Mt. Moriah, Rowan County, 1950-52; Shades Valley, Birmingham, Ala., 1952-56; Redeemer, Houston, Texas, 1956-62; St. Mark's, Corpus Christi, Texas, 1962-64; Lutheridge, full-time Program Director, 1964-66; Bethany, Memphis, Tenn., 1966-75; Secretary, Southeastern Synod, Atlanta, Ga., 1975-79; Assistant to the President-Bishop, Southeastern Synod, 1979-83; retired 1983. Interim pastor, Cross of Life, Roswell, Ga., 1983-84. Chaplain, Goldkist Corporation, Atlanta, Ga., 1984-89; Pastor for homebound, Redeemer, Atlanta, Ga., 1987-92. Transferred to North Carolina Synod 1992 and served as supply pastor for various congregations.

Other: Summer internship, Spindale Mission Congregation, 1948; Kure Beach Mission Congregation, 1949; delegate to United Lutheran Church in America and Lutheran Church in America Conventions; President, Alabama Conference, Georgia-Alabama Synod, 1954; President, Eastern and Southern Conferences, Texas- Louisiana Synod, 1952-53, 1962-63; Dean, Cumberland District, Southeastern Synod, 1973-75; Executive Board, Lutheridge, 1971-75; President, Tennessee Association of Churches, 1980-82; Secretary, Georgia Interchurch Association, 1977-79; Freedom Foundation, Valley Forge, recipient of George Washington Honor Medal, 1966; Chaplain, National Boy Scout 50th Anniversary Jamboree, 1960; Recipient of Lamb Award; Recipient of Silver Beaver Award, 1988. Lions Club, Cherryville, Vice President, 1997-.

MOTHERSHED, MARY VIRGINIA

Date/Place of Birth: April 9, 1954; Columbia, S.C.

Parents: James Walter Mothershed and Lois (Durham) Mothershed.

Education: Lenoir-Rhyne, A.B. 1976; Southeastern Seminary, M.Div. 1978; Lutheran Theological Southern Seminary, 1980; Substance Abuse Chaplaincy Internship: The Earle E. Morris Alcohol and Drug Addiction Treatment Center, Columbia, S.C., 1980; Kensington University, Oxford, England and Glendale, Calif., Ph.D. Philosophy

Ordination: September 14, 1980 by North Carolina Synod.

Calls: Holy Trinity, Gastonia, 1980-82; Ebenezer, Catawba, 1983-85; Holy Cross, Lincolnton, 1988-91; Director of Pastoral Services, Cedar Cross Institute for Life Enrichment, Inc., Charlotte, 1991-.

Other: Board, Lenoir-Rhyne, 1987-; Task Force on Liturgical Renewal, 1987-90; Vice President, Lincoln Lutheran Pastors' Association, 1987-91; Lutheran-Episcopal Dialogue, 1986; University of North Carolina at Charlotte Lutheran Campus Ministry Development, 1986; Lutheran-Roman Catholic Dialogue, 1980, 1990.

MOURITSEN, JOHN COREY

Date/Place of Birth: December 3, 1969; Bridgeport, Conn.
Parents: Robert John Mouritsen and Lynn Ruth (Henson) Mouritsen.
Spouse/Marriage Date: Kristen (Nagle) Mouritsen; August 15, 1992.
Child: Kieran John.
Education: Wittenberg University, B.A. 1992; Herzen Pedagogical Institute, Leningrad; Gettysburg Seminary, M.Div. 1996.
Ordination: June 16, 1996 by North Carolina Synod.
Calls: St. John, Hudson, 1996-.

MOZINGO, HUGH LEE, III

Date/Place of Birth: November 5, 1948; Mecklenburg County, N.C.
Parents: Hugh Lee Mozingo, II and Faye (Poovey) Mozingo.
Education: Lenoir-Rhyne, B.A. 1971; Lutheran Theological Southern Seminary, M.Div. 1977.
Ordination: July 3, 1977 by North Carolina Synod.
Calls: Good Hope, Hickory, 1977-79.
Other: Transferred to Florida Synod in 1979.

MULLEN, LESTER ALFRED, II

Date/Place of Birth: February 3, 1942; Lincoln County, N.C.
Parents: Lester Alfred Mullen, Sr. and Florence Ermintrude (Little) Mullen.
Spouse/Marriage Date: Beverly Kay (Lingle) Mullen; December 22, 1963 in Faith, N.C.
Children: The Reverend Patrick Shannon, Laura Ann.
Education: Davidson College, B.S. Biology 1963; High Point and Catawba College, Teacher Certification, 1980; Lutheran Theological Southern Seminary, M.Div. 1967; Lutheran General Hospital, C.P.E. 1972.
Ordination: June 1967 by North Carolina Synod.
Calls: Messiah, Hannahan, S.C., 1967-71; Trinity, Vale, 1972-81; St. Luke, Tyro, 1981-88; Ebenezer, Catawba, 1992-98; Chaplain, Abernathy Center, Newton, 1998-. Vice Pastor at various congregations.
Other: Chemistry teacher at Lincolnton High School, 1988-95; Teacher of the Year, Lincoln County, 1992; Science/Math Teacher of Year, Lincolnton High School, 1993-94; Camp Committee; Chair, Environmental Concerns Committee.

MULLEN, PATRICK SHANNON
Date/Place of Birth: January 8, 1968; Charleston, S.C.
Parents: The Reverend Lester Alfred Mullen, II, and Beverly Kay (Lingle) Mullen.
Spouse/Marriage Date: Kay Marie (Kinard) Mullen; April 20, 1991.
Child: Justice Patrick.
Education: Davidson College, B.A. *cum laude* 1990; Lutheran Theological Southern Seminary, M.Div. with honors, 1995.
Ordination: October 1, 1995 by North Carolina Synod.
Calls: Shepherd of the Sea, Atlantic Beach, 1995-.

MURDOCK, CHARLES LEWIS
Date of Birth: June 25, 1947.
Parents: Edd Fuller Murdock and Ella (Young) Murdock.
First Spouse/Marriage Date: Jennifer (Fox) Murdock; July 8, 1967.
Children of First Marriage: Julie, Lori.
Second Spouse/Marriage Date: Lena (Smith) Murdock; May 15, 1984.
Education: Gardner Webb, B.S. 1989; Lutheran Theological Southern Seminary, M.Div. 1994.
Ordination: July 3, 1994 by North Carolina Synod.
Calls: Antioch, Dallas, 1994-98; Grace, Washington, 1998-.

MURRAY, DONALD ALLEN
Date/Place of Birth: August 15, 1950; Jacksonville, Fla.
Parents: Allen Amos Murray and Juanita Edge (Lee) Murray.
Spouse/Marriage Date: Elizabeth Ann (Morefield) Murray; September 29, 1979 in Rural Hall, N.C.
Child: Philip Allen.
Education: Newberry, A.B. 1972; Lutheran Theological Southern Seminary, M.Div. 1978; Drew University, D.Min. 1988.
Ordination: June 19, 1978 by Florida Synod.
Calls: Nazareth, Rural Hall, 1978-82; Coble's, Julian, 1982-91; retired October 1991.
Other: Article for *Partner's Magazine* on positive use of the children's sermon.

MURRAY, WALDO EMERSON
Date/Place of Birth: November 26, 1862; Dedham, Mass.
Parents: Walter Murray and Jane (Huggan) Murray.
Spouse/Marriage Date: Clara (Diralla) Murray; 1910.
Child: Grace.
Education: Thiel College, A.B. 1890, A.M.; Philadelphia Seminary, 1893.
Ordination: 1893 by Pittsburgh Synod.
Calls: In Ontario, N.Y., and Nova Scotia, 1893-1915; transferred to Tennessee Synod 1915 and served Holy Trinity, Hickory, 1915-19; transferred to New York Synod, 1920 and served St. Peter, Verona, N.Y., 1919-22.
Other: President, Nova Scotia Synod, 1906-09.
Date of Death/Burial Location: January 9, 1922; Verona, N.Y.

NAGLE, DANIEL KEITH

Date/Place of Birth: August 24, 1951; Jamestown, N.Y.
Parents: Don Allen Nagle and Janice Diane (Bulow) Nagle.
Spouse/Marriage Date: Donna Marie (Hogan) Nagle; August 30, 1975.
Children: Ingrid Elizabeth, Meredith Kristine.
Education: Rochester Institute of Technology, A.A.S. Chemistry, 1971; North Park College, B.A. Philosophy, 1973; Chicago Seminary, M.Div. 1977; Duke University, Th.M. Ethics 1989.
Ordination: June 19, 1977 by Upper New York Synod.
Calls: Trinity, Castleton-on-Hudson, N.Y., 1977-81; Chaplain, United States Army, 1981-, with service at Ft. Bragg, 1985-88, 1993-.

NAGLE, JOHN ROBERT

Date/Place of Birth: December 18, 1943; Meyersdale, Pa.
Parents: The Reverend Robert Smith Nagle and Rebecca Neff (Phillippi) Nagle.
Spouse/Marriage Date: Elaine Ann (Hartzell) Nagle; June 12, 1965 in Gettysburg, Pa.
Children: Kristen Sue Mouritsen, Gretchen Elisabeth.
Education: Gettysburg College, B.A. 1965; Gettysburg Seminary, M.Div. 1969; Drew University, D.Min. 1988.
Ordination: May 25, 1969 by Southeastern Pennsylvania Synod.
Calls: Christ the King, Cary, 1969-.
Other: Contributor to various church daily devotional services; author of book of sermons, *The Story I Love to Tell*; contributor to book of sermons, *A Daisy A Day*; Executive Board; District Secretary, 1971-73.

NAHOUSE, RICHARD GRAHAM

Date/Place of Birth: May 22, 1938; Passaic, N.J.
Parents: Richard Arthur Nahouse and Ottie (Robinson) Nahouse.
Spouse/Marriage Date: Nancy Elizabeth (Fritts) Nahouse; May 1, 1976 in Lexington, N.C.
Children: Elizabeth Rose, Mary Katherine, Graham Robinson.
Education: University of Richmond, B.A. 1959; Southeastern Baptist Seminary, B.D. 1962; Lutheran Theological Southern Seminary, Certificate, 1964.
Ordination: June 14, 1964 by North Carolina Synod.
Calls: Nazareth, Rural Hall, 1964-69; Our Redeemer, Greenville, 1969-91; Contact Pastor at East Carolina University, Greenville, 1969-91; Exchange Pastor with Christus Kirche, Syke, Germany, July-October 1990; Trinity, Landis, 1991-; Vice Pastor at various congregations.

NAU, WALTER THEODORE
Date/Place of Birth: March 5, 1908; Crishnagiri, Travancore, British India.
Parents: The Reverend Henry Nau and Helen (Hempfing) Nau.
Spouse/Marriage Date: Elizabeth Ann (Esch) Nau; August 22, 1932 in East St. Louis, Ill.
Children: Lanay Marie Hartman, William Henry, James Michael.
Education: Concordia College (Mo.), A.B. 1925; Concordia Seminary (Mo.), B.D. 1930; Guilford College, B.A. 1933; Duke University, M.A. 1942, Instructor and Fellow in Romance Languages, 1942-45, Ph.D. 1949.
Ordination: July 20, 1930 by Central Illinois District, The Lutheran Church-Missouri Synod.
Calls: Bethany, Waynesboro, Va., and St. John, Louisville, Ill., 1928-32; St. Mark, China Grove, 1938-44; First, Lexington, 1944-46; Supply, St. Matthew, Kings Mountain 1951 and numerous other churches; retired 1975 to Hickory, N.C.
Other: Faculty, Liberty High School, Liberty, 1933-36; Professor of French and German and Head of Department, Lenoir-Rhyne, 1945-94; author, *Main Currents of French Literature,* 1952; Chaplain, Hickory Unit of the North Carolina Lutheran Homes. District Governor, Rotary International.
Date of Death/Burial Location: December 2, 1996; Oakwood Cemetery, Hickory, N.C.

NEASE, SHADRACK LABAN
Date/Place of Birth: March 10, 1865; Effingham County, Ga. A descendant of the Salzburger Lutheran colonists in Georgia.
Parents: Frederick L. Nease and Mary E. (Dasher) Nease.
Spouse/Marriage Date: Maggie (Lowman) Nease; September 14, 1894 in Lexington County, S.C.
Children: Lowell Lanier, Ruth, George Lowman, Elizabeth, William Lomm, Hilma.
Education: Newberry College; Lutheran Theological Southern Seminary, 1892.
Ordination: 1892 by Tennessee Synod.
Calls: In South Carolina and Georgia; in North Carolina: Mt. Calvary, Claremont, 1921-24; transferred to Virginia Synod, 1924; St. James-Zion, near Waynesboro, Va., was his last charge. Of his more than forty years as an ordained Lutheran minister, more than twenty were served in the Tennessee and North Carolina Synods.
Date of Death/Burial Location: March 14, 1941; Waynesboro, Va.

NEHLS, TIMOTHY WALTER
Date/Place of Birth: January 18, 1942; Fremont, Ohio.
Parents: Mr. and Mrs. Alvin F. Nehls.
Spouse/Marriage Date: Beverly Ann (Martin) Nehls; July 7, 1962.
Children: Joseph Frederick, Deborah Ann.
Education: Bowling Green State University; Capital University, Columbus, Ohio, B.A., 1965; Evangelical Lutheran Theological Seminary, Columbus, Ohio, B.D., 1969; University of North Carolina, Charlotte, N.C., M.Ed., 1975.
Ordination: June 8, 1969 by American Lutheran Church.
Calls: Good Shepherd, Charlotte, 1969-77; Palms, Palm Harbor, Fla., 1978-.

NEIFFER, JACOB GRABENSTEIN

Date/Place of Birth: January 23, 1840; near Philadelphia, Pa.

Parents: Christian Neiffer and Cathrine Barbara (Grabenstein) Neiffer.

Education: Gettysburg College, two years; Franklin & Marshall College, A.B. 1865, A.M. 1871; Philadelphia Seminary, 1868; Wittenberg University, D.D. 1903.

Ordination: 1868 by Ministerium of Pennsylvania.

Calls: In Richmond, Va., 1868-70; in North Carolina: St. John, Salisbury, 1870-75; Beth Eden, Newton, 1873-75; transferred to Ohio Synod 1875 and served churches at Lima, Dayton, and Toledo, Ohio, 1875-1908.

Other: Secretary, North Carolina Synod, 1871-72; President, Ohio Synod, 1902-05.

Date of Death/Burial Location: July 29, 1924; Toledo, Ohio.

NELSON, DAVID PAUL

Date/Place of Birth: February 17, 1935; Pittsburgh, Pa.

Parents: The Reverend John Emil Nelson and Lillie Dorothy (Engdahl) Nelson.

Spouse/Marriage Date: Mary Anne (Petrea) Nelson; June 29, 1963 in Salisbury, N.C.

Children: Vaughn Paul, Ken-Erik.

Education: Upsala College, A.B. 1957; Philadelphia Seminary, M.Div. 1960; graduate work, East Carolina University, 1963, and Wake Forest University and North Carolina Baptist Hospital, Clinical Training in Pastoral Care and Counseling, 1974.

Ordination: June 15, 1960 by New York and New England Synod.

Calls: St. Timothy, Havelock-Shepherd of the Sea, Atlantic Beach, 1960-64; Bethany, Kannapolis, 1964-68; Resurrection, Augusta, Ga., 1968-71; St. Timothy, Forest Park, Ga., 1971-73; St. James, Rockwell, 1974-79; St. John, Salisbury, 1979-82; Chief Chaplain, Lutheran Services for the Aging, Salisbury, 1982-90; St. Mark, Claremont, 1991-97; retired in 1997 to Salisbury, N.C.; Vice Pastor at various congregations.

Other: Attended Helsinki assembly of Lutheran World Federation, 1963; Secretary, Eastern District, 1962-64; Fellow and Certified Chaplain in the College of Chaplains, 1987; Certified Chaplain in North Carolina Chaplains' Association, 1985; Commendation from Veterans Administration Medical Center for service as part-time Chaplain, 1982; *Who's Who in Executives and Professionals*, 1996; Music and Worship Committee, 1962-67; Social Ministry Committee, 1966-67.

NELSON, ELOF GUS

Date/Place of Birth: April 11, 1924; Minneapolis, Minn.

Parents: John W. Nelson and Ruth Lind Nelson.

Spouse/Marriage Date: Marette (Johnson) Nelson; August 23, 1947 in Rice Lake, Wis.

Children: Susan Johnson, Janice, Carol, Peter, Ann Norris.

Education: Gustavus Adolphus, B.A. 1948; United States Medical School, Certificate, two years; Luther Northwestern Seminary, M.Th. 1953; Andover Newton, D.Min. 1960; San Francisco Seminary, S.T.D. 1973.

Ordination: June 5, 1953 by Southern Minnesota District, Evangelical Lutheran Church.

Calls: McVille Lutheran Parish, McVille, N.D., 1953-57; Chaplain, Fairview Lutheran Hospitals, Minneapolis, Minn., 1958-72; Christ, Cape Coral, Fla., 1988-91; retired in 1989 to Asheville, N.C.

Other: Professor of Religion and Health, University of Minnesota Medical School, 1971-88, Professor Emeritus; Lutheran Association of Pastoral Counselors; Florida Lutheran

Council on Aging; American Lutheran Church Reserved Task Force on Medical Ethics; Pastor, Preaching Mission - Joint Lutheran- Episcopal, 1993-94; author, *Your Life Together,* 1965; *Keeping Love Alive,* 1972; *Bio-Medical Ethics,* 1974; National Lutheran Consultant for Lutheran Clinical Pastoral Education; Lutheran Church Research Program, 1962-81; Teacher, Pastoral Psychology, Luther Seminary Graduate Program; taught senior citizens at University of North Carolina at Asheville; taught at Red Cross.
Date of Death/Memorial Service: March 25, 1998; Memorial service held at St. Mark, Asheville, N.C.

NELSON, GEORGE W.

Date/Place of Birth: April 21, 1894; Brooklyn, N.Y.
Education: Muhlenberg College, A.B. 1918; Lutheran Theological Southern Seminary, 1921.
Ordination: 1921 by North Carolina Synod.
Calls: St. Luke, Summerville, S.C., 1921-26.
Other: Supply for Calvary, Morganton, 1918.
Date of Death/Burial Location: 1926; Charleston, S.C.

NELSON, JOHN EMIL

Date/Place of Birth: December 2, 1884; Varberg, Sweden.
Parents: Nils Anton Nelson and Amelia Josephina Nelson.
First Spouse/Marriage Date: Lillie Dorothy (Engdahl) Nelson; June 24, 1922 in Port Byron, Ill.
Children: Dorothy Elaine Meeker, Bryon Emil, the Reverend David Paul.
Second Spouse/Marriage Date: Ruth A. M. (Armstrong) Nelson; August 1, 1942 in Pittsburgh, Pa.
Third Spouse/Marriage Date: Ruth Amelia (Swanson) Nelson, April 29, 1967 in Kannapolis, N.C.
Education: Upsala Academy and Junior College, 1916; Upsala College, A.B. 1919; Augustana Seminary, B.D. 1922; University of Pittsburgh, M.Ed. 1937.
Ordination: June 18, 1922 by Augustana Synod.
Calls: First, Waltham, Mass., 1922-30; Friendship, Pittsburgh, Pa., 1930-43; Salem, Norwich and Ebenezer, Willimantic, Conn., 1943-49; Grace, Schenectady, N.Y., 1949-57; Bethlehem, Hampton, Conn., 1957-59; retired 1957 to Claremont, N.C.; transferred to North Carolina Synod in 1962; Supply, East Hampton, Conn., 1957-59; Supply, Ebenezer, Catawba County, 1960-62.
Other: President, Boston and Pittsburgh Districts, Augustana Synod; member of boards of several Augustana Synod institutions.
Date of Death/Burial Location: May 4, 1985; Mt. Calvary Cemetery, Claremont, N.C.

NELSON, THOMAS EDWARD, II

Date/Place of Birth: September 24, 1945; Nueces County, Texas.
Parents: Thomas Edward Nelson, Sr. and Esther Lucile (Gunderson) Nelson.
Spouse/Marriage Date: Darlene Nelson; 1980.
Education: University of Tennessee, B.S. 1968; Chicago Seminary, M.Div. 1979.

Ordination: May 27, 1979 by Southeastern Synod.
Calls: Holy Trinity, Raleigh, 1979-84; Assistant Pastor, Christ the King, Cary, 1988-.
Other: Lutheran Church in America Delegate, Southeastern Synod, 1972, 1974; Consulting Committee, World Hunger Appeal, 1972-75.

NEWBY, WILBUR VERNON

Date/Place of Birth: February 16, 1916; Newberg, Ore.
Parents: Ross A. Newby and Clarice (Newlin) Newby.
Spouse/Marriage Date: Juanita (Horton) Newby; June 6, 1947 in Baltimore, Md.
Education: Pacific College, B.A. 1938; Hartford Theological Seminary, B.D. 1942; Mt. Airy Seminary, S.T.M. 1943; Johns Hopkins University; Union Seminary (N.Y.).
Ordination: May 26, 1943 by Maryland Synod.
Calls: Grace, Easton and St. Paul, Cordova, Md., 1943-47; Salem, Catonsville, Md., 1947-60; First, Collingdale, Pa., 1960-61; Our Saviour, Seaside, Ore., 1961-65; Immanuel, Centralia, Wash., 1965-70; Gloria Dei, North Vancouver, British Columbia, 1970-71; Redeemer, Charlotte, 1971-76; Grace, Liberty, 1976-81; retired May 1, 1981.
Date of Death/Burial Location: April 20, 1988; Rowan Memorial Park, Salisbury, N.C.

NICHOLS, DAVID BRENT

Date/Place of Birth: May 26, 1954; Winston-Salem, N.C.
Parents: David E. Nichols and Esther (Brown) Nichols.
Spouse/Marriage Date: Lynn (Wilson) Nichols; August 17, 1985 in North Augusta, S.C.
Children: David Wilson, Andrew Brent, Elizabeth Anne.
Education: Wingate College, A.S. 1974; North Carolina State University, A.B. Sociology, 1979; Lutheran Theological Southern Seminary, M.Div. 1986.
Ordination: May 29, 1986 by North Carolina Synod.
Calls: Prince of Peace, Salisbury, 1986-90; St. Paul, Pomaria, S.C., 1990-; Vice Pastor at various congregations.

NIEWOEHNER, RICHARD DEAN

Date/Place of Birth: July 21, 1949; Columbus, Ohio.
Parents: Richard W. Niewoehner and Alice (Golden) Niewoehner.
Spouse/Marriage Date: Alice (Hook) Niewoehner; August 11, 1973 in Morristown, Ind.
Children: Richard Addison, Daniel Robert.
Education: Pennsylvania State, Maryville College, B.A. 1972; Philadelphia Seminary, M.Div. 1976.
Ordination: June 13, 1976 by Western Pennsylvania-West Virginia Synod.
Calls: Shiloh, Lewisville, 1976-79; First, Warren, Pa., 1979-.
Other: Transition Team for Western Pennsylvania-West Virginia Synod; Transition Team for Northwestern Pennsylvania Synod; President, Warren Pastoral Counseling Board; Bishop's Resource Team.

NILSEN, NORMAN M.
Date/Place of Birth: August 14, 1933; Philadelphia, Pa.
Parents: Mr. and Mrs. Nils Joseph Nilsen.
Spouse/Marriage Date: Margaret Paul (Haedrich) Nilsen; June 12, 1954.
Children: Eric Norman, Alan Ralph, Amy Lynn.
Education: Drexel University, Philadelphia, Pa., Diploma, 1960; Evangelical Lutheran Theological Seminary, Columbus, Ohio, B.A., 1967.
Ordination: June 18, 1967 by American Lutheran Church.
Calls: St. Luke, Taylorsville, 1967-71, 1971-75; Mt. Pisgah, Hickory, 1967-71; Assistant Pastor, St. John, Columbus, Ohio, 1975-77; St. John, Columbus, Ohio, 1977-80 (called twice); Prince of Peace, Richmond, Va., 1980.
Other: U.S. Navy, four years.

NORDSIEK, GERALD ALAN, JR.
Date/Place of Birth: May 6, 1962; Jacksonville, Fla.
Parents: Gerald Alan Nordsiek, Sr. and Kathleen (Gooding) Nordsiek.
First Spouse/Marriage Date: Susan Dianne Nordsiek; July 27, 1985 in Columbia, S.C.
Second Spouse/Marriage Date: Carol A. (McLamb) Nordsiek; April 13, 1996.
Education: Lenoir-Rhyne, A.B. Psychology/Business Administration 1984; Lutheran Theological Southern Seminary, M.Div. 1988.
Ordination: June 5, 1988 by North Carolina Synod.
Calls: St. Matthew, Wilmington, 1988-94; First, Greensboro, 1994-95.
Other: Member of Synod Council; Secretary, Coastal Conference; Copy Editor of *Soli Deo Gloria.*

NORDSIEK, PAUL KENNETH
Date/Place of Birth: May 19, 1910; Beardstown, Ill.
Parents: Henry Nordsiek and Marie Anna (Ring) Nordsiek.
Spouse/Marriage Date: Dorothy May (Fess) Nordsiek; October 12, 1938 in Chicago, Ill.
Children: Gerald Alan, Janet May Hilton.
Education: Carthage, A.B. 1932; Chicago Seminary, B.D. 1935; Newberry, D.D. 1962.
Ordination: May 19, 1935 by Wartburg Synod.
Calls: Martin Luther, Chicago, Ill., 1935-39; Trinity, Des Plaines, Ill., 1939-42; Redeemer, Aurora, Ill., 1942- 51; St. Mark, Jacksonville, Fla., 1951-64; St. John, Winter Park, Fla., 1964-72; Living Word, Lantana, Fla., 1972-77; retired March 1, 1977 to Jacksonville, Fla.; transferred to North Carolina Synod January 20, 1983; Vice Pastor at various congregations in North Carolina; transferred to Florida-Bahamas Synod, January 1998.

NORMAN, CLARENCE EDWARD
Date/Place of Birth: March 12, 1892; Prosperity, S.C.
Parents: Victor Louis Norman and Nina Gustelle (Wheeler) Norman.
Spouse/Marriage Date: Lottie Lee (Wyse) Norman; June 20, 1917 in Columbia, S.C.
Children: Rebecca Wyse Leager, Kathryn Wheeler Howell.

Education: University of North Carolina, A.B. 1912; Lutheran Theological Southern Seminary, 1917, B.D.; graduate school at Kennedy School of Missions, Hartford, Conn., 1924.

Ordination: May 13, 1917 by North Carolina Synod.

Calls: Missionary in Japan for General Council, 1917-18, then for United Lutheran Church in America 1918-33; Managing Director, interdenominational office of Newspaper and Correspondence Evangelism, Fukuoka, Japan, 1925-31; Treasurer, Japan Lutheran Mission, several years. Churches served in North Carolina: Holy Trinity, Raleigh, and Pastor to Lutheran students in Raleigh colleges, 1933-49; supplied services for Lutherans in Goldsboro before Good Shepherd was developed, 1937-38; St. Luke-Morning Star, Monroe, 1949-54; St. Luke only, 1954-61; retired 1961 at Cary, N.C.; in retirement has supplied churches from Mt. Holly to Atlantic Beach.

Other: High School math teacher for two years; Secretary, Board, Lutheran Theological Southern Seminary, 1938-47; contributed sermon, "The Secret of Greatness" to "Victim or Victor?" (Lenten sermons, United Lutheran Publishing House);   Historical Works Committee, North Carolina Synod, 1963-66; compiler, under direction and with cooperation of Historical Works Committee, of most sketches in *Life Sketches of Lutheran Ministers, North Carolina-Tennessee Synods, 1773-1965*.

Date of Death/Burial Location: September 23, 1981; Mount Lawn Cemetery, Raleigh, N.C.

NORMAN, WADE NOLEN

Date/Place of Birth: November 13, 1938; Guilford County, N.C.

Parents: Fred Nolen Norman and Mary Ella (Bottoms) Norman.

Spouse/Marriage Date: Barbara Jeanne (Presson) Norman; July 4, 1965 in Charleston, S.C.

Education: Lenoir-Rhyne, A.B. 1962; Lutheran Theological Southern Seminary, B.D. 1965.

Ordination: June 6, 1965 by North Carolina Synod.

Calls: St. Paul, Crouse-Bethel, Gaston County, 1965-68.

Other: Demitted Ministry January 11, 1970.

NORRIS, JEFFERSON LEANDER

Date/Place of Birth: April 19, 1898; Boone, N.C.

Parents: Millard H. Norris and Ida (Davis) Norris.

Spouse/Marriage Date: Mae (Throneburg) Norris; October 10, 1928 in Hudson, N.C.

Children: Jefferson Lawrence, Ida Mae Elliot, Marion Theresa Yoder (married the Reverend John Y. Yoder, Jr.).

Education: Lenoir-Rhyne, A.B. 1923, D.D. 1951; Lutheran Theological Southern Seminary, B.D. 1927; graduate study, University of South Carolina.

Ordination: February 1927 by North Carolina Synod.

Calls: St. Martin, Maiden-Luther's Chapel-Salem, Lincoln County, 1927-37; Kimball Memorial, Kannapolis, 1937-46; Macedonia, Burlington, 1947-58; Grace, Hendersonville, 1958-60; retired January 1, 1967; Vice Pastor at various congregations.

Other: Executive Director, North Carolina Lutheran Homes, 1960-67, and Acting Superintendent, Hickory Unit, North Carolina Lutheran Homes, 1962-65; Fund raiser for

Unit near Albemarle; Secretary, Board, Lenoir- Rhyne, 1935-55; President, Western Conference, 1935-36; President, Southern Conference, 1946; First Chair, Board, North Carolina Lutheran Homes, 1958-60.
Date of Death/Burial Location: September 1, 1974; Catawba Memorial Cemetery, Hickory, N.C.

NORRIS, LAWRENCE DARRELL

Date/Place of Birth: September 16, 1954; Rowan County, N.C.
Parents: Clemmie Elwood Norris and Frances (Meacham) Norris.
Spouse/Marriage Date: Kathy Anne (Liles) Norris; May 2, 1981 in China Grove, N.C.
Children: John Matthew, Paul Christopher.
Education: Catawba College, B.A. 1976; Lutheran Theological Southern Seminary, M.Div. 1980.
Ordination: May 25, 1980 by North Carolina Synod.
Calls: Bethel, Lincolnton, 1980-82; Mt. Zion, Richfield, 1982-92; Union, Salisbury, 1992-; Vice Pastor at various congregations.
Other: Member, Consulting Task Force - Minority Ministry, North Carolina Synod, 1981.

NUECHTERLEIN, ANNE MARIE

See Thalheimer, Anne Marie Nuechterlein
Date/Place of Birth: August 7, 1954; Saginaw, Mich.
Parents: Duane C. Nuechterlein and Audrey A. Nuechterlein.
Spouse/Marriage Date: Dana R. Thalheimer; March 16, 1985.
Children: Sonja Marie, Sarah Grace.
Education: Valparaiso University, B.A. Theology and Social Work 1976; University of North Texas, M.Ed. Counseling and Student Services 1982; Christ Seminary-Seminex, M.Div. 1983; Texas Women's University, Doctor of Philosophy in Marriage and Family Therapy, 1986.
Ordination: June 23, 1985 by Texas Synod.
Calls: Deaconess, Messiah Lutheran Church, St. Louis, Mo., 1976-79; Lutheran Campus Minister, St. Paul and University Center, Denton, Texas, 1979-82; Assistant Pastor, Christ the Servant, Denton, Texas, 1983-84; Associate Pastor, St. Luke, Richardson, Texas, 1984-85; Pastoral Counselor, Raleigh, 1991-.
Other: Instructor, North Texas State University, Old Testament and World Religions, 1979-82; Associate Professor of Contextual Education, Wartburg Seminary, 1986-93; Interim Director, Tokyo Community Counseling Services, Tokyo, Japan, 1990; Visiting Professor, Duke University, Pastoral Theology and Spirituality, 1991-; American Association of Pastoral Counselors; Fellow, American Association of Marriage and Family Therapy, Clinical Member and Supervisor; Editor, Alban Institute Editorial Board, 1989-90; Editor, Journal of Ministry in Addiction and Recovery Editorial Board, 1991-. Various articles in journals.   Author of various books: *Improving Your Multiple Staff Ministry,* 1989; *Male/Female Church Staffs: Celebrating the Gifts, Confronting the Challenges,* 1990; *Families of Alcoholics,* 1993; *Relating as Women and Men; Effective Leadership.*

NUSSMANN, ADOLPH (ADOLPHUS NUSMANN)

Date of Birth: July 1739.

Parents: Joan Nussmann and Joanna Marie (Hilleke) Nussmann.

First Spouse/Marriage Date: Elizabeth (Rintelmann) Nussmann, daughter of "Delegate" Christopher Rintelmann; 1774.

Children of First Marriage: Paul, Margaret, Elizabeth.

Second Spouse: Barbara (Layrle) Nussmann, daughter of "Delegate" Christopher Layrle.

Children of Second Marriage: John, Daniel, Catherine, Barbara.

Education: Received instruction in Lutheran Theology at Goettingen University, where he registered April 30, 1772 with a scholarship from the Consistory in Hannover.

Ordination: Unknown.

Calls: Pastor Nussmann lived on his 200 acre farm near St. John, Cabarrus County, was pastor of three congregations, and had supervision of the entire North Carolina mission of some twenty congregations.

Other: Baptized July 12, 1739 in Liebfrauen Roman Catholic Church in Muenster, Westphalia and converted to the Lutheran faith from the Franciscan Order shortly before he received the North Carolina call. Because he actively supported the American Patriots, he suffered physical torture from Tories. There were times when he had to hide to save his life. He recognized himself as a Lutheran missionary on the "most distant border of the civilized world," with a parish of seven hundred square miles and at a time when horseback was the only means of travel. His first residence was in Rowan County, near Second Creek (Organ) Church. At the end of his first year, he decided to move to the Buffalo Creek area (St. John Church, Cabarrus County) where he lived during the rest of his ministry. First Lutheran pastor in Rowan County, 1772. Chair, Helmstaedt Society; strong believer in catechetical instruction, sponsored schools, and published eight textbooks for North Carolina. Largest school was at St. John, Cabarrus County; The General Assembly of the State of North Carolina named Pastor Nussmann as member of the Board of Trustees which was commissioned to establish an academy in Salisbury, 1785; took steps toward establishing Lutheran libraries in North Carolina and asked for a printing press, urging sponsors to supply hymnals for the North Carolina congregations.

Date of Death/Burial Location: November 3, 1794 of cancer at the age of 55; St. John Cemetery, Concord, N.C.

NYE, WILLIAM ELWOOD, II

Date/Place of Birth: March 15, 1918; Wilmington, Del.

Parents: Robert C. Nye and Catherine Maguire Nye.

First Spouse/Marriage Date: Martha Macy E. (Brick) Nye; May 29, 1943.

Children of First Marriage: John Robert, Stephen George, The Reverend Paul Andrew.

Second Spouse/Marriage Date: Martha J. (Frye) Nye; June 25, 1974 in Hickory, N.C.

Step Children: Barbara Marie Terry, Ruth Elizabeth Terry, Julia Kneeburg Terry, Glenn Roger Terry.

Education: Susquehanna University, A.B. 1940; Philadelphia Seminary, M.Div. 1943, S.T.M. 1959; graduate studies in Gerontology at Michigan State and North Texas State.

Ordination: May 26, 1943 by Ministerium of Pennsylvania.

Calls: St. John, Shenandoah, Pa., 1943-44; Chaplain, U.S. Naval Reserve, 1944-46; Salem, Philadelphia, Pa., 1946-52; Zion, Flourtown, Pa., 1956-69; Lutheran Social Mission Society, Philadelphia, Pa., 1970-71; Lutheran Social Services of New Jersey, Trenton, N.J., 1971-75; retired February 28, 1978 to North Wilkesboro, N.C.; Vice Pastor at various congregations.

Other: Board, Lutheran Home at Germantown, Philadelphia, Pa.; Board, Lutheran Social Mission Society, Philadelphia, Pa.; Program Director, Haverford Center of Philadelphia and as Consultant for the Aging for Lutheran Social Services of New Jersey; Delegate, Constituting Convention, L.C.A.; Convention Chaplain; Delegate to 1970 White House Conference on Aging.
Date of Death/Burial Location: November 19, 1996; Holy Trinity, Hickory, N.C.

OBERLY, FRANK CLARENCE
Date/Place of Birth: March 14, 1869; Catasauqua County, Pa.
Parents: John W. Oberly and Alamida (Snyder) Oberly.
Spouse: Addie M. (Sherman) Oberly.
Children: Henry, Robert.
Education: Muhlenberg College, A.B. 1889, A.M. 1892; Philadelphia Seminary, 1892.
Ordination: 1892 by Ministerium of Pennsylvania.
Calls: Transferred to Tennessee Synod 1893 and served St. Mark, Luray, Va., 1893-95; transferred to Chicago Synod, 1896; served churches in Illinois (First English, Decatur), Ohio, and Pennsylvania (Holy Trinity, Greenville; Christ, Pittsburgh; First English, Butler), and last at First Church, Washington, Pa., 1920-22.
Other: Board, Philadelphia Seminary, 1915-22.
Date of Death/Burial Location: March 22, 1922; Washington County, Pa.

OFFMAN, DAVID ISAIAH
Date/Place of Birth: April 18, 1864; New Market, Va.
Parents: Frederick Offman and Hannah Cline (Caldwell) Offman.
First Spouse/Marriage Date: Mary Elizabeth (Jones) Offman; December 21, 1892 in Randolph County, N.C.
Children of First Marriage: David Orlo and Otho Frederick (twins), Ruth Hannah, Mina Etta.
Second Spouse/Marriage Date: Mrs. Fannie (Albright) (Johnson) Offman; May 20, 1920.
Education: Polytechnic Institute, New Market, Va., A.B. 1886; theology under the Reverend Socrates Henkel.
Ordination: 1889 by Tennessee Synod.
Calls: In North Carolina: Coble's, Guilford County-Melanchthon, Randolph County-Mt. Pleasant, Alamance County, 1890-1902, 1913-21; Mt. Moriah-St. Mark, Rowan County, 1903-12; Coble's-Low's, Guilford County-Mt. Pleasant-St. Paul, Alamance County, 1921-40; retired 1940 to Burlington; supplied Mt. Pleasant-St. Paul, 1940-46.
Other: Secretary, Tennessee Synod, 1913-18; operated a small printery at Julian for church and public job printing; taught school in Virginia and North Carolina; served in North Carolina General Assembly, 1903; writer of notes for Sunday School lessons in "Our Church Paper;" noted compiler of genealogical data (unpublished) of families in Guilford, Randolph, Alamance, and other counties.
Date of Death/Burial Location: September 8, 1954; Melanchthon Church, Randolph County, N.C.

OGBURN, HERMAN KAPP, III

Ordination: May 31, 1985 by North Carolina Synod.
Other: Transferred to Northeast Pennsylvania Synod in 1985. Removed from roll October 1992 in Winston- Salem, N.C.

OLSON, CARL JAY

Date/Place of Birth: November 28, 1938; Dade County, Fla.
Parents: Albert Jacob Olson and Elizabeth Ann (Palo) Olson.
Spouse/Marriage Date: Barbara Edith (Hanna) Olson; July 30, 1966 in Gastonia, N.C.
Children: Jonathan Andrew, Laura Anne.
Education: Thiel College, B.A. 1962; Gettysburg, B.D. 1966.
Ordination: June 9, 1966 by Western Pennsylvania-West Virginia Synod.
Calls: Hope, Evans City (now Mars), Pa., 1966-74; Redeemer, Gastonia, 1978-82.
Other: Dropped from roll, 1982.

ONEY, WILLIAM BURNS

Date/Place of Birth: December 4, 1849; near Lexington, Ky.
First Spouse: Catherine (Groseclose) Oney; near Wytheville, Va.
Children of First Marriage: Cora (died at 16), Sara, Thomas Wiggins, the Reverend Elbert E., Forest Andrew (died at 16).
Second Spouse: Jenette (Remine) Oney; Washington County, Va.
Children of Second Marriage: Margaret L., Willie S.
License/Ordination: Licensed 1881 and ordained 1882 by Southwest Virginia.
Calls: Served churches in Virginia; transferred to North Carolina Synod, 1897; St. Matthew-St. Peter, Rowan County, 1897-98; St. Andrew, Concord-Center Grove-Mt. Hermon, Cabarrus County, 1898-1900; transferred to Virginia Synod, 1900 serving churches in Virginia, Ohio and Maryland; retired 1929.
Date of Death/Burial Location: August 11, 1939; Thornrose Cemetery, Staunton, Va.

ONSTAD, AMARETTA "AMY" (JONES)

Date/Place of Birth: April 1, 1949; Billings, Mont.
Parents: William A. Jones and Pauline M. Jones.
Spouse/Marriage Date: The Reverend George L. Onstad; December 26, 1970.
Children: Dana Lynn, Terri Kay.
Education: University of Montana, B.A. 1970; Lutheran Theological Southern Seminary, M.Div. 1982; Kansas State University, M.S. Family Life Education 1994.
Ordination: May 1982 by Southeastern Synod.
Calls: Our Saviour, West Columbia, S.C., 1982-83; Baptist Medical Center, Cola, S.C., Hospice and Oncology Chaplain, 1983-88; Frankfurt, Germany, Chapel Program from Evangelical Lutheran Church in America Church Council, 1990; Mary and Martha, Durham, 1995-97; Vice Pastor at various congregations. Moved to Georgia.

OPGRAND, MARK

Date/Place of Birth: November 3, 1948; Medford, Ore.
Spouse: Carol Lynne (Thysell) Opgrand.

Education: Pacific Lutheran University, B.A. Education, 1970; Luther Seminary, M.Div. 1979.
Ordination: April 22, 1979 by Oregon Synod.
Calls: Assistant Pastor, St. Paul, Wilmington, 1997-.
Other: Elizabeth, Caldwell, Texas, 1979-81; United Campus Minister, Odessa, Texas, 1981-84; Lutheran Campus Pastor, Purdue University, 1984-95; Lutheran Disaster Response Coordinator, Wilmington, 1996-97.

ORINSON, EDWARD HOWARD
Date/Place of Birth: December 7, 1910; Cleveland, Ohio.
Parents: William Fred Orinson and Caroline Amelia (Horn) Orinson.
Spouse/Marriage Date: Marjorie Jean (Eich) Orinson; September 2, 1943 in Nevada, Ohio.
Children: The Reverend Edward Luther, Marjorie Ann.
Education: Wittenberg University, A.B. 1938; Hamma Divinity School, S.T.M. 1942; University of Michigan, M.A. 1939.
Ordination: June 19, 1942 by Ohio Synod.
Calls: In Ohio: Nevada, Nevada, 1942-48; First St. Mark, Toledo, 1944-48; Messiah, Urbana, 1948-53; Auburn, Springfield, 1958-64; in North Carolina: Zion, Catawba County, 1964-72; St. Mark, Salisbury, 1972-82; retired June 15, 1982; Vice Pastor at various congregations.

ORINSON, EDWARD LUTHER
Date/Place of Birth: September 10, 1944; Bucyrus, Ohio.
Parents: The Reverend Edward Howard Orinson and Marjorie Jean (Eich) Orinson.
Spouse/Marriage Date: Janis Nell (Brittain) Orinson; May 17, 1967 in Hickory, N.C.
Children: Marc Samuel, Kara Michele.
Education: Lenoir-Rhyne, A.B. 1967; Lutheran Theological Seminary, Columbus, Ohio, M.Div. 1971; graduate work at University of Tennessee in German.
Ordination: June 6, 1971 by North Carolina Synod.
Calls: St. Mark, Cherryville, 1971-73; Advent, Charlotte, 1973-77; Campus Minister to students at the University of North Carolina at Charlotte, 1973-77.
Date of Death/Burial Location: February 19, 1978; ashes interred at Evergreen Cemetery, Charlotte, N.C.

OSTLUND, ARNOLD E., SR.
Date/Place of Birth: February 19, 1919; Beltrami County, Minn.
Parents: Axel Ostlund and Hilda (Anderson) Ostlund.
Spouse/Marriage Date: Margrethe E. (Herum) Ostlund; January 23, 1942 in Minneapolis, Minn.
Children: Arnold, Jr., Alan, Arlynne.
Education: Augsburg College, B.A. 1942; Augustana Seminary, M.S. 1945; University of Nebraska, M.A. 1950; graduate work at Universities of Colorado and Columbia.
Ordination: June 10, 1945 by Augustana Synod.

Calls: New Bethlehem, Temple City, Calif., 1945-47; Saronville, Saronville, Nev., 1947-50; Mt. Calvary, Boulder, Colo., 1950-57; retired in March 1984; moved to Asheville and transferred from New York Synod in March 1984 and transferred to Grand Canyon Synod, 1990.

Other: Assistant Professor, Hartwick College, Oneonta, N.Y., 1957-59; Dean of Men, Wagner College, Staten Island, N.Y., 1959-61; Island Development Center, Chaplain, Staten Island, N.Y., 1961-82.

Date of Death: July 22, 1994.

OVERCASH, KAY EUGENE

Date/Place of Birth: July 30, 1943; China Grove, N.C.

Parents: Paul Alexander Overcash and Nita Evelyn (Garver) Overcash.

Spouse/Marriage Date: Glenda Gail (Holshouser) Overcash; August 8, 1965 in China Grove, N.C.

Children: Timothy Roland, Philip Alan, Rodney Aaron.

Education: University of North Carolina at Chapel Hill, A.B. Sociology 1965; Lutheran Theological Southern Seminary, M.Div. 1969.

Ordination: June 1, 1969 by North Carolina Synod.

Calls: St. Paul, Farmers Branch, Texas, 1969-80; Emmanuel, West Columbia, S.C., 1980-.

OXNER, JASON WITHERSPOON

Date/Place of Birth: September 22, 1883; Saluda, Edgefield County, S.C.

Spouse: Julia (Ector) Oxner.

Education: Newberry College, A.B. 1905; Lutheran Theological Southern Seminary, 1908, B.D. 1925; Chicago Seminary, B.D. 1919; graduate study, University of South Carolina.

Ordination: 1908 by Georgia Synod.

Calls: In Georgia, 1908-10; in South Carolina, 1910-18; Camp Pastor for Lutheran soldiers, Camp Jackson, S.C., 1918; Tennessee Synod, 1920-23, (Mt. Tabor, West Columbia, 1918-26; St. Luke, Florence, 1926-31) but data of churches served not always available; did mission work in Georgetown (1939-40) and served other churches of South Carolina Synod until 1947 except for service as Chaplain in U.S. Army, 1943-45; retired with rank of Lieutenant Colonel.

Date of Death/Burial Location: July 7, 1958; Wittenberg Church, Leesville, S.C.

PALMER, SAMUEL C.

Ordination: Ordained Deacon by Tennessee Synod at Blue Springs Church, Greene County, Tenn. 1835.

Calls: Served churches in Sullivan County, Tenn.

Other: Voluntarily withdrew from Synod, 1844.

PALUMBO, PAUL KEVIN

Date/Place of Birth: March 15, 1958; Hyattsville, Md.

Parents: Paul C. Palumbo and Yvonne (Rice) Palumbo.

Spouse/Marriage Date: Virginia (Wagner) Palumbo; July 11, 1981 in Bowie, Md.

Children: Marguerite Hannah, Samuel Robert, Rosa Yvonne, Emma Maureen.

Education: Guilford College, B.A. 1980; Duke Divinity School, M.Div. 1984; graduate work at Gettysburg Seminary, 1986.
Ordination: January 1, 1989 by North Carolina Synod.
Calls: Abiding Savior, Durham, 1989-1999.

PARK, GEORGE HENRY CALVIN

Date/Place of Birth: July 28, 1890; Rowan County, N.C.
Parents: Jesse Franklin Park and Margaret Jane (Trexler) Park.
Spouse/Marriage Date: Mary Ina (Ballentine) Park; October 24, 1917 in Lexington, S.C.
Children: Conrad B. (Ph.D., once professor at Lenoir-Rhyne and Dean of Newberry College), The Reverend Harold F. (Professor at Lutheran Theological Southern Seminary), Robert G. (died in 8th month), The Reverend Karl Monroe, Rachel Jane.
Education: Roanoke College, A.B. 1911; Lutheran Theological Southern Seminary, 1914.
Ordination: 1914 by North Carolina Synod.
Calls: First Pastor, built church, Kimball Memorial, Kannapolis, 1914-22; first full-time Pastor, built church, Lutheran Chapel, Gastonia, 1922-26; served churches in South Carolina at Orangeburg, Chapin, Whitmire and Blythewood, and in Birmingham, Ala.; retired 1957 at Columbia, S.C.
Other: Chair, Parish Education Committee of North Carolina, Georgia-Alabama, and South Carolina Synods, in which synods was home mission Pastor for 27 years; North Carolina Synod Archivist, 1925-26.
Date of Death/Burial Location: May 10, 1969; Organ Church Cemetery, Salisbury, N.C.

PARK, KARL MONROE

Date/Place of Birth: June 30, 1924; Gastonia, N.C.
Parents: The Reverend George Henry Calvin Park and Mary Ina (Ballentine) Park. Older brothers are Conrad B. Park, Ph.D., Professor of Chemistry at Lenoir-Rhyne and Dean of Newberry College, and The Reverend Harold F. Park, Assistant Professor of Christian Education at Lutheran Theological Southern Seminary.
Spouse/Marriage Date: Miriam Virginia (Horton) Park; August 23, 1950 in Salisbury, N.C.
Children: Mary Jane, Theresa Rachel Hannon, Robert Horton, Karl Henry.
Education: Clemson University, 1942-44; Lenoir-Rhyne, A.B. 1949; Lutheran Theological Southern Seminary, M.Div. 1952, also graduate study, 1955-56; graduate work at Michigan State University, 1966-68, summer classes.
Ordination: June 1, 1952 by South Carolina Synod.
Calls: Ridge Parish (Bethlehem, Enon, St. Peter), Lexington County, S.C., 1952-54; Reformation, Lancaster, S.C., 1954-57; Mission Developer, Murfreesboro, Tenn., 1957-59; in Murfreesboro, Tenn., contact pastor for National Lutheran Council at Veterans Administration Hospital and Middle Tennessee State College; St. Mark, Rowan County, 1959-63; St. Martin, Stanly County, 1963-72; also one of two pastors assisting Lutheran chaplain at Seward Air Force Base in preaching and pastoral ministry to personnel and their

families; Grace, Hendersonville, 1972-83; Daniel's, Lincolnton, 1983-87; Vice Pastor at various congregations; retired June 30, 1987.

Other: United States Army Air Corps, 1944-46; writer of one week's devotions, *Light For Today,* July 1962; Evangelism, Stewardship (Chair), Social Ministry, Town and Country Church, and Publicity Committees; Chair, Historical Works Committee; President's Salary, Justice and Social Change, Child Care, Christian Education Task Forces; Secretary, Board, Lutheran Children's Home of the South; Steering Committee to set up Lutheran Family Services; First Board, Lutheran Family Services; Associate Editor and Editor-pro tem., *North Carolina Lutheran;* since June 1987 Archives helper and Assistant Archivist for North Carolina Synod; delegate to North Carolina Council of Churches and on its Town and Country Church and Executive Committees; Lutheran Church in America Consulting Committee on Stewardship, two years; Governor, North Carolina District West, Civitan International, 1989-90; North Carolina District West Honor Key, two times; Civitan International Foundation Fellow.

PARKER, EMMANUEL P.

Date/Place of Birth: November 9, 1836; Rowan County, N.C.
Parent: Father was Drew Parker.
Spouse/Marriage Date: Margaret Matilda (Lentz) Parker; May 13, 1858 in Rowan County, N.C.
Children: Laura C., Lawson D., Martin L., Sarah A., The Reverend Theodore C., Francis R., Walter L., Charles A., Maggie L., Flora H.
Ordination: 1872 by North Carolina Synod.
Calls: Coble's-Low's, Guilford County, 1871-82, Richland, Liberty, 1872-81; Nazareth-Shiloh, Forsyth County, 1882-87; Reformation-St. Matthew, Davie County, 1892-94, Bethany, Davidson County, perhaps at same time; Frieden's-Sharon (site bought and church built), Gibsonville, 1895-1901.
Date of Death/Burial Location: August 9, 1912; Frieden's Church, Guilford County, N.C.

PARKER, THEODORE CALVIN

Date/Place of Birth: November 18, 1866; Rowan County, N.C.
Parents: The Reverend Emmanuel P. Parker and Margaret Matilda (Lentz) Parker.
Spouse/Marriage Date: Mary Etta (Kegley) Parker; July 3, 1901 in Wytheville, Va.
Children: Lentz Kegley, Lawson D., Theodore Charles, Marguerite E., Stephen E.
Education: North Carolina College, A.B. 1896, Honorary A.M. 1899; Gettysburg Seminary, 1899.
Ordination: 1899 by Southwest Virginia Synod.

Calls: In Virginia, 1899-1902; transferred to North Carolina Synod, 1903; St. John, Cabarrus County, 1902-05; St. Luke, Bear Poplar-Concordia, Rowan County, 1905-07; Lebanon-Providence, Rowan County-St. Matthew, Davie County, 1907-12; St. Michael, Troutman-Amity-St. Paul, Iredell County, 1912-15; again in Virginia, 1915-25; Giles County Parish, 1915-21; Neuse River Parish, Montgomery County, 1915-23; St. Paul-Grace, Gilbert, S.C., 1925-27; St. Mark-St. Andrew, Blythewood, S.C., 1927-30; retired 1930 at Pembroke, Va.

Other: Secretary, North Carolina Synod, 1912-15.
Date of Death/Burial Location: August 11, 1960; St. John Church, Wythe County, Va.

PARRY, DANIEL WILLIAM

Date/Place of Birth: October 12, 1948; Burlington, Iowa.
Parents: Daniel Doe Parry and Janet Irene Parry.
Spouse/Marriage Date: The Reverend Beverly (Hardgrove) Parry; May 25, 1990.
Children: Ed Hardgrove, Will Hardgrove.
Education: Western Illinois University, B.S. Chemistry 1970; University of Iowa, B.S. Psychology 1977; Fuller Seminary, M.Div. Theology 1981; University of Colorado, M.S. Physical Chemistry 1972.
Ordination: June 14, 1981 by Iowa Synod.
Calls: Associate Pastor, Trinity, Sheridan, Wyo., 1981-84; U.S. Navy Chaplain, 1985-; Interim Pastor at various congregations; Ship Chaplain, Charleston, S.C., 1985-87; Battalion Chaplain, Camp Lejeune, 1987-91; Navy Weapons Station Command Chaplain, Concord, Calif., 1991-94; U.S. Marine Corps Air Station, New River Command Chaplain, Jacksonville, N.C., 1994-.
Other: Served in Desert Storm with Marines in Saudi Arabia, 1990-91.

PATTEN, CHESTER M.

Date/Place of Birth: December 23, 1923; Butler, Pa.
Parents: Mr. and Mrs. Lee O. Patten.
Spouse/Marriage Date: Mary Jane (Frey) Patten; August 22, 1948.
Children: David Lee, Carol Beth, Mary Anne, Janet Lou.
Education: Capital University, Columbus, Ohio, A.B., 1945; Evangelical Lutheran Theological Seminary, Columbus, Ohio, B.D., 1948.
Ordination: September 12, 1948 by American Lutheran Church.
Calls: Immanuel, Moses Lake, Wash., 1948-51; Assistant Youth Director, American Lutheran Church, Columbus, Ohio, 1951-59; Youth Director, American Lutheran Church, Columbus, Ohio, 1959-60; Assistant Youth Director, American Lutheran Church, Minneapolis, Minn., 1961; Pastor, Ascension, Eau Gallie, Fla., 1961-69; Pastor, Mt. Zion, Conover, 1969-78; Senior Pastor, Emanuel, Sequin, Texas, 1978-.
Other: Lutheran Council in the U.S.A.; American Representative to International Youth Directors' meeting near Nurnberg, Germany, 1960.

PATTERSON, CHARLES ROBERT, SR.

Date/Place of Birth: May 4, 1895; Cabarrus County, N.C.
Parents: Charles C. Patterson and Amanda Elizabeth (Bostian) Patterson.
Spouse/Marriage Date: Frances Ruth (Miller) Patterson, sister of the Reverends L. D. and P. L. Miller; May 22, 1921 in Lenoir, Caldwell County, N.C.
Children: Dorothy Elaine Bray, Charles Robert, Jr., Dr. Joe Miller.

Education: Lenoir-Rhyne, A.B. 1918; Lutheran Theological Southern Seminary, 1921; graduate study, University of South Carolina, 1919-21.
Ordination: November 10, 1921 by Georgia Synod.
Calls: Zion Parish, Effingham County, Ga., 1921-22; St. Martin-Salem-Luther Chapel, Maiden, 1922-26; St. Mark, China Grove, 1926-38; Grace, Thomasville, 1938-47; St. Stephen, Hickory, 1947-53; Mission Developer/Pastor, Messiah, Hickory, 1953-66; retired August 31, 1966; Vice Pastor to various congregations.
Other: Board, Lenoir-Rhyne; delegate to two United Lutheran Church in America conventions and attended at own expense all others except one from 1921 to 1955, as of date of reporting; Board, North Carolina Lutheran Homes; Chair, Pensions Committee for nine years.
Date of Death/Burial Location: March 4, 1977; Catawba Memorial Park, Hickory, N.C.

PATTERSON, RICHARD SADELLER

Date/Place of Birth: August 21, 1866; Concord, N.C.
Parents: Robert Patterson and Annie C. (Rogers) Patterson. A half brother of the Reverend C. A. Rose.
Spouse/Marriage Date: Clara Elizabeth (Schwartz) Patterson; September 6, 1892 near Gettysburg, Pa.
Children: Mrs. J. Ira Land, Mrs. Fred A. Hoffman, Winnifred.
Education: Gettysburg College, A.B. 1889; Gettysburg Seminary, 1892; D.D.
Ordination: 1892 by Maryland Synod.
Calls: Woodsboro, Maryland Charge, 1892-99; Trinity, Berlin, Pa., 1899-1906; Immanuel, Philadelphia, Pa., 1906-08; Trinity, Coatesville, Pa., 1908-13; again in Woodsboro Charge, Md., 1917-25; Salem Charge, Westminster, Md., 1925-30.
Other: General Secretary, Home Mission Board, United Synod South, 1913-17, being a member of North Carolina Synod during that period.
Date of Death/Burial Location: February 26, 1930; Gettysburg, Pa.

PATTERSON, ROBERT LEONIDAS

Date/Place of Birth: February 20, 1871; China Grove, N.C.
Parents: Ibsen Franklin Patterson and Maria Louisa (Low) Patterson.
First Spouse/Marriage Date: Virginia A. (Blackwelder) Patterson; January 1, 1895 in Mt. Pleasant, N.C.
Children of First Marriage: Frank Bernard, George Richard, Ruth Roberta (died at age 15), Virginia Lee, Luther Weidner.
Second Spouse/Marriage Date: Nellie Virginia (Rhoades) Patterson; February 28, 1942 in St. Petersburg, Fla.
Education: North Carolina College, A.B. 1891, A.M. 1894; Gettysburg Seminary, 1894; Chicago Seminary, B.D. 1901; Susquehanna University, D.D. 1911.
License/Ordination: 1894 by Maryland Synod.
Calls: Union Bridge, Md., 1894-99; Osborne, Ohio, 1901-02; Somerset, Pa., 1902-08; St. Mark's, Charlotte, 1908-14; Union, Rowan County, 1914-15; Atchison, Kan., 1915-20; Selinsgrove, Pa., 1921-22; Supply, St. Luke's, Charlotte, 1928-29; Holy Trinity, Charlotte, 1934-36, and Pastor Emeritus, 1936; retired 1936 at Charlotte, N.C.

Other: Professor, Western Seminary, Fremont, Neb., 1923-28;   Visiting Professor, Hartwick Seminary, 1929-30; Visiting Professor, Lutheran Theological Southern Seminary, 1933-34.
Date of Death/Burial Location: July 18, 1944; China Grove, N.C.

PATTON, WILLIAM RANKIN, JR.

Date/Place of Birth: January 21, 1933; Orlando, Fla.
Parents: William Rankin Patton, Sr. and LaNell (Moye) Patton.
Spouse: Laura Carolyn (McCleneghan) Patton; May 7, 1950 in Moncks Corner, S.C.
Children: William R., Sherri LaNell, Matthew Eric.
Education: Duke University, A.B. 1957; Philadelphia Seminary, B.D. 1960; Duke Divinity School, Th.M. 1965.
Ordination: 1960 by South Carolina Synod.
Calls: Trinity, St. Petersburg, Fla., 1960-63; Part-time Pastor to Lutheran students, Duke University, 1963-65; Lutheran Chaplain, Duke University, and University of North Carolina at Greensboro, 1965-69, under direction of the Lutheran Student Foundation of Durham, which is participated in also by the American Lutheran Church.
Other: Demitted the Ministry in 1969.

PAUL, ALVY CURTIS

Date/Place of Birth: September 4, 1935; Monessen, Pa.
Parents: Alvy H. Paul and Helen E. (Dunlop) Paul.
Spouse/Date of Marriage: Margaret Rebecca (Miller) Paul; June 8, 1956 in Belle Vernon, Pa.
Children: Timothy Allan, Kristin Anne Paul Ruth.
Education: California University, B.S. 1957; Northwestern Seminary, M.Div. 1960; graduate work at Dropsie University, 1962-63; University of Minnesota, M.S. Library Science 1969.
Ordination: June 1, 1960 by Pittsburgh Synod.
Calls: Associate Pastor, Calvary, Pittsburgh, Pa., 1960-61; Redeemer, Philadelphia, Pa., 1961-63.
Other: Northwestern Seminary, Librarian-Assistant to the President, 1963-76; Director, Learning Resources, Lenoir-Rhyne, Hickory, 1976-; St. Luke, Lincolnton, Interim, 1982-.

PAYNE, C. ARNOLD

Date/Place of Birth: April 6, 1917; Calmar, Iowa.
Parents: Claude Franklin Payne and Gena Amelia (Veme) Payne.
Spouse/Marriage Date: Rosalie (Ortolani) Payne; May 22, 1950 in Chicago, Ill.
Children: Gena, Adele-Alys.
Education: Aurora College, B.A. 1934; Chicago Lutheran Seminary (Maywood), 1943.
Ordination: May 24, 1944 by Illinois Synod.
Calls: Unity-St. Andrew-Christ Mission, Chicago, Ill., 1944-47; Zion, St. Louis, Mo., 1964-67; The Lutheran Church-Missouri Synod Parish, Taylorsville, N.C., 1970-72; The Lutheran Church-Missouri Synod Parish, Danville, Va., 1972-74; The Lutheran Church-Missouri Synod Parish, Sedgewickville, Mo., 1974-77; Ebenezer, Catawba, 1977-78; The

Lutheran Church-Missouri Synod Parish, Boonville, Mo., 1978-80; Vice Pastor at Holy Trinity, Reidsville, 1981.
Other: Dropped from roll, 1982.

PEDERSON, DALE LAIRUS

Date/Place of Birth: September 22, 1946; Thief River Falls, Minn.
Parents: William E. Pederson and Clara (Kilen) Pederson.
Spouse/Marriage Date: Pamela Kay (Hudson) Pederson; June 8, 1969.
Children: Jason Lairus, Katrina Ann, Monica Jane.
Education: Appalachian State University, B.A. Philosophy and Religion 1971; Lutheran Theological Southern Seminary, M.Div. 1975.
Ordination: June 8, 1975 by North Carolina Synod.
Calls: Messiah, Salisbury, 1975-79; St. Paul, Statesville, 1979-83; Cedar Grove, Vale, 1985-.

PEELE, JERALD MICHAEL

Date/Place of Birth: August 7, 1942; High Point, N.C.
Parents: Clyde Vernon Peele and Bloomfield (Smith) Peele Spencer.
First Spouse/Marriage Date: Ina Ruth (Ingram) Peele; February 12, 1963 in Myrtle Beach, S.C.
Children of First Marriage: Roger Spencer Victor, Matthew Martin.
Second Spouse/Marriage Date: Melanie (Baxley) Peele; April 12, 1975.
Children of Second Marriage: Andrew Griffin, John Barry Byrd (stepson).
Education: Cincinnati Conservatory of Music, B.S. 1964; University of Tennessee, M.A. 1966; Lutheran Theological Southern Seminary, M.Div. 1979.
Ordination: March 25, 1979 by North Carolina Synod.
Calls: St. John, Taylorsville, 1979-80; St. Martin, Albemarle, 1980-88; Our Father, Greensboro, 1988-91; Holy Cross, Lincolnton, 1991-97; St. Peter, Salisbury, 1996-97; St. Paul, Hamlet, 1997-99.
Date of Death/Burial Location: January 1, 1999; Rose Hill Cemetery, Marion, S.C.

PEELER, DAVID GENE

Date/Place of Birth: January 8, 1943; Faith, N.C.
Parents: Nevin Glenn Peeler and Rose (Baker) Peeler.
Spouse/Marriage Date: Norma Kay (Crotts) Peeler; June 16, 1968 in Lexington, N.C.
Child: Brent David.
Education: Catawba College, A.B. 1966; Lancaster Seminary, B.D. 1969, M.Div. 1973.
Ordination: June 10, 1979 by North Carolina Synod.
Calls: Memorial United Church of Christ, Lexington, 1969-78; Frieden's, Gibsonville, 1978-86; First, Lexington, 1990-91; Mt. Moriah, China Grove, 1991-.

PEELER, J. L.
Date/Place of Birth: August 10, 1925; Rowan County, N.C.
Parents: Thomas Calvin Peeler and Elizabeth Ellen (Lyles) Peeler.
Spouse/Marriage Date: Ethel Loraine (Sloop) Peeler; May 17, 1946 in Salisbury, N.C.
Children: Carl Andrew, Paul Cromer, Timothy Welker.
Education: Lenoir-Rhyne, A.B. 1947; Lutheran Theological Southern Seminary, B.D. 1950.
Ordination: June 25, 1950, by North Carolina Synod.
Calls: Red Bank Parish, Lexington County, S.C., 1950-51; Prosperity, Cabarrus County, 1952-55; Mission Developer/Pastor, Holy Trinity, Reidsville, 1956-59; Bethlehem, Catawba County, 1959-87; Chaplain, Lutheran Home, Hickory Unit, 1988-95; retired September 17, 1987 to Newton, N.C.
Other: Author, *A Time of Pain, a Time of Hope, a Time of Assurance;* World Missions Committee, 1965-69; Parish Education Committee; Education for Ministers Committee; Nominations Committee, 1962; Auxiliaries Committee.

PEERY, JOHN CARNAHAN, SR.
Date/Place of Birth: February 24, 1876; Burkes Garden, Va.
Parents: Captain Thomas Peery and Sarah Henrietta (Repass) Peery. An older brother was the Reverend R. B. Peery.
First Spouse/Marriage Date: Alean Emma (Martin) Peery; September 6, 1905 in Blacksburg, Va.
Children of First Marriage: The Reverend John C., Jr. (Missionary in India), Thomas Martin, Alean Elizabeth.
Second Spouse/Marriage Date: Pearle Miller (Powlas) Peery, youngest sister to wives of the Reverends L. P. Boland and O. W. Aderholt and of Misses Maude and Annie Powlas, missionaries in Japan; August 4, 1920 in Rowan County, N.C.
Children of Second Marriage: The Reverend William Powlas (Missionary in India, 1945-87), James Brown.
Education: Roanoke College, A.B. 1900; instructor there two years; M.A. 1902; Lutheran Theological Southern Seminary, 1905; Lenoir-Rhyne, D.D. 1919.
License/Ordination: 1905 by Southwest Virginia Synod.
Calls: Holy Trinity, Lynchburg, Va., 1904-11; St. Andrew, Hickory, 1917-20; supplied Mt. Calvary, Claremont, 1924-25; Redeemer, Newberry, S.C., 1925-31; St. Michael, Irmo, S.C., 1932-39.
Other: President of Marion Junior College, 1905-11; President, Elizabeth College, Salem, Va., 1911-17; President, Lenoir-Rhyne, 1920-25.
Date of Death/Burial Location: December 5, 1939; Oakwood Cemetery, Hickory, N.C.

PEERY, ROBERT NELSON, JR.
Date/Place of Birth: March 17, 1942; Greene County, Tenn.
Parents: The Reverend Robert Nelson Peery, Sr. and Leota (Cobble) Peery.
Education: University of North Carolina at Chapel Hill, A.B. 1965; Philadelphia Seminary, B.D. 1968.

Ordination: June 30, 1968 by North Carolina Synod.
Calls: Mission Developer, Wading River, N.Y.
Other: Executive Committee of Lutheran Church in America Luther League, 1962-64; President, North Carolina Luther League, 1962-63; President, Lutheran Church in America Luther League, 1962-64; removed from roll in 1971.
Date of Death: March 12, 1986.

PEERY, ROBERT NELSON, SR.

Date/Place of Birth: February 1, 1910; Burkes Garden, Va.
Parents: Stephen Leonard Peery and Josephine (Shawyer) Peery.
Spouse/Marriage Date: Leota (Cobble) Peery; January 22, 1939 in Midway, Tenn.
Child: The Reverend Robert Nelson, Jr.
Education: Roanoke College, A.B. 1933; Lutheran Theological Southern Seminary, B.D. 1938.
License/Ordination: Licensed 1938 and ordained January 26, 1939 by Virginia Synod.
Calls: Mosheim Parish, Midway, Tenn., 1939-42; organized Holy Trinity, Newport, Tenn., 1942-48; First Pastor, Trinity, Roanoke, Va., 1948-49; Beth Eden, Newton, 1950-70.
Other: Delegate, 1960 United Lutheran Church in America and 1962 (merger) United Lutheran Church in America/Lutheran Church in America conventions; President, Board, North Carolina Lutheran Homes; Board, North Carolina Council of Churches; Stewardship Committee; Social Ministry Committee; in Virginia Synod: Board, Sipe's Orchard Home, 1960; Secretary and Vice President, Western Conference, 1952-58.
Date of Death/Burial Location: January 17, 1971; Sinking Springs Cemetery, Midway, Tenn.

PEERY, RUFUS BENTON

Date/Place of Birth: April 9, 1868; Burkes Garden, Va.
Parents: Captain Thomas Peery and Sara Henrietta (Repass) Peery. A younger brother was the Reverend John C. Peery.
Spouse/Marriage Date: Annie Letitia (Rich) Peery; August 21, 1895 in Wytheville, Va.
Children: Harold Rich, the Reverend Thomas Benton, Rob Roy, Paul Denver, William Wallace, Donald Lee.
Education: Roanoke College, A.B. 1890, M.A. 1895; Gettysburg Seminary, 1892; Gettysburg College, Ph.D. 1897; Midland College, D.D. 1909.
Ordination: 1892 by Southwestern Virginia Synod.
Calls: First Missionary of United Synod South to Japan, 1892-1903, and Co-founder of the mission with the Reverend J. A. B. Scherer; Immanuel, Philadelphia, Pa., 1904-05; St. Paul, Denver, Colo., 1905-12; St. Mark, Polo, Ill., 1919-20; St. Andrew, Hickory, 1920-24; Holy Trinity, Raleigh, 1931-33; Zion, Wooster, Ohio, 1924-31; retired 1933 at Raleigh, N.C.
Other: Professor of Philosophy, Lenoir-Rhyne, 1920-24; President, Rocky Mountain Synod, 1908; Board, Tabitha Home; Board, Wittenberg College; President, Midland College, Atchison, Kan., 1912-19; Author, *The Gist of Japan* (eight editions), *Lutherans in Japan*, in Japanese *Religion a Necessity to Man* and *Addresses to Young Men;* translated into Japanese *The Common Service* and *Orders for Ministerial Acts,* used for 25 years

without revision; assisted in financial appeals for Carthage, Lenoir- Rhyne, and Wittenberg Colleges.
Date of Death/Burial Location: October 25, 1934; Montlawn Cemetery, Raleigh, N.C.

PEERY, WILLIAM POWLAS

Date/Place of Birth: May 21, 1922; Hickory, N.C.
Parents: The Reverend John Carnahan Peery, Sr. and Pearle Miller (Powlas) Peery.
Spouse/Marriage Date: Marinelle (Fridy) Peery of Spartanburg, S.C.; March 17, 1947 in Guntur, India.
Children: William Michael, James Robert.
Education: Newberry College, A.B. 1943; Lutheran Theological Southern Seminary, B.D. 1945; Vanderbilt University, M.A. 1959; Duke University, Ph.D. 1972; Lenoir-Rhyne, D.D. 1966.
Ordination: September 30, 1945 by South Carolina Synod.
Calls: Board of Foreign Missions, United Lutheran Church in America - appointed to the Andhra Evangelical Lutheran Church, India, 1945; Pastor, Tummrukota Parish, West Guntur Synod, 1946-51; Lutheran Seminary, Rajahmundry - Lecturer, 1952-64, Bursar, 1956-64, Acting Principal at various times; Andhra Christian Theological College, Rajahmundry - Lecturer and Bursar, 1966-69; Executive Director, Inter-Church Service Agency, Madras, 1969-70; United Theological College, Bangalore, Professor, 1971-87; retired May 1987 to Durham, N.C.; Vice Pastor to various congregations.
Other: Vice President, 1953-55, President, 1959-63, 1966-69, 1973-75, of Council of the India Mission of the Lutheran Church in America.

PENCE, C. H.

Place of Birth: Rockingham County, Va.
Ordination: 1892 by Joint Synod of Ohio.
Calls: Transferred 1912 to Tennessee Synod from Chicago Synod; Mt. Moriah-St. Mark, Rowan County, 1912-14; served churches in Ohio, Illinois and Indiana.
Date of Death/Burial Location: 1947; Wabash, Ind.

PENCE, EDGAR ZIRKLE, SR.

Date/Place of Birth: May 8, 1893; Rockingham County, Va.
Parents: The Reverend Martin Luther Pence and Annie (Zirkle) Pence.
Spouse/Marriage Date: Ethel (Evans) Pense; May 8, 1918 in Manassas, Va.
Children: Annie Vivian, Marie Elizabeth, Edgar Zirkle, Jr., Robert Luther.
Education: Lenoir-Rhyne, A.B. 1913, D.D. 1941; Chicago Seminary, 1916.
Ordination: 1916 by Tennessee Synod.
Calls: Bethel, Manassas, Va., 1916-23; St. Jacob Parish, Chapin, S.C., 1923-27; Holy Trinity, Little Mountain, S.C., 1927-42; Trinity, Greenville, S.C., 1942-53.
Other: President, South Carolina Synod, 1937-43; United Lutheran Church in America Parish and Church School Board, twelve years; organized first Lutheran kindergarten and parochial school in South Carolina at Greenville; Adviser, Alcoholics Anonymous for City of Greenville, S.C.
Date of Death/Burial Location: September 14, 1953; Greenville, S.C.

PENCE, MARTIN LUTHER
Date/Place of Birth: September 22, 1865; Broadway, Rockingham County, Va.
Parents: John P. Pence and Mary Elizabeth (Shutters) Pence. Two brothers were ministers, and two sisters married ministers.
Spouse/Marriage Date: Annie Rebecca (Zirkle) Pence; February 5, 1889 in New Market, Va.
Children: Seven, of whom four died in childhood or youth; the others were: The Reverend Edgar Zirkle, Arthur L., and Edith (married the Reverend Paul C. Sigmon).
Education: Lenoir-Rhyne, A.B. 1896; also theological courses under the Reverend R. A. Yoder.
Ordination: 1896 by Tennessee Synod.
Calls: Daniel's, Lincoln County-St. Mark, Gaston County-Grace, Catawba County, 1896-99; Toms Brook, Va., five churches, 1899-1908; Trinity, Vale-Cedar Grove-David Chapel, Lincoln County-Sardis, Catawba County, 1908-14; St. Peter Parish, Chapin, S.C., 1914-18; Orkney Springs, Va., four churches, 1918-24; Friendship-Shiloh-St. John, Alexander County, 1924-26.
Other: President, Virginia Conference of the Tennessee Synod, 1918-24; lead in merger that part of the merged synod (North Carolina and Tennessee Synods) with the Virginia Synod in 1924; United North Carolina Synod Committee to Set Bounds of Conferences, 1921; Tennessee Synod delegate to United Lutheran Church in America merger (1918) convention.
Date of Death/Burial Location: Died in pulpit, while preaching, at Friendship Church, April 25, 1926; Solomon Church, near Forestville, Va.

PEPER, JAMES MICHAEL
Date/Place of Birth: September 6, 1942; Napoleon, Ohio.
Parents: Robert B. Peper and Ann (Wilscam) Peper.
Spouse/Marriage Date: Kala Ann Peper; January 28, 1983.
Children: Karan Lyn, Wesley Emerson Boggs, Jamie Mitchelle.
Education: Lenoir-Rhyne, B.A.; Hamma Seminary.
Ordination: September 21, 1969 by North Carolina Synod.
Calls: Ebenezer, Catawba, 1969-70; Messiah, Ft. Wayne, Ind., 1970-87; First English, Goshen, Ind., 1987-; Messiah, Skidway Island, Ga., 1998-.
Other: *North Carolina Lutheran* Committee, 1969-70.

PERRY, FRANK CASTON, SR.
Date/Place of Birth: July 19, 1924; Kannapolis, N.C.
Parents: Joseph Franklin Perry and Ida Virginia (Caston) Perry.
Spouse/Marriage Date: Martha Anne (McDaniel) Perry; June 20, 1951 in Anderson, S.C.
Children: Martha Anne Brashear, Elizabeth Lee Godfrey, Frank Caston, Jr.
Education: Furman University, A.B. 1948; Lutheran Theological Southern Seminary, B.D., 1955; Duke University, Th.M. 1965; Lenoir-Rhyne, D.D., 1981.
Ordination: June 12, 1955 by North Carolina Synod.

Calls: Mission Developer/Pastor, Prince of Peace, Kinston, 1955-59; Holy Trinity, Chapel Hill, and Chaplain to Lutheran students at University of North Carolina, 1959-65; Holy Trinity, Chapel Hill, 1965-84; Pastor/Developer, Reconciliation, Wilmington, 1984-90; retired June 30, 1990 to Wilmington; Vice Pastor at various congregations.

Other: Worship Committee, 1958-62; Press, Radio and Television Committee, 1960-63; Board, Lutheran Theological Southern Seminary, 1966-67; Executive Board, 1967-70, 1970-73; District Dean, Northern District and Eastern District, 1971-72, 1973; President's Task Force, Priority Program; Board, Lutheran Family Services of the Carolinas; Lutheran Student Foundation, 1969-72; Education Committee for Ministers, 1962; Lutheran Church in America Delegate, 1972.

PERRY, RICHARD J., JR.

Date/Place of Birth: July 31, 1948; Ashland, Ky.
Parents: Richard J. Perry, Sr. and Ethyl (Ross) Perry.
Spouse/Marriage Date: Theresa Marie (Cosby) Perry; December 21, 1974 in Chicago, Ill.
Child: Rashida.
Education: Carthage College, B.A. 1973; Chicago Seminary, M.Div. 1977, Th.M. 1989.
Ordination: June 12, 1977 by Michigan Synod.
Calls: Calvary, Gary, Ind., 1977-80; Director, Inclusive Ministry, North Carolina Synod, 1980-88; Director, Black Ministries, Commission for Multicultural Ministries, Evangelical Lutheran Church in America, 1988-89. Transferred from faculty, Chicago Seminary, to Central States Synod.
Other: Assistant Professor, Church and Society, Lutheran School of Theology at Chicago, 1996-; Secretary and President of LHRAA; Chicago Seminary Alumni Senate; article published in *Theology and the Black Experience;* delegate to 7th Assembly of Lutheran World Federation and delegate to various Lutheran Church in America Conventions.

PERRYMAN, GARY ALLEN

Date/Place of Birth: July 28, 1946; Chicago, Ill.
Parents: Donald E. Perryman and Marilyn Perryman.
Spouse/Marriage Date: Nancy Edith (MacKenzie) Perryman; December 28, 1968 in Atlanta, Ga.
Children: Brian Edward, Adam Brandt.
Education: Lenoir-Rhyne, A.B. 1968; Lutheran Theological Southern Seminary, M.Div. 1972.
Ordination: June 4, 1972 by North Carolina Synod.
Calls: Christ, Elkin, 1972-78; Emmanuel, High Point, 1978-94; Vice Pastor at various congregations.
Other: Consultant, American Missions Committee, 1974-77; Education Ministry Committee; dropped from roll, 1994.

PERSAUD, PATRICK M.

Date/Place of Birth: June 12, 1941; Guyana, South America.
Parents: Priam Persaud and Sanicherie Persaud.
Education: Carthage, B.A. Philosophy 1965; Chicago Seminary, B.D. 1968, S.T.M., Th.D., 1972.

Ordination: May 22, 1968 by Illinois Synod.
Calls: Chaplain, University of Puerto Rico, 1968-72; Christ The Mediator, Chicago, Ill., 1972-76; St. Mark, Chicago, Ill., 1976-81; Clinical Pastoral Resident, Northwestern Memorial Hospital, Chicago, Ill., and St. Luke Episcopal Hospital in Houston, Texas, 1981-82; Chaplain, Duke University Hospital, Durham, 1984-89; Director, Clinical Pastoral Education of the Cleveland Clinic Foundation, 1988-.
Other: Lecturer in New Testament Language and Theology, Chicago Seminary.

PESCHAU, FERDINAND WILLIAM ELIAS

Date/Place of Birth: February 17, 1849; Clausthal-Tellerfeld, Hannover, Germany.
Parents: Henry Andrew Christian Frederick Peschau and Wilhelmina (Muehlhahn) Peschau.
Spouse/Marriage Date: Clara J. (Myers) Peschau; June 3, 1873 in York Springs, Pa.
Children: Margaret Wilhelmina, Linda Augusta, Cora Elizabeth, Ferdinand Henry Edward, Clara Beta, Andrew Luther. A grandson is the Reverend Kenneth P. Otten.
Education: Gettysburg College, A.B. 1872; Gettysburg Seminary, 1876; North Carolina College, D.D. 1891.
License/Ordination: Licensed 1873 and ordained 1876 by Pittsburgh Synod.
Calls: Nebraska City, Neb., and Nashville, Tenn., 1876-82; St. Paul, Wilmington, 1882-92; began Sunday school, 1890, built church, and organized St. Matthew, Wilmington, 1892, the Reverend G. D. Bernheim becoming its first pastor; Greensburg, Pa., 1893-1900; Miamisburg, Ohio, 1900-16.
Other: President, North Carolina Synod, 1886-90; President, General Synod South, 1886-87; Board, North Carolina College; Member of special committee, North Carolina Synod, to organize its four Negro pastors and their congregations into a synod (The Alpha Synod of the Evangelical Lutheran Church of Freedmen in America), May 1889; Secretary, Nebraska Synod and Middle Tennessee Synod.
Date of Death/Burial Location: March 9, 1916; Miamisburg, Ohio.

PETERS, MARY CLINE (McGHEE)

Date/Place of Birth: August 3, 1953; Roanoke, Va.
Parents: Robert I. McGhee and Billie F. McGhee.
Spouse/Marriage Date: David C. Peters, deceased.
Education: James Madison University, B.S. Speech Pathology 1975; Lutheran Theological Southern Seminary, M.Div. 1994; Chaplaincy Program, Duke University Medical Center, 1997-98.
Ordination: June 26, 1994 by Virginia Synod.
Calls: Trinity, Shamokin, Pa., 1994-96; St. John, Salisbury, 1998-.
Other: Special education teacher in Roanoke City school system; Volunteer Chaplain, Visiting Nurses Association Hospice, Shamokin, Pa.

PETERSON, JESSE REUBEN
Date/Place of Birth: July 15, 1821; Gaston County, N.C.
Spouse/Marriage Date: Mary A. (Detter) Peterson; March 10, 1842.
Children: Jane Frances, J. Alonzo, Henry Melchoir Muhlenberg, Melville Brown, Alice Cornelia.
License/Ordination: Licensed 1843 and ordained 1846 by Tennessee Synod.
Calls: Lutheran Chapel (built new church, 1872), Gastonia, 1840-83; Philadelphia, Gaston County, 1845-97; St. Mark, Crouse, 1847-65; St. Luke, Lincoln County, 1848-54; Christ's, Stanley, 1857-97; supplied Mt. Moriah, Rowan County, 1871; organized and built church, St. Matthew, Kings Mountain, 1876-79; Daniel's, Lincoln County, 1876-82; Good Shepherd, Mt. Holly, 1884-92; Holy Communion, Dallas, 1891-92, 1893-97.
Other: Secretary, Tennessee Synod, seven times, 1849-73; President, five times, 1863-83.
Date of Death/Burial Location: May 15, 1897; Christ Church, Stanley, N.C.

PETERSON, MARY E.
Education: University of Northern Iowa, B.A., German/Teaching 1969; Wartburg Theological Seminary, M.Div. 1976.
Ordination: August 15, 1976.
Calls: Interim Pastor for North Texas-North Louisiana Synod, 1986-88; Lutheran Campus Ministry, Winona, Minn., 1989-92; First English Evangelical Lutheran and Campus Ministry, Richmond, Va., 1993-96; Interim Pastor, St. Andrew, New Bern, 1996. Trinity, Gresham, Ore., 1998-.
Other: High School German teacher, 1969-71; Board, Young Women's Christian Association; Iowa Commission on the Status of Women; Dorothy Day Roman Catholic Worker House Shelter; CARITAS, ecumenical project to house homeless; Women's Resource Center.

PETREA, BRUNNER EUGENE
Date/Place of Birth: August 22, 1884; Cabarrus County, N.C.
Parents: William Osborne Petrea and Anna Nancy (Lyerly) Petrea. A younger brother is the Reverend H. Smith Petrea.
Spouse/Marriage Date: Anna (Umberger) Petrea; October 1, 1919 in Wytheville, Va.
Children: Anna Elizabeth (married the Reverend Herman W. Cauble), Margaret Lyerly Guenther.
Education: Mount Pleasant Collegiate Institute, Newberry College, A.B. 1908; Lutheran Theological Southern Seminary, 1913; Lenoir-Rhyne, D.D. 1951.
Ordination: 1913 by North Carolina Synod.
Calls: St. John-Lebanon, Wytheville, Va., 1913-19; St. Paul-Winters-Bost-Mt. Union, Uniontown, Md., 1919-21; St. Matthew, Wilmington, 1921-28; St. Paul (Hardin)-Antioch-Philadelphia, Gaston County, 1928-32; Union, Rowan County, 1932-49; Nazareth, Rural Hall-Shiloh, Lewisville, 1949-54; retired 1955 near Concord, N.C.

Other: Taught public school two years in South Carolina; Statistical Secretary, North Carolina Synod, 1933-58; Editor and Business Manager, *North Carolina Lutheran,* 1937-50; Board, Lutheran Theological Southern Seminary, 1933-37; delegate, six United Lutheran Church in America conventions between 1918 and 1952; Executive Board, North Carolina Synod.

Date of Death/Burial Location: October 2, 1965; St. John Church, Cabarrus County, N.C.

PETREA, HENRY MATTHEW

Date/Place of Birth: January 7, 1868; Cabarrus County, N.C.
Parents: Laban Petrea and Frances Petrea.
First Spouse: Name unknown.
Children of First Marriage: seven children.
Second Spouse: Viola (Swartzwelder) Petrea.
Children of Second Marriage: three children.
Education: North Carolina College, A.B. 1887; Philadelphia Seminary, 1891.
Ordination: 1892 by North Carolina Synod.
Calls: Trinity Mission, Richmond, Va., 1891-93. Transferred 1893 to Allegheny Synod; served parishes in Pennsylvania (Addison, Berrysburg, Roy's Hill, Loransville, and Breezewood) and West Virginia (Brandonville). Retired 1945.
Date of Death: August 11, 1956.

PETREA, HENRY SMITH

Date/Place of Birth: November 1, 1888; Cabarrus County, N.C.
Parents: William Osborne Petrea and Anna Nancy (Lyerly) Petrea. An older brother was the Reverend B. E. Petrea.
Spouse/Marriage Date: Lavinia Gaynell (Crapps) Petrea; November 29, 1916 in Columbia, S.C.
Child: Nell McCreery.
Education: Mount Pleasant Collegiate Institute, Newberry College, A.B. 1912, D.D. 1935; Lutheran Theological Southern Seminary, 1915.
Ordination: 1915 by North Carolina Synod.
Calls: White Rock Pastorate (Bethel, Mt. Vernon, Mt. Olivet, Mt. Hermon), S.C., 1915-18; Graniteville and Aiken, S.C., 1918-23; Elloree, S.C., 1923-28; Mt. Horeb, Chapin and St. John and Bethlehem, Irmo, S.C., 1928-38; Grace, Rock Hill (also pastor to Lutheran students at Winthrop College), S.C., 1938-54; Saluda County, S.C., 1954-59; retired 1959 at Prosperity, S.C.; Supply Macedonia, Prosperity, S.C., 1961-63; Mt. Tabor, Little Mountain, S.C., 1965-67; St. John, Lexington, S.C., 1968-72.
Other: Statistical Secretary, South Carolina Synod, 1920-45; Executive Committee, 1920-45; Editor-Manager, *South Carolina Lutheran,* 1937-53; Editorial Committee, *History of the Lutheran Church in South Carolina;* Outstanding Alumnus Award, Newberry College, 1976.
Date of Death/Burial Location: October 19, 1978; Elmwood Cemetery, Columbia, S.C.

PETREA, RAYMOND ALLEN
Date/Place of Birth: August 10, 1930; High Point, Guilford County, N.C.
Parents: Luke Parker Petrea and Raymelle (Palmer) Petrea.
Spouse/Marriage Date: Beatrice Lea (Coble) Petrea; August 13, 1954 in Julian, N.C.
Children: Sylvia Greeson, Arleen Oldham, Louisa Bowman.
Education: Lenoir-Rhyne, A.B. 1952; Lutheran Theological Southern Seminary, M.Div. 1955.
Ordination: June 12, 1955 by North Carolina Synod.
Calls: St. Timothy, Catawba County, 1955-59; St. James, Brunswick, Ga., 1959-61; Faith, Warner Robins, Ga., 1961-65, which became the first "white" Lutheran Church in America congregation in the South to receive black members; Holy Trinity, Reidsville, 1965-66; Christ, Winston-Salem, 1981-85; Grace, Liberty, 1991-96; retired December 1996 to Greensboro; Vice Pastor at various congregations.
Other: Director of Public Relations, Roanoke College, 1966-74; Director of Information Services and Campus Pastor for Lutheran students, High Point University, 1974-81; Director of Development and first President, Lutheran Services for the Aging Foundation, Inc. 1985-91; contributor to numerous church, professional and commercial periodicals, including "Resource," "Salt," "YA Idea Book," "Lutheran Men," and "Luther League Topics;" published book: *The Communicating Congregation*, 1982; Interim editor of the *North Carolina Lutheran,* 1980; top professional award from the College News Association of the Carolinas, 1980.

PETREA, ROBERT WILLIAM
Date/Place of Birth: November 23, 1844; Cabarrus County, N.C.
Spouse/Marriage Date: Sophia Louisa (Bostian) Petrea; May 1877 in China Grove, N.C.
Children: Charles A., John Calvin, Joseph Allen.
Education: North Carolina College and Philadelphia Seminary.
Ordination: 1876 by North Carolina Synod.
Calls: Ebenezer, Rowan County, 1876-77; St. John, Cabarrus County, 1876-87; organized and built church, Mt. Olive, 1878-82; organized and built church, Prosperity, 1879-87; Cold Water, 1887; Pilgrim-St. Luke, Davidson County, 1883-85; Murphysboro, Ill., 1887-91; Pawnee City and Hardy, Neb., 1891-1903.
Date of Death/Burial Location: September 13, 1903; Pawnee City, Neb.

PETRY, JOHN LEWIS, III
Date/Place of Birth: June 24, 1952; Louisville, Ky.
Parents: Clifton Lamar Petry and Amy Lou (Young) Petry.
Spouse/Marriage Date: Katherine Lynn (Richards) Petry; September 1, 1979 in Indianapolis, Ind.
Child: Kristen Michelle.
Education: University of Kentucky, B.S. 1976; Lutheran Theological Southern Seminary, M.Div. 1982.
Ordination: May 20, 1982 by Indiana-Kentucky Synod.
Calls: Trinity, Vale, 1982-84; Christ, Charlotte, 1984-88; St. John, Walhalla, S.C., 1988-96; Emmanuel, High Point, 1996-.

PFLUM, HENRY JACOB, JR.

Date/Place of Birth: December 28, 1892; Reading, Pa.
Parents: Henry J. Pflum, Sr. and Ida (Eshelman) Pflum.
Spouse/Marriage Date: Florence (Wessell) Pflum; September 7, 1921 in Wilmington, N.C.
Child: Henry C.
Education: Roanoke College, A.B. 1918, D.D. 1930; Philadelphia Seminary, B.D. 1921; Columbia University, M.A. 1923; Muhlenberg College, D.D. 1959.
Ordination: 1921 by Ministerium of Pennsylvania.
Calls: Holy Trinity, Rockville Center, N.Y., 1921-24; Holy Trinity, Buffalo, N.Y., 1924-43; Christ, Allentown, Pa., 1943-62, Pastor Emeritus; retired 1962 at Wilmington, and transferred to North Carolina Synod; Vice Pastor of various congregations in North Carolina.
Other: Board, 1932-44, President, 1938-44, American Missions; Board of Foreign Missions, 1955-62; Committee on *Common Service Book*, 1932-50; Board of Education and Home Missions Board of the New York Synod; Board, Good Shepherd Home, Allentown, Pa.; Board, Home Missions, Ministerium of Pennsylvania, serving as President; Chaplain, 1964, convention of North Carolina Synod. Author and contributor to *Professional Journals.*
Date of Death/Burial Location: March 23, 1970; Grandview Cemetery, Allentown, Pa.

PHIFER, DANIEL WOODROW

Ordination: June 2, 1968 by Southeastern Synod.
Calls: Holy Trinity, Marietta, Ga., 1968. Chaplain. Vice Pastor St. James, Fayetteville, 1977.

PHIFER, W. PHILO

Place of Birth: Maryland.
Spouse: Hattie (Boger) Phifer.
Children: Willie, Hugh, Mattie.
License/Ordination: *History of the Lutheran Church in North Carolina,* (1803-1953) says he was licensed by Maryland Synod; Jensson's Biographies says he was baptized, instructed and confirmed by the Reverend David James Koontz, a fellow Negro Lutheran minister. Ordained April 28, 1890 at Charlotte by North Carolina Synod.
Calls: Ministered to his congregation at Concord; organized St. Paul Church, Charlotte; Lexington.
Other: Later moved to Baltimore, Md. An organizer of the Alpha Synod in 1889 and its first secretary.
Date of Death/Burial Location: 1911; Baltimore, Md.

PHILLIPPI, ALEXANDER

Date/Place of Birth: July 25, 1833; Wythe County, Va.
Parents: John Phillippi and Mollie (Wisely) Phillippi.
Spouse/Marriage Date: Cynthia (Brown) Phillippi; 1860 in Wytheville, Va.
Education: Roanoke College, A.B. 1857; Gettysburg Seminary; Pennsylvania College, D.D.

License/Ordination: Licensed 1859 by North Carolina Synod; transferred to and ordained by Southwest Virginia Synod, 1861.

Calls: First Pastor of St. Mark's, Charlotte, 1859-61; Lynchburg, Va. and Trinity-St. John, Wytheville, Va., the latter parish for fifty years to his death; retired to Wytheville, Va.

Other: For 21 years, operated Trinity Hall, Wytheville, Va., a school for boys and girls; Board, Roanoke College.

Date of Death/Burial Location: November 28, 1915; Wytheville, Va.

PHILLIPS, CHARLES ARTHUR

Date/Place of Birth: November 12, 1878; Concord, N.C.

Parents: John W. Phillips and Jennie Lou (Correll) Phillips.

First Spouse/Marriage Date: Minnie (Hiller) Phillips; June 7, 1907 in Plains, Ga.

Children of First Marriage: Charles Hiller (died at age two), Rosalie, the Reverend George Arthur.

Second Spouse/Marriage Date: Mrs. Mary C. (Coogle) Phillips; 1955 in Oglethorpe, Ga.

Education: North Carolina College, B.S. 1899; Lutheran Theological Southern Seminary, 1902.

Ordination: 1902 by North Carolina Synod.

Calls: Nazareth-Shiloh, Forsyth County, 1902-04; Zion Parish, Marlow, Ga., 1904-06; Plains Parish, Plains, Ga., 1906-17; Ascension, Chattanooga, Tenn., 1917-20; Camp Pastor, Camp Wheeler and Fort Oglethorpe, Ga., under National Lutheran Commission for Soldiers and Sailors Welfare; again in Georgia, at Oglethorpe and Plains, 1921-26; Grace, Prosperity, S.C., 1926-27; St. Mark's, Mooresville, 1927-33; Haven, Salisbury, 1935-50; organized and supplied Atonement, North Wilkesboro, 1951; retired 1950 at Hickory and from 1954 lived at Oglethorpe, Ga.

Date of Death/Burial Location: February 16, 1960; Catawba Memorial Park, Hickory, N.C.

PHILLIPS, DONALD MYRON

Date/Place of Birth: February 26, 1953; Hickory, N.C.

Parents: Paul Vaughan Phillips, Sr. and Arthelia Pauline (Lowman) Phillips.

Spouse/Marriage Date: Patricia Leigh (Stamey) Phillips; July 28, 1974 in Wilkesboro, N.C.

Children: Callie Elizabeth, Kathryn Leigh.

Education: Lenoir-Rhyne, A.B. Religious Studies, *magna cum laude*, 1974; Lutheran Theological Southern Seminary, M.Div., *cum laude*, 1978.

Ordination: June 11, 1978 by North Carolina Synod.

Calls: Lutheran Chapel, China Grove, 1978-84; Faith, Conover, 1984-89; St. Luke, Lexington, 1989-; Vice Pastor at various congregation.

Other: Chair, Stewardship Committee, Stewardship Interpreter; Historical Works Committee; Family Life Committee; Staff at Lutheran Church in America National Youth Gathering, 1985; Adjunct Faculty at Davidson County Community College (Religion), 1998-.

PHILLIPS, GEORGE ARTHUR
Date of Birth/Burial Location: September 12, 1915; Plains, Ga.
Parents: The Reverend Charles Arthur Phillips and Minnie F. (Hiller) Phillips.
Spouse/Marriage Date: Mary Elizabeth (Hallman) Phillips; September 7, 1940 in Columbia, S.C.
Children: Charles Luther, Paul Douglas, Elizabeth Dee Ashcraft.
Education: Catawba College, A.B. 1937; Lutheran Theological Southern Seminary, B.D. 1940, also graduate study; Chicago Seminary and Lutheran Theological Southern Seminary.
Ordination: May 30, 1940 by North Carolina Synod.
Calls: Bethlehem-New Jerusalem, Catawba County, 1940-43; Mt. Calvary-St. Luke, Claremont, 1944-46, Mt. Calvary only, 1946-47; St. Andrew's, Charleston, S.C., 1947-50; Mt. Pleasant, Saluda, S.C., 1950-51; Missionary in India, 1951-58, in Western Godavari Synod of Andhra Lutheran Church, chiefly among illiterates of jungle area tribes; Christiana, Granite Quarry, 1958-61; St. Mark, Luray, Va., 1961-63; Faith, Conover, 1963-66; Holy Trinity, Mt. Pleasant, 1967-70; Ebenezer, Pierson, Fla., 1970-73; Vice Pastor at various congregations.
Other: Stewardship Committee, 1964-66; Pensions Committee, 1968-71.
Date of Death/Burial Location: March 24, 1987; Oakdale Cemetery, Deland, Fla.

PIPHO, STEPHEN L.
Education: Pepperdine University, Master of Human Resources Management, 1978; Naval Postgraduate School, Electrical Engineer, 1983; Gettysburg Seminary, M.Div. 1997; University of Virginia, Foreign Affairs, 1972.
Ordination: May 30, 1997 by North Carolina Synod.
Calls: Redeemer, Charlotte, 1997-.

PITTS, TERRY FULMER
Date/Place of Birth: July 11, 1947; Lancaster, Pa.
Parents: Lewis C. Pitts and Alice Rebecca (Fulmer) Pitts.
Spouse/Marriage Date: Barbara Jane (Keck) Pitts; May 16, 1970 in Hickory, N.C.
Children: Alyssa Virginia, Eric Michael.
Education: Lenoir-Rhyne, B.A. 1969; Waterloo Seminary, M.Div. 1973; graduate work at McCormick Seminary.
Ordination: June 24, 1973 by Eastern Canada Lutheran Church in America Synod for the North Carolina Synod.
Calls: Christ, Windsor, Ontario, 1973-76; St. Mark, Kitchener, Ontario, 1976-79; Rose Bay Parish, Rose Bay, Nova Scotia, 1979-82; St. Matthew, Granite Falls, 1987-88; Bethlehem, Hickory, 1988-98; Vice Pastor to various congregations.
Other: Director of Alumni Affairs, Lenoir-Rhyne, 1982-87; Worship and Music Committee, Chair, Eastern Canada; Parish Life Committee, Eastern Canada; Planning Committee, *Lutheran Book of Worship*, Introduction, Eastern Canada.

PLESS, CHARLES RAHN
Date/Place of Birth: October 2, 1878; Concord, N.C.
Parents: John Lawson Pless and Mary Ruth (Walker) Pless.
Spouse/Marriage Date: Hallie Kate (Miller) Pless; May 3, 1904 in Rowan County, N.C.
Children: Charles Miller, the Reverend John Albert, Paul David.
Education: North Carolina College, A.B. 1900; Lutheran Theological Southern Seminary in Mt. Pleasant, S.C., 1903; Chicago Seminary, B.D. 1904.
Ordination: 1904 by North Carolina Synod.
Calls: Mt. Zion-Luther's-New Bethel, Richfield, 1904-07; St. Michael, Troutman-Amity-St. Paul, Iredell County, 1907-09; St. Andrew-Mt. Hermon, Concord, 1909-11; St. John-Cold Water, Cabarrus County, 1912-15; Union, Rowan County, 1915-18; Wittenberg-Immanuel, Granite Quarry, 1918-22; St. James, Rockwell, 1919-22; St. Luke, St. Luke-Pilgrim, Davidson County, 1922-30: St. Luke-Morning Star, Monroe, 1930-33; St. Luke-Pilgrim, Davidson County, 1933-40; retired 1940 because of ill health at Kannapolis, N.C.
Date of Death/Burial Location: July 1, 1962; Carolina Memorial Park, Concord, N.C.

PLESS, JOHN ALBERT
Date/Place of Birth: April 16, 1917; Rowan County, N.C.
Parents: The Reverend Charles Rahn Pless and Hallie Kate (Miller) Pless.
Spouse/Marriage Date: Beatrice (Rentz) Pless; November 27, 1938 in Columbia, S.C.
Children: The Reverend John Edward, Joanna Bea.
Education: Mount Pleasant Collegiate Institute, Roanoke College, two years, Duke University, A.B. 1937; Lutheran Theological Southern Seminary, B.D. 1940.
Ordination: May 30, 1940 by North Carolina Synod.
Calls: Pilgrim-St. Luke, Davidson County 1940-51 succeeding his father; built a new church at Pilgrim after fire, 1943, and educational building at St. Luke, 1950; St. Luke only, 1951-67; Vice Pastor at various congregations.
Other: Board, North Carolina Lutheran Homes, 1962-67, President, 1964-65; Chair, Operational Committee on Evangelism, 1962-65; North Carolina Council of Churches, 1962-63; Executive Director, North Carolina Lutheran Homes, 1967-78.
Date of Death/Burial Location: March 28, 1978; Carolina Memorial Park, Concord, N.C.

PLESS, JOHN EDWARD
Date/Place of Birth: December 20, 1948; Winston-Salem, N.C.
Parents: The Reverend John Albert Pless and Beatrice (Rentz) Pless.
Spouse/Marriage Date: Linda (Russell) Pless; February 9, 1975 in Aurora, Ill.
Children: John Aaron, Sarah Elizabeth.
Education: Lenoir-Rhyne, A.B. Economics, 1971; Lutheran Theological Southern Seminary, M.Div. 1975.
Ordination: June 8, 1975 by North Carolina Synod.
Calls: St. Peter, Salisbury, 1975-84; Holy Trinity, Little Mountain, S.C., 1984-92; Organ, Salisbury, 1992-; Vice Pastor at various congregations.

PLEXICO, THURMOND CLAUDE
Date/Place of Birth: October 10, 1928; Columbia, S.C.
Parents: Claude Goode Plexico and Lida Mae (Denny) Plexico.
Spouse/Marriage Date: Mary Katherine (Wilhelm) Plexico; July 6, 1952 in Salisbury, N.C.
Child: Byron Kent.
Education: Lenoir-Rhyne, A.B. 1948; Lutheran Theological Southern Seminary, B.D. 1951. Graduate study: Lutheran Theological Southern Seminary; University of South Carolina, 1949; Princeton Seminary, 1953; Institute of Advanced Pastoral Studies, Bloomfield Hills, Mich., 1964; World Center of Liturgical Studies, Florida; Lutheran Theological Southern Seminary Scholars Program and Pastor's Institute; Parish Leadership Seminars, Indiana.
Ordination: June 1951 by South Carolina Synod.
Calls: Union, Rowan County, 1951-53; Mission, Lutheran Church of Our Savior, Jacksonville, and Ministry to military personnel and their families in the form of the Lutheran Service Center, 1953-63; St. James, Concord, 1963-88; St. Martin, Concord, 1988-97; retired, May 1997. Vice Pastor at various congregations.
Other: President (Dean), Eastern District of the Lutheran Church in America, three years; Chaplain, Luther League Convention, 1952; World Council of Church meetings, Evanston, Ill., 1954; Lutheran World Federation Meeting in Helsinki, Finland, 1963; Dean, Chaplain, Lutheran Church in America Lutheridge Institute of Church Music, 1966; Chaplain, Convention of the North Carolina Synod, 1971; Chaplain/Preacher, Convention of the Lutheran Council in the U.S.A., Minneapolis, Minn., 1972; one of sixteen representatives of the Lutheran Church in America to the Lutheran Council in the U.S.A., three terms; Lenoir-Rhyne Synod Covenant Committee; Evangelism Committee; Member and Chair, Publicity Committee; Chair, Worship- Music-Fine Arts, six years; Key '73 Task Force; Chair, Professional Services Committee, 1978-81; Professional Leadership Cabinet; Secretary, American Missions Committee; Presidential Induction Committee, 1978; President of Ministerial Associations in Salisbury, Jacksonville, and Concord; Charter President, Jacksonville Rotary Club; President, Onslow County-Camp Lejeune United Fund; Chair, Jacksonville Civic Council; Vice Chair and Chair, American Red Cross in Jacksonville and in Concord; District Chair, Boy Scouts in Eastern Carolina; First Chair of the Cabarrus County Human Relations Commission; District Governor of Rotary for Central North Carolina; twice as Personal Representative of the President of Rotary International at District Conventions of Rotary; Paul Harris Fellow of the Rotary Foundation; *Who's Who in the South and Southwest*, twice; *Who's Who in America in Religion*, 1978; *International Who's Who in Community Service*, third edition; writings: contributor to "A Mighty Fortress," "The Home Altar," columnist in *The North Carolina Lutheran*; contributor to *Today*, edited by Dr. Reuben Youngdahl; author of *The Church Wedding* with excerpts published in Journal of Church Music; A Journey in Faith - The History of St. Martin Lutheran Church, (1797-1994).

PLONK, GARY STEVEN
Date/Place of Birth: March 4, 1954; Charlotte, N.C.
Parents: Clarence Samuel Plonk and Julia (Pollock) Plonk.
Spouse/Marriage Date: Karen (Sparks) Plonk; August 7, 1976 in Kings Mountain, N.C.
Children: Stephanie Lynn Ellen, Samuel Robert Benjamin, William Charles Thomas.

Education: Lenoir-Rhyne, A.B. 1976; Lutheran Theological Southern Seminary, M.Div. 1980; Clemson University, M.Ed. 1994.
Ordination: May 25, 1980 by North Carolina Synod.
Calls: Morning Star, Matthews, 1980-83; University Lutheran, Clemson, S.C., 1984-.

POLENZ, LESTER FREDERICK
Date/Place of Birth: November 5, 1924; Leigh, Neb.
Parents: Louis H. P. Polenz and Sophia A. (Dasenbrock) Polenz.
Spouse/Marriage Date: Nancy Lee (Graves) Polenz; June 1, 1953 in Marysville, Ohio.
Children: Timera Ann Holly, Lennita S. P. Danford, John, Leslie, Michele.
Education: Capital University, B.A. 1950; Trinity Seminary, B.D. 1953.
Ordination: June 28, 1953 by Iowa Synod.
Calls: St. John, Steubenville, Ohio, 1953-55; Good Shepherd, Pittsburgh, Ohio, 1955-65; Biscayne Boulevard, Miami, Fla., 1965-67; St. Paul, Bridgeport, Ohio, 1967-71; Grace, Centersburg, Ohio, 1971-78; Zion, Hartford County, Ind., 1978-80; Training School, Fla., 1981-84; Putnam Correctional Institute, State of Florida, 1984-91; Correctional Chaplain, State of Florida, 1981-91; retired January 31, 1991 from Florida- Bahamas Synod to Franklin, N.C.

POPE, CARL MORRIS, JR.
Date/Place of Birth: October 9, 1945; Iredell County, N.C.
Parents: Carl Morris Pope, Sr. and Pauline Anna (Ford) Pope.
Spouse/Marriage Date: June Gail (Robinson) Pope; October 9, 1976 in Charlotte, N.C.
Education: Lenoir-Rhyne, A.B. 1972; Lutheran Theological Southern Seminary, M.Div. 1976.
Ordination: June 13, 1976 by North Carolina Synod.
Calls: Luther's, Richfield, 1976-77; Mt. Olive, Mt. Pleasant, 1977-79; Philadelphia, Granite Falls, 1979-81.
Other: Dropped from roll June 2, 1985.

POWELL, EUGENE MARION
Date/Place of Birth: October 24, 1937; Springfield, Ohio.
Parents: Andrew J. Powell and Esther Powell.
Spouse/Marriage Date: Delphine M. (Robinson) Powell; August 4, 1974 in Chicago, Ill.
Children: Wendell Landon, Eugenia Delphine.
Education: New Mexico Highlands University, AS-AA, 1964, B.A. 1970; Hamma School of Theology, M.Div. 1974; graduate work at Chicago Seminary, 1975.
Ordination: December 30, 1973 by Illinois Synod.
Calls: Assistant Pastor, St. John Missionary Baptist Church, Springfield, Ohio, 1968-73; Campus Pastor, Bethel, Chicago, Ill., 1974-79; Pastor/Developer Hope, Raleigh, 1979-82. Assistant to the Bishop, Southeastern Synod, Evangelical Lutheran Church in America.
Other: Board, Church Federal of Greater Chicago; Lutheran Representative to The Task Force for World Peace; Co-Author, *Ministry to Black People in Higher Education: A Lutheran View*.

PREHN, ROGER HENRY
Date/Place of Birth: September 17, 1944; Madison, Wis.
Parents: Vince E. Prehn and Clara (Hinze) Prehn.
Spouse/Marriage Date: Andrea (Wanotke) Prehn; September 3, 1970 in Toledo, Ohio.
Children: Jill Catherine Hudkins, Meredith Ann.
Education: Wartburg College, B.A. 1966; Chicago Seminary, M.Div. 1970; graduate work at Gettysburg Seminary.
Ordination: June 7, 1970 by Wisconsin-Upper Michigan (Lutheran Church in America) Synod.
Calls: Mt. Zion, Trade City, Pa. and Salem, Smicksburg, Pa., 1970-72; St. Matthias, Greensburg, Pa., 1973- 84; Bethlehem, Grand Rapids, Mich., 1984-88; Assistant to the Bishop, Northwest Lower Michigan Synod- Evangelical Lutheran Church in America, 1988-92; St. Paul, Durham, 1992-.
Other: Certificate of Recognition for Refugee Resettlement given by The National Conference of Roman Catholic Bishops; Evangelical Lutheran Church in America-Episcopal Adult Catechumenate Training Team.

PRICE, EVERETT RAY
Date/Place of Birth: May 16, 1935; Catawba County, N.C.
Parents: Floyd T. Price and Ila M. (Adams) Price.
Spouse/Marriage Date: Bernice L. (Mathias) Price; August 10, 1958 in West Columbia, S.C.
Child: Scottie Lee Marsh.
Education: Lenoir-Rhyne, A.B. 1956; Lutheran Theological Southern Seminary, B.D. 1959.
Ordination: June 7, 1959 by North Carolina Synod.
Calls: Mission Developer/Pastor, Holy Cross, Lincolnton, 1959-67; Mission Developer/Pastor, Our Shepherd, Hartsville, S.C., 1968-85; Faith, West Columbia, S.C., 1985-.

PRICE, JAMES PRESLEY
Date/Place of Birth: June 30, 1856; Lexington County, S.C.
Parents: Joseph Price and Elizabeth Price.
First Spouse/Marriage Date: Rebecca Ann (Sox) Price; December 12, 1877 in Lexington County, S.C.
Children of First Marriage: Martha Catherine, Lucy Agnes, Mamie Rebecca, Jason Ambrose, Lelia Eudora, James Robert, Joseph Lloyd.
Second Spouse: Mrs. Elizabeth (Leonard) Price in Lincoln County, N.C.
Education: Concordia College, in both literary and theological courses, graduating in 1888.
License/Ordination: Licensed May 1888 and ordained December 1888 by Tennessee Synod.
Calls: Mt. Gilead-St. Martin, Cabarrus County and St. Martin, Stanly County, 1888-1900; Daniel's, Lincoln County and Grace, Catawba County, 1901-06; Shiloh, Alexander County, 1907-09; Philadelphia, Granite Falls and Mt. Hebron, Hildebran, 1907-13; retired 1913 at Hickory; supplied St. John, Hudson, 1919, and other churches.
Other: Was noted for his memory of the Scriptures.
Date of Death/Burial Location: September 9, 1935; Oakwood Cemetery, Hickory, N.C.

PROPST, JOHN CALLOWAY

Date/Place of Birth: October 28, 1948; Concord, N.C.

Parents: Earl Wilson Propst and Frances (Calloway) Propst.

Spouse/Marriage Date: Elizabeth (Aberle) Propst; June 5, 1971 in Concord, N.C.

Children: Jenni, Brian, J. Austin.

Education: Lenoir-Rhyne, B.A. 1971; Lutheran Theological Southern Seminary, M.Div. 1975.

Ordination: June 8, 1975 by North Carolina Synod.

Calls: St. Paul, Fullerton, Calif., 1975-77; Augustana, Phoenix, Ariz., 1977-83; Mission Developer/Pastor, Desert Cross, Tempe, Ariz., 1983-89; Spirit of Joy, Weddington, 1989-; Vice Pastor at various congregations.

Other: Dean, Arizona District, Pacific Southwest Synod; Spiritual Director, Via de Cristo; Mission Outreach Committee; Spirituality Committee; Chair, Pacific Southwest Synod Youth Committee.

PUOTINEN, ARTHUR G.

Date/Place of Birth: September 7, 1941; Crystal Falls, Mich.

Parents: Kaleva Puotinen and Ines Pauline Puotinen.

Spouse/Marriage Date: Judith Cathleen (Kapoun) Puotinen; August 8, 1964 in West St. Paul, Minn.

Children: Anne Marie, Marjetta Lee, Sara Lynne.

Education: Suomi, A.A. 1961; Augustana, B.A. 1963; Chicago Seminary, M.Div. 1967; University of Chicago, Divinity School, M.A. 1969, Ph.D. 1973; Wake Forest University, M.B.A. 1984.

Ordination: March 1967 by Wisconsin-Upper Michigan Synod.

Calls: Trinity, Chicago, Ill., 1968-70.

Other: Assistant Professor of Religious Studies, Central Michigan University, 1971-74; Dean of Faculty, Suomi College, 1974-78; Vice President of Academic Affairs, Lenoir-Rhyne, 1978-83; Associate Academic Dean, Roanoke College, 1983-84; Executive Director, Lutheran Educational Conference of North America, 1984-88; President, Grand View College, 1988-96; Vice President and Provost, Suomi College, 1996-; author of one book and numerous articles and reviews concerning religion, history, and education; Board, Central Iowa Health Systems; Board, Suomi College; Board, Ballet Iowa; Board, Lutheran Educational Conference of North America; Des Moines Rotary Club; Union Park Neighborhood Association Steering Committee; Des Moines Lutheran Coalition Council; Iowa Association of Independent Colleges and Universities; Iowa College Foundation; Greater Des Moines Committee; Southeastern Iowa Synod of the Evangelical Lutheran Church in America Clergy.

QUANSTROM, CONRAD L.

Date/Place of Birth: August 4, 1945; McLean County, Ill.

Parents: Richard C. Quanstrom and Wilhelmine S. (Keim) Quanstrom.

Spouse/Marriage Date: Linda G. (Burgin) Quanstrom; July 11, 1967 in Hickory, N.C.

Children: Todd Aaron.

Education: Lenoir-Rhyne, B.A. 1967; Hamma Seminary, B.D. 1971.

Ordination: July 9, 1971 by Southeastern Synod.

Calls: Assistant Pastor, Holy Trinity, Raleigh, 1971-74; Wittenberg, Granite Quarry, 1974-78.

Other: Resigned March 9, 1981.

RADCLIFF, JAMES MORETZ
Spouse/Marriage Date: Alice Radcliff.
Ordination: June 1, 1969 by North Carolina Synod.
Calls: Shiloh, Lewisville, 1969-72.
Other: Resigned from Ministry, 1972 to become Vocational Rehabilitation Counselor with State of North Carolina.

RADLOFF, MARK PAUL
Date/Place of Birth: May 23, 1953; Columbus, Ohio.
Parents: Paul Robert Radloff and Marilyn (Saylor) Radloff.
Spouse/Marriage Date: Sandra (Tregoning) Radloff; April 7, 1984 in Bradenton, Fla.
Children: Megan Elizabeth.
Education: Capital University, B.A. 1975; Luther-Northwestern Seminary, M.Div. 1979; University of Georgia, M.Ed. 1988.
Ordination: February 10, 1980 by Michigan District, American Lutheran Church.
Calls: Associate Pastor, St. John, Farmington, Mich., 1980-83; Interim Pastor, Zoar, Perrysburg, Ohio, 1983- 84; Church of the Savior, Newland, 1984-87; Lutherock Outdoor Ministry, Newland, 1984-92; Assistant to the Bishop, Indiana-Kentucky Synod, 1992-.
Other: American Alliance of Leisure and Recreation award for article, "The Future Family: Key to the Future of the Church," 1988.

RAHN, SHEPPARD SENECA
Date/Place of Birth: February 14, 1845; Effingham County, Ga.
Parents: Cletus Rahn and Eliza Hannah Rahn.
First Spouse/Marriage Date: Martha Ida (Campbell) Rahn; January 26, 1875 in Cross Hill, S.C.; died July 13, 1877.
Children of First Marriage: Robert Campbell (lived 38 days).
Second Spouse/Marriage Date: Sallie Waring (Parker) Rahn; December 27, 1881 in Columbia, S.C.; died January 3, 1888.
Children of Second Marriage: Richard Parker (died in second year), Joseph Albion, Sarah Alice.
Third Spouse/Marriage Date: Frances Henrietta (Parker) Rahn; April 20, 1897 in Jacksonville, Fla. ; died June 7, 1905.
Education: Newberry College, A.B. 1872, A.M. 1875, D.D. 1900; Lutheran Theological Southern Seminary, 1874; Plummer College, Ph.D. 1892.
License/Ordination: Licensed 1874 and ordained 1874 by Georgia and Adjacent States Synod.
Calls: In Georgia, 1874-1885, 1894-97; in Virginia at St. John, Wytheville, 1889-92 and organized Christ, Radford in 1891; in South Carolina, Bethlehem-St. John, Pomaria, 1874-76; transferred to North Carolina Synod at Ebenezer, Rowan County, 1878-79; transferred back to South Carolina to Sandy Run, and others in Lexington County, and in Newberry County, 1885-89; transferred to Tennessee Synod; Holy Communion, Dallas, 1892-93; supplied Lutheran Chapel, Gastonia, 1894; St. Luke-Morning Star, 1896-97; St. John, Jacksonville, Fla., 1897-1911.

Other: In Georgia Confederate States Army Cavalry, 1862-65; North Carolina College, 1877-79; Professor, Greek and Modern Languages, Newberry College, 1880-85; Co-principal, Gaston College, 1892-93; wrote for various Lutheran periodicals.
Date of Death/Burial Location: July 1, 1911; Columbia, S.C.

RALL, TIMOTHY GRAVES

Date/Place of Birth: July 13, 1963; Chisholm, Minn.
Parents: The Reverend E. Eugene Rall and Geraldine Rall.
Spouse/Marriage Date: Elizabeth (Graves) Rall; June 22, 1996.
Education: Luther College, B.A. Music, 1985; Gettysburg Seminary, M.Div. 1995; graduate work at University of Northern Iowa, 1987.
Ordination: August 15, 1996 by North Carolina Synod.
Other: Youth ministry work in Iowa, Pennsylvania, Maryland and North Carolina.
Calls: Associate Pastor, Kimball Memorial, Kannapolis, 1996-.

RAMSEUR, FRED MANLEY, JR.

Date/Place of Birth: February 12, 1925; Durham, N.C.
Parents: Fred Manley Ramseur, Sr. and Beulah Mae (Propst) Ramseur.
Spouse/Marriage Date: Vera Mae (Tichenor) Ramseur of Catawba County, N.C.; November 11, 1942 in York, S.C.
Children: John David, Fred Manley, III.
Education: Lenoir-Rhyne, A.B. 1954; Lutheran Theological Southern Seminary, B.D. 1957.
Ordination: June 9, 1957 by North Carolina Synod.
Calls: St. Stephen, Hickory, 1957-60; Emmanuel, Lincolnton, 1960-64; Holy Trinity, Charlotte, 1964-78; disability retirement, 1978-79; Ascension, Wilson, 1979-83; retired, 1983; Vice Pastor at various congregations.
Other: Evangelism Committee, 1962-66; Secretary, Southwest District, 1962-64; Campus Ministry, 1968; Nominating Committee, 1966.

RANKIN, WILLIAM C.

License/Ordination: Licensed by Presbyterian Church; ordained Pastor by Tennessee Synod in Buehler's Church, Sullivan County, Tenn., September 9, 1831.
Other: At the convention of the Tennessee Synod in Phaniel Church, Rowan County, he was charged with deviation from the Augsburg Confession. He withdrew from the Synod and went back to the Presbyterian Church. His name was removed from the roll of the Tennessee Synod on September 15, 1832.

RAU, HARRY LEE, JR.
Date/Place of Birth: May 26, 1925; Macon, Bibb County, Ga.
Parents: Harry Lee Rau, Sr. and Mary E. (Rogers) Rau.
Spouse/Marriage Date: M. Barbara (Schwarz) Rau; August 22,
1952 in Jacksonville, Fla.
Children: Karl Frederick, Kurt Luther, and two sons who died
in infancy.
Education: Newberry College, A.B. 1949; Lutheran Theological
Southern Seminary, B.D. 1952.
Ordination: June 1, 1952 by Georgia-Alabama Synod.
Calls: Holy Trinity, Elberton, Ga., 1952-55, Mt. Zion-St. Luke,
Oglethorpe-St. John, Macon County, Ga., 1955-56; Holy Trinity, Elizabethton, Tenn.,
1957-59; Good Shepherd, Walterboro, S.C., 1959-64; Lutheran Chapel, China Grove,
1964-79; Chaplain, North Carolina Lutheran Homes, Salisbury, 1979-82; Vice Pastor at
various congregations; retired 1983.
Other: Veteran of World War II; participated in the Normandy campaign; Adviser, Rowan
County Services for the Aging; Rowan County Choral Society.
Date of Death/Burial Location: July 19, 1996; Macon Memorial Park, Macon, Ga.

RAUCH, MICHAEL
Date/Place of Birth: October 6, 1780; perhaps in Lexington District, S.C.
Children: John (Treasurer, South Carolina Synod), 1847-55.
License/Ordination: Licensed 1812 in Lau's (Low's) Church, Guilford County, and
ordained 1819 in St. John, Cabarrus County, by North Carolina Synod.
Calls: Churches served were all in South Carolina, congregations of North Carolina Synod
until 1824 when he and five other North Carolina Synod pastors organized the South
Carolina Synod; served some thirteen churches in Lexington District, S.C., until about 1856.
Date of Death/Burial Location: February 26, 1869; Lexington County, S.C.

RAUSHER, TODD
Spouse: Barbara Rausher.
Children: Nichole Elizabeth, Daniel Jonathan.
Education: Duquesne University, B.S. Business Administration, 1987; Drexel University,
MBA in Operations Management, 1990; Lutheran Theological Southern Seminary, M.Div. 1997.
Ordination: May 30, 1997 by North Carolina Synod.
Calls: Friendship, Taylorsville, 1997-.
Other: Alexander County Prison Ministry; Meals on Wheels; Youth Baseball Coach;
Certified Baseball Umpire.

RAY, KENNETH LYLE
Date/Place of Birth: December 31, 1958; Raleigh, N.C.
Parents: Graham Steverson Ray and Elaine (Husketh) Ray.
Spouse/Marriage Date: Deborah (Falls) Ray; April 16, 1983.
Children: Richard Cameron, Chandler Graham.
Education: University of North Carolina, B.A. 1980; Duke University, M.Div. 1995;
graduate work at Lutheran Theological Southern Seminary.

Ordination: May 19, 1995 by North Carolina Synod.
Calls: Christ the King, Cary, 1995-.

RECK, JOHN B.

Education: Began his theological studies under his missionary brother, Abraham, and then enrolled for studies under the Reverend Samuel Simon Schmucker at New Market, Va.
Ordination: 1826 by North Carolina Synod in Zion Church, Botetourt County, Va.; Lutheran churches in Southwest Virginia at that time were members of the North Carolina Synod.
Calls: St. Michael, Troutman, 1825-30; St. John, Salisbury-Union, Rowan County, 1826-31; transferred to Maryland Synod, 1831; was appointed missionary in the West, which meant Ohio and adjacent states.
Other: Was a brother of the Reverend Abraham Reck who was born in Littlestown, Pa., and ordained by the Pennsylvania Ministerium. Secretary of North Carolina Synod, 1828-30.

REICHARD (REICHERT OR RIEGERT), JOHN MICHAEL

License: Licensed by North Carolina Synod in Lau's (Low's) Church, Guilford County, 1821.
Other: No further reference to him in Synod's *History of the Lutheran Church in North Carolina,* (1803-1953). It appears that soon after 1821 he moved to South Carolina. In 1824 a John Riegert of Monroe County, Ala., sought ordination by the South Carolina Synod, but after examining him, the Synod concluded he was not adequately prepared for ordination.

REICHLEY, GLENN CARLTON

Date/Place of Birth: April 19, 1927; Perkasie, Pa.
Parents: Francis Daub Reichley and Florence (Reese) Reichley.
Spouse/Marriage Date: Evelyn Margreta (Clarke) Reichley; June 17, 1950 in Philadelphia, Pa.
Children: Darryl Glenn, Richard Thomas, Phyllis Jean Fujita.
Education: Muhlenberg College, A.B. 1947; Philadelphia Seminary, M.Div. 1950; graduate work at Philadelphia Seminary.
Ordination: June 1950 by Ministerium of Pennsylvania.
Calls: Spies-Oley Parish, Oley, Pa., 1950-55; St. Paul, Hawley, Pa., 1955- 59; Old Goshenhoppen, Woxall, Pa., 1959-63; Assistant Pastor, Trinity, Lansdale, Pa., 1963-65; St. Paul, Sassamansville, Pa., 1965-71; Lebanon, Cleveland, 1973-78; New Bethel, Richfield, 1978-87; Upper Frankford Parish, Newville, Pa., 1987-89; Vice Pastor various congregations in North Carolina; retired to Salisbury.
Other: Board of Inner Missions, Ministerium of Pennsylvania; Board, Social Ministry, Southeast Pennsylvania Synod; Boy Scouts of America, in Pennsylvania and North Carolina; teacher of physically handicapped children in Norristown, Pa.

REITZEL, CHRISTIAN GUIDO

Date/Place of Birth: March 30, 1805; Guilford County, N.C.
Parents: Henry Reitzel and Katrina (Moser) Reitzel.

First Spouse/Marriage Date: Delilah (Ingold) Reitzel; November 15, 1827 in Orange County (now Alamance County), N.C.

Children of First Marriage: Anderson Alexander, Mary Ann, Tempe Catherine, Turley Magdaline, Lucinda Caroline, Sylvina Lucinda, Margaret Julian, Henry John, Lydia Sarah, Jane Camellia, Jerome Cass.

Second Spouse/Marriage Date: Susan (Shook) Reitzel; December 17, 1857.

Children of Second Marriage: Rufus Reuben, Titus Silvanus, Philo Lareston, Candace Ellen, Plato Samuel.

Ordination: 1835 as Deacon and 1841 as Pastor by Tennessee Synod.

Calls: Coble's, Guilford County-Mt. Pleasant, Alamance County-Melanchthon, Randolph County, 1835-37; St. Peter, Catawba County, 1839-49; Friendship, Alexander County, 1842-44; Zion, Catawba County, 1840-47; Miller's, Hickory, 1841-49; St. Martin, Cabarrus County, 1843-45; St. Stephen, Hickory, 1845-49; Supply, with the Reverends J. R. Moser and P. C. Henkel, St. Paul, Newton (Startown), 1847-48.

Date of Death/Burial Location: October 25, 1870; St. Peter Church, Catawba County, N.C.

RENDLEMAN, CHRISTOPHER HENRY

Date/Place of Birth: March 18, 1935; Fort Wayne, Ind.

Parents: David Atwell Rendleman, Sr. and Grace Gertrude (Aaron) Rendleman. An older brother is the Reverend Toby A. Rendleman.

Spouse/Marriage Date: Susan Joan (Atherton) Rendleman; August 30, 1958 in Spartanburg, S.C.

Children: Christopher Martin, Susan Lynn Faggion.

Education: Davidson College, two years, Lenoir-Rhyne, A.B. 1956; Lutheran Theological Southern Seminary, B.D. 1959.

Ordination: June 7, 1959 by North Carolina Synod.

Calls: Assistant Pastor, First, Norfolk, Va., 1959-61; Redeemer, Bristol, Tenn., 1961-67; Messiah, Hickory, 1967; retired to Hickory, N.C., 1997; Vice Pastor at various congregations.

Other: District Secretary, 1970.

RENDLEMAN, TOBY AARON

Date/Place of Birth: July 11, 1927; Salisbury, N.C.

Parents: David Atwell Rendleman, Sr. and Grace Gertrude (Aaron) Rendleman. A younger brother is the Reverend C. H. Rendleman.

First Spouse/Marriage Date: Theresa Audry (Thue) Rendleman; August 3, 1948 in Woodlyn, Pa.

Children of First Marriage: Henry Stephen, Jane Ellen Cotner, Donna Margaret, Karen Eleanor Blue.

Second Spouse/Marriage Date: Mary Jo Rendleman; June 17, 1979.

Education: Catawba College, A.B. 1950; Lutheran Theological Southern Seminary, B.D. 1953.

Ordination: June 14, 1953 by North Carolina Synod.

Calls: Trinity, Cabarrus County, 1953-57; St. Matthew, Delphi, Ind., 1958-63; Mission Developer/Pastor, Redeemer, Somerset, Ky., 1964-70; Trinity, Logansport, Ind., 1971-77; Holy Cross, Kokomo, Ind., 1977-; retired to Russiaville, Ind.

RENNINGER, THOMAS

Date/Place of Birth: July 16, 1942; Lehigh County, Pa.
Parents: Jesse B. Renninger and Myrtle (Herbst) Renninger.
Spouse/Marriage Date: Carol L. (Lange) Renninger; August 28, 1965 in Gettysburg, Pa.
Children: Jodi Kristen, Eric Thomas, Kristen Andrea Ruth.
Education: Muhlenberg, A.B. 1964; Gettysburg, B.D. 1967.
Ordination: May 28, 1967 by Eastern Pennsylvania Synod.
Calls: New Jerusalem, Lexington, 1967-70; Nazareth, Rural Hall, 1970-72; Atonement, Wilkesboro, 1973- 81; Vice Pastor at various congregations.
Other: Resigned May 4, 1981.

REPASS, ELLIS ARTHUR

Date/Place of Birth: August 21, 1874; Rural Retreat, Wythe County, Va.
Parents: Luther Kurtz Repass and Margaret Ann (Crabtree) Repass.
Spouse/Marriage Date: Mary Florence (Burch) Repass; August 28, 1900 near Salem, Va.
Children: John H.
Education: Roanoke College, A.B. 1897, D.D. 1936; Philadelphia Seminary, 1900; Central University, Indianapolis, Ind., Ph.D. 1904.
Ordination: 1900 by Ministerium of Pennsylvania.
Calls: Augusta, Shenandoah, and Rockingham Counties, Va., 1900-17; Bethel-St. Paul, Rowan County, 1917-18; Mercersburg, Lancaster, and Columbia, Pa., 1918-41; retired 1941 at Columbia, Pa.
Other: Author of pamphlet, "Home Training;" contributor to *Pennsylvania Poems;* Secretary, Virginia Synod, 1913-17; Trustee, Elizabeth College, Salem, Va., 1915-17.
Date of Death: January 13, 1959.

RHOADS, DAVID MICHAEL

Date/Place of Birth: November 17, 1942; Altoona, Pa.
Parents: Luke H. Rhoads and Virginia (Andrews) Rhoads.
Spouse/Marriage Date: Sandra (Roberts) Rhoads, Evangelical Lutheran Church in America Pastor, now Chaplain, Kenosha County Jail; September 12, 1964 in Frederick, Md.
Children: Tania Donata, Jessica Sanders.
Education: Gettysburg College, B.A. 1963; Oxford University, M.A. 1965; Gettysburg Seminary, B.D. 1966; Duke University, Ph.D. 1973.
Ordination: May 5, 1968 by North Carolina Synod.
Calls: St. John, Asheboro, 1968-70; Vice Pastor at various congregations.
Other: Professor, Carthage College, Kenosha, Wis., 1973-88; Chicago Seminary, 1988-; Publications: *Israel in Revolution, Mark as Story, The Challenge of Diversity;* American Missions Committee, North Carolina Synod, 1969-70.

RHOADS, HAROLD EMMETT
Date/Place of Birth: November 25, 1908; Middletown, Ohio.
Parents: Jesse Harley Rhoads and Lillie Mae (Geering) Rhoads, who were Baptists.
Education: Wittenberg University, A.B. 1950 doubling in theology at Hamma Divinity School for two years; Lutheran Theological Southern Seminary, B.D. 1951.
Ordination: July 8, 1951 by North Carolina Synod.
Calls: Assistant Pastor, St. John, Salisbury, 1951-55; Mission Developer, Holy Trinity, Reidsville, 1955; Mission Developer/Supply Pastor, Gloria Dei, Salisbury, 1960-61; Chaplain - Veterans Administration Hospitals, Salisbury, N.C. and Downey, Ill., 1955-57; retired 1957 at Salisbury; Vice Pastor at various congregations.
Date of Death/Burial Location: June 1, 1987; Woodhill Cemetery, Franklin, Ohio.

RHOADS, RICHARD ARTHUR
Date/Place of Birth: November 6, 1963; Cleveland, Ohio.
Parents: Earl Frederick Rhoades and Eleanor Rose (Badners) Rhoades.
Spouse/Marriage Date: Corrine Marie (Priebe) Rhoads, daughter of the Reverend Dr. Kenneth Priebe, Bishop of Ohio District, American Lutheran Church; May 23, 1987 Circleville, Ohio.
Children: Cindy Marie.
Education: Capital University, 1982-83, Ohio State University, B.S. Genetics, 1985; Trinity Seminary, M.Div. 1990.
Ordination: June 10, 1995 by Southern Ohio Synod.
Calls: Grace, Curwensville; Olanta, Olanta; Salem, New Millport, Pa., 1990-92; Frieden's, Gibsonville, 1992-.

RHODES, CLARENCE KILLIAN, SR.
Date/Place of Birth: December 15, 1886; Dallas, N.C.
Parents: Oliver Peterson Rhodes and Sarah Alice (Hoffman) Rhodes.
Spouse/Marriage Date: May Marguerite (Rhyne) Rhodes; October 7, 1913 in Charlotte, N.C.
Children: Clarence Killian, Jr., Henry Oliver, Georgie May Crigler.
Education: Lenoir-Rhyne, A.B. 1910; Lutheran Theological Southern Seminary, 1913.
Ordination: October 5, 1913 by Tennessee Synod.
Calls: Rockingham, Va., Parish, 1913-19; St. Mark-Corinth, Saluda, S.C., 1919-22; St. Paul-Antioch-Philadelphia, Gaston County, 1922-28; Madison, Va. Parish, 1928-45; retired 1945 near Charlotte; transferred back to North Carolina Synod, 1948; supplied St. Mark's, Charlotte, and other churches.
Other: Board of Directors, Shenandoah Lutheran School, New Market, Va., 1913-21.
Date of Death/Burial Location: August 18, 1963; Sharon Memorial Park, Charlotte, N.C.

RHODES, GEORGE HEILIG, JR.
Date/Place of Birth: January 28, 1881; Gouldsboro, Pa.
Parents: The Reverend George Heilig Rhodes, Sr. and Margaret (Walker) Rhodes. Father died when he was just over two months of age.
Spouse/Marriage Date: Mary May (Flowers) Rhodes; June 25, 1908 in Gouldsboro, Pa.
Children: Paul H. (M.D.), Virginia, (married the Reverend Albert H. Keck, Jr.).
Education: Muhlenberg College, A.B. 1904; Philadelphia Seminary, 1907; Lenoir-Rhyne, D.D. 1939.
Ordination: 1907 by Southwest Virginia Synod.
Calls: Woman's Memorial, Pulaski, Va., 1907-09; Grace, Rural Retreat, Va., 1909-20; St. John, Knoxville, Tenn., 1920-22; First, Albemarle, 1927-48; retired 1949 at Albemarle; supplied churches, including Ebenezer, Rowan County, and Holy Trinity, Raleigh.
Other: Secretary, Treasurer, and President, Southwest Virginia Synod; Superintendent of Virginia Synod, 1922-27; after retiring, served as Business-Circulation Manager of the *North Carolina Lutheran;* delegate to five United Lutheran Church in America conventions; Board, Lutheran Theological Southern Seminary, 1939-47; Dean of Summer School for Church Workers, before Lutheridge was established.
Date of Death/Burial Location: August 8, 1958; Albemarle Cemetery, Albemarle, N.C.

RHODES, JOHN
Date/Place of Birth: August 19/20, 1820; Lincoln (now Gaston) County, N.C.
Parents: Christian Rhodes and Magdalene (Rhyne) Rhodes.
Ordination: Deacon 1841 by Tennessee Synod.
Date of Death/Burial Location: September 3/4, 1842 age 22 years, fourteen days, in typhoid fever epidemic. Buried in family cemetery on South Fork River, near Dallas and Vestal's Ford, N.C.

RHODES, STEPHEN RAY
Date/Place of Birth: February 17, 1956; Grand Rapids, Mich.
Parents: O. L. Rhodes and Gail (Christianson) Rhodes.
Spouse/Marriage Date: Elizabeth Anne Rhodes; February 1, 1986 in Columbia, S.C.
Children: Gregory, Christina Gayle.
Education: Newberry College, University of South Carolina, B.A. 1982; Lutheran Theological Southern Seminary, M.Div. 1987.
Ordination: January 10, 1988 by North Carolina Synod.
Calls: Lebanon, Cleveland, 1987-90; Resurrection, Greensboro, 1990-92.
Other: On leave from call, 1992. Not on roll in 1996.

RHYNE, ALFRED DICKSON
Date/Place of Birth: June 17, 1932; Gastonia, N.C.
Parents: Aldice Roscoe Rhyne and Frances Ethel (Thornburg) Rhyne.
Spouse/Marriage Date: Mabel Llewellyn (Graham) Rhyne; December 23, 1951 in Gastonia, N.C.
Children: John Lingle, Dana Marie Walters, Michael Graham.
Education: Clemson University, two years, Lenoir-Rhyne, A.B. 1955; Lutheran Theological Southern Seminary, M.Div. 1958.
Ordination: June 8, 1958 by North Carolina Synod.
Calls: Good Shepherd, Brevard, 1958-65; Faith, Faith, 1965-88; Luther's, Richfield, 1990-; retired 1988 to Faith, N.C.; Vice Pastor at various congregations.
Other: Social Ministry Committee, 1963-65.

RHYNE, GEORGE LAMAR
Date/Place of Birth: October 21, 1950; Dallas, N.C.
Parents: Phillip M. Rhyne and Addie Mae Rhyne.
Spouse/Marriage Date: Vicki Dianne (Wilcox) Rhyne; August 5, 1973 in Dallas, N.C.
Education: Gaston College, A.A. 1970; Lenoir-Rhyne, B.A. 1972; Lutheran Theological Southern Seminary, M.Div. 1977.
Ordination: June 12, 1977 by North Carolina Synod.
Calls: Co-Pastor, Beth Eden, Newton, 1977-83; St. Mark, Salisbury, 1983-91; Assistant to the Bishop, North Carolina Synod, Salisbury, 1991-; Vice Pastor at various congregations.

RHYNE, JOHN OSKER, JR.
Date/Place of Birth: March 14, 1948; Gaston County, N.C.
Parents: John Osker Rhyne, Sr. and Etta Elizabeth (Rudisill) Rhyne.
Education: Lenoir-Rhyne, A.B. History 1970; Lutheran Theological Southern Seminary, M.Div. 1975.
Ordination: October 3, 1976 by North Carolina Synod.
Calls: Prince of Peace, Salisbury, 1976-81; Ebenezer, Catawba County, 1981-83.
Other: Lay Supply Pastor, New Jerusalem, Lexington, 1975-76. Dropped from roll June 2, 1985.

RHYNE, MARVIN JACK
Date/Place of Birth: May 16, 1931; Vale, Lincoln County, N.C.
Parents: William Grady Rhyne and Annie Gladys (Workman) Rhyne.
First Spouse/Marriage Date: Betty Jeanette (King) Rhyne; August 19, 1956 in Concord, Cabarrus County, N.C.; deceased 1971.
Children of First Marriage: Cheryl Elizabeth, Mark Timothy, Lisa Antoinette, Betty Suzanne.

Second Spouse/Marriage Date: Colleen (Hawkins) (Sisk) Rhyne; December 2, 1972 in Lincolnton, N.C.
Children: Gayle Denise Sisk (step daughter).
Education: Appalachian State Teachers College, two years, Lenoir-Rhyne, B.S. Religious Education 1956; Lutheran Theological Southern Seminary, B.D. 1959.
Ordination: June 7, 1959 by North Carolina Synod.
Calls: St. Timothy, Hickory, 1959-63; Holy Cross, Mocksville, 1963-67; St. Luke-Salem, Lincolnton, 1967- 74; Salem, Lincolnton, 1974-; Vice Pastor at various congregations.
Other: Camping Committee, two terms.

RHYNE, RICHARD WAKEFIELD

Date/Place of Birth: June 13, 1941; Mecklenburg County, N.C.
Parents: Robert R. Rhyne, Sr. and Sue Betty (Finger) Rhyne.
First Spouse/Marriage Date: Mary Ruth (Mauney) Rhyne, daughter of the Reverend Jacob Luther Mauney, Sr.; January 30, 1965 in Roanoke, Va.
Children of First Marriage: Deborah Elizabeth, Mary Malisa.
Second Spouse/Marriage Date: Virginia (Soberg) Rhyne; November 1, 1980.
Children of Second Marriage: Erik Richard, Siri Megan.
Education: North Carolina A. & T. State University; Lenoir-Rhyne, B.A. 1964; Lutheran Theological Southern Seminary, M.Div. 1969; graduate work at A&T State University and University of South Carolina; University of North Carolina Law School, 1964-65.
Ordination: June 1, 1969 by North Carolina Synod.
Calls: Mission Developer/Pastor, Warnersville Mission, Prince of Peace, Greensboro, 1969-73; Administrative Assistant to the President, North Carolina Synod, 1973-78; Director, Social Ministries, Lutheran Council in the United States of America, New York, 1978-83.
Other: President, Southwestern District, Luther League of North Carolina, 1959-60; Social Ministry Committee, 1971-73; Task Force on Justice and Social Change, 1970-73; Delegate to North Carolina Council of Churches, 1971-73; removed from roll, May 1986.

RHYNE, SIDNEY WHITE, SR.

Date/Place of Birth: January 25, 1894; Charlotte, N.C.
Parents: Aaron Sidney Rhyne and Mary Margaret (White) Rhyne.
Spouse/Marriage Date: Ruth Naomi (Dry) Rhyne; June 19, 1928 in Concord, N.C.
Children: Sidney White, Jr., Charles Sylvanus.
Education: Davidson College, Roanoke College, A.B. 1918, D.D. 1938; Lutheran Theological Southern Seminary, 1922; graduate study, Grenoble University, France, 1918, and Northwestern University, 1927 and 1928; Lenoir-Rhyne, L.L.D.
1961.
Ordination: 1922 by North Carolina Synod.
Calls: Field Missionary, North Carolina Synod, for Eastern North Carolina, organizing and serving Trinity, Rocky Mount, 1922-26; retired 1962 at Philadelphia, Pa. to Clemson, S.C.; transferred 1965 from North Carolina Synod to South Carolina Synod.

Other: Board, Parish Education: Field Secretary (six Southern synods), 1926-31; and Executive Secretary, 1931-62; Literary contributions: many articles on parish education in United Lutheran Church in America, other church and interdenominational journals, and United Lutheran Church in America church school curricular and parish education promotional materials.
Date of Death: October 19, 1986.

RHYNE, WILLIAM RUDISILL, SR.
Date/Place of Birth: November 17, 1942; Charlotte, N.C.
Parents: Alfred Leonard Rhyne and Nella (Rudisill) Rhyne.
Spouse/Marriage Date: Susan M. (Davis) Rhyne; August 10, 1963 in Kings Mountain, N.C.
Children: William Rudisill, Jr., Sara Lane, Nella Jo.
Education: University of North Carolina at Chapel Hill, Lenoir-Rhyne, B.A. 1964; Lutheran Theological Southern Seminary, M.Div. 1968.
Ordination: June 9, 1968 by North Carolina Synod.
Calls: Bethel, Salisbury, 1968-75; Low's, Liberty, 1976-90; retired October 1990 to Burlington, N.C.; Vice Pastor at various congregations.
Other: Northern Conference Dean and Secretary; Board, Lutheran Children's Home of the South; Board, Lutheran Family Services; Board, Lutheran Outdoor Ministries.

RICKERT, JOHN MICHAEL
See also Reichard, (Reichet or Riegert), John
License: Licensed October 22, 1804 by North Carolina Synod, at second convention, held in Pilgrim Church, Davidson County. He preached some, but not regularly, and was never ordained.
Other: No account of churches he served, or reference to him after 1815.

RICKS, EDWIN LEE
Date/Place of Birth: January 4, 1937; Rocky Mount, N.C.
Parents: Edwin Burton Ricks and Margaret (Waters) Ricks.
Education: Lenoir-Rhyne, A.B. 1959; Lutheran Theological Southern Seminary, B.D. 1962; attended U.S. Army Chaplain School.
Ordination: June 17, 1962 by North Carolina Synod.
Calls: Grace, Bessemer City, 1962-65; Assistant Pastor, St. Matthew, Charleston, S.C., 1965-70; Staff, Lutheran Church in America Board of Parish Education, 1970-82.
Other: North Carolina Council of Churches, 1962-63; Auxiliaries Committee, 1962-63; Youth Ministry Committee, 1963-64.
Date of Death: June 27, 1982.

RIDDLE, PATRICK WENDELL
Date/Place of Birth: May 6, 1959; Havelock, N.C.
Parents: Wendell Riddle and Georgia R. Riddle.
Spouse/Marriage Date: Janet (Holton) Riddle; June 30, 1984 in Wilmington, N.C.
Children: Savannah Corbin, Mary Victoria (twins).

Education: Virginia Wesleyan College, B.A. History 1981 *cum laude*; Lutheran Theological Southern Seminary, M.Div. 1985; graduate work at Gordon-Conwell Seminary.

Ordination: May 31, 1985 by Virginia Synod.

Calls: Good Shepherd, Goldsboro, 1985-89; Friendship, Taylorsville, 1989-1999; St. Stephen, Lexington, S.C., 1999-; Vice Pastor at various congregations.

Other: Outreach Committee, 1988-94; PLMD Committee, 1986-88; Omicron Delta Kappa Leadership and Honor Society; Phi Alpha Theta Honor Society (History); Outstanding Young Man of America, 1984.

RIDENHOUR, CHARLES ELMORE

Date/Place of Birth: April 4, 1893; Cabarrus County, N.C.

Parents: Luther Alexander Ridenhour and Alice Elizabeth (Barringer) Ridenhour.

Spouse/Marriage Date: Addie Marguerite (Cline) Ridenhour; May 22, 1919 in Cabarrus County, N.C.

Children: Charles Edward, Alice Victoria (married the Reverend W. David Wise) and Lillian Adelaide Cline (twins).

Education: Mount Pleasant Collegiate Institute, Newberry College, A.B. 1916; Lutheran Theological Southern Seminary, 1919.

Ordination: 1919 by North Carolina Synod.

Calls: St. Paul-Bethel, Rowan County, 1919-28; Reformation, Davie County, 1919-25; Lutheran Chapel, China Grove-Center Grove Kannapolis, 1928-45; Holy Communion, Dallas, 1945-54; Mission Developer/Pastor, Redeemer, Charlotte, 1954-58; retired 1958 at Charlotte; Vice Pastor at various congregations.

Other: Board, Lenoir-Rhyne; Board, Lutheran Theological Southern Seminary; Board, Children's Home.

Date of Death/Burial Location: April 4, 1971; St. John Lutheran Church Cemetery, Concord, N.C.

RIDENHOUR, DAVID EFIRD

Date/Place of Birth: August 3, 1950; Richfield, N.C.

Parents: Bernard Lefler Ridenhour and Myrtle L. (Efird) Ridenhour.

First Spouse/Marriage Date: Rose (Harrison) Ridenhour; October 5, 1968 in Chesterfield, S.C.

Children: Daniel David

Second Spouse/Marriage Date: Katherine R. (Gering) Ridenhour of Mercer County, N.J.; March 29, 1980 in Albemarle, N.C.

Children: Katherine Elizabeth.

Education: Pfeiffer College, B.A. Religion 1979; Lutheran Theological Southern Seminary, M.Div. 1984.

Ordination: May 25, 1984 by North Carolina Synod.

Calls: Pilgrim, Lexington, 1984-87; St. Matthew, Salisbury, 1987-94; Old St. Paul, Newton, 1994-; Vice Pastor at various congregations.

Other: Stewardship Committee, 1988-1994, Chair, 1992-93; Editor, Stewardship Newsletter, 1992; wrote screenplay for Synod Stewardship Video, 1992; wrote Good Friday Chancel Drama, 1987.

RIDENHOUR, ERNEST WINFORD, JR.

Date/Place of Birth: December 22, 1925; Albemarle, N.C.
Parents: Ernest Winford Ridenhour, Sr. and Alice Rosetta (Goodman) Ridenhour. A younger brother is the Reverend W. J. Ridenhour.
Spouse/Marriage Date: Evelyn Alma (Wise) Ridenhour; August 26, 1950 in High Point, N.C.
Children: Sharon Marie Bost, Joel Ernest, The Reverend Steven Paul, Mark Wayne, Crystal Annette.
Education: Duke University, Lenoir-Rhyne, A.B. 1948; Lutheran Theological Southern Seminary, B.D. 1951, also graduate study.

Ordination: July 8, 1951 by North Carolina Synod.
Calls: Mt. Hermon-Sharon, Iredell County, 1951-53; Sharon only, 1953-55; St. Paul, Startown, 1955-62; St. Paul, Iredell County, 1962-64; Organ, Rowan County, 1964-74; Nativity, Arden, 1974-89; Retired 1989 to Arden, N.C.; Vice Pastor for various congregations.
Other: Chair, Pastors' Salary Committee; Delegate, Lutheran Church in America Convention; 33 years on volunteer staff at Lutheridge; Board, North Carolina Lutheran Homes, Vice Chair; Board, Crescent View; President, Asheville-Buncombe Community Christian Ministry; Board, Hospice.

RIDENHOUR, MARTIN LUTHER

Date/Place of Birth: October 10, 1880; Cabarrus County, N.C.
Parents: John M. Ridenhour and Mary J. (Petrea) Ridenhour.
Spouse/Marriage Date: Mary Virginia (Schaeffer) Ridenhour; June 12, 1910 in Barber, N.C.
Children: Mary Kathleen, John Franklin, Elizabeth Fisher, Charles Edward, Joseph Conrad, Robert Lee, Sarah Schaeffer (married the Reverend E. R. Lineberger, Jr.).
Education: Mount Pleasant Collegiate Institute, Lenoir-Rhyne, A.B. 1906; Lutheran Theological Southern Seminary, 1909.
Ordination: 1909 by North Carolina Synod.
Calls: St. Luke, Bear Poplar-Concordia, Rowan County, 1908-11; Bethel-St. Paul, Rowan County, 1911-16; Reformation, Davie County, 1915-16; St. Stephen-Mt. Olive, Cabarrus County, 1917-19; Supply Immanuel, Rowan County, 1918; Organ-Ebenezer, Rowan County, 1919-22; Kimball Memorial, Kannapolis, 1922-37.
Date of Death/Burial Location: May 10, 1937; St. John Church, Cabarrus County, N.C.

RIDENHOUR, STEVEN PAUL

Date/Place of Birth: May 21, 1956; Newton, N.C.
Parents: The Reverend Ernest W. Ridenhour, Jr. and Evelyn (Wise) Ridenhour.
Spouse/Marriage Date: LaRue (Bomberger) Ridenhour; June 17, 1978.
Children: Matthew Steven, Jacob Luke.
Education: Lenoir-Rhyne, A.B. 1978; Lutheran Theological Southern Seminary, M.Div. 1982.
Ordination: June 6, 1982 by North Carolina Synod.
Calls: St. Paul-St. Luke, Shenandoah, Va., 1982-84; Trinity, Pulaski, Va., 1984-94; Holy Trinity, Wytheville, Va., 1994-.

Other: Alumni Board, Lutheran Theological Southern Seminary, 1988-95; Evangelical Lutheran Church in America Assembly Voting Member, 1995; visited as a member of the North Carolina Synod's Delegation to visit our companion synod - The Islands District-Papua, New Guinea.

RIDENHOUR, THOMAS EUGENE, SR.

Date/Place of Birth: November 11, 1937; Concord, N.C.
Parents: Clarence A. Ridenhour and Elizabeth (Webb) Ridenhour.
Spouse/Marriage Date: Mary Anna (Glass) Ridenhour; August 19, 1961.
Children: The Reverend Thomas Eugene, Jr., Mary Elizabeth, William Clarence.
Education: Davidson College, A.B. History, Honors, 1960; Lutheran Theological Southern Seminary, B.D. *cum laude*, 1965; Duke University, Ph.D. Religion 1972.
Ordination: July 27, 1969 by North Carolina Synod.
Calls: Resurrection, Greensboro, 1969-74.
Other: Faculty Gettysburg Seminary, 1974-91; Faculty and later Dean, Lutheran Theological Southern Seminary, 1991-; Management Committee, DPL of Lutheran Church in America, 1982-87, Chair, 1984-87; Board, Division for Ministry Evangelical Lutheran Church in America; Word and Witness Instructor, Lutheran Church in America; Development team for Renewing Project, Division for Parish Services, Lutheran Church in America; Preaching from Commitment, Lutheran Church in America - development team and instructor; Examining Committee, North Carolina Synod; Examining Committee of Western Pennsylvania-West Virginia Synod; Transition Task Force for Ministry for formation of Evangelical Lutheran Church in America.

RIDENHOUR, VICTOR CLARENCE

Date/Place of Birth: May 14, 1871; Cabarrus County, N.C.
Parents: Daniel Hazelius Ridenhour and Josephine (Petrea) Ridenhour.
Spouse/Marriage Date: Jessie Miriam (Layton) Ridenhour; October 14, 1903 in Creston, S.C.
Children: William Leighton.
Education: North Carolina College, A.B. 1899;Lutheran Theological Southern Seminary, 1902; Lenoir-Rhyne, D.D. 1933.
Ordination: 1902 by North Carolina Synod.
Calls: St. Michael, Troutman-Amity-St. Paul, Iredell County, 1902-05; St. Andrew's-St. Michael, near Columbia, S.C., 1905-06; St. John, Knoxville, Tenn., 1906-12; First, Albemarle, 1912-23; Emmanuel, Lincolnton-St. Luke, Lincoln County, 1923-30; Holy Trinity, Hickory, 1930-41.
Other: Board, Lenoir-Rhyne, 1928-41; Board, Lutheran Theological Southern Seminary.
Date of Death/Burial Location: June 20, 1941; Oakwood Cemetery, Hickory, N.C.

RIDENHOUR, WILLIAM JACOB

Date/Place of Birth: May 29, 1930; Albemarle, N.C.
Parents: Ernest Winford Ridenhour, Sr. and Alice Rosetta (Goodman) Ridenhour. An older brother is the Reverend E. W. Ridenhour, Jr.

Spouse/Marriage Date: Grace Allen (Huffman) Ridenhour; June 6, 1953 in Rowan County, N.C.
Children: Carroll William, David Jacob, Alice Jo, John Nugent.
Education: Lenoir-Rhyne, A.B. 1952; Lutheran Theological Southern Seminary, M.Div. 1955.
Ordination: 1955 by North Carolina Synod.
Calls: Holy Communion, Dallas, 1955-58; St. Paul, Rowan County, 1958-63; Mission Developer/Pastor, St. Andrew, Portsmouth, Va., 1963-69; Mission Developer/Pastor, King of Kings, Fairfax, Va., 1969-91; Interim Pastor at various congregations; retired 1995 to Fairfax, Va.
Other: Worked with Alcohol Abuse Programs; Camp Committee, North Carolina Synod, 1963.

RIEMENSCHNEIDER, GEORGE HENRY

Place of Birth: Germany (another source says in Pendleton County, Va.).
Education: Goettingen University, Germany.
License/Ordination: Licensed 1808 and ordained 1818 by Ministerium of Pennsylvania.
Calls: Transferred in 1824 to Tennessee Synod from Maryland Synod. In Virginia, he served Trinity, Augusta County, 1810-1823; Salem, Mt. Sidney, Augusta County, 1811-1820; Peaked Mountain, Rockingham County, 1812-1817; and was in Pendleton County, W.Va., 1821-1834. No record is available of his connection with Tennessee Synod after 1834. His son was the Reverend John Junius of the Virginia Synod.

RILEY, EBER LEROY, JR.

Date/Place of Birth: March 31, 1948; Columbia, S.C.
Parents: Eber LeRoy Riley, Sr. and Alice (Fritz) Riley. A younger brother is the Reverend Michael Fritz Riley.
First Spouse/Marriage Date: Brenda Kay (Amick) Riley; August 15, 1970 in Columbia, S.C.
Children of First Marriage: Eber LeRoy, III, Mary Alison.
Second Spouse/Marriage Date: Elizabeth F. (Pryor) Riley; April 13, 1996.
Step-children: Christopher Stuart Pryor, David Pryor.
Education: Lenoir-Rhyne, B.A. English *cum laude* with Honors in English, 1970; Lutheran Theological Southern Seminary, M.Div. 1974; Upsala College, D.D. 1994; Lenoir-Rhyne, D.D. 1996.
Ordination: June 2, 1974 by South Carolina Synod.
Calls: Co-Pastor, Augsburg, Winston-Salem, 1974-80; Assistant to the Bishop, New Jersey Synod, Lutheran Church in America, 1980-87; Assistant to the Bishop, New Jersey Synod, Evangelical Lutheran Church in America, 1988-91; Bishop, New Jersey Synod, Evangelical Lutheran Church in America, 1991-.
Other: North Carolina Synod: PLMD Task Force; Youth Ministry Committee; Director, Lutheran Church in America Strength For Mission Appeal, 1977-79; Board, Lenoir-Rhyne, 1979-80; Division for Parish Services, Lutheran Church in America Shared Staff for Stewardship Development Program, 1982-87; Lutheran Church in America Convention Voting Representative, 1984, 1986; Evangelical Lutheran Church in America Constituting Convention Voting Representative, 1987.

RILEY, MICHAEL FRITZ
Date/Place of Birth: October 31, 1949; Columbia, S.C.
Parents: Eber Leroy Riley, Sr. and Alice (Fritz) Riley. Older brother is Bishop Eber Leroy Riley, Jr. of the New Jersey Synod.
Spouse: Betty (Bollinger) Riley.
Children: Teresa Michelle, Bryna Gail, Christopher Michael.
Education: Lenoir-Rhyne, A.B. 1971; University of South Carolina, M.Ed. 1974; University of North Carolina at Greensboro, Ed.D. 1990; Lutheran Theological Southern Seminary, M.Div. 1998.
Ordination: June 6, 1998 by North Carolina Synod.
Calls: Calvary, Morganton, 1998-.

RIMMER, JOHN PAUL
Date/Place of Birth: April 12, 1921; Troutman, N.C.
Parents: John Franklin Rimmer and Lizzie Lavina (Troutman) Rimmer.
Spouse/Marriage Date: Eva Bryte (Bess) Rimmer; April 8, 1944 in Cherryville, N.C.
Children: The Reverend John Thomas, Martha Jane Cadwallader, Jerry Franklin.
Education: Appalachian State Teachers College, one year, Lenoir-Rhyne, A.B. 1943; Hamma Divinity School, 1945; graduate work at Lutheran Theological Southern Seminary.
Ordination: February 18, 1945 by Ohio Synod.
Calls: Hopeful-Hebron, Florence, Ky., 1945-47; Grace, Bessemer City, 1948-52; Mt. Hermon, Cabarrus County, 1952-59; Immanuel, Rowan County, 1959-67; Prince of Peace, Kinston, 1967-78; Mission Developer/Pastor, Messiah of the Mountains, Burnsville, 1978-82; retired December 31, 1982 in Cherryville, N.C.; Vice Pastor at various congregations.
Other: Camp Committee, 1965-70; Nominating Committee, 1968-69; Evangelism Committee, 1969-71.

RIMMER, JOHN THOMAS
Date/Place of Birth: May 7, 1945; Kenton County, Ky.
Parents: The Reverend John Paul Rimmer and Eva Bryte (Bess) Rimmer.
Spouse/Marriage Date: Reeda (Hampton) Rimmer; August 26, 1967 in Rockwell, N.C.
Children: Justin Thomas.
Education: Lenoir-Rhyne, A.B. 1968; Lutheran Theological Southern Seminary, M.Div. 1972.
Ordination: June 4, 1972 by North Carolina Synod.
Calls: Christ, East Spencer, 1972-78; Vice Pastor at various congregations.
Other: Dropped from Roll, 1982.

RINEHART, MICHAEL WARREN
Date/Place of Birth: August 2, 1961; Columbus, Ohio.
Parents: The Reverend Warren W. Rinehart and Patricia L. Rinehart.
Spouse/Marriage Date: Susan Elise (Warne) Rinehart; August 13, 1988.

Child: John David.
Education: Valparaiso University, B.Music, 1983; Trinity Seminary, M.Div. 1988.
Ordination: June 19, 1988 by Southeastern Iowa Synod.
Calls: St. Paul, Davenport, Iowa, 1988-94; Christ, Charlotte, 1994-97; Grace, Conroe, Texas, 1997-.
Other: Confirmation Curriculum for Augsburg Fortress, Publishers; led music at three The Lutheran Church- Missouri Synod National Youth Events.

RINN, RONALD ALLEN

Date/Place of Birth: September 15, 1945; Stamford, Texas.
Parents: Roland Alfred Rinn and Alvine (Kainer) Rinn.
Spouse/Marriage Date: Cynthia (Heinemeier) Rinn; August 27, 1967 in San Antonio, Texas.
Children: Mary Elizabeth, Erin Aine.
Education: Texas Lutheran College, B.A. 1968; Lutheran Theological Southern Seminary, M.Div. 1972, D.Min. 1992.
Ordination: June 18, 1972 by Florida Synod.
Calls: Christ the King, South Miami, Fla., 1972-75; St. Matthew, Jacksonville, Fla., 1975-89; Augsburg, Winston-Salem, 1989-.

RISER, GEORGE ALBERT

Date/Place of Birth: About 1875; Newberry County, S.C. An older brother was the Reverend Sidney T. Riser.
Spouse: Miss Chapman in Newberry County, S.C.
Education: Newberry College, A.B. 1897; Lutheran Theological Southern Seminary, (while at Newberry), 1898.
Ordination: 1898 by North Carolina Synod.
Calls: Mt. Olive-St. Stephen, Cabarrus County, 1898-99; Salem, near Mt. Sidney, Va., 1899-1902.
Date of Death/Burial Location: 1902; Thornrose Cemetery, Staunton, Va., beside his older brother, who had served as Pastor there.

RISER, WILBER HOUCK

Date/Place of Birth: December 4, 1868; Orangeburg, S.C.
Parents: William D. Riser and Carrie (Haigler) Riser.
Spouse/Marriage Date: Zenith (Layton) Riser; May 18, 1898 in St. Matthews, S.C.
Children: Thelma, Virginia, Zenith.
Education: Newberry College, A.B. 1895; Lutheran Theological Southern Seminary, 1898; graduate study, Chicago Seminary.
Ordination: 1898 by Virginia Synod.
Calls: Wardensville, W.Va., 1898-99; near Woodstock, Va., 1899-1901; First, Norfolk, Va., 1901-11; St. Mark, China Grove, 1911-17; transferred to Virginia Synod, 1917, serving at Lynchburg for short while until health failed; South Carolina Synod, 1917-24; St. Stephen, Lexington, 1917-20; St. Matthew, Lexington County, 1919-20, and St. Peter, Chapin, 1921-23; St. John, Pomaria, 1921-22, retired 1922 at Columbia, S.C.
Date of Death/Burial Location: March 17, 1924; Orangeburg, S.C.

RISER, YANCEY VON ALLEN
Date/Place of Birth: January 13, 1873; Saluda County, S.C.
Parents: J. H. Riser and Elizabeth (Etheredge) Riser.
Spouse/Marriage Date: Jessie (Summer) Riser; November 27, 1902 in Newberry, S.C.
Children: Rupert Summer.
Education: Newberry College, A.B. 1895; Lutheran Theological Southern Seminary, 1898; graduate study, Philadelphia Seminary.
Ordination: 1898 by South Carolina Synod.
Calls: Sumter, Florence, Newberry and Lexington Counties, S.C., 1898-1916; Frieden's-Sharon, Gibsonville, 1916-21; transferred to South Carolina Synod, 1929; retired 1927 near Pomaria, S.C.
Other: Taught in schools and operated a dairy farm after retiring.
Date of Death/Burial Location: February 23, 1962; Summer Family Cemetery, near Pomaria, S.C.

RISINGER, PAUL DAVID
Date/Place of Birth: May 18, 1870; Leesville, S.C.
Parents: Wesley Risinger and Rosa (Shealy) Risinger.
First Spouse/Marriage Date: Ida Mae (Brown) Risinger of Iredell County, a sister of the Reverend Charles L. Brown, D.D., missionary in Japan, and later a Secretary of United Lutheran Church in America Board of Foreign Missions; July 19, 1899 in Monroe, N.C.
Second Spouse/Marriage Date: Grace (Caughman) Risinger of Leesville, S.C.; January 30, 1941 in Columbia, S.C.
Education: Lenoir-Rhyne, Newberry College, A.B. 1897; Lutheran Theological Southern Seminary, 1898.
Ordination: 1897 by Tennessee Synod.
Calls: St. Luke-Morning Star, Monroe, 1897-99; Holy Communion-Antioch-Philadelphia, Dallas, 1907-11; Trinity-Concordia, Landis, 1922-24; St. Stephen-St. John, Lenoir, 1924-28; Holy Trinity, Troutman, 1928-36; St. Paul, Iredell County, 1928-30, 1932; Lone Star and Elloree (1899-1904), Ehrhardt (1917-22), Lexington (1911-16), and Johnston (1904-07) in South Carolina; Senoia and Haralson, Ga.; retired 1936 at Leesville, S.C., and supplied churches in that area; again active, 1941-47, Silverstreet, and one year in Saluda County, S.C.; retired again 1948 at Leesville, S.C.
Other: Chair, Board, Summerland College.
Date of Death/Burial Location: November 12, 1950; Leesville, S.C.

RITCHIE, CARL LAEMMLE
Date/Place of Birth: March 28, 1932; Charlotte, N.C.
Parents: Hubert Edmund Ritchie and Gertrude Eloise (McKenzie) Ritchie.
Spouse/Marriage Date: Mary Frances (Brown) Ritchie; August 20, 1955 in Danville, Va.
Children: Mary Eloise Gilreath, Luther Hubert, Deborah Ruth Fox, Martha Elizabeth Mountain.

Education: Lenoir-Rhyne, A.B. History/Religion 1954; Lutheran Theological Southern Seminary, M.Div. 1957.

Ordination: June 9, 1957 by North Carolina Synod.

Calls: Mt. Calvary, Claremont, 1957-60; Mission Developer/Pastor, Church of Our Father, Greensboro, 1960-62; St. John, Jacksonville, Fla., 1962-66; Christ the King, Temple Terrace, Fla., 1966-69; First, Lexington, 1970-81; St. Michael, High Point, 1981-86; Interim, A Mighty Fortress, Summerville, S.C., 1986-89; retired December 31, 1987 in Charlotte, N.C.; Vice Pastor at various congregations.

Other: Florida Synod: Dean, Northern District, 1965-67; Youth Ministry Committee, 1965-67; Contact Pastor, University of South Florida, 1967-69; Parish Education Committee, 1965-66; Youth Action Adults Coordinator for Youth Expo, 1969; Delegate, Lutheran Church in America Convention, 1968; North Carolina Synod: Evangelism Committee, 1970-82; Board, North Carolina Lutheran Family Services, 1984-86.

RITCHIE, CLARENCE ROSS, JR.

Date/Place of Birth: September 25, 1932; Rocky Mount, N.C.

Parents: The Reverend Clarence Ross Ritchie, Sr. and Barbara Ada (Brady) Ritchie. A great-grandson of the Reverend George H. Cox.

Spouse/Marriage Date: Jo Anne (Hall) Ritchie; May 22, 1955 in Salisbury, N.C.

Children: Janice Brady Barbee, Clarence Ross, III, Joanna Kirk Britt, Barbara Kathryn Lippard, Camilla Hall Berger.

Education: Lenoir-Rhyne, A.B. 1954, D.D. 1980; Lutheran Theological Southern Seminary, M.Div. 1957, S.T.M. 1967.

Ordination: June 9, 1957 by North Carolina Synod.

Calls: Good Shepherd, Goldsboro, 1957-60; St. Andrew's, Columbia, S.C., 1960-66; First, Albemarle, 1966- 71; Augsburg, Winston-Salem, 1971-88; Director, Planning Giving, Lutheran Theological Southern Seminary, 1988-91; retired December 31, 1991 in Chapin, S.C.; Vice Pastor at various congregations.

Other: North Carolina Synod: Secretary, Eastern Conference, 1958-60; Board, Lutheran Services for the Aging, Inc.; Executive Board, 1976-82; Board, Lutheran Theological Southern Seminary, 1967; Board, Lenoir- Rhyne, 1968-76; Stewardship Committee, Chair; Nominating Committee, Chair; Delegate to Lutheran Church in America Conventions; South Carolina Synod: Executive Board, 1965-66; Evangelism Committee, 1962-65; Church Vocations Committee, 1962-66; Contributor to *Light for Today, Luther Life, Lutheran Men, The Home Altar;* writer of series of lessons and Teacher's Guides for Young People and Adults in the Augsburg Series of the Lutheran Church in America Sunday Church School Curriculum. Attended Lutheran World Federation Assembly in Budapest, Hungary, July 1984.

RITCHIE, CLARENCE ROSS, SR.
Date/Place of Birth: October 18, 1900; Concord, N.C.
Parents: John Henry Ritchie and Effie Best (Cox) Ritchie.
Mother was a daughter of the Reverend George H. Cox.
Spouse/Marriage Date: Barbara Ada (Brady) Ritchie; June 14, 1928 in Columbia, S.C.
Children: Barbara Ada (married the Reverend Wayne S. Allran), the Reverend Clarence Ross, Jr.
Education: Mount Pleasant Collegiate Institute, Lenoir-Rhyne, A.B. 1924, D.D. 1952; Lutheran Theological Southern Seminary, B.D. 1927; University of South Carolina, M.A. 1927; Harvard University Chaplain School, 1942.
Ordination: 1927 by North Carolina Synod.
Calls: Trinity, Rocky Mount, 1927-39; First, Lexington, 1939-50, on leave 1942-46, as U.S. Army Chaplain (Major), with service in European Theater; supplied Lebanon, Davidson County, 1947-48; Mission Developer/Pastor, Good Shepherd, Morristown, Tenn., 1959-62.
Other: Superintendent, Lutheran Southern Mountain Mission Work, Konnarock, Va., 1951-59; Director, Christian Higher Education Year Appeal, North Carolina Synod, 1949-50; literary contributions: *American Standard of Living,* M.A. thesis, bound copy in University of South Carolina library; pamphlet, *Facts on Southern Mountain Work;* Editor, *Konnarock Echoes,* 1951-59.
Date of Death/Burial Location: July 15, 1962; Holy Trinity Church, Little Mountain, S.C.

RITCHIE, EDWARD LEE
Date/Place of Birth: March 27, 1876; Cabarrus County, N.C.
Parents: George E. Ritchie and Lundie Elizabeth (Barrier) Ritchie.
Spouse/Marriage Date: Edith Pearl (Ryan) Ritchie; June 7, 1911 in Washington, D.C.
Children: Lucile Elizabeth, Josephine Love, Margaret Lee.
Education: North Carolina College, A.B. 1901; Lutheran Theological Southern Seminary, 1905, B.D. 1927.
Ordination: 1905 by North Carolina Synod.
Calls: Organized Calvary, Spencer-Christ, East Spencer, 1905-07; Burkes Garden, Va., Bristol, Tenn., and Waynesboro, Va., 1907-22; also in Pennsylvania, 1922-38; retired 1938 and supplied in York County, Pa., to 1940, and in Washington, D.C., 1940-42.
Date of Death/Burial Location: December 5, 1943; Fort Lincoln Cemetery, Washington, D.C.

RITCHIE, GROVER OSCAR, SR.
Date/Place of Birth: February 12, 1886; Cabarrus County, N.C.
Parents: Solomon Monroe Ritchie and Mary (Cress) Ritchie.
Spouse/Marriage Date: Alma (Ridenhour) Ritchie; December 28, 1910 in Cabarrus County, N.C.
Children: Harold A., Voigt, Eugene, Grover Oscar, Jr., Paul E.
Education: Mount Pleasant Collegiate Institute, Newberry College, A.B. 1909; Lutheran Theological Southern Seminary, 1913.
Ordination: 1913 by North Carolina Synod.

Calls: Salem-Grace, Rowan County, 1913-18; Faith-Immanuel, Faith, 1918-19, Faith only, 1919-26; supplied Wittenberg, Granite Quarry, 1922-26; Grace, Thomasville, 1926-37.
Other: Board, Children's Home of the South, 1931-37.
Date of Death/Burial Location: February 8, 1937; St. John Church, Cabarrus County, N.C.

RITCHIE, HOKE HENDERSON, SR.

Date/Place of Birth: September 20, 1916; Rowan County, N.C.
Parents: Gilbert Henderson Ritchie and Ila C. (Brown) Ritchie.
First Spouse/Marriage Date: Clara Eunice (Cook) Ritchie; June 20, 1944 in Kannapolis, N.C.
Children of First Marriage: Mirian Brown Gillespie, John David, Hoke Henderson, Jr., Martha Ila.
Second Spouse/Marriage Date: Betty Louise (Sechler) (Ballard) Ritchie; June 6, 1987.
Education: Lenoir-Rhyne, A.B. 1941; Lutheran Theological Southern Seminary, B.D. 1944.
Ordination: July 16, 1944 by North Carolina Synod.
Calls: Holy Trinity-Mt. Pleasant, Mt. Zion,-Old Mt. Pleasant, Watauga County, 1944-46; Daniel's, Lincoln County-Grace, Catawba County, 1946-51; Trinity, Rocky Mount, 1951-66; Grace, Thomasville, 1966-83; retired December 31, 1983 to Concord, N.C.; Vice Pastor to various congregations.
Other: American Missions Committee, 1962-63; Stewardship Committee, 1969; Board, Lutheran Theological Southern Seminary, 1954-60; Statistician, North Carolina Synod, 1959-62; Executive Board, North Carolina Synod, 1959-73; Board, North Carolina Lutheran Homes, 1974-83; North Carolina Synod delegate, Lutheran Church Conventions, 1956, 1958, 1960, 1962; Secretary and President, Southern Conference; Civitan Club; Chaplain, Hospice of Cabarrus County, Inc.; President, Thomasville Ministerial Association.

RITCHIE, JOHN ALEXANDER

Date/Place of Birth: September 13, 1908; Rowan County, N.C.
Parents: Charles E. Ritchie and Lillie (Bost) Ritchie.
First Spouse/Marriage Date: Julia Kidd (Whitener) Ritchie of Hickory; July 1932 in York, S.C.
Children of First Marriage: John Kidd.
Second Spouse/Marriage Date: Ama Lee (Boyd) Ritchie; August 2, 1942 in Corydon, Ind.
Children of Second Marriage: Mary Lee Levitt.
Education: Lenoir-Rhyne, B.S. 1931; Lutheran Theological Southern Seminary, B.D. 1935; graduate study, University of North Carolina; Presbyterian Seminary, Louisville, Ky.; Biblical Seminary; Philadelphia Seminary, S.T.M. 1939; Union Seminary and Columbia University, M.A. Religious Education 1953; graduate work at Duke University, New York University and Yale University.
Ordination: 1935 by North Carolina Synod.

Calls: Mt. Olive, Hickory, 1935-37; Supply, First, Greensboro, 1939-40; St. David, Kannapolis, 1947-51; Supply, Pilgrim, Davidson County, 1951-52; Supply, Charleston, W.Va.; Corydon and Milan, Ind., 1942-45; Supply, Laurel and Louisville, Miss., 1945-47; inactive in ministry, 1951-56; supply, St. John, Taylorsville, 1956-65, full time, 1965-73; retired September 13, 1973; Vice Pastor at various congregations.
Other: Part-time instructor (Bible), Lenoir-Rhyne, 1961-; Literary contributions: *Revelation in Rhyme,* a small book of Biblical poetry; *Thus Saith the Lord,* a popular theology for the laity; and *The Father-Son Revelation,* a teaching outline for Bible study.
Date of Death/Burial Location: August 10, 1983; Concordia Lutheran Church Cemetery, China Grove, N.C.

RITCHIE, WILEY WASHINGTON JOSEPHUS

Date/Place of Birth: September 24, 1867; Faith, N.C.
Parents: Peter Alexander Ritchie and Elizabeth Camilla (Brown) Ritchie. A half brother of the Reverends C. L. T. and J. H. C. Fisher.
Spouse/Marriage Date: Anna Maria (Henkel) Ritchie, daughter of Dr. Solon P. C. Henkel, October 25, 1899 in New Market, Va.
Children: Charles Mathias, Frederick Henry, Miller Alfred Franklin.
Education: North Carolina College, 1896; Lutheran Theological Southern Seminary, 1899.
Ordination: 1898 by Virginia Synod, and transferred 1900 to North Carolina.
Calls: Macedonia, Burlington-Peace, Guilford County, 1899-1903; transferred 1903 to Virginia Synod; Mt. Hermon, Newport, Augusta County, 1903-05; St. Peter, Churchville, Augusta County, 1905-14; Kimberling, Wythe County, 1914-16; retired at Churchville, Va.
Date of Death/Burial Location: September 27, 1953; Green Hill Cemetery, Churchville, Va.

ROBBE, RANDY STEPHEN

Date/Place of Birth: March 16, 1947; Tooele County, Utah.
Education: Stanford University, A.B. 1969; Lutheran Theological Southern Seminary, M.Div. 1973.
Ordination: May 17, 1973 by Southeastern Synod.
Calls: Assistant Pastor, St. James, Fayetteville, 1973-75; Mt. Moriah, China Grove, 1975-82.
Other: Resigned July 25, 1982.

ROBERTSON, AUSTIN FULTON, JR.

Date/Place of Birth: October 30, 1936; Columbia, S.C.
Parents: Austin Fulton Robertson, Sr. and Margaret (Wise) Robertson.
First Spouse/Marriage Date: Betty Jo (Meredith) Robertson of Anderson, S.C.; June 29, 1957 in West Columbia, S.C. His parents were Methodists, hers Baptists.
Children of First Marriage: Rachel Elizabeth Simmons, Bruce Meredith, Jo Margaret.
Second Spouse/Marriage Date: Mary Worth (Burton) Robertson; March 4, 1979.
Step-Children of Second Marriage: James Burton Chesnutt, Catherine Rogers Chesnutt, Elizabeth Marshall Chesnutt.
Education: University of South Carolina, B.A. 1958, M.Ed. 1972; Lutheran Theological Southern Seminary, M.Div. 1961.

Ordination: May 28, 1961 by South Carolina Synod.
Calls: Grace, Liberty, 1961-62; Holy Cross, Charleston Heights, S.C., 1962-67; St. John, Pomaria, S.C., 1967-72; St. Mark, Blythewood, S.C., 1982-90; Mt. Pleasant, Saluda, S.C., 1990-95; retired October 1996 to Columbia, S.C.
Other: Counseling, Midlands Technical College, Columbia, S.C., 1973-82; Chaplain, U.S. Naval Reserves, 1962-69.

ROBERTSON, GEORGE GASTON

Date/Place of Birth: November 27, 1916; Greensboro, Guilford County, N.C.
Parents: James W. Robertson, Sr. and Netta B. (Cook) Robertson.
Spouse/Marriage Date: Zerma Plinia (Smith) Robertson; December 27, 1946 in Cramerton, N.C. His and his wife's parents were Methodists.
Children: Sylvia Lee, Megan Zerma Walck.
Education: Lenoir-Rhyne, A.B. 1949, following war service; Lutheran Theological Southern Seminary, B.D. 1952; Pastoral Care, North Carolina Baptist Hospital, Winston-Salem, 1964-65.
Ordination: June 15, 1952 by North Carolina Synod.
Calls: Christ, East Spencer, 1952-56; Grace, Bessemer City, 1956-61; Trinity, Concord, 1961-64; Chaplain, Veterans Administration, Tomah, Wis., 1965-82.
Other: U.S. Army Medical Corps, 30th Infantry Division, World War II, four and a half years to June 1945; wounded three times in combat; received Bronze Star, and five combat stars; North Carolina Council of Churches, 1962-63.
Date of Death/Burial Location: July 25, 1986; Oakgrove Memorial Gardens Cemetery, Tomah, Wis.

ROBERTSON, WILLIAM ELLIS, JR.

Date/Place of Birth: April 28, 1953; Hendersonville, N.C.
Parents: William Ellis Robertson, Sr. and Billie (Rose) Robertson.
Spouse/Marriage Date: Ann Blair (Lindsey) Robertson; September 11, 1982 in Lynchburg, Va.
Children: Paul, Sam, Anne Virginia.
Education: Davidson College, B.A. 1975; Harvard Divinity School, M.Div. 1980; additional courses, Lutheran Theological Southern Seminary.
Ordination: September 17, 1982 by North Carolina Synod.
Calls: Co-Pastor, St. Mark's, Charlotte, 1982-85; Reformation, Philadelphia, Pa., 1985-87; The Covenant Center (Special Call), Western Carolina Center, Morganton, 1987-95.

ROBINSON, CARROLL LEE

Date/Place of Birth: May 20, 1937; Gastonia, N.C.
Parents: John Hall Robinson and Robylee (Davis) Robinson.
First Spouse/Marriage Date: Marie Anita (Beatty) Robinson; August 16, 1958 in Charlotte, N.C.
Children of First Marriage: Michael William, Yvonne Carol, Gail Lanora, Lisa Deann.
Second Spouse/Marriage Date: Patricia (Bradbury) Robinson; July 31, 1977 in Salisbury, N.C.
Children of Second Marriage: Jennifer Lynn Crisp.
Third Spouse/Marriage Date: Barbara Anne (Boland) Robinson; October 11, 1992.

Child of Third Marriage: Daniel Pettus Boland Robinson.
Education: Warren Wilson Junior College, 1956; Lenoir-Rhyne, A.B. History 1958; Lutheran Theological Southern Seminary, B.D. 1962.
Ordination: June 17, 1962 by North Carolina Synod.
Calls: Holy Trinity, Reidsville, 1962-64; Ascension, Wilson, 1964-68; St. Paul, Dallas, 1968-71; Our Savior, Dallas, 1971-74; Salem, Salisbury, 1975-89; Lebanon, Cleveland, 1990-; Vice Pastor at various congregations.
Other: World Missions Committee, 1967-68.

ROBINSON, CARROLL LEONARD

Date/Place of Birth: August 14, 1940; Gastonia, N.C.
Parents: William Leonard Robinson and Isabel Elizabeth (Lewis) Robinson Hoffman.
Spouse/Marriage Date: Greta Gail (Ball) Robinson; June 15, 1962.
Children: Teresa Gail Ratliff, Dana Lea, Carol Edith.
Education: Lenoir-Rhyne, A.B. 1962; Lutheran Theological Southern Seminary, M.Div. 1966; University of Kentucky School of Medicine, Clinical Pastoral Education, 1970, Intensive Training Certificate, 1974; Institute for Advanced Study in Relations Psychotherapy, Intensive Training Certificate, 1976.
Ordination: June 5, 1966 by North Carolina Synod.
Calls: St. Philip, Newberry, S.C., 1966-68; Holy Communion, Spartanburg, S.C., 1969-70; Advanced Chaplain Intern, Clinical Pastoral Education, St. Luke Episcopal Hospital, Houston, Texas, 1971; Director of Pastoral Care, Clinical Chaplain II, South Carolina Department of Mental Health, 1982-; Interim Pastor: House of Prayer, Lake City, Texas; Prince of Peace, Salisbury; Lutheran Church of the Living Word, Laurinburg; St. Mark, Lumberton, New Bethel, Richfield; Pomaria, Pomaria, S.C.
Other: Founder of Columbia Association for Rational Thinking; Rational Emotive Behavioral therapist for children and adults; Synod Christian Education Committee.

ROBINSON, D. TIMOTHY

Date/Place of Birth: July 19, 1927; Hagerstown, Md.
Parents: Ralph C. Robinson and Margaret (Rohrer) Robinson.
Spouse/Marriage Date: Gwendolyn (Witt) Robinson; October 25, 1952 in Lake City, Fla.
Children: Mary Juanita Walker, Gwen Lynn Liebenrood, Martha Kim Stephenson.
Education: Newberry College, B.S. English Language and Literature 1953; Gettysburg Seminary, B.D. 1960.
Ordination: 1960 by Central Pennsylvania Synod.
Calls: St. John, Espy, Pa., 1960-61; Trinity, Camp Hill, Pa., 1961-63; Holy Communion, Yeagertown, Pa., 1963-65; Christ, Dallastown, Pa., 1965-70; Advent, York, Pa., 1970-80; Chester-York Lutheran Parish, York, S.C., 1980-83; St. Mark, Isle of Palms, S.C., 1983-86; retired 1987 to Calabash, N.C.
Other: Military Service - U.S. Navy, 1945-47; Sermon contributor to *Ministers Annual,* 1987-90; President, The Lutheran Camping Corporation; Board, The Lutheran Social Services; Mifflin County Youth Probation Board; President, Mifflin County, Pa. Ministerium; President, Lewistown Area Pastoral Association; Commission on Camping Executive Board; Chaplain, U.S. Steel Workers Convention, 1975; Father of the Year, Greater Harrisburg, Pa., 1962; *Who's Who Outstanding Religious Leaders of America,* 1978; College campus preacher and guest lecturer.

ROBINSON, HARRY HOOVER, JR.
Date/Place of Birth: June 12, 1924; High Shoals, Gaston County, N.C.
Parents: Harry Hoover Robinson, Sr. and Lois (Hovis) Robinson.
Spouse/Marriage Date: Maxine E. (Heafner) Robinson; June 18, 1946 in Dallas, Gaston County, N.C.
Children: Pacita Yvonne Luckey, wife of the Reverend Ronald G. Luckey, Harry Hoover, III, Tori Lilje Barnard.
Education: Lenoir-Rhyne, A.B. 1948, D.D. 1982; Lutheran Theological Southern Seminary, B.D. 1951; Wake Forest Seminary, D.Min. 1977.
Ordination: June 1951 by North Carolina Synod.
Calls: Holy Comforter, Belmont, 1951-63; St. Paul, Durham, 1963-84; Director, Lutheran Family Services Public Relations, Publicity and Development, 1984-87; retired December 1987 to Durham, N.C.
Other: Board, North Carolina Lutheran Homes; Chair, Committee on Social Ministry, 1965-67; Chair, Lutheran Student Foundation, Durham; organized the Durham County Community Living Program for Mentally Retarded Adults; began the first camping experience for the mentally retarded at Burnsville, N.C. while serving as Chair of the Social Ministry Committee; Outstanding Civic Service Award by Durham Civitan Clubs, 1980; Man of Year, Chamber of Commerce, Belmont, 1963. Retired December 1987 to Durham, N.C., later moving to Myrtle Beach, S.C.

ROEVER, ELDON DIETRICH
Date/Place of Birth: August 4, 1919; Janesville, Iowa.
Parents: William Henry Roever and Maria (Voigts) Roever.
Spouse/Marriage Date: Martha Louise (Teeter) Roever; June 24, 1945 in Conover, N.C.
Children: Brenda Steed, Sylvia Myers, Eldon David, John Timothy.
Education: Wartburg College, B.A. 1942; Wartburg Seminary, B.D. 1945.
Ordination: June 10, 1945; Iowa Synod.
Calls: St. Paul, Hampton, Iowa, 1945-47; Mt. Zion, Conover, 1947-69; Beck's, Lexington, 1969-89; Vice Pastor at various congregations.
Other: World Missions Committee; Board, Lutheran Triad Ministerial Association; Secretary, Lexington Ministerial Association; President, Lexington Diabetic Association.
Date of Death/Burial Location: April 1, 1989; Beck's Lutheran Church Cemetery, Lexington, N.C.

ROGERS, JAMES EDWARD
Date/Place of Birth: January 14, 1939; Canton, Ohio.
Parents: Joseph Edward Rogers and Thelma Gertrude (Lucas) Rogers.
Spouse/Marriage Date: Marlene Sue (Vest) Rogers; June 25, 1966 in Roanoke, Va.
Children: Shannon Christine.
Education: St. Andrew's Presbyterian College, B.A. 1968; Lutheran Theological Southern Seminary, M.Div. 1972.
Ordination: June 11, 1972 by Virginia Synod.
Calls: Nazareth, Rural Hall, 1972-78; Lutheran Church of the Living Word, Laurinburg, 1978-85; Morning Star, Matthews, 1985-88.
Other: President, Forsyth Lutheran Council; Synodical Worship and Music Committee.
Date of Death/Burial Location: November 2, 1988; ashes interred at Sharon Memorial Park, Charlotte, N.C.

ROGERS, LOUIS VICTOR
Date/Place of Birth: December 3, 1930; Wilmington, Del.
Parents: Dr. Victor C. Rogers and Jennie F. Rogers.
Spouse/Marriage Date: Lois Jane (Wittchen) Rogers; June 19, 1954 in Wilmington, Del.
Children: Jeffrey Scott, Gregory Dean, Jonathan Todd.
Education: Gettysburg College, B.A. 1953; Philadelphia Seminary, B.A. 1957; University of North Carolina at Chapel Hill, M.A. 1973.
Ordination: May 26, 1957 by Eastern Pennsylvania Synod.
Calls: St. Luke, Noxen, Pa. and Reformation, Harvey's Lake, Pa., 1957-59; Nescopeck Parish, Nescopeck, Pa., 1959-62; Campus Pastor, University of Delaware, Newark, Del., 1963-66; Chaplain, Lenoir-Rhyne, 1966- 76; Pastor/Developer, Prince of Peace, Columbia, Miss., 1977-81; New Hope, Sallis, Miss., 1981-83; St. Mark, Lumberton, 1983-84.
Date of Death/Burial Location: August 30, 1984; Miller's Lutheran Church Cemetery, Hickory, N.C.

ROOF, EDWIN F. K.
Date/Place of Birth: September 19, 1888; Calhoun County, S.C.
Parents: Edwin J. Roof and Ann (Kyzer) Roof.
First Spouse: First wife died not long after marriage.
Second Spouse/Marriage Date: Mary Ellen (Wilson) Roof; September 19, 1918 in Walhalla, S.C.
Children of Second Marriage: Edwin, Mary Ellen.
Education: Newberry College, A.B. 1910; Lutheran Theological Southern Seminary, 1914; Philadelphia Seminary, B.D. 1921.
Ordination: 1914 by South Carolina Synod.
Calls: Ehrhardt, S.C., 1914-17; Oglethorpe, Ga., 1917-19; Rincon, Ga., 1919-22; St. James-Immanuel, Rockwell, 1922-25; Lutheran Chapel-Center Grove, China Grove, 1925-28; St. Matthew, Wilmington, 1928-29; St. Paul, Grafton, W.Va., 1929-53; Silver Valley-Lebanon, Davidson County, 1953-54.
Other: Secretary, 1941-44, President, 1944-47, West Virginia Synod.
Date of Death/Burial Location: October 24, 1954; Walhalla, S.C.

ROOF, FRANCIS KEITT

Date/Place of Birth: October 17, 1877; Lexington County, S.C.
Parents: Daniel James Roof and Jane Esther (Buff) Roof.
Brothers were the Reverends W. H. and W. J. Roof; a sister was
Mattie Anna who married the Reverend Enoch Hite.
First Spouse/Marriage Date: Mary Etta (Campbell) Roof;
August 1894 near Lexington, S.C.
Children of First Marriage: Naomi Alliene, Lila Fay (married
the Reverend Victor D. Derrick), the Reverend Francis Kearney,
Gladys Evelyn.
Second Spouse/Marriage Date: Claudia Ella (Yount) Roof of
Catawba County, N.C.; November 29, 1928 in Charleston, S.C.
Education: Lenoir-Rhyne, Newberry College, A.B. 1897; Lutheran Theological Southern
Seminary, 1900, B.D. 1927.
Ordination: 1900 by Tennessee Synod.
Calls: St. Timothy-St. Paul and Old St. Paul, Catawba County, 1900-12; Beth Eden,
Newton, 1900-05; Supply, St. Luke, Catawba County, 1904, and St. James, Catawba
County, 1905; Calvary, Morganton-Mt. Hebron, Hildebran, 1920-24; Cedar Grove and St.
James, Leesville, Lexington County, S.C., 1913-20; Mt. Hermon, Emmanuel, and St.
David's, West Columbia, S.C., 1924-38.
Date of Death/Burial Location: December 31, 1938; Mt. Hermon Church Cemetery, near
West Columbia, S.C.

ROOF, LESTER ODA, JR.

Date/Place of Birth: July 25, 1931; Leesville, S.C.
Parents: The Reverend Lester Oda Roof, Sr. and Virgie Eula
(Sandel) Roof.
Spouse/Marriage Date: Carolyn Doris (Lackey) Roof; June 4,
1955 in Kings Mountain, N.C.
Children: Carol Elizabeth Eanes, Rebecca Jo Gladden.
Education: Lenoir-Rhyne, A.B. 1953; Lutheran Theological
Southern Seminary, B.D. 1956.
Ordination: June 10, 1956 by North Carolina Synod.
Calls: Trinity, Sanford, 1956-67; Faith, Conover, 1967-83; St.
Paul, Salisbury, 1983-89; St. Martin, Maiden, 1989-97; retired January 1, 1998 to Newton;
Vice Pastor at various congregations.
Other: Board, Lutheran Services for the Aging; Stewardship Committee; Synodical
Western District Secretary; President, East Catawba County Cooperative Christian
Ministry; Advisory Board, United Fund; Drug Awareness Task Force; Chair, World
Missions Committee; Pastors' Support Committee; Chair, Nominating Committee.

ROOF, LESTER ODA, SR.
Date/Place of Birth: January 13, 1900; Lexington, S.C.
Parents: Scott Elmore Roof and Plumie Elizabeth (Mathias) Roof.
Spouse/Marriage Date: Virgie Eula (Sandel) Roof; December 23, 1929 in Chapin, S.C.
Children: The Reverend Lester Oda, Jr., Lowell Sandel, Betty Eula Conner.
Education: Lenoir-Rhyne, A.B. 1926; Lutheran Theological Southern Seminary, B.D. 1929.
Ordination: May 26, 1929 by South Carolina Synod.
Calls: Cedar Grove-St. James, Lexington County, S.C., 1929-45; Nazareth-Shiloh, Forsyth County, 1945-48; Holly Grove-New Jerusalem, Davidson County, 1948-55; Wittenberg, Granite Quarry, 1956-66.
Other: Secretary, President, Lexington County Ministerial Association; Chaplain, Civitan; Granite Quarry Recreation Committee.
Date of Death/Burial Location: August 13, 1979; Mt. Hermon Lutheran Church Cemetery, West Columbia, S.C.

ROOF, WALTER JAMES
Date/Place of Birth: February 17, 1880; Lexington County, S.C.
Parents: Daniel James Roof and Jane Esther (Buff) Roof. Two older brothers were the Reverends W. H. and F. K. Roof; a sister was Mattie Anna who married the Reverend Enoch Hite.
Spouse/Marriage Date: Lila Buist (Clute) Roof; September 28, 1910 in Mt. Pleasant, S.C.
Children: James Wilbur, Jack Buist, Simons Lucas, Catherine Lucas.
Education: Lenoir-Rhyne, A.B. 1907; Lutheran Theological Southern Seminary, 1910; Newberry College, M.A. 1915; graduate study, University of South Carolina and Biblical Seminary.
Ordination: 1910 by Tennessee Synod.
Calls: St. Jacob and Mt. Horeb, Chapin; Mayer Memorial, Newberry, S.C., 1910-15; St. Barnabas, Charleston, S.C., 1923-34; Grace, Rock Hill, S.C. and as Pastor to Lutheran students at Winthrop College, 1934-38; St. Stephen, Lenoir, 1915-18; Emmanuel, Lincolnton-St. Luke, Lincoln County, 1918-23; Trinity, Vale-Cedar Grove, Lincoln County-Sardis, Catawba County, 1938-50; Sharon-Peace, Gibsonville, 1950-52; retired 1952 at Mt. Pleasant, S.C. and later Rock Hill, S.C.
Other: Author of *History of the Lutheran Churches of Charleston, South Carolina*, (1927).
Date of Death/Burial Location: January 3, 1962; Laurelwood Cemetery, Rock Hill, S.C.

ROOF, WILLIE HARDEE

Date/Place of Birth: February 17, 1866; Lexington County, S.C.
Parents: Daniel James Roof and Jane Esther (Buff) Roof. Two brothers were the Reverends F. K. and W. J. Roof; a sister was Mattie Anna who married the Reverend Enoch Hite.
Spouse/Marriage Date: Corrie Magdalene (Price) Roof; June 13, 1897 in Gilbert, S.C.
Children: Edna Mary, James Emerson, Ruth Magdalene, William Voigt, Frances Jane, Sara Elizabeth, Martha Price.
Education: Lenoir-Rhyne, A.B. 1894; Lutheran Theological Southern Seminary, 1906.
Ordination: 1895 by Tennessee Synod.
Calls: Cedar Grove, Leesville and St. Paul, Gilbert, Lexington County, S.C., 1897-1904; Holston Synod in Tennessee: Blountville, 1906-13; and Greeneville, 1913-17; St. Lukes, Prosperity, S.C., 1917-22; again at Blountville, Tenn., 1922-26; Daniel's, Lincoln County, Grace, Catawba County, 1926-39; retired 1939 near Lincolnton.
Other: President, Holston Synod, 1913-17; taught school, 1894-97; Home Mission Board, United Synod South, three years.
Date of Death/Burial Location: May 5, 1952; Daniel's Church Cemetery, Lincoln County, N.C.

ROSCHEN, ARNOLD

Date/Place of Birth: January 27, 1761; Bremen, Germany. The third German pastor called for ministry to Lutheran churches in North Carolina.
Parents: Ludwig Roschen and Margarete (Harffs) Roschen.
Spouse/Marriage Date: Married a woman from Bremen; 1788.
Children: No record of any children.
Education: Goettingen University, Germany, also studying theology there, 1780-85, and under the Reverend Professor Nicolai in Bremen, 1785-88.
Ordination: Ordained 1788 in Germany.
Calls: Beck's-St. Luke, St. Luke, Davidson County-Dutchman's Creek, Davie County-Nazareth-Shiloh, Forsyth County, 1789-1800.
Other: Arrived in Charleston, S.C. on November 28, 1788 and arrived in North Carolina on February 20, 1789. Bought farm of 200 acres and built log house, near Beck's Church, Davidson County. With Pastors Nussmann, Arends, Storch, and Bernhardt, took part in ordination of Robert Johnston Miller May 20, 1794 as an Episcopal minister. He and his wife returned to Germany in 1800 and served a Lutheran congregation in Mulaum-Harsefeld, 1800-22.
Date of Death/Burial Location: March 13, 1822; Mulaum-Harsefeld, Germany.

ROSE, CHARLES ALEXANDER

Date/Place of Birth: March 11, 1857; Rowan County, N.C.
Parents: W. A. Rose and Ann Kathern (Rodgers) Rose. A half-brother was the Reverend Richard S. Patterson.
Spouse/Marriage Date: Maria Susan (Patterson) Rose; May 25, 1882 in Cabarrus County, N.C.
Children: J. A., Lizzie, R. S., Mary E., C. A., H. G., Annie C.

Education: North Carolina College, A.B., 1880, A.M.; Lutheran Theological Southern Seminary, 1883.
Ordination: 1883 by Southwest Virginia Synod.
Calls: Floyd, Va., 1882-84; St. Paul-Bethel, Rowan County, 1884-99; Christ, East Spencer, 1884-97.
Other: President, North Carolina Synod, 1898-99.
Date of Death/Burial Location: July 2, 1899; Lutheran Chapel Church, China Grove, N.C.

ROSENMILLER, DAVID P.

Date/Place of Birth: June 22, 1809; York, Pa.
Parents: Louis Rosenmiller and Rebecca P. Rosenmiller.
Spouse/Marriage Date: Mary Eliza (Sheffer) Rosenmiller.
Education: Gettysburg College; Gettysburg Seminary, 1829.
License/Ordination: Licensed 1830 and ordained 1831 by North Carolina Synod.
Calls: Beck's-Pilgrim-St. Luke, St. Luke, Davidson County, 1830-31; Nazareth-Shiloh, Forsyth County, 1830-32; St. John, Salisbury, 1831-32; transferred to Pennsylvania Synod, 1832; served churches in Pennsylvania, 1832-80 except for one parish in Ohio, 1840-49.
Date of Death/Burial Location: September 26, 1880; Lancaster, Pa.

ROTH, GARY

Date/Place of Birth: June 30, 1948.
Spouse/Marriage Date: Eleanore L. (Huber) Roth
Children: Jeffrey B., Lucen.
Education: Capital University, B.A. English 1971; Trinity Seminary, M.Div. 1978; graduate work at Loyola University.
Ordination: January 14, 1979.
Calls: St. Peter, Baltimore, Md., 1979-86; Zion, Coraopolis, Pa., 1986-96; St. Andrew, New Bern, 1998-.
Other: Chaplain, Maryland School for Boys, 1984-86; Chaplain, Mariner Home, Coraopolis, Md., 1987-96; Southwest Pennsylvania Synod Peace Task Group; Habitat for Humanity; Newsmaker of the Year, Coraopolis, Md., 1995; Founder, Cornell Community Advisory Council; West Hills Ministerial Association.

ROTH, HERBERT CARL

Date/Place of Birth: February 18, 1922; Pittsburgh, Pa.
Parents: Julius Roth and Louise (Kasenter) Roth.
Spouse/Marriage Date: Gene Isabel (Kingman) Roth; May 26, 1946 in Santa Anna, Calif.
Children: Timothy, Gary, Mark, Sharon Schrafft, David.
Education: Capital University, B.A. 1943; Trinity Seminary, B.D. 1945.
Ordination: September 16, 1945 by California Synod.
Calls: Newport Harbor, Newport Beach, Calif., 1945-53; Bethlehem, Pittsburgh, Pa., 1953-71; St. Mark, Morristown, N.J., 1971-84; retired 1984; transferred to North Carolina Synod, 1988.
Other: President, Pittsburgh City Mission Society, 1955-71; President, New Jersey Conference, 1970-72; Chair, Foreign Missions, Eastern District, American Lutheran Church, 1962-64; Board, New Jersey Lutheran Social Services, 1976-82.

ROTH, PHILIP
License: Licensed by North Carolina Synod, 1812.
Calls: Preached in Guilford County, 1812-24.
Date of Death/Burial Location: 1824; Guilford County, N.C.

ROTH, RICHARD PAUL
Date/Place of Birth: November 6, 1941; Springfield, Ill.
Parents: William W. Roth and Sara (Swartley) Roth.
First Spouse/Marriage Date: Susan Bunham (Schmeltzer) Roth; June 6, 1964 in Springfield, Ill.
Children of First Marriage: Deborah Susan, Rachel Linda.
Second Spouse/Marriage Date: Olivia Kay (Crowe) Roth; April 12, 1980 in Shelby, N.C.
Education: Wittenberg University, A.B. 1963; Hamma School of Theology, M.Div. 1967.
Ordination: May 1967 by Illinois Synod.
Calls: Friedens, Covington, Ohio, 1967-72; Oak Grove, Zelienople, Pa., 1973-76; First, Chadwick, Ill., 1977- 82; Shiloh, Lewisville, 1982-97.
Other: Board and Finance Committee, Lutheran Social Services of the Miami Valley, 1968-72; Board and three committees, Thiel College, 1973-76; Synod Parish Education Committee, 1973-76. Retired in 1997.

ROTH, ROBERT PAUL
Date/Place of Birth: December 8, 1919; Milwaukee, Wis.
Parents: The Reverend Paul Wagner Roth and Rose Marie (Schulzke) Roth.
Spouse/Marriage Date: Margaret (Beckstrand) Roth, daughter of the Reverend O. Garfield Beckstrand of Rockford, Ill.; June 17, 1943.
Children: Erik Beckstrand, Maren Rumari Hood, Maarja Kristin Cappetta, John Mark, Sonja Anne Frederick.
Education: Carthage College, BA. 1941; Northwestern Seminary, M.Div. 1945; University of Illinois, M.A. 1942; University of Chicago, Ph.D. 1947; Roanoke College, D.D. 1959.
Ordination: March 1945 by Northwest Synod.
Calls: Epiphany, Milwaukee, Wis., 1945-46; St. Paul, Red Wing, Minn., 1949-53.
Other: Professor, Luthergiri Seminary, Rajahmundry, India, 1946-48; Associate Professor, Augustana College, Rock Island, Ill., 1948-49; Lecturer, St. Olaf College, Northfield, Minn., 1952-53; Professor (New Testament) and Dean of Graduate School, Lutheran Theological Southern Seminary, and member of North Carolina Synod, 1953-61; Professor, Northwestern Seminary, Minneapolis, Minn., 1961-90; Dean, Northwestern Seminary, 1968-76; Editor in Chief of *Areopagus,* Global Missions Magazine of Tao Forg Shan Christian Center, Hong Kong, 1990-91; literary contributions: "Commentaries on I Peter and II Peter" in "The Biblical Expositor" series; contributed to symposium, "Stewardship in Contemporary Theology;" many articles in various Lutheran periodicals, such as *The Lutheran, The Lutheran Church Quarterly, Sursum Corda, The Lutheran Companion,* and Luther League periodicals, also *Religion in Life* and *Christianity Today;* Chair, Commission on Church Architecture, 1956-64; Chair, Commission on Worship, Lutheran Church in America, 1968-78; Chair, Fortress Press, Lutheran Church in America Board of Publications, 1978-86; Author, *Meaning and Practice of the Lord's Supper, Story and Reality,* 1973; *The Theater of God,* 1985. Contributions to thirteen books and 75 articles; Translator and Editor, *New International Version of the Bible,* 1978.

ROTHROCK, SAMUEL

Date/Place of Birth: November 26, 1809; near Salem, Forsyth County, N.C., fifth of nine children, of Huguenot ancestry.

First Spouse/Marriage Date: Mary (Hoke) Rothrock, Adams County, Pa.; July 30. 1833 daughter of Conrad Hoke. She died August 21, 1836 near end of his pastorate in Pennsylvania, day after bearing a son, who died also.

Child of First Marriage: Unnamed son who died shortly after birth.

Second Spouse/Marriage Date: Amelia Rosetta (Arey) Rothrock, September 14, 1837; daughter of Peter Arey and Phoebe (Thomas) Arey, and a sister of the Reverend Benjamin Arey. Died April 30, 1890.

Children of Second Marriage: Lewis Hazelius, (1839-1923), who served in Confederate States Army, became a schoolmaster, taught at North Carolina College, and was Principal of Mt. Pleasant Female Seminary, 1876-82, Milas Luther (1840-1842) and Charlotte Lucetta Jane (1847-1851).

Education: Gettysburg College, and Gettysburg Seminary, 1829-33, twice walking round trip from home (400 miles); University of North Carolina, D.D. 1888.

License/Ordination: Licensed 1833 and ordained 1834 by North Carolina Synod.

Calls: Union, Rowan County and St. John, Salisbury, 1833-35; Franklin and Fulton Counties, Pa., (16 months) 1835-36; again in North Carolina, 1836-89, two or three times in some churches (total years each in parenthesis): eleven in Rowan County: Union (6); St. Paul (7); Luther's (5); St. John, Salisbury (4); St. Matthew and Bethel (1 or 2); Salem and organized St. Luke, Bear Poplar, (6); St. Peter (14); Ebenezer (6); and longest, Organ (3 times for nearly 33 years, 1844-86); also, St. Stephen, Cabarrus County, (14); New Bethel, Stanly County, (1 or 2); and supply, Frieden's, Guilford County-St. Paul, Alamance County, (1 or 2).

Other: Parts of his diary in English (December 8, 1834-February 3, 1863 with gaps covering more than five years) are in Synod's archives at Salisbury. He preached in German and in English, sometimes in both at the same service. He was president of North Carolina Synod ten terms, 1840-80; secretary five terms,1837-45, and treasurer five terms, 1834-79; Board, Western Carolina Male Academy, and of its successor, North Carolina College; twice President of Southern General Synod, 1849 and 1867. Fellow members of synod in 1883 presented him a gold-headed cane.

Date of Death/Burial Location: November 2, 1894; Union Church, Rowan County, N.C.

Note: The reader desiring more information on Pastor Rothrock may wish to consult the sketch in the earlier version of *Life Sketches*. The reader may also see *The Samuel Rothrock Diaries, 1834-1893, Volume I* transcribed and indexed by Bernard William Cruse, Jr. and *The Samuel Rothrock Diaries, Volume II: Annotations and Commentary*, by Harriet Arey Davidson, both published by the Authority of Historical Works Committee of the North Carolina Synod, Evangelical Lutheran Church in America.

RUDISILL, DORUS PAUL, SR.
Date/Place of Birth: April 30, 1902; Cherryville, N.C.
Parents: John Henry Rudisill, Sr. and Sarah Frances (Rudisill) Rudisill.
Spouse/Marriage Date: Robbie Ione (Stevenson) Rudisill; August 30, 1935 in Abbeville, S.C.
Children: Dorus Paul, Jr., Barbara Ione.
Education: Lenoir-Rhyne, A.B. 1922; Philadelphia Seminary, one year, Lutheran Theological Southern Seminary, B.D. 1925; University of Pennsylvania, University of South Carolina, M.A. 1925; Hartford Seminary, S. T. M. 1932; Duke University, Ph.D. 1945.
Ordination: January 20, 1926 by South Carolina Synod.
Calls: Holy Communion, Dallas-Christ's, Stanley-Bethel, Iron Station, 1925-31; re-organized and built church, Calvary, Morganton-Mt. Hebron, Hildebran, 1933-38; Calvary only, 1938-42. Mission Developer/Pastor to University of North Carolina Lutheran students, Chapel Hill, 1942-46, developing and organizing Trinity, Sanford, 1943, and Holy Trinity, Chapel Hill, 1946; Supply, St. John, Alexander County, 1946-54; retired July 1970.
Other: Professor (Bible, Philosophy), Lenoir-Rhyne, 1946-73; Professor Emeritus, Lenoir-Rhyne, 1973-78; Board, Lutheran Theological Southern Seminary, 1942-43, 1955-58; Distinguished Service Citation, Lenoir- Rhyne Alumni Association, 1972; Executive Committee, four years; North Carolina Synod Representative at National Council of Churches Conventions, 1950, 1952; Examining Committee, 1969-70; author: articles for church publications and three books; *Who's Who Among Authors and Journalists* and *Who's Who in America*; Rotary Club and Catawba Valley Executive's Club.
Date of Death/Burial Location: August 10, 1978; Oakwood Cemetery, Hickory, N.C.

RUDISILL, JOHN ANDERSON
Date/Place of Birth: May 28, 1856; Long Shoals, near Lincolnton, N.C.
Parents: Absalom Rudisill and Louisa Matilda (Speagle) Rudisill.
Spouse/Marriage Date: Mary Alice (Gilbert) Rudisill; December 16, 1886 in Mooresville, N.C.
Children: Evan Leon, Winnie Ethel, Loy Alvin, John Arthur.
Education: Rutherford College; Gaston College; Catawba College, Concordia College, A.B. 1880, also studying theology there.
Ordination: October 17, 1883 by Tennessee Synod.
Calls: Ministry was for a period of twelve years, 1883-95: Bethphage, Trinity, Sardis and Lutheran Chapel, Burke County; Sardis and St. Paul, Catawba County; organized and served Cedar Grove, Lincoln County, 1883-95; David Chapel, Lincoln County, 1892-95; St. Mark, Crouse, 1894-95; preached at Mt. Pleasant, Watauga County, Blowing Rock, Valle Crucis, 1884, 1885, 1889, 1892 and at other times; Daniel's, Lincoln County, 1884-95; St. Luke, Lincoln County; and Trinity, Vale, 1883-95; Antioch, Gaston County, 1883-95; Lutheran Chapel (East Gastonia), Gaston County; Glen Alpine, Burke County, (forerunner of Calvary, Morganton), with other pastors, 1883-95.
Other: Taught school at Ridge Academy, Vale; Secretary, Tennessee Synod, 1893-94.
Date of Death/Burial Location: July 21, 1895 of typhoid fever; Trinity Church, Vale, N.C.

RUECKWALD, PAUL T.

Date/Place of Birth: August 28, 1910; Lockport, N.Y.
Parents: The Reverend and Mrs. Max M. Rueckwald.
Spouse/Marriage Date: Gladys Ida (Luke) Rueckwald; June 28, 1932.
Children: Marie, Ruth, Martha.
Education: Martin Luther College, Buffalo, N.Y., B.M., 1928; Capital University, Columbus, Ohio; Evangelical Lutheran Theological Seminary, Columbus, Ohio, Diploma, 1932.
Ordination: June 12, 1932 by American Lutheran Church.
Calls: Cleveland Hill, Buffalo, N.Y., 1932-33; Emmanuel, East Pittsburgh, Pa., 1933-39; St. Luke, Venus, Pa., 1939-45; Jerusalem, Columbiana, Ohio and Zion, New Waterford, Ohio, 1945-48; St. Paul, Zelienople, Pa. and St. John, Connoquenessing, Pa., 1948-53; Christ, Pittsburgh, Pa., 1953-57; Good Shepherd, Charlotte, 1960-64; Holy Trinity, Vallejo, Calif., 1964-75.
Date of Death/Burial: June 15, 1996.

RUNGE, B. HENRY W.

Date/Place of Birth: January 2, 1864; presumably in Wilmington, N.C.
Parents: G. H. W. Runge and Johanna Dorothea (Shultz) Runge, natives of Germany. They lived in Wilmington, and are buried in Oakdale Cemetery there.
Education: Newberry College, North Carolina College, 1890; Philadelphia Seminary.
Ordination: June 2, 1895 by North Carolina Synod, after he had been called to serve churches in Sullivan County, Tenn., left vacant by the death of the Reverend Abel J. Brown, D.D.
Date of Death/Burial Location: Died thirteen days after ordination, June 15, 1895; Oakdale Cemetery, Wilmington, N.C.

RUPP, JOHN CHARLES FRANCIS

Date/Place of Birth: June 23, 1856; Dayton, Pa.
Spouse/Marriage Date: Zelie (Hill) Rupp; June 15, 1886.
Children: Louis William, John Hill.
Education: Gettysburg College, A.B., A.M. 1878; Gettysburg Seminary, 1883.
Ordination: 1884 by Pittsburgh Synod.
Calls: Served churches in Pennsylvania, Ontario, Canada, and Ohio, 1890-1933.
Other: Member of North Carolina Synod, 1885-87, serving as Professor at North Carolina College; transferred back to Pittsburgh Synod, 1887; Principal, Connoquenessing Academy, Zelienople, Pa., 1887-90; Co-editor, *Commentary for Teachers on Sunday School Lessons,* 1897-1923.
Date of Death/Burial Location: 1933; Leechburg, Pa.

SAARINEN, MARTIN FREDRICK

Date/Place of Birth: July 6, 1929; Portland, Ore.
Parents: John Fredrick Saarinen and Eliza (Toppari) Saarinen.
First Spouse/Marriage Date: Maryann (Pietila) Saarinen; December 29, 1953 in Fairport Harbor, Ohio.
Children of First Marriage: Randall Featherston, Leveristi Pursey, Melanie Ehler, Kevin Featherston, Mary Moser, Paul Kristman, Beth Marie, Erik John.

Second Spouse/Marriage Date: Marilyn Joan (Culy) Saarinen; July 1, 1990 in Columbia, S.C.
Education: University of Minnesota, B.A. 1955; Suomi Seminary, B.D. 1958; Wisconsin State University, M.Ed. 1958; Hamma School of Theology, D.Min. 1974.
Ordination: July 19, 1955 by Suomi Synod.
Calls: Evangelical, Bruce, Wis., 1955-58; Campus Pastor, Registrar, Instructor, Suomi College, 1958-60; Bethany, Ashtabula, Ohio, 1960-67; Assistant to President, Ohio Synod, Lutheran Church in America, Columbus, Ohio, 1967-72; assigned to North Carolina Synod while at Lutheran Theological Southern Seminary; Vice Pastor at various congregations; retired July 1, 1990; transferred to Virginia Synod in 1997.
Other: Professor, Church and Ministry and Director of Doctor of Ministry and Continuing Education Programs, Lutheran Theological Southern Seminary, 1972-90; Dean, Northeast District, Ohio Synod; Chair, Board, Suomi Seminary; Examining Committee, Western Pennsylvania/West Virginia Synod; Chair, Leadership Development, Ohio Council of Churches; Radio Reader, South Carolina Commission for the Blind; author: *The Life Cycle of a Congregation;* co-author, *Why Churches Don't Grow*; author of several monographs, articles and unpublished papers; organized two mission congregations, Orr, Minn. and Iron River, Wis.; Church Consultant in Ministry Planning, Conflict Resolution, Team building; United States Marine Corps at end of World War II and during the Korean War.

SACHTLEBEN, CARL RONALD

Date/Place of Birth: September 17, 1943; Chicago, Ill.
Parents: Carl Henry Sachtleben and Helen Elsa Sachtleben.
Spouse/Marriage Date: Ann Marie (Dietz) Sachtleben; June 25, 1966 in Cheyenne, Wyo.
Children: Michael Carl, Stephen Mark.
Education: Valparaiso University, B.A. 1965; Concordia Seminary, M.Div. 1969, S.T.M. 1970.
Ordination: July 5, 1970 by The Lutheran Church-Missouri Synod.
Calls: Assistant Pastor, Concordia, Wilmington, Del., 1974-77; Director of Pastoral Services, Delaware Cancer Network, Wilmington, Del., 1977-79; St. Mark, Wilmington, Del., 1979-91; St. John, Salisbury, 1991-.
Other: Director, Resident Field Education, Concordia Seminary, 1970-74; Director, CONTACT, Wilmington and Concordia Family Life Center, Wilmington, Del., 1974-77; Pastoral Counselor, Tressler Center for Human Growth, Wilmington, Del., 1976-90; Pastoral Counselor, Care and Counseling, Inc., St. Louis, 1970-72; Candidate Placement Committee, The Lutheran Church-Missouri Synod, 1970-73; Delaware/Maryland Synod Council, 1982-87; Dean, Delmarva Conference, 1987-90; Delaware-The Lutheran Church-Missouri Synod Committee on Calls to Special Ministry, 1980-87; Intern Supervisor, Lutheran Theological Southern Seminary, 1991-92; Presentation Team for Lutheran Church in America, *Statement on Death and Dying,* 1978.

SAFRIT, DONALD LYNN, SR.

Date/Place of Birth: November 23, 1935; Rowan County, N.C.
Parents: Luther Lynn Safrit and Catherine Alice (Bost) Safrit.
Spouse/Marriage Date: Dolores Imogene (Page) Safrit; September 19, 1956 in Landis, N.C.
Children: Donald Lynn, Jr., (died on fifth day), Mary Catherine Hancock, Donald Lynn, III.
Education: Lenoir-Rhyne, A.B. 1959; Lutheran Theological Southern Seminary, B.D. 1962, also graduate study.

Ordination: June 1962 by North Carolina Synod.

Calls: Christ's, Columbia, S.C., 1962-63; St. Paul, Dallas, 1963-68; Bethany, St. Enoch, Kannapolis, 1968- 75; Shiloh, Hickory, 1975-80; Developer/Pastor, Christ the King, Dalton, Ga., 1980-85; Lutheran Church of Our Savior, Albany, Ga., 1985-87; Pomaria, Pomaria, S.C., 1988-92; Christ, East Spencer; Interim, Center Grove, Kannapolis; reorganized, Ebenezer, Catawba, 1958-59; Supply at various congregations; retired April 1, 1995 to China Grove, N.C.

Other: Luther League: North Carolina Southern District President, 1955-57, Luther League of America Caravanner - 1953-54; National President, Kappa Chi Fraternity, 1955-57; Association of Lutheran Seminarians, 1959-62, National President, 1960-62; Association of Lutheran Clergy Lutheran Church in America, Steering Committee, 1970-74, President, 1973-74; Lutheran Church in America Delegate from North Carolina Synod, 1974; Board, Lutheridge, 1973-80, Secretary, 1977-80; Southern District Secretary, North Carolina Synod, 1971-75; Nominating Committee Chair, North Carolina Synod, 1967; Environmental Concerns Committee, North Carolina Synod, 1977-80; Board, Lutheran Ministries of Georgia, 1983-87; YOUTHEXPO Promotional Agent, 1969; Active in Boy Scouts on state and national levels.

Date of Death/Burial Location: October 31, 1997; Mt. Moriah Lutheran Church Cemetery, China Grove, N.C.

SAFRIT, DONALD RAY

Date/Place of Birth: January 18, 1942; Salisbury, N.C.

Parents: Earl Ray Safrit and Alice (Albright) Safrit.

Spouse/Marriage Date: Theresa (Lyerly) Safrit; August 1, 1965 in China Grove, N.C.

Children: Lewis Ray, Gregory Harold.

Education: Lenoir-Rhyne, B.A. Sociology, 1964; Lutheran Theological Southern Seminary, M.Div. 1969.

Ordination: June 6, 1969 by North Carolina Synod.

Calls: Churchville Parish, Augusta County, Va., 1969-71; Good Hope, Hickory, 1971-77; Christiana, Salisbury, 1977-91; St. Luke, Shallotte/Ocean Isle Beach, 1991-; Trinity, Rocky Mount.

Other: District Dean, Coastal Conference, 1995; Board, LSA, Inc., 1980-86; Board, Salisbury Retirement Center, 1984-1990; Board, Rowan Helping Ministries, 1982-90; Board, Hope Harbor Woman's Shelter of Brunswick County, 1992-95.

SAFRIT, GARY LEE, SR.

Date/Place of Birth: March 26, 1938; Rowan County, N.C.

Parents: George Adam Safrit and Margie Viola (Park) Safrit.

Spouse/Marriage Date: Brenda Ann (Arcuri) Safrit; October 16, 1965 in Hickory, N.C.

Children: Gary Lee, Jr.

Education: Lenoir-Rhyne, A.B. Sociology 1960; Lutheran Theological Southern Seminary, M.Div. 1964.

Ordination: June 14, 1964 by North Carolina Synod.

Calls: St. Timothy, Catawba County, 1964-68; St. Johannes, Charleston, S.C., 1968-72; Our Saviour, Greenville, S.C., 1972-.

Other: First recipient of the John Benjamin Bendenbaugh Award for Distinguished Pastoral Leadership from the Alumni Association of Lutheran Theological Southern Seminary, 1994; Youth Ministry Committee, 1966- 68; Chair, Architecture and Fine Arts Committee, 1967-68; in South Carolina Synod: Chair, Worship Committee; Executive Board; Bishop's Blue Ribbon Committee; Dean, Piedmont District; Delegate, 1986 Lutheran Church in America Convention; Voting Member, Constituting Convention of the Evangelical Lutheran Church in America; Synod's Committee on Congregational Life.

SAHL, THOMAS JAMES
Date/Place of Birth: May 29, 1945; Minneapolis, Minn.
Parents: Mr. and Mrs. Theodore O. Sahl.
Spouse/Marriage Date: Sandra Diane (Williams) Sahl; September 1, 1970.
Children: Kimberly Beth.
Education: University of Minnesota, Augsburg College, Minneapolis, Minn., B.A. 1967; Luther Seminary, St. Paul, Minn., M.Div. 1971.
Ordination: June 27, 1971 by American Lutheran Church.
Calls: Calvary, Merrill, W.Va., 1971-75; Associate Pastor, Our Saviour and Pleasant Valley, Park River, N.D., 1975-76; Zion, McGrath, Minn., 1976-80; Saron, Minot, Md., 1980-1985; Peace, Burlington, 1980-85; St. Paul, Hickory, 1985-86; Avoca, Neb., 1987-.

SAIN, ROBERT ALLEN
Date/Place of Birth: October 26, 1954; Lincolnton, N.C.
Parents: Paul Edward Sain and Myrtle (Davis) Sain.
Spouse/Marriage Date: Rebecca (Fritz) Sain; July 8, 1978 in Columbia, S.C.
Children: Douglas Allen, Karl Edward, Jordan Richard.
Education: Lenoir-Rhyne, A.B. Religion, 1977; Lutheran Theological Southern Seminary, M.Div. 1981.
Ordination: May 24, 1981 by North Carolina Synod.
Calls: Good Shepherd, Brevard, 1981-85; Pastor/Developer, Our Saviour, Jonesboro, Ark., 1985-89; Holy Communion, Dallas, 1989-94; transferred to South Carolina Synod, St. Lukes, Prosperity, 1994; Messiah, Hickory and Interim at various congregations, 1998-.

SALTZER, CRAIG DAVIS
Date/Place of Birth: June 13, 1950; York, Pa.
Parents: Clark Warren Saltzer and Frances Jeanne (Steward) Saltzer.
Spouse/Marriage Date: Marian Faye (Hovis) Saltzer; June 19, 1985 in Stanly County, N.C.
Education: Cornell University, B.A. 1972; Columbia University Teachers College, M.A. 1973; Gettysburg Seminary, M.Div. 1984.
Ordination: June 24, 1984 by North Carolina Synod for Central Pennsylvania Synod.
Calls: Grace, Thomasville, 1984-; Vice Pastor for various congregations.

SALZGERBER, ROBERT L.
Date/Place of Birth: September 30, 1947; Chicago, Ill.
Spouse/Marriage Date: Susan G. Salzgerber.

Children: Jennie R., Jason R., Ericka, Katie.

Education: Luther College, B.A. History/Political Science 1970; Northwestern Seminary, M.Div., 1974; Pittsburgh Seminary, D.Min. 1987; Word and Witness Bible Study Program, 1987-95.

Ordination: June 9, 1974.

Calls: Bethany, Siren, Wis., 1974-77; Luther Point Camp, Grantsburg, Wis., 1977-79; Camp Lutherlyn, Prospect, Pa., 1979-84; Grace, Butler, Pa., 1984-92; St. Luke, Pittsburgh, Pa., 1992-95; St. Matthew, Wilmington, 1995-.

Other: Radio Broadcast weekly on spirituality; received Richard J. Rapp Memorial Prize in Doctor of Ministry Studies; conceived, planned and implemented county-wide Helpline; planned and presented Junior/Senior High School Assembly series dealing with self esteem, motivation, identity, vocations, sexuality, conformity, substance abuse, and relationships. Author: *Christian Community, Individualism and Work in Butler, Pa.; Inklings and Tidbits: Hot Fudge Sundae and Other Delectable Faith Stories; Assayings: Theological Faith Testings; Poison Ivy Island; Mental health delegate in county;* Camp design team land use specialist.

SANGER, LAWRENCE OSCAR

Date/Place of Birth: December 20, 1919; Chili, Wis.

Parents: Ernest Sanger and Emma (Franke) Sanger.

Spouse/Marriage Date: Gloria (Linder) Sanger; June 15, 1946 in Cleveland, Ohio.

Children: Cheryl Rose Bartlette, Cynthia Dawn Gwin, Reed Christian.

Education: Wartburg, B.A. 1943; Wartburg Seminary, M.Div. 1946; Southeastern Baptist Seminary, M.S. Theology, 1972.

Ordination: June 30, 1946 by Wisconsin District, American Lutheran Church.

Calls: St. John, Akron, Ohio, 1945-56; three parishes in Wisconsin, 1946-56; U.S. Army Chaplain, Fort Slocum, N.Y., 1956, Fort Dix, N.J., 1956-57, Orleons, France, 1957, Captieux, France, 1958-59, Fort Bragg, 1960-65, Thailand, 1965-66, Fort Ord, Calif., 1966-68, Vietnam, 1969-72, Augsburg, Germany, 1972-75, Fort Bragg, 1975-76, Augusta, Ga., 1976. North Carolina Department of Corrections Chaplain, Lillington, 1977-87; supply for various congregations; retired February 1, 1987.

Other: Service Awards - Legion of Merit, Meritorious Service Medal, Bronze Star, two awards of the Army Commendation Medal; represented Bishop on several North Carolina Prison-related Committees such as Yokefellow, Prison Fellowship and the North Carolina Commission on Ministry in Prisons.

SANNER, LYNN M.

Spouse/Marriage Date: Barry Sanner.

Children: Kathryn Anne

Education: Pennsylvania State University, B.S. Agriculture/Environmental Science; Gettysburg Seminary, M.Div. 1989.

Ordination: 1989.

Calls: Faith, Somerset, Pa.; St. Matthew, Wilmington, 1997-.

Other: Bishop's Convocation in Allegheny and Northwestern Pennsylvania Synods; Somerset County Children's Task Force; Somerset County Board of Family Services; Homeless Shelter Advisory Board of Somerset County.

SATERBAK, ALLEN JAMES
Date/Place of Birth: October 25, 1940; La Crosse, Wisc.
Parents: Mr. and Mrs. Elvin M. Saterbak.
First Spouse: Cordella Marie (Gotoski) Saterbak.
Children of First Marriage: Julie, Kurt.
Second Spouse/Marriage Date: Julie (Steinke) Saterbak; January 30, 1977.
Education: Luther College, Decorah, Iowa, B.A. 1962; Luther Seminary, St. Paul, Minn., M.Div., 1971.
Ordination: March 14, 1971 by American Lutheran Church.
Calls: Christ, Greensboro, 1971-74.
Other: U.S.A.F. for five years; University of Wisconsin Office of Development. Removed from ministry December 31, 1977.

SCHAACK, EDWARD ROBERT, JR.
Date/Place of Birth: December 9, 1939; Charleston, S.C.
Parents: Edward Robert Schaack, Sr. and Willa (Martin) Schaack.
Spouse/Marriage Date: Ellen Elizabeth (Brown) Schaack; July 9, 1966 in Rural Retreat, Va.
Children: Virginia Elizabeth, Edward Martin, Catherine Louise.
Education: Newberry College, 1962; Lutheran Theological Southern Seminary, 1967.
Ordination: May 26, 1967 by South Carolina Synod.
Calls: Christ, Elkin, 1967-71; Churchville Parish, Augusta County, Va., 1971-77; Kimberling Parish, Va., 1980-87; Arroway-Kimberling Parish, Va. 1987-.
Other: Executive Director, Hungry Mother Lutheran Retreat Center, 1987-; Lutheran Mountain Ministries, 1980-.

SCHAEFFER, FREDERICK WILLIAM
Date/Place of Birth: November 22, 1883; New York, N.Y.
Parents: John Christian Schaeffer and Amalia Melvina (Gunterberg) Schaeffer.
Spouse/Marriage Date: Else Evelyn (Brahe) Schaeffer; July 3, 1918 in Brooklyn, N.Y.
Children: Donald William, Evelyn Elizabeth Diers.
Education: Wagner College, A.B. 1902; Philadelphia Seminary, 1905; Hartford Seminary, S. T. M. 1932.
Ordination: 1905 by Ministerium of Pennsylvania.
Calls: First, Lock Haven, Pa., 1905-07; Home Missionary, Ascension Lutheran Church, Brooklyn, N.Y., 1907-11; Missionary in India, 1911-14; Principal of boys' school in Peddapur, India; St. John, Lynbrook, Long Island, N.Y. and Emanuel, New Haven, Conn., 1915-17; Reformation, New Britain, Conn., 1917-52; retired 1952 to Hendersonville, N.C.; transferred to North Carolina Synod 1962 when Lutheran Church in America was formed.
Date of Death/Burial Location: May 29, 1976; Tulocay Cemetery, Napa, Calif.

SCHAEFFER, GEORGE FRANCIS

Date/Place of Birth: January 3, 1830; Carmel, Preston County, W.Va.

Education: Gettysburg College; received D.D. degree.

License/Ordination: Licensed 1861 and ordained 1865 by Allegheny Synod.

Calls: Preached in Cumberland, Md., in nearby churches, several years; Parishes in Pennsylvania, at Bloomfield and Newport; Parish at Apollo, Pa., 1878-82; First, Albemarle-Mt. Carmel, Cabarrus County, 1883-84; Mt. Hermon, Cabarrus County, 1884; St. James, Concord, 1885-86.

Other: Taught at Cumberland, Md.; Vice-principal, Lutherville, Md., Female Seminary, two years; in business several years before becoming Principal of Somerset, Pa., Academy, 1857-60 also serving there 1864-66 and 1874-78; came to North Carolina, as Professor at North Carolina College, and Mont Amoena Seminary, 1860-61. When these institutions closed because of the War Between the States, he returned North. Returned to North Carolina as Principal, Mont Amoena Seminary, 1882-83; President, North Carolina College 1883-87; retired 1887 and lived at Monroe, Ga. until 1902 then at White Stone near Spartanburg, S.C.

Date of Death/Burial Location: September 27, 1916; buried presumably at Spartanburg, S.C.

SCHAEFFER, HARRY BRENT

Date/Place of Birth: August 30, 1891; Newberry, S.C.

Parents: The Reverend William Carl Schaeffer, Sr. and Jane (Hahn) Schaeffer. An older brother was the Reverend William Carl Schaeffer, Jr.

First Spouse/Marriage Date: Lora (Neas) Schaeffer; August 28, 1916 in Parrottsville, Tenn.

Children of First Marriage: Dorothy Clare (married the Reverend John H. Koch), the Reverend William Brent, Margaret Elizabeth (married the Reverend F. G. Sturm).

Second Spouse: Lois (McCartha) Schaeffer in Leesville, S.C.

Education: Newberry College, A.B. 1910, D.D. 1927; Lutheran Theological Southern Seminary, 1915, B.D. 1924.

Ordination: 1915 by Holston Synod.

Calls: Ascension, Chattanooga, Tenn., 1915-18; St. Matthew-St. Luke, Kings Mountain, 1919-23, and organized Ascension, Shelby, 1923; St. Matthew, Charleston, S.C., 1923-26; Memorial, St. Augustine, Fla., 1934-36; Trinity, Kansas City, Kan., 1936-38; Trinity, Jackson, Miss., 1938-52; Wittenberg, Leesville, S.C., 1952-57; organized churches at Elberton, Ga., 1938, and at Chester and York, S.C., 1957-58; supplied Mt. Olivet, Chapin, S.C., 1959-63.

Other: President, Lenoir-Rhyne, 1926-34; Schaeffer Hall (women's dormitory) there is named in his honor; last Secretary, Tennessee Synod 1920-21 and first Secretary, United North Carolina Synod, 1921-23; President, Mississippi Synod, 1939-48; Board of Education, United Lutheran Church in America, 1950-53; Commission on Study of Structure, United Lutheran Church in America, 1953-54; Board, Newberry College, 1953-ff; Camp Pastor, World War I, Atlanta, Ga., 1918; Director in South, Anniversary Appeal of Board of American Missions, United Lutheran Church in America, 1938; State Chair for Mission of Southern Regional Council, 1946-50; President, Jackson (Mississippi)

Juvenile Council, 1944-46; Honorary Member, Mississippi Poetry Society, 1952-; retired at Leesville, S.C.
Date of Death/Burial Location: January 31, 1975; Wittenberg Cemetery, Leesville, S.C.

SCHAEFFER, JACOB M.
Ordination: Ordained Deacon 1843 by Tennessee Synod.
Calls: St. James, Greene County, Tenn.; Daniel's, Lincoln County, 1846; reported to have served congregations in Monroe, McMinn and Knox counties in Virginia.
Other: One of seven Tennessee Synod pastors who organized the Holston Synod, 1860-61. Grandfather of Reverends W. C. Davis and H. Grady Davis.
Date of Death: 1885.

SCHAEFFER, WILLIAM BRENT
Date/Place of Birth: August 11, 1918; Chattanooga, Tenn.
Parents: The Reverend Harry Brent Schaeffer and Lora (Neas) Schaeffer.
Spouse: Mary Ethelyn (Riser) Schaeffer.
Education: Newberry College, A.B., 1938; Lutheran Theological Seminary, Gettysburg, Pa., B.D., 1946; Glasgow University, 1945; Virginia Polytechnic Institute, 1943-44; University of Stockholm and Uppsala University, 1947; Furman University, M.A., 1948-52.
Ordination: 1948 by Mississippi Synod.
Calls: In South Carolina, St. Michael, Greenville, 1948-51; Holy Trinity, North Augusta, 1951-58. In North Carolina Synod, Vice Pastor, Good Shepherd, Brevard, 1985; in South Carolina, St. Matthias, Easley, 1978-82. Retired in 1982. Vice Pastor, Living Waters, Cherokee, 1991; Assisting Minister, Grace, Hendersonville.
Other: Senior Representative in the United Kingdom for the Lutheran World Federation, 1958-65. Transferred to Maryland Synod, 1965-78. U.S. Army, 1942-46.

SCHAEFFER, WILLIAM CARL
Date/Place of Birth: January 19, 1882; Richmond, Va.
Parents: The Reverend William C. Schaeffer and Jane (Hahn) Schaeffer. A younger brother is the Reverend H. B. Schaeffer.
Spouse/Marriage Date: Edith G. (Wagner) Schaeffer of Allentown, Pa.; June 10, 1936 in Hendersonville, N.C.
Education: Newberry College, A.B. 1901, Honorary M.A., D.D.; Lutheran Theological Southern Seminary, 1904; graduate study at Leipzig and Berlin Universities, 1904-05; Muhlenberg College, D.D.
Ordination: 1904 by Georgia Synod.
Calls: Assistant Pastor, St. Mark's, Charlotte, 1906-08; Redeemer, Atlanta, Ga., 1909-18, also organizing congregations in Lakeland, Fla., Birmingham, Ala., and Chattanooga, Tenn.; St. John, Allentown, Pa., 1919-53; Mission Developer/Pastor, St. John, Winter Park, Fla., 1954-60.
Other: Professor (Religion, Philosophy), Elizabeth College, Charlotte, 1906-08; President, Georgia and Adjoining States Synod, 1913-18; Secretary, National Lutheran Commission for Soldiers and Sailors, 1917-18. In United Lutheran Church in America: Board of

Deaconess Work, 1924-32; President, Parish and Church School Board, 1920-42; President, Board of American Missions, 1942-52; Chair, Committee on Church Architecture, 1945-49; Counselor, National Lutheran Council, 1944-48; Board, Philadelphia Seminary, 1932-52.
Date of Death/Burial Location: January 18, 1960; Allentown, Pa.

SCHAIDT (SCHAID), JOHN GEORGE

Date/Place of Birth: July 31, 1846; Lonaconing, Md.
Parents: Casper Schaidt and Christiana Schaidt.
Spouse/Marriage Date: Anna (Stansill) Schaidt; 1881.
Children: No record of children.
Education: Muhlenberg College, A.B. 1872; Philadelphia Seminary, 1875; received D.D.
Ordination: 1875 by Ministerium of Pennsylvania, and transferred to Holston Synod.
Calls: Served a bilingual church (German-English), Knoxville, Tenn., 1875-87; transferred 1888 to North Carolina Synod; transferred 1889, to Tennessee Synod; transferred to South Carolina Synod, serving St. John, Walhalla, S.C., 1895-1903; St. Peter (Piney Woods), near Chapin, S.C., 1903-08; served St. John, Saltsburg, Pa., 1908-09.
Other: President and Professor, North Carolina College, 1857-89; Professor (Latin, German), Concordia College, 1889-95; President, Holston Synod, 1879; author: *Luther's Translation of the Bible,* 1882.
Date of Death/Burial Location: August 6, 1909; New Haven, W.Va.

SCHECK, JOHN D.

License/Ordination: Licensed 1827 and ordained 1830 by South Carolina Synod. Came to South Carolina from Maryland.
Calls: Organized Mt. Calvary, Johnston, and St. Mark, Lexington County, S.C., 1828; Sandy Run, Swansea, S.C., 1830; Mt. Pleasant, Ehrhardt, S.C., 1831-35; in Georgia, 1832-37; in Alabama, 1838; St. Nicholas, Fairfax, S.C., 1836-39; transferred 1841 to North Carolina Synod, serving St. John, Salisbury, 1840-44; St. Matthew, Rowan County, 1841-43; St. John, Cabarrus County, 1844-57; Lutheran Chapel, China Grove; New Bethel, Stanly County, 1856-57; Frieden's, Guilford County-St. Paul, Alamance County, 1859-64; transferred to Eastern Pennsylvania Synod, 1865.
Other: First regularly called Missionary of the South Carolina Synod, 1827. Postmaster at China Grove (renamed *Lutherville* during his term), 1844-49, while Pastor at Lutheran Chapel; Secretary, North Carolina Synod, 1841; President, 1842, 1845, 1861.
Date of Death/Burial Location: 1868; Old Lutheran (St. John) Cemetery, Salisbury, N.C.

SCHERER, DANIEL

Date/Place of Birth: September 12, 1790; Guilford County, N.C.
Parents: Frederick Scherer and Barbara (Smith) Scherer. An older brother was the Reverend Jacob Scherer. Father was a soldier in American Revolutionary forces.
Spouse/Marriage Date: Rachel (Kaempffer) Scherer; August 2, 1815.
Children: The Reverend Jacob, Helena, John W. F., Susan Barbara, Louise R. (married the Reverend Mr. Lesher), Maria, Daniel M., Sophia L. (married the Reverend J. Matthew

Lingle), Rebecca Adaline, Julia Lavinia (married the Reverend Elias Schwartz), Sarah A. M. who married the Reverend Martin Luther Kaempffer.

License/Ordination: Licensed 1816 and ordained 1821 by North Carolina Synod.

Calls: Lutheran Chapel, China Grove, 1820-30; St. John, Cabarrus County, 1821-31; Organ, Rowan County, 1823-29, Luther's, Rowan County, 1828-30; New Bethel, Stanly County, 1824-31; from 1832 to his death (1852), still a member of North Carolina Synod, he exercised a pioneer missionary ministry in Southern Illinois, organizing many churches; long-time pastorates were in Hillsboro, Ill., twelve years, and Mt. Carmel and Jordan Creek, Wabash County, Ill., 1843-52.

Other: Preached in both the German and English languages; earned his living by farming, and for a while kept a store.

Date of Death/Burial Location: April 4, 1852; Sand Hill Cemetery, Mt. Carmel, Ill.

SCHERER, GIDEON

Date/Place of Birth: About 1815 or 1817; Guilford County, N.C.

Parents: The Reverend Jacob Scherer and Elizabeth Scherer. A younger brother was the Reverend Simeon Scherer.

License/Ordination: Licensed 1840 by North Carolina Synod. One of four North Carolina pastors in Virginia (the others, Jacob Scherer and Elijah Hawkins (ordained) and John Jacob Greever (licensed), who with two other pastors organized Southwest Virginia Synod, 1842; was ordained at organizing convention.

Calls: St. Peter, Cripple Creek, Wythe County, Va., 1841-42; Botetourt Parish (Brick Union, St. Mark), Botetourt County, Va., 1842-1846; Roanoke Parish, Zion, Roanoke, Va., 1842-51. Ministerial services in Texas, 1852-53.

Other: Co-Founder of Colorado College, Columbus, Texas. Was instrumental in having Virginia Collegiate Institute named Roanoke College in Salem, Va.

Date of Death: 1861; Texas.

SCHERER, JACOB

Date/Place of Birth: February 7, 1785; Guilford County, N.C.

Parents: Frederick Scherer and Barbara (Smith) Scherer. A younger brother was the Reverend Daniel Scherer. Father served in American Revolutionary forces.

Spouse: Elizabeth Scherer.

Children: The Reverend Gideon, the Reverend Simeon, the Reverend John Jacob.

License/Ordination: Licensed 1810 and ordained 1813 by North Carolina Synod.

Calls: Frieden's-Low's, Guilford County-Richland, Liberty-St. Paul, Alamance County, 1810-28; organized Cobles, Guilford County, 1812-29; served in Virginia and West Virginia in the 1830s, 1840s and early 1850s; later ministry, 1855-60 was in Texas.

Other: Associate Missionary with the Reverend Robert J. Miller in early period of ministry. As a pastor of North Carolina Synod, one of six pastors to organize Southwestern Virginia Synod in 1842. Served seven one-year terms as Secretary of North Carolina Synod between 1815 and 1827; and as President, 1824, 1835.

Date of Death/Burial Location: March 2, 1860; Columbus, Texas.

SCHERER, MELANCHTHON GIDEON GROSECLOSE

Date/Place of Birth: March 16, 1861; Catawba County, N.C.
Parents: The Reverend Simeon Scherer and Sarah Ann Jemimah (Roseman) Scherer. Mother died when he was four years old. The Reverend Jacob Scherer was his grandfather and the Reverend Daniel Scherer his uncle.
Spouse/Marriage Date: Alice M. C. (Ehrman) Scherer; October 20, 1886 in Catawba County, N.C.
Children: Boy (stillborn), Mary (died at age 6), the Reverend Paul Ehrman.
Education: Roanoke College, A.B. 1881, A.M. 1886, D.D. 1902; Southern Seminary at Salem, Va., 1882, first honor.
License/Ordination: Licensed 1882 and ordained 1883 by Virginia Synod.
Calls: In Virginia, 1882-86; Grafton, W.Va., 1886-90; Mt. Holly Springs, Pa., 1890-93; St. James, Concord, 1893-96; Mt. Hermon, Cabarrus County, 1895-99; Redeemer, Newberry, S.C., 1899-1901; St. Andrew's, Charleston, S.C., 1905-18.
Other: President, North Carolina College, 1896-99; Professor, Lutheran Theological Southern Seminary, 1901-05; first Secretary, United Lutheran Church in America, and *ex officio* Member of Executive Board, 1918-32; last President, United Synod South, 1914-18; Joint Committee to Propose Constitution of United Lutheran Church in America, and Ways and Means Committee to Arrange Merger in 1918 of General Council, General Synod, and United Synod South, into United Lutheran Church in America; (at his death he was the last surviving President of the three general bodies); *Common Service Book* Committee until 1931; Celebration of 400th Anniversary of Reformation Committee in 1917; took part in organizing National Lutheran Council 1918 and was a Commissioner to it from United Lutheran Church in America, 1918-32; Statistical and Church Yearbook Committee, United Lutheran Church in America, 1925-32; Board of Editors, *Lutheran World Almanac* from 1924; American Society of Church History; Board of Managers and Versions Committee, American Bible Society; Board, American Tract Society; Board, Newberry College; Board, Lutheran Theological Southern Seminary; Delegate to the first World Universal Christian Conference on Faith and Order, Stockholm, Sweden, 1925, and the first World Conference, Lausanne, Switzerland, 1927; author, *Christian Liberty and Church Unity,* 1932, and co-author of Key Series, *Our Church Paper,* 1924; contributed to *What is Lutheranism?*, 1930).
Date of Death/Burial Location: November 9, 1932; Magnolia Cemetery, Charleston, S.C.

SCHERER, SIMEON

Date/Place of Birth: October 29, 1819; Guilford County, N.C.; was baptized by the Reverend C. A. G. Storch. From age seven was brought up in Virginia.
Parents: The Reverend Jacob Scherer and Elizabeth Scherer. An older brother was the Reverend Gideon Scherer.
First Spouse/Marriage Date: Mary Ann (Davis) Scherer; July 24, 1851 in Salisbury, N.C.; died February 5, 1853.
Children of First Marriage: Sarah E. V.
Second Spouse/Marriage Date: Sarah Ann Jemimah (Roseman) Scherer; February 6, 1855 in Catawba County, N.C.; died February 13, 1865.
Children of Second Marriage: Four sons, among them the Reverend Melanchthon Gideon Groseclose.

Third Spouse/Marriage Date: Mrs. Harriet Isabel (Brown) James Scherer, daughter of Michael and Marie Brown, Rowan County, April 3, 1867.

Children of Third Marriage: Two sons, the older had died before July 1874; the other, the Reverend James A. B. Scherer.

Education: Classical and Theological Institute, Lexington, S.C., (forerunner of Newberry College, and Lutheran Theological Southern Seminary), 1841-42; Polytechnic Institute, New Market, Va., 1843; Gettysburg Seminary, 1846.

License/Ordination: Licensed 1848 and ordained 1850 by Southwestern Virginia Synod.

Calls: Giles County, Va., 1848-51; Union, Rowan County, 1851-53, again 1869-72; St. John, Salisbury, 1852-55, again with the Reverend W. H. Cone, 1867-72; Bethel, Rowan County, 1862-72; Salem, Rowan County, 1863-68; St. Peter, Rowan County, 1868-70; Organ, Rowan County, 1869-70, in several of which Pastor Cone assisted; while in second pastorate at Union, organized both Christiana 1871 and Christ (previously called Smith's Schoolhouse), East Spencer, 1870-75; Frieden's-Coble's-Low's, Guilford County-St. Paul, Alamance, 1855-58; St. Michael, Troutman, 1853-56; Beth Eden, Newton, 1860-61; and St. Paul, Alamance County, again, 1873-76.

Other: While getting education and later serving churches, taught school at times to supplement income; also toured in Maryland, Virginia, and North Carolina as agent for Roanoke College; in 1858 planned to move to Texas and serve with father and brothers (brother John was President of Colorado College), but for family reasons plan was abandoned; Secretary, North Carolina Synod, 1856; President, 1860; in his synodical file is a copy of *Notes On Life and Ministry of Rev. S. Scherer, Written by Himself,* to July 15, 1874.

Date of Death/Burial Location: July 11, 1876; Frieden's Church, near Gibsonville, N.C.

SCHILLINGER, SYLVANUS LEDEBUR

Date/Place of Birth: March 31, 1908; Mercer County, Pa.

Parents: The Reverend Paul D. Schillinger and Ida (Ledebur) Schillinger.

Spouse/Marriage Date: Esther Jane (Lincoln) Schillinger; June 25, 1935.

Education: Capital University, B.A. 1928; Evangelical Lutheran Theological Seminary, Columbus, Ohio, B.D. 1932; Hartwick Seminary, Oneonta, N.Y.; Union Seminary; Jewish Seminary; Lenoir-Rhyne College, D.D. 1969.

Ordination: August 28, 1932 by American Lutheran Church.

Calls: Martin Luther, Bergton, Va., 1932-33; Cedarhurst, N.Y., 1936-43; St. Paul, Hickory and Old St. Paul, Newton, 1944-56; St. Paul, Hickory, 1956-83.

Other: Professor of Classical Languages, Outlook College, Outlook, Saskatchewan, Canada; Co-author of *Facing the Cross.*

Date of Death: October 23, 1983.

SCHIMEL, MARY ANNA (BADER)

See: Mary Anna Bader.

SCHMIDT, CHARLES Z. M.
Ordination: 1812 by North Carolina Synod at Lincolnton.
Calls: Received into North Carolina Synod in 1811 with nine congregations being served in Tennessee: New Haven, Blountville; Zion, Bristol; Solomon, St. James, and Blue Springs, Greene County; Miller, Knox County; Sinking Springs, Midway; Immanuel, Millingport; and one other.
Other: Along with two other school teachers, Jacob Zink and Adam Miller, served as early workers for Lutheran Church in East Tennessee, in late 18th and early 19th centuries.
Date of Death/Burial Location: 1814; Tennessee.

SCHMIDT, EDWIN R.
Date/Place of Birth: October 23, 1928; Gackle, N.D.
Parents: John Schmidt and Christina Schmidt.
Spouse/Marriage Date: Jean (Galliart) Schmidt; October 12, 1952 at Dubuque, Iowa.
Children: Beth, Paula, Eric, Stephen.
Education: Wartburg College, B.A. 1949; Wartburg Seminary, M.Div. 1952.
Ordination: June 1952 by American Lutheran Church.
Calls: Mission Developer/Pastor, Salem, Stanton, N.D., 1952-56; St. John, Arthur, N.D., 1956-62; Trinity, Cooperstown, N.D., 1962-71; St. Olaf, Devil's Lake, N.D., 1971-77; Mission Developer/Pastor, Christ, Vernon Hills, Ill., 1977-93; retired 1993; Vice Pastor, Shepherd of the Hills, McHenry, Ill.; Interim Assistant Pastor for Nurturing of New Members, St. Mark's, Charlotte, 1996.
Other: Chaplain for Police Department and at Mercy Hospital, Devil's Lake, N.D.; Chaplain, Countryside Fire Protection District, Ill.; in the Eastern North Dakota District, American Lutheran Church: Youth Committee, Bible Camp Committee, Town and Country Higher Education Committee; District Council, Eastern North Dakota District representative on the National Board of Missions and Chair of the New Missions Subcommittee.

SCHMITT, HERMAN M. J.
Date/Place of Birth: June 13, 1913; Anamoose, N.D.
Parents: The Reverend J. Schmitt and Johanna Schmitt.
Spouse/Marriage Date: Ollie (Monk) Schmitt; October 15, 1938 in Illinois.
Children: Paul H., Donald M., Joanne M.
Education: Wartburg College, B.A. 1935; Wartburg Seminary, M.Div. 1938; University of Illinois, M.S. 1942.
Ordination: June 1938 by South Dakota Synod.
Calls: Emmanuel, New Leipzig, N.D., 1938-41; Trinity, Shumway, Ill., 1941-49; Good Shepherd, Wells, Minn., 1949-64; Christ, Corpus Christi, Texas, 1964-70; Zion, Peoria, Ill., 1970-80; retired 1980 to North Carolina; transferred to Colorado in 1988.
Date of Death/Burial Location: March 8, 1998; Littleton, Colo.

SCHMUCKER, GEORGE
Parents: The Reverend John Nicolas Schmucker, whose two brothers, John George and John Peter, were also Lutheran ministers. Father was for many years pastor of the Woodstock, Va., congregation.
Ordination: 1857.
Calls: Transferred to Tennessee Synod 1858 and served churches in Pendleton and Hardy Counties, Va. He and two other Tennessee Synod pastors, the Reverends James E. Seneker and Henry Wetzel, with their congregations, organized the Concordia Synod in Virginia, 1867; short-lived, in a few years it became a district of Joint Synod of Ohio.

SCHMUCKER, JOHN PETER
Date and Place of Birth: Was born soon after family came from Germany in 1781 and settled in Lehigh County, Pa. for one year, and in Lancaster County, Pa., for another; then moved to valley of Virginia near Woodstock.
Parent: John Christopher Schmucker. Younger brother of the Reverends John George and John Nicolas Schmucker. A nephew, George, son of the Reverend John Nicolas Schmucker, also became a Lutheran minister.
License/Ordination: Licensed 1813 at Lincolnton, N.C.; was ordained in 1820 by the North Carolina Synod when twenty congregations in Virginia, served by him and itinerant pastors, were received into North Carolina Synod.
Calls: Served North Carolina Synod churches located in Virginia: Solomon, Forestville, 1814-20; St. Matthew, New Market, 1817-18; Supply, Zion, Edinburg.
Other: No further data available concerning his ministry or life.

SCHOBER, GOTTLIEB
Place of Birth: November 1, 1756; Bethlehem, Pa. He would grow up to be an "industrial and business pioneer, lawyer, state senator, postmaster and church official." (Brawley, *Dictionary of North Carolina Biography*, 5, 399).
Parents: Andreas Schober and Hedwig (Schubert) Schober.
Education: Received education in the Moravian school at Bethlehem, Pa., called Nazareth Hall. In 1769 was sent by his parents along with a group of other Moravian boys to Bethabara, Wachovia, in North Carolina, to learn a trade. He was apprenticed to a leather maker in the new settlement of Salem.

He earned the displeasure of church officials at Salem by taking in outside work, rather than confining himself to the work assigned him by his supervisor. In 1770 began his study of the pipe organ. In 1779 served three years as a teacher in the school in Salem. In 1782 became an assistant in the Salem store, selling among other things, leather breeches of his own manufacture and began making frequent trips to Charleston, S.C., to trade for articles not manufactured in Salem. In 1785 left the leather store to learn the trade of tinsmith and opened a tinware shop in Salem in 1786. In 1787 added house painting to the services he was prepared to offer. In 1789 secured permission from the Moravian leaders to build and operate a plant in Salem designed to produce paper, and when the mill became operational in 1791 was the first of its kind in North Carolina. In 1792 the first post office was established in Salem in Schober's house, and he was the Postmaster. He and his sons, Nathaniel and Emanuel, occupied this post for a total of 52 years. In 1794 on the basis of his private study of the law, Schober was admitted to the bar in Stokes and Rowan Counties. As the only lawyer in the Moravian settlement, he handled all of their legal concerns. Because of disputed titles to lands in Wilkes County, Schober was often in court in Statesville, Morganton and Raleigh In 1795 became a land speculator, purchasing more than 100,000 acres in Surry, Stokes, and Yadkin counties, but failed to realize a profit from it. He ended up giving a large tract of it to Gettysburg Seminary and other tracts to his sons. In May 1799 was named one of three persons to handle the community's music program. In 1800 was named a member of the *Helfer Conferenz*, a group overseeing the religious and secular affairs of the Salem community. In 1802 became the Justice of the Peace for Salem and in 1805 was elected to the State Senate, being re-elected in 1808.

Spouse/Marriage Date: Maria Magdalena (Transou) Schober; December 17, 1782. Died June 13, 1835.

Children: Nathaniel, Johanna Sophia, Emanuel, Anna Pauline, Hedwig Elizabeth, Benjamin, Maria Theresa.

Ordination: In 1773 felt called to enter the ordained ministry, but the Moravian community selected its ministerial candidates by lot and the lot went against him. In 1809 was traveling to Charleston, S.C. in the company of his friend, the Reverend Charles [C. A. G.] Storch of Rowan County, and his conversations with Storch rekindled his interest in becoming an ordained minister. Was reared in the Moravian Church and continued all his life as a member, yet was ordained October 21, 1810 by North Carolina Synod at its annual convention. The Moravians permitted him to continue to live in Old Salem and attend services as a Moravian. After a time, they also permitted him to resume his services as an organist at Home Church.

Calls: As a Lutheran, he provided supply services for churches in Davie, Davidson and Forsyth counties. In the year of his ordination, 1810 at age 56 he was elected Secretary of the North Carolina Synod, a post to which he was returned for eight years. In 1812 he was elected the first Treasurer of the North Carolina Synod and kept this post until 1831. On September 1, 1816 he established a Sunday School at Hopewell, four miles from Salem, which was one of the first, if not indeed the first such school to be established in the state of North Carolina. He then proceeded to establish similar schools in each of the churches he served. A Moravian record of February 7, 1813 speaks of Pastor Schober's serving Bethlehem and Beaverdam Lutheran Churches, near Salem, N.C., every four weeks, "and on the other Sundays free school is held there and the young people are instructed in reading and singing; adults also attend" (an early type of Sunday School). Nazareth-Shiloh, also Hopewell, Forsyth County, 1810-30; Davidson County: Beck's and New Jerusalem 1815-31 and supplied St. Luke and Pilgrim, 1816.

Other: In 1817 he was asked to prepare for publication a history of the Reformation and Luther's writings accompanied by an explanation of their meaning. The manuscript was approved by the Synod and 1,500 copies published. The book, *Luther,* became involved in the dispute which culminated in the creation of the Tennessee Synod. Theological differences between David Henkel, ardent and strict confessional Lutheran, and Schober, a Moravian ordained to serve Lutheran congregations, were pronounced, and contributed to the split in North Carolina Synod in 1820, resulting in organization of Tennessee Synod. In 1820 was North Carolina Synod's representative at the organizational meeting of the General Synod and played a significant role in drafting the organization's initial constitution. Was named to that organization's committee on preparing a hymn book and a catechism for the use of its member synods. In 1821 was elected President of the North Carolina Synod and was annually re-elected until 1831.   Credited with saving some Lutheran churches from disintegrating, among them St. John, Salisbury. He was one of three persons responsible for presenting to the North Carolina Synod and the Episcopal Convention a "Plan of Union" which called for delegates of each denomination to attend the annual convention of the other. Schober called a halt to this exchange when, at a Lutheran celebration of the Eucharist, Schober concluded that the Episcopalians did not regard the ordination of their Lutheran brethren as valid. Served on Board of Directors, General Synod theological school at Gettysburg, Pa. In 1828 helped to organize the interdenominational Stokes County Sunday School Union to support the growing Sunday School movement and for four years served as the organization's first President.

Date of Death/Burial Location: June 29, 1838; God's Acre, Old Salem, Winston-Salem, N.C.
(Sources: James S. Brawley, "Gottlieb Shober," *Dictionary of North Carolina Biography*, William S. Powell, Ed. 5, 339-40, 1994; Jerry L. Surrat, *Gottlieb Schober of Salem*, 1983.)

SCHOENBERG, JOHN C. A.

Place of Birth: Pennsylvania.
License/Ordination: Licensed by South Carolina Synod at organizational convention, 1824. Transferred 1826 to North Carolina and was ordained in 1828 by North Carolina Synod.
Calls: Supplied Kimberling parish, Rural Retreat, Va., one year; was sent in 1827 to do missionary work in Illinois. Returned in 1828 reporting that: "There were hundreds of Lutherans scattered through Illinois, Indiana, and Missouri, entirely destitute of preaching by our ministers." First pastor of Union Church, near Anna, Ill., 1827-29, and continued ministry in that state, as member of North Carolina Synod. Note: Illinois Synod was organized in 1851.

SCHOOLFIELD, DANIEL S.

Ordination: Licensed in 1835; ordained Deacon 1837 by Tennessee Synod in Blue Springs Church, Greene County, Tenn.
Calls: Monroe, Blount, Greene Counties, Tenn., 1835-39; Koiner's Church, Augusta County, Va., 1839; further record of ministry not available.
Other: Name not listed on synodical roll after 1845.

SCHOTT, GEORGE FREDERICK, JR.

Date/Place of Birth: November 3, 1913; Newport News, Va.
Parents: George Frederick Schott, Sr. and Ingeborg Elizabeth (Nielsen) Schott.
Spouse/Marriage Date: Violet Ruth (Cauble) Schott, sister of the Reverend Herman W. Cauble; August 7, 1940 in Salisbury, Rowan County, N.C.
Children: The Reverend George Frederick, III.
Education: Lenoir-Rhyne, A.B. 1937, D.D. 1958; Lutheran Theological Southern Seminary, B.D. *cum laude* 1942; Chicago Seminary, S. T. M. 1961.
Ordination: June 4, 1942 by North Carolina Synod.

Calls: St. Andrew's-St. Michael, near Columbia, S.C., 1942-44; first full-time pastor, Calvary, Spencer, 1944-52; retired 1981.

Other: Professor of Systematic Theology, Lutheran Theological Southern Seminary, 1952-81; Board, Lenoir- Rhyne, 1949-75, Vice Chair, 1950-59; Secretary, North Carolina Synod, 1949-53; North Carolina Synod Historical Works Committee, 1949-55, 1961-63; contributed four articles to *Lutheran Encyclopedia* of the Lutheran World Federation; Lutheran chaplain, World Boy Scout Jamboree, 1947; awarded Silver Beaver, Boy Scouts of America, 1950; Commission on Marriage, United Lutheran Church in America, 1954-56; Chair, Evsor Forest Housing Development Corporation (Housing for the Elderly), 1983-; Chair, Senior Catering Supplies, Meals on Wheels; Board, Richland-Lexington Drug and Alcohol Council, ten years; Chair, Seminary Ridge Community Council, eight years.

SCHRODER, HENRY ANDREW, SR.

Date/Place of Birth: August 7, 1896; Charleston, S.C.

Parents: Julius N. Schroder and Emily M. (Lesemann) Schroder.

Spouse/Marriage Date: Pauline (Boozer) Schroder, daughter of the Reverend V. Y. Boozer; August 7, 1923 at Madison, Va.

Children: Margaret Pauline (married the Reverend Herbert C. Wolf), Henry Andrew, Jr.

Education: Newberry College, before, and College of Charleston, after service (1917-18) in U.S. Navy in World War I; Lutheran Theological Southern Seminary, 1923.

Ordination: 1923 by South Carolina Synod.

Calls: As student, organized Ascension, Danville, Va., 1922; organized and built church, Grace, Rock Hill, S.C., 1923-31; St. Paul, Durham, 1931-63, Pastor Emeritus, 1963-76; Pastor to Lutheran students at Duke University; Pastor to Lutheran students at University of North Carolina at Chapel Hill, 1937-42, before Holy Trinity, Chapel Hill, was developed; visiting pastor to Lutheran patients at Duke Hospital and to servicemen at Camp Butner during World War II; Vice Pastor at various congregations.

Date of Death/Burial Location: February 25, 1976; Maplewood Cemetery, Annex B, Durham, N.C.

SCHULTZ, LANELL

Calls: Providence, Winston-Salem, 1975-1980.

SCHWARTZ, JOHN WILLIAM

Date/Place of Birth: January 8, 1834; Gettysburg, Pa.

Parents: William P. Schwartz and Isabella S. Schwartz.

Education: Gettysburg College, A.B., D.D. 1891; Gettysburg Seminary; received private tutoring in theology.

First Spouse/Marriage Date: Kate C. (Gemberling) Schwartz; December 27, 1859 at Selinsgrove, Pa.

Children of First Marriage: Mrs. M. M. Albeck, William K., Fred K.

Second Spouse/Marriage Date: Philomena (Keller) Schwartz; April 22, 1891 at Kelleysburg, Pa.

License/Ordination: Licensed and ordained for Tennessee Synod by the Reverends Socrates Henkel and David M. Henkel; Licensed by Western Pennsylvania Synod. Ordained by the Eastern Pennsylvania Synod in 1860.

Calls: Name first found on Tennessee Synod roll in 1855 though absent at 1855 convention, and absent and excused at conventions in 1856 and 1857; dismissed to Joint Synod of Ohio 1857 and served churches in Ohio, 1857-59; served three pastorates in Pennsylvania, 1859-1919, with the first at Berwick, Pa., and the last at Worthington, 1867-1919; Lycoming County, Pa., 1861-62.

Other: Instructor, Johnstown (Pennsylvania) Academy, 1862-65; accepted similar appointment at Martinsburg, Pa., 1965. Trustee, Gettysburg Seminary, 1893-1913.

Date of Death/Burial Location: January 23, 1919 (one source says May 23); Worthington, Pa.

SCHYLER, JULIUS C. W.

License: Licensed 1827 by North Carolina Synod in St. Paul Church, Lincoln (now Catawba) County.

Calls: Served in Stokes County, 1827-28; name not on synodical roll after 1828.

Other: Assistant to President of North Carolina Synod, 1827-28.

SEABOCH, JACOB AUGUSTUS

Date/Place of Birth: May 13, 1905; Hickory, N.C.

Parents: Lee Jones Seaboch and Ida (Huffman) Seaboch.

Spouse/Marriage Date: Martha (Taylor) Seaboch; August 14, 1931 at Haralson, Ga.

Children: Richard Taylor, Stephen Lowell.

Education: Lenoir-Rhyne, A.B. 1926; Lutheran Theological Southern Seminary, B.D. 1929; graduate study, Emory University and University of Georgia.

Ordination: Ordained 1929 by North Carolina Synod.

Calls: Haralson and Senoia, Ga., 1929-35; Good Shepherd, Savannah, Ga., 1943-50; St. Mark, Rowan County, 1950-59; Pilgrim, Davidson County, 1959-63; Grace, Liberty, 1964-70; retired 1970; Vice Pastor at various congregations.

Other: Principal, Haralson Junior High School, and Molena High School, Ga., 1935-43; Board, Lutheran Theological Southern Seminary, 1948-51; President, Ebenezer Conference of the Georgia Synod, 1948-49.

Date of Death/Burial Location: September 21, 1975; Gilmore Memorial Park, Julian, N.C.

SEAGLE, HENRY L.

Date/Place of Birth: January 16, 1877; Reidsville, N.C.

Education: Educated in Theology at Lutheran Theological Southern Seminary, 1905.

Ordination: 1905 by Holston Synod.

Calls: Transferred 1906 to Tennessee Synod, and served Mt. Gilead and St. Martin Churches, Cabarrus County, 1906-08; Virginia Synod History says he served Miller and Zion Churches, Knox County, Tenn., 1905-06, having succeeded the Rev. J. C. Wessinger;

his address in 1908 was Lincolnton, and in 1909-17 was Charleston, S.C., but no record is found of churches he served; member of Tennessee Synod in 1918.

SEAMAN, RALPH WITSON

Date/Place of Birth: January 3, 1918; Baldwin, N.Y.
Parents: Wilfred M. Seaman and Anita (Southard) Seaman.
Spouse/Marriage Date: Mary E. (Strickland) Seaman; August 15, 1943 in Baldwin, N.Y.
Children: Lois Anne, Linda Jeanne.
Education: Muhlenberg College, A.B. 1939; Lutheran Theological Seminary (Philadelphia), B.D. 1942; S.T.M., 1944.
Ordination: June 3, 1942, by New York and New England Synod.
Calls: Trinity, Castleton-on-Hudson, N.Y., 1944-47; Bethany, North Bergen, N.J., 1947-51; St. Paul, Beachwood, N.J., 1951-56; St. Paul, Millville, N.J., 1956-71; Grace, North Arlington, N.J., 1971-74; Ebenezer, China Grove, 1974-79; Atonement, Wilkesboro, 1979-83; retired March 1, 1983; Unit Chaplain at Lutheran Home, Salisbury, 1985-88; transferred to New Jersey Synod, 1988; Vice Pastor at various congregations.

SECHRIST, ANDREW

License/Ordination: Licensed June 1821 in Lau's (Low's) Church, Guilford County, by North Carolina Synod, and ordained May 1831 in Organ Church, Rowan County.
Calls: Listed in Virginia Synod History at Marion-Ebenezer Parish (then of North Carolina Synod), Smyth County, Va., in 1820. Statements as to his synodical membership are conflicting, as that after being Licensed in 1821 by North Carolina Synod, was ordained Deacon in 1823 by Tennessee Synod; then ordained as Pastor in 1831 by North Carolina Synod, but membership was severed in May 1835. In September 1935 he reunited with Tennessee Synod, and was a member until September 1837. However, *History of the Lutheran Church in North Carolina,* (1803-1953) lists him as serving Richland Church (Tennessee Synod), Randolph County, 1852-54.

SEEGERS, JOHN CONRAD

Date/Place of Birth: October 6, 1867; Columbia, S.C.
Parents: John C. Seegers and Mary Dorothea (Schroeder) Seegers.
Spouse/Marriage Date: May Erwin (Ide) Seegers; February 14, 1893 in Richmond, Va.
Children: John Conrad (President, Muhlenberg College), Virginia May, Florence H., L. Walter, Sarah C., Ernest F.
Education: Newberry College, A.B. 1888, D.D. 1909; Philadelphia Seminary, 1891; Muhlenberg College, Honorary M.A. 1907.
Ordination: 1891 by Holston Synod.
Calls: First, Richmond, Va., 1891-94; Redeemer, Albany, N.Y., 1895-1901; St. John, Easton, Pa., 1901-11; Trinity, Reading, Pa., 1911-14; St. Paul, Wilmington, 1918-21.
Other: Professor of Practical Theology, Lutheran Theological Southern Seminary, 1914-18; Professor, Philadelphia Seminary, 1921-36; President, Home Missions Board, United Synod South, 1916-18; Vice President, Board of American Missions, United Lutheran Church in America, 1918-24; served on committees of synods, and of General Council, United Synod South, and United Lutheran Church in America; Co-author, *An Explanation*

of The Common Service; author, *The Church for the Ages;* and co-editor, *The Lutheran Church Review,* and *Gospel Preaching for the Day* (2 volumes).
Date of Death/Burial Location: June 23, 1936; Philadelphia, Pa.

SELL, JOHN W.

Date/Place of Birth: December 31, 1931; Milwaukee, Wis.
Parents: Hamlin G. Sell and Dolores (Windfelder) Sell.
Spouse/Marriage Date: Cathy (Truss) Sell; June 17, 1978 in Milwaukee, Wis.
Children: William Krzyzanowski, Lauri Elli Sell, Sarah (Sell) Rathcamp, Peter Sell, Greg Krzyzanowski.
Education: University of Wisconsin, Carthage College, B.S. 1957; Luther Seminary, M.Div. 1960.
Ordination: May 1960 by Northwest Synod, ULCA.
Calls: Cross of Christ, Minneapolis, Minn., 1960-62; Trinity, Kenosha, Wis., 1962-64; Advent, Cedarberg, Wis., 1964-70; Milwaukee Council on Alcoholism, Administrative Chaplain, 1970-84; Epiphany, Milwaukee, Wis., 1970-86; Christ, Charlotte, 1987; Ebenezer, China Grove, 1987-92; Redeemer, Kannapolis, 1992-95; Interim Pastor at various congregations. Retired October 1997.

SENEKER, JAMES E.

Place of Birth: Sullivan County, Tenn., a son of Zion Church.
Ordination: Ordained Deacon by Tennessee Synod 1852 and Pastor 1857.
Calls: Beck's-New Jerusalem-Pilgrim, Davidson County, 1860-62; from 1863 to 1866 served Tennessee Synod churches in Virginia; with other pastors of Virginia Special Conference of Tennessee Synod, helped to organize Concordia Synod in 1866 with permission of Tennessee Synod. However, at scheduled date for first convention, only he and two other pastors (George Schmucker and Henry Wetzel) showed up. The new synod failing to thrive, they petitioned Joint Synod of Ohio in 1869 to receive it as its Concordia District. Sixteen years later (1884), after multiple requests, Wetzel was received back into Tennessee Synod, but the other two pastors never returned.

SENEKER, JOHN A.

Place of Birth: Sullivan County, Tenn., son of Zion Church.
Ordination: Ordained Deacon 1852 and Pastor 1857 by Tennessee Synod, along with James E. Seneker.
Calls: Solomon Church, Greene County, Tenn.; appears to have been one of ten organizers of Holston Synod, December 1860-January 1861.
Other: For unknown reason, was deposed from Holston Synod in 1870.
Burial Location: Virginia.

SENTER, JONAS MICHAEL

Date/Place of Birth: November 11, 1863; Gaston County, N.C.
Parents: Jonas Senter and Malinda (Carpenter) Senter.
Spouse/Marriage Date: Barbara D. (Hunt) Senter, daughter of the Reverend George L. Hunt; April 2, 1891 in Newton, N.C.
Children: Olive Winifred, Lillian Ruth, Ella Grace, Herman Frederick, William Edward, George Loy, Karl Winfield, Kathryn Theodosia (died in infancy).
Education: Gaston College, Dallas, and St. Paul Practical Seminary, Hickory; Newberry College, D.D. 1924.
License/Ordination: Licensed and ordained 1890 by Joint Synod of Ohio.
Calls: Four churches, Petersburg, W.Va., 1890-1902; Bethel-Luther's Chapel, Lincoln County-St. Paul, Gaston County, 1902-12; transferred 1912 to Tennessee Synod, bringing Luther's Chapel with him; Beck's-Holly Grove-New Jerusalem, Davidson County, 1912-18; St. Martin-Mt. Hermon-Sharon, Iredell County, 1915-20; in South Carolina, Tennessee Synod: Bethlehem-Mt. Horeb-St. John, Chapin, 1920-26; in 1922 he and churches at Chapin, along with other North Carolina Synod churches and pastors in South Carolina, were transferred to South Carolina Synod; Salem, Rowan County, 1926-32; again, in South Carolina at Pomeria and St. Matthew, Pomaria, 1932-34; retired in 1934.
Other: Board, Newberry College.
Date of Death/Burial Location: August 11, 1946; Bethel Church, Gaston County, N.C.

SETTLEMYRE, DANIEL J.

Date/Place of Birth: October 19, 1851; near Hickory, N.C.
Parents: Paul Settlemyre and Clara (Smith) Settlemyre.
Spouse/Marriage Date: Hester Ann (Carpenter) Settlemyre; April 25, 1883 in Lincoln County, N.C.
Children: Ocie Clara Elenora, Polycarp Plato, Myrtle May, Laura Ann, Lillian Gertrude, Chloe Edith, Paul Hubert, Emma Blanche, Philip Adolphus.
Education: Concordia College, studied theology under the Reverends P. C. Henkel, R. A. Yoder, and J. M. Smith.
Ordination: 1883 by Tennessee Synod.
Calls: Mt. Moriah, 1883-86, 1892-94, and St. Mark, 1890-92, 1893-94, Rowan County; Friendship, Alexander County-Philadelphia, Granite Falls, 1886-87; Sharon-St. Martin, Iredell County, 1886-91; organized with eight members, St. John, Statesville, and built church, 1888-92; mission churches of Tennessee Synod in Alabama, four years; Coble's, Guilford County-Melanchthon, Randolph County-Mt. Pleasant, Alamance County, 1903-1911; retired 1911 in Hickory.
Other: Taught school at times to supplement income for family support.
Date of Death/Burial Location: June 5, 1917; New Jerusalem Church, Catawba County, N.C.

SETZER, CHARLES PETER

Date/Place of Birth: March 28, 1938; Brunswick, Ga.

Parents: The Reverend Roy Baxter Setzer and Harriet (Teufel) Setzer. An older brother was the Reverend John Schoneberg Setzer; the Reverend Charles M. Teufel, D.D., was his grandfather.

Spouse/Marriage Date: Donna Sue (Mullin) Setzer; July 10, 1966 in Lincolnton, N.C.

Children: David Peter, Joy Suzanna.

Education: Washington University, Iowa State University, Colorado University, B.A. 1961; Lutheran Theological Southern Seminary, M.Div. *cum laude* 1965; Lenoir-Rhyne, D.D., 1987.

Ordination: June 6, 1965 by North Carolina Synod.

Calls: Mission Developer/Pastor, Lutheran Church of the Living Word, Laurinburg, 1965-70; Holy Trinity, Gastonia, 1970-87; St. Mark's, Charlotte, 1987-; Vice Pastor at various congregations.

Other: Adult Member at Large of North Carolina Luther League, 1966-67; Committee on Auxiliaries, 1967- 70; Youth Ministry Committee; Board, Lenoir-Rhyne, 1973-81; President, Task Force - Priority Program, 1970-72; first recipient of Walton Harlowe Greever Award from Lutheran Theological Southern Seminary; Founders Award from Heart Association; Outstanding Young Man of the Year from Jaycees; Good Neighbor Award from Mental Health Association; Service to Mankind Award from Sertoma Club; Spiritual Director, National Lutheran Secretariat of Via de Cristo, 1994-96; General Chair, North Carolina Synod's Lutheran Homes Appeal, 1985-87; Founded the Youth Ministry Camp with the Retarded; Chair, Region 9 Steering Committee; Executive Board, North Carolina Synod 1981-86 Synod Council, 1993-.

SETZER, DENNIS LEE, JR.

Date/Place of Birth: August 23, 1944; Lincoln County, N.C.

Parents: Dennis L. Setzer, Sr. and Mable (Robinson) Setzer.

Spouse/Marriage Date: Gloria Jean (Miller) Setzer; July 17, 1964, in York, S.C.

Children: Dennis Lee, III, Kirk Monroe, Trevor Kolby, John Robinson.

Education: Lenoir-Rhyne, A.B. 1966; Lutheran Theological Southern Seminary, M.Div. 1970.

Ordination: June 7, 1970 by North Carolina Synod.

Calls: St. Paul, Burlington, 1970-76; Zion, Hickory, 1976-81; Grace, Bessemer City, 1982-86; Cross of Christ, Concord, 1986-89; Church of the Resurrection, Rocky Mount, 1989-92; transferred to South Carolina Synod in 1992. Was serving St. Philip, Myrtle Beach, S.C. in 1999.

SETZER, JOHN SCHONEBERG

Date/Place of Birth: May 1, 1934; Brunswick, Ga.

Parents: The Reverend Roy Baxter Setzer and Harriet (Teufel) Setzer. Was the older brother of the Reverend C. Peter Setzer; the Reverend Charles M. Teufel, D.D., was his grandfather.

Spouse/Marriage Date: Rossina (Vrionides) Setzer; August 9, 1964 in Deer Park, N.Y.

Education: University of Louisville, 1951-54, St. Olaf, B.A. *cum laude* 1955; Lutheran Theological Southern Seminary (middle year at Chicago Seminary), B.D. *cum laude* 1958; Duke University, Ph.D. in Systematic Theology 1963.

Ordination: June 1958 by Illinois Synod.

Calls: Union, Rowan County, 1958-61; Emmanuel, Lincolnton, 1964-67; Vice Pastor at various congregations; transferred to Upper New York Synod, 1967.
Other: Teacher at Hartwick College, Oneonta, N.Y.
Date of Death/Burial Location: November 25, 1976; New York.

SETZER, ROY BAXTER, SR.

Date/Place of Birth: June 24, 1900; Catawba County, N.C.
Parents: David Pinkney Setzer and Mary Ida (Hahn) Setzer.
Spouse/Marriage Date: Harriet (Teufel) Setzer, daughter of the Reverend Charles M. Teufel; January 3, 1932 in Staunton, Va.
Children: The Reverend John Schoneberg, Carole Elizabeth, the Reverend Charles Peter, Fred Teufel, Roy Baxter, Jr., Mary Fonda Boye (wife of the Reverend Richard E. Boye), Diane Grondahl Schroeder.
Education: Lenoir-Rhyne, B.A. 1927; Lutheran Theological Southern Seminary, B.D. 1930; graduate study, University of South Carolina and Union (New York City) Seminary.
Ordination: 1930 by North Carolina Synod.
Calls: St. James, Brunswick, Ga., 1930-38; Salem-Luther Memorial, Cocke County, Tenn., 1938-42; St. John, Anderson, Ind., 1942-47; Memorial, Louisville, Ky., 1947-55; Mizpah, St. Louis, Mo., 1955-58; Hope, Pueblo, Colo., 1958-64; Alamance, Alamance, 1964-70; retired September 1970; Vice Pastor at various congregations.
Other: Pastor/Evangelist in United Lutheran Church in America, through its Department of Evangelism, holding many preaching missions in the U.S.; Board, Home for the Aged, Jeffersontown, Ky.; Welfare Director of Brunswick, Ga., and associate judge; started the first Boys Club in the South for underprivileged children.
Date of Death/Burial Location: July 26, 1979; Alamance Lutheran Church Cemetery, Alamance, N.C.

SHANER, MARTIN LUTHER

Date/Place of Birth: June 6, 1910; Staunton, Va.
Parents: Jacob Luther Shaner and Maggie Boyd (Hiserman) Shaner.
Spouse/Marriage Date: Grace Aline (Mayer) Shaner; May 26, 1933 in Columbia, S.C.
Children: Virginia Carolyn Lehman, Robert Luther, Loretta Jo Grose, Jacob Lindsay, Janet Lois Fitzgibbon.
Education: Roanoke College, A.B. 1932; Lutheran Theological Southern Seminary, B.D. 1935.
Ordination: July 21, 1935 by Virginia Synod.
Calls: Giles Parish, Giles County, Va., 1935-40; New River Parish, Cambria, Va., 1940-41; U.S. Air Force Chaplain, 1941-63, at Seymour Johnson Air Force Base, Goldsboro, 1959-63; retired from Chaplaincy, 1963; Advent, Toledo, Ohio, 1963-68; organized Triumphant Cross, Trotwood, Ohio, 1968-74; retired 1974; supplied Melanchthon Chapel, 1974-86; retired again for health reasons.
Date of Death/Burial Location: April 28, 1993; Staunton, Va.

SHAW, CHARLES PIERSON, JR.
Date/Place of Birth: August 18, 1964; Winston-Salem, N.C.
Parents: Charles Pierson Shaw, Sr. and Maude M. (Thrower) Shaw.
Spouse/Marriage Date: The Reverend Lois Paulette (Stavely) Shaw; December 3, 1994.
Education: Appalachian State University, B.S. Music 1987; Lutheran Theological Southern Seminary, M.Div. 1994.
Ordination: June 3, 1994 by North Carolina Synod.
Calls: Sharon Evangelical, Statesville, 1994-98; Christ, Winston-Salem, 1998-

SHAW, LOIS PAULETTE (STAVELY)
Spouse/Marriage Date: The Reverend Charles Pierson Shaw; December 3, 1994.
Education: Tusculum College, B.A. Management, 1989; Lutheran Theological Southern Seminary, M.Div. 1994.
Ordination: 1997 by North Carolina Synod.
Calls: St. Michael, High Point, 1997-.
Other: Counselor, Mitchell Community College, Statesville.

SHEALY, CHARLES JACKSON, JR.
Date/Place of Birth: April 6, 1919; Prosperity, S.C.
Parents: The Reverend Dr. Charles J. Shealy, Sr. and Elizabeth (Voigt) Shealy.
Spouse: Sara (Paysinger) Shealy.
Children: Charles J., III, Margaret Amanda Randall, Sara Ann Duncan.
Education: Newberry College, B.A. English Literature 1940; Lutheran Theological Southern Seminary, B.D. 1943.
Ordination: June 20, 1943 by South Carolina Synod.
Calls: St. Paul, Aiken, S.C., 1943-48; Campus Pastor at Duke University, Durham, 1948-50; St. Luke, Thunderbolt, Ga., 1950-58; Grace, Rock Hill, S.C., 1959-69; Bethlehem, Pomaria, S.C., 1969-82; retired September 1, 1982; Vice Pastor at various congregations.
Other: Lieutenant Colonel, U.S. Army Reserve.
Date of Death/Burial Location: August 9, 1996; memorial service at The Lutheran Church of the Redeemer, Newberry, S.C., with the body being donated to the Medical University.

SHEALY, GUY HUBERT
Date/Place of Birth: May 13, 1945; Lexington, S.C.
Parents: Gaston G. Shealy and Ruby Lee (Swygert) Shealy.
Spouse/Marriage Date: Linda Kathryn (Smith) Shealy; August 31, 1974 in Columbia, S.C.
Children: Paul Gaston, Elizabeth Frances.
Education: Newberry, A.D. 1967; Lutheran Theological Southern Seminary, M.Div. 1971; Columbia Seminary, D.Min. 1996; Winthrop University, M.Ed. 1980.
Ordination: June 27, 1971 by South Carolina Synod.
Calls: Messiah, Hanahan, S.C., 1971-73; Catawba Mental Health Center, 1973-86; Lutheran Family Services, 1986-88; The Saluda Center, 1988-.

SHEALY, JAMES FRANKLIN

Date/Place of Birth: November 3, 1939; Little Mountain, S.C.
Parents: Andrew Floyd Shealy and Myrtle Katherleen (Lake) Shealy.
Spouse/Marriage Date: Belva (Betty) (Stuck) Shealy; June 13, 1965 in Pomaria, S.C.
Children: James Matthew, Edie Elizabeth, David Stuck.
Education: Newberry College, A.B. English 1961; Lutheran Theological Southern Seminary, M.Div. 1965; graduate work, Lutheran Theological Southern Seminary, 1968, and Trinity Seminary, 1992-93.
Ordination: June 6, 1965 by South Carolina Synod.
Calls: St. Luke, Bear Poplar, 1965-73; Bachman Chapel, Prosperity, S.C., 1973-.
Other: Evangelism Committee, South Carolina Synod; Dean, Newberry District, South Carolina Synod; Past Officer in Lutheran Ministers of Newberry; Officer in Mid-Carolina Ministers Association; President, Mid- Carolina Lions Club; leader in sermon study group of local Lutheran pastors.

SHEALY, JEFFERSON DAVIS

Date/Place of Birth: February 22, 1862; near Leesville, S.C.
Parents: Wiley Shealy and Jemima (Hallman) Shealy.
Spouse: Katherine R. (Greene) Shealy.
Education: Newberry College; presumably attended Lutheran Theological Southern Seminary.
Ordination: 1891 by South Carolina Synod.
Calls: St. Andrew-Mt. Hermon-Cold Water, Concord, 1894-95; served some fourteen churches in South Carolina in four counties: Lexington, Newberry, Saluda, and Aiken Counties.
Date of Death/Burial Location: October 9, 1926; Leesville, S.C.

SHEALY, PERRY EDGAR

Date/Place of Birth: September 2, 1880; Prosperity, S.C.
Parents: Samuel Luther Shealy and Sarah Catherine (Kinard) Shealy.
Spouse/Marriage Date: Pearl Mae (Moody) Shealy; November 13, 1910 in Mt. Pleasant, S.C.
Children: Mildred Mae.
Education: Lenoir-Rhyne, one year, Newberry College, A.B. 1907, M.A. 1914; Lutheran Theological Southern Seminary, 1910; Chicago Seminary, B.D. 1918.
Ordination: 1910 by Georgia Synod.
Calls: Rincon, Ga., 1910-12; St. James, Beth Eden and Colony, Newberry, S.C., 1912-16; in North Carolina: Trinity, Landis-Concordia, Rowan County, 1916-17; from 1918 in South Carolina (Orangeburg, Orangeburg, 1918-21), Virginia, and Tennessee; last at Fincastle, Va., 1949-58; retired 1958 near Fincastle, Va., later near Winchester, Va.
Date of Death/Burial Location: February 22, 1967; Mt. Hebron Cemetery, Winchester, Va.

SHEAROUSE, OSWALD BENJAMIN

Date/Place of Birth: August 31, 1861; Springfield, Ga.
Parents: Joshua Christopher Shearouse and Emma (Dasher) Shearouse.

Spouse/Marriage Date: Frances Jane (Black) Shearouse; November 28, 1895 in Saluda County, S.C.
Children: Junius Bernard, Floyd Noah, Louise, Eleanor.
Education: Newberry College, A.B. 1890; Lutheran Theological Southern Seminary, 1892.
Ordination: 1892 by Synod of Georgia and Adjacent States.
Calls: In South Carolina, congregations of South Carolina and Tennessee Synods, in Edgefield, Lexington, and Newberry Counties, 1892-1912; St. Enoch, Enochville-Trinity, Cabarrus County, 1912-17; St. John, Pisgah, Providence and Nazareth, Lexington, S.C., 1917-34.
Date of Death/Burial Location: January 8, 1934; Providence Church Cemetery, Lexington, S.C.

SHEEKS, BRUCE CHARLES

Date/Place of Birth: April 14, 1955; Salisbury, N.C.
Parents: Walter Howard Sheeks and Eula Kinard (Park) Sheeks.
Spouse/Marriage Date: Kim Elaine (Ledbetter) Sheeks; October 6, 1979 in Hickory, N.C.
Children: Charles Cameron.
Education: Lenoir-Rhyne, B.A. 1977; Lutheran Theological Southern Seminary, M.Div. 1981.
Ordination: May 24, 1981 by North Carolina Synod.
Calls: Immanuel, Rockwell, 1981-.

SHEETS, WELDON ROBERT

Date/Place of Birth: October 5, 1924; Augusta County, Va.
Parents: George E. Sheets and ? (Wine) Sheets.
Spouse/Marriage Date: Nancy M. Sheets; June 1950 in Hickory, N.C.
Children: Debbie Blakenburg, Gary, Kent, Kevin, Terri Ball.
Education: Lenoir-Rhyne, A.B. 1950; Philadelphia Seminary, M.A. 1967.
Ordination: May 1967 by Eastern Pennsylvania Synod.
Calls: Immanuel, Bluefield, W.Va., 1967-73; St. Andrew, Portsmouth, Va., 1973-81; Gloria Dei, Huntingdon Valley, Pa., 1981-83; Immanuel, Bluefield, W.Va., 1983-85; transferred from Virginia Synod at retirement in 1985; Vice Pastor at various congregations in North Carolina.

SHELBY, ROBERT FITZHUGH, JR.

Date/Place of Birth: September 30, 1911; Harperville, Miss.
Parents: Robert Fitzhugh Shelby, Sr. and Mae (McGinnis) Shelby.
Spouse/Marriage Date: Cornelia Elizabeth (Caldwell) Shelby; April 17, 1938 in Gastonia, N.C.
Child: The Reverend Robert Fitzhugh, III.
Education: Lenoir-Rhyne, A.B. 1933, D.D. 1967; Lutheran Theological Southern Seminary, B.D. 1936, and also graduate work.
Ordination: May 28, 1936 by North Carolina Synod.

Calls: Holy Comforter, Belmont, 1936-41; Home Mission Pastor, Redeemer, Macon, Ga., 1941-47, also military service pastor; Kimball Memorial, Kannapolis, 1947-55; St. Paul, Columbia, S.C., 1955-64; Holy Comforter, Belmont, 1964-78, Pastor Emeritus, 1982; retired September 1, 1978; Vice Pastor at various congregations.

Other: Secretary, Service Pastors Association, NLC, 1941-47; President of Northern Conference, Georgia/Alabama Synod, 1944-47; Executive Committee of Georgia/Alabama Synod, 1942-47; Advisor and Counselor in Domestic and Juvenile Problems for Cabarrus County, 1948-55; Chair, Lutheran Student Work of the South Carolina Synod, 1958-64; Chaplain, University of South Carolina Football Team, 1956-60; Chair, Inner Missions Committee of South Carolina Synod, 1958-64; Chair, North Carolina Synod Radio and TV Committee, 1947-55; Dean, Southwestern District of North Carolina Synod, 1964-70; Board, Lenoir-Rhyne, 1951-56; Board, Lutheran Theological Southern Seminary; Publicity Chair, United Lutheran Hour (radio), 1952-54; North Carolina Lutheran Homes Committee, 1964-70; Trustee, Gaston Children's Center, 1964-78; President, Belmont Rotary Club, 1968-69; delegate to Lutheran Church in America Convention, 1944, 1954, 1970; three times winner of the George Washington Honor Medal, presented by Freedom Foundation Valley Forge, for outstanding sermons, 1960, 1962, 1966; Citizen of the Year for Outstanding Community Service, Belmont, 1978; The American Legion Award for Christian Dedication to Mankind, 1978.

SHELBY, ROBERT FITZHUGH, III

Date/Place of Birth: May 20,1942; Macon, Ga.

Parents: The Reverend Dr. Robert Fitzhugh Shelby, Jr. and Cornelia Elizabeth (Caldwell) Shelby.

Spouse/Marriage Date: Virginia Williamette (Black) Shelby; June 12, 1965 in Cherryville, N.C.

Children: Robert Fitzhugh, IV, Virginia Elizabeth.

Education: Lenoir-Rhyne, B.A. Social Studies, 1964; Lutheran Theological Southern Seminary, M.Div. 1968.

Ordination: June 9, 1968 by North Carolina Synod.

Calls: St. John, Hudson, 1968-95; Faith, Conover, 1995-.

Other: Synod Communications Committee, 1985-92; Strength for Mission Appeal Cluster Director; Key '73 Council Visitation Team Member; Outdoor Ministries Council Visitation Team Member, LRC Strategy for the 1970s; Synod Convention Elections Committee, two years; TV Techniques Workshop Director, 1990 Carolinas Evangelism Conference; Hudson Community Development Association Chair, Charter Member, Foothills Performing Arts Board of Directors, six years; South Caldwell High School Advisory Committee, seven years; Vice Chair and Chair, Caldwell County Schools Advisory Committee, 1991-1992; South Caldwell High School Student Assistance Program Board, Community Representative, 1993-95; LRC Parents Association Executive Committee, 1994-.

SHELL, AUSTIN FOCHT
Date/Place of Birth: June 23, 1922; Montgomery County, Ohio.
Parents: Arthur Ray Shell and Mary Edith (Focht) Shell.
First Spouse/Marriage Date: Lois Jeanne (Rugh) Shell, daughter
of the Reverend Meade A. Rugh; June 19, 1946 in Charleroi, Pa.
Children of First Marriage: Kathleen Lucile (deceased),
Michael Austin, Margaret Ellen Jay, Martin Christopher.
Second Spouse/Marriage Date: Elizabeth Anne (Bartlett) Shell;
July 28, 1979 in Columbia, S.C.
Step Children of Second Marriage: Michael David Blanck,
Cynthia Blanck Eldridge, Linda Blanck Propst.
Education: Wittenberg University, A.B. 1944; Hamma School of Theology, B.D. 1945;
Ohio University, M.A. 1961; Boston University, Ph.D. 1972.
Ordination: November 25, 1945 by Ohio Synod.
Calls: Sulphur Springs, Ohio, 1945-50; St. Mark, Mansfield, Ohio, 1951-55; Mission
Developer/Pastor, Christ, Athens, Ohio, and pastor to Lutheran students, Ohio University,
1956-61; retired 1989.
Other: Professor, Pastoral Care, Director of Field Education, Lutheran Theological
Southern Seminary, 1965-69; Director of Internship, 1966-75, 1986-89; Professor of
Pastoral Care, Emeritus, 1989; Secretary, 1947-49, and President, 1950-52, Central
Conference, Ohio Synod; Commission on Evangelism, Lutheran Church in America, 1967-
72; Continuing Education and Professional Leadership Committee, North Carolina Synod;
Consultant in evangelism and professional leadership for Lutheran Church in America
Synods of Southeast; Evangelism consultant for Lutheran Church in America Key '73 and
for Word and Witness program. Author, along with John Steven Kerr, *Word and Witness:
Telling the Good News;* author of other articles; Clinical Member of Association for
Clinical Pastoral Education; Southeast Region Certification Committee; Southeastern
Region and Association Certification Committee; Fellow of American Association of
Pastoral Counselors; Chair, Southeast Region Association Ethics Committee; Chair,
Southeast Region, Association Finance Committee; Institutional Review Board, Richland
Memorial Hospital, Columbia, S.C., 1985-94; transferred 1965 to North Carolina Synod.

SHENK, ELONZO ASHBY
Date/Place of Birth: September 24, 1868; Luray, Va.
Parents: William J. Shenk and Elizabeth (Shutters) Shenk.
Spouse/Marriage Date: Katharine (Pifer) Shenk; October 18,
1899 in Gravel Springs, Va.
Children: Katharine E.
Education: Roanoke College, A.B. 1892; Philadelphia Seminary,
1895.
License/Ordination: Licensed 1894 and ordained 1895 by
Virginia Synod.
Calls: Bethlehem, Waynesboro, Va., 1894-96; Trinity, Newport
News, Va., 1898-1908; Augsburg, Winston-Salem, 1908-15; Incarnation, Baltimore, Md.,
1915-18; First, Greensboro, 1918-35; retired 1935 at Greensboro, later at Kings Mountain,
N.C.; Supply, Grace, 1937, 1939-41 and Richland, 1940-41, Liberty, and St. Luke, Bear
Poplar.

Other: Inner Mission Board, General Synod, while in Baltimore, Md., 1916-18; Board, Children's Home of the South, and Chair, North Carolina Commission to raise $150,000 for new buildings.

Date of Death/Burial Location: November 14, 1944; Kings Mountain, N.C.

SHENK, JACOB ERNEST

Date/Place of Birth: June 18, 1860; Luray, Va.

Parents: John Adam Shenk and Anna (Hershberger) Shenk.

Spouse/Marriage Date: Bertha Gertrude (Henkel) Shenk; 1890 in Waynesboro, Va.

Children: Ernest Merlin, Gordon Harry, Jay Ernest, Luther Virgil, Anna Henkel, Virginia Marie. (In 1914 sons had name changed from Shenk to original of Schenck, but presumably he made no change for himself).

Education: Polytechnic Institute, New Market, Va.; in law at University of Virginia, and practiced five years; studied theology privately, perhaps.

License/Ordination: Licensed 1888 and ordained 1890 by Virginia Synod.

Calls: Bethlehem, near Waynesboro, Va., 1889-90; organized Grace, Waynesboro, Va., 1891-94; organized First, Norfolk, Va., 1894-1901; Woodstock, Va., 1901-05; St. James, Concord, 1905-10; First, Greensboro, 1910-15; retired 1916 at Greensboro.

Date of Death/Burial Location: February 4, 1916; Waynesboro, Va.

SHEPPARD, JOHN DILLON

Date/Place of Birth: April 23, 1900; Rowan County, N.C.

Parents: Moses L. Sheppard and Bulah (Coggin) Sheppard.

Spouse/Marriage Date: Georgia Erma (Arndt) Sheppard, a lineal descendant of Johann Gottfried Arends (Arndt); June 4, 1929 in Claremont, N.C.

Children: Sonya Ann McKay.

Education: Mount Pleasant Collegiate Institute, Lenoir-Rhyne, A.B. 1925; Lutheran Theological Southern Seminary, 1928.

Ordination: May 20, 1928 by North Carolina Synod.

Calls: St. Luke-Morning Star, Monroe, 1928-30; St. James-Immanuel, Rockwell, 1930-35; Bethany, Kannapolis, 1935-43, also developing, organizing, and building small chapel, St. David, Kannapolis, 1937; Ascension, Shelby, 1943-53; Mission Developer, St. Andrew, Homestead, Fla., 1953-54; Mission Developer/Pastor, St. Matthew, Jacksonville, Fla., 1954-65; retired in 1965 at Conover, N.C., and was Vice Pastor at various congregations.

Other: Promoted in the depression years the raising of rabbits and growing of lespedeza by rural parishioners; Board, Children's Home of the South; Board, Lowman Home; helped to resettle European refugees after World War II in area of Shelby.

Date of Death/Burial Location: April 17, 1977; Claremont Lutheran Cemetery, Claremont, N.C.

SHIPMAN, RONALD JAMES

Date/Place of Birth: May 15, 1945; Williamsport, Pa.
Parents: James F. Shipman and Mildred E. (Culp) Shipman
Spouse/Marriage Date: Susan Christine (Blomquist) Shipman; September 12, 1964 in Williamsport, Pa.
Children: Evan Scott, Maren Heather.
Education: Pennsylvania State University, 1965; Mansfield State College, B.A. 1979; Gettysburg, Pa., M.Div. 1983.
Ordination: June 10, 1983 by Central Pennsylvania Synod.
Calls: St. Matthew, Salisbury, 1983-86; Epiphany, Woodbridge, Va., 1986-; serving Atonement, Sacramento, Calif., 1998-.

SHIPTON, CALVIN LEE

Date/Place of Birth: June 18, 1909; Rowan County, N.C.
Parents: Calvin Sylvester Shipton and Dallie Victoria (Hodge) Shipton. A great-great-great-grandson of Adolph Nussmann, first Lutheran pastor in North Carolina.
Spouse/Marriage Date: Frances Margaret (Estes) Shipton; June 14, 1934 in Columbia, S.C.
Children: Lois Evelyn (died in childhood), Paul Louis, Ann Marie Lentz.
Education: Lenoir-Rhyne, A.B. 1931; Lutheran Theological Southern Seminary, B.D. 1934.
Ordination: May 24, 1934 by North Carolina Synod.
Calls: Luther's-Mt. Zion-New Bethel (supplied last two, 1932-33), Richfield, 1934-38; Alamance, Alamance, 1938-49; Supply, St. Paul, Alamance County, 1947-49; St. John, Cabarrus County, served by his ancestor Nussmann (1774-94), 1949-65; Friendship, Taylorsville, 1965-74; retired in June 1974; Vice Pastor at various congregations.
Date of Death/Burial Location: September 4, 1993; Immanuel Lutheran Church Cemetery, Rockwell, N.C.

SHIREY, JOHN DANIEL

Date/Place of Birth: May 15, 1836; at or near Staunton, Va.
Parents: Peter Shirey and Julia Ann (Kizer) Shirey.
Spouse/Marriage Date: Margaret Catherine (Shaver) Shirey; February 26, 1863 in Botetourt County, Va.
Children: Julia, Ella Belle, Luther S., Alma Cook (served as treasurer of United Lutheran Church in America Women's Missionary Society for a number of years). A granddaughter of Pastor Shirey is Sister Miriam Shirey.
Education: Roanoke College (2nd graduating class), A.B. 1857; Honorary A.M., D.D. 1895; Gettysburg Seminary, 1860.
License/Ordination: Licensed 1860 and ordained 1861 by Virginia Synod.
Calls: Mt. Tabor, near Staunton, Va., 1860-67; Floyd County, Va., 1867-70; Beth Eden Parish, near Newberry, S.C., 1870-82; Grace, Rowan County, 1882-87; St. Luke-Salem, Rowan County, 1882-89; with the Reverend C. L. T. Fisher, supplied Holy Trinity, Mt. Pleasant, 1890-92.

Other: President, North Carolina College, 1889-96. Secretary 1872, 1877, and President 1878, South Carolina Synod. Active in promotion of home and foreign missions in the Rowan County churches he served through the first women's societies in North Carolina Lutheran churches formed in 1885 leading to organizing of synodical society.
Date of Death/Burial Location: April 5, 1896; Mt. Pleasant, N.C.

SHOFFNER, ROBERT HUNTER

Date/Place of Birth: November 17, 1944; Tallahassee, Fla.
Parents: Robert Lucine Shoffner and Helen Joyce (Newnam) Shoffner.
Spouse/Marriage Date: Joy Elizabeth (Kirk) Shoffner; September 5, 1970 in China Grove, N.C.
Children: Adrienne Joy, Lauren Hunter.
Education: University of North Carolina at Chapel Hill, B.A. Zoology 1967; Lutheran Theological Southern Seminary, M.Div. 1974.
Ordination: May 31, 1974 by North Carolina Synod.
Calls: Assistant Pastor, 1974-75, Team Pastor, 1975-78, Holy Trinity, Hickory; Parish Life Ministries Assistant to the Bishop, North Carolina Synod, 1967-82; Assistant to the President, Luther College, Decorah, Iowa, 1982-91; Interim Vice Pastor, Zion, Clayton Center, Iowa, 1983-86; Holy Trinity, Hickory, 1991-.
Other: President of Luther League, North Carolina Synod, 1966-67; Member, Lutheran Church in America Luther League Executive Committee, 1966-67; Board, Lutheran Theological Southern Seminary, 1977-80, 1981-82; Delegate to 1980 Lutheran Church in America Biennial Convention; Board, Lenoir-Rhyne, 1992-; contributor to *Learning Wits*; author of sermon in 1977 *Augsburg Sermons;* Peace Corps Volunteer, Malawi, Africa, 1967-69; *Who's Who in Colleges and Professional Schools,* 1974; *Outstanding Young Men of America,* 1979; Rotary Club Paul Harris Fellow, 1995.

SHORES, SAMUEL W., III

Spouse: Nadine Shores.
Children: Jeffery Scott, Summer Michelle, Jennifer E.
Education: Barton College, 1973; Philadelphia Seminary, M.Div. 1997.
Ordination: September 7, 1997.
Calls: Grace, Liberty, 1997-.
Other: Homeless Shelter, Habitat for Humanity.

SHUFORD, GEORGE WASHINGTON

Date/Place of Birth: February 22, 1925; Lincoln County, N.C.
Parents: Joseph Monroe Shuford and Beulah Era (Michael) Shuford. A descendant of the Reverend Johann Gottfried Arends (Arndt).
Spouse/Marriage Date: Orpha Christine (Ford) Shuford of Caldwell County; August 25, 1959 in Neuendettelsau, Bavaria, Germany.
Children: Michael George, Mark David.
Education: Lenoir-Rhyne, B.S. Chemistry 1950; Lutheran Theological Southern Seminary, B.D. 1953; Lutheran World Federation scholarship, Neuendettelsau, Germany, 1958-59; graduate study, Duke University.
Ordination: June 14, 1953 by North Carolina Synod.

Calls: St. Mark, Caldwell County-Holy Communion, Banner Elk, 1953-54; Holy Communion, Banner Elk-Holy Trinity, Deep Gap-Bethany, Boone, 1954-58; Chaplain (part-time) for Lutheran students at Duke University, 1959-63; Morning Star, Mecklenburg County, 1963-66; Grace, Bessemer City, 1966-69; Peace, Gibsonville, 1969-77; St. Luke, Conover, 1977-78.

Other: Publications and Publicity Committee, 1967-69; Editor, *North Carolina Lutheran,* 1969-78; Delegate, North Carolina Council of Churches, 1979; Historical Works Committee, 1975-78; Task Force on the 175th Anniversary, 1973; Delegate to the 1970, 1972, 1974, and 1976 biennial conventions of the Lutheran Church in America; Board, Lenoir-Rhyne, 1975-78; Distinguished Service Award from Lenoir-Rhyne, 1976.

Date of Death/Burial Location: June 2, 1978; Woodlawn Memorial Cemetery, Hickory, N.C.

SHUMATE, THOMAS JOSEPH

Date/Place of Birth: October 15, 1929; Staunton, Va.
Parents: The Reverend Alfred Ritchie Shumate and Ellen (Burkholder) Shumate.
First Spouse/Marriage Date: Frances Ann (Peninger) Shumate; June 14, 1953 in Concord, N.C.
Children of First Marriage: Toni Walther, Alfred Glenn, Jeffrey Joseph.
Second Spouse/Marriage Date: Elizabeth (Johnson) Shumate; June 16, 1974.
Education: Lenoir-Rhyne, A.B. 1951; Lutheran Theological Southern Seminary, B.D. 1954; St. Mary Seminary and University, D.Min. 1984.
Ordination: May 30, 1954 by Virginia Synod.
Calls: Union, Rowan County, 1954-58; St. John, Roanoke, Va., 1958-62; First, Portsmouth, Va., 1962-71; Assistant Pastor, St. Paul, Hampton, Va., 1975-77; Walker Mountain Parish, Wytheville, Va., 1977-. Now retired in Wytheville, Va.

SIDES, FLOYD EUGENE, SR.

Date/Place of Birth: August 23, 1940; Stanly County, N.C.
Parents: George Henry Sides and Lily Esther (Morgan) Sides.
Spouse/Marriage Date: Barbara Louise (Holshouser) Sides; February 25, 1961 in Hickory, N.C.
Children: Kimberly Leigh Havird, Floyd Eugene, Jr.
Education: Pfeiffer College, Lenoir-Rhyne, A.B. Sociology, 1962; Lutheran Theological Southern Seminary, B.D. 1966.
Ordination: June 6, 1966 by North Carolina Synod.
Calls: Mission Developer/Pastor, Research Triangle Park, Durham, Christus Victor, 1966-74; Mayer Memorial, Newberry, S.C., 1974-.
Other: Stewardship Committee, North Carolina Synod, 1969-72; Social Ministry Committee, South Carolina Synod; Parish Life and Ministry Development, South Carolina Synod.

SIEG, PAUL, SR.

Date/Place of Birth: March 12, 1866; Churchville, Va.

Parents: Henry Bingham Sieg and Martha Anna (Davies) Sieg.

Spouse/Marriage Date: Clara Frances (Groseclose) Sieg; August 20, 1902 in Wytheville, Va.

Children: Paul, Jr., Katharine Groseclose, Martha Davies.

Education: Roanoke College, A.B. 1887, A.M. 1892; Philadelphia Seminary, 1892.

Ordination: 1892 by Virginia Synod.

Calls: Wytheville, Radford, Buena Vista, and Danville, Va., and at Bristol, Tenn., 1893-1912.

Other: Professor and Treasurer, 1912-22, and Acting President, Elizabeth College, Salem, Va. 1918-22; Business Manager and Treasurer, Lenoir-Rhyne, 1922-26, and member of North Carolina Synod; Instructor, Roanoke College, 1887-89, following graduation; Secretary, Southwestern Virginia Synod, 1905-12; Chair, Board, Marion College, 1905-12; President, Board, Children's Home of the South, 1912-22; contributor to *Lutheran Church Visitor* and *Lutheran Church Review;* retired 1929 in Churchville, Va.

Date of Death/Burial Location: December 19, 1945; Churchville, Va.

SIFFERD, CALVIN WRIGHT

Date/Place of Birth: November 4, 1850; China Grove, N.C.

Parents: Dr. Paul Sifferd and Margaret (Peeler) Sifferd.

Spouse/Marriage Date: Mary Rebecca (Henkel) Sifferd, daughter of the Reverend David M. Henkel; May 2, 1875 at St. John, Cabarrus County, N.C.

Children: Paul A., William D., Mary M., Calvin S., Lillian H., Charles L. (fatally burned at age 3).

Education: North Carolina College; Philadelphia Seminary; Wittenberg University, D.D. about 1897.

Ordination: 1875 by North Carolina Synod, and transferred to Southern Illinois Synod.

Calls: None in North Carolina; served in Illinois, Kansas, Oklahoma, and Indiana from 1876 to his death.

Other: President, Miami Synod; Member, Board, Carthage College; Board, Wittenberg College; Michigan Synod published his address on "The Call to the Ministry."

Date of Death/Burial Location: June 12, 1925; Ebenezer Church, Rowan County, N.C.

SIFFORD, CLARENCE EUGENE, JR.

Date/Place of Birth: October 2, 1935; Cabarrus County, N.C. Great-great grandson of the Reverend Timothy Moser.

Parents: Clarence Eugene Sifford, Sr. and Mary R. (Moser) Sifford Bonds. His Great-Great-Grandfather was The Reverend Timothy Moser.

Spouse/Marriage Date: Margaret Faye (Brunson) Sifford; January 20, 1961 in Summerton, S.C.

Children: Susanne Marie Edwards, Jonathan Carl.

Education: Lenoir-Rhyne, A.B. 1957; Lutheran Theological Southern Seminary, M.Div. 1960.

Ordination: June 5, 1960 by North Carolina Synod.

Calls: New Jerusalem, Davidson County, summers of 1958-59, 1960-64; Mt. Hermon, Cabarrus County, 1964-73; at New Jerusalem promoted and guided dissolving of union arrangement, originally begun in 1856 with three other congregations, and since 1923 in effect with an Evangelical and Reformed (now United Church of Christ) congregation,

which in October 1962, bought equity of New Jerusalem in the property. New Jerusalem then by synod's authority began using property of disbanded Silver Valley congregation, which synod conveyed to it by deed in February 1963; Bethphage, Lincolnton, 1974-90; Salem, Salisbury, 1990-; Vice Pastor at various congregations.
Other: Secretary, Synod Evangelism Committee; Chair, Synod Outreach Committee; Voting Member at Convening Convention Evangelical Lutheran Church in America, 1987; Synod Council-Synod Executive Committee.

SIGMAN, WALTER AUGUSTUS, SR.
Date/Place of Birth: October 3, 1905; Newton, Catawba County, N.C.
Parents: Walter Vernon Sigman and Mertie Lula (Sigmon) Sigman.
Spouse/Marriage Date: Emma Lee (Cathey) Sigman; May 24, 1931 in Andrews, N.C.
Children: Marie Lee, Walter A., Jr., Vernon R., Stephen Douglas.
Education: Lenoir-Rhyne, A.B. 1928; Lutheran Theological Southern Seminary, B.D. 1931.
Ordination: September 1931 by North Carolina Synod.
Calls: Vale Parish (Trinity, Cedar Grove, Sardis, Vale), 1931-37; Mt. Olive, Hickory, 1937-42; Chaplain, U.S. Army, 1943-46; Helton Parish (Faith, Helton, St. John, Attoway), Whitetop, Va., 1946-50; Orkney Springs Parish (St. Paul, Morning Star, Powder Springs), Orkney Springs, Va., 1950-52, 1969-72; Mt. Calvary, Johnston, S.C., 1952-57; St. James, Leesville, S.C., 1957-60; Wardensville Parish (St. Peter, Ebenezer, Hebron), W.Va., 1960-65; Bethlehem-Waynesboro, Melanchthon Chapel, Weyers Cave, Waynesboro, Va., 1965-69; retired 1972.
Date of Death/Burial Location: January 27, 1981; Pinelawn Cemetery, Clinton, S.C.

SIGMON, CRAIG EUGENE
Date/Place of Birth: February 13, 1961; Iredell County, N.C.
Parents: Ted E. Sigmon and Janice J. Sigmon.
Spouse/Marriage Date: Susan (Moore) Sigmon; August 7, 1982.
Children: Benjamin Craig, Katie Marie, Betsy Elaine.
Education: Appalachian State University, B.A., B.S. Bus.Ad. 1983; Lutheran Theological Southern Seminary, M.Div. 1996.
Ordination: August 15, 1996 by North Carolina Synod.
Calls: St. James, Rockwell, 1996-.

SIGMON, JOHN HENRY, JR.
Date/Place of Birth: October 6, 1921; Hickory, N.C.
Parents: John Henry Sigmon, Sr. and Sallie (Miller) Sigmon.
Spouse: Vivian Leona (Miller) Sigmon; June 9, 1946 in Hickory, N.C.
Children: John Henry, III, David Gerald, Timothy Miller, Mary Beth Young.
Education: Lenoir-Rhyne, B.S. 1942; Lutheran Theological Southern Seminary, B.D. 1949.

Ordination: June 5, 1949 by North Carolina Synod.

Calls: Calvary, Morganton, 1949-83; retired December 31, 1983 to Hickory, N.C.; Vice Pastor at various congregations.

Other: Board, North Carolina Lutheran Homes, 1965-71, 1972-81; President and Vice President, Western Conference; Secretary, Western District; Christian Education Committee; Board, Lutherock; Lutheran Church in America Delegate, 1972.

SIGMON, PAUL CROMER

Date/Place of Birth: May 17, 1896; Catawba County, N.C.

Parents: Daniel Elias Sigmon and Dorcas Emily (Rhodes) Sigmon. Younger brother of the Reverend R. Bruce Sigmon.

Spouse/Marriage Date: Edith (Pence) Sigmon, daughter of the Reverend M. L. Pence and sister of the Reverend E. Z. Pence; October 19, 1921 in Orkney Springs, Va.

Children: Ruth Elizabeth, Carl Pence.

Education: Catawba College, two years, Lenoir-Rhyne, A.B. 1918; Lutheran Theological Southern Seminary, B.D. 1926; University of South Carolina, M.A. 1921; Vanderbilt and Duke Universities.

Ordination: 1921 by Synod of Georgia and Adjacent States.

Calls: Reformation, Savannah, Ga., 1921-22; Orangeburg, S.C., 1922-25; Philadelphia, Granite Falls-St. John, Hudson-St. Matthew, Caldwell County, 1925-29; St. Paul, Durham, 1929-31; Calvary-Christ, Spencer, 1931-32.

Date of Death/Burial Location: October 25, 1932; Newton, N.C.

SIGMON, ROBERT BRUCE

Date/Place of Birth: December 27, 1892; Catawba County, N.C.

Parents: Daniel Elias Sigmon and Dorcas Emily (Rhodes) Sigmon. Older brother of the Reverend Paul C. Sigmon.

Spouse/Marriage Date: Illion Katherine (Stamey) Sigmon; April 20, 1920 in Lawndale, N.C.

Children: Robert Stamey, Bruce Rhodes.

Education: Catawba College, Lenoir-Rhyne, A.B. 1916; Lutheran Theological Southern Seminary, 1919; graduate study University of South Carolina, 1916-17.

Ordination: September 12, 1919 by Tennessee Synod.

Calls: Beck's-Holly Grove-Lebanon-New Jerusalem, Davidson County, 1919-28; Mt. Calvary, Claremont-St. Luke, Catawba County, 1928-43; Philadelphia, Granite Falls-St. John, Hudson-St. Matthew, Caldwell County, 1943-49; Grace-Richland, Liberty, 1949-50; Reformation, Taylorsville, 1950-59; retired 1959 at Newton, N.C.; Vice Pastor at various congregations.

Other: Board, Children's Home of the South, 1930-40; Board, Sipe's Orchard Home, 1952-60.

Date of Death/Burial Location: July 2, 1984; St. James Lutheran Church Cemetery, Newton, N.C.

SIKES, JAMES R.
Date/Place of Birth: March 29, 1832; Guilford County, N.C.
Parents: Nathan N. Sikes and Prudence (Andrews) Sikes.
First Spouse/Marriage Date: Clarissa (Reid) Sikes; June 2, 1853 in Ashland, Pa.
Second Spouse/Marriage Date: Addie M. (West) Sikes of Ohio, a sister to the Reverend J. N. West, a missionary to India; November 6, 1884.
Education: Chiefly by self-study.
License/Ordination: Licensed 1860 and ordained 1861 by North Carolina Synod.
Calls: Nazareth-Shiloh, Forsyth County, 1862-64; in 1864 transferred to a synod of General Synod, and served churches in Pennsylvania, New Jersey, New York, and Ohio, presumably until 1893; Frieden's, Guilford County, 1893-95; organized with eight members, Sharon, Gibsonville, October 28, 1894 preaching last on December 5, 1894.
Date of Death/Burial Location: January 21, 1895; Frieden's Church, Guilford County, N.C.

SIMMEL, FREDERICK WILLIAM
Date/Place of Birth: March 3, 1933.
Spouse/Marriage Date: Kathryn A. Simmel.
Children: Jon-Frederick, Karry, Kirk, Klint, James.
Education: U.S. Naval Academy, Electrical Engineering, 1956; Baylor University, B.A., History, Minor in Education, 1958; Gettysburg Seminary, M.Div. 1961; Pittsburgh Pastoral Institute in Counseling Certification, 1964; Frostburg State University, M.Ed. 1966; Gettysburg Seminary, Advanced Pastoral Care, 1971; North East Center for Transactional Analysis, 1972; Correctional Officers Academy Certification, 1993; Academy for Prison Chaplaincy Certification, 1993.
Ordination: June 4, 1961 by Lower Susquehanna Synod.
Calls: Mt. Calvary, Westernport, Md., 1961-63; Mt. Olivet, Pittsburgh, Pa., 1964-65; Center Township (Van Kirk and Faith), Monaca, Pa., 1965-71; St. John, Thurmont, Md., 1971-75; Pastor/Developer, Christ-Hope-St. Peter, Erie, Pa., 1975-77; Pastor/Developer, St. Luke's-Monessen-Trinity, Donora, Pa., 1977-80; Christ, Beaver Falls, Pa., 1980-88; Chaplain, Breezewood Trucker-Traveler, Breezewood, Pa., 1988-92; Chaplain, Franklin County Prison, Chambersburg, Pa., 1992-96; retired to Ocean Isle, N.C. and transferred to North Carolina Synod from West Virginia-Western Maryland Synod, 1996.

SIMMONS, GEORGE LEE
Date/Place of Birth: November 6, 1942; Cabarrus County, N.C.
Parents: Guy Everette Simmons and Margaret Cornelis (Sweet) Simmons.
Spouse/Marriage Date: Mary Josephine (Carter) Simmons; June 26, 1966 in West Columbia, S.C.
Children: Mary Jennifer, Carole Leigh.
Education: Lenoir-Rhyne, A.B. English 1965; Lutheran Theological Southern Seminary, M.Div. 1969.
Ordination: June 1, 1969 by North Carolina Synod.
Calls: Luther's, Richfield, 1969-75; Resurrection, Greensboro, 1975-83; Trinity, Rocky Mount, 1983-96; St. Andrew, Andrews, 1996-; Vice Pastor at various congregations.
Other: Parish Education, 1971-72.

SIMS, GEORGE LEE

Date/Place of Birth: March 29, 1948; Richland County, Columbia, S.C.
Parents: Jesse Lee Sims and Erma Carolyn (Fulmer) Sims. Step-mother: Bernice (Chapman) Sims.
Spouse/Marriage Date: Ann Scott (Paetzell) Sims; May 26, 1978 in Columbia, S.C.
Children: Kristen Ann, David Christopher.
Education: Newberry, B.A. 1971; Lutheran Theological Southern Seminary, M.Div. 1975.
Ordination: June 1, 1975 by South Carolina Synod.
Calls: Trinity, Rocky Mount, 1975-79; Our Father, Greensboro, 1979-81; Good Shepherd, Columbia, S.C., 1981-84; Christ the King, Columbia, S.C., 1984-88; Reformation, New Market, Va., 1988-.
Other: Educational Ministry Committees, North Carolina and South Carolina Synods; Lutheran Campus Ministry Committee for University of South Carolina; Board, Newberry College.

SIMS, ROBERT FREDERICK

Date/Place of Birth: November 6, 1936; Spartanburg, S.C.
Parents: Joe L. Sims and Hester (Moser) Sims.
Spouse/Marriage Date: Mary Frances (Carpenter) Sims; May 6, 1958 in Salisbury, N.C.
Children: Laura Cameron, Mary Scott, Joseph C.
Education: Lenoir-Rhyne, A.B. 1958; Lutheran Theological Southern Seminary, M.Div. 1961, D.Min. 1978.
Ordination: June 11, 1961 by North Carolina Synod.
Calls: Ascension, Shelby, 1961-67; Redeemer, McLean, Va., 1967-73; Ebenezer, Columbia, S.C., 1973-; Serving the Lutheran Church of the Redeemer, Atlanta, Ga. in 1999.
Other: Social Ministry Committee, 1965-66; Board, Lutheran Theological Southern Seminary; Board, Lowman Home.

SIMS, TIMOTHY CALHOUN

Date/Place of Birth: October 15, 1948; Gainesville, Fla.
Parents: Dr. James H. Sims and Ruth Elizabeth (Gray) Sims.
Spouse/Marriage Date: Rebecca Lynne (Banks) Sims; June 20, 1976 in Lexington, S.C.
Children: Joshua Luke-Gregory, Rachel Anna-Katherine, Adam Mark-Nicholas.
Education: University of North Carolina at Chapel Hill, B.A. English, 1973; Lutheran Theological Southern Seminary, M.Div. 1978; Duke University Divinity School, Th.M. Ethics 1989.
Ordination: June 11, 1978 by North Carolina Synod.
Calls: Messiah, Knoxville, Tenn., 1978-80; Trinity, Rocky Mount, 1980-82; U.S. Navy Chaplain Corps, 1982-present; Command Chaplain, U.S.S. Prairie, 1982-85; Pastoral Counselor Navy Family Service Center, NCBC Port Hueneme, Calif., 1985-86; Command Chaplain, Naval Support Force Antarctica, 1986-88; Senior Protestant Chaplain, Naval Air Station, Patuxent River, Md., 1989-91; Command Chaplain, U.S.S. Belleau Wood, 1991-93; Regimental Chaplain, U.S. Marine Corps Recruit Depot, San Diego, Calif., 1993-96; Command Chaplain, U.S.S. Blue Ridge, Yokosuka, Japan, 1996-.

Other: Secretary, American Missions, 1981-82; Articles in *Partners, Christian Century;* Awards: Navy Commendation Medal, two awards, Navy Achievement Medal, Antarctic Service Medal, Sea Service Deployment Ribbon, three awards.

SIMUNDSON, DANIEL JOHN
Date/Place of Birth: February 14, 1933; Seattle, Wash.
Parents: The Reverend Kolbeinn Simundson and Groa (Thorsteinson) Simundson.
Spouse/Marriage Date: Sally Ann (Mueller) Simundson; June 23, 1962 in St. Louis, Mo.
Children: Susan, Ann Marie.
Education: Stanford University, B.A. 1955; Chicago Seminary, M.Div. 1959; Harvard University, Ph.D. 1971.
Ordination: May 1959 by Pacific Synod of United Lutheran Church in America.
Calls: Salem, Mendon, Ill., 1959-61; Chaplain, Washington University Medical Center, St. Louis, Mo., 1961- 67. Transferred from Illinois Synod, 1971.
Other: Professor, Appalachian State University, Boone, N.C., 1971-72; Professor, Luther Seminary, St. Paul, 1972-; Author: *Faith Under Fire, Where is God in My Suffering?, Where is God in My Praying?, The Message of Job, Hope for All Seasons.*

SINK, HENRY RAY
Date/Place of Birth: January 6, 1934; Lexington, Davidson County, N.C.
Parents: John Raymond Sink and Gurlah Mae (Michael) Sink.
First Spouse/Marriage Date: Martha Joanne (Frye) Sink; August 4, 1956 in Kannapolis, N.C.
Children of First Marriage: Martha Elizabeth, Sarah Catherine.
Second Spouse/Marriage Date: Susan (Brant) Sadtler; October 13, 1979.
Step-Children: Gradson Wesley Pruitt, III, Howard Matthias Pruitt.
Education: Lenoir-Rhyne, A.B. 1956; Lutheran Theological Southern Seminary, M.Div. 1959; graduate work, North Carolina State University, 1966-67.
Ordination: June 7, 1959 by North Carolina Synod.
Calls: St. David, Kannapolis, 1959-63; Mission Developer/Pastor, Christ the King, Cary, 1963-68; Messiah, Burlington, 1969-72; Mt. Pleasant, Burlington, 1973-76; Shiloh, Lewisville, 1979-82; United, Lock Haven, Pa., 1982-88; Pastor/Developer, St. Mary, Bartlett, Tenn., 1988-91; Interim Pastor at various congregations; Grace, Bessemer, Ala., 1992-96; Peace-Sharon, Gibsonville, 1996-.
Other: North Carolina Synod - Nominating Committee, Evangelism Committee; Christian Education Committee; Secretary, Raleigh-Durham Area Institutional Chaplaincy Advisory Committee; Secretary and President, Forsyth County Lutheran Council. Central Pennsylvania Synod - Committee on Parish Life; Parish Life Steering Committee; Committee on Development of Lay Ministry; Chair, Committee for Development of Intentional Ministry; Executive Board, Central Valleys District Cabinet. Upper Susquehanna Synod - Transition Team Preparing for 1988 Merger; Constitutional Committee. Southeastern Synod - Minutes Committee; Memphis Cluster Area Mission Strategy Team; Board, Lutheran Social Services of Memphis; Board, Lutheran Village

Cooperative; Lutheran Village Cooperative Special Advisory Committee; Lutheran Social Services of Memphis Personnel Committee; Congregational Life Committee; Secretary-Treasurer, Alabama Conference. Board, Lock Haven Day Care Center, Clinton County Children and Youth Social Services, Gallery Players of Burlington, Clinton County Arts Council, Clinton County United Way, Rock Haven Rotary Club (Vice President and President), Bartlett Rotary Club (Charter Member, Vice President). Initiated plans for and chaired special committee (ecumenical) for re-settling of refugees in Lewisville, N.C.; Chair, Special Committee for formation of "Parents Anonymous" in Lock Haven, Pa.; Memphis South Rotary Club; Cursillo in North Carolina and Pennsylvania; *Who's Who in the South and Southwest, 1991*; Mensa.

SINK, OLIN WARD
Date/Place of Birth: September 1, 1907; Lexington, Davidson County, N.C.
Parents: Abner Julian Sink and Augusta (Beck) Sink. An older brother of the Reverend Voigt Mock Sink.
Spouse/Marriage Date: Betty Hofmann (Holt) Sink; November 17, 1935 in Atlanta, Ga.
Children: Elizabeth Beck (married the Reverend M. Thomas Sublett), Martha Holt Bloh.
Education: Guilford College, Lenoir-Rhyne, A.B., 1930; Lutheran Theological Southern Seminary, M.Div. 1933.
Ordination: June 11, 1933 by Georgia-Alabama Synod.
Calls: Assistant Pastor, Redeemer, Atlanta, Ga., 1933-35; Holy Trinity, Charlotte, 1935-64; St. Andrew, New Bern, 1964-68; Messiah, Salisbury, 1968-75; retired January 1975; Vice Pastor at various congregations.
Other: Board, Lenoir-Rhyne; Board, Nazareth Children's Home; Board, Lutheran Theological Southern Seminary; Board, Lutheran Nursing Home; World Missions Committee, 1964-66.
Date of Death/Burial Location: March 4, 1997; Pilgrim Lutheran Church Cemetery, Davidson County, N.C.

SINK, VOIGT MOCK
Date/Place of Birth: February 25, 1917; Lexington, Davidson County, N.C.
Parents: Abner Julian Sink and Augusta Belle (Beck) Sink. A younger brother of the Reverend Olin Ward Sink.
First Spouse/Marriage Date: Emily L. (Smith) Sink of Greenville, S.C.; December 26, 1940 in Charlotte, N.C.
Children of First Marriage: Emily Rosemary Crum, Carole Voigt White, Richard Thomas, Daniel Alan, last two, twins.
Second Spouse/Marriage Date: Waldtraut Livia (Timmerman) Sink; April 5, 1977.
Education: Lenoir-Rhyne, A.B. 1938;Lutheran Theological Southern Seminary, M.Div. 1941; Auburn University, M.Ed. Counseling.
Ordination: June 1, 1941 by North Carolina Synod.

Calls: Good Shepherd, Walterboro, S.C., 1941-43; Chaplain, U.S. Air Force, 1943-70; Nativity, Shreveport, La., 1970-71; Our Redeemer, Montgomery, Ala., 1971-75; New Hope, Sallis, Miss., 1976-80; St. John, Johnston, S.C., 1980-.

Date of Death/Burial Location: January 25, 1994; Edgefield, S.C.

SIPE, G. WAYNE

Date/Place of Birth: January 27, 1941; Newton, N.C.

Parents: Glenn Woodrow Sipe and Minnie Rosa (Boggs) Sipe.

Spouse/Marriage Date: Emily Carol (Guckenberger) Sipe; June 14, 1969.

Children: Christopher Wayne, Nathaniel Wayne, Michelle Anne.

Education: Lenoir-Rhyne, B.A. 1966; Evangelical Lutheran Theological Seminary (Ohio), M.Div. 1970.

Ordination: July 12, 1970 by Eastern District, American Lutheran Church.

Calls: Bethel, Northeast Maryland, 1970-72; Trinity, Akron, N.Y., 1972-81; Stewart Avenue, Pittsburgh, Pa., 1981-85; Reformation, Culpeper, Va., 1985-89; St. Luke, Woodstock, Va., 1989-95; Concordia, China Grove, 1996-.

Other: President, Lutheran Mission Society of Western New York, 1977-79; Service and Mission Committee, Eastern District, American Lutheran Church, 1976-81; Virginia Synod Global Missions Committee, 1984-95; Board, Good Samaritan Connections of Shenandoah County, Va., 1993-94; Western New York Conference Clergy Representative (Eastern District/American Lutheran Church) to 1976, American Lutheran Church Churchwide Convention in Washington, D.C.; Chaplain, Faith and Science Week at Carolina Furnace Lutheran Camp, Fort Valley, Va., 1993-95; Chaplain, Fairview-St. Luke Ruritan Club, Woodstock, Va., 1990-95.

SIPE, RICHARD VARNER, JR.

Date/Place of Birth: February 13, 1914; Newton, N.C.

Spouse/Marriage Date: Constance (Graff) Sipe; 1974.

Education: Lenoir-Rhyne, B.A. 1971; Evangelical Lutheran Theological Seminary (Ohio), M.Div. 1976.

Ordination: 1976 by American Lutheran Church.

Calls: St. Paul, Glenford, Ohio, 1976-79; Good Hope, Glenford, Ohio, 1976-79; Bethel, Northeast Maryland, 1979-82; Trinity, East Rochester, N.Y., 1982-86; Chaplain, U.S. Navy; transferred from Virginia Synod in 1994 to Conover, N.C.; Chaplain, Veterans Administration in Vancouver, Wash.

SKINNER, HAROLD GILBERT

Date/Place of Birth: December 20, 1927; Rocky Mount, N.C.

Parents: Edgar D. Skinner and Lillian (Heilig) Skinner.

Spouse/Marriage Date: Nancy E. (Foil) Skinner; August 1, 1953 in Kannapolis, N.C.

Children: Elizabeth Heilig, David Lee, Mark Foil.

Education: Lenoir-Rhyne, A.B. 1952; Chicago Seminary, M.Div. 1956; graduate work at Lutheran Theological Southern Seminary.

Ordination: June 10, 1956 by North Carolina Synod.

Calls: Pastor/Mission Developer, Christ, Cheyenne, Wyo., 1956-58; Trinity, Canon City, Colo., 1958-62; St. Michael, Greenville, S.C., 1962-73; Wittenberg, Leesville, S.C., 1973-82, and concurrently Director, Karl W. Kinard Conference Center, Leesville, S.C., 1973-81; St. John's, Cherryville, 1982-92; retired January 1992 to Hickory, N.C.

Other: South Carolina Synod Executive Board, two terms; Chaplain, South Carolina Synod Convention; North Carolina Synod Council, two terms; two funeral sermons published in *In Sure and Certain Hope*; Dean, Piedmont District and Western District, South Carolina Synod; Dean, Southwestern District, North Carolina Synod.

SLICE, PAUL OWENS

Date/Place of Birth: July 1, 1932; Chapin, S.C.
Parents: George Bailey Slice and Louise (Summer) Slice.
Spouse/Marriage Date: Karilyn Louise (Slye) Slice; September 13, 1957 in Columbia, S.C.
Children: Stephen Paul, Kristeen Elizabeth.
Education: Newberry College, A.B. 1954; Lutheran Theological Southern Seminary, M.Div. 1957.
Ordination: June 9, 1957 by South Carolina Synod.
Calls: St. Luke, Bear Poplar, 1957-59; Mt. Hermon, West Columbia, S.C., 1959-67; Holy Trinity, Anderson, S.C., 1967-. Retired in 1998 to Anderson, S.C.
Other: Chair, South Carolina Synod Stewardship Committee; Chair, South Carolina Synod Social Ministry Committee; Board, Lowman Home, 22 years; Delegate, Convention of the Lutheran Church in America, 1976, 1978; Dean, Piedmont District of the South Carolina Synod; President, Anderson County Literacy Association; President (two terms) of the Anderson Memorial Hospital Clergy Staff.

SLOOP, DAVID ARTHUR

Date/Place of Birth: September 29, 1951; Salisbury, N.C.
Parents: Frank Brown Sloop, Sr. and Gladys (Eudy) Sloop.
Spouse/Marriage Date: Sally Elizabeth (Clark) Sloop; June 12, 1976 in Ridgewood, N.J.
Children: Elizabeth Clark, Peter David. Legal Guardian for Scott Alan Friberg, John Carl Friberg, Karen Clark Friberg.
Education: University of North Carolina at Chapel Hill, B.A. Religion/American Studies 1973; Harvard Divinity School, M.T.S. 1975; Gettysburg Seminary, M.Div. 1978.
Ordination: June 11, 1978 by North Carolina Synod.
Calls: Macedonia, Burlington, 1978-82; Pastor/Developer, Good Shepherd, Raleigh, 1982-; Vice Pastor at various congregations.
Other: Justice and Social Change Committee, 1979-83; World Hunger Committee, 1979-81; Director, Camp with Differently Abled, 1979-88; Board, Lutheran Family Services, 1980-92; delegate and to church assemblies, 1985, 1988; Voting Member, 1995; Chaplain, Division for Mission in North America Pastor/Developer School, 1986; Winner of Kennedy Foundation Family of Distinction for North Carolina, 1992

SLOOP, HENRY ELI HALL

Date/Place of Birth: March 25, 1862; near China Grove, N.C.
Parents: Abraham Sloop and Delilah (Bostian) Sloop.

Spouse/Marriage Date: Mary Edna (Ketchie) Sloop, daughter of the Reverend W. R. Ketchie; March 9, 1897.

Children: Four sons, of whom two were Lutheran ministers; three daughters of whom Lois and Ruth married ministers.

Education: North Carolina College, 1891; Gettysburg Seminary, 1894; Chicago Seminary, B.D. 1925.

Ordination: Licensed by Maryland Synod, 1893; ordained 1894 by North Carolina Synod.

Calls: St. Matthew-Reformation, Davie County-Providence, Rowan County, 1894-96; transferred to Synod of Georgia and Adjacent States, 1896; nine different pastorates in Georgia, Mississippi, Tennessee (Cocke and Greene counties, 1905-07), West Virginia and Virginia, 1896-1931, except 1907-09, serving St. Stephen-Mt. Olive, Cabarrus County; retired 1931.

Other: Principal, Beth Eden (Mississippi) Collegiate Institute, while pastor there; Co-principal of school in Smith County, Mississippi; President, Holston Synod.

Date of Death/Burial Location: March 30, 1943; Greenlawn Cemetery, China Grove, N.C.

SLOOP, JERRY LEE

Date/Place of Birth: March 7, 1952; Mooresville, N.C.

Parents: Eustace Lee Sloop and Dorothy Ruth (Cauble) Sloop.

Spouse/Marriage Date: Maribeth (Morgan) Sloop; March 13, 1971.

Children: Donnie Lee, Daniel Heath.

Education: University of North Carolina at Charlotte, Rowan County Community College, Pfeiffer College, B.A. 1985; Lutheran Theological Southern Seminary, M.Div. 1989.

Ordination: June 2, 1989 by North Carolina Synod.

Calls: Bethany, Kannapolis, 1989-94; Bethel, Salisbury, 1994-98; Vice Pastor at various congregations.

Other: Secretary/Treasurer, Cabarrus-Stanly Lutheran Ministers Association, 1992-94; Kannapolis-Concord CROP Walk Coordinator, 1990, 1991; Rowan Ministerial Association; Lutheran Outdoor Ministry Committee; Rowan Umpire Association; junior varsity baseball coach at North Rowan High School; U.S. Air Force.

Date of Death/Burial Location: October 20, 1998; Grace, Salisbury, N.C.

SLOOP, LUTHER RANKIN

Date/Place of Birth: August 14, 1921; Cabarrus County, N.C.

Parents: Charles Marks Sloop and Margaret Ruth (Goodman) Sloop.

Spouse/Marriage Date: Mary Louise (Frye) Sloop; June 13, 1948 in Newton, Catawba County, N.C.

Children: David Luther, Wayne Franklin, Barbara Louise, Mary Ann Carriker.

Education: Lenoir-Rhyne, A.B. 1945; Lutheran Theological Southern Seminary, B.D. 1948, M.Div. 1972.

Ordination: April 7, 1948 by North Carolina Synod.

Calls: Lebanon-Providence, Rowan County-Amity, Iredell County-St. Matthew, Davie County, 1948-50; St. Martin-Cold Water, Cabarrus County, 1950-57; Zion, Catawba

County, 1957-64; Frieden's, Guilford County, 1964-71; St. Martin, Maiden, 1971-83; retired 1983 to Newton, N.C.; Vice Pastor at various congregations.

SLOOP, PERRY L.

Date/Place of Birth: November 29, 1941; Landis, N.C.
Parents: Gray Alexander Sloop and Lucille (Mullis) Sloop.
Spouse/Marriage Date: Mary Jo (Warren) Sloop; August 21, 1965 in Charlotte, N.C.
Children: Christina Maria.
Education: Catawba College, B.A. 1964; University of Tennessee, 1965; Lutheran Theological Southern Seminary, M.Div. 1970; Frye Regional Hospital, Hickory, Chaplain Service, 1988.
Ordination: June 6, 1970 by North Carolina Synod.
Calls: New Bethel, Richfield, 1970-74; Holy Cross, Yoakum, Texas, 1974-76; Trinity, Miles, Texas, 1976-80; St. Paul, Darrouzett, Texas, 1980-82; Holy Trinity, Houston, Texas, 1982-84; Trinity, Vale, 1985-90; retired August 1990 to Lincolnton, N.C.
Other: Chaplain, Trinity Nursing Home in Shiner, Texas, and Frye Regional Hospital, Hickory.

SLOOP, RICKY LYNN

Date/Place of Birth: May 21, 1959; Mooresville, N.C.
Parents: Eustace Lee Sloop and Ruth (Cauble) Sloop.
Spouse: Sharon Sloop.
Education: Pfeiffer College, B.A. Religion 1992; Lutheran Theological Southern Seminary, M.Div. 1996.
Ordination: December 13, 1996 by North Carolina Synod.
Calls: Messiah, Salisbury, 1996-.
Other: Habitat for Humanity; Youth Baseball Coach.

SMELTZER, JOSIAH PIERCE

Date/Place of Birth: September 10, 1819; Carroll County, Md.
First Spouse/Marriage Date: Harriet A. (Buffington) Smeltzer; October 22, 1848 in Taneytown, Md.
Second Spouse/Marriage Date: Anna Eliza (Eichelberger) Smeltzer; June 17, 1851, in Walhalla, S.C.
Education: Gettysburg College, A.B. 1846; Gettysburg Seminary, 1847; Erskine College, D.D. 1873.
Ordination: 1848 presumably by Maryland Synod; transferred 1857 to Virginia Synod, 1860, to Southwestern Virginia Synod, 1861, to South Carolina Synod, and 1878 to Tennessee Synod.
Calls: St. John, Harper's Ferry, W.Va., 1848-60; St. Peter, Shepherdstown, W.Va., 1852-60; in South Carolina, Luther Chapel (Church of the Redeemer), Newberry, 1861-68. In Tennessee Synod: St. Jacob-St. Thomas-Bethlehem, near Chapin, S.C., 1878-86.
Other: Roanoke College, 1860-61; Newberry College, in the War Between the States years, serving as President and Professor, and doubling as Dean and Teacher in Lutheran Theological Southern Seminary, then connected with the college, 1861-77. In early

ministry in Newberry, baked bread in home kitchen for sale for a livelihood, since college and church could pay him little. President, South Carolina Synod, 1872-73; Vice President, 1882-83; Corresponding Secretary, 1861-71. Founder and Principal of Walkalla Female College, 1877, 1885.
Date of Death/Burial Location: October 31, 1887; St. John Church, Walhalla, S.C.

SMITH, HARWOOD TURRENTINE, JR.
Date/Place of Birth: September 28, 1937; Brooklyn, N.Y.
Parents: Harwood Turrentine Smith, Sr. and Virginia Ella (Smithers) Smith.
Spouse/Marriage Date: Barbara Ann (Harrison) Smith of Dallas, Texas; July 9, 1960 at Tuscaloosa, Ala.
Children: Joseph Leigh, Carolyn Eva.
Education: University of Alabama, B.A. 1959; Philadelphia Seminary, B.D. 1962.
Ordination: June 1962 by New York-Northeastern Synod.
Calls: Sharon, Gibsonville, 1962-67; Holy Trinity, Troutman, 1967-78; St. Matthew, Kings Mountain, 1978- 93; Bethany, Boone, 1993-99; retired August 1999. Vice Pastor at various congregations.
Other: American Missions Committee, 1968.

SMITH, JACK EVERETT
Date/Place of Birth: July 2, 1927; China Grove, Rowan County, N.C.
Parents: Mack Henry Smith and Mardre (Horne) Smith.
Spouse/Marriage Date: Christine (Heller) Smith, daughter of the Reverend Dr. Mark Owen Heller; June 11, 1949 in Woxall, Pa.
Children: Maria Christine, Michael Craig, Mark Clifton, Melodie Celeste.
Education: Lenoir-Rhyne, A.B. 1948; Philadelphia Seminary, M.Div. 1951; Lutheran Theological Southern Seminary, S.T.M. 1968.
Ordination: July 8, 1951 by North Carolina Synod.
Calls: St. Martin, Stanly County, 1951-52; Coble's (Zion), Guilford County, 1952-56; Grace, Thomasville, 1956-59; St. Mark, Asheville, 1959-68; St. John's, Cherryville, 1968-81; retired in 1981; Vice Pastor at various congregations.
Other: Executive Board, North Carolina Synod.

SMITH, JASPER JAY
Date/Place of Birth: January 13, 1924; Taylorsville, Alexander County, N.C.
Parents: Thomas Boyd Smith and Laura L. (Austin) Smith. Younger brother of the Reverend W. Leo Smith.
First Spouse/Marriage Date: Sarah Ann (Zimmerman) Smith; July 17, 1954 in Rowan County, N.C.
Children: Stephen Jay, Michael Freeman, Renee Ann Sauer.

Second Spouse/Marriage Date: Lou (Hulon) Smith; February 28, 1987.

Education: Appalachian State Teachers College, 1941-42; drafted into Army 1942; Lenoir-Rhyne, A.B. 1948; Lutheran Theological Southern Seminary, M.Div. 1951; graduate study, Union Seminary.

Ordination: July 8, 1951 by North Carolina Synod.

Calls: Bethel, Rowan County-St. Matthew, Davie County, 1951-54; St. Andrew, New Bern, 1954-56; Chaplain, U.S. Air Force, 1956-84; retired 1984 and served Augsburg, Union, S.C., 1984-92, half-time.

Other: Served in World War II and Vietnam; received four Bronze stars, Meritorious Service Medal, Air Force Commendation Medal, American Campaign Medal, Asiatic-Pacific Camp Medal, Good Conduct Medal, Air Force Outstanding Unit Award, Republic of Vietnam Gallantry Cross.

Date of Death/Burial Location: June 17, 1991; Bethel Cemetery, Salisbury, N.C.

SMITH, JOHN LEWIS

Date/Place of Birth: March 13, 1879; Rowan County, N.C.

Parents: Elias Leroy Smith and Delilah Virginia (Bostian) Smith.

First Spouse/Marriage Date: Margaret Alice (Rodgers) Smith; October 20, 1901 in Rowan County, N.C.

Children of First Marriage: Eugene.

Second Spouse/Marriage Date: Mary Louise (Porter) Smith; June 8, 1911 in Salisbury, N.C.

Children of Second Marriage: Margaret Delilah.

Education: Mount Pleasant Collegiate Institute, Lenoir-Rhyne, A.B. 1908; Lutheran Theological Southern Seminary, 1911.

Ordination: 1911 by North Carolina Synod.

Calls: St. Luke-Pilgrim, Davidson County-Reformation, Davie County, 1911-12; transferred 1912 to Southwestern Virginia Synod; served parish at Rural Retreat, Va., and other parishes at Florence, S.C. (St. Luke, 1914-17), Harrisonburg, Va., Bristol, Tenn., Greenville, S.C. (Trinity, 1923-26), and two in Ohio, 1912-41; retired 1941 to Salisbury.

Date of Death/Burial Location: September 28, 1943; St. Enoch Church, Rowan County, N.C.

SMITH, JOHN MELANCHTHON

Born: November 19, 1830.

License/Ordination: Licensed 1856 and ordained 1858 by Tennessee Synod.

Calls: St. Martin, Iredell County, 1857-70; Sharon, Iredell County, 1858-74; Friendship, Alexander County, 1867-77; St. Peter, Catawba County, 1856-62, 1865-76; Zion, Hickory, 1870-81; St. James, Newton, 1870-79; St. John, Conover and St. Paul, Newton, 1870-94; St. Stephen, Hickory, 1873-77.

Other: Treasurer, Tennessee Synod, five terms between 1860 and 1880, Secretary in 1861, 1863, 1876; President in 1864, 1868, 1873, and 1885; Joint Commission (North Carolina and Tennessee Synods) to submit "terms for union," 1871, adopted by both synods, but not effected. With the Rev. P. C. Henkel, led in founding Conover High School in 1878 sponsored by Tennessee pastors of that area. In 1880 Tennessee Synod adopted, chartered, and renamed it Concordia College. In 1897 went to The Lutheran Church-Missouri Synod; living in 1910 at Claremont, N.C.

Place of Death/Burial Location: May 1913 Conover, N.C.; St. John Church, Catawba County, N.C.

SMITH, RONALD COLEMAN, SR.
Date/Place of Birth: July 6, 1929; Lexington, N.C.
Parents: Z. Griff Smith and Mary (Swing) Smith.
Spouse: Lillie Joyce (Massey) Smith.
Children: Ronald, Jr., Robert Griff.
Education: Lenoir-Rhyne, A.B. 1964; Lutheran Theological Southern Seminary, B.D. 1968.
Ordination: June 9, 1968 by North Carolina Synod.
Calls: Trinity, New Smyrna, Fla., 1968-69; St. Paul, Mt. Pleasant, S.C., 1969-70.
Date of Death/Burial Location: August 15, 1970; Lutheran Cemetery, Mt. Pleasant, S.C.

SMITH, THOMAS BRUCE
Date/Place of Birth: March 28, 1949; Miami, Fla.
Parents: Thomas John Smith and Eleanor Olean (Goodman) Smith. Great-great-great-great grandson of The Reverend Adolphus Nussmann.
Spouse/Marriage Date: Anna Virginia (Loope) Smith; May 26, 1973 in Buchanan, Va.
Education: Miami Dade Junior College and University of Miami, B.S. Electrical Engineering 1971; Lutheran Theological Southern Seminary, M.Div. 1975; Drew University, D.Min. 1993.
Ordination: June 22, 1975 by Florida Synod.
Calls: Faith, Tampa, Fla., 1975-82; Mt. Hermon, Concord, 1982-97; Vice Pastor at various congregations; transferred to Southeast Synod, 1997. Christ the King, Cumming, Ga., 1997-.
Other: Chair, Service to Leadership; Associate Chaplain, Cabarrus Memorial Hospital, Concord; Women, Church and Society Committee, Florida Synod, 1976-81; Commission of Personnel Services, Florida Synod, 1979-81; Board, Lutheran Theological Southern Seminary, Florida Synod, 1980-82; Strength for Mission - Action Group Director, 1978.

SMITH, TIMOTHY MARCUS
Date/Place of Birth: January 20, 1960; Lenoir, N.C.
Parents: Dr. Marcus C. Smith and Dorothy (Walker) Smith. Grandson of the Rev. James Ernest Walker.
Spouse/Marriage Date: Wendy (Weisner) Smith; December 18, 1983 in Roanoke Rapids, N.C.
Children: Matthew Marcus, Isaac David, Ruth Anna.
Education: University of North Carolina at Chapel Hill, Master of Arts with Honors in Religion, 1982; Gettysburg Seminary, M.Div. 1986; Drew University, D.Min. 1992.
Ordination: 1986 by North Carolina Synod.
Calls: St. Paul, Startown, 1986-93; Grace, Boone, 1993-.
Other: President, Catawba Valley Lutheran Ministerial Association; President, Eastern Catawba Cooperative Christian Ministry and Board, Head Start Program; Secretary, Western Piedmont Conference; Chair, Youth Ministry Committee; Board, Lutheran Services for the Aging in North Carolina, Chair, Finance Committee; Evangelism Committee, Board, Vice President, "Hospitality House" in Boone; Seminary Intern Supervisor; High Country Coalition of Churches and Watauga County Ministerial Association; Committee for Eco-Justice.

SMITH, WILBERN LEO
Date/Place of Birth: August 3, 1912; Taylorsville, N.C.
Parents: Thomas Boyd Smith and Laura L. (Austin) Smith.
Older brother of the Reverend Jasper J. Smith.
Spouse/Marriage Date: Evelyn Lena (Patterson) Smith; May 18,
1940 in China Grove, N.C.
Children: Carolyn Elaine, Edwin Leo, Harold Eugene.
Education: Lenoir-Rhyne, A.B. 1933; Lutheran Theological
Southern Seminary, B.D. 1937, S.T.M. 1959 (first, with the
Reverend Hoyle L. Whiteside, to receive that degree from
Lutheran Theological Southern Seminary); graduate work, Union
Seminary (N.Y.), 1954.
Ordination: May 26, 1937 by North Carolina Synod.
Calls: St. David (organized 1938)-Redeemer (organized 1939 and built church),
Kannapolis, 1937-43; Zion, Catawba County, 1943-45; St. Andrew, Andrews, 1945-47; St.
Paul, Dallas, 1947-62; New Jerusalem, Catawba County, 1962-79; retired December 1979;
Bethany, Hickory, Retired Assistant, 1980, Pastor Emeritus, 1987; Vice Pastor at various
congregations.
Other: Lowman Home Board, 1959-66, Secretary, 1965-66; Publications and Publicity
Committee, 1967-68; North Carolina Council of Churches, 1962-63; Northwestern District
Dean, 1970-77; Chair, Auxiliaries, 1969-72; Executive Board of North Carolina Synod,
1975-79; Chair, Convention Committee, 1976; Delegate, United Lutheran Church in
America Conventions, 1960, 1962; Coordinator, North Carolina Synod Conventions, 1970-
86; Member of the Boy Scouts of America as Troop Committee Member, Camp Counselor,
and Chaplain for 25 years; Startown Lions Club.

SMITH, WILLIAM ELMER
Date/Place of Birth: September 16, 1931; Hickory, N.C.
Parents: William Franklin Smith and Zora Lee (Hilton) Smith.
Spouse/Marriage Date: Ruby (Haywood) (Harker) Smith;
August 30, 1961 in Norwood, N.C.
Stepchildren: Naia Dawn and Terry Randolph Harker.
Education: Lenoir-Rhyne, A.B. 1953; Lutheran Theological
Southern Seminary, M.Div. 1956; Clinical Pastoral Education -
Gaston Memorial Hospital, 1976.
Ordination: June 10, 1956 by North Carolina Synod.
Calls: Mission Developer, Charlotte, 1956-57; Miller and Zion,
Knoxville, Tenn., 1957-58; Sinking Springs, Midway, Tenn.-Blue Springs, Mosheim,
Tenn.-Luther-Zion, Limestone, Tenn., 1958-59; Mt. Zion-New Bethel, Richfield, 1960-62;
Bethany, Boone-Holy Trinity, Deep Gap, 1962-64; Salem-St. Luke, Lincoln County, 1964-
66; St. Mark, Cherryville, 1966-70, 1973-76; Good Shepherd, Hickory, 1971-73; St.
Stephen, Gold Hill, 1976-83; Messiah, Burlington, 1983-84; retired 1985 in Crouse, N.C.

SMITH, WILLIAM JACOB
Date/Place of Birth: March 31, 1845; Boonsboro, Md.
Spouse/Marriage Date: Alice (Kizer) Smith; probably about 1880 in Rowan County, N.C.

Children: Two sons, the Reverends Frisby D. and Edwin B.; three or four daughters, one of whom married the Reverend J. H. Richard. Two nephews were Lutheran pastors, and also college Presidents, the Reverends Charles J. Smith (Roanoke College) and G. Morris Smith (Susquehanna University).

Education: Roanoke College, AB 1875; Lutheran Theological Southern Seminary, 1878.

Ordination: 1878.

Calls: St. John, Salisbury, 1878-83; Christ, East Spencer, 1881-82; in Virginia (St. Mark, Roanoke, 1883-85; Gravel Spring Parish, Frederick and Shenandoah counties, 1885-1911).

Other: Secretary, North Carolina Synod, 1881-83; President, Virginia Synod, 1899.

Date of Death/Burial Location: February 19, 1911; Bloom, Va.

SMITHDEAL, JOHN L.

Date of Birth: 1836.

License: Licensed 1858 by North Carolina Synod.

Calls: Bethel-St. Paul, Rowan County, 1858-60; Frog Level (old name for Prosperity), S.C., 1860-61; St. Paul, Iredell County-Beth Eden, Newton, 1862-65; later in Montoursville, Lycoming County, Pa., 1866.

Date of Death/Burial Location: May 1, 1871; Ancram, N.Y.

SMYRE, ELI E.

Ordination: Ordained by a special committee (the Reverends A. J. Fox, J. M. Smith and Timothy Moser) of Tennessee Synod in Phaniel Church, Rowan County, third Sunday in December 1860.

Calls: St. Martin, Stanly County, 1860-63; Madisonville, Tenn., about 1866.

Date of Death/Burial Location: 1869; presumably buried in Tennessee.

SMYTH, RICHARD THOMAS

Date/Place of Birth: September 22, 1943; Chicago, Ill.

Parents: William Astrup Smyth and Marjorie (McCann) Smyth.

Spouse/Marriage Date: Nancy Elizabeth (Baker) Smyth; June 15, 1968 in Spartanburg, S.C.

Children: April Joy, Marjorie Hope.

Education: Newberry, A.B. 1965; Lutheran Theological Southern Seminary, M.Div. 1969; Appalachian State University, M.A. 1975; Luther Rice Seminary, D.Min. 1981.

Ordination: June 1, 1969 by North Carolina Synod.

Calls: St. Timothy, Hickory, 1969-74; Holy Cross, Lincolnton, 1974-83; Vice Pastor at various congregations.

Other: On leave from call in 1983; in 1987 was in Monetta, S.C.; Instructor in Psychology at Lenoir-Rhyne, 1974-75; Organizer/Chair, Lincoln County Nursing Home Advisory Board, 1979-83; founded and organized Lincoln County Pastor's Support Group, 1978-83; organized and founded Lincoln County Law Enforcement Chaplaincy, 1978-83; founded and organized Church School for Developmentally Delayed, 1975-83; Board, Christian Ministries of Lincoln County, 1974-83; received First Pilot Good Citizenship Award, 1982; honored by Senior Citizens of Lincoln County, 1979; Jaycee Community Service Award, 1978; PTA Citizenship Awards, 1976-77; author of Augsburg Fortress, Publishers Sunday School materials and devotional pamphlets; *Role of the Police Chaplain*, North Carolina

Department of Corrections, 1979; *Some Miracles of the Old Testament,* 1969; President, Association for Retarded Citizens; President, Mental Health Association; Board, Kidney Foundation.

SNAPP, PHILIP LOY

Date/Place of Birth: December 22, 1873; St. Paris, Ohio.
Spouse/Marriage Date: Henrietta Pearl (Sharp) Snapp of Driscoll, W.Va.; November 28, 1900.
Children: Leo Philip, Ralph Coffman, Mildred Sharp.
Education: St. Paul Seminary, Hickory.
Ordination: 1899 by Joint Synod of Ohio, at Baltimore, Md.
Calls: (Joint Synod) Driscoll, W.Va., 1899-1900 and Highland County, Va., 1899-1908; Tennessee Synod: Beth Eden-Grace-Morning Star-Mt. Calvary, Page County, Va., 1909-20; Virginia Synod: Augusta and Wythe Counties, Va., 1920-39; retired 1939.
Date of Death/Burial Location: February 14, 1940; Rural Retreat, Va.

SNYDER, HARMON MILTON

Education: Carthage College, A.B. and A.M.; Hamma Divinity School, B.D.; University of Chicago, Ph.D. 1925.
Calls: Served churches at Detroit, Mich., Chicago, Ill., and Hays, Kan.; transferred to North Carolina Synod, 1925 from Kansas Synod.
Other: Professor and head of department (Sociology, Economics), Lenoir-Rhyne, 1925-28; previously, Supply Professor, 1923-24, Assistant Professor, 1924-25, (Philosophy, Sociology, Education, Religious Education), Wittenberg University; American Sociological Society; transferred to Eastern Pennsylvania Synod, 1931; retired at Norristown, Pa. in 1965.

SNYDER, WILLIAM ALFRED

Date/Place of Birth: December 31, 1870; Waterloo, Ontario, Canada.
Parents: Thomas Snyder and Lorene (Stahlschmidt) Snyder.
Spouse/Marriage Date: Emma Louise (Specker) Snyder of Berlin (now Kitchener), Ontario, Canada; October 6, 1897.
Children: Margaret Louise, John Harold, William Louis.
Education: McGill University; Philadelphia Seminary, 1897; Lenoir-Rhyne, D.D. 1911.
Ordination: 1897 by Ministerium of Pennsylvania.
Calls: In Pennsylvania, 1897-1904, at West Reading and Wernersville; St. Paul, Wilmington, 1904-12; in New York, 1912-21, at St. Luke, Brooklyn.
Other: Board, Social Missions, United Lutheran Church in America, 1918-21; Committee of Book of Worship, United Synod South; contributed to *The American Lutheran Survey,* Columbia, S.C.
Date of Death/Burial Location: July 13, 1921; Greenwood Cemetery, Brooklyn, N.Y.

SOMMERS, HEIDI JO

Date/Place of Birth: December 31, 1967; Milwaukee, Wis.
Parents: James Winston Sommers and Nancy Jean (Holyfield) Sommers.

Education: Lenoir-Rhyne, B.A. Psychology/Sociology 1990; Lutheran Theological Southern Seminary, M.Div. 1994.
Ordination: December 11, 1994 by North Carolina Synod.
Calls: Calvary, Clarkston, Mich., 1994-95; First, Albemarle, 1997-.
Other: Lutheran Youth of North Carolina Network Chair, 1996-.

SONDHAUS, MARTIN
Date/Place of Birth: May 21, 1820; Erfurt, Prussia, Germany, and came to this country as a young man.
Education: Gettysburg College, A.B. 1842; Gettysburg Seminary, 1844.
License/Ordination: Licensed 1844 by Western Pennsylvania Synod, and ordained 1850 by Ministerium of Pennsylvania.
Calls: In Pennsylvania, 1844-55; transferred 1855 to Tennessee Synod; served churches in Hardy and Pendleton Counties, Va., 1855-59; in Ohio (New Bremen), Illinois (Lemont and Summit), and Missouri (St. Louis), 1859-78.
Other: Preached in both German and English.
Date of Death: April 4, 1878; St. Louis, Mo.

SORENSEN, PAUL MATT
Date/Place of Birth: March 22, 1938; Sault St. Marie, Chippewa County, Mich.
Parents: Albert S. Sorensen and Anna L. (Johnson) Sorensen.
Spouse/Marriage Date: Mary Ellen Ida (Koski) Sorensen; December 29, 1962 in L'Anse, Mich.
Children: Phillip Andrew, Nathan Paul.
Education: Luther Junior College, A.A. 1959; Bethany College, B.A. 1961; Chicago Seminary, B.D. 1965.
Ordination: June 20, 1965 by Wisconsin-Upper Michigan Synod.
Calls: Lebanon, and Mission Developer, Our Saviour, Welcome, Davidson County, 1965-70; Bay Shore, Milwaukee, Wis., 1970-74; Our Redeemer, Menasha, Wis., 1974-83; Fristad, Centuria, Wis., 1983-88; St. Mark, Cudahy, Wis., 1988-.
Other: Youth Committee, Educational Ministry Committee, Secretary, Dean of District; local clergy organizations; Ad Hoc Committees on Alcohol, Drugs; delegate to National Convention, 1982; Advisory Committee, Lutheran Social Services.

SOWERS, ROBERT REEVES
Place of Birth: Floyd County, Va.
Parents: Druss W. Sowers and Manerva (Williams) Sowers.
First Spouse/Marriage Date: Hettie A. (Spangler) Sowers; December 9, 1891 in Floyd, Va.
Children of First Marriage: Zada Ione, Willie Alnora, Jennie Mabel, Lillian Bowling, Robert Easter, Mattie Manie.
Second Spouse/Marriage Date: Mary L. (Brown) Sowers, daughter of the Reverend H. M. Brown, Rowan County; October 10, 1911.
Children of Second Spouse: Harry Brown, Jack R., Edgar R.
Education: No formal college or seminary training.
License/Ordination: Licensed 1898 and ordained 1901 by Southwest Virginia Synod.

Calls: In Gladesboro and Ceres, Va.; transferred 1903 to North Carolina Synod; Low's-Coble's, Guilford County-St. Paul, Alamance County, 1903-05; First, Albemarle, 1905-06; St. Michael, Troutman-Amity-St. Paul, Iredell County, 1906-07; Bethel-St. Paul, Rowan County, 1907-11; Wittenberg-Christiana, Granite Quarry-St. James, Rockwell, 1911-13; Organ-Ebenezer, Rowan County, 1914-18; in Tennessee (Greene County, 1918-1919) and South Carolina (Ft. Motte, Irmo and Columbia, 1920-23; Lone Star and Elloree, 1922- 23).
Date of Death/Burial Location: June 7, 1924; Zion Church, Floyd, Va.

SOX, CHARLES JASON

Date/Place of Birth: September 27, 1873; Lexington County, S.C.
Education: Lenoir-Rhyne, A.B. 1902; Lutheran Theological Southern Seminary, 1905.
Ordination: 1905 by Southwest Virginia Synod.
Calls: Gladesboro, Carroll County, Va., 1905-06; Mt. Pleasant, Saluda, S.C., 1906-07; transferred 1907 to Tennessee Synod; Mt. Hermon-Sharon-St. Martin, Iredell County, 1907-10; transferred 1910 to North Carolina Synod; Frieden's-Sharon, Gibsonville, 1910-13; transferred 1917 to South Carolina Synod, Bethany, Lexington, 1919-38; St. James, Lexington, 1921-24. Retired 1939.
Date of Death/Burial Location: 1947; St. Stephen Cemetery, Lexington, S.C.

SOX, DAVID ADAM

Date/Place of Birth: October 13, 1856; Edmund, S.C.
Education: Studied at Concordia College and Theology at North Carolina College.
Ordination: Ordained 1883 by Tennessee Synod in Concordia College Chapel, with the Reverends J. A. Rudisill and D. J. Settlemyre.
Calls: Tennessee Synod churches at Oak Level and Edwardsville, Ala.; Concordia-Grace, Rowan County, 1887-88; transferred 1898 to Synod of Georgia and Adjacent States; later served in South Carolina: Mt. Calvary-St. John, near Johnston; Good Hope, Saluda County; organized (1908) and served twice, Holy Trinity, New Brookland (West Columbia) 1907 to death.
Other: Was an inventor.
Date of Death/Place of Burial: Early in 1922; Elmwood Cemetery, Columbia, S.C.

SOX, ENOCH JEFFERSON

Date/Place of Birth: February 20, 1866; Lexington County, S.C.
Parents: Conrad Samuel Sox and Sarah Ellen (Baughman) Sox.
Spouse/Marriage Date: Allie Lula Irene (Roof) Sox, sister of the Reverends F. K., W. H., and W. J. Roof; September 6, 1891 in Lexington County, S.C.
Children: Rosa, J. Loy, the Reverend Samuel L., Irene, Edith, Louise, Mildred, Everette, Harold.
Education: Lenoir-Rhyne, A.B. 1896, A.M. 1901, D.D. 1922; theology there also; Chicago Seminary; Newberry College, D.D.
Ordination: 1895 by Tennessee Synod.
Calls: Daniel's, Lincoln County-Grace, Catawba County, 1895-96; St. James, Lincoln County-St. Paul, Newton-Mt. Zion, Caldwell County, 1897-99; Mt. Olive, 1899-1901, 1914-20; St. Stephen, Hickory, 1903-05, 1914-20; in South Carolina, early in ministry,

Tennessee Synod churches: St. John, near Pomaria; St. Peter, near Chapin; St. Paul, Gilbert; St. James, Summit; and Holy Trinity, Little Mountain; again in North Carolina: Supply, with the Reverends R. L. Fritz and J. L. Cromer, Shiloh, Alexander County, 1896-1907; Mt. Calvary, Claremont, 1920-21; Bethlehem, Catawba County, 1925-26; Friendship, Alexander County-St. John, Hudson, 1926-27, 1931; St. Paul, Catawba County, 1928; and Mt. Hebron, Hildebran, 1932.

Other: Lenoir-Rhyne, Professor (Mathematics and Greek), 1898-1905, (Bible and Religion), 1919-34; Treasurer, Endowment Fund, 1914-23. In Tennessee Synod: Secretary, 1902-03, President, 1906-08, Statistical Secretary, 1909-14, and Treasurer, 1914-21.

Date of Death/Burial Location: February 22, 1934; Hickory, N.C.

SOX, SAMUEL LUND, SR.

Date/Place of Birth: June 7, 1905; Chapin, S.C.

Parents: The Reverend Enoch Jefferson Sox and Allie Lula Irene (Roof) Sox, sister of the Reverends F. K., W. H., and W. J. Roof.

Spouse/Marriage Date: Nellie Viola (Coulter) Sox; January 14, 1931 in Newton, N.C.

Children: Samuel Lund, Jr., Harold David, Sylvia.

Education: Lenoir-Rhyne, A.B. 1926, D.D. 1965; Lutheran Theological Southern Seminary, B.D. 1929.

Ordination: May 29, 1929 by North Carolina Synod.

Calls: St. Paul, Startown-Mt. Hebron, Hildebran, 1929-32; Supply, Calvary, Morganton, 1931; Bethany, Hickory, 1932-40; First (relocated in former First Baptist Church building, renovated), Greensboro, 1940-70. Pastor to Lutheran students at local institutions, chiefly University of North Carolina at Greensboro; retired in 1970; Vice Pastor at various congregations.

Other: Board, Lenoir-Rhyne; Board, Lowman Home.

Date of Death/Burial Location: November 21, 1989; Westminster Memorial Garden, Greensboro, N.C.

SPEAGLE, FREDERICK MARTIN LUTHER

Birth/Place of Birth: November 25, 1883; Henry, Catawba County, N.C.

Parents: William P. Speagle and Mary (Houser) Speagle.

Spouse/Marriage Date: Maud Ellen (Townsend) Speagle; September 8, 1911 in Hickory, N.C.

Children: Paul Cedric, Mary Ellen.

Education: Lenoir-Rhyne, A.B. 1911; Lutheran Theological Southern Seminary, 1914.

Ordination: 1914 by Tennessee Synod.

Calls: St. Martin-Salem-Luther Chapel, Maiden, 1914-17; Supply, Sardis, Catawba County, 1915; St. Mary-Solomon, Forestville, Va., 1917-25; St. Paul, Crouse-St. Mark-Bethel, Gaston County-Bethphage, Lincoln County, 1923-28; Calvary, Concord, 1928-32; St. Paul, Hardin-Antioch-Philadelphia, Gaston County, 1932-47; Holy Trinity-Mt. Pleasant-Old Mt. Pleasant-Mt. Zion, Watauga County, 1947-51; retired 1951 in Cherryville.

Other: Taught high school Forestville, Va., 1920-22.
Date of Death/Burial Location: June 5, 1954; St. Mark Church, near Crouse, N.C.

SPIGGLE, GEORGE W.

Date/Place of Birth: December 4, 1855; Salem, Va.
First Spouse: Mary (Boon) Spiggle; Salem, Va.
Children of First Marriage: The Reverend Krauth, Elizabeth, Georgia, Beulah, Lula.
Second Spouse/Marriage Date: Ina Catherine (Kegley) Spiggle; June 24, 1920 in Wytheville, Va.
Education: Roanoke College, A.B. 1878; Lutheran Theological Southern Seminary, 1881.
Ordination: 1881 by Southwestern Virginia Synod.
Calls: In Virginia, about fourteen years, with congregations in Giles and Craig counties, Pembroke and Newport, Mt. Tabor, 1885-94, Wytheville, 1918-23; in Pennsylvania, about fourteen years, in Kittanning, Youngstown and Penn, 1894-1917; transferred 1908 to North Carolina Synod, from Pittsburgh Synod; First, Lexington, 1909; transferred 1910 back to Pittsburgh Synod; served again in Pennsylvania, and in Wytheville, Va., about fifteen years. Retired in 1923.
Date of Death/Burial Location: October 1, 1925; St. John Church, Wytheville, Va.

SPRACHER, LEVI BITTLE

Date/Place of Birth: March 3, 1873; Burkes Garden, Va.
Parents: Erastus Spracher and Joanna Spracher.
Spouse/Marriage Date: Nora C. (Price) Spracher; November 14, 1906 in Newport, Va.
Children: Elinor (died in infancy and buried at Union Church, Rowan County).
Education: Roanoke College, A.B. 1902; Lutheran Theological Southern Seminary, 1905.
Ordination: 1905 by Southwestern Virginia Synod.
Calls: Craig Parish, Craig, Va., 1904-08; Union-Christiana, Rowan County, 1908-09, then Union only, 1909-14; transferred 1915 to Holston Synod, serving Ascension, Chattanooga, Tenn., October 1, 1914-January 14, 1915.
Date of Death/Burial Location: January 14, 1915 of smallpox after a few days of illness; Forest Hill Cemetery, Chattanooga, Tenn., because health regulations prohibited his body being sent to Graham, Va., his hometown. Burial was "without ceremony, by a squad from the health office, detailed for that duty during the epidemic." Later a memorial service was held at his grave by Ascension congregation, led by the Reverends A. D. R. Hancher and B. S. Brown, Jr.

STACKEL, ROBERT WILLIAM

Date/Place of Birth: February 23, 1913; Rochester, N.Y.
Parents: William H. Stackel and Lillian Rose (Reuter) Stackel.
Spouse/Marriage Date: Virginia Marie (Gehr) Stackel; June 24, 1943 in Bethlehem, Pa.
Children: David Frederick, John Robert, Andrew William, Martha Lois Felts.
Education: Hamilton College, 1935; Philadelphia Seminary, 1938; Thiel College, D.D. 1951.
Ordination: June 15, 1938 by New York Synod.

Calls: St. Paul, Dansville, N.Y., 1938-43; Emmanuel, Rochester, N.Y., 1943-47; First English, Pittsburgh, Pa., 1947-55; Holy Trinity, Akron, Ohio, 1958-72; retired 1980; part-time staff member, St. Mark's, Charlotte.

Other: Director, Lutheran Evangelism Mission, United Lutheran Church in America, 1955-58; Executive Director, Division for World Missions and Ecumenism, Lutheran Church in America, 1972-74; Director, World Hunger Appeal, Lutheran Church in America, 1974-80; U.S.A. National Committee of the Lutheran World Federation, Lutheran Council in the U.S.A., Governing Board of the National Council of Churches of Christ in the U.S.A.; Delegate from Lutheran Church in America to Third Assembly of the World Council of Church in New Delhi, India; Executive Board, United Lutheran Church in America, 1958-66; Commission on Stewardship and Congregational Life, Lutheran World Federation, 1958-65; Board, Wittenberg University; Board, Hamma School of Theology; Board of Theological Education, Lutheran Church in America, 1958-72; President, Akron Rotary Club, 1969; President, United Community Council, Akron, Ohio, 1968-70; General Board, National Council of Churches of Christ in the U.S.A., 1972-74; Executive Committee, National Lutheran Council, 1972-74. In North Carolina Synod: Board, Lenoir-Rhyne College, 1982-91, 1993-94; Board of Visitors, Lutheran Theological Southern Seminary, 1988-91; Chair, Stewardship Committee, 1988-91; Presenter, Stewardship Practicums, Lutheran Laity Movement, 1979-94; Clergy Co-Chair, synod-wide Lenoir- Rhyne Centennial Renewal Campaign; author of six books and contributions to many others; monthly contributor to the magazine, *The Clergy Journal;* Chaplain, 1970, National Convention of the Lutheran Church in America; Chaplain, 1989 Assembly of the North Carolina Synod.

Date of Death/Burial Location: October 17, 1994; Sharon Memorial Park, Charlotte, N.C.

SQUIRE, PHILLIP MYRON

Date/Place of Birth: February 11, 1950; Toledo, Ohio.
Parents: Myron Guy Squire and Laretta Fay Squire.
Spouse/Marriage Date: Mary Anne (Roberts) Squire; June 24, 1978 in Nashville, Tenn.
Education: Purdue University, B.A./B.S. 1972; Gettysburg Seminary, M.Div. 1976.
Ordination: June 13, 1976 by Michigan Synod.
Calls: Associate Pastor, First, Nashville, Tenn., 1976-79; Holy Trinity, Hickory, 1979-83; Resurrection, Kings Mountain, 1983-88; King of Glory, Clemmons, 1988-.
Other: Worship and Music Committee; Spirituality Task Force and Committee; Northern Conference Coordinator for "Love in Action" Appeal; Heilig Media Center Advisory Committee.

STALEY, MAURICE EDWARD

Date/Place of Birth: September 4, 1927; Alamance County, N.C.
Parents: William Alfred Staley and Fannie Belle (Curtis) Staley.
Spouse/Marriage Date: Patsy Ruth (Carter) Staley; April 2, 1950 in Alamance, N.C.
Children: Roger Neal, Carol Lynne.
Education: Elon College, B.A. Religion 1963; Lutheran Theological Southern Seminary, B.D. 1966.
Ordination: June 5, 1966 by North Carolina Synod.

Calls: New Bethel-Mt. Zion, Richfield, 1966-69; Mt. Zion, Richfield, 1966-81; Center Grove, Kannapolis, 1981-94; retired in 1994 to Kannapolis, N.C.; Vice Pastor at various congregations.
Other: Ministry to Prisons Committee, 1974-81.

STAMM, BRIAN JAMES

Date/Place of Birth: February 17, 1964; Ellwood City, Pa.
Parents: Daniel L. Stamm and Monna H. Stamm.
Education: Thiel College, B.A. 1987; Gettysburg Seminary, M.Div. 1991; U.S. Navy Chaplains School, 1994.
Ordination: November 7, 1991 by North Carolina Synod.
Calls: Calvary, Spencer, 1991-94; Chaplain, U.S. Navy, 1994-.
Other: South East Asia Service Medal; National Defense Service Medal; Sea Service Deployment Ribbon.

STANGER, JOHN

Date/Place of Birth: June 10, 1765; Kircheim Uber Teck, Germany and later family moved to Stuttgart, Germany in 1779.
Parent: Johannes Stanger.
Spouse/Marriage Date: Anna Magdelene (Wampler) Stanger, died 1846; December 25, 1791.
Children: Five daughters and four sons.
Education: Studied theology at the University of Tuebingen before coming to America in December of 1784; arrived in Charleston, S.C. at Easter of 1785; in August 1787 Stanger is reported to be a "catechist." By June of 1790 he had settled in Wythe County, Va.
License/Ordination: Received authorization to perform marriages according to the Lutheran rite in 1790 at the Wythe County, Va., Court. In 1791 was present when the ordained Lutheran pastors in North Carolina met and organized the North Carolina "Ministerium." At that time was ordained and entrusted with the oversight of "four charges in Virginia on the New River."
Calls: Is credited with service at Zion, Cripple Creek, Wythe County, Va. until 1824; Elk Creek congregation, Grayson County; and St. Peter, New River; Stanger gave the land for the church building at Zion and served as their pastor from 1791 to 1824. Retired from ministry in 1824.
Other: Elected to represent Wythe County in the House of Deputies at Williamsburg, Va. He also represented the Wythe-Pulaski District for one term, 1839-40. Montgomery County records note weddings he performed there during the first decade of his service as a pastor.
Date of Death: October 14, 1848; Zion, Cripple Creek, Wythe County, Va. Zion Lutheran Church Cemetery, Wythe County, Va.

STARR, CHARLES MARION
Date/Place of Birth: May 31, 1925; Hickory, N.C.
Parents: Charles Burton Starr and Annie Iona (Abernethy) Starr.
Spouse/Marriage Date: Mary June (Hollar) Starr; January 25, 1948 in Hickory, N.C.
Children: Carol Ann Townsend, Charles Emery, Mary June Dudde.
Education: Lenoir-Rhyne, A.B. 1945, D.D. 1973; Lutheran Theological Southern Seminary, M.Div. 1948.
Ordination: April 7, 1948 by North Carolina Synod.
Calls: St. Paul, Hamlet, 1948-52; Calvary, Spencer, 1952-58; Redeemer, Charlotte, 1958-66; Kimball Memorial, Kannapolis, 1966-76; St. Paul, Wilmington, 1976-83; St. Mark, Asheville, 1983-1990; retired 1990; Vice Pastor at various congregations.
Other: Board, Lutheridge, 1959-69; Chaplain of 1963 North Carolina Synod Convention; Executive Board, North Carolina Synod, 1969-78; Examining Committee, 1963-73; Board, Lenoir-Rhyne, 1980-89, Secretary, 1982-89; Dean, Southern District, 1963-70; Board, Lutheran Services for Aging, 1990-; Board, Crescent View Retirement Center, 1991-, Chair; delegate to numerous assemblies of United Lutheran Church in America and Lutheran Church in America; listed in two editions of *Who's Who in Religion*; United Way Board of Directors in Cabarrus and New Hanover Counties; Senior Man-of-Year, Kannapolis, 1973; Adjunct Chaplain, St. Joseph's Hospital, Asheville.

STECK, CHARLES F., JR.
Date of Birth: September 14, 1890; Muncie, Ind.
Parents: The Reverend Charles F. Steck, Sr. and Florence G. (Jones) Steck.
Spouse/Marriage Date: Marie (Hansen) Steck; May 1, 1918 in Grand Rapids, Mich.
Children: Charles F., III, Richard Hansen, Jean Marie Sherwood.
Education: Wittenberg University, 1915; Hamma Divinity School, 1918.
Ordination: 1918 by Ohio Synod.
Calls: None in North Carolina, but 1918-33 at Upper Sandusky and Dayton, Ohio, Bluefield, W.Va., Knoxville, Tenn., and Detroit, Mich.; Chaplain, U.S. Army, 1936-50; Mission Developer at Tampa, Fort Lauderdale, and Sebring, Fla., 1950-57; retired 1957 at Cherryville, N.C.; transferred 1962 to North Carolina Synod.
Other: Superintendent, William Hansen School for Boys; Secretary, Florida Synod; Industrial Chaplain for Carolina Freight Carriers Corporation, 1957-59; compiled *Three Hours on The Cross,* a Good Friday devotional service, 1926.
Date of Death/Burial Location: July 29, 1966; Riverview Cemetery, Waynesboro, Va.

STEFFEY, SIDNEY DAVID
Date/Place of Birth: August 6, 1867; Rural Retreat, Va.
Parents: Franklin Steffey and Jane (Buck) Steffey.
Spouse/Marriage Date: Lillian (Jones) Steffey; March 18, 1888 in Rural Retreat, Va.
Children: No record of children.
Education: Wartburg College, 1887; theology there also, 1890; studied under the tutelage of the Rev. J. B. Greiner.

License/Ordination: Licensed 1889 and ordained 1890 by Southwest Virginia Synod.

Calls: Damascus and Blue Ridge Springs, Va., 1890-96; St. John, Cabarrus County, 1896-1901; Prosperity (now Cross of Christ), Cabarrus County, 1896; Mt. Olive, Cabarrus County, 1896-97; transferred 1901 to Holston Synod and preached at Berea Church in Virginia, serving churches in Tennessee (Immanuel, Blountville, 1901-05), and later in Ohio, Illinois, and Indiana, 1901-32.

Other: When the Synodical Convention was held in Hawkins Chapel in 1893 the visiting pastors preached in the different churches in the community, as was the custom, and Mr. Steffey preached in the church owned by the African-American citizens. President, Southern Illinois Synod.

Date of Death/Burial Location: April 25, 1932; Rockcreek Cemetery, near Camden, Ind. (Another source says burial is at Mt. Pisgah, Ind.)

STELLING, THOMAS OSBORNE

Date/Place of Birth: March 14, 1923; Augusta, Ga.

Parents: Carl Henry Stelling, Sr. and Lucy Ellen (Osborne) Stelling.

Spouse/Marriage Date: Geneva (Harrison) Stelling; February 1954.

Education: Augusta Junior College, 1941; Newberry College, A.B. 1943; Lutheran Theological Southern Seminary, 1945; Kennedy School of Missions, Hartford Seminary, one year; Student (pre-med) Emory University, and (medicine) Medical College, Augusta, Ga., 1954-58; University of Florida, M.R.C. 1964-5.

Ordination: September 1945 by Georgia-Alabama Synod.

Calls: United Lutheran Church in America Missionary in Liberia, West Africa, 1945-50; Chaplain, U.S. Air Force, 1951-53; Mission Developer, Good Shepherd, College Park, Ga., 1953-54; Mission Developer, St. Andrew, Hurst, Texas, 1959-60; Supply, Waco, Texas, 1962; St. Andrew, New Bern, 1962-63; retired in 1965 because of physical disability.

Other: Medical research work, while awaiting a call, 1960-61.

Date of Death/Burial Location: December 25, 1996; Westover Cemetery, Augusta, Ga.

STENDER, WILLIAM HAROLD, SR.

Date/Place of Birth: January 5, 1906; Charleston, S.C.

Parents: John Fred W. Stender and Anna C. (Mencken) Stender.

Spouse/Marriage Date: Roberta Elise (MacDougall) Stender; September 20, 1933 in Columbia, S.C.

Children: Anne Elise, Roberta MacDougall, William Harold, Jr.

Education: Newberry College, A.B. 1927; Lutheran Theological Southern Seminary, B.D. 1930; University of South Carolina, M.A. 1942.

Ordination: 1930 by South Carolina Synod.

Calls: Chaplain, South Carolina State Hospital, Columbia, S.C.; St. Paul, Columbia, S.C., 1930-32; St. James, Sumter, S.C., 1933-45; St. Matthew, Kings Mountain, 1945-50; Resurrection-St. Matthew, Cameron, S.C., 1950-56; Emmanuel, Atlanta, Ga., 1956-67; retired 1967.

Other: Lecturer at Pastors' School, Sandershausen, Bavaria, Germany. Parish Education Committee, Evangelism Committee, Examining Committee; President, Southern Conference; President, Central Conference; Dean, Western Georgia District; Delegate, School of World Order, Oneonta, N.Y.; District Governor Kiwanis International; Young Mens' Christian Association Board; President, Ministerial Association; author of "Student Attitudes Toward Religion" (unpublished M.A. thesis); published: *Pastor's Treatment of the Abnormal,* and *Travelogue of Three Months European Travel and Study.*

STEPHENSON, JAMES RAY

Date/Place of Birth: November 24, 1928; Roanoke, Va.
Parents: Robert L. Stephenson and Pauline (Burton) Stephenson.
Spouse/Marriage Date: Loretta (Darr) Stephenson; June 3, 1955 in Columbia, S.C.
Children: Deborah Gywn Hoover, James Gregory, Mary Elizabeth Hilliard.
Education: Roanoke College, B.A. 1952; Lutheran Theological Southern Seminary, M.Div. 1955; Lenoir-Rhyne, D.D. 1984.
Ordination: June 26, 1955 by Virginia Synod.
Calls: Assistant Pastor, St. John, Salisbury, 1955-58; St. Mark, Clarksburg, W.Va., 1958-62; St. Peter, Miami, Fla., 1967-75. Holy Trinity, Hickory, 1975-1990; Pastor/Developer, Prince of Peace, Kinston, 1990-93; retired 1993; Vice Pastor at various congregations.
Other: Associate Director, Commission on Evangelism, Lutheran Church in America, (Field Service), Decatur, Ga., 1962-67; Dean, Mountain District, Western Pennsylvania-West Virginia Synod, 1962-63; Board, Old People's Home, Zelienople, Pa., 1962-63; delegate to merging convention forming Lutheran Church in America; Chair, March of Dimes; Civitan Club; Missioner, Lutheran Evangelism Mission; Chair, City Clarksburg Commission on Human Relations; President, Harrison County Ministerial Association; Chair, Building Fund Campaign for Young Mens' Christian Association; Part-time Chaplain for Veterans Administration Hospital; Kiwanis Club; Dean, Greater Miami District; Executive Council of Florida Synod; President, Cooperative Christian Community Service Agency; delegate, Lutheran Church in America Convention; Lutheran Council, Dade County; President, Hickory Rotary Club - Paul Harris Fellow; Board, Lenoir-Rhyne; Pastor Evangelist/Director, Lutheran Church in America; Board, Hickory Soup Kitchen and Shelter for the Homeless; Board, Ten Broeck Hospital; Board, Catawba County Chamber of Commerce; Board, Hickory Community Theatre; Chaplain, Catawba County Sheriff's Department; Board, Lutheran Services for the Aging for North Carolina, Vice Chair, and later Chair, Foundation Board; Board, Genesis Communications, Philadelphia, Pa.; Board, Academy of Preachers, Philadelphia Seminary; Chair, Synod's Committee on Evangelism; Introduction Team, *Lutheran Book of Worship*; Chair, Evangelism Committee; Vice Chair, Lutheran Services for the Aging; Volunteer Chaplain Hospice; Volunteer of the Year; Governor's Volunteer of the Year; Kinston Rotary Club; Volunteer Chaplain, Lenoir Memorial Hospital; Lenoir County United Way Budget Committee; Executive Committee Friends of the Homeless - President Elect, 1993; Lenoir Community College Program Advisory Board; Board, Boys and Girls Club of Lenoir County, President Elect, 1993. Evangelism Consultant, North Carolina Synod; Board, Sylvia B. Whitener - LINC; Board, High Hope School; Steering Committee, Cooperative Christian Ministry Fund Appeal.

STEVENS, MARTY E.

Date/Place of Birth: June 28, 1953; Greensboro, N.C.
Parents: Herman K. Stevens, Jr. and Ruby (Mason) Stevens.
Education: University of North Carolina at Charlotte, B.S. Accounting 1974; Lutheran Theological Southern Seminary, M.Div. 1993; Certified Public Accountant, C.P.A. 1976; graduate work at Union Seminary, (Va.), 1997-.
Ordination: May 21, 1993 by North Carolina Synod.
Calls: St. John, Salisbury, 1993-1997.

STICKLEY, VASTINE RINKER

Place of Birth: Near Waynesboro, Va.
First Spouse: Emma (Martin) Stickley in Blacksburg, Va.
Second Spouse: Carrie (Keister) Stickley, a niece of his first wife.
Children: No children of either marriage.
Education: Roanoke College, A.B. 1873; Lutheran Theological Southern Seminary, 1874.
License/Ordination: Licensed 1873 and ordained 1876 by Southwestern Virginia Synod.
Calls: In Virginia, (Giles and Craig counties) 1873-76, (Newport and Waynesboro) 1884-91, (Shenandoah County) 1904-05; Salem-St. Luke-Grace (organized 1880), Rowan County, 1876-82; Bethel, Rowan County-Christ, East Spencer, 1882-84; St. Enoch, Rowan County-Trinity, Cabarrus County, 1892-1903; Nazareth-Shiloh, Forsyth County, 1906-07; St. Andrew (Supply), Concord-Mt. Hermon, Cabarrus County, 1907-08; Coble's-Low's, Guilford County-Richland, Randolph County-St. Paul, Alamance County, 1909-13; Lebanon-Providence, Rowan County-St. Matthew, Davie County, 1915-20.
Other: President, North Carolina Synod, 1881, 1896, 1897.
Date of Death/Burial Location: 1921; Waynesboro, Va.

STINGLEY, JAMES DAVID

Date/Place of Birth: August 11, 1815; Lexington County, S.C.
Parents: John Stingley and Sally (Bernhard) Stingley.
Spouse/Marriage Date: Jane Campbell (Casey) Stingley; April 14, 1853 in Richland County (?), S.C.
Children: John Jacob, Robert Cayce, David Bernhard, Betty Rea, Charley Edwin, James Campbell, Bachman, Sarah Wyse.
Education: Theology at Lutheran Theological Southern Seminary, 1846.
License/Ordination: Licensed 1846 and ordained 1849 by South Carolina Synod.
Calls: St. Paul-St. John, near Pomaria, S.C., 1853-55, and again in 1855-60; St. Michael and Bethel (High Hill), Richland County, S.C., 1849-50; in Mississippi, 1850-53; transferred 1861 from Mississippi Synod to North Carolina Synod; St. Michael, Troutman-St. Paul, Iredell County, 1860-62.
Other: One of the organizers of the Mississippi Synod in 1855.
Date of Death/Burial Location: April 4, 1866; New Hope Lutheran Cemetery, Sallis, Miss.

STIREWALT, ARTHUR JULIUS

Date/Place of Birth: February 5, 1881; Stony Man, Page County, Va.

Parents: The Reverend John Nathaniel Stirewalt and Emily Ann (Hershberger) Stirewalt. A cousin of the Reverend M. L. Stirewalt, Sr.

Spouse/Marriage Date: Alice Marie (Wulbern) Stirewalt; August 5, 1914 in Charleston, S.C.

Children: Meta Elise, Ruth Emily, Alice Wulbern.

Education: Lenoir-Rhyne, A.B. 1902, D.D. degree was offered but declined in 1913 (later accepted), because he felt too young and not worthy of the honor; Chicago Seminary, 1905; graduate study, Columbia University, 1921-22.

Ordination: 1905 by Tennessee Synod.

Calls: Missionary in Japan of United Synod South, 1905-18, same United Lutheran Church in America, 1918-52, engaged in evangelistic, educational, and social work in Kumamoto, Saga, and Tokyo.

Other: A founder of boys school (Kyushu Gakuin) in Kumamoto, and Dean, 1916-20 also teacher in theological department. After 1923 earthquake and fire he founded and operated in Tokyo Home for Widows and Children, 1925-32, also Old Peoples Home, 1923-41; frequent terms as President, Secretary, and Treasurer of Japan Lutheran Mission, and member of its Executive Committee; Joint Executive Committee of Mission and Japan Lutheran Church; President and Treasurer, Federation of Christian Missions; Vice President, National Christian Council of Japan; still in Japan on December 7, 1941 (Pearl Harbor Day), was allowed by government to occupy own home, and later was repatriated, in exchange of nationals, on Swedish S. S. Gripsholm; retired 1952 at Kobe, Japan, and taught in Lutheran Bible Institute, a school of the Lutheran Mission from Norway; awarded by Emperor Hirohito Fourth Order of the Sacred Treasurer July 4, 1952 in recognition of service to the Japanese people, and three days later was received in audience by Emperor for half-hour of conversation.

Date of Death/Burial Location: September 24, 1968; Luray Memorial Cemetery, Luray, Va.

STIREWALT, JACOB

Date/Place of Birth: August 17, 1805; Rowan County, N.C.

Parents: John N. Stirewalt and Mary Elizabeth (Rendleman) Stirewalt, Sr. Father served in War of 1812 with rank of Captain; moved to North Carolina in early manhood. An older brother was the Reverend John N. Stirewalt (1802-36).

Spouse/Marriage Date: Henrietta (Henkel) Stirewalt; January 8, 1833 in New Market, Va.

Children: Four sons, of whom two, the Reverends John Nathaniel and Jerome Paul, were the fathers, respectively, of the Reverends A. J. and M. L. Stirewalt, Sr., and six daughters.

License/Ordination: Licensed 1837 and ordained 1838 by Tennessee Synod.

Calls: Chiefly in Shenandoah County, Page County, Rockingham County, Va. including Rader, Timberville, Va., 1837-39, 1858-69; Emmanuel, New Market, Va., 1833-43; St.

Peter, Rowan County, 1840; preached often at Tennessee Synod Conventions held in North Carolina, Virginia, South Carolina, and Tennessee.

Other: On committee, with the Reverends Ambrose Henkel and Jacob Killian to compile a Liturgy for Use in Tennessee Synod churches, 1838-39; author, *Grades in the Ministry* (concerning the Ministerial Office and Ordination), published posthumously in 1881; collaborated in translating *Luther's Large Catechism* for the *Book of Concord* (1851).

Date of Death/Burial Location: August 21, 1869; Emmanuel Church, New Market, Va.

STIREWALT, JAMES COUNCIL

Date/Place of Birth: May 25, 1927; China Grove, Rowan County, N.C.

Parents: Murril Henderson Stirewalt and Ruby Clara (Blackwelder) Stirewalt.

Spouse/Marriage Date: Martha Alma (Arthurs) Stirewalt; May 29, 1955 in Iredell County, N.C.

Children: Anna Christine, Lisa Ruth, John David, Emily Grace.

Education: Catawba College, A.B. 1951; Lutheran Theological Southern Seminary, M.Div. 1956; graduate work at Yale, 1952.

Ordination: June 10, 1956 by North Carolina Synod.

Calls: Cedar Grove, Vale, Lincoln County, 1956-59; Holy Trinity, Reidsville, 1959-61; Ascension, Danville, Va., 1961-67; Salem, Salisbury, 1967-74; Trinity, Landis, 1974-87; Vice Pastor at various congregations; retired 1987.

Other: Board, North Carolina Lutheran Homes, 1970; District Dean, 1970-72; District Secretary, 1969.

STIREWALT, JEROME PAUL

Date/Place of Birth: April 11, 1850; New Market, Va.

Parents: The Reverend Jacob Stirewalt and Henrietta (Henkel) Stirewalt.

Spouse/Marriage Date: Tirzah A. (Coffman) Stirewalt; October 6, 1878 in Shenandoah County, Va.

Children: William J., the Reverend Martin Luther, Sr.

Education: New Market Polytechnic Institute; received A.M. degree; studied theology under pastors in Tennessee Synod; Lenoir-Rhyne, D.D. 1914.

Ordination: 1873 by Tennessee Synod.

Calls: Fourteen churches in three pastorates, in Shenandoah, Augusta, and Rockingham Counties, Va., 1874-1920; the longest, Rader, 1882-1920 and organized St. Paul, 1889-1920 near Timberville; organized, Morning Star, 1887-93, and Salem, near Hamburg, 1898; retired 1920 at New Market, Va. where he continued to write and manage his farm.

Other: Of Tennessee Synod, Secretary six terms, Treasurer four terms, President four terms; Examining Committee, 22 years; Address, *The Pioneers Of Synod,* at the Tennessee Synod's centennial convention (1920) was published in the minutes; contributor to *Our Church Paper, Our Sunday School, Lutheran Church Visitor,* and secular periodicals; wrote notes for Lutheran Lesson Quarterly (General Council); contributed the article on Tennessee Synod in *The Lutherans of America*, edited by E. J. Wolf, D.D.

Date of Death/Burial Location: May 28, 1934; Emmanuel Cemetery, New Market, Va.

STIREWALT, JOHN DAVID
Date/Place of Birth: September 3, 1959; Gastonia, N.C.
Parents: The Reverend James Council Stirewalt and Martha Alma (Arthurs) Stirewalt.
Spouse/Marriage Date: Deborah Lieselotte (Moore) Stirewalt; August 22, 1987 in Columbia, S.C.
Children: Hannah Michelle, Clara Grace.
Education: Lenoir-Rhyne, Psychology 1981; Lutheran Theological Southern Seminary, M.Div. 1988.
Ordination: November 27, 1988 by North Carolina Synod.
Calls: St. Stephen, Gold Hill, 1988-91; Associate Pastor, Redeemer, Columbia, S.C., 1991-. Mission Developer/Pastor, Christ Our Redeemer, Austin, Texas, 1997.
Other: Convener, Dutch Fork Cluster Cabinet, South Carolina Synod, 1991; Exchange Pastor, Hamburg, Berlin, Germany, 1994; published in *South Carolina Lutheran* and in *Faithworks,* South Carolina Synod Social Ministry Committee magazine; formed first AIDS Care Congregational Team in the South Carolina Synod; headed effort through Lutheran Family Services and Redeemer to support a refugee from Sarajevo.

STIREWALT, JOHN N.
Date/Place of Birth: August 7, 1802; Rowan County, N.C.
Parents: The Reverend John N. Stirewalt (Captain in War of 1812 and Lutheran minister) and Mary Elizabeth (Rendleman) Stirewalt. A younger brother was the Reverend Jacob Stirewalt.
Spouse: Name unknown.
Children: Four.
Education: Was taught by his parents and took literary and classical courses of study.
License/Ordination: Licensed 1827 and ordained 1829 by Tennessee Synod.
Calls: Little is known of his ministry, less than ten years long; Mt. Moriah, Rowan County, 1834-36.
Other: Secretary, Tennessee Synod, 1832; bought farm near New Market, Va., shortly before death, to which family moved after his death.
Date of Death/Burial Location: Died from lung trouble, August 13, 1836; Lutheran Chapel Church, China Grove, N.C.

STIREWALT, JOHN NATHANIEL
Date/Place of Birth: February 21, 1844; New Market, Va.
Parents: The Reverend Jacob Stirewalt and Henrietta (Henkel) Stirewalt. A younger brother was the Reverend Jerome Paul Stirewalt.
Spouse/Marriage Date: Emily Ann (Hershberger) Stirewalt; November 3, 1870 in Luray, Va.
Children: A son is known, the Reverend Arthur Julius, Lutheran missionary in Japan.
Education: New Market (Va.) Academy; Roanoke College; studied theology under father.
License/Ordination: Licensed 1869 and ordained 1871 by Tennessee Synod.
Calls: First resident Lutheran pastor in Page County, Va., where in the Stony Man parish spent his entire ministry 1871-1907 except 1892-93, spent at East Germantown (now Pershing), Ind.; developed and organized four churches in Page County, Va.
Other: President, 1896, Treasurer, 1873, 1883-85, 1887-92, of Tennessee Synod.
Date of Death/Burial Location: January 11, 1907; Luray, Va.

STIREWALT, JULIUS LUTHER
Parents: John N. Stirewalt and Hannah R. (Henkel) Stirewalt. Mother was a daughter of the Reverend Paul Henkel and Elizabeth (Negeley) Henkel. An older brother was the Reverend Paul J. Stirewalt. A great-great-grandson of the original John Stirewalt, who came from Germany in 1749 and died in North Carolina in 1796. Two cousins were the Reverends John Nathaniel and Jerome Paul Stirewalt.
Education: Capital University.
Ordination: Ordained Deacon for Tennessee Synod 1854 by the Reverends A. Henkel and Henry Wetzel, in St. Peter Church, Lexington County, S.C., and ordained Pastor in 1856.
Calls: In 1857 visited pastorless churches in Indiana; in 1858 was serving Zion, East Germantown (now Pershing), Ind. In New Germantown, Ohio in 1871-72 and died there.
Date of Death/Burial Location: June 16, 1872; Pershing, Ind.

STIREWALT, MARTIN LUTHER, JR.
Date/Place of Birth: June 9, 1913; Hickory, N.C.
Parents: The Reverend Martin Luther Stirewalt, Sr. and Caroline (Dentzer) Stirewalt.
Spouse/Marriage Date: Frances Louise (Miller) Stirewalt, daughter of the Reverend L. D. Miller, Sr.; August 17, 1937 in Concord, N.C.
Children: Anna Carolyn Gilbo, Martin Luther, III.
Education: Lenoir-Rhyne, A.B. 1934; Duke University, M.A. 1937, Ph.D. 1945; Gettysburg Seminary, B.D. 1946.
Ordination: 1947 by North Carolina Synod.
Other: Professor (Classical Languages, Bible and Philosophy), Lenoir-Rhyne, 1937-59, Department Chair, 1950-59; for North Carolina Synod: Archivist, Student Work Committee, Examining Committee, Commission on Negro Work, Lenoir-Rhyne Alumni Board; Professor (New Testament Theology, Classical Languages and Literature), Hamma Divinity School, Wittenberg University, 1959-75, Dean of Curriculum, 1970-75; author: Studies in *Ancient Greek Epistolography,* 1993; *Segregation and the Church; A Bible Study;* retired 1976 to Hillsborough, N.C.

STIREWALT, MARTIN LUTHER, SR.
Date/Place of Birth: July 24, 1882; New Market, Va.
Parents: The Reverend Jerome Paul Stirewalt and Tirzah Amelia (Coffman) Stirewalt.
Spouse/Marriage Date: Caroline (Dentzer) Stirewalt; December 24, 1907 in Chicago, Ill.
Children: Sister Catharine Amelia, Ruth Elizabeth, the Reverend Martin Luther, Jr., Mary Caroline.
Education: Lenoir-Rhyne, A.B. 1902, D.D. 1921; Chicago Seminary, B.D. 1906; graduate study, University of Chicago, University of Virginia, Northwestern University, A.M. 1928.

Ordination: 1907 by Chicago Synod.

Calls: St. Paul, Frankfort, Ind., 1915-16; St. James, Concord, 1916-22; St. John, Salisbury, 1930-38.

Other: Institutions served: Instructor, Weidner Institute, Mulberry, Ind., 1906-09; Professor (Bible, Ancient Languages), Lenoir-Rhyne, 1909-15; Professor (Practical Theology), Chicago Lutheran Seminary, 1922-30; Professor (Systematic Theology) and sometime Dean, Lutheran Theological Southern Seminary, 1938-51; retired 1951 at Hickory; Associate Professor (Bible, Philosophy), Lenoir Rhyne, 1955-59. Board, Lenoir- Rhyne, 1921-22, 1932-60 and Chair, 1935-51; Vice President, North Carolina Synod, 1917-22; Secretary, Joint Commission on Merger of North Carolina and Tennessee Synods, 1919-21; in United Lutheran Church in America: Board of Education, 1930-40; from 1918 member of Committee on *Common Service Book*; Court of Adjudication and Interpretation; author of *The Curricula of Lutheran Theological Seminaries in the United States;* contributed sermon to *Gospel Preaching for the Day,* and articles in Lutheran magazines.

Date of Death/Burial Location: March 10, 1960; Emmanuel Church, New Market, Va.

STIREWALT, MILES J.

Ordination: Ordained Deacon 1858 by Tennessee Synod in Zion Church, Lexington County, S.C. and Pastor 1859 in Bethlehem Church, Augusta County, Va.

Calls: Coble's, Guilford County-Melanchthon, Randolph County-Mt. Pleasant, Alamance County, 1859-62; Mulberry, Ind.

Other: Secretary, 1862, Treasurer, 1861, 1863-65, of Tennessee Synod; in 1868 living then and for a number of years thereafter at Augusta Station, Ind., was dismissed to the English District, Joint Synod of Ohio.

Date of Death: 1904 in Mulberry, Ind.

STIREWALT, PAUL J.

Date/Place of Birth: March 12, 1828; at or near New Market, Va.

Parents: The Reverend John N. Stirewalt and Hannah R. (Henkel) Stirewalt. Mother was daughter of the Reverend Paul Henkel and Elizabeth (Negeley) Henkel. An older brother was the Reverend Julius L. Stirewalt, and cousins were the Reverends John Nathaniel and Jerome Paul Stirewalt.

Education: University of Virginia.

Ordination: Ordained Deacon by Tennessee Synod in 1853 in Emmanuel Church, New Market, Va., and Pastor in 1855 in same church.

Calls: Lima, Ohio, 1854-59; also preached at some churches in Indiana.

Date of Death/Burial Location: March 21, 1859; New Market, Va.

STIVER, STANLEY LOUIS, JR.
Date/Place of Birth: June 29, 1921; Youngstown, Ohio.
Parents: Stanley L. Stiver, Sr. and Alta (Baun) Stiver.
Spouse/Marriage Date: Mary (Anderson) Stiver; February 20, 1949 in New Orleans, La.
Children: John Mark, David James.
Education: Capital University, A.B. 1944; Trinity Seminary, B.D. 1947.
Ordination: June 29, 1947 by Texas District - American Lutheran Church.
Calls: St. Luke, New Orleans, La., 1947-51; St. Mark, Wheeling, W.Va., 1951-59; St. Mark, Claremont, 1959-90; retired October 1990; Vice Pastor at various congregations.
Other: District Youth Committee, Evangelism Committee, served as a Luther League Leadership School Lecturer, invited to serve at Evangelistic Lutheran Missions.

STOCKMAN, JAMES EDGAR, SR.
Date/Place of Birth: June 16, 1899; Lexington County, S.C.
Parents: J. T. Stockman and Anna (Bickley) Stockman. The Reverend Enoch D. Stockman is a younger brother.
Spouse/Marriage Date: Eula Mae (Carlisle) Stockman; November 11, 1930 in Greenville, S.C.
Children: James Edgar, Jr., Jane Carlisle, Eliza Anna.
Education: Lenoir-Rhyne, A.B. 1920; Lutheran Theological Southern Seminary, 1923, B.D. 1924; University of South Carolina, M.A. 1923; Roanoke College, D.D. 1963.
Ordination: 1923 by North Carolina Synod.
Calls: St. Luke-Morning Star, Monroe, 1923-26; Trinity, Greenville, S.C., 1926-41; Chaplain, U.S. Army, 1941-46; St. Mark, Roanoke, Va., 1946-65; retired at Roanoke, Va.
Other: Executive Council, Virginia Synod, 1954-58.
Date of Death/Burial Location: 1966; Mt. Horeb, Chapin, S.C.

STONER, JOHN DOWIE
Date/Place of Birth: March 26, 1907; Rowan County, N.C.
Parents: John Knox Stoner and Mittie Belle (Morgan) Stoner.
Education: Lenoir-Rhyne, A.B. 1936; Lutheran Theological Southern Seminary, 1939.
Ordination: 1939 by North Carolina Synod.
Calls: Lebanon-Providence, Rowan County-Amity, Iredell County-St. Matthew, Davie County, 1939-44; Lebanon-Providence, only 1944-45.
Other: From 1945 engaged in secular work; name removed from roll, 1963.
Date of Death/Burial Location: Unknown.

STORCH, CARL AUGUST GOTTLIEB
Date/Place of Birth: June 16, 1764; Helmstedt, Germany.
Parents: Georg Frederich Storch and ? (Von Asseburg) Storch.
Education: Gymnasium and University of Helmstedt, 1782-85.
Ordination: Ordained in 1788 and arrived in North Carolina in September of 1788.

Spouse/Marriage Date: Christine (Beard) (Bahrt) Storch; January 14, 1790 in Salisbury, N.C.

Children: Of eleven children only two, Anna and Theophilus, survived infancy. The latter (name had been changed to Stork) was distinguished as preacher, pastor, scholar, educator, and author, and served (1859-60) as first President of Newberry College. A grandson was the Reverend Charles Augustus Stork, D.D.

Calls: St. John, Salisbury (1788-?)-Organ (1788-23)-Union (1788-1810), Rowan County; Lutheran Chapel, Rowan County, 1789-1820; St. John, Cabarrus County, 1796-97; 1800-21; first Pastor, New Bethel, Stanly County, 1806-14, 1819-23; Cold Water, Cabarrus County, 1810-?.

Other: Was private tutor, three years. Was next pioneer pastor to come to North Carolina from Germany after Nussmann, Arends, and Bernhardt. Declined call to St. John's, Charleston, S.C., in 1814 because of great need of pastors in North Carolina. One of four pastors, who with fourteen laymen, organized in 1803 the North Carolina Synod; its third President, 1806-12, and elected twice later, serving a total of fourteen years. Latter part of life he lived on his farm in Rowan County, a mile north of present Ebenezer Church; retired 1823 due to physical infirmities.

Date of Death/Burial Location: March 29, 1831; Organ Church, Rowan County, N.C.

STORM, RALPH WARREN

Date/Place of Birth: August 29, 1930; Buffalo, N.Y.

Parents: John Storm and Antoinette (Anderson) Storm.

Spouse/Marriage Date: Juanita Jean (Corrigall) Storm; June 19, 1954 in Buffalo, N.Y.

Children: Naomi Ruth Howard, Tracy Ellen Phillips.

Education: Hartwick College, B.A. 1951; Philadelphia Seminary, M.Div. 1954; graduate work at Union Seminary and New York University.

Ordination: June 16, 1954 by New York and New England Synod.

Calls: St. Mark, Elmsford, N.Y., 1954-65; Holy Trinity, Elmira, N.Y., 1965-70; St. Matthias, Greensburg, Pa., 1970-72; Messiah, Wesleyville, Pa., 1972-76; Trinity, Meadville, Pa., 1976-84; Holy Trinity, Newport, Tenn., 1985-88; retired in 1988 to Hendersonville, N.C.; Interim pastor at various North Carolina congregations.

Other: In Upper New York Synod: Chair, World Missions Committee; Secretary, Southern Tier District; in Western Pennsylvania-West Virginia Synod: Secretary, Church Vocations-Examining Committee; Camp Director, Harris Hill Ecumenical Camp in Elmira, N.Y.; Camp Director, Camp Chi Rho in Upper New York Synod; Executive Director, Haywood Christian Ministry, Inc. 1988-92; *Who's Who in Religion*, two editions; President, Phelp's Memorial Hospital Chaplains Association, two terms; President, Chemung County Ministerial Association; President, Erie County Lutheran Pastor's Association; President, Greater Meadville Clergy Association.

STOUDEMAYER, GEORGE ABNER

Date/Place of Birth: May 31, 1879; Edgefield County, S.C.

Parents: George B. Stoudemayer and Elvira (Chapman) Stoudemayer.

Education: Newberry College, A.B. 1914; Lutheran Theological Southern Seminary, 1917; Philadelphia Seminary, B.D. 1924.

Ordination: 1917 by Tennessee Synod.

Calls: Tennessee Synod: Grace-St. Paul, Gilbert-St. John-Holy Trinity, Pelion, S.C., 1917-23; in Pennsylvania (Mifflinville Parish, 1923-24), Georgia (Macon County Parish, 1925-26), West Virginia (Hampshire County, 1927-30), Virginia (Shenandoah County, 1930-40). Retired in 1940.
Date of Death/Burial Location: November 20, 1949; Good Hope Church, Ward, S.C.

STOUDEMAYER, JOHN M.

Date/Place of Birth: October 6, 1950; Cook, Ill.
Parents: T. C. Stoudemayer and Mabel A. (Boone) Stoudemayer.
Spouse/Marriage Date: Stephanie Stoudemayer; June 1, 1985 in Charleston, S.C.
Children: Zachary Benjamin.
Education: Furman University, B.A. 1972; Lutheran Theological Southern Seminary, M.Div. 1987.
Ordination: September 2, 1987 by South Carolina Synod.
Calls: St. Paul, Statesville, 1987-90; Kimball Memorial, Kannapolis, 1990-93; transferred to South Carolina Synod, 1993. In 1998 serving Faith, Batesburg, S.C.

STOUDENMIRE, WILLIAM

Place of Birth: South Carolina Synod History lists him as a member, 1878-80 and says he was a son of Trinity Church, Elloree, S.C., presumably indicating that he was reared at or near Elloree.
License/Ordination: Licensed by Southwestern Virginia Synod in 1878 and ordained in 1880.
Calls: Supplied St. Paul, Newport, Va., 1876; supplied St. Matthew, Calhoun County, S.C.; transferred 1884 to North Carolina Synod from Maryland Synod; served St. John, Salisbury, 1884-86; letter of transfer issued to East Ohio Synod, 1886.

STOWE, LAWSON DOUGLAS

Date/Place of Birth: March 5, 1942; Charlotte, N.C.
Parents: Lawson Hendrix Stowe and Helen Louise (Rhyne) Stowe.
Spouse: Sally (Osborne) Stowe.
Ordination: November 30, 1969 by North Carolina Synod.
Education: Lenoir-Rhyne, A.B. 1964; Lutheran Theological Southern Seminary, M.Div. 1969; graduate work in in-depth counseling at Memphis Institute of Medicine and Religion, Memphis, Tenn., 1968.
Calls: Gloria Dei, Hampton, Va., 1969-.
Other: Project Director, Neighborhood Youth Program at Reformation, Columbia, S.C.; Coordinator/Planner for "A Happening," nationally recognized youth program in occupational vocations sponsored by the North Carolina Lutheran Synod, 1967; Consultant, Southeastern Synod Planning Committee for "Youth Happening" in the Memphis, Tenn. area; Rotary Club Award, Mt. Holly, 1960; awards for outstanding services to Lenoir- Rhyne; Iota Epsilon Omega Honorary Journalistic Fraternity; *Who's Who in American Colleges and Universities*, 1964. Board of Trustees, Lutheran Theological Southern Seminary; Board of Directors, Eastern Cluster of Lutheran Seminaries, 1998-2000.

STRICKLER, JAMES WILLIAM

Date/Place of Birth: November 25, 1856; Madison County, Va.
Parent: James Francis Strickler and Sarah Jane (Cullen) Strickler.
Spouse/Marriage Date: Mary Chloe (Cole) Strickler; 1884 in Marion, Va.
Children: The Reverend Luther Warren, Mabel Freelove. The Reverend Luther Warren Strickler, II, is a grandson.
Education: Roanoke College, A.B. 1878; Lutheran Theological Southern Seminary, 1882.
Ordination: 1882 by Southwestern Virginia Synod.
Calls: In Carroll County, Va., 1882-84; Washington, Bland, Rockingham and Frederick counties, Va., 1888- 1905; Waynesboro and Newport, Va., 1909-16; in North Carolina, Union-Christiana, Rowan County, 1884-88; St. Andrew-Mt. Hermon, Concord, 1905-07; Nazareth-Shiloh, Forsyth County, 1907-09.
Date of Death/Burial Location: November 29, 1916 at Middlebrook, Va.; Waynesboro, Va.

STROBEL, PHILIP A.

Date/Place of Birth: September 16, 1812; Charleston, S.C.
Parents: Captain John Strobel and Mary Grace (Beard) Strobel.
Spouse/Marriage Date: Carolina (Wilson) Strobel; January 1, 1835.
Education: Under tutelage of Dr. John Bachman, pastor of St. John's, Charleston, S.C.; Lutheran Theological Southern Seminary, 1836.
License/Ordination: Licensed 1836 by South Carolina Synod; transferred 1837 and ordained 1838 by North Carolina Synod.
Calls: Mt. Pleasant, Ehrhardt, S.C.; organized, built church, St. Enoch, Rowan County, 1835-41; Cold Water, Cabarrus County, 1837; New Bethel, Stanly County, 1838-41; organized St. Stephen, Cabarrus County, 1837-41; transferred 1841 to South Carolina Synod; served Ebenezer, Columbia, S.C., 1841; in Georgia: Ebenezer, Jerusalem 1844-49; at Macon organized congregation, 1848; served churches in New York, New Jersey, and Maryland; again in North Carolina: Organ, Rowan County; St. Stephen, Cabarrus County; transferred 1876 from North Carolina Synod to Hartwick, New York Synod.
Other: Secretary, North Carolina Synod, 1840; in 1843 founded school for girls at Savannah, Ga.; Principal and Professor at Female Institute, Americus, Ga., 1849-55; Secretary, New York Synod, 1857, 1859; Principal and Professor, Mont Amoena Seminary, Mt. Pleasant, 1874-75; Board, North Carolina College; wrote *History of The Salzburgers in Georgia*, (1855).
Date of Death/Burial Location: November 1882; Dansville, N.Y.

STROHECKER, THOMAS HAMLIN

Date/Place of Birth: April 13, 1847; Charleston, S.C.
First Spouse: Mattie (Williams) Strohecker of Albany, Ga., who died about five years later.
Second Spouse: Julia Stockton (Davidson) Strohecker of Charlotte.
Children of Second Marriage: Five sons and two daughters.
Education: Wofford College, 1867; Philadelphia Seminary. Practiced law at Albany, Ga., before entering ministry.
Ordination: 1879 by Ministerium of Pennsylvania.
Calls: Transferred 1882 to North Carolina Synod; St. Mark's, Charlotte, 1881-82; St. Matthew-St. Peter-Luther's, Rowan County, 1881-86; churches in Illinois, three years; St.

Michael, Troutman-Amity-St. Paul, Iredell County, 1889-90; St. Luke-Pilgrim, Davidson County, 1896.

Other: Moved to Davidson for children to attend Davidson College; studied medicine there, graduating with first honor; later moved to Salem, Va., and practiced until health failed.

Date of Death/Burial Location: June 1, 1916 in Washington, D.C.; Elmwood Cemetery, Charlotte, N.C.

STROUP, BRADY LEE

Date/Place of Birth: August 26, 1876; Gaston County, N.C.

Parents: Cephas Stroup and Josephine (Hanks) Stroup.

Spouse/Marriage Date: Blanche Irene (Yoder) Stroup, daughter of the Reverend R. A. Yoder; November 27, 1906 in Lincolnton, N.C.

Children: Richard Weidner, Irene Elizabeth, Rose Fisher, Josephine Adele, Ruth Louise (died in third year), Brady Leon, Robert Paul.

Education: Lenoir-Rhyne, A.B. 1903; Chicago Seminary, B.D. 1906.

Ordination: 1906 by Tennessee Synod.

Calls: Cedar Grove-St. James, Lexington County, S.C., 1906-09; St. Peter-St. John, near Chapin, S.C., 1919-21; Beth Eden, Newton-New Jerusalem-Zion, and Supply (1913); St. Paul, Startown, 1909-15; transferred 1915 to Chicago Synod, and served churches in Indiana and Ohio; retired 1946 at Logansport, Ind.

Other: Secretary, Tennessee Synod 1909-1911 and Treasurer four months in 1911.

Date of Death/Burial Location: July 1, 1954; Mt. Hope Cemetery, Logansport, Ind.

STROUP, HERBERT WILSON, JR.

Date/Place of Birth: June 28, 1919; Harrisburg, Pa.

Parents: Herbert Wilson Stroup, Sr. and Nada C. (Keefer) Stroup.

Spouse/Marriage Date: Barbara (Kirkpatrick) Stroup; December 26, 1942 in Harrisburg, Pa.

Children: Kirk Michael, Barbara Katharine.

Education: Gettysburg College, A.B. 1940; Gettysburg Seminary, B.D. 1943; S.T.M. 1949; George Washington University, M.A. 1963; Union Seminary, (Va.), Ph.D. 1972.

Ordination: May 26, 1943 by Central Pennsylvania Synod.

Calls: St. John, Mercersburg, Pa., 1943-50; U.S. Navy Chaplain, 1944-46; Holy Trinity, Raleigh, 1950-52; Holy Trinity, Camp Hill, Pa., 1952-60; retired in 1989 to Gettysburg, Pa.

Other: Taught and coached at Mercersburg Academy; Professor of Pastoral Theology, Gettysburg Seminary, 1960-89; Dean of Students and Professor of Pastoral Care, Gettysburg Seminary, 1965; author of two books, 26 articles and numerous book reviews for *Christian Century*; Licensed by Pennsylvania as Psychologist and private practice of Marriage and Family Counseling; teacher of Pastoral Counseling at St. Mary's Seminary, Emmitsburg, Md., the only Protestant on the faculty of 23 priests.

STUTTS, WILLIAM HENRY

Date/Place of Birth: February 11, 1866; Buffalo, N.Y.

Parents: Rudolph Stutts and Anna Louise (Strubbe) Stutts.

First Spouse: Cora May (Spencer) Stutts.

Children of First Marriage: Lillian, Maude Spencer.
Second Spouse: Anna May (Suling) Stutts.
Education: Hartwick Academy; Hartwick Seminary; D.D. Hartwick College, about 1915.
Ordination: 1893 by North Carolina Synod.
Calls: Transferred to New York Synod, 1894; all calls in New York, with last one at Epiphany, Brooklyn, 1908-35.
Other: Retired 1935 at Laurens, N.Y.
Date of Death/Burial Location: November 21, 1946; Milford, N.Y.

SUBLETT, MARVIN THOMAS

Date/Place of Birth: May 26, 1935; Asheville, N.C.
Parents: Marvin Timothy Sublett and Gladys Delilah (Poovey) Sublett.
Spouse/Marriage Date: Elizabeth Beck (Sink) Sublett, daughter of the Reverend Olin W. Sink; August 22, 1959 in Charlotte, N.C.
Children: Katherine Elizabeth Minardi, Karol Elaine Hoffman.
Education: Lenoir-Rhyne, A.B. 1957; Lutheran Theological Southern Seminary, B.D. 1960; McCormick Seminary, D.Min. 1975.
Ordination: June 5, 1960 by North Carolina Synod.
Calls: Good Shepherd, Hickory, 1960-64; St. Paul, Tampa, Fla., 1964-71; Martin Luther, Charleston, S.C., 1971-74; Trinity, Jacksonville, Fla., 1974-88; Grace, Ormond Beach, Fla., 1988-.
Other: North Carolina Synod: District Secretary, 1962-64; Florida Synod: Vice President, 1979-87; Executive Board, 1977-87; Board, Lutheran Theological Southern Seminary, 1967-68, Board, Bishop's Representative, Newberry College, 1980-88; Board, Lenoir-Rhyne, 1989-97; Churchwide Assembly Delegate 1980, 1984, 1986, 1987.

SUGG, CLAYTON WALTER, SR.

Date/Place of Birth: September 18, 1921; Snow Hill, N.C.
Parents: Samuel Clayton Sugg and Olive Elizabeth (Yount) Sugg. The Reverend J. Alonzo Yount was his grandfather, and the Reverends Noah D. and Walter N. Yount are uncles.
Spouse/Marriage Date: Leona (Council) Sugg of Hoke County; December 19, 1942 at Enid, Okla.
Children: The Reverend Clayton Walter, Jr., Paul Timothy.
Education: Lenoir-Rhyne, A.B. 1947; Philadelphia Seminary, B.D. 1950, S.T.M. 1961; Clinical Pastoral Education University of Iowa, 1966; School of Alcohol Studies, Rutgers University, 1969; School of Theology, Dubuque, Iowa, D.Min. 1977.
Ordination: May 24, 1950 by Ministerium of Pennsylvania.
Calls: Advent, Mt. Ephraim, N.J., 1950-52; organized Gloria Dei, New Milford, N.J., 1952-54; First, Lafayette, La., and organized Trinity, New Iberia, La., 1954-59; Grace, Amarillo, Texas, 1959-61; Christ, Durham, 1961-65. Began Lutheran social mission work by monthly visitation in Louisiana State Penitentiary, Angola, La., 1954-59. Veterans Administration hospital Chaplain, 1965-81. Retired June 1981 to Knoxville, Iowa. Supply Pastor to various congregations.
Other: U.S. Army Air Force, 1942-45.

SUMMERS, DANIEL BARRETT

Date/Place of Birth: July 9, 1916; Elon College, Guilford County, N.C.

Parents: George Andrew Summers and Lelia Virginia (Brown) Summers.

Spouse/Marriage Date: Lula Catherine (Apple) Summers; June 6, 1942 in Guilford County, N.C.

Children: Lelia Ann Moore, Dennis Andrew, Lou Ellen Runyan, David Nathan.

Education: Elon College, A.B. 1938; Lutheran Theological Southern Seminary, B.D. 1942.

Ordination: June 4, 1942 by North Carolina Synod.

Calls: Nazareth-Shiloh, Rural Hall, 1942-45; Zion, Hickory, 1945-49; Beck's, Lexington, 1949-68; Coble's, Julian, 1968-81; retired in 1981; Vice Pastor to various congregations.

Other: Board, Lowman Home, 1959-63; Vice President, Eastern Conference; President, Northern Conference; World Missions Committee.

Date of Death/Burial Location: November 25, 1991; Frieden's, Gibsonville, N.C.

SUNDLIE, ELMER DENNIS

Date/Place of Birth: March 28, 1934; Forman, N.D.

Parents: Elmer M. Sundlie and Maghnild (Nockleby) Sundlie.

Spouse/Marriage Date: Jean Raye (Spikes) Sundlie; December 7, 1957 in Winston-Salem, N.C.

Children: Karen Elizabeth, Mark William.

Education: North Dakota University, B.S. 1961; Lutheran Theological Southern Seminary, B.D. 1965.

Ordination: June 6, 1965 by North Carolina Synod.

Calls: Good Shepherd, Brevard, 1965-67; Daniel's, Lincolnton, 1967-68; Vice Pastor at various congregations.

Other: Removed from roll in 1980 at Sauk Rapids, Minn.

SUSKOVIC, SCOTT J.

Spouse: Gretchen Suskovic.

Children: Hannah, Nathan.

Education: St. Olaf, B.A. Religion; 1983; Northwest Seminary, M.Div. 1987; Boston University School of Theology, D. Min. 1995.

Ordination: June 21, 1987.

Calls: First, White Bear Lake, Minn.; Christ, Charlotte, 1998-.

SWANEY, DENNIS D.

Date/Place of Birth: March 13, 1819; Page County, Va., a son of Mt. Calvary Church, Stony Man, Va.

Ordination: Ordained Deacon by Tennessee Synod 1842 in Trinity Church, Lincoln County, and Pastor 1848 in Solomon Church, Shenandoah County, Va.

Calls: Philippi, Va. (now W.Va.), two years. Transferred 1851 to Ohio Synod; Nokomis, Ill., 1867-76.

Date of Death/Burial Location: December 28, 1876; Nokomis, Ill.

SWANEY, WILLIAM H.
Date/Place of Birth: July 13, 1824; Page County, Va.
Spouse/Marriage Date: Mrs. Rebecca (Lichliter) Swaney; August 19, 1845.
Children: Five sons and three daughters.
Education: Studied theology under the Reverends Ambrose and Socrates Henkel.
Ordination: 1868 by Tennessee Synod in Salem Church, Lincoln County, N.C.
Calls: New Market, Va., 1867-69; transferred 1869 to English District, Joint Synod of Ohio, and served churches in Ohio to 1880.
Date of Death: October 3, 1885.

SWANSON, REUBEN JOSEPH
Date/Place of Birth: April 15, 1917; Rockford, Ill.
Parents: Joseph Emanuel Swanson and Esther Lorenza (Carlson) Swanson. Great grandfather was the Reverend L. P. Stenstrom.
First Spouse/Marriage Date: Edna Maria (Carlson) Swanson; June 5, 1943 in Chicago, Ill.
Children of First Marriage: Robert Winfield, The Reverend Timothy Richard, Susan Maria.
Second Spouse/Marriage Date: Marian Helen (Mellgren) Swanson; April 9, 1976.
Education: Gustavus Adolphus College, A.B. 1942; Augustana Seminary, B.D. 1945; Yale University, S.T.M. 1951, Ph.D. 1956; University of California, Berkeley, Chinese Language Study, 1946.
Ordination: June 1945 by Augustana Lutheran Church.
Calls: Initial Mission Developer, St. John, Antioch, Calif.; Immanuel, Wakefield, Mich.-Zion, Mellen, Wis., 1946-49; St. Paul, Ansonia, Conn., 1949-53; Trinity, Washington Depot, Conn., 1949-54; Tabor, Branford, Conn., 1954-58; Initial Mission Developer for Shepherd of the Hills, Sylva; Vice Pastor at various congregations in North Carolina; retired in June 1982 to Camarillo, Calif.
Other: Professor (Bible), Grand View Seminary, Des Moines, Iowa, 1958-60; Professor and Head of Department, (Religious Studies), Lenoir-Rhyne, 1960-68; Professor of Philosophy and Religion, Professor Emeritus, Western Carolina University, 1968-82; Patristics Committee, International Greek New Testament Project; Senior Mentor and Adjunct Professor, California Lutheran University, 1982-84; Adjunct Professor of Bible and Greek, St. John's Seminary, Camarillo, Calif.; author, *The Horizontal Line Synopsis of the Gospels, Roots Out of Dry Ground.* Apostolic Blessing from Pope John Paul II for contributions to Biblical study for the preparation of the Synopses; translator and writer for the American Bible Society's publication of *The Apocrypha; New Testament Greek Manuscripts. Variant Readings Arranged in Parallel Lines Against Codex Vaticanus,* Volumes 1-5; articles in various publications; Mayor of the Town of Dillsboro, N.C., 1973-75; Co-founder and President, *Western North Carolina Press,* 1975-82; Distinguished Alumni Citation in the field of Theology from the Gustavus Alumni Association, 1996; Board, American Scandinavian Society-Thousand Oaks, 1986-91; Board, Chief Financial Officer, Scandinavian American Cultural and Historical Foundation, 1985; Scripps Research Council.

SWANSON, TIMOTHY RICHARD
Date/Place of Birth: July 31, 1946; Chicago, Ill.
Parents: Dr. Reuben Joseph Swanson and Edna Maria (Carlson) Swanson.

Spouse/Marriage Date: Sherry L. (Cooper) Swanson; July 15, 1973.
Children: Jessica Kimberly, Christine Alisa, Erik Christopher.
Education: Gustavus Adolphus, B.A. 1968; Philadelphia Seminary, M.Div. 1972.
Ordination: June 4, 1972 by North Carolina Synod.
Calls: Holy Trinity, Manasquan, N.J., 1972-76; Cross of Glory, Matawan, N.J., 1976-84; Epiphany, Warren, N.J., 1984-90; St. Mark, Wapakoneta, Ohio, 1990-93; Holy Cross, Fairfield, Ohio, 1993-.
Other: New Jersey Synod - Chair, Young Adults in Transition Task Force; Chair, Recreational Ministry Committee; Chair, Beisler Camping and Retreat Center Committee.

SWICEGOOD, DERMONT FRITZ
Date/Place of Birth: August 29, 1910; Lexington, N.C.
Parents: Charles Franklin Swicegood and Martha Jane (Fritz) Swicegood.
First Spouse/Marriage Date: Eloise (Efird) Swicegood; May 31, 1935 in Albemarle, N.C.
Children of First Marriage: The Reverend Dermont Luther, Gaynell Hubbs, Brenda Mae, David Efird.
Second Spouse/Marriage Date: Lois (Winemiller) Swicegood; November 15, 1986.
Education: Lenoir-Rhyne, A.B. 1932; Lutheran Theological Southern Seminary, M.Div. 1935, also graduate study.
Ordination: May 23, 1935 by North Carolina Synod.
Calls: St. Mark, Rowan County, 1935-38; St. Enoch, Enochville, 1938-45; Center Grove, Kannapolis, 1945-51; Mt. Tabor, West Columbia, S.C., 1951-60; St. Stephen, Hickory, N.C., 1960-69; Pisgah, Lexington, S.C., 1969-80; retired 1980 in West Columbia, S.C.; Vice Pastor at various congregations.
Other: Sipe's Orchard Home Committee, 1963-66; Stewardship Committee of North Carolina and South Carolina Synods; Allocations Committee of United Lutheran Church in America; Chair, Vocations Committee, South Carolina Synod; active in scouting for 25 years; Progress Director, Conference and Camping Appeal, South Carolina Synod; received the "Lutheran Men in Mission" Award of the South Carolina Synod, 1990; Committee of Aging, South Carolina Synod.

SWICEGOOD, JOHN
Date/Place of Birth: December 30, 1806; Davidson County, N.C.
Parents: Philip Swicegood and Macdolena (Harmon) Swicegood.
Spouse: Sarah Crouch (or Crouse) Swicegood.
Children: Daniel, Maria E., Charles Gice, Philip, John R., Martin L., (last three died at ages of one, seven, and thirteen years, respectively).
Education: Gettysburg Seminary.
License/Ordination: Licensed 1836 and ordained 1851 by North Carolina Synod.
Calls: Hopewell, Browntown, and other places in Davidson County, 1837-47; Nazareth-Shiloh, Forsyth County, 1847-53, 1865-67; supply, with the Reverend Simeon Scherer, St. Michael, Troutman, 1853-56; Beth Eden, Newton, 1855; Low's, Guilford County-Richland, Randolph County, 1854-55; St. Paul, Iredell County, 1855-56; Bethany, Davidson County, 1860-67.

Date of Death/Burial Location: September 9, 1870; Bethany Church, Shady Grove, Davidson County, N.C.

SWICEGOOD, OLIN GRAY
Date/Place of Birth: June 6, 1910; Lexington, Davidson County, N.C.
Parents: Aldine Keiffer Swicegood and Viola Mae (Michael) Swicegood.
Spouse/Marriage Date: Willie Mae (Eargle) Swicegood; May 26, 1935 in Columbia, S.C.
Children: Leila Mae Bost, Rebecca Gray Massey.
Education: Lenoir-Rhyne, A.B. 1930; Lutheran Theological Southern Seminary, M.Div. 1933.
Ordination: June 25, 1933 by North Carolina Synod.
Calls: Mt. Hermon-Sharon-St. Paul, Iredell County, 1933-35; Amity, Iredell County-Lebanon-Providence, Cleveland, Rowan County-St. Matthew, Davie County, 1935-37; St. Andrew, Andrews, 1937-38; St. Matthew-St. Peter, Rowan County, 1938-47; Holy Trinity, Troutman, 1947-68; Mt. Olive, Mt. Pleasant, 1968-76; retired in 1976; Vice Pastor to various congregations.
Other: Dean, Secretary, Central Conference; Board, Children's Home of the South twenty-eight years and Vice President for fourteen years; American Missions Committee, fourteen years; delegate to several conventions of United Lutheran Church in America.
Date of Death/Burial Location: January 26, 1991; St. Michael Cemetery, Troutman, N.C.

SWIDZINSKI, LARRY ALBERT
Date/Place of Birth: March 22, 1950; Butler, Pa.
Parents: Albert Swidzinski and Betty (Yost) Swidzinski.
Spouse/Marriage Date: Carol (King) Swidzinski; June 17, 1972 in Miami Springs, Fla.
Children: Christine Carol, Jamianne Lara, Debra Lynn.
Education: Capital University, B.S. Social Work, 1972; Trinity Seminary, M.Div. 1976.
Ordination: August 22, 1976 by Eastern District, Pennsylvania Synod.
Calls: Prince of Peace/Immanuel, Williamson, Texas, 1976-85; St. Luke, Taylorsville, 1985-.

SWING, STAFFORD LEROY
Date/Place of Birth: April 3, 1922; Davidson County, N.C.
Parents: William Henry Swing and Florence (Beck) Swing.
Spouse/Marriage Date: Dorothy Elaine (Ketner) Swing; November 25, 1947 in Salisbury, N.C.
Children (by adoption): Paul Ray, Donald Leigh, Debra Allene.
Education: University of North Carolina, two years, Lenoir-Rhyne, A.B. 1944; Lutheran Theological Southern Seminary, B.D. 1946.
Ordination: July 19, 1946 by North Carolina Synod.
Calls: Assistant Pastor, St. John, Salisbury, 1946-47, Redeemer, Kannapolis, 1947-50; St. Michael, Irmo, S.C., also serving as Parish Education-Youth Worker for South Carolina Synod, 1950-53; Mt. Olive, Hickory, 1953-59; Assistant Pastor, Luther Memorial,

Madison, Wis., 1959-63; Peace, San Antonio, Texas, 1963-67; Reformation, Columbia, S.C., 1967-80.
Other: Assistant Editor, *North Carolina Lutheran*, 1955, Editor Pro Tem, 1956.
Date of Death/Burial Location: August 28, 1980; City Memorial Cemetery, Salisbury, N.C.

SWYGERT, GEORGE DAVID, SR.
Date/Place of Birth: October 5, 1941; Chapin, S.C.
Parents: Carroll Verner Swygert and Roslyne (Bouknight) Swygert.
Spouse/Marriage Date: Marilyn Mae (Bopp) Swygert; June 8, 1963 in Clemson, S.C.
Children: George David, Jr., Martha Lynn Park, Michael Luther.
Education: Newberry College, A.B. 1963; Lutheran Theological Southern Seminary, M.Div. 1967.
Ordination: May 26, 1967 by South Carolina Synod.
Calls: St. James, Leesville, S.C., 1967-70; Grace, Bessemer City, 1970-81; Organ, Salisbury, 1981-92; St. Mark, China Grove, 1992-.
Other: Youth Ministry Committee, 1971.

SWYGERT, ROBERT LEE
Date/Place of Birth: October 20, 1921; Lexington County, S.C.
Parents: George William Swygert and Cattie Inez (Caughman) Swygert.
Spouse/Marriage Date: Dolores A. (Wiley) Swygert, native of Iowa; January 20, 1946 in Leesville, S.C.
Children: Gary Dennis, Duane Merrill.
Education: Newberry College, B.S. 1954; Lutheran Theological Southern Seminary, B.D. 1957.
Ordination: June 9, 1957 by South Carolina Synod.
Calls: Bethany, Newberry County, S.C., 1957; St. Jacob Parish, Chapin, S.C., 1957-58, St. Jacob only, 1958-61; Prosperity (now Cross of Christ), Cabarrus County, 1961-64; Mission Developer, St. Michael, Moncks Corner, S.C., 1964-66; Mission Developer, St. Timothy, Goose Creek, S.C., 1964-66; Holy Trinity, Springfield, Ga., 1966-68; Greene County Parish, Greeneville, Tenn., 1968-71; Pine Grove, Lone Star, S.C., 1971-82; Faith, West Columbia, S.C., 1982-84; retired 1984 to Lone Star, S.C.
Other: In South Carolina Synod: Secretary, Southern District, 1972-74; Dean, Amelia District, 1974-79; Executive Board, 1981-84.

TABLER, JOHN THOMAS
Place of Birth: Traptown, Md.
Spouse/Marriage Date: Matilda (Brown) Tabler; April 16, 1835.
Education: Studied theology at Gettysburg Seminary, 1829-32.
License/Ordination: Licensed by North Carolina Synod in 1832; transferred to and ordained by Virginia Synod in 1833.
Calls: Pilgrim-St. Luke, Davidson County, 1831-33; supplied St. John, Salisbury, 1832-33; St. Michael, Troutman, 1832; also reported to have served some churches in Virginia (Zion, Floyd County, 1835-42; New St. Peter, Montgomery County, 1835-39; St. John, Wytheville, 1837-39), before and after his ordination, some years conflicting with terms of

service in North Carolina; Virginia Synod records state that he was transferred back to North Carolina Synod in 1838; name does not appear in the records after September 1841.

TAIPALE, JOYCE ELIZABETH

Date/Place of Birth: October 30, 1952; Painesville, Ohio.
Parents: John Edwin Taipale and Beverly Jean (Tegner) Taipale.
Education: Lakeland Community College, Hiram College, B.A. History 1975; Trinity Seminary, M.Div. 1990; graduate work at Case Western Reserve University, MSLS Archival Specialty, 1997-98.
Ordination: October 27, 1990 by Northeastern Ohio Synod.
Calls: Emmanuel, High Point, 1990-92; St. Paul, Burlington, 1992-.
Other: Chair, Worship and Music Committee; Chaplain, Women of the Evangelical Lutheran Church in America-North Carolina Assembly, 1995.

TAKIMOTO, KOCHICHIRO

Place of Birth: Wakayama, Japan.
Education: Began career as primary school teacher; baptized in December 1882. Graduated from Pacific Seminary (Presbyterian), Calif.
Ordination: Previously ordained as Church of Christ Minister in 1903. Transferred to Lutheran Church in July 1911; ordained 1917 (? 1912), by order of North Carolina Synod.
Calls: In Japan served at Wakayama as evangelist of The Church of Christ in Japan (united body in which five Presbyterian and Reformed Missions were working); then in Hawaii. Back in Japan, Pastor at Wakayama, also taught English in school there. Became pastor at Kumamoto, also teaching in our seminary there. In August 1918 succeeded first native Lutheran Pastor in Japan, the Reverend Ryohei Yamanouchi, at Momodani, Osaka. President of Japan Lutheran Church, 1920-, visiting all congregations in 1924 in a three-month period. Last church served, Sumiyoshi, Osaka, 1931-38.
Other: Japanese President, Joint Consortium, 1926; Member, Joint Executive Committee, 1926; Joint Examining Committee, 1929; Delegate to National Christian Council, 1929; Board of Trustees for Evangelical Lutheran Church in Japan in Kieyushu Gaubin, 1929.
Date of Death: December 8, 1945 at son's home in Nagano Prefecture.

TALLENT, JOSEPH EDWARD

Date/Place of Birth: November 17, 1947; Toluca, N.C.
Parents: Dock Howard Tallant and Margaret Hazel (Mull) Tallant.
Spouse/Marriage Date: Patricia Ann (Freeman) Tallent; August 13, 1983 in Raleigh, N.C.
Children: Randall Joseph.
Education: Wake Forest University, Lenoir-Rhyne, A.B. Sociology 1975; Philadelphia Seminary, M.Div. 1985.
Ordination: May 31, 1985 by North Carolina Synod.
Calls: Lord of Life, Garner, 1985-.
Other: North Carolina Synod Social Ministry Cabinet and Committee; Spiritual Director, Teens Encounter Christ; Clergy Presenting Couple/Contact, Lutheran Marriage Encounter; worked in field of drug and alcohol abuse, organizing a youth crisis center, developing educational and training materials and working at state level to develop, plan, and evaluate programs.

TAYLOR, DICKSON WALTER
Date/Place of Birth: June 15, 1918; Leesville, S.C.
Parents: Pickens C. Taylor and Bertha (Addy) Taylor.
Spouse/Marriage Date: Jeanne (Setzer) Taylor; May 23, 1942 in Hickory, N.C.
Children: Margaret Jeanne Oglesbee, John.
Education: Lenoir-Rhyne, B.A. 1938; Lutheran Theological Southern Seminary, M.Div. 1941.
Ordination: August 17, 1941 by South Carolina Synod.
Calls: St. Matthew, Konnarock, Va., 1941-43; Christ, Radford, Va., 1943-49; First, Portsmouth, Va., 1950-56; Muhlenberg, Harrisonburg, Va., 1956-64; Good Shepherd, Virginia Beach, Va., 1964-80; retired to Hickory, N.C., July 1, 1980; transferred to North Carolina Synod in 1980.

TAYLOR, JOHN FRANKLIN, JR.
Date/Place of Birth: April 2, 1932; Landis, N.C.
Parents: John Franklin Taylor, Sr. and Mariette (Goodman) Taylor.
Spouse/Marriage Date: Barbara Jean (Sigmon) Taylor; November 28, 1959 at Statesville, N.C.
Children: John Mark, Phillip Wayne, Paul Eugene.
Education: Lenoir-Rhyne, A.B. 1955; Lutheran Theological Southern Seminary, B.D. 1958; graduate work at Emory University and Syracuse University.
Ordination: June 8, 1958 by North Carolina Synod.
Calls: Gold Hill Parish (Mt. Olive-St. Stephen), Gold Hill, 1959-63; Peace, Gibsonville, 1963-68; Grace, Newton, 1969-73; Trinity, Martinsburg, W.Va., 1974-. Retired to Edinburg, Va.
Other: Rural Parish Committee, 1961-62; World Missions Committee, 1963-68; President, Piedmont All Lutheran Pastors' Conference, 1967-68; Chaplain, Area I Alcoholics Anonymous, 1970-73.

TAYLOR, MICHAEL HOYLE, SR.
Date/Place of Birth: January 16, 1944; Lincolnton, N.C.
Parents: Hoyle Taylor and Mary (Bangle) Taylor.
Spouse/Marriage Date: Emilia Carol (Buffaloe) Taylor; July 2, 1966 in Raleigh, N.C.
Children: Laurel Allison, Michael Hoyle, Jr.
Education: Lenoir-Rhyne, B.A. 1966; Lutheran Theological Southern Seminary, M.Div. 1970; Graduate Theological Foundation, M.B.A., D.Min.
Ordination: June 7, 1970 by North Carolina Synod.
Calls: Good Shepherd, Savannah, Ga., 1970-73; Ascension, Savannah, Ga., 1973-76; Abiding Presence, Beltsville, Md., 1980-.

TEED, RONALD EDWIN
Date/Place of Birth: May 8, 1944; Newberry County, S.C.
Parents: Adelbert Y. Teed and Bertha Mae (Hall) Teed.
Spouse/Marriage Date: Karen Sue (Bolch) Teed; September 12, 1970 at Hickory, N.C.
Children: Cynthia Leanne, Jennifer Christine.

Education: Lenoir-Rhyne, A.B. 1966; Trinity Seminary, M.Div. 1971; University of Tennessee, M.S.S.W. 1981; Candidate for D.Min., Lutheran Theological Southern Seminary.
Ordination: August 19, 1971 by American Lutheran Church, Southeastern Synod.
Calls: Martin Luther/Zion Parish, Bergton, Va., 1971-74; Mountain Lutheran Parish, Bergton, Va., 1973-74; Ascension, Waycross, Ga., 1977-80; Messiah, Charles City, Iowa, 1983; Developer, Family of Faith, Concord, 1983-87.
Other: Removed from Roll, 1992; North Carolina Alliance for Mentally Ill, Inc. in Raleigh, N.C.; Habilitation Specialist, Neuse Mental Health, Mental Retardation and Substance Abuse Service Program, New Bern, N.C.

TERRY, ROGER HAROLD, JR.
Date/Place of Birth: February 3, 1925; East Spencer, N.C.
Parents: Roger Harold Terry, Sr. and Marie (Kneeburg) Terry.
First Spouse/Marriage Date: Martha Jean (Frye) Terry; June 30 1948 in Hickory, N.C.
Children: Barbara Marie, Ruth Elizabeth, Julia Kneeburg, Glenn Roger.
Second Spouse/Marriage Date: Kathryn (Wagoner) (Koontz) Terry; November 22, 1973 at Salisbury, N.C.
Education: Lenoir-Rhyne, A.B. 1945, Doctor of Sacred Music, 1973; Lutheran Theological Southern Seminary, B.D. 1948; Union Seminary, S.T.M. 1955; graduate work at Columbia University and Temple University.
Ordination: April 7, 1948 by North Carolina Synod.
Calls: Assistant Pastor, St. John, Salisbury, 1948-50; Augustana Lutheran Church, Emanuel, Ridgefield Park, N.J., 1950-53, while studying at Union Seminary; St. Mark, China Grove, 1953-59; Worship and Music Resources Editor, United Lutheran Church in America Board of Parish Education, 1959-62, Lutheran Church in America, 1962-77, edited three church school hymnals, for pre-school, grades 1-6, and youth and adults; helped develop Long-Range Program of Christian Education; Peace, Gibsonville, 1977-83; Macedonia, Burlington, 1983-84; Nazareth, Rural Hall, 1985-87; retired in 1987; Vice Pastor at various congregations.
Other: Author/Editor: *Church School Hymnal for Children; Young Children Sing; Music Resource Book; Music in Christian Education; Sing! Hymnal for Youth and Adults; Children Sing, Books 1-3; Celebrate;* numerous other resources, print and audio-visuals for all age levels; Author: *Lutheran Hymnody in North America,* major essay in *Hymnal Companion to the Lutheran Book of Worship*; arranged hymn tune for *Let All Things Now Living,* LBW. Helped develop the *Lutheran Book of Worship* as Lutheran Church in America staff representative to the Inter-Lutheran Commission on Worship; Ecumenical Member, Commission on Church Music, Episcopal Diocese of Pennsylvania; Chaplain, Program Director, Workshop Leader, Program Committee of Lutheridge Music Week; conducted synodical workshops on lifestyle simplification for World Hunger Task Force, 1980s; North Carolina Synod Executive Board, 1982-85; Co-editor, *Soli Deo Gloria,* North Carolina Synod Journal of worship, music and the arts, 1993-95; Board, Secretary, Admissions Committee, Lowman Home; Chair, Youth Committee, 1949-50; Organizational Chair and first President, Ridgefield Park, New Jersey Council of Churches, 1952; Chair, Evangelism, chaired study and proposal which led to first synodical full-time

Secretary for stewardship and evangelism; Chair, Worship Committee, planned and coordinated program of introduction for the *Service Book and Hymnal,* 1958; delegate to Harrisburg and Toronto United Lutheran Church in America Conventions; American Guild of Organists, Association of Lutheran Church Musicians, Hymn Society of the United States and Canada (former member of national Executive Committee and Research Committee) and formerly, Music Educators National Conference, Pennsylvania Music Educators Association, and Department of Worship, United Lutheran Church in America; *Who's Who in Religion; Who's Who in the World;* President, China Grove Rotary Club; volunteer construction worker and fund raiser for Hurricane Hugo victims, 1992.

THALHEIMER, ANNE MARIE (NEUCHTERLEIN)
See: Neuchterlein, Anne Marie (Thalheimer)

THOMAS, EDWARD L.
Ordination: Request received from Rocky Mountain Synod for ordination by North Carolina Synod, 1995.
Calls: Bethlehem, Los Alamos, N.M., 1995-.

THOMAS, LUTHER ALEXANDER, SR.
Date/Place of Birth: August 8, 1888; Rowan County, N.C.
Parents: Albert David Thomas and EvAnn S. (Miller) Thomas.
Spouse/Marriage Date: Fannie S. (Brown) Thomas of Granite Quarry, sister of the Reverend P. D. Brown; August 6, 1914 in Rowan County, N.C.
Children: Grace Brown Kale, Luther Alexander, Jr., Karl Miller.
Education: Mount Pleasant Collegiate Institute, Roanoke College, A.B. 1911; Lutheran Theological Southern Seminary, 1914; graduate study, Northwestern University, 1926; Lenoir-Rhyne, D.D. 1929.
Ordination: May 5, 1914 by North Carolina Synod.
Calls: St. Stephen, Lexington, S.C., 1914-17; St. Mark's, Mooresville-St. Luke, Bear Poplar, 1917-20; St. Mark's only, 1920-22; St. James, Concord, 1922-30; Grace, Winchester, Va., 1930-36; Emmanuel, Lincolnton, 1936-45, Pastor Emeritus, 1961; Holy Trinity, Miami, Fla., 1945-50; Epiphany, Miami Beach, Fla., 1950-57; retired 1957 at Lincolnton, N.C.; Vice Pastor at various congregations.
Other: President, Florida Synod, 1947-49; Board of Trustees Educational Institutions, 1925-30; Board of Deaconess Work, United Lutheran Church in America, 1930-42.
Date of Death/Burial Location: June 16, 1978; Christiana Lutheran Cemetery, Salisbury, N.C.

THOMPSON, ROBERT HAROLD, II
Date/Place of Birth: October 6, 1944; Elyria, Ohio.
Parents: Robert Harold Thompson, Sr. and Lola Pearl (Pickett) Thompson.
Spouse/Marriage Date: Thelma Nadine (Broome) Thompson; September 10, 1966 in Kannapolis, N.C.

Children: Robert Harold, III, Stephanie Nadine.
Education: Pfeiffer, A.B. 1971; Lutheran Theological Southern Seminary, M.Div. 1975; Union Seminary, D.Min. 1980; Andersonville Baptist Seminary, Th.D. 1994.
Ordination: June 8, 1975 by North Carolina Synod.
Calls: Reformation, Taylorsville, 1975-81; St. John, Walhalla, S.C., 1981-88; St. Peter, Chapin, S.C., 1988-.
Other: North Carolina Synod - Western District Youth Advisor, Synodical Professional Services Committee, Confirmation Ministry Task Force, Educational Ministry Committee; North Carolina and South Carolina Synod - Carolinas' Evangelism Conference Small Group Leader; publications: *Word In Season* devotional writer; South Carolina Synod - District Dean, Educational Ministry Committee, Synodical Evangelism Committee, Confirmation Task Force, Spiritual Advocates Committee. Associate Faculty, Newberry College.

THORNBURG, J. LEWIS
Date/Place of Birth: February 5, 1900; High Shoals, Gaston County, N.C.
Parents: Lorenzo A. Thornburg and Susan Ida (Plonk) Thornburg.
Spouse/Marriage Date: Mary Lee (Barnhardt) Thornburg; August 3, 1927 in Salisbury, N.C.
Children: Martha Reid Cauble.
Education: Lenoir-Rhyne, A.B. 1920, D.D. 1951; Lutheran Theological Southern Seminary, 1923; Philadelphia Seminary, B.D. 1924; University of South Carolina, M.A. 1923; also graduate study, University of Pennsylvania, Columbia University, Duke University, and University of North Carolina.
Ordination: November 11, 1923 by North Carolina Synod.
Calls: St. Paul, Durham, and pastor to Lutheran students at Duke University, 1923-30; also, pastor to Lutheran students, University of North Carolina at Chapel Hill, 1924-27; St. John, Statesville, 1930-45; supplied St. Paul, Iredell County, 1938; St. Mark, China Grove, 1945-49; Executive Director, Lutheridge Assembly, 1949-67; Good Shepherd, Brevard, 1968-75; retired 1966; Vice Pastor to various congregations.
Other: President, Eastern and Northern Conferences; Board, Lenoir-Rhyne, 1947-52; Board, Lutheran Theological Southern Seminary, 1952-53; Delegate to United Lutheran Church in America Convention in Philadelphia and Cleveland, Ohio; United Lutheran Church in America Nominating Committee, four years; Guest Preacher at Philadelphia Convention; Registrar, Summer School for Church Workers; Delegate to Lutheran Brotherhood Convention, Allentown, Pa.; Delegate, Convo on Aging, Pittsburgh, Pa.; Synodical Task Force on Aging. Boy Scouts of America; Executive Board of Piedmont Council; received Beaver Award, the Lamb Award, and the Pro Deo Patria Award; contributor to Lutheran periodicals, *Parish School Magazine*, and of sermon in Lenten volume, *Victim or Victor* (Muhlenberg Press).
Date of Death/Burial Location: June 7, 1987; Oakwood Cemetery, Statesville, N.C.

THUESEN, THEODORE JOHANNES, JR.

Date/Place of Birth: March 7, 1928; Cedar Falls, Iowa.
Parents: Theodore Johannes Thuesen, Sr. and Christine (Jensen) Thuesen.
Spouse/Marriage Date: Mary Caroline (Wise) Thuesen; May 29, 1968.
Children: Erik Daniel, Peter Johannes, Sarah Caroline.
Education: Grand View College, A.A. 1947; Augustana College, B.A. 1949; Chicago Seminary, M.Div. 1956; University of Iowa, M.A. Sociology, 1955; graduate study at University of Oregon, University of Washington, Appalachian State University.
Ordination: August 19, 1956 by American Evangelical Lutheran Church (Danish).
Calls: Bethesda, Newark, N.J., 1959-59; Hope, Enumclaw, Wash., 1959-63; retired June 1994 to Hickory, N.C.
Other: Instructor in Sociology, Pacific Lutheran University, 1963-67; Professor of Sociology, Lenoir-Rhyne, 1967-94, Professor Emeritus of Sociology, 1994; received the Raymond M. Bost Distinguished Professor Award, Lenoir-Rhyne, 1981; public School teaching in Anamosa, Iowa, 1949-50; U.S. Army, 1951-53; Danish American Heritage Society.

TILLEY, GEORGE EDWARD

Date/Place of Birth: May 17, 1951; Durham, N.C.
Parents: George S. Tilley, Jr. and Faye (Hewell) Tilley.
Education: Concordia College, A.A.; Concordia Senior College, (Ind.), B.A.; Concordia Seminary (SEMINEX), M.Div.; Columbia University, M.S.
Ordination: 1979 by North Carolina Synod.
Calls: Calvary, Spencer, 1979-81; St. Matthew, Charleston, S.C., 1981-82; Holy Redeemer, Brooklyn, N.Y., 1981-.
Other: Removed from roll 1990 in New York.

TOEDTMAN, WILLIAM HENRY

Date/Place of Birth: March 25, 1900; Miamisburg, Ohio.
Parents: Mr. and Mrs. Charles Toedtman.
Spouse/Marriage Date: Margaret (Langenfelder) Toedtman; October 11, 1930.
Children: Janice Elaine.
Education: Ohio State University, Columbus, Ohio; Capital University, B.A. 1923; Evangelical Lutheran Theological Seminary, Columbus, Ohio, B.D. 1927; Princeton Seminary, M.St. 1928; Lenoir-Rhyne, D.D. 1940.
Ordination: April 1928 by American Lutheran Church.
Calls: St. Luke, Baltimore, Md., 1928-32; St. John, Sweet Air, Md., 1928-32; Miller's, Hickory, 1932-49; Oceanside, Long Island, N.Y., 1949-67.
Other: President, Concordia Conference, two years; Urban Church Committee, Eastern District; Eastern District Youth Committee; Secretary, Koinoia Society, New York City; Board of Regents, Capital University, 1961-66.

TOLER, ELIZABETH JOY
Date/Place of Birth: June 20, 1953; Chelyan, W.Va.
Parents: Edward Harrison Toler and Eileen Alice Toler.
Education: Lenoir-Rhyne, A.B. 1981; Lutheran Theological Southern Seminary, M.Div. 1985.
Ordination: December 2, 1985 by North Carolina Synod.
Calls: Prince of Peace, Kinston, 1985-89; Mt. Gilead, Mt. Pleasant, 1989-.
Other: Multicultural Ministry Committee, 1986-90, Chair, 1989-90; Board, Lutheran Services for the Aging, 1993-; Credentials and Enrollment Committee, 1986, Chair, 1994; Conduct of Elections Committee, 1987, 1995.

TONNESEN, KENNETH
Date/Place of Birth: October 12, 1938; Elizabeth, N.J.
Parents: Einar Tonnesen and Elsie (Corneliusen) Tonnesen.
Spouse/Marriage Date: Carol (Kolbjornsen) Tonnesen; August 18, 1962 in Staten Island, N.Y.
Children: Laureen Wacenske, Philip.
Education: Concordia College, (Minn.), B.A. History 1960; Luther Seminary, M.Div. 1964.
Ordination: June 1964 by Eastern District, Florida Synod, American Lutheran Church.
Calls: Advent, Orange Park, Fla., 1964-71; Hope, Selden, N.Y., 1971-75; Grace, Raleigh, 1975-90; Mt. Pisgah, Hickory, 1990-.

TONNESEN, PHILIP TODD
Date/Place of Birth: November 3, 1967; Green Cove Springs, Fla.
Parents: Kenneth Tonnesen and Carol Tonnesen.
Spouse/Marriage Date: Debra (Janisko) Tonnesen; July 30, 1988 in Delray Beach, Fla.
Children: Julie Laureen, Gregory Todd.
Education: Lenoir-Rhyne, B.A. History, 1989; Lutheran Theological Southern Seminary, M.Div. 1993.
Ordination: May 21, 1993 by North Carolina Synod.
Calls: Cross and Crown, Matthews, 1993-97; Bishop's Assistant, Salisbury, 1997-.

TOWNSEND, PAUL DAVID
Date/Place of Birth: April 21, 1954; Tandil, Argentina.
Parents: The Reverend Noah Earl Townsend and Virginia Carolina (Morgan) Townsend, daughter of the Reverend Dr. F. G. Morgan.
First Spouse/Marriage Date: Joyce (Murphy) Townsend; January 1, 1977 in Reidsville, N.C.
Children of First Marriage: Benjamin Thomas, Katherine Murphy.
Second Spouse/Marriage Date: Carol (Starr) Townsend, daughter of the Reverend C. Marion Starr; August 11, 1990.
Stepchildren: Joshua Scott Ballard, Katherine Starr Ballard.
Education: University of North Carolina at Greensboro, B.A. Philosophy 1976; Lutheran Theological Southern Seminary, M.Div. 1982.
Ordination: June 6, 1982 by North Carolina Synod.
Calls: St. Peter, Southport, 1982-88; Gloria Dei, Salisbury, 1988-92; St. Mark's Temple, Clifton Heights, Pa., 1992-95; St. Michael, Sellersville, Pa., 1995-.
Other: Assisted at Hispanic Mission, Nueva Creacion, Philadelphia, Pa., 1995-96.

TOWNSEND, NOAH EARL

Date/Place of Birth: March 7, 1923; Valle Crucis, Watauga County, N.C.

Parents: Noah A. Townsend and Sarah C. (Barger) Townsend.

Spouse/Marriage Date: Virginia Caroline (Morgan) Townsend, daughter of the Reverend F. Grover Morgan; December 20, 1946 in Hickory, N.C.

Children: Rebeca Lucia, Sara Leticia, Margarita Virginia, The Reverend Paul David, Henry Martin, Amalia Argentina, Alicia Carolina.

Education: Lenoir-Rhyne, A.B. 1946; Lutheran Theological Southern Seminary, B.D. 1949; Syracuse University, M.A. in Religious Journalism, 1962.

Ordination: June 5, 1949 by North Carolina Synod.

Calls: Missionary in Argentina of United Lutheran Church in America Board of Foreign Missions, 1949-67, and since, of Lutheran Church in America Board of World Missions; in Buenos Aires: Good Shepherd, Tandil, 1949-55; Our Saviour, Olavarria, 1956-58; Redeemer, Buenos Aires (Interim Pastor and Chaplain of its 600-pupil parochial school), 1965-66; Director of Office of Evangelism and Literature for United Evangelical Lutheran Church in Argentina, 1958-66; Holy Trinity, Reidsville, 1967-77; Good Shepherd, Weehawken, N.J., 1977-85; retired July 16, 1985; Vice Pastor at various congregations.

Other: Author of articles, sermons, stories, pageants, etc., published in twenty periodicals and newspapers in the United States, Argentina, and Puerto Rico; Editor, *Obras Navidenas,* a book of Christmas dramas, 1966; wrote, translated and published many Christian Educational materials in Spanish for use throughout Latin America; Director, Senior Citizens at First, Greensboro, 1987-93; Vice President, Secretary, and Statistician of Argentina Lutheran Synod and Secretary of Ecumenical Council of Churches; writer and translator from English into Spanish for Lutheran Church magazine *Luz y Verdad (Light and Truth),* also for Lutheran Church in America Committee on Spanish Publications; North Carolina Synod - Stewardship Committee, Social Ministry Committee, Companion Synod Committee, and Global Missions Committee; Chair, Communications Task Force; Chair, Committee on Publications and Publicity; Secretary, Northern District; Assistant Editor, *North Carolina Lutheran,* 1970-76; Spanish instructor at Rockingham Community College, 1971; presenter, two Global Mission Events; New Jersey Synod - Christian Education Committee and Educational Resource Team; participant in Lutheran Church in America Transcultural Seminars in Cincinnati and Chicago; Participant, Lutheran Church in America Hispanic Conferences in New York, Miami, San Antonio and Puerto Rico; Urban Pastors' Conference, 1979; fact-finding mission to Cuba, 1980; Committee to open an office for the resettlement of Mariel Boatlift Cubans in the early 80s.

TRETHEWAY, JACK EVANS

Date/Place of Birth: November 16, 1923; Ironwood, Mich.

Parents: Gideon Thomas Tretheway and Clara Justine (Peterson) Tretheway.

Spouse/Marriage Date: Donna Jean (Joneson) Tretheway; December 27, 1949 at Rock Island, Ill.

Children: Sue Ellen Brewer, Thomas Roy, Erik Dean.

Education: Lutheran Bible Institute, Seattle, Wash., 1946; Business College, Seattle, Wash.; Augustana College, A.B. 1950; Institute of Pastoral Care, Augustana Hospital,

Chicago, Ill., six weeks, 1951; Augustana Seminary, B.D. 1954; Garrett Biblical Institute, Evanston, Ill., summer 1958.
Ordination: June 20, 1954 by Augustana Lutheran Church.
Calls: Augustana-Lund-Upsala, Detroit Lakes, Minn., 1954-57; First-Esther, Parkers Prairie, Minn., 1957-60; Chaplain, U.S. Navy, Camp Lejeune, 1960-64; First, Des Moines, Iowa, 1964-70; Chief, Chaplain Service, Veterans Administration Medical Center, Madison, Wis., 1970-75; Chief, Chaplain Service, Veterans Administration Medical Center, Milwaukee, Wis., 1975-83; Chief, Chaplain Service, Veterans Administration Medical Center, Salisbury, 1983-88; retired February 29, 1988 to Salisbury, N.C.; Chaplain, Lutheran Home, 1988-.

TREXLER, BERNARD LITTLETON
Date/Place of Birth: December 17, 1917; Granite Quarry, N.C.
Parents: William Roedel Trexler and Carrie (Cauble) Trexler-Plyler. The Reverend Leroy C. Trexler is a younger brother.
Spouse/Marriage Date: Dorothy (Caughman) Trexler; November 1, 1941 in Columbia, S.C.
Children: Bishop William Bernard, John David.
Education: Lenoir-Rhyne, A.B. 1938, D.D. 1991; Lutheran Theological Southern Seminary, B.D. 1941.
Ordination: 1941 by North Carolina Synod.
Calls: Holy Comforter, Belmont, 1941-43; Trinity, Rocky Mount, 1943-49; St. Mark, Asheville, 1949-59; St. Mark, Corpus Christi, Texas, 1959-61; Trinity, Greenville, S.C., 1961-83, Pastor Emeritus, 1983; Vice Pastor for various congregations.
Other: Board, Lutheran Children's Home of the South; Chair, Board, Lutheridge, 1958-59; Chair, Lutheran Theological Southern Seminary Trustees, 1975-87; Camping and Conference Committee, South Carolina Synod, 1967-80; Lutheridge Camp and Conference Center and Kinard Conference Center; Chair, Parish Education Committee, South Carolina Synod, 1962-68; Chair, Continuing Education for Pastors, South Carolina Synod, 1970-76; delegate, United Lutheran Church in America Convention, 1956; delegate, Lutheran Church in America Convention, 1970, 1972, 1980.
Date of Death/Burial Location: April 4, 1996; Union Lutheran Church Cemetery, Salisbury, N.C.

TREXLER, EDGAR RAY, JR.
Date/Place of Birth: September 17, 1937; Salisbury, N.C.
Parents: The Reverend Edgar Ray Trexler, Sr. and Eula Belle (Farmer) Trexler.
Spouse/Marriage Date: Emily Louise (Kees) Trexler; August 21, 1960 in Raleigh, N.C.
Children: David Ray, Mark Raymond, Karen Emily.
Education: Lenoir-Rhyne, A.B. English 1959, Litt.D. 1978; Lutheran Theological Southern Seminary, M.Div. *cum laude* 1962; graduate work at Boston University, 1962; Syracuse University, M.A. Religious Journalism, 1964; Midland, Litt.D. 1990; Wittenberg, D.D. 1994; study leaves, Lutheran World Federation, Geneva, Switzerland, 1977, 1981.

Ordination: 1962 by North Carolina Synod.

Calls: St. John, Lyons, N.Y., 1962-65; Features Editor, Associate Editor, Editor of *The Lutheran (Lutheran Church in America)*, 1965-87; Editor, *The Lutheran (Evangelical Lutheran Church in America)*, 1987-99. Retired to Hendersonville, N.C. in 1999..

Other: Award of Merit, Associated Church Press, editorial writing, 1991; articles in mission magazines, 1974; Board, Lenoir-Rhyne, 1975-84; Author: *Anatomy of a Merger, Lutheran World Federation-6, New Face of Missions, Creative Congregations, Ways to Wake Up Your Church;* Lenoir-Rhyne Distinguished Alumnus Award, 1991; Newberry College Distinguished Service Award, 1992; Lutheran Theological Southern Seminary Bachman Distinguished Leadership Award, 1993; extensive travel and coverage of Lutheran Church in America/Evangelical Lutheran Church in America overseas missions, ecumenical outreach, including the Vatican and the Ecumenical Partriarchate.

TREXLER, EDGAR RAY, SR.

Date/Place of Birth: May 29, 1896; Rowan County, N.C.
Parents: Luther C. Trexler and Sallie (Brown) Trexler.
Spouse/Marriage Date: Eula Belle (Farmer) Trexler; October 2, 1928 in Faith, N.C.
Children: The Reverend Edgar Ray, Jr.
Education: Lenoir-Rhyne, A.B. 1924; Lutheran Theological Southern Seminary, 1927; University of South Carolina, M.A. 1927.
Ordination: 1927 by North Carolina Synod.
Calls: Mt. Zion-New Bethel-Luther's, Richfield, 1927-31; Mt. Moriah, Rowan County, 1931-50; Holy Trinity, Mt. Pleasant, 1950-59; Daniel's, Lincoln County, 1959-63, Pastor Emeritus, 1963; retired 1964 near Lincolnton, N.C.
Other: Secretary, Board, Lowman Home, 1940-56; Scoutmaster's Key, 1952; Veteran of World War II; Department Chaplain of the State Department of the American Legion, 1947
Date of Death: June 6, 1974; Daniel's Cemetery, Lincolnton, N.C.

TREXLER, FLOYD COLUMBUS

Date/Place of Birth: October 28, 1922; Rowan County, N.C.
Parents: Luther L. Trexler and Mary (File) Trexler.
Spouse/Marriage Date: Maurine (Rehm) Trexler; October 10, 1946 in Milwaukee, Wis.
Children: Deborah Leigh Houlette, Donna Lynn Fisher, David Lee, Danny Luke.
Education: Catawba College, A.B. 1952; Lutheran Theological Southern Seminary, B.D. 1953.
Ordination: June 1953 by North Carolina Synod.
Calls: Bethany, Kannapolis, 1953-60; St. Mark's, Mooresville, 1960-65; Our Savior, Jacksonville, 1965-66; Bethany, Hickory, 1966-69; transferred to Indiana-Kentucky Synod, 1969.
Other: Stewardship Committee, 1967; Officers and Staff Salaries Committee, 1966-67. A community leader in efforts to open lines of communications between black and white residents of Hickory, N.C., following the murder of Martin Luther King, Jr.
Date of Death/Burial Location: July 4, 1998; Evergreen Cemetery, Louisville, Ky.

TREXLER, HENRY ALEXANDER

Date/Place of Birth: December 22, 1855; near Rockwell, N.C.
Parents: Caleb Trexler and Elizabeth Levinia (Lyerly) Trexler.
First Spouse/Marriage Date: Eltha Geva (Van Poole) Trexler;
October 27, 1887 in Rowan County, N.C.
Children of First Marriage: Daisy E., Duke C., Charles Otho,
Clarence W., two who died young, Luther M., Eltha Gideon.
Second Spouse/Marriage Date: Sarah Elizabeth (Lippard)
Trexler; January 6, 1903 at Barium Springs, N.C.
Education: North Carolina College, one year, Roanoke College,
two years, A.B. 1882, A.M. 1885; Lutheran Theological
Southern Seminary, one year, Philadelphia Seminary, 1886; Chicago Seminary, B.D. 1911.
Ordination: 1886 by Ministerium of Pennsylvania.
Calls: St. Matthew-St. Peter-Luther's, Rowan County, 1886-92; Bethany, Davidson
County-Nazareth-Shiloh, Forsyth County, 1892-97; Salem-Grace-Lebanon, Rowan
County, 1897-1907; Organ-Ebenezer, Rowan County, 1907-14; St. Matthew-St. Peter,
Rowan County, (Supply, 1909-10), 1914-20; Mt. Zion-Luther's-New Bethel, Richfield,
1920-24; Christiana, Granite Quarry, 1924-31; retired 1931 at Rockwell, N.C.
Date of Death/Burial Location: May 1, 1945; St. Peter Church, Rowan County, N.C.

TREXLER, LEROY CAUBLE, SR.

Date/Place of Birth: August 9, 1922; Granite Quarry, N.C.
Parents: William Roedel Trexler and Carrie (Cauble) Trexler.
The Reverend Bernard L. Trexler is an older brother.
Spouse/Marriage Date: Mable (Shealy) Trexler; September 27,
1945 at Columbia, S.C.
Children: Baby girl (deceased), Nancy Eileen, Robin (deceased),
Leroy Cauble, Jr., Joel Claude.
Education: Lenoir-Rhyne, A.B. 1943; Lutheran Theological
Southern Seminary, B.D. 1945.
Ordination: October 7, 1945 by North Carolina Synod.
Calls: Good Shepherd, Goldsboro, 1945-49; Mt. Hermon, Cabarrus County, 1949-51; St.
John's, Cherryville, 1952-58; St. Paul, Sarasota, Fla., 1958-65; St. Paul, Columbia, S.C.,
1965-75; St. Stephen, Lexington, S.C., 1975-78; St. John, Hollywood, Fla., 1978-81; Good
Shepherd, Boca Raton, Fla., 1981-83; Wittenberg, Leesville, S.C., 1983-86; retired October
1986 to Cherryville, N.C.; Interim, Bethphage, Lincolnton, and St. Mark, Cherryville.

TREXLER, ROY LEON

Date/Place of Birth: June 23, 1930; Salisbury, Rowan County, N.C.
Parents: Nat Francis Harr Trexler and Clara Ethel (Morgan) Trexler.
Spouse/Marriage Date: Dorothy Elizabeth (Shealy) Trexler; June 13, 1956 at Batesburg,
S.C.
Children: Mary Katherine Collins, Martha Ruth Van Sciver, Paul Andrew.
Education: Lenoir-Rhyne, A.B. 1953; Lutheran Theological Southern Seminary, B.D.
1956, also graduate study; University of North Carolina at Charlotte, M.Ed. 1972.
Ordination: June 10, 1956 by North Carolina Synod.

Calls: Prosperity (now Cross of Christ), Cabarrus County, 1956-60; St. Andrew, Andrews, 1960-61; Bethel-St. Paul, Crouse, 1961-64; St. Mark, Rowan County, 1964-68; Cold Water, Concord, Tent-making ministry, 1969-80; Vice Pastor at various congregations.
Other: Dropped from roll, 1984.

TROUTMAN, CARLSON BERNARD

Date/Place of Birth: March 14, 1928; Statesville, N.C.
Parents: Nathan Wesley Troutman and Zella Mae (Lippard) Troutman.
Spouse/Marriage Date: Jenny Lind (Hottle) Troutman; June 12, 1949 at Toms Brook, Va.
Children: Thomas Carl, Barbra Lind Humphrey.
Education: Lenoir-Rhyne, A.B. 1950; Lutheran Theological Southern Seminary, M.Div. 1953.
Ordination: June 14, 1953 by North Carolina Synod.
Calls: In Virginia: Salem, Mt. Sidney, 1953-58; Holy Trinity, Martinsville, 1958-61; Hebron-Mt. Nebo, Madison, 1961-70; Reformation, New Market, Va., 1970-87; Salem, Mt. Sidney, Va., 1987-90; retired in 1990 in New Market, Va.
Other: Chaplain, Virginia Synod Convention, 1962; delegate to Lutheran Church in America Convention, 1968; Trustee, Vice President of Board, Virginia Synod Lutheran Homes, Inc. for six years; Chair, Shenandoah Valley Lutheran Housing, Inc.; Chaplain, Virginia State Firemen's Association for fourteen years; Chaplain, Northern Virginia Firefighters' Association for 23 years; Shenandoah County Interchurch Planning Service; Weekday Religious Education Council of Shenandoah County.

TROUTMAN, EDWIN FLAVIUS

Date/Place of Birth: October 18, 1897; Troutman, N.C.
Parents: Elliot J. Troutman and Isabelle (Stevenson) Troutman.
Spouse/Marriage Date: Estelle (Brown) Troutman; June 7, 1927 in Troutman, N.C.
Children: The Reverends Edwin Nosker and Gerald Stevenson.
Education: Lenoir-Rhyne, A.B. 1923; Lutheran Theological Southern Seminary, 1926.
Ordination: February 23, 1927 by North Carolina Synod.
Calls: Lebanon-Providence, Rowan County-Amity, Iredell County-St. Matthew, Davie County, 1926-29; St. Andrew, Andrews, 1929-37; Grace, Thomasville, 1937-38; Grace, Boone-St. Mark, Blowing Rock-Holy Communion, Banner Elk, 1938-52, Grace only, 1953-65, Pastor Emeritus of Grace; Campus pastor to Lutheran students, Appalachian State Teachers College, Boone, 1938-66; retired 1965 at Troutman, N.C.; Vice Pastor at various congregations.
Date of Death/Burial Location: June 29, 1978; St. Michael Cemetery, Troutman, N.C.

TROUTMAN, EDWIN NOSKER

Date/Place of Birth: May 10, 1928; Statesville, Iredell County, N.C.
Parents: The Reverend Edwin Flavius Troutman and Estelle (Brown) Troutman. The Reverend Gerald S. Troutman is his younger brother. Great-great-great-great grandson of Adolph Nussmann.
Spouse/Marriage Date: Faye (Creech) Troutman; June 16, 1951 at Jacksonville, Fla.

Children: Edwin Richard, Gretchen Creech, Sarah Neal, Ashlie Brown, Carol Estelle.
Education: Appalachian State Teachers College, B.S. 1948; Lutheran Theological Southern Seminary, M.Div. 1954.
Ordination: June 20, 1954 by North Carolina Synod.
Calls: Emmanuel, Roanoke, Va., 1954-55; Mission Developer/Pastor, Good Shepherd, Morristown, Tenn., 1956; Mission Developer/Pastor, Peace, Alexandria, Va., 1957-60; Washington County Parish, Chilhowie, Va., 1960-62; St. James, Jacksonville, Fla., 1962-65; St. Peter, Shenandoah, Va., 1965-68; Luther Memorial, Blacksburg, Va., 1968-80; Mission Developer/Pastor, Christ, Wise, Va., 1980-88; Christ, Jonesville/Elkin, 1988-90; retired in 1990 to Advance, N.C.; Vice Pastor at various congregations.
Other: Organizer of Ecumenical Food Bank of Wise County, Inc., 1985; Citizen of the Year, Wise County, Va., 1985.

TROUTMAN, GERALD STEVENSON, SR.
Date/Place of Birth: December 16, 1933; Andrews, N.C.
Parents: The Reverend Edwin Flavius Troutman and Estelle (Brown) Troutman. The Reverend Edwin N. Troutman is his older brother.
Spouse/Marriage Date: Marihope (Shirey) Troutman; August 19, 1959 at Newnan, Ga.
Children: Gerald Stevenson, Jr., Lee Shirey, Francus Brown Harris.
Education: Lenoir-Rhyne, A.B. 1956; Lutheran Theological Southern Seminary, M.Div. 1960; Candler School of Theology, Emory University, D.Min. 1987; Newberry College, D.D. 1976..
Ordination: June 1960 by North Carolina Synod.
Calls: Reformation, Greeneville, Tenn., 1960-63; St. John, Atlanta, Ga., 1963-69; first full-time Secretary, Southeastern Synod, 1969-75; President-Bishop, Southeastern Synod, Lutheran Church in America, 1975-87; Division for Ministry and Department for Synodical Relations, Evangelical Lutheran Church in America, 1988-; Lutheran Ministries of Georgia, 1993-.
Other: Board, Lenoir-Rhyne; Board, Newberry College; Chair, Protestant Radio and Television Center Board; Chair, Management Committee, Office for Administration and Finance, Lutheran Church in America; President, Board of American Missions, Lutheran Church in America; Board, Lutheran Theological Southern Seminary; Board, Lutheridge; Board, Williams-Henson Lutheran Home for Children; Conference of Bishops; Chaplain, Greeneville Fire Department, Lions Club, Ministerial Association in Greeneville; President, Atlanta Lutheran Pastors Association; Board, Druid Hills Civic Association; Executive Committee, Christian Council of Metropolitan Atlanta; Board, Georgia Interchurch Association; Committee of American Red Cross, Dekalb- Rockdale Advisory; Board of Visitors, Interdenominational Theological Center, Atlanta, Ga.; *Who's Who in Atlanta, Georgia; Personalities of The South; Who's Who in Religion; Who's Who in America,* 43rd edition; Pastor-in-Residence, Lenoir-Rhyne; writer for *Pericope Partners;* Editor, *Epiphany Meditations* Booklet.

TROUTMAN, ROBERT LOVE

Date/Place of Birth: March 4, 1932; Statesville, Iredell County, N.C.

Parents: Percy Love Troutman and Nonnie (Larue) Troutman.

Spouse/Marriage Date: Margaret Ruth (Lineberger) Troutman; June 3, 1956 in Stanley, N.C.

Children: Robert David.

Education: Lenoir-Rhyne, B.A. 1954; Lutheran Theological Southern Seminary, M.Div. 1957; Newberry College, D.D. 1982.

Ordination: June 9, 1957 by North Carolina Synod.

Calls: Sharon, Gibsonville, 1957-61; Bethel, Rowan County, 1961-67; Secretary, Christian Education, North Carolina Synod, 1967-69; Executive Director, Lutheridge, 1969-90; Director of Church Relations, Lutheran Family Services, 1991-; Vice Pastor at various congregations.

Other: Committee, Parish Education, 1964-67, Chair, 1965-67; Publications and Publicity Committee, 1962- 65; District Secretary, 1964-67; Lutheran Church in America Delegate, 1970; Examining Committee, 1972-75, Secretary, 1972-75; Committee for Professional Preparation, 1975-83, Registrar, 1975-82, Chair, 1982-83; Board, Lenoir-Rhyne College Alumni Association, 1992-95, Vice President, 1995-96; Director of Church Relations, Lutheran Family Services, to retirement, Arden, 1997.

TROUTMAN, ROY TAYS

Date/Place of Birth: July 15, 1888; Iredell County, N.C.

Parents: Adam Carmi Troutman and Barbara L. (Collins) Troutman.

First Spouse/Marriage Date: Laura Jeanette (Bradford) Troutman; June 5, 1918 (died early in 1920), in Iredell County, N.C.

Children of First Marriage: Geraldine Grey Killinger.

Second Spouse/Marriage Date: Mary Ella (Cline) Troutman; June 15, 1921 at Concord, N.C.

Education: Lenoir-Rhyne, A.B. 1915; Lutheran Theological Southern Seminary, 1918, B.D. 1924; Chicago Seminary, S.T.M. 1924.

Ordination: 1918 by North Carolina Synod.

Calls: Salem-Grace, Rowan County, 1918-20; St. John, Cabarrus County, 1921-23; Holy Trinity, Charlotte, 1924-27; College Church, Salem, Va., 1927-34; Bethany, Lexington, Va., 1934-42; Resurrection, Daytona Beach, Fla., 1942-46; Bedford County Parish, Tenn., 1946-48; Bethel Parish, Springfield, Ga., 1948-53; St. James, Lexington, S.C., 1953-58; retired 1958 and transferred 1960 to North Carolina at Concord; Supply, St. Martin-Cold Water, Cabarrus County, several years.

Other: Board, Children's Home of the South, Salem, Va., 1943-44; Secretary, Georgia-Alabama Synod, 1951-53; President, Roanoke Conference of Virginia Synod, 1930-31.

Date of Death/Burial Location: December 30, 1967; St. John, Cabarrus County, N.C.

TRULL, BILLY GENE

Date/Place of Birth: October 15, 1932; Concord, N.C.

Parents: L. C. Trull and Tessie Lee (Underwood) Trull.

Spouse/Marriage Date: Sara Nancy (Carpenter) Trull; August 18, 1956 at Concord, N.C.

Children: Virginia Anne, Alicia Lynne.
Education: Lenoir-Rhyne, A.B. 1956; Lutheran Theological Southern Seminary, B.D. 1959.
Ordination: 1959 by North Carolina Synod.
Calls: St. Mark-St. John, Caldwell County, 1959-61; St. Mark, Gaston County, 1961-64; St. Martin, Maiden, 1964-70.
Other: Evangelism Committee, 1970; demitted the ministry, 1971.

TUCKER, JOHN BRYANT

Date/Place of Birth: August 15, 1960; Washington, D.C.
Parents: Leonard B. Tucker and E. Johanne (Crow) Crafton.
Spouse/Marriage Date: Jeanne Marie (Watson) Tucker; June 16, 1990.
Children: Kayla Marie, Zachary Bryant.
Education: Salisbury State College, Maryland, B.A. Social Work 1982; Gettysburg Seminary, 1985; Lutheran Theological Southern Seminary, M.Div. 1994.
Ordination: October 23, 1994 by South Carolina Synod.
Calls: In Maryland: Reformation, Baltimore, 1983-85; St. Luke, Silver Spring, 1985; Good Shepherd, Gaithersburg, 1986-90. In South Carolina: Synod Office, 1991-94; Bethlehem, Leesville, S.C., 1994-98; St. John, Salisbury, 1998-.
Other: Youth Ministry Coordinator, South Carolina Synod; Lay Associate Minister, Good Shepherd, Gaithersburg, Md., four years; Interim Director of Youth Ministry, St. Luke, Silver Spring, Md.; Parish Worker, Reformation, Baltimore, Md.

TYLER, WARREN A.

Date/Place of Birth: August 10, 1945; Cook, Ill.
Parents: Gerald Harold Tyler and Alpha Marie (Byrd) Tyler.
First Spouse/Marriage Date: Marilyn Tyler; June 3, 1967 in Roselle, Ill.
Children of First Marriage: Anna Kathleen Howard, Peter Joseph.
Second Spouse: Cathy S. Tyler.
Step-children: Charles L. Borders, III, Jonathan Mark Borders.
Education: Concordia College, Illinois, B.A. 1967; Concordia Seminary, Illinois, M.Div. 1971; University of North Carolina at Chapel Hill, M.S. Social Work.
Ordination: June 1971 by Illinois Synod.
Calls: Macedonia, Burlington; St. Johns, Bridgeton, N.J., 1971-78; Redeemer, Burlington, 1978-85; Administrator, Lutheran Retirement Center, Burlington, 1987-88; Administrator, Lutheran Retirement Center, Alamance, 1988; transferred to North Carolina Synod in 1988; Vice Pastor at various congregations.
Date of Death/Burial Location: May 10, 1996; Alamance, Memorial Park, Alamance, N.C.

VANDERFORD, BILLY LEE

Date/Place of Birth: November 20, 1934; Rowan County, N.C.
Parents: G. N. Vanderford and Mary Pauline (Rogers) Vanderford.
Spouse/Marriage Date: Jo Ann (Critcher) Vanderford; July 6, 1958 at Boone, N.C.
Children: Lisa Ann, Linda Lee, Judy Renee, John Paul.
Education: Lenoir-Rhyne, A.B. 1957; Lutheran Theological Southern Seminary, B.D. 1960.
Ordination: June 5, 1960 by North Carolina Synod.

Calls: Mt. Hermon, Iredell County, 1960-62; Redeemer, Kannapolis, 1962-69; A Mighty Fortress, Charlotte, 1969-74; St. Luke, Lexington, 1974-77.
Date of Death/Burial Location: September 22, 1977; St. Paul Cemetery, Salisbury, N.C.

VAN DEURSEN, ADIN PRESTON

Date/Place of Birth: November 11, 1954; Philadelphia, Pa.
Parents: Charles Van Deursen and Christina (Warren) Van Deursen.
Spouse/Marriage Date: Brenda Lee (Shambaugh) Van Deursen; January 28, 1984.
Children: Ashley Nicole, Allison Lee, Aaron W.
Education: Lenoir-Rhyne, B.A. Sociology 1976; Lutheran Theological Southern Seminary, M.Div. 1980.
Ordination: May 19, 1980 by North Carolina Synod.
Calls: Jewett-Sherrodsville Parishes, Jewett and Sherrodsville, Ohio, 1981-84; First, Plymouth, Ohio, 1984- 89; First, Bellefontaine, Ohio, 1989-95; Department of Pastoral Care, Masonic Homes, Elizabethtown, Pa., 1995-.

VAN DEUSEN, ROBERT ELDON

Date/Place of Birth: April 1, 1909; St. Johnsville, N.Y.
Parents: The Reverend Robert J. Van Deusen and Nettie May (Groff) Van Deusen.
Spouse/Marriage Date: Ruth (Brown) Van Deusen; July 8, 1935; died 1997.
Children: Robert John, Elizabeth Jean.
Education: Hartwick College, A.B. 1932, D.D. 1963; Hartwick Seminary, 1935; Syracuse University, M.A. 1948; American University, Ph.D. 1968.
Ordination: 1935 by New York Synod.
Calls: Rhinebeck, N.Y., 1935-38; Richmondville, N.Y., 1938-40; St. Paul, Tampa, Fla., 1941-44; Bureau of Service to Military Personnel, Kansas City, Mo., 1944-45; Bureau of Service to Military Personnel, Washington, N.C., 1945-48; Secretary, National Lutheran Council, Washington, D.C., 1948-75; Ebenezer, Columbia, S.C., 1975-78; retired in 1975 to Columbia, S.C. and later to Charlotte.
Other: Washington column in *The Lutheran* for twelve years; Editor, *Focus*.

VAN HORNE, ROBERT MARION, JR.

Date/Place of Birth: June 5, 1943; Jackson, Ky.
Parents: Robert Marion Van Horne, Sr. and Elizabeth Mize (Riddell) Van Horne.
Spouse/Marriage Date: Mary Stobo (Bradham) Van Horne; July 27, 1967 in South Carolina.
Children: Katherine McDowell McMillan, William Bernard, Robert Stobo.
Education: University of Kentucky, B.A. 1965; Lutheran Theological Southern Seminary, M.Div. 1970.
Ordination: June 1, 1970 by South Carolina Synod for the Indiana-Kentucky Synod.
Calls: Redeemer, Charleston, S.C., 1970-81; Christ, Cape Coral, Fla., 1981-84; Holy Trinity, Hickory, 1984- 86; Redeemer, Newberry, S.C., 1986-96; Trinity, St. Petersburg, Fla., 1996-.

VARN, KARL MICHAEL
Date/Place of Birth: October 11, 1946; Columbia, S.C.
Parents: Claude Harold Varn and Lila Mae (Roof) Varn.
Spouse/Marriage Date: Lynette Bridget (Kuran) Varn; August 22, 1970 in Durham, N.C.
Children: Meredith Leigh, Lydia Christine.
Education: Lenoir-Rhyne, A.B. Sociology 1971; Lutheran Theological Southern Seminary, M.Div. 1975; McCormick Seminary, D.Div. 1995.
Ordination: June 1, 1975 by South Carolina Synod.
Calls: St. Mark, Isle of Palms, S.C., 1975-79; Holy Comforter, Belmont, 1979-.
Other: Board, Lutheran Services for the Aging; Ecumenical Affairs Committee, Credentials and Enrollment Committee; PLMD Task Force Committee; Church Council Retreat Coordinator; *Ecumenical Handbook;* led sixteen volunteers for clean-up of the Great Flood of '93 in LaGrange, Mo.,'94 Flood of Albany, Ga., and '95 Flood of East St. Louis, Ill.

VAUGHAN, DAVID BARRY
Date/Place of Birth: May 2, 1941; Los Angeles, Calif.
Parents: Clarence Marvin Vaughan and Emily (Riser) Vaughan Salazar.
Spouse/Marriage Date: Diane (Roby) Vaughan; April 24, 1965 in Savannah, Ga.
Children: Meredith Ruby, Stephen Thorpe, Ashley Werner.
Education: Pasadena City College, A.A. 1963; Lenoir-Rhyne, B.A. 1974; Lutheran Theological Southern Seminary, M.Div. 1978.
Ordination: June 11, 1978 by North Carolina Synod.
Calls: St. Paul, Hamlet, 1978-83; St. David's, West Columbia, S.C., 1983-87. Transferred to another denomination.

VERSPRILLE, CRAIG W.
Date/Place of Birth: December 29, 1953; Monroe County, N.Y.
Parents: Fred Versprille and Irene Versprille.
Spouse/Marriage Date: Linda (Foy) Versprille; October 7, 1977 in Rochester, N.Y.
Parents: Kristen Marie, William Abraham, John Patrick.
Education: University of Rochester, B.S. Chemical Engineering 1977; Lutheran Theological Southern Seminary, M.Div. 1985, and graduate work.
Ordination: May 1985 by South Carolina Synod.
Calls: Ascension, Richland, S.C., 1985-90; St. Thomas, Charlotte, 1990-95. In 1999 was in Harrisburg, N.C.
Other: Dean, South Carolina Synod, 1988-90.

VOELKER, LINDA (PROPST)
Date/Place of Birth: February 16, 1946; Hickory, N.C.
Parents: Hal Edwin Propst and Annie (Lail) Propst.
First Spouse/Marriage Date: Dan Allan Hopkins; August 24, 1968.
Children of First Marriage: Camille Denise Hopkins, Cheri Barrett Hopkins.
Second Spouse/Marriage Date: The Reverend Robert Allen Voelker; February 13, 1993.
Education: Appalachian State University, B.S. 1968, M.A. 1970; Lutheran Theological Southern Seminary, M.Div. 1995.

Ordination: May 30, 1997 by North Carolina Synod.
Calls: Co-Pastor, Wittenberg, Granite Quarry, 1997-.
Other: Chaplain, Richland Hospital, Columbia, S.C.; Teacher at Wayne Community College, junior high school in North Carolina, and high school in New Orleans, La.

VOELKER, ROBERT ALLEN

Date/Place of Birth: January 24, 1943; Palmer, Kan.
Parents: Elmer Walter Voelker and Helen Delia (Moddelmog) Voelker.
First Spouse/Marriage Date: Darlene May (Worthy) Voelker; 1965.
Children of First Marriage: Tamara Diane, Cheri Renee, Bethany Anne.
Second Spouse/Marriage Date: The Reverend Linda (Propst) (Hopkins) Voelker; February 13, 1993.
Education: Concordia College (Neb.), B.S. Ed. 1965; Catawba College; Lutheran Theological Southern Seminary, M.Div. 1997; University of Nebraska, M.S. Zoology, 1967; University of Texas, Ph.D. Zoology 1970.
Ordination: May 30, 1997 by North Carolina Synod.
Calls: Co-Pastor, Wittenberg, Granite Quarry, 1997-.
Other: Worked in Research Triangle Park in genetics, molecular biology and evolution.

VOIGT, ANDREW GEORGE

Date/Place of Birth: January 22, 1859; Philadelphia, Pa.
Parents: Andreas George Voigt and Anna K. (Dehnhardt) Voigt.
Spouse/Marriage Date: Clara Mathilda (Eisenhardt) Voigt; January 10, 1884 at Philadelphia, Pa.
Children: Professor Gilbert Paul, Clara Louise, twins Caroline and Elizabeth (married the Reverend Charles J. Shealy), a daughter dying in infancy.
Education: University of Pennsylvania, A.B. 1880; Philadelphia Seminary, 1883, third year at Erlangen University, Germany.
Honorary degrees: Newberry College, A.M. 1889; Roanoke College, D.D. 1895; Lenoir-Rhyne, L.L.D.
Ordination: 1883 by Ministerium of Pennsylvania.
Calls: St. Paul, Mt. Holly-Zion, Riverside, N.J., 1883-85; St. Paul, Wilmington, 1898-1902; supplied with the Reverend Professor L. G. M. Miller, Holy Trinity, Charlotte, 1916-17 and many others.
Other: Professor of Modern Languages, Newberry College, and Professor of Theology, Lutheran Theological Southern Seminary, 1885-89, 1891-98; Professor and acting President, Thiel College, 1889-91; Dean (President) and professor (Systematic Theology), Lutheran Theological Southern Seminary, 1903-32; President, United Synod South, 1906-10, 1924-26; Commission on Adjudication, United Lutheran Church in America, 1918-33, except for two years; Commission on Organizing of Lutheran World Convention (now Federation); published *Why We are Lutherans,* and other pamphlets; also Biblical Dogmatics: *Between God and Man,* based on his seminary course; contributed to *The Lutheran Commentary* and *The Lutheran Cyclopedia,* and edited *The Lutheran Church Visitor* a few years, while at Newberry, S.C.
Date of Death/Burial Location: January 2, 1933; Elmwood Cemetery, Columbia, S.C.

VOGEN, NORMAN PAUL

Date/Place of Birth: November 7, 1928; Newark, Ill.
Parents: Peter Vogen and Grace Thomasine (Nelson) Vogen.
Spouse/Marriage Date: Joann Mae (Oppelt) Vogen; June 28, 1952.
Children: Krista Louise Knight, Karen Ruth Gayle, Sonja Marie Baertsch, Eric Lloyd.
Education: University of Illinois, B.S. 1950; Luther Seminary, M.Div. 1954.
Ordination: June 20, 1954 by ELC, Eastern District.
Calls: East Side, Sioux Falls, S.D., 1954-57; Our Savior, Stoughton, Wis., 1957-62; Calvary, Beloit, Wis., 1962-72; Christ the King, Delafield, Wis., 1972-81; South Miami, Miami, Fla., 1981-94; retired May 31, 1994 to Mooresville; Vice Pastor at various congregations. Interim Pastor, St. Thomas, St. Mark's, A Mighty Fortress, Charlotte.
Date of Death/Burial Location: September 7, 1997; Helmar Lutheran Cemetery, Helmar, Ill.

WADE, PEYTON J.

Date/Place of Birth: August 26, 1847; Floyd County, Va.
Parents: Owen Wade and Levinia (Pflieger) Wade.
Spouse/Marriage Date: Susanah P. (Hylton) Wade; December 26, 1876 in Willis, Va.
Children: Edward W., the Reverend William A., Lena E.
Education: Poor health prevented his preparing for ministry at Roanoke College; first a merchant; later studied theology under his pastor.
License/Ordination: Licensed 1889 by Southwest Virginia Synod and ordained 1891 by Virginia Synod.
Calls: In West Virginia and Virginia, 1891-98; Pilgrim-St. Luke, Davidson County-Cherry Hill, Davie County, 1898-1905; Frederick, Md., 1905-17; retired in 1917.
Date of Death/Burial Location: September 13, 1925; Mt. Olivet Cemetery, Frederick, Md.

WAGNER, JAMES M.

Ordination: Ordained Deacon 1844 by Tennessee Synod and Pastor in 1847.
Calls: Mt. Moriah, Rowan County, 1848; Beck's-Pilgrim, Davidson County, 1854-60; New Jerusalem (first pastor, from 1856), Davidson County, 1856-60.
Other: One of organizers of Holston Synod, 1860-61; Sinking Springs, Greene County, Tenn., 1870-77; listed in its minutes at following places in Tennessee: Millwood, Knoxville, Telford, Midway, Madisonville, and Troutman (last time in 1890); taught at Hiwassee College, Mosheim Institute, and other institutions; Treasurer, Tennessee Synod, 1854, 1856, 1858; Secretary, 1857. President, Holston Synodical College, 1877-1882.
Died: 1890.

WAGSCHAL, FRANCIS KIRKEGAARD

Date/Place of Birth: March 18, 1919; Stone Arabia, N.Y.
Parents: The Reverend Louis F. Wagschal and Agnes Marie (Kirkegaard) Wagschal.
Spouse/Marriage Date: Edna Belle (Weygandt) Wagschal; June 1, 1944 in Uniontown, Ohio.
Children: Karen Marie Montaperto, Paul Frederick, Mark Edward, Linda Elizabeth Frado.
Education: Wittenberg University, B.A. 1941; Philadelphia Seminary, M.Div. 1944; graduate work at Chicago Seminary, 1949-52; Hartwick College, D.D. 1968.

Ordination: June 7, 1944 by New York Synod.
Calls: Zion, Oldwick, N.J., 1944-47; St. Mark, Middleburgh, N.Y., 1947-55; Messiah, Lewiston, N.Y., 1955- 59; Executive Director of Lutheran Student Foundation and Lutheran Counselor at Columbia University, New York City, N.Y., 1959-63; Chaplain, Waterloo Lutheran University, Waterloo, Ontario, Canada, 1963-66; Redeemer, Scarsdale, N.Y., 1966-74; Resurrection, St. Albans, N.Y., 1974-77; Director of Faith and Life Institute, Lutheran Church in America/Division for Mission in North America/Church in Society, New York City, N.Y., 1977-87; retired, 1987; transferred to North Carolina Synod in 1991.

WALCHER, DANIEL
License: Licensed 1816 by North Carolina Synod, but not ordained.
Calls: Beck's-Pilgrim-St. Luke, Davidson County, 1817-21.
Other: Name removed from the clerical roll in 1823.

WALCK, CLARENCE GEORGE, JR.
Date/Place of Birth: March 3, 1936; Eckley, Pa.
Parents: Clarence George Walck, Sr. and Auvilla Fern (Whitebread) Walck.
Spouse/Marriage Date: Dorothy Louise (Arnold) Walck, daughter of the Reverend Dr. Paul Elmer Arnold); August 21, 1960 in West Palm Beach, Fla.
Children: Charlotte Louise Anspach, Clarence George, III.
Education: Lenoir-Rhyne, B.A. 1962; University of South Carolina, M.Ed./Counseling 1974, advanced doctoral courses; Lutheran Theological Southern Seminary, M.Div. 1965; University of North Carolina at Charlotte, courses in advanced counseling.
Ordination: May 26, 1965 by Florida Synod.
Calls: Bethlehem, Hallandale, Fla., 1965-68; Holy Trinity, Somerset, Pa., 1968-69; St. Philip, Newberry, S.C., 1969-78; Concordia, China Grove, 1979-89; St. Martin, Albemarle, 1989-; Vice Pastor at various congregations; retired to New London, N.C.
Other: Board, Camping Ministry for Florida, Pennsylvania, North Carolina and South Carolina Synod; started church senior citizen center in North Carolina, South Carolina, Florida, Pennsylvania; Boy Scout Adult Leader, 1956-; started learning centers in South Carolina (2), Pennsylvania, and North Carolina; started full scout programs in Washington State, Florida, Pennsylvania, South Carolina, North Carolina (2).

WALES, DIANNE MARIE
Date/Place of Birth: May 1, 1945; Los Angeles, Calif.
Parents: James Wales and Donna Marie (Rhode) Wales.
Education: Wheaton College; California State, San Jose, Calif., B.A. Math 1976; Gettysburg Seminary, M.Div. 1984.
Ordination: May 24, 1985 by Maryland Synod.
Calls: Chaplain, U.S. Army, Ft. Bragg, 1984-89, Germany, 1989-. Was in Fayetteville, N.C. in 1998.

WALKER, JAMES ERNEST

Date/Place of Birth: February 14, 1902; Cabarrus County, N.C.
Parents: John Davis Walker and Minnie R. (Faggart) Walker.
Spouse/Marriage Date: Frances Margaret (Aderholdt) Walker; October 28, 1930 in Hildebran, N.C.
Children: Dorothy Aderholdt Smith, Martha Louise Erwin, William Davis.
Education: Mount Pleasant Collegiate Institute, 1923, Lenoir-Rhyne, A.B. 1925; Lutheran Theological Southern Seminary, B.D. 1929; graduate study, University of South Carolina, 1927-28.
Ordination: May 29, 1929 by North Carolina Synod.
Calls: Assistant Pastor, Messiah, Philadelphia, Pa., 1920-30; St. Martin, Cabarrus County and St. Martin, Stanly County, 1930-35; St. James-Immanuel, Rockwell, 1935-42; St. Martin-Salem-Luther Chapel, Maiden, 1942-47, St. Martin alone, 1947-51; Grace, Rowan County, 1951-67; Vice Pastor at various congregations.
Other: President, Western Conference of North Carolina Synod, 1954.
Date of Death/Burial Location: January 27, 1987; St. John Church Cemetery, Concord, N.C.

WALKER, ROBERT GLENN, JR.

Date/Place of Birth: June 25, 1929; Norfolk, Va.
Parents: Robert Glenn Walker, Sr. and Randi Lillian (Mathisen) Walker Comer.
Spouse/Marriage Date: Cecelia Mary (Cone) Walker; June 23, 1951 in Raleigh, N.C.
Children: Kathryn Marie Chatfield, Victoria Elizabeth.
Education: Lenoir-Rhyne, A.B. 1951, D.D. 1985; Chicago Seminary, B.D. 1954; Florida State University, M.S. 1964, and additional graduate work.
Ordination: May 19, 1954 by Illinois Synod.
Calls: Mission Developer/Pastor, Christ, St. Petersburg, Fla., 1954-57; Mission Developer/Pastor, St. Stephen, Tallahassee, Fla., 1957-61; Chaplain, Lenoir-Rhyne, 1961-66; National Lutheran Campus Ministry, Southern Region Director, 1966-93; Church of Good Shepherd, Galax, Va., 1993-; retired in 1993.
Other: *Hacawa*, Lenoir-Rhyne, dedicated to him in 1965; National Council on Family Relations; National Association of College and University Chaplains; College and University Work Committee, 1962-66; Church Vocations Committee, 1962-71; Board, Lutheran Theological Southern Seminary, 1969-72, Chair 1986-98; Candidacy Committee.

WALLACE, GERALD PATRICK

Date/Place of Birth: April 19, 1946; Concord, N.C.
Parents: Bryce Fleetwood Wallace and Myrtle M. (Austin) Wallace. Brother of the Reverend Ralph J. Wallace.
Spouse/Marriage Date: Nancy (Caughman) Wallace; August 22, 1970 in West Columbia, S.C.
Children: Kerri Elaine, Brett Patrick.
Education: Lenoir-Rhyne, B.A. 1968; Lutheran Theological Southern Seminary, M.Div. 1972.

Ordination: June 4, 1972 by North Carolina Synod.
Calls: Holy Cross, Mocksville, 1972-74; Ascension, Shelby, 1974-78; St. Mark's, Mooresville, 1978-85; Our Saviour, Southern Pines, 1985-87; Our Saviour, West Columbia, S.C., 1987-.

WALLACE, RALPH JUSTIN

Date/Place of Birth: October 12, 1935; Greensboro, N.C.
Parents: Bryce Fleetwood Wallace and Myrtle Margie (Austin) Wallace. Brother of the Reverend Gerald Patrick Wallace.
Spouse/Marriage Date: Sarah Frances (Huddle) Wallace, daughter of the Reverend K. Y. Huddle; June 7, 1958 in Newton, N.C.
Children: Leslie Carol, Christopher Alan.
Education: Lenoir-Rhyne, A.B. 1958; Lutheran Theological Southern Seminary, M.Div. 1961; Newberry College, D.D. 1989.
Ordination: June 11, 1961 by North Carolina Synod.
Calls: Ascension, Wilson, 1961-64; St. Paul, Hamlet, 1964-67; Emmanuel, Lincolnton, 1967-72; Macedonia, Burlington, 1972-77; St. Paul, Columbia, S.C., 1977-91; Faith, Knoxville, Tenn., 1991-; Vice Pastor at various congregations.
Other: Represented the Lutheran Church in America on *The Protestant Hour*, 1975; one of the first Pastor/Evangelists of Lutheran Church in America; Chaplain for North Carolina and South Carolina Synod Assemblies; Delegate to Lutheran Church in America Convention in Boston; contributor to *The Human Chain of Divine Grace* and author of *What Does He Mean by "A Little While"?*; Parish Education, 1962-63; Sub-Committee on *The Lutheran*, 1964-67, 1968; Publications and Publicity Committee, 1968-71; Nominating Committee, 1963; Evangelism Committee, 1967.

WALLACE, WILLIAM EDWARDS

Date/Place of Birth: May 22, 1951; Salisbury, Rowan County, N.C.
Parents: William McKinley Wallace, Jr. and Lucy (French) Wallace.
Spouse/Marriage Date: France Burns (Edwards) Wallace; December 27, 1970 in Ansonville, N.C.
Children: Jennifer Ann.
Education: Appalachian State University, Lenoir-Rhyne, B.A. 1975; Lutheran Theological Southern Seminary, M.Div. 1980; graduate work at Yale University, 1975.
Ordination: May 25, 1980 by North Carolina Synod.
Calls: Associate Pastor, St. Paul, Savannah, Ga., 1980-81; Our Saviour, Southern Pines, 1981-84; transferred to Georgia Synod in 1984.
Other: Resigned in 1990 in Waltham, Mass.

WALTHER, MARTIN

Date/Place of Birth: Powell's Fort, east of Woodstock, Va.
License/Ordination: First licensed 1815 by Ministerium of Pennsylvania, to serve as catechist under his former teacher, the Reverend Paul Henkel. Licensed 1817 by North Carolina Synod and ordained 1821 in Low's Church, Guilford County, N.C.

Calls: Botetourt, Montgomery, and Shenandoah Counties, Va., among them St. Jacob, Fincastle; Zion, Burkes Fork; St. David. Transferred to Virginia Synod, 1829.
Date of Death/Burial Location: October 30, 1834; Virginia.

WANG, SHOU SHAN
See Wang, Yung Sheng

WANG, YUNG SHENG (May also be known as Wang, Shou Shau)
Place of Birth: Tsimo, Shantung, China.
Ordination: Was approved in 1937 by North Carolina Synod for ordination by the Reverend L. Grady Cooper, after Dr. Cooper's return to China following furlough.
Calls: Name first appeared in synod's roll of pastors in 1939. Served several years in TsangKou, suburb of Tsingtao.
Other: In 1954-62, lived in Tsimo, China. In 1974 was forced to leave TsangKou and return to his old home, Chou Chang. Pastor Douglas E. Erickson writes: "There his relatives kept him and he engaged in such agricultural work as he was able until his death."
Date of Death: 1976.

WANNEMACHER, JOHN HENRY
Date/Place of Birth: April 10, 1866; Carrollton, Ohio.
Parents: Ulrich Wannemacher and Anna Margarethe (Grieser) Wannemacher.
Spouse/Marriage Date: Lula Geneva (Yoder) Wannemacher; 1894 in Hickory, N.C.
Children: Margaret (mother of the Reverend Harold G. Deal, Jr.), Catherine, Ernest.
Education: Capital University, A.B. 1890; St. Paul Seminary, Hickory, 1894.
Ordination: Ordained 1894 by Joint Synod of Ohio.
Calls: Ebenezer (preceded St. Paul, Crouse)-Luther's Chapel, Lincoln County-Bethel, Gaston County, 1895- 1899, St. Martin-Salem-Luther Chapel, Maiden, 1914-17; Supply, Sardis, Catawba County, 1915; St. Mary-Solomon, Forestville, Va., 1917-25; St. Paul, Crouse, 1894-96; Newburg, W.Va., 1897-98; Churches of Joint Synod in Kansas, and of General Council in Ohio and Pennsylvania, 1900-11; transferred 1911 to Tennessee Synod from Pittsburgh Synod; Holy Trinity, Hickory, 1911-15; with the Reverend R. S. Patterson, supplied services at Hendersonville, 1914-15.
Other: Professor, St. Paul Seminary, Hickory, 1898-1900; First Joint Commission (North Carolina and Tennessee Synods) to Consider Proposition to Unite all Lutherans in North Carolina, 1914-15; Editor and Business Manager, *The Catawba Lutheran*, 1913-15.
Date of Death/Burial Location: March 18, 1915; Hickory, N.C.

WARD, MICHAEL ROBERT
Date/Place of Birth: February 25, 1971; Philadelphia, Pa.
Parents: Thomas Ward and Harriet Ward.
Spouse/Marriage Date: Hannah (Fye) Ward; June 19, 1993.
Education: Appalachian State University, B.S. Business Administration, 1993; Trinity Seminary, M.Div. 1997.
Ordination: May 30, 1997 by North Carolina Synod.
Calls: St. Mark's, Charlotte, 1997-.
Other: Program Director, Camp Lutherock, 1993-94.

WARREN, CARL WAYNE

Date/Place of Birth: July 4, 1941; Hickory, N.C.
Parents: Carl Wesley Warren and Annie Lee (Sipe) Warren.
Spouse/Marriage Date: Myra Gertrude (Seitz) Warren; August 9, 1964 in Newton, N.C.
Children: Carveth Wesley.
Education: Lenoir-Rhyne, B.D. 1963; Lutheran Theological Southern Seminary, M.Div. 1967.
Ordination: June 4, 1967 by North Carolina Synod.
Calls: Jerusalem, Rincon, Ga., 1967-69; Associate Pastor, St. Mark's, Charlotte, 1969-74; St. Timothy, Forest Park, Ga., 1974-92; St. James, Brunswick, Ga., 1992-94; Prince of Peace, Fernandina Beach, Fla., 1994-.
Other: Youth Ministry Committee, 1968-69; Social Ministry Committee, 1968-69.

WASA, TSUNENARI

Place of Birth/Education: June 10, 1852; no specific data are available as to his education, and other facts of his life and ministry.
Ordination: Was a Buddhist priest before conversion to Christianity. Instructed by the Reverend J. B. Hail of the Cumberland Presbyterian Mission and was baptized May 7, 1882. Studied theology under the Reverend R. B. Perry. Ordained March 10, 1918 at Kurume, Japan, by order of Tennessee Synod.
Calls: Evangelist in Lutheran Church in 1897; Saga City and in Saga Prefecture, where in 1892, the Reverends R. B. Peery and J. A. B. Scherer began United Synod South mission work in Japan; Hida; Nogara, Ogi. Retired March 1930.
Date of Death: October 11, 1937.

WAUGH, E. FRANKLIN

Date/Place of Birth: March 23, 1959; Buncombe County, N.C.
Parents: Edward G. Waugh and Carol C. (Jarvis) Waugh.
Spouse/Marriage Date: Jill (Alsop) Waugh; August 25, 1984 in Columbia, S.C.
Children: John Franklin, Mark Taylor.
Education: University of North Carolina at Chapel Hill, B.S. 1981; Lutheran Theological Southern Seminary, M.Div. 1987.
Ordination: July 26, 1987 by North Carolina Synod.
Calls: Reformation, Taylorsville, 1987-92; St. John, Highland, Pa., 1992-.

WEANT, GARY ALAN

Date/Place of Birth: August 10, 1950; Rowan County, N.C.
Parents: Harvey Arthur Weant and Margaret (Stirewalt) Weant.
Spouse/Marriage Date: Linda Marie (Morgan) Weant; July 2, 1972 in Salisbury, N.C.
Children: Rebekah Marie, Jonathan Alan.
Education: Lenoir-Rhyne, A.B. 1972; Lutheran Theological Southern Seminary, M.Div. *cum laude* 1976.
Ordination: May 31, 1976 by North Carolina Synod.
Calls: Philadelphia, Dallas, 1976-; Vice Pastor at various congregations.
Other: Task Force on ministry with the handicapped, 1977-78; Educational Ministry Resource Team, 1977- 81; Chair, Religious Inventory Task Force in Gaston County, 1979-

80; Co-author, *A Study of Religion in Gaston County;* Professional Preparations Committee, 1978-84; President, Lutheran Support Group of Gaston, Inc., 1983-85; Adjunct Chaplain, Gaston Memorial Hospital, 1981-; area Lutheran Coordinator for Gaston County recycling projects for World Hunger, 1981; assisted in resettling Hmong-Laotion refugee families and Viet Namese-Laotian families; Gaston County Community Based Alternative Task Force, 1982; Charter Member, Dallas Area Yokefellow Prison Ministry, 1982-; Chair, North Carolina Synod Task Force on Peace, 1983-; Coordinator, "Listening to the People Conference," 1983-; Moderator, Peace Symposium, 1985; Board, Lenoir-Rhyne, 1984; Vice President, Dallas Ministerial Association, 1986-; President, Greater Gastonia Ministerial Association, 1987-; Stewardship Task Force, 1994-; Co-convener of The Theological Work Group and co-editor of *Seeking Common Ground for the Good of All: A Biblical and Theological Critique of Issues Regarding Public Education in a Pluralistic Democracy,* 1994; Conference Dean, 1976-89; Gaston County Children's Council, 1988-91; Chair, Social Ministry Committee, 1990-93; Advisory Committee, Chaplain's and Pastoral Care Departments, Gaston Memorial Hospital, 1991-; Family Advocate of the Year Award, 1993.

WEANT, WILLIE BAXTER

Date/Place of Birth: December 17, 1918; Rowan County, N.C.
Parents: Andrew Manco Weant and Lou Rejina (Hodge) Weant.
Spouse/Marriage Date: Frances Engenia (Wilhelm) Weant; October 3, 1944 in Rowan County, N.C.
Education: Pfeiffer Junior College, 1940; Lenoir-Rhyne, A.B. 1946; Lutheran Theological Southern Seminary, B.D. 1949; Newberry College, D.D. 1963.
Ordination: June 5, 1949 by North Carolina Synod.
Calls: Union, Rowan County, 1949-50; St. Mark, Coral Gables, Fla., 1950-59.
Other: U.S. Army Air Force, bomber pilot three years and eight months, in World War II; Vice President, Florida Synod, 1954-60; Mission Superintendent, Florida Synod 1960-63; Regional Secretary, Lutheran Church in America Board of American Missions for South Carolina, Florida, and Caribbean Synods, 1963-85; Distinguished Service Award, Newberry College.
Date of Death/Burial Location: March 15, 1991; Grace Lutheran Cemetery, Salisbury, N.C.

WEAVER, JOHN FRANKLIN

Date/Place of Birth: February 4, 1935; Hickory, N.C.
Parents: Gordon Jacob Weaver and Pearl (Whitener) Weaver.
Spouse/Marriage Date: Barbara Joan (Aull) Weaver; July 23, 1960 in Beaufort, S.C.
Children: Michael Gordon, Jennifer Joan Walrath.
Education: Lenoir-Rhyne, A.B. 1958; Lutheran Theological Southern Seminary, M.Div. 1961; graduate work at University of Pennsylvania, Boston University and Wake Forest University.
Ordination: June 11, 1961 by North Carolina Synod.
Calls: Sharon, Iredell County, 1961-65; Chaplain, U.S. Navy, 1965-84; retired with rank of Captain, 1984; Summer Memorial, Newberry, S.C., 1984-. Retired at Newberry, S.C.
Other: U.S. Marine Corps service in Korean Conflict, three years.

WEBB, DAVID GLENN

Date/Place of Birth: August 1, 1950; McDowell County, N.C.
Parents: Carl Glenn Webb and Lola Belle (Wiseman) Webb.
Spouse/Marriage Date: Judith (Parkison) Webb; May 27, 1978 in Hickory, N.C.
Children: Asher Glenn, Luke Thomas, Silas Liddell.
Education: Lenoir-Rhyne, B.A. 1972; Lutheran Theological Southern Seminary, M.Div. 1978.
Ordination: June 11, 1978 by North Carolina Synod.
Calls: Bethany, Boone, 1978-84; Ebenezer, China Grove, 1984-87; Shepherd of the Hills, Sylva, 1987-; Vice Pastor at various congregations.
Other: Southern Highland Area Mission Strategy Team, 1984; minister in the National Parks System (Glacier, Mont.), 1975; author: *A Strategy for a Lutheran Witness in the Southern Highlands of North Carolina.*

WEBER, PAUL D.

Spouse/Marriage Date: Florence (Jowers) Weber.
Children: Erin Christine, Jeffrey Michael, Amanda Kate.
Education: Concordia Senior College (Ind.), B.A. Music 1971; Christ Seminary, M.Div./Worship 1975; Washington University, M.Music/Organ and Composition, 1974; Yale University; M.M.A./Composition, 1979; University of Iowa, D.M.A./Choral Conducting 1988.
Ordination: July 29, 1979.
Calls: Holy Trinity, Hermitage, Pa.; Special Call by North Carolina Synod, Co-Chair, Sacred Music Department, Lenoir-Rhyne, 1996-.
Other: CROP Walk; Community Food Warehouse; clergy associations; arts organizations; Little League; Visiting Choral Director, The College of Idaho, 1989; Instructor in Organ/Theory, Concordia College, (N.Y.), 1974.

WEDDINGTON, GUION THOMAS

Date/Place of Birth: October 21, 1925; Faith, N.C.
Parents: Robert Lee Weddington and Geneva Lorraine (Hess) Weddington.
Spouse/Marriage Date: Naomi Hettie (Steinmetz) Weddington, native of Baltimore, Md.; April 17, 1953 in Guntur, India.
Children: Sarah Ruth Smith, Mary Martha Poetker, Raymond Steinmetz.
Education: Lenoir-Rhyne, B.A. 1949; Lutheran Theological Southern Seminary, B.D. 1952, and graduate work.
Ordination: January 11, 1953 by North Carolina Synod.
Calls: While awaiting ordination, supplied Lutheran Chapel, Gastonia, September 1952-January 1953; Lutheran Church in America missionary in India, serving in Andhra Evangelical Lutheran Church, 1952-74; Evangelistic Missionary, Language Study, East Godavari District, Andhra Pradesh, 1953-55; Penumudi and Kuchinapudi Parishes, East Guntur Synod, 1955-58; Evangelistic Missionary, Polavaram and Koyyakannapuram, Special Area of West Godavari Synod, 1959-65; Evangelistic Missionary, Parvatipuram-Saluri, Godavari Synod, 1966-73; Edinburg Parish (Zion-Bethel-St. Jacob) Virginia Synod,

1974- 79; Amity, Cleveland, 1980-85; Reformation, Taylorsville, 1985-87; retired 1987 in Taylorsville, N.C.; Vice pastor at various congregations.

WEDEKIND, RONALD GEORGE

Date/Place of Birth: February 13, 1946; Bronxville, N.Y.
Parents: Fred George Wedekind and Elsa Wedekind.
Spouse/Marriage Date: Karen Sue (Blackman) Wedekind; August 18, 1973 in West Liberty, Iowa.
Children: Jason Patrick, Susan Elizabeth.
Education: Luther College, B.A. 1968; Wartburg Seminary, M.Div. 1974; Pittsburgh Seminary, Th.M. 1980; Clinical Pastoral Education, University of Virginia, 1981.
Ordination: August 4, 1974; Eastern District, American Lutheran Church.
Calls: Peace Evangelical, Greenock, Pa., 1975-80; Chaplain, United Hospital, Grand Forks, N.D., 1981-87; Chaplain, New Hanover Regional Medical Center, Wilmington, 1987-.

WEE, DANIEL MARSDEN

Date/Place of Birth: October 13, 1941; Madison, Wisc.
Parents: Mr. and Mrs. Morris Wee.
Spouse/Marriage Date: Kristin Karen (Borsgard) Wee; May 27, 1966.
Education: St. Olaf College, Northfield, Minn., B. A. 1963; Luther Seminary, St. Paul, Minn., B.D. 1968.
Ordination: September 22, 1968 by American Lutheran Church.
Calls: Grace, Raleigh, 1968-74; Grace, Scarsdale, N.Y., 1974-77; Immanuel, New Rochelle, N.Y., 1974-77; Lord of Life, Waterloo, Iowa, 1977-.

WEEKS, MICHAEL AYERS

Date/Place of Birth: February 8, 1954; Clinton, Sampson County, N.C.
Parents: Bennie Elmond Weeks and Hazel Catherine (Hinson) Weeks.
Spouse/Marriage Date: Carol (Austin) Weeks, August 14, 1976 in Charlotte, N.C.
Children: Carol Elizabeth.
Education: Appalachian State University, B.Mus. 1978; Philadelphia Seminary, M.Div. 1989.
Ordination: June 2, 1989 by North Carolina Synod.
Calls: Good Shepherd, Hickory, 1989-92; Good Shepherd, Charlotte, 1992-97.
Other: Music Director, Director of Christian Education, St. Luke's, Charlotte, 1980-84; American Guild of Organists.
Date of Death/Burial Location: May 25, 1997; Sharon Memorial Park, Charlotte, N.C.

WEEKS, WILLIAM GERALD

Date/Place of Birth: November 12, 1945; Knox County, Tenn.
Parents: William Oscar Weeks and Mildred Grace (Haun) Weeks.
Spouse/Marriage Date: Marian Elizabeth (McCauley) Weeks; August 6, 1967 in Knoxville, Tenn.
Children: Tonja Ashe Eichelberger, Stephanie Elaine Behrens.

Education: Maryville College, B.A. 1967; Gettysburg Seminary, Pa., Yale Divinity School, M.Div. 1971; graduate work at University of North Carolina at Chapel Hill; Princeton Seminary, Th.M. 1986.

Ordination: July 18, 1971 by Southeastern Synod.

Calls: Immanuel, Blountville, Tenn., 1971-75; Our Redeemer, Montgomery, Ala., 1976-78; Resurrection, Kings Mountain, 1978-83; Bethany, Hickory, 1983-85; Trinity, Hixson, Tenn., 1988-90; First, Topeka, Kan., 1990-96; St. Paul, Hampton, Va., 1996-.

Other: Dean, Central States Synod; Social Ministry Unit, Southeastern Synod; Justice and Social Change Committee, North Carolina Synod; Social Ministry Consulting Team; North Carolina Lutheran Homes Capital Funds Consultation Team; Youth Ministry Committee; President, Catawba Valley Lutheran Ministers' Association; Lutheridge Program Committee; Lutheran Outdoors Ministries Capital Funds Consultation Team; Secretary, Alabama-Mississippi District, Southeastern Synod; Social Ministry Committee, Southeastern Synod; Lutheran Church in America Task Force for Minority Ministry in Alabama; World Missions Committee, Southeastern Synod; Parish Education Committee, Chair, Southeastern Synod; Parish Education Consultant, Southeastern Synod; Convention Committee, 1977, Southeastern Synod; Secretary, Tennessee Valley District, Southeastern Synod; Board, The Community Kitchen, Chattanooga, Tenn.; Board, Lutherhaus, Hickory; Cooperative Christian Ministry, Hickory; Catawba County Ministerial Association, Hickory; President and Vice President, Kings Mountain Ministerial Association; Board, Little Theater, Kings Mountain; Rotary Club, Kings Mountain; Board, Food Bank, Kings Mountain; Board of Directors, IMPACT of Alabama; Montgomery Ministerial Alliance, Montgomery, Ala.; Central Heights Ruritan, Blountville, Tenn.; President, Vice President and Treasurer, Blountville Ministerial Association, Tennessee; Kingsport Ministerial Association, Kingsport, Tenn.

WEEKS, ROBERT MARTIN

Date/Place of Birth: January 5, 1935; Columbia, S.C.

Parents: The Reverend Thomas H. Weeks and Pauline (Martin) Weeks.

Spouse/Marriage Date: Sylvia (Metz) Weeks; August 21, 1958 in Mt. Tabor, West Columbia, S.C.

Children: Kristi Lynn Wade, Tanya Marie.

Education: Roanoke College, Newberry College, B.S. 1957; Lutheran Theological Southern Seminary, M.Div. 1960; Princeton Seminary, Th.M. 1977.

Ordination: May 22, 1960 by South Carolina Synod.

Calls: St. Michael, Columbia, S.C., 1960-64; St. James, Sumter, S.C., 1964-66; Chaplain, U.S. Navy, 1966-92, joining North Carolina Synod in 1985; retired 1992 in New Orleans, La.

WEINBACH, JOHN PHILIP

Date/Place of Birth: March 20, 1938; Buffalo, N.Y.

Parents: William Weinbach and Lydia Weinbach.

Spouse/Marriage Date: Rhoda Marie (Schroder) Weinbach; August 17, 1963.

Children: Joel, Chris, Andrew, Paula.

Education: State University of New York at Buffalo, Concordia College (N.Y.), Concordia Senior College (Ind.), B.A. 1960; Concordia Seminary (Mo.), M.Div. 1964.

Ordination: June 1964 by The Lutheran Church-Missouri Synod.

Calls: Good Shepherd, Lansing, Mich., 1964-67; Prince of Peace, Virginia Beach, Va., 1968-74; St. Luke, Croydon, Pa., 1976-78; Lutheran Social Ministries of New Jersey, Evangelical Lutheran Church in America, 1988-94; Abiding Presence, Fuquay-Varina, 1994-.

WEINELT, RONALD HENRY

Date/Place of Birth: March 6, 1933; Baltimore, Md.
Parents: John Henry Weinelt and Martha H. (Meyn) Weinelt.
Spouse/Marriage Date: Patricia Dorothy (Riley) Weinelt; June 11, 1955 in Lansdowne, Md.
Children: Kurt Martin, Erik Luther.
Education: Gettysburg College, B.A. 1955; Gettysburg Seminary, M.Div. 1958.
Ordination: May 28, 1958 by Maryland Synod.
Calls: Mission Developer/Pastor, Christ, Lexington Park, Md., 1958-61; Gloria Dei, Salisbury, 1961-63; Kure Memorial, Kure Beach, 1963-70; Redeemer, Houston, Texas, 1970-76; Bethany, Memphis, Tenn., 1976-81; Living Word, Jonesboro, Ga., 1981-89; St. John, Rincon, Ga., 1991-94; Advent, Doraville, Ga., 1994-.
Other: Parish Education, 1962-63; Camp Committee, Chair, North Carolina Synod, 1963-69; Worship Committee, Southeastern Synod, Chair, six years; Chair, Lutheran Ministries of Georgia Task Force on Clinical Health; Clinical Coordinator of LMG Counseling Service; Founder, Association of Battered Clergy; Charter Medical, Addiction Counselor, 1989-90; Parkside Recovery Place, Addiction Counselor, Atlanta, Ga., 1990; retired 1995 in Baltimore, Md.

WEISNER, ANDREW FRANKLIN

Date/Place of Birth: April 22, 1957; Winston-Salem, N.C.
Parents: William Franklin Weisner and Mildred (Mahaffey) Weisner.
Spouse: Claudia Patricia (Earle) Weisner.
Children: Step-daughter Amanda Juilliet Lemons Earle.
Education: Lenoir-Rhyne, A.B. Philosophy 1979; Gettysburg Seminary, M.Div. 1983; Chicago Seminary, Th.M. 1991, A.B.D. 1994; graduate work at Catholic University of America, Washington Theological Union, Catholic Theological Union in Chicago, University of Chicago.
Ordination: November 7, 1983 by North Carolina Synod.
Calls: Resurrection, Greensboro, 1983-89; Interim pastor at various congregations; Chaplain-College Pastor, Lenoir-Rhyne, 1995-.
Other: Published Book Reviews in *Lutheran Partners, Currents in Theology and Mission, Anglican and Episcopal History;* articles in *Gettysburg Seminary Bulletin, Soli Deo Gloria.*

WENDT, MICHAEL D.

Date/Place of Birth: November 15, 1940; Kansas City, Mo.
Parents: Bernard H. Wendt and Kordula M. Wendt.
Spouse/Marriage Date: Lucinda D. Wendt; December 11, 1971 in Jacksonville, Fla.
Children: Keri D., Joy D., Holly D., Benjamin M. M.
Education: St. Paul Junior College, A.A. 1961; Concordia Senior College, B.A. 1963; Concordia Seminary, M.Div. 1967.

Ordination: September 10, 1967; Western District - The Lutheran Church-Missouri Synod. *Calls*: Lutheran Metropolitan Ministry, Jacksonville, Fla., 1967-75; Abiding Savior, Durham, 1975-89; The Dispute Settlement Center of Durham, 1983-98.

WERTZ, JOHN ELBERT, SR.

Date/Place of Birth: March 30, 1944; Pulaski, Va.
Parents: The Reverend Lester A. Wertz, Sr., D.D. and Mary Sara (Anderson) Wertz. A brother of the Reverend Lester A. Wertz, Jr.
Spouse/Marriage Date: Nancy Lucile (Caldwell) Wertz; December 23, 1967 in Aiken, S.C.
Children: John Elbert, Jr., Robert Allen, Mary Jo.
Education: University of South Carolina, A.B. 1966; Lutheran Theological Southern Seminary, M.Div. 1971; graduate work at Auburn University.
Ordination: June 6, 1971 by South Carolina Synod.
Calls: St. Michael, Moncks Corner, S.C., 1971-77; Christ's, Stanley, 1977-83; transferred to Illinois Synod, 1984. In 1998 was serving St. Paul, Aiken, S.C.
Other: South Carolina Synod - Publicity Committee, Media Coordinator for Evangelical Outreach, Editor, Synod Convention Newsletter, Parish Education Committee, Chair of the Trident Area Title XX Program, Vice Chair of the Area Program on Aging for three years, Human Resources Committee of the Council of Governments; Executive Committee of the Charleston Area Senior Citizens; Planning Committee of the Trident Area United Way, President of the Berkeley County Ministerial Association; *Who's Who in Religion in America*.

WERTZ, JOSEPH QUINCY, SR.

Date/Place of Birth: December 12, 1853; Saluda County, S.C.
Parents: The Reverend J. H. W. Wertz and Caroline (Derrick) Wertz.
Spouse/Marriage Date: Martha Virginia (Houseal) Wertz; 1881 in Newberry, S.C. As widow, became second wife of the Reverend W. A. Lutz.
Children: Lillian Elizabeth, Joseph Quincy, Jr., Viola Mayer, Augustus Houseal.
Education: Newberry College, A.B. 1877; Lutheran Theological Southern Seminary, 1881.
Ordination: 1881 by South Carolina Synod.
Calls: Salem-St. Mark, Lexington County, St. Stephen, Lexington, and Pine Grove, St. Matthew, S.C., 1881- 89; Christiana (1889-94)-Union (1890-93), Rowan County; St. John, (1894-96)-Mt. Olive (1894), Cabarrus County; St. Mark, China Grove, 1896-1902; Center Grove, Kannapolis, 1896-98, 1902-07; Lutheran Chapel, China Grove, 1896-1907.
Date of Death/Burial Location: August 10, 1907; Lutheran Chapel Church, China Grove, N.C.

WESSINGER, BENJAMIN DAVID

Date/Place of Birth: October 24, 1878; near Chapin, S.C.
Parents: David F. Wessinger and Julia C. (Frick) Wessinger. An older brother was the Reverend J. C. Wessinger.
Spouse/Marriage Date: Nancy Virginia (Caughman) Wessinger; November 10, 1903 in Lexington, S.C.
Children: Julia, Elaine, George D., Louise Elizabeth.

Education: Lenoir-Rhyne, A.B. 1899; Philadelphia Seminary, 1903. His widow says he declined D.D. degree.

Ordination: 1903 by Tennessee Synod.

Calls: St. Peter, Newberry County, S.C., 1903-04; Cedar Grove, Lexington County, S.C., 1904-05; St. Paul-St. John-Grace, Lexington County, S.C., 1906-13; St. John's, Cherryville, 1913-23, assisted in organizing Ascension, Shelby, 1923; Grace, Lakeland, Fla., 1924-36. Retired 1936 at Lakeland, Fla. ; at Kure Beach, conducted services in community chapel two summers before organization of Kure Memorial (1951).

Other: President, Tennessee Synod, 1918-21; First President of Florida Synod; Board, Lenoir-Rhyne; Board, Newberry College; Commission to Recommend Conference Borders for the Merged (North Carolina and Tennessee) Synod, 1921; contributed frequently to several church papers.

Date of Death/Burial Location: December 11, 1951; St. Thomas Church near Chapin, S.C.

WESSINGER, BERNICE JUSTUS

Date/Place of Birth: December 22, 1895; Chapin, S.C.

Parents: J. S. Wessinger and Anna (Seay) Wessinger.

Spouse/Marriage Date: Florence Ethel (Beam) Wessinger; October 20, 1920 in Cherryville, N.C.

Children: The Reverend Charles Samuel, Mary Roof.

Education: Lenoir-Rhyne, A.B. 1917; Lutheran Theological Southern Seminary, 1920.

Ordination: 1920 by Tennessee Synod.

Calls: Two (Tennessee Synod) churches at Pelion, S.C., 1920-22; Trinity-Cedar Grove-Sardis, Vale, 1922-26; Haven, Salisbury, 1927-33; Calvary, Spencer-Christ, East Spencer, 1933-44; Bethlehem-New Jerusalem (church rebuilt after fire in 1948), Catawba County, 1944-50; New Jerusalem alone, 1950-58.

Other: Board, Children's Home of the South, Salem, Va., 1937-51; Chair, local weekday religious radio broadcasts while serving in Salisbury and Catawba County.

Date of Death/Burial Location: June 17, 1958; Evergreen Cemetery, Charlotte, N.C.

WESSINGER, CARROLL LEROY

Date/Place of Birth: July 12, 1931; Chapin, S.C.

Parents: Ben L. Wessinger and Zola (Stuck) Wessinger.

Spouse/Marriage Date: Gloria Ann (Smith) Wessinger; June 23, 1956 in Charlotte, N.C.

Children: Mark Haywood, Beth Ann Cochran.

Education: Newberry College, A.B. 1953; Lutheran Theological Southern Seminary, M.Div. 1956; graduate work at Chicago Seminary, 1957, 1959, San Francisco Theological Seminary.

Ordination: June 10, 1956 by South Carolina Synod.

Calls: St. John, Springfield, Ohio, 1956-59; Prince of Peace, Indianapolis, Ind., 1959-64; Nativity, Arden, 1964-70; Division for Mission in North America, Regional Director for Appalachian Region, Virginia Synod, 1970-.

Other: Camp Committee, 1966-70. Retired in Wytheville, Va.

WESSINGER, CHARLES SAMUEL

Date/Place of Birth: September 9, 1921; Pelion, S.C.

Parents: The Reverend Bernice Justus Wessinger and Florence Ethel (Beam) Wessinger.

Spouse/Marriage Date: Alice Elizabeth (Young) Wessinger, sister of the Reverend Jacob H. Young; June 8, 1945 in Charlotte, N.C.

Children: Anna Mary Scott, Elizabeth Ellen Doulgerakis, Samuel Young.

Education: Lenoir-Rhyne, A.B. in languages 1942; Lutheran Theological Southern Seminary, M.Div. 1945; graduate work at Philadelphia Seminary, Medical University of South Carolina; Newberry College, D.D. 1971.

Ordination: April 4, 1945 by North Carolina Synod.

Calls: Mt. Pleasant-Good Hope-Trinity, Saluda County, S.C., 1945-47; Grace, Thomasville, 1947-56; Supply, Silver Valley, Davidson County, 1947-49; St. Andrew's, Charleston, S.C., 1956-76; Peachtree Road, Atlanta, Ga., 1976-83; retired 1983 to Chapin, S.C.; Interim Pastor at various congregations.

Other: Assistant Editor and Editor, *North Carolina Lutheran;* 1955-56; published articles in *The Lutheran* and other United Lutheran Church in America magazines; conducted weekly column on Religion in *The Saluda Standard* and *Thomasville Tribune*. In North Carolina Synod: Chair, Publicity Committee; Parish Education Committee; North Carolina Representative on Lutheran Hour Committee; Chair, Radio and TV Committee. In South Carolina Synod: Executive Board, for three terms; Little Joint Commission on Lutheran Unity Committee; Examining Committee; delegate to three conventions of United Lutheran Church in America and Lutheran Church in America; Chair, Stewardship Committee; Chair, Committee on Publications; Chair, Campus Ministry Committee; Board, Lutheran Theological Southern Seminary; Dean, Southern District; Board, Franke Home. In Southeastern Synod: Dean, Metro Atlanta North District; Finance Committee; Chair, Examining Committee; Board, Newberry College; President, Lions Clubs in Thomasville, N.C. and Charleston, S.C., and Board in Atlanta, Ga. and Columbia, S.C.; Board, Atlanta Council of Churches; Davidson County Board of Public Welfare; Thomasville Recreation Commission; South Carolina State Guard; President, Charleston Area Senior Citizens Board and President, Trident Aging Commission; President, Ministerial Associations in Thomasville and Charleston; Chair, Planning Commission, Town of Chapin; Advisory Committee, Irmo-Chapin Recreation Commission; Advisory Committees, School Boards in Thomasville and Charleston; publications: Histories of Grace Church, Thomasville, N.C.; St. Andrew's, Charleston, S.C.; Mt. Horeb, Chapin, S.C.; Mt. Tabor, West Columbia, S.C.; articles in *Luther Life, The Lutheran, the New Days Word,* and *Lutheran Men.* Jaycee Young Man of the Year; Civitan Club Award; President, delegate to international conventions for Lions Club; Boy Scout Leader; Clergy Advisor to South Carolina Lutheran Men in Mission. Board, Shepherd's Center and Irmo-Chapin Recreation Board.

Date of Death/Burial Location: December 13, 1996; Evergreen Cemetery, Charlotte, N.C.

WESSINGER, ELMORE LAFAYETTE

Date/Place of Birth: January 10, 1870; near Chapin, S.C.

Parents: James Daniel Wessinger and Adaline (Fulmer) Wessinger.

Spouse/Marriage Date: Alice (Hartman) Wessinger; October 10, 1900 in Lancaster, Pa.

Children: Lewis Hartman.

Education: Concordia College, 1888-91; Newberry College, A.B. 1892; Philadelphia Seminary, 1896.

Ordination: 1896 by Ministerium of Pennsylvania.
Calls: St. John, Shiremanstown, Pa., 1896-1903; Tennessee Synod, 1903-08; Emmanuel-Mt. Zion, New Market, Va.; transferred back to Ministerium of Pennsylvania, 1908; Advent, Lancaster, Pa., 1908-28; Zion, Marietta, Pa., 1931-47; retired 1947 at Lancaster, Pa.
Other: President, Tennessee Synod, 1904-05; President, Virginia Conference, Tennessee Synod, 1904-07.
Date of Death/Burial Location: March 20, 1967; Greenwood Cemetery, Lancaster, Pa.

WESSINGER, JACOB CALVIN, SR.

Date/Place of Birth: April 5, 1868; near Chapin, S.C.
Parents: David F. Wessinger and Julia C. (Frick) Wessinger. A younger brother was the Reverend B. D. Wessinger.
Spouse/Marriage Date: Mary Lula (Shealy) Wessinger; December 5, 1895 in Little Mountain, S.C.
Children: Jacob Calvin, Jr., Mary Virginia, Camilla Estelle.
Education: Concordia College, Lenoir-Rhyne, A.B. 1893, Honorary M.A.; Lutheran Theological Southern Seminary, 1904; graduate study, Philadelphia Seminary and University of South Carolina.
Ordination: 1893 by Tennessee Synod.
Calls: Manassas, Va., Parish, 1893-94; Daniel's, 1894-95; Trinity-Bethphage-Cedar Grove-David Chapel, Lincoln County, 1895-1903; Sardis, Catawba County, 1899-1902; Beck's-Lebanon-New Jerusalem, Davidson County, 1904-05; Miller Chapel-Zion-Bethel, Knox County, Tenn., 1903-04; churches of both Tennessee and South Carolina Synods in Newberry and Lexington Counties, S.C., and of Georgia-Alabama Synod in Effingham County, Ga., 1905-30; retired 1930 at Rincon, Ga.
Date of Death/Burial Location: August 21, 1940; Holy Trinity Church, Little Mountain, S.C.

WESSINGER, JOSEPH SAMUEL

Date/Place of Birth: July 30, 1882; near Chapin, S.C.
Parents: J. Austin Wessinger and Eady F. (Shealy) Wessinger.
Spouse/Marriage Date: Jessie Lee (Oxner) Wessinger; May 28, 1911 in West Columbia, S.C.
Children: Retha Elizabeth, Mildred Arlene, Margaret Verl, John Bruce, James Arnold, Junie Erlene, Tommy Joe.
Education: Clemson College, B.S. Agriculture 1908; Lutheran Theological Southern Seminary, 1911.
Ordination: 1911 by Tennessee Synod.
Calls: Toms Brook, Va., 1911-15; Mt. Moriah-St. Mark, Rowan County, 1915-27, St. Mark only, 1940-47; St. Martin, Cabarrus County-St. Martin, Stanly County, 1947-50; Newberry County, S.C., 1927-34; Lexington County, S.C., 1934-40; Mt. Pilgrim-Mt. Tabor, Newberry County, S.C., 1950-61; retired at Newberry, S.C.
Date of Death/Burial Location: July 29, 1978; St. Peter Cemetery, Chapin, S.C.

WESTENBARGER, B. L.

Ordination: Presumably ordained by the Joint Synod of Ohio.

Calls: Bethel, Gaston County-Luther's Chapel, Lincoln County, 1912; Ebenezer (preceded St. Paul) (1902), Crouse, 1891-95; Antioch (about 1882)-St. Paul (1912), Gaston County, 1896-98. Living in retirement in Magnolia, Ohio in 1929.

WETZEL, HENRY

Date/Place of Birth: December 13, 1815; Wythe County, Va.

Parents: George Wetzel and Margaret Wetzel.

Spouse/Marriage Date: Mary Catherine (Staubus) Wetzel; December 5, 1839 in Augusta County, Va.

Children: Francis Jane Victoria, Martin Luther (accepted as student for ministry, died 1865 at age 24), Mary Catherine Hilker (died at age 13), Rebecca Parnelia Ann, Henrietta Virginia, and two daughters, whose names are not known.

Education: Attained proficiency in literature and theology, through diligence in study, as well as in church history and dogmatics.

Ordination and Calls: Ordained Deacon, 1837 and served St. Peter, Rowan County, 1839; ordained 1841 by Tennessee Synod; Tennessee Synod granted permission to pastors of its Virginia Special Conference to organize a synod of their churches. In 1867 at the announced time only three pastors, Henry Wetzel, James E. Seneker, and George Schmucker, attended. They and their lay delegates formed the Concordia Synod, which was too weak to survive long. Ten years later it became the Concordia District of Joint Synod of Ohio. Pastor Wetzel served churches of the three synods in Virginia, including: St. Paul, Augusta County, 1841-61; and for varying periods, from 1842 to 1872, in Rockingham County; organized Bethany (St. Jacob), "Peaked Mountain Church" Trinity, and Phaniel; and from 1861 to 1875 in Shenandoah County, Va.: Zion, St. Matthew, and St. David. Some churches he served after 1867 had followed the three pastors out of Tennessee Synod, and several he had organized out of separating groups. After making pleas over a period of years, he was received back into Tennessee Synod in 1885 at which time he was holding monthly services in Manassas, Va. He also served churches in West Virginia and Baltimore, Md.

Other: President, Virginia Special Conference, Tennessee Synod, 1856; selected as translator into English of the *Epitome* of the *Book of Concord* for publication, and also third volume of *Luther's Church Postil on the Epistles*.

Date of Death/Burial Location: March 3, 1890; Zion Church, near Edinburg, Va.

WHITE, BYRON WILBUR, SR.

Date/Place of Birth: December 26, 1949; Yonkers, N.Y.

Parents: Byron Leo White and Dorothy Rose (Johnston) White.

Spouse/Marriage Date: Deborah Suellen (Stanford) White; June 5, 1971 in Burlington, N.C.

Children: Byron Wilbur, Jr., Betty Rose.

Education: Greensboro College, B.A. Philosophy and Religion 1971; Lutheran Theological Southern Seminary, M.Div. 1975.

Ordination: June 8, 1975 by North Carolina Synod.

Calls: Calvary, Spencer, 1975-79; First, New Port Richey, Fla., 1979-82; Pastor/Developer, Lamb of God, San Carlos Park, Fort Myers, Fla., 1982-94; Faith, Deland, Fla., 1994-.

Other: Chair, Leadership Support Committee, Florida-Bahamas Synod, 1990-93; Dean, Flagler-Volusia Conference, Florida-Bahamas Synod, 1995.

WHITE, JAMES BLAIR

Date/Place of Birth: September 29, 1960; Salisbury, N.C.
Parents: John W. White and Dora Elaine (McSherry) White.
Spouse/Marriage Date: Holley Denise (Henry) White; January 1, 1984 in Cayce, S.C.
Children: Joshua Andrew, Katie Elizabeth.
Education: Wingate College, B.S. 1982; Lutheran Theological Southern Seminary, M.Div. 1986.
Ordination: May 19, 1986 by North Carolina Synod.
Calls: Sardis, Hickory, 1986-90; Concordia, China Grove, 1990-95; Pilgrim, Lexington, 1995-.
Other: Publication: *Bible Survey* with the Reverend James Campbell for first year confirmation students.

WHITE, MUSSER DIVEN

Date/Place of Birth: January 14, 1917; Harrisburg, Pa.
Parents: Musser D. White and Ruth (Lautenschlager) White.
First Spouse/Marriage Date: Grace (Getman) White; 1943.
Children of First Marriage: Robert Musser, John Kenneth, Richard Royce.
Second Spouse/Marriage Date: Iris Elizabeth (Anderson) White; August 8, 1970 in Riverdale, Md.
Children of Second Marriage: Wade Eric, Rebecca Styers.
Education: Gettysburg College, 1936; Gettysburg Seminary, 1939.
Ordination: 1939 by Maryland Synod.
Calls: St. Mark-Incarnation, Washington, D.C., 1939-1948; Mission Developer/Pastor, St. John, Riverdale, Md., 1948-72; Redeemer, Pittsburgh, Pa., 1972-80; Vice Pastor, Christ, Elkin, and Interim Pastor, Nazareth, Rural Hall; retired in 1980.
Other: President, Stewardship Committee, Maryland Synod; Chair, Missions Committee, Maryland Synod; Secretary, National Lutheran Home for Aged.
Date of Death/Burial Location: July 22, 1984; Nazareth Church Cemetery, Rural Hall, N.C.

WHITENER, BOYCE DANIEL, SR.

Date/Place of Birth: July 28, 1934; Catawba County, N.C.
Parents: James Reid Whitener and Maude Hettie (Wike) Whitener.
Spouse/Marriage Date: Joyce Blondelle (Amick) Whitener; September 3, 1960 in White Rock, S.C.
Children: The Reverend Boyce Daniel, Jr., Patti Whitener Arey.
Education: Lenoir-Rhyne, A.B. 1957, D.D. 1993; Lutheran Theological Southern Seminary, B.D. 1960.
Ordination: June 5, 1960 by North Carolina Synod.
Calls: Pastor Developer/Pastor, Holy Cross, Mocksville, 1960-63; Trinity, Vale, 1963-67; Developer/Pastor, Good Shepherd, Florence, Ala., 1967-71; Alamance, Alamance, 1971-76; Bethany, Hickory, 1976-82; Regional Director, Division for Mission in North America for North Carolina and South Carolina, Charlotte, 1982-88; Evangelical Lutheran Church in America Mission Director, Outreach, 1988-97; retired July 1997 to Newton.
Other: Co-Executive Director, North Carolina Lutheran Men in Mission.

WHITESIDE, HOYLE LEE, SR.
Date/Place of Birth: June 25, 1926; Lincolnton, N.C.
Parents: Arnold Lee Whiteside and Ethel (Bumgarner) Whiteside.
Spouse/Marriage Date: Anne (Coffey) Whiteside; June 28, 1950 in Granite Falls, N.C.
Children: Susan Rebekah Martin, Hoyle Lee, Jr.
Education: Lenoir-Rhyne, A.B. 1948; Lutheran Theological Southern Seminary, M.Div. 1950, S.T.M. 1959; graduate work at University of South Carolina, Yale University, and Rutgers University; Elon College, D.D. 1968.
Ordination: June 25, 1950 by North Carolina Synod.
Calls: Bethlehem, Catawba County, 1950-53; Lutheran Chapel, Gastonia, 1953-60; Our Redeemer, Montgomery, Ala., 1960-61; Macedonia, Burlington, 1961-72; St. John, Statesville, 1973-89; retired June 1989 to Statesville, N.C.
Other: He and the Reverend W. Leo Smith were the first two S.T.M. graduates of Lutheran Theological Southern Seminary; thesis subject: "The Doctrine of the Real Presence in the Sacrament of the Altar;" Board, Lutheran Theological Southern Seminary; Board, Lenoir-Rhyne College; North Carolina Synod Council; Delegate to Lutheran Church in America Convention; Chair, Synod Evangelism Committee; Board, North Carolina Lutheran Homes; Chair, Synodical Stewardship Committee; Chair, Professional Leadership Committee; received The Lamb Award - Boy Scouts of America; 1966; served as Contact Pastor for Maxwell Air Force Base and the Air University, Gunter Air Force Base, Elon College, and Mitchell College; Burlington Distinguished Citizenship Award.

WHITLEY, JOY ROBIN
Date/Place of Birth: May 24, 1961; Charlotte, N.C.
Parents: Buford Whitley and Joann Whitley.
Education: Pfeiffer College, B.A. Church Music 1983; Lutheran Theological Southern Seminary, M.Div. 1994.
Ordination: November 5, 1995 by North Carolina Synod.
Calls: Advent, Charlotte to on leave from call.

WHITTECAR, GEORGE RICHARD, SR.
Date/Place of Birth: August 22, 1910; Peabody, Kan.
Parents: Lair J. Whittecar and Ruth J. (White) Whittecar.
Spouse/Marriage Date: Ruth Elizabeth (Livers) Whittecar, daughter of the Reverend Ralph W. Livers, D.D.; June 16, 1936 in Council Bluffs, Iowa.
Children: Ruth Elaine Matkins, Margaret Lair Garrison, Elizabeth Ann Hull, George Richard, Jr.
Education: Midland College, A.B. 1932; Western Seminary, Fremont, Neb., B.D. 1935; graduate study, Tulsa University; Lenoir-Rhyne, D.D. 1963.
License/Ordination: Licensed 1934 and ordained May 1, 1935 by Kansas and Adjacent States Synod.

Calls: Zion, Beloit, Kan., 1934-39; First, Tulsa, Okla., 1939-51; St. James, Concord, 1951-62.

Other: Secretary, Synod of Kansas and Adjacent States, 1941-42; President, 1942-45; Stewardship Secretary, 1948-51; Board of Social Missions, United Lutheran Church in America, 1950-62; Department for Evangelism, 1955-60; Department of Christian Life and Mission, 1969-72; Board of Social Ministry, Lutheran Church in America, 1950-64; Lutheran Church in America Board of American Missions, 1966-72; Delegate to six United Lutheran Church in America conventions, 1938-58, and ex-officio to Lutheran Church in America conventions as North Carolina Synod President; President, Tulsa Council of Churches 1941-42; accredited visitor from United Lutheran Church in America to Second Assembly, World Council of Churches, Evanston, Ill., 1954; Vice President, North Carolina Council of Churches, 1961-65; President, 1963-65; Board, Lenoir-Rhyne, 1978-94; first President, North Carolina Synod of Lutheran Church in America, 1962-78, with the title changing from President to Bishop in 1980; Director, Conference and Camping Ministries Appeal, 1981-83; retired 1978.

Date of Death/Burial Location: August 4, 1984; St. John Cemetery, Concord, N.C.

WICK, LAWRENCE W.

Date/Place of Birth: August 12, 1939; Sterling, Ill.
Parents: Maurice L. Wick and Alice C. (Johannsen) Wick.
Spouse/Marriage Date: Sherill A. (Carlson) Wick June 18, 1969 in Rockford, Ill.
Children: Anders Christopher, Annika Christina.
Education: Wartburg College, B.A. 1961; Chicago Seminary, M.Div. 1966; Institute of Pastoral Care, Elgin, Ill., Certified 1965; Purdue University, M.S. 1973; Chicago Seminary, D.Min. 1976; graduate work at Seabury- Western Theological Seminary, Princeton University and Oxford University in Oxford, England.
Ordination: May 25, 1966; Illinois Synod.
Calls: Grace, Richmond, Ill., 1966-70; House of Prayer, Country Club Hills, Ill., 1970-74; Wilmette, Wilmette, Ill., 1974-84; St. Mark's, Charlotte, 1984-86; Kountze Memorial, Omaha, Neb., 1984-. In 1998 serving Grace, Woodstock, Ill.
Other: Who's Who in Religion, 1977, 1985; various articles and sermons published; Governor's Commission on Mental Health; Board, Rotary International; Boy Scouts of America Area Council Treasurer; Salvation Army Service Unit Treasurer; Wilmette Public Library Board, Secretary, Vice President; Rotary International Scholarship Committee, Foundation Committee and Invocation Committee; Alumni Board, Wartburg College, President; Board, AIDS Interfaith Network Treasurer and Chair; United Way-CHAD Appeal, Division Chair; Omaha Police Department, Chief's Advisory Committee. Illinois Synod: Camping Committee, American Missions Committee, Special Missions Committee, Lutheran Social Services of Illinois Development Committee; Lutheran Research and Planning Council for Illinois; Task Force on Pastoral Compensation, Chair, 1979-84; Lutheran Church in America: Lutheran School of Theology at Chicago Instructor, Lutheran Church in America Foundation Board, Chair, 1981-87, Division for World Missions and Ecumenism, Study Trip to the People's Republic of China; North Carolina Synod: Carolinas Evangelism Conference Planning Committee, Professional Services Committee, Church Management Seminary Presenter. Nebraska Synod: Budget and Finance Committee, Immanuel Hospital Foundation Board, Secretary, Church Management Seminar Presenter, Synod Task Force of Stewardship; Board, Immanuel Hospital, Lutheran Family Services of Nebraska, Co-Chair of Special Fund Appeal;

Evangelical Lutheran Church in America: Evangelical Lutheran Church in America Foundation, Advisory Board, Augustana College, Board of Trustees.

WICKS, EDWIN HAROLD

Date/Place of Birth: February 22, 1953; Orlando, Fla.
Parents: Harold Edwin Wicks and Florence (Weidig) Wicks.
Spouse/Marriage Date: Lucy (McHugh) Wicks; July 12, 1975 in Winter Park, Fla.
Children: Margaret Kathleen, Emily Louise, Sarah Ruth.
Education: University of Central Florida, B.S.B.A. 1976; Lutheran Theological Southern Seminary, M.Div. 1980.
Ordination: May 24, 1981 by South Carolina Synod.
Calls: Ehrhardt Memorial, Ehrhardt, S.C., 1981-82; Prince of Peace, Kinston, 1982-84; Chaplain, U.S. Navy, 1985-93; Interim, St. John, Yutan, Neb., 1993-94; Grace, Walton, Neb., 1994-.

WIKE, JACOB

Date/Place of Birth: January 1, 1867; near Hickory, N.C.
Parents: Miles Wike and Sarah (Setzer) Wike. An older brother was the Reverend Polycarp Cyprian Wike.
Spouse/Marriage Date: Jessie Esther (Frank) Wike; October 11, 1893 in Davidson County, N.C.
Children: Everette P., Ethel L., Keith S., Grady M., Sarah E., Mabel L., Jesse M., Martin L.
Education: Concordia College, A.B. 1890; theology there, also; studied medicine at Davidson Medical College some time between 1897 and 1910; no data as to graduation or practice.
Ordination: 1891 by Tennessee Synod.
Calls: Mt. Pleasant, Watauga County 1890-91 with others supplied, 1898; Beck's-Lebanon-Pilgrim, Davidson County, 1891-93; New Jerusalem, 1892-94, and Holly Grove, 1893-94, Davidson County; Bethlehem, near Irmo, and St. Jacob, near Chapin, S.C.; Sallis, Beth Eden, Forest, and Homewood, Miss., 1910-1918; Wallace, Ind., 1919-22; retired 1923 at Walnut Ridge, Ark., and later at St. Louis, Mo.
Date of Death/Burial Location: April 17, 1958; Walnut Ridge, Ark.

WIKE, POLYCARP CYPRIAN

Date/Place of Birth: September 1, 1858; near Hickory, N.C.
Parents: Miles Wike and Sarah (Setzer) Wike. A younger brother was the Reverend Jacob Wike.
Spouse/Marriage Date: Mary (Ramey) Wike; 1900.
Children: Irene, Luther, Weidner, Gladys.
Education: Lenoir-Rhyne; Chicago Seminary, 1898.
Ordination: 1886 by Tennessee Synod.
Calls: Supplied with the Reverend C. H. Bernheim, Mt. Pleasant, Watauga County, 1883-84, and with the Reverends Jacob Wike and J. L. Cromer, 1898; Toms Brook and New Market, Va., 1886-89, also Maurertown, Va., 1890-; transferred to Chicago Synod, 1899; churches served to 1926 in Indiana, New Jersey, Ontario, Canada and Illinois.

Other: Secretary, 1892, and President, 1895, Tennessee Synod; Financial Secretary, Weidner Institute.
Date of Death/Burial Location: August 4, 1953; Chicago, Ill.

WILHELM, MARK ERIK
Date/Place of Birth: April 26, 1968; Concord, N.C.
Parents: Vaughn A. Wilhelm and Nancy A. Wilhelm.
Spouse/Marriage Date: Julia (Smith) Wilhelm; July 19, 1990.
Education: University of North Carolina at Charlotte, B.A. Psychology, 1990; Lutheran Theological Southern Seminary, M.Div. 1996.
Ordination: May 31, 1996 by North Carolina Synod.
Calls: Church of Our Saviour, Dallas, 1996-.

WILLIAMS, FRANKIE WAYNE
Date/Place of Birth: July 30, 1943; New Bern, N.C.
Parents: Frank B. Williams and Marie B. Williams.
Spouse/Marriage Date: Cecilia (Page) Williams; September 23, 1967.
Children: Kristin Leigh, Kelley Lynne.
Education: Lenoir-Rhyne, B.A. 1965; Lutheran Theological Southern Seminary, M.Div. 1969.
Ordination: June 1, 1969 by North Carolina Synod.
Calls: St. John, Abingdon, Va., 1969-72; Director of Outdoor Ministries, Virginia Synod, 1972-90; Executive Director, Lutheridge-Lutherock Ministries, 1990-93; Executive Director, Sequanota Lutheran Conference Center and Camp, Virginia, District of Columbia and West Virginia Synods, 1993-; supply to various congregations.
Other: Regional Coordinator, Outdoor Ministries, Lutheran Church in America, 1986-87, and Evangelical Lutheran Church in America, 1987-93.

WILLIAMS, GREGORY BRUCE
Date/Place of Birth: December 8, 1957; Manchester, England.
Parents: Harold Bruce Williams and Patricia (Pinson) Williams.
Spouse/Marriage Date: Brenda (Elliott) Williams; June 26, 1982 in Durham, N.C.
Children: Rachel Anne, Elliott Bruce.
Education: Wake Forest University, B.A. Chemistry 1979; Lutheran Theological Southern Seminary, M.Div. 1986.
Ordination: May 30, 1986.
Calls: Shiloh, Hickory, 1986-90; Holy Trinity, Gastonia, 1990-95; Bethany, Hickory, 1995-; Vice Pastor at various congregations.
Other: Director, North Carolina Synod Youth Ministry Committee's Servant Camp with the Differently Abled, 1989-94; organized and participated in Care Team for persons living with AIDS, 1993-95; Youth Ministry Committee, 1988-92; Spiritual Director, Western North Carolina Via de Cristo, 1989-91; Spiritual Director, Hand-in-Hand Teens Encounter Christ; Pastoral Advisor, Synod Lutheran Men in Mission, 1989-90.

WILSON, JAMES HERBERT

Date/Place of Birth: April 16, 1854; Williamston, S.C.
Parents: Parents, who died when he was three years old, were Delany L. Wilson and Hannah (Barrett) Wilson.
Spouse/Marriage Date: Mary Elizabeth (Dunlop) Wilson; August 1879 in Salem, Va.
Children: Lawrence Livingstone, Mary Salome, Hannah Barrett, Roberta Pauline, Robert Dunlop.
Education: Newberry College, A.B. 1877, honorary A.M. 1880, D.D. 1905; Lutheran Theological Southern Seminary, 1880.
Ordination: 1880 by South Carolina Synod.
Calls: In South Carolina, 1880-1903; St. James, Graniteville, Prospect and Early Branch, 1881-1883; Mt. Lebanon and St. Matthew, Cameron, 1883-1888; Mt. Pleasant, Ehrhardt and St. Nicholas, Fairfax, 1888-1902. St. John, Salisbury, 1903-06; Ascension, Savannah, Ga., 1907-10; Orangeburg and Sumter, S.C., 1911-1919.
Other: President, South Carolina Synod, 1889-91, 1898-99; Board, Newberry College; President, Board of Lutheran Theological Southern Seminary; Financial Agent, Children's Home of the South, Salem, Va., 1907-08; Financial Agent, Marion College.
Date of Death/Burial Location: July 17, 1919; Mt. Pleasant Church, near Ehrhardt, S.C.

WINGARD, EMANUEL ALBERT

Date/Place of Birth: July 29, 1849; Lexington County, S.C.
Parent: Mother was Elizabeth (Muller) Wingard.
Spouse/Marriage Date: Virginia Morris (Kizer) Wingard; October 1876 in Salem, Va.
Children: Albert Kenneth, Hannah Virginia, Mary Elizabeth, Emma A., Irene Lockwood.
Education: Newberry College, A.B. 1872, D.D.; Lutheran Theological Southern Seminary, 1875.
Ordination: 1875 by South Carolina Synod.
Calls: St. Mark's, Charlotte, 1876-81; in South Carolina until 1900; first regular pastor, St. Paul, Columbia, S.C., 1887-1900.
Other: President, South Carolina Synod, 1885, 1889; author of poems, publishing two books; *Echoes and Other Poems*, and *For Church and State*.
Date of Death/Burial Location: November 26, 1900; Columbia, S.C.

WINKLE, DAVID LEN

Date/Place of Birth: May 18, 1956; Webster Parish, La.
Parents: Ralph E. Winkle and Mary Ann (Ogle) Winkle.
Spouse/Marriage Date: Mari Jo (Efferding) Winkle; November 21, 1987 in Rincon, Ga.
Children: Ellen Jennifer, Adrienne Lee, Megan Elizabeth, Heather Patricia.
Education: University of Tennessee, B.A. 1982; Lutheran Theological Southern Seminary, M.Div. 1986.
Ordination: May 25, 1986 by Southeast Synod.
Calls: St. John, Effingham, Ga., 1986-90; Augsburg, Winston-Salem, 1990-96; Chaplain, U.S. Army, Columbia, S.C., 1997-.

WINTERS, ROBERT WILLIAM, SR.

Date/Place of Birth: October 17, 1903; Catawba County, N.C.
Parents: Frank Winters and ? (McRee) Winters.
Spouse/Marriage Date: Helen (Boggs) Winters; May 18, 1933 in Claremont, N.C.
Children: Robert William, Jr., Patricia Helen, Paul David, Sylvia Helen.
Education: Concordia College, A.B. 1926; Capital University, M.Div. 1929.
Ordination: August 29, 1929 by Ohio Synod.
Calls: First English, Newton Falls, Ohio, 1929-31; St. John, Ellicott City, Md., 1933-37; St. John and Trinity, Akron, N.Y., 1941-50; Holy Trinity, Grove City, Erie, Pa., 1950-70; retired 1969 as member of North Carolina Synod.

WISE, CURTIS KERR, JR.

Date/Place of Birth: August 14, 1932; Columbia, S.C.
Parents: The Reverend Curtis Kerr Wise, Sr. and Ruby Caroline (Ropp) Wise.
Spouse/Marriage Date: Martha Ann (Bost) Wise; April 25, 1959 in Concord, N.C.
Children: Teresa Ann Morley, Stephen Curtis, Maria Elizabeth Brown.
Education: Newberry College, A.B. 1954; Lutheran Theological Southern Seminary, B.D. 1957.
Ordination: June 9, 1957 by North Carolina Synod.
Calls: Cold Water-St. Martin, Cabarrus County, 1957-58; Amity, Iredell County, 1959-63; St. Stephen-Mt. Olive, Cabarrus County, 1963-68; Trinity, Vale, 1968-72; Philadelphia, Dallas, 1972-74; Mt. Gilead, Mt. Pleasant, 1974-81; retired in 1981.
Other: Chaplain, Concord Optimist Club.
Date of Death/Burial Location: November 21, 1981; Oakwood Cemetery, Concord, N.C.

WISE, CURTIS KERR, SR.

Date/Place of Birth: April 1, 1897; Rowan County, N.C.
Parents: Daniel Franklin Wise and Mary Laura (Kluttz) Wise.
Spouse/Marriage Date: Ruby Caroline (Ropp) Wise; October 12, 1926 in Columbia, S.C.
Children: Rebecca Marie (married the Reverend Curtis E. Derrick), Sarah Ropp Benbow, the Reverend Curtis Kerr, Jr., Mary Caroline (married the Reverend Theodore J. Thuesen).
Education: Lenoir-Rhyne, A.B. 1923 interrupting course to serve in U.S. Army in World War I; Lutheran Theological Southern Seminary, B.D. 1926; graduate study, University of South Carolina, 1923-24.
Ordination: 1927 by North Carolina Synod.
Calls: Good Hope, Hickory, Student Developer, 1923-26, Pastor, 1926-32; Supply, Sardis, Catawba County, 1931; St. Luke, Columbia, S.C., 1932-49; Faith Mission, West Columbia, S.C., 1941-45; Social Missions Pastor, South Carolina Synod, 1949-51; Zion-Pilgrim-Providence, Lexington County, S.C., 1951-54; St. Peter, Rowan County, 1954-58; Grace, Catawba County, 1958-59; retired October 1959.
Date of Death/Burial Location: May 10, 1960; Salem Church, Rowan County, N.C.

WISE, GERALD CLIFFORD

Date/Place of Birth: February 27, 1924; Kent, Ill.
Parents: Porter L. Wise and Elma (Wolford) Wise.
Spouse/Marriage Date: Bertha A. (Pilson) Wise; August 29, 1948 in Dubuque, Iowa.
Children: Stephen Andrew, The Reverend Robert Frederick.
Education: University of Dubuque, B. A. 1950; Chicago Seminary, B.D. 1953.
Ordination: May 20, 1953 by Illinois Synod.
Calls: Holy Trinity, Fredericksted, Virgin Islands, 1953-56; Immanuel, Camanche, Iowa, 1956-60; Holy Trinity, Key West, Fla., 1960-61; St. Paul, Tampa, Fla., 1961-64; St. Andrew, Mt. Airy, 1964-68; Emanuel, Woodstock, Va., 1968-81; St. Peter/St. Matthew, Toms Brook Parish, 1981-84; retired 1984 in Plant City, Fla.

WISE, JERRY RITCHIE

Date/Place of Birth: August 22, 1941; Rowan County, N.C.
Parents: John R. Wise and Creola (Kepley) Wise.
Spouse/Marriage Date: Linda (Johnson) Wise; July 7, 1969.
Children: Tanya, Suzanne.
Education: Lenoir-Rhyne; Lutheran Theological Southern Seminary; University of Michigan, M.S.; Certification as social worker and marriage counselor.
Ordination: August 25, 1968 by Lutheran Church in America.
Calls: St. Paul, Detroit, Mich.; clinical pastoral work on Long Beach, Calif., Rap Line, Farmington, Mich.; social treatment worker in Garden City, Mich.
Date of Death/Burial Location: November 25, 1986; Salem Church Cemetery, Salisbury, N.C.

WISE, ROBERT FREDERICK

Date/Place of Birth: June 10, 1959; Clinton, Iowa.
Parents: The Reverend Gerald Clifford Wise and Bertha Anna (Pilson) Wise.
Spouse/Marriage Date: Kathleen Lynn (Nizer) Wise; January 22, 1986.
Children: Daniel Scott, Rebekah Lynn, Elizabeth Rose.
Education: Lord Fairfax Community College, A.S. Business Administration, 1979; Roanoke College, B.S. Biology, 1981; Gettysburg Seminary, M.Div. 1990.
Ordination: July 15, 1990 by North Carolina Synod.
Calls: Mt. Olive, Mt. Pleasant, 1990-94; Reformation, Lakeland, Fla., 1994-.

WISE, ROY THOMAS

Date/Place of Birth: July 18, 1944; Plains, Ga.
Parents: J. C. Wise, Jr. and Mary Virginia (Easterlin) Wise.
Spouse/Marriage Date: Susan Faith (Tamsberg) Thomas; June 29, 1968 in Georgetown, S.C.
Children: Kristin Rebecca, Mary Catherine.
Education: University of Georgia, B.S. 1966; Lutheran Theological Southern Seminary, M.Div. 1970.
Ordination: July 25, 1970 by Southeastern Synod.
Calls: Associate Pastor, St. Paul, Savannah, Ga., 1970-77; Center Grove, Kannapolis, 1977-81; resigned 1984.
Other: Vice President, Lutheran Theological Southern Seminary Alumni Association, 1975-77.

WISE, WALTER DANIEL

Date/Place of Birth: May 12, 1880; Courtland, Miss.

Parents: Cornelius Lorenzo Wise and Sarah Ann (Wyant) Wise.

Spouse/Marriage Date: Fannie Lavinia (Frick) Wise; October 5, 1909 in Chapin, S.C.

Children: The Reverend Bernard Frick, Evelyn Ruth Harr, the Reverend Worth David.

Education: Lenoir-Rhyne, A.B. 1905; Lutheran Theological Southern Seminary, 1908.

Ordination: September 26, 1908 by Tennessee Synod.

Calls: St. James-Ebenezer, Catawba County, 1908-12; Mt. Calvary, Claremont, 1908-11, 1912-18; St. Martin-Luther Chapel-Salem, Maiden, 1918-21; Cedar Grove-St. James, Lexington, Lexington County, S.C. 1921-28, St. John, 1922-24, and Salem, 1923-25, Lexington County, S.C.; Silverstreet, Silverstreet-Corinth, Saluda, S.C., 1928-36; Summer Memorial, Newberry, S.C., 1930-36; Immanuel-Zion-New Haven, Sullivan County, Tenn., 1936-44; Kimberling-Corinth, Wythe County, Va.-Pleasant Hill, Smyth County, Va., 1944-47; retired 1947; transferred 1962 to North Carolina Synod.

Other: Secretary, 1914-16, President, 1917-19, North Carolina Conference, Tennessee Synod.

Date of Death/Burial Location: April 11, 1964; Mt. Horeb Church Cemetery, Chapin, S.C.

WISE, WORTH DAVID

Date/Place of Birth: February 23, 1924; Leesville, S.C.

Parents: The Reverend Walter Daniel Wise and Fannie Lavinia (Frick) Wise. The Reverend Bernard Frick Wise was a brother.

Spouse/Marriage Date: Alice Victoria (Ridenhour) Wise, daughter of the Reverend Charles E. Ridenhour, August 5, 1950 in Dallas, N.C.

Children: Robert David, Rebekah Elizabeth Bumgarner.

Education: Lenoir-Rhyne, A.B. 1945; Lutheran Theological Southern Seminary, B.D. 1948.

Ordination: April 7, 1948 by North Carolina Synod.

Calls: St. Mark, Rowan County, 1948-50; St. Andrew, Concord, 1950-54; St. John, Asheboro, 1954-61; Mt. Calvary, Claremont, 1961-77; St. Mark, Cherryville, 1977-86; retired 1986.

Other: Secretary, 1958-60, Stewardship Committee, 1954-62; Delegate, National Stewardship Conference, New York City, 1960; Board, Lutheridge, 1965-71; Lion of the Year Award by Asheboro Lions Club, 1956; Parish Education Committee, 1961-68; Board, Lutheran Children's Home of the South; Delegate, Lutheran Church in America, 1968.

Date of Death: January 28, 1994.

WITTENBERG, VIRGIL OTTO

Date/Place of Birth: March 23, 1934; Napoleon, Ohio.

Parents: Mr. and Mrs. Otto Wittenberg.

Spouse/Marriage Date: Janet (Wise) Wittenberg; August 31, 1958.

Children: Julia Clare, Paul Stuart.

Education: Capital University, Columbus, Ohio, B.A., 1956; Evangelical Lutheran Theological Seminary, Columbus, Ohio, B.D., 1960.

Ordination: June 12, 1960 by American Lutheran Church.

Calls: Trinity, East Rochester, N.Y., 1960-69; Abiding Savior, Durham, 1969-74; Trinity, Gibsonia, Pa., 1974-. Retired.

Other: Eastern District Parish Education Board, 1961-67; Board of Directors of St. John's Home for Aging, Rochester, N.Y., 1964-66; Research and Planning Committee, Rochester Council of Churches, 1964-74; Sub- Committee Urban Renewal, East Rochester, 1967-74; Vice President, Lutheran Church in America and American Lutheran Church Inner Mission Society, 1967-74; Lutheran Church-Missouri Synod, Lutheran Church in America and American Lutheran Church Program Committee Coordinator, 1967-74.

WOLF, J. MICHAEL

Ordination: One source says that he was ordained by North Carolina Synod in 1860 but mentions no churches served in North Carolina; moved to Pennsylvania, and preached at Altoona, 1867-75, and Lancaster, 1878-80; and in Schenectady, N.Y., 1876-77; *History of the Lutheran Church in North Carolina,* (1803-1953) refers to him as M. Wolf and lists him only in the clerical list on p. 381: Ordained 1860 (synod not named); first received into North Carolina Synod 1890 from New York and New Jersey Synod.

Date of Death/Burial Location: 1899; Poplar Mount, N.C.

WOOD, DEBORAH JEAN (BRAUNWARTH)

Date/Place of Birth: December 12, 1941; Philadelphia, Pa..

Parents: Charles L. Braunwarth and Marion A. (Biggerstaff) Braunwarth.

Spouse/Marriage Date: Lawrence R. Wood, Jr.; June 22, 1963.

Children: Janet Lorraine, Lawrence Robert, III.

Education: Gettysburg College, B.A. History, 1963; Lutheran Theological Southern Seminary, M.Div. 1987; Clemson University, M.Ed. 1976.

Ordination: January 8, 1989 by South Carolina Synod.

Calls: Trinity, Georgetown, S.C., 1989-93; Our Saviour, Welcome, 1995-.

Other: Board, Lutheran Homes of South Carolina, 1990-93; Division for Outreach, South Carolina Synod, 1994-95; Continuing Education Committee, South Carolina Synod, 1989-92.

WOOD, ROGER WAYNE

Date/Place of Birth: October 5, 1941; Spartanburg, S.C.

Parents: Osborne Glenn Wood, Sr. and Eunice Mae Wood.

First Spouse/Marriage Date: Clara Ruth (Coleman) Wood; December 24, 1965 in Columbia, S.C.

Children of First Marriage: Teresa Lena Smith, Debra Renee Smith, Janet Gail.

Second Spouse/Marriage Date: Suzanne Elinor (Ebright) (Shelton) Wood; August 8, 1977 in Jasper, Ark.

Children of Second Spouse: Heidi Marie Shelton, Wendi Noelle Shelton.

Education: Wofford, A.B. 1963; Duke Divinity School, M.Div. 1967; graduate work at Gettysburg Seminary, Lutheran Theological Southern Seminary and Vanderbilt University Divinity School.

Ordination: June 4, 1967 by North Carolina Synod.

Calls: Christ, East Spencer, 1967-70; St. Mark, Lumberton, 1970-73; Mission Developer/Pastor, Shepherd of the Hills, Sylva, 1973-76; Christ, Durham, 1977-81. Transferred to Illinois Synod, 1981.

Other: Social Ministry Committee, 1968-70; American Missions Committee, 1974-76; Professional Development Committee.

WOOD, WILLIAM COLLINS, SR.
Date/Place of Birth: August 20, 1927; Vero Beach, Fla.
Parents: Fletcher Bart Wood and Rosa Edna (Lipsey) Wood.
Spouse/Marriage Date: Margaret Lois (Howell) Wood; March 15, 1947 in Lakeland, Fla.
Children: William Collins, II, John Robert.
Education: Florida Southern College, A.B. 1950; Pittsburgh-Xenia Seminary, 1952; Oberlin Graduate and Candler (Emory University) Schools of Theology; Lutheran Theological Southern Seminary, B.D. 1960.
License/Ordination: Licensed 1944 and ordained May 22, 1950 by Florida Methodist Conference; ordained Lutheran Pastor 1960 by Florida Synod.
Calls: First Methodist, Brandon, Fla., 1950-53; Bloomingdale Methodist Parish, Bloomingdale, Ohio, 1953-55; First Methodist, Moore Haven, Fla., 1955-58; First Methodist, Bushnell, Fla., 1958-66; Shiloh, Lewisville, 1960-63; Pilgrim, Lexington, 1963-71; Christ, Winston-Salem, 1971-77; Mt. Calvary, Claremont, 1977-90; retired 1990 to Newton, N.C.; Vice Pastor at various congregations.

WOOD, WILLIAM COLLINS, II
Date/Place of Birth: September 14, 1948; Lakeland, Fla.
Parents: The Reverend William Collins Wood, Sr. and Margaret Lois (Howell) Wood.
Spouse/Marriage Date: Linda Carol (Mangum) Wood; December 27, 1969 in Wake County, N.C.
Children: Laura Kathryn, Patricia Ann.
Education: Lenoir-Rhyne, A.B. 1970; Lutheran Theological Southern Seminary, M.Div. 1974; University of Virginia, M.E. 1980.
Ordination: May 30, 1974 by North Carolina Synod.
Calls: Associate Pastor, Grace, Winchester, Va., 1974-79.
Other: Resigned from ministry, 1982.

WOODARD, JOHN NELSON
Date/Place of Birth: June 15, 1948; Luray, Va.
Parents: Conrad Woodard and Margaret C. Woodard.
Spouse/Marriage Date: Marsha (Williams) Woodard; November 17, 1973 in Newberry, S.C.
Children: Ashley Elizabeth.
Education: Bethany College, Kansas, B.A. English 1970; Lutheran Theological Southern Seminary, M.Div. 1974.
Ordination: June 10, 1974 by Virginia Synod.
Calls: Christ, Ft. Lauderdale, Fla., 1974-75; Our Saviour, Dallas, 1975-78; Wittenberg, Granite Quarry, 1978-; in 1998 was at Miller's, Hickory. Pastor at various congregations.

WOOLLY, DONALD EDGAR

Date/Place of Birth: August 12, 1932; High Point, N.C.

Parents: Clyde Edgar Woolly and Mattie Princess (Moose) Woolly Hatley.

Spouse/Marriage Date: Anne Judith (Rumley) Woolly; July 12, 1958 in Greensboro, N.C.

Children: Mary Elizabeth Trump, Page Ellen Putnam, The Reverend Donald Rhodes.

Education: Lenoir-Rhyne, A.B. 1955; Lutheran Theological Southern Seminary, M.Div. 1958; McCormick Theological Seminary, D.Min. 1981.

Ordination: June 8, 1958 by North Carolina Synod.

Calls: Low's, Guilford County, 1958-61; St. John, Asheboro, 1961-67; Lutheran Chapel, Gastonia, 1967-73; St. Andrew's, Columbia, S.C., 1973-94; retired 1994.

Other: Delegate to Lutheran Church in America Convention; Board, Lutheridge; Executive Council of South Carolina Synod; Dean and Secretary, Dutch Fork District; Chaplain, North Carolina Synod Convention; Board, Red Cross; Board, Young Mens' Christian Association; Board, Family Services of Gastonia; Rotary Club for 25 years, serving as Secretary and President; President of three Ministerial Associations; received South Carolina's highest civilian award - The Order of the Palmetto - for outstanding service to the community and state, particularly in underprivileged ministries; in North Carolina Synod: Stewardship Committee, Evangelism Committee, Youth Committee, District Secretary; in South Carolina Synod: Professional Leadership Preparation Committee, Stewardship Committee, Youth Committee, Evangelism, Nominations Committee.

WORTMANN, HEINRICH BURCHARD GABRIEL

Place of Birth: Mittelnkirchen bei Stade, Germany.

Education: Goettingen University, April 21, 1738.

Calls and Other: Served a parish near Hamburg, Germany. Arrived in Philadelphia on the *Queen of Denmark* in November 1752. He is credited with service at Alsace Lutheran, Berks County, Pa. In 1753 he served several months in Lancaster, then moved to Trinity, Reading. In July 1753 he was "dismissed" at Reading and moved to Virginia. H. M. Muhlenberg called him a *cholericus*, but another source says "family troubles" prompted his removal to Virginia. In 1757-58 he was resident pastor at Upper Peaked Mountain, McGaheysville, Va., and is believed also to have served Rader, Fort Run. Served St. John's, Charleston, S.C., for two years following the death of Pastor John George Friedrichs (d. 1760). The fact that Muhlenberg was told when he visited Charleston in 1774 that, following his ministry at St. John's, Wortmann "went farther into the country" lends credence to the suggestion that he is the "Waterman" who is believed to have served the Lutherans on Crim's Creek (St. John, Pomaria, S.C.) following the pastorate of John G. Luft. It has been reported that Wortmann also served for a time as Pastor of Ascension, Savannah, Ga. In 1772 a Moravian minister, Mr. Soelle, reported that "Pastor Wartmann is ... living in the Dutchman's Creek neighborhood, having been born in Hanover, and being an educated, ordained minister." Dutchman's Creek (Reformation, Mocksville) was clearly a functioning congregation as early as 1766 and may well date back to the settlement of the Heidelberg community around 1760. Just when Wortmann arrived in Rowan (now Davie) County is not known, nor how long he stayed. It seems clear that he was the first ordained Lutheran minister to reside in North Carolina, since John Caspar Stoever was not ordained at the time of his residence in Craven County and Adolph Nussmann did not arrive to begin his ministry until 1773. The Rowan County records indicate that Wortmann was still in the area as late as December 1773 at which time he joined Daniel Little, a Salisbury Lutheran, in witnessing a will. "A Journeyman, John Wartmann by name, was employed to assist in the [Henkel] printery in 1810 and the firm's name was changed to Ambrose Henkel and Company." John is reportedly a son of Pastor Wortmann.

WRAY, JACK CLARK
Date/Place of Birth: June 3, 1945; Burlington, N.C.
Parents: Wade N. Wray and Nadine H. Wray.
Spouse/Marriage Date: Karen Virginia (Chalfant) Wray; May 29, 1971 in Columbia, S.C.
Children: J. Derek.
Education: Lenoir-Rhyne, A.B. 1967; Lutheran Theological Southern Seminary, M.Div. 1971.
Ordination: 1971 by North Carolina Synod.
Calls: Zion, Guyton, Ga., 1971-73; St. Matthew, Rossville, Ga., 1973-79; First, Nashville, Tenn., 1979-82; Redeemer, Savannah, Ga., 1982-86.
Other: Southeastern Synod: Social Ministry Committee; Coordinator, Social Ministry Resource Network; Coordinator, Peacemaking Network.

WUEBBENS, PETER JOHN
Date/Place of Birth: July 24, 1935; Gogebic County, Mich.
Parents: The Reverend Hilbert J. Wuebbens and Virginia C. (Kelly) Wuebbens.
Spouse/Marriage Date: Lola Anne (Bland) Wuebbens; December 27, 1957 in Zanesville, Ohio.
Children: Stephanie Ann, Karen Adele, William Bruce, Joan Lynne, Ellen Beatrice.
Education: Capital University, B.A. 1957; Trinity Seminary, B.D. 1960; graduate work at Union Seminary (N.Y.), Harvard Divinity School, Weston College, and Interfaith Institute at Wildacres.
Ordination: April 4, 1961 by American Lutheran Church, Eastern District Synod.
Calls: St. Paul, Waldo, Ohio, 1961-64; Peace, Wayland, Mass., 1964-68; Our Saviour, Edison, N.J., 1968-78; Good Shepherd, Charlotte, 1978-91; Holy Trinity, Leesburg, Va., 1991-.
Other: "Founding Father" of Lake Wylie Lutheran Church, Fort Mill, S.C., 1979-80; American Lutheran Church-Lutheran Church in America Joint Communion Practices Committee, 1974-76; Chair, Martin Luther Camp Corp. (Koinonia) Highland Lake, N.Y., 1974-78; American Lutheran Church's Eastern District Council, 1976-80; American Lutheran Church's Southeastern District Council-Convener, Mission Secretary, 1984-87; North Carolina Transition Team, Chair, Structure for Mission-Ministry, 1986-87; Dean, Southern District of North Carolina Synod, 1988-; Chair, Charlotte Area Clergy Association, 1985; Planning Committee, GCAR Interfaith Institute at Wildacres, 1986-; Chair, Charlotte-Mecklenburg Community Relations Committee, 1990; Charlotte-Eastern Kiwanis Club.

WYRICK, HERMAN PEERY, SR.
Date/Place of Birth: October 26, 1896; Rural Retreat, Va.
Parents: Walter Winfield Wyrick and Ollie Ora (Brown) Wyrick.
Spouse/Marriage Date: Jane Hearne (Hennies) Wyrick; August 10, 1921 in Columbia, S.C.
Children: Herman Peery, Jr.

Education: Roanoke College, A.B. 1918; Lutheran Theological Southern Seminary, 1921.
License/Ordination: Licensed 1918 and ordained 1921 by Southwest Virginia Synod.
Calls: Luther Memorial, Blacksburg, Va., 1921-22; Macedonia, Burlington, 1922-29; first regular pastor, church built (1930), education building (1948), St. Luke's, Charlotte, 1929-53; St. Paul, Hamlet, 1953-58.
Other: Secretary, Board, Lutheran Theological Southern Seminary, 1946-52.
Date of Death/Burial Location: July 28, 1958; Forest Lawn Cemetery, Charlotte, N.C.

WYSE, JOHN HOPE

Date/Place of Birth: February 14, 1861; Lexington County, S.C.
Spouse/Marriage Date: Grace (Henderlite) Wyse; 1889.
Education: Roanoke College, A.B. 1885; Philadelphia Seminary, 1888.
Ordination: 1888 by Ministerium of Pennsylvania.
Calls: First, Albemarle, 1889; Holy Trinity, Mt. Pleasant, 1888-89; Bethlehem, St. Matthew-St. Philip, Newberry County-Corinth, Saluda County-Macedonia, Lexington County-St. Mark, near Fort Motte, S.C., 1890-98; Central Church, Burkes Garden, Va., 1898-1904; Mt. Tabor Parish, Augusta County, Va., 1904-08.
Date of Death/Burial Location: March 25, 1908; Staunton, Va.

YODER, DAVID DEAN

Date/Place of Birth: February 9, 1942; Elkhart County, Ind.
Parents: Huber A. Yoder and L. Edith (Thompson) Yoder.
Spouse/Marriage Date: Adeline Kay (Amstutz) Yoder; September 29, 1967 in Mussoorie, India.
Children: Karmen Kay.
Education: Goshen College, B.A. History, 1964;Lutheran Theological Southern Seminary, M.Div. 1982; graduate work at Christian Theological Seminary.
Ordination: June 26, 1983 by North Carolina Synod on behalf of Ohio Synod.
Calls: Holy Trinity, Reidsville, 1982-90; Gethsemane, Indianapolis, Ind., 1990-.
Other: Missionary/Teacher in India under the Mennonite Board of Missions at Woodstock School, Mussoorie, India.

YODER, HAROLD MONROE

Date/Place of Birth: November 23, 1922; Hickory, N.C.
Parents: Monroe Craig Yoder and Ethel Katherine (Setzer) Yoder.
Spouse/Marriage Date: Selena Frances (Kime) Yoder; October 20, 1951 in Liberty, N.C.
Children: Eric Monroe, Frances Kathryn, William Craig, Mary Ann Watson.
Education: Lenoir-Rhyne, A.B. Pre-Med 1943; University of North Carolina, 1943; Gettysburg Seminary, M.Div. 1950; graduate work at Washington, D.C. School of Psychiatry and University of North Carolina at Chapel Hill; Lutheran Theological Southern Seminary, D.Min. 1983.
Ordination: June 25, 1950 by North Carolina Synod.
Calls: Grace, Liberty, 1950-52; Good Shepherd, Goldsboro, 1952-57; Director, Department for Institutional Ministry, Council of Churches National Capitol Area, Washington, D.C., 1957-62; Chaplain, St. Elizabeth Hospital, Washington, D.C., 1962-64; Chaplain, Lutheran Hospital of Maryland, Baltimore, Md., 1964-72; Director, Department for Pastoral

Services, Richland Memorial Hospital, Columbia, S.C., 1972-86; Associate Director for Clinical Pastoral Education, Richland Memorial Hospital, Columbia, S.C., 1986-; retired. *Other*: Offices in local Ministerial Associations; Chair, Institutional Ministry Committee, North Carolina Council of Churches, 1952-57; Washington Seminar on Religion and Psychiatry, 1957-63; Regional Director, Mid-Atlantic Region, Association for Clinical Pastoral Education, Inc. 1967-72; Committee on Church Vocations, Maryland Synod, 1970-72; Coordinator, Lutheran Parish Intern Cluster, Baltimore Area, 1969-72; Chair, Baltimore Area Lutheran Evaluation Committee, Lutheran Council in the U.S.A., 1967-72; Columbia Area Lutheran Evaluation Committee, Lutheran Council in the U.S.A., Chair, 1983-ff.

YODER, JACOB LARRY

Date/Place of Birth: May 26, 1943 at Lincolnton, N.C.
Parents: Jacob Ralph Yoder and Mary Katheryn (Miller) Yoder.
Spouse/Marriage Date: Marianne (Howard) Yoder; June 19, 1966.
Children: Nathan Howard, Joshua Howard, David Howard.
Education: Lenoir-Rhyne, A.B. 1965 *magna cum laude;* Lutheran Theological Southern Seminary, M.Div. 1969, cum laude; Duke University, Ph.D. 1978.
Ordination: June 1, 1969 by North Carolina Synod.
Calls: Associate Pastor, Christ in Pacific Beach, San Diego, Calif., 1969-72; St. Paul, Durham, 1975-76; Chaplain, Lenoir-Rhyne, 1977-82; Interim Pastor of Grace, Newton, 1993-; Vice Pastor at various congregations.
Other: Synod Council; Executive Board; Chair, Social Ministry, Ecumenical Affairs, Youth Ministry Committees; Chair, Lenoir Rhyne Faculty Assembly, 1993-; Director, Center for Theology, Lenoir-Rhyne College, 1998-; Director, Lineberger Center for Cultural and Educational Renewal, Lenoir-Rhyne, 1980; Director of Honors, Lenoir-Rhyne, 1983-87, 1991-; Dean, Graduate Studies and Honors, Lenoir-Rhyne, 1988-91; Roediger Distinguished Service Professorship, 1995-96; Jefferson Cup, award for distinguished service to Lenoir-Rhyne, 1986; Bost Distinguished Professor Award for Excellence in Teaching, 1985; Student Government President's Award, 1980; Evangelical Lutheran Church in America - Task Force on Human Sexuality, 1989-, Constituting Convention Delegate, 1987, Voting Member of the Constituting Convention and the Assemblies in 1989 and 1993; Long-Range Planning Sub-Committee on Curriculum and Program, Lutheran Theological Southern Seminary; Steering Committee for Theological Conversations, Southeast District of The Lutheran Church-Missouri Synod and North Carolina Synod, 1985-87; Lutheran-Episcopal Dialogue, 1984-87; New Lutheran Church Task Force, Chair, 1984, 1986, 1987; Delegate, Lutheran Church in America Convention 1984, 1986; Task Force on Peace, 1984-87; Mission Audit Committee, 1983; Campus Ministry Committee, 1977-80; Bioethics Task Force, 1979; Pacific Southwest Synod - Youth Ministry Committee, Youth Convo Planner and Coordinator; San Diego District Youth Ministry Committee, Chair, 1969-72; fourteen academic committees and assignments; Hickory Humanities Forum, 1981, and three other conferences; nineteen published lectures, articles and papers.

YODER, JOHN YATES, JR.

Date/Place of Birth: October 13, 1930; Salisbury, N.C.
Parents: John Yates Yoder, Sr. and Leah (Miller) Yoder.

Spouse/Marriage Date: Marian Theresa (Norris) Yoder, daughter of the Reverend J. L. Norris; August 17, 1954 in Burlington, N.C.
Children: Susan Annette, Sandra Carolyn, John Yates, III, Sharon Theresa.
Education: Lenoir-Rhyne, A.B. 1952; Lutheran Theological Southern Seminary M.Div. 1955, also graduate study; Georgia State University, M.P.A.
Ordination: July 1955 by North Carolina Synod.
Calls: Frieden's, Guilford County, 1955-58; Redeemer, Kannapolis, 1958-61; Mission Developer/Pastor, Epiphany, Winston-Salem, 1961-64; Committee on College and University Student Work, 1962-65; Chaplain-Intern, John Umstead Hospital, Butner, 1964-65; demitted ministry 1965 for psychiatric counseling service.
Other: Board, Lutheran Theological Southern Seminary, 1977-82; Board, Lenoir-Rhyne, 1984-89.

YODER, ROBERT ANDERSON

Date/Place of Birth: August 16, 1853; Lincoln County, N.C.
Parents: Solomon Yoder and Sarah (Seagle) Yoder.
Spouse/Marriage Date: Rosa Elizabeth (Fisher) Yoder; May 9, 1878 in Rowan County, N.C.
Children: Mary Pearl, Lela Fisher (married the Reverend John Hall), Maud Elizabeth, Blanche Irene (married the Reverend Brady L. Stroup), Margaretta Anna, Robert Able, Paul Allison.
Education: Hahn and Little Classical School, Hickory Taverns, Hickory, 1871; North Carolina College, 1872-74, A.B. 1877, D.D. 1899; Lincoln University, Indiana, 1874-75; theology under the Reverends A. J. Fox, P. C. Henkel, and J. M. Smith, and at Philadelphia Seminary, 1883-85.
Ordination: 1879 by Tennessee Synod.
Calls: Served churches of North Carolina Conference of Tennessee Synod in three counties, often three or four at same time; in Catawba County: Concordia Chapel, Conover, 1879-83; St. James, 1879-96, 1901-05; Grace, 1884-95; St. Andrew, Hickory, 1896-1901, 1905; Sardis, 1896-99; St. Martin, Maiden, 1898-1900, 1901-05; Ebenezer, 1901-05; organized Mt. Calvary, Claremont, 1902-05; Mt. Olive, 1905; Beth Eden, Newton, 1894-96, 1905; in Watauga County: Mt. Pleasant, 1881, with the Reverend J. P. Miller, 1888; in Lincoln County: Salem, 1884-99; Emmanuel, Lincolnton, 1905-11.
Other: Official positions in Tennessee Synod: Secretary, 1885; President, 1886; Corresponding Secretary, 1887; Treasurer, beneficiary fund, 1890-91; Treasurer of Synod, 1894-1911; Delegate to United Synod South, 1888-1910. In United Synod South: Vice President, 1900-02; President, 1902-06; President, Board, Home Missions and Church Extension, 1909-10. Educational positions: in Concordia High School, teacher and head, 1878-83; after it became Concordia College, Professor and President, 1888-91. With the Reverends A. L. Crouse, W. P. Cline, and J. C. Moser, and layman J. G. Hall, trustee of the Walter W. Lenoir property, founded Lenoir-Rhyne in 1891; President of same, 1891-1901, also lecturing in such subjects as logic, psychology, mathematics, and ethics; designer of "Old Main" at Lenoir-Rhyne College, and a number of churches; Board, Concordia College; Board, Lenoir-Rhyne College, 1899-1901; author of many doctrinal and practical papers and pamphlets which were published chiefly in *Our Church Paper* and *Lutheran Church Visitor,* including: "From the Human to the Divine," "What Type of Lutheranism

Should Prevail in the South," "The Situation in North Carolina," "The Call to the Work of the Gospel Ministry," and "The Biblical Basis of Missions-Our Marching Orders."
Date of Death/Burial Location: May 16, 1911; Daniel's Churchyard, near Lincolnton, N.C.

YONTS, MARTIN LUTHER, SR.

Date/Place of Birth: March 11, 1926; Thomasville, N.C.
Parents: Lloyd Oran Yonts and Bernice Maggie (Sink) Yonts.
Spouse/Marriage Date: Hazel Onella (Collins) Yonts; June 25, 1946 in Thomasville, N.C.
Children: Martin Luther, Jr.
Education: University of North Carolina at Chapel Hill, 1943; Lenoir-Rhyne, A.B. 1946, D.D. 1991; Temple University, 1945; Philadelphia Seminary, B.D. 1948.
Ordination: June 14, 1948 by North Carolina Synod.
Calls: Trinity, Homer City-Luther Chapel, Coral, Pa., Brush Valley, Brush Valley, Pa., 1948-53; Wittenberg, Granite Quarry, 1953-56; Good Shepherd, Dallas, Texas, 1956-60.
Other: Secretary, Home Missions and Stewardship, Texas-Louisiana Synod, 1960-63; Regional Secretary (Ohio and Michigan), Board of American Missions, Lutheran Church in America, 1963-65; Assistant Executive Secretary, Board of American Missions, 1965-73; Regional Director, Division for Mission in North America, Texas-Louisiana Synod, 1973-87; Bishop, Southeastern Texas-Southern Louisiana Synod, 1987-91; retired January 1992 to Hendersonville, N.C.; Director of Development, Lutheran Hospital, Inc., Houston, Texas, 1992-93; published writings in *The Lutheran, Light for Today, Word in Season, Home Altar, Augsburg Sunday School Lessons*.

YOOS, HERMAN ROBERT, III

Date/Place of Birth: January 1, 1952; Concord, N.C.
Parents: Herman Robert Yoos, Jr. and Cynthia (Swenson) Yoos.
Spouse/Marriage Date: Cindy (Parker) Yoos; July 14, 1984.
Children: Sarah Kristin, Andrew Jordan, Elizabeth Joy.
Education: University of North Carolina at Chapel Hill, B.A. Speech and Political Science 1974; Lutheran Theological Southern Seminary, M.Div. 1979; Columbia Theological Seminary, D.Min. 1997.
Ordination: June 10, 1979 by North Carolina Synod.
Calls: Associate Pastor, St. Mark's, Charlotte, 1979-82; Redeemer, Charleston, S.C., 1982-96; Good Shepherd, Columbia, S.C., 1996-.
Other: South Carolina Synod Council, 1989-94; Chair, Commission on Inclusion, 1989-94, Region 9 Multicultural Chair, Intern Supervisor, 1985-89; Professional Leadership Committee for Continuing Education; President of Christian Jewish Council; Founding Member of Charleston Congress of Religion; Pastoral Advisor of Lutheran Social Services, 1989-96; Hospice Chaplain.

YOST, CARL RUSSELL

Date/Place of Birth: April 17, 1955; Salisbury, N.C.
Parents: The Reverend Dr. John L. Yost, Jr. and K. Sue (Caughman) Yost. Grandson of The Reverend Dr. John L. Yost, Sr. and The Reverend Dr. Carl B. Caughman; brother to the Reverend John L. Yost, III.
Spouse/Marriage Date: Debra Lynn (Query) Yost; December 28, 1980.

Children: Allison Rebecca, Jacob Russell, Laura Kathryn.

Education: Lenoir-Rhyne, B.A. History 1979; Lutheran Theological Southern Seminary, M.Div. 1983; Clinical Pastoral Education, Richland Memorial Hospital, 1983; U.S. Army Chaplain School, 1986.

Ordination: May 27, 1983 by South Carolina Synod.

Calls: Holly Grove, Lexington, 1983-86; Shades Valley, Birmingham, Ala., 1986-92; Pilgrim, Lexington, S.C., 1992-.

Other: North Carolina Synod Education Committee, 1984-86; Southeastern Synod Council, two terms as Alabama representative, 1988-92; U.S. Army Guard-Reserve Chaplaincy, 1985-; Lexington Interfaith Community Service, 1985-.

YOST, JOHN LEWIS, III

Date/Place of Birth: September 14, 1948; Savannah, Ga.

Parents: The Reverend Dr. John L. Yost, Jr. and Kathryn Sue (Caughman) Yost. Grandson of The Reverend Dr. John L. Yost, Sr. and The Reverend Dr. Carl B. Caughman; brother to the Reverend Carl Russell Yost.

Spouse/Marriage Date: Brenda (Wyke) Yost; November 26, 1970.

Children: Joshua Aaron, Jennifer Lauren.

Education: Lenoir-Rhyne, A.B. 1970; Lutheran Theological Southern Seminary, M.Div. 1974.

Ordination: May 31, 1974 by North Carolina Synod.

Calls: Emmanuel, Naples, Fla., 1974-76; Mission Developer/Pastor, Christus Victor, Bonita Springs, Fla., 1976-83; Messiah, Mauldin, S.C., 1983-.

Other: Florida Synod: Chair, Camping and Retreat Committee, 1979-82; Commission for Congregational Life, 1979-81; Evangelical Outreach Team; Stewardship Cluster Leader; Youth Ministry Committee. South Carolina Synod: Professional Leadership Preparation Committee; Board, Lutheran Theological Southern Seminary.

YOST, JOHN LEWIS, SR.

Date/Place of Birth: March 9, 1893; Rowan County, N.C.

Parents: John Monroe Yost and Laura Jane (May) Yost.

Spouse/Marriage Date: Eva Louise (Dunning) Yost; May 24, 1917 in Columbia, S.C.

Children: The Reverend John Louis, Jr., Elizabeth Louise.

Education: Mount Pleasant Collegiate Institute, Roanoke College, A.B. 1914, L.L.D. 1959; Lutheran Theological Southern Seminary, 1917; Newberry College, D.D. 1935.

Ordination: 1917 by North Carolina Synod.

Calls: Redeemer, Bristol, Tenn., 1917-21; St. Luke, Bear Poplar, 1921-23; and Holy Trinity, Gastonia, 1923-29; Redeemer, Atlanta, Ga., 1929-45.

Other: President, Lutheran Theological Southern Seminary, 1945-60; retired January 1, 1961, at Columbia, S.C.; President, Georgia-Alabama Synod, 1942-45; Board of Foreign Missions, United Lutheran Church in America, twelve years; official visitor of same to Japan mission field, 1947; transferred back to North Carolina Synod, 1960; new administration building at Lutheran Theological Southern Seminary is named "John Lewis Yost Administration Building" in his honor.

Date of Death/Burial Location: March 6, 1985; Elmwood Cemetery, Columbia, S.C.

YOST, JOHN LOUIS, JR.
Date/Place of Birth: April 27, 1921; Bear Poplar, N.C.
Parents: The Reverend Dr. John Lewis Yost, Sr. and Eva Louise (Dunning) Yost.
Spouse/Marriage Date: Kathryn Sue (Caughman) Yost, born at Rajahmundry, India, daughter of the Reverend Carl B. Caughman; September 27, 1945 in Columbia, S.C.
Children: The Reverend John Louis, III, Kathryn Susan Gragg, The Reverend Carl Russell.
Education: Newberry College, A.B. 1943; Lutheran Theological Southern Seminary, B.D. 1945; Lenoir-Rhyne, D.D. 1964.
Ordination: October 7, 1945 by Georgia-Alabama Synod.
Calls: Holy Trinity, Lynchburg, Va., 1945-47; St. Paul, Savannah, Ga., 1947-52; Secretary, Board of Foreign Missions, United Lutheran Church in America, 1952-54; Haven, Salisbury, 1954-59; Holy Trinity, Hickory, 1959-75; St. Matthew, Charleston, S.C., 1975-86, Pastor Emeritus; retired 1986.
Other: Chair, North Carolina Synod Operational Committee, ("Little JCLU"), 1961-62; first President, North Carolina Synod, Lutheran Church in America, at constituting convention in 1962 but declined, choosing to continue as pastor; Executive Board, North Carolina Synod, 1962-67, 1970-73; Dean, Northwestern District, 1973-80; Trustee, Michael Peeler Fund; Executive Committee, Board of World Missions Lutheran Church in America, 1962-; Board, Lenoir-Rhyne, 1967-70; B.W.M. - Lutheran Church in America, Secretary, 1962; Delegate, Lutheran Church in America, 1962, 1966, 1968, 1970, 1972; Campus Ministry Committee, 1967-70; World Missions Committee, 1962-68; South Carolina Synod Executive Board and Dean; Chair of Board, Newberry College; Delegate, Lutheran World Federation Assembly, in Tanzania, Africa.

YOUNG, JACOB HOSEA, JR.
Date/Place of Birth: August 14, 1925; Charlotte, N.C.
Parents: Jacob Hosea Young, Sr. and Geneva (Basinger) Young.
First Spouse/Marriage Date: Martha Ann (Edwards) Young; August 5, 1950 in Burkes Garden, Va.
Children of First Marriage: David.
Second Spouse/Marriage Date: Barbara Jean (Spidal) Young; October 7, 1979 in Kure Beach, N.C.
Step-daughter: Edith Marie.
Education: Lenoir-Rhyne, A.B. 1947; Lutheran Theological Southern Seminary, B.D. 1950.
Ordination: June 25, 1950 by North Carolina Synod.
Calls: Sharon-St. Matthew-Red Oak, Bland County, Va., 1950-51; Zion, Catawba County, 1951-56; Philadelphia, Granite Falls, 1956-61; Holy Trinity, Martinsville, Va., 1961-75; Kure Memorial, Kure Beach, 1975-90; retired August 26, 1990.

YOUNG, ROBERT GLENN
Date/Place of Birth: July 15, 1945; Salisbury, N.C.
Parents: Eddie Linz Young and Lala Mae (Agner) Young.

Spouse: Barbara Jean (Beaver) Young; December 18, 1966.
Children: David Neil; Barbara Suzanne.
Education: Catawba College, B.A. 1967; Lutheran Theological Southern Seminary, M.Div. 1971.
Ordination: June 6, 1971 by North Carolina Synod.
Calls: Morning Star, Matthews, 1971-77; Grace, Boone, 1977-92; Resurrection-St. Matthew Parish, Cameron, S.C., 1992-.
Other: North Carolina Synod: Parish Education Committee, Campus Ministry Committee, American Missions Committee, Appalachian Consultation Committee, Internship Supervising Pastor. South Carolina Synod: First Call Theological Education Colleague Group Leader, Ministry Team for Rostered Leaders.

YOUNG, ROBERT LINDEN

Date/Place of Birth: June 17, 1935; Davidson County, N.C.
Parents: Robert Chester Young and Blanche Marie (Everhart) Young.
Spouse/Marriage Date: Andrea Louise (McNaughton) Young; September 1, 1963 in Charleston, S.C.
Children: Robert Andrew, Stephanie Lynn.
Education: One year at North Carolina State University, Lenoir-Rhyne, A.B. 1958; Lutheran Theological Southern Seminary, B.D. 1964; University of North Carolina at Chapel Hill, MSPS 1974; Vanderbilt University, D.Min. 1983.
Ordination: June 14, 1964 by North Carolina Synod.
Calls: Amity, Iredell County, 1964-67; Good Hope, Hickory, 1967-71; Messiah, Burlington, 1973-74; Campus Pastor, Christ the King, Houston, Texas, 1975-76; Advent, Spindale, 1977-80; Interim at various congregations; dropped from roll, 1984.
Other: North Carolina Chaplains' Association; Veterans of Foreign Wars Chaplain; American Association of Pastoral Counselors, Association for Clinical Pastoral Education, Inc., Ecumenical Social Ministry of Davidson County, Lions Clubs, International; Chaplains Association Program, Lexington Memorial Hospital; Ministerial Association of Davidson County; author, *Eucharistic Themes for Pastoral Care*.

YOUNGBLOOD, JAMES ROBBINS

Date/Place of Birth: July 17, 1947; Charlotte, N.C.
Parents: D. K. Youngblood and Violet (Robbins) Youngblood.
Spouse/Marriage Date: Linda Ruth (Crawford) Youngblood; June 12, 1971 in Charlotte, N.C.
Children: Kelly, Robbin.
Education: Clemson University, B.S. Electrical Engineering 1970; Lutheran Theological Southern Seminary, M.Div. 1975; Syracuse University, M.Social Work; graduate work at University of North Carolina at Charlotte.
Ordination: 1975 by South Carolina Synod.
Calls: Antioch, Dallas, 1975-78; Chaplain, Western State Hospital, Staunton, Va., 1980-81; Supply, St. Paul, Mt. Solon, Va., 1986-; resigned June 1984 in Staunton, Va.

YOUNT, ADOLPHUS LEROY

Date/Place of Birth: May 28, 1853; Catawba County, N.C.

Parents: Noah Yount and Elizabeth (Herman) Yount. A younger brother was the Reverend J. Alonzo Yount.

Spouse/Marriage Date: Leah Ellen (Henkel) Yount, daughter of the Reverend David Melanchthon Henkel and Helleah Anna Maria (Henkel) Henkel; June 13, 1877.

Children: David Leroy, the Reverend John Arndt, Mary Helen (died at age 15), the Reverend Paul Luther, Carl Cossman, M.D., Frederick (died at age 3), Anna Elizabeth (died at age 10), Hilda Margaret, William Leonard (died at age 10).

Education: North Carolina College and by private teachers; received D.D., presumably from North Carolina College.

License/Ordination: Licensed 1876 and ordained 1877 by Tennessee Synod.

Calls: Supplied St. Mark's, Charlotte, 1874-76; transferred after ordination to Illinois Synod, 1877; served churches in Illinois, Nova Scotia, and Pennsylvania, including First Church, Greensburg, Pa.

Date of Death/Burial Location: December 14, 1914; Greensburg, Pa.

YOUNT, ADRIAN KENNETH

Date/Place of Birth: January 26, 1902; Catawba County, N.C.

Parents: Davis Emmanuel Yount and Alice Leona (Miller) Yount. An older and a younger brother, respectively, are the Reverends Carroll N. and Wade D. Yount.

Spouse/Marriage Date: Audrey Elizabeth (Shumate) Yount; June 11, 1929 in Churchville, Va.

Education: Lenoir-Rhyne, A.B. 1925; Lutheran Theological Southern Seminary, B.D. 1928; University of South Carolina, M.A. 1928.

Ordination: May 1928 by North Carolina Synod.

Calls: Ascension, Danville, Va., 1928-39; Forestville, Mt. Jackson, Va., 1939-44; Mt. Tabor, Middlebrook, Va., 1944-51; St. Paul, Connersville, Ind., 1951-55; Trinity, Lebanon, Ind., 1955-59; Jacob-Zion Parish, Edinburg, Va., 1959-66; retired February 1967.

YOUNT, CARROLL NOAH

Date/Place of Birth: November 1, 1891; Catawba County, N.C.

Parents: Davis Emmanuel Yount and Alice Leona (Miller) Yount. Two younger brothers are the Reverends A. K. and W. D. Yount.

Spouse/Marriage Date: Ethel Marguerite (Porter) Yount; June 10, 1918 in Barium Springs, N.C.

Children: Mary Alice (married the Reverend Stanley B. Jennings), Kathryn Schultz Wirick, Brent Porter, Carroll Thomas.

Education: Lenoir-Rhyne, A.B. 1915; Lutheran Theological Southern Seminary, 1918 B.D. 1924; University of South Carolina, M.A. 1918.

Ordination: 1918 by Georgia and Adjacent States Synod.

Calls: St. James, Brunswick, Ga., 1918-19; Holy Communion-St. Paul-Philadelphia-Antioch, Gaston County, 1919-22; Holy Communion-Christ-Bethel, Gaston County, 1922-25; St. Stephen-Mt. Olive, Hickory, 1925-35, Supply, 1935-36; Faith, Faith, 1935-53; first full-time Pastor, Atonement, North Wilkesboro, 1953-60; Mission Developer, Elkin Mission, 1960-61; retired 1962 near Statesville; Vice Pastor for various congregations.

Other: Board, Lutheran Theological Southern Seminary, 1934-37, 1943-46; Board, Lowman Home, 1953-55; Committee member, teacher, secretary, treasurer, dean, and director, at various times, Summer School for Church Workers, 1925-34; promoter of first organized district leadership training schools in the synod, 1935- 41; Examining Committee, 1951-54; Chair, 1956-69, Historical Works Committee, 1952-69, assisting in publishing and managing sales of History of the Lutheran Church in North Carolina, (1803-1953).
Date of Death/Burial Location: February 3, 1972; Iredell Memorial Park, Statesville, N.C.

YOUNT, GLENN ANTHONY, SR.
Date/Place of Birth: April 9, 1922; Hickory, N.C.
Parents: Hugh Preston Yount and Myrtle Vesta (Seaboch) Yount.
Spouse/Marriage Date: Doris Maenell (Sigmon) Yount; April 6, 1947 in Startown, N.C.
Children: Glenn Anthony, Jr., Susan Gaye.
Education: Lenoir-Rhyne, B.A. 1941; Lutheran Theological Southern Seminary, M.Div. 1944, also graduate study and at Chicago Seminary.
Ordination: July 16, 1944 by North Carolina Synod.
Calls: St. Paul, Startown, 1944-49; Immanuel, Rockwell, 1949-54; Bethphage-Cedar Grove, Lincoln County, 1954-56; Bethphage alone, 1956-60; St. Luke, Bear Poplar, 1960-64; Shiloh, Alexander County, 1964-74; Tent Ministry, St. Matthew, Granite Falls, 1975-81, Vice Pastor through 1984; retired 1984; Vice Pastor at various congregations.
Other: American Missions Committee, 1968-70; Presidential Priority Committee, 1969-72; Delegate, Lutheran Church in America, 1968; Nominating Committee, 1963.

YOUNT, JOSHUA ALONZO
Date/Place of Birth: December 17, 1864; near Conover, N.C.
Parents: Noah Yount and Elizabeth (Herman) Yount. Three nephews are the Reverends C. N., A. K., and W. D. Yount.
First Spouse/Marriage Date: Sarah Lugene (Miller) Yount; 1889 in Catawba County, N.C.
Children of First Marriage: Mattie (died in 1927), the Reverend Noah David, Paul (died in 1910), Ella, Olive (mother of the Reverend Clayton W. Sugg), Lillie, the Reverend Walter N., John L.
Second Spouse/Marriage Date: Louise (Glendmeyer) Yount; April 28, 1912 in Baltimore, Md.
Education: Concordia College, Lenoir-Rhyne, studied theology there, also.
Ordination: 1900 by Tennessee Synod.
Calls: All in North Carolina except in Pittsburgh Synod, 1904-05, some of them more than one pastorate; his records, Dr. Jacob L. Morgan's, and *History of the Lutheran Church in North Carolina*, (1803-1953) are conflicting, and dates are uncertain. In Catawba County: organized St. Luke; St. Stephen; Sardis; and perhaps St. Peter and Salem. In Alexander County: Friendship (three times); Shiloh; and organized, served twice, St. John. In Caldwell County: Philadelphia, Granite Falls (twice); St. Stephen, Lenoir; organized, served twice, St. John, Hudson; and St. Mark, near Blowing Rock. In Watauga County:

Holy Communion (twice); Mt. Pleasant (three or four times); Old Mt. Pleasant; Mt. Zion (twice); Grace, Boone; and Holy Trinity. In Lincoln County: Trinity, Vale-Cedar Grove. In Cabarrus County: Mt. Olive-St. Stephen. In Rowan County: supplied Immanuel. Retired 1939 on farm near Conover; supplied Mt. Pleasant and Holy Trinity in Watauga County. *Date of Death/Burial Location:* June 4, 1943; St. Timothy Lutheran Church Cemetery, Catawba County, N.C.

YOUNT, LAWRENCE EDWIN

Date/Place of Birth: February 1, 1936; Mecklenburg County, N.C.
Parents: Robert Alvin Yount and Lillie Bell (Cansler) Yount.
Spouse/Marriage Date: Barbara Ann (Herndon) Yount; August 23, 1959 in Hickory, N.C.
Children: Mark C., Alice Y., Karl S., Michael W.
Education: Lenoir-Rhyne, A.B. Religious Education 1958; Lutheran Theological Southern Seminary, M. Div. 1961; currently working on Th.D. Degree.
Ordination: June 11, 1961 by North Carolina Synod.
Calls: Sardis, Catawba County, 1961-62; Mt. Hermon, Iredell County, 1962-; Vice Pastor at various congregations.

YOUNT, NOAH DAVID

Date/Place of Birth: February 24, 1892; near Conover, N.C.
Parents: The Reverend Joshua Alonzo Yount and Sarah Lugene (Miller) Yount. A younger brother is the Reverend Walter N. Yount.
Spouse/Marriage Date: Rena Bertie (Simmons) Yount; November 10, 1936 in Conover, N.C.
Children: John David, Sara Ella.
Education: Lenoir-Rhyne, A.B. 1915; Lutheran Theological Southern Seminary, 1918, B.D. 1925.
Ordination: November 6, 1918 by Tennessee Synod.
Calls: In North Carolina, Watauga, Avery, Ashe, and Caldwell Counties; Four, Holy Communion (Watauga Parish); Mt. Pleasant (rebuilt 1922 on new site after fire in 1920); Mt. Zion; and organized (1918) Holy Trinity; three preaching points: Boone, Blowing Rock (Bailey's Camp), and Banner Elk. (Part of Mt. Pleasant in 1922 organized Old Mt. Pleasant and built on old site). Field missionary for Western North Carolina, 1923-25, surveying territory, developing and organizing missions: Ascension, Shelby; St. Mark, Asheville; and St. Andrew, Andrews; Ascension, Shelby-Grace, Bessemer City, 1925-32; Grace only, 1932-37; St. John, Hollywood, Fla., 1937-55; Augsburg, Union-St. Timothy, Whitmire, S.C., 1955-1964.
Other: Tennessee Synod Delegate, United Lutheran Church in America merger convention, 1918. In Florida Synod: Statistician, President, Secretary; Board, Children's Home and Lowman Home; retired 1964 residing at Conover and supplying churches; transferred 1965 to North Carolina Synod.
Date of Death/Burial Location: October 1, 1980; Conover Cemetery, Conover, N.C.

YOUNT, ROBERT WALTER

Date/Place of Birth: July 14, 1922; Lincoln County, N.C.
Parents: Samuel Walter Yount and Flossie Richardson (Ramsey) Yount.
Spouse/Marriage Date: Ima Jean (Newton) Yount; December 24, 1942 in Vale, N.C.
Children: Robert Gary, Barbara Jean Beaver, Joyce Ann Poovey.
Education: Lenoir-Rhyne, A.B. 1959, D.D. 1982; Lutheran Theological Southern Seminary, B.D. 1962.
Ordination: June 17, 1962 by North Carolina Synod.
Calls: St. John-St. Mark, Caldwell County, 1962-65; Trinity, Cabarrus County, 1965-81; Sharon, Statesville, 1981-93; retired June 1993 to China Grove, N.C.; Vice Pastor at various congregations.
Other: Parish Education Committee, 1971-72; World Missions Committee, 1970; Board, Lenoir-Rhyne, 1961-74; Distinguished Service Award, Lenoir-Rhyne, 1971.
Date of Death: December 8, 1996.

YOUNT, ROYALL AUSTIN, JR.

Date/Place of Birth: June 4, 1947; Tampa, Fla.
Parents: The Reverend Dr. Royall Austin Yount, Sr. and Martha (Townsend) Yount.
Spouse/Marriage Date: Joyce C. Yount.
Children: Keren E., Jeremy R.
Education: Newberry College, B.A. Philosophy, 1969; Chicago Seminary, M.Div. 1973; graduate work at Chicago Seminary
Ordination: June 1, 1973 by Arkansas-Oklahoma Synod.
Calls: Christ, San Diego, Calif., 1973-75; Christ the King, Tequesta, Fla., 1975-79; Prince of Peace, Hot Springs, Ark., 1979-96; Holy Trinity, Raleigh, 1996-.
Other: In Arkansas-Oklahoma Synod: Transition Team, 1986-87; Synod Council, 1988-91; Consultation Committee, 1988-91; Dean, Mid-Arkansas Conference, 1987-94; Mutual Ministry Committee, 1988-91; Chair, Planning Committee for two Synod Conventions, 1990, 1994; President, Vice President, Treasurer of Hot Springs Ministerial Alliance; Board, Hot Springs Community Foundation.

YOUNT, ROYALL AUSTIN, SR.

Date/Place of Birth: May 19, 1922; Hickory, N.C.
Parents: Floyd Stephen Yount and Lottie May (Austin) Yount.
Spouse/Marriage Date: Martha Lee (Townsend) Yount; June 14, 1945 in Hickory, N.C.
Children: The Reverend Royall Austin, Jr., John Timothy.
Education: Lenoir-Rhyne, A.B. 1942, L.L.D., 1987; Lutheran Theological Southern Seminary, M.Div. 1945; graduate work, Chicago Seminary; Newberry College, D.D. 1956.
Ordination: April 4, 1945 by North Carolina Synod.
Calls: St. Paul, Tampa, Fla., 1945-52; President, Florida Synod, United Lutheran Church in America, 1949-50; President, Florida Synod, Lutheran Church in America, 1950-62; retired 1987; Vice Pastor at various congregations.
Other: Parish Education, Lutheran Church in America; Pensions Board, Secretary, 1984-86; Commission on Function and Structure; National Lutheran Council; Lutheran Council, U.S.A.; Division for Service to Military Personnel, Lutheran Council in the United States of America; Consulting Committee on Military Chaplaincy; Board, Newberry College; Board, Lutheran Theological Southern Seminary; Conference of Bishops; Lutheran

Ministries of Florida; National Council of Churches; President, Florida Council of Churches.

YOUNT, WADE DAVIS

Date/Place of Birth: June 28, 1909; Catawba County, N.C.
Parents: Davis Emmanuel Yount and Alice Leona (Miller) Yount. Older brothers are the Reverends C. N. and A. K. Yount.
Spouse/Marriage Date: Nora Charline (Deal) Yount; May 20, 1936 in Conover, N.C.
Children: Max Hoffman, Kenneth Davis, Johanna Wells Baldwin.
Education: Lenoir-Rhyne, A.B. 1933;Lutheran Theological Southern Seminary, B.D. 1936.
Ordination: May 27, 1936 by North Carolina Synod.
Calls: Grace-Melanchthon-Richland, Liberty, 1936-37; Supply, Kimball Memorial and St. Enoch, Kannapolis, 1937-38; St. Mark, Rowan County, 1938-40; Nazareth-Shiloh, Rural Hall, 1940-41; Christ, Evansville, Ind., 1944-46; Sardis, Catawba County-Salem, Lincoln County, 1950-53; retired 1953 near Conover; Supply, St. John, Alexander County, 1954-56; Supply, Salem, Lincoln County, 1956-61.
Date of Death/Burial Location: June 10, 1989; St. Timothy Lutheran Church Cemetery, Hickory, N.C.

YOUNT, WALTER NICHOLAS, SR.

Date/Place of Birth: September 7, 1905; near Conover, N.C.
Parents: The Reverend Joshua Alonzo Yount and Sarah Lugene (Miller) Yount. An older brother is the Reverend Noah D. Yount.
First Spouse/Marriage Date: Virginia (Turner) Yount of Concord, N.C.; June 13, 1928 in Boone, N.C.
Children of First Marriage: Walter N., Jr., Philip Clair, Martha Ann Phillips.
Second Spouse: Jessie (Isenhour) (Corl) Yount.
Step-children: Larry Corl
Education: In business before entering college. Mount Pleasant Collegiate Institute, Lenoir-Rhyne 1931-32, D.D. 1982; Lutheran Theological Southern Seminary, 1935.
Ordination: 1935 by North Carolina Synod.
Calls: Nazareth-Shiloh, Forsyth County-Bethany, Stokes County, 1935-40; Bethphage-St. Mark-St. Paul, Lincoln County-Bethel, Gaston County, 1940-42; St. John, Asheboro, 1942-51; Calvary, Concord, 1951-71, Pastor Emeritus; retired 1972; Vice Pastor at various congregations.
Other: Board, Lenoir-Rhyne, 1961-74; Chair, Committees on Pensions, and on Christian Vocation, 1961-72; delegate to three conventions; Board, Quickle Scholarship Foundation; Distinguished Service Award, Lenoir- Rhyne, 1971; Executive Director, North Carolina Lutheran Men; Lodge at Agape Camp dedicated in his honor; President, Alumni Association of Lutheran Theological Southern Seminary; President, Concord Ministers Association, Cabarrus County Ministers Association, and Cabarrus County Lutheran Ministers Association. Contributor to *Light for Today* and *The Lutheran;* Synod Examining

Committee; Distinguished Service Award from the Board of Trustees of Lenoir-Rhyne College, 1971.

Date of Death/Burial Location: December 8, 1996; Carolina Memorial Park Mausoleum, Kannapolis, N.C.

ZIELINSKI, TODD ALLEN

Date/Place of Birth: May 3, 1969; Clinton, Iowa.

Parents: Edward Zielinski (Dennis S. Roberts, Stepfather) and Cheri L. (Roberts) Zielinski.

Spouse/Marriage Date: Tracie Leigh Zielinski; December 18, 1993.

Education: West Virginia University at Parkersburg; Marshall University, B.A. Psychology 1994; Gettysburg Seminary, M.Div. 1999.

Ordination: June 10, 1999 by North Carolina Synod.

Calls: Mission Development in Charlotte, N.C., 1999-.

Other: Design team for Young Adult Ministry Convo, 1999 National Assembly; sang, recorded and published for Youth Gathering, Year 2000 in St. Louis.

ZIMBECK, SILAS A.

Ordination: 1893 by Indiana Synod.

Calls: In Pennsylvania, 1897-1901. Transferred 1912 to North Carolina Synod from Eastern Pennsylvania Synod, and served St. Andrew-Mt. Hermon, Cabarrus County, 1912-14. Transferred 1915 to Georgia and Adjacent States Synod; served in Florida and Illinois.

Date of Death/Burial Location: 1931; Sharon, Wis.

ZIMMERMAN, CHARLES MERCER

Date/Place of Birth: March 5, 1948; Bethesda, Md.

Parents: Charles W. Zimmerman and Dorothy M. Zimmerman.

Spouse/Marriage Date: Margaret Kay (Plemmons) Zimmerman; June 10, 1972 in Asheville, N.C.

Children: Michael Kurt, Scott William.

Education: University of Maryland, B.S. 1970; Lutheran Theological Southern Seminary, M.Div. *cum laude* 1974.

Ordination: June 14, 1974 by Maryland Synod.

Calls: St. Paul, Statesville, 1974-78; First, Greensboro, 1979-.

ZIMMERMAN, JAMES PHILIP

Date/Place of Birth: February 27, 1938; Moulton, Ohio.

Parents: Elmer Edward Zimmerman and Ruth Aileen (Kaiser) Zimmerman.

Spouse/Marriage Date: Paula Marie (Schellhase) Zimmerman; August 7, 1965 in Parma, Ohio.

Children: Lisa Marie, Kristen Michelle, Heather Lynne.

Education: Capital University, B.A. 1960; Trinity Seminary, M.Div. 1964.

Ordination: June 28, 1964; Ohio District, The American Lutheran Church.

Calls: Faith, Arlington, Va., 1964-70; Christ, East Northport, N.Y., 1970-79; Mt. Zion, Conover, 1979-.

Other: Publication of *The Bereaved Parent* in *Acute Grief,* 1981.

ZINK, JACOB, SR.
Date/Place of Birth: June 10, 1756; probably in Stoney Creek, Shenandoah County, Va.
Parents: Johann Gottlief Zink and Barbara (Funkhouser) Zink.
Spouse: Mary Margaret Zink (maybe the second spouse).
Children: Jacob, Jr., Sarah Miller, Daniel, Mary Frances Parrish, Mary Catherine Ganote, Rebecca Hollowell, Elizabeth Scott, Lavinia.
License/Ordination: On May 5, 1806 was granted a license to perform marriages in Jefferson County, Ky. Licensed 1815 by North Carolina Synod in Organ Church, Rowan County; ordained 1820 at organizational convention of Tennessee Synod in Solomon Church, Greene County, Tenn.
Calls: One of seven North Carolina Synod ministers who organized German Lutheran Tennessee Conference or Tennessee Synod. Churches served in East Tennessee, and Virginia, including Zion, Sullivan County, Tenn., Solomon, Greene County, Tenn., and Sugar Grove, Bristol, Va. Performed marriages and preached in the area of Abingdon from February 1791 to April 1802. First minister of St. Paul at Bardstown, Ky., and one of the first ministers of the Jeffersontown Lutheran Church, also in Kentucky. Organized Rich Valley Church, later known as Sugar Grove Church, one mile east of Benham's on Aberam's Creek in Washington County.
Other: Preached his sermons in German. Made at least one extensive missionary tour, as indicated in the following statement: "A letter from the Rev. Jacob Zink, received at the third convention (Tennessee Synod, 1822), stated that he had baptized twenty-eight adults and sixty-nine infants in the State of Louisiana and many more than that number in the State of Indiana." (p. 77, *History of the Lutheran Church in North Carolina*, (1803-1953)). Made journeys extending from Louisiana to Indiana and as far west as Cape Girardeau, Mo.
Date of Death/Burial Location: February 13, 1829; Zion Church Cemetery, near Harristown and Salem in Washington County, Ind.

ZINK, P. E.
License/Ordination: Licensed 1872 in Organ Church, Rowan County, N.C.; ordained 1873 in St. Paul, Rowan County, by North Carolina Synod.
Calls: In 1873 assisted the church's pastor, the Reverend J. D. Bowles, in reorganizing Dutchman's Creek Church as Reformation Church, Davie County; served Pilgrim-St. Luke, Davidson County, 1878-1883; no further record of his service.
Date of Death/Burial Location: December 23, 1892; Old Chapel Cemetery, near Tyro, Davidson County, N.C.

ZIPPERER, DEWEY WILLIAM
Date/Place of Birth: December 21, 1898; Marlow, Ga.
Parents: John Theophilus Zipperer and Salome Margaret (Waldhour) Zipperer.
Spouse/Marriage Date: Beulah (Walborn) Zipperer of Van Vert, Ohio; August 25, 1925 in Raleigh, N.C.
Children: Ellen Jacquelyn.
Education: Lenoir-Rhyne, A.B. 1922; Lutheran Theological Southern Seminary, B.D. 1925; University of South Carolina, M.A. 1925.

License/Ordination: Licensed 1925 by Virginia Synod and ordained 1926 by Virginia Synod. *Calls*: Forestville Parish, Mt. Jackson, Va., 1925-31, 1950-53; Blacksburg Parish, Blacksburg, Va., 1931-37; Zion-St. James, Waynesboro, Va., 1937-50; Mt. Moriah, Rowan County, 1953-61; St. James-Solomon, Greene County, Tenn., 1961-64. Retired at Mt. Jackson, Va.
Other: Secretary, New Market Conference, Virginia Synod, 1926-31; Secretary, Roanoke Conference, Va., 1934-35, President, 1936-37; Secretary, Staunton Conference, Va., 1945-49. *Date of Death*: August 20, 1985.

ZORB, GLENN M.

Date/Place of Birth: June 30, 1953; Takoma Park, Md.
Parents: Irving S. Zorb and Doris (Sessler) Zorb.
Spouse/Marriage Date: Susan (Crowell) Zorb; October 10, 1981 in Columbus, Ohio.
Education: Wittenberg University, A.B. 1975; Philadelphia Seminary, M.Div. 1979; graduate work at Ohio State University.
Ordination: July 1, 1979 by Maryland Synod.
Calls: Associate Pastor, Holy Trinity, Columbus, Ohio, 1979-83; Haven, Salisbury, 1983-88; Resurrection, Horsham, Pa., 1988-; serving All Saints, Worthington, Ohio, 1998-.

HEFNER, DOUGLAS EDWARD

Date/Place of Birth: October 1, 1964; Hickory, N.C.
Spouse/Marriage Date: Lori Ann (Van Ravestein) Hefner; May 23, 1992.
Children: Elizabeth Grace, Matthew Douglas.
Education: North Carolina State University, B.S. Premed/Zoology; 1987, Lutheran Theological Southern Seminary, M.Div., 1992; Clinical Pastoral Education, Richland Hospital, S.C. 1992; Graduate Work at University of North Carolina at Charlotte in counseling.
Ordination: October 18, 1992 by South Carolina Synod.
Calls: Silverstreet, Silverstreet, 1992-96; Associate Pastor, St. Stephens, Lexington, S.C. 1996-98; transferred to North Carolina Synod in January, 1999; Co-Pastor, St. Peter, Salisbury, N.C. 1998-.
Other: Eagle Scout, leader in scouting; Medical in Army National Guard; Camp Counselor at Lutheridge; Chaplain at Western Carolina Center; Newberry, S. C. Alcohol/Drug Abuse Committee, 1993-96; in South Carolina Synod - Campus Ministry Committee, Social Ministry Committee, Ministry Committee, Chair of Campus Ministry and Social Ministry Synod Committees, Ministry Team for Outreach, Chair for Advisory Council for Lutheran Counseling and Enrichment Center; Lexington, S.C. Interfaith Community Services Board;
Counseling/Enrichment Center (LFS) Advisory Board; Midlands CROP Walk Planning Committee; Chaplain, Lexington, S.C. Medical Center Hospital; Campfirmation Cluster at Lutheridge.

HEFNER, LORI ANN (VAN RAVESTEIN)

Date of Birth: August 31, 1962.
Spouse/Marriage Date: Douglas Edward Heffner; May 23, 1992.
Children: Elizabeth Grace, Matthew Douglas.

Education: University of North Carolina - Greensboro, B.S./Nutrition 1985, M. Ed. 1987; Lutheran Theological Southern Seminary, M.Div. 1995.

Ordination: August 18, 1996 by South Carolina Synod.

Calls: Associate Pastor, St. Stephens, Lexington, S.C. 1996-98; transferred to North Carolina Synod, 1999; Co-pastor, St. Peter, Salisbury, 1998-.

Other: Nutrition Education Specialist, 1986; Neutritionist, Davis Community Hospital, Statesville, N.C. 1987-89; Food Ministry Director, Marietta, Ga. 1989-92; Dietary Service Director, Hilhaven Nursing 1989; began first CROP Walk for Newberry County, S.C.; in South Carolina worked for Interfaith Community Services and Manna House (food bank); Hospital Chaplain for Lexington, S.C. Medical Center 1996-98; Lutheran Brotherhood Area Educator, Lexington, S.C.1998; South Carolina Synod Learning Ministry Committee; South Carolina Synod Lutheran Conference and Retreat Center Board 1998; Chaplain, South Carolina Department of Corrections, women's Prison 1994-95.

INDEX

Barringer, Continued

Elaine Elizabeth	17
Ellen (Kesler)	94
Evelyn E. (McLemore)	17
George Herbert	16
Hubert Paul	17
Hugh Perry	17
Jackson Lee	16
John Daniel	17
Joseph Allen	16
Larry Edward	17
Lena (Rudisill)	17
Lorena Smith (Arndt)	16
Mamie (Rowland)	17
Margaret	144
Marshall Otho	16
Martha Sue	17
Paul Arndt	16
Perry L.	17
Sheila Ann	17

Bartholomew

C. Earl	17
Christopher	17
Craig E.	17
Laura O.	17
LaVaughn (Boyle)	17

Bartlett

Elizabeth Anne	438

Bartlette

Cheryl Rose (Sanger)	415

Barton

Linda Carolyn	305
Barton College	441

Bartos

Andrew	18
Carl Ann (Bayer)	18
Elizabeth Ann	18
Helen (Gribbon)	18
James Andrew	18
Jeffrey Andrew	18
Timothy Scott	18

Bartuseviz

Emilia	306

Basinger

Geneva	538

Basis and Constitution for Merger

Joint Commission on	110

Basnight

Hope	81

Bass

Frieda	1

Bates

Bates, Continued

Margaret	172

Bathier

Margaret	319

Baton Rouge Parish Senior Citizens

Commission	89

Battalion Chaplain, Camp Lejeune, N.C.

	357

Batterman

Alice Christina (Anderson)	18
Henry Otto	18
Mary Amy (Matthews)	18
William Henry	18
Battle of Brandywine	319
Battle of Gettysburg	209
Battle of Long Island	319
Battle of Valley Forge	319
Battle of White Plains	319

Bauer

B. Susan (Bilton)	18
Donna Celeste (Gantt)	161
Esther I. (Brown)	18
Jason David	18
Louis E., Sr.	18
Louis Edwin, Jr.	18
Megan Elizabeth	18

Baughman

Sarah Ellen	461

Baumgartner

Andrew Conrad	19
Carla Frances	19
Frances (Wisdom)	19
Hugh E., Sr.	19
Hugh Edward, Jr.	19
Hugh Eric	19
Patricia Lee Bowles	19
Paul Wisdom	19
Thelma (Conyers)	19
William Edward	19

Baun

Alta	475

Baver

Linda S. (Ehlers)	132
Wendy (Moebius)	325

Baxley

Melanie	360
Bay Shore, Milwaukee, Wis.	460

Bayer

Carl Ann	18
Baylor University	446

Bayne

Carrie Viola (McDowell)	19

Brown, Continued

David Solomon	58
Dora	56
Edna	54
Edna Propst	56
Elizabeth (Killian)	54
Ellen Elizabeth	416
Ellen Gladys	58
Emily Athalinda (Propst)	56
Estelle	497, 498
Esther	346
Esther I.	18
Eugene Luther	54
Evelyn Christian	56
Fannie S.	489
Florence Adelle (Bodenhorn)	57
Florence Earhart	59
Frank Hatcher	54
Harriet Isabel	422
Henry Maxwell	56-58, 314, 460
Herman Alexander	56
Ida Mae	395
Ila C.	398
Janice Adelle	57
Jason S.	56
Jennie Bass	58
Joe	54
John D. A.	56
John Daniel	56, 94, 95
John Richard	58
Joseph	58
Josephine Virginia	59
Julia (Teeter)	54
Julia Ann	66
Karen Cox	56
Kathy Marlene	237
Ladye L.	57
Lala Cladora	56
Laura M.	16
Lelia Virginia	481
Lewis D. Henry	58
Lillian	54
Lillian Luetta	182
Lillie Eudora	56
Lizzie	54
Lois Elizabeth	57
Louise	100
Lucetta Jane (Fisher)	56
Lucy Ashton (Dillard)	58
Lucy Mabon	58
Lular Rosa	56
Marcus Calvin	58

Brown, Continued

Margaret (Earhart)	59
Margaret L.	14
Maria Elizabeth (Wise)	526
Marie	422
Mary (Kistler)	54
Mary Catherine	54, 55
Mary Catherine (Brown)	54, 55
Mary Elizabeth	54
Mary Eve (Cassell)	59
Mary Frances	395
Mary L.	460
Mary L. R.	58
Mary Lucetta	56
Matilda	485
Mattie Jordan	58
Maxwell Melanchthon	58
Michael	58, 422
Monica	54
Myron Day	54
Myrtle M.	56
Nancy (Teeter)	54
Nancy E. (Agner)	58
Nathan	57
Nathan Maxwell	56
Nellie	88
Ollie Ora	532
Oscar L.	57
Paul Cassell	59
Peter Marchman	57
Pleasant David	56-58, 489
Rebecca	95
Richard L.	56-58, 142, 144-146
Robert Hall	56
Robert Meredith	57
Rosa S. (Agner)	57
Rufus	59
Ruth	501
Sallie	495
Sarah (Hudson)	58
Sarah Cladora (Fisher)	56
Sarah Josephine	58
Serena Louise	258
Solomon	56, 58
Susan Carol	12
Susan Dale (Cauble)	71
Thelma Ruth	56
Thomas Shannon, Jr.	58
Timothy	57
Tomas Shannon, Sr.	58
William Roedel	xi, 59
Browntown, Davidson County	483

N.C. (North Carolina), Continued

Hudson   1, 31, 68, 78, 86, 109, 330, 340, 348, 376, 437, 445, 462, 541

Huntersville   229

Iredell County   7, 9, 11, 20, 22, 29, 56, 68, 76, 102, 124, 129, 130, 139, 141, 151, 164, 168, 169, 179, 182, 188, 193, 194, 199, 212, 218, 220, 236, 237, 239, 244, 245, 251, 269, 271, 279, 285, 286, 306, 308, 311, 319, 320, 322, 329, 334, 337, 339, 356, 373, 375, 390, 391, 395, 431, 444, 452, 455, 458, 461, 469, 471, 475, 479, 484, 490, 497, 499, 501, 510, 526, 539, 542

Iron Station   9, 410

Jacksonville   17, 51, 182, 206, 207, 237, 298, 307, 357, 374, 495

Jonesville   498

Julian   22, 341, 351, 369, 428, 481

Kannapolis   2, 13, 55, 56, 69, 70, 75, 81, 83, 88-91, 94, 101, 104, 106, 117, 121, 125, 140, 149, 156, 159, 161, 166, 169, 176, 177, 206, 209, 215, 223, 229, 232, 234, 237, 262, 266, 274, 282, 289, 293, 294, 296, 301, 312, 317, 321, 334, 335, 344, 345, 348, 355, 364, 373, 379, 389, 390, 398, 399, 413, 430, 437, 439, 448, 450, 452, 457, 465, 466, 477, 483, 485, 490, 495, 501, 515, 527, 535, 544, 545

Kings Mountain   4, 5, 25, 31, 39, 70, 76, 77, 89, 90, 102, 111, 112, 118, 125, 143, 145, 151, 152, 157, 161, 163, 183, 208, 216, 273, 299, 300, 302, 323, 328, 343, 367, 374, 388, 404, 417, 438, 439, 454, 464, 467, 513

Kinston   67, 87, 195, 364, 393, 468, 492, 523

Kure Beach   17, 52, 70, 86, 212, 223, 261, 276, 296, 299, 339, 514, 516, 538

N.C. (North Carolina), Continued

Lake Norman Area   229

Landis   11, 55, 107, 109-111, 138, 144, 184, 271, 332, 333, 342, 395, 412, 435, 453, 471, 487

Laurinburg   17, 21, 60, 183, 204, 401, 403, 432

Lawndale   445

Lenoir   20, 41, 61, 109, 110, 114, 133, 147, 217, 224, 232, 241, 283, 307, 311, 315, 317, 319, 357, 395, 405, 456, 541

Lenoir County   468

Lewisville   261, 272, 346, 367, 378, 408, 449, 530

Lexington   14, 22, 40, 44, 55, 77, 82, 86, 96, 100, 101, 113, 115, 136, 138, 141, 145, 159, 160, 165, 168, 170, 177, 208, 214, 215, 241, 257, 307, 312, 322, 342, 343, 360, 370, 371, 383, 386, 389, 396, 397, 402, 448, 449, 456, 463, 481, 483, 484, 501, 520, 530, 537

Liberty   16, 20, 37, 114, 142, 150, 265, 343, 400, 438, 441, 445, 533, 544

Lillington   415

Lincoln (now Catawba) County   336, 338, 428

Lincoln (now Gaston) County   238, 385

Lincoln County   2, 3, 8, 9, 17, 19, 31, 51, 55, 67, 68, 70, 76, 98, 102, 103, 109, 111, 115, 124, 130, 148, 151, 152, 158, 159, 162, 167, 171, 178, 180, 188, 191, 195, 196, 199, 200, 202, 206, 208, 218, 231, 238, 244, 247, 249, 271-273, 275, 277, 282, 298, 309, 311, 319, 324, 336, 340, 348, 364, 367, 376, 386, 391, 398, 405, 406, 410, 418, 431, 432, 441, 457, 461, 462, 471, 481, 482, 495, 508, 518, 519, 535, 541-544

Lincolnton   3, 8, 9, 23, 26, 31, 34, 54, 76, 77, 88, 93, 98, 99, 103, 110, 115-117, 123, 141, 167, 171, 177, 180, 187, 192, 198, 199, 201, 208, 213, 214,

N.C. (North Carolina), Raleigh,
  Continued
                362, 363, 375, 377, 380, 385,
                425, 448, 451, 479, 486-488,
                492, 494, 506, 512, 543, 546
Randolph County   99, 100, 114,
                148, 153, 169, 173, 180, 189,
                199, 226, 295, 330, 336, 338,
                351, 382, 429, 431, 469, 474,
                                          484
Reidsville   81, 328, 360, 361,
                369, 384, 401, 428, 471, 492,
                                     493, 533
Rhodhiss   98
Richfield   90, 122, 124, 125, 143,
                152, 159, 228, 241, 252, 254,
                267, 284, 294, 320, 321, 328,
                329, 334, 335, 349, 373, 375,
                381, 386, 389, 401, 440, 446,
                453, 457, 465, 495, 496
Richlands   206, 207
Richmond County   189
Ridgeway   288
Roanoke Rapids   93, 456
Robbinsville   138
Rockingham   161, 258, 493
Rockingham County   138
Rockwell   12, 36, 143, 144, 147,
                157, 270, 276, 293, 310, 312,
                320, 321, 344, 373, 393, 403,
                436, 439, 440, 444, 461, 496,
                                     506, 541
Rocky Mount   79, 127, 187, 209,
                210, 262, 288, 302, 330, 387,
                388, 396-398, 413, 432, 446,
                447, 450, 494
Rose Vale   331
Rowan (now Davie) County   531
Rowan County   2, 7-10, 14, 16,
                17, 20, 21, 28, 29, 31, 36-40,
                42, 44, 45, 54-56, 58, 59, 61,
                62, 66, 69, 71, 74, 76, 80, 82-
                84, 89, 90, 94, 95, 97, 99-
                101, 103, 106, 108-112, 115,
                119, 124, 126, 129-131, 138-
                140, 143-145, 147, 151, 152,
                156, 160, 167, 169, 171, 174,
                175, 177-180, 182, 187, 188,
                192-194, 197, 199, 203, 212,
                213, 215, 216, 218-221, 223,
                226, 227, 229, 236, 237, 239,
                241, 244-246, 248, 250, 251,

N.C. (North Carolina), Rowan County,
  Continued
                257-261, 263-265, 269, 270,
                272, 277, 278, 281-286, 289,
                295, 309, 310, 312-314, 317,
                318, 320, 327, 329, 332-334,
                336-339, 349-352, 355, 356,
                358, 361, 363, 367, 369, 373,
                374, 378, 381, 383, 385, 389,
                390, 392, 393, 398, 406, 407,
                409, 412, 413, 419, 420, 422,
                425, 426, 428, 431, 433, 435,
                439-443, 452, 454, 455, 457,
                458, 461, 463, 469-472, 475,
                476, 478, 483, 484, 489, 495-
                497, 499, 500, 504, 506, 507,
                509, 510, 515, 518, 519, 526-
                528, 532, 535, 537, 542, 544,
                                     546, 547
Rowan County (now a part of
  Davie County)   198
Rural Hall   8, 61, 173, 287, 317,
                332, 341, 342, 367, 383, 403,
                                481, 488, 520, 544
Rutherfordton   210
Salem   409, 424-426
Salem community   425
Salisbury   2, 3, 5, 7, 8, 14, 23,
                27, 29, 33, 37, 39, 42, 43, 45,
                46, 53, 54, 57-59, 63, 64, 68,
                71, 72, 75, 80, 82, 84-86, 90,
                92, 95, 100, 102, 104, 107,
                112, 118, 130, 131, 134, 137,
                138, 141, 142, 144-147, 150,
                152, 156, 157, 159, 160, 170,
                174, 182, 188, 192, 198, 200,
                203, 204, 208-210, 213-215,
                219-221, 225-227, 236, 237,
                240, 241, 245, 252, 254, 256,
                258, 261, 264-268, 272, 278,
                279, 283-286, 288, 301, 302,
                307, 308, 310-312, 314, 317,
                319, 321, 322, 330-335, 338,
                344, 346, 349, 350, 353, 355,
                360, 361, 366, 371, 373, 374,
                380-382, 384, 386, 388, 389,
                396, 400, 401, 404, 407, 409,
                412, 413, 419, 421, 422, 426,
                429, 436, 440, 444, 447, 449,
                451-453, 455, 458, 468, 469,
                471, 474, 476, 477, 484, 485,
                488-490, 492, 494, 496, 500,

Ohio, Continued

	360, 493
Circleville	384
Cleveland	62, 64, 138, 225, 274,
	305, 353, 384, 415, 490
Collamer	32
Collins	228
Columbiana	411
Columbus	30, 34, 50, 69, 121,
	132, 193, 196, 208, 218, 250,
	254, 255, 305, 311, 324, 325,
	346, 347, 353, 357, 378, 393,
	491, 529, 547
Council of Churches	412
Covington	408
Crestline	153
Cuyahoga	92, 117
Cuyahoga County	67, 274
Darrtown	256
Dayton	18, 115, 133, 155, 324,
	344, 466
Defiance	324
Deshler	30, 35
District	35, 545
Elyria	5, 162, 489
Euclid	248
Fairfield	483
Fairport Harbor	411
Findlay	256, 324
Fort Recovery	193
Fostoria	35
Franklin	384
Galion	246
Germantown	196
Glenford	255, 450
Greenville	351
Hamilton	251
Hamilton County	148
Jewett	501
Johnsville	206
Joint Synod	15
Joint Synod of	11
Lancaster	18
Lewisburg	196
Lima	344, 474
Lithopolis	175
Lodi	156
London	206
Lorain	282
Lucas	133
Luckey	155
Magnolia	519

Ohio, Continued

Malinta	245
Mansfield	324, 438
Mapleton	255
Marion	206
Marysville	375
Miami	256
Miamisburg	366, 491
Middle Point	85
Middletown	384
Mifflin	202
Montgomery County	438
Moulton	545
Napoleon	364
Nevada	353
New Bedford	132
New Bremen	460
New Germantown	473
New Waterford	411
Newark	206, 256
Newton Falls	526
North Lima	324
North Olmsted	202
Northwood	113
Osborne	358
Painesville	486
Paris	255
Parma	254, 545
Paulding	138
Perry County	196
Perrysburg	378
Pittsburgh	375
Plymouth	501
Portsmouth	193
Ravenna	246, 305
Sandusky	335
Shaker Heights	256
Sherrodsville	501
Silver Run	188
Solon	305
Somerset	132
Springfield	74, 353, 375, 516
St. Paris	459
Stark County	228
Steubenville	375
Sugar Grove	116
Sulphur Springs	438
Summit County	120
Toledo	35, 57, 113, 117, 172,
	315, 344, 353, 376, 433, 464
Trotwood	433
Uniontown	251, 504